New Jersey

Andi Marie Cantele & Mitch Kaplan

The Countryman Press ✳ Woodstock, Vermont

We welcome your comments and suggestions. Please contact Explorer's Guide Editor, The Countryman Press, P.O. Box 748, Woodstock, Vermont 05091; or e-mail countrymanpress@wwnorton.com.

New Jersey: An Explorer's Guide
ISBN 978-0-88150-840-6

Maps by Moore Creative Designs, © 2005 The Countryman Press
Book design by Bodenweber Design
Text composition by PerfecType, Nashville, TN

Published by The Countryman Press, P.O. Box 748, Woodstock, Vermont 05091

Distributed by W. W. Norton & Company, Inc., 500 Fifth Avenue, New York, NY 10110

Printed in the United States of America

10 9 8 7 6 5 4 3 2 1

DEDICATION

In memory of Vincent "V. J." Fusco, brother and friend
—A. M. C.
For Penny, always.

And, with special thanks to Pat Turner Kavanaugh, without whom the end might never have come into sight.
—M. K.

BOOKS BY ANDI MARIE CANTELE

52 Weekends in Connecticut
Connecticut: An Explorer's Guide
Backroad Bicycling in Connecticut
Backroad Bicycling in Western Massachusetts
Backroad Bicycling in New Hampshire

BOOKS BY MITCH KAPLAN

52 Weekends in New Jersey
The Unofficial Guide to the Mid-Atlantic with Kids
The Cheapskate's Guide to Myrtle Beach
The Golf Book of Lists

EXPLORE WITH US!

Welcome to the second edition of *New Jersey: An Explorer's Guide,* a detailed and comprehensive travel guide to the Garden State. All entries in this book—restaurants, hotels, museums, galleries, and attractions—are included solely on merit, not paid advertising. We select each one based on personal experience, extensive research, repeated visits, and the advice of the many local residents we encounter during our travels throughout New Jersey.

The layout of this guide is designed to be simple and easy to use. We have divided New Jersey into six geographic regions, which are organized into several chapters apiece. Each chapter begins with an introduction to the area, followed by individual listings starting with places to see, things to do, and outdoor attractions, moving on to lodging and dining, then ending with entertainment options and selective shopping. Closing each chapter is a list of special events that take place in the region. The following points will help you get started on your way.

WHAT'S WHERE

In the beginning of the book you'll find an alphabetical listing of special highlights, with important information and advice that you can reference quickly either while planning a trip to New Jersey or during your travels.

LODGING

Please don't hold us or the respective innkeepers responsible for the rates, which are listed as of press time. Some changes are inevitable. Keep in mind that many establishments often require a 2- or 3-day minimum stay on weekends and holidays. At the time of this writing, New Jersey has a 6 percent state room tax, an additional 5 percent state occupancy fee, and local taxes and fees that vary town by town. Prices given in this book do not include tax or gratuity.

RESTAURANTS

In each chapter, please note a distinction between *Dining Out* and *Eating Out.* Restaurants in *Dining Out* tend to be more expensive, while those listed under *Eating Out* are generally more casual and inexpensive. At the end of each listing, the price range given is for à la carte dinner entrée prices; prix fixe menus are specified. Remember that prices are likely to change, and many restaurants change their menus seasonally. Use the descriptions as a general guide to the type of cuisine an establishment serves.

KEY TO SYMBOLS

- ❦ **Special value.** The special value symbol appears next to lodging, restaurants, and attractions that combine quality and moderate prices.
- ♿ **Wheelchair.** The wheelchair symbol appears next to establishments that are partially or fully handicapped accessible.
- ✎ **Child-friendly.** The child-friendly symbol appears next to lodging, restaurants, attractions, and events of special appeal to youngsters or families with young children.

- ❦ **Pet-friendly.** The pet-friendly symbol denotes lodgings that welcome pets, which most of the time means dogs. Even if an establishment accepts pets, it's always a good idea to give advance notice. Some places might charge an extra fee, require a deposit, or accept pets only at particular times of the year.

- ▼ **Gay-friendly.** The inverted triangle symbol indicates establishments that make an extra effort to cater to a gay clientele.

- ∞ **Weddings.** The wedding symbol appears next to venues that are experienced with hosting weddings.

- "T" **Wi-Fi.** Locations that offer wireless Internet

- ↬ **Ecofriendly establishments.** In the case of lodgings, denotes certified participants in the Florida Green Lodging Program. In the case of other businesses, properties noted by the authors as taking special initiatives to reduce, reuse, and recycle.

We would appreciate your comments and corrections about places you visit or know well in the state. You may address your correspondence to Explorer's Guide Editor, The Countryman Press, P.O. Box 748, Woodstock VT 05091; countrymanpress@wwnorton.com.

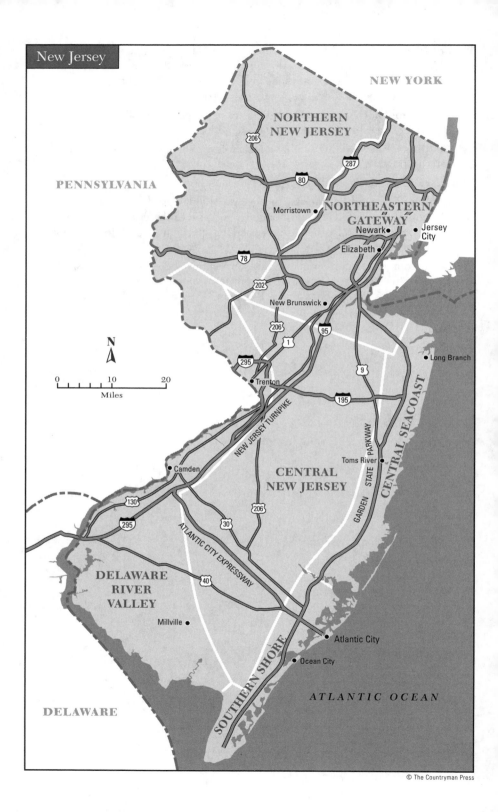

New Jersey

NEW YORK

NORTHERN
NEW JERSEY

PENNSYLVANIA

Morristown

NORTHEASTERN
GATEWAY

Newark

Jersey
City

Elizabeth

New Brunswick

Long Branch

Trenton

Camden

CENTRAL
NEW JERSEY

Toms River

CENTRAL SEACOAST

GARDEN STATE PARKWAY

NEW JERSEY TURNPIKE

ATLANTIC CITY EXPRESSWAY

DELAWARE
RIVER
VALLEY

Millville

SOUTHERN SHORE

Atlantic City

Ocean City

ATLANTIC OCEAN

DELAWARE

N

0   10   20
Miles

206   287   80   78   202   206   95   1   295   9   195   130   295   30   206   40

© The Countryman Press

CONTENTS

11   INTRODUCTION
18   WHAT'S WHERE IN NEW JERSEY

1 The Northeastern Gateway / 37
39   THE PALISADES TO HOBOKEN
66   THE NEWARK AND JERSEY CITY REGION
90   WEST OF THE PARKWAY
122 THE SOUTHERN GATEWAY

2 Northern New Jersey / 143
144 THE NORTHERN HIGHLANDS
167 THE UPPER DELAWARE RIVER
185 THE HILLS: FLEMINGTON TO MORRISTOWN

3 The Delaware River Valley / 221
223 RIVER TOWNS: MILFORD TO TITUSVILLE
245 THE TRENTON AND CAMDEN AREA
273 THE DELAWARE BAY REGION

4 Central New Jersey / 297
298 THE PRINCETON REGION
320 THE PINELANDS REGION

5 The Central Seacoast / 341
343 SANDY HOOK TO BELMAR
374 SPRING LAKE TO BAY HEAD
395 BARNEGAT BAY
411 LONG BEACH ISLAND: BARNEGAT LIGHT TO HOLGATE

6 The Southern Shore: Atlantic City to Cape May / 433
434 THE ATLANTIC CITY REGION
476 OCEAN CITY TO WILDWOOD
515 THE CAPE MAY PENINSULA

550 INDEX

INTRODUCTION

Welcome to the Garden State, and the second edition of the most comprehensive guide to the famous places, diverse landscape, rich history, and hidden gems that make traveling in New Jersey such an unexpected pleasure. From the rugged hills along the Delaware River and the charming Victorian streets of Cape May to the amusement piers along the Jersey Shore, the rolling farmland of Hunterdon County, the museums, theaters, and first-class restaurants in the Northeastern Gateway region, and the glitz of Atlantic City's casino skyline, New Jersey truly offers something to satisfy everyone. This guide is filled with pages of practical information to help visitors navigate their way around, and decide where to stay and what to do. It is also designed to be a useful resource for New Jerseyans looking for a new part of their home state to discover, or needing ideas on how or where to entertain out-of-state guests. We have selected hundreds of lodgings, restaurants, attractions, and shops that represent a broad range of tastes and budgets. Perhaps most importantly, we hope that this guide reveals the "other" New Jersey to travelers who assume that clogged highways, suburban sprawl, and industrial landscapes define the entire state.

Each chapter focuses on a particular region, and begins with an overview to familiarize visitors with its flavor, history, and unique features. Then we offer practical information on getting to and around each area, as well as tourism contacts and places to go in the event of an emergency. Following that is a detailed list of the region's worthwhile attractions, from historic homes and lighthouses to museums and zoos. From there we move on to things to do, such as bicycling, hiking, kayaking, ice-skating, and skiing, and also list a wide variety of spectator sports, from minor-league baseball and NFL football to thoroughbred racing. Next, we have included a variety of options for enjoying nature, in a well-manicured suburban park or a historic garden, from the top of the state's loftiest peaks, on a pristine barrier beach, or in a wildlife refuge spread across thousands of wild acres.

Most vacation plans start with choosing a place to stay, and we have included lodgings around the state that will appeal to a wide range of visitors. New Jersey's specialty is the charming Victorian bed & breakfast. Hundreds of the turn-of-the-20th-century homes on the shoreline and around the state—particularly in the Victoriana hotbeds of Cape May and Ocean Grove—have been meticulously restored and opened to overnight guests. Most have wraparound porches, ornate antiques, formal parlors, and wicker rocking chairs; some boast soaring turrets, fanciful gingerbread trim, and cheerful multihued exteriors. Other lodging options include historic inns, resorts, and full-service hotels, as well as motels and campgrounds. So it goes with restaurants in New Jersey. The range of culinary options is mouth-watering, from upscale dining rooms in fine inns and sleek SoHo-style bistros (listed under *Dining Out*) to authentic ethnic eateries that feature everything from Thai and Indian to Cuban, Turkish, Ethiopian, and Middle Eastern cuisine. Chrome diner cars serving no-frills fare hark back to New Jersey's designation as the Diner Capital of the World, and classic seafood houses along the shore serve the freshest just-off-the-boat fish anywhere (listed under *Eating Out*). Boardwalk treats like pizza, frozen custard, saltwater taffy, and hand-whipped fudge, plus classic delis, brewpubs and coffeehouses, and wonderful bakeries (listed under *Snacks*), round out the offerings. Finally, we've included local theaters, concerts halls, and other entertainment venues, plus galleries, specialty shops (not a complete listing, but a sampling of what the area has to offer), and some of each region's best annual festivals and special events.

As you plan your trip, keep scale in mind. As the nation's fifth-smallest state, New Jersey stretches 166 miles north to south, and just 65 miles east to west at its widest point. That is good news for the explorer who wants to experience the Garden State's rich diversity, even when given only a short amount of time. You can get from the rugged Delaware Water Gap in the northwestern corner of the state to the tip of the Cape May peninsula on the Atlantic Ocean in just a few hours; from the New York City metropolitan region it's no more than a couple hours to anyplace in the state.

Regardless of its relatively small size, New Jersey boasts a surprising wealth of geographic, historical, and cultural diversity, which comes as a surprise to first-time visitors expecting the urban sprawl that the state is unfortunately identified with. We have tried to weave the state's little-known images into the familiar ones, not only to paint a broad picture of what New Jersey has to offer but also to debunk the negative stereotypes that unfairly characterize this much-maligned state. These stereotypes have served as fodder for many a stand-up comic, resulting in many would-be visitors dismissing "Joizy" as simply joke material. Those who have discovered the "real" New Jersey—the one beyond the New Jersey Turnpike, the "What exit are you from?" quips, and *The Sopranos*—know that there are hidden gems all around the state. New Jersey, they will tell you, is nicknamed the Garden State for a reason.

Contrary to its popular image, New Jersey is full of rural areas and open spaces, although they are steadily shrinking. Statistically speaking, it's the most densely populated state in the nation; but close to 90 percent of the 8.7 million residents live in urban areas. That leaves plenty left to explore. It may come as a surprise to learn that 40 percent of the state is blanketed in forest, or that there are more than 800 lakes and ponds, 117 wildlife management areas, and some 800,000 acres of farmland—from South Jersey's sprawling produce farms to the small family-owned wineries and organic farms in the northern hills. New Jersey is a peninsula, so coastlines figure prominently in the landscape. Except for its 38-mile border with New York State, it's entirely surrounded by water. In fact, the earliest European settlers mistook New Jersey for an island. The long, eastern shoreline along the Atlantic Ocean leads south to Delaware Bay and the Delaware River, which forms the state's western boundary with Pennsylvania.

Keep in mind that New Jersey was one of young America's original 13 colonies, so its history is rich and far-reaching. As a result, there is a wealth of historic sites, battlefields, and centuries-old homes that are open to visitors looking for a fix on the past. You can see the remnants of 18th-century iron forges and furnaces, tour working farms open as living-history museums, climb to the top of historic lighthouses, or tour grand Victorian mansions that look just as they did at the turn of the 20th century.

The original New Jerseyans were the Lenni-Lenape Indians who for centuries lived and farmed in small villages throughout the state, and traveled into the mountains and to the coast to hunt and fish. In 1524, Italian navigator Giovanni da Verrazano reached Newark Bay near what is now Sandy Hook. He was the first European to explore the coast, and almost a century would pass before English explorer Henry Hudson sailed his *Half Moon* through New York Harbor and up his namesake river for the Dutch East India Company, claiming the entire region for the Netherlands in 1609. A few years later, Dutch navigator Cornelius Mey sailed into the mouth of the Delaware River, and even though he never landed on the lovely peninsula jutting into the bay and the Atlantic, he named it Cape Mey, a spelling that would eventually change to Cape May.

English, Dutch, and Swedish settlers farmed the colony for more than 100 years before the Revolutionary War. In the late 17th century, New Jersey was divided into two colonies—West Jersey and East Jersey—each with its own capital and royal governor. William Penn had considered settling his Quaker followers in New Jersey but, dismayed by the confusion, he crossed the Delaware River, founded Philadelphia, and transformed it into a city that rivaled New York.

Key battles in the American Revolution—most notably the battles of Trenton, the battle of Princeton, and the battle of Monmouth—were fought on New Jersey soil, earning it the nickname Cockpit of the Revolution. During the war, George Washington spent a lot of time, roughly a quarter of the entire conflict, in New Jersey—more time, in fact, than in any other state. Visitors can go to Washington Crossing State Park in Titusville to see where the general and his Continental army made their famous Christmas-night crossing of the icy river in 1776, the scene immortalized in Emanuel Leutze's famous painting *Washington Crossing the Delaware*. Trenton has erected a war monument where the patriots defeated the Hessians; the battlefields in Princeton and Monmouth are hauntingly well preserved; and Morristown National Historical Park—the country's first national park—is the site of Jockey Hollow, the military encampment where thousands of Continental troops spent the bitter winters of 1776–77 and 1779–80. Historic homes that Washington used as military headquarters, including the Ford Mansion in Morristown, the Wallace House in Somerville, and the Dey Mansion in Wayne, are open for tours.

New Jersey has been an industrial pioneer since the 1700s, from whaling, fishing, and shipbuilding on the seacoast, to glassmaking and cranberry harvesting in the Pinelands, to iron smelting and copper mining in the rugged northern hills, to the tanneries in Newark and textile factories in Paterson—the nation's first planned industrial city built on the Great Falls of the Passaic River. Wheaton Village in Millville, Batsto Village in Wharton State Forest, and Waterloo Village in Stanhope are some of New Jersey's historic industrial centers that have been recreated or preserved; in Paterson, the industrial heritage of the "Silk City" will soon be the centerpiece of one of New Jersey's newest national parks.

The 1830s brought a wave of canal building, as the Morris Canal and the Delaware and Raritan Canal were cut across northern New Jersey. The canals' pioneering system of locks provided a quick route for flat-bottomed barges to make the journey from the Delaware River to the East Coast, laden with Pennsylvania coal. Benjamin Franklin once called New Jersey "a barrel tapped at both ends," for its location tucked between Philadelphia and New York. In Hoboken, John Stevens launched his horseless "steam carriage," which was the country's first railroad. Industrial belts were forming along the Delaware River between Trenton and Camden, and in cities like Elizabeth and Jersey City on the Hudson. People began moving from their rural farms to work alongside millions of European immigrants in the factories of Newark, Paterson, and Elizabeth. The age of telecommunications was born when Samuel Morse developed the telegraph at the Speedwell estate in Morristown in 1838. Nearby in Menlo Park, Thomas Edison was hard at work in his "invention factory," where the prolific inventor created the phonograph, the incandescent light bulb, the motion picture camera, and the first system of manufacturing and distributing electricity. Today New Jersey is known as the Workshop of the Nation, just behind Texas in chemical production, and first in the country for pharmaceuticals and cleaners. Many of the state's 4 million workers are employed at some of the world's top petrochemical industries, high-tech computer labs, corporate world headquarters, and research facilities like Bell Labs. Pharmaceutical giants Johnson & Johnson, Bristol-Myers Squibb, Merck, and Hoffmann-La Roche produce medications for diabetes, AIDS, cancer, and heart disease.

To guide you through all of this diversity, we've organized New Jersey into six regions: the Northeastern Gateway nearest New York City; the rural lake-studded hills of Northern New Jersey; the long and scenic Delaware River valley; the Central New Jersey region; and the Central Seacoast and the Southern Shore regions, covering the state's famous shoreline. Each has its own unique flavor, as you'll find.

The Northeastern Gateway is the sprawling metropolitan region where most New Jersey residents live, a heavily industrialized area just across the Hudson River from Manhattan. Here the suburbs and the state's largest cities are linked by a seemingly endless web of interstates and overpasses. Newark Liberty International Airport is one of the busiest airports in America; Newark and Elizabeth are massive seaports, each handling more cargo than New York City. Their gritty harbor terminals greet visitors arriving from New York, as does the industrial swath of factories and smokestacks that follows the New Jersey Turnpike through the region. This is the image that many people unfortunately assign to the entire state.

This region can't deny its connection to New York City. Many residents commute to jobs in Manhattan every day, and the dramatic skyline seems to be everywhere, from Frank Sinatra Park in Hoboken to Liberty State Park in Jersey City, where ferries shuttle visitors into New York Harbor to see the Statue of Liberty and Ellis Island. There's much to offer travelers. Ethnic eateries abound in places like Washington Street in Hoboken and the Ironbound District in Newark. The Newark Museum owns the largest holding of Tibetan art in the Western Hemisphere, the Montclair Art Museum has a fine collection of 19th-century American landscape paintings, and historic sites like Paterson's Lambert Castle and Elizabeth's Boxwood Hall satisfy history buffs. Madison is home to one of the top Shakespeare theaters in the country; Union City hosts the nation's longest-running Passion Play; and the State Theatre in New Brunswick, the New Jersey Performing Arts Center in Newark, and the Paper Mill Playhouse in Millburn offer top-flight performances. Those visitors flock to Newark's Branch Brook Park in springtime to see the profusion of cherry blossoms that is bigger than the famous display in

Washington, DC. Visitors wishing to escape the crowds can explore the rugged Palisades, the dramatic cliffs along the Hudson River that are laced with miles of hiking trails, go birding in the vast Hackensack Meadows and Great Swamp National Wildlife Refuge, or hike the forested reservations in the suburbs of Essex County. Polished enclaves like Summit and Montclair, with grand turn-of-the-20th-century mansions built by merchants who made their fortunes in New York City, also offer fine dining and worthwhile attractions of their own.

Northern New Jersey is one of the state's biggest surprises, a rural region of high rolling farmland and rugged wooded mountain ridges. Here is Lake Hopatcong, the state's largest at 4 square miles; High Point, New Jersey's aptly named highest peak at 1,803 feet; and the magnificent Delaware Water Gap National Recreation Area, a spectacular gorge along the Delaware River and a mecca for camping, hiking, canoeing, and fishing. Historic sites include colonial-era iron forges at Ringwood Manor and Long Pond Ironworks, picturesque wineries that welcome visitors to tour the vineyards and sample their vintages, and organic farms where you can pick your own fruits, vegetables, flowers, and herbs. Two off-the-beaten-path gems that shouldn't be missed are the New Jersey State Botanical Garden, a lovely oasis tucked high in the wooded hills at Ringwood State Park; and Layton Village, one of the country's top fine-crafts schools in a serene rural setting. You can easily spend a couple of days in the Morristown area, exploring its historic homes, museums, Revolutionary War sites, and Fosterfields, a 19th-century living-history farm.

In the Delaware River valley, historic towns like Milford, Frenchtown, Stockton, and Lambertville started as trading posts and commercial centers for surrounding farms. Today they are charming and upscale weekend destinations, strung like jewels along the riverbank, their streets lined with historic inns, art galleries, antiques shops, and trendy bistros and coffeehouses. Their outskirts remain delightfully rural, where crop fields, barns, and winding back roads punctuate the hills. In Trenton, the state capital since 1790, visitors can tour the grand gold-domed state house, get a fix on military history at the Old Barracks, and stroll the outdoor galleries at the eclectic Grounds for Sculpture. Camden is an industrial city shaped by its proximity to Philadelphia just across the river. Joseph Campbell started the Campbell Soup Company here in the late 19th century, selling canned condensed soup made from locally grown meats and vegetables. Walt Whitman spent the last years of his life in Camden, where he entertained the literary stars of his day and often wandered the streets of his beloved city. His house is open to visitors, who can also check out Adventure Aquarium (formerly the New Jersey State Aquarium) and Pomona Hall, a fine local-history museum run by the Camden County Historical Society.

Parts of the quiet Delaware Bay region draw comparisons to rural New England. It's also the least-populated and least-visited part of the entire state. Old-fashioned towns like Salem and Greenwich, where 18th-century residents staged their own equivalent of the Boston Tea Party in the village square, are full of well-preserved historic homes and surrounded by wide-open expanses of farmland dotted with small communities. Bridgeton has the state's largest historic district, with more than 2,000 Colonial, Federalist, and Victorian homes and buildings. The region is also known for its rich maritime heritage, from the history of oystering on the bay to the grand mansions built by prosperous sea captains along the Maurice River in Mauricetown, another New England–like village. In Bivalve, visitors can board the *A. J. Meerwald,* an authentically restored oyster schooner and New Jersey's official tall ship, for peaceful sails on Delaware Bay.

In Central New Jersey, the home of Ivy League Princeton University offers all the usual amenities one expects to find in a college town: friendly coffeehouses, interesting shops, a great bookstore, lively pubs, and restaurants offering everything from pancakes and tempeh to haute French cuisine and sushi. You can tour the noteworthy collections at the Princeton Art Museum; explore Drumthwacket, the official New Jersey governor's residence; and watch regattas on Lake Carnegie, the university's private lake built by industrialist Andrew Carnegie so that Princeton's crew teams could have a decent place to row. At more than a million acres, the Pinelands National Reserve is the largest expanse of wilderness between Boston and Washington, DC. The sandy-bottomed forest of white cedar, pitch pine, swamps, and cranberry bogs starts in the central part of the state and covers much of South Jersey. For visitors, it offers hiking trails, a preserved farming and ironworks village, a re-created glass factory and the country's largest glass museum at Wheaton Village, and creeks and rivers for fishing and paddling. It's home to the fabled New Jersey Devil (no, it's not just a hockey team), the part-man, part-horse creature that supposedly resides deep in the forest; and a massive 17-trillion-gallon underground aquifer, one of the largest in the world, containing pure glacial water.

The Jersey Shore remains the popular tourist destination that it has been since the 1800s, when boardwalks and grand hotels were built up and down the coast. Every summer millions of families, couples, and young singles go "down the shore" to the beaches and barrier islands that stretch from Sandy Hook to Cape May, strung with dozens of shore towns, all unique in flavor.

The Central Seacoast region is like a montage of diverse images woven together, from crowded boardwalks, surfers, and tacky souvenir shops to lovely Victorian neighborhoods and white-sand beaches and dunes. The region starts at the Sandy Hook peninsula, with its historic military fortification and the oldest working lighthouse in America; following that is Long Branch, the turn-of-the-20th-century "summer White House" to several U.S. presidents that's now an urban shore community; the hip town of Red Bank, with a historic downtown on the Navesink River filled with antiques shops, boutiques, jazz clubs, and trendy bistros; Asbury Park, whose boardwalk and Stone Pony rock club were put on the map by Bruce Springsteen; the historic Methodist summer community of Ocean Grove, now a charming family-friendly Victorian resort; the amusement-packed boardwalks of Point Pleasant Beach and Seaside Heights; and Long Beach Island, where the Barnegat Lighthouse, or "Old Barney," has stood sentry over Barnegat Inlet since the 19th century. Its distinctive red-and-white-banded light tower is a popular subject of artists and photographers, and beckons the adventurous to climb its 217 steps for a commanding view of the Atlantic.

The Southern Shore region starts in Atlantic City, the famous casino city that was America's first resort and continues to be one of the most-visited destinations in the country. Eleven gambling palaces offer thousands of slot machines and gaming tables for those who come seeking fortune on the casino floor. The city that has hosted the Miss America Pageant from the 1920s until 2005 and whose streets inspired the board game Monopoly offers many options for its nongambling visitors. There's swimming and sunbathing on wide sandy beaches, the only ones in the state—along with Wildwood's—that are free; strolling on the old-time wooden boardwalk; and exploring Absecon Lighthouse. Nearby in Margate City, Lucy the

Elephant has been drawing curious visitors to the unique pachyderm-shaped structure since 1881.

To the south, Ocean City is a bustling family-friendly resort with an 8-mile beach and summer concerts on the boardwalk's music pier; Wildwood is known for its rollicking amusement piers, incredibly wide beaches, and the largest collection of 1950s-era doo-wop architecture in America. Cape May attracts hordes of birders who come to witness the spectacular pageant of tens of thousands of shorebirds, songbirds, and raptors during their spring and fall migrations. Most visitors, however, come to see one of America's largest collections of Victoriana, and to dine in some of the state's best gourmet restaurants. The entire resort is a historic district of more than 600 beautifully restored turn-of-the-20th-century homes, many of which are elegant inns and bed & breakfasts that welcome guests.

There are a number of quiet corners for those wishing to get away from the noise and neon of the amusement piers or the height-of-summer beach crowds—places like Island Beach State Park, one of the last remaining pristine barrier beaches on the East Coast; and Barnegat Bay, whose quiet waters border an intricate coastline of inlets, salt marshes, and shallow tidal creeks, perfect for kayaking, birding, and crabbing for blue claws. The 40,000-acre Edwin B. Forsythe National Wildlife Refuge stretches along the coast from Barnegat to Atlantic City, and is open to motorists, paddlers, and cyclists. The Cape May peninsula is blanketed in wildlife refuges and bird sanctuaries, pockets of beauty that welcome nature lovers all year, and perfect places to discover the natural glories that New Jersey has to offer.

ACKNOWLEDGMENTS

We are grateful to everyone who contributed their expertise, suggestions, and advice on various parts of New Jersey. We rely on countless people—from tourism directors to New Jerseyans we meet in our travels—who each offered something that found its way into the book. It would be impossible to name them all, but each gave us the benefit of their knowledge in a wide variety of subjects, from taffy shops along the Jersey Shore to organic farms in the Highlands.

For their contributions, we owe thanks to Barbara W. Steele of Ocean County Public Affairs, Susan Ricciardi of the Atlantic City Convention and Visitors Authority, Carmen Gonzales of the South Jersey Tourism Corporation, Jeanne DeYoung of the Monmouth County Department of Economic Development and Tourism, Jenn Heinold of the Mid-Atlantic Center for the Arts in Cape May, Donna Csolak of the Garden State Wine Growers Association, Lois Hetfield of the Ocean Grove Chamber of Commerce, Dana Loschiavo of the New Jersey Department of Environmental Protection, and Beverly Trapp of the Greater Wildwoods Tourism Improvement and Development Authority.

At The Countryman Press, we are indebted to Lisa Sacks for her tremendous patience and guidance through the editing and production process. Thanks also to Kermit Hummel, Fred Lee, and Gail Cohen for help with this revised edition, and to Clare Innes, Kelly Thompson, and Jennifer Thompson, who guided the first edition. All of you helped make this book possible.

WHAT'S WHERE IN NEW JERSEY

AREA CODES New Jersey has nine area codes: Area codes **201** and **551** serve the Northeastern Gateway region; **609** covers the Southern Shore region, including Atlantic City, the Wildwoods, and Cape May, as well as portions of the Delaware Bay and Pinelands regions, Princeton, and Trenton; **732** and **848** serve the central shoreline, and parts of central New Jersey and the Gateway region; **856** covers the Pinelands, Delaware Bay, and the Camden region; **908** serves the northern New Jersey region; **973** and **862** are the area codes for northern New Jersey as far east as Newark.

AGRICULTURAL FAIRS The **Agricultural Fair Association of New Jersey** (www.njagfairs.com) publishes an online directory of 20 old-fashioned county fairs with agricultural exhibits, carnival rides, animals, live entertainment, food, and midway games held throughout the state from May to September. The **Warren County Farmers' Fair** in Harmony has been an annual event in northern New Jersey for 75 years, with tractor pulls, horse shows, and hot-air balloons. There are also two state fairs: In Sussex County, the **New Jersey State Fair** in Augusta is a traditional country fair; **State Fair Meadowlands** is a 2-week-long fair at the Meadowlands Sports Complex in East Rutherford in July.

AIRPORTS AND AIRLINES
Newark Liberty International Airport (973-961-6000; parking information: 888-397-4636; www.panynj.com) in Newark is New Jersey's largest airport, served by more than 40 major carriers, including American Airlines (800-433-7300), British Airways (800-247-9297), Continental Airlines (800-525-0280), Delta Airlines (800-221-1212), United Airlines (800-241-6522), and US Airways (800-428-4322). **AirTrain Newark** (888-397-4636; www.airtrainnewark.com) provides rail service between airport terminals and mass transit, including New Jersey Transit and Amtrak trains as well as New York and Newark's Penn Stations. **Atlantic City International Airport** (609-645-7895; www.acairport.com), Exit 9 on the Atlantic City Expressway in southern New Jersey, is served by Spirit Airlines (800-772-7117). Out-of-state options near the Northeastern Gateway region include **John F. Kennedy International Airport** (718-244-4444; www.kennedyairport.com) and **LaGuardia International Airport** (718-533-3400; www.laguardiaairport.com) in New York City. **Philadelphia International Airport** (215-937-6937; www.philadelphia-phl

18

.com) in Pennsylvania is near western New Jersey. Click on **www.njaviation.com** for a complete list of the state's local, regional, and international airports.

AMUSEMENT PARKS New Jersey's largest and best-known amusement park is **Six Flags Great Adventure** (732-928-1821; www.sixflags.com) on Route 537 in Jackson, with rides and attractions in the theme park, waterslides at Hurricane Harbor, and exotic animals at Wild Safari. Others include **Mountain Creek Waterpark** (973-827-2000; www.mountaincreekwaterpark.com) in Vernon, **Tomahawk Lake** (973-398-7777; www.tomahawklake.com) in Sparta, **Fantasy Island Amusement Park** (609-492-4000; www.fantasyislandpark.com) in Beach Haven, and **Clementon Amusement Park and Splash World** (856-783-0263; www.clementonpark.com) in Clementon. Several parks cater specifically to families with young children, including **Wild West City** (973-347-8900; www.wildwestcity.com) in Netcong, **Land of Make Believe** (908-459-9000; www.lomb.com) in Hope, and **Storybook Land** (609-641-7847; www.storybookland.com) in Cardiff. **Point Pleasant Beach, Seaside Heights,** and **Wildwood** are some of the resort towns along the Jersey Shore that sport their own amusement piers on the boardwalk.

ANTIQUING Antiques dealers and shops are found virtually throughout New Jersey, but certain regions—in particular the towns of **Frenchtown** and **Lambertville** on the Delaware River, **Mullica Hill** in the Delaware Bay region, and **Red Bank** near the Jersey Shore—have many antiques shops in concentrated areas. In addition, New Jersey has a variety of antiques marketplaces, auctions, and flea markets where collectors and browsers can conveniently see merchandise from a variety of dealers in one location. For listings of statewide antiques dealers and a calendar of antiques shows and events, click on **www.newjerseyantiques.net**.

APPALACHIAN TRAIL The 2,174-mile-long **Appalachian National Scenic Trail** runs through New Jersey and 13 other states on its route from Mount Katahdin in Maine to Georgia's Springer Mountain. The 72.4-mile New Jersey section is more rugged and remote than one might expect from the nation's most densely populated state, and has an active bear population. The white-blazed trail—or "AT" as hikers call it—crosses the Delaware River on the busy Delaware Bridge between New Jersey and Pennsylvania, and winds along trout streams, through hemlock ravines, and across rocky ridges on its way to New York State. Particular sections of the trail like the **Delaware Water Gap National Recreation Area, Sunfish Pond,** and **Mohican Point** with its 360-degree panorama are extremely popular with day- and weekend hikers. For more information, contact the **Appalachian Trail Conservancy** (304-535-6331; www.appalachiantrail.org), 799 Washington St., P.O. Box 807, Harpers Ferry, WV 25425-0807.

AQUARIUMS The state's largest is **Adventure Aquarium** (856-283-0545; www.adventureaquarium.com), in Camden (formerly the New Jersey State Aquarium). The city's riverfront aquarium boasts a West African river exhibit with hippos and crocodiles, a shark tank with a 40-foot walk-through tunnel, a 760,000-gallon Deep Atlantic Open Ocean Tank that is home to two-dozen sharks, as well as sea turtles and stingrays; and some 80 permanent exhibits featuring seals, penguins, and thousands of fish. **Jenkinson's Aquarium** (732-892-0600; www.jenkinsons.com/aquarium) on the boardwalk in Point Pleasant Beach has sharks, seals, penguins, and a touch tank. The **Ocean Life Center** at Historic Gardner's Basin (609-348-2880; www.oceanlifecenter.com) in Atlantic City is a fisherman's museum and educational marine center with a shark- and tropical fish–filled aquarium, touch tanks, and interactive exhibits.

ART MUSEUMS The **Princeton University Art Museum** (609-258-3788; www.artmuseum.princeton.edu) holds the university's topflight collection, with 60,000 works of art that span centuries. At the shore, **Noyes Museum of Art** (609-652-8848; www.noyesmuseum.org) in Oceanville contains exhibits of contemporary art, American folk art, and crafts. In Clinton, **Hunterdon Museum of Art** (908-735-8415; www.hunterdonartmuseum.org) is a 19th-century gristmill on the Raritan River, with three galleries of contemporary art. The **African Art Museum of the Society of African Missions** (201-894-8611; www.smafathers.org) in Tenafly has a unique collection of art and crafts from sub-Saharan Africa. The **Hiram Blauvelt Art Museum** (201-261-0012; www.blauveltmuseum.com) in Oradell is one man's collection of wildlife art and big game. The **Newark Museum** (973-596-6550; www.newarkmuseum.org) in Newark isn't devoted exclusively to art, but boasts the largest collection of Tibetan art and artifacts in the Western Hemisphere and one of America's top collections of 18th- to 20th-century American art. In Montclair, the **Montclair Art Museum** (973-746-5555; www.montclairartmuseum.org) is New Jersey's first public museum, with a noted collection of

American Indian art and artifacts. Rutgers University has on its campus in New Brunswick the **Jane Voorhees Zimmerli Art Museum** (732-932-7237; www.zimmerlimuseum.rutgers.edu), which displays American and European art.

ARTS COUNCILS Jersey Arts (1-800-843-2787; www.jerseyarts.com) is a comprehensive online guide to arts and culture in New Jersey, with events listings, links to local and national arts organizations, and information on artists who live and work in New Jersey. **South Jersey Cultural Alliance** (609-645-2760; 888-704-7522; www.sjca.net) publishes a comprehensive listing of arts and cultural events and sites in eight South Jersey counties, from ecotourism and historical sites to theater, music festivals, museums, and galleries.

BALLOONING Scenic hot-air balloon rides are available year-round throughout New Jersey, and many are concentrated in rural Hunterdon County, in communities like **Clinton, Whitehouse Station,** and **Readington.** Flights generally begin around sunrise or sunset, when the wind is calmest, and last about an hour. Most companies suggest you make a reservation well in advance; weekend-evening flights tend to be the most popular. The annual summertime **Quick Chek Festival of Ballooning** (800-468-2479; www.balloonfestival.com) in Readington features more than 100 hot-air balloons plus entertainment and fireworks. Check the index, or look under *To Do—Ballooning* in relevant chapters for companies in a particular region.

BEACHES New Jersey's 127-mile shoreline is a lively jumble of boardwalk amusements, pristine natural areas, and white-sand beaches stretching along the Atlantic Ocean, beloved by surfers, anglers, beachcombers, and sunbathers. The northernmost ocean beach on the shoreline is in **Gateway National Recreation Area—Sandy Hook Unit,** Fort Hancock (732-872-5970); **Island Beach State Park** (732-793-0506) in Seaside Park is a 10-mile swath of untouched sand dunes between the Atlantic Ocean and Barnegat Bay. More than 30 of the state's town beaches charge entrance fees; the beaches in Atlantic City and the Wildwoods, however, are free. New Jersey beaches aren't considered an exotic vacation destination, but they are within driving distance of millions of people. The best times to drive to the shore during the summer are late Friday evening or very early on Saturday morning. The heaviest beach-bound traffic is Friday after work until around 10 PM; avoid traveling to the shore on Saturday from 9 AM to 3 PM. Dogs are prohibited from most New Jersey beaches from May to September. For information on local beaches, including access fees and regulations, contact the local municipal clerk's office. Most communities require beachgoers to purchase a badge for access to their beaches.

BED & BREAKFASTS B&Bs throughout New Jersey include charming Colonial farmhouses, ornate Victorian homes, and elegant mansions that welcome overnight visitors. B&Bs can be found along the shoreline and the Delaware River, in the northern rural hills, and in historic towns scattered throughout the state. The **B&B Innkeepers Association of New Jersey** (732-449-3535; 866-449-3535; www.njinns.com), P.O. Box 108, Spring Lake 07762, publishes a directory with brief descriptions of more than 80 B&Bs and inns around the state.

BICYCLING The **New Jersey Department of Transportation** (www.state.nj.us/transportation) publishes a series of full-color guides to rides throughout the state that can be downloaded from their Web site, where you can also order a water-resistant version. Other free materials include information on New Jersey paths and rail-trails, cycling clubs, bike events, and bike commuting tips. Before setting out on your own, drop by a local bike shop for supplies, repairs, advice on planning a route, or information on local group rides.

BIRDING The Pinelands, the Delaware Bay region, and the southern shore are prime areas for bird-watching in New Jersey, especially during the spring and fall migrations. The vast expanses of hardwood swamps and salt marshes along the Delaware River, like those in Tuckahoe's **Lester G. MacNamara Wildlife Management Area** (609-628-3219), are a busy feeding and resting ground for bald eagles, peregrine falcons, and hundreds of other bird species. Birders from around the country come to the Cape May region in May, when birds feast on horseshoe crab eggs at **Higbee Beach Wildlife Management Area** (609-628-2103). Hawks and owls live in the woods and fields of **Assunpink Wildlife Management Area** (609-259-2132), one of the top bird-watching areas in central New Jersey. Just outside of Atlantic City, the 44,000-acre **Edwin B. Forsythe National Wildlife Refuge** (609-652-1665) is a pristine swath of islands, bays, and inlets on the Atlantic Flyway, the route for tens of thousands of migrating birds. Herons and egrets nest at the **Stone Harbor Bird Sanctuary** (609-368-5102), the only municipally funded heronry in America. Also in Stone Harbor, the **Wetlands Institute**

(609-368-1211) leads guided birding walks through coastal wetlands and upland marshes. Just to the south, Cape May is a premier birding center. During the summer, hundreds of bird species nest at the **Cape May Bird Observatory** (609-884-2736; birding hotline: 609-898-2473), which sponsors the New Jersey Audubon Society's **World Series of Birding,** a popular 24-hour birding contest. Many birds pass through **Cape May Point State Park** (609-884-2159), where fall is the best time to observe the migration of waterfowl, raptors, shorebirds, and songbirds. The **New Jersey Audubon Society** (908-204-8998; www.nj audubon.org) works to raise environmental awareness and protect New Jersey's wildlife and natural habitats. The society maintains nine staffed nature centers throughout the state; they are described in each chapter.

BOARDWALKS Atlantic City, Ocean City, Wildwood, Point Pleasant Beach, and other resort towns on the Jersey Shore are famous for their long wooden boardwalks, each with a unique flavor. Some, like in **Seaside Heights,** are virtual kiddie amusement parks offering a barrage of activities, kitschy souvenir shops, food stands, and carnival rides. Others, like the one in historic **Ocean Grove,** are quiet and charming beachfront walkways perfect for leisurely strolls.

BOATING New Jersey offers many opportunities for boating on lakes, ponds, rivers, and the Atlantic Ocean. The New Jersey Department of Environmental Protection's **Division of Fish and Wildlife** (609-292-2965; www.njfishandwildlife.com) has information on boating on inland and tidal waterways, including a list of boat access sites. Children under 17 operating a boat must complete a boating safety course; anyone operating a

motorized boat on inland waters must be licensed. All motorboats must be registered with the Department of Motor Vehicles.

BUS SERVICES Greyhound (800-231-2222; www.greyhound.com) serves more than a dozen communities at terminals and at stops with limited services: Newark, Ho-Ho-Kus, Ridgewood, Mahwah, Waldwick, Ramsey, Somerville, Paramus, and Hackettstown in northern New Jersey; Camden, Trenton, Mount Laurel, and Atlantic City in the southern regions. **Peter Pan** (800-343-9999; www.peterpanbus.com) stops in Camden, Mount Laurel, and Newark. **New Jersey Transit** (973-275-5555; 800-955-2321; www.nj transit.com) provides local bus service on nearly 200 routes around the state.

CAMPING For a free campground map and guidebook of New Jersey's public and private campgrounds and RV parks, contact the **New Jersey Campground Owners Association** (609-465-8444; 800-222-6765; www .njcampgrounds.com;), 29 Cooks Beach Rd., Cape May Court House, NJ 08210. There are 19 state forests, parks, and recreation areas with camping facilities for tents and trailers; these public campgrounds do not provide hook-ups. Several of them offer furnished rental cabins, with running water, electricity, bathrooms, kitchens, and fireplaces or wood-burning stoves. Others offer lean-tos, rustic wilderness campsites, and yurts—circular, wood-framed tents with a wood floor and deck. For information and reservations regarding these sites, contact the state park or forest directly. Pets are not allowed in state camping facilities.

CANOEING AND KAYAKING A number of outfitters offer guided kayak and canoe tours, while others have boat rentals available; they are described in each chapter. Rentals are also available at some state parks. For information, contact the **Department of Environmental Protection, Division of Parks and Forestry** (609-984-0370; 800-843-6420), P.O. Box 402, Trenton 08625-0402.

CASINOS More than 30 million visitors descend on Atlantic City every year, the majority of whom come to try their luck at one of the 11 casinos at this world-famous Jersey Shore gambling mecca. They are **Atlantic City Hilton Casino Resort** (609-347-7111; www.hiltonac.com), **Bally's Atlantic City** (609-340-2000; www.ballysac .com), **Borgata Hotel Casino and Spa** (609-317-1000; www.theborgata .com), **Caesars Atlantic City** (609-348-4411; www.caesarsac.com), **Harrah's Atlantic City Casino Hotel** (609-441-5000; www.harrahs.com), **Resorts Casino Hotel** (609-344-6000; www.resortsac.com), **Showboat Casino Hotel** (609-343-4000; www.harrahs .com), **Tropicana Casino and Resort** (609-340-4000; www.tropicana.net), **Trump Marina Hotel & Casino** (609-441-2000; www.trumpmarina .com), **Trump Plaza Hotel and Casino** (609-441-6000; www.trumpplaza .com), and **Trump Taj Mahal Casino Resort** (609-449-1000; www.trumptaj .com).

CHILDREN, ESPECIALLY FOR Throughout this book the ✐ symbol designates child-friendly attractions, lodgings, dining, and special events. Kids love boats and trains, especially the antique steam-powered **Pine Creek Railroad** (732-938-5542) in Allaire State Park and the **Black River & Western Railroad** (908-782-9600), which runs between Ringoes and Flemington. Also in Flemington, **Northlandz** (908-782-4022) is billed as the world's largest model train

exhibit, with a life-sized working steam train. In Bivalve, kids can sail on the restored oyster schooner *A. J. Meerwald* (856-785-2060), New Jersey's official tall ship. Jersey City's **Circle Line Ferry** (201-435-9499) to Ellis Island and the Statue of Liberty is another child pleaser. New Jersey's minor-league ballparks cater to kids. The **New Jersey Jackals** (973-746-3131) play **Yogi Berra Stadium** at Montclair State University in Little Falls (the **Yogi Berra Museum** is a good stop before the game). The **Somerset Patriots** (908-252-0700) play in an old-fashioned ballpark in Bridgewater. In Trenton, the **Trenton Thunder** (609-394-3300) has New Jersey's only minor-league stadium with a hand-operated scoreboard. A vintage-looking brick stadium on the Delaware River is home to the **Camden Riversharks** (856-963-2600), and at **Lakewood BlueClaws** (732-901-7000) home games, spectators can picnic on the outfield lawn. For a peek at living history, **Howell Living History Farm** (609-737-3299) in Titusville is an old-fashioned horse-powered farm with a lively barnyard, and demonstrations like spring planting, cider making, and maple sugaring. **Wild West City** (973-347-8900) in Netcong looks like 19th-century Dodge City, Kansas, with live action shows, stagecoach rides, and gold panning. Kids can watch bull riding, steer wrestling, and barrel racing at the **Cowtown Rodeo** (856-769-3200) in Pilesgrove. Museums designed just for children, with fun hands-on exhibits and make-believe play stations, include Cherry Hill's **Garden State Discovery Museum** (856-424-1233) and the **New Jersey Children's Museum** (201-262-5151) in Paramus. **Liberty Science Center** (201-200-1000) in Jersey City has more than 250 interactive exhibits on health, the environment, and inventions—and the largest IMAX dome screen in the country. New Jersey's rugged northern hills comprise the "Fluorescent Mineral Capital of the World," with two rock and mineral museums: **Franklin Mineral Museum** (973-827-3481) in Franklin and **Sterling Hill Mining Museum** (973-209-7212) in Ogdensburg, where you can explore a real underground zinc mine. At the shore, **Ripley's Believe It or Not! Museum** (609-347-2001) in Atlantic City features Robert Ripley's infamously bizarre collection of unusual finds. Nearby, **Lucy the Elephant** (609-823-6473) is a 65-foot-tall national historic landmark, and the only elephant statue of its size in the world. Live animals can be seen in their natural surroundings at **Turtle Back Zoo** (973-731-5800) in West Orange, the largest zoo in northern New Jersey, and at **Space Farms Zoo and Museum** (973-875-5800) in Sussex, the most extensive private collection of North American wildlife in the world. Other zoos include Paramus's **Bergen County Zoo** (201-262-3771) with a walk-through aviary and a 19th-century farmyard; **Popcorn Park Zoo** (609-693-1900) in Forked River, **Cape May County Park and Zoo** (609-465-5271) in Cape May Courthouse, and **Cohanzick Zoo** (856-455-3230) in Bridgeton. **Adventure Aquarium** (856-365-3300) in Camden is home to two-dozen sharks, thousands of fish, and rare South African penguins. **Jenkinson's Aquarium** (732-899-1659) at Point Pleasant Beach and the **Ocean Life Center** (609-348-2880) in Atlantic City have aquariums, touch tanks, and interactive exhibits. The Jersey Shore boardwalks are lined with kid-friendly attractions: **Jenkinson's Pavilion and Amusement Park** (732-892-0600) at Point Pleasant Beach has arcades, rides, and bumper cars; the **Seaside Park Boardwalk**

(732-914-0100) boasts an antique carousel and carnival games; **Funtown Amusement Pier's Tower of Fear** (732-830-7437) is the tallest ride on the Jersey Shore; **Atlantic City's Steel Pier** (609-345-4893) is lined with food stands, rides, and games; **Gillian's Wonderland Pier** (609-399-7082) in Ocean City has dozens of tame rides catering to children and families; and **Morey's Piers and Water Parks** (609-522-3900) in Wildwood has it all, from roller coasters to carousels. Off the boards, **Six Flags Great Adventure** (732-928-1821) in Jackson has extreme rides for the older kids, **Bugs Bunny Land** and the **Looney Tunes Seaport** for the younger set; **Clementon Amusement Park** (856-783-0263) in Clementon has a nostalgic antique carousel, classic Ferris wheel, and one of the longest log flume rides in the country; and **Mountain Creek Waterpark** (973-827-2000) in Vernon has whitewater tubing rides for big kids, **Half Pint Harbor** for the little ones. A few old-fashioned theme parks cater to families with very young children. **Land of Make Believe** (908-459-9000) in Hope has low-key carnival rides, a water park, and a petting zoo, and **Storybook Land** (609-641-7847) in Cardiff is an amusement park with a collection of whimsical storybook-themed buildings.

CLIMATE New Jersey is one of the smallest states in the nation, but its climate varies widely, from the cool Kittatinny Mountains in the north, the mild Delaware Bay region in the south, and the moderate temperatures along the shoreline. In the Northern Highlands, where elevations reach 1,800 feet, it snows an average of 40 to 50 inches from mid-October to April, and temperatures are about 10 degrees colder than on the coast. The south receives only 10 to 15 inches of snowfall from mid-November to mid-April. Sea breezes off the Atlantic keep the temperature flux on the Jersey Shore in check, with cooler summers and warmer winters than in interior regions. In the vast interior known as the Pine Barrens, the scrub pine and oak forest with its sandy soil (which doesn't absorb sunlight) keeps the air cool and dry.

COLLEGES AND UNIVERSITIES

For information on the state's colleges and universities, contact the **New Jersey Commission on Higher Education** (609-292-4310; www.state.nj.us/highereducation), 20 West State St., P.O. Box 542, Trenton 08625-0542. The commission publishes a comprehensive online directory of New Jersey's 56 state colleges and universities, independent 4-year institutions, theological seminaries, and community colleges.

COTTAGE RENTALS

Most cottage rentals in New Jersey are in the shore towns along the 127-mile Atlantic coastline, although others can be found on the shores of the state's many lakes and ponds, especially in the northern hills. Contact the tourism organizations listed under *Guidance* in each chapter, or real estate agents in the region you plan to visit.

CRAFTS

The **Peters Valley Craft Education Center** (973-948-5200; www.petersvalley.org) in Layton is a nationally known school for fine craftsmanship in the picturesque Delaware Water Gap National Recreation area. In spring and summer, instructors lead seminars and intensive workshops for beginner to advanced students who want to learn about and create fine crafts, from photography and ceramics to blacksmithing and woodworking. One of the largest crafts shows in

America is held here in September. The gallery and gift store feature contemporary crafts, on display and for sale, by more than 300 artists from around the country. In Madison, the **Museum of Early Trades and Crafts** (973-377-2982) mounts exhibits and workshops on 18th- and 19th-century craftsmen and craftswomen, and hosts special crafts events and demonstrations for children.

DINERS

New Jersey is the unofficial Diner Capital of the World, an homage to the classic late-night eateries that sprang up along the state's roadsides when the phenomenon spread up and down the East Coast. To travelers, diners promise a quick cup of joe or a cheap, hearty meal. New Jersey's glowing neon and polished chrome diners are living postcards from 1950s America, with streamlined exteriors typical of the era's futuristic designs. Inside, customers sit in Naugahyde booths or at Formica-topped counters, and hash browns, meatloaf, and lemon meringue pie are still on the menu. Many of the prefab roadside eateries were built in New Jersey and wound up alongside the state's highways (a few companies here still manufacture them). Some of the 2,000 or so diners once in New Jersey still survive, serving up old-fashioned home-style cooking as they have for decades, notably: Jersey City's **White Manna Hamburgers, Forked River Diner** in Forked River, **Short Stop Diner** in Bloomfield, **Mastori's Diner** in Bordentown, **Tick-Tock Diner** in Clifton, and **Burlington Diner** in Burlington. For more information on these Garden State icons, click on www.njdiners.com.

EMERGENCIES

Call **911** from anywhere in New Jersey in an emergency. Hospital and emergency numbers are listed at the beginning of each chapter.

EQUESTRIAN SPORTS The horse is New Jersey's official state animal, and the history of equestrian sports here is long. **Freehold Raceway** (732-462-3800; www.freeholdraceway .com) in Freehold dates to the 19th century; today it has live daytime harness racing for pacers and trotters as well as simulcast races from tracks around the country. In Oceanport, **Monmouth Park Racetrack** (732-222-5100; www.monmouthpark.com) has live and simulcast thoroughbred racing. The million-dollar **Haskell Invitational Thoroughbred Race** in August draws some 50,000 spectators to see the world's top champions. **Meadowlands Racetrack** (201-935-8500; www.meadowlandsracetrack .com) in East Rutherford is known for its live world-class harness racing, particularly the **Hambletonian Festival of Racing,** whose $1.7 million purse makes this the highest-stakes trotting race in the world. The headquarters of the **United States Equestrian Team** (908-234-1251) is in Gladstone, with an Olympic training facility and a summertime **Festival of Champions** horse show that attracts the world's best Olympic-caliber riders, and horses that compete in show jumping, dressage, driving, and other events in a country fair atmosphere. In Allentown, the **Horse Park of New Jersey** (609-984-4389; www.horseparkof newjersey.com) hosts the **Festival of Horses** in August, a popular family event.

EVENTS This guidebook lists a variety of regional special events at the end of each chapter. The **New Jersey Office of Travel and Tourism** (800-847-4865); www.visitnj.org) maintains an online events calendar and can mail travel literature that features events around the state.

FALL FOLIAGE The hills and forests of New Jersey put on a fiery autumn foliage display that rivals any in New England. Peak viewing is usually from early to mid-October in the higher northern elevations; by mid- to late October the central and southern regions are ablaze in vibrant color. Some of the best places for leaf peeping are in the state parks and forests; see the *Green Space* listings in each chapter. The **summit of High Point** (in High Point State Park), along the **Delaware and Raritan Canal** (from the Delaware River to New Brunswick), and **Pinelands National Reserve** are popular spots. The best way to see the spectacle is by exploring back roads. For twice-weekly updated foliage reports throughout the season, click on www.foliagenetwork.com; New Jersey is included in their Northeast United States report.

FARMER'S MARKETS There are more than 100 open-air farmer's markets scattered around New Jersey during the growing season, which usually runs from early summer to October. They are often held on Saturday and Sunday mornings, or on evenings during the week. The markets that were originally intended to provide local farmers with an additional source of income have provided an economic boost to many downtowns across the state. Their popularity in New Jersey is part of a nationwide revival, thanks to a growing interest in organic and locally grown produce. Strawberries, tomatoes, corn, asparagus, blueberries, eggplant, herbs, and lettuce are among the state's more prolific crops. For a comprehensive listing of all community farmer's markets in New Jersey, log onto the state **Department of Agriculture** Web site, www.state.nj.us/ jerseyfresh.

FERRIES In Jersey City, the **Statue of Liberty Ferry** (877-523-9849; www.statuecruises.com) provides service between Liberty State Park and the Statue of Liberty and Ellis Island. **New York Waterway** (800-533-3779; www.nywaterway.com) links Weehawken, Hoboken, and Jersey City to New York City. **Liberty Park Water Taxi** (201-985-8000) runs between Jersey City and Manhattan. **SeaStreak** (800-262-8743; www.seastreak.com) connects Atlantic Highlands and Highlands to New York City. On the Delaware River, **RiverLink Ferry** (215-925-5465; www.riverlinkferry.org) runs from mid-March to November between Adventure Aquarium in Camden and Penn's Landing in Philadelphia. **Three Forts Ferry** (302-834-7941; www.threeforts.com) operates from April to October, offering service from Fort Mott State Park in Pennsville to three historic forts along the Delaware River. On the Cape May peninsula, the **Cape May–Lewes Ferry** (800-643-3779; www.capemay lewesferry.com) is a toll ferry that connects Cape May to Lewes, Delaware, via Delaware Bay, and is popular with commuters and tourists.

FILM Hollywood may be synonymous with the film industry, but it all began in New Jersey. Thomas Edison invented the motion picture at his laboratory in West Orange and tested his equipment at the nation's first film studio, the Black Maria. Shortly thereafter, the silent-film industry was born in America's original Hollywood, Fort Lee, where by 1914 most American movies were made with stars like Mary Pickford and Paul Robeson. Screen legend Marlon Brando made Hoboken famous when he starred in *On the Waterfront*, which was shot at locations around the city. Jack Nicholson, Meryl Streep, Danny DeVito, and Susan Sarandon are all Garden State natives who went on to big-screen fame. Many movies and television shows are filmed here, including *Law & Order: SVU*, which shoots in North Bergen and other New Jersey locations. New Jersey native Kevin Smith is a well-known independent filmmaker who shot *Clerks* in Leonardo and *Jersey Girl*, in Paulsboro. South Orange native Zach Braff wrote, directed, and starred in *Garden State*, which he filmed in and around his hometown. The **New Jersey International Film Festival** (732-932-8482; www.njfilmfest.com) at Rutgers University in New Brunswick is a 2-month-long celebration of American independent films and international releases that includes film screenings and guest directors.

FISHING, INLAND There are more than 4,000 lakes, rivers, ponds, streams, and reservoirs in New Jersey. Inland waters are stocked with three-quarters of a million fish. A fishing license is required for residents aged 16 to 69, and all nonresidents 16 or older, who fish on inland waterways. Visitors can obtain the license in advance from the **New Jersey Division of Fish and Wildlife** (609-292-2965; www.njfishandwildlife.com); a trout stamp is required if you're planning to fish for trout. The **Pequest Trout Hatchery and Natural Resources Education Center** (908-637-4125) in Oxford raises hundreds of thousands of brook, rainbow, and brown trout each year for release in more than 200 of New Jersey's lakes and rivers. In addition to the hatchery, the education center has interactive exhibits and films on the state's natural resources.

FISHING, SALTWATER Tuna, **bluefish, Atlantic mackerel,** and **marlin** are some of the common species found in the Atlantic Ocean off the coast of New Jersey. Hundreds of charter- and party fishing boats are available to take anglers out on the open water on day trips to fish for **blues and bottom fish,** or on long-distance excursions for **cod, tuna,** and other species. For **party-boat and charter-boat services,** see the *To Do—Fishing* sections throughout this guidebook. *Party boats* are usually 60 to 100 feet long and carry 20 to 150 passengers; they accept anglers on an individual, first-come basis until the boat is filled. *Charter boats* are smaller vessels—most carry six to eight people, and are reserved by a group in advance. No license is required to fish in the Atlantic Ocean. **Surf fishing** for **striped bass** and **bluefish** is popular onshore. Information on tide charts, solar and lunar tables, marinas, and tackle shops, as well as a comprehensive list of New Jersey's party and charter boats is available from the **Department of Environmental Protection's Division of Fish and Wildlife** (609-292-2965; www.nj fishandwildlife.com). Crabbing and clamming are popular along New Jersey's 83 miles of bay shores. **Clamming** is allowed from June to September; a license is required. The season for **blue crabs** runs from mid-March to December, and varies depending on location. **Bay scallops, mussels,** and **oysters** can be harvested without a license.

GARDENS New Jersey earns its Garden State nickname in part from its wide variety of lovely botanical gardens, arboretums, and parks that boast stunning blooms, as well as numerous commercial flower and herb nurseries with their own winning displays. The **New Jersey State Botanical Garden** (973-962-9534; www.njbg.org) in Ringwood State Park is a 100-acre mountaintop oasis of formal borders, naturalized gardens, and European-

style parterres surrounding the magnificent Skylands Manor. In Upper Montclair's **Presby Memorial Iris Gardens** (973-783-5974; www .presbyirisgardens.org), more than 40,000 irises explode in a springtime profusion of color. Some of the species date to the 1500s. The **Reeves-Reed Arboretum** (908-273-8787; www .reeves-reedarboretum.org) in Summit features 12 acres of rose, herb, wildflower, daylily, and rock gardens in an estate setting. In Swainton, the highly regarded **Leaming's Run Botanical Gardens** (609-465-5871; www .leamingsrungardens.com) has the largest annual garden in the country. The **Garden Conservancy's Open Days program** (888-842-2442; www .gardenconservancy.org) provides the public with a rare glimpse of private New Jersey gardens each summer.

GOLF New Jersey has more than 200 golf courses, and more than 140 of them are open to the public. This guide describes only those courses that are open to the public. Click on www .njsga.org for the **New Jersey State Golf Association's** list of tournaments, courses, golf news, and volunteering opportunities. High-rated golf courses are found all over New Jersey, but the Atlantic City region has the state's top courses. The **Greater Atlantic City Golf Association** (800-465-3222; www.gacga.com) offers golf packages and advance tee times at nine public courses in the area, as well as maps and information about lodging and dining. For true golf aficionados, the **United States Golf Association Museum and Archives** (908-234-2300; www.usgamuseum.com) in Far Hills features exhibits on the history of golf, vintage golf equipment, and personal memorabilia from some of the game's greatest players.

HANDICAPPED ACCESS Throughout this book, the ঙ symbol indicates restaurants and lodgings that are handicapped accessible.

HIGHWAY TRAVEL New Jersey is served by three major toll roads. The **Garden State Parkway** (732-442-8600) runs north and south, paralleling the coast for 173 miles from the New York State Thruway to Cape May. The **New Jersey Turnpike** (732-247-0900) travels 137 miles from the northeast corner of the state at the George Washington Bridge to the Delaware Memorial Bridge in southeastern New Jersey. The 44-mile-long **Atlantic City Expressway** (609-965-6060) connects Atlantic City to Route 42 in Gloucester County, just east of the New Jersey Turnpike. Other major interstates include **287, 280, 80, 78,** and **195.** Contact the **New Jersey Division of Travel and Tourism** (800-847-4865; www.visitnj.org) to request a free official state driving map. For lane closures, holiday congestion, roadwork, or similar travel news regarding New Jersey highways, click on **www.nj commuter.com.**

HIKING AND WALKING There is a wealth of places to hike and walk in New Jersey, ranging from easy jaunts through coastal nature preserves along the shore to moderate hikes through the rural Pinelands and strenuous excursions along the ridges and thickly forested hills of the northern Highlands. Most of the state's parks, forests, recreation areas, wildlife refuges, and nature preserves have hiking trails; see individual listings under the *To Do— Hiking* and *Green Space* sections of each chapter. The **Appalachian Trail (AT)** cuts through the rugged northwestern corner of the state (see *Appalachian Trail* in this section) and can be accessed via many side trails. In

the Pinelands, the **Batona Trail** meanders 50 miles from Brendan T. Byrne State Forest in Pemberton to Bass River State Forest in New Gretna, passing through a rural landscape of cranberry bogs, swamps, and pine forests. The **Highlands Trail,** an under-construction long-distance trail system, will stretch 150 miles from the Hudson River in New York to the Delaware River in New Jersey. Some sections of the trail are open; others are still being cleared. The **New York–New Jersey Trail Conference** (201-512-9348; www.nynjtc.org) is an organization of more than 100 hiking clubs and environmental organizations that build and maintain marked hiking trails. Their Web site posts news on trail closures and other information useful to hikers.

HISTORIC HOMES AND SITES As one of America's 13 original colonies, New Jersey is rich in history, particularly of the Revolutionary War era. State parks protect battlefields, military forts, and encampments across the state. Nearly 60 preserved historic homes and structures are open to the public; see *To See—Historic Homes and Sites* in each chapter for sites in a particular region. In the Delaware Bay region, **Bridgeton** has the state's largest historic district, with more than 2,200 registered colonial-, federal-, and Victorian-era historic landmarks. The seaside resort town of **Cape May** is a national historic landmark, with more than 600 restored Victorian buildings. Re-created historic villages like **Batsto, Allaire,** and **Whitesbog,** and living-history farms, including **Howell** and **Fosterfields,** give visitors a glimpse of New Jersey life as it was centuries ago. The **New Jersey Historical Society** (973-596-8500; www.jerseyhistory.org), 52 Park Place, Newark 07102, is an excellent resource.

HORSE RACING See *Equestrian Sports.*

HUNTING For information on hunting in New Jersey, contact the state **Department of Environmental Protection, Division of Fish and Wildlife** (609-292-2965; www.njfish andwildlife.com), P.O. Box 402, Trenton 08625-0402.

INFORMATION The **New Jersey Division of Travel and Tourism** (609-777-0885; 800-847-4865; www .visitnj.org), 20 West State St., Trenton 08625, publishes a state travel guide, specialized brochures, and the official state map, and will send them on request. There are six regional tourism councils that also provide a wealth of travel information for their areas: **Greater Atlantic City** (866-719-8687), **Delaware River** (856-757-9400), **Gateway** (877-428-3930), **Shore** (732-506-5050), **Skylands** (800-847-4865), and **Southern Shore** (800-227-2297).

INFORMATION CENTERS There are 13 state welcome centers located throughout New Jersey on major highways and at other sites. There are two on the Atlantic City Expressway, in **Atlantic City** (609-383-2727) and in **Hammonton** (609-965-6316). On the New Jersey Turnpike, the **Molly Pitcher Welcome Center** (609-655-1610) is southbound in Cranbury at mile marker 71.9; another welcome center is in **Liberty State Park** (201-915-3401), off Exit 14B on the New Jersey Turnpike in Jersey City. Two are on the Garden State Parkway: northbound at mile marker 172 in **Montvale** (201-391-5737) and at mile marker 18.3 in **Ocean View** (609-624-0918). A welcome center in **Deepwater** (856-299-5272) is on I-295 northbound, a mile from the Delaware

Memorial Bridge. The **Knowlton Welcome Center** (908-496-4994) is on I-80 eastbound at mile marker 7, near the Delaware Water Gap in Columbia. At **Newark Liberty International Airport** (973-624-1014) an information booth is in Terminal B at international arrivals. In Flemington, the **Liberty Village Premium Outlets** (908-788-5729) has a welcome center; another is in **Bridgewater** (908-725-1552). In Trenton there are two welcome centers: the **State House Annex** (609-777-2719) on West State Street and the **Trenton Convention and Visitors Bureau** (609-777-1770) at Lafayette and Barrack streets.

LIGHTHOUSES New Jersey has 11 lighthouses along the coast that are accessible to the public. The **New Jersey Lighthouse Society** (www.njlhs .org), P.O. Box 332, Navesink 07752-0332, offers information on past and current lighthouses along the Atlantic coast, in New York Harbor, and in the Delaware Bay, as well as events and information for visitors. The **Twin Lights of Navesink,** a medieval-style brownstone beacon named for its double light, was built in 1862 and boasts panoramic views of Manhattan from the top. **Sandy Hook Lighthouse** is the oldest operating lighthouse in America, built in 1764 and standing sentinel over New York Harbor at the Sandy Hook Unit of Gateway National Recreation Area. The 1896 **Sea Girt Lighthouse** is part of a refurbished Victorian building. Built in 1835, **Barnegat Lighthouse,** known locally as "Old Barney," overlooks Barnegat Bay and Island Beach State Park on Long Beach Island. Visitors can climb 217 steps to the top. **Tucker's Island Light,** at the working maritime village of Tuckerton Seaport, is a replica of the original 1868 lighthouse that collapsed into the Atlantic Ocean in the 1920s. Atlantic City's **Absecon Lighthouse** is a 171-foot-tall beacon built in 1857. The 1859 **Cape May Lighthouse** looms above Cape May Point State Park, a natural area popular with migrating butterflies and birds. **Hereford Inlet Lighthouse,** built in North Wildwood in 1874, is surrounded by a charming flower and herb garden. **East Point Lighthouse** in Heislerville, built in 1849, overlooks Delaware Bay. New Jersey has two rear-range lighthouses that were built inland to operate in conjunction with front-range lights to guide vessels through the Delaware River's shipping channel. The 1880 **Tinicum Rear Range Lighthouse** stands in Paulsboro; and Pennsville's **Finns Point Rear Range Light** was built in Buffalo, New York, then transported by train and wagon in 1876.

MUSEUMS As you might expect from a state whose roots are in the colonial era, New Jersey has a bounty of small local history museums, mostly in well-preserved 18th- and 19th-century homes. There is also a fine collection of top-notch museums that covers a wide assortment of subjects, from arts and sciences to maritime, industrial, and agricultural history. Some of the best include **Liberty Science Center** (201-200-1000; www.lsc.org) in Jersey City, a four-story family science museum with more than 250 interactive exhibits on health, the environment, and inventions; and the **Old Barracks Museum** (609-396-1776; www.barracks .org) in Trenton, with the only original French and Indian War barracks in America, and where Washington defeated Hessian troops during the American Revolution. Also in Trenton, the **New Jersey State Museum** (609-292-6464) has Native American artifacts, a cast of the first complete dinosaur skeleton found in America, and an extensive collection of African American art. At the **Battleship Memorial and Museum** (856-966-1652; 866-877-6262; www.battleship newjersey.org) in Camden, visitors can tour the **battleship *New Jersey*,** a floating museum and the most highly decorated battleship in the U.S. Navy. The **Morris Museum** (973-971-3700; www.morrismuseum.org) in Morristown is one of New Jersey's largest museums, a 1912 Georgian-style mansion with an eclectic mix of some 48,000 pieces. The state has world-class art museums (see *Art Museums*), and a number of museums that are beloved by children (see *Children, Especially for*).

MUSIC Professional orchestras perform at various venues throughout New Jersey; they include the **New Jersey Symphony Orchestra** (973-624-3713), the **Garden State Philharmonic** (732-451-0064), and the **Greater Trenton Symphony Orchestra** (609-394-1338). Summertime music festivals bring nationally known musicians to stages around the state. Starting in May, the **Cape May Music Festival** (609-884-5404; 800-275-4278) is a month-long extravaganza of jazz bands, chamber music, orchestras, world music, and opera at various locations around town. Two other major festivals come in June: the **Appel Farm Arts and Music Festival** (800-394-1211) in Elmer is a day-long outdoor concert on two stages; and in Bridgeton, the **Bridgeton Folk Festival** (856-451-9208; 800-319-3379) draws nationally known folk musicians to the Delaware Bay region. **Knowlton Riverfest** (908-496-4816) in Knowlton is a 3-day festival of country, jazz, bluegrass, and blues along the banks of the Delaware River in August. Many towns—especially along the Jersey Shore—host weekly free outdoor concerts in July and August; they are listed in individual chapters under *Entertainment—Music*.

NATIONAL PARK AREAS The **Delaware Water Gap National Recreation Area** (570-828-2253; www.nps.gov/dewa) in Columbia cuts a dramatic swath through the Kittatinny Mountains, in some places soaring a quarter mile above the river. The 70,000-acre park stretches for 40 miles along the Delaware River in the rural hills of Warren County. Outdoor enthusiasts flock here to canoe, kayak, and fish; waterfalls, deep ravines, and steep ridges in this spectacular area beckon hikers and campers. **Morristown National Historical Park** (908-766-8215; www.nps.gov/morr) in the hills above Morristown—the first national park in America—is where George Washington and his troops spent the winter of 1779–80 during the Revolutionary War. On the grounds is Washington's headquarters, and the soldiers' quarters in Jockey Hollow. **Gateway National Recreation Area—Sandy Hook Unit** (732-872-5970; www.nps.gov/gate) sits on a barrier peninsula at the northern tip of the Jersey Shore. This is one of the nation's first urban national parks, with a unique combination of Manhattan skyline views, historic **Fort Hancock, Sandy Hook Lighthouse**—the oldest operational lighthouse in America—and wide, sandy ocean beaches with trails leading through dunes. In central New Jersey, the vast **Pinelands National Reserve** (609-894-7300; www.nps.gov/pine) is a 1.1-million-acre preserve of pine and oak forest, cranberry bogs, and Atlantic white cedar swamps that's one of the largest natural areas east of the Mississippi River.

NATURE PRESERVES New Jersey has more than 500,000 acres protected as state land in parks, forests, recreation areas, and natural areas. Nearly 300,000 acres are preserved within 117 wildlife management areas, which are large swaths of land used mostly by paddlers, birders, anglers, and hunters. Some have visitors centers and nature trails; others are largely undeveloped. **The Nature Conservancy,** a nationwide environmental conservation organization, has helped to preserve 54,000 acres throughout the state. And, of course, there's the 1.1 million acres protected in the massive **Pinelands National Reserve,** which covers about 25 percent of New Jersey. A variety of nature preserves are described in each chapter under *Green Space*.

PETS, TRAVELING WITH Throughout this book, the 🐾 symbol indicates lodgings, parks, and other places where pets are welcome.

PICK-YOUR-OWN More than 150 farms across New Jersey welcome visitors into the fields to pick their own fruits, berries, vegetables, herbs, flowers, and Christmas trees. The growing season stretches from mid-April to mid-November, with the majority of crops ready for picking from June to September. For a detailed listing of pick-your-own farms and a harvest schedule, click on **www.pickyourown .org** or on the **New Jersey Department of Agriculture Web site (www.state.nj.us/jerseyfresh);** you can find a farm in a particular region or search for a certain type of crop. It's advised that you phone a farm before visiting to check if the fields are open. Pick-your-own farms in each region are listed by chapter under *Selective Shopping—Farms and Gardens*.

POPULATION New Jersey's population, according to the 2006 U.S. Census estimate, is 8,724,560.

RAILROAD EXCURSIONS See *Children, Especially for.*

REST AREAS See *Information Centers.*

RESTAURANTS Many New Jersey restaurants have a bring-your-own alcohol policy. If "BYOB" appears in the text of a restaurant listing, it means that alcohol is not served on the premises, but patrons may bring their own wine. You might be able to bring your own wine to a restaurant with a liquor license, if, for example, the bottle isn't on their wine list; but you will likely be charged a corkage fee. It's best to phone ahead to be sure.

SKIING, CROSS-COUNTRY High Point (973-702-1222) in Sussex has groomed cross-country ski trails and snowmaking from mid-November to March. Many trails are above 1,600 feet in elevation, which almost guarantees snowy conditions in winter. In Newton, **Fairview Lake Ski Touring Center** (201-383-9282) has 600 acres of woodlands and open fields with 12 miles of marked, groomed trails and a ski lodge.

SKIING, DOWNHILL New Jersey has three major ski areas, all with snowmaking capability, night skiing, snowboarding, ski shops, and groomed trails ranging from easy novice to challenging expert terrain; all are within a 1-hour drive from the metropolitan New York area. **Mountain Creek** (973-864-8000; www.mountaincreek .com) in Vernon has 45 trails, nine lifts, seven terrain park trails, and eight tubing lanes, as well as lodging, dining,

and shopping on-site. Also in Vernon **Hidden Valley** (973-764-4200; www .hiddenvalleynj.com) has been a family ski resort for 35 years, with skiing on a dozen trails, snowboarding, and snow tubing in a tubing park with a 600-foot snow chute. **Campgaw Ski Area** (201-327-7800; www.skicampgaw.com) in Mahwah has five beginner and intermediate ski and snowboarding trails on a mountain with a 275-foot vertical drop; two double chairlifts, six 800-foot snow tubing runs with surface lifts, and a freestyle terrain park.

STATE PARKS AND FORESTS New Jersey has 41 state parks, 11 state forests, and three state recreation areas that offer a variety of activities, from camping and hiking to canoeing, biking, and historic sites. For more information, contact the **New Jersey Division of Parks and Forestry** (609-984-0370; 800-843-6420; www .nj.gov/dep/parksandforests), 501 East State St., P.O. Box 404, Trenton 08625.

THEATER The **New Jersey Theatre Alliance** (973-731-6582; www.nj theatrealliance.org), a consortium of the state's nonprofit professional theaters, features information, an events calendar, and special offers. Click on **www.njartstix.org** for deeply discounted day-of-show tickets to concerts, dance performances, and plays at affordable prices at close to 40 New Jersey theaters. The alliance also sponsors **Family Week at the Theatre,** with more than 120 theater events for children at venues throughout the state; most events are free. Theaters are listed under *Arts Centers* or *Theater* in the *Entertainment* section of each chapter.

TIDES Click on **www.saltwater tides.com** to view tide tables for locations around New Jersey, including the Hudson River; the shoreline from Sandy Hook to Cape May, including Barnegat Bay and other major bays; Delaware Bay; and the state's tidal rivers.

TRAIN SERVICES **Amtrak** (800-872-7245; www.amtrak.com) routes from New York's Penn Station to points south and west pass through New Jersey; most trains serve Newark and Trenton, some make stops at Newark Liberty International Airport, Iselin, New Brunswick, and Princeton Junction. **New Jersey Transit** (973-275-5555; www.njtransit.com) trains serve much of the state on a commuter rail network of 11 rail and light rail lines. **Port Authority Transit Corporation (PATCO)** (856-772-6900; www.drpa.org) runs a high-speed rail line linking southern New Jersey and Philadelphia. **Port Authority Trans Hudson (PATH)** (800-234-7284; www.panynj.com) provides rail service between the Newark metropolitan area and Manhattan. **Southeastern Pennsylvania Transportation Authority (SEPTA)** (215-580-7800; www.septa .org) links Trenton and the Camden area with greater Philadelphia.

VINEYARDS AND WINERIES
Wine making in New Jersey is a tradition that dates more than 200 years. London's Royal Society of the Arts recognized two New Jersey vintners in 1767 for producing the first bottles of quality wine from grapes grown and harvested in Colonial America. In the 1800s, a grape-growing industry producing wine and grape juice was based in **Vineland** in South Jersey. Early explorers gave Vineland its name because of the abundance of grape vines.

Wine grapes are one of the Garden State's most profitable crops. There are 33 wineries—many family-owned and -operated—that together produce about a million gallons of wine a year in more than 40 varieties, from sparkling wines and fruit wines to dry red and white wines. All are open for tours and tastings; many host festivals and special events attended by more than a quarter-million visitors every year. In addition to their wines, together they preserve thousands of acres of open space. The **Garden State Wine Growers Association** (609-588-0085; www.newjerseywines.com) has information on festivals, wineries, wine trails, day trip suggestions, and the history of New Jersey wine making. Wineries are located all around the state in beautiful areas of pristine farmland or surrounded by rural scenery; some are housed in historic buildings or converted barns. Many are collecting national and international awards at prestigious wine competitions. Among them, **Alba Vineyard** (908-995-7800) in Finesville boasts spectacular views as well as a tasting room in a rustic 1805 stone barn. **Four Sisters Winery** (908-475-3671) in Belvidere is on the grounds of a working farm. In Ringoes, **Unionville Vineyards** (908-788-0400) sits on 90 acres spread across picturesque central New Jersey countryside. In southern New Jersey, **Renault Winery** (609-965-2111) in Egg Harbor City is one of the oldest continually operating wineries in America, established in 1864. **Tomasello Winery** (800-666-9463) in Hammonton is the state's largest winery, with a selection of 40 wines. **Cream Ridge Winery** (609-259-9797) in Cream Ridge specializes in award-winning wines made from cherries, apricots, plums, cranberries, and many other fruits.

WHALE AND DOLPHIN WATCHING

In Atlantic City, *Cruisn 1* (609-347-7600) hosts 2-hour dolphin-watch trips with an onboard marine naturalist. *Silver Bullet* **Speedboat and Dolphin Watch** (609-522-6060) in Wildwood offers daily whale- and dolphin-watch excursions. In Wildwood Crest, **Captain Sinn's Marine Center** (609-522-3934) takes passengers on whale-watching excursions. In Cape May, the **Cape May Whale Watch and Research Center** (609-898-0055; 888-531-0055) and the *Cape May Whale Watcher* (609-884-5445; 1-800-786-5445) sail from March to December to view humpback whales, finback whales, and bottlenose dolphins.

The Northeastern Gateway

THE PALISADES TO HOBOKEN

THE NEWARK AND JERSEY CITY
REGION

WEST OF THE PARKWAY

THE SOUTHERN GATEWAY

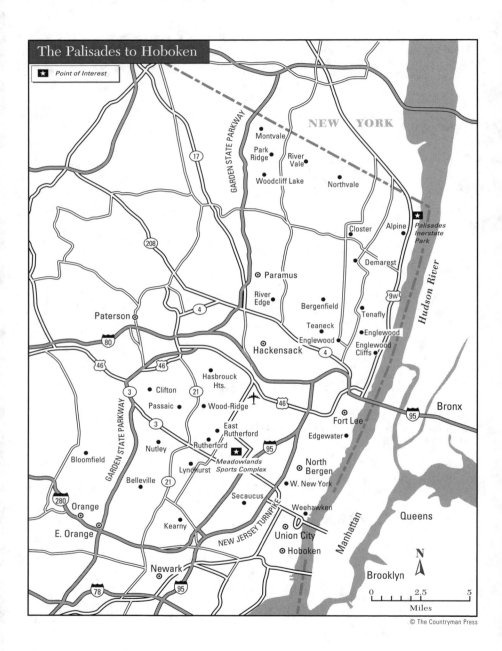

The Palisades to Hoboken

★ Point of Interest

NEW YORK

GARDEN STATE PARKWAY

17

Montvale

Park
Ridge

River
Vale

Woodcliff Lake

Northvale

208

Closter

Alpine

★ Palisades
Inerstate
Park

Demarest

Paramus

River
Edge

Bergenfield

9W

Tenafly

Paterson

4

Teaneck

Englewood

Englewood

80

Hackensack

4

Englewood
Cliffs

Hudson River

46

46

Hasbrouck
Hts.

3

Clifton

21

Passaic

Wood-Ridge

46

US 46

East
Rutherford

Fort Lee

Bronx

95

Nutley

Rutherford

Edgewater

95

Bloomfield

★

Meadowlands
Sports Complex

North
Bergen

GARDEN STATE PARKWAY

Lyndhurst

21

Belleville

W. New York

280

Secaucus

Orange

Weehawken

Manhattan

Queens

E. Orange

Kearny

NEW JERSEY TURNPIKE

Union City

N

Newark

Hoboken

Brooklyn

78

95

0   2.5   5
Miles

© The Countryman Press

THE PALISADES TO HOBOKEN

Perched across the Hudson River from New York City is the New Jersey that fans of *The Sopranos,* the hit HBO mob-family drama set in the Northeastern Gateway region, know and quickly recognize. This is the extreme northeast corner of the state, and it's planted firmly in the sprawling New York City metropolitan region, one of the most densely populated and developed areas in America. More people live in Bergen County than any other county in New Jersey; in fact, the population here is larger than that of six states in the U.S. It's also one of the nation's most affluent counties, a ranking it can also credit to its location in the shadow of the Big Apple.

It's an unfortunate reality that out-of-state visitors—even many residents—write off this part of New Jersey as simply a place to pass through as quickly as possible in order to get someplace better. And can you blame them? From congested highways, motorists take in chemical dumps and a concrete landscape fanning into suburbia, the kind of urban sprawl that has earned the Garden State its much-undeserved bad rap.

What few realize is that the Northeastern Gateway region uses its proximity to the world's most famous metropolis to its advantage. The urban sprawl is sprinkled with hidden treasures—from chic restaurants and museums to galleries and topflight cultural and sporting venues—that are convincing many visitors (and increasing numbers of residents) to skip the trip into Manhattan and spend the day, evening, or weekend in New Jersey. You can easily make a day out of a visit to Palisades Interstate Park, where you can hike the famous bluffs, launch a kayak into the Hudson River, tour a Revolutionary War–era fort, and bike along a historic road tucked between the soaring cliffs and the riverbanks with the New York City skyline contributing a stunning-yet-surreal backdrop. Hoboken aims to please everyone, with outdoor summertime concerts and films in Pier A waterfront park, beautifully preserved brownstones in historic tree-lined neighborhoods, and Washington Street, a bustling thoroughfare of trendy boutiques, old-fashioned bakeries, ethnic eateries, and ultrahip bistros and bars.

Revitalization is taking place up and down the industrial landscape along the New Jersey waterfront. Astute developers are converting and rehabbing one of the world's busiest railway and shipping centers—not to mention prime Hudson River real estate—into gleaming office towers, green linear parks, and factory buildings–turned–luxury lofts.

Midtown Manhattan is just a stone's throw away, by commuter ferry, the

Holland and Lincoln tunnels, the George Washington Bridge, and the PATH trains out of Hoboken's historic Erie Lackawanna Train Terminal, a stately Beaux-Arts landmark on the waterfront. Commuters and tourists have hustled through this busy ferry and train station since it was built in 1907. Its lofty Tiffany glass ceiling, gleaming wood, intricate terrazzo floor, and copper roof weathered to a rich green patina are all suggestive of an earlier era.

In the early 1800s, Hoboken was considered quite fashionable by illustrious Manhattanites, who were known to row across the Hudson just to spend a Sunday afternoon in Elysian Fields, the city's historic riverfront park. Few people realize that the first brewery in the United States opened in Hoboken in 1642. Sports fans could probably tell you that the city hosted the country's first organized game of baseball in the summer of 1846. Movie buffs know it as the gritty setting for Marlon Brando's Academy Award–winning classic *On the Waterfront*. But just about everyone knows that Hoboken is Francis Albert Sinatra's hometown. Sinatra—the Chairman of the Board, Ol' Blue Eyes, the city's hometown hero—emerged from Hoboken in the 1940s and went on to croon "New York, New York," run around with the Rat Pack, and launch a career in music and film that would last for decades. His birthplace at 415 Monroe Street is gone, but his boyhood home still stands.

It took Hoboken nearly 300 years to evolve from tidal wetlands sandwiched between the Hudson River and the Palisades to an industrial center and seaport to a hip urban residential and commercial city. The earliest Dutch settlers bought the area from the Lenni-Lenape Indians, and sold it to Colonel John Stevens for $90,000. He laid out the city in 1804, built the world's first steam locomotive here in 1825, and transformed Hoboken into a major railroad and shipping hub. His ancestors established the Stevens Institute of Technology at the site of their family estate atop a promontory that features a Civil War–era cannon and a stunning view of the Manhattan skyline at the Castle Point lookout area.

THE SOPRANOS

HBO's award-winning hit series *The Sopranos* is a New Jersey–based mob drama that explores the ongoing angst of troubled boss Tony Soprano and his dysfunctional family and associates. It casts a humorous light onto the world of organized crime while helping to solidify the stereotypes already established in many people's minds about what New Jersey—and New Jerseyans—are like.

Die-hard fans regularly make the pilgrimage to the Garden State to see the gritty and familiar real-life places where the series was filmed. **On Location Tours** (212-209-3370) offers narrated excursions aboard coach buses on Saturdays and Sundays. The tours, which leave at 2 PM and generally last about 4 hours, include more than 40 northern New Jersey locales where episodes have been shot. You'll pass Bada Bing's, Pizzaland, and Satriale's Pork Store while hearing colorful commentary about the show and its locations. These trips run year-round (leaving from Manhattan) and are very popular; reservations are required.

After weathering its share of downswings in the past two centuries, Hoboken is heading back up again. The mile-square port city of some 40,000 residents is attracting more and more young families and twentysomethings who are realizing that the city offers an attractive mix of history, culture, and urban chic minus the big-city prices. They're settling into a mix of well-preserved brownstones in old neighborhoods and luxury apartments along the waterfront, right across the river from Greenwich Village. Sprawling brick factories and warehouses that once produced everything from Maxwell House coffee to Lipton tea are now stylish SoHo-style lofts, health clubs, and office space. Washington Street's sophisticated eateries, Euro-chic sidewalk cafés, and hip cocktail lounges are packed with legions of young professionals who work across the river in Manhattan, just a mile away.

Behind the waterfront is a string of workaday towns and cities, home to a patchwork of ethnic communities that stretch back generations. Visitors can sample their rich heritage through a year-round schedule of international parades, festivals, and cultural events. And, of course, there's the food. In this region you can hear languages from far-flung corners of the globe, and smell and taste the exotic flavors of a variety of homelands. The region's Latino community is centered in Union City, while more than 300 Cuban, Mexican, and Peruvian eateries and shops line the streets in West New York. In North Bergen you can dine on Cuban, African, Indian, and Middle Eastern cuisine. Every October, Union City's Hispanic State Parade draws 200,000 to see cultural dances, bands, and floats that display the proud culture and unique traditions of dozens of countries.

Today's industrial landscape makes it easy to forget that New Jersey's roots lie deep in America's earliest days. Visitors should keep in mind that New Jersey was one of the 13 original colonies, and some of the first European settlers carved out farms and lives in the regions that are now Bergen and Hudson counties. Tucked amid the shopping malls, freeways, and housing developments are places like Fort Lee, a Revolutionary War–era signal station that allowed General George Washington and his Continental army to keep tabs on British-occupied New York. Later, Fort Lee would be known as Hollywood East, home to Thomas Edison's Black Maria, the nation's first film studio. Along with the light bulb, Edison invented the motion picture camera. From 1907 to 1917 Fort Lee was the hub of the nation's film industry in its earliest days, when icons like Mary Pickford and Paul Robeson were the stars of the silent screen.

Historic New Bridge Landing Park was the site of a vital Revolutionary War–era supply line, river crossing, military headquarters, encampment ground, and intelligence-gathering post on the Hackensack River. It was here, at the 18th-century Steuben House, that Thomas Paine stood with George Washington and watched the bedraggled Continental army retreat from Fort Lee, with British troops on their heels. The event inspired Paine's *American Crisis* essay and the now famous phrase, "These are the times that try men's souls."

In places like Park Ridge and Clifton, Dutch-style houses and barns dating from the early 18th century have been meticulously restored, filled with period artifacts, and opened to visitors, some with demonstrations of open-hearth cooking by docents in period dress. The Dutch settlers were farming Bergen County's then-rural valleys in the 1600s—sharing space with the Manhattans, Tappans, and Hackensacks, the region's earliest residents—long before the American Revolution. Hackensack's historic town green is still framed by the steep spire of a stately old church, and the courthouse and jail built in 1716. Hackensack is also home to the New Jersey Naval Museum and the restored USS *Ling,* permanently berthed in the Hackensack River as a living tribute to the era of American diesel-powered submarines.

When most people talk about the Meadowlands, they're likely discussing sports and not bird-watching. So while Hackensack Meadows is a vital ecosystem for more than 265 species of native and migratory birds, it's better known for East Rutherford's Meadowlands Sports Complex, home to the New York Giants and New Jersey Nets. For decades the 18,000-acre tract of marshland and swamp along the Hackensack River earned an unfortunate reputation as one of the most polluted dumping grounds in the country, scarred by mountains of toxic waste, industrial debris, and household refuse. For years it has been a colossal trash heap, as well as fodder for stand-up comedians and an eyesore for commuters on the New Jersey Turnpike, who could smell as well as see the contamination.

Today ambitious efforts are underway by environmental groups, politicians, and developers to turn the watery Meadowlands around and restore the once-green habitat. Abandoned landfills are being capped and transformed into retail and office space, condos, and wildlife sanctuaries. The New Jersey Meadowlands Commission maintains an environmental center and 110-acre nature preserve protecting tidal marshes, an Atlantic white cedar swamp, and wildflower meadows that are important to native wildlife and thousands of migratory birds that use the Meadowlands to rest and feed. A massive billion-dollar redevelopment plan calls for condominiums, shops, restaurants, golf courses, a hotel—even a marina on the Hackensack River. It's all part of a statewide effort to preserve open space that's particularly important here, where New Jersey's industrial history has scarred the landscape, but not irrevocably. Hopes for a new urban oasis are high.

Just to the northeast, the Palisades loom high above the Hudson River, a line of majestic dark basalt cliffs marching west toward New York State. Palisades Interstate Park is the result of 19th-century lobbying to protect the 190-million-year-old cliffs that were being destroyed by heavy quarrying. The park shields a desolate 13-mile stretch of riverfront—some 2,500 acres—from the George Washington Bridge and into New York State. Hikers are rewarded with spectacular views of upper Manhattan and the Hudson River from atop the cliffs, where one of a dozen official state hawk-watch sites is located. Birders come from around the country in the fall to observe the annual spectacle as thousands of hawks and other birds of prey wing their way over northern New Jersey on the Atlantic Flyway, the busy migratory route along the East Coast. For visitors, there are 30 miles of hiking trails

THE USS *LING* SUBMARINE IS PERMANENTLY BERTHED AND OPEN FOR TOURS AT THE NEW JERSEY NAVAL MUSEUM IN HACKENSACK.
Courtesy of the New Jersey Naval Museum

through rugged woodland, the Hudson River for kayaking, a scenic bike route, historic sites, and a parkway with three overlooks that offer commanding views of the Manhattan skyline.

Another set of cliffs just south of the Palisades in Weehawken was the site of many duels, a method of choice for settling disputes in America's early days. But the most famous duel in young America's history took place here on July 11, 1804, when bitter political and personal rivals Aaron Burr and Alexander Hamilton met on the dueling ground in 1804. They were two of the most prominent leaders of the time: Hamilton, America's first secretary of the treasury under George Washington, and author of *The Federalist Papers;* Aaron Burr, vice president of the United States. Hamilton was shot and later died of his wounds, while Burr's career began a spiral that ended with accusations of treason a few years later. Today the site is designated by a historical marker in a small park in Weehawken.

Entries in this section are arranged in roughly geographic order, from north to south.

AREA CODES 201, 973.

GUIDANCE The **Hoboken Chamber of Commerce** (201-222-1100; www .hobokenchamber.com), P.O. Box 349, Hoboken 07030, maintains a comprehensive online directory of information for visitors. Click on the Web site for city maps, a calendar of events, bus and train schedules, and a list of restaurants, shops, and other businesses.

A state travel information center (201-391-5737) is located in Montvale on the Garden State Parkway northbound at mile marker 172 and is well stocked with maps, brochures, and other tourism literature. The **Vince Lombardi Travel Plaza** (201-943-8757) is located on the New Jersey Turnpike at mile marker 116 in Ridgefield.

The **Meadowlands Liberty Convention and Visitors Bureau** (1-877-652-8287; www.meadowlandslibertycvb.com), 201 Rt. 17 N., Rutherford, maintains an extensive directory of travel information on its Web site for visitors.

GETTING THERE *By air:* **Newark Liberty International Airport** (973-961-6000; parking information: 888-397-4636; www.panynj.com) in Newark is served by more than 40 major carriers. **AirTrain Newark** (888-397-4636; www.airtrain newark.com) provides rail service between airport terminals and mass transit, including New Jersey Transit and Amtrak trains as well as New York's and Newark's Penn Stations. **John F. Kennedy International Airport** (718-244-4444; www.kennedyairport.com) and **LaGuardia International Airport** (718-533-3400; www.laguardiaairport.com) in New York City are both close to the Northeastern Gateway region.

By bus: **Greyhound** (800-231-2222; www.greyhound.com) makes a limited-service stop (no terminal) in Paramus. **New Jersey Transit** (800-955-2321; 973-275-5555; www.njtransit.com) provides local bus service on nearly 200 routes around the state.

By rail: **New Jersey Transit** (800-772-2222; 973-762-5100; www.njtransit.com) commuter trains run between Hoboken's magnificent 1907 Erie Lackawanna Terminal and the northern New Jersey suburbs. Some New Jersey Transit lines go directly to New York's Penn Station via Secaucus Junction without stopping in

Hoboken. The Pascack Valley Line runs north through Rutherford, Hackensack, and other communities in this chapter to the New York state line. **PATH** (Port Authority Trans Hudson) train service (800-234-7284; www.panynj.com) from Manhattan connects to Hoboken. The Hudson–Bergen Light Rail Line connects Hoboken Terminal to Jersey City and Bayonne.

By ferry: **New York Waterway** (800-533-3779; www.nywaterway.com) provides daily service to and from New York City via 10 New Jersey terminals.

By car: The **New Jersey Turnpike (I-95)** and the **Garden State Parkway** are the two major highways through this region. The **Holland Tunnel** connects lower Manhattan to Jersey City, where **Routes 1/9** and **I-78** lead to the New Jersey Turnpike. The **Lincoln Tunnel** connects midtown Manhattan to the New Jersey Turnpike; **Route 3** continues west to the **Garden State Parkway.** The **George Washington Bridge (GWB or "The GW") (I-95)** connects New York with New Jersey in Fort Lee. From the GW Bridge, the **Palisades Interstate Parkway** and **Route 9 West** follow the Hudson River north to New York State, and **Route 4** cuts west to the Garden State Parkway. When exploring this area by car, it's wise to carry a detailed road map.

GETTING AROUND *Taxis:* Taxi services in Hoboken include **Hoboken Taxi** (201-420-1480), **Hoboken Yellow Taxi** (201-420-8294), and **United Taxi** (201-795-9149). **East Coast Car Company** (201-944-6800) serves most of the region.

MEDICAL EMERGENCY **Pascack Valley Hospital** (201-358-3000), 250 Old Hook Rd., Westwood. The emergency number is 201-358-3100.

Bergen Regional Medical Center (201-967-4000), 230 East Ridgewood Ave., Paramus. The emergency number is 201-967-4141.

Hackensack University Medical Center (201-996-2000), 30 Prospect Ave., Hackensack. The emergency number is 201-996-2300.

Englewood Hospital and Medical Center (201-894-3000), 350 Engle St., Englewood. The emergency number is 201-894-3440.

Meadowlands Hospital Medical Center (201-392-3100), 55 Meadowlands Pkwy., Secaucus. The emergency number is 201-392-3210.

Clara Maass Medical Center (201-955-7000), 206 Bergen Ave., Kearny. The emergency number is 201-955-7040.

St. Mary Hospital (201-418-1000), 308 Willow Ave., Hoboken. The emergency number is 201-418-1900.

✹ To See

ART MUSEUMS **The African Art Museum of the Society of African Missions** (201-894-8611; www.smafathers.org), 23 Bliss Ave., Tenafly. Open daily 9–5. Free admission. The history of African culture is traced through a unique collection of art, ceremonial masks, crafts, and other artifacts of sub-Saharan Africa. This is one of five such art museums that the Society of Catholic Missionaries maintains around the world. Call about a schedule of lectures and concerts.

Hiram Blauvelt Art Museum (201-261-0012; www.blauveltmuseum.com), 705 Kinderkamack Rd., Oradell. Open Wed.–Fri. 10–4; Sat. and Sun. 2–5; closed holidays. Free admission. With his personal collection of wildlife art and big-game specimens, conservationist Hiram Blauvelt founded this unique museum in 1957 to raise public awareness of the issues facing the natural world. An ornate 19th-century shingled carriage house with turrets contains a series of small galleries with dioramas, mounted animals, and natural-history and wildlife exhibits that showcase the work of artists inspired by nature. The permanent exhibit features works by John James Audubon, Frederic Remington, and other noted wildlife artists. The museum's upper level houses the North American mammal and big-game collection, including rare and extinct species. Changing exhibitions are mounted in the outdoor sculpture garden as well as in the galleries. Call about a schedule of lectures, painting demonstrations, and artist roundtables.

HISTORIC HOMES AND SITES Wortendyke Barn (201-930-0124), 13 Pascack Rd., Park Ridge. Open May–Oct., Wed., Sat., and Sun. 1–5 and by appointment. Free admission. Wortendyke Farm was a working Dutch family farm from 1735 until 1851; today the barn (the last surviving relic of the 460-acre farm) is one of the only original New World Dutch-style barns in existence. These barns, crafted of heavy timber with the door built into the gable end, dotted farm fields all over Bergen County in the 18th and 19th centuries. Inside, farms tools, implements and horse-drawn vehicles from the 1700s and 1800s are on display, along with exhibits on Bergen County's agricultural past and Revolutionary War–era history.

Kearney House (201-768-1360; www.njpalisades.org), Alpine Picnic Area, Palisades Interstate Park, Alpine. Open for self-guided tours May–Oct., Sat., Sun., and holidays noon–5, or by appointment. Free admission. The stone Kearney House was part of a remote-yet-thriving 19th-century settlement on the Hudson River known as Closter Landing. Rachel Kearney was a local widow who raised eight children in what was then a two-room house. The tavern she ran out of her home was frequented by the dockworkers, quarrymen, and boat crews that passed through. Rachel lived in the house until she died in 1870 at the age of 90. At the turn of the 20th century the house was used in springtime by fishermen working the river's shad run; later it served as headquarters for the park police. The house would have been demolished in the 1920s, if not for the widely believed (and later discounted) story that Lieutenant General Charles Cornwallis used it as his military headquarters while planning a surprise raid on the Continental army at Fort Lee in 1776. Visitors are welcome to explore the house's furnished rooms, including the rustic kitchen—with hand-hewn beams and massive hearth—which dates to the mid-1700s.

Historic New Bridge Landing Park (201-487-1739; www.newbridgelanding .org), 1209 Main St., River Edge. Grounds are open daily. The **Steuben House** is open Wed.–Sat. 10–noon and 1–5; Sun. 2–5. The **Campbell-Christie House** is open on the second Sunday of the month. The **Demarest House** is open by appointment only. A historic museum village and Revolutionary War site along the west bank of the Hackensack River whose 17th- and 18th-century Dutch Colonial–style sandstone houses, common in colonial-era northern New Jersey, hold the museum collections of the **Bergen County Historical Society.** The 18-acre site was first a Native American encampment, later a European fort, and finally a prosperous mill town and landing, where sloops were loaded with iron from northern

New Jersey's furnaces and sent to New York City. During the Revolutionary War, New Bridge served as a military headquarters as well as a battleground; the bridge itself was a strategic river crossing. It was here in 1776 that Thomas Paine and General George Washington watched the bedraggled Continental army cross the bridge, with General Cornwallis and his British troops in close pursuit, following a surprise attack at Fort Lee. The scene inspired the famous phrase, "These are the times that try men's souls," which appeared later in Paine's *American Crisis* essays, written to rekindle Americans' flagging support of the war effort. The 1774 **Campbell-Christie House** was a farmhouse, a tavern, and a blacksmith shop. The 1678 **Demarest House** has Dutch furnishings from the 1600s and 1700s, and other relics of Bergen County's past. The 1752 **Steuben House** is the best and oldest example of Dutch Colonial–style architecture. Inside, a vintage toy collection includes the circa-1700 wax doll that's considered the oldest doll in the country. The park's other historic features include the **New Bridge,** the oldest iron-truss swing bridge in New Jersey, an English-style barn, and an authentically replicated out-kitchen (early American kitchens were built away from the main house) with a smokehouse and a beehive oven. Call about their year-round schedule of special events, which includes guided tours, book sales, colonial concerts, festivals, Revolutionary War roundtables, workshops and lectures.

Hamilton House Museum (973-744-5707), 971 Valley Rd., Clifton. The house is open for tours and special events from Mar. to Dec., Sun. 2–4. An early-19th-century sandstone farmhouse built by John and Anna Vreeland in 1817 has been restored and filled with period furnishings. Guides in period costume demonstrate open-hearth cooking and other domestic routines of the early 1800s.

MUSEUMS ✄ **New Jersey Children's Museum** (201-262-5151; www.njcm .com), 599 Valley Health Plaza, Paramus. Open Mon.–Fri. 10–6; Sat. and Sun. 10–6 (Oct.–Apr.) and 10–5 (May–Sept.); closed Thanksgiving and Christmas. Admission $10; children under 1, free. More than 30 hands-on interactive exhibits that promote learning and play for toddlers and preschool-age children. Real-life play areas include an office, a fire engine, a pizzeria, a grocery store, a medieval castle, and a prehistoric cave. Science and technology activities are geared toward first-graders.

Aviation Hall of Fame and Museum of New Jersey (201-288-6344; www .njahof.org), Teterboro Airport, 400 Fred Wehran Dr. (Rt. 46), Teterboro. Open Tues.–Sun. 10–4; closed Mon. and major holidays. Adults $6; seniors and children $4. A retired control tower at busy Teterboro Airport has been transformed into a unique museum that chronicles New Jersey's ties to 200 years of aviation history. Watch private and commuter planes and listen to a live radio broadcast where air traffic controllers once worked. The education center has artifacts and films on military aviation and space travel, a simulated control tower, rocket engines, preserved airplanes, and a Hall of Fame room honoring aviation greats from Amelia Earhart to astronaut (and New Jersey native) Buzz Aldrin. The M.A.S.H. exhibit—with Korean War–era military vehicles, an authentically replicated surgical suite, and a Bell 47C helicopter—is the only one of its kind in the country.

✄ **Meadowlands Museum** (201-935-1175), 91 Crane Ave., Rutherford. Open Sept.–June, Mon., Wed., and Sat. 1–4, Sun. 2–4; July and Aug., Mon.–Thurs. 1–4, Sun. 2–4. Admission by donation. A local history museum housed in a restored

NEW JERSEY NAVAL MUSEUM
(201-342-3268; www.njnm.com), Borg Park, 78 River St., Hackensack. Open for tours Sat. and Sun. 10–4; last tour leaves at 3:15 pm. Closed weekdays and major holidays. Adults $8; children 11 and under, $3. The World War II–era USS *Ling,* restored and permanently berthed in the Hackensack River, is a living tribute to the era of American diesel-powered submarines. Visitors can descend into the torpedo rooms as well as the engine and control rooms to get a firsthand idea of the tight quarters a 95-person crew lived in. The 312-foot-long, 2,500-ton *Ling* was commissioned in 1945 near the end of World War II and patrolled the Atlantic before serving as a Brooklyn-based training vessel during the 1960s. The museum also has a Vietnam War–era patrol boat (the only one in the Northeast), a World War II–era Japanese torpedo and two-person German coastal defense submarine, and personal memorabilia and photographs.

19th-century farmstead. The story of the Meadowlands region is told through an eclectic mix of exhibits, from historical photographs and artifacts to vintage toys, a Colonial kitchen, and New Jersey rocks and minerals. Workshops on historical crafts and lectures by guest speakers are among the special events scheduled throughout the year.

✍ **Hoboken Historical Museum and Cultural Center** (201-656-2240; www.hobokenmuseum.org), 1301 Hudson St., Hoboken. Open Tues.–Thurs. 2–9; Fri. 1–5; Sat. and Sun. noon–5; closed Mon. Suggested donation $2; children, free. The story of Hoboken is told through a permanent collection of local memorabilia, photographs, and artifacts, as well as changing exhibits, lectures, family programs, festivals, and garden and walking tours.

ZOO 🐾 ✍ **Bergen County Zoological Park** (201-262-3771), Van Saun County Park, 216 Forest Ave., Paramus. Open year-round, daily 10:30–4:30; from Apr. to Sept., Sat. and Sun. 9:30–5. Admission May–Oct.: adults $2; seniors and children 12–17, $1; children 11 and under, free. Free admission Nov.–Apr. An interesting mix of wild and domestic animals resides at this county zoo that attracts half a million visitors a year. The **North American Wetlands Aviary** is a walk-through area with a wide variety of birds, including rare and endangered species. Chickens, cows, geese, and sheep roam the 19th-century farmyard. There are picnic facilities and a butterfly garden that hums with activity during the summer.

✳ To Do

BICYCLING **Palisades Interstate Park** (201-768-1360; www.njpalisades.org), River Rd., Edgewater. Open Apr.–Oct. during daylight hours. Cyclists (ages 15 and older only) are allowed on a 7-mile stretch of historic **Henry Hudson Drive** that follows the Hudson River. The scenic road was built between 1916 and 1940, and winds along the river through Palisades Interstate Park. From River Road in Edgewater the road dips and rises along the spectacular Palisades, runs under the George Washington Bridge, and goes past picnic areas that boast views of the river, the soaring cliffs, and the New York City skyline before ending at the **Alpine Picnic Area.** Bikes are also allowed on the **old Route 9 West**—now closed to auto traffic—from Route 9 to the **State Line Lookout.** This popular biking area is an oasis in one of the most densely populated places in America, so you'll be sharing the road with many other cyclists at any given time.

🚲 **HoBiken** (201-963-0909; www.hobiken.com), at Symposia Bookstore, 510 Washington St., Hoboken. Open Mon.–Fri. 11–9; Sat. and Sun. 1–9. A community bicycle project offers low-cost ($5) daily bike rentals for visitors; bike use is available for Hoboken residents by donation. The fleet of bikes is rebuilt from donated or recovered bicycles.

BIRDING State Line Hawk Watch (201-768-1360; www.njpalisades.org), State Line Lookout, Palisades Interstate Park, Alpine. Open late Aug.–Nov., daily 9–5. Every autumn, the world's largest raptor migration takes place as the birds travel down the eastern seaboard toward their wintering grounds as far away as South America. It's a natural pageant that is nothing short of spectacular, and thousands of nature lovers, birders, and professional ornithologists come to watch as kestrels, hawks, eagles, falcons, ospreys, vultures, and other birds of prey wing pass over this segment of the Atlantic Flyway. Along with the nonprofit **Hawk Migration Association of North America (HMANA),** park workers monitor hawk migration over the Palisades, one of a dozen official hawk-watch sites in New Jersey. The 14 species of hawks spotted every year include the **red-tailed hawks** that reside year-round in the Palisades.

Richard W. DeKorte Park (201-460-8300), Two DeKorte Park Plaza, Lyndhurst. The park is open daily 8 AM–dusk; the **Meadowlands Environment Center** is open Mon.–Fri. 9–5; Sat. and Sun. 10–3. This wildlife preserve in the Meadowlands draws birders from around the country. An enclosed viewing area at the nature center looks out over the wildlife preserve, but for an up-close look pick up a brochure and take a self-guided tour of the grounds. A 1.1-mile boardwalk trail passes through a salt marsh wetland along Kingsland Creek, where many species of local and migratory waterfowl and other birds are often spotted as they rest here on their journey along the Atlantic Flyway. The wildlife-viewing blinds and benches along the trail are good vantage points.

BOAT EXCURSIONS Horizon Cruises (201-385-9400; 877-368-4685; www.horizoncruisesinc.com), Lincoln Harbor Marina, 1500 Harbor Blvd., Weehawken. Public dinner cruises daily; lunch trips on Sat. and Sun. Reservations are recommended. Harbor cruises aboard a luxury yacht with gourmet cuisine, live entertainment, and commanding views of the New York City skyline.

Spirit Cruises (866-211-3805; www.spiritcruises.com), Lincoln Harbor Marina, Harbor Blvd., Weehawken. Open year-round; reservations are recommended. Lunch and dinner cruises—complete with live entertainment and dancing— aboard the *Spirit of New Jersey* pass through New York Harbor and all its world-famous sights, from the Statue of Liberty and Ellis Island to the Empire State Building and the Brooklyn Bridge.

Classic Sail (973-966-1684; www.classicsail.com), Lincoln Harbor Yacht Club, Weehawken. Cruises on the Hudson River aboard the schooner **Richard Robbins**, a majestic two-masted, gaff-rigged wooden sailboat built in 1902.

CANOEING AND KAYAKING In **Palisades Interstate Park,** paddlers can launch canoes and kayaks from the picnic areas at the **Alpine Boat Basin** (201-768-9798) on Alpine Approach Road in Alpine, the **Englewood Boat Basin** (201-894-9510) on Dyckman Hill Road in Englewood Cliffs, and **Hazzard's Launching Ramp** (201-768-1360) beneath the George Washington Bridge in Fort Lee. All are open May through October; there's a $10 fee to launch from Hazzard's Launching Ramp. The beaches and picnic areas at the boat basins make for a good post-paddle stop.

GOLF Several public 18-hole golf courses are tucked into this heavily developed region. Most of them feature practice facilities and a clubhouse with a pro shop and a snack bar, often a restaurant. They include **River Vale Country Club** (201-391-2300), 660 Rivervale Rd., and **Valley Brook Golf Club** (201-664-5886), 15 Riverdale Rd., River Vale; **Overpeck Golf Course** (201-837-3020), East Cedar La., Teaneck; and **Hendricks Field Golf Course** (973-751-0178), 220 Franklin Ave., Belleville.

HIKING **Flat Rock Brook Nature Center** (201-567-1265; www.flatrockbrook .org), 443 Van Nostrand Ave., Englewood. The trails and picnic area are open daily from dawn to dusk; the nature center is open Tues.–Fri. 9–5; Sat. and Sun. 1–5. Free admission. A 150-acre wildlife sanctuary and environmental education center on the western flank of the Palisades. Trails lead through a diverse landscape of wildflower meadows, wetlands, forest, and ponds, all teeming with birds and wildlife in their natural habitats. The sanctuary was founded in 1974 by a group of conservation-minded local residents who wanted to protect a quickly disappearing natural landscape in northern New Jersey, including one of the last tracts of forest in the region.

Richard W. DeKorte Park (201-460-8300), Two DeKorte Park Plaza, Lyndhurst. Grounds and trails are open daily; pick up a trail guide at the **Meadowlands Environment Center** before you start exploring. Free admission. The 1.1-mile **Marsh Discovery Trail** leaves from the parking-lot entrance and follows a board-walk along Kingsland Creek—watch for native and migratory birds and waterfowl that flock to the reeds and grasses in this salt marsh wetland. This trail leads to another path that follows a dike along the **Saw Mill Creek Wildlife Management Area,** with scenic overlooks and a rare sense of solitude in this urban area. Visitors are amazed to learn that the landscaped hill they climb on the **Kingsland Overlook Trail** is a former landfill. The expansive view from here includes the Manhattan skyline off in the distance.

SPECTATOR SPORTS **Meadowlands Sports Complex** (201-935-3900; www .meadowlands.com), 50 Rt. 120, East Rutherford. The sports and entertainment complex that's also known as the Meadowlands and The Big M attracts millions of visitors to see the world's top athletes and performers. The 600-plus events every year include World Cup soccer and NBA championships as well as flea markets, family shows, and the Meadowlands State Fair. The Pope has been a headliner; so has Bruce Springsteen, who has played the Meadowlands 60 times. The complex includes four major venues: **Giants Stadium** (201-935-3900), home to the New York Jets, New York Giants, and the Red Bulls professional soccer team; **Meadow-lands Racetrack** (201-843-2446; 800-227-4480; www.thebigm.com), with live and simulcast thoroughbred racing and harness racing, including the world-famous trotting race, the **Hambletonian Festival of Racing** (see *Special Events*); the **IZOD Center**, which hosts the Seton Hall Pirates and New Jersey Nets (until they move to Brooklyn) as well as professional ice-skating and family entertainment; and the **Theater at IZOD Center**, an intimate venue with concerts, theater, and family shows.

✳ Green Space

NATURE PRESERVES ✐ **Lost Brook Preserve** (201-568-6093; www.tenafly naturecenter.org), Tenafly Nature Center, 313 Hudson Ave., Tenafly. The grounds and trails are open daily from dawn to dusk; the nature center is open daily 9–5, closed holidays. Free admission. This pristine 380-acre preserve is a rare urban oasis, a peaceful upland forest that offers 6 miles of trails. The landscape is dotted with streams and ponds, home to birds, deer, rabbits, and other small animals. Kids love the nature center's butterfly habitat, nature store, hands-on displays, and natural-history exhibits.

Flat Rock Brook Nature Center (201-567-1265; www.flatrockbrook.org), 443 Van Nostrand Ave., Englewood. Grounds and trails are open daily from dawn to dusk. The nature center is open Tues.–Fri. 9–5; Sat. and Sun. 1–5. Free admission. A 150-acre preserve and environmental education center on the western slopes of the Palisades. The sanctuary's pristine landscape is teeming with wildlife and laced with more than 3 miles of hiking trails that lead to ponds, quarry cliffs, wildflower meadows, woodlands, and a rushing stream. Boardwalk and picnic area.

PARKS **Clifton Municipal Sculpture Park** (973-471-0222; www.sculpture.org), 900 Clifton Ave., Clifton. Open daily from dawn to dusk. A beautiful 24-acre town park doubles as an outdoor art gallery. A permanent collection of sculpture is scattered throughout the grounds; new pieces are always being added.

Fort Lee Historic Park (201-461-1776), Hudson Terrace, Fort Lee. Grounds open year-round, daily 8 AM–sunset; a $5 parking fee is charged during special events. The visitors center is open Wed.–Sun. 10–5; free admission. In 1776, British and American forces were fighting the Revolutionary War, and Fort Lee— named for General Charles Lee, whose troops defended New York City—was one of the fortifications built that summer to defend the city and the Hudson River. In November, the British captured some 2,000 Continental soldiers at New York's Fort Washington as the rest fled across the Hudson to Fort Lee. General Cornwallis and 5,000 British troops followed, and launched a surprise attack on the Americans that forced General George Washington and his troops to abandon the Palisades fort and begin their famous retreat across New Jersey, all the way to the Pennsylvania side of the Delaware River. Washington would change the course of the war that Christmas, when he led his troops back across the Delaware to New Jersey, and to victory over the Hessians in Trenton. Today, the fort sits on a 33-acre site on top of the Palisades. The visitors center has exhibits on Fort Lee's role in the Revolutionary War, and a well-stocked bookstore. Paths leading past a reconstructed 18th-century soldiers' hut and gun batteries offer panoramas of the Hudson River, the George Washington Bridge, and the Manhattan skyline.

✐ **Richard W. DeKorte Park** (201-460-8300), Two DeKorte Park Plaza, Lyndhurst. Grounds open daily; the **Meadowlands Environment Center** is open

PALISADES INTERSTATE PARK

(201-768-1360; www.njpalisades.org), Alpine. Grounds are open daily, year-round from dawn to dusk. The 2,500-acre park straddling the New Jersey–New York border along the Hudson River is a rugged natural retreat in one of the most developed urban areas in America. It was created in 1900, thanks to the efforts of local preservationists trying to protect the towering black cliffs threatened by destruction from aggressive 19th-century quarrying. There are plenty of trails for hikers to explore; before heading out, pick up a trail guide at park police headquarters on Alpine Approach Road, or a copy of the topographical maps available at Lookout Inn at the State Line Lookout Area. Two main trails, the Long Path and the Shore Trail, are federally designated National Historic and Recreational Trails. They follow most of the park's 13-mile length from north to south over easy to moderate terrain. There are also a half-dozen cross-country ski trails that are open for hiking. The aqua-blazed **Long Path** starts at the **Fort Lee–Rockefeller Lookout** and follows the crest of the majestic cliffs, with panoramic views of the Hudson, all the way to the New York state line. The **Shore Trail** follows the riverbank north and climbs to the top of the cliffs via the **Giant Stairs,** a challenging section that's part hike, part rock scramble. It passes **waterfalls, a beach,** and the historic **Kearney House,** a restored 18th-century home that is open to visitors. Some believe that British general Cornwallis used the house as his headquarters during a surprise attack on the Continental army at Fort Lee in 1776. The **Old Alpine Trail** follows the route Cornwallis and his soldiers took up the cliffs.

Mon.–Fri. 9–5; Sat. and Sun. 10–3. An award-winning wildlife preserve with hiking and nature trails through the Meadowlands beloved by birders and solitude seekers. The center is a New Jersey Meadowlands Commission facility operated by Ramapo College of New Jersey, and features nature exhibits and an enclosed viewing area looking out over the marshes, swamps, and wildflower meadows. This 110-acre oasis sits in the most urbanized part of New Jersey, with hundreds of acres of reclaimed landfills and restored wetlands along the Hackensack River. The environmental education center has a year-round schedule of nature programs for children and adults, including guided nature walks. The butterfly garden is a peaceful spot, as is **The Cove,** where a panorama of the Meadowlands and the New York City skyline is reflected in a porcelain enamel plaque honoring those who lost their lives on September 11, 2001.

Pier A Park (201-420-2349), 100 Frank Sinatra Dr., Hoboken. A city park built on a former shipping pier jutting out over the Hudson River next to the historic Erie Lackawanna Terminal. An amphitheater at the end of the pier is the setting for Movies Under the Stars, a popular free summertime film series. Crowds come here to picnic on the tree-studded lawns, fish off the pier, and bike along the paths.

THE MEADOWLANDS ENVIRONMENT CENTER IS A NEW JERSEY MEADOWLANDS FACILITY OPERATED BY RAMAPO COLLEGE OF NEW JERSEY.

Elysian Park (201-420-2349), 1001 Hudson St., between 10th and 11th Sts., Hoboken. In the 19th century, Manhattanites would muscle a rowboat all the way across the Hudson River just to spend an afternoon at the leafy riverfront park. In 1846, the city park, known then as **Elysian Fields** (see sidebar, next page), hosted the world's first ball game. Hoboken's famous 1954 flick *On the Waterfront* was filmed here. It's a good spot away from the crowds, with a nice view of the Empire State Building, lively basketball courts, and a very popular dog run.

✳ Lodging

HOTELS & ✎ **Hilton Woodcliff Lake** (201-391-3600; 800-258-9621; www.hiltonwoodclifflake.com), 200 Tice Blvd., Woodcliff Lake 07677-9998. One of Hilton's luxury properties sits on 21 beautifully landscaped acres surrounded by woodland. A recent multimillion-dollar renovation has given the place the look and feel of a country hotel with the amenities of a full-service Hilton. Guest rooms are nicely spiffed up and now come with free, wireless high-speed Internet access. A variety of dining options includes **Saffron,** a casual restaurant serving creative, healthy cuisine at three meals; a coffee shop; a convivial lounge; and seasonal poolside dining. Active travelers who don't want to put their workout routine on hold while they're away will appreciate the state-of-the-art health and fitness facility with indoor and outdoor pools, tennis and racquetball courts, a jogging track, a putting green, a playground, and a fitness trail. The spa offers massage, body treatments, facials, and many other indulgences. $245 and up.

& **Clinton Inn Hotel** (201-871-3200; 800-275-4411; www.clinton-inn.com), 145 Dean Dr., Tenafly 07670. The 119 guest rooms are clean and comfortable. They feature standard amenities plus high-speed Internet access, work desks with ergonomic chairs, a complimentary daily newspaper, and turndown service. **Palmer's Crossing** is a restaurant and bar serving three meals daily. $229 and up.

🐾 ✏ ♿ **Sheraton Meadowlands Hotel and Conference Center** (201-896-0500; 800-325-3535; www.sheraton meadowlandshotel.com), Two Meadowlands Plaza, East Rutherford 07073. This 21-story hotel and conference center is adjacent to the Meadowlands Sports Complex. The 427 rooms and suites have all the usual amenities; there's also a fitness room, gift shop, and video arcade. The indoor heated pool and whirlpool tub occupy a bright and airy space whose glass walls afford a spectacular view of the Manhattan skyline. The **Chairman's Grill** is a stylish and casual eatery serving American cuisine all day; there's also a lounge in the lobby. $134 and up.

♿ **Renaissance Meadowlands Hotel** (201-231-3100; 800-851-6028), in the Meadowlands Corporate Park, 801 Rutherford Ave., Rutherford 07070. This 163-room Marriott hotel is right next to the Meadowlands Sports Complex. **CK's Steakhouse** (201-231-3141) is a sophisticated and polished steakhouse with an award-winning wine list. It's open daily for three meals but is best known for its top-notch aged steaks and chops. Rooms and suites have the usual features plus cordless phones, flat-screen TVs, high-speed Internet access, a free daily newspaper, and Starbuck's coffee; some have upgrades like whirlpool tubs and balconies. A fitness center, indoor pool, and whirlpool round out the amenities. $229 and up.

✏ ♿ **Meadowlands Plaza Hotel** (201-272-1000; 866-272-0060; www .meadowlandsplazahotel.com),

THE FIRST BASEBALL GAME—ELYSIAN FIELDS

America's first recorded baseball game—the world's first game of organized baseball—was played at Hoboken's Elysian Fields, known today as Elysian Park, on June 19, 1846. Taking the field were two local teams, the New York Nine and the Knickerbocker Baseball Club. It was the first baseball game to follow set rules, developed the year before by Alexander Cartwright, "the Father of Baseball," who umpired the historic game. His guidelines introduced the baseball diamond, home plate, a 21-pace distance between bases, and the concept of three strikes in half an inning. Some of his rules have changed, however. That day in Elysian Fields, there were two nine-man teams, pitching was underhanded, and a team had to score 21 points to win. The New Yorks won handily, scoring 23 runs in four innings (the Knickerbockers earned one run). It was the beginning of what would become the biggest all-American pastime ever.

There are some who dispute Hoboken's claim to baseball history. Newspaper articles published in 1823 refer to a game of "base ball" played in Manhattan. Furthermore, historians in Pittsfield, Massachusetts, claim that an 18th-century city bylaw suggests that baseball was played there as early as 1791.

40 Wood Ave., Secaucus 07094. A full-service hotel near the Meadowlands Sports Complex with 176 guest rooms ranging from standard-sized accommodations with two queen beds to two-room suites with a king bedroom, parlor with sleeper sofa, refrigerator, microwave, and bathroom with whirlpool tub. **La Reggia** serves authentic Italian specialties for lunch and dinner in an elegant dining room, and the casual lounge features weekend entertainment. A 24-hour fitness center, local shuttle, and business services are among the many amenities. $139 and up.

🐾 ✂ ♿ **Sheraton Suites on the Hudson** (201-617-5600; 888-625-5144), 500 Harbor Blvd., Weehawken 07086. An all-suite riverfront hotel that's just a half mile from Manhattan—naturally, the views are stunning. The New York Waterway ferry stops right outside the hotel, a convenience that draws many guests who would normally stay in Manhattan (and spend a lot more on a room). Each nicely furnished and spacious suite has a parlor with a sleeper sofa, two phone lines, and a wet bar with refrigerator, coffeemaker, and microwave. Amenities include a fitness room, an indoor pool, and a business center; babysitting services are available. The new **Harbor Bar and Brasserie** overlooks the New York City skyline and serves French bistro–inspired cuisine for breakfast, lunch, and dinner daily. $179 and up.

W Hotel (201-253-2400; 877-946-8357; www.whotels.com/hoboken), 225 River St., Hoboken 07030. The newest W Hotel debuted along the banks of the Hudson River in Hoboken in 2009. It's a W Hotel and Residences property, which combines the W's trademark sleek see-and-be-seen boutique hotel (225 rooms) with luxury apartments (40 upscale residences). It promises to be as stylish and superchic as its Manhattan counterparts across the river, with the W's famously luxe amenities, including a Bliss Spa, 24-hour fitness and business facilities, and a lounge boasting a skyline panorama, something the Manhattan properties can't offer. $369 and up.

✳ Where to Eat

DINING OUT

In Hoboken

🍴 **Augustino's** (201-420-0104; www.augustinosrestaurant.com), 1104 Washington St. Open for dinner Mon.–Sat.; closed Sun. Reservations are required. Locals love this buzzy, charming place, where the smell of Italian cooking wafts through the tiny dining room and greets you at the door. It's a homey and comforting welcome, and a sign of good things to come. Angelo "Buddy" Yandoli runs the kitchen, and his wife, Sharon, is in charge of the dining room, where she treats her guests like family. Augustino's trademark is its homespun Southern Italian classics, from house-made bruschetta and mussels steamed in white wine, to pork chops with roasted peppers in a red wine sauce, and a dozen or so specialty pizzas. There are just 10 tables, so there are no more than two-dozen people eating at a time. The vintage photos of Hoboken, gilt-edged mirrors adorning exposed brick walls, and a pressed-tin ceiling, lend the long, narrow space an Old World feel. No credit cards. $14–35.

City Bistro (201-963-8200; www.citybistrohoboken.com), 56–58 14th St. Open for lunch Mon.–Sat.; dinner daily; Sun. brunch. Reservations are recommended. The rooftop deck bar of this swank and trendy downtown bistro boasts one fine view of the Manhattan skyline. Inside is a handsome bar, where expertly crafted elixirs are

AMANDA'S
(201-798-0101; www.amandasrestaurant.com), 908 Washington St., Hoboken. Open daily for dinner; brunch on Sat. and Sun. An elegant brownstone with a series of intimate rooms decorated in rich fabrics and fine art create the most romantic of backdrops for an evening of fine dining. This sophisticated downtown spot—named for the granddaughter of the restaurant's founder—is where people come when they're looking for impeccable service and creative, flawless American cuisine. A recent menu featured starters like endive salad with smoked trout and lemon vinaigrette, risotto with butternut squash, caramelized onions, and sage, and seared pepper-crusted tuna with black beluga lentils. For dinner, there was roasted monkfish with warm potato salad and shallot reduction; pan-seared cod with chorizo, eggplant caviar, and fennel confit; and roasted duck breast with pear-potato puree, figs, and wilted greens. The weekend brunch menu is lighter but equally inventive; think warm mushroom and goat cheese salad, poached eggs with crab hash and orange hollandaise sauce, or creamy polenta with apricot compote. The extensive and well-chosen wine list includes many reasonably priced bottles. $19–34.

doled out to an oh-so-hip crowd, while others like to take in the Hoboken street scene from a sidewalk table. The sleek red-and-black color scheme sets the tone for creative Mediterranean-accented New American fare. $20–32.

Robongi (201-222-8388; www.robongi .com), 520 Washington St. Open daily for lunch and dinner. This simple and stylish storefront eatery is the kind of place where regulars dine at least once a week—the food is that good and the prices that reasonable. They come for the attentive service and artful Japanese cuisine, from the expertly crafted sushi and sashimi to the fresh fish straight from Manhattan's Fulton Fish Market. Starters include *edamame* with a sprinkling of sea salt, or *oshinko* (pickled daikon, cucumber, and other vegetables). The menu features a long list of tempura and teriyaki, but many go for the blackboard specials, which come with soup and salad. Save room for sweet endings like ginger ice cream

and fried bananas, or just a satisfying cup of green tea. BYOB. $11–23.

Dining Room at Anthony David's (201-222-8359; www.anthonydavids .com), 111 Tenth St. Open Tues.–Sun. for dinner; brunch daily. When an upscale market like Hoboken's Anthony David's opens a dining room, authorities like *Gourmet* magazine take notice. It's a place to savor seriously ambitious and inventive cuisine. The menu changes often, and might offer appetizers like broiled oysters with mascarpone, scallions, and radicchio, or beef carpaccio with shaved truffles and parmesan in a lemon vinaigrette. For dinner, saffron risotto comes with Maine lobster, prawns, mussels, and clams; and braised rabbit is bedecked with capers, pancetta, and wilted greens. Don't leave without browsing the market's selection of exquisitely prepared foods and haute foodstuffs. BYOB. $24–36.

Frankie & Johnnie's (201-659-6202), 163 14th St. Open daily for dinner. Reservations are recommended. This old-school steakhouse is a Hoboken institution, known for its chops and dry-aged New York–style steaks seasoned with their secret blend of spices. The bar sports its original pressed-tin ceiling and tile floor, along with antique mirrors, a hand-carved cherry bar, and a vintage streetlamp and clock. The restaurant dates to 1926, when it took over a 19th-century longshoremen's saloon, a gritty history that was reflected in the classic Hoboken film *On the Waterfront*. Scenes for the movie were shot here. Today, the soft candlelight and live piano and jazz make it as chic and sophisticated as its Manhattan counterparts. Clams casino, chilled oysters, and tuna tartare are popular starters that lead to diver scallops, red snapper, and, of course, steaks of all sizes and persuasions. $20–40.

Cucharamama (201-420-1700; www .cucharamama.com), 233 Clinton St. Open for dinner Tues.–Sat.; brunch and dinner Sun.; closed Mon. Reservations are recommended. Foodies are buzzing about this chic South American hot spot. *Cucharamama* means "mother spoon," and fittingly, the kitchen turns out chimichurri, tamales, empanadas, and other homey Latin-inspired dishes from a wood-fired adobe oven. $15–30.

Lua (201-876-1900; www.luarestaurant .com), 1300 Sinatra Dr. Open daily for dinner; Sun. brunch. This pan-Latin eatery in the Shipyard development along the Hudson River is one of the city's hottest eateries at the moment. They bill the cuisine as Nuevo Latino, a popular culinary trend, but here it's well executed. Inventive Latin fusion cuisine (ceviche is a specialty) keeps pace with ultra-modern surroundings, which include a 360-degree elliptical bar. $19–36.

In Rutherford and East Rutherford

Café Matisse (201-935-2995; www .cafematisse.com), 167 Park Ave., Rutherford. Serving dinner Tues.–Sun.; closed Mon. Reservations are recommended. Contemporary American and European cuisine in an 1898 firehouse converted into elegant dining rooms and a wine shop. The walls are painted in bold hues with faux works by Matisse, and there's a romantic garden outside for summer dining. Chef-owner Peter Loria gets high marks for blending modern twists with time-honored techniques. Start with pan-seared, clove-scented scallops with caramelized apricots and zinfandel syrup; or duck confit with wild mushrooms and cashews atop a scallion pancake with orange-cardamom syrup. Next, you might try pan-roasted lamb with feta, curried eggplant, and mint-basil yogurt sauce; or charred filet mignon with pumpkin risotto and chestnut honey-roasted shrimp. Desserts are homemade and sublime. BYOB. Prix fixe $60–95.

&. **Park & Orchard Restaurant** (201-939-9292; www.parkandorchard.com), 240 Hackensack St., East Rutherford. Serving lunch Mon.–Fri.; dinner daily. Reservations are accepted. What began as a humble storefront eatery has morphed into a success story of epic proportions. This huge, and hugely popular, restaurant near the Meadowlands Sports Complex is considered one of the top restaurants in New Jersey for its eclectic American and international cuisine. Only 100 or so restaurants around the world earn the prestigious annual *Wine Spectator* Grand Award, and Park & Orchard has won it numerous times. The extensive something-for-everyone menu is so overwhelming that the close-your-eyes-and-point method works well, since you really can't go wrong with anything. There are homey all-American classics like chicken meatloaf and mashed potatoes; Mexican, Cajun, and French specialties, a huge list of creative stir-fries, and a daily changing list of grilled meats that might feature quail and ostrich. But let's talk dessert: The ever-changing menu features a couple dozen selections, perhaps pecan-crusted chocolate torte with butterscotch sauce, or grilled pineapple slices drizzled with honey. $16–29.

Mignon Steak House (201-896-0202), 72 Park Ave., Rutherford. Open daily for lunch and dinner. Generous cuts of aged prime steak without the Manhattan price tag. Overwhelmed by the extensive menu? Start with crab ravioli or tuna carpaccio, then order the signature dish: savory filet mignon. Desserts are rich finales: flourless chocolate torte with mocha sauce, key lime pie served in a martini glass, and classic cheesecake. BYOB. $17–45.

Elsewhere

∞ **Stony Hill Inn** (201-342-4085; www.stonyhillinn.com), 231 Polifly Rd., Hackensack. Open for lunch Mon.–Fri.; dinner daily. Reservations are suggested. A centuries-old Georgian estate boasting an excellent staff and top-notch French and Italian cuisine. The dining room gets its elegance from white linen, plush drapes, and soaring windows, an opulent setting makes this a sought-after wedding venue. Plans are in the works for an on-site hotel. $20–40.

Paula at Rigoletto (201-422-9500; www.paulaatrigoletto.com), 3706 Park Ave., Weehawken. Open for dinner Tues.–Sun.; Sun. brunch; closed Mon. Paula Frazier, Bruce Springsteen's former chef, now helms her own cozy Italian restaurant. Authentic northern

Italian dishes are simply yet expertly prepared; the walls are hung with the work of local artists. Killer desserts like chocolate-walnut torte alone are worth the trip. BYOB. $18–22.

Arthur's Landing (201-867-0777; www.arthurslanding.com), at Port Imperial, Pershing Rd., Weehawken. Open daily for dinner; brunch on Sat. and Sun. Reservations are recommended. A plum spot on the Hudson River waterfront offers spectacular Manhattan skyline views and elegant American cuisine. To start, try the caramelized shallot ravioli, or seared Hudson Valley foie gras. Dinner might be grilled bass with butternut-ginger puree and broccoli rabe; or cider-glazed duck breast with pomegranate syrup. With the pre-theater package, you dine here then hop aboard a ferry to take in a Broadway show. $23–32.

Madeleine's Petite Paris (201-767-0063; www.madeleinespetitparis.com), 416 Tappan Rd., Northvale. Open for lunch Tues.–Fri.; dinner Tues.–Sat.; Sun. brunch. Reservations are accepted. Gaspard and Madeleine Caloz's warm and inviting restaurant has the feel of a stylish European bistro. Gaspard is a highly touted Swiss chef, and Madeleine is in charge of the dining room. Together they have worked magic for more than three decades, in which time their classic French cooking and impeccable service have earned an impressive list of rave reviews and a legion of loyal fans. Prix fixe $29; entrées $28–37.

&. **Harvest** (201-750-9966; www.harvestbistro.com), 252 Schraalenburgh Rd., Closter. Open for lunch Tues.–Fri.; dinner Tues.–Sun.; Sun. brunch. Reservations are recommended, especially on weekends. It's hard to choose where to eat—the dining room is elegant and chic, with a soaring cathedral ceiling, dramatic stone fireplace, and French doors; but the outdoor deck overlooking the woods is lively, energetic, and fun. Either way, the service is pleasant and the classic French cuisine is top-notch, and accompanied by a well-selected wine list. Start with Provençal fish soup, move on to coq au vin or bouillabaisse, and end with crêpes or profiteroles. Prix fixe $35; entrées $20–35.

& **The Restaurant** (201-678-1100; www.therestaurant.net), 160 Prospect Ave., Hackensack. Reservations are suggested. Open for lunch Tues.–Fri.; dinner Tues.–Sun.; Sun. brunch. Don't be fooled by the generic name—this is one of the hottest dining rooms in the state. The airy space with dramatic vaulted wood-beam cathedral ceilings and gilt-edged oil paintings is reminiscent of a medieval church, a sophisticated backdrop for the stellar Continental cuisine with accents of Northern Italy. The menu changes seasonally to take advantage of the freshest ingredients, and gets high marks for artistic presentation. Entrées range from aged prime steaks and chops prepared by the in-house butcher, to honey-coriander-crusted Atlantic salmon, or free-range Canadian duckling. Sunday brunch is an extraordinary event, and **The Gourmet Pantry** (see *Snacks*) sells fresh soups, prepared foods, and home-baked breads and desserts. Entrées $20–36.

Chengdu 46 (973-777-8855), 1105 Rt. 46 E., Clifton. Open for lunch Tues.–Fri.; dinner Tues.–Sun.; Sun. prix fixe luncheon. A stylish and upscale Chinese restaurant known for its authentic Szechuan cuisine—fish, shellfish, chicken, beef, pork—accented with spices and seasonings imported from China. Chengdu 46 has consistently garnered enthusiastic praise and accolades from food critics, and has been considered one of the top Chinese restaurants in the state for the past two decades. Ask about their special wine-tasting dinners. $15–25.

Chakra (201-556-1530; www.chakra restaurant.com), 144 W. Rt. 4, Paramus. Open for dinner Mon.–Sat.; closed Sun. Hip young diners love this dimly lit space named for the body's energy centers. The dining room, dressed in bold hues and lush fabrics, is vibrant and stylish. Seasonal New American dishes have Asian and Italian touches (think seared shallot-crusted tuna, steak tartare, burgundy-braised short ribs). There's also a high energy bar and lounge. $19–35.

EATING OUT

In Hoboken

✧ **Leo's Grandevous Restaurant** (201-659-9467; www.leosgrandevous .com), 200 Grand St. Open for lunch Mon.–Fri.; dinner daily. Leo's has been dishing out traditional Italian cuisine since 1939, and although founder Leo DiTerlizzi retired in 1999, the restaurant is still in his family, making it one of Hoboken's oldest family-run establishments. It's proudly old school, from the jukebox to the collection of Frank Sinatra photos and memorabilia lining the walls. Start with a hot antipasto or a plate of roasted peppers and smoked mozzarella; next, try the homemade ravioli, pasta with meatballs, or veal, chicken, and steak. Eat in the casual and intimate dining area or at the large bar, where you can choose from two-dozen bar pies, around $7. No credit cards. $12–18.

Bangkok City (201-792-6613), 335 Washington St. Open daily for lunch and dinner. A warm and inviting spot with traditional Thai décor and the classic earthy and exotic cuisine of Thailand. Start with *tom yum koong* (shrimp soup with lemongrass and hot pepper) or barbecued beef salad with lime juice and chili pepper. Move on to pad Thai; grilled sirloin with lemon sauce, chili pepper, and fresh garlic; steamed salmon in green curry sauce with coconut milk and eggplant; or a variety of curry dishes, from mild to fiery. $11–19.

Maxwell's (201-653-1703; www.max wellsnj.com), 1039 Washington St. Serving dinner Mon.–Fri. until midnight; Sat. and Sun. until 1 AM. Maxwell's has been a neighborhood landmark since it opened on the corner of 11th Street in 1978. It's legendary for its live music, but the food is decent, too. A long, narrow dining area with windows overlooking the street is quieter than the bar area, which also has tables. The lofty pressed-tin ceiling, tile floor, brick walls, and long wood bar lend an old-time tavern feel. A dependable menu of quesadillas, soups, burgers, burritos, and daily specials like pasta and seafood. $9–20.

Baja (201-653-0610), 104 14th Street. Open for lunch Fri.; dinner daily; brunch on Sat. and Sun. Reservations are recommended, especially on weekends. A loud, lively café frequented by a young clientele, who come for the freshly prepared Mexican fare and the 120 varieties of tequila behind the bar. There's an equally impressive list of margaritas, but the strawberry is a must since it's the only flavor made with fresh fruit. Choose from Tex-Mex standards like enchiladas and tacos, or creative specialties like red snapper in an avocado-tomatillo sauce. Huevos rancheros and breakfast burritos at brunch. $10–22.

❦ **Schnackenberg's Luncheonette** (201-659-9836), 1110 Washington St. Open Mon.–Sat. for breakfast and lunch. The menu (egg cream, malted milk, liverwurst), décor (linoleum, chrome, vinyl), and prices add up to a trip back in time in this old-fashioned luncheonette with remnants-of-a-bygone-era ambience. It opened in 1931, and hasn't changed much since. The antique cash register stands proudly behind the counter. Meals around $7.

In Union City

❦ **El Artesano Restaurant** (201-867-7341; www.elartesanorestaurant.com), 4101 Bergenline Ave. Open daily for breakfast, lunch, and dinner. Reservations are accepted. Nuevo Latino cuisine has been supertrendy in recent years, but this Union City institution is the real deal—a no-frills eatery serving authentic Cuban cuisine in a casual family-style atmosphere. Traditional Spanish dishes like paella and shrimp in wine sauce come with bargain prices, making it possible to be adventurous and try a little of everything. You might start with avocado salad, red bean soup, chicken empanada, or a tamale wrapped in corn husks. Next, try the savory pot roast in red sauce, Cuban-style beef stew, fried red snapper, or crispy pork rinds and mashed green plantains. $8–20.

Beyti Kebab (201-865-6281), 4105 Park Ave. Open daily for lunch and dinner. Reservations are required for Saturday night. Behind an unassuming storefront lies some of the most authentic Turkish, Middle Eastern, and Mediterranean cuisine around. On Saturday night, everyone dines in a large banquet hall where they're entertained by belly dancing and live traditional Turkish music. Start with creamy tabbouleh, silky smooth hummus, stuffed grape leaves, or fried eggplant with garlic yogurt. Move on to the namesake kebabs—veal, lamb, or chicken, marinated in herbs and spices, then grilled—or minced lamb patties or roasted beef. Soft pita bread and cool mint and yogurt sauces are refreshing accompaniments to the exotic seasonings. Traditional desserts like baklava or *kadayif,* shredded wheat with walnuts. BYOB. $13–24.

Elsewhere

Village Gourmet (201-438-9494), 75 Park Ave., Rutherford. Asian-inspired American dishes (General Tao's chicken the specialty) are on the menu of this bustling café. There's a wine shop on the premises in case you forget to bring a bottle. BYOB. $13–22.

Café Angelique (201-541-1010), One Piermont Rd., Tenafly. Open daily. A charming café in a restored train depot. Many regulars come here for decadent grown-up treats (think warm chocolate soufflé) designed to help you embrace your sweet tooth. Not in the mood for dessert? There's a menu of omelets and other standards for breakfast, as well as salads, soups, and sandwiches for lunch.

White Manna Hamburgers (201-342-0914), 358 River Rd., Hackensack. Open Mon.–Sat. for breakfast, lunch, and dinner. This beloved art deco relic from New Jersey's diner days is the quintessential greasy spoon. There were several White Mannas in northern New Jersey at one time; today this is one of only two that remain (the other is in Jersey City). The shoebox-sized interior sports a curved counter with stools, behind which burgers sizzle on the grill. They're good and tasty (greasy and fattening) and come with piping-hot fries. Affectionately known as "sliders," they're served plain or smothered in onions and cheese. $4–8.

& **East** (201-837-1260), 1405 Teaneck Rd., Teaneck. Open daily for lunch and dinner; reservations are recommended. A bustling, noisy, and energetic Japanese restaurant that's part of an equally popular Manhattan restaurant chain. Sit around the large sushi bar for the *kaiten-zushi,* a revolving

selection of self-serve plates of expertly prepared sushi—a common dining tradition in Japan. $12–20.

La Riviera Trattoria (973-478-4181), 421 Piaget Ave. (Rt. 46 E.), Clifton. Open for lunch Tues.–Fri.; dinner Tues.–Sun.; closed Mon. A longtime local favorite for homey Italian fare. Many come here for the homemade pasta, or the signature Seafood Riviera, in which calamari, scallops, clams, and shrimp are broiled and drizzled with olive oil. Ricotta cheesecake and cannoli are among the traditional and satisfying desserts. $12–24.

SNACKS

In Hoboken

Dom's Bakery Grand (201-653-1948), 506 Grand St. Open daily. Some 2,000 loaves are formed every day by hand and baked in a vintage coal-fired oven. Dominick and Flo Castellitto's landmark bakery churns out European breads, French loaves, round *panella* breads, rolls, focaccia, and sausage bread.

Antique Bakery (201-714-9323), 122 Willow Ave. Open daily. Coal-fired brick ovens turn out close to 3,000 loaves and rolls daily, using the same traditional methods that have worked for more than 70 years. Most of the breads are shipped to restaurants and sandwich shops in New York City and to area businesses. Loyal customers come in for the popular peasant bread, or *pagnotta,* a crusty round loaf of chewy white bread. Others line up for soft focaccia, baguettes, round *panella* breads, and breads stuffed with sausage, pepperoni, and peppers.

Carlo's Bake Shop (201-659-3671), 95 Washington St. Open daily. A family-run Italian bakery in business for close to a century, known for its hot coffee and delicious pastries—cheesecake, crumb cake, Danish, traditional

Italian cookies and treats like biscotti, *torrone,* and *struffoli.*

The Hoboken Gourmet Company (201-795-0110), 423 Washington St. Open Mon.–Fri. 6 AM–9 PM; Sat. and Sun. 6 AM–7 PM. Step down from the street into this charming and cozy shop with wood floors and a pressed-tin ceiling. Old-fashioned glass jars are filled with sweets, from huge slabs of biscotti to chocolate-covered pretzels. Breakfast is omelets, fluffy belgian waffles, and egg sandwiches; salads, soups, and wraps later on. It's also a good place to stop in for an espresso or cappuccino. Work by local artists hangs on the brick walls. $7–15.

Fiore House of Quality (201-659-1655), 414 Adams St. A bustling deli and local meeting place with the usual selection of sandwiches, but the special—shaved roast beef, fresh mozzarella, and gravy served hot on Italian bread—is what people line up for. Everything is wonderfully fresh, familiar, and appealing, and the prices are gentle.

Elsewhere
Balthazar Bakery (201-503-9717), 214 South Dean St., Englewood. Open Mon.–Sat. You can buy the handcrafted artisan breads made for the posh SoHo brasserie of the same name. Exquisite, Old World–style breads are baked in a hearth oven, like their signature hearty *pain de seigle boule* and *pain au levain,* or a classic baguette. Flaky croissants, rich brioche, seasonal fruit tarts, and other desserts.

The Gourmet Pantry (201-968-9378), at The Restaurant, 160 Prospect Ave., Hackensack. Open Tues.–Sun. People come in the morning for muffins, turnovers, croissants, omelets, and egg sandwiches; later on for the fresh soups and made-to-order gourmet sandwiches. The pantry features close to two dozen varieties of freshly baked breads, homemade pasta, and desserts. $6–15. (See also *Dining Out.*)

Rutt's Hut (973-779-8615), 417 River Rd., Clifton. A well-known institution that gives the region's hot-dog hot spots a run for the money. Deep-fried hot dogs, known here as "rippers," are generously smothered with chili, sauerkraut, hot or sweet relish, and other classic condiments.

Vitamia & Sons (973-546-1140), 206 Harrison Ave., Lodi. Open daily. Tradi-

🍴 ♿ TICK-TOCK DINER

(973-777-0511; www.tictockdiner.com), 281 Allwood Rd. (Rt. 3), Clifton. Open around the clock for breakfast, lunch, and dinner. In a state that's unofficially but commonly known as the Diner Capital of America, this chrome-sided landmark in Clifton is a real treasure and considered one of the best. Their motto is "Eat heavy," and the kitchen does all it can to ensure that you do. They serve heaping portions of just about anything you can imagine eating in a diner. The meatloaf comes in thick slabs smothered in gravy; the cheese blintzes are sweet and well stuffed; and the chicken noodle soup comes steaming-hot. If you arrive with a hankering for breakfast, you're in luck— there are a few dozen varieties of omelets, not to mention pancakes, waffles, and all the other standbys. All cakes and pastries are baked on the premises. Since 1949. $7–18.

tional Italian pastries, each more sinfully tempting than the one before, fill gleaming cases in this tidy shop that evolved from a family business started in Sicily in 1829. Fresh ravioli is handmade here every day; a dozen or so varieties come with decadent fillings like lobster, but the simple cheese ravioli is the best seller.

ICE CREAM ✿ **Bischoff's** (201-836-0333), 468 Cedar Lane, Teaneck. Open daily year-round. This old-fashioned ice-cream parlor, luncheonette, and candy store has been a landmark in the center of town since it opened in 1934. Homemade ice cream comes in 40 flavors and is served on cones, in sundaes, and in milkshakes.

✿ **Family Scoops** (201-533-1337), 320 Washington St., Hoboken. Open daily 11–11. People line up at this take-out window at the heart of Washington Street for frozen yogurt, gelato, ice cream, and Italian ice—all homemade. Italian ice comes in flavors like mango and honeydew; gelato includes chocolate-hazelnut, pistachio, and tiramisu.

✳ Entertainment

Meadowlands Exposition Center (201-330-7773; www.mecexpo.com), Harmon Meadow, 355 Plaza Dr., Secaucus. A 61,000-square-foot expo center with a year-round schedule of trade shows, festivals, nationally known speakers, and cultural events.

✿ **Bergen Performing Arts Center** (201-227-1030; www.bergenpac.org), 30 N. Van Brunt St., Englewood. The former John Harms Center offers a full schedule of music, dance, theater, comedy, and programs for children.

ARTS CENTERS ✿ **Williams Center for the Arts** (201-939-6969; www.williamscenter.org), One Williams Plaza, Rutherford. A nonprofit multi-

cultural performing-arts center that offers a wide variety of shows throughout the year. The center is housed in the 1920s-era **Rivoli Theater**—a former silent-film house—and named for the Pulitzer Prize–winning poet William Carlos Williams, who once lived in the neighborhood. Performances range from ballet and opera to Broadway musicals and music festivals. The resident children's theater presents classic plays and holiday shows.

Monroe Center for the Arts (201-795-3767; www.monroecenter.com), 720 Monroe St., Hoboken. A multidisciplinary arts center whose painters, potters, photographers, sculptors, and other local artists open their studios to the public on the first Sunday of every month. The **Monroe Center Gallery's** year-round rotating exhibits feature the work of artists from the New York City metropolitan region.

MUSIC Free outdoor concerts along the Hudson River waterfront are easy to come by in the summertime. Hoboken's **Summer Enchanted Evening Concert Series** (201-420-2207) takes place at Shipyard Park on 13th Street on Tuesday and at Frank Sinatra Park on Thursday. All shows begin at 7 PM and feature Latin, jazz, rock, swing, R&B, or opera. In Weehawken, the **Hudson River Performing Arts Center** (201-716-4540) hosts concerts in Lincoln Harbor Park from late June to mid-September. Performances begin at 7 PM—bring a lawn chair or blanket.

THEATER **DeBaun Auditorium: The Center for Performing Arts** (201-216-8937; www.debaun.org), Edwin Stevens Hall, Stevens Institute of Technology, Fifth and Hudson Sts., Hoboken. Theater, music, children's programs, modern dance, and special events and series.

PARK PERFORMING ARTS CENTER—THE PASSION PLAY
(201-865-6980; www.passionplayusa.org), 560 32nd St., Union City. The show-piece of the theater's full schedule of multicultural musical productions and performances is the longest-running Passion Play in America. The story of Jesus Christ's last days on earth, also known as the Greatest Story Ever Told, has been staged in Union City since 1915; first in a school auditorium, later at this 1,400-seat Broadway-style theater built in 1931 especially for the Passion Play. During the Easter season, professional actors and members of the local community stage weekend matinees of the musical theater production, which is modeled after the original Passion Play that has been performed every 10 years in Oberammergau, Germany, since 1634. The Union City play was developed as a peaceful response to the international discord surrounding World War I; today the theater is the sole survivor of what was once a thriving downtown theater district.

FILM Movies and Music Under the Stars (201-592-3663; www.fortleefilm .org), Constitution Park, Linwood Ave., Fort Lee. A free summer film series on Wednesdays, with live music at 7 PM followed by a movie at sunset.

Movies Under the Stars (201-420-2207), Pier A Park, First St. and Frank Sinatra Dr., Hoboken. A popular free summer film series takes place every Wednesday evening from June to August; bring a blanket or a lawn chair and a picnic.

✳ Selective Shopping

ART GALLERIES Center Gallery (201-767-7160), Old Church Cultural Center School of Art, 561 Piermont Rd., Demarest. A year-round schedule of changing exhibitions showcases the work of regional artists and craftspeople. The annual pottery show and sale in December has been a popular event for more than 30 years.

Arielle's Gallery (201-894-0405), 20 North Dean St., Englewood. Fine art, sculpture, and American crafts in a downtown gallery.

B.A.M.A. Galleries (201-659-8873), 946 Bloomfield St., Hoboken. A bright and airy storefront gallery showcasing the work of national artists in changing exhibits. Classes in yoga, dance, painting, and drawing.

Richard W. DeKorte Park (201-460-8300), Valley Brook Ave., Lyndhurst. Open daily. The **Flyway Gallery** features monthly changing exhibits of paintings, photographs, sculptures, and graphic art.

BOOKSTORE Symposia Bookstore (201-963-0909), 510 Washington St., Hoboken. Open daily noon–6; often stays open late. A small independent bookstore that doubles as a community center. The shop floor is living-room cozy, with works by local artists on the walls, couches and chairs, a chessboard, maybe a card game or a jigsaw puzzle set up; Internet access is available by donation. They even rent bicycles.

FACTORY OUTLET Secaucus Outlets (201-348-4780; 877-688-5382), Meadowlands Parkway (off Rt. 3), Secaucus. Open daily. Donna Karan,

Eileen Fisher, Reebok, Yves Saint Laurent, Pierre Deux, Nine West, and other designer duds for sale.

FLEA MARKET Meadowlands Flea Market (201-935-5474), Giants Stadium, Meadowlands Sports Complex, 50 Rt. 120, East Rutherford. Open year-round, Sat. 8–3; additional holiday hours. Over 600 vendors offering an ever-changing selection of collectibles, crafts, produce, and fresh-cut flowers.

SPECIAL SHOPS Mrs. Hanna Krause Candy (201-843-0337; 888-657-2873), Rt. 17 S., Paramus. A family-owned confectioner since 1929 that still makes its old-time candies by hand. Caramel, nougat, marzipan, and other fillings are first cooked, then hand dipped in chocolate one piece at a time. They specialize in traditional homemade chocolates, butter crunch, creams, cordial cherries, and nut bark. Seasonal items include tens of thousands of chocolate bunnies every Easter.

Demarest Farm (201-266-0472), 244 Werimus Rd., Hillsdale. Open May to late-Nov., daily 8–6. A family farm established in 1886 has evolved into a something-for-everyone destination: pick-your-own produce, seasonal hayrides, potted plants, and a country store.

Mitsuwa Marketplace (201-941-9113), 595 River Rd., Edgewater. Open daily 9:30–8. A sprawling market with a huge selection of imported Japanese, Korean, and Chinese groceries. The food court features authentic Japanese pastry, steaming bowls of noodles, and freshly prepared sushi.

Corrado's Family Affair (973-340-0628), 1578 Main Ave., Clifton. Open daily. A massive store featuring food and wine from around the world and a large selection of European meats and cheeses. The bakery section sells freshly baked loaves from more than a dozen area bakeries, from Italian loaves to baguettes, fresh Middle Eastern pita bread, and Portuguese rolls. You hear all kinds of languages spoken by the shoppers that crowd the store on weekends.

Anthony David's Gourmet Market (201-222-8399), 953 Bloomfield St., Hoboken. A stylish corner neighborhood market with upscale deli items and imported gourmet groceries. An intimate dining room offers creative haute cuisine.

Aaraa (201-386-0101), 628 Washington St., Hoboken. Upscale home accessories and gifts in a lovely, inviting shop. Handmade paper, jewelry, fabrics, bedding, tablecloths, delicate silk shawls, scarves, and handbags.

✷ Special Events

February: **New Jersey Spring Home Show** (201-330-7773; www.mecexpo.com), Meadowlands Exposition Center, Secaucus.

March: **The Passion Play** (201-865-6980), Park Performing Arts Center, Union City (see *Entertainment—Theater*). The longest-running Passion Play in the country. **St. Patrick's Day Parade** (201-420-7842), 14th and Washington Sts., Hoboken.

May: **Hoboken Arts Music Festival** (201-420-2207), Washington St., Hoboken. **Hooked on the Hudson** (201-768-0379), Palisades Interstate Park, Alpine. A spring celebration of the Hudson River with a shad bake, a fishing tournament, crafts, food, and environmental exhibits.

June: ✄ **State Fair Meadowlands** (973-984-3000; www.njfair.com), Giants Stadium, Meadowlands Sports Complex, East Rutherford. Stage shows, rides, fair food, and circus acts.

Tour of Hoboken's Secret Gardens (201-656-2240), Hoboken Museum, Hoboken.

July: ✿ **St. Ann's Italian Street Festival** (201-200-5505), St. Ann's Square, Eighth and Jefferson Sts., Hoboken. A weeklong celebration with traditional Italian foods, games, nightly live entertainment, and rides for kids. The festival has been a tradition for more than a century and draws more than 20,000 visitors.

August: **The Hambletonian Festival of Racing** (201-935-8500), Meadowlands Racetrack, East Rutherford. An American harness horse-racing tradition since 1926, and the highest-stakes trotting race in the world. Watch the best trotters and drivers compete for a $1.5 million purse.

September: **Hoboken Italian Festival** (201-216-0252), Hoboken.

October: **Hispanic Day Parade** (1-877-428-3930), Union City. **Hispanic State Parade of New Jersey** (1-877-428-3930), Bergenline Ave., West New York. ✿ **Harvest Festival** (201-420-2207), Frank Sinatra Park, Hoboken. Festivities include hayrides, live music, storytelling, pumpkin painting, rides, and a petting zoo. **Hoboken House Tour** (201-656-2240), Hoboken. A self-guided tour of some of the city's finest homes.

THE NEWARK AND
JERSEY CITY REGION

N ewark and Jersey City are the state's two largest cities, presiding over a highly developed industrial, retail, and residential swath that has just about paved over this entire region. Together, they are a gateway to New York City as well as one of the most important trade centers in the world, with a major airport, the world's largest containership port, and a bustling manufacturing hub. A number of revitalization projects are underway, however, that are sprucing up the waterfront and bringing in visitor-friendly attractions, from a world-class science and technology museum to greenways along the Hudson River and New York Harbor.

Newark is New Jersey's largest city and one of its oldest, settled in 1666. Before that, Lenni-Lenape Indians, followed by European settlers, were using the harbor for fishing and transportation; by 1661 they had a ferry service up and running. Newark was one of the first cities in America—only Boston and New York are older. It quickly became an industrial hub in the young republic for many pioneering advances. Experimental use of asphalt began in 1870, making Newark the first city in the nation to pave its streets. So many products were being manufactured here in the 19th century that city leaders organized the Newark Industrial Exhibition in 1872. It was the first such exhibition in the country to showcase products made exclusively in one city. Today, the Newark region is home to Fortune 500 companies, high-tech labs, and major world headquarters, including Prudential Financial, the country's largest life insurance company.

Newark may not leap to mind when we think of vacation destinations—many still remember the violent race riots of the 1960s that made the city a poster child for inner-city decay. Today, however, it's a revitalized city with a lot to offer visitors. The downtown arts district is packed with theaters and restaurants; most noteworthy are the authentic Spanish, Portuguese, and Brazilian eateries packed into the Ironbound District, named for its location amid railroad tracks. It's a lively and energetic neighborhood with a city-within-a-city feel, and the streets are often filled with boisterous crowds of people out for a night of fun. The Newark Museum is one of the most highly regarded fine-arts museums in the country, and boasts the largest collection of Tibetan art and artifacts in the Western Hemisphere. The elegant Ionic-columned Newark Symphony Hall is the oldest and largest performance space in New Jersey. The New Jersey Performing Arts Center opened in 1997 and is a venue for world-class theater, headlining entertainers, and

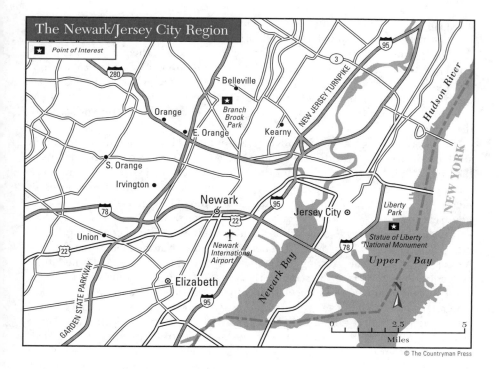

The Newark/Jersey City Region

★ Point of Interest

the New Jersey Symphony Orchestra. The city's professional baseball legacy dates to 1902, when the Newark Indians were formed. They eventually became the Newark Bears, who now play at the city's Riverfront Stadium. The Prudential Center, the city's new state-of-the-art arena, is now home to the New Jersey Devils hockey franchise. For those who make more than a day trip to Newark, there are thousands of hotel rooms that cater to businesspeople during the week, and therefore offer great rates on weekends.

New Jersey's second largest city sits just across the Hudson River from Manhattan. Jersey City was once America's rail shipping center; the many warehouses lining the waterfront served the nearby freight yards. Pavonia, as it was first known, was settled by Dutch fur traders in the 1630s. What began as a fishing and farming village transformed itself into a gritty factory town in the 1800s, one of the cities leading the way during the Industrial Revolution. This success peaked at the turn of the 20th century before the city suffered the same postwar decline in the 1950s that the rest of America suffered from. Rail lines, factories, and warehouses seemed to shut down overnight, and the city decayed quietly, until its leaders and investors launched a renaissance in the 1980s that is still building momentum.

Abandoned industrial buildings and freight warehouses along the waterfront were razed to make room for office, retail, and residential developments, while historic factories and warehouses were saved and converted into luxury lofts and condos. The world's largest passenger-train shed once occupied the site that's now known as Exchange Place, a major financial center where shiny, new office buildings occupy the old rail yards. The sole remaining historic structure is 15 Exchange Place, which was once New Jersey's tallest building. Today that distinction goes to the 876-foot-tall Goldman Sachs office tower, comparable in height to the tallest buildings in Lower Manhattan. Jersey City has been dubbed Wall Street West for the number of finance, commerce, and real estate giants who have moved across the river from Manhattan. The waterfront is known as the Gold Coast for the same reason; it's also known as "the sixth borough" for its ties to the metropolis across the Hudson.

Just past Exchange Place is a moving September 11th monument that features a steel girder from the World Trade Center and an image of the old skyline across the river. While you're here, look for the Colgate Clock, a massive 1920s-era timepiece with a dial that's a staggering 50 feet in diameter (the minute hand moves 23 inches every minute). When it was perched atop the old Colgate-Palmolive warehouses at this site, New Yorkers could see it from across the river.

Furthermore, Jersey City is fast positioning itself as a cultural center for the arts. The Powerhouse Arts District, a neighborhood of historic factories and warehouses, is a vibrant and growing arts community that is already home to the largest concentration of artists in the state. Early-20th-century brick warehouses have been converted into studio space and lofts to give artists a place to live and work. The relative affordability and proximity to Manhattan are big draws. Resident artists and city leaders are pushing for more arts-related development, including museums, galleries, and performance spaces that will attract visitors. The arts district—named for the 1908 Hudson & Manhattan Railroad powerhouse—revolves around the P. Lorillard Tobacco Company warehouse, a rambling historic structure at 111 First Street that has been converted into artists' studios used by an eclectic mix of artists, musicians, designers, and writers. Fast becoming one of the city's biggest events is the Jersey City Artist Studio Tour, when artists open their doors to collectors, dealers, and the general public. The tour features the work of Jersey City–based artists, as well as those from around the state and New York City.

One of Jersey City's crown jewels is Liberty State Park, a greenway along New York Harbor that is one of the most visited state parks in America and attracts millions of visitors every year. The park's Liberty Science Center, fresh off a multi-million-dollar expansion, boasts the largest IMAX dome screen in the country, and is now one of the region's top science and technology museums. The long-abandoned terminal of the Central Railroad of New Jersey was rescued and brought back to its former glory. At this grand historic building, park visitors catch the Circle Line ferry for an up-close view of the two most famous symbols of democracy, freedom, and opportunity in the world—the Statue of Liberty and Ellis Island. There's nothing perhaps more recognizable than Lady Liberty presiding above New York Harbor with her torch held high. Ellis Island holds the historic processing center where more than 12 million immigrants first stepped foot into their new lives in the United States. Today, nearly 40 percent of all Americans can trace an element of their family history to Ellis Island. The monuments are on the New Jersey side of New York Harbor, but since New York was granted possession of the islands in 1833, the statue is considered to be in New York; the two states share Ellis Island.

Below Newark is a string of historic industrial waterfront communities. Elizabeth is a major shipping port whose docks bustle with cargo ships from around the world. For visitors, there's Jersey Gardens Mall, the state's largest indoor outlet mall, and historic Boxwood Hall, a restored 18th-century mansion that's a rare

FAMOUS NEW JERSEYANS

An impressive number of icons in entertainment, sports, literature, and history have roots in New Jersey. Of course there's Frank Sinatra of Hoboken, and Rumson's Bruce Springsteen, perhaps New Jersey's most famous native son. His home state figures prominently in many of his classic songs, and the public library in Asbury Park owns the world's most extensive collection of written material on the Boss.

But did you know that Shaquille O'Neal and Joe Pesci are from Newark, or that Danny DeVito once worked at a hair salon in Asbury Park? Music stars hailing from the Garden State include Paul Simon, Jon Bon Jovi, the Jonas Brothers, Bette Midler, Dionne Warwick, Sarah Vaughan, Connie Francis, Frankie Valli, and jazz great and Red Bank native William "Count" Basie, who played his big-band hits at resorts and clubs along the Jersey Shore.

Most film and television stars are from someplace other than Hollywood, like Jack Nicholson, who was born in Neptune, Michael Douglas of New Brunswick, and Bruce Willis, who grew up in Carney's Point. Susan Sarandon is an Edison native (as is Brittany Murphy), and John Travolta, Meryl Streep, and Tom Cruise all have roots here. Independent filmmaker Kevin Smith shot cult classics like *Clerks* on his home turf in Leonardo, while South Orange native Zach Braff, star of the NBC sitcom *Scrubs,* wrote, directed, and starred in *Garden State,* a film that was shot in and around his hometown.

New Jersey native Buzz Aldrin was the second person to walk on the moon. Aviator Charles Lindbergh is as famous for his son's 1932 kidnapping and murder (Flemington's "Trial of the Century") as he is for completing the world's first solo flight across the Atlantic. He and wife, the writer Anne Morrow Lindbergh, lived on a farm outside Princeton in Hopewell. Princeton native Paul Robeson was a true Renaissance man—civil rights activist, athlete, singer, and actor. In the sports world, New Jersey claims Yogi Berra of Montclair, as well as Phil Rizzuto and track star Carl Lewis.

There's the Bud Abbott (Asbury Park) and Lou Costello (Paterson) comedy duo, fellow comedian Jerry Lewis (Newark), and Asbury Park resident Stephen Crane, author of the seminal Civil War novel *The Red Badge of Courage.* Physician and Pulitzer prize–winning poet William Carlos Williams wrote about life in Passaic and Rutherford, Beat-generation poet Allen Ginsberg hailed from Paterson, and Charles Addams, creator of *The Addams Family* TV show, is also from the Garden State.

And finally, there's Tony Soprano. The crime-family don is fictitious, of course, but the star of the former New Jersey–based hit HBO mob series *The Sopranos* is portrayed by native son and Rutgers alumnus James Gandolfini. Joe Pantoliano, one of his third-season costars, is from Hoboken.

remnant of Elizabeth's days as New Jersey's colonial capital city. Bayonne is a working-class industrial city on a peninsula jutting into New York Harbor that boomed in the early- to mid-20th century with shipping terminals, factories, and some of the world's largest oil refineries. Many of its residents are descendants of the first European immigrants that came here right from Ellis Island. Royal Caribbean International's *Explorer of the Seas* is based at Bayonne's former World War II–era military terminal, renamed Cape Liberty Cruise Port after the famous statue in the harbor.

Entries in this section are arranged in roughly geographic order.

AREA CODES 973, 908, 201, 732.

GUIDANCE A **state welcome center** (973-624-1014) is located at Newark Liberty International Airport in the International Arrivals area of Terminal B. In Jersey City, a state-run **tourism information center** is located at Liberty State Park (201-915-3400) in the historic Central Railroad of New Jersey Terminal. It's open daily year-round and well stocked with travel literature and information.

The Hudson County Chamber of Commerce (201-386-0699; www.hudson chamber.org), 660 Newark Ave., Suite 220, Jersey City. Their Web site is full of useful travel information, from lodging and dining options to transportation information, attractions, and activities.

GETTING THERE *By air:* **Newark Liberty International Airport** (973-961-6000; 888-397-4636; www.panynj.com), Newark. **AirTrain Newark** (888-397-4636; www.airtrainnewark.com) provides rail service between airport terminals and mass transit, including New Jersey Transit and Amtrak trains, New York's and Newark's Penn Stations, and downtown Newark.

By rail: Newark is 15 minutes from Manhattan by train. Newark's Penn Station and Broad Street Station are serviced by **PATH** (Port Authority Trans Hudson) trains (800-234-7284; www.panynj.gov) and **New Jersey Transit** commuter trains (973-275-5555; 800-955-2321; www.njtransit.com). The Hudson–Bergen Light Rail Line connects Bayonne and Jersey City to Hoboken Terminal.

Amtrak (800-872-7245; www.amtrak.com) stops at the Metropark commuter rail station in Iselin (100 Middlesex–Essex Turnpike) and at Penn Station in Newark, where there are commuter-rail and bus connections. Amtrak trains connect to Newark Liberty International Airport via a monorail.

By bus: **Greyhound** (800-231-2222; www.greyhound.com) stops at the Penn Central Railroad Terminal on Market Street in Newark.

By car: If exploring this area by car, it's wise to carry a detailed road map. The **Garden State Parkway** and the **New Jersey Turnpike** are the two major highways running through the region. Others include east–west **I-78,** which starts in Jersey City and cuts across northern New Jersey. Lower Manhattan is connected to Jersey City by the **Holland Tunnel.** Toll bridges from Staten Island link to Perth Amboy (Outerbridge Crossing Bridge), Bayonne (Bayonne Bridge), and Linden (Goethals Bridge) via the **Staten Island Expressway.**

By ferry: **New York Water Taxi** (212-742-1969; www.nywatertaxi.com) ferry service links the Paulus Hook Pier in Jersey City to Pier 11 near Wall Street in

THE NEW JERSEY TURNPIKE

For better or worse, New Jersey's identity is irrevocably linked to its name-sake turnpike. Simon and Garfunkel lyricized it and many a commuter has cursed it, both for its oft-clogged conditions and the less-than-pleasing industrial landscape. Not only is the New Jersey Turnpike a favorite punching bag for stand-up comedians, it's also, however unjustly, the basis of most out-of-state motorists' impressions of the entire state.

When work on the superhighway began in 1950 with 10,000 laborers, more than 100 contractors, and 130 construction contracts, it was the biggest such project of its kind. The original 118-mile, four-lane highway cost $255 million and opened in November 1951. New Jersey sits squarely between Manhattan and Philadelphia, two of the Northeast's biggest cities. The need for a major link between them became paramount in the 1940s and '50s when America's system of freeways began booming. The original turnpike was built along a busy transportation corridor that dated to colonial times, when the trip was made by stagecoach. Eventually both ends of the road were extended to connect the Delaware Memorial Bridge, which gave access to Delaware, with the George Washington Bridge, which linked New Jersey to New York City, and the roadway was widened to 14 lanes in some places. It's a massive interstate, as wide as the length of a football field, and the country's most heavily traveled toll highway. In 1952 tolls were $1.75, and 17.9 million vehicles—49,000 a day, on average—traveled on it. Today, of course, is a different story. Every year, some 205 million motorists use the turnpike; that's about 560,000 a day.

Each of the 12 rest stops along the turnpike honors a famous New Jerseyan from the area, and a brass plaque at each site explains the individual's historical and cultural contributions to the Garden State. Among the historical figures are Alexander Hamilton, Quaker settler John Fenwick, and Declaration of Independence signer Richard Stockton. Two are named for presidents—Woodrow Wilson, former state governor and Princeton University president; and Grover Cleveland, the first U.S. president born in New Jersey. Others are named for poets Joyce Kilmer and Walt Whitman, inventor Thomas Edison, *Last of the Mohicans* novelist James Fenimore Cooper, Revolutionary War heroine Molly Pitcher, American Red Cross founder Clara Barton, and football legend Vince Lombardi.

Manhattan. The canary yellow high-speed catamarans shuttle passengers on the short but scenic trip across New York Harbor. **New York Waterway** (800-533-3779; www.nywaterway.com) ferry service runs between the Colgate Ferry Terminal at Exchange Place in Jersey City, from Liberty Harbor, and from Harborside Financial Center in Jersey City.

GETTING AROUND *Taxis:* Taxi stands are located at terminals A, B, and C at **Newark Liberty International Airport** in Newark. **ABC Taxi Limo** (888-222-5459) serves the Newark region. **Grove Taxi** (201-434-8566) and **Budget Limo & Taxi** (201-222-8000) serve Jersey City.

Bus services: **New Jersey Transit** (973-275-5555; 800-955-2321; www.njtransit .com) provides local bus service throughout the region.

MEDICAL EMERGENCY Saint Michael's Medical Center (973-877-5000), 268 Dr. Martin Luther King Blvd,, Newark. The emergency number is 973-877-5500.

Jersey City Medical Center (201-915-2000), 50 Baldwin Ave., Jersey City. The emergency number is 201-915-2200.

Trinitas Hospital (908-994-5000), 225 Williamson St., Elizabeth. The emergency number is 908-994-5057.

Bayonne Hospital (201-858-5000), 29th St. at Avenue E, Bayonne. The emergency number is 201-858-5258.

Robert Wood Johnson University Hospital (732-381-4200), 865 Stone St., Rahway. The emergency number is 732-499-6100.

✴ To See

CHURCH Cathedral Basilica of the Sacred Heart (973-484-4600), 89 Ridge St., Newark. Open daily 9–7; tours on the first Sunday of the month at 1 PM or by appointment. The cornerstone of Newark's spectacular French Gothic cathedral was laid in June 1899. The national historic landmark is the fifth-largest cathedral in the United States, so naturally everything about it is on a grand scale, from the magnificent rose window (second largest in the country) to the largest church organ in New Jersey.

HISTORIC HOMES AND SITES Boxwood Hall State Historic Site (908-282-7617), 1073 East Jersey St., Elizabeth. Open Mon.–Fri. 9–5. Call for admission prices. Boxwood Hall is a rare remnant of Elizabeth's proud past as New Jersey's colonial-era capital, whose residents and distinguished guests helped shape the young nation. The circa-1750 mansion was home to Elias Boudinot—lawyer, diplomat, director of the U.S. Mint, and president of the Continental Congress that ratified the peace treaty with England. George Washington dined here in 1789 on the way to his inauguration in New York; other prominent visitors included the Marquis de Lafayette and a young Alexander Hamilton. Boudinot married Hannah Stockton, sister of Declaration of Independence signer Richard Stockton; in 1795 he sold Boxwood Hall to Jonathan Dayton, another signer of the Constitution. The mansion served as a boardinghouse and a senior citizens' home, then was slated for demolition before it was restored and opened to the public in 1943. Colonial–and Revolutionary War–era antiques, furnishings, and portraits reflect the lives of the Boudinot and Dayton families.

MUSEUMS ✐ New Jersey Historical Society Museum (973-596-8500; www .jerseyhistory.org), 52 Park Place, Newark. Open Tues.–Sat. 10–5; closed Sun. and Mon. Admission $4. A research library of 80,000 volumes and 1 million manuscripts, and a museum dedicated to New Jersey history, sit at the heart of Newark's growing arts district. Together they boast the most extensive collection of New Jersey–related objects and artifacts anywhere. Exhibits tell the story of the Garden State, through paintings, photographs, maps, memorabilia, ethnic costumes, and New Jersey–made goods from the colonial era to the 20th century. There's even an interactive display on the New Jersey Turnpike.

✦ **Liberty Science Center** (201-200-1000; www.lsc.org), Liberty State Park, 251 Philip Dr., Jersey City. Open Tues.–Fri. 9–4; Sat. and Sun. 9–5; closed Mon., Thanksgiving, and Christmas Day. Adults $15.75; seniors, and children 2–12, $11.50; children under 2, free. This is an impressive family science and technology museum—a four-story facility with more than 250 interactive exhibits on health, the environment, and inventions, and an **Omni Theater** whose towering six-story screen is the largest IMAX dome screen in the country. A recent $109 million expansion and renovation doubled the size of the original facility.

Photo from the collections of the New Jersey Historical Society
THE NEW JERSEY HISTORICAL SOCIETY WAS FOUNDED IN 1845; WITH ITS MUSEUM, LIBRARY, AND ARCHIVES IT IS THE OLDEST CULTURAL INSTITUTION IN THE STATE.

✦ **Jersey City Museum** (201-413-0303; www.jerseycitymuseum.org), 350 Montgomery St., Jersey City. Open Wed.–Fri. 11–5; Sat. noon–5; closed Sun.–Tues. Adults $4; children, students, and seniors $2; children 11 and under, free. More than 20,000 objects—from drawings and prints to decorative arts, maps, and industrial artifacts—represent the extensive permanent collection of this first-rate museum, which also showcases the work of emerging and established artists. Jersey City's own August Will, a 19th-century illustrator and landscape painter, has more than 300 paintings and works on paper in the collection.

Afro-American Historical Society Museum (201-547-5262), at the Greenville Public Library, 1841 John F. Kennedy Blvd., Jersey City. Open Mon.–Sat. 10–5; closed Sun.; reduced summer hours. Free admission. The displays exhibit both the history and heritage of New Jersey's African American residents in interesting and thoughtful ways. Among the notable pieces are African paintings and sculpture, African American crafts, artifacts from African American churches, and relics from the civil rights era through the 1960s.

✳ To Do

BICYCLING Liberty State Park (201-915-3400; www.libertystatepark.org), Morris Pesin Dr., Jersey City. The park is open daily 6 AM–10 PM. Biking is allowed on

⚓ NEWARK MUSEUM AND BALLANTINE HOUSE

(973-596-6550; www.newarkmuseum.org), 49 Washington St., Newark. Open Wed.–Fri. noon–5; Sat. and Sun. 10–5; closed major holidays. Adults $10; seniors, students, and children $6. Newark boasts one of the most highly regarded fine-arts museums in the country, and the largest museum complex in New Jersey. Its permanent display of art from North Africa, sub-Saharan Africa, Asia, the Pacific, and North and South America represents some 74,000 specimens, as well as 12,000 fossils, 2,000 seashells, a superb collection of 18th- and 19th-century American painting, sculpture, and decorative art, and the largest assemblage of Tibetan art and artifacts in the Western Hemisphere. When the museum was founded in 1909 it occupied the top floor of the Newark Library. Today there are 80 art and science galleries. The **Education Center** offers lectures, concerts, gallery tours, films, and theater productions; there are workshops and classes for adults, and scavenger hunts, art-making projects, museum tours, and other programs especially for kids. The **Dreyfuss Planetarium** has a solar telescope and special programs on the night sky and the cosmos. The **Victoria Hall of Science** has an excellent natural-science collection of more than 10,000 specimens covering natural history, as well as exhibits that include a tropical rainforest, the African savanna, and the Arctic tundra. There's a mini-zoo, and the **Alice Ransom Dreyfuss Memorial Garden,** a lovely courtyard garden with an 18th-century schoolhouse and a 19th-century carriage house with exhibits on firefighting.

Attached to the museum is the Ballantine House, a restored 1885 limestone and brick mansion that functions as a wing of the museum. The Ballantines were not only famous beer brewers, they were also one of Newark's most prominent families. Two floors of galleries and period rooms provide a glimpse at the Ballantines' high-society life in Victorian-era Newark, and house a world-class collection of American art, decorative arts, and domestic artifacts from the mid-1600s to the present. The mansion is a national historic landmark.

the 2-mile-long **Liberty Walk promenade** along New York Harbor and on the network of paths through the 88-acre **Green Park.** The best times to ride are during the week, early in the morning, or in the evening, when the walkway is less crowded; other times, you'll likely be sharing the promenade with a considerable number of people.

BIRDING **Liberty State Park** (201-915-3400; www.libertystatepark.org), Morris Pesin Dr., Jersey City. There is an observation book at the **Interpretive Center** where you can read about past sightings by fellow birders and contribute your own observations. Before setting out, pick up a birding pamphlet that contains a checklist of the 239 species—many threatened or endangered—of birds in the park. While some species make the park their year-round home, most visit for one or more seasons. Migratory shorebirds flock to the waterfront in spring and fall. In summer, herons can be seen in the park's salt marshes. Wintertime brings ducks, geese, swans, owls, gulls, and birds of prey like hawks, kestrels, and falcons.

BOAT EXCURSION ✍ **Circle Line Statue of Liberty Ferry** (201-435-9499) leaves from Liberty State Park in Jersey City, making stops at the **Ellis Island Immigration Museum** on Ellis Island and the **Statue of Liberty National Monument** on Liberty Island. Boats run daily year-round except for Christmas Day, stopping first at Ellis Island, then at the Statue of Liberty. The ticket office is in the Central New Jersey Railroad Terminal near the ferry dock.

BOATING In Jersey City, **Liberty State Park** maintains a boat launch at the first parking area on Morris Pesin Drive. The ramp is open daily year-round, and provides access to the Hudson River, Upper New York Bay, and the Atlantic Ocean. A fee is charged from April to October. (See also *Green Space—Park.*)

Liberty Landing Marina (201-985-8000), Liberty State Park, Jersey City. A full-service marina with 200 slips, lunch and dinner cruises, a restaurant, and a sailing school.

FISHING In Jersey City, you can launch a boat in New York Harbor or cast a line from Liberty State Park. Most anglers come for the **shad, bluefish,** and **striped bass;** crabbers come for the **blue claw crabs.** The park's designated fishing areas are on the piers near the park office; you can also fish off the 2-mile-long **Liberty Walk promenade.** A license is not required.

SPECTATOR SPORTS ✍ **Newark Bears** (973-483-6900; 866-554-2327; www .newarkbears.com), Riverfront Stadium, Bridge St. (off Rt. 21), Newark. The season runs from May to Sept. This 6,200-seat minor-league ballpark—a handsome brick old-style stadium—on the Passaic River opened in 2000. It's easy to get to: New Jersey Transit's Broad Street Station is right across the street. When the original Newark Bears played in the city during the 1930s and '40s, Yogi Berra was a member of the well-known Yankees farm team. Today the Bears are in the Atlantic League, an organization of professional regional teams that play many of their games on nights and weekends. The focus here is clearly on family entertainment, from the play area for children (complete with pitching booth) to the regular fireworks displays.

Prudential Center (info: 973-757-6000; tickets: 201-507-8900; www.pru center.com), 165 Mulberry St., Newark. The city's new state-of-the-art arena, also known as The Rock, is home to the New Jersey Devils and the Seton Hall Pirates.

THE NEWARK BEARS PLAY THEIR HOME GAMES AT RIVERFRONT STADIUM IN NEWARK.

Courtesy of the Newark Bears

STATUE OF LIBERTY NATIONAL MONUMENT AND ELLIS ISLAND IMMIGRATION MUSEUM

Getting there: ✐ The Circle Line Statue of Liberty Ferry (212-269-5755), Liberty State Park, Jersey City. Ferries run daily year-round, 8:30–4, except Christmas Day. Adults $10; seniors and children 4–12, $8; $4; children 3 and under, $4. Admission to the islands is free.

The Statue of Liberty on Liberty Island and the Ellis Island Immigration Museum are two of America's most prized national monuments. Together they comprise the **Statue of Liberty National Monument** and attract 6 million visitors a year. Although most people associate the famous landmarks with New York City, Ellis Island is jointly owned by New York and New Jersey. The small harbor islands were granted to New York in 1833, before the immigration port opened and the statue was unveiled. Ownership squabbles between the states went to the U.S. Supreme Court, which decided in 1998 to divide ownership of Ellis Island between the two states, settling the controversy once and for all.

The regal image of Lady Liberty with her torch raised high is one of the world's most recognizable symbols of personal freedom and democracy, for locals and tourists as well as for immigrants (for Native Americans, it's a symbol of power) seeking a new life in the Land of Opportunity. She was a gift from France to commemorate 100 years of American independence and democracy. Work began on the bronze statue in 1876—sculptor Frédéric-Auguste Bartholdi was aided by Eiffel Tower architect Alexandre-Gustave Eiffel—and it was dedicated in 1886. A plaque at the statue's base depicts the immortalized words of Emma Lazarus:

> *Give me your tired, your poor,*
> *Your huddled masses yearning to breathe free,*
> *The wretched refuse of your teeming shore.*
> *Send these, the homeless, tempest-tost to me,*
> *I lift my lamp beside the golden door!*

For more than 12 million immigrants that sailed into New York Harbor, the immigration processing station on Ellis Island was the final hurdle; here it was decided whether they would be allowed into the United States. Dur-

✳ Green Space

GARDENS Alice Ransom Dreyfuss Memorial Garden (973-596-6550), 49 Washington St., Newark. A peaceful spot tucked behind the Newark Museum and surrounded by brick walls features 20th-century American sculpture, an 18th-century schoolhouse (the oldest in the city), and a 19th-century carriage house that contains the **Newark Fire Museum.** There's also a popular free lunchtime summer concert and performance series.

ing the peak years from 1892 to 1924, some 6,000 people passed through every day. For newly arrived immigrants (only steerage and third-class passengers were required to go through the station), it was the link between the Old World and America. From the grand Registry Room, the busy way station known for its long inspection lines, immigrants could see the Manhattan skyline and Lady Liberty out the hall's arched windows. Today more than 100 million Americans can trace their ancestry to immigrants who entered the United States at Ellis Island.

The museum occupies the majestic Beaux Arts–style **Main Building,** where visitors can tour the **Great Hall,** the **Registry Room,** and other smaller halls with exhibits showcasing various aspects of how immigrants were processed. Moving displays feature black-and-white photographs, passports, foreign currency, clothing, stacks of steamer trunks, and the personal belongings of some of the multitudes that passed through the halls. For families researching their ancestral roots, there's the **American Family Immigration History Center,** with passenger records and photos of the ships that came to the island. The **American Immigrant Wall of Honor** is inscribed with the names of more than 600,000 immigrants. Plans call for the renovation of the island's complex of three-dozen deteriorating buildings, including the quarantine pavilions and hospital wards where 1 in 10 immigrants either died or was deemed too ill to be allowed entry into the country. Free ranger-led tours of the Main Building are available, as well as live performances, a documentary film, and a food court and gift shop.

The historic **Central Railroad of New Jersey Terminal** at Liberty State Park is a worthwhile destination in itself. For about 8 million immigrants processed at Ellis Island, the brick rail terminal was the last stop on their long journey into America. During the turn-of-the-20th-century peak immigration years, it was a bustling commuter and freight transportation center, with ferries and trains transporting tens of thousands of commuters and newly arrived immigrants to New York, New Jersey, and points beyond. Use declined in the 1950s as more and more commuters turned to the brand-new bridges and tunnels spanning the Hudson River, and the terminal closed in 1967. Today the grand building is undergoing restoration, and exhibits tell the story of American immigration and New Jersey's railroad and transportation history.

Bible Gardens of Israel (732-634-2100), Rt. 1, Woodbridge. Open daily from dawn to dusk. Free admission. This Jewish cemetery in **Beth Israel Memorial Park** features four unique themed gardens planted exclusively with trees, shrubs, and plants that are mentioned in the Bible. The gardens were established in the 1950s with plants, rocks, and shrubs imported from Israel. Today, bay, myrtle, figs, olives, and pomegranates grow here—each specimen is labeled for easy identification.

BRANCH BROOK PARK

(973-268-3500; www.branchbrookpark.org), Franklin Ave., Belleville and Newark. Open daily from dawn to dusk. This historic county park—the first in America—was designed by Central Park's famous landscape architect, Frederick Law Olmsted. Most people come in April for the city's Cherry Blossom Festival (see *Special Events*), when 2,700 Japanese cherry trees burst into a pink and white profusion of bloom that heralds the start of spring. Essex County is appropriately nicknamed Cherry Blossom Land, since there are more cherry blossoms here than in the tidal basin of Washington, DC. The 2-week-long celebration has been a tradition for more than 30 years. In addition to concerts, dances, carriage rides, and a food festival, there are Japanese cultural activities, arts and crafts, a 10K run and a bike tour—all planned to coincide with the peak bloom, which lasts for a brief time. The cherry trees stretch through the park for 2 miles, a spectacular collection that began with the donation of one tree by the mayor of Tokyo.

PARK ✿ **Liberty State Park** (201-915-3400; www.libertystatepark.org), Morris Pesin Dr., Jersey City. Open daily year-round, 6 AM–10 PM. Visitors can pick up the shuttle that connects sites within the park to the nearby PATH train stop. A 1,212-acre oasis in one of the country's most densely populated metropolitan regions, just across New York Harbor from Manhattan. All the usual state park activities are here, from boating, fishing, and swimming to picnicking, biking, and tennis. The undeniable centerpiece of the park is its namesake, the **Statue of Liberty National Monument,** which includes the venerable international symbols of freedom, the **Statue of Liberty** and **Ellis Island.** A year-round ferry brings visitors to Lady Liberty and Ellis Island's rambling immigration buildings. No doubt, it's an unforgettable trip, but perhaps the most dramatic vista of both is from **Liberty Walk,** the park's 2-mile-long promenade that stretches along the harbor. From there, the two islands sit just offshore, and the New York City skyline provides an impressive backdrop.

Sitting quietly in the background at the center of the park is a 60-acre salt marsh that is teeming with birds and crisscrossed with nature trails and wildlife viewing areas. A nature path near the **Interpretive Center** (on Freedom Way) has signs that identify plants along the way. There's a full schedule of environmental education programs for children and adults, from sensory walks and insect safaris to programs on raptors, bats, and others, which explore the wetlands around New York Bay.

From 1889 to 1967, the historic **Central Railroad of New Jersey Terminal** was a major hub for just-arrived immigrants from Ellis Island and millions of New Jersey residents commuting to jobs in New York City. The dilapidated train platforms have been restored. **Liberty Science Center** (201-200-1000) is the park's state-of-the-art science and technology museum (see *To See—Museums*); its **Omni Theater** has the largest IMAX dome screen in the country.

79

THE NEWARK AND JERSEY CITY REGION

✳ Lodging

HOTELS

In Newark

✦ **Hilton Newark Penn Station** (973-622-5000), Gateway Center, Raymond Blvd., Newark 07102-5107. A downtown hotel at the heart of the business district (3 miles from Newark Liberty International Airport) and conveniently connected by a walkway to Penn Station's New Jersey Transit, PATH, and Amtrak trains, and the Gateway Center. Guest rooms are nicely furnished with contemporary décor; business travelers appreciate the oversized work desks and dual-line phones with voice mail and data ports. Upgraded accommodations include one-bedroom suites, junior suites, and top-floor executive suites with a private lounge, complimentary continental breakfast, and evening hors d'oeuvres. A full-service business center, fitness center, and seasonal outdoor pool round out the amenities. **Market Street Bar and Grill** has casual fare. $249 and up.

✦ **Newark Liberty Marriott** (973-623-0006; 800-882-1037; www.newarkairportmarriott.com), Newark Liberty International Airport, Newark 07114. There are numerous hotels and motels in the area, but travelers like this property because it's the only place to stay on the airport grounds. The 591 guest rooms and six suites were recently renovated; hotel amenities include a fitness center with whirlpool tub and sauna, a connecting indoor-outdoor pool, a pub, a casual grill, and a steakhouse. $249 and up.

In Jersey City

✦ **Hyatt Regency Jersey City** (201-469-1234; 800-233-1234; www.jerseycity.hyatt.com), Two Exchange Place, Jersey City 07302. Jersey City's Hyatt is a nine-story luxury hotel perched on the Harborside Financial Center's south pier, jutting out over the Hudson River. It's located at the heart of the financial district, directly across the river from Lower Manhattan and Wall Street. It couldn't be easier to get to and from the hotel—it's right next to the Exchange Place PATH station, and a short walk to the Paulus Hook Pier ferry terminal. The 336 guest rooms and 14 suites are stylishly decorated, and each boasts a view of either the Statue of Liberty, New York Harbor, or the New York City skyline. Amenities include Internet access, in-room safes, and refrigerators; most of the suites have outdoor balconies. The fully equipped health club has an indoor lap pool. **Vu** restaurant is an upscale steakhouse, seafood restaurant, and lounge, with an especially dramatic view of the skyline at night. $339 and up.

✦ **Doubletree Club Hotel** (201-499-2400; 800-222-8733), 455 Washington Blvd., Jersey City 07310. An all-suite hotel with 198 two-room suites that's a short walk to the PATH trains and ferries to Manhattan. Each suite has a living room, a bedroom, a wet bar with coffeemaker, refrigerator, and microwave, a two-line phone, and two TVs; high-speed Internet access is available in all rooms, for a fee. Corner

ROBERT TREAT HOTEL

(973-622-1000; reservations: 800-569-2300; www.rthotel.com), 50 Park Place, Newark 07102. This landmark hotel in the downtown arts district is on the National Register of Historic Places and named for Captain Robert Treat, the former Connecticut governor who founded Newark. President Woodrow Wilson stayed here shortly after the hotel opened in 1916; today it hosts business travelers, parents of Rutgers University students, and visitors here for the nearby Newark Museum and the New Jersey Performing Arts Center, just across the street. Each of the 173 guest rooms and suites comes with standard amenities, plus free high-speed Internet access. **Maize** is a stylish and chic dining room serving breakfast, lunch, and dinner (see *Dining Out*); the **Starlight Roof** lounge has good cocktails and nightly live entertainment. The free hotel shuttle stops at Newark Liberty International Airport and Newark's Penn Station. $100 and up.

suites are more spacious than standard units, and the best views of the New York skyline are from the top floors. There's a fitness room and a business center; valet laundry service is available during the week, when the hotel is full of business travelers. **Harsimus Cove Bar and Grill** serves New American cuisine at breakfast, lunch, and dinner every day. Complimentary weekend local shuttle service. $279 and up.

Candlewood Suites—Exchange Place

(201-659-2500; 877-226-3539), 21 Second St., Jersey City 07302. An all-suite hotel near Exchange Place that caters to business travelers and guests on extended stays. Studios and one-bedroom suites come with a combined living and sleeping area, small kitchen, and bathroom. The laundry facilities (free for guests) are a nice plus; there's also a fitness center, a complimentary CD and video library, and a round-the-clock convenience store. PATH trains to Manhattan are close by. $229 and up.

Westin Jersey City Newport (201-626-2900; www.westin.com/jerseycity), 479 Washington Blvd., Jersey City 07310. Jersey City's newest hotel opened in the financial district in 2009. It's a block from the PATH station and adjacent to the Newport Centre Mall. There are 414 guest rooms and 15 suites, fitness and business centers, an indoor pool, and a stunning view of Manhattan, thanks to the Hudson River waterfront locale. **Fire & Oak** serves contemporary American cuisine; **Half Moon** is a casual lounge. $299 and up.

CAMPGROUND

Liberty Harbor Marina & RV Park (201-386-7500; 800-646-2066; www.libertyharborrv.com), 11 Marin Blvd., Jersey City 07302. Open year-round. A new concept in camping: views of the Statue of Liberty and the New York skyline from your RV site. There are 55 sites with full hook-ups, and easy access to Manhattan-bound buses, trains, and ferries. Keep in mind that the campground is located in a parking lot behind a marina, not on the waterfront as the name might suggest. If you want to see the views from your site, be sure to request it. $50–60.

✳ Where to Eat

DINING OUT

In Newark

&. **Maize** (973-733-2202; www.maize restaurant.com), at the Robert Treat Hotel, 50 Park Place. Open daily for breakfast, lunch, and dinner. Reservations are suggested. A stylish and urbane dining room in the **Robert Treat Hotel** (see sidebar, previous page) serving upscale American and Mediterranean cuisine. Many people stop at Maize for dinner before catching a show across the street at the New Jersey Performing Arts Center. Start with crab spring rolls with lemongrass soy sauce, then move on to the filet mignon with mushroom risotto and a merlot demi-glace, or the seared red snapper with grilled pineapple and tomato ragout. The fresh herbs used in the kitchen are grown through a local community service initiative. Extensive wine list. $22–37.

&. **Theater Square Grill** (973-642-1226; www.theater-square-grill.com), One Center St., at the **New Jersey Performing Arts Center** (see sidebar, page 86). Open for lunch Mon.–Fri.; prix fixe dinner if there's a performance); Sat. and Sun. brunch. Reservations are strongly recommended. Theatergoers fill the dining room for the sophisticated takes on New American and international cuisine, or head to the casual lounge for a light preshow meal. The three-course dinner menu might start with smoked salmon and baked Brie with truffled crème fraîche, or prosciutto-wrapped shrimp with Grand Marnier sauce. The pan-seared cod with broccoli rabe and chorizo, and the grilled lamb with mushroom risotto are popular entrées. End with the chocolate peanut butter truffle torte or Frangelico crème brûlée with hazelnut biscotti. The bistro serves a lighter menu. $15–45.

27 Mix (973-648-0643; www.27mix.com), 27 Halsey St. Open Mon.–Sat. for lunch and dinner; closed Sun. A lively bar and narrow dining room of exposed brick walls and small tables is intimate and stylish, a good place for a date. The creative Southwestern-influenced menu promises freshness, from both ingredients and ideas. It includes grilled shrimp tacos for an appetizer; jerk-spiced chicken with black bean sauce or pan-seared salmon with sweet corn salsa for an entrée. In summer, live jazz on the patio makes this one of the top al fresco spots around. $15–25.

Forno's of Spain (973-589-4767; www.fornosrestaurant.com), 47 Ferry St. Open daily for lunch and dinner. A casual Spanish eatery in a Portuguese neighborhood in Newark's Ironbound District. The menu of traditional Spanish dishes includes several renditions of paella, made with various combinations of fish, shellfish, chicken, and sausage. The dining room tends to be busy and loud, especially on weekends, making it a good place for a celebration or dinner with a group rather than a quiet romantic dinner. The seasonal outdoor dining provides a more relaxed, laid-back setting, if that's what you're looking for. Don't miss Forno's signature sangria. $15–25.

Adega Grill (973-589-8830; www.adegagrill.com), 130 Ferry St. Open for lunch Mon.–Fri.; dinner daily. Reservations are recommended. A charming, Old World–style bistro in the Ironbound District, serving huge portions of top-notch Spanish and Portuguese cuisine. *Adega* is Portuguese for "wine cellar," and the grill lives up to its name with a list of some 200 bottles. The dining-room décor—from the wall sconces and candlelight to the wrought-iron cellar gates—is reminiscent of a centuries-old wine cellar. Dishes are listed by their Spanish or

Portuguese names and are accompanied by a brief description so you know what you're getting. You might start with *chouriço assado*, Portuguese sausage served flambé at tableside; or *camārao à guilho*, shrimp sautéed in garlic. Next, try the *gambas recheadas*, crabmeat-stuffed prawns; or the *mar e terra*, a combination of grilled lobster and beef tenderloin. Next door, the **Adega Lounge** is sleek and modern with a SoHo vibe and a young, hip crowd. $21–43.

Other Spanish and Portuguese restaurants in the Ironbound District that are worth a mention (and a visit) include **Chateau of Spain** (973-624-3346), 11 Franklin St.; **Iberia Peninsula** (973-344-5611), 63–69 Ferry St.; **Brasilia Grill** (973-589-8682), 99 Monroe St.; and **Vila Nova do Sol Mar** (973-344-8540), 267 Ferry St.

In Jersey City

Marco & Pepe (201-860-9688; www.marcoandpepe.com), 289 Grove St. Open for brunch and dinner Tues.–Sun.; Sat. and Sun. brunch only; closed Mon. A casual-yet-upscale café in a former bodega that attracts a sophisticated, city-slick crowd. The menu of global bistro fare includes gazpacho with basil oil, and *pommes frites* with roasted-garlic dipping sauce, for starters. Entrées—which come in half portions ideal for grazing and sharing—feature grown-up comfort food like macaroni and cheese with mushrooms, bacon, and aged Gruyère and goat cheese; grilled steak with Asian vegetables and a sake soy-ginger syrup; and duck confit with white bean ravioli. There's also a decent selection of homey desserts, such as warm chocolate cake with hazelnut gelato and chocolate ganache. The entire menu is also available at the bar, plus dessert wines, single-malt scotch, and after-dinner drinks. $15–25.

Confucius Asian Bistro (201-386-8898), 558 Washington Blvd. Open daily for lunch and dinner. A popular pan-Asian eatery near the waterfront with a dramatic soaring interior done in linen wall panels, brush-painted scrolls, and rich tapestries. The predominately Chinese and Thai menu features refreshingly eclectic renditions of the usual Chinese restaurant fare. Fried rice, for example, is infused with green tea; and sweet-and-sour red snapper is an interesting takeoff from the traditional sweet-and-sour chicken and shrimp. The house specialty dish, appropriately called Confucius, is a savory blend of lobster and seafood over Asian noodles. Save room for the homemade mango ice cream. The bar attracts a young, trendy crowd. $14–34.

Casa Dante Restaurant (201-795-2750; www.casadante.com), 737 Newark Ave. Open daily for lunch and dinner. Reservations are recommended. This Old World Italian fine-dining spot is a Jersey City landmark. It's also a hidden gem, tucked off the street, which is fine by the legions of regulars who prefer to have it to themselves like a closely guarded secret. Business types, movers and shakers, and first dates flock to the elegant mahogany-walled dining room for the refined atmosphere, professional service, and fine Southern Italian classic cuisine. The menu is a list of perfectly executed classics, from the paper-thin beef carpaccio to the tender veal marsala. Families will feel comfortable here, too. $21–34.

Puccini's (201-432-4111; www.puccinisrestaurant.com), 1064 West Side Ave. Open daily for lunch and dinner. Authentic northern Italian fare in an elegant dining room that attracts a loyal clientele. The menu is an extensive list of the dependable dishes you expect to find in a classic Italian restaurant—veal parmesan, seafood *fra diavolo*, linguine with clam sauce, chicken marsala—but Chef Pasquale's expert preparation and fresh ingredients elevate them above the run-of-the-mill. Ask the maître d' if there's something you want that doesn't appear on the menu; the kitchen likes to accommodate special requests whenever possible. $21–35.

Grand Banks Restaurant (201-521-1800; www.gbcafe.com), 75 Montgomery St. Open for lunch Mon.–Fri.; dinner daily; Sat. and Sun. brunch. Reservations are suggested. A seafood house and bar with an extensive menu of sushi and sashimi. Classic dishes like blackened salmon and fried jumbo shrimp are eclipsed by the Grand Banks Seafood Supreme, a colossal feast of Asian-style lobster tail, mussels, shrimp, crab, and scallops stir-fried with ginger and scallions. The Japanese combination plates—teriyaki and tempura dishes accompanied by miso soup, salad, and a sushi roll—are a bargain. There's also a decent selection of meat, pasta, and vegetarian dishes. $10–29.

Edward's Steak House (201-761-0000; www.edwardssteakhouse.com), 239 Marin Blvd. Open for lunch Mon.–Fri.; dinner Mon.–Sat.; closed Sun. Weekend reservations are a must. An elegant building, first an 1870s townhouse, later a Prohibition-era speakeasy. Today, classic steakhouse fare is given a creative spin and served in stately surroundings. The filet mignon carpaccio with truffle oil is a nice way to start off, and the sirloin au poivre, pork mignon, and porterhouse steak are as hearty as you'd expect steakhouse fare to be. $22–75.

Porto Leggero (201-434-3200; www.portoleggero.net), Five Harborside Financial Center. Open for lunch Mon.–Fri.; dinner Mon.–Sat.; closed Sun. Reservations are recommended. Tuscan-inspired cuisine is served at this dramatic waterfront hot spot that melds hip with good taste. The high-ceilinged dining room is decked with white linen and velvet drapes, and the kitchen's talent more than matches the sophisticated surroundings. Classic Italian dishes (shrimp scampi) are paired with more stylish inventions (potato-crusted striped bass). Service is masterful; menu choices, elegant. All the plates are lovely, and there's a good wine list to boot. $20–40.

Ox (201-860-4000; www.oxrestaurant.com), 176 Newark Ave. Open for dinner Tues.–Sun.; closed Mon. Reservations are recommended. Here's a super-cool spot with a big-city feel that will make you forget you're not in Manhattan. The name is a nod to Paul Bunyan, and the cuisine is as American as the larger-than-life folk hero. The décor is stylish and urbane, the vibe, fun and friendly. $14–26.

⊙ **Liberty House Restaurant** (201-395-0300; www.libertyhouserestaurant.com), 76 Audrey Zapp Dr. Open for lunch Tues.–Sat.; dinner Tues.–Sun.; Sun. brunch; closed Mon. This elegant dining room is the best spot in the city for formal dining. Soaring windows frame views of the Hudson River and the New York skyline, which is particularly dramatic at night. The stellar cuisine befits its stunning location: seafood, a specialty, is prepared with an expert hand yet kept simple. $20–36.

Elsewhere
Spanish Pavillion (973-485-7750; www.spanishpavillion.com), 31 Harrison Ave., Harrison. Open for lunch Mon.–Fri.; dinner daily. Reservations are recommended for dinner on weekends. Jerry and Mike Fernandez run this warm and friendly eatery near the New Jersey Performing Arts Center,

serving authentic Spanish dishes. It has been in the family for three generations; when their grandparents first opened the doors in 1963, it was New Jersey's first Spanish restaurant. Since then, many similar eateries have followed in their footsteps, but this is still a local favorite because customers are treated like family and the cuisine hasn't flagged. The seafood here is incredibly fresh, and runs the gamut from broiled lobster tails to paella studded with mussels, squid, shrimp, and clams. Meats include the familiar pork chops, veal cutlets, and steaks but also specialties like sautéed calves' liver or stewed tripe with Spanish sausage. Extensive wine list. $16–43.

Amici's Restaurant (201-437-4299; www.amicirestaurant.com), 184 Broadway, Bayonne. Open daily for lunch and dinner. Reservations are suggested. *Amici* is Italian for "friends," and this lovely fine-dining restaurant and lively martini lounge is indeed friendly, with an extensive menu of Old World Italian specialties and impeccable service. Generous portions and reasonable prices. $13–27.

& **Casa Giuseppe** (732-283-9111; www.casagiuseppe.com), 487 Rt. 27, Iselin. Open for lunch Tues.–Fri.; dinner Tues.–Sun.; open Mon. for lunch and dinner in Dec. only. Reservations are accepted. This fine-dining gem is a local favorite, serving authentic and perfectly executed Italian and northern Italian classics in a charming and romantic atmosphere. Start with one of the house specialties—eggplant baked with portobello mushrooms, chopped shrimp, and mozzarella with homemade tomato sauce. Move on to grilled Chilean sea bass with polenta in an orange-ginger sauce; or their signature lemon sole crusted with pine nuts and bread crumbs, served over sautéed spinach. $21–32.

Restaurant David Drake (732-388-6677; www.daviddrakes.com), 1449 Irving St., Rahway. Open for dinner Mon.–Sat.; closed Sun. This is New Jersey celebrity chef's eponymous restaurant, and you won't go wrong if Drake is in the kitchen. The setting (a converted early 19th-century house) is intimate and sophisticated, and the food is simply magnificent. Modern American cuisine with French touches means elegant appetizers like crispy potato gnocci and fluke sashimi; sautéed skate wing, braised short ribs, and other well-executed entrées; coffee panna cotta, lemon-scented chocolate tart, and other exquisite desserts. The experience isn't cheap, but for a special night out, this is worth the splurge. Prix fixe $85; entrées $23–40.

EATING OUT

In Newark
Hobby's Delicatessen and Restaurant (973-623-0410), 32 Branford Place. Open Mon.–Sat.; closed Sun. This family-owned and -operated downtown deli is a New Jersey treasure, widely considered one of the best delis in the state. Hobby's has been in business for more than 80 years. It's perpetually filled with lunchtime regulars from the nearby courthouse and surrounding businesses. Loyal patrons willingly line up for pastrami on rye and other deli standbys. $6–14.

Dickie-Dee Pizza (973-483-9396), 380 Bloomfield Ave. Open daily. A no-frills order-at-the-counter pizzeria that serves up huge sandwiches (round loaves of Italian bread stuffed with cheese, meats, fried peppers and onions, and such), grilled cheesesteaks, classic thin-crust pizza, and deep-fried hot dogs. A legion of regulars has haunted this neighborhood joint for more than 50 years. $6–15.

In Jersey City

Baja (201-915-0062), 117 Montgomery St. Open Mon.–Fri. for lunch and dinner; Sat. and Sun. for brunch and dinner. Reservations are accepted. A lively Mexican eatery in a stylish brick-store-front space filled with paintings and sculpture by local artists. The kitchen serves up well-prepared, authentic Mexican fare, from burritos and flautas to tacos, chimichangas, and a long list of seafood specials. A young, hip crowd comes for the live weekend entertainment and the extensive selection of tequilas, margaritas, and sangrias. $10–22.

♪ **Brownstone Diner & Pancake Factory** (201-433-0471; www.brownstonediner.com), 426 Jersey Ave. Open daily for breakfast, lunch, and dinner. Breakfast is any time you want it, notably pancakes in every incarnation imaginable. Standard diner fare such as sandwiches, salads, and steaks fills the rest of the menu. Service is fast, informal, and friendly, and the portions are generous. At press time, a major expansion was underway. $8–24.

Elsewhere

&. **Belmont Tavern** (973-759-9609), 12 Bloomfield Ave., Belleville. Open for dinner Wed.–Mon.; closed Tues. A family-friendly neighborhood tavern where people dine together at communal tables on just-like-mom-used-to-make comfort food. The atmosphere is lively and loud, and the staff is curt at times, but the food is delicious. The house specialty is Chicken Savoy, which is coated in a savory blend of oregano, parmesan, and garlic and tossed with balsamic vinegar. Huge bowls of ziti, *cavatelli,* and other pastas are popular crowd pleasers here. No credit cards. $12–24.

Little Food Café (201-436-6800), 330 Kennedy Blvd., Bayonne. Open for breakfast, lunch, and dinner

Mon.–Fri.; breakfast and lunch on Sat.; closed Sun. An inviting family-run neighborhood eatery with an eclectic menu of healthy soups, sandwiches, and salads made with fresh ingredients. At mealtime, the café is bustling and packed, mostly with locals. The homemade desserts are not to be missed. $8–12.

♪ **Tops Diner** (973-481-0490; www.thetopsdiner.com), 500 Passaic Ave., Harrison. Open Sun.–Thurs. 6 AM–1 AM; Fri. and Sat. 6 AM–4 AM. An eatery, bar, and bakery with the usual something-for-everyone diner fare, plus lots of cocktails and housemade desserts. The voluminous menu offers serious food dished out in generous portions, or just that quintessential diner order—hot coffee and a slab of pie. $9–30.

♠ ♪ **Jose Tejas Restaurant** (732-283-3883), 700 Rt. 1, Iselin. Open daily for lunch and dinner. A casual and friendly Mexican eatery serving authentic Tex-Mex cuisine at unbelievably low prices. Fresh salsa comes with warm tortilla chips; standards like fajitas, enchiladas, and blackened chicken are well prepared and generously portioned. Nights and weekends get very busy; be prepared to wait. $8–10.

&. *♠* **Mie Thai** (732-596-9400), 34 Main St., Woodbridge. Open daily for lunch and dinner. This small and charming Thai restaurant next to Woodbridge's New Jersey Transit rail station offers freshly prepared and tasty authentic Thai dishes at bargain prices. Start with shrimp and pork summer rolls wrapped in rice paper; or *tom yum,* a hot-and-sour soup with fresh chilies and lemongrass with chicken, pork, or seafood. Their house version of pad Thai, Thailand's national dish, features shrimp, roast pork, and chicken with fried rice, ground peanuts, tofu, and egg in a light bean

NEW JERSEY PERFORMING ARTS CENTER

(973-642-8989; box office: 888-466-5722; www.njpac.org), One Center St., Newark. One of the state's best-known arts centers boasts two theaters, two restaurants, and **Theater Square,** a beautifully landscaped outdoor venue where the annual summertime free music series is staged. The year-round schedule runs the gamut from classical music, jazz, and pop to opera, dance, and theater. World-class entertainers grace the stage, as do New Jersey's top performers, including the **New Jersey Symphony Orchestra.** Performances are held in the spectacular, four-tiered 2,750-seat **Prudential Hall** or in the intimate 514-seat **Victoria Theater.** The **Center Stage gift shop** features the work of local artists and designers, and the **Theater Square Grill** serves pre-performance lunch and dinner (see *Dining Out*).

THE NEW JERSEY PERFORMING ARTS CENTER, OR NJPAC, FEATURES ARTISTS FROM NEW JERSEY AND AROUND THE WORLD AT THE VICTORIA THEATER AND PRUDENTIAL HALL.

Photo courtesy of the New Jersey Performing Arts Center, © Jeff Goldberg/Esto

sauce. There's an extensive vegetarian menu, and many dishes can be prepared without meat, on request. BYOB. $10–15.

SNACKS Riviera Bakery (973-491-9000), 124 Ferry St., Newark. After dinner in the Ironbound District, do as the locals do: stroll over here for coffee and dessert. Gleaming cases are filled with every confection imaginable, each more tempting than the one before it.

Pecoraro Bakery (201-798-0111), 279 Newark Ave., Jersey City. They've been making bread in the brick oven here since 1923. Some 2,000 loaves a day include baguettes, whole wheat loaves, Italian *panellas,* and stuffed breads. If you phone ahead, and they aren't too busy, they may even make you a pizza.

Jerry's (908-355-4242), 906 2nd Ave., Elizabeth. The hot dogs here are famously boiled then finished on a griddle. Those with big appetites should order theirs smothered in sauerkraut and homemade chili. Next door, **Tommy's** (908-351-9831) prepares their deep-fried dogs Italian style, served on pizza bread and topped with sautéed onions, peppers, and potatoes.

✳ Entertainment

ARTS CENTER Barron Arts Center (732-634-0413), 582 Rahway Ave., Woodbridge. An active community arts center housed in a magnificent 19th-century cathedral-like building complete with clock tower and lovely stained-glass windows. The full schedule includes concerts, drawing classes, poetry readings, and a lecture series. The art gallery mounts changing exhibitions showcasing the work of nationally known artists and craftspeople as well as New Jersey artists.

MUSIC AND THEATER

In Newark

Prudential Center (info: 973-757-6000; tickets: 201-507-8900; www.prucenter.com), Rt. 21 S. New Jersey's newest arena hosts headlining entertainment as well as the New Jersey Devils and Seton Hall Pirates.

New Jersey Symphony Orchestra (973-624-3713; box office: 800-255-3476; www.njsymphony.org), Two Central Ave. The state's top orchestra—established in the 1920s—is based at the **New Jersey Performing Arts Center** (see sidebar, page 86) but per-

forms at venues around the state, including summer events like outdoor pops concerts and Amadeus festivals celebrating Mozart. It's the only orchestra in the world that plays vintage rare stringed instruments, part of their renowned historic Golden Age Collection.

♪ **Newark Symphony Hall** (973-643-4550; box office: 973-643-8009; www.newarksymphonyhall.org), 1020 Broad St. The elegant Ionic-columned Salaam Temple, built by the Shriners in 1925, is home to New Jersey's oldest and largest arts facility. A full schedule of new and classic plays, concerts, dance performances, and seasonal family shows are staged in the 2,800-seat **Sarah Vaughan Concert Hall** and in an intimate 200-seat theater.

Jazz in the Garden Summer Concert Series (973-596-6550), Alice Ransom Dreyfuss Garden, 49 Washington St. Free summertime concerts are held every Thursday afternoon in this brick-walled garden behind the Newark Museum.

In Jersey City

Jazz for Lunch (201-547-4322) is a summer concert series at Exchange Place. Free noontime concerts on Thursday feature R&B, jazz, salsa, and swing. Liberty State Park (201-915-3400) hosts the annual **Summerfest** music series at the historic Central Railroad of New Jersey Terminal, with Dixieland jazz, big-band, and classical music on Tuesday and Sunday evenings.

Loew's Jersey Theatre (201-798-6055; www.loewsjersey.org), 54 Journal Square. This long-neglected 1929 baroque-style movie palace has been restored to its original grandeur. Today it's a performing arts space with a full roster of films, concerts, plays, and children's programs.

✴ Selective Shopping

ART GALLERIES

In Newark

Aljira, A Center for Contemporary Art (973-622-1600), 591 Broad St. A gallery at the heart of Newark's downtown arts district. Changing exhibits feature contemporary visual art.

Paul Robeson Gallery (973-643-6877), Paul Robeson Campus Center, Rutgers University—Newark, 350 Dr. Martin Luther King Blvd. Changing exhibitions by faculty, students, and other renowned artists.

In Jersey City

Chamot Gallery (201-610-1468), 111 First St., 4th floor. Open Tues.–Sun. noon–6 and by appointment; closed Mon. Changing exhibits in art, sculpture, photography, and design.

Art Center on First, 111 First St. This is the largest artists' community west of the Hudson River, and home to more than 100 full-time working artists, painters, photographers, sculptors, furniture designers, musicians and composers, graphic designers, and jewelry designers. Collectors and arts lovers from around the world flock here in October, when the artists open their studio doors during the **Jersey City Artist Studio Tour**.

In Rahway

Arts Guild of Rahway (732-381-7511), 1670 Irving St. Sculpture, photography, and other changing exhibits. The annual juried **Union County Art Show** features the work of artists that live or work in Union County. A popular jazz series takes place from October to May.

OUTLETS AND MALLS ✤ **Jersey Gardens** (908-354-5900; www.jersey gardens.com), 651 Kapkowski Rd. (exit 13A off the New Jersey Turnpike), Elizabeth. Open daily. New Jersey's largest outlet mall is as massive, sprawling, and overwhelming as you'd expect a 1.3-million-square-foot indoor retail space to be. More than 200 outlets include big-name retailers like **Banana Republic, Nike, Victoria's Secret, Brooks Brothers, Saks Fifth Avenue,** and **Benetton,** plus megastores like **Bed Bath & Beyond** and **Old Navy.** You'll find last season's couture at relatively low prices at **Neiman Marcus Last Call.** There's also a **20-screen movie theater complex,** a **food court, restaurants,** and a **children's play area.**

Newport Centre Mall (201-626-2025), 30 Mall Dr. W., Jersey City. Open Mon.–Sat. 10–9:30; Sun. 11–6. This is the only enclosed, regional shopping center in Hudson County. More than 140 retail stores are anchored by **JCPenney, Macy's,** and **Sears;** there's also a 1,000-seat food court and an 11-screen movie theater complex. The mall is linked to Manhattan and New Jersey by PATH trains and by New Jersey Transit commuter buses and trains.

FARMER'S MARKETS

In Newark

The **Common Greens Farmer's Market** (973-733-9333) is held in Military Park at the corner of Broad Street and Raymond Boulevard. The open-air market runs from June to October, Thursday 10:30–5.

In Jersey City

There are four seasonal farmer's markets in Jersey City where local farmers sell their New Jersey–grown produce. The **Journal Square Farmer's Market** is an open-air market open Wednesdays from July to November. It has been here for more than a decade, and is popular with thousands of commuters who catch the nearby buses and PATH trains. The **Van Vorst**

Farmer's Market at Jersey Avenue and Montgomery Street runs from June to November on Saturdays. The **Newport Pavonia Farmer's Market** on Pavonia East Street operates from July to December, Thursday 11:30–6:30. The **Harvest Square Farmer's Market** at St. Patrick's Church runs from July to October on Tuesdays.

✱ Special Events

March: **St. Patrick's Day Parade** (973-733-4781), South Orange Ave., Newark. This lively celebration, the oldest in New Jersey, has been a city tradition for 75 years.

April: ✐ **Branch Brook Cherry Blossom Festival** (973-268-3500), Branch Brook Park, Lake St., Newark. Japanese cultural demonstrations, concerts, art shows, races, and family activities are held throughout the 3-week-long festival. Thousands of visitors come to marvel at the serene beauty of more than 2,700 Japanese cherry trees in bloom. The park boasts more blossoms than the famous cherry trees in Washington, DC.

June: **Strawberry Festival** (201-935-7479), Town Hall Park, Lyndhurst. All things strawberry, hosted by the Lyndhurst Historical Society.

July: **Summer Food, Art, and Craft Fair** (908-874-5247), Jersey City. More than 100 fine-art and crafts vendors, plus food from area restaurants. **Newark Food and Brew Festival** (973-655-6483), downtown Newark. **Lincoln Park Music Festival** (973-242-4144), Newark. An annual downtown festival featuring a series of free evening outdoor concerts with a diverse array of sounds, including Latin jazz, R&B, and traditional music from Haiti, Africa, and Brazil. **Newark Black Film Festival** (973-596-6493), Newark Museum, Newark. America's longest-running black film festival, showcasing African and African American film and history since 1974.

August: ✐ **La Festa Italiana** (201-795-0120), the Church of Our Lady of the Most Holy Rosary, Jersey City. New Jersey's first Italian parish, established in 1885. Masses are still celebrated in Italian at this 1885 Romanesque church. The street festival features homemade Italian specialties, from Italian ice and *panini* to *zeppoli* and cannoli. Live music, games of chance, and carnival rides.

September: **Liberty Rhythm & Blues and Jazz Festival** (888-556-5299), Liberty State Park, Jersey City. The Statue of Liberty is the backdrop for this well-attended music festival.

October: **Jersey City Artists Studio Tour** (201-547-4333), Jersey City. Hundreds of artists open their studio doors to collectors, dealers, and the general public. The tour features painting, sculpture, glassmaking, performance arts, and works in other media by Jersey City–based artists, as well as artists from around the state and New York City. **Liberty Boat Show** (212-984-7000; www.liberty boatshow.com), Liberty Landing Marina, Liberty State Park, Jersey City. Motorboats, sailboats, boating seminars, and live entertainment. **Newark Open Doors** (973-643-1625; www.newarkarts.org), Newark. Self-guided tour of artists' studios and art galleries.

WEST OF THE PARKWAY

T his region running along the Garden State Parkway is a curious contradiction. It's undoubtedly planted firmly in New Jersey's densely populated Northeastern Gateway region, but it has enough parks, public gardens, nature preserves, cultural attractions, and historic sites—even a national wildlife refuge—to make you feel like you're far from one of the country's most densely populated metropolitan areas.

This was the homeland of the Lenni-Lenape before Dutch settlers moved in and carved the landscape into farmland in the 17th and 18th centuries. A passenger-rail line was built through the region in the 1890s, bringing wealthy New Yorkers who came to the rolling hills for a respite from the rigors of fast-paced city life. Many chose to stay, building so many grand country estates in the hills that the area earned a legendary reputation as the Newport of New Jersey. Today, Somerset and Essex counties are peppered with wealthy suburbs like Montclair, Summit, Glen Ridge, Maplewood, South Orange, and Short Hills. Visitors looking for luxe accommodations head to the Hilton at Short Hills, or to Summit's Grand Summit Hotel, a highbrow Tudor-style country accommodation built at the site of The Blackburn House, which was *the* place for a genteel 19th-century getaway.

You can spend days trying to see all of the well-preserved historic sites and top-rate museums. In Ho-Ho-Kus, the Hermitage is a restored 18th-century stone manor and national historic landmark that counts George Washington, Alexander Hamilton, the Marquis de Lafayette, James Madison, and Aaron Burr among its distinguished guests. The lush gardens surrounding the 18th-century Durand-Hedden House in Maplewood boast one of the largest collections of herbs in the Northeast. In Fair Lawn, the Garretson Farm County Historic Site was the location of a forge and furnace that operated well before the American Revolution; today it's a living-history museum of the early Dutch colonial period. There's a museum in Montclair devoted to baseball great and hometown hero Yogi Berra, and a national historic site in West Orange at the site of Menlo Park, Thomas Edison's famous invention factory, where he developed the motion picture camera, incandescent light bulb, and 1,000 other patented machines and gadgets.

Perched alongside the Great Falls of the Passaic River is Paterson, New Jersey's third-largest city and the nation's first planned industrial city. It was the vision of Alexander Hamilton, who first saw the thundering falls when he visited the area in the 18th century with George Washington. In 1778, Hamilton proposed that a city be built of industries that could harness the tremendous waterpower at the 77-foot

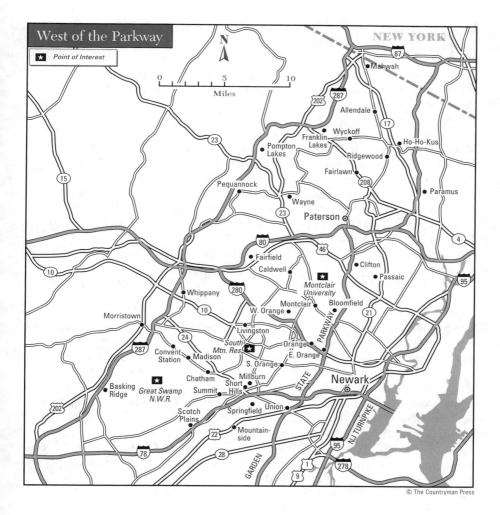

falls. In terms of volume, it's the second-largest waterfall east of the Mississippi. The city was established a few years later and named for New Jersey governor William Paterson. It quickly earned the nickname Silk City, known for its silk- and textile-manufacturing plants as well as its locomotive industries. In 1906, Cooke Locomotive Works produced the locomotive that helped build the Panama Canal. Later, the Silk City Diner Company produced the ubiquitous shiny chrome diner cars that were scattered along roadsides throughout New Jersey and around the country. The modern-day submarine and the Colt revolver were also developed here.

Hundreds of Paterson's original buildings were destroyed by fire and flood in the early 1900s, but a historic district was established to preserve the remaining mills and houses from the city's manufacturing heyday. The Paterson Museum has a permanent exhibit on the city's industrial past, while the American Labor Museum honors the thousands of working-class immigrants who powered the mills. Paterson's industrial landscape inspired artists, including the poet William Carlos

Williams, who immortalized the city in his writings; Beat-generation icon Allen Ginsberg, who was a Paterson native; Edward Hopper, who painted it; and Jack Kerouac, who made references to the city in his seminal novel *On the Road.* Today Paterson's residents represent more than 75 ethnic groups. Naturally, the city's restaurants are a melting pot of exotic cuisines, from Lebanese and West Indian to Creole and Turkish.

Montclair is affluent and artsy, and visitors shouldn't miss a stroll down eclectic Bloomfield Avenue, shopping and dining along Church Street, an afternoon at the Montclair Art Museum, or a performance in the community's summer parks concert series that attracts international musicians. Plainfield is home to New Jersey's oldest community symphony orchestra as well as the Plainfield Shakespeare Garden, one of only a few gardens dedicated to the Bard in the United States. In Upper Montclair, the Presby Memorial Iris Gardens is a National Historic Trust Site with 100,000 plants that erupt into a spectacular springtime show. Millburn's Paper Mill Playhouse was founded in the 1930s as one of America's first regional theaters; today it's New Jersey's official state theater, offering Broadway-caliber musicals and plays.

Essex County's network of 26 parks and reservations is America's first county park system, the 19th-century vision of landscape architect Frederick Law Olmsted Sr., whose pièce de résistance was New York City's Central Park. His sons, the famous Olmsted brothers design duo, helped their father with the pioneering project. South Reservation, tucked between the first and second ridges of the Watchung Range, includes a zoo, skating rinks, and three public golf courses. Eagle Rock Reservation is known for its spectacular views of the New York City skyline, and for Highlawn Pavilion, one of the top gourmet restaurants in the state. Union County maintains the Watchung Reservation, a 1,000-acre wooded preserve near the Great Swamp National Wildlife Refuge, which encompasses 7,600 acres of federally protected wetlands less than 30 miles from Times Square. The refuge is the result of efforts by a local environmental group who fought the proposed development of an airport here in the 1970s. The Great Swamp isn't a swamp, per se, but rather a mix of meadows, marshes, woodland, brush-filled swamps, and wetlands. The diverse habitat is home to a variety of wildlife, from fox and deer to more than 250 species of native birds.

Entries in this section are arranged in roughly geographic order, from north to south.

AREA CODES 732, 908, 201.

GUIDANCE A **state welcome center** (201-391-5737) is located at mile marker 172 on the Garden State Parkway northbound in Montvale. You'll find all sorts of helpful travel literature here, from brochures to maps, and a knowledgeable staff to field your questions.

The **Somerset County Chamber of Commerce** operates a visitors center (908-725-1552) at 360 Grove St. (at Rt. 22) in Bridgewater.

GETTING THERE *By air:* **Newark Liberty International Airport** (973-961-6000; 888-397-4636; www.panynj.com) in Newark is served by more than 40 major carriers. **AirTrain Newark** (888-397-4636; www.airtrainnewark.com) provides rail service between airport terminals and mass transit, including New Jersey Transit and Amtrak trains as well as New York's and Newark's Penn Stations. **John F. Kennedy International Airport** (718-244-4444; www.kennedyairport.com) and **LaGuardia International Airport** (718-533-3400; www.laguardiaairport.com) in New York City are both close to the Northeastern Gateway region.

By rail: **Amtrak** (800-872-7245; www.amtrak.com) serves Penn Station in Newark. **New Jersey Transit** (973-275-5555; 800-955-2321; www.njtransit.com) commuter trains reach many communities in this region. The Bergen County and Main lines run to Hoboken, where **PATH** (Port Authority Trans Hudson) train service (800-234-7284; www.panynj.com) continues on to Manhattan. The Morris & Essex and the Montclair–Boonton lines go directly to Penn Station in Manhattan.

By bus: **Greyhound** (800-231-2222; www.greyhound.com) stops at the Short Line terminal in Ridgewood and makes limited-service stops (no terminal) in Waldwick, Ramsey, Mahwah, Ho-Ho-Kus, and Allendale. From there, **New Jersey Transit** buses and commuter trains head into the suburbs.

By car: The **Garden State Parkway** runs from north to south along the eastern edge of this region. Other major highways include **I-287,** which cuts a wide arc around the New York City metropolitan region from New York State (and the Tappan Zee Bridge) to the **New Jersey Turnpike (I-95)** in Edison. **I-80** and **I-78** start in this region and run east–west across northern New Jersey to Pennsylvania.

GETTING AROUND *Taxis:* **Madison Livery** (973-377-6843) in Madison, **Paterson Area Taxi** (973-628-8333), and **Wayne Taxi & Limo** (973-742-5808) in Wayne; and **West Orange & Orange Taxi** (973-672-5252) and **Eagles Taxi Service** (973-675-3017) in Orange serve the region.

Bus services: **New Jersey Transit** (800-772-2222; www.njtransit.com) buses serve the entire region.

MEDICAL EMERGENCY **Chilton Memorial Hospital** (973-831-5000), 97 West Pkwy., Pompton Plains. The emergency number is 973-831-5111.

Wayne General Hospital (973-942-6900), 224 Hamburg Tpke., Wayne. The emergency number is 973-956-3300.

Barnert Hospital (973-977-6600), 680 Dr. Martin Luther King Jr. Hwy., Paterson. The emergency number is 973-977-6603.

St. Joseph's Regional Medical Center (973-754-2000), 703 Main St., Paterson. The emergency number is 973-754-2222.

The Valley Hospital (201-447-8000), 223 North Van Dien Ave., Ridgewood. The emergency number is 201-447-8300.

Union Hospital (908-687-1900), 1000 Galloping Hill Rd., Union. The emergency number is 908-687-1900.

✳ To See

COLLEGES AND UNIVERSITIES Many area colleges and universities have art exhibits, concerts, lectures, and cultural events in theaters, arts centers, and galleries that are open to the public. They include **Drew University** (973-408-3000; www.drew.edu), Madison; **William Paterson University** (877-978-3923; www

.wpunj.edu), Wayne; **Montclair State University** (973-655-4000; www.montclair
.edu), Montclair; **Seton Hall University** (973-761-9000; www.shu.edu), South
Orange; **Ramapo College** (201-684-7500; www.ramapo.edu), Mahwah; and **Fairleigh Dickinson University** (201-692-2000; www.fdu.edu), Teaneck.

HISTORIC HOMES **Dey Mansion** (973-696-1776), 199 Totowa Rd., Wayne.
Open Wed.–Fri. 1–4; Sat. and Sun. 10–4; closed Mon. and Tues. Admission $1;
children under 10, free. George Washington used this brick and fieldstone Georgian-style mansion as his military headquarters in 1780 during the American Revolution. One of the home's front rooms served as his office, where he met with his
aides and worked on battle strategy. While Washington and his personal guards
stayed in the house, thousands of Continental soldiers camped in tents on the
property. Although his wife, Martha, stayed with him at times during the war, on
this occasion she stayed at the Ford Mansion in Morristown. The circa-1740 home,
built by Dirk Dey and son Colonel Theunis Dey, contains period artifacts and
Queen Anne- and Chippendale-style furnishings.

Van Riper–Hopper House (973-694-7192), 533 Berdan Ave., Wayne. Open by
appointment; admission by donation. A handsome Dutch Colonial farmhouse built
in 1786 by Uriah Van Riper is the headquarters of the **Wayne Historical Commission** and the **Wayne Township Museum.** It's a fine example of the early New Jersey architecture typical of this region in the 1700s. The original six fireplaces are still
here, as are the wide-plank floors, rough-cut hand-hewn beams, and thick fieldstone
walls. Also on the property is the **Mead–Van Duyne House,** a circa-1740 stone
Colonial farmstead that was moved here to save it from a highway construction project. A six-lane highway—Route 23 South—now passes over its original site.

✍ MONTCLAIR ART MUSEUM

(973-746-5555; www.montclair-art.org), Three South Mountain Ave., Montclair. Open Wed.–Sun. noon–5; closed Mon., Tues., and major holidays;
reduced summer hours. Adults $12; seniors and students $10; children 11 and
under, free. This stately Greek Revival–style building houses permanent and
changing exhibits of top-notch American and Native American art in New
Jersey's first public museum, which opened in 1913. There's an excellent rep-
resentation of 18th- and 19th-century American artists, including impressionists **Childe Hassam, John Singer Sargent, John Singleton Copley, Winslow
Homer,** and Montclair native **George Inness.** In the 1800s, the Newark-born
landscape artist was known for his rural scenes, especially the hill country in
the Delaware Water Gap region and the countryside around Montclair. His
early landscapes were influenced by his association with the 19th century
Hudson River school of painters, famous for their dramatic vistas of New
York's Hudson River valley and the western frontier. Later he developed his
own signature style, what he called "civilized landscapes," hazy, dreamlike
images that emphasized the serenity of nature but also contained a human
element—a house or a barn, perhaps—that implied the presence of people.

THE HERMITAGE

(201-445-8311; www.thehermitage.org), 335 N. Franklin Tpke., Ho-Ho-Kus. Guided tours Wed.–Sun. 1–4; the last tour leaves at 3:15 PM. Closed Mon., Tues., and major holidays. Adults $5; seniors $4; children 6–12 $2; 5 and under, free. The original dwelling, a circa-1740 brownstone, was built by high-ranking British military officer James Prevost, who counted George Washington, Alexander Hamilton, the Marquis de Lafayette, James Madison, and Aaron Burr among his distinguished guests. In July 1778 General Washington used the home as his military headquarters, where he and his Continental troops regrouped after the bloody battle of Monmouth. Following the death of Captain Prevost, Burr married Prevost's widow, Theodosia, here in 1782. Local industrialist and physician Elijah Rosegrant (from the Dutch, Rosenkrantz) purchased the home in 1807; his son, Elijah Rosecrantz Jr., transformed it into the Gothic Revival–style manor that stayed in the family for 163 years, until 1970. Today, the whimsical gingerbread-style stone house is a national historic landmark, and the only restored 18th-century structure in Bergen County. Displays of clothing, furnishings, personal items, and documents are a window into the Rosencrantzes' high-class Victorian-era lifestyle. A museum shop sells gifts and reproductions. Vintage auto festivals, crafts and antiques shows, and military encampments and reenactments are held on the grounds throughout the year.

Grover Cleveland House (973-226-0001), 207 Bloomfield Ave., Caldwell. Open Wed.–Fri. 9–6; Sat. 9–5; Sun. 1–6; closed Mon., Tues., and major holidays. Free admission. This is the birthplace of America's 22nd and 24th president, born on March 18, 1837. Grover Cleveland was a man of firsts: the first Democrat elected after the Civil War, the only U.S. president elected to two nonconsecutive terms, the only president born in New Jersey, the first one to marry in the White House, and the first to publicly admit to fathering an illegitimate child. He moved to Princeton following his presidency in 1897, and is buried in Princeton Cemetery.

Durand-Hedden House and Garden (973-763-7712), Grasmere Park, 523 Ridgewood Rd., Maplewood. Limited hours; phone ahead. A restored circa-1790 farmhouse on 2 acres with one of the largest collections of herbs in the Northeast. When Ebenezer Hedden bought the property around 1740, it encompassed more than 70 acres; his son Obadiah built a farmhouse here after the American Revolution. It's part of the present house, including the kitchen, with its original sandstone fireplace and reconstructed beehive oven, and an upstairs bedroom. His son Henry bought the house in 1812; it was then passed on to his son James Madison Durand, a prominent Newark jeweler, who introduced the decorative Greek Revival and Italianate features—peaked gables with rounded-top windows and the ornate front doorframe. These were added in the mid-1800s, around the time that the front room, porch, back parlor, and bedrooms were constructed. The award-winning Victorian flower and herb garden is maintained by the **Maplewood Garden Club,** and is the setting for an annual summertime garden party, tours, educational programs, and open-house events.

HISTORIC SITES 130 in "The Southern Gateway" for a description of the **Edison National Historic Site,** located in West Orange.

Garretson Farm County Historic Site (201-797-1775; www.garretsonfarm.org), 402 River Rd., Fair Lawn. Open Sun. 1–4. The Garretson forge and farm is one of Bergen County's oldest historic sites. It was established half a century before the American Revolution by one of the first Dutch families to settle and farm the region. The sandstone house was built in 1719, and six generations of the Garretson family resided on the sprawling farm along the banks of the Passaic River. Today the remaining 2-acre site is a living-history museum of the early Dutch colonial period; the original sections of the house show the crude building methods and materials of the time—the sandstone blocks were held together with a

GREAT FALLS NATIONAL HISTORIC LANDMARK DISTRICT

Paterson's historic landmark district is a nod to its rich manufacturing heritage and proud history as the first planned industrial city in America. The Society for the Establishment of Useful Manufactures (S.U.M.) was founded in 1791 to develop Alexander Hamilton's vision of an industrialized nation. Massive factories and millraces were built along the banks of the Passaic River to harness the tremendous waterpower of the Great Falls, where a billion gallons a day tumble over a 77-foot cliff. By the 19th century, Paterson's mills were producing, silk, cotton, bricks, jewelry, and shoes; more than 6,000 locomotives were built (second only to the number produced in Philadelphia); and Samuel Colt was manufacturing his famous revolvers in the city's Old Gun Mill. Thousands of immigrants came to the "Silk City" to work on the factory floors for low wages as mill owners got rich.

Paterson's 118-acre industrial historic site includes the city's Beaux-Arts-style city hall, the Phoenix mill complex, the 19th-century home of silk manufacturer John Ryle, the 1835 Benjamin Thompsen House, and the Thomas Rogers Locomotive Erecting Shop, home to the **Paterson Museum** (973-321-1260; www.thepatersonmuseum.org), Two Market St. The museum is open Tues.–Fri. 10–4; Sat. and Sun. 12:30–4:30; closed Mon. and holidays. Adults $2; children free. Exhibits reflect the evolution of Paterson's 19th-century heyday as one of America's leading industrial centers. They tell the story of inventor and local schoolteacher John Holland, "the Father of the Modern Submarine," who produced two experimental subs here. The hulls are part of the museum's permanent collection, as are exhibits on mineralogy (including New Jersey's famous fluorescent minerals in a replica mine), mortar made from river mud and straw, and the pipes were made of clay. The carriage house was built in the 1800s, and the gambrel roof was added at the turn of the 20th century. Special events include programs on colonial horticulture, agriculture, and crafts.

MUSEUMS See also **Paterson Museum** (See sidebar, these pages).

American Labor Museum (973-595-7953), Botto House National Landmark, 83 Norwood St., Haledon. Open Wed.–Sat. 1–4; closed Sun.–Tues. and holidays (open on Labor Day). Adults $1.50; children, free. This 1908 Victorian home with restored period rooms is a national historic landmark, with exhibits, photos, artifacts, and a research library that trace Paterson's industrial history and labor-union past, and the culture of its working-class citizens. Pietro and Maria Botto were Italian immigrants who worked in Paterson's silk mills in the early 20th century. In 1913 the massive Paterson Silk Strike put 20,000 mill employees out of work; the Botto home was the nerve center where union leaders would rally the hardworking immigrants that ran the mills.

local archaeology, and 200,000 photographs and negatives. Changing exhibits feature the work of local and regional contemporary artists.

Hamilton never got to see his dream come true—he was shot and killed in a duel with longtime political and personal rival Aaron Burr in 1804. A memorial statue of Hamilton stands overlooking the Great Falls.

THE GREAT FALLS OF THE PASSAIC RIVER INSPIRED FOUNDING FATHER ALEXANDER HAMILTON'S VISION OF TURNING PATERSON INTO AMERICA'S FIRST PLANNED INDUSTRIAL CITY, FOLLOWING HIS CREATION OF THE SOCIETY OF USEFUL MANUFACTURES (S.U.M.) IN 1791.

Photo courtesy of Joe Costa

LAMBERT CASTLE MUSEUM

(973-247-0085; www.lambertcastle.com), Three Valley Rd., Paterson. Open
Wed.–Sun. 1–4. Adults $3; seniors $2; children 12–18, $1.50. Grounds are
open daily from dawn to dusk; the research library is open by appointment.
The opulent 19th-century estate of silk baron Catholina Lambert is now
home to the Passaic County Historical Society. Lambert built this monument
to his success high atop Garrett Mountain, where it could stand sentinel
over the "Silk City" mills where his vast fortune was taking shape. When his
sandstone and granite home was built in 1892, it was modeled after Warwick Castle, one of many royal estates Lambert often saw as a boy in England. The future tycoon was the son of poor cotton-mill workers, and seeing
the castles perched above humble homes like his own inspired him to pur-
sue success in America, where the dream of building his own castle could
come true. Visitors can tour the castle and see period rooms, local-history
exhibits, and Lambert's impressive collection of European artwork.

✐ **Yogi Berra Museum and Learning Center** (973-655-2378; www.yogiberra
museum.org), Montclair State University, Eight Quarry Rd., Little Falls. Open
Wed.–Sun. noon–5 (until 7 during New Jersey Jackals home games); closed Mon.,
Tues., and major holidays. Adults $6; students $4; children 4 and under, free. If
you're heading to a New Jersey Jackals baseball game, arrive early and spend some
time at this worthwhile site. It's a museum dedicated to Lawrence Peter "Yogi"
Berra's stellar career. He began as one of baseball's greatest catchers in the 1950s
and was a 15-time All-Star and a three-time Most Valuable Player; later he did a
stint as a major-league manager for the Yankees and the Mets. The museum features nostalgic memorabilia-filled displays on the history of baseball, the story of
the New York Yankees, New Jersey's role in the history of major-league baseball,
and, of course, the longtime Montclair resident who coined such familiar phrases
as "It ain't over till it's over," and "It's déjà vu all over again."

Israel Crane House Museum (973-744-1796), 108 Orange Rd., Montclair. Open
for guided tours Fri. and Sat. 1–4; Sun. 2–5. Adults $5; children 10 and under, $2.
A handsome 1796 Federal-style mansion—one of the few remaining in northern
New Jersey—is not just a museum; it also includes a 19th-century general store
and post office, a farmhouse, a library, and herb and flower gardens. Montclair
founding father Israel Crane was known as King Crane, not only for building the
first toll road into central New Jersey but also for his role as a prominent local
tycoon. He ran several mills, a general store, and prosperous brownstone quarries,
and built the mansion—which was quite opulent by 18th-century standards—when
he was only 22. Three generations of the Crane family lived here; the Ionic
columns and other Greek Revival details were added circa 1840. Rooms contain
18th- and 19th-century furniture, rugs and quilts, paintings, tools, and household
items—even an 1816 painted bedroom set owned by Paul Revere. Special events
include open-hearth cooking and beehive oven baking demonstrations in the
reconstructed vintage kitchen.

✇ **Whippany Railway Museum** (973-887-8177; www.whippanyrailwaymuseum .net), One Railroad Plaza, Whippany Rd. and Rt. 10 W., Whippany. Open Apr. to mid-Oct., Sun. noon–4, and select days in December; phone ahead for a schedule of seasonal train excursions and to make a reservation. Admission to the museum and grounds: Adults $1; children 11 and under, 50 cents. New Jersey's railroad history is on display in changing exhibits of railroad artifacts, memorabilia, photographs, and rare documents—even antique train bells and whistles—in a restored turn-of-the-20th-century freight house. The **Whippanong Valley Railroad,** a 30-foot-long model-train layout, is one of the largest such exhibits in New Jersey. Outside in the old Morristown & Erie Railway yard is a **1942 steam engine** built for the U.S. military, historic locomotives, restored passenger cars and cabooses, and coal loaders. The museum offers seasonally themed train rides through scenic Morris County aboard their enclosed passenger cars and a 1940s-era parlor car pulled by a vintage diesel-powered locomotive. Annual excursions include the **Easter Bunny Express, Halloween Express,** and the **Santa Claus Special,** with Santa and his elves on board.

✇ **Museum of Early Trades and Crafts** (973-377-2982; www.metc.org), Main St. (Rt. 124) and Green Village Rd., Madison. Open Tues.–Sat. 10–4; Sun. noon–5; closed Mon. Adults $5; seniors, students, and children $3; children 5 and under free. A unique museum recognizing the art of ordinary people—18th- and 19th-century craftsmen and craftswomen—in preindustrial New Jersey. The permanent collection includes an exhibit of rural New Jersey farm life in the early 1800s, another on the history of blacksmithing (which goes back about 3,000 years), and displays featuring local 19th-century tradesmen, including a cabinetmaker, cooper, distiller, and shoemaker. The museum shop sells children's toys and books, handcrafted pottery and glass, and other crafts.

Tunis-Ellicks Historic House and Museum (973-292-0161), Village and Millbrook roads, New Vernon. Limited hours; phone ahead. The **Harding Historical Society** maintains this circa-1800 farmhouse as a museum depicting life on a typical 19th-century New Jersey farm. A re-creation of an authentic 19th-century parlor garden surrounds the house with 120 varieties of perennials and herbs.

Liberty Hall Museum (908-527-0400; www.kean.edu/libertyhall), Kean University, 1003 Morris Ave., Union. Open Wed.–Sat. 10–4, Sun. noon–4; closed major holidays. Call for a schedule of guided tours. Adults $10; seniors $8; students $5; children two and under, free. This stately 1772 mansion—built by William Livingston, New Jersey's first governor—and 23 manicured acres of lawns, formal English gardens, and ponds is a national historic site that doubles as a rare oasis in this heavily developed part of the New York City metropolitan region. Seven generations of the royal governor's family occupied the magnificent house for 225 years. The Georgian-style manor–turned–Victorian Italianate mansion hosted such illustrious guests over the centuries as George and Martha Washington, Alexander Hamilton, Theodore Roosevelt, and Ulysses S. Grant, as well as several 20th-century U.S. presidents. The visitors center in the restored 18th-century Blue House has an orientation video that's worth seeing before you explore the museum. Exhibits trace New Jersey history and the history of the family from the colonial era to the early 20th century. Exquisitely restored rooms are furnished with art, antiques, and memorabilia. Some of the original outbuildings still stand, including a wagon shed, carriage house, and icehouse, all filled with artifacts.

Photo courtesy of Liberty Hall Museum

GENERATIONS OF THE LIVINGSTON AND KEAN FAMILIES HAVE LIVED AT LIBERTY HALL SINCE 1772, WHEN THE GEORGIAN MANSION WAS BUILT BY WILLIAM LIVINGSTON, NEW JERSEY'S FIRST GOVERNOR.

ZOO ✪ **Turtle Back Zoo** (973-731-5800; www.turtlebackzoo.com), 560 Northfield Ave., West Orange. Open daily 10–3:30; extended hours during the summer. Adults $6; children 2–12 and seniors, $3. The 2,000-acre **South Mountain Reservation** is home to this popular zoo—the largest in northern New Jersey—where wild and domestic animals live in their natural surroundings. Hundreds of animals representing more than 200 species inhabit the zoo, which gets its unusual name from a rock formation, located in the picnic area, that resembles a turtle shell. The resident wildlife includes timber wolves, bobcats, penguins, monkeys, cougars, prairie dogs, birds of prey, and black bears. Children love the petting zoo with barnyard animals and pony rides, and the miniature-train ride through the reservation.

✳ To Do

AMUSEMENT PARK ✪ **Bowcraft Playland** (908-389-1234; www.bowcraft .com), 2545 Rt. 22 W., Scotch Plains. Open Apr.–Oct.; closed Nov.–Mar. The arcade is open daily year-round. Free admission to the park; tickets must be purchased for the rides. An old-fashioned amusement park that's ideal for younger children and families. Amusement rides, a video arcade, mini golf, a miniature-train ride, games of chance, and a food court are among the attractions.

GOLF The Northeastern Gateway region's suburban sprawl is surprisingly dotted with many well-regarded public 18-hole golf courses. Most have a clubhouse with a snack bar or a restaurant, a pro shop, and instruction or practice facilities. They include **Darlington Golf Course** (201-327-8770), 277 Campgaw Rd., Mahwah; **High Mountain Golf Club** (201-891-4653), 845 Ewing Ave., Franklin Lakes;

Sunset Valley Golf Course (973-835-1515), 47 West Sunset Rd., Pompton Plains; **Passaic County Golf Course** (973-881-4921), 207 Totowa Rd., Wayne; **Meadows Golf Club** (973-696-7212), 79 Two Bridges Rd., Lincoln Park; **Francis Byrne Golf Course** (973-736-2306), 1100 Pleasant Valley Way, West Orange; **Pinch Brook Golf Course** (973-377-2039), 234 Ridgedale Ave., Florham Park; **New Jersey National Golf Club** (908-781-2575), 579 Allen Rd., Basking Ridge; **East Orange Golf Club** (973-379-7190), 440 Parsonage Hill Rd., Short Hills; **Ash Brook Golf Course** (908-756-0414), 1210 Raritan Rd., Scotch Plains; **Oak Ridge Golf Course** (732-574-0139), 136 Oak Ridge Rd., Clark; and **Green Knoll Golf Course** (908-722-1300; 908-722-1301), 587 Garretson Rd., Bridgewater.

HIKING **Ramapo Valley County Reservation** (201-825-1388), Rt. 202, Mahwah. A network of hiking trails connects a series of lakes in this 3,300-acre tract of wooded terrain. For an easy walk, follow the trail around **Scarlet Oak Pond;** for a challenge, take the trail up Rocky Mountain to **Bear Swamp Lake,** a remote mountaintop lake. Pick up a trail map at the park entrance.

Eagle Rock Reservation (973-268-3500), West Orange. Bridle paths and hiking trails lace this wooded Essex County park in the Watchung Mountains. Mostly easy to moderate hiking trails lead to stunning views of Manhattan, from the Verrazano-Narrows Bridge to the George Washington Bridge. As its name implies, **Lookout Point** provides visitors with a spectacular view of the New York City skyline, including the George Washington Bridge and the Empire State Building.

South Mountain Reservation (973-268-3500), West Orange and Millburn. This is an inviting forest with surprisingly rough terrain, considering its location at the heart of suburbia. Most visitors stick to the 27-mile network of gravel carriage roads, which are easy to follow and make for rewarding hiking. There are 19 miles of trails—the yellow-blazed Lenape Trail and the white-blazed Rahway Trail—which are inconsistently marked and sometimes hard to follow. First-time visitors should contact the park for guidance before heading out on the trails. Highlights include panoramas from atop the Watchung ridgeline, the beautiful **Hemlock Falls,** and the **Maple Falls Cascade,** a dramatic 25-foot plunge into a steep, narrow canyon.

Watchung Reservation (908-789-3670), 452 New Providence Rd., Mountainside. A network of dirt roads, nature trails, and bridle paths winds through the Watchung Reservation. Pick up a free trail map at the **Trailside Nature and Science Center;** from there you can leave on a variety of hikes of varying degrees of length and difficulty. One of the most popular is the white-blazed Sierra Trail, an 8.5-mile loop that circles the reservation on dirt roads, bridle trails, boardwalks, and footpaths. Along the way, you'll pass an 18th-century cemetery, the brick ruins of an old mill, picturesque **Surprise Lake,** and the deserted village of **Feltville,** an abandoned 19th-century mill village.

✍ **Great Swamp National Wildlife Refuge** (973-425-1222), 241 Pleasant Plains Rd., Basking Ridge. Grounds open year-round daily from sunrise to sunset; headquarters open Mon.–Fri. 8–4:30. This refuge is more popular among birders than hikers. Trails are short and easy, ideal for families with young children or those looking for a relaxing nature walk. The Orange Trail and the Red Trail are the two main mile-long trails that start behind the visitors center and follow a series of boardwalks and footpaths through marshy areas. Summertime brings a lot of people and a lot of mosquitoes; it's wise to carry insect repellent to avoid the bugs and to visit early in the morning to avoid the crowds. The best time to hike here is at the height of the annual bird migration in the fall, when thousands of songbirds and raptors pass through.

SPECTATOR SPORTS ✔ **New Jersey Jackals** (973-746-7434; www.jackals .com), Yogi Berra Stadium, Montclair State University, One Hall Dr., Little Falls. Games are played from late May to mid-Sept. This is the smallest minor-league ballpark in New Jersey, and the only one named for a person. The stadium and outfield lawn have seating for 7,000 spectators. The adjacent **Yogi Berra Museum and Learning Center** (see *To See—Museums*) is a good stop before the game.

✔ **Somerset Patriots** (908-252-0700; www.somersetpatriots.com), Commerce Bank Ballpark, One Patriots Park (off E. Main St.), Bridgewater. Games are played May–Sept.; call for a schedule. The Patriots are a professional minor-league baseball team in the Atlantic League. Their 6,100-seat stadium is a state-of-the-art facility with the feel of an old-fashioned ballpark; it features 20 luxury suites, an alcohol-free family section, and a picnic area that's open before games.

STARGAZING Sperry Observatory (908-276-2730; events hotline: 908-276-7827), on the campus of Union County College, 1033 Springfield Ave., Cranford. The observatory is open to the public for free Friday-evening lectures followed by an observation session. Most talks—on various astronomy-related topics—are given by members of **Amateur Astronomer, Inc.,** one of the largest astronomy clubs in America. The observatory's two telescopes are among the largest telescopes on the East Coast available for amateur use.

✳ Green Space

GARDENS James Rose Center (201-446-6017; www.jamesrosecenter.org), 506 E. Ridgewood Ave., Ridgewood. Open for self-guided tours from mid-Apr. to Oct. Admission $8. James Rose was a leading landscape architect during the 1930s, known for his pioneering design ideas. With a plan he conceived while serving in the South Pacific during World War II, Rose built his Ridgewood main house, guesthouse, and studio in 1953. Its blend of architecture, art, and landscape—with wall murals, gardens, and an Asian-style roof garden—was revolutionary in modern American design. Rose lived here for 40 years, and after his death a foundation was established to restore and preserve the complex.

Avis Campbell Gardens (973-746-9614), 60 South Fullerton Ave., Montclair. Gardens open daily. Free admission; a fee is charged for some programs. Lovely English-style gardens maintained by volunteers from the **Garden Club of Montclair**—the largest garden club in New Jersey—include an herb garden, a rose garden, and a formal walled garden surrounding a central fountain. Many plants are labeled, a gesture that's appreciated by visitors who see something they want to plant in their gardens back home.

Van Vleck House and Gardens (973-744-4752; www.vanvleck.org), 21 Van Vleck St., Montclair. Gardens are open daily 10–5. The gardens represent the work of three generations of gardeners in the Van Vleck family. The 6-acre estate is lush with azaleas, rhododendrons, and wisteria, and well-manicured formal gardens surrounding a 1916 Mediterranean-style villa.

Brookdale Park Rose Garden (973-268-3500), Brookdale Park, Grove St., between Summit and Wildwood avenues, Upper Montclair. During the month of June, close to 100 species of roses erupt in a profusion of bloom in this 121-acre suburban park on the border of Montclair and Bloomfield. The rose garden was established here in 1959 with a donation of 750 rosebushes by the **North Jersey Rose Society.**

Florence and Robert Zuck Arboretum (973-408-3000), on the campus of Drew University, 36 Madison Ave., Madison. Pick up a trail guide at the entrance to the arboretum, located on the southwest part of Drew's 186-acre campus. The brochure describes numbered sites along the nature trail that passes along two glacial ponds, popular stopovers for migrating herons and waterfowl. Visitors can take a self-guided walk through this serene woodland retreat, created and named for Drew faculty members Florence and Robert Zuck.

Reeves-Reed Arboretum (908-273-8787; www.reeves-reedarboretum.org), 165 Hobart Ave., Summit. Grounds are open daily, dawn to dusk. Free admission. An arboretum at the former Reeves-Reed family estate, on the National Register of Historic Places, is a center for environmental and horticultural education. The 12-acre landscape of open meadows, woodlands, and sweeping lawns surrounding formal gardens was designed in the 19th and 20th centuries, and the plantings were coordinated to deliver a succession of blooms from spring to fall. Springtime begins with a cheerful profusion of color from bulbs, wildflowers, flowering trees, rhododendrons, and azaleas. Summertime brings roses, herbs, and daylilies, while perennial beds and rock gardens put on a continuous show. There's a botanical library, and maple syrup demonstrations in late winter and early spring.

Greenwood Gardens (973-258-4026; www.greenwoodgardens.org), 274 Old Short Hills Rd., Short Hills. Open for guided tours; reservations are required.

PRESBY MEMORIAL IRIS GARDENS

(973-783-5974), Mountainside Park, 474 Upper Mountain Ave., Upper Montclair. Grounds are open daily 10–8 during the blooming season, which peaks between mid-May and mid-June. Free admission. Frank H. Presby was one of America's leading horticulturalists and a founder of the American Iris Society, not to mention a prominent Montclair resident. He began planting irises here in 1927, and today his legacy is one of the finest collections of irises in the world. Each spring more than 40,000 irises—4,500 historic and new varieties—blanket this National Historic Trust Site in a profusion of vivid color. The gardens include tall bearded specimens; Japanese, Siberian, and dwarf varieties; and species that produce a second bloom in late September and October. Iris growers from around the world have donated plants to the gardens, which are maintained by hundreds of volunteers. Extensive written records support the history of the collection and trace some species to the 1500s. It's believed that other varieties date back thousands of years. Special events like iris identification classes, art exhibits, and concerts take place mostly while the irises are in bloom.

This once-opulent private estate fell into complete neglect; today it's one of a dozen restoration projects of the Garden Conservancy. The 22 acres includes stately Italianate gardens, grottos, and walkways.

Plainfield Shakespeare Garden (908-753-3000), Cedar Brook Park, Park Dr., Plainfield. The garden is open year-round but reaches its peak in early June. Plainfield's Shakespeare Garden—one of only a few such gardens in the United States—was established in 1927 and is maintained by the **Plainfield Garden Club.** More than 40 flowers, herbs, and shrubs appear in the Bard's works, and they're all here—old-fashioned roses, peonies, herbs such as rosemary and lemon balm, and topiary-style clipped shrubs, including yew and holly. The garden features a sundial, a honeysuckle-covered arbor, and 19 flower beds edged in brick, as was customary in Shakespearean-era English gardens. Scattered throughout the plantings are markers giving the common and botanical names of each plant, plus quotations from Shakespeare's writings about each one. The annual **Shakespeare in Bloom festival** features lectures, tours, and demonstrations.

NATURE CENTERS ✍ **James A. McFaul Environmental Center** (201-891-5571), Crescent Ave., Wyckoff. Grounds are open daily from dawn to dusk; the museum is open Mon.–Fri. 8–4:45; Sat., Sun., and holidays 1–4:45. Free admission (some programs charge a fee). An environmental center with live animals, a wildlife exhibit hall overlooking a waterfowl pond, and a full schedule of workshops, demonstrations, and programs for children and adults. Outside, nature trails wind through 81 acres of woodland, grassy hillsides, and gardens. The grounds put on a spectacular display in springtime, when some 25,000 daffodils create an explosion of color in open meadows.

✍ **Great Swamp Outdoor Education Center** (973-635-6629), 247 Southern Blvd., Chatham. Open daily 9–4:30. Free admission (some programs might charge a fee). A 40-acre outdoor education center on the eastern fringe of the **Great Swamp National Wildlife Refuge**, maintained by the Morris County Parks Commission. Hikers and bird-watchers come for the 2 miles of trails that follow footpaths and a boardwalk through the natural area. Ask about their educational programs, interesting nature activities, and guided nature walks; they offer programs for adults as well as children.

✍ **Somerset County Environmental Education Center** (908-766-2489; www.somersetcountyparks.org), 190 Lord Stirling Rd., Basking Ridge. The center is open daily 9–5; trails are open year-round, dawn to dusk. Free admission. Pick up a trail map and explore some of the 8 miles of boardwalks and footpaths through this pristine natural area adjacent to the **Great Swamp National Wildlife Refuge** in Lord Stirling Park. The nature center is maintained by the Somerset County Parks Commission, which offers workshops, programs, and nature-themed special events, as well as environmental education classes and guided field trips.

✍ **Trailside Nature and Science Center** (908-789-3670; www.ucnj.org/parks), at the Watchung Reservation, 452 New Providence Rd., Mountainside. Open daily 1–5. Admission by donation. New Jersey's first nature center is tucked into the wooded 2,000-acre **Watchung Reservation** and maintained by the Union County Department of Parks and Recreation. This is a great place for families; young children love the hands-on **Discovery Room** with its live reptiles and interactive exhibits. There are permanent and changing displays on the food chain, geology, pond life, birds of prey, and other environmental topics. The center also has a **small planetarium** and a bird observation area. Outside, the 13-mile network of trails satisfies hikers, while the herb, butterfly, and wildflower gardens are ideal subjects for nature photographers.

NATURE PRESERVES ✔ **Lorrimer Sanctuary** (201-891-2185), 790 Ewing Ave., Franklin Lakes. The trails and visitors center are open Wed.–Fri. 9–5; Sat. 10–5; Sun. 1–5; closed Mon., Tues., and major holidays. Lucine Lorrimer donated her estate to the **New Jersey Audubon Society** in 1956. The 18th-century main house is a visitors center with programs on birding and photography, nature-study workshops for adults, and Saturday nature classes for children. Kids love the hands-on exhibits and interpretive displays; there's also a well-stocked gift shop with field guides, nature-themed gifts, natural-history books, bird feeders, and T-shirts. Go outside and check out the winter bird-feeding area before heading out on the nature trails that lace through 14 acres of serene evergreen and hardwood forest.

Cora Hartshorn Arboretum and Bird Sanctuary (973-376-3587; www.hartshorn arboretum.org), 324 Forest Dr. South, Short Hills. Open daily from dawn to dusk. Free admission. This lovely arboretum encompasses 16 acres of native woodland habitat donated by Cora Hartshorn in 1958. Her hope was to create a nature sanctuary to raise public awareness and respect for nature and New Jersey's native flora and fauna. Today, the sanctuary protects more than 150 species of wildflowers and rare ferns, 45 species of trees (including 275-year-old tulip trees), and 100 species of birds. The arboretum is an official monarch butterfly tagging site as well as a milkweed habitat and butterfly habitat observation site. If you've come here to hike, you can pick up a trail map on the door to the **Stone House** (stop inside to see the mounted animal and bird specimens) and head out on the 3 miles of trails that traverse hilly terrain and pass through a natural amphitheater carved by glaciers.

✔ **Great Swamp National Wildlife Refuge** (973-425-1222), 241 Pleasant Plains Rd., Basking Ridge. Grounds are open year-round, daily from dawn to dusk; headquarters are open Mon.–Fri. 8–4:30. Free admission. Morris County's Great Swamp was formed when the Wisconsin Glacier melted and retreated some 25,000 years ago. The land was purchased by English settlers from the Delaware Indians in the early 1700s, and cleared and farmed for the next couple centuries before reverting to woods and swampland. In the 1960s the refuge was established, and the eastern half of the 7,600-acre tract became a federally designated wilderness area. It's a prime feeding and resting area for migratory birds—more than 244 species have been seen here—and a popular spot for viewing deer, muskrats, beavers, foxes, and reptiles as well as birds. Many visitors come on spring and fall weekends to see the refuge's wildlife. It's far more rewarding to visit during the week, in the early morning or late afternoon. There are walking trails and board-walks, plus a wildlife overlook and two bird blinds. Those opting to stay in the car can drive along Pleasant Plains Road, where wildlife is often seen. Guided walks, informative programs, and activities for children are hosted by Friends of the Great Swamp Refuge. There are also two environmental centers at the refuge— the **Somerset Environmental Education Center** and the **Great Swamp Outdoor Education Center**—that offer nature classes and guided tours.

RESERVATIONS Eagle Rock Reservation (973-268-3500), West Orange. The mountain was named in the early 1800s, when bald eagles were said to nest in the steep cliffs. When the reservation was formed later in the century, it was kept largely undeveloped, except for a network of hiking paths and bridle trails criss-crossing the wooded terrain, and a historic cobblestone road winding up the mountain. A rustic structure built at the top is now **Highlawn Pavilion** (see *Where to Eat—Dining Out*), the park's landmark mountaintop restaurant that's renowned for its gourmet cuisine and stunning views of the Empire State Building and other icons on the Manhattan skyline.

South Mountain Reservation (973-268-3500), West Orange, Maplewood, and Millburn. A sprawling Essex County park, established in 1895 after a decade of political wrangling, covers 2,047 acres in the Watchung range and spreads across several communities. The Civilian Conservation Corps built a network of trails and footbridges here in the 1930s. The paths are still popular with hikers, while other visitors come for the fishing and rock climbing, or to see the wild residents of **Turtle Back Zoo**. There's even a Revolutionary War–era site, high up on the mountain. General George Washington ordered the construction of a signal station that would allow his Continental army to keep tabs on British forces occupying New York City. Today an observation area at the site affords visitors a panorama of the Hudson River and New York City beyond it.

Loantaka Brook Reservation (973-326-7600), Loantaka Way, Chatham Township. This 570-acre reservation, part of the Morris County park system, was formed in the 1950s when several local property owners donated their land for public use. *Loantaka,* the Native American name given to the stream that runs through the park, means "place of the cold winter." There are 5 miles of trails shared by hikers, cyclists, joggers, and equestrians; the reservation also has a recreation area with ball fields, a fitness station, a picnic area, and a playground.

Watchung Reservation (908-527-4911), 452 New Providence Rd., Mountainside. Nature trails, picnic areas, playgrounds, ponds for ice-skating, and hiking trails—all in a 2,000-acre natural setting. The beautiful pine forest was planted in the 1930s by the Civilian Conservation Corps. The reservation is the well-known location of the **deserted village of Feltville,** a settlement founded in 1845 by David Felt, a New York City entrepreneur who wanted to attract people to work in his paper mill in the Watchung Mountains. A small village of a dozen homes, and a building that functioned as a school, general store, and post office, thrived for about 30 years before it was abandoned. Remnants of the 19th-century village, including houses and a cemetery, are on the National Register of Historic Places and are undergoing restoration.

✳ Lodging

HOTELS ♿ **Hotel Westminster** (973-533-0600; 800-388-2741; www .westminsterhotel.net), 550 W. Mount Pleasant Ave. (Rt. 10 West), Livingston 07039. A full-service hotel set amid the many Fortune 500 companies in the Morristown, Short Hills, and Parsippany area. Naturally, business amenities are state-of-the-art, as are all those extras that are conducive to relaxation after a long day in the office or the boardroom. There's a top-rate fitness center, an indoor heated pool, and massage therapies and facials in the spa. The 187 guest rooms and suites boast sophisticated and contemporary décor, with luxe touches like triple-sheeted beds, comfy duvets, feather or down pillows, plush robes, and upscale bath products. Suites have a separate parlor/dining area, and a choice of a kitchenette or an additional bedroom. Rooms and suites have oversized work areas, high-speed Internet access, fully stocked minibars, three phones, TV, and an in-room safe. **Strip House** serves top-notch steaks, chops, and seafood in a lavish setting. The hotel provides a complimentary shuttle to the ultra-exclusive Mall at Short Hills. $199 and up.

♿ **Hamilton Park Hotel & Conference Center** (973-377-2424; 800-321-6000; www.hamiltonparkhotel.com), 175 Park Ave., Florham Park 07932. Corporate headquarters are a dime a dozen in this part of New Jersey, and many of their clients and business associates stay here, where the around-the-clock computer center and 40 meeting rooms help them take care of business. Leisure travelers and families like to stay here, too. The 219 tastefully decorated guest rooms and suites—some boast handsome antique reproduction armoires and four-poster beds—have high-speed Internet access, work areas, and dual phone lines. The hotel sits on 13 acres of pleasantly landscaped grounds complete with walking trails, gardens, a fountain, and an in-ground pool. Inside there's another pool, a fitness center, whirlpool tubs, saunas, and racquetball, tennis, basketball, and volleyball courts. **Vanderbilts** is a lively sports bar and game lounge with big-screen TVs, billiards tables, shuffleboard, and live music; **STIR** is a new martini and wine bar. $229 and up.

✶ ♿ **The Hilton at Short Hills** (973-379-0100; 800-445-8667; www.hilton shorthills.com), 41 John F. Kennedy Pkwy., Short Hills 07078. A luxury hotel in a parklike suburban setting,

with 304 guest rooms and suites. Standard rooms are nicely furnished in pleasing natural tones and have two-line phones, plush robes, and a complimentary daily newspaper. The suites, which have a bedroom and a living room connected by a French door, come with thoughtful touches like umbrellas and lint brushes. The executive suites on the top floors are elegantly appointed and have their own concierge, as well as continental breakfast, evening hors d'oeuvres, and late-night desserts. A full-service spa pampers guests with luxurious facials, massages, and body treatments, and the state-of-the-art fitness center has a Jacuzzi tub, an indoor pool, and personal trainers. Outside there's a tennis court and a lagoon pool with a seasonal patio bar and grill. The Hilton obviously has travelers in mind: their amenities include airport shuttles and foreign-currency exchange as well as a shoe-shine stand and airline and car-rental desks. **The Terrace** serves light bistro fare; **The Retreat** lounge serves afternoon tea. The hotel is just across the street from the upscale Mall at Short Hills, and provides a free shuttle to and from the boutiques. $275 and up.

♿ **Grand Summit Hotel** (908-273-3000; 800-346-0773; www.grand summit.com), 570 Springfield Ave., Summit 07901. A magnificent brick Tudor-style country hotel two blocks from downtown and within walking distance of the New Jersey Transit train station. In 1868 this was The Blackburn House, an elegant country resort where wealthy Manhattanites came to relax and recover from the fast pace of city life. The Summit Suburban Hotel was built at the site in 1929, just before the stock market crash. It stayed in business largely because of the ill fortune of many wealthy residents, who were forced to sell their estates and move into the hotel. European craftsmen created a stately lobby with vaulted beams, a massive stone fireplace, stained glass, and richly gleaming wood. Today, some of the 150 individually decorated guest rooms are upgraded with a fireplace and French doors; turndown service with homemade cookies is a nice touch. The **Hunt Club** steak and seafood grill serves breakfast, lunch, dinner, and Sunday brunch. Shoppers appreciate the free shuttle to the Mall at Short Hills. $165 and up.

∞ **Olde Mill Inn** (908-221-1100; 800-585-4461; www.oldemillinn.com), 225 Rt. 202, Basking Ridge 07920. A pretty country inn surrounded by a brick courtyard and landscaped grounds in a lovely country setting not far from I-287. The 102 guest rooms and two suites are spacious and comfortable, outfitted with marble baths and elegant décor. The deluxe rooms add a king four-poster bed and wet bar with microwave and refrigerator. The suites have living and dining areas, Jacuzzi tubs, and wet bars; one has a fireplace. Guests mingle and relax in common areas that are at once gracious and cozy—the formal piano lounge, the lobby with its grand circular staircase, the mahogany-paneled library, and the light-filled conservatory, where breakfast is served. The **Grain House Restaurant** serves traditional American cuisine for lunch, dinner, and Sunday brunch in a charming 18th-century building with antiques-filled dining rooms and a convivial pub with live music on weekends. Continental breakfast. $179 and up.

& **Hotel Indigo Basking Ridge** (908-580-1300; 877-846-3446; www .hotelindigo.com), 80 Allen Rd., Basking Ridge 07920. A newly renovated inn, formerly the Inn at Somerset Hills, with the amenities of a full-service hotel. There are 120 guest rooms, suites, and efficiencies. Standard rooms are simple and comfortable; junior suites have a bedroom, living area, and kitchenette; king suites are the roomiest accommodations, with Jacuzzi tubs, living and dining areas, and a kitchenette. **Phi** serves American cuisine in a contemporary setting; **The Golden Bean** and **The Tap Room** offer more casual fare. There's a 24-hour exercise room, a library with laptop computers, guest laundry facilities, dry-cleaning services, and a free local shuttle. Continental breakfast. $150 and up.

& **Somerset Hills Hotel** (908-647-6700; 800-688-0700; www.shh.com), 200 Liberty Corner Rd., Warren 07059. A 111-room hotel in a pleasant setting tucked into the rolling Watchung Mountains and adjacent to a wildlife sanctuary. The standard rooms, efficiencies, and Jacuzzi suites have traditional décor and thoughtful amenities; guests have use of an outdoor pool and an exercise room. The **Tap Room** has a full menu, a casual bar and nightly entertainment. $180 and up.

& **Kenilworth Inn** (908-241-4100; 800-775-3645; www.kenilworthinn .com), Kenilworth Blvd. and South 31st St., Kenilworth 07033. The 112 guest rooms and suites are clean and comfortable with traditional décor and custom cherry furnishings, as well as TV, phone, refrigerator, and high-speed Internet access. The nicely landscaped grounds have an in-ground pool and a gazebo, and the **Fireside Lounge** serves light meals at dinner. Continental breakfast. $99 and up.

Best Western Westfield (908-654-5600; 800-688-7474), 435 North Ave. W., Westfield 07090-1433. A longtime downtown lodging within walking distance of Westfield's charming shops and restaurants. All the standard amenities are here, with one notable addition: **Chez Catherine**, one of the state's top French restaurants (see *Dining Out*). Continental breakfast. $140 and up.

BED & BREAKFASTS Les Saisons (973-762-3416; www.lessaisonsinn .com), 304 Elmwood Ave., Maplewood 07040. The Christensen family's elegant circa-1840 Second Empire French Victorian offers eight antiques-filled guest rooms and suites, a comfy sitting room with fireplace, and lovely grounds that invite strolling. Full breakfast. $100–185.

☃ ✿ **The Pillars of Plainfield** (908-753-0922; 888-745-5277; www.pillars2 .com), 922 Central Ave., Plainfield 07060-2311. This majestic 1870 Victorian-Georgian mansion tucked behind a wrought-iron gate on parklike grounds is a secluded escape, yet convenient to many places in the Northeastern Gateway region, including

Newark Liberty International Airport and Manhattan. The interior is striking, with many original features like a circular stairway, fireplaces, and stained-glass windows. There are four guest rooms, two suites, and a studio apartment (ideal for extended stays), all with private bath, phone, air-conditioning, TV and VCR, robes, and turndown service. Each room is uniquely and thoughtfully decorated—the Clementine Yates Room is wonderfully sunny and bright—but the suites are extra-special and worth the splurge. Complimentary chocolates, cookies, and refreshments are served in addition to a full Swedish breakfast of home-baked goods. $125–190.

✳ Where to Eat

DINING OUT Saddle River Inn (201-825-4016; www.saddleriverinn .com), Two Barnstable Court, Saddle River. Open for lunch Wed.–Fri.; dinner Tues.–Sat.; closed Sun. and Mon. Reservations and jackets are required at dinner. This romantic spot serving

THE PILLARS OF PLAINFIELD BED AND BREAKFAST INN, AN 1870 VICTORIAN-GEORGIAN MANSION TUCKED AWAY ON A SECLUDED ACRE OF LAND IN NEW JERSEY'S BUSY NORTHEASTERN GATEWAY REGION.

Photo courtesy of Chuck Hale

impeccable French cuisine is where people come for special occasions. It's part of Barnstable Court, a former 19th-century country estate, and the restaurant occupies a restored mill house. The seasonally changing menu features expertly prepared and artfully presented French cuisine with Swiss touches. Appetizers might be smoked salmon with crème fraîche, or escargot baked in brandy and herb butter. Move on to the roasted filet of beef with chestnut puree, served with either *roesti* or spaetzle, or the Maine lobster with cognac-champagne sauce and potato gnocchi. BYOB. $29–36.

The Chef's Table (201-891-6644; www.chefstablenj.com), Franklin Square Shopping Center, 754 Franklin Ave., Franklin Lakes. Open for lunch Tues.–Fri.; dinner Tues.–Sun.; closed Mon. Reservations are required. An intimate and charming bistro serving classic French cuisine. Lobster thermidor is a signature dish, as is rack of lamb baked in puff pastry; daily specials might be bouillabaisse, cassoulet, or braised lamb shank. Crêpes, tarts, and crème brûlée for dessert. BYOB. $19–30.

Chez Catherine (908-654-4011; www.chezcatherine.com), at the Best Western Westfield (see *Lodging—Hotels*) 431 North Ave. W., Westfield. Open for lunch Tues.–Fri.; dinner Tues.–Sat.; closed Sun. and Mon. Chez Catherine's fare wins high marks for authenticity and tops readers' polls on a regular basis. The kitchen re-creates the classics with fresh ingredients and solid techniques. The short but well-executed menu features appetizers like leek soup and foie gras; entrées include osso buco and Dover sole. Service is attentive and impeccable. Prix fixe $59.

Il Capriccio (973-884-9175; www.ilcapriccio.com), 633 Rt. 10 E., Whippany. Open for lunch Mon.–Fri.; dinner Mon.–Sat.; closed Sun. Reser-

vations are recommended. Old World elegance on the outside—topiary, urns, and statues—hints at the goings-on inside. The regional Italian cuisine of chef Antonio Grande has been a local favorite for more than a decade. In the dining room, an impressive tapestry depicts Venice, and the menu is printed on exquisite Florentine paper. A signature dish is the veal tenderloin in *salsa agrodolce,* a vinaigrette of balsamic vinegar, lemon, pine nuts, and raisins. Much of the fish and shellfish is imported from the Mediterranean, and much of the produce comes from their own organic farm. Keep in mind that a meal here is a pricey proposition. $26–45.

& **Fascino** (973-233-0350; www.fascinorestaurant.com), 331 Bloomfield Ave., Montclair. Open for dinner Mon.–Sat.; closed Sun. Reservations are suggested, and should be made well in advance for a weekend. The seasonal cuisine in this family-run hot spot is Italian with hints of American and French, so the menu can feature just about anything. It's near impossible to choose; as you read the menu, each dish sounds more interesting than the one before it. The sophisticated dining room and impeccable service make you feel like you're dining in a chic private club. Entrées are a short but interesting selection of meats and seafood, and might include sage and garlic chicken breast with braised escarole and mascarpone polenta fries; or East Coast halibut with a salad of shaved fennel, kalamata olives, grapefruit, and a blood-orange reduction. Dessert shouldn't be missed, whether it's something homey like pistachio praline bread pudding or the decadent molten chocolate cake. BYOB. $22–29.

CulinAriane (973-744-0533; www.culinariane.com), 33 Walnut St., Montclair. Open for dinner Wed.–Sat.; closed Sun.–Tues. Reservations are recommended. Chef-owner Ariane Duarte appeared on Bravo's Emmy-winning reality show *Top Chef.* Her tiny storefront restaurant features eclectic modern American cuisine. The brief but well selected seasonal menu might include pecan-crusted chicken with apricot cheddar risotto, creamy goat cheese polenta with roasted imported mushrooms, and for dessert, chocolate truffle cake with Jamaican rum custard. BYOB. $22–34.

Osteria Giotto (973-746-0111), 21 Midland Ave., Montclair. Open for lunch Mon. and Wed.–Fri.; dinner Wed.–Mon.; closed Tues. Reservations are recommended. A tiny and cozy eatery known for its generous portions of gnocchi, ravioli, and other homey Italian dishes. It can be tough to get a table at this lovely spot, aptly named for a thirteenth-century painter. Even if you have a reservation, you might have to wait (it's worth it). BYOB. $20–35.

Epernay (973-783-0447; www.epernay nj.com), Six Park St., Montclair. Open for dinner Tues.–Sun.; closed Mon. A French bistro that's regarded as one of the best of Montclair's many restaurants. In a town with a solid reputation for dining, and dozens of restaurants, it's no small feat. Daily specials range from bouillabaisse and cassoulet to braised short ribs. BYOB. $19–33.

Mesob (973-655-9000; www.mesob restaurant.com), 515 Bloomfield Ave., Montclair. Open Tues.–Sun. for lunch and dinner; closed Mon. At this stylish and chic eatery, diners enjoy the exotic cuisine in true Ethiopian fashion—without utensils. A *mesob* is the traditional small woven table that holds communal platters of food. *Injera,* the country's national bread, is sometimes used to hold food; you can also tear off pieces to scoop up whatever you're eating. The menu features many stewed meats, simmered in garlic, ginger, and *berbere* (Ethiopian curry), cut into pieces small enough to scoop with bread. End your meal with a cup of tea infused with cloves, ginger, and cardamom. BYOB. $14–26.

Highlawn Pavilion (973-731-3463; www.highlawn.com), Eagle Rock Reservation, West Orange. Open for lunch Mon.–Fri.; dinner daily. Jackets are required at dinner. The former Old Casino built on an overlook in the reservation in 1911 is now one of the best gourmet restaurants in New Jersey. Spectacular views of the Manhattan skyline, grand architecture, and 15th- and 16th-century antiques all blend into a romantic and elegant setting that truly can't seem to be topped. Take away the setting, and you're left with gourmet European cuisine that would still be worth coming for. You might start with the warm duck salad with marinated asparagus, grape tomatoes, and red currant vinaigrette, or citrus-cured Atlantic salmon with jumbo lump crabmeat and caviar. Entrées run the gamut from tamarind-glazed rack of lamb with black truffle cassoulet, to a grilled veal chop with sweet potato puree and beet salsa. Desserts are exquisite works of art, especially the key lime cheesecake mousse with pistachio syrup and berry confit. The piano bar features gourmet pizzas from the Italian brick wood-burning oven. $27–38.

Basilico (973-379-7020; www.basilico millburn.com), 324 Millburn Ave., Millburn. Serving lunch and dinner Tues.–Sun.; closed Mon. Reservations are recommended. A stylish storefront eatery with impeccable service and decent prices. The extensive menu takes traditional northern Italian seafood, pasta, and meat dishes, and gives them a creative twist. Start with fresh mussels and clams in Pernod

sauce with fennel, or their signature creamy wild mushroom soup. Next, try the calamari and shrimp over polenta, or the grilled whole Mediterranean sea bass. The house specialty is osso buco served over fettuccine. BYOB. $18–29.

♿ **Restaurant Serenade** (973-701-0303; www.restaurantserenade.com), Six Roosevelt Ave., Chatham. Open for lunch Mon.–Fri.; dinner daily (à la carte Sun.–Thurs.; prix fixe Fri. and Sat.). Reservations are recommended. Many words have been used to describe chef James Laird's restaurant: stylish, chic, sophisticated, are just a few. Whatever you call it, this lovely spot is a gem, critically acclaimed for both its romantic surroundings and the food. The menu has many decidedly French touches, from the calves' liver with a bacon-onion tartlet and cassis sauce to the dijon-crusted salmon with chanterelles, potato gnocchi, and fennel. Desserts are part elegance, part comfort food. Try the roasted Bosc pear with butterscotch ice cream and cocoa reduction or the Tahitian vanilla crème brûlée. Entrées $23–38; prix fixe $80.

♿ **THE MANOR**

(973-731-2360; www.themanorrestaurant.com), 111 Prospect Ave., West Orange. Open Tues.–Sun. for lunch and dinner; Sun. brunch; closed Mon. Reservations are recommended, and jackets are required at dinner. Dinner here is truly a world-class experience—so is lunch, for that matter. Critics include the restaurant and its contemporary New American cuisine among their personal favorites. The setting is a magnificent manor house surrounded by 20 beautifully landscaped acres that include exquisite formal gardens; the kitchen makes regular use of the property's herb garden. This landmark restaurant—in business for more than half a century—is considered one of the top dining experiences in New Jersey, equal parts haute cuisine, impeccable service, and romantic surroundings. The dining room and lobby are furnished in rare antiques that set an elegant stage for the food, which is as gourmet as you'll find anywhere in New Jersey. You might begin with grilled quail with thyme goat cheese risotto, or house-smoked salmon with caviar crème fraîche. Next comes a seared veal chop and roasted artichoke and asparagus ragout in a shallot vinaigrette, or caramelized scallops with roasted-corn risotto and sweet pepper sauce. Buffets are a specialty here, too, from the acclaimed Sunday brunch to the sumptuous lobster dinner buffet offered from Wednesday through Saturday. Desserts are equally stunning. Profiteroles are filled with white chocolate and dark chocolate mousse, warm Valrhona chocolate cake comes glazed in a berry compote, and Tahitian vanilla crème brûlée is paired with iced almond-rum cake. The menu is accompanied by a wine cellar with more than 500 bottles. The **Terrace Lounge** has live piano music, and the elegant 80-seat **Le Dôme** rooftop nightclub has live music and dancing every Friday and Saturday night, and a monthly **Cabaret Soirée** series that draws top performers. $26–45.

Scalini Fedeli (973-701-9200; www
.scalinifedeli.com), 63 Main St.,
Chatham. Open for lunch Mon.–Fri.;
dinner Mon.–Sat.; closed Sun. Expert
service and flawless cuisine makes this
formal dining room one of New Jersey's top Italian restaurants. At the
helm is chef-owner Michael Cetrulo,
who also runs the more casual **Il
Mondo Vecchio** (973-301-0024) in
Madison. A French influence is seen in
dishes like sliced duck breast with
seared foie gras. Signature mascarpone
cheesecake for dessert. Prix fixe $52;
entrées $22–35.

**Stage House Restaurant and Wine
Bar** (908-322-4224; www.stagehouse
restaurant.com), 366 Park Ave., Scotch
Plains. Open for lunch Mon.–Fri.; dinner daily. Reservations are recommended. Four-star French dining at
fireside tables in a circa-1737 Early
American brick mansion. In warm
weather, you can dine on the outdoor
patio complete with kitchen herb garden and bubbling fountain. The innovative New American and French
cuisine is a longtime favorite of local
foodies and nationally known gourmands. The seasonal menu might start
with butternut squash soup with
Granny Smith apple and pumpkin seed
oil, or a risotto of Bosc pear and roasted prawns with golden raisins, braised
Napa cabbage, and lemon verbena.
Dinner could feature roasted Atlantic
halibut with baby beet risotto, or
grilled filet mignon with green pepper
sauce and glazed vegetables. A signature dessert is the passion fruit *panna
cotta*. Entrées $18–36; prix fixe
$15–55.

Lorena's (973-763-4460; www
.restaurantlorena.com), 168 Maplewood Ave., Maplewood. Open for dinner Wed.–Sun.; closed Mon. and Tues.
This highly touted restaurant is named
for Lorena Perez, who is in charge of

the dining room. It's widely considered
one of the best French restaurants in
northern New Jersey, and it's as charming and romantic as you'd expect a
jewel box of a restaurant to be. The
classic French cuisine is elegant and
expertly prepared. Atlantic monkfish
comes with mussels and fingerling
potatoes; filet mignon is accompanied
by braised onions in a black truffle
sauce; and Maine skate wing is paired
with brown butter cider emulsion.
Sweet endings include lavender-scent-
ed crème brûlée. BYOB. $26–34.

Verjus (973-378-8990; www.verjus
restaurant.com), 1790 Springfield Ave.,
Maplewood. Open for lunch Tues.–
Fri.; dinner Tues.–Sun.; Sun. brunch;
closed Mon. Reservations are request-
ed. Critics rave about the contemporary French cuisine, which changes
daily and with the seasons. You might
start with roasted pumpkin soup with
smoked prosciutto, then choose steak
au poivre with green peppercorn
sauce, ending with molten chocolate
almond truffle cake. $23–33.

Roots Steakhouse (908-273-0027;
www.rootssteakhouse.com), 401
Springfield Ave., Summit. Open daily
for dinner. Feeling carnivorous? *Meat*
is the word at this urbane chophouse
and bar that stands out in a region rich
in gourmet dining options. Generous
hand-cut rib eyes, filets, and strip
steaks are served with a choice of
sauces—horseradish cream, au poivre,
hollandaise, or bearnaise. The atmosphere is reminiscent of an old-school
Manhattan steakhouse, perpetuated by
the sophisticated dining room and
mahogany-beamed bar. $25–40.

Café Panache (201-934-0030; www
.cafepanachenj.com), 130 E. Main St.,
Ramsey. Open for lunch Mon.–Fri.;
dinner daily. Chef-owner Kevin Kohler
recently gave his longtime restaurant a
refreshing facelift, much to the delight

of the regulars that crowd in for his farm-fresh cuisine. The kitchen takes full advantage of the region's seasonal flavors in dishes that blend creative American fare with international flavors. If seafood soup is on the daily menu, be sure to order it; ditto for the crispy wasabi halibut. BYOB. $25–36.

& **Trap Rock Restaurant and Brewery** (908-665-1755; www.traprock restaurant.net), 279 Springfield Ave., Berkeley Heights. Open for lunch Mon.–Sat.; dinner daily. Reservations are recommended. An upscale eatery offering innovative dishes and a half dozen or so of their own brews daily. Start with the wild mushroom and Roquefort strudel with black truffle vinaigrette, then the pan-seared scallops and crab fritters or the slow-braised short ribs with horseradish potato puree. End with warm caramel-pumpkin bread pudding with ginger-vanilla cream. You can eat at the bar that overlooks the brewery and serves a lighter menu. Outdoor patio dining in-season. $22–33.

Restaurant MC (973-921-0888; www.restaurantmc.com), 57 Main St., Millburn. Open for lunch Tues.–Fri.; dinner daily; brunch on Sat. and Sun. This chic American bistro is one of New Jersey's hot new restaurants, the go-to place for pasta, pizza, seafood, and steak prepared with regional ingredients in a wood-burning stone oven. The sashimi and salads will satisfy those looking for something lighter. A sommelier is on hand to guide you through the award-winning wine list. $18–32.

Stone House at Stirling Ridge (908-754-1222; www.stirlingridgeevents .com), 50 Stirling Rd., Warren. Open for dinner Tues.–Sun.; Sun. brunch; closed Mon. A dress up and dine kind of place, whose stellar modern American cuisine keeps pace with the rustic

yet elegant surroundings reminiscent of a grand western-style lodge. Chef Jerry Villa puts a sophisticated spin on familiar favorites, using high-quality ingredients to create gracious country cuisine. Starters like sea scallop carpaccio lead to entrées like seared Chilean sea bass and peppercorn-dusted sirloin. Service is knowledgeable, professional, and efficient. Live jazz on weekends. $25–40.

EATING OUT ⊘ & **E&V Ristorante** (973-942-4664; www.evrestaurant .com), 320 Chamberlain Ave., Paterson. Open for lunch Tues.–Fri.; dinner Tues.–Sun.; closed Mon. A family-friendly restaurant serving huge portions of homemade Italian cuisine in casual surroundings for nearly 40 years. You're apt to be dining alongside longtime regulars anytime you're here. There's a long list of house specialties, along with the regular menu—the chef's special features shrimp, mushrooms, and artichokes prepared with prosciutto, butter, and white wine and served over homemade fettuccine. No credit cards. $10–20.

Thai Chef (973-783-4994), 664 Bloomfield Ave., Montclair. Open daily for lunch and dinner. A popular BYOB where the exotic and aromatic cuisine of Thailand is prepared with French accents. If you're familiar with Thai cuisine, the menu is fairly standard—satays, pad Thai, and meats and seafood with earthy flavors like lemongrass, chili, cilantro, and ginger. Other locations in Somerville and Hackensack. BYOB. $12–18.

⊘ **Ritz Diner** (973-533-1213), 72 E. Mount Pleasant Ave., Livingston. Open daily for breakfast, lunch, and dinner. One of the fancier diners in New Jersey, not the traditional chrome-and-neon kind of place, but the same quick, satisfying, no-frills food. Breakfasts are homey and filling; if you come for lunch or dinner, don't miss a slice of their famous apple pie. A popular place that's always packed with locals. $9–15.

🦞 🐟 **Pals Cabin** (973-731-4000), 265 Prospect Ave., West Orange. Open daily for lunch and dinner. Reservations are accepted. What started as a hot dog stand in 1932, opened by Martin Horn and his "pal" Roy Sale, is now a casual roadside family restaurant, and a local favorite serving a huge menu of homey comfort food. They've got half-pound burgers and foot-long hot dogs for a quick, light meal; entrées like Idaho rainbow trout, and sautéed calves' liver (topped with fried onions and bacon, on request) if you're in the mood for something more. Desserts include freshly baked apple pie, and homemade caramel custard. $11–35.

Sweet Basil's Café (973-325-3340; www.sweetbasilscafe.com), 641 Eagle Rock Ave., West Orange. Open daily for breakfast, lunch, and brunch. A longtime favorite spot for creative lunches now serves breakfast and brunch: think French toast, fluffy pancakes, and omelets stuffed with just-picked fruits and veggies. $7–15.

The Huntley Taverne (908-273-3166), Three Morris Ave., Summit. Open for lunch Mon.–Fri.; dinner daily. An upscale bistro in a mission-style building, serving grilled fish, chops, and other New American fare. The upstairs Arts and Crafts–style dining room overlooks the bar, where a lighter menu of sandwiches, appetizers, and pizza out of the wood-burning oven is served. $14–34.

Raagini (908-789-9777), 1085 Rt. 22 E., Mountainside. Open for lunch Mon.–Fri.; dinner daily. This popular Indian restaurant is always at the top of readers' polls, and earns its spot

there with attentive service and well-prepared authentic dishes that fill the room with exotic aromas. Chicken, lamb, and seafood are marinated in spices and sauces of varying degrees of spiciness, from cool yogurt and mint to fiery curries. Start with the veggie-stuffed *dosas*, a typical southern India dish, then pick from the curries or kebabs, or the delicacies from the tandoor oven. Traditional breads like *naan* are baked to order. $13–32.

Van Gogh's Ear Café (908-810-1844; www.vangoghsearcafe.com), 1017 Stuyvesant Ave., Union. Open daily. A coffeehouse and café where an artsy crowd gathers all day. In the evening, the café showcases the talent of comedians, musicians, and other local artists with a full schedule of art exhibits and live entertainment. A coffee bar serves the usual; the eclectic lunch and dinner menus include lots of vegetarian options. BYOB. $8–12.

Star Tavern & Pizzeria (973-675-3336), 400 High St., Orange. Open daily. Nothing fancy, but legions of hungry fans drive long distances for the crispy thin-crust pizza. Here's a tip: order a whole pizza for yourself (many proclaim a steadfast devotion to the plain cheese variety) and ask for it well done. The repertoire isn't limited to pizza, however. Fried calamari, pasta dishes, and eggplant parmesan are among the Italian staples on the menu. $9–20.

Indigo Smoke (973-744-3440; www.indigosmoke.com), 387 Bloomfield Ave., Montclair. Open daily for lunch and dinner. A Kansas City–style barbecue joint where the ribs are smoked long and slow. Accompaniments are straight out of the South: corn bread, collard greens, and whipped sweet potatoes. Sandwiches and salads accommodate small appetites. $8–21.

Raymond's (973-744-9263; www .raymondsnj.com), 28 Church St., Montclair. Open for breakfast and lunch Mon.–Fri.; dinner daily; brunch Sat. and Sun. Vintage-inspired décor lends the feel of a 1930s brasserie. Corn-batter pancakes, omelets, and French toast at breakfast; later on, dishes such as mussels marinara, burgers, and steak frites lead to decadent desserts like Valrhona chocolate torte. BYOB. $10–23.

Dimaio's Cucina (908-464-8585; www.dimaios.com), 468 Springfield Ave., Berkeley Heights. Open daily for lunch and dinner. Chef/owner Sal Passalacqua, a longtime guest chef on the Food Network, has cooked with chefs around the world. Fittingly, his southern Italian cooking is influenced by global flavors, from the pizza with asiago cheese and truffled mushrooms to the barbecued salmon with pine nuts and raisins. $15–30.

ℰ **Country Pancake House** (201-444-8395), 140 E. Ridgewood Ave., Ridgewood. Open daily for breakfast, lunch, and dinner. Befitting its name, this local institution serves huge portions of pancakes that come in more than 100 varieties. You'll have ample time to ponder your choice as you wait to be seated; tables are in constant demand. $8–15.

SNACKS 🍴 **Libby's Lunch** (973-278-8718), 98 McBride Ave., Paterson. Open daily until 1 AM. Locals flock to this friendly eatery near the Passaic Falls for the tasty dogs with a host of toppings, including Libby's special sauce. It was opened in 1936 by William Pappas, who was the first to sell Hot Texas Wieners, one of many in Paterson to eventually do so. The Texas Wiener—a deep-fried hot dog smothered in mustard, onions, and fiery chili sauce—actually originated in

New Jersey. There are several varieties of the original, all perfectly paired with piping-hot french fries. $4–10.

Millburn Deli (973-379-5800), 328 Millburn Ave., Millburn. Open daily 8–6. The usual soup, salad, sandwich roster is available, but most come in for the sloppy joes. In fact, it's not unusual to see regulars lined up when the deli opens to order them. Here, the sandwich doesn't consist of the ubiquitous ground beef and tomato sauce on a bun; rather it's a triple-decker sandwich with turkey, ham, or roast beef, Swiss cheese, Russian dressing, and homemade coleslaw tucked between freshly sliced rye bread.

The Bread Company (973-509-2525), 113 Walnut St., Montclair. Open Tues.–Sat.; closed Sun. and Mon. A small organic bakery (they cater to vegans and customers with wheat allergies) that gets many ingredients from local farms. Freshly baked muffins and scones, homemade soup, and of course, earthy, whole grain breads. The Walnut Street Loaf is studded with dates, nuts, raisins, and figs; and the Celebration Bread—a fruit, spice, nut, and seed-studded loaf more appropriate as a dessert than as a sandwich—is wildly popular. Enjoy your treats at an outdoor table, when the weather allows.

Belgiovine's Italian Delicatessen (973-744-2221), 714 Bloomfield Ave., Montclair. Open Tues.–Sun.; closed Mon. Close to the Montclair Art Museum. A busy family-owned take-out deli for 25 years. Loyal regulars come for the handmade pastas, sausages, antipasti, mozzarella, and fresh bread.

Café Eclectic (973-509-9179), 444 Bloomfield Ave., Montclair. Open daily until midnight; until 2 AM on Sat. Coffee and coffee drinks pair nicely with cakes, pies, and other desserts. Cozy and comfortable, with décor—and a clientele—that lives up to its name. Live jazz and folk music on Monday and Tuesday nights.

Summit Cheese Shop (908-273-7700), 75 Union Place, Summit. Open Mon.–Sat.; closed Sun. This is a tiny shop, but it manages to display about 100 varieties of cheeses from around the world, including an entire case devoted to goat cheese. The cheeses are hand-cut when they're ordered from whole wheels. There's also a deli with fresh meats and homemade desserts.

Towne Deli (908-464-5400), 810 Old Springfield Ave., Summit. Across from the New Providence railroad station. A big selection of take-out sandwiches. Grab a sandwich before you grab the train.

Bovella's Pastry Shoppe (908-232-4149), 101 E. Broad St., Westfield. The Mastroianni family's old-school Italian bakery is a neighborhood institution, where ricotta pies, biscotti, macaroons, and other traditional favorites put Grandma's to shame. Come summer, Bovella's is also a popular stop for gelato, granita, and sorbet.

Café Beethoven (973-635-0005), 262 Main St., Chatham. Open daily for breakfast, lunch, and dinner. A likable little place, where you can lunch on inventive sandwiches and salads, or order a cup of tea and sample the decadent desserts. Reading, working, and general lingering is encouraged.

Johnny & Hanges (201-791-9060), 23-20 Maple Ave., Fair Lawn. This hot dog joint, in business since 1939, is a New Jersey favorite for top-notch frankfurters. Order yours "all the way," which means topped with mustard, onions, and their signature chili sauce.

Jimmy Buff's (973-325-9897), 60 Washington St., West Orange. also in East Hanover, Irvington, and Scotch Plains. Today, "Italian hot dogs," topped with potatoes, onions, and peppers and tucked onto Italian bread, can be found all over New Jersey. In the 1930s, however, Jimmy "Buff" Racioppi was credited with dreaming up the sinfully good sandwich.

Donna Toscana (908-272-4380), 19 Eastman St., Cranford. Open Wed.–Sun.; extended summer hours. Chocoholics, rejoice! What's not to love about a café devoted to the cocoa bean? This chocolaty oasis is full of decadent grown-up treats designed to help you embrace your sweet tooth. Chocolates and truffles are filled with old faves like hazelnut as well as of-the-moment flavors from lemon and basil to nutmeg and balsamic vinegar. In addition to these handmade wonders, the lounge also serves chocolate fondue, gelato, cheesecake, and frozen hot chocolate.

ICE CREAM Holsten's Brookdale Confectionery (973-338-7901), 1063 Broad St., Bloomfield. Open daily. An old-time ice-cream parlor serving homemade candy and ice cream. Hot fudge sundaes, burgers, classic diner standbys.

✳ Entertainment

ARTS CENTERS Luna Stage Company (973-744-3309; www.lunastage .org), 695 Bloomfield Ave., Montclair. A professional theater in Montclair's bustling town center, offering musicals, classical and contemporary theater, and concerts. The intimate performance space consists of three state-of-the-art venues, one seating 99 people, the others seating around 50. Special performance series include concerts, live comedy, storytellers, and local musicians and artists at informal open-mike nights. The theater is within walking distance of many downtown restaurants.

◆ **Oskar Schindler Performing Arts Center** (973-669-7385; www.ospac .org), Four Boland Dr., West Orange. The outdoor amphitheater and 3 surrounding acres were donated by local resident Larry Pantirer to found the only performance center in the country named for the man who saved the lives of more than a thousand Jews— including Pantirer's father—during the Holocaust. A full schedule of ethnic celebrations, music festivals, arts workshops for children and adults, film festivals, and concerts.

◆ **The Watchung Arts Center** (908-753-0190; www.watchungarts.org), 18 Stirling Rd., Watchung. A nonprofit arts center showcasing visual, performing, and creative arts. There's a concert series featuring classical, jazz, and acoustic folk rock, art programs for adults and children, and photography workshops and exhibits.

Shea Center for the Performing Arts (973-720-2371; www.wpunj.edu), at William Paterson University, 300 Pompton Rd., Wayne. Live music, theater, family programs, lectures, and art exhibits.

South Orange Performing Arts Center (973-275-1114; www.sopacnow .org), One SOPAC Way, South Orange. A new venue offering family shows, music, dance, and plays; there's also a five-screen cineplex.

MUSIC *◆* **Opera at Florham** (973-443-8620; www.operaatflorham.com), at the Florham Madison campus of Fairleigh Dickinson University, 285 Madison Ave., Madison. Oct.–Apr. A professional regional opera company in residence at Fairleigh Dickinson's Madison campus. Their schedule offers fully staged operas, cabaret recitals, children's productions, lectures, and vocal competitions.

◆ **Plainfield Symphony** (908-561-5140; www.plainfieldsymphony.org), 176 Watchung Ave., at E. Seventh St., Plainfield. Concert schedule runs from Nov.–Apr. This is the oldest community orchestra in New Jersey, together for nearly 90 years. Classical performances, as well as pops and children's concerts, are held in Plainfield at the Crescent Avenue Presbyterian church.

Westfield Symphony Orchestra (908-232-9400; www.westfield symphony.org), 224 E. Broad St., Westfield. Performances from Oct. to mid-May. A professional orchestra that presents five concert series a year at the Union County Arts Center in Rahway and the Presbyterian Church in Westfield.

Trumpets Jazz Club (973-744-2600; www.trumpetsjazz.com), Six Depot Square, Montclair. A popular spot for live jazz, blues, and world music.

Shanghai Jazz (973-822-2899), 24 Main St., Madison. Reservations are essential. This always-packed downtown hot spot offers live jazz Wednesday through Sunday; it's also a supper club serving pan-Asian cuisine.

Wellmont Theatre (973-783-9500), Five Seymour St., Montclair. The area's newest music venue in a fully restored historic 1922 theater.

THEATER *◆* **12 Miles West Theatre Company** (973-259-9187; www .12mileswest.org), Playwrights Theatre, 33 Green Village Rd., Madison. This award-winning professional theater is New Jersey's first resident theater company. It's also home to the **New Jersey School of Dramatic Arts,** a theatrical education program for kids and adults. An annual one-act play festival showcases playwrights from New

Jersey, and the guest-artist series features tango dancers, cabaret, and concerts by regionally and nationally known musicians.

✒ Paper Mill Playhouse—The State Theatre of New Jersey (973-376-4343; www.papermill.org), 22 Brookside Dr., Millburn. The playhouse was founded in 1934 as one of the first regional theaters in the country; in 1972 it was designated New Jersey's official state theater. Today it offers Broadway-caliber classic American musicals, children's productions, concerts, and a wide variety of plays, including new material. The art gallery showcases the work of more than 500 regional artists every year.

✒ Chatham Community Players (973-635-7363; www.chathamplayers .org), 23 North Passaic Ave., Chatham. Offering the public high-quality theater since 1922. There are three main plays and musicals each year, plus children's shows in the **Fantasy Theater. Jersey Voices** is a series of one-act plays by New Jersey playwrights, staged during the summer.

✒ Forum Theatre Company (732-548-0582; www.forumtheatrecompany .com), 314 Main St., Metuchen. Performances Nov.–June. The 1920s-era theater was built as a vaudeville house and later became a movie theater; then the Forum Theatre Company turned it into a regional arts center. Today they stage performances of musicals, comedies, and dramas, including new works by New Jersey artists.

✳ Selective Shopping
ART GALLERIES Ramapo College Art Galleries (201-684-7575), Ramapo College of New Jersey, 505 Ramapo Valley Rd., Mahwah. Rotating exhibits of contemporary art by faculty members and international artists. Exhibits are mounted at the **Berrie**

Center Art Galleries, Potter Library Galleries, and the **Selden Rodman Gallery of Popular Arts.**

Ben Shahn Galleries (973-720-2654), at William Paterson University, Pompton Rd., Wayne. Open Sept.–June, Mon.–Fri. 10–5. A dozen exhibits mounted during the academic year showcase the work of contemporary artists working in photography, sculpture, painting, and other media. Also on display are permanent collections of Oceanic and African art, and an outdoor sculpture exhibit. Call for a schedule of their popular lectures.

Visual Arts Center of New Jersey (908-273-9121; www.artcenternj.org), 68 Elm St., Summit. Galleries open daily. Adults $5; children $3. An art school, founded in 1933 by a group of local artists, with galleries and outdoor exhibition space devoted to contemporary art. The public is welcome to attend the lectures, demonstrations, juried shows, and performances, or to take a docent-led tour to have a look around.

University Art Galleries (973-655-3382), Montclair State University, Valley Rd., Montclair. A series of three indoor galleries and a sculpture garden, this establishment features changing exhibits by students and professional artists, at least one international show every year, and an annual juried show. The permanent collection includes contemporary American paintings and sculpture, African art, and 17th- and 18th-century European paintings. A lecture series brings students and the public together with professional artists.

✒ Atelier Gallery (973-377-3660), Creative Hands Art Studio, 14 Kings Rd., Madison. Open Mon.–Sat. 10–3; closed Sun. A year-round schedule of changing exhibitions featuring the work of emerging and established

THE SHAKESPEARE THEATRE OF NEW JERSEY

(973-408-5600; www.shakespearenj.org), Drew University, 36 Madison Ave., Madison. Main-stage productions from June–Dec. New Jersey's only Shakespeare theater—one of the top such theaters in the country—features a professional group of actors devoted to the Bard (they present other classic works, too). It's the longest-running Shakespeare theater on the East Coast, presenting Shakespeare's best-known works, from *Hamlet* and *Macbeth* to *Romeo and Juliet,* as well as some of Shakespeare's more obscure plays. Most productions are at the **F. M. Kirby Shakespeare Theatre** at Drew University, which has a well-regarded drama program of its own. The theater also holds a variety of unique Shakespeare-themed events, from wine tastings and lectures to art exhibits.

artists from the New Jersey and New York area. An art studio offers classes for adults and children.

BOOKSTORES ♪ **Bookends Bookstore** (201-445-0726), 232 E. Ridgewood Ave., Ridgewood. A full-service independently owned bookshop with a wide selection of titles and an extensive schedule of discussions and signings by best-selling authors. Ask about their story-time program for children.

Montclair Book Center (973-783-3630; www.montclairbookcenter.com), 219–221 Glenridge Ave., Montclair. This is the largest new and used bookstore in New Jersey, with more than a million books in stock and a collection of rare books and first editions. It's also one of the largest independent bookstores in the state, with a diverse selection of books on New Jersey, Americana, military history, children's literature, and sports, plus many author-signed books.

Watchung Booksellers (973-744-7177), 54 Fairfield St., in Watchung Plaza, Montclair. Everything an independent bookshop should be: weekly signings and readings by local authors, in-house book groups, and lots of staff picks.

Chatham Bookseller (973-822-1361), Eight Green Village Rd., Madison. This welcoming shop has a book-savvy staff and shelves crammed with used and out-of-print books of all genres.

SPECIAL SHOPS The Mall at Short Hills (973-376-7359; www.shop shorthills.com), 1200 Morris Tpke. (Rt. 24), Short Hills. Open Mon.–Fri. 10–9; Sat. 10–7; Sun. noon to 6. Luxury shopping in an upscale mall with more than 175 chic specialty stores and restaurants. All the venerable boutiques are here: Tiffany & Co., Gucci, Versace, and Cartier, anchored by Nordstrom, Saks Fifth Avenue, Neiman Marcus, Bloomingdale's, and Macy's.

Montclair Antique Center (973-746-1062), 34 Church St., Montclair. Period furniture, estate jewelry, and one-of-a-kind home accessories.

The Outdoor Store (973-746-5900), 30 Church St., Montclair. An independent shop with enough hiking, trail running, and backpacking gear, plus clothing and accessories, to rival the big box stores.

Pumpkins and Petunias (908-654-1600), 258 E. Broad St., Westfield. Funky clothing for "hip mamas and babes," which means AC/DC T-shirts for toddlers and stylish maternity frocks.

NURSERY AND FARM MARKET
Waterford Gardens (201-327-0721), 74 E. Allendale Rd., Saddle River. Open daily Apr.–Aug.; Mon.–Sat. during the rest of the year. The focus of this nursery spread along the banks of the Saddle River is water gardening. A profusion of tropical plants bloom in a series of artfully planted ponds. They sell a diverse selection of lotuses, night-blooming water lilies, and other exotic plants.

✳ Special Events

✿ *February:* **Maple Sugaring Festival** (973-635-6629), Great Swamp Outdoor Education Center, Chatham. Tree-tapping demonstrations, syrup tasting, games, and crafts (see *Green Space—Nature Centers*). **Antiques Show** (973-744-1796), Upper Montclair. Sponsored by the Montclair Historical Society. 24 dealers.

May: **Montrose in May** (973-763-1880), Montrose Park, South Orange. A vintage-trolley tour of South Orange's 19th- and early-20th-century homes.

June: ✿ **New Jersey Renaissance Festival and Kingdom** (732-271-1119), South Mountain Reservation, South Orange. A popular renaissance festival with medieval food and games, crafts, and performances; puppet shows, comedy troupes, and fairy-tale reenactments for children. **Spring Fine Art and Crafts at Brookdale Park** (908-874-5247), Brookdale Park, Montclair. An arts-and-crafts festival with close to 200 exhibitors.

July: **Jazzfest** (1-800-303-6557), Drew University, Madison. A 2-day outdoor jazz festival hosted by the New Jersey Jazz Society. ✿ **Fourth of July Parade** (908-753-3000), North Plainfield. The oldest parade in central New Jersey attracts close to 100,000 spectators. ✿ **Passaic County 4-H Fair** (973-831-7788), Wayne Civic Center, Wayne. Music, crafts, food, farm animals, and children's activities. ✿ **Fourth of July Celebration,** Memorial Park, Maplewood. Independence Day festivities include traditional events like pie-eating contests and an old-time circus.

September: ✿ **Harvest Festival** (908-527-4900), Trailside Nature and Science Center, Mountainside. A colonial and Native American celebration. **Great Falls Festival** (973-278-4019), Paterson. A Labor Day weekend multicultural celebration that attracts tens of thousands of visitors. ✿ **Art in the Park** (908-874-5247), Anderson Park, Upper Montclair. More than 200 artists plus live music, crafts, games, and international cuisine. **Fine Art and Crafts at Verona Park** (908-874-5247), Verona Park, Verona. Some 150 exhibitors featuring photography, crafts, sculpture, and fine art.

December: ✿ **First Night** celebrations in Summit (908-522-1722), South Orange (973-763-4778), and Montclair (973-509-4910) feature music, entertainment, and food on New Year's Eve in a family-friendly environment. **Candlelight Mansion Tours** (908-527-0400), Liberty Hall Museum, Kean University, Union.

THE SOUTHERN GATEWAY

New Brunswick was a colonial hub for trade and commerce ever since it was first established in 1730 by Dutch and English settlers venturing down from Manhattan. It kept that mantle during the Industrial Revolution, when the Delaware and Raritan Canal and rail lines reached the city, and factories and warehouses set up shop in the 19th century. In 1885 the three Johnson brothers opened a factory in New Brunswick, producing medical bandages, adhesive tape, and gauze. Johnson & Johnson is now one of the largest producers of medical supplies worldwide, and retains its global headquarters in downtown New Brunswick.

Rutgers University was the eighth college to be founded in the colonies when it was established in New Brunswick in 1766. It was also the only state university in existence before the American Revolution. Visitors flock to its prestigious New Jersey Film Festival, which showcases the new works of Garden State filmmakers. Also on campus is the Jane Voorhees Zimmerli Art Museum, with permanent and changing exhibits of American and European art, and the New Jersey Museum of Agriculture, which tells the story of 300 years of agricultural history in the Garden State. For culture and entertainment, head to George Street, home to chic bistros and the State Theatre—New Jersey's largest performing-arts center—and the George Street Playhouse, New Brunswick's first professional theater.

In Holmdel, Longstreet Farm is a living-history farm, restored to reflect rural life on a 19th-century working family farm, where interpreters in period dress demonstrate daily chores in the barnyard, the crop fields, and in the Victorian farmhouse. Next door, the Holmes-Hendrickson House is a well-preserved 1754 farmhouse and a classic example of the early Dutch Colonial architecture common in Monmouth County before the American Revolution. Somerville's Old Dutch Parsonage was built by the Dutch Reformed Church in 1751 and later occupied by Jacob Hardenbergh, the founder of Queens College, a colonial-era institution that later became Rutgers University. John Wallace was a prominent local merchant who built the Wallace House, where he later hosted General Washington while the Continental army was encamped during the winter of 1778–79.

Somerville is the Somerset County seat, and its downtown streets are filled with antiques shops, interesting eateries, and well-preserved grand Victorian-era homes and 18th- and 19th-century commercial buildings. There's a street named in honor of former resident Paul Robeson, opera singer, actor, all-American football star, civil rights activist, and scholar. Robeson's father was a minister at the tiny white church along this street.

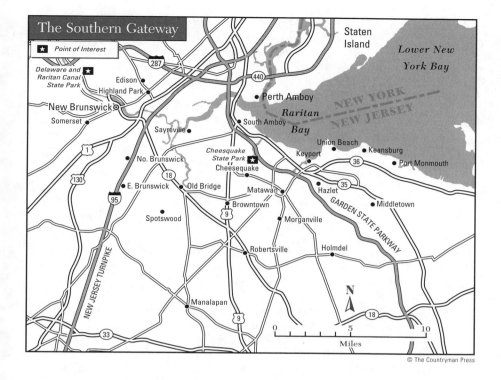

Perth Amboy, an industrial city and port of entry at the mouth of the Raritan River, bustles with freighters, tankers, barges, cargo ships, and tugboats. Waterfront redevelopment is underway, including The Landings, a proposed $600 million entertainment, residential, and retail waterfront district. The city was incorporated in 1683, and became the colonial capital of East Jersey in 1686. Perth Amboy's city hall, established in 1685, is the nation's oldest City Hall building in continuous use. It's a Victorian-style building today, but it retains some original elements that date to the 1700s.

The city's Proprietary House is the only colonial-era royal governor's mansion still intact within the 13 original colonies. The proprietors of East Jersey built the residence in 1762 for Governor William Franklin, son of Benjamin Franklin. It's open to visitors, along with Kearny Cottage, a small clapboard house next door that was home to the Kearnys, one of Perth Amboy's most politically prominent Loyalist families before the American Revolution.

Keyport is a 19th-century seaport town that bustled with oystering and shipbuilding at the turn of the century. Today it's a quaint old-time community that draws visitors with a small commercial district near the Raritan Bay waterfront; its streets are clustered with antiques shops, specialty stores, and eateries. Front Street, laid out in the 1830s, retains much of its original architecture. Just outside downtown, Keyport Harbor is dotted with pleasure boats.

Delaware and Raritan Canal State Park features one of central New Jersey's most popular multi-use recreational trails, following the towpath of the historic

19th-century canal that was dug across New Jersey so that Pennsylvania coal, pulled by mule-driven barges, could quickly make the journey between Philadelphia and New York City. The 70-mile linear path is part of the National Recreational Trail system, and is a popular haven for joggers, cyclists, hikers, and equestrians. Cheesequake State Park, located here along with several of the top arboretums in the state, provides a welcome respite throughout the year.

Entries in this section are arranged in roughly geographic order.

AREA CODES 732, 908.

GUIDANCE **The Middlesex County Cultural and Heritage Commission** (732-745-4489), 703 Jersey Ave., New Brunswick. Open Mon.–Fri. 8:30–4:15; Tues. 8:30–6:30. Request a copy of the county cultural calendar, a 200-page biannual directory of museum events, performing arts, history, and special events and festivals.

The East Brunswick Chamber of Commerce (732-257-3009), 21 Brunswick Woods Dr., East Brunswick, has information on restaurants, lodging, parks, attractions, and a calendar of cultural events. Open Mon.–Fri., 9–4.

GETTING THERE *By air:* **Newark Liberty International Airport** (973-961-6000; 888-397-4636; www.panynj.com) in Newark is served by more than 40 major carriers. **John F. Kennedy International Airport** (718-244-4444; www.kennedy airport.com) and **LaGuardia International Airport** (718-533-3400; www .laguardiaairport.com) in New York City are both convenient to the Southern Gateway region.

By bus: **Greyhound** (800-231-2222; www.greyhound.com) stops at the Somerset Hotel (908-725-2737) in Somerville. **New Jersey Transit** (973-275-5555; www .njtransit.com) provides local bus service throughout the region.

By rail: **Amtrak** (800-872-7245; www.amtrak.com) stops at the train station in New Brunswick, where there are connections to New Jersey Transit bus and rail service. **New Jersey Transit** (973-275-5555; www.njtransit.com) commuter trains connect Penn Station in Manhattan to stations in the Southern Gateway region, including Perth Amboy, South Amboy, and Matawan on the North Jersey Coast Line, and Edison and New Brunswick on the Northeast Corridor Line.

By car: The **Garden State Parkway** and the **New Jersey Turnpike** cross paths in the northern boundary of this region. The turnpike **(I-95)** heads southwest toward New Brunswick, and the parkway continues southeast toward the shoreline.

GETTING AROUND *Taxis:* **ABC Taxi** (732-247-1200), **Express Taxi and Limo Service** (732-296-3030), and **Victory Taxi Association** (732-545-6666), all in New Brunswick, and **American Taxi** (908-526-0055) and **Sky-View Taxi** (908-725-2233) in Somerville serve the region.

MEDICAL EMERGENCY **Somerset Medical Center** (908-685-2200), 110 Rehill Ave., Somerville. The emergency number is 908-685-2920.

Bayshore Community Hospital (732-739-5900), 727 North Beers St., Holmdel. The emergency number is 732-739-5924.

✳ To See

COLLEGES AND UNIVERSITIES Rutgers, The State University (732-445-4636; www.rutgers.edu), George St., New Brunswick. The school was founded in 1766 as Queens College; today it's New Jersey's state university. It consists of five colleges spread across 2,800 acres on the Raritan River in New Brunswick and Piscataway. The campuses are linked by a free bus service. For visitors, the university offers art museums, an agricultural museum, display gardens, and the **New Jersey Film Festival,** the Garden State's longest-running and largest film festival.

HISTORIC HOMES ✐ **Cornelius Low House** (732-745-4177), 1225 River Rd., Piscataway. Open Tues.–Fri., and Sun. 1–4; closed Mon., Sat., and holidays. Free admission. The **Middlesex County Museum** is a repository of art and New Jersey history, and it's housed in one of the best-preserved classic Georgian-style homes in the state. Prominent local merchant Cornelius Low built the majestic mansion high on a bluff in 1741. Back then this was the settlement known as Raritan Landing, an early-colonial-era port community on the Raritan River. The museum presents changing exhibits on New Jersey history and culture, a lecture series, and workshops for children.

Kearny Cottage (732-826-1826), 63 Catalpa Ave., Perth Amboy. Call for hours. This quaint 18th-century cottage is a rare surviving historic house in highly urbanized Perth Amboy. Michael Kearny built the little cottage around 1780, right next to the **Proprietary House,** the royal governor's mansion. The Kearnys were a successful family descended from Irish gentry, and became just as prominent and influential upon arriving in the colonial capital. Kearny's wife, Elizabeth Lawrence, known in Perth Amboy as Madam Scribblerus, was a popular writer and socialite in the early days of the republic. The cottage has been Perth Amboy's local museum since the 1920s; it's full of historical memorabilia.

Proprietary House (732-826-5527; www.proprietaryhouse.org), 149 Kearny Ave., Perth Amboy. The mansion is open for tours Wed. 10–4. Afternoon tea is held every Wed. from 1 to 4. Tours $1.50; afternoon tea $3.50. In the 1760s, the proprietors of East Jersey (in the days when there was an East Jersey and West Jersey) commissioned an official governor's residence to be built in Perth Amboy, the colonial capital. Within the original 13 colonies, this is the only royal governor's mansion still in existence. William Franklin—who, as it turned out, would be New Jersey's last royal governor—lived here with his wife until 1776, when the American Revolution broke out and he was arrested and removed from Perth Amboy. The mansion has since gone through a succession of transformations—from private residence to hotel to Presbyterian retirement home; in 1967 it was taken over by the state, and the Proprietary House Association was charged with restoring it to its former glory. Today part of the magnificent historic property is a museum, and the rest of the building has been converted into professional office space. A gift shop is located in what was once the housekeeper's room.

Buccleuch Mansion Museum (732-745-5074), Buccleuch Park, Easton Ave., New Brunswick. Open Sun. June–Oct.; tours and exhibits are run by the local chapter of the **Daughters of the American Revolution.** A stately 1739 Georgian

Photo courtesy of the Proprietary House

THE PROPRIETARY HOUSE IN PERTH AMBOY WAS COMMISSIONED BY THE PROPRIETORS OF THE 18TH-CENTURY COLONY OF EAST JERSEY AS THE OFFICIAL RESIDENCE OF WILLIAM FRANKLIN, THE LAST APPOINTED ROYAL GOVERNOR OF NEW JERSEY.

mansion—built for the daughter of royal governor Lewis Morris and her husband, a Revolutionary War officer—is a historic house museum that is considered New Brunswick's finest example of Colonial architecture. George Washington was a regular visitor to the estate, which overlooks the Raritan River, until British troops seized the house when they occupied New Brunswick in 1777. After the Revolution, prominent New Brunswick families lived here for more than 150 years; it's best known as the birthplace of poet Joyce Kilmer. Today, the mansion—on the National Register of Historic Places—is beautifully restored with Colonial-, Federal-, and Victorian-era furnishings and antiques, and original details like Federal-style mantels and whimsical Parisian-style wall coverings.

Holmes-Hendrickson House (732-462-1466), 62 Longstreet Rd., Holmdel. Open May–Oct., Thurs.–Sat. 1–4. Free admission. A carefully restored 18th-century Dutch-style red-clapboard farmhouse next door to Longstreet Farm (see *Historic Sites*). William Holmes, a farmer of Dutch and English descent, built the house in 1754 as the centerpiece of his family's prosperous farm. It's a fine example of the early Dutch Colonial architecture common in pre–Revolutionary War New Jersey, and features period furnishings and displays on early farm life. Ask about a schedule of spinning and weaving demonstrations and other special programs.

HISTORIC SITES East Jersey Olde Towne Village (732-745-3030), 1050 River Rd., Piscataway. Open Tues.–Fri. 8:30–4:15; Sun. 1–4; closed Mon. and Sat.; guided tours Tues.–Fri., and Sun. at 1:30 PM. Guided tours of original, reconstructed, and replicated 18th- and 19th-century buildings typical of an early New Jersey farming and merchant community. There's also a full schedule of lectures, workshops, concerts, storytelling, and seasonal programs to educate the public on life in the Raritan Valley centuries ago.

The Meadows Foundation (732-828-7418; www.themeadowsfoundation.org), 1289 Easton Ave., Somerset. A nonprofit group that preserves and restores historic sites, with an emphasis on early Dutch and American heritage. They maintain seven historic homes in Franklin Township: The **1722 Van Wickle House,** the **1810 Hageman Farm,** the **1835 Blackwells Mills,** the **1755 Van Liew-Suydam house,** the **1752 Franklin Inn,** the **1892 Tulipwood,** and the **1705 Wyckoff-Garretson House.** A variety of special programs—holiday festivals, house tours, concerts, and historical demonstrations—take place at these sites throughout the year.

✐ LONGSTREET FARM

(732-946-3758), Holmdel Park, 44 Longstreet Rd., Holmdel. The farm is open daily 9–5 from Memorial Day to Labor Day; daily 10–4 during the rest of the year. The farmhouse is open Mar.–Dec., Sat., Sun., and holidays, noon–3:30. Free admission. An 1890s farm adjacent to the Holmes-Hendrickson House (see *Historic Homes*) is a living-history museum, restored to reflect rural life on a 19th-century working family farm in Monmouth County. Costumed interpreters dressed as farmhands demonstrate daily and seasonal chores around the Victorian-style house and 9-acre farm. Visitors can watch blacksmithing, planting and harvesting in the fields, livestock care in the barnyard and Dutch-style barn, and cooking in the 19th-century kitchen.

LONGSTREET FARM WAS SETTLED BY ONE OF THE AREA'S EARLIEST DUTCH FAMILIES IN THE MID-1700S.

Courtesy of Ann V. Loftus

OLD DUTCH PARSONAGE AND WALLACE HOUSE STATE HISTORIC SITE
(908-725-1015), 71 Somerset St., Somerville. Open Wed.–Sat. 10–noon and
1–4; Sun. 1–4; closed Mon., Tues., and major holidays. Free admission. The
Reverend John Frelinghuysen and the Dutch Reformed Church built the Old
Dutch Parsonage as a seminary in 1751, but second owner Jacob Hardenbergh was better known for founding Queens College here in 1766. It eventually became Rutgers University and was designated New Jersey's state
university in 1945. The spartan brick house was moved here from its original
site on the banks of the Raritan River.

Across the street is the Wallace House, built in 1776 as part of Hope
Farm, the rural spread belonging to wealthy Philadelphia merchant John
Wallace. General Washington used the house as his military headquarters
from December 1778 to June 1779; his Continental army spent the winter
nearby at the Middlebrook Winter Encampment. The house is a fine example of original Georgian architecture; it boasts many original architectural
details and its rooms are full of period furnishings.

Old Millstone Forge Museum (732-873-2803; www.oldmillstoneforge.org),
North River St., Millstone. Open on Sun. 1–4 from Apr. to June and from Oct. to
Dec. Free admission. This is one of the oldest continually operating blacksmith
shops in America, with a forge dating to the Revolutionary War and in operation
until 1959. Today, amateur blacksmiths demonstrate old-time techniques. Among
the 18th-century blacksmithing implements on display are handmade tools, a pair
of 17th-century Dutch anvils, and 20th-century hand-operated equipment.

Jane Voorhees Zimmerli Art Museum (732-932-7237; www.zimmer
limuseum.rutgers.edu), on the campus of Rutgers University, 71 Hamilton St.,
New Brunswick. Open Tues.–Fri. 10–4:30; Sat. and Sun. noon–5; closed Mon.
Adults $3; children free. Permanent and changing exhibits of American and Euro-
pean art, including nonconformist Russian historical art. Special collections include
stained glass, sculpture, paintings, original illustrations for children's literature, and
American and French contemporary and turn-of-the-20th-century prints.

Museum of the American Hungarian Foundation (732-846-5777), 300 Somerset St., New Brunswick. Open Tues.–Sat. 11–4; Sun. 1–4; closed Mon. Suggested
donation $5. Hungarian folk art, sculpture, photography, and other art forms that
illustrate the rich history and culture of Hungarian immigrants in America. Changing art and photography exhibits are mounted in addition to displays from the
museum's permanent collections of paintings, coins, and rare medieval manuscripts.

Rutgers University Geology Museum (732-932-7243), 85 Somerset St., New
Brunswick. Open Mon. 1–4; Tues.–Fri. 9–noon; phone ahead for weekend hours.
Free admission. The natural history of New Jersey is told through exhibits of Indi-
an artifacts, dinosaur fossils, mummies, minerals, and mastodons.

New Jersey Museum of Agriculture (732-249-2077; www.agriculturemuseum
.org), on the campus of Cook College, Rutgers University, 103 College Farm Rd.

(just off US 1), North Brunswick. Open Tues.–Sat. 10–5; closed Sun., Mon., and major holidays. Adults $4; students and seniors $3; children 4–12, $2; children 3 and under, free. A critically acclaimed museum devoted to three centuries of agricultural history on rural farms in the Garden State, from precolonial days to the present. The permanent collection includes the massive 8,000-piece **Wabun C. Krueger Collection of Agricultural, Household, and Scientific Artifacts.** Displays of vintage farm equipment include hay rakes, reapers, fodder choppers, and plows, and a 19th-century horse treadmill and a thresher. The collection of antique farm vehicles includes market wagons, surreys, tractors, and sleighs. The reproduction tin shop is full of vintage tools used by Early American carpenters; there's also a fully stocked old-fashioned general store and a large-scale replica of a Lenni-Lenape wigwam. You can see kitchen gadgets, like the butter churn, and the turn-of-the-20th-century electrical appliances, like irons and washing machines, that changed domestic life forever. The museum also boasts thousands of vintage and contemporary photographs, prints, and negatives dating to the 19th century, and the largest observation beehive in the Northeast—home to a live colony of more than 25,000 honeybees.

New Jersey Vietnam Veterans' Memorial and Vietnam Era Educational Center (732-335-0033; 800-648-8387; www.njvvmf.org), One Memorial Lane, next to the PNC Bank Arts Center, Holmdel. Open Tues.–Sat. 10–4; closed Sun. and Mon. Adults $4; students and seniors $2; veterans, active military personnel, and children 10 and under, free. The memorial is open year-round, 24 hours a day. The Educational Center is the only museum in America solely devoted to the Vietnam War, with film footage, newspaper stories, photographs, and the personal letters of New Jersey soldiers stationed in Southeast Asia. The adjacent New Jersey Vietnam Veterans' Memorial is an open-air pavilion in remembrance of the more than 1,500 New Jersey residents who died or were missing in action in the Vietnam War. The names of the dead and the missing are engraved on 366 polished black granite panels. The tree-lined walkways symbolize the road patrols soldiers conducted in Vietnam's rural countryside. Special programs include ceremonies, readings, discussions, and a film and lecture series.

✳ To Do

BICYCLING Delaware and Raritan Canal State Park (609-924-5705; www.dandrcanal.com), various locations. Open daily sunrise to sunset. New Jersey's longest state park is a narrow, linear greenway stretching some 70 miles along the Delaware and Raritan Canal, the historic constructed waterway that links the Delaware River in Frenchtown to the Raritan River in New Brunswick. In the 19th century it was a bustling freight transportation link between New York City and Philadelphia; today the historic towpath is part of the **National Recreational Trail system,** one of central New Jersey's most popular multi-use trails, and a great route to explore on a bike. The trail is perfect for all ages and abilities; the flat, easy terrain is ideal for beginners, and the distance will satisfy experienced cyclists.

✂ Cheesequake State Park (732-566-2161), 300 Gordon Rd., Matawan. This is one of the only places in the region where you can ride a bike off-road. Most of the park's trails are off-limits to mountain bikes, but cyclists are welcome on the white-blazed multi-use trail, a 3.5-mile route with a number of short climbs and

THOMAS A. EDISON MEMORIAL TOWER AND MENLO PARK MUSEUM
(732-549-3299; www.menloparkmuseum.com), 37 Christie St., off Rt. 27, in the
Menlo Park section of Edison. Open Thurs.–Sat. 10–4; closed Sun.–Wed.
Free admission. A 131-foot tower topped with a 13-foot light bulb marks the
site of Menlo Park, the "invention factory" and "birthplace of recorded
sound" where Thomas Alva Edison, regarded as the world's most gifted
inventor, lived and worked from 1876 to 1887. His famous laboratory was the
world's first modern research and development facility, and it was here that
some of his most famous inventions took shape, from the phonograph (the
first recording, "Mary Had a Little Lamb," was accomplished in 1877) and
the incandescent light bulb to the motion picture camera, electric railway
car, and film projector. The museum features some of his inventions, memorabilia related to the prolific inventor's life, and products created by the
Thomas A. Edison Company. In all, Edison acquired more than 1,000 patents
for his inventions, creations that continue to make everyday 21st-century life
easier. He once said, "I never perfected an invention that I did not think
about in terms of the service it might give others." While he's most famous
for the light bulb and the phonograph, his development of the carbon trans-
mitter and the first system of manufacturing and distributing electricity was
even more revolutionary but not nearly as high-profile as some of his other
inventions.

Eventually Edison outgrew Menlo Park and moved his laboratory into a
larger facility in West Orange, where he made improvements to the telegraph, telephone, and phonograph, and created Black Maria, the first film
studio. Today, it's the **Edison National Historic Site** (see *To See—Historic
Sites* in "West of the Parkway.") In addition to the laboratories, the site
includes **Glenmont,** Edison's 23-room Queen Anne mansion, furnished much
as it was when the inventor lived there.

A side note: Thomas Edison's first phonograph played records that
were cylindrical; the familiar flat disk was developed later by a Camden
repair-shop owner who was inspired while repairing one of the original Edi-
son-designed phonographs. Eldridge Johnson made his fortune when he
founded the Victor Talking Machine Company in 1901 and began producing
records and phonographs. The company eventually became **RCA Victor,** and
his phonograph was called the Victrola.

descents. The surface alternates between pavement, gravel, and dirt, so it's best to ride a hybrid or mountain bike. The trail is ideal for a short easy ride, or for families with children. The trail isn't long enough for an all-day ride; many local cyclists come here to take a quick after-work spin before heading home. You can hear the cars on the Garden State Parkway, but the park is about as far from civilization as you'll get in this area, where green space is a rarity.

BOAT EXCURSIONS **Cornucopia Cruise Line** (732-697-9500; 800-924-8477; www.cornucopiacruise.com), Cornucopia Perth Amboy Pier, Riverview Dr., Perth Amboy. Year-round excursions; reservations are required. Lunch, brunch, dinner, and moonlight cruises aboard the *Princess* and the *Destiny*. The luxury dinner liners cruise between New Jersey and Manhattan—dinner and Saturday lunch cruises sail into New York Harbor, and the Sunday brunch cruises head up the Raritan River to the Verrazano-Narrows Bridge. There's a DJ on the lunch and brunch cruises, and a DJ or live band and dancing at night.

CANOEING AND KAYAKING **Delaware and Raritan Canal State Park** (609-924-5705; www.dandrcanal.com), various locations. Open sunrise to sunset. The linear state park follows the historic 1830s canal across New Jersey, from the Delaware River in Trenton to New Brunswick. For those paddling the canal for the first time, it's best to launch in Griggstown, where there's an outfitter that can supply rentals and offer advice on exploring the canal. **Griggstown Canoe and Kayak Rental** (908-359-5970), 1076 Canal Rd., rents canoes and kayaks from Apr. to Oct. (see also "The Princeton Region" in "Central New Jersey").

Cheesequake State Park (732-566-2161), 300 Gordon Rd., Matawan. Six-acre Hooks Creek Lake is open to boaters from the day after Labor Day to the day before Memorial Day weekend. Canoes, kayaks, and small boats with electric motors are allowed on the lake; only car-top launching is permitted.

FISHING **Delaware and Raritan Canal State Park** (609-924-5705; www.dandrcanal.com), various locations. Open sunrise to sunset. Fishing for catfish, perch, pickerel, bass, and trout is allowed along the entire length of the canal. The state division of fish and wildlife stocks the canal with trout in the spring. Anglers must have a state fishing license, and an additional stamp for trout fishing.

Cheesequake State Park (732-566-2161), 300 Gordon Rd., Matawan. Freshwater fishing on Hooks Creek Lake for sunfish, trout, catfish, and largemouth bass; a New Jersey fishing license is required. There's also a bridge near the lake parking area that allows crabbing.

GOLF Public 18-hole golf courses in the area include **Quail Brook Golf Course** (732-560-9528), 625 New Brunswick Rd., Somerset; **Spooky Brook Golf Course** (732-873-2242), 582 Elizabeth Ave., Somerset; **Charleston Springs Golf Course** (732-409-7227), 101 Woodville Rd. (Rt. 527), Millstone; **Rutgers University Golf Course** (732-445-2631), 777 Hoes Lane W., Piscataway; and **Tamarack Golf Course** (732-821-8881), 97 Hardenburg Lane, East Brunswick (36 holes). Each facility has a clubhouse with a pro shop and snack bar, and a driving range.

HIKING **Delaware and Raritan Canal State Park** (609-924-5705; www.dandr canal.com), various locations. A 70-mile network of trails follows the entire length of the 19th-century canal, from the Delaware River in Frenchtown to the Raritan River in New Brunswick. Hikers can follow the canal along the old towpath, which has been converted into a popular multi-use trail.

Cheesequake State Park (732-566-2161), 300 Gordon Rd., Matawan. There are five blazed trails in the park that offer easy to moderate hikes. The white-blazed route is a multi-use trail designated for hiking and mountain biking. Four other marked trails are exclusively for walkers and hikers, ranging in length from just over a mile to 3.5 miles.

HORSEBACK RIDING ✍ **Washington Riding Stables** (732-249-2471; www .washingtonstables.com), 3701 Bordentown Ave., Sayreville. Open year-round (weather permitting), Sat. and Sun. 8–4:30; weekdays by reservation only. Guided western-style trail riding for adults and children (ages 9 and up). The stable has horses for all levels of riders, from greenhorns to seasoned equestrians. Rides last from 30 to 90 minutes, and explore 500 acres of wooded trails and open fields. Hand-led pony rides are available for younger children, ages 2 and up.

SPECTATOR SPORTS **Old Bridge Township Raceway Park** (732-446-7800; www.etownraceway.com), 230 Pension Rd., Old Bridge. Open Mar.–Nov. Raceway Park has been catering to race fans for more than 40 years with drag racing and motocross competitions, including the National Hot Rod Association's **Super Nationals,** one of the NHRA's top events, and the **Import and Low Rider Summer Slam**. It's one of the top drag strips in the country, and one of three in New Jersey. The racing complex includes a road course and a motocross course.

SWIMMING **Cheesequake State Park** (732-566-2161), 300 Gordon Rd., Matawan. Swimming is permitted in Hooks Creek Lake from Memorial Day weekend to Labor Day, when lifeguards are on duty. There's a bathing area with a concession stand and bathhouse facilities.

✳ Green Space

GARDENS **Colonial Park Arboretum** (732-873-2459), 156 Mettlers Rd., East Millstone. A 144-acre arboretum specializing in native shade and flowering trees, shrubs, and evergreens. Come in the spring, when the 200 lilac shrubs put on a spectacular show. There's a gazebo surrounded by 5 acres of perennials, and a circular fragrance and sensory garden with 80 species of plants growing in easy-to-reach raised beds. The **Rudolf W. van der Goot Rose Garden** is a 1-acre formal display of 4,000 roses representing nearly 300 varieties, from antique roses to exquisite miniature blooms. The garden is a tribute to the first horticulturalist to work in Somerset County's parks.

Holmdel Arboretum (732-946-9562), Holmdel Park, Longstreet Rd., Holmdel. Open year-round, daily 8 AM–dusk. The arboretum was established in 1963, with hundreds of flowering and ornamental-specimen trees, shrubs, cultivars, and plant species in Monmouth County's 564-acre Holmdel Park. A color-coded map at the entrance to the arboretum identifies the collections, which include cedars and several varieties of weeping trees.

RUTGERS GARDENS

(732-932-8451; www.rutgersgardens.rutgers.edu), 112 Ryders Lane, Cook College, Rutgers University, New Brunswick. Open daily May–Sept., 8:30 AM–dusk; Oct.–Apr., daily 8:30–4:30. Guided tours by appointment. This 50-acre public arboretum contains a series of botanical gardens that date to 1932. There are thousands of native and exotic species, from perennials and annuals to ornamental shrubs, shade trees, a bamboo forest, and the world's largest collection of American holly. An outdoor classroom features landscaping plants in various settings, and the annual open house in July is geared especially for gardeners, with vegetable and flower plots, display gardens, and special presentations. Marked walking trails wander through a virgin stand of forest.

NATURAL AREA William L. Hutcheson Memorial Forest (732-932-9631), Amwell Rd., East Millstone. The forest is open to the public for guided tours from spring to fall. Free admission. One of the few remaining uncut forests in the mid-Atlantic states. The land was first purchased by Dutch settlers in 1701 and has white oak trees as old as 350 years. The sanctuary protects the old forest and provides a nationally known living laboratory for research, maintained by Rutgers University. **Mettler's Woods** is a 26-acre stand of mixed oak that's one of the last primeval forests in North America. It is also New Jersey's last-remaining uncut upland forest and a federally designated natural landmark. Tours are led by Rutgers faculty members and touch on topics such as forest ecology, natural history, and conservation.

STATE PARK Delaware and Raritan Canal State Park (609-924-5705; www.dandrcanal.com), various locations. In 1830 the Delaware and Raritan Canal Company was chartered to dig a canal across New Jersey that would connect the Delaware and the Raritan rivers, thereby allowing commercial barge traffic to pass between New York City and Philadelphia. When the canal was completed in 1834 it was an engineering marvel, with 15 lift locks and two guard locks designed to compensate for the changes in terrain along the hilly course. A feeder canal followed the Delaware River from Milford to Trenton, where the main canal continued east for 44 miles across central New

THE HISTORIC DELAWARE AND RARITAN CANAL IS THE CENTERPIECE OF NEW JERSEY'S LONGEST LINEAR STATE PARK, A 70-MILE GREENWAY STRETCHING FROM THE DELAWARE RIVER IN FRENCHTOWN TO THE RARITAN RIVER IN NEW BRUNSWICK.
Photo by Jonathan Carlucci

Jersey to the Raritan River in New Brunswick. Teams of mules guided the cargo-laden barges along on the canal from a towpath along the riverbank. It was an active waterway until the 1930s, and the canal was added to the National Register of Historic Places when Delaware and Raritan Canal State Park was established in the 1970s. Today, the 70-mile linear park is one of the busiest recreation sites in central New Jersey. On weekends, the old towpath is packed with cyclists, joggers, hikers, and equestrians. Anglers fish from the canal's banks, and canoeists and kayakers paddle up and down the calm waterway. History lovers come to see the handcrafted 19th-century bridges, bridge-tender dwellings, stone culverts, canal locks, and cobblestone spillways. Most of the main canal and feeder canal—close to 60 miles—is still intact.

✳ Lodging

HOTELS ✵ ₺ **Sheraton Edison Hotel—Raritan Center** (732-225-8300; 888-625-5144), 125 Raritan Center Pkwy., Edison 08837. The 276 guest rooms are outfitted for business travelers, complete with ergonomic desk chairs, dual-line phones, and voice mail; the hotel maintains a round-the-clock business center. The indoor pool, fitness center, and sauna were recently spruced up, and there's a jogging path and sundeck outside. **The Chairman's Grill and Bar** serves American cuisine in a bistrolike setting, and **Whispers Lounge** offers cocktails in the atrium every evening. $159 and up.

₺ **Crowne Plaza Edison** (732-287-3500; 800-424-6423; http://cpedison .com), 2055 Lincoln Hwy. (Rt. 27), Edison 08817. A chain hotel that's several significant notches above the norm. The 169 guest rooms include deluxe suites with Jacuzzi tubs and wet bars. Even the standard rooms are unusually spacious, not to mention clean and nicely furnished. All rooms have two phones with voice mail and data ports, TV, and generously sized work desks. The fitness center is open day and night; there's also a business center, a laundry and dry-cleaning service, and a gift shop. **Christie's Steakhouse** serves three meals in a sophisticated setting of polished mahogany, black leather, and

white linen. Continental breakfast. $159 and up.

The Heldrich Hotel & Spa (732-729-4670; 866-609-4700; www.the heldrich.com), 10 Livingston Ave., New Brunswick 08901. Downtown's sleek new hotel, spa, and conference center has 248 rooms and 14 suites done up in stylish and simple décor. All rooms have ample work space; suites have separate parlors. **Christopher's Restaurant & Bar** is chic and modern; **Daryl** is a wine bar that keeps pace. Works by New Jersey artists hang in the bar, the lobby, and the guest rooms. $189 and up.

₺ **Hyatt Regency New Brunswick** (732-873-1234; 800-633-7313; www .newbrunswick.hyatt.com), Two Albany St., New Brunswick 08901. A convention and conference center hotel within walking distance of downtown's upscale eateries, theaters, and shops, and close to Rutgers University and New Jersey Transit. There's a heated pool, a whirlpool, a sauna, and an exercise room in the hotel, and two tennis courts outside. **Glass Woods Tavern** serves regional American cuisine; a lounge serves snacks and light meals. $199 and up.

₺ **Hilton East Brunswick** (732-333-3610), Three Tower Center Blvd., East Brunswick 08816. A sophisticated and modern chain hotel located within the Tower Center Business Complex and surrounded by several major company headquarters, including Johnson & Johnson and Canon. The guest rooms, parlor suites, and oversized executive rooms have all been recently renovated. Business services, a gift shop, foreign-currency exchange, and assistance with car rental and activity planning. The health club has an indoor pool, a sauna, spa services, and an on-site personal trainer. **The Café** serves three meals in a casual setting; there's also a sports bar and a relaxing piano lounge in the hotel atrium. The coffee shop in the lobby serves light meals at breakfast and lunch. $149 and up.

CAMPGROUND Cheesequake State Park (732-566-2161), 300 Gordon Rd., Matawan 07747. Open Apr.–Oct. The 53 tent and trailer sites come with fire rings and picnic tables; showers and flush toilets are within

walking distance of every site. Individual sites $20; group sites $25.

✳ Where to Eat
DINING OUT

In New Brunswick
The Frog and the Peach (732-846-3216; www.frogandpeach.com), Hiram Square, 29 Dennis St. Lunch Mon.–Fri.; dinner daily. Reservations are recommended. Fine dining in a renovated 19th-century factory building–turned–elegant restaurant tucked among New Brunswick's Federal-style downtown town houses. The chic décor is a mix of architectural salvage pieces, stained glass, and fresh flowers. The cuisine, combined with attentive service and a stellar wine list, has earned the restaurant a long list of accolades, including the America's Top Tables award from *Gourmet* magazine. The kitchen uses classic French techniques but gives them a fresh spin, while borrowing

---

CHEESEQUAKE STATE PARK
(park: 732-566-2161; interpretive center: 732-566-3208), 300 Gordon Rd., Matawan. Grounds are open year-round, dawn to dusk; the interpretive center is open daily 8–4 from Memorial Day to Labor Day; Wed.–Sun. 8–4 during the rest of the year. The name Cheesequake, incidentally, is from the Native American *Cheseh-ch-ke,* meaning "upland." At 1,284 acres, this is a decent-sized park for such a highly developed part-urban, part-suburban area. There's plenty to do: hiking, mountain biking, winter sports, canoeing, crabbing for blue claws, even camping. Most visitors come for the swimming at Hooks Creek Lake, where there's a sandy beach with a bathhouse, a concession stand, and lifeguards on duty during the summer. What makes this park a real gem, however, is its unique natural diversity, a feature that goes largely unnoticed. The various ecosystems found throughout northern and southern New Jersey are all here. There's hardwood forest, white cedar swamp, freshwater- and salt marsh, meadows, and pine barrens. This wonderful diversity is best seen from the hiking trails; pick up a map at the interpretive center, explore the park, then stop back later to see the exhibits on wildlife, history, Native Americans, and the park's natural habitats.

flavors from American regional cuisine. Begin with duck and smoked foie gras terrine with pistachio brioche; or tuna sashimi and cucumber salad in lemongrass broth. Move on to pumpkin seed–crusted Chilean sea bass with red onion confit and sage brown butter sauce. Or try the beef tenderloin with buttermilk whipped potatoes, braised collard greens, and applewood bacon demi-glace. A lighter menu is served in the bar and on the patio, in-season. $25–40.

Clydz (732-846-6521; www.clydz .com), 55 Paterson St. Reservations are suggested. A mix of Rutgers students and well-heeled diners gravitate here for the lively bar scene and well-executed and artfully presented American cuisine. Treat yourself to the Kobe beef tenderloin, if you must, but don't miss the crème brûlée and other excellent desserts. The bar has good cocktails, especially the Cajun martini. $19–34.

Hotoke (732-246-8999; www.hotoke restaurant.com), 350 George St. Open for lunch Mon.–Fri.; dinner daily; sushi bar open late Thurs.–Sat. Reservations are recommended. A sleek and stylish pan-Asian restaurant, cocktail lounge, and sushi bar popular with young professionals and theatergoers. The wine list is impressive, as are the braised short ribs, crispy whole fish, and wok-seared scallops and beef. $24–40.

Panico's (732-545-6100; www.panicos restaurant.com), 103 Church St. Open daily for lunch and dinner. Reservations are recommended. Fine Italian cuisine in a formal and elegant setting within walking distance from the downtown theater district. The seasonal menu revolves around classic Italian dishes like veal chops and homemade pasta. A recent menu featured grilled beef tenderloin with a vegetarian tart in a roasted-garlic sauce; and grilled

whole fish served with new potatoes, leeks, tomatoes, and spinach. Impressive wine list. $24–36.

Catherine Lombardi (732-296-9463; www.catherinelombardi.com), Three Livingston Ave. Open daily for dinner. Simple yet satisfying plates of Italian-American cuisine served in elegant surroundings upstairs from the venerable Stage Left. The kitchen excels with refined twists on homey standards such as eggplant parmesan, osso buco, and house-made pastas and sauces. Be sure to try the lasagna with meatballs and sausage—even if it means skipping dessert. Entrées: $20–40; prix fixe $50.

& **The Old Bay Restaurant** (732-246-3111; www.oldbayrest.com), 61–63 Church St. Serving dinner Mon.–Sat.; closed Sun. Southern Louisiana cooking, whether it's Creole or Cajun, is one of the most interesting of America's regional cuisines. Creole was born in New Orleans but is rooted in African, Italian, French, Spanish, and Native American cuisine. Cajun cooking was brought to the Mississippi Delta by French immigrants in the 18th century. This New Orleans–style bistro offers traditional and contemporary renditions of both. Start with seafood and sausage gumbo, then have some shrimp étouffée or seafood jambalaya. Weekends are lively and fun, with live blues bands and mint juleps, hurricanes, and other Southern cocktails. $14–26.

& **SoHo on George** (732–296-0533; www.sohoongeorge.com), 335 George St. Open for lunch Mon.–Fri.; dinner daily. Reservations are recommended. An eclectic bistro near the State Theatre, popular with everyone from college students to theatergoers. The attractive dining room is handsome and dimly lit, with wine posters on the walls, a lively bar, and a view of the bustling open kitchen. An interesting

STAGE LEFT

(732-828-4444; www.stageleft.com), Five Livingston Ave., New Brunswick. Open for lunch on Fri.; dinner daily. In December, lunch is served daily. One of New Jersey's most highly regarded restaurants and a consistent winner of readers' polls is also one of the top restaurants in the country. It's near the theater district, as the name implies. A series of elegant, intimate dining rooms sets the stage for Chef Anthony Bucco's flawless contemporary American cuisine that uses fresh local ingredients. A *fromager* is in charge of the extensive selection of artisanal cheeses. The extensive, topflight wine list of 1,000 bottles consists of mostly estate-bottled wines, many hard to find. Diners choose either the prix fixe tasting menu, or order from the equally top-notch à la carte selections. You could begin with chilled Maine lobster with fingerling-potato salad, creamed leeks, and a truffle cream sauce, or seared Hudson Valley foie gras. For an entrée, wood-grilled filet mignon comes with wilted spinach and potato gratin in a wild mushroom and shallot demi-glace; lamb is accompanied by fava beans, chanterelle mushrooms, grits, and a blackberry port sauce. A signature dish is the aged 3-pound porterhouse for two, grilled over a wood fire. Desserts like bread pudding with hibiscus sauce and ice cream are divine. A bistro-style menu of burgers, sandwiches, and light meals is served in the bar. Entrées $22–49; prix fixe $35–89.

menu, stylish surroundings, and a well-chosen wine list keep the place crowded. Dishes boast a creative blend of upscale ingredients, from tuna tartare and Guinness-braised short ribs to seared foie gras and scallop ceviche. Desserts are outstanding, whether it's a homey warm fruit tart or an exquisite chocolate mousse tower. $19–40.

Elsewhere

Origin (908-685-1344; www.originthai.com), 25 Division St., Somerville. Open for lunch Tues.–Sat.; dinner Tues.–Sun.; closed Mon. A charming storefront eatery in a high-ceilinged historic building serving authentic Thai cuisine with global accents. One of the more interesting starters is the peking duck salad studded with fruits and nuts. Pad Thai is a standout among the main dishes that feature fresh ingredi-ents, flavorful sauces, and lots of seafood. Desserts include apple spring rolls with butterscotch sauce and passion fruit ice cream. The dining room has an open kitchen in the rear, where cooks bustle to feed the loyal fans that crowd this place just about every night. BYOB. $15–30.

Wasabi Asian Plates & Sushi Bar (908-203-8881), 12 W. Main St., Somerville. Artfully prepared authentic Japanese cuisine that successfully blends flavors, textures, and colors. It's a favorite spot with area sushi and sashimi lovers; the regular menu—including shredded wakame seaweed in sesame sauce, garlic chili grilled beef, and mango tofu pudding—is equally gratifying. $12–25.

7 Hills of Istanbul (732-777-9711; www.7hillsofistanbul.com), 441 Raritan

Ave., Highland Park. In a Turkish neighborhood with several authentic Turkish restaurants, this one stands out. Start with the grilled eggplant salad with chickpea puree. Main courses are a variety of grilled meats, seafood, flavorful kebabs, and vegetarian dishes, accompanied by bulgur pilaf, couscous, or rice. Desserts are sweet and syrupy. BYOB. $14–25.

🐾 ♿ **Sophie's Bistro** (732-545-7778; www.sophiesbistro.net), 700 Hamilton St., Somerset. Serving lunch Tues.–Fri.; dinner Tues.–Sun.; closed Mon. Reservations are recommended on weekends. A casual and low-key French bistro with expertly prepared cuisine, attentive service, and reasonable prices. The menu is a short but interesting mix of house dishes and specials that might include shrimp bisque, a tart of shallots and oven-roasted tomatoes, a cassoulet of beans and garlic sausage, or tender and flavorful coq au vin. House-made desserts include crème brûlée and a decadent molten chocolate cake. The well-chosen wine list features mostly French wines. $16–25.

EATING OUT

In Somerville
Cedars Restaurant (908-722-8686), 45 W. Main St. Open for lunch Mon.–Sat.; dinner daily. Reservations are recommended for weekends. A lively and vibrantly decorated Lebanese restaurant that caters to a diverse crowd. Aromatic spices and flavors enhance baba ghanouj, kebabs, tabbouleh, hummus, and other familiar and exotic dishes. Live music and belly dancing. BYOB. $14–25.

Shumi (908-526-8596), 30 S. Doughty Ave. Open for lunch and dinner Tues.–Sat.; dinner Sun.; closed Mon. When you want the freshest sushi and sashimi, this is where you should go—locals say Shumi has some of the best anywhere. The dining room is intimate, peaceful, and oft-filled with regulars, who come for the attentive service and top-quality authentic Japanese cuisine at moderate prices. BYOB. $12–20.

Thai Chef (908-253-8300), 24 E. Main St. Lunch Mon.–Sat.; dinner daily. Reservations recommended on weekends. Authentic Thai cuisine in a casual setting across from the Somerville courthouse. The spacious dining room is dominated by a sushi bar in the center, where you can watch the chef deftly prepare fresh hand rolls. Start with wild mushroom soup, move on to one of their fiery curries or traditional noodle dishes. The mango sorbet is an exotic and refreshing dessert. This is one of three locations in New Jersey. BYOB. $12–23.

In Edison
Jack Cooper's Celebrity Deli (732-549-4580), 1199 Amboy Ave. Open daily for breakfast, lunch, and dinner. An old-time family-run delicatessen serving homemade versions of traditional Jewish delicacies. From the deli, potato latkes, hot pastrami on rye, chicken soup with matzo balls, and herring in cream sauce are house specialties. For dinner, try the baked chicken meatloaf with gravy and mashed potatoes, corned beef and cabbage, or fish-and-chips with malt vinegar. $9–20.

In Keyport
Drew's Bayshore Bistro (732-739-9219; www.bayshorebistro.com), 58 Broad St. Open for dinner Tues.–Sun.; closed Mon. Fans of Cajun cuisine frequent this relative newcomer to tuck into crawfish étouffée, jambalaya, gumbo, and other signature dishes. Chef-owner Andrew Araneo cooks up generously portioned down-home favorites, a little slice of New Orleans in New Jersey. BYOB. $18–28.

In New Brunswick

Harvest Moon Brewery and Café
(732-249-6666), 392 George St. Open
daily for lunch and dinner; closed
major holidays. A menu of creative
American dishes accompanied by a
seasonally changing selection of their
own handcrafted brews. You can dine
on burgers, gourmet pizza, sandwiches,
buffalo-style wings, and other pub
standards. For something more eclectic, try the miso soup with tofu, seaweed, and scallions, or the roasted
pepper and smoked-mozzarella ravioli
with sautéed baby arugula, shallots,
and roasted garlic. End with a jumbo
ice-cream sandwich made with homemade chocolate chip–pecan cookies.
The **Moonlight Lounge** has late-
night food, drinks, and live entertainment. $15–28.

Stuff Yer Face (732-247-1727), 49
Easton Ave. Open daily. Patrons here
have been digging into stromboli—or
'boli, as aficionados of the Italian
stuffed sandwich refer to it—for more
than 30 years. Pizza, sandwiches, and
bar bites appear on the lengthy menu,
but it's the generous amounts of quality meats and cheeses stuffed into
freshly baked breads that most people
make the trip for. And with more than
75 international brews on the menu,
they offer one of the most impressive
beer lists around. $7–15.

Old Man Rafferty's (732-846-
6153), 106 Albany St. Open daily for
lunch and dinner. A relaxed and casual
downtown hangout frequented by a
college-aged crowd. On weekends,
expect a wait to get in. Generous portions of pub fare, from appetizers to
burgers; the tomato basil soup is a specialty. $10–20.

In North Brunswick

Seafood Empire (732-398-9090),
2205 US 1 S. Open daily for lunch and
dinner. A way-above-average Chinese
restaurant that's popular with locals,
despite its no-frills surroundings and
its location on a busy highway. Regulars know that the cuisine more than
compensates. Tender dumplings
stuffed with flavorful pork are a good
starter, followed by fresh seafood,
some of which comes directly from the
restaurant's tank after you place your
order. The Thai seafood casserole flavored with curry and chili is a house
specialty. BYOB. $12–20.

✷ Entertainment

The Garden State Exhibit Center
(732-469-4000), 50 Atrium Dr., Somerset, and the **New Jersey Convention
and Exposition Center** (732-417-
1400), Raritan Center, 97 Sunfield
Ave., Edison, host numerous special
events and consumer shows throughout the year (see *Special Events*).

ARTS CENTERS **Mason Gross
Performing Arts Center** (732-932-
7511; www.masongross.rutgers.edu), at
Rutgers University, 85 George St.,

✎ STATE THEATRE

(732-246-7469; 877-782-8311; www
.statetheatrenj.org) 15 Livingston
Ave., New Brunswick. Central New
Jersey's largest performing-arts
center is housed in a majestic theater that opened in 1921 as a 1,800-
seat vaudeville theater. A $3 million
renovation restored the theater to
its original grandeur and added
new state-of-the-art sound and
lighting systems. Today there's a
full schedule of opera, international dance companies, popular
music, Broadway musicals, concerts, live comedy, and children's
programs.

New Brunswick. Hundreds of cultural events throughout the year, from opera and dance to student jazz ensembles and theater groups.

PNC Bank Arts Center (732-203-2500; hotline: 732-335-8698; www.artscenter.com), Telegraph Hill Park, Holmdel. Performances scheduled from May to Sept. The arts center is the scene of a popular summerlong entertainment series. The 6,900-seat open-air pavilion is surrounded by 10,600 lawn seats. Headlining entertainment, symphonies, concerts, opera, dance, and ethnic-heritage festivals.

DANCE American Repertory Ballet Company (732-249-1254; www.arballet.org), 80 Albany St., New

AMY IRVING STARRED IN THE WORLD PREMIERE PRODUCTION OF *CELADINE* AT THE GEORGE STREET PLAYHOUSE IN NEW BRUNSWICK.

Photo courtesy of George Street Playhouse/T. Charles Erickson

Brunswick. The resident dance company at the **New Brunswick Cultural Center** is a nationally recognized ballet troupe and the state's leading dance company. When they're not on stage here, they're either performing around New Jersey or off on a national or an international tour.

MUSIC An annual free summer outdoor concert series is held at the **East Brunswick Municipal Complex** (732-390-6797), One Jean Walling Civic Center, East Brunswick. Ragtime, jazz, brass bands, country, and '50s-era music. Bring a blanket or lawn chairs.

THEATER ✔ **Plays in the Park** (732-548-2884; www.playsinthepark.com), Roosevelt Park Amphitheater, Pine Dr., Edison. Outdoor performances June–Sept.; indoor shows Oct.–May. Theatergoers crowd the park for dramas, comedies, and musicals sponsored by the Middlesex Department of Parks and Recreation, a summertime tradition in Edison since 1963. The season finishes with a musical revue, dance concerts, or a well-known play. In the fall, the backstage area is converted into an intimate 150-seat theater space, where children's performances are mounted.

George Street Playhouse (732-246-7717; www.gsponline.org), Nine Livingston Ave., New Brunswick. Six main-stage productions are mounted from September to April. When the George Street Playhouse was founded in 1974 as New Brunswick's first professional theater, it occupied a vacant supermarket. A decade later, it moved to its present location, the former New Brunswick YMCA. Today, it's a 375-seat theater, dedicated to the production of established plays, innovative and challenging new works, reimagined classics, revivals of Tony Award–winning musicals, and world-premiere musicals.

Crossroads Theatre (732-545-8100; www.crossroadstheatrecompany.org), Seven Livingston Ave., next to the George Street Playhouse, New Brunswick. Tony-winning theater devoted to works by African American artists; the annual Genesis Festival spotlights young playwrights.

✧ **Villagers Theatre** (732-873-2710; www.villagerstheatre.net), 475 DeMott Lane, Somerset. A year-round schedule of musicals, plays, and productions for children is performed by a community-theater group founded in 1960.

✳ Selective Shopping

ANTIQUES **Keyport's Antiques District** has about a dozen shops in restored 19th-century brick buildings near the bay, including **Keyport Antique Emporium** (732-888-2952), 46–52 W. Front St.; **Keyport Antique Market** (732-203-1001), 17–21 W. Front St.; **Antique Station** (732-739-3377), 89 Broad St.; **North River Antiques** (732-264-0580), Two W. Front St.; and **Grandma's Olde and New Shoppe** (732-335-4190), 34 W. Front St.

Lloyd's (908-526-4344), 130 W. Main St., Somerville. Open Mon.–Sat. 10–6; Sun. noon–5. A sophisticated shop stocked with European antiques, reproductions, and home accessories. Just around the corner at 14 Davenport St., **Lloyd's French Shop** (908-526-7788) has rustic and charming Provence-style goods.

✳ Special Events

January: **New Jersey Trailer and Camping Show** (732-417-1400), New Jersey Convention Center, Edison. This popular show has featured the lat-

est recreational vehicles for the past 45 years.

February: The **Garden State Home Show** (800-332-3976) is held at the Garden State Convention Center in Somerset. The **New Jersey Flower & Garden Show** (800-332-3976) and the **New Jersey Boat Show** (732-417-1400) are held at the New Jersey Convention Center in Edison.

Spring: **New Jersey Film Festival** (732-982-8482; www.njfilmfest.com), Rutgers University, New Brunswick. New Jersey's longest-running and largest film festival is a 3-month-long celebration of American independent films, new international releases, documentaries, experimental features, and other works. Activities include film screening, workshops, and guest directors and speakers.

March: **Winter Sugarloaf Crafts Festival** (800-210-9900), Garden State Convention Center, Somerset. More than 250 fine craftspeople and artists, plus crafts demonstrations, food, and entertainment.

April: ✧ **New Jersey Folk Festival** (732-932-5775), Rutgers University, New Brunswick.

Dancing, music, children's activities, workshops, ethnic foods, and a juried crafts show. ✧ **Ag-Field Day** (732-932-9559), Cook College, New Brunswick. A popular Rutgers University festival with agricultural exhibits, food, farm animals, and a variety of demonstrations and tours. A tradition for 90 years.

May: **Tour of Somerville Cycling Series** (908-725-7223), Manville. Four days of professional and amateur cycling races with more than 500 riders; a racing tradition since 1940.

June: **New Jersey Quilt Convention** (732-591-0257), New Jersey Convention Center, Edison. More than 400 judged quilts in the state's largest quilt show, plus lectures, workshops, vendors, and demonstrations. **Rose Day** (732-873-2459), Colonial Park, East Millstone. The award-winning **Rudolf W. van der Goot Rose Garden's** 4,000 roses—some 300 species—at the peak of bloom, as well as lectures and workshops.

July: **Perth Amboy Waterfront Festival** (732-442-7400), Perth Amboy. Food, vendors, and games attract 50,000 visitors a year. ✺ **Independence Day** celebrations with family activities and fireworks in East Brunswick (732-390-6797) and Piscataway (732-745-4489). ✺ **Americana Festival of Sails** (732-946-2711), Keyport. A colorful sailboat parade in Keyport Harbor, and a festival with a chowder cook-off, live entertainment, crafters, and seafood.

September: ✺ **The PNC Bank Arts Center** (732-442-9200) in Holmdel hosts two popular fall heritage festivals—the **African American Arts and Heritage Festival** and the **German Festival.** Both celebrations showcase the unique traditions of each culture, including ethnic foods, crafts,

dancing, music, and games. **Keyport Fall Festival** (732-946-2711), W. Front St., Keyport. Crafts, an antiques auction, and baking contests.

Autumn: **New Jersey Film Festival** (732-932-8482), Rutgers University, New Brunswick. Like the university's springtime film festival, this one features American independent films, documentaries, experimental features, new international releases, and other works. More than 100 film screenings, lectures, and workshops are held in various locations.

November: **Fall Sugarloaf Crafts Festival** (1-800-210-9900), Garden State Exhibit Center, Somerset. Crafts demonstrations, food, entertainment, and 250 fine craftspeople and artists. ✺ **Turkey Trot and Cross Country Race** (732-390-6797), East Brunswick. A variety of competitions, including crawling and toddling races for young participants.

Mid-November through December: **Holiday Light Spectacular** (732-335-8698), PNC Bank Arts Center, Holmdel. A drive-through park with a dazzling display of holiday lights.

Northern New Jersey

THE NORTHERN HIGHLANDS

THE UPPER DELAWARE RIVER

THE HILLS: FLEMINGTON TO
MORRISTOWN

THE NORTHERN HIGHLANDS

The state's rural and hilly northern reaches, known alternately as the Highlands or the Skylands, is a sprawling oasis of postcard countryside that can make first-time visitors—even born-and-bred New Jerseyans—forget they're in the nation's most densely populated state. Along quiet back roads is a patchwork of rolling hills, thickly forested ridges, and farmland dotted with shimmering lakes and streams. Hikers, campers, cross-country skiers, and birders flock to the state parks and forests spread across 60,000 virtually untouched acres. The highest peaks are in the rugged Kittatinny and Ramapo mountains and are laced with a web of hiking trails, including the Appalachian Trail—the well-trodden Georgia-to-Maine route that snakes through northern New Jersey for 70 miles. Visitors are often amazed that many places here are only 50 or so miles from New York City, and that some of the most remote hiking areas afford views of the Manhattan skyline on clear days.

It comes as a surprise to even longtime residents, how time has so dramatically passed by this rural region, which maintains more similarities to New England than to the rest of New Jersey. The Highlands and New England have a shared colonial history and geography, out-of-the-way villages and old mill towns with vintage buildings, and a quiet appeal, all of which evoke a bygone era. Roads lined with historic homesteads, barns, and produce stands wind past rural crop fields and elegantly restored bed & breakfasts that sit in relative obscurity, far off the well-beaten tourist path. Family farms sell organic herbs and eggs, artisan cheeses, and heirloom tomatoes, and welcome passersby into their fields to pick berries, flowers, and pumpkins.

Visitors to this rural region may find it hard to imagine that it was a thriving industrial center in the 18th and 19th centuries, when mines, furnaces, and forges were in the big business of extracting iron ore from the hills. Ironworks in Boonton, Ringwood, and Hanover supplied America's earliest wars with arms and ammunition, from the American Revolution to the Civil War. Today the mines are filled in, but remnants of the historic furnaces remain in towns like Boonton, and in Ringwood and Long Pond Ironworks state parks, centers of the iron industry in the 1700s. Ringwood State Park also boasts a trio of historic gems—the opulent Ringwood Manor and Skylands Manor, and the lovely New Jersey State Botanical Garden, a 96-acre collection of spectacular plantings high in the hills. In Stanhope, Waterloo Village is a well-preserved 18th-century iron industry settlement that enjoyed a renaissance when the Morris Canal opened in the 1800s. There's also a re-created 17th-century Lenni-Lenape village of authentic longhouses, an homage

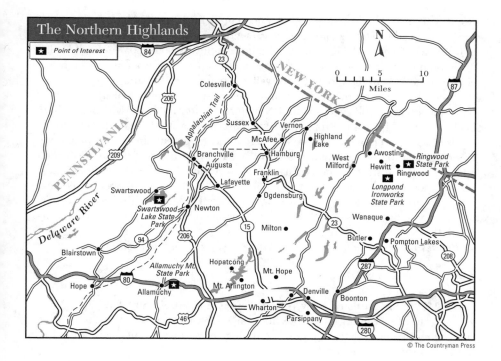

to the Native Americans who hunted and fished the northern hills long before the first European settlers arrived. As of press time, the historic village is closed for renovations; call before visiting.

The original 18th-century village of Boonton lies beneath the surface of the Jersey City Reservoir, but by the 1830s a new Boonton was a flourishing ironworks village on the Morris Canal. Its well-preserved historic downtown buildings house antiques shops, specialty stores, and a historical society museum, along with handsome colonial- and Victorian-era houses. Sussex is home to the Tri-State Actors Theater, a regional professional equity theater based in a 19th-century Beaux Arts building downtown. Newton is the Sussex County seat, and its Greek Revival courthouse is perched on a hill above a historic green framed by shops. During the summer, visitors swarm to Augusta to see the New Jersey State Fair and the Sussex County Farm and Horse Show. Together they celebrate the state's agricultural heritage with all the trappings of an old-fashioned country fair.

Sussex County was known around the world in the 19th century for its rich supply of zinc ore and unique fluorescent minerals. Included in the more than 350 minerals extracted here—the greatest diversity of species in the world—are rare varieties found nowhere else on earth. Today two historic mines are popular museums. The Franklin Mineral Museum has exhibits of local minerals—including franklinite—and a replica of its original mine. Nearby in Ogdensburg, the Sterling Hill Mining Museum leads visitors on underground tours of New Jersey's last operating zinc mine.

The Highlands seem to cater to families, with a variety of amusements that appeal to young children. Some, like the Old West–style Wild West City and the daytime resort of Tomahawk Lake, are old-fashioned family fun spots that have been around for many decades. The region's newest attractions, particularly in Vernon, are decidedly upscale. Crystal Springs Resort is a sprawling luxury hotel, spa, and golf facility, while Mountain Creek—known for its popular ski area—boasts a four-season resort village at the base of the mountain, as well as a popular water park.

Some residents fret over high-profile changes such as these, fearing the suburban sprawl that has plagued much of New Jersey. After all, the Highlands sit in the backyard of the largest metropolitan region in America. In the past decade, thousands of acres of open space were lost here to development, and the population is creeping west, particularly along the I-80 and I-287 corridors. But the area's rural appeal is holding strong. The Highlands Conservation Act provides federal funds for land conservation efforts, and in recent years, 22,000 acres of open space have been preserved. There may be fewer acres of farmland than in the past, but there are more working farms, mostly small-scale family operations. For the visitor, this is still the New Jersey of long ago.

Entries in this section are arranged in roughly geographic order.

AREA CODES 908, 973.

GUIDANCE Skylands of New Jersey Tourism Council (800-475-5263; www.skylandstourism.org), P.O. Box 464, Belvidere, maintains a Web site with comprehensive information on lodging, dining, attractions, events, and things to do in northwestern New Jersey.

The Warren County Convention & Visitors Bureau (908-835-9200; www .visitwarren.com) offers detailed visitor information on their Web site. You can also phone the office for assistance or to request travel literature.

GETTING THERE *By air:* **Newark Liberty International Airport** (973-961-6000; 888-397-4636; www.panynj.com) in Newark serves the entire state. Those traveling to New Jersey also use **John F. Kennedy International Airport** (718-244-4444; www.kennedyairport.com) and **LaGuardia International Airport** (718-533-3400; www.laguardiaairport.com) in New York City.

By rail: **New Jersey Transit** (973-275-5555; www.njtransit.com) runs commuter rail service from Hoboken (connect to Penn Station in Manhattan via **PATH** trains) to Lake Hopatcong, with stops including Netcong, Denville, Dover, Mountain Lakes, and Boonton.

By bus: **New Jersey Transit** (973-275-5555; www.njtransit.com) provides bus service between West Milford, Ringwood, Wanaque, and Greenwood Lake.

By car: **I-80** is one of northern New Jersey's two major east–west interstates and cuts across the southern edge of this region. It's a convenient route, but often plagued with traffic snarls, the result of thousands of residents commuting to and from the New York metropolitan area. If possible, avoid travel during the morning and afternoon rush, which can reach a standstill that stretches for miles. A scenic, less-traveled option is **Route 23,** which connects **I-287** in Morris County with **I-84** in New Jersey's extreme northwest corner.

GETTING AROUND *Taxis:* In Stanhope, **Area Taxi Service** (973-347-5256); in Netcong, **Classic Taxi** (973-691-9280) and **Taxi Service** (973-398-6756).

MEDICAL EMERGENCY **Saint Clare's Hospital** has three locations in the northwest Highlands region. *In Denville* (973-625-6000; emergency 973-625-6063) at 25 Pocono Rd.; *in Boonton* (973-316-1800; emergency 973-625-6150) at 130 Powerville Rd.; and *in Sussex* (973-702-2714; emergency 973-625-6150), at 20 Walnut St.

Newton Memorial Hospital (973-383-2121), 175 High St., Newton. The emergency number is 973-579-8500.

✳ To See

HISTORIC HOMES AND SITES **Skylands Manor** (973-962-7527), Ringwood State Park, Morris Rd., Ringwood. A magnificent Tudor-style manor house offers visitors a glimpse of the good life enjoyed by New Jersey's elite in the early 20th century. The opulent mountaintop retreat was built on 1,100 acres in 1927 for New Jersey inventor and financier Clarence McKenzie Lewis, and designed by noted architect John Russell Pope, whose high-profile work includes the Jefferson Memorial and the National Gallery of Art in Washington, DC. The Lewis family clearly spared no expense—many of the elaborate architectural and decorative elements were imported and assembled from historic European castles and châteaus. The dining room's rich oak paneling comes from England, the green marble in the breakfast room is from Italy. Light filters in through Bavarian and Swiss stained-glass medallions, and the elaborately carved oak study is from Germany. The Lewises lived here until 1953, and a private college occupied the estate for a time before the state purchased it in 1966. Today it's a popular venue for weddings and other private functions; the grounds are a lovely place to stroll and explore. The extensive gardens—some 96 acres—make up the stunning **New Jersey State Botanical Garden** (see sidebar, page 156).

Ringwood Manor (973-962-7031; www.ringwoodmanor.com), Ringwood State Park, Sloatsburg Rd., Ringwood. Open for tours Wed.–Sun. 10–3. Free admission.

RINGWOOD MANOR IN RINGWOOD STATE PARK WAS THE GRAND HOME OF THE 19TH-CENTURY IRONMASTERS WHO PRESIDED OVER THE AREA'S FURNACES AND FORGES.

Photo courtesy of Ringwood Manor

Ringwood Ironworks thrived in New Jersey's northern hills from colonial times into the 20th century. A succession of ironmasters lived near the Ringwood Company's bustling mines, forges, and furnaces in the Ramapo Mountains. The grand mansion standing today was the opulent summer estate of the Cooper-Hewitt family, one of America's wealthiest and most influential 19th-century families. From 1854 to 1936 ironmaster Abram S. Hewitt used some of his considerable fortune to create a magnificent 51-room Victorian-era country house, complete with 250 windows, 24 fireplaces, and 28 bedrooms. The rooms reflect an eclectic variety of styles, from the masculine and dark Gothic Revival wood-paneled great hall to the whimsical French drawing room with Louis XVI furnishings. Throughout the mansion are the Hewitt family's fine antiques, American 19th-century paintings, and furnishings, as well as relics from the iron industry and the ironmasters who once lived here. The landscaped grounds and European-inspired formal gardens are charming and serene, well worth a visit even when the house isn't open. The Hewitts donated Ringwood Manor to the state in 1939.

Long Pond Ironworks Historic District (973-657-1688; www.longpondiron works.org), Long Pond Ironworks State Park, 1334 Greenwood Lake Tpke. (Rt. 511), West Milford. Museum and visitors center open Apr.–Nov., Sat. and Sun. 1–4; open the rest of the year on Sat. and Sun. by appointment. When German ironworkers built a colonial-era furnace here in 1766, it would be the beginning of a thriving village that grew with the addition of two larger furnaces during the Civil War. A succession of ironmasters operated the ironworks in the 18th and 19th centuries, supplying the American Revolution, the War of 1812, and the Civil War with weapons and other iron products. This was one of many iron-smelting villages in the Highlands, fueled by water power supplied by Greenwood Lake; in colonial times the lake was known as Long Pond. The preserved 175-acre site contains the ruins of forges, workers' housing, blast furnaces, a country store, and other commercial buildings. The 5.7-mile **Hasenclever Iron Trail** follows an 18th-century road that linked the ironworks at Long Pond with those at Ringwood (see previous listing). Historic sites along the way include remains of a lime kiln, the site of a Hewitt-family hunting camp, remnants of an iron mine, and the site of Peter's Mine, one of Long Pond's largest and oldest mines, built in 1740.

Waterloo Village (973-347-0900), Allamuchy Mountain State Park, 525 Waterloo Rd. (Rt. 604), Stanhope. Note: As of press time, the buildings are closed indefinitely; call before visiting. The 400-acre site on the banks of the Musconectcong River is an authentically restored Early American mill village. During the Revolutionary War, this was an ironworks known as Andover Forge; but when the Morris Canal was opened in 1831, it became a bustling inland port. A general store, stagecoach inn, apothecary, tavern, gristmill, and blacksmith shop are among the village's 18th- and 19th-century buildings. Two other sites include **Rutan Farm,** a rustic 19th-century farmstead with one of New Jersey's only preserved log cabins; and a **re-created 1625 Lenni-Lenape tribal village** on an island in Waterloo Lake.

MUSEUMS Van Bunschooten House and Museum (973-875-5335), 1097 Rt. 23, Sussex. Open mid-May through mid-Oct., Thurs. and Sat. 1–4. Adults $2, children $1. In 1787 the Reverend Elias Van Bunschooten built this white-clapboard Colonial farmhouse, where he would spend the next 40 years living and working in what was then the wilds of northern New Jersey. The minister was sent by the

✐ FRANKLIN MINERAL MUSEUM

(973-827-3481; www.franklinmineralmuseum.com), 32 Evans St., Franklin. Open weekends in Mar.; Apr.–Nov., Mon.–Sat. 10–5; Sun. 11–5; closed Dec.–Feb. Guided mine tours daily. Adults $7; seniors $5; children 3–12, $4. A unique rock and mineral museum in the hilly northern region of New Jersey known as the Fluorescent Mineral Capital of the World. The museum features more than 4,000 mineral specimens—the world's largest single collection—extracted from local mines and around the world. A unique exhibit of brilliant fluorescent minerals glows under ultraviolet light, including franklinite, a locally discovered mineral found only in New Jersey. The New Jersey Zinc Company opened a mine here in the 1840s and operated for more than 100 years, extracting zinc from the underground mine for use as a paint additive. The original mine is gone, but a two-story replica includes materials salvaged from the original structure. The museum features natural history exhibits of gemstones, fossils, and Native American stone tools and artifacts. A well-stocked gift shop sells rocks, gems, mineral lights, and jewelry.

Dutch Reformed Church to serve the region's faithful; he remained here until his death in 1815. Docents in colonial dress lead tours through rooms containing the home's original furnishings, Revolutionary War–era weapons, and period clothing. Outbuildings include a barn, icehouse, and wagon house with antique farm tools and a vintage carriage.

Lake Hopatcong Historical Museum (973-398-2616), Hopatcong State Park, Landing. Open Mar.–May and Sept.–Nov., Sun. noon–4. Free admission. A rustic 19th-century building that once housed the Morris Canal's lock tender is a small museum of local history. Permanent exhibits illustrate the history of New Jersey's largest lake, from the early days of Lenni-Lenape settlement (when Hopatcong comprised two smaller lakes) and the building of the Morris Canal, to the turn of the 20th century, when city folk flocked to grand resort hotels and amusement parks lining the lakeshore.

Boonton Historical Society and Museum (973-402-8840), in the historic John Taylor building, 210 Main St., Boonton. Open Sat. 1–4 and by appointment. Admission by donation. The restored 1897 home of a local doctor, reflecting the styles of the Victorian, Gothic, and Colonial Revival eras, hosts the Boonton Historical Society. Their small museum features local photographs and artifacts of Boonton's history from 1741 to 1903, during which time it was America's largest iron manufacturing center, employing close to 700 workers who made Boonton the nation's largest producer of nails. On Saturdays, guided walking tours of the old ironworks, the Morris Canal, or historic neighborhoods, leave from various locations in town.

BREWERY High Point Wheat Beer Co. (973-838-7400), 22 Park Place, Butler. Open Mar. to Dec. on the second Sat. of the month from 2 to 4 and by appoint-

✎ STERLING HILL MINING MUSEUM

(973-209-7212; www.sterlinghillminingmuseum.org), 30 Plant St., Ogdens-burg. Open daily Apr.–Nov.; weekends and by appointment Mar. and Dec.; closed Jan. and Feb. Guided mine tours daily at 1 PM; mineral collecting on the last Sunday of the month during the season. Adults $10; seniors $9; children 12 and under, $7.50. This is the only place in New Jersey where you can explore a real underground zinc mine. Tours of the quarter-mile tunnel—where temperatures hover in the 50s—are especially popular on rainy days. New Jersey's northern hills were renowned in the 18th century for their rich mineral deposits. More than 340 minerals have been found in this area, including the world's largest number of fluorescent varieties. When the operation closed in 1986, it was the state's last working mine. The mining museum features tools, artifacts, and minerals in indoor, outdoor, and underground exhibits, and historical buildings spread across 30 hilly acres above the Wallkill River.

ment. This was the first brewery in America to exclusively produce wheat beer using authentic German brewing techniques. The German-style beer, called weiss, is the highest-rated dark wheat beer. Ingredients like wheat and barley imported from Bavaria are mixed in the brew house's massive stainless steel tanks, creating a beer that's rich, creamy, and full of flavor.

ZOO ✎ **Space Farms Zoo and Museum** (973-875-5800; www.spacefarms.com), 218 Rt. 519, Sussex. Open May–Oct., daily 9–5. Adults $13.50, seniors $12.50, children $9. This sprawling 400-acre museum and zoo—the largest in the state—is home to the most extensive private collection of North American wildlife in the world. Some 500 animals representing 100 different species—including tigers, buffalo, timber wolves, and jaguars—live in a natural setting that has evolved dramatically since the Space family opened a wild-animal shelter here in 1927 (ask about their ongoing programs to restore endangered and threatened wildlife). The museum complex has a staggering menagerie of items, including locally mined fluorescent minerals, Revolutionary War– and Civil War–era weapons, Native American artifacts and vintage cars, wagons, carriages, and sleighs. Visitors can also picnic, play mini golf, tour the blacksmith shop, or browse in the old-time country store.

✳ To Do

AMUSEMENTS ✎ **Mountain Creek Waterpark** (973-864-8444; www.mountain creekwaterpark.com), Rt. 94, Vernon. Open daily, late June through mid-Sept. Adults $35; children and seniors $25; children 2 and under, free. A 39-acre water park carved out of a mountainside with two-dozen waterslides, wave pools, rides, rope swings, and whitewater tubing rides. The High Anxiety ride features a four-story plunge and a 90-foot tunnel; H2-OH-NO is a 99-foot-long speed slide; and Cannonball Falls is an enclosed body slide that ejects riders 12 feet above the water. Half Pint Harbor has pools, a play area, and water rides for small children.

✒ **Tomahawk Lake** (973-398-7777; www.tomahawklake.com), 153 Tomahawk Trail, off Rt. 15, Sparta. Open weekends Memorial Day through mid-June; daily mid-June through Labor Day. Adults $11; children 8 and under, $10 (cash only). Since 1952, this 20-acre lake with a white-sand beach, swimming, picnicking, and boating has been a popular daytime resort destination for families. The water park features 10 waterslides, water rides, a racing slide, and a water play area for small children. Activities from horseshoes and volleyball to mini golf, plus a ball field and an arcade.

✒ **Wild West City** (973-347-8900; www.wildwestcity.com), Rt. 206, Netcong. Open May through Columbus Day. An authentic western heritage theme park celebrating cowboys, horses, and other icons of the 19th-century American West is a reproduction of the frontier town of Dodge City, Kansas. Actors depict real-life historical characters in thrilling live-action western shows from stagecoach and bank robberies to gunfights at the OK Corral. Re-created 19th-century buildings—including a schoolhouse, blacksmith shop, saloon, and chapel—and museums and shops line the historic unpaved Main Street. Children love the stagecoach and pony rides, narrated train ride, and petting zoo; they can also play mini golf and pan for gold.

BIRDING **Paulinskill Valley Trail** (973-786-6445), Kittatinny Valley State Park. Pick up the trail on Rt. 206 in Andover or Rt. 663 in Lafayette. About 20 percent of New Jersey's known species of birds—or 560 different species—have been spotted along this linear recreational trail. It was built on a former rail bed along the route of the New York, Susquehanna, and Western Railway, which means easy walking on relatively flat terrain.

BOATING See also *Canoeing and Kayaking.*

The following state parks and forests offer boating on lakes and ponds: **Long Pond Ironworks State Park** (973-962-7031), Greenwood Lake Tpke. (Rt. 511), West Milford, has two boat launches on Monksville Reservoir; **Ramapo Mountain State Forest** (973-962-7031), Oakland, has a mountaintop lake; **Wawayanda State Park** (973-764-1030), 885 Warwick Tpke., in Hewitt has a public boat launch and rents canoes, paddleboats, and rowboats. Sailboats, sailboards, and boats with electric motors are allowed on the lake.

Lake Hopatcong is New Jersey's largest lake, a mecca for boaters of all persuasions, and extremely busy during the summer months. Various marinas and shops carry fishing and boating gear, or have public launches, including: **Lake's End Marina** (973-398-5707), 91 Mount Arlington Blvd., Landing; **Hopatcong Boathouse** (973-663-7990), 156 Rt. 181, Lake Hopatcong; and **Lee's County Park Marina** (973-398-5199), 443 Howard Blvd., Mount Arlington.

CANOEING AND KAYAKING **Greenwood Lake** is a 7-mile-long lake straddling the New Jersey–New York border within Greenwood Lake State Park in Hewitt. **South Shore Marina** (973-728-1681), 1880 Greenwood Lake Tpke. (Rt. 511), rents canoes and kayaks.

Shepherd Lake in Ringwood State Park is a 74-acre spring-fed lake just below the New York state line. The Shepherd Lake Recreation Area boathouse (973-962-6999) rents canoes, rowboats, and small sailboats; there's also a public boat ramp.

Wawayanda Lake is a picturesque mile-long lake surrounded by forested hills along the New York–New Jersey border at Wawayanda State Park (973-764-1030) in Hewitt. Paddle to the north shore, where Double Pond, a 19th-century industrial town, once presided. Visitors can see the remains of the charcoal blast furnace, raceways, and foundations where an iron-smelting industry once thrived. Canoes can be rented at the park facility near the beach and picnic areas.

At Swartswood State Park, **Row Your Boat Rentals** (973-383-4200) rents sailboats, canoes, paddleboats, kayaks, and rowboats on **Swartswood Lake**.

Monksville Reservoir (973-962-7031), Long Pond Ironworks State Park, Greenwood Lake Tpke. (Rt. 511), West Milford. The 1,819-acre park offers canoeing and kayaking, and canoe rentals.

Lake Aeroflex and Gardner's Pond, Kittatinny Valley State Park (973-786-6445), Limecrest Rd. (Rt. 669), Andover. Lake Aeroflex has a boat ramp; Gardner's Pond is accessible on foot from the parking area at Aeroflex-Andover Airport.

FISHING The numerous fishing spots in this rural region include the following lakes and ponds, where a New Jersey fishing license is required: In Lockwood, **Allamuchy Pond** and **Cranberry Lake** at Allamuchy Mountain State Park (908-852-3790); in Andover, **Lake Aeroflex** and **Gardner's Pond** at Kittatinny Valley State Park (973-786-6445); in Hewitt, **Wawayanda Lake** in Wawayanda State Park (973-853-4462); in Oakland, trails lead to **Ramapo Lake** at Ramapo Mountain State Forest (973-962-7031); in Ringwood, **Monksville Reservoir** at Long Pond Ironworks State Park (973-962-7031), and **Shepherd Lake** at Ringwood State Park (973-962-7031); and in Swartswood, **Swartswood Lake** and **Little Swartswood Lake** at Swartswood State Park (973-383-5230). In Landing, **Lake Hopatcong** at Hopatcong State Park (973-398-7010) is one of the state's top spots for **ice fishing.**

GOLF Crystal Springs Golf and Spa Resort (973-827-5996) in Hamburg is northern New Jersey's premier golf resort. It offers five award-winning 18-hole courses—Crystal Springs, Ballyowen, Wild Turkey, Black Bear, and Minerals—each with its own amenities. There's a luxury hotel and lodge for overnight guests (see *Lodging—Resorts*).

Other 18-hole public golf courses in the region include **Apple Mountain Golf and Country Club** (908-453-3023; 800-752-9465), 369 Hazen–Oxford Rd. (Rt. 624), Belvidere; **Rolling Greens Golf Club** (973-383-3082), 214 Newton–Sparta Rd., Newton; **Sky View Golf Club** (973-726-4653), 226 Lafayette Rd., Sparta; **Bowling Green Golf Club** (973-697-8688), 53 Schoolhouse Rd., Milton (a course designed for walking); and **Great Gorge Country Club** (973-827-5757), Rt. 517, McAfee.

HIKING Wawayanda State Park (973-853-4462), 885 Warwick Tpke., Hewitt. This 16,679-acre state park along the New York–New Jersey border has an extensive 40-mile network of hiking and nature trails through wooded terrain punctuated with rock outcroppings and wetlands. Some pass by the park's lakes and ponds; others skirt undisturbed natural areas, including a steep hemlock ravine, a rare Atlantic white cedar swamp, and a mixed hardwood forest that's home to barred owls, red-shouldered hawks, and other threatened species. A trail up **Wawayanda**

THE 2,050-MILE-LONG APPALACHIAN TRAIL CUTS THROUGH THE REMOTE NORTHWESTERN CORNER OF NEW JERSEY FOR 73.6 MILES BETWEEN NEW YORK STATE AND THE DELAWARE RIVER ALONG THE PENNSYLVANIA BORDER.

Mountain leads to an observation area with phenomenal views of the Highlands region. A narrow and rocky 19.6-mile section of the white-blazed **Appalachian Trail** also passes through the park.

Ringwood State Park (973-962-7031), 1304 Sloatsburg Rd., Ringwood. A 40-mile network of multi-use and hiking-only trails through 5,237 acres of varied terrain. Hikers can explore Shepherd Lake or climb to rocky vistas. A 5.76-mile trail linking **Ringwood Manor** and **Long Pond Ironworks** features historic sites from the region's 18th- and 19th-century ironworks (see *To See—Historic Homes and Sites*).

Ramapo Mountain State Forest (973-962-7031), Skyline Dr., Oakland. More than 40 miles of trails cut through rugged mountainous terrain. The Ramapo Lake Trail is a 4.5-mile wooded and hilly route that passes through a historic iron-mining area along the former Cannonball Road, a key route for transporting munitions during the American Revolution. The trail climbs past waterfalls on its way to a 120-acre mountaintop lake; from there, you can hike to the ruins of **Van Slyke Castle** perched above the lake.

The Highlands Trail is a 150-mile hiking trail under construction from Storm King Mountain on the Hudson River in New York through northern New Jersey to the Delaware River in Phillipsburg. Members of the **New York–New Jersey Trail Conference (NYNJTC)** are creating the trail, marked with turquoise diamond-shaped blazes, by connecting existing footpaths and old logging roads with new sections of trail. Some sections are open; hikers should contact the NYNJTC for information (201-512-9348). **Wyanokie High Point,** a scenic vista along the trail in northern Passaic County, affords stunning views of the Manhattan skyline and the Hudson River valley.

Paulinskill Valley Trail and Sussex Branch Trail (973-786-6445) are multi-use recreational trails in rural Warren and Sussex counties that pass through Kittatinny

Valley State Park. Each was built on a former rail bed—the Paulinskill trail along the route of the New York, Susquehanna and Western Railway, and the Sussex trail on the old Sussex Railroad line. Together they provide about 47 miles of relatively flat terrain on cinder and gravel paths, ideal for easy walks and longer, moderate hikes. Both trails are known for their bucolic surroundings and opportunities for wildlife viewing.

Mahlon Dickerson Reservation (973-326-7600), Weldon Rd., Jefferson. Pick up a trail guide at the Saffin Rock Rill Visitors Center, or inquire about guided hikes. The reservation has a total of 20 miles of trails over a variety of terrain, ideal for both beginners and advanced hikers. The Pine Swamp Trail is a 4-mile loop trail that passes through rhododendron groves, forest, and swamp, and climbs to 1,300-foot **Headley Overlook,** with spectacular views of Lake Hopatcong. Other trails circle scenic Saffin Pond and follow the rail bed of the 19th-century Ogden Mine Railroad; the 150-mile **Highlands Trail** also passes through the reservation.

HORSEBACK RIDING Echo Lake Stables (973-697-1257; www.echolake stables.com), 55 Blakely Lane, Newfoundland. Open Fri.–Tues.; closed Wed. and Thurs. Trail rides, old-fashioned hayrides, and night rides to an outdoor western-style barbecue.

Spring Valley Equestrian Center (973-383-3766; www.springvalleyequestrian center.com), 56 Paulinskill Lake Rd., Newton. Reservations are required. Guided trail rides along the Paulinskill Valley Rail Trail.

MOUNTAIN BIKING Diablo Freeride Park (973-209-3388), Mountain Creek Resort, 200 Rt. 94, Vernon. Open May–Oct., Sat. and Sun. 9–4; July and Aug. open daily. Mountain Creek is widely known as a ski resort, but during the summer the mountain bike park draws intermediate to advanced downhill riders. Unlike traditional mountain biking, downhill riding involves steep rocky terrain and various obstacles on trails often accessed by a chairlift. For cross-country mountain bikers, there are 12 miles of technical single track on the back side of Vernon Peak.

Many parks and forests in the Highlands region have trails open to mountain bikes, notably **Ringwood State Park** (973-962-7031) in Ringwood, **Mahlon Dickerson Reservation** in Jefferson, **Stephens and Allamuchy Mountain state parks** north of Hackettstown, **Ramapo Mountain State Forest** (973-962-7031) in Ringwood, and **Kittatinny Valley State Park** (973-786-6445) in Andover.

SAILING South Shore Marina (973-728-1681), 1880 Greenwood Lake Tpke. (Rt. 511), Hewitt. A sailing school at the southern tip of 7-mile-long Greenwood Lake, a picturesque glacial lake straddling the New Jersey–New York border in the Bearfort Mountains. Lessons for beginners; experienced sailors can rent Sunfish or Catalina sailboats.

SWIMMING ∮ **Wawayanda State Park** (973-853-4462), 885 Warwick Tpke., Hewitt. Lifeguards are on duty from Memorial Day weekend to Labor Day. The swimming area at 255-acre Lake Wawayanda has a white-sand beach, a bathhouse, lifeguards, changing rooms, and a snack bar. Inner tubes, rafts, and other flotation devices are not allowed in the swimming area. The beach often gets crowded on summer weekends; it's best to arrive early.

✦ **Shepherd Lake Recreation Area** (973-962-7031), Ringwood State Park, Shepherd Lake Rd., Ringwood. The swimming area is staffed by lifeguards from Memorial Day weekend to Labor Day. A cool spring-fed lake surrounded by 4,000 acres of forested hills on the New Jersey–New York border. The swimming area has a sandy beach, a playground, changing rooms, and a concession stand selling food and beach supplies.

✦ **Hopatcong State Park** (973-398-7010), Landing Blvd., Landing. A lawn slopes down to the shore of Lake Hopatcong, where there's a swimming area with a concession stand and a bathhouse, and lifeguards are on duty.

✳ Winter Sports

DOWNHILL SKIING ✦ **Hidden Valley** (973-764-4200; www.hiddenvalleynj .com), 44 Breakneck Rd., Vernon. Day- and nighttime skiing daily in-season. A small family-oriented ski area with a dozen trails with a 620-foot vertical drop and three lifts, including a triple chairlift. Ski and snowboard programs for children, as well as rentals and instruction.

✦ **Mountain Creek Ski Resort** (973-864-8128; www.mountaincreek.com), 200 Rt. 94, Vernon. New Jersey's largest ski area offers day- and nighttime skiing and snowboarding on 45 trails and in a terrain park spread across four mountains. The nine lifts include an eight-passenger open-air gondola and four quad lifts. Mountain Creek also boasts the region's only Olympic-caliber **superpipe** for snowboarding. Spend the night at **The Appalachian** lodge or in a condo at **Black Creek Sanctuary**.

✦ **Campgaw Mountain Ski Center** (201-327-7800; www.skicampgaw.com), 200 Campgaw Rd., off Rt. 202, Mahwah. This is a small ski area—eight trails and five lifts—but it offers the amenities of a much larger facility. There's snowmaking on all trails, a freestyle snowboard park, snow tubing runs with lifts, and nighttime skiing, snowboarding, and snow tubing. Lessons and rentals.

CROSS-COUNTRY SKIING High Point Cross Country Ski Center (973-702-1222; www.xcskihighpoint .com), 1480 Rt. 23, Sussex. Open daily 8–4 in-season. At a top elevation of 1,803 feet, these are the highest (and snowiest) cross-country ski trails in the state. Snowmaking on nearly half of the 16-kilometer network of trails that is a mix of beginner and expert terrain

MOUNTAIN CREEK IS A YEAR-ROUND RESORT IN THE VERNON VALLEY OF NORTHERN NEW JERSEY OFFERING DAY AND NIGHT SKIING AND SNOWBOARDING.
Photo courtesy of Mountain Creek Ski Resort

groomed for skate skiing and classic skiing. A separate 8-kilometer trail is designated for snowshoeing. Ski and snowshoe rentals, lessons, and a rustic lodge where you can enjoy homemade light meals and snacks in front of the fireplace.

Fairview Lake Ski Touring Center (201-383-9282), 1035 Fairview Lake Rd., Newton. The Fairview Lake YMCA Camp has 12 miles of marked and groomed trails spread across 600 acres of woodlands and open fields surrounding 110-acre Fairview Lake. The ski lodge has equipment rentals and information on lessons.

Parks and forests with trails open to cross-country skiing include **Stephens and Allamuchy Mountain state parks** (908-852-3790) in Hackettstown, **Ringwood State Park** (973-962-7031) and **Ramapo Mountain State Forest** (973-962-7031) in Ringwood, **Wawayanda State Park** (973-853-4462) in Hewitt, **Silas Condict County Park** (973-326-7600) in Kinnelon, **Tourne Park** (973-326-7600) in Denville, **Mahlon Dickerson Reservation** (973-326-7600) in Jefferson, and **Abram S. Hewitt State Forest** (973-853-4462) in Hewitt.

✳ Green Space

STATE FORESTS **Norvin Green State Forest** (973-962-7031), Sloatsburg Rd., Ringwood. More than 4,300 acres of rugged, virtually undisturbed forest, part of the **Wyanokie Wilderness Area,** is laced with miles of trails and old logging roads for hiking only. **Weis Ecology Center** (973-835-2160) is an environmental education center in the forest, run by the New Jersey Audubon Society, with hikes, camping, outdoor activities, and environmental education programs on the state's Highlands region. Adjacent to Ringwood State Park.

Abram S. Hewitt State Forest (973-853-4462), 885 Warwick Tpke., Hewitt. A 2,000-acre tract of marshland and hemlock and oak forest donated to New Jersey by the family of one of the region's most prominent 19th-century ironmasters. The rugged and remote terrain is accessible only on foot; the trails are popular for hiking and cross-country skiing. The **Appalachian Trail** passes through here just below the New York–New Jersey border. Adjacent to Wawayanda State Park.

NEW JERSEY STATE BOTANICAL GARDEN
(973-962-9534; www.njbg.org), Ringwood State Park, Morris Rd., Ringwood. Gardens open year-round, daily 8–8; garden tours on Sun. at 2 PM. New Jersey's official state botanical garden is spread across 96 mountaintop acres at the magnificent Tudor-style **Skylands Manor** (see *To See—Historic Homes and Sites*). A stunning and unique variety of horticultural displays, from naturalized woodland plantings to formal perennial borders and European-style parterres, all surrounded by over 1,000 acres of forests and open meadows. Individual gardens are devoted to tree peonies, lilacs, wildflowers, heather, rhododendrons, and azaleas, as well as trees, annuals, and perennials. An eclectic collection of garden ornaments and statues, some centuries old, can be seen throughout the gardens.

Ramapo Mountain State Forest (973-962-7031), Skyline Dr., Oakland. A 4,200-acre wooded and remote mountainous tract laced with more than 40 miles of challenging hiking trails. The pristine **Ramapo Lake Natural Area** has a mountaintop lake for fishing and birding, and rocky trails leading to outcroppings and ledges with rewarding views.

STATE PARKS **Wawayanda State Park** (973-853-4462), 885 Warwick Tpke., Highland Lakes. A rugged 16,679-acre tract of wetlands and forest sprinkled with rocky outcroppings, adjacent to Abram S. Hewitt State Forest. Most visitors come here for **Wawayanda Lake,** a pristine 255-acre lake that offers fishing, swimming, and boating. In the 19th century, an iron-smelting village occupied the north shore. There's also a 40-mile network of trails for hiking, horseback riding, mountain biking, and cross-country skiing. Some of the paths are the old logging roads cut in the early 20th century by the New Jersey Zinc Company. A third of the park is protected in undisturbed natural areas that are home to many endangered and threatened plant and wildlife species, such as timber rattlesnakes and bog turtles.

Ringwood State Park (973-962-7031), 1304 Sloatsburg Rd., Ringwood. A 5,237-tract in the Ramapo Mountains where the Ringwood Company's blast furnaces and iron forges flourished in the 18th and 19th centuries. A succession of ironmasters lived at Ringwood Manor, ending with prominent American industrialist Abram S. Hewitt, whose family donated the land to the state in 1936. Nearby, Skylands Manor, the opulent 20th-century summer estate of Clarence Lewis, is home to the spectacular **New Jersey State Botanical Garden** (see sidebar, previous page). Fishing, boating, and swimming at pristine spring-fed **Shepherd Lake;** an extensive web of hiking and multi-use trails lace through the park.

Swartswood State Park (973-383-5230), Rt. 619, Swartswood. Swimming, fishing, and boating on **Swartswood Lake**. Trails for hiking, cross-country skiing, and snowshoeing.

Kittatinny Valley State Park (973-786-6445), Limecrest Rd. (Rt. 669), Andover. A linear state park with boating and fishing on **Lake Aeroflex** and **Gardner's Pond.** Trails for hiking, horseback riding, mountain biking, and cross-country skiing include the **Paulinskill Valley Rail Trail and Sussex Rail Trail** (see *To Do—Hiking*).

Stephens and Allamuchy Mountain State Parks (908-852-3790), Hackettstown. Two adjoining state parks with 7,000 acres intersected by Interstate 80. Most visitors come here to tour **Waterloo Village** (see *To See—Historic Homes and Sites*), a restored 19th-century industrial village on the Musconectcong River. The fishing, hiking, camping, and boating are good, too.

Hopatcong State Park (973-398-7010), Lakeside Blvd., Landing. When the Morris Canal was carved through northern New Jersey, Lake Hopatcong was one of its major water suppliers. Later on, during America's era of grand resort hotels in the late 19th and early 20th centuries, New Jersey's largest lake became a bustling summertime vacation destination. Thousands of tourists escaped the stifling heat of Manhattan and Philadelphia by flocking to the sprawling hotels dotting the shoreline. Today, the small state park offers swimming, fishing, and boating; a museum in a restored 19th-century canal tender's house has interesting exhibits on local history (see **Lake Hopatcong Historical Museum** under *To See—Museums*).

NATURAL AREA **Pyramid Mountain Natural Historic Area** (973-334-3130), Boonton Ave. (Rt. 511), Montville Township. A 1,000-acre wilderness tract of fields, forest, and wetlands are laced with a network of rugged trails and rock outcroppings popular for bouldering. Most hikers trek up **Pyramid Mountain** to see **Tripod Rock,** a spectacular glacial erratic deposited here by the Wisconsin Glacier more than 18,000 years ago. The unique multi-ton rock formation—also known as Three Pillar Rock—is made of gneiss and balanced atop three smaller boulders. A pair of similar formations, called **Solstice Stones,** is believed to be a remnant of a Native American ceremonial site. Nearby on the edge of a swamp is massive **Bear Rock,** another Wisconsin Glacier–era boulder that's one of the largest in New Jersey.

✳ Lodging

RESORTS ♂ ⟨ **Crystal Springs Resort** (973-827-5996; www.crystal golfresort.com), Two Chamonix Dr., off Rt. 94, Vernon 07462. A luxury resort, spa, and golf complex with two unique lodging options. **Minerals Resort & Spa** (973-827-2222) is named for the historic abundance of minerals in the northern New Jersey hills. Most of the 175 rooms boast views of the golf greens and surrounding mountains; condominium-style units adjacent to nearby **Mountain Creek Ski Resort** (see *To Do—Downhill Skiing*) are ideal for families or couples traveling together. The hotel-style guest rooms are decorated in a mountain theme, and many rooms have stone fireplaces and comfortable sitting areas; luxury suites have a dining area and wet bar. **Elements Spa** offers unique mineral therapies, indulgent body treatments, skin care, massage, even treatments designed especially for golfers. **Minerals Sports Club** features tennis, racquetball, basketball, seven indoor and outdoor pools, a steam room and sauna, and a fitness center. Rooms at the new Adirondack-style **Grand Cascades Lodge** (973-823-6500) nearby in Hamburg boast fireplaces and private balconies with lovely views. $169 and up; inquire about condominium rates.

♂ **Mountain Creek Resort** (973-864-8000; 888-767-0762) 200 Rt. 94, Vernon 07462. In winter, Mountain Creek is New Jersey's largest ski area (see *To Do—Downhill Skiing*); in summer, the focus is on mountain biking, golf, and the resort's water park. The new 100-room **Appalachian** has comfy studios and suites on the mountain; if you're looking for more room, **Black Creek Sanctuary** offers beautifully furnished one-, two-, and three-bedroom town houses. All units—many are slope side—feature gas fireplaces, fully equipped gourmet kitchens, high-speed Internet access, and digital TVs in the living room and bedrooms. Outside there are heated pools, hot tubs, fire pits, a playground, and a gazebo. Call about ski-, golf-, and water-park packages. $159–519.

INN ⟨ ∞ **The Inn at Panther Valley** (908-852-6000; www.panthervalley inn.com), 1627 Rt. 517, Hackettstown 07840. A charming New England–style country inn with 100 comfortable and well-appointed guest rooms in the main lodge or in one of the homey cottagelike buildings. Both the standard rooms and two-room suites have private bath, cable TV, air-conditioning, and high-speed Internet access. The lovely and well-kept grounds include a pond with resident geese, and a courtyard with gazebo. Many guests choose the inn for its picturesque surroundings, which are conveniently close to I-80. Fitness center. $129–180.

♿ APPLE VALLEY INN BED & BREAKFAST

(973-764-3735; www.applevalleyinn.com), 967 Rt. 517, P.O. Box 302, Glenwood 07418. An elegant 1831 Colonial mansion is a warm and inviting bed & breakfast whose name is a nod to the apple orchards that once dotted the Pochuck Valley. The seven individually decorated guest rooms are country comfortable. Most have either fireplaces or woodstoves and four-poster beds; some have lovely architectural details like hand-carved mantelsand intricate moldings. The first-floor Gala Room, with original wood beams and a floor-to-ceiling brick fireplace, is wheelchair accessible. Guests like to linger in the cozy parlor and sitting area, or on one of the rambling porches, with views of the lovely gardens and the countryside beyond. For hikers, the **Appalachian Trail** is a mile down the road. The full breakfast might include the inn's signature poppy seed bread or banana nut buttermilk pancakes. $130–160.

APPLE VALLEY INN BED AND BREAKFAST IS A COZY RETREAT IN A 19TH-CENTURY COLONIAL MANSION IN RURAL SUSSEX COUNTY, MINUTES FROM THE APPALACHIAN TRAIL IN GLENWOOD.

Photo courtesy of Apple Valley Inn

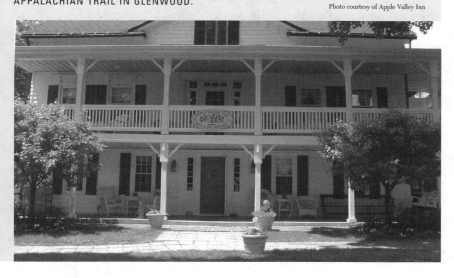

BED & BREAKFASTS Glenwood Mill Bed & Breakfast (973-764-8660; www.glenwoodmill.com), 1860 Rt. 565, Glenwood 07418. A 200-year-old mill on Pochuck Brook has been transformed into a unique and charming bed & breakfast surrounded by lovely perennial gardens. The mill was in operation up until World War I, powered by the spectacular waterfall nearby. Each of the four guest rooms and suites is decorated with antiques and mill artifacts. Rooms have private bath with bubble jet tubs, gas fireplaces, and queen beds; the suites also have sitting areas and a separate shower. A full breakfast is served in the rustic wood-beamed great room. $145–225.

Alpine Haus Bed & Breakfast (973-209-7080; 877-527-6854; www.alpine hausbb.com), 217 Rt. 94, Vernon 07462. A 19th-century Federal-style inn and adjacent carriage house offer cozy and thoughtfully decorated accommodations. The eight guest rooms are named for mountain wildflowers and decorated with period antiques; all have private bath, phone, and TV. Guests can relax in the formal parlor and cozy family room, or enjoy the spectacular views of the Pochuck Mountains from the second-floor covered porch, where breakfast is sometimes served. Next to the ski slopes and water park at Mountain Creek resort. $110–155.

&. **The Wooden Duck Bed & Breakfast** (973-300-0395; www.woodenduck inn.com), 140 Goodale Rd., Newton 07860. Innkeepers Beth and Karl Krummel's Cape Cod–style bed & breakfast is on 17 acres of woodland and open meadows, with 1,600 more acres next door at **Kittatinny Valley State Park**. Nine guest rooms—six in the main house, three in the carriage house—all have private baths, queen beds, air-conditioning, and armoires. Some of them also have a fireplace, a soaking tub, or a private balcony. Common areas include a game room with a double-hearth fireplace and a cozy living room. Guests can help themselves to the video library and refreshments in the pantry. Outside there's an inground pool and a brick patio, where a full breakfast is served when the weather allows. $125–299.

∞ **Crossed Keys Inn** (973-786-6661; www.crossedkeys.com), 289 Pequest Rd., Andover 07821. This 1790 farmhouse is so romantic, many couples choose to tie the knot here. The inviting common areas—living room, library, and sunporch—are tastefully decorated with Oriental rugs, antiques and reproductions. The 12-acre property features a formal garden, a stream and pond, and an antiques-filled artist's studio with shuffleboard, books, and a pool table. The five guest rooms have private baths; if you don't stay in one with a fireplace, don't fret—there are five fireplaces in common areas

throughout the house. The honeymoon suite in the lovely stone cottage has a Jacuzzi tub for two. Full breakfast. $150–185.

The Whistling Swan Inn (973-347-6369; 888-507-2337; www.whistling swaninn.com), 110 Main St., Stanhope 07874. Liz Armstrong's beautifully restored 1905 Queen Anne Victorian is a charming village B&B. She offers seven lovely guest rooms and two suites with period décor (one room has a stained-glass window), private baths, queen featherbeds, TV/VCR (watch a classic film from the in-house library), and phones. The suites have fireplaces and whirlpool tubs. Guests can relax outside in one of the hammocks, on a porch swing overlooking the Victorian garden, or inside by the fire. Fresh-baked breads, cookies, and other complimentary refreshments. A full buffet breakfast is served in the elegant dining room. $105–249.

CAMPGROUNDS ✸ ✿ **Pleasant Acres Farm Campground** (973-875-4166; 800-722-4166; www.pleasant acres.com), 61 DeWitt Rd., off Rt. 23, Sussex 07461. Open year-round. A 300-acre campground in the Kittatinny Mountains exclusively for recreational vehicles, travel trailers, pop-up trailers, and motor homes. Along with the usual camping amenities, there are live country-and-western bands and dancing, horse-drawn hayrides, farm animals to pet and feed, and activities like cow milking and sheep shearing. Meals are included during the week. Sites $52.

✿ **Green Valley Beach Campground** (973-383-4026; www.green valleybeach.com), 68 Phillips Rd., Newton 07860. More than 200 open and wooded sites; amenities range from an Olympic-sized swimming pool, game room and playground, to a lake for fishing and swimming. Sites $36–41.

🐾 ✆ ♿ **Panther Lake Camping Resort** (973-347-4440; 800-543-2056), Six Panther Lake Rd., Andover 07821. Open Apr.–Oct. A family campground with 435 sites on a 45-acre private lake with boating, fishing, and a sandy beach for swimming. In-ground pool and hot tub, camp store, and snack bar. Lots of activities and special events. Sites $39–44.

Camping is also available in some of the region's state parks, including **Swartswood State Park** (973-383-5230) in Swartswood, **Wawayanda State Park** (973-853-4462) in Hewitt (group camping only), and **Stephens State Park** (908-852-3790) in Hackettstown. The **Mahlon Dickerson Reservation** (973-663-0200) in Jefferson has campsites with tent platforms and rustic shelters, and wooded trailer sites.

✳ Where to Eat

DINING OUT Andre's Restaurant & Wine Boutique (973-300-4192; www.andresrestaurant.com), 188 Spring St., Newton. Open for dinner Wed.–Sun.; closed Mon. and Tues. Andre and Tracey de Waal's popular downtown restaurant offers an ever-changing menu of innovative European and American cuisine. Simple, elegant dishes feature locally grown organic produce. You might start with a hearty soup of white beans, toasted walnuts, and crisp bacon; or duck confit with roasted garlic and black truffles. For dinner, try the grilled wild king salmon with cabernet mashed potatoes, or pork tenderloin with jerk seasoning and grilled pineapple. Ask about their wine tastings and monthly themed dinners. $24–33.

Bula World Cuisine (973-579-7338; www.bularestaurant.com), 134 Spring St., Newton. Reservations are recommended. *Bula* is a Tahitian word

meaning "life," which this eclectic and fun restaurant is full of. The imaginative menu is brimming with unique global twists. Appetizers range from a roasted asparagus and spring radish salad with horseradish champagne vinaigrette, to Caribbean shrimp cakes with chipotle rémoulade and mango salsa. Entrées might include grilled summer vegetables tossed with light cream, goat cheese, and pine nuts; or a traditional Hungarian chicken and pork paprikash with handmade dumplings. The artwork on the walls is by local artists; the lounge offers live jazz. BYOB. $15–30.

The Montville Inn (973-541-1234; www.montvilleinn.com), 167 Rt. 202, Montville. Open for lunch and dinner Tues.–Sun.; closed Mon. A colonial inn with Revolutionary roots, fresh off a $3 million facelift, is now modern and cozy. Comfort-food favorites are given a gourmet kick, in the form of house-smoked prime rib, top-notch steaks, and old-fashioned donuts for dessert. Creative cocktails and California wines in the inviting dark-paneled bar. $17–30.

✆ **Berta's Chateau** (973-835-0992; www.bertaschateau.com), Seven Grove St., Wanaque. Open daily for dinner. Reservations are recommended. This longtime favorite dishes up hearty portions of northern Italian cuisine accompanied by a top-notch wine list. Santina and Pietro Berta opened the restaurant in 1927 in a former carriage barn. The atmosphere is country casual, the menu is full of classics. $18–43.

South City Grill (973-335-8585; www.southcitygrill.com), 60 Rt. 46, Mountain Lakes. Lunch Mon.–Fri.; dinner daily. Reservations are recommended. This South Beach, Miami-inspired seafood grill is one of three locations in New Jersey; others are in Rochelle Park (201-845-3737) and

Jersey City (201-610-9225). The dining room is urbane and coolly hip, the lively bar has a view of the open kitchen, and the wine list and seafood are topflight. The menu is heavy on fish (wood-grilled) and shellfish (a stop at the oyster bar is a must), with American and Asian touches. Desserts like peanut butter mousse with chocolate ganache and peanut brittle topped with vanilla and chocolate sauce are pure decadence. $20–30.

Restaurant Latour (973-827-0548), at Crystal Springs Resort, One Wild Turkey Way, off Rt. 94, Hamburg. Open for dinner Thurs.–Sun.; closed Mon.–Wed. Reservations are required. Quite possibly the most elegant and upscale hotel dining in New Jersey. The dining room gets its elegance from the luxe décor, flawless service, and an impressive contemporary American menu. Presentation is big here, and it's always interesting to see the dramatic arrangements on the plates that come out of the kitchen. Expect big-ticket ingredients like truffles, foie gras, and game meats. The 50,000-bottle cellar is sure to satisfy wine aficionados, and desserts like citrus-scented cheesecake are delicious works of art. Prix fixe $62–100.

Mohawk House Restaurant (973-729-6464; www.mohawkhouse.com), Three Sparta Junction, Sparta. Open daily for dinner. The seasonally changing New American cuisine more than keeps pace with the stately yet rustic surroundings. Punched-up favorites include roasted lobster and corn bisque, and cider-glazed grilled pork with sweet potato puree. $22–32.

EATING OUT ✐ **Taco of the Town** (973-875-9892), 54 Main St., Sussex. Open for lunch Tues.–Sat.; dinner Tues.–Sun.; closed Mon. Vicki and Joey Gonzales's casual and friendly downtown Mexican eatery is a local favorite. The dependable menu of authentic burritos, enchiladas, and, of course, the namesake tacos, relies on family recipes they brought to New Jersey from Southern California. $10–18.

✐ ♿ **Bella Montagna** (973-728-4664), 1131 Greenwood Lake Tpke. (Rt. 511), Ringwood. Serving dinner Tues.–Sun.; closed Mon. Reservations are recommended on weekends. A friendly little trattoria in a strip-mall setting, serving generous portions of fresh, well-prepared Italian cuisine. The menu blends traditional *frutti di mare* and chicken parmigiana with creative pasta dishes, all accompanied by tasty, home-baked bread. The staff is pleasant and helpful, the prices reasonable. $12–24.

✐ **Krogh's Restaurant and Brew Pub** (973-729-8428; www.kroghs.com), 23 White Deer Plaza, Sparta. Open daily for lunch and dinner. Reservations are recommended. The Krogh family opened their restaurant and tap room on Lake Mohawk more than 80 years ago. Today, the 1920s-era building is a national historic landmark. The menu offers straightforward comfort food and pub standards. The pub features handcrafted beers, a good selection of microbrews, and live music. $12–23.

✐ **The Homestead Restaurant** (973-383-4914; www.homesteadrest.com), 294 N. Church St. (Rt. 94), Sparta. Open daily for lunch and dinner; breakfast on Sat. and Sun. Country-western-themed family restaurant, popular après-ski stop (Mountain Creek is fifteen minutes down the road), sit at wooden tables, drink from mason jars, nosh on burgers, wings, steaks, and other comfort food staples. $14–27.

The Tea Hive (973-579-7177), 310 Rt. 94, Newton. Open Wed.–Sat. 11–3;

closed Sun.–Tues. Phone ahead before visiting, as the property was for sale at press time. A visit to this Victorian-style tearoom in an 18th-century farmhouse on the rural outskirts of Newton makes for a relaxing and fun afternoon. You can choose from the changing lunch menu, a variety of traditional afternoon teas, or just enjoy a cup of tea with one of their exquisite desserts, which might include chocolate-dipped strawberries or flourless chocolate cake. The **Bee's Knees** is a quaint gift shop in the barn behind the wildflower garden. $3–19.

Black Forest Inn (973-347-3344; www.blackforestinn.com), 249 Rt. 206 North, Stanhope. Open for lunch Mon., and Wed.–Fri.; dinner Wed.–Mon.; closed Tues. When it comes to serving traditional German fare, the kitchen here has it going on. Authentic specialties are robust and hearty—weiner schnitzel, spaetzle, and herring with apples and sour cream. Desserts are what you'd expect in a German restaurant: Black Forest cake and apple strudel. $12–24.

Millside Café (973-383-1611), 12 Morris Farm Rd., Lafayette. Open daily for breakfast and lunch. A cozy neighborhood café, in an old general store, known for its homey fare: hearty soups, creative sandwiches, and pies, as well as breakfast all day. Antiquers pack in on weekends. $8–15.

Holland American Bakery (973-875-5258), 246 Rt. 23, Sussex. Open Tues.–Sat.; closed Sun. and Mon. You can't miss the windmill, or the brick building behind it. Inside, traditional Dutch treats such as stollen, linzer tortes, and windmill cookies share space with Dutch cheeses and other imported groceries.

✹ Entertainment

THEATER ✐ **Tri-State Actors Theater** (973-875-2950; www.tristateactors theater.org), Fountain Square, 74 Main St., Sussex. The **Crescent Theater** occupies a 1917 Beaux-Arts brick building that once presented silent films and live vaudeville. Today it's a nonprofit professional equity theater with actors from New Jersey, New York, and Pennsylvania. They present new and classic plays along with holiday performances, shows for families, new play readings, and special events.

Darress Theatre (973-334-9292; www.darresstheater.com), 615 Main St., Boonton. Films (silent, classic, independent, foreign, new releases) and live performances (stand-up comedy, musicals, concerts, plays) in a restored 1922 vaudeville theater. The theater was designed backward, so patrons enter a door by the screen instead of from the back of the room.

✹ Selective Shopping

ANTIQUES **Lafayette Mill Antiques Center** (973-383-0065; www.millantiques.com), 12 Morris Farm Rd., off Rt. 15, Lafayette. Open Thurs.–Mon; closed Tues. and Wed. A historic collection of buildings on the Paulinskill River, centered on a retired gristmill that operated in the 19th century. Today more than 50 dealers occupy 23,000 square feet of space on three floors, selling country furniture, folk art, vintage jewelry, china, Victoriana, and collectibles.

Great Andover Antique Company (973-786-6384), 124 Main St. (Rt. 206), Andover. Open Wed.–Sun. 10–5; closed Mon. and Tues. A multidealer shop spread across three buildings. A wide variety of 18th- and 19th-century antiques, from pottery and furniture to French textiles and Victorian-era goods; some modern 20th-century pieces.

ART GALLERIES **Flying Pig Gallery** (973-875-8487), 15 Main St., Sussex. A storefront gallery featuring contemporary painting, sculpture, furniture, and other works by local and international artists. Ask about a schedule of painting and drawing classes.

Barn Gallery (973-962-2252), Ringwood State Park, 1304 Sloatsburg Rd., Ringwood. A gallery run by the Ringwood Manor Association of Arts features changing exhibits of work by regional artists.

Lake Mohawk Gallery (973-512-2057), 21 White Deer Plaza, Sparta. A Lake Mohawk gallery displaying original works by local, national, and international artists in every medium. A year-round schedule of solo and group shows; limited-edition prints, designer jewelry, local memorabilia, and artful home décor for sale in the gift gallery.

SPECIAL SHOPS **Olde Lafayette Village** (973-383-8323; www.lafayette villageshops.com), at the junction of Rts. 15 and 94, Lafayette. Open daily. Specialty shops, factory-outlet stores, and eateries line winding paths in a quaint village-like setting.

Frogmore Country Store (973-347-6259), 238 Rt. 206, Andover. Specialty foods, home and bath products, candles, and gifts in a delightful shop.

FARMS AND GARDENS

In Wantage
Fair Acres Farms (973-875-6613), 1343 Rt. 23. Open Apr.–Oct.; closed Nov.–Mar. A lovely nursery occupying a Victorian farm in the rolling hills just south of High Point State Park. A historic barn, housing a garden shop, is surrounded on all sides by fanciful display gardens that will inspire both first-time gardeners and professionals. There's an interesting selection of annuals, perennials, shrubs, and trees,

as well as unique garden pottery from Mexico.

Stephens Farm (973-875-2849), 467 Rt. 284. Open year-round, Thurs.–Sat.; call ahead for hours. Ted and Annemarie Stephens' organic farm is in a peaceful, rural setting right on the **Appalachian Trail.** They carry everything from farm-fresh chicken, pork, and bacon to eggs from free-range chickens. Their small farm market features fresh herbs, fruit, vegetables, and heirloom tomatoes—all organic, of course.

Needmore Farm (973-875-0565), 24 Wantage School Rd. Open year-round. Gail Fatum raises close to 100 goats on her small northern New Jersey dairy farm. They provide ample milk for the homemade fresh goat cheese, creamy fudge, and natural soaps that you can pick up at the farm's self-serve store.

✎ **The Farmer's Wife** (973-702-7614), 383 Rt. 519. A farm stand selling farm-fresh eggs, cut-your-own flowers, homemade salad dressing, jams and jellies, and old-fashioned candy and cookies. Kids love to pet the resident goats, sheep, calves, and other farm animals.

In Lafayette
The Family Farm (973-875-1447), 136 Pelletown Rd. This seventh-generation dairy farm has been in the same family since 1845. The farm's small self-serve store sells fresh herbs and perennials, homemade pesto, jams, herb vinegars, and freshly baked old-fashioned cookies.

PICK-YOUR-OWN FARMS **Sussex County Strawberry Farm** (973-579-5055), 565 Rt. 206, Andover. Open in June, daily 8–6. Strawberries and pumpkins for picking in the fields.

Pochuck Valley Farm (973-764-4732), 962 Rt. 565, Glenwood. Homemade pies and apple cider in the farm market; pick your own apples, pears, pumpkins, plums, and Christmas trees.

Lucey's Berry Farm (973-383-4309), 41 Beaver Run Rd., Lafayette. Open June–Oct., daily 9–5. Raspberries and blueberries.

Bear Creek Berry Patch (908-979-1451), 1087 Dark Moon Rd., Newton. Open June–Oct.; call ahead for crop and weather conditions. Several varieties of raspberries.

Windy Brow Farms (973-579-9657), 359 Ridge Rd., Newton. Open Mar.–Dec. Apples.

✳ Special Events

May: **Garden State Horse Show** (www.gardenstatehorseshow.org), Sussex County Fairgrounds, Augusta. World-class equestrians compete in New Jersey's largest horse show for a $50,000 purse.

June: **Spring Festival** (973-691-6990), Stanhope. **Crawfish Fest** (973-948-5500), Sussex County Fairgrounds, Augusta. The cuisine of the Deep South and the music of Louisiana. Listen to New Orleans R&B, gospel, funk, and zydeco and feast on grilled alligator, jambalaya, fried catfish, crawfish, and shrimp Creole. The festival cooks up 10,000 pounds of crawfish every year. **Lake Hopatcong Yacht Club Antique and Classic Boat Show** (973-663-1408), Lake Hopatcong. An annual 2-day event held for over 30 years. More than 100 boats built between 1920 and 1970 are judged on their appearance and the authenticity of their renovation; the next day, they gather for a parade around the lake.

August: ✍ **New Jersey State Fair/Sussex County Farm and Horse Show** (973–948-5500), at the Sussex County Fairgrounds, Augusta. Horse shows, livestock, a carnival,

food, live entertainment, fireworks, farm tractor pulls, lumberjack competitions, exhibits, and more.

September: **18th Century Living History Weekend** (973-657-1688; www.longpondironworks.org), Long Pond Ironworks, West Milford. **Antique Fire Apparatus Muster and Flea Market** (973-335-8704), New Jersey Firemen's Home, Boonton.

Late September through early October: **Geraldine Dodge Poetry Festival** (973-540-8443), Waterloo Village, Stanhope. Internationally known poets, storytellers, and musicians at the largest poetry festival in North America. It's a biennial event held in even-numbered years.

BOBOLINK DAIRY AND BAKEYARD (973-764-4888; www.cowsoutside .com), 42 Meadowburn Rd., Vernon. Farm store open year-round, Wed.–Sun.; reservations are required for farm tours. Nina and Jonathan White's grass-fed dairy cows provide the milk they use to craft their artisanal raw-milk cheeses that are aged in "caves" or cellars on the farm. Outside is a wood-fired brick oven where the Whites make rustic handcrafted breads out of organic stone-ground flour, fresh herbs, and dried fruits and nuts. They also sell eggs and pasture-raised beef. Ask about tastings, tours, and classes in bread baking and cheese making.

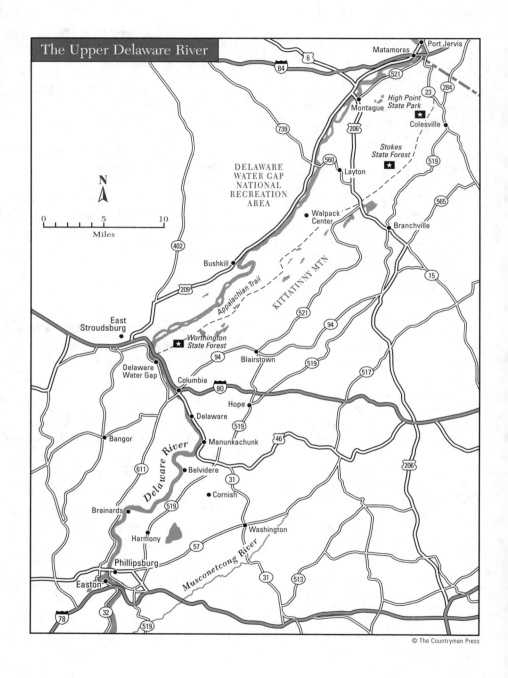

The Upper Delaware River

© The Countryman Press

THE UPPER DELAWARE RIVER

New Jersey's longest river flows through a spectacular area of rugged mountains and deep woods on its way to the Atlantic Ocean. The Delaware River lazes smooth and wide as it twists through the Delaware Water Gap National Recreation Area to the gap itself, a craggy 2-mile-long gorge that's one of the state's most impressive natural wonders. It slices through the Kittatinny Mountains, in some places soaring a full quarter of a mile above the river. The 70,000-acre park stretches for 40 miles along both sides of the Delaware River; in New Jersey, it drifts inland into dreamy forest-clad hills that often seem like a mere painted backdrop.

The Delaware is part of America's Wild and Scenic River system, one of the last large free-flowing rivers in the contiguous 48 states, and the last undammed river left in the eastern part of the country. Millions of New Jersey residents rely on the river's exceptional water quality for drinking water as well as a pristine place to play. Here it is a centerpiece rather than a boundary, where boaters paddle and float on sun-sparkled water, anglers cast for trout and shad, birders track autumn's awe-inspiring hawk migration, and hikers climb high into the Kittatinny Range, where they may encounter fellow trekkers passing through on New Jersey's 73-mile section of the Appalachian National Scenic Trail. The state's extreme northwest corner harbors its highest peak, the aptly named High Point, whose war monument at the 1,803-foot summit affords panoramic vistas of the Pennsylvania and New York mountains, with the gentler rolling terrain of Sussex and Warren counties' farmland trailing away to the south and east. Here barns, silos, and dairy cows still punctuate a landscape of crop fields, quiet back roads, and picturesque historic towns. But most of this region is a collection of public lands enveloped in one massive swath of green—an impressive small use of big space in an area that's just 90 minutes from the largest metropolitan region in America. It's a refuge for outdoors enthusiasts and solitude seekers, who may find it hard to believe that these mountains once hummed with industry, and that the thickly forested ridges and hills were almost entirely cleared just a century and a half ago.

The Lenni-Lenape inhabited this area long before European pioneers and fur traders arrived from the Hudson River valley as early as the 1600s. They grew tobacco, pumpkins, and corn on small plots in the fertile valley, and hunted the densely wooded mountains. English and Dutch settlers began farming the region in the early 1700s—remnants of these early farmsteads are scattered throughout the forests. The relationship between the Lenni-Lenape and the new settlers wasn't idyllic, and fearing an alliance with British forces, George Washington stepped in. On the general's order, colonial troops defeated the tribes, essentially ending their existence along the Delaware River.

The Revolutionary War brought about a wave of settlement, soon followed by an era of industrial growth in the 1800s that would, for a time, change the face of the mountains. The long-ago riverfront settlement of Brontzmanville flourished with mills, homes, quarries, a school, and a post office (today it's a quiet camping area in Worthington State Forest). Like similar villages, it needed fuel and lumber—as did the mills, limestone and slate quarries, and copper mines—and turned to the abundance of natural resources at its disposal. Huge swaths were clear-cut for lumber, fuel, and the production of charcoal, literally ravaging the forest to meet the needs of a growing population.

The turn of the 20th century saw a shift back toward preservation, however, as New Jersey's influential families and leaders gave huge tracts of land near the river to the state to preserve for future generations. The prominent Kuser family donated the land that became High Point State Park. Former New Jersey governor Edward Stokes's gift of 500 acres evolved into the forest that now bears his name and spreads across 12 miles of the Kittatinny Ridge, linking High Point State Park in the northeast to the Delaware Water Gap National Recreation Area in the southwest. From his private game reserve, industrialist Charles Worthington helped reestablish New Jersey's white-tailed deer population, which was virtually wiped out by rampant deforestation and hunting in the 19th century.

Today deer thrive in Worthington State Forest, whose pristine glacial lake is considered one of New Jersey's little-known gems. Locals know that the best places to fish are hidden in these hills—places like Ghost Lake, Dunnfield Creek, and Sunfish Pond—not to mention the Delaware River itself. The region is noteworthy for its hiking and camping, but it's equally appealing in winter, when you can cross-country ski and snowshoe along miles of hauntingly quiet trails. Keep in mind that most of New Jersey's bear population lives in this region; commonsense steps like properly storing food while camping make unwanted encounters far less likely.

Warren and Sussex counties remain largely agricultural, not with the huge-scale truck farms typical of South Jersey, but instead dotted with small, family-run specialty farms. This is the Garden State, remember, and it is to the surprise and delight of many first-time visitors that residents of this part of New Jersey live by the nickname. Wineries in Montague and Belvidere open their doors to the public for tours, tastings, and seasonal festivals. Other farms sell their bounty—from organic eggs and honey to peaches, apples, and berries—at quaint produce stands and farm markets along rural back roads. Many invite visitors into the fields and orchards to pick what they want from the colorful tapestries of fruits and vegetables. The Warren County Farmers' Fair in Harmony hasn't changed much since an agricultural fair was first held here in 1859. Thousands of people still come to see livestock, locally grown fruits and vegetables, farm equipment, baked goods, and horse shows. The hot-air balloons, carnival rides, and demolition derby are among the nods to the 21st century; but at its heart the fair is a celebration of the region's agricultural heritage, which is still alive and well.

The picture-postcard village of Hope was built alongside a millstream in 1769 by a Protestant Moravian sect from central Europe whose members were drawn to the rural surroundings. It was one of the country's first planned communities, but it lasted for less than half a century. The Moravians were forced to leave Hope in the early 1800s, when many of the church's settlements in the United States were folding under financial constraints. They left behind an assortment of finely crafted buildings, with the thick limestone walls and steeply pitched roofs characteristic of Moravian architecture. Their church, or *Gemeinhaus,* is now a bank; the general store, or *Leinbach,* is a real estate office. An 1803 school has been converted into offices, and the massive 1769 gristmill is an elegant inn and restaurant.

Like most of New Jersey's off-the-beaten-path gems, Hope is not completely undiscovered. Retirees and weekenders from Manhattan are buying up the old farmsteads, lured by the rural landscape and convenient location off Interstate 80. Regardless, this tiny community remains peacefully stuck in time. Quaint village shops sell antiques, gifts, and handmade crafts. On the outskirts of town, wooded rolling hills, horse pastures, old dairies, and farm fields are dotted with clapboard farmhouses and vintage barns.

From its strategic location at the confluence of the Delaware and the Lehigh rivers, Phillipsburg was once a booming transportation hub, served by five railroads and supporting numerous foundries and factories. In 1824, the Morris Canal and Banking Company began work on the 102-mile freight canal that would connect the Delaware River at Phillipsburg to the Passaic River in Newark and the Hudson River in New York. In Phillipsburg's heyday, 18 tracks ran through town, and barges laden with Pennsylvania coal floated along the canal behind South Main Street on the beginning of their journey across New Jersey. As it did in many of New Jersey's urban centers, the economy took a big hit when manufacturing jobs all but vanished in the 20th century, and now Phillipsburg is banking on its industrial and transportation heritage to lure visitors back. A volunteer-run museum is devoted to the city's rich history, and an antique diesel-powered locomotive takes passengers on scenic excursions along the Delaware River. Downtown commercial buildings are in a hopeful state of transition, with an eclectic mix of shops and eateries filling once-vacant storefronts and lending a polish that Warren County's largest community hasn't seen in a long time.

For those who stubbornly cling to the tired clichés about New Jersey, a visit to any of these places will shatter that illusion. To begin exploring this rural and back-roaded oasis, you could get off Interstate 80 just before the Delaware River and head north into Worthington State Forest and the Delaware Water Gap National Recreation Area. Old Mine Road is one of the earliest byways in the area, traversing the forest for miles along the Delaware River. Accounts differ on who actually developed the original road. Some believe it was built by Dutch prospectors who drifted down from New York to mine the Kittatinny Ridge for copper as early as the 1600s. Historians maintain that, like many colonial roads, it parallels an old Native American path that was well trod by German, Scottish, and English settlers and fur traders as a route from the Hudson River valley region. Route 560 in Layton leads to Peters Valley Craft Education Center, a nationally known arts education center whose talented faculty and inspiring natural surroundings attract the country's top artists and craftspeople. Route 206 traces the path of a historic Native American trade route through Culver Gap in Stokes State Forest. Back at I-80, Route 521 leads straight into Hope's historic center, where Route 519 rambles south through Jenny Jump State Forest into Belvidere, the 19th-century seat of Warren County. Its historic courthouse square and leafy town green include the redbrick county courthouse and three stately churches, and neighborhood streets are neatly lined with splendid old Victorian structures.

Entries in this section are arranged in roughly geographic order, from north to south.

AREA CODE 908, 973

GUIDANCE **The Knowlton Welcome Center** (908-496-4994) is located at mile marker 7 on I-80 eastbound in Columbia, 7 miles east of the Delaware Water Gap. It's well stocked with travel literature and has public restrooms.

Skylands of New Jersey Tourism Council (800-475-9526; www.skylandstourism .org) has a comprehensive Web site and will mail brochures, maps, and information on request.

GETTING THERE *By air:* **Newark Liberty International Airport** (973-961-6000; 888-397-4636; www.panynj.com) in Newark serves the entire state. **John F. Kennedy International Airport** (718-244-4444; www.kennedyairport.com) and **LaGuardia International Airport** (718-533-3400; www.laguardiaairport.com) in New York City are also convenient to northern New Jersey.

By car: Two east–west interstates, **I-80** and **I-78,** connect the Upper Delaware River area to Pennsylvania and the metropolitan New York region.

MEDICAL EMERGENCY **Warren Hospital** (908-859-6700), 185 Roseberry St., Phillipsburg. The emergency number is 908-859-6767.

Saint Clare's Hospital (973-702-2714), 20 Walnut St., Sussex. The emergency number is 973-625-6150.

Newton Memorial Hospital (973-383-2121), 175 High St., Newton. The emergency number is 973-579-8500.

✴ To See

HISTORIC HOMES **Foster-Armstrong House** (973-293-3106), 320 River Rd., Montague. Open in summer for tours; phone ahead. A restored 18th-century home on the National Register of Historic Places is the headquarters of the

---

NEW JERSEY STATE SYMBOLS
Motto: liberty and prosperity
Tree: red oak
Dinosaur: Hadrosaurus foulkii (unearthed in Haddonfield in 1858)
Animal: horse (petitioned by New Jersey schoolchildren in 1977)
Flower: purple violet
Bird: eastern goldfinch
Insect: honeybee
Fruit: blueberry (grown in the Pinelands)
Shell: knobbed whelk
Folk dance: square dance
Fish: brook trout
Ship: A. J. Meerwald (a historic oyster schooner based in Bivalve)

Montague Historical Society. Julius Foster built the neat and trim white-clapboard building around 1790; his son-in-law James Armstrong expanded it in the early 1800s. A walk through the house reveals an interesting mix of artifacts and memorabilia on local history from the 1700s to the early 1900s. A military room contains historic uniforms, personal letters, and newspaper accounts from the Civil War to World War II. Other rooms in the house have Victorian furnishings and clothing, Native American artifacts, and antique weaving looms with handmade quilts and linens.

Neldon-Roberts Stonehouse (973-293-3106), 501 Rt. 206, Montague. Open for tours on Sun. in summer; call for hours. This rustic shuttered stone house was built alongside a quiet country road in the early 1800s. It was occupied by several Montague families, including the Neldons and Robertses; it even served the small rural community as a schoolhouse for a time. The second floor, where art exhibits are now showcased, once provided a living space for the resident schoolteacher. The house retains many of its original architectural elements, from the fireplace and wide-plank floors to the unusual deep-set windows. Exhibits depict life in rural 19th-century New Jersey; a period herb garden grows out back.

MUSEUMS **Warren County Historical Society Museum** (908-475-4246), 313 Mansfield St., Belvidere. Call ahead for hours. A circa-1848 brick town house containing exhibits of treasures from homes around Warren County. Family furnishings, antiques, and memorabilia reflect centuries of farm life and industrial progress in one of New Jersey's most rural regions.

New Jersey Transportation Heritage Center (908-859-1277; www.njthc.org), 178 S. Main St., Phillipsburg. Open Sat. and Sun.; call ahead for hours. Phillipsburg's downtown Union Station was once a bustling passenger stop for the Delaware, Lackawanna & Western Railroad and the Central Railroad of New Jersey. Today the historic station is a new volunteer-run museum and information center. Exhibits tell the story of New Jersey's diverse transportation history, from the steam-, diesel-, and electric locomotives used to haul passengers and freight, to the mule-drawn boats that plied the Morris Canal, and the trolleys, streetcars, and buses that shuttled city folks around the state's urban centers. Museum holdings include an extensive collection of photos, maps, artifacts, and other memorabilia, as well as antique railcars, trucks, buses, and other transportation vehicles.

WINERIES **Westfall Winery** (973-293-3428; www.westfallwinery.com), 141 Clove Rd., Montague. Open for tastings Sat. and Sun. noon–5; closed in Jan. A beautiful 350-acre horse farm in rural Sussex County near High Point State Park is home to one of New Jersey's newest wineries, specializing in Italian-style dry wines. The tasting room features some of Westfall's handcrafted wines—chianti, pinot grigio, and cabernet, as well as light-tasting fruit varieties. One of their popular fruit wines is a chardonnay made from New Jersey peaches.

WOLF PRESERVE **Lakota Wolf Preserve** (1-877-733-9653; www.lakotawolf.com), at Camp Taylor Campground, 89 Mount Pleasant Rd., Columbia. Open daily May–Aug.; closed Mon., Sept.–Apr. Adults $15; children 11 and under, $7. Reservations are required; inquire about special photography and video tours.

FOUR SISTERS WINERY AT MATARAZZO FARMS
(908-475-3671; www.foursisterswinery.com), 783 Rt. 519, Belvidere. Open
daily 9–6 for tastings; wine cellar tours on weekends and holidays; market
open daily May–Oct. The winery at this 230-acre working farm is named for
the Matarazzos' four daughters. More than two-dozen varieties of wine are
produced here. All are made from lambrusca and French-American hybrid
grapes, and many have won regional, national, and international awards.
Visitors can bring a picnic lunch and eat on the deck, which has panoramic
views of the vineyards and the rolling hills of Warren County. Fun events like
grape-crushing parties, moonlit hayrides, and murder-mystery dinners are
very popular. The country market sells jams, sauces, dressings, light lunches, and fresh-baked pies and pastries.

Wolf-watches are held in summer at 10:30 AM and 4 PM, in fall and winter at 10:30
AM and 3 PM. Packs of timber-, arctic-, and tundra wolves live in compounds surrounding a viewing area. From there, visitors learn about their living habits and
the social structure of the pack while watching and listening to them play and
interact in a natural setting. The preserve is also home to bobcats and foxes. A
unique and unforgettable experience, especially if you're lucky enough to hear a
wolf's haunting, otherworldly howl.

✳ To Do

AMUSEMENTS ✐ **Land of Make Believe** (908-459-9000; www.lomb.com), 354
Great Meadows Rd. (Rt. 611), Hope. Open May through Labor Day. Adults $21;
children 2–18, $23; seniors $19; children 2 and under, free. While most amusement parks specialize in high-adrenaline thrills, this old-fashioned family-fun park
features safe, low-key rides designed for young children. Pirate's Cove is a pirate-
themed water park where kids can get wet, with tubing, tame waterslides, and a
wading pool. Amusements include a variety of nursery-rhyme rides, a carousel,
carnival games with prizes, a petting zoo at Old McDonald's Farm, and rides on a
replica Civil War–era locomotive. The park also has a gift shop and a spacious area
for picnicking.

BALLOONING **Have Balloon Will Travel** (800-608-6359; www.haveballoon
willtravel.com), 57 Old Belvidere Rd., Phillipsburg. Hot-air balloon trips year-
round; call for reservations at least a week in advance. Hour-long scenic hot-air
flights over rural Hunterdon and Warren counties leave either at sunrise or 2
hours before sunset (when the wind is calmest), and are followed by a champagne
picnic.

Balloonatics and Aeronuts (908-454-3431; 877-438-6359; www.aeronuts.com),
Seven Harmony Brass Castle Rd., Phillipsburg. Flights are available daily year-
round, and reservations are required. One-hour champagne balloon trips over the
Delaware River valley launch at sunrise or a few hours before sunset. Balloons
hold two to three passengers, but larger groups can be accommodated.

BIRDING New Jersey's rugged northwest corner along the Delaware River is located along a major raptor flyway; it's known as one of the top raptor-spotting areas in the country. From late August to early December, birders swarm to several observation sites along the Kittatinny Ridge—armed with binoculars, spotting scopes, and bird identification field guides—to witness the world-famous annual migration of hawks, kestrels, harriers, vultures, eagles, ospreys, and other birds of prey. If you're lucky, you might spot some of the hummingbirds, monarch butterflies, and songbirds that also pass through the region on their long journey to South America and other warm climes. Some of the best places to watch from include **Scott's Mountain Hawk Watch,** on the western shore of Merrill Creek Reservoir off Route 57, north of Phillipsburg; **Sunrise Mountain** at Stokes State Forest in Branchville; and **Raccoon Ridge** in Blairstown. This spectacular natural phenomenon—at the peak of migration, thousands of birds glide overhead in a single day—draws an equally interesting mix of casual observers and serious raptor spotters, who will often be more than happy to share their knowledge with you. For more information, contact the **New Jersey Audubon Society** (908-204-8998; www.njaudubon.org) or the **Hawk Migration Association of North America** (www.hmana.org).

BOATING See also *Canoeing, Kayaking, Tubing, and Rafting.*

Stokes State Forest (973-948-3820), Rt. 206, Branchville. There's no boat ramp, but small boats with electric motors are permitted on **Lake Ocquittunk.**

There are several boat ramps and launch sites on the New Jersey side of the Delaware River; all are free unless otherwise indicated. In the **Delaware Gap National Recreation Area** (570-588-2440), there's a launch site on Old Mine Road, 9.3 miles north of the Delaware Water Gap; it's open to car-top boats from mid-April to mid-October and charges a fee. There's also a ramp about a mile south on Old Mine Road. Boat ramps are also at **Kittatinny Beach,** below the I-80 bridge; in **Worthington State Forest** (908-841-9575), 4 miles north of I-80 off Old Mine Rd., near the forest office; **Belvidere access** (908-852-4317), downstream from the Belvidere Bridge; and the **Phillipsburg Boat Ramp** (908-454-7281), Riverside Way, Phillipsburg. The **Holland Church** access site (908-735-8793), 1 mile south of the Riegelsville Bridge off River Road in Holland Township, is open to car-top boats; large boats are not recommended.

CANOEING, KAYAKING, TUBING, AND RAFTING From the tri-state junction of New Jersey, New York, and Pennsylvania to the southern part of this region near Phillipsburg, the Delaware River glides along—sometimes peacefully, other times quickly—as it twists past New Jersey's rugged northwestern border. This pristine federally designated scenic waterway is well known for its first-rate fishing, kayaking, canoeing, rafting, and tubing. It's also dotted with pristine islands; the ones with tent sites accessible only by boat make for a unique overnight experience (see **Delaware Water Gap National Recreation Area** under *Lodging—Campgrounds*).

Lazy River Outpost (570-242-8020; www.lazyriveroutpost.com), Four Union Square, Phillipsburg, puts visitors on the river with kayaks, rafts, canoes, and tubes, with a free shuttle to the drop site.

Several outfitters just over the New Jersey state line also rent canoes, kayaks, tubes, and/or rafts for the Delaware, including: **Indian Head Canoes** (800-874-2628), Barryville, NY; **Kittatinny Canoes and Rafts** (800-356-2852), Dingmans Ferry, PA; **Chamberlain Canoes** (800-422-6631), Minisink Hills, PA; and **Adventure Sports** (570-223-0505; 800-487-2628), Marshalls Creek, PA.

FISHING The **Delaware River** is one of New Jersey's top fishing destinations. Shad, smallmouth bass, perch, walleye, catfish, and muskies are among the species that thrive here; a New Jersey fishing license is required. See *Boating*, above, for a listing of public boat ramps and launch sites along the river.

Stokes State Forest (973-948-3820), Rt. 206, Branchville. The lakes and streams in the forest are known among local anglers for offering some of the best trout fishing in the state. **Stony Lake** and **Lake Ocquittunk,** as well as **Big Flat Brook** and its tributaries, are stocked annually with trout.

Worthington State Forest (908-841-9575), Old Mine Rd., Columbia. Anglers come here for the **Delaware River's** spring shad run as well as the panfish and bass fishing. A ramp for small boats is located near the forest office. **Dunnfield Creek** is a designated Wild Trout Stream and a good place to fish for brook trout. The picturesque creek tumbles over rocks from its source high on Mount Tammany to the Delaware River. **Sunfish Pond** is a pristine alpine lake with yellow perch, bullheads, pickerel, and, of course, sunfish.

Ghost Lake and Mountain Lake (908-459-4366) at Jenny Jump State Forest in Hope are notable fishing spots. At Ghost Lake, anglers can try for catfish, largemouth bass, and sunfish; there's a boat launch for car-top boats only. It's an artificial, fairly shallow lake—about 10 feet deep at most—and gets choked with weeds later in the season. The state fish and wildlife division stocks Mountain Lake with trout; a public boat launch allows boats with electric motors only.

GOLF **Apple Mountain Golf and Country Club** (908-453-3023), 369 Hazen–Oxford Rd. (Rt. 624), Belvidere. An 18-hole golf course in business for more than 30 years. The clubhouse has a restaurant and golf shop; the fairways boast spectacular views of Warren County's rolling farmland and the Pocono Mountains beyond.

The Architects Golf Club (908-213-3080), 700 Strykers Rd., Lopatcong, is an 18-hole public golf course with an eye for history. Each hole reflects the trademark design style of some of the world's premier golf architects from the 19th and early 20th centuries. Facilities include a clubhouse with golf shop and pub-grill, practice area with driving range and putting green, and snack bar.

HIKING **The Appalachian Trail.** A 73-mile portion of the Appalachian National Scenic Trail passes through the northwest corner of New Jersey. It enters the state from Pennsylvania just above the Delaware Water Gap, where thru-hikers come in over the Delaware River along busy I-80. The trail leaves civilization quickly behind when it climbs into Worthington State Forest and the Kittatinny Mountains. It follows the high ridge through the Delaware Water Gap National Recreation Area, Stokes State Forest, and High Point State Park, then snakes across northern New Jersey to the New York state line at Greenwood Lake. Contact the

Appalachian Mountain Club (212-986-1430; www.amc-ny.org) for information on hiking along the trail in New Jersey.

High Point State Park (973-875-4800), 1480 Rt. 23, Sussex. As the name implies, this northernmost state park boasts the state's loftiest peak. High Point has 11 marked trails for all abilities, from short easy walks to challenging rocky terrain; but few hikers leave here without climbing to the highest point in New Jersey. From the top of **High Point Monument** at the 1,803-foot summit, the three-state panoramic view encompasses the Kittatinny Range, the Catskill and Pocono mountains, Lake Marcia, and the Delaware River. The granite monument tower is a 220-foot-tall stone obelisk, completed in 1930 to honor the state's war veterans.

Stokes State Forest (973-948-3820), Rt. 206, Branchville. In addition to a 12.5-mile section of the **Appalachian Trail,** the forest maintains a 33-mile network of marked trails. They vary widely in difficulty, from short, level walks to longer routes over rocky terrain. Most hikers who come here choose either to scale the 1,653-foot summit of **Sunrise Mountain** or to explore **Tillman Ravine,** a deep hemlock-filled gorge. The peak of Sunrise Mountain affords spectacular panoramas of the Delaware River and Kittatinny valleys. The ravine is in the Tillman Ravine Natural Area, a 525-acre natural area that's home to endangered plants and wildlife. A web of trails leads into the dramatic gorge, whose precipitous walls are covered in an evergreen forest. From one of the parking areas, walk down to the series of small waterfalls carved out of sandstone and shale by the spring-fed waters of Tillman Brook. Look for **the Teacup,** a unique swirling rock formation. Over time, moving sand and stones, combined with the force of water, created the smooth hole.

Worthington State Forest (908-841-9575), Old Mine Rd., Columbia. In the Delaware Water Gap National Recreation Area. The state forest has some 24 miles of marked trails, including 7.8 miles of the **Appalachian Trail.** Most hikers go to the undisturbed **Sunfish Pond Natural Area** or, more specifically, its lovely 41-acre lake, a tarn set at the crest of the Kittatinny Ridge. The spring-fed pond is a national natural landmark, one of the few remaining glacially carved alpine lakes in the Appalachian Highlands. The 1.5-mile trail circling the lake is peppered with scenic overlooks. In the pristine **Dunnfield Creek Natural Area,** the 3.5-mile Dunnfield Creek Trail follows the rushing waters of Dunnfield Creek and traverses a deep ravine thick with rhododendron and mountain laurel that put on a spectacular springtime display. You can also take a 1.3-mile trail to the 1,527-foot peak of **Mount Tammany,** high above the Delaware River, or explore several miles of old forest roads.

HORSEBACK RIDING ✍ **Double D Guest Ranch** (908-459-9044; www .doubledguestranch.com), 81 Mount Hermon Rd., Blairstown. (See also *Lodging—Other Lodging.*) Open daily from 9 AM year-round; closed on Christmas Day. Reservations are required. A variety of riding excursions: Beginners and children like the 1-hour rides, which explore the open pastures and wooded trails on Phil Dukes's 75-acre ranch. Two-hour trips follow the **Paulinskill Valley Trail,** a 26-mile converted railbed known for its rich wildlife habitat and pristine natural surroundings. Half- and full-day trips explore the quiet woodlands in nearby **Allamuchy Mountain and Swartswood state parks.**

STARGAZING **Greenwood Observatory** (908-459-4909), Jenny Jump State Forest, Far View Rd., Hope. Public programs Apr.–Oct., Sat. at 8 PM. Admission by donation. Members of the United Astronomy Clubs of New Jersey present astronomy programs and lectures that, weather permitting, are followed by an observing session. The observatory is perched high in the forest, at around 1,100 feet, where the telescope is pointed at an area whose dark-sky location (a night sky with little light pollution) is most ideal for gazing at the heavens.

SWIMMING ✌ **Stony Lake** (973-948-3820), Rt. 206, Branchville. A swimming area in Stokes State Forest with a sandy beach, bathhouse, playground, picnic area, and food concessions. Lifeguards are on duty from Memorial Day weekend to Labor Day.

✌ **Lake Marcia** (973-875-4800), High Point State Park, Rt. 23, Sussex. Lifeguards are on duty from Memorial Day weekend to Labor Day. A cool, spring-fed 20-acre lake in New Jersey's highest state park. The beach has a food concession and bathhouse.

TRAIN RIDE ✌ **Belvidere & Delaware River Railroad** (908-454-4433; 877-872-4674; www.nyswths.org), station and ticket office on Market St., next to the Morris Canal arch, Phillipsburg. Train rides year-round on Sat. and Sun.; Thurs.–Sun. in July and Aug.; and on Memorial Day, July 4th, and Labor Day. Trains leave on the hour from 11 to 3. Reservations are recommended. Scenic 1-hour excursions aboard restored old-time trains are a treat for young and old railroad buffs. You'll leave Phillipsburg and journey south along the Delaware River to Carpentersville on the tracks of the Belvidere & Delaware River, or "Bel-Del" Railway. An antique diesel locomotive pulls 1940s- and 50s-era passenger cars. Special events include holiday-themed trips. Operated by the **New York, Susquehanna and Western Technical and Historical Society.**

✳ Winter Sports

CROSS-COUNTRY SKIING **Stokes State Forest** (973-948-3820), **Worthington State Forest** (908-841-9575), and **Jenny Jump State Forest** (908-459-4366) open some trails to cross-country skiing and snowshoeing in winter.

✳ Green Space

NATIONAL RECREATION AREA **Delaware Water Gap National Recreation Area** (visitors center: 908-496-4458; information line: 570-426-2452; www.nps.gov/dewa); headquarters are on River Rd., off Rt. 209, Bushkill, PA 18324. Day-use areas are open year-round, daily from dawn until dusk. The **Kittatinny Point Visitor Center** (908-496-4458), Exit 1 off I-80 at the Delaware Water Gap, is open daily in summer; Wed.–Sun. in Sept. and Oct.; weekends until mid-Nov. The National Park Service maintains this spectacular 70,000-acre natural area in New Jersey and Pennsylvania along a 40-mile stretch of the Delaware River. A rugged landscape of forest-clad mountain ridges, rivers, lakes, and rushing waterfalls stretches along the New Jersey side to the impressive Delaware Water Gap at the southern end of the park. The gap is a dramatic gorge that is more than a mile wide where the river bends sharply east into the Appalachians. It can be viewed from the visitors center, but the best vantage point is from the river itself. The recreation area has a network of trails for hiking, mountain biking, and winter sports, and there is swimming, fishing, and boating in the river. You can spend the night outdoors in a variety of ways, from an established campground with modern facilities to backcountry camping along the **Appalachian Trail** to primitive river-front sites exclusively for boaters.

STATE FORESTS **Stokes State Forest** (973-948-3820), One Coursen Rd., off Rt. 206, Branchville. This 15,432-acre rugged and beautiful state forest was established in 1907 and named for former New Jersey governor Edward C. Stokes, who donated the first 500 acres of land to the state. In addition to the trail network, many of the cabins, shelters, and roads were built in the 1930s by members of the Civilian Conservation Corps (CCC), President Franklin Roosevelt's initiative that gave employment to young men during the Great Depression. All manner of outdoors enthusiasts flock here, and there's something to please just about all of them. Swimming and canoeing on **Stony Lake,** picnicking along **Stony Brook,** trout fishing on **Lake Ocquittunk** and **Big Flat Brook,** and excellent trails for hiking, mountain biking, horseback riding, and cross-country skiing. Spend the night under the stars at a campsite or in one of the rustic cabins.

Worthington State Forest (908-841-9575), Old Mine Rd. (3 miles north of I-80), Columbia. A 6,200-acre forested oasis on the Delaware River, just off I-80. Many visitors head right to the **Sunfish Pond Natural Area,** whose 41-acre alpine lake was named one of the seven Natural Wonders of New Jersey in 1978. The pristine lake gets its name from one of the few hardy species of fish that can tolerate the water's high acidity. You can also hike along the park's network of trails and old woods roads, or camp on an island that's accessible only by canoe.

Jenny Jump State Forest (908-459-4366), State Park Rd., Hope. This 2,427-acre preserve features 10 miles of marked trails that snake up 1,134-foot **Jenny Jump Mountain,** from which there are panoramic views of the Pequest Valley, the

HIGH POINT STATE PARK

(973-875-4800), 1480 Rt. 23, Sussex. Entrance fee charged from Memorial Day weekend to Labor Day; weekdays $5; weekends $10. New Jersey's highest peak is actually the nation's 10th-lowest state high point. Regardless, the climb to the 220-foot granite monument is exhilarating, and the 360-degree panorama from 1,803 feet is rewarding. Just north of the peak in the **Dryden Kuser Natural Area** is a pristine swamp filled with **rare Atlantic white cedar**—the highest-elevation swamp (1,500 feet above sea level) of its kind in the world. **Lake Marcia** is a spring-fed lake at the base of the mountain with good fishing. The thickly forested mountains in this 15,328-acre preserve attract an abundance of wildlife, from resident deer and black bear to the hawks, eagles, falcons, and other raptors that fly overhead during their annual migration (see *To Do—Birding*). Much of the parkland was designed by Boston's Olmsted brothers, the dynamic landscape-architecture duo whose father, Frederick Law Olmsted, designed Central Park.

Kittatinny Mountains, and the Delaware Water Gap. Some of the rock outcroppings you'll see from the trails are estimated to be 1.6 billion years old. There are two lakes for fishing and boating, and trails for mountain biking and winter sports. **Ghost Lake** is known for its superb bass fishing.

✳ Lodging

BED AND BREAKFAST Alexander Adams Homestead (908-459-4018; www.alexanderadamshomestead.com), 31A Auble Rd., Blairstown 07825. A Quaker family, one of many who settled northern New Jersey centuries ago, built this lovely collection of 18th-century buildings. Today they are part of a private estate that welcomes guests who are fortunate enough to find this gem. The circa-1730 stone cottage, one of Warren County's oldest homes, is a romantic retreat frequented by honeymooners and others seeking rural seclusion. It's furnished with tasteful antiques, 19th-century portraits, and fine linens; the original wide-planked floorboards and stone fireplace are charming touches. There's a kitchenette, bedroom, bathroom, and a cozy sitting room with fireplace. The homestead also includes a renovated

✦ ✦ INN AT MILLRACE POND

(908-459-4884; 800-746-6467; www.innatmillracepond.com), 313 Hope Johnsonburg Rd. (Rt. 519), P.O. Box 359, Hope 07844. A stone gristmill built by the Moravian sect that founded Hope in the 18th century is a lovely and romantic inn. The massive four-story gristmill operated from 1770—around which time it produced flour that supplied George Washington's Continental troops—until the early 1950s. The 23-acre grounds are steeped in history, from the hand-cut slate millrace channeling water from the pond to the mill to the carefully preserved mill buildings where innkeepers Charles and Cordie Putcamra provide simple-yet-elegant accommodations. In all, there are 17 individually decorated guest rooms with private bath, Colonial reproduction furnishings, handmade oriental rugs, and original architectural details like hand-hewn beams and wide-plank pine floors. The two guest rooms in the stone cottage—once home to the wheelwright who looked after the gristmill—have either a whirlpool tub or double whirlpool tub. In the gristmill itself, nine guest rooms with canopy beds and/or whirlpool tubs are spread across three floors. The six guest rooms in the Millrace House, where the miller lived, share a cozy parlor as common space. An 1830 home, moved to the property to save it from demolition, contains a small conference center, library, and parlor with fireplace. A candlelit dinner at the inn's critically acclaimed restaurant is a must (see *Dining Out*). Continental breakfast. $175–255.

19th-century carriage house with two suites, one with a private deck and patio, the other with a kitchenette and sitting area. In the morning, breakfast (continental during the week, full on weekends) is dropped off at the cottage and in the suites. Guests can use the outdoor pool during the summer. $130–245.

CAMPGROUNDS **High Point State Park** (973-875-4800), Rt. 23, Sussex. Individual tent sites available Apr.–Oct.; other camping facilities available mid-May through mid-Oct. There are 50 tent sites with picnic tables and fire rings along **Sawmill Lake;** flush toilets are within walking distance. Two group campsites, with pit toilets and drinking water, accommodate up to 35 people each. Rustic cabins along the eastern shore of **Steenykill Lake** include a pair of three-bedroom cabins, and a group cabin that sleeps 28 people.

Stokes State Forest (973-948-3820), Rt. 206, Branchville. Campsites open year-round; cabins available from Apr. to mid-Dec. Tent sites for individuals and large groups, as well as lean-tos and trailer sites with bathroom facilities and drinking water (no water, electric, or sewer hook-ups), are located in several areas throughout the forest. In addition, there are 16 rustic cabins that accommodate between 4 and 12 people. The cabins are in such high demand that reservations are doled out via lottery; contact the forest office for details.

🐾 🐕 ♿ **Kymer's Camping Resort** (973-875-3167; 800-526-2267), 69 Kymer Rd., Branchville 07826. Open Apr.–Oct. A family campground with 250 sites on 200 acres and all the standard amenities. Olympic-sized pool, kiddie pool, and hot tub; fishing in a stocked pond; mini golf and tennis.

Weekend entertainment ranges from live country-and-western music to bingo and horseshoe tournaments. Sites $30; cabins $75.

In **Delaware Water Gap National Recreation Area**, **Dingmans Campground** (507-828-1551; 877-828-1551; www.dingmanscampground.com) is located on the Pennsylvania side of the river, off Rt. 209 and just south of the Dingman's Ferry Bridge in Layton. Backcountry camping is allowed in the park on the **Appalachian Trail** for extended trips of 2 or more days. Primitive waterfront campsites along the river are available on a first-come, first-served basis for boaters and canoeists traveling along the river; 1-night stays only. The **River Bend group campsite** near Millbrook is available for nonprofit organizations. Also within the recreation area is **Worthington State Forest**, Old Mine Rd., Columbia. There are 69 riverfront tent and trailer sites with modern bathrooms, showers, and drinking water (no hook-ups) open from Apr. to Dec. Three group campsites accommodate 35 people each, and tent sites on Labar and Tocks islands in the Delaware River are accessible by canoe only.

Jenny Jump State Forest (908-459-4366), State Park Rd., Hope. From Apr. to Oct., 22 tent and trailer sites with showers and toilets are available. A series of rustic shelters near the top of Jenny Jump Mountain—with furnishings, bunk beds, and woodstoves—are open year-round. Sites $20.

🐕 **Triple Brook Family Camping Resort** (888-343-2267; www.triple brook.com), 58 Honey Run Rd., off Rt. 80, Hope (mailing address: 58 Honey Run Rd., Blairstown 07825). Open Apr.–Oct. A family resort with wooded campsites and rustic cabins on a bucolic 250-acre working farm, which means farm animals to feed and hayrides through the fields. Two outdoor pools, one with a heated whirlpool spa just for adults. A full schedule of special events and activities. In the Kittatinny Mountains, close to the Delaware Water Gap. Campsites $33–42; cabins $65–75.

✔ **Delaware River Family Campground** (908-475-4517; 800-543-0271), 100 Rt. 46, P.O. Box 142, Delaware 07833. All the usual campground amenities are here—game room, mini golf, pool, volleyball—but the real draw is the Delaware River. You can swim, fish (New Jersey license required), or just get out on the water any number of ways. If you don't have your own boat, you can rent just about anything, from a tube or raft to a canoe, a single or double kayak, a boat with trolling motor—even a cargo tube to tow your cooler along. Tubers float downstream for 4 miles, and there are various excursions for canoes, kayaks, and rafts. Campsites $35–39; cabins $85 and up.

✹ ✔ **Camp Taylor Campground** (908-496-4333; 800-545-9662; www .camptaylor.com), 85 Mount Pleasant Rd., Columbia 07832. Open year-round. A family campground perhaps best known for the **Lakota Wolf Preserve** (see *To See—Wolf Preserve*), a unique sanctuary where timber-, arctic-, and tundra wolves can be observed in a natural setting. The campground is an ideal base for hikers; trails lead directly from the campground into 72,000 acres of forested state and federal land, including the **Delaware Water Gap National Recreation Area** and the **Appalachian National Scenic Trail.** Boating, fishing, and swimming on a private 2-acre lake. Kids love the game room, playground, and mini golf. Campsites $25–33; cabins $70 and up.

✳ Where to Eat

DINING OUT

In Walpack

✔ & **Walpack Inn** (973-948-3890; www.walpackinn.com), Rt. 615. Open Fri. and Sat. for dinner; lunch and dinner on Sun. Reservations are only taken for large groups, so be prepared to wait. The Walpack Inn is a local institution, known for its hearty portions of dependable fare—grilled seafood, prime rib, and other classic American and Continental dishes. It was opened in 1949 by the Heigis family, and the second generation still runs the place. The two large dining rooms have tall windows that take full advantage of the stunning Kittatinny Mountains in the near distance. The country-style décor includes a collection of vintage agricultural and household items lining the walls. Dinner comes with their signature whole wheat bread laced with molasses. Homemade pies for dessert. $21–44.

In Phillipsburg

The Union Station Grill (908-387-1380; www.theunionstationgrill.com), Nine Union Square. Open daily for lunch and dinner. For years this was known as the Wardell (taken from "Warren County" and "Delaware River"), a landmark 1920s-era hotel at the foot of the Phillipsburg Free Bridge just south of Main Street. A hotel actually stood here in the mid-19th century, opening as the Lenni Lenape Hotel in 1854. The latest incarnation is a top-notch steak and seafood house in a meticulously restored antique railroad dining car, the old Penn Central coach No. 1420. Snazzy black-and-white-striped awnings and cascading window boxes grace the entrance to the building. $16–28.

In Hope

Inn at Millrace Pond (908-459-4884; www.innatmillracepond.com), 313 Hope Johnsonburg Rd. (Rt. 519). Dinner nightly in the main dining room; dinner in the tavern Mon.–Fri. The Inn at Millrace Pond is as historic and lovely as Hope, where the restaurant finds its home at the heart of the 18th-century village. Elegant fine dining by candlelight and firelight in the massive gristmill, where you can also spend the night (see *Lodging—Inn*). The rustic and charming décor includes the mill's original massive beams and grain chute. The colonial tavern, downstairs past the old waterwheel, has a cozy fireplace and a wine cellar with numerous vintages. Service is personal and attentive, the cuisine is American and traditional. French Brie wrapped in puff pastry with fresh fruit and a Grand Marnier honey reduction, or chilled strawberry mint soup, might be included among the starters. For dinner, try the filet mignon with black peppercorn brandy sauce, or grilled sea scallops and shrimp with cilantro lime vinaigrette. Desserts are homey and satisfying. $23–33.

EATING OUT ❧ **Thisilldous Eatery** (908-475-2274), 320 Front St., Belvidere. Open for breakfast daily; lunch Mon.–Sat. The menu promises "good food for all," and this downtown eatery delivers with homemade comfort food in cozy no-frills surroundings. Hearty breakfasts, burgers, salads, and sandwiches at lunch. A local haunt for more than 20 years. BYOB. $6–14.

Café Verde (908-454-7477), 60 S. Main St. Open for lunch and dinner Wed.–Fri.; dinner Sat. and Sun.; Sun. brunch; closed Mon. and Tues. A friendly and casual café in a lovely row house overlooking the Delaware River.

Check out the revolving exhibits of local art. BYOB. $12–20.

✇ ♿ **Ryan's Parkside** (908-454-6620), on Shappell Park, 371 S. Main St., Phillipsburg. Open daily for lunch and dinner; Sun. breakfast and brunch. Reservations are recommended. A convivial neighborhood eatery with an extensive menu of American, Continental, and Italian classics. Hand-cut steaks, seafood, chicken, veal, and pasta are well prepared and generously portioned. The salads, soups, and desserts—including their signature apple pie and cherry cheesecake—are all homemade. $9–20.

❧ **Simplicity Café** (908-387-1770), Four Union Square, Phillipsburg. Open Tues.–Sun. for breakfast and lunch; closed Mon. A no-frills eatery in a former train depot overlooking the Delaware River. Creative breakfast and lunch fare; egg casserole and pancakes in the morning, crêpes, quiches, and wraps later on. Homemade baked goods. In good weather, eat on the deck with views of the river and the Phillipsburg-Easton bridge. $6–10.

✸ Entertainment

THEATER ♪ **Country Gate Players** (908-475-1104; www.countrygate.org), 114 Greenwich St., Belvidere. This nonprofit community theater group is the oldest and most active arts organization in Warren County. They mounted their first musical, *The King and I*, in 1973; in the 30 years since then, membership has grown to nearly 100 local actors. They present five main stage productions every year—dramas, comedies, musicals, and children's productions—in a 1930s-era art deco–style movie theater.

PETERS VALLEY CRAFT EDUCATION CENTER

(973-948-5200; www.petersvalley.org), 19 Kuhn Rd. (at Rt. 615), Layton. A unique artistic community and education center tucked away in the beautiful natural surroundings of the Delaware Water Gap National Recreation Area since 1970. In spring and summer, nationally recognized instructors lead seminars and intensive workshops for beginner to advanced students on photography, ceramics, blacksmithing, fibers, woodworking, and fine metals. Workshops run usually 3 to 5 days, and are open to anyone wishing to learn about and create fine crafts. In summer, artists open their studio doors to the public, and the center hosts one of the largest crafts shows in America. **Peters Valley Store and Gallery** (973-948-5202) is open year-round most days from 11–5, but their hours change seasonally, so it's best to phone ahead. Contemporary crafts by resident artists and faculty, as well as more than 300 works by artists from around the country are on display and for sale.

PETERS VALLEY CRAFT EDUCATION CENTER IN LAYTON IS A NATIONALLY RECOGNIZED CENTER FOR FINE CRAFTS, WHERE ARTISTS TEACH WORKSHOPS AND COURSES FOR BEGINNING AND ADVANCED STUDENTS IN A PEACEFUL, RURAL ENVIRONMENT.

Photo courtesy of Peters Valley Craft Education Center

✳ Selective Shopping

ANTIQUES AND SPECIAL SHOPS **C&C Collectibles and Antiques** (908-459-4122), 1292 Bridgeville Rd. (Rt. 519), Hope. Open Fri.–Sun. 11–5 and by appointment. A barn full of china, glassware, lighting, and pottery, as well as an assortment of formal, country, and primitive furniture. Fun items like costume jewelry and unique pieces of art.

The Nest (908-459-5461), Two Walnut St., in the Long House, Hope. Open Fri. and Sat. 10–5; Sun. 11–5. Unique vintage home furnishings, from linens and rugs to artwork and primitives.

ARTISTS AND ARTISANS **Neldon-Roberts Stonehouse** (973-293-3106), 501 Rt. 206, Montague. On Sunday during the summer, the work of artists and crafters is on display in an early-19th-century stone house that's a small museum of local history (see *To See—Historic Homes*).

Lafayette Clayworks (973-948-3987), 22 Wantage Ave., Branchville. Open Mon., and Wed.–Sat., 10–5; closed Sun. and Tues. Artist and owner Joyce Maurus-Sullivan's bright and airy gallery features lovely displays of her specialty—handmade stoneware pottery. Bowls, cups, dishes, vases, and pitchers are among her functional and beautiful works of art. Students' work is also on display, from hand-painted pieces to eclectic sculpture and decorative pottery. Joyce teaches pottery classes for adults and children, as well as seasonal workshops in raku and wood firing.

Gallery 23 (908-362-6865; www.gallery23.com), 23 Main St., Blairstown. Open Mon.–Sat. 10–5; Sun. noon–4. An art gallery representing 30 regional artists working in a variety of media, from painting and photography to woodworking, jewelry, and sculpture.

PICK-YOUR-OWN FARMS AND FARM MARKETS **Flatbrook Farm** (973-948-2554), Two Degroat Rd., Rt. 206, Montague. Call ahead for hours. A rural farm selling organic meat—turkey, chicken, and beef—and farm-fresh eggs.

✐ **Marshall's Farm Market** (908-475-1989), 114 Rt. 46, Delaware. Open daily. A combination market and country store close to the Delaware Water Gap. The market features just-picked apples (18 varieties), pumpkins and gourds, and freshly pressed apple cider. The old-fashioned country store sells a good selection of farm products, from fruit butters and unique jams to smoked meats, pies, and a dozen varieties of honey. Call for a schedule of weekend fall hayrides that begin in late September.

Matarazzo Farms (908-475-3872), Rt. 519, Belvidere. Country market open daily May–Oct. The country market at this 230-acre working farm sells jams, sauces, dressings, light lunches, freshly baked pies and pastries, and their own handcrafted wines. **Four Sisters Winery** is open daily for tastings and leads wine-cellar tours on weekends (see sidebar, page 172). Pick your own raspberries, apples, and pumpkins.

✐ **Mackey's Orchard** (908-475-1507), 284 Rt. 519. Open daily April through Christmas Eve. Devlen and Holly Mackey grow 100 varieties of apples in their 96-acre orchard on farmland that's been in the Mackey family for eight generations. The farm market, a renovated dairy barn, sells a wide variety of fruits and vegetables, freshly pressed apple cider, fresh eggs, maple syrup, jams, and jellies. The inventory changes with the seasons, from ice cream and potted plants in summer to pumpkins and Christmas wreaths at the end of the year. The farm's bounty is baked into fruit pies and pastries, including their signature apple cider donuts and double-crust apple pies. In-season, visitors can pick their own berries, cherries, apples, plums, pears, and pumpkins.

Strawberry Hill Farm (908-453-2374), 388 Hazen–Oxford Rd. (Rt. 624). Open daily during the season (usually the month of June) from 8 to 6. Pick your own strawberries.

Stoneyfield Orchards (908-475-5209), Five Orchard St. Op en June–Oct., daily 9–5:30. Pick your own sour cherries, peaches, apples, and pears.

✳ Special Events

late July to early August: ✐ **Warren County Farmers' Fair** (908-859-6563), Warren County Fairgrounds, Rt. 519, Harmony. An old-fashioned country fair for 70 years. Hot-air balloon festival, food and games on the midway, agricultural exhibits, entertainment, tractor- and truck-pull competitions, and horse shows. Kids love the animal exhibit barn, and the special activities and entertainment just for them. Demolition derby, mud-bog races, and a parade of antique tractors.

August: ✐ **Knowlton Riverfest** (908-496-4816), Rt. 46, Delaware. A 3-day music festival along the banks of the Delaware River that's one of the largest family-oriented music festivals in northwestern New Jersey. Country,

jazz, bluegrass, rock, and blues acts, as well as food, crafts, games, and exhibits.

September: **Peters Valley Crafts Fair** (973-948-5200), Peters Valley Craft Education Center, Layton. One of the largest crafts fairs in the country has been going on in the Delaware Valley for 40 years. The work of more than 150 contemporary and traditional craftspeople is on display, and there are crafting demonstrations and opportunities to talk with the artisans. **Victorian Days** (908-475-4124), Belvidere. Historic house tours, antique cars, antiques and crafts, garden parties, a vintage fashion show, and entertainment honor Belvidere's Victorian heritage. **Art Across the River** (908-496-8020), Columbia and Portland, PA. Antiques, fine art and crafts, and traditional folk art on display in communities on opposite banks of the Delaware River, linked by bridge. **Warren County Antiques Fair & Festival** (908-459-4122), Warren County Fairgrounds, Rt. 519, Harmony.

October: **Hope and Dreams Film Festival** (908-459-5797), Hope. A weekend of screenings and talks featuring local, national, and international films and filmmakers.

December: **Christmas Craft Market** (908-459-5127), Hope. Juried holiday crafts show and sale.

THE HILLS:
FLEMINGTON TO MORRISTOWN

T racing its roots to the early 1700s, Morristown is named one of America's Dozen Distinctive Destinations by the National Trust for Historic Preservation for its well-preserved historic district of Greek Revival–, Federal-, and Victorian-era homes and its picturesque town green. The Morristown Green is a lovely town square—like the ones that define New England villages—surrounded by wide streets, a 19th-century Federal-style brick county courthouse, and well-preserved vintage commercial buildings with an interesting mix of shops and eateries. Modern office buildings and apartment complexes are tucked among its 18th- and 19th-century structures, but Morristown still retains a decidedly historic flavor.

Less than an hour's drive from Manhattan, Morristown is close enough to be touched by metropolitan sprawl yet harbors some 31 historic sites virtually untouched by the hand of the 21st century. It's a true crossroads of history and progress, where chic urban émigrés feel at home among galleries and bistros a stone's throw from places like Historic Speedwell and Acorn Hall that date to the 1800s, and Fosterfields Living Historical Farm, a working farm that uses turn-of-the-20th-century farming methods. It's a point of local pride that Morristown—whose hills sheltered the Continental army through two harsh winters during the Revolutionary War—has the first national historic park in America. It's no Grand Canyon, but it is picturesque enough to attract 400,000 visitors annually, and preserves one of the most significant sites in the history of the American War of Independence.

During the bitter winters of 1777 and 1779–80, Morristown's outlying hills protected the main encampments of the American Continental army and served as General George Washington's military headquarters. Washington chose Morristown for its strategic location—there were good roads for supply lines and quick communication with Philadelphia and Congress, sheltering terrain, a supportive local community (nearly 50 iron forges and furnaces in Morris County supplied the Continental army with ammunition), and an advantageous distance—just 30 miles—from British-occupied New York. While the commander in chief lived in relative luxury in the Ford Mansion, his 10,000 troops—in worse condition than they were at Valley Forge—were bunked down in crude log huts in Jockey Hollow. Morristown National Historical Park preserves more than 1,000 acres of open meadows and woodlands that surround the encampments' most significant sites:

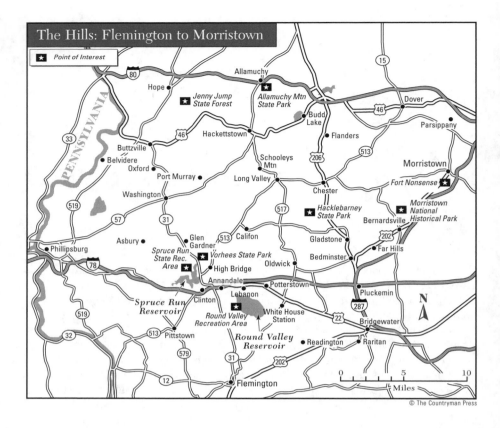

Washington's headquarters at the Ford Mansion; reconstructed soldiers' huts and 27 miles of hiking trails at Jockey Hollow; the 18th-century Wick Farm, which served as Major General Arthur St. Clair's command center; and "Fort Nonsense," where Washington's soldiers built a fortification atop Mount Kemble to protect Morristown from the threat of a British invasion.

New Jersey's 19th-century transformation from agricultural region to industrial hub was hastened by America's canal boom. Scottish immigrant and entrepreneur George P. Macculloch envisioned a constructed waterway that could traverse the state's rugged northern hills from the Delaware River in western New Jersey to the Hudson River in New York. The result was the Morris Canal, where boats loaded with Pennsylvania iron and coal negotiated changes in elevation via Macculloch's revolutionary system of 23 inclined planes and 23 lift locks along the canal's 102-mile route. Today the Morristown mansion built by the Father of the Morris Canal is New Jersey's top house museum, full of 18th- and 19th-century European and American fine art and furnishings. Macculloch Hall is perhaps best known for its collection of works by Thomas Nast, the famous *Harper's Weekly* political cartoonist who introduced 19th-century America to the Republican Elephant, Democratic Donkey, Uncle Sam, and the modern version of Santa Claus, indelible caricatures that remain among the most recognizable images in modern culture.

During the Industrial Revolution, the only constant in New Jersey was change, and despite Macculloch's cutting-edge engineering, the canal was eclipsed in short

order by the faster, more efficient railroad. By the mid-1800s, the Morris & Essex
Lines cut through a rural farming region that was now readily accessible to the
outside world. Mills sprung up along rivers and streams, and Colonial farmhouses
were slowly replaced by ornate Italianate, Victorian, and Gothic Revival mansions.
Many have been lovingly restored and can be seen along back roads and in historic
village centers like Clinton and Hackettstown. Some are local-history museums;
others are hospitable bed & breakfasts.

After the Civil War the Gilded Age reached Morris County, as wealthy Manhattanites realized that the cool, rolling countryside just outside their city would make
a fine summer retreat. They built opulent manor houses in Morristown, Far Hills,
and Bedminster, and in Bernardsville's lavish "mountain colony" enclave, where
multimillionaires resided in palatial mansions and brought socialites from Manhattan to the country. A whirlwind social season of polo matches, glittering high-society parties, and debutante balls were de rigueur, until the stock market crashed in
1929. For many residents of the colony, the party was essentially over, and many of
their mansions were neglected or sold, paving the way for upscale residential
developments. After World War II the landscape changed once again, as suburban
housing tracts started dotting the region in a trend that hasn't yet stopped. Today,
this area contains New Jersey's most rapidly growing counties. Farms are evolving
into shopping malls and housing developments, with traffic congestion an unfortunate daily ritual.

America's first factory-outlet village is in Flemington, a few blocks from the historic Main Street lined with handsome Victorian homes and commercial buildings.
Flemington enjoyed a fleeting moment of fame in 1935, when the county courthouse hosted the trial of Bruno Hauptmann, who was convicted in the kidnap-
murder of aviator Charles Lindbergh's baby son. The Trial of the Century made
headlines around the world, and journalists reported the daily courtroom drama
from across the street at the landmark Union Hotel. The 1854 Black River &
Western Railroad takes passengers on nostalgic jaunts through Flemington's scenic
countryside on an 1854 steam-powered locomotive.

River towns like Clinton and Chester retain their old-time flavor with well-preserved main streets that attract swarms of visitors on weekends. Clinton's vintage
downtown buildings house an eclectic jumble of shops, galleries, and eateries. The
town's much-photographed landmark Red Mill resides next to a waterfall on the
south branch of the Raritan River. It was built around 1812 as a woolen mill, and
in the next century would serve as a gristmill, a talc factory, and a stone-processing
plant—even peach baskets were made here. Today it's part of a museum village
along with a blacksmith shop, limestone quarry, and one-room schoolhouse. On
the opposite bank, the Hunterdon Museum of Art displays the work of regional
artists in a vintage stone mill. The hills around Clinton are a hub for hot-air ballooning, one of the most breathtaking and peacefully low-tech means of enjoying
New Jersey's rural landscape. Several outfitters take passengers on champagne
flights around sunrise and sunset—when wind conditions are calmest—to float
above farmland and wooded hills at about 5 miles an hour. Every summer in Readington, the New Jersey Festival of Ballooning draws more than 100 hot-air balloons and some 175,000 spectators to the largest summertime balloon festival in
North America.

Chester was settled as a farming and mill town along the Black River in the
early 1700s. Its boom period coincided with the mining of iron ore in the 19th

century, when many of its historic downtown commercial buildings were built. Today, Main Street has excellent shopping, packed with unique stores, cafés, crafts galleries, and antiques shops. Chester's rural outskirts are dotted with small family farms that sell their bounty in roadside markets; many let visitors pick their own raspberries, peaches, and apples, or take an old-fashioned autumn hayride into their pumpkin patches.

The rural town of Long Valley was first known as German Valley, named for the region's early settlers who first planted the fields and whose meticulous stonework can still be seen around town. The Long Valley Pub and Brewery, housed in a 200-year-old stone barn, features their handiwork and is a convivial pub whose hand-crafted brews pay tribute to the region's history and culture. Sprinkled throughout this region are numerous topflight restaurants—notably, The Bernards Inn and Le Petit Château in Bernardsville—that offer some of the most elegant and sophisticated fine dining in New Jersey.

Without doubt, this region is somewhat suburbanized, but large tracts of open space still remain. Morris County alone maintains 14,000 acres of open space with an impressive string of parks that offer everything from camping and fishing to hiking trails that boast spectacular views of the Manhattan skyline. A handful of state parks, recreation areas, and wildlife preserves protect pristine forestland laced with trails for hiking, mountain biking, horseback riding, and cross-country skiing. Some of the area's grand estates—Duke Farms (home of former tobacco heiress Doris Duke, "the Richest Little Girl in the World"), Frelinghuysen Arboretum, and Willowwood Arboretum, among them—were exclusive retreats for the privileged few nearly a century ago; their spectacular gardens and extraordinary natural surroundings can now be enjoyed by everyone.

Entries in this section are arranged in roughly geographic order, from south to north.

AREA CODES 973, 908.

GUIDANCE A **New Jersey state welcome center** (908-782-8550) is located at Liberty Village Premium Outlets, One Church St., Flemington. It's well stocked with official state tourism literature as well as menus, maps, and brochures on area attractions, museums, lodgings, and events.

Skylands of New Jersey Tourism Council (800-475-9526; www.skylandstourism .org) maintains a Web site with information on visiting the region. On request, they will mail out literature and information on travel in northwestern New Jersey.

Morris County Visitors Center (973-631-5151; www.morristourism.org), Six Court St., Morristown. Open Mon.–Fri. 9–4:30; Sat. 9–1 from June–Aug. A very friendly and helpful staff runs this extremely well-stocked information center in downtown Morristown near the courthouse. Maps, events listings, and brochures on historic sites, lodging and dining, museums, parks, walking tours, and recreation are among the diverse travel literature they carry.

GETTING THERE *By air:* **Newark Liberty International Airport** (973-961-6000; 888-397-4636; www.panynj.com) in Newark is New Jersey's largest airport, served by more than 40 major carriers. **John F. Kennedy International Airport** (718-244-4444; www.kennedyairport.com) and **LaGuardia International Airport** (718-533-3400; www.laguardiaairport.com) in New York City are other options.

By rail: **New Jersey Transit** (973-275-5555; 800-955-2321; www.njtransit.com)
provides commuter service from Hoboken (commuters connect to Manhattan via
PATH trains) as far as Hackettstown and High Bridge.

By bus: **Greyhound** (800-231-2222; www.greyhound.com) makes a stop in Hackettstown; there is no terminal or passenger service. **New Jersey Transit** (973-275-
5555; 800-955-2321; www.njtransit.com) provides bus service throughout this
region. The **Morris County Metro** bus line (973-829-8101) serves Morris County
with several bus routes that operate from Monday through Saturday.

By car: **I-80** and **I-78** cut through this area on their routes from the metropolitan
New York City area west to Pennsylvania. Both interstates are connected by **I-287,**
which runs north to south along the eastern edge of this region.

GETTING AROUND *Taxis:* **P & P Taxi** (973-539-5903), **Comfort Cab** (973-
267-1700), and **Bumblebee Taxi** (973-683-1313) are all based in Morristown and
serve the surrounding communities.

MEDICAL EMERGENCY **Hunterdon Medical Center** (908-788-6100), 2100
Wescott Dr., Flemington. The emergency number is 908-788-6183.

Hackettstown Community Hospital (908-852-5100), 651 Willow Grove St.,
Hackettstown. The emergency number is 908-850-6800.

Morristown Memorial Hospital (973-971-5000), 100 Madison Ave., Morristown.
The emergency numbers are 973-971-6102 (children) and 973-971-5007 (adults).

Saint Clare's Hospital (973-989-3000), 400 West Blackwell St., Dover. The
emergency number is 973-989-3200.

✳ To See

HISTORIC HOMES **Acorn Hall** (973-267-3465; www.acornhall.org), 68 Morris
Ave., Morristown. Gardens open daily from dawn to dusk; docent-led mansion
tours Mon. and Thurs. 10–4; Sun. 1–4; closed major holidays; tours by appointment. Adults $6; seniors $5; students $3; children 11 and under, free. The **Morris
County Historical Society** is headquartered in this lovely 1853 Italianate mansion that still features most of its original Victorian-era furnishings. Exhibits feature
period clothing, textiles, and decorative objects. The landscaped Victorian gardens
surrounding the house are planted with flowering trees, bulbs, and shrubs. The
Victorian research library—New Jersey's only such facility—is open to the public by appointment.

Schuyler-Hamilton House (973-267-4039), Five Olyphant Place, Morristown.
Open for tours Sun. 2–4 and by appointment. Adults $4; children $2. This trim
white-clapboard house was built in 1760 by Dr. Jabez Campfield, who was best
known as George Washington's personal physician. The house's name, however,
derives from a widely believed but unproven romantic legend. During the winter
of 1779–80, John Cochran, surgeon general of the Continental army, was a guest at
the house. So was Alexander Hamilton, who supposedly met and courted Betsy
Schuyler, Cochran's niece, at Campfield's home. Local historians believe the
romance really happened, although no documentation exists to prove it. The
house, one of the only remaining 18th-century buildings left in Morristown, has
period furnishings and is maintained by a local chapter of the Daughters of the
American Revolution.

HISTORIC SITES Cooper Gristmill (908-879-5463), Black River Park, 66 Rt. 513, Chester. The visitors center is open Apr.–Oct., Sat. and Sun. 10–5; in July and Aug. it's also open Wed.–Fri. Admission by donation. A gristmill has been in operation on the Black River since the Revolutionary War; this one was built by Nathan Cooper in 1826. Today it is New Jersey's only restored water-powered gristmill, and it's on the National Register of Historic Places. This part of Chester was once known as Milltown, a flourishing industrial village of miners, millers, and farmers on the Black River. It was rich with natural resources—waterpower from the river, fertile soil for farming, plenty of iron ore in the hills, and forests thick with timber. During 45-minute tours of the gristmill, guides in period dress operate the mill's restored machinery. You'll see how water from the river turns the 6-ton waterwheel, which powers the gears and shafts that turn the 2,000-pound grinding stones that reduce coarse grain into soft flour. In 1 hour, the massive millstones can churn out as much as 800 pounds of flour, and a system of belts and elevators moves flour throughout the mill in a move toward automation—cutting-edge technology in the 19th century. For a donation, visitors can take home some of the organic stone-ground whole wheat flour and cornmeal produced at the mill.

HISTORIC SPEEDWELL

(973-285-6550, 333 Speedwell Ave. (Rt. 202), Morristown. Open Apr. to Oct., Wed.–Sat. 10–5; Sun. noon–5; closed Mon. and Tues. Free admission. Special events and programs are held on weekends; call for a schedule. The estate of 19th-century ironmaster Stephen Vail has been known as the **Birthplace of the Telegraph** ever since his son Alfred, along with **Samuel F. B. Morse,** developed a working model of the electromagnetic telegraph here in 1838. That January, they held the first public demonstration of the revolutionary device in the estate's factory building. But Speedwell has historical significance on many levels. **Speedwell Iron Works** thrived from the early- to mid-1800s; here the elder Vail developed the steam engine for the SS *Savannah,* the world's first transatlantic steam-powered ship. Today the collection of historic buildings—some originally on-site, others moved here to save them from demolition—is a museum of early-19th-century life, with displays of vintage farm implements, antique vehicles, colonial furnishings, and relics from Vail's ironworks. You can see the restored 24-foot waterwheel that once powered the mill still turning in the wheelhouse, or take a guided tour of the restored 1840s **Vail House,** furnished with elegant period furnishings as well as portraits painted by Morse. The 1849 **Homestead Carriage House,** one of Speedwell's original buildings, contains a museum shop, exhibits on Speedwell Iron Works and its role in the Industrial Revolution, and early communications equipment. The early-19th-century **L'Hommedieu House** has a visitors center and gift shop.

✎ **Fosterfields Living Historical Farm** (973-326-7645), 73 Kahdena Rd., at Rt. 510, Morristown. Open Apr.–Oct., Wed.–Sun. 10–5; closed Mon. and Tues. Special events and demonstrations are held on weekends. Free admission to the farm; there's a charge for programs. New Jersey's first living-history farm is devoted to turn-of-the-20th-century farming and domestic life. Most visitors come to this national register historic site for the weekend demonstrations by costumed interpreters. They go about a day's farmwork—raising livestock, milking cows by hand, tilling fields—following the schedule that Charles Foster recorded in his journals. His daughter Caroline donated her beloved family farm to the Morris County Park Commission after living there for a century (she died at 102). Visitors can help out with chores like cooking, tending crops, cleaning harnesses, and churning butter, all the while learning what life was like for a farm foreman and his family a century ago. High on a hill overlooking the farm is **The Willows,** the ornate Gothic Revival mansion that Joseph Warren Revere (Paul Revere's grandson) built for the Fosters in 1854. It's open for guided tours, furnished and restored to how it looked from 1880 to 1910.

MUSEUMS ✎ **Northlandz** (908-782-4022; www.northlandz.com), 495 Rt. 202 South, Flemington. Open year-round, Mon., Wed.–Fri. 10:30–4; Sat. and Sun. 10:30–5:30; closed Tues. Adults $13.75; seniors $12.50; children $9.75; steam train rides $2.75. The **Great American Railway** is the world's longest miniature railroad, but this museum is anything but small. It took Bruce Zaccagnino 25 years (and millions of dollars) to complete the masterpiece that sprung from his passion for trains. Today, 8 miles of railroad track wind through cities and around 35-foot-tall mountains, over hundreds of bridges—some up to 40 feet long—and past thousands of intricate, handcrafted buildings. There are 10,000 freight cars, and about 100 trains run on the tracks every day. Even though it's indoors, the walking tour through this amazing world is a mile long. Outside, a replica of the **Raritan River Railway steam train** takes visitors on a ride through the woods. Northlandz isn't just for railroad buffs, however. An on-site museum has more than **200 collectible dolls and a 100-room dollhouse.** There's also an **art gallery** and a **music hall with a 2,000-pipe organ.**

Red Mill Museum Village and Hunterdon Historical Museum (908-735-4101; www.theredmill.org), 56 Main St., Clinton. Open Apr. through mid-Oct., Tues.–Sat. 10–4, Sun. noon–5; closed Mon. and major holidays. Adults $8; seniors $6; children 6 and older $5; children under 6, free. More than 40,000 relics of Hunterdon County's industrial and agricultural history are on display in Clinton's landmark Red Mill, a local icon that appears often on official New Jersey maps and tourism posters. The vast collection of objects—from Victorian household items and clothing to farm equipment and tools—is displayed on a rotating basis in exhibit galleries spread across several floors. The four-story circa-1810 gristmill was built on the south branch of the Raritan River, where it produced wool, grain, talc, peach baskets, graphite, and plaster before closing in 1928. Other restored buildings in the 10-acre village include an old-fashioned general store, a blacksmith shop, a post office, the circa-1860 one-room Bunker Hill Schoolhouse, a replica log cabin and springhouse, and the remnants of a 19th-century limestone quarry. This is a popular location for Civil War reenactments, music festivals, car shows, militia musters, and seasonal events (see *Special Events*).

National Park Service photo by T. Winslow

DURING THE AMERICAN REVOLUTION THE FORD MANSION IN MORRISTOWN
NATIONAL HISTORICAL PARK SERVED AS GEORGE WASHINGTON'S HEADQUARTERS
FROM DECEMBER 1779 TO JUNE 1780.

MORRISTOWN NATIONAL HISTORICAL PARK

(headquarters: 973-539-2016; Jockey Hollow Visitor Center: 973-543-4030;
www.nps.gov/morr), 30 Washington Place, Morristown. Open year-round, daily
9–5; closed Thanksgiving, Christmas, and New Year's Day. Museum admission
$4. The site where George Washington and his Continental army spent the bit-
ter winter of 1779–80 during the American Revolution is the first national historical park in America. Washington chose the rolling hills southwest of
Morristown for their advantageous location, close to British-occupied New
York City.

George and Martha Washington stayed at Jacob Ford Jr.'s newly built
Georgian-style mansion that winter. Ford was a prominent mill-, mine-, and
forge owner; he was also a colonel in the New Jersey militia. He died before

Hunterdon Museum of Art (908-735-8415; www.hunterdonartmuseum.org),
Seven Lower Center St., Clinton. Gallery open Tues.–Sun. 11–5; closed Mon.
Admission $5. A highly regarded contemporary art museum housed in a 19th-cen-
tury fieldstone gristmill on the south branch of the Raritan River, opposite the Red
Mill Museum Village (see previous listing). Three galleries mount changing
exhibits of a wide variety of works, from paintings and lithographs to videos and
furniture. Art classes for adults and children, and outdoor art festivals and other
events are among the museum's offerings.

Washington arrived, so his wife hosted the general, his wife, and army officers. Ford Mansion was the nerve center of military operations, where Washington met with his officers and with diplomats, local residents, and even spies.

Meanwhile, eight infantry brigades spent the harsh winter crowded into tiny huts in the **Jockey Hollow** encampment, the "wintering ground" for more than 10,000 Continental soldiers. Some 600 acres of forest were cleared to build enough shelters. In December 1779, most soldiers were still sleeping in tents; but by February, as many as 1,200 log huts lined the hills. The shelters were cramped and conditions generally deplorable. Soldiers were forced to steal food from local farms; some soldiers simply deserted. The ones that stayed spent 7 grueling months at Jockey Hollow. Today tours, reenactments, and special events are held year-round at the site of the winter encampment, where visitors can see five reconstructed soldiers' huts. Most of the park's 400,000 annual visitors come for Jockey Hollow's 27 miles of hiking and equestrian trails; there's also an auto tour on a 2-mile loop road.

At the same time, Major General Arthur St. Clair and his officers used Henry and Mary Cooper Wick's 18th-century farmhouse as their winter headquarters. The 1,400-acre **Wick Farm** was the central command center for St. Clair's 2,000 Pennsylvania soldiers. Henry Wick was a volunteer with the Morris County cavalry during the war, so his wife and daughter lived on the farm during the encampment. According to legend, young Temperance Wick once hid her horse inside the farmhouse to keep it from being taken by Continental troops. Programs and tours are often held at the house and in its period herb garden.

In the spring of 1777, Washington ordered troops to build a fort on top of **Mount Kemble** to protect Morristown from a potential British invasion. The attack never came and, according to legend, the soldiers who built the structure called it Fort Nonsense because they doubted its strategic value, even suggesting the general ordered the project simply to give them something to do. Today the earthen fort is gone, but stones mark the location of the walls, a period cannon rests at the site, and the view from the 597-foot peak of Mount Kemble is lovely.

Shippen Manor Museum (908-453-4381), Eight Belvidere Ave., Oxford. Open on the first and second Sun. of each month, 1–4; closed on major holidays. Admission $3. A gracious circa-1754 Georgian-style stone mansion owned by William and Joseph Shippen—doctors, brothers, and gentlemen farmers from a prominent Philadelphia family. They founded **Oxford Furnace,** the area's biggest ironworks and employer, on their 4,000-acre estate. Pick up a brochure that describes a self-guided walking tour of the Oxford Furnace industrial historic district. You can also take a docent-guided tour of the 18th-century ironmasters' residence, or explore it on your own. Summer lawn concerts, military encampments, and an annual heritage festival are held at the museum throughout the year (see *Special Events*).

Morris Museum (973-971-3700; www.morrismuseum.org), Six Normandy Heights Rd., Morristown. Open Wed., Fri., and Sat. 11–5; Thurs. 11–8; Sun. 1–5; closed Mon., Tues., and major holidays. Adults $10; seniors and children $7; free admission Thursday 5–8. A 1912 Georgian-style mansion is home to one of New Jersey's largest museums, a staggering collection of some 48,000 pieces acquired over the past century. Today they fill an eclectic mix of permanent and changing exhibits—Native American artifacts, dinosaurs and fossils, rocks and minerals, dolls and toys, vintage clothing, 19th- and 20th-century American and European painting and sculpture, and visual and performing arts, to name just a few. The museum shop has a good selection of quality items, and the **Bickford Theatre** mounts musicals, dramas, and comedies.

Macculloch Hall Historical Museum (973-538-2404; www.macullochhall.org), 45 Macculloch Ave., Morristown. Open for tours Sun., Wed., and Thurs. 1–4; group visits at other times by appointment. Admission by donation. This early-19th-century Federal-style brick mansion is considered one of New Jersey's finest historic house museums, with 10 period rooms and four galleries with changing exhibits. It was built for **George P. Macculloch, "the Father of the Morris Canal."** The Scottish immigrant and entrepreneur was one of the masterminds behind the world-famous engineering marvel, which stretched 102 miles across northern New Jersey from the Delaware River to the Hudson River, built to quickly haul Pennsylvania coal and iron to New York City. Local philanthropist **W. Parsons Todd** acquired the Old House, as it was known by Macculloch's descendants, in 1949. In time, he restored it to its original 19th-century magnificence and filled it with his considerable collection of 18th- and 19th-century English and American art and antiques. The museum is perhaps best known for Todd's treasure trove of paintings, letters, drawings, and political cartoons by **Thomas Nast.** The artist who created the modern image of Santa Claus, Uncle Sam, the Republican Elephant, and the Democratic Donkey was the country's leading political cartoonist in the 19th century; his sharp wit was an influential force in the turbulent world of poli-

UNITED STATES GOLF ASSOCIATION MUSEUM AND ARCHIVES (908-234-2300; www.usgamuseum.com), 77 Liberty Corner Rd., Far Hills. Open Tues.–Sun. 10–5; closed Mon. and major holidays. Adults $7; children 13–17, $3.50; children 12 and under, free. The rich history of golf is on display at **Golf House,** the Georgian mansion that headquarters the United States Golf Association (USGA), an organization dating to 1894. More notably, it's home to the world's largest collection of golf equipment, memorabilia, books, photos, art, and artifacts, featured in changing and permanent exhibits that trace the development of the game. The museum's most unusual piece is perhaps the famous "moon club," the folding 6-iron Admiral Alan Shepard Jr. took to the moon during his *Apollo XIV* mission in 1971. There's also vintage equipment, clubs used by USGA champions, and a replica club maker's studio. A theater shows continuous classic footage of the game's most famous players, and special rooms are devoted to golf greats Francis Ouimet, Ben Hogan, and Bobby Jones.

tics. The Nast collection spans 50 years, from his first drawings as a teenager to a sketch he completed before leaving on the diplomatic mission to South America from which he would never return (he died in Ecuador of yellow fever in 1902). The mansion's 2-acre seasonally blooming garden, planted since the mid-1700s, is the oldest in Morris County. Today it has been restored with original plantings and 40 varieties of heirloom roses.

The Stickley Museum at Craftsman Farms (973-540-1165; www.stickley museum.org), 2352 Rt. 10 West, Parsippany. Grounds open year-round, dawn to dusk. Guided house tours Apr. through mid-Nov., Wed.–Fri. noon–3; Sat. and Sun. 11–4; mid-Nov. through Mar., Sat. and Sun. 11–4. Adults $6; seniors and students $5. Pioneering architect and furniture designer Gustav Stickley was a leader in the Arts and Crafts movement that swept America in the early 1900s. Stickley became famous for the clean lines and simple, straightforward design of his finely built Craftsman homes and mission-style furniture. Culturally, the movement was a dramatic rebellion against the formality and the excesses of the Victorian period. For many, fine craftsmanship was a welcome departure from the Victorian era's mass production of low-quality decorative objects. Stickley's unique T-shaped log house is the only residence he designed for his own use; today it's a national historic landmark. Construction began in 1911 with local fieldstone and chestnut logs, natural materials intended to blend into the surroundings. Exhibits feature relics from the Arts and Crafts movement; the museum shop sells contemporary crafts, books, and gifts.

TROUT HATCHERY ✔ **Pequest Trout Hatchery and Natural Resources Education Center** (908-637-4125), 605 Pequest Rd. (Rt. 46), Oxford. Open Mon.–Fri. 10–4; closed holidays. Free admission. Ask about the year-round schedule of programs on wildlife and natural resource issues. Take a self-guided tour of the fish hatchery, where more than 600,000 brook trout, rainbow trout, and brown trout are raised each year for release in more than 200 of New Jersey's lakes and rivers. A 15-minute video explains the trout-rearing process, from gathering eggs to stocking waterways. In addition to the hatchery, the state Department of Environmental Protection maintains an education center with interactive displays, an exhibit on New Jersey's endangered wildlife, and films on the state's natural resources. Outside there are picnic areas and hiking trails, including a self-guided interpretive nature trail.

✳ To Do

BALLOONING **In Flight Balloon Adventures** (888-301-2383; www.balloonnj .com), 23 Belvidere Ave., Clinton. Open daily year-round. Reservations are required. A variety of scenic hot-air balloon rides over the rural hills near Spruce Run Reservoir. Special trips for groups and couples include bed & breakfast getaways, sunrise and sunset trips, and dinner flights.

Sky Sweeper Balloon Adventures (800-462-3201), off I-78, Clinton. Open daily year-round. Reservations are recommended. Scenic hot-air balloon flights launch at sunrise and sunset just west of Clinton, and float over picturesque Hunterdon County. When skies are clear, views of the Manhattan skyline can often be seen.

Alexandria Balloon Flights (888-468-2477; www.njballooning.com), Sky Manor Airport, 42 Sky Manor Rd. (off Rt. 615), Pittstown. Reservations are recommended, especially for sunset trips on weekends. Scenic champagne balloon flights over the rolling hills and rural farmland of Hunterdon County. Trips leave around dawn and just before sunset, weather permitting.

Balloons Aloft (908-996-3333; 866-800-4386; www.njballoon.com), Sky Manor Airport, 42 Sky Manor Rd. (off Rt. 615), Pittstown. Reservations are required. Champagne and continental breakfast for sunrise flights; champagne and hors d'oeuvres after sunset trips. Rides last about 1 hour, depending on wind conditions. The airport has a restaurant and a gift shop.

Hunterdon Ballooning Inc. (908-788-5415; www.hunterdonballooning.com), 111 Locktown–Flemington Rd., Flemington. Reservations are required—at least 2 weeks in advance for weekends, a week in advance for weekday trips. Scenic hot-air balloon champagne flights over rural Hunterdon County's hills, farms, and villages. Trips last about 45 minutes and launch around dawn and sunset.

Tewksbury Balloon Adventures (908-439-3320; www.tewksburyballoon.com), 29 Oldwick Rd., Whitehouse Station. Open daily May–Oct. Hot-air balloon trips over northwestern New Jersey's rural farms and hills since 1972.

BICYCLING **The Morris County Parks Commission** (973-326-7600) maintains two multi-use recreational trails that are pleasant for bicycling, and ideal for beginners and for families with children. These popular trails can be very busy on weekends. In Morris Township, you can reach the **Patriot's Path Recreation Trail** from Inamere Road and Lake Valley Road; call for locations of other access points. The 20-mile-long Patriot's Path links trails in several local, county, state, and federal parks from Morristown to Mendham and Bernardsville. The surface ranges from crushed stone to gravel or dirt, mixed with some paved sections and the cinder beds of old rail lines. The **Traction Line Recreation Trail** runs from Morristown to Madison through **Morristown National Historical Park** (see sidebar, page 192) on the abandoned trolley line of the Morris County Traction Company. The 2.5-mile paved path parallels New Jersey Transit's Morris & Essex Lines. In Morristown, you can access the trail on Morris Avenue at I-287.

Some state and local parks in this region open their trails to mountain bikes, including **Spruce Run State Recreation Area** (908-638-8572) in Clinton, **Voorhees State Park** (908-638-6969) in Glen Gardner, **Lewis Morris County Park** (973-326-7600) in Morris Township, and **Round Valley Recreation Area** (908-236-6355) in Lebanon.

In Hillsborough, you can pedal through the sprawling **Duke Farms** (908-722-3700; www.dukefarms.org) estate (see sidebar, page 203). Twilight and Saturday morning guided excursions on a seven-mile loop through the landscape are offered from spring to fall.

BOATING **Silas Condict County Park** (973-326-7600), 53 East Hanover Ave., Kinnelon. The picturesque lake at this park named for a local Revolutionary War hero has a boat dock. On weekends and holidays from Memorial Day weekend to Labor Day, visitors can rent rowboats and paddleboats.

Round Valley Reservoir (908-236-6355), at Round Valley Recreation Area, 1220 Lebanon–Stanton Rd. (Rt. 629), Lebanon. There's a public launch for sailboats, motorboats, and canoes.

Spruce Run State Recreation Area (908-638-8572; boat rentals: 908-638-8234), One Van Syckels Rd., Clinton. Because of its favorable wind conditions, **Spruce Run Reservoir** is a mecca for sailboarders and sailors; a local sailing club hosts many events on the water. Canoes and small motorboats are also allowed on the reservoir; all boats must launch from the public ramp at the day-use area.

Schooley's Mountain County Park (908-876-4294), 91 E. Springtown Rd. (off Rt. 517), Washington Township. Rowboats and paddleboats can be rented from the boathouse on **Lake George** on weekends from Memorial Day to Labor Day.

FISHING Spruce Run Reservoir (908-638-8572), Spruce Run State Recreation Area, One Van Syckels Rd., Clinton. The reservoir, along with **Mulhockaway Creek** and **Spruce Run Creek,** is home to nearly 30 species of fish. The state division of fish, game, and wildlife stocks the waters with striped bass, northern pike, and trout; native species include catfish, largemouth bass, carp, and yellow perch.

Round Valley Reservoir (908-236-6355), at Round Valley Recreation Area, 1220 Lebanon–Stanton Rd. (Rt. 629), Lebanon. There are close to 20 species of fish in the reservoir, including native lake trout, largemouth and smallmouth bass, and the brown and rainbow trout that are stocked every year.

Allamuchy Pond (908-852-3790), Allamuchy Mountain State Park, 800 Willow Grove St., Hackettstown. Fishing for warm-water species, including perch, pickerel, sunfish, and largemouth bass.

Black River (908-638-6969), Hacklebarney State Park, 119 Hacklebarney Rd., Long Valley. Trout fishing in the Black River Gorge on the Black River and two of its tributaries, **Trout Brook** and **Rinehart Brook.** The Black River is stocked with trout in the spring. In addition to the state park access, you can also fish the Black River from the Black River Wildlife Management Area in Chester, and Black River Park in Chester, near the Cooper Gristmill.

The south branch of the **Raritan River** is considered one of the state's most pristine trout streams. You can access the river at South Branch Linear Park in Clinton and Flemington, at the Ken Lockwood Gorge Wildlife Management Area in Califon, and at Califon Park in Califon.

Stephens State Park (908-852-3790), 800 Willow Grove St., Hackettstown. The Musconectcong River is a boulder-strewn freshwater river that flows through the state park and is known locally as a prime trout-fishing stream. Each spring the New Jersey fish and wildlife division stocks the waters with rainbow trout, brook trout, and brown trout.

GOLF Several 18-hole golf courses in the region are open to the public, most with a clubhouse, pro shop, and driving range. Among them are **Beaver Brook Country Club** (908-735-4022), 25 Country Club Dr., Annandale; **Hillsborough Country Club** (908-369-3322), 146 Wertsville Rd., Flemington; **Royce Brook Golf Club** (888-434-3673), 201 Hamilton Rd., Hillsborough; **Flanders Valley Golf Course** (973-584-5382), 81 Pleasant Hill Rd., Flanders (36 holes); **Mine Brook Golf Club** (908-979-0366), 500 Schooley's Mountain Rd., Hackettstown; and **High Bridge Hills Golf Club** (908-638-5055), 203 Cregar Rd., High Bridge.

HIKING Round Valley Recreation Area (908-236-6355), at Round Valley Reservoir, 1220 Lebanon–Stanton Rd. (Rt. 629), Lebanon. Four marked trails cover a variety of terrain; all leave from the day-use area. Two mile-long trails wander gently through a pine forest; these pleasant walks are ideal for seniors or families with small children. Lower Cushetunk Trail is a 3-mile-long hike to the wilderness campsites at the eastern edge of the reservoir. The rugged Cushetunk Trail is a 9-mile out-and-back trail through the **Cushetunk Mountains** that passes through thick woods and open meadows. The steep and rocky terrain will challenge experienced hikers, mountain bikers, and equestrians.

Hacklebarney State Park (908-638-6969), 119 Hacklebarney Rd., Long Valley. Hiking trails in the park's rugged 465-acre natural area offer spectacular views of the Black River as it cascades over boulders in the **Black River Gorge,** a steep ravine whose slopes are thick with hemlocks. A trail leads down into the base of the ravine, where the cool and shady forest floor protects rare plant species such as leatherwood and Virginia pennywort. Other trails follow tributaries of the Black River, including Trout Brook, which has a **picturesque waterfall.**

Jockey Hollow (973-543-4030; 973-539-2016), Morristown National Historical Park, Tempe Wick Rd., Morristown. Pick up a trail map at the visitors center. An extensive 25-mile network of hiking trails traverses this park, where George Washington's Continental army spent the winter of 1779–80 (see sidebar, page 192). One of the more popular routes is the blue-blazed trail from the visitors center parking lot to the top of **Mount Kemble.** It's an easy to moderate 3-mile loop, and on clear days the spectacular view from the top of Mount Kemble includes the Manhattan skyline. Near the historic cannon are stones that mark the site of the Revolutionary War–era **"Fort Nonsense,"** which was built during the encampment of George Washington's Continental army during the winter of 1779–80.

Schooley's Mountain County Park (908-876-4294), 91 East Springtown Rd. (off Rt. 517), Long Valley. A popular hike in this Morris County park is to **the falls on Electric Brook.** From the park's Springtown Rd. entrance, walk along the road that goes around Lake George. Just before the dam, follow the blue-blazed Falling Waters trail (it's rocky in places) a short distance to the falls. From here, there are a few options: You can head back the way you came, but if you want to hike some more, continue past the falls to Patriot's Path. Follow this white-blazed trail to the right to the **Long Valley overlook.** At 892 feet, this isn't the park's highest elevation, but the views are rewarding. From here you can retrace your steps or continue past the overlook to the steep and rocky **Boulder Gorge Trail,** which will bring you back to Electric Brook and give you a different view of the falls. The trail will lead you back to the lodge near the parking lot where you began.

SPECTATOR SPORTS Island Dragway (908-637-6060; www.islanddragway .com), Main St. (Rt. 46 West), Great Meadows. Open Fri.–Sun., Mar.–Oct.; Sat. and Sun. in Nov. A family-owned drag strip operating here for 45 years. It's the smallest of New Jersey's three drag strips but offers a full schedule of drag-racing events.

Hamilton Farm (908-234-1251; www.uset.com), 1040 Pottersville Rd. (Rt. 512), Gladstone. The stable is home to the U.S. Equestrian Team, which trains Olympic and world-class athletes. The public is welcome to attend competitions, including show jumping and dressage, from April to October.

STARGAZING **Paul Robinson Observatory** (908-638-8500; www.njaa.org), Voorhees State Park, Observatory Rd. (off Rt. 513), Glen Gardner (see also *Green Space—State Parks*). Open Memorial Day through Oct. on Sat. evening and Sun. afternoon; shorter hours in the off-season. Admission by donation. The observatory was built in 1965 by the **New Jersey Astronomical Association.** Perched at 840 feet above sea level, it sits at the highest point in the park. The public is invited to observe the night sky through a massive 28-inch Newtonian reflector telescope—one of the largest privately owned telescopes in the state—and through several smaller scopes. The visitors center and space-education center have archives and changing astronomical exhibits, as well as regularly scheduled lectures and films on the cosmos.

SWIMMING ✄ **Round Valley Reservoir** (908-236-6355), at Round Valley Recreation Area, 1220 Lebanon–Stanton Rd. (Rt. 629), Lebanon. Lifeguards are on duty from Memorial Day weekend to Labor Day. The scenic 4,003-acre artificial lake has a sandy beach with restrooms, showers, and changing areas. Food and beach supplies are available in the concession building. Two playgrounds and volleyball nets are near the beach. Rafts, inner tubes, and other flotation devices are not allowed in the swimming area.

✄ **Spruce Run State Recreation Area** (908-638-8572), One Van Syckels Rd., Clinton. Swimming is allowed during the summer when lifeguards are on duty. The swimming beach has a concession area selling food and beach-related items, and the bathhouse has restrooms, changing areas, showers, and a first-aid station. Inner tubes, rafts, and other floats are not permitted.

TRAIN RIDE ✄ **Black River & Western Railroad** (908-782-9600; www .brrht.org), Rt. 12 and Stangl Rd., Flemington. Open May–Oct., Sat., Sun., and holidays. A nostalgic excursion through Hunterdon County on a restored steam- and diesel-powered locomotive. The 11-mile scenic round-trip between Ringoes and Flemington takes just over an hour. Excursions begin at the station in Turntable Junction, behind the Liberty Village Premium Outlets center. The train stops in Ringoes, where there's a **railroad museum** and picnic area. Special events include the **Railroad Days** celebration in summer and holiday trips with Santa at Christmas.

✳ Winter Sports

CROSS-COUNTRY SKIING Many state and local parks in this region offer their trails and open fields to cross-country skiers during the winter. You need to bring your own skis and equipment. These parks include **Hunterdon County Arboretum** (908-782-1158), Lebanon; **Spruce Run State Recreation Area** (908-638-8572), Clinton; **Round Valley Recreation Area** (908-236-6355), Lebanon; **Lewis Morris County Park** (973-326-7600), Mendham; **Bamboo Brook Outdoor Education Center** and **Willowwood Arboretum** (973-326-7600), Chester; **Hedden County Park** (973-326-7600) in Dover; **Frelinghuysen Arboretum** (973-326-7600), Morris Township. Morris County's two multi-use recreational trails, **Patriot's Path Recreational Trail** and the **Traction Line Recreational Trail,** are open to cross-country skiers.

ICE-SKATING ✍ **Hollydell Ice Arena** (609-582-1234), Hollydell Dr. and East Holly Ave., Washington Township. Skating parties, rentals, group lessons, and ice hockey.

✍ **Lewis Morris County Park** (973-326-7600), 270 Mendham Rd. (Rt. 24), Mendham. Ice-skating on Sunrise Lake.

✍ **William G. Mennen Sports Arena** (973-326-7650), 161 E. Hanover Ave., Morristown. Open year-round; call for public skating hours. This busy indoor facility—home to the **New Jersey Colonials** hockey club—offers 2-hour public skating sessions daily. The skate shop has rentals, and the snack bar has a fireplace to warm up by.

✍ **Hedden County Park** (973-326-7600), 124 Reservoir Ave., Dover. Ice-skating on the park's 6-acre lake; there's a fireplace near the lake that blazes for warmth during the skating season.

✳ Green Space

GARDENS Leonard J. Buck Garden (908-234-2677), 11 Layton Rd., Far Hills. Open Mon.–Fri. 10–4; Sat. 10–5; Sun. noon–5. Admission by donation. Leonard Buck was a geologist and trustee of the New York Botanical Gardens in the 1930s, and an avid gardener in his own right. When he wanted to plant a garden in a rugged glacial-stream valley running through his property, he envisioned naturalistic plantings that would grow in harmony with the landscape. The result is a stunning woodland garden—actually a variety of small, individual gardens—that blends naturally with rock outcroppings, ponds, and a woodland stream. The garden is beautiful any time of year, but in spring the azaleas, rhododendrons, and dogwoods put on a spectacular display.

Cross Estate Gardens (www.crossestategardens.org), Old Jockey Hollow Rd., Bernardsville. Open daily from sunrise to sunset. Free admission. This grand 1905 country estate was once the centerpiece of Queen Anne Farm, part of Bernardsville's famed "mountain colony" enclave of opulent summer mansions. The estate's second owners, W. Redmond and Julia Newbold Cross (Julia was president of the New York Horticultural Society), surrounded the house with lavish English country-style beds and borders. Today, brick walkways meander through a variety of beautiful gardens. There's a formal walled garden, a shade garden, a mountain laurel allée, borders of ornamental grasses, woodland plantings, and groves of shrubs and trees.

Willowwood Arboretum (973-326-7600), 300 Longview Rd., Chester. Open daily dawn to dusk. Free admission. A stately 1783 Federal-style mansion surrounded by two formal gardens and 130 acres of rolling farmland has been a public arboretum since 1950. This lovely spot was once known as Paradise Farm, but when brothers Robert and Henry Tubbs purchased the property in 1908 they renamed it for the abundance of willows that flourished here. The Tubbs brothers were well-known and respected gardeners in international horticultural circles, and friends and fellow gardeners from around the world introduced them to many of the rare and exotic species that still grow here. Today, more than 3,500 varieties of native and exotic plants, shrubs, and trees grow on the grounds. Walking paths meander through meadows and woodlands blanketed in wildflowers, among displays of lilacs and magnolias, and within theme gardens dotted with antique garden statuary.

FRELINGHUYSEN ARBORETUM

(973-326-7600; www.arboretumfriends.org), 53 East Hanover Ave., Whippany. The Haggerty Education Center is open daily 9–4:30; the grounds are open daily 9 AM–dusk. Guided tours from late Apr. to Oct., Sat. and Sun. at 2 PM. Free admission. Matilda Frelinghuysen donated her family's spectacular country estate—with its 19th-century Colonial Revival mansion and lovely formal gardens—as a public arboretum. The 127-acre summer estate, also known as the old Whippany Farm, is a nationally recognized horticultural center whose English-style landscape attracts both fledgling gardeners and professionals who come here for inspiration. Close to the mansion are flowering cherry and crabapple trees, a marsh meadow garden, dogwoods and peonies, gardens of ferns and roses, and well-manicured perennial borders. An assortment of more than a dozen home-demonstration gardens shows visitors how to design a four-season garden, water and rock gardens, and gardens that feature roses, vegetables, or evening blooms. Nature trails lead into the woodlands and open meadows, where you can see an extensive collection of labeled shrubs and trees, as well as ferns and wildflowers flourishing next to a cypress swamp. The blue trail passes between a long meadow and a cool hemlock and cedar forest to reach the Pinetum, a collection of evergreens from around the world, including pines, redwoods, and spruces. The Frelinghuysen Mansion is the headquarters of the **Morris County Parks Commission;** the **Haggerty Education Center** has a horticultural reference library and hosts horticulture programs, art and photography exhibits, and garden and flower shows, including the **New Jersey Daffodil Show** in April.

NATURAL AREAS Fairview Farm Wildlife Preserve (908-234-1852), 2121 Larger Cross Rd., Bedminster. Open daily from dawn to dusk. A picturesque former 170-acre farm is maintained by the Upper Raritan Watershed Association as a wildlife preserve. A 5-mile network of trails through the property is popular with hikers and birders. The meadows are a rich habitat for deer, fox, hawks, and several species of threatened and endangered animals. Painted turtles and a variety of bird species can be spotted at the pond, and butterflies and hummingbirds are often seen hovering around the gardens.

Scherman-Hoffman Sanctuary (908-766-5787), 11 Hardscrabble Rd., Bernardsville. Open daily from dawn to dusk. A pristine 276-acre tract of forest and open fields is home to more than 200 species of wildlife and maintained by the **New Jersey Audubon Society. The Patriot's Path Recreational Trail** links the sanctuary with Cross Estate Gardens and Jockey Hollow in Morristown National Historical Park, and Lewis Morris County Park. A nature store sells an interesting selection of books and gifts, an exhibit room has displays of native birds, and an observation window looks out on the often-busy bird feeding area.

NATURE CENTER **Bamboo Brook Outdoor Education Center** (973-326-7600), 170 Longview Rd., Chester. The education center is adjacent to Willowwood Arboretum (see *Gardens*). Fields, forests, and a formal garden are spread across a 100-acre natural area that once was the home of Martha Brookes Hutcheson, one of the country's first female landscape architects. She designed the garden here in the late 1920s with native and exotic plants, water features, and a white cedar allée. The walking trails that follow the brook and wind through the fields are peaceful and lovely.

PARKS ✂ **Schooley's Mountain County Park** (908-876-4294), 91 E. Springtown Rd. (off Rt. 517), Washington Township. Another link in the Morris County Park Commission's extensive network of open space. This 782-acre park is named for the Schooleys, a prominent Quaker family who settled in the area around 1790. It was a resort area at the turn of the 20th century, then a YMCA camp from the 1920s until the 1950s. There's a network of blazed trails for hiking and horseback riding; other activities include boating and ice-skating on Lake George, and sledding and cross-country skiing. Kids love the playground and ball fields.

✂ **Lewis Morris County Park** (973-326-7600), 270 Mendham Rd. (Rt. 24), Mendham. A picturesque community park named for Lewis Morris, who was elected the first governor of the New Jersey colony in 1738. Swimming, fishing, and boating at the Sunrise Lake Beach Club, several miles of hiking trails, and sledding and cross-country skiing through the open fields in winter.

STATE PARKS **Round Valley Recreation Area** (908-236-6355), at Round Valley Reservoir, 1220 Lebanon–Stanton Rd. (Rt. 629), Lebanon. The reservoir was built in the 1950s to meet New Jersey's rapidly growing demand for water; the recreation area opened to the public in 1977. Today the 1,288-acre site attracts a variety of outdoors enthusiasts. People can cross-country ski, picnic, and stay overnight at wilderness campsites. Trails are open for hiking, horseback riding, and mountain biking. The centerpiece is undoubtedly the 4,003-acre reservoir, which offers swimming, paddling, boating, fishing—even scuba diving and skin diving.

Spruce Run State Recreation Area (908-638-8572), One Van Syckels Rd., Clinton. A 600-acre multi-use recreation area 4 miles north of the center of Clinton. Most visitors come for the swimming, boating, sailing, windsurfing, and fishing at the 1,290-acre reservoir; there's also camping and picnicking.

Voorhees State Park (908-638-6969), 251 County Rd. (Rt. 513), Glen Gardner. Former New Jersey governor Foster Voorhees donated Hill Acres, his 325-acre northern Hunterdon County farm, to the state in 1929. Today the 640-acre state park offers picnicking, hiking, cross-country skiing, camping, mountain biking, a fitness circuit with exercise stations—even stargazing. The New Jersey Astronomical Association runs the park's **Robinson Observatory** (see *To Do—Stargazing*), which hosts viewing sessions and programs open to the public.

Hacklebarney State Park (908-638-6969), 119 Hacklebarney Rd., Chester. A couple stories explain the unusual name of this rugged 892-acre forest. One cites the Lenni-Lenape term *hackiboni*, meaning "bonfire." Another dates to the 19th century, when the area was mined for iron ore. According to local legend, a foreman named Barney Tracey was oft-harassed by his workers. Their practice of "heckling Barney" might have evolved into the name Hacklebarney. From the parking area, you can hike to the Black River, which rushes past boulders as it slices through a spectacular hemlock-lined ravine, a favorite haunt of local anglers. Even on summer's hottest days, the **Black River Gorge** is refreshingly cool, thanks to the magnificent dark green hemlocks that block sunlight from the steep walls of the ravine. This quiet park is home to several endangered and threatened species, including barred owls and Cooper's hawks.

Stephens State Park (908-852-3790), 800 Willow Grove St., Hackettstown. A 727-acre state park just north of Hackettstown. Remnants of the 19th-century **Morris Canal,** including one of its locks and part of the canal towpath, can be seen at Saxton Falls. Trout fishing on the **Musconectcong River,** 6 miles of multi-use trails, and rustic campsites.

DUKE FARMS

(908-722-3700; www.dukefarms.org), 80 Rt. 206 South, Hillsborough. A variety of guided tours are available for the manor house, grounds, gardens, and greenhouses; reservations are required. The greenhouses at Duke Farms have been open to visitors since 1964; it wasn't until 2003—a decade after Doris Duke's death—that the public could sneak a glimpse at the world of one of the wealthiest families in history. Doris Duke was the only child of James Buchanan "Buck" Duke, the tycoon who founded the American Tobacco Company and endowed Duke University. In 1893 he began creating Duke Farms, the sprawling 2,700-acre oasis that his daughter inherited, along with his vast fortune, when he died in 1925. Throughout the rest of her life, Duke would be known as the Richest Little Girl in the World. The heiress's famous reclusion surrounded her with an air of mystery; she was rarely seen in public, even though she owned houses around the world and spent much of her life globe-trotting with the 20th-century jet set.

The Duke Farms Foundation has maintained Duke's suburban oasis of privilege in the decade since her death, and access to the grounds is tightly controlled. A 700-acre area of Duke Farms is open to the public in a guided trolley tour that winds through the parklike grounds with ornate fountains and statuary reminiscent of England's beautifully manicured parks. The fine landscaping includes lakes, artificial waterfalls, grottoes, a couple million trees, and meadows and woodlands laced with stone walls and bridges. The grounds are similar in design to New York City's Central Park, but nearly three times the size. During the winter, the collection of greenhouses known as **Duke Gardens** is open to the public. The displays are akin to a horticultural world tour, lush with rare and exotic specimens from Duke's travels around the world.

✳ Lodging

HOTELS

In Morristown 07960

&. **Hyatt Morristown at Headquarters Plaza** (973-647-1234; 888-591-1234; http://morristown.hyatt.com), Three Headquarters Plaza. A sharp downtown hotel that's frequented by business travelers; it's also a convenient base for visitors coming to see Morristown's historic sites. The 256 recently renovated guest rooms are each traditionally decorated; all are equipped with large work desks, high-speed Internet connections, CD players, robes, and the like. The two luxurious suites are richly outfitted in luxe fabrics, gleaming mahogany, and overstuffed furniture, and add such amenities as living rooms and dining rooms, and wet bars. The health club—with an indoor running track, a pool, personal trainers, and massage therapy—is a few notches above the usual hotel fitness amenities. The **Eclectic Grill** serves contemporary American cuisine in modern surroundings, while **Qube Lounge** is a popular hangout. Continental breakfast. $129 and up.

&. **The Madison Hotel** (973-285-1800; 800-526-0729; www.themadison hotel.com), One Convent Rd. With its glass-enclosed conservatory, sweeping landscaped grounds, and stylishly appointed guest rooms, this Georgian-style, cupola-topped hotel is one of Morristown's premier places to spend the night. Its location next to the New Jersey Transit train station makes this an ideal base for visitors from Manhattan and for others not traveling by car. The lobby is at once polished and cozy, especially inviting when the fireplace is blazing. The 185 guest rooms and suites aren't overly luxurious, but they're individually furnished in traditional décor and tasteful reproduction

antiques. The hotel restaurant, **Rod's Steak and Seafood Grille,** serves very good steakhouse fare in handsome surroundings of polished brass and gleaming wood. For a unique treat, dine in one of the elegantly restored turn-of-the-20th-century parlor cars. Other amenities include a fitness center and an indoor pool. Continental breakfast is served near the fireplace in the lobby. $119–369.

&. **The Westin Governor Morris** (973-539-7300; 866-716-8117; www .westingovernormorris.com), Two Whippany Rd. The new lobby of Morristown's Westin is more reminiscent of a chic boutique-style hotel than a link in a national chain. A $15 million facelift has given the 224 guest rooms and suites an urbane polish with thoughtful, luxurious touches. Bathrooms are outfitted with oversized towels, plush robes, Aveda bath products, and dual showerheads. The suites have upgraded amenities like Bose sound systems, plasma TVs, and living-room and dining areas. The beautifully designed hotel restaurant, **Copeland,** offers upscale New American cuisine, an extensive wine list, a Sunday seafood brunch, and a top-notch raw bar. Everything else has been thought of: a top-of-the-line fitness center, airport limousine service, a pool, and a handy 24-hour business center. There's a chic new martini lounge, and a cappuccino and espresso bar in the lobby. Service is warm and accommodating, from the bellhops and porters to the front-desk staff. $129 and up.

Best Western Morristown Inn (973-540-1700; reservations: 800-688-7474; www.bestwesternnewjersey.com), 270 South St. Location, location, location is all-important in the hotel business; this one is close to the Morristown Green and a blink away from I-287. Better yet, this Best Western is a cupola-topped Georgian-style building that looks nothing like a chain hotel. The lobby and common areas, with colonial antiques, rich drapes, wall sconces, and a portrait of George Washington over the mantel, suggest a classic country inn. The 60 guest rooms are clean and comfortable, done up in traditional, colonial, or contemporary décor; efficiencies and a suite have spacious sitting areas. Amenities include an exercise room with sauna, laundry facilities, and a restaurant serving breakfast, lunch, and dinner daily. Continental breakfast. $179 and up.

Elsewhere

🦞 🍴 ♿ **Hampton Inn** (908-284-9427), 14 Royal Rd., Flemington 08822. This standard no-frills hotel is clean and comfortable, a perfectly good option for families or visitors coming to Flemington's renowned factory outlets. The 83 guest rooms have the expected amenities—cable TV, phone, and air-conditioning. The heated indoor pool, whirlpool spa, and fitness center make this hotel stand out among other similarly priced options. Continental breakfast. $119 and up.

🍴 ♿ **Holiday Inn Select** (908-735-5111; www.hisclinton.com), 111 W. Main St. (Rt. 173), Clinton 08809. This Holiday Inn is nice enough, but the little touches are what set it apart from its run-of-the-mill peers. How many chain hotels offer front-porch rocking chairs, lemonade, coffee, and fresh-from-the-oven cookies? Details like these, plus a warm and friendly staff, make this hotel as charming as the historic Victorian town it's a part of. The 142 guest rooms and minisuites have the usual amenities, plus nice extras like robes, morning newspaper delivery, and nightly turndown service. The country-style **Main Street Garden Café** serves three meals daily (brunch on Sunday), and guests and locals socialize at **Jitterbugs nightclub.**

There's a fitness center, high-speed Internet access in all common areas, and an indoor heated pool with Jacuzzi. $110 and up.

INN ♿ ⊗ **The Bernards Inn** (908-766-0002; 888-766-0002; www.bernardsinn.com), 27 Mine Brook Rd., Bernardsville 07924. A charming 1907 inn across from the Bernardsville train station that's part mission-style hotel, part Edwardian manor house, and part historic American country inn. The décor, service, and amenities are reminiscent of a small European luxury hotel. The antiques-filled common areas are elegant and relaxing, with nice moldings and other historic architectural details lending a charming touch. The 20 guest rooms and suites are up to the same standards: tastefully decorated with pastoral-themed artwork, country antiques, and imported linens. All are equipped with plush robes, stocked minibar, two phones, and large work desks. Then there are the complimentary shoe shines and the nightly turndown service with chocolates. The historic country inn and restaurant is known for its gourmet American cuisine and award-winning wine list (see *Dining Out*). Continental breakfast is served in the lovely Garden Room. $249 and up.

BED & BREAKFASTS Main Street Manor Bed & Breakfast (908-782-4928; www.mainstreetmanor.com), 194 Main St., Flemington 08822. Donna and Ken Arold's neat and trim 1901 Queen Anne–style Victorian manor is an elegant gem in Flemington's historic district. Outdoors are a cozy front porch and beautifully landscaped grounds. Inside is all turn-of-the-20th-century charm and elegance, from the foyer's crystal chandelier and grand staircase to the formal front parlor with fireplace and quaint side parlor with antiques, books, and sherry. The five guest rooms have an elegant B&B feel, with antiques, handmade quilts, and walls dressed up in florals and toile, plus modern amenities like private bath and central air-conditioning. Each room offers something unique, such as a four-poster rice bed, a stained-glass window, or a private porch. Full breakfast is served in the paneled dining room. $130–215.

☙ ⚲ Silver Maple Organic Farm Bed & Breakfast (908-237-2192; www.silvermaplefarmbandb.com), 483 Sergeantsville Rd., Flemington 08822. A lovely historic stone farmhouse with a homey vibe that invites relaxation. Innkeeper Steven Noll offers five guest rooms and suites with unique décor inspired by world travels and local history. Outside, there's a tennis court, swimming pool, hot tub, even resident goats. Full breakfast. $99–175.

⁀ı⁀ The Riverside Victorian (908-238-0400; www.riversidevictorian .com), 66 Leigh St., Clinton 08809. This circa-1870 mansard-style Victorian, which sits a block from the shops and restaurants in historic Clinton, is a warm and relaxing bed & breakfast. The six guest rooms (two can be combined into a suite) are decorated with carefully chosen period furnishings, family heirlooms, and reproductions, and original details like wide-plank floors. One guest room has an ornately carved Gothic-style bed; others have wardrobes, armoires, or fanciful cast-iron beds. Modern amenities like TV, Wi-Fi Internet access, air-conditioning, and phone are in each room, and all but one have private baths. Guests like to gather on the front porch for afternoon refreshments, and business travelers have use of a fax machine and laser printers. A full breakfast features the inn's signature Irish soda bread. $95–130.

♿ Holly Thorn House Bed and Breakfast (908-534-1616; www .hollythornhouse.com), 143 Readington Rd., Whitehouse Station 08889. Guests are always amazed that this lovely inn, a replica of an elegant English manor house, was once a decidedly unsophisticated cow barn. There are four guest rooms and one suite; some done in light and sunny pastels, others decorated in rich, dark hues. All are outfitted in antiques and amenities that include private bath, phone, desks, and data ports. Guests like to congregate in the massive great room, which has two fireplaces, a piano, an open kitchen, and walls hung with family photos and paintings. A sitting room with leather sofas has a warm, clubby feel. The billiard room has a complimentary wine bar, and the library is well stocked with books, games, and snacks. Outside, guests can relax in and around the in-ground pool, or stroll the herb garden and expansive grounds. The inn is not appropriate for children under 14. Full breakfast. $125–175.

The Neighbour House Bed & Breakfast (908-876-3519; www.neigh bourhouse.com), 143 West Mill Rd. (Rt. 513), Long Valley 07853. This elegant Greek Revival–style farmhouse on the New Jersey Register of Historic Places is a quiet and romantic retreat. The house is perched high on a sloping lawn with distant views of the south branch of the Raritan River, and the 3-acre grounds are surrounded by 800 acres of farmland. Unlike most rural farmhouses, it boasts the graceful architecture and charming details of a finely crafted home, from the eight fireplaces and a grand staircase to the folding shutters, heart pine floors, and pocket doors. Innkeepers Rafi and Iris Kadosh offer four guest rooms that are lovely and tastefully furnished. They often host small weddings, as well as businesspeople who are relocating to the area. The brick veranda and the columned porch are relaxing places to enjoy complimentary snacks and refreshments; inside, the common areas are cozy and spacious. Full breakfast. $85–135.

✧ **The Raritan Inn at Middle Valley** (908-832-6869; www.raritaninn .com), 528 Rt. 513, Califon. A charming 275-year-old inn noted for its use of green technology, from geothermal heating to solar energy. Five guest rooms are outfitted in antiques and luxe linens; all have air conditioning and a private bath, some have a gas stove or spa tub. Outside, the south branch of the Raritan River runs through the property; guests can also walk to the Columbia Trail, a popular destination for hiking, biking, and cross-country skiing. Full breakfast. $139–279.

CAMPGROUNDS Round Valley Reservoir (908-236-6355), at Round Valley Recreation Area, 1220 Lebanon–Stanton Rd. (Rt. 629), Lebanon. Open Apr.–Oct. Reservations are recommended for holiday weekends. Outdoors enthusiasts who want to experience wilderness camping without leaving New Jersey love these primitive campsites at the far eastern shore of the reservoir. There are only two ways of getting here—on foot or by boat—which is just fine, since most people who camp here aren't fans of crowded campgrounds anyway. By trail it's a 3-mile hike to get to the closest site; from there, 84 other sites (with fire rings only) are scattered throughout the woods. If you require modern amenities, planned activities, and your car close by, this definitely is not the place for you. But if you savor peace and quiet, and don't mind hauling in your gear, then this is a real find. Sites $17.

♪ **Spruce Run State Recreation Area** (908-638-8572), One Van Syckels Rd., Clinton. Open Apr.–Oct. The 67 family campsites at Spruce Run Reservoir are conveniently close to the boat-rental facilities. Sites have picnic tables and grills; modern restrooms and

THE NEIGHBOUR HOUSE BED AND BREAKFAST IN LONG VALLEY IS A METICULOUSLY PRESERVED GREEK REVIVAL–STYLE FARMHOUSE SURROUNDED BY 800 ACRES OF RURAL FARMLAND IN MORRIS COUNTY.

Photo courtesy of Iris Kadosh

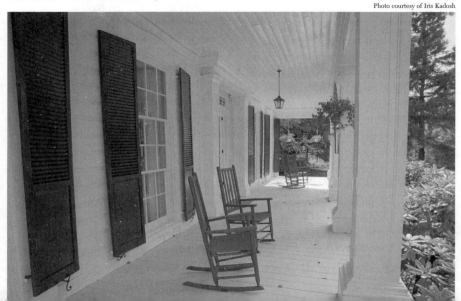

showers are located at either end of the campground. $15.

Voorhees State Park (908-638-6969), 251 County Rd. (Rt. 513), Glen Gardner. Open Apr.–Oct. Reservations are required for group campsites. Fifty wooded sites for tents, tent trailers, and RVs—all equipped with picnic tables and fire rings. Drinking water, modern restrooms with hot showers, a dumping station for trailers, and a playground are all on-site. Two group camping areas hold 50 campers each. Individual sites $20; group sites $50.

Stephens State Park (908-852-3790), 800 Willow Grove St., Hackettstown. Open Apr.–Oct. Forty campsites are ideal for tents or small trailers. Amenities include fire rings, picnic tables, and flush toilets within walking distance of the sites. Sites $20.

✳ Where to Eat

DINING OUT

In Flemington

55 Main (908-284-1551; www.55main .com), 55 Main St. Open for lunch Mon.–Fri.; dinner Wed.–Sat.; closed Sun. Reservations are recommended. Chef Jonas Gold's creative New American cuisine is full of the kind of unique culinary twists that make dining out fun. A recent menu featured tortellini stuffed with Vidalia onion and goat cheese, a salad of grilled Jersey peaches with prosciutto and blue cheese, garlic and lime-roasted chicken, and homemade pumpkin cheesecake. BYOB. $15–26.

Fusion (908-788-7772; www.fusionon main.com), 123 Main St. Open daily for lunch and dinner. A stylish antiques-filled space serving adventurous Asian fusion dishes with French influences. Foodies rave about and flock to this place for dishes like wok-seared venison, grilled wild boar, and

lemon-crusted lobster. All the traditional pan-Asian flavors—tamarind, curry, ginger, garlic, coriander—are well represented. BYOB. $22–32.

Matt's Red Rooster Grill (908-788-7050; www.mattsredroostergrill.com), 22 Bloomfield Ave. Open for dinner Tues.–Sun.; closed Mon. Reservations are recommended. A restored Victorian where American cuisine is described as upscale comfort food. The kitchen's creative side emerges in the cedar-planked roasted salmon with a soy honey and pomegranate glaze, and the coconut-crusted beef short ribs. Dessert is a short selection of satisfying endings, from apple-caramel cheesecake to vanilla bread pudding. In good weather, try for one of the sought-after tables on the rambling porch. BYOB. $22–34.

In Bernardsville

Due Terre (908-221-0040; www.due terre.com), 107 Morristown Rd. Open for lunch Mon.–Fri.; dinner daily. Contemporary Italian cuisine in an elegant setting. Regardless of what meal you eat here, this is top-notch dining at its finest. The specialty handmade pastas are a must; a variety of tasting menus are also available. Luscious desserts are made in house. $18–35.

Le Petit Château (908-766-4544), 121 Claremont Rd. Open for lunch Tues.–Fri.; dinner Tues.–Sun.; closed Mon. Reservations are recommended; jackets are required at dinner. Le Petit Château is widely considered one of New Jersey's most elegant and sophisticated hot spots for its big-city-quality fine dining in a well-heeled suburban setting. Chef-owner Scott Cutaneo's menu blends haute French classics and contemporary dishes. Start with pan-seared foie gras, then indulge in filet mignon or roasted seafood or game. The wine cellar is stocked with a staggering collection of French, American, and international vintages—some 22,000 bottles in all. There's an intimate bar that's popular with locals. $23–38.

The Bernards Inn (908-766-0002; www.bernardsinn.com), 27 Mine Brook Rd. Open daily for dinner; reservations are recommended. Chef Edward Stone's innovative New American dishes are known for their unique French accents, seasonal fresh ingredients, and fine sauces. The elegant restaurant in a romantic Edwardian inn (see *Lodging—Inn*) is furnished with centuries-old portraits. You can choose from two dining rooms—one plush and sophisticated, the other rustic and handsome with a fieldstone fireplace and gleaming mahogany. Entrées might include slow-roasted Atlantic salmon with sun-dried tomato ragout and saffron gnocchi, or prime tenderloin of beef with polenta and vegetable terrine. The signature crème brûlée and the fallen chocolate soufflé cake are both excellent ways to end a meal. The convivial bar features live jazz pianists in the evening. More than 8,000 French and American vintages in the award-winning wine cellar. $28–44.

In Morristown
& **The Grand Café** (973-540-9444; www.thegrandcafe.com), 42 Washington St. Lunch Mon.–Fri.; dinner Mon.–Sat.; closed Sun. and holidays. Reservations suggested. An elegant and sophisticated dining room paired with flawless French-American cuisine makes for one of Morristown's most memorable culinary experiences. You can choose from the highbrow opulence and formality of the dining room, or eat outdoors in the intimate flower-filled allée, when the weather allows. Dinner could begin with escargot baked in a puff pastry shell, or mussels in a lemongrass shallot broth. Move on to the New York sirloin steak with

asparagus and truffle demi-glace, or roasted Long Island duck in a honey-ginger glaze. Save room for their signature Grand Marnier soufflé. A perennial favorite for more than 20 years. $25–42.

& **Pazzo Pazzo** (973-898-6606; www.pazzopazzo.com), 74 Speedwell Ave. Open for lunch Mon.–Fri.; daily for dinner. Reservations are suggested. This chic Italian eatery is right off the Morristown Green, but you'll feel like you're in a sleek Manhattan restaurant once you step inside. The bar is as hip as the young patrons who frequent it. The dining room, with its gold sculptures, modern artwork, and soft light given off by hundreds of candles, is sophisticated and romantic. The menu revolves around pasta, gourmet pizza, and other regional Italian dishes. $26–50.

Mehndi (973-871-2323; www.mehtani restaurantgroup.com), 88 Headquarters Plaza, Three Speedwell Ave. Mehndi offers some of the best—and priciest—Indian cuisine in the state, and a glam setting to boot. Traditional dishes, ranging from mildly seasoned to fiery-hot, win high marks for authenticity and tops readers' polls on a regular basis. Next door, SM23 is a stylish lounge where martinis come in flavors ranging from grilled pineapple and cardamom to apple and thyme. If noise and crowds are not your penchant, dine early to avoid the thriving bar scene. $18–35.

Elsewhere
The Perryville Inn (908-730-9500; www.theperryvilleinn.com), 167 Perryville Rd., Perryville. Open for lunch Tues.–Fri.; dinner Tues.–Sun.; closed Mon. Classic French and contemporary American fare in a restored 19th-century Federal-style tavern. Today, a series of old-fashioned and romantic dining rooms features cuisine that gets

high marks for its elegant touches, artistic presentation, and fresh ingredients. Dinner could start with jumbo lump crabmeat salad with chilled gazpacho vinaigrette, or grilled lamb atop a potato goat cheese pancake. You can't go wrong with the entrées, but the oven-dried tomato and lobster ravioli and the Maine lobster with bread pudding and vanilla chive sauce are among the kitchen's signature dishes. Finish with something from the seasonal dessert menu, which might offer hazelnut truffle Napoleon or a caramelized banana tart. $24–35.

La Casa Bianca (908-534-8384; www.lacasabianca.net), 144 Main St., Whitehouse Station. Open for lunch Tues.–Fri.; dinner Tues.–Sun.; closed Mon. For truly authentic cuisine from Italy and the Mediterranean, step through the door of this former post office into a casual and friendly space with trattoria-like charm. Dishes are familiar, delicious, and generously portioned: calamari, seafood, pasta, veal. Tuscan-style brick-oven pizzas are works of art: inventive toppings include broccoli rabe, scallops, and grilled squash. $15–30.

Pluckemin Inn (908-658–9292; www.pluckemininn.com), 359 Rt. 202 South, Bedminster. Open for lunch Mon.–Fri.; dinner Tues.–Sat.; closed Sun. The original inn of the same name welcomed 19th-century guests; today, an elegant Napa-inspired interior sets the tone for exquisite contemporary American cuisine. The kitchen shows off its smarts, and creativity, in dishes like king salmon with chestnut-porcini puree; braised lamb shank with olive puree and gremolata; and sautéed tilefish with sweet and sour broth. They take wine seriously here: more than 15,000 bottles are dramatically displayed in a soaring glass tower. $29–46.

Dora (908-735-4171), 17 Main St., Clinton. Open daily for lunch and dinner. Loyal patrons fill this center-of-town eatery. It has all the charm of a warm and friendly Italian trattoria, complete with local artwork, and crisp blue-and-white décor. The inventive pasta dishes are a must; traditional Italian dishes range from veal scaloppini to chicken Florentine. $15–27.

EATING OUT

In Flemington

Shaker Café (908-782-6610; www.shakercafe.com), 31 Main St. Open daily for breakfast, lunch, and dinner. An eclectic spot known for its creative twists on breakfast and lunch café standards (think omelets stuffed with ham, Brie, and raspberry jam; southwestern chicken wraps with guacamole and chipotle mayo). Mexican dishes at dinner. $5–12.

🐟 **Blue Fish Grill** (908-237-4528; www.thebluefishgrill.com), Nine Central Ave. Whether you eat in or take out, this casual eatery is a good place to rest and recharge during a busy day of shopping at Flemington's outlets. From the menu at the open kitchen, you order your choice of fresh fish, which is cooked on a wood-fired grill. Other dishes range from fish and chips to seafood tacos. BYOB. $8–12.

Max's Bistro (908-782-5947), 161 Main St. Open for lunch Tues.–Fri.; dinner Tues.–Sun.; closed Mon. A casual bistro-style eatery serving well-prepared Italian classics in the dining room or outside in the sidewalk café. Dinner entrées are divided equally— half feature traditional pasta dishes like capellini *putanesca* with plum tomatoes, anchovies, capers, olives, garlic, and basil. The other half is chicken, veal, shrimp, and steak. They sell New Jersey wines, or you can bring a bottle of your own. $17–25.

Elsewhere

& **Cloves** (973-347-9290), 61 International Dr., Budd Lake. Open Wed.–Mon. for lunch and dinner; closed Tues. A casual Indian restaurant that's simply and pleasantly furnished with traditional Indian décor. From the dining room you can see the busy glass-enclosed kitchen with its tandoori ovens busily churning out the cuisine known for its exotic and earthy spices in varying degrees of intensity. To start, you can try the hearty lentil soup or one of the traditional samosas, stuffed with spicy ground lamb or a filling of potatoes and peas. The extensive menu features chicken korma, tender chicken in a light and creamy sauce with cashews; tandoori lamb as well as the more traditional tandoori chicken; and the not-for-the-timid lamb vindaloo in a fiery tomato sauce. Vegetarians will appreciate the ample selection of meatless dishes. BYOB. $14–29.

& **Long Valley Pub and Brewery** (908-876-1122; www.longvalleypuband brewery.com), One Fairmount Rd. (Rt. 517), Long Valley. Open daily for lunch and dinner; Sun. brunch. A beautiful 200-year-old stone barn built by some of the region's earliest settlers at the foot of Schooley's Mountain is a lively pub and brewery. Their handcrafted ales—German Valley Amber, Grist Mill Golden Ale, and Black River Brown Ale—pay tribute to local icons. Eat outside in the summer, by the fireplace in winter. The American menu features traditional pub fare alongside creative dishes. Desserts are a collection of homey favorites, from the carrot cake with cream cheese frosting to the deep-dish apple crumb pie and warm brownie sundae. $11–30.

The Old Riverhouse (908-735-4141; www.oldriverhouserestaurant.com), 49 Main St., Clinton. Open daily for breakfast, lunch, and dinner. Reserva-

tions are recommended for dinner on weekends. A casual café whose terrace is a prime spot in warm weather, with its lovely view of the Raritan River and Clinton's historic Red Mill. Among the many great salads at lunch, a standout is the Café Salad, made with grapes, apples, toasted pecans, blue cheese, and bacon with mandarin orange dressing. Dinner is dressed up a bit, with satisfying and well-prepared steak, chicken, and seafood dishes. $14–28.

Sally Lunn's (908-879-7731; www .sallylunns.com), 15 Perry St., Chester. Open Tues.–Sun.; closed Mon. This charming restaurant and Victorian tearoom has been a downtown gem for a quarter century. An interesting selection of light meals includes homemade soups, fresh salads, and sandwiches. For an unusual treat, try the traditional English-pub fare, from cottage pie to cornish pasties stuffed with ground lamb, turnips, potatoes, and leeks. Save room for one of the homemade desserts, especially the buttermilk scones (the recipe is a secret, so don't ask) that come with clotted cream and strawberries. Don't leave without browsing through the tea-related antiques, china, and collectibles. $8–14.

Redwoods Grill & Bar (908-879-7909; www.redwoodsgrillandbar.com), 459 Main St., Chester. Open for lunch Mon.–Sat.; dinner Fri.–Sun. They try to make everyone happy here, and according to regulars, they pull it off. There's light pub fare, plus a long repertoire of steaks, chops, and seafood prepared on a six-foot-long wood-burning grill. In season, the patio is a delightful place to dine. $16–33.

Black Horse Tavern (973-543-7300), One W. Main St., Mendham. Dinner in the tavern Tues.–Sun.; lunch and dinner daily in the pub; Sun. brunch. In the 18th century, this was a busy stagecoach stop; today it's a charming tavern and pub serving traditional and hearty American cuisine. You might start with smoked brook trout, chilled lobster cocktail, or baked stuffed clams. Dinner ranges from shrimp and lobster scampi to a variety of dry-aged steaks and grilled seafood. Locals frequent the convivial pub, which serves burgers, pizzas, seafood, and snacks, and hosts live music on weekends. $16–29. *The Butler's Pantry Trackside* (908-234-9404), at the Far Hills train station, Rt. 202 North, Far Hills. Open Mon.–Sat. for breakfast, lunch, and dinner; closed Sun. A casual spot that bustles with commuters during the day, and packs in families later on for fried seafood platters and interesting specials at dinner. $10–20.

Frank and Sheri's (973-285-5554), 19–21 Market St. (US 202 North), Morristown. Serving lunch Mon.–Fri.; dinner Mon.–Sat.; closed Sun. Reservations are recommended. A stylish and casual eatery whose specialty is the authentic cuisine of Portugal. Start with *alentejana,* a soup made with fresh garlic, crusty bread, and a poached egg; or grilled *chourico,* homemade smoked Portuguese sausage with port wine and brandy. Paella comes two ways—with seafood, or with lobster, chicken, and Portuguese sausage. Among the homemade desserts, their specialty is *beirao,* milk chocolate espresso mousse topped with white chocolate mousse and Portuguese herbal orange liqueur. BYOB. $16–27.

SNACKS

In Flemington
Basil Bandwagon (908-788-5737; www.basilbandwagon.com), 276 Rt. 202/31. A natural food store and café offering good-for-you vegan and vegetarian dishes. Smoothies come jam-packed with amino acids and antioxidants, by way of organic fruits and veggies. The store has a complete line of health food products and vitamins, as well as fresh produce and organic eggs.

Vienna Bake Shop (908-788-2677), 26 Main St. The warm and sweet smell of freshly baked delicacies drifts out the door of this quaint little shop in the heart of town. They're known for beautiful special-occasion cakes, but there's a lot to offer someone wandering in. Homemade cheesecakes, tortes (sacher, mocha, linzer), cookies, and chocolate and vanilla cakes with rich hazelnut butter cream are among the temptations on display.

Lisa's Deli & Restaurant (908-782-5253), 21 Rt. 12. Open Mon.–Sat. from 7 AM; closed Sun. A good stop for a hearty bacon-and-eggs breakfast, and deli classics like club sandwiches, hot and cold subs, burgers, hot dogs, and salads at lunch. Generous and filling portions, popular with locals. $5–12.

Country Griddle (908-788-8779), 285 Rt. 202. Open daily for breakfast, lunch, and dinner. An old-fashioned family diner that's extremely popular on weekends. At breakfast, you can choose from the usual morning meal standbys, or go for it with omelets stuffed with goat cheese, asparagus, and other creative fillings. $8–15.

Elsewhere
Wasabi (908-238-9300), Five Main St., Clinton. A tiny eatery that gets raves for its top-notch sushi and huge specialty rolls. Most regulars come in for take-out. BYOB.

Coco Luxe (908-781-5554; www.cocoluxepastry.com), 161 Main St., Peapack. Open Tues.–Sun.; closed Mon. Food-savvy locals flock to this boutique French pastry shop for its decadent cookies, cakes, tarts, and croissants. Not in the mood for sweets? There's a menu of sandwiches, quiche, and soups, as well as espresso and tea.

In Morristown
L'Appetito (973-539-8844), 23 Washington St. Open Mon.–Fri. 7–4; closed Sat. and Sun. Daily soups and specials. Eat in or take to go. This little eatery bustles in the morning with the gourmet coffee-and-pastry crowd hurrying off to work; the breakfast sandwiches are delicious and filling. Lunch is equally busy, with gourmet salads, sandwiches, and wraps. The sloppy joes are a triple stack of ham or roast beef with turkey, topped with Swiss cheese, coleslaw, and homemade Russian dressing on rye.

COFFEE AND TEA

In Clinton
Dani & Jonny's Cappuccino (908-735-7737), Three Main St. As you'd expect, you can get a really good cappuccino here, but that's not nearly all. They offer homemade pastries and healthy snacks, and a full menu of coffees, teas, and juices.

Citispot Coffee and Tea House (908-735-0307), 51 Main St. This heart-of-the-village shop is a good place to start the day, if only for its homey baked goods and excellent coffee. You can also get a good cup of tea or cocoa.

In Chester
La Sierra Coffee Roasters (908-879-0313), 35 Perry St. A variety of delicious international and flavored coffees, specialty coffee drinks, and yummy treats to go with them.

K.C.'s Coffee Place (908-879-9932), 56 Main St. A gourmet coffee bar that's fun, friendly, and popular with locals as well as shoppers from out of town. A full menu of lattes, espressos, cappuccinos, and other hot and cold coffee and tea drinks. Coffee-related items and lovely gift baskets for sale throughout the shop.

✴ Entertainment
ARTS CENTERS Printmaking Council of New Jersey (908-725-2110; www.printnj.org), 440 River Rd., Branchburg. An arts center devoted to regional artists pursuing the fine art of printmaking. Changing themed and juried exhibitions of original prints and artwork. In addition to the exhibits, many other programs are open to the public, from printmaking demonstrations and guided gallery tours to printmaking classes and workshops and the center's annual holiday sale.

Myhelan Cultural Arts Center (908-876-5959), 18 Schooley's Mountain Rd., Long Valley. A local arts organization that celebrates the "cultural mosaic of our world," mainly through art, music, and film. The year-round schedule features art exhibits, concerts, workshops, and an annual independent-film festival.

THEATER Famous Trials Theater (908-782-2610; www.famoustrials .com), 13 Chapel View Dr., Flemington. The kidnapping and murder of aviator Charles A. Lindbergh's infant son, and the subsequent conviction and execution of Bruno Hauptmann, made for one of history's most notorious courtroom sagas. The drama unfolded at the Hunterdon County Courthouse in Flemington, where today actors bring the Trial of the Century back to life in a dramatic reenactment. The play is based on original court transcripts, and the 6-week trial is whittled down to 2 hours, making for a dramatic, fast-paced performance. The audience sits in the original public stalls; seats are even available in the jury box. Other historic courtroom dramas and fictional plays are also presented, and tours of the courthouse and county jail are offered. A unique theater experience.

Hunterdon Hills Playhouse (800-447-7313; www.hhplayhouse.com), 88 Rt. 173 West, Perryville. A former 80-acre country estate is a popular professional dinner theater featuring New York–area actors on stage. A full year-round season of musicals, comedies, musical revues, and holiday performances. Dinner is traditional American fare—roast turkey with stuffing, Yankee pot roast, and roast leg of lamb, followed by a buffet of homemade desserts.

✐ **Bickford Theatre** (973-971-3706; www.morrismuseum.org), Six Normandy Heights Rd., Morristown. Award-winning dramas, comedies, and musicals presented by a local professional company in a 312-seat theater at the **Morris Museum**. A year-round schedule of performances for adults and children.

✐ **Community Theatre** (973-539-8008; www.mayoarts.org), at the Mayo Center for the Performing Arts, 100 South St., Morristown. One of New Jersey's premier arts centers for both local and touring performance artists and companies. A full season with a wide range of offerings: pop, blues, jazz, and classical artists, as well as comedy, dance, theater, symphony orchestras, children's productions, and holiday shows.

Dover Little Theatre (973-328-9202; www.doverlittletheatre.org), Elliot St., Dover. A longtime community theater group—established in 1933—gives local actors, producers, directors, and volunteers the opportunity to be involved in theater, whether on stage or behind the scenes. Four plays a year

are presented in Dover's intimate 108-seat theater.

Lackland Performing Arts Center (908-979-0900; www.centenarystage co.org), Centenary College, 400 Jefferson St., Hackettstown. When this new state-of-the-art facility opens in late 2009, it will be home to the **Centenary Stage Company,** a nonprofit professional-equity theater group with a year-round schedule of classic revivals and new works.

✐ **Pax Amicus Castle Theatre** (973-691-2100; www.paxamicus.com), 23 Lake Shore Dr., Budd Lake. This 200-seat theater was built on the shore of New Jersey's largest spring-fed lake in the 1940s. When it was renovated in the 1970s, the new façade was modeled after a 15th-century French château, hence the name. The **Pax Amicus** (Latin for "Peace, Friend") arts organization, founded in 1970, presents Broadway and off-Broadway revivals and comedies, and children's productions.

✐ **The Growing Stage** (973-347-4946; www.growingstage.com), at the Palace Theatre, Seven Ledgewood Ave. (Rt. 183), Netcong. In its early days, the circa-1919 Palace Theatre offered vaudeville and silent films. In the 1930s new works were tested on audiences here before heading to Broadway. Today, a theater group of professional and community actors stages high-quality productions for young people and families here, and has done so for more than 20 years. The season includes Shakespeare's plays, staged versions of novels, and family classics like *Alice in Wonderland* and *Babes in Toyland.*

✳ **Selective Shopping**

ANTIQUES Washington Antique Center (908-689-1900), 44 E. Washington Ave. (Rt. 57), Washington.

Antique furniture (primarily 19th- and 20th-century; some reproductions), as well as pottery, art, china, linens, rugs, and collectibles.

Long Valley Antiques (908-876-1333; www.longvalleyantiques.com), 20 Schooleys Mountain Rd., Long Valley. Fine vintage furniture, plus an eclectic assortment of antiques, architectural elements, and reasonably priced collectibles.

Chester Antique Mall (908-879-7836), 427 Rt. 24, Chester. More than two-dozen dealers sell a little of everything here. You can spend a good part of the day attempting to peruse it all, from furniture, antiques, and linens to jewelry, china, glassware, and primitives.

Chester Antique Center (908-879-4331), 32 Grove St., Chester. More than 30 dealers offer an extensive collection of American antique furniture, plus a variety of unique vintage lighting, including oil lamps, early electric chandeliers, and gasoliers.

Pegasus Antiques (908-879-4792), 98 Main St., Chester. A shop crammed with almost everything, from antique clocks and toys to Depression glass, silver, and vintage bottles and signs. A fun place to browse and reminisce.

ART GALLERIES Clinton Falls Frame and Art (908-735-7220), Main and Lehigh streets, Clinton. As the name implies, this gallery is next to Clinton's picturesque falls. Original works and limited-edition prints by local artists, as well as fine handcrafted furniture, gifts, and framing and restoration services.

Johnson Gallery (908-234-2345), 2020 Burnt Mills Rd., Bedminster. The **Somerset Art Association** hosts several exhibitions a year, featuring the work of local and regional artists. Galleries, workshops, classes. Call for a schedule.

Grace Fine Art Gallery (973-538-6700), 142 South St., Morristown. An elegant gallery with an extensive collection of American and European oil paintings, with an emphasis on 20th-century impressionists. Four rooms in the gallery display more than 100 paintings.

BOOKSTORES Twice Told Tales (908-788-9094), 14 Bloomfield Ave., Flemington. Marilyn Theile's bookshop carries a good selection of new titles plus thousands of used books. Trade-ins are accepted. She also runs **Moonstone Mystery Bookstore,** a bookshop next door that specializes in mysteries, and used and new titles.

Clinton Book Shop (908-735-8811), 33 Main St., Clinton. An independently owned bookstore at the heart of Clinton's Victorian downtown. They have an impressive selection of books on New Jersey, from glossy coffee-table books with Garden State images to travel guides, books on New Jersey history, and titles published by local independent publishers.

Old Book Shop (973-538-1210), Four John St., Morristown. Browsing the old books, magazines, postcards, and catalogs is akin to a trip back in time. Used books, some rare and collectible.

The Book Worm (908-766-4599), 99 Claremont Rd., Bernardsville. A friendly shop with lots of events and book signings.

FACTORY OUTLETS ✿ Liberty Village Premium Outlets (908-782-8550), One Church St., Flemington. Open daily. This is the first factory-outlet village of its kind in the country. A former artisan's village now has more than 60 shops in an old-fashioned setting, and hosts a summer music series featuring New Jersey musicians. Top designer retailers include Brooks

Brothers, Calvin Klein, Tommy Hilfiger, L.L. Bean, Jones New York, and an L.L. Bean Factory Store. The outlets are conveniently within walking distance of Flemington's downtown restaurants. Next to Liberty Village is **Turntable Junction** (908-782-7071), another complex of specialty shops, outlets, and eateries at the heart of Flemington's historic district.

FLEA MARKET Dover Flea Market (973-989-7870), 18 W. Blackwell St., Dover. Open Apr.–Dec., Sun. 9–4. A large outdoor flea market stretching through several blocks in historic downtown Dover.

SPECIAL SHOPS

In Long Valley
Schooley's Mountain General Store (908-852-4943), 250 Schooley's Mountain Rd., Long Valley. The oldest continuously operating general store in New Jersey. The old-fashioned redclapboard building with a wide front porch houses a post office and store with a deli, gifts, and groceries.

In Chester
Black River Candy Shoppe (908-879-1233), 44 Main St. An old-time sweet shop featuring more than 600 varieties of candy—from gourmet lollipops and Lindt chocolates to rock candy and saltwater taffy. Customers love the huge selection of nostalgic candy—when was the last time you had red-hot dollars, candy buttons, circus peanuts, or a Sugar Daddy? They stock them all, plus hard-to-find goodies like chocolate-covered molasses paddles and Fruit Stripe gum. More than 200 varieties of bulk candy can be bought by the pound; other goodies fill nostalgic gift tins.

✿ **Mangel's Homemade Chocolates** (908-879-5640), 115 Rt. 206. Since 1959, Mangel's has been making old-

fashioned chocolates by hand using natural ingredients and their own tried-and-true recipes. Today the shelves in this local institution are lined with chocolate-dipped cherries, truffles, and other traditional favorites alongside novelty and seasonal chocolates. Vintage photos of Chester and work by local artists on the walls add to the charm and nostalgia in this quaint shop, which is frequented by many longtime regulars.

Chester Crafts and Collectibles (908-879-2900), 28 Main St. Fine crafts by more than 70 regional artisans are on display in a gallery-like setting. The ever-changing selection of unique handcrafted pieces includes furniture, sculpture, framed art, jewelry, pottery, clothing, porcelain dolls, and traditional crafts.

The Whistling Elk (908-879-2425), 44 Main St. A sophisticated shop with European country-style home furnishings, art, and decorative objects. You can find beautiful antique and reproduction furniture here, but the real gems are the accessories that lend a home its signature style. Luxurious throws, pillows, and bedding; elegant lamps and chandeliers; and scented aromatherapy candles are some of the finds.

Clothes Call (908-879-4130; www.clothescall.com), 58 Main St. Stylish women's apparel and accessories.

Caravan Traders (908-879-2064), Perry St. An eclectic collection of gifts and home décor from around the world. They specialize in handmade American and European furnishings, from armoires and cedar chests to rustic farm tables, plus a huge selection of high-quality area rugs.

Elsewhere
Enjou Chocolat (973–993-9090), Eight DeHart St., Morristown. Check

your willpower at the door. The shelves of this shop are lined with all manner of gourmet temptations—some homey and nostalgic, others delicate works of edible art—all smothered in gourmet chocolate. Truffles, nonpareils, chocolate-covered Oreos and pretzels, and chocolate caramel apples by the piece, by the pound, or arranged in a basket for the ultimate gift.

Oldwick General Store (908-439-2642), 57 Main St., Oldwick. A local gathering spot for homemade meals, baked goods, and the morning papers.

FARMS AND GARDENS

In Long Valley

✿ **Ort Farms** (908-876-3351), 25 Bartley Rd. Open daily 9–7. An old dairy farm—in the family for six generations—now grows tomatoes, corn, and other fruits and vegetables for sale at the farm stand. In the fall, look for the enormous pumpkin sign—that's when gourds, Indian corn, apples, and hardy mums are ready, and visitors can take a free tractor-pulled hayride to the pumpkin patch. Kids love the donkey, goats, lamb, ducks, and other residents of the barnyard.

✿ **Valley Shepherd Creamery** (908-876-3200; www.valleyshepherd.com), 50 Fairmount Rd. Shop open Thurs.–Sun. 10–5; guided tours Sat. and Sun. From some 460 sheep come artisan cheeses using Old World techniques and recipes. Ask about monthly cheese-making classes. A small shop is stocked with cheeses, wool blankets, and sheepskins. Tours touch on milking, cheese making, and sheep shearing. In the fall, a wagon ride takes visitors to the cave where cheese is aged.

In Chester

✿ **Alstede Farms** (908-879-7189; www.alstedefarms.com), 84 Rt. 513.

Open year-round, Mon.–Sat. 9–6; Sun. 10–5. A lovely family farm where you can pick your own strawberries, peaches, raspberries, pumpkins, and apples in-season. They grow and sell a staggering amount of fruits and vegetables, from the earliest asparagus in May to the berries, peaches, corn, and tomatoes of summer to autumn's gourds, Indian corn, and winter squash. Kids love the friendly farm animals and, in autumn, the corn maze and weekend hayrides. The farm store also sells freshly baked fruit pies as well as annuals and perennials.

✿ **Riamede Farm** (908-879-5353; www.riamede.com), 122 Oakdale Rd. Open daily 9–4:30 in fall. A scenic farm where you can pick your own apples in an old-fashioned 50-acre orchard, take a free weekend hay-wagon ride, pick pumpkins, and enjoy freshly pressed apple cider.

✿ **Stony Hill Farm Market and Gardens** (908-879-2696; www.stony hillgardens.com), Eight Rt. 24. Open daily 9–6. Two farms selling fruits, vegetables, and seasonal garden plants. There are 18,000 square feet of greenhouses spread across 40 acres, with the area's largest selection of orchids (as many as 700 in bloom at one time), as well as annuals and perennials from early spring well into summer. Pick-your-own pumpkins, plus hayrides and a massive corn maze (300,000 cornstalks and 10,000 feet of pathways) in the fall; poinsettias, wreaths, and Christmas trees around the holidays.

Elsewhere

Melick's Town Farm (908-439-2318; www.melickstownfarm.com), 472 Rt. 523, Califon. Open Apr.–Dec., daily 9–6. The farm stand features the bounty of the fields, from fruits and vegetables to pies, apple cider, honey, jams, farm-fresh eggs, and other dairy products. In-season, you can pick your own peaches (summer), and apples and pumpkins (fall).

⚘ **Donaldson Farms** (908-852-9122; www. donaldsonfarms.net), 345 Allen Rd., Hackettstown. Open May–Nov. Pick your own strawberries, flowers, and pumpkins, or simply visit the farm stand for just-picked produce.

Peaceful Valley Orchards (**908-730-7748**; www.peacefulvalleyorchards .com), 150 Pittstown Rd., Pittstown. Pick your own strawberries in the spring; the farm market sells freshly baked pies and produce from the fields.

Wightman's Farms (973-425-1727; www.wightmansfarms.com), 1111 Mt. Kemble Rd., Morristown. Depending on the season, you can pick your own apples and peaches, or explore a corn maze. The farm market is well stocked with produce, baked goods, and locally produced food items, from honey to wine.

✳ Special Events

February: **Morristown Antiques Show** (973-682-4844), at the National Guard Armory, 430 Western Ave., Morristown.

April: **New Jersey Daffodil Show** (973-326-7600), Frelinghuysen Arboretum, Morristown. Hundreds of daffodils and other flowers in competition and on display. **Civil War Era Weekend** (908-735-4101), Red Mill Museum Village, Clinton. Union and Confederate reenactors set up camps, demonstrate weaponry, and other period skills; live Civil War–era music.

May: **Warren County Heritage Festival** (908-453-4381), Oxford. The **Raritan River Music Festival** (908-213-1100) takes place at various locations in northwest New Jersey. Musicians play at historic venues in a variety of country settings.

June: **Morristown Fine Arts and Crafts Festival** (973-267-1722), Vail Mansion, Morristown. More than 100 artists and artisans. **Bonnie Brae Polo Classic** (908-580-0051), Fieldview Farm, Pittstown. **Spring Chester Craft Show** (973-377-3260), Municipal Field, Chester. One of the top crafts shows in the country, featuring more than 150 regional artisans and their fine art and country crafts, from furniture and handmade paper to watercolors and pottery. Entertainment and live crafts demonstrations.

July: ⚘ **New Jersey Festival of Ballooning** (800-468-2479), Solberg Airport, Readington. This long-weekend celebration, which features more than 125 hot-air balloons and some 175,000 spectators, is the largest summertime balloon festival in North America.

WELL-SWEEP HERB FARM (908-852-5390; www.wellsweep .com), 205 Mount Bethel Rd., Port Murray. Open year-round, Mon.–Sat. 9–5; closed Sun. and holidays. Call ahead Jan.–Mar. The Hyde family's nationally known gardens boast a staggering variety of herbs and one of the largest herb collections in the country. They grow around 1,700 varieties of herbs here, from common kitchen herbs to many rare and exotic species. There are more than 100 kinds of thyme and more than 80 types of fragrant lavender. Brick walkways meander past a variety of display areas, from butterfly gardens and rock gardens to perennial gardens. The quaint garden shop has dried wreaths, garden supplies, and books on herbs and gardening.

During the day, family activities, live entertainment, and an arts-and-crafts marketplace; at night fireworks and a stunning balloon glow.

🖉 **Independence Day Celebration** (973-539-2016), Morristown. Fireworks, family activities, and a public reading of the Declaration of Independence.

🖉 **Family Film and Fun Festival** (908-284-0121), Flemington. On Wednesdays in July, a family film on the Flemington Green follows live music. Spectators bring lawn chairs, blankets, and picnics.

🖉 **Morris County Fair** (973-285-8301), Chubb Park, Rt. 24, Chester. A traditional fair with agricultural exhibits, horse shows, a petting barn, a pet show, a talent show, hayrides, and kiddie rides.

August: 🖉 **Anderson House Seafood Festival** (908-534-5818), Deer Path Park, Flemington. Live entertainment, crafts, children's rides, and lots of seafood, from lobster and clam cakes to fish-and-chips.

🖉 **Scandinavian Fest** (610-868-7525; www.scanfest.org), Vasa Park, Budd Lake. Entertainment, kids' activities, crafts, and food.

September: 🖉 **Fall Festival** (973-455-1133), Morristown. Community celebration with food, entertainment, rides, and historic exhibits on and around the Morristown Green. **Fall Chester Craft Show** (973-377-3260), Municipal Field, Main St., Chester.

October: **Apple Harvest Festival,** Chester.

December: **Holly Walk** (973-539-2016), Morristown National Historical Park, Morristown. Tour historic homes decorated for the holidays and depicting traditional holiday festivities of the 18th, 19th, and early 20th centuries. **Holiday Crafts at Morristown** (973-455-0338), at the National Guard Armory, Morristown. Nationally recognized artists and artisans.

🖉 **First Night Morris County** (973-455-0708), on the Morristown Green, Morristown. Family activities and entertainment on New Year's Eve.

The Delaware River Valley

RIVER TOWNS:
MILFORD TO TITUSVILLE

THE TRENTON AND CAMDEN AREA

THE DELAWARE BAY REGION

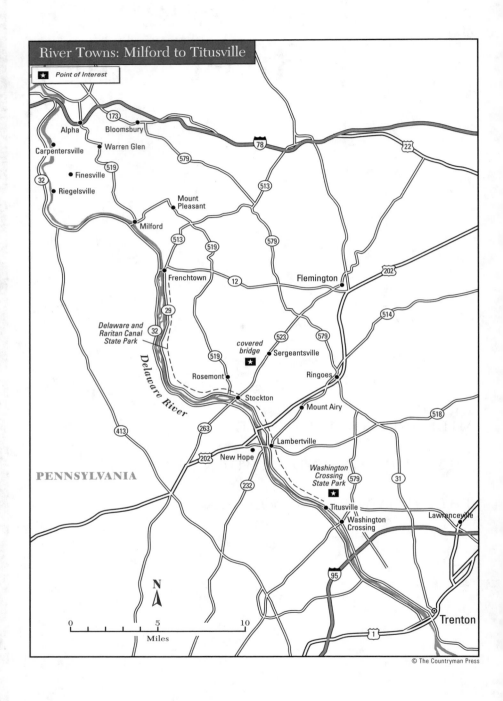

River Towns: Milford to Titusville

★ Point of Interest

RIVER TOWNS:
MILFORD TO TITUSVILLE

The quaint historic towns along the Delaware River's east bank are beloved destinations for regular visitors, a pleasant surprise to those stumbling upon them for the first time. Centuries-old Milford, Frenchtown, Stockton, and Lambertville are strung like jewels between scenic Route 29 and the river. They're the kinds of places that challenge the well-worn clichés about New Jersey; although it's the most densely populated state in America, here the Garden State resembles a quiet corner of New England.

The hills of Hunterdon and Warren counties comprise a rural tableau of crop fields and forest, nothing like the urbanized New Jersey implanted in most people's minds. A network of lovely back roads winds past quintessential country scenes of hay fields, dairy farms, and historic farmhouses, where drivers still share the road with tractors and other farm vehicles. Historic sites are plentiful here, too. You'll find places like Titusville's Howell Living History Farm, a circa-1900 horse-powered operation; and Washington Crossing State Park, where General George Washington and his Continental troops landed after their famous crossing of the icy Delaware on Christmas night 1776, a pivotal turning point in the Revolutionary War. But the places that draw thousands of visitors annually are the well-preserved downtown streets at the heart of New Jersey's riverside communities.

In many ways, these villages do not differ much from one another in character. People shop for antiques, dine, stroll, and admire grand old homes. Each one has a main thoroughfare called Bridge Street that predictably leads to a bridge that crosses to the Pennsylvania side of the river.

On the other hand, while Milford has a quaint one-street downtown, Lambertville's historic streets are lined with fine restaurants, upscale country inns, and coolly hip boutiques and coffeehouses that cater to city-slick weekenders who come to escape their frenetic world but don't want to rough it, per se. Stockton and Frenchtown are somewhere in between, achieving a comfortable mix of authentic rural charm with a hint of polish—bistros, art galleries, and friendly markets that cater to both locals and tourists.

On the fringes of these towns, the landscape is magnificent, and well worth exploring. At the very least, visitors should walk along the Delaware and Raritan Canal, the waterway that changed the face of this area when it was built by immigrants in 1832, bringing a world of commerce and industry to these rural farming communities. The abandoned railroad line along the river and canal stretches for 30 miles from Frenchtown south to Trenton, where it turns east and heads another 36 miles across the state to New Brunswick. Today, the canal is the centerpiece of New Jersey's longest state park, with a multi-use path shared by hikers, cyclists, and equestrians. Of course there's also the river, offering fishing, paddling, tubing, and rafting.

You cross a small bridge to reach the tiny hamlet of Milford, blessedly untouched by progress, and bordered by the Delaware River to the west and red shale cliffs to the east. Its tiny cemetery has headstones dating to the 1700s, and its main street is lined with antiques shops, unique stores, a bakery, and a handful of markets. On foot you can head down Bridge Street, cross the bridge to the Pennsylvania side, and return—a nice stroll to enjoy after dinner at the town's authentic British pub or at the charming seafood house by the railroad tracks.

Like Milford, Frenchtown is an old-fashioned square-mile riverfront town. Grover Cleveland, the only Garden State native to be president, once fished the waters here. Most of the art galleries and boutiques are in historic buildings clustered on Bridge and Race streets. It's a laid-back blue-collar town that's popular with antiques hunters, cyclists who ride the canal path, and foodies who haunt the gourmet markets and upscale bistros. Side streets are lined with centuries-old clapboard homes, Greek Revival and Italianate mansions, and historic mills. Visitors who flock here on weekends can spend the night in a bed & breakfast or inn.

In the 18th century, this spot had little more than a ferry service across the Delaware when Paul Henri Mallot-Prevost came to Sherrod's Ferry (as it was called then). The French-speaking Swiss immigrant and banker, who was also an officer in the Revolutionary War–era French army, had fled to America and wound up on the Delaware River. He bought land, persuaded family and friends to settle here, and built houses and commercial buildings (including the Frenchtown Inn on Bridge Street), and the town was eventually named for the language spoken by its new residents. Frenchtown prospered as a mill town after the Civil War, evidenced by its many Victorian homes, now proudly restored. Race Street is named for the millrace that channeled water through here 200 years ago to fuel the town's mills, which produced peach baskets, ceramics, furniture, and wagon wheels. Today, a summertime Bastille Day celebration honors Frenchtown's founding father.

In Stockton, visiting gourmands and honeymooners haunt the lovely Stockton Inn, whose charming environs inspired a famous Broadway tune. Prallsville Mills, a complex of lovingly preserved historic mills and barns, is an active performing-arts center. Historic homes sit cheek by jowl on Main Street. behind picket fences and hedgerows, while shops and eateries line nearby Bridge Street. As in Frenchtown, cyclists and hikers trundle through on the canal path. Stockton attracts its share of tourists on weekends but remains decidedly low-key in comparison to its bustling neighbors.

Farther downstream is Lambertville, another river town that hasn't seen much change since the 19th century. It was settled in 1732 by Emanuel Coryell, who ran a busy tavern and inn while operating a ferry service across the Delaware River to New Hope, Pennsylvania. For a time, settlements on both sides of the river were known as Coryell's Ferry, the midpoint on the 2-day stagecoach journey between Philadelphia and New York City. During the American Revolution, Washington's troops crossed the Delaware here, and before the battle of Monmouth in 1778, the general stayed at the Holcombe Farm while his troops camped in an orchard at Union and Bridge streets. In 1810, the town was renamed after Captain John Lambert, who built a stone inn and tavern called the Lambertville House that still takes in lodgers and diners. That same year, a bridge was built across the river.

Lambertville became a thriving industrial center in the 1800s, due in large part to the new Delaware and Raritan Canal that barges navigated to transport coal from the Pennsylvania mines to New York City. The next decades brought rapid change. In the 1850s, the Belvidere–Delaware Railroad was built along the canal, and mills churned out freight cars, locomotives, hairpins, wagon wheels, and rubber products. The merchants and factory owners who subsequently prospered built the grand mansions that now make up Lambertville's noteworthy historic district.

Today the railroad is gone and the mills are closed, and Lambertville has successfully reinvented itself into the Antique Capital of New Jersey. Nowhere else in the state will you find such a large and diverse collection of antiques shops, whose inventory runs the gamut from Turkish rugs, folk art, Chinese porcelain, and 18th-century European furniture to eclectic home décor and high-end French antiques. Its large historic district is perfect for strolling, full of pretty Federal row houses and ornate Victorian homes with well-tended gardens. Bridge Street has some of the town's earliest houses and public buildings; many are restored and house antiques shops as well as inns, restaurants, unique specialty stores, and art galleries. The D&R Canal runs through town, a popular destination for joggers, bikers, cross-country skiers, hikers, and canoeists.

Long before the first Europeans came along, Native American tribes—notably the local Lenni-Lenape—had hunted and fished along the river valley for generations. At Lambertville's statewide famous Shad Festival, which celebrates the return of shad to the Delaware River, New Jersey's only remaining commercial shad fishermen demonstrate the traditional hauling and preparation methods that Native Americans handed down to settlers centuries ago.

A few miles inland, Sergeantsville is little more than a rural junction, where a single blinking traffic light marks the heart of town. The general store at this historic crossroads has served the community since the 1800s; today it offers homemade Chinese food along with the usual coffee, sandwiches, and groceries. Across the street, the Sergeantsville Inn serves gourmet fare in a rustic 18th-century roadside building. Clapboard Victorians, a tiny post office and town hall, and a stone church with a gleaming white steeple and beautiful stained-glass windows, complete the scene. Sergeantsville boasts the lone remaining public covered bridge in New Jersey—a weathered gray structure that has spanned Wickecheoke Creek since 1872.

As much as this area's charm may surprise even born-and-bred New Jerseyans, it's far from undiscovered. Summer folk have been seeking refuge in hotels and inns here since the railroad tracks were laid down; nowadays, theatrical celebrities and Wall Street execs spend quiet weekends in grand restored Colonials and Federal-style mansions. But the wealth of hidden treasures in these river towns makes visitors feel as if they are the first to discover them. Consider the well-preserved relics of history such as the Holcombe-Jimison Farmstead—the oldest farmstead in Hunterdon County—the Vermont-esque Green Sergeants covered bridge, the antiques and art of Lambertville, the funky charm of Frenchtown and Stockton, and summer plays and music performances under the stars in Washington Crossing State Park. If you expect to have the quaint downtown streets and lovely corner bistro to yourself on a Saturday afternoon, be forewarned: Many others will have the same idea as you. To avoid disappointment, make lodging and dinner reservations well in advance whenever possible.

Entries in this section are arranged in roughly geographic order.

AREA CODE 609.

GUIDANCE Frenchtown Visitors Bureau (800-989-3388; www.frenchtown .com), P.O. Box 425, Frenchtown 08825, will send local tourism literature and give advice on visiting the Frenchtown region. You can also click on www.frenchtowner .com, an online local travel guide.

Lambertville Area Chamber of Commerce (609-397-0055; www.lambertville .org), 239 N. Union St., Lambertville 08530. The office answers phone queries Mon.–Fri. 9–2, and on request will send a tourism information packet with brochures on local businesses and attractions.

Hunterdon County Chamber of Commerce (908-735-5955; www.hunterdon-chamber.org) maintains a Web site with visitor information and an online magazine, *Hunterdon Living.*

The Lambertville Historical Society (609-397-0770; www.lambertvillehistorical society.org) leads walking tours from Apr. to Oct. on the first Sunday of the month at 2 PM, and at other times by appointment. Guided tours leave from the Marshall House Museum at 62 Bridge St. and include historic homes and sites throughout Lambertville.

GETTING THERE *By air:* **Newark Liberty International Airport** (973-961-6000; parking information: 888-397-4636; www.panynj.com) in Newark serves the entire state. **Philadelphia International Airport** (215-937-6800; www.philadelphia -phl.com) in Pennsylvania is convenient to western New Jersey.

By bus: **Trans-Bridge Lines** (908-730-6552; 800-962-9135; www.transbridge bus.com) provides daily bus service from Bethlehem, Pennsylvania, to Newark Liberty International Airport, Port Authority Bus Terminal, and JFK International Airport in New York City. The bus stops in Lambertville on Bridge St., between Main St. and Rt. 179, and in Frenchtown on Front St., at the junction of Bridge St. **New Jersey Transit** (973-275-5555; www.njtransit.com) runs daily between Lambertville and Trenton.

By car: There are no major highways in this rural region, but two interstates are close by: **I-78** passes through Phillipsburg north of Milford, and **I-95** cuts between Titusville and Trenton. **Rt. 29,** a scenic two-lane road running parallel to the Delaware River, is the main north–south route through this area, connecting Milford, Frenchtown, Stockton, Lambertville, and Titusville.

MEDICAL EMERGENCY Capital Health Systems—Fuld Campus (609-394-6000), 750 Brunswick Ave., Trenton. The emergency number is 609-394-6101.

Capital Health Systems—Mercer Campus (609-394-4000), 446 Bellevue Ave., Trenton. The emergency number is 609-394-4022.

Saint Francis Medical Center (609-599-5000), 601 Hamilton Ave., Trenton. The emergency number is 609-599-5210.

COVERED BRIDGE **Green Sergeants covered bridge,** Rt. 604, Sergeantsville. This colonial-era landmark is the last-remaining public-access covered bridge in New Jersey. The original bridge was built in 1872 over Wickecheoke Creek, a tributary of the Delaware River. It was dismantled in 1960 after sustaining heavy damage and rebuilt with some of the original materials. Today it's a one-lane bridge—drivers heading toward Rosemont pass over the boards; those going to Sergeantsville use the road that passes alongside the bridge, which features a timber floor and hand-split cedar shakes.

HISTORIC SITES **Prallsville Mills** (609-397-3586), Rt. 29, Stockton. Call for a schedule of arts and cultural events. This site along the Delaware River was a thriving industrial center from the 18th to the 20th century. John Prall Jr. purchased a wooden gristmill at the confluence of the Delaware River and Wickecheoke Creek in 1794, and the operation soon included a sawmill, a new stone gristmill, a store, and other buildings. Together with the stone quarry and fisheries along the Delaware, Prall's mill complex turned this rural farming region into a prosperous commercial center. Today the well-preserved of historic mill buildings in Delaware and Raritan Canal State Park is an active cultural center with a full schedule of community events, concerts, art exhibits, and antiques shows. Among the picturesque buildings maintained and restored by the Delaware River Mill Society is an 1877 stone gristmill with original mill machinery, an 1850 wagon shed, a tiny scale house, a red-clapboard sawmill, and an art gallery for local artists in a circa-1794 linseed oil mill (see *Entertainment—Arts Centers*). The mills are a sought-after location for weddings and other special events.

MUSEUMS **Holcombe-Jimison Farmstead Museum** (609-397-2752; www .holcombe-jimison.org), 1605 Daniel Bray Hwy. (Rt. 29), just north of Lambertville. Open May–Oct., Wed. 9–noon, Sun. 1–4. The circa-1711 John Holcombe house is open several times a year for tours; call for a schedule. Adults $5; seniors and students $3. John Holcombe's farm is believed to be the oldest in rural Hunterdon County. He was certainly Lambertville's first resident, and his stone farmhouse served as George Washington's headquarters for a time during the American Revolution. Today the farmstead's three-story-bank barn (built into a hillside to make all levels accessible from the ground) is a museum of Hunterdon County farm life from 1800 to 1900. Period displays include vintage farming equipment, a rural post office, a farmhouse kitchen, the office of a country doctor and blacksmith, print, and carpentry shops. Demonstrations in woodworking, period herb gardening, blacksmithing, cider making, and other facets of rural country life centuries ago.

Marshall House Museum (609-397-0770; www.lambertvillehistoricalsociety.org), 62 Bridge St., Lambertville. Open Apr.–Oct., Sat. and Sun. 1–4 and by appointment. Admission by donation. Guided walking tours of town start here on the first Sunday of the month at 2 PM. A well-stocked museum of local history was the boyhood home of James Wilson Marshall, a leader of the historic California gold rush of 1849. Marshall's Federal-style house was built in 1816 of locally produced brick. The original 5-acre (or 44-perch) property once had a smokehouse, barn, and wagon shop. The Marshall family lived here until 1834; today it's the headquarters of the **Lambertville Historical Society,** with rooms full of period furnishings, and permanent and changing exhibits on local history and culture, from the shad industry to vintage quilts.

WINERIES AND BREWERIES **Alba Vineyard and Winery** (908-995-7800; www.albavineyard.com), 269 Rt. 627, in the Finesville section of Milford. Open year-round for tours and tastings, Wed.–Sun., noon–5. A rustic tasting room and art gallery along with modern wine-making facilities in a converted 1805 stone barn with limestone walls, old oak beams, and an impressive wood bar. The winery is surrounded by the rolling hills of the Musconetcong Valley. The fine-art gallery displays the work of established and emerging local artists, and the **Alba Concert Series** features jazz, folk, and blues performances. The **Grand Harvest Wine Festival** (see *Special Events—October*) and other events are held throughout the year.

Hopewell Valley Vineyard (609-737-4465; www.hopewellvalleyvineyards.com), 46 Yard Rd., Pennington. Open daily noon–5 PM, Fri. noon–8 PM. Call or see the Web site for their schedule of tastings and special events. Sergio and Barbara Neri's award-winning wines blend three generations of family wine-making experience with the philosophy that great wines are "born in the vineyard and raised in the winery." Vinifera like pinot grigio and chardonnay—traditional grapes native to Italy—and other homegrown grapes go into the Neri's handcrafted wines. The wine shop sells wine and wine-related gifts, books, and gift baskets; the rustic tasting-room has a copper bar, a wood-burning stove, and windows overlooking the vineyards on the Neri's farm.

River Horse Brewery (609-397-7776; www.riverhorse.com), Lambert Square, 80 Lambert Lane, Lambertville. Open daily noon–5 for tours and samples. Visitors to the region's only microbrewery can see how handcrafted beers are kegged and bottled in this family-owned facility housed in a former cracker factory. Handcrafted lagers, ales, and seasonal brews for sampling in the tasting room and retail shop.

🐏 🦆 HOWELL LIVING HISTORY FARM

(609-737-3299; www.howellfarm.org), 101 Valley Rd. (off Rt. 29), Titusville. Open Feb.–Nov., Tues.–Fri. 10–4; Sat. 10–4 (programs 11 AM–3 PM); Sun. noon–4 from Apr. to Nov. for self-guided tours only; closed Mon. Free admission. An old-time family homestead reminiscent of the area's farms circa-1900. Pick up a guidebook and tour the apple orchard, farm buildings, and barnyard, home to pigs, geese, ducks, and guinea hens. Saturday farming demonstrations using period farming tools and techniques show the seasonal cycles of life on an animal-powered farm. Visitors can take part in special events like the annual game of old-fashioned town ball, a historic version of baseball.

ALBA VINEYARD PRODUCES MANY AWARD-WINNING WINES AT THEIR WINERY IN THE HILLS ABOVE THE DELAWARE RIVER IN THE FINESVILLE SECTION OF MILFORD. THE VINEYARD HOSTS MANY FESTIVALS THROUGHOUT THE YEAR, AND IS OPEN FOR TOURS.

✳ To Do

BICYCLING Delaware and Raritan Canal State Park (732-873-3050; www.dandrcanal.com) has a recreational path on a converted towpath along the Delaware River and its feeder canal from Frenchtown to Trenton, where it joins the main canal to New Brunswick. There is cycling, running, walking, and horseback riding on the 30-mile crushed-gravel path from Frenchtown to Trenton. From Frenchtown, the trail heads south past Bulls Island Recreation Area and historic Prallsville Mills, through Stockton, Lambertville, and Titusville. You can access the path from several points along Rt. 29, including the parking area off Bridge St. in Frenchtown, Bulls Island Recreation Area, Prallsville Mills in Stockton, Holcombe-Jimison Farmstead Museum in Lambertville, and Washington Crossing State Park in Titusville. Several bridges cross the river into Pennsylvania making easy loop rides; you can also ride along the path, then return on Rt. 29, which has a wide shoulder good for cycling.

Cycle Corner of Frenchtown (908-996-7712; www.thecyclecorner.com), 52 Bridge St., Frenchtown, rents mountain bikes, tandems, and recumbent bikes.

BOATING (See also *Canoeing and Kayaking* and *Tubing and Rafting.*)

Boaters can access the **Delaware River** from Rt. 29 at the Kingswood access ramp (609-984-1401), 1 mile south of Frenchtown; a fishing license or state-issued boat ramp permit is required and a fee is charged. **Delaware and Raritan Canal State Park** (732-873-3050; www.dandrcanal.com) has three boat ramps that are free: one on Rt. 29, 3.4 miles north of Stockton in Byram; another on Rt. 29 at Bulls Island Recreation Area (609-397-2949); and one off Bridge St. in Lambertville. Only canoes and boats with electric motors are allowed on the canal.

CANOEING AND KAYAKING (See also *Tubing and Rafting.*)

Both the **Delaware River** and the **Delaware and Raritan Canal** are naturals for paddling. Local outfitters include:

✍ **Bucks County River Country** (215-297-5000; www.rivercountry.net), Two Walters Lane, Point Pleasant, PA. Open daily in summer; Thurs.–Mon. from mid-Sept. until the end of Oct. Reservations are recommended. Kayaking and canoeing trips on the Delaware River that last 2 to 4 hours.

CARRIAGE RIDES Stockton Carriage Tours (609-397-9066), P.O. Box 493, Stockton 08559. Call for a schedule of public rides. Take an elegant, horse-drawn open carriage ride through a rural New Jersey landscape. About once a week, they open to the general public for 20-minute tours that leave from Prallsville Mills and other locations around Stockton. Otherwise, they bring private groups (up to 12 people) on a variety of scenic tours—some cross the picturesque **Green Sergeants covered bridge** (see *To See—Covered Bridge*); others will take passengers to an area restaurant or inn for dinner.

Bucks County Carriages (215-862-3582; www.buckscountycarriages.com), 2586 N. River Rd., New Hope, PA. Most of their tours are in Bucks County, Pennsylvania, but their horse-drawn antique carriages also take passengers on tours through Lambertville, starting at Lambertville Station.

FISHING The **Delaware River** is wildly popular with anglers, who fish for trout, rock bass, stripers, and shad from boats or along the shore or by fly-fishing in the shallows. Fishing is also permitted on the **Delaware and Raritan Canal** for perch, catfish, pickerel, and sunfish; the canal is stocked with trout in the spring. There are many access points along Rt. 29, including **Washington Crossing State Park** (609-737-0623) in Titusville; **Bulls Island Recreation Area** (609-397-2949) in Stockton, which has good fishing holes just below the wing dam, near the pedestrian bridge; and near the bridge in Frenchtown, where Nishisakawick Creek empties into the Delaware River. A fishing license is required, as is a trout stamp for trout fishing.

HIKING In Titusville, **Washington Crossing State Park** (609-737-0623), 355 Washington Crossing–Pennington Rd. (Rt. 546), has 15 miles of moderately challenging trails that crisscross nearly 2,000 acres of forest and natural areas along the Delaware River.

✍ The **Delaware and Raritan Canal State Park** (732-873-3050; www.dandr canal.com) The 34-mile Main Canal Trail and the 31.5-mile Feeder Canal Trail are multi-use, flat, crushed-gravel surface paths that are good for easy hiking and ideal for families with young children.

TUBING AND RAFTING ✍ **Delaware River Tubing** (908-996-5386; 866-938-8823), 2998 Daniel Bray Hwy. (Rt. 29), Frenchtown. Open Memorial Day–Labor Day, Mon.–Fri. 10–7; Sat. and Sun. 9–7. Reservations suggested. Caters to families, with trips that last 3 to 4 hours and end with a barbecue lunch. They also have a limited number of rafts for rent.

✍ **Bucks County River Country** (215-297-5000), Two Walters Lane, Point Pleasant, PA. Open daily in summer; Thurs.–Mon. from mid-Sept. until the end of Oct. Reservations are recommended. Tubing and rafting trips on the Delaware River that last 2 to 4 hours.

✐ WASHINGTON CROSSING STATE PARK

(609-737-0623), 355 Washington Crossing–Pennington Rd. (Rt. 546; off Rt. 29), Titusville. Grounds open daily sunrise to sunset; buildings open Wed.–Sun. This 1,000-acre park on the banks of the Delaware River was intended to be a historical park but is equally popular for its recreation offerings. On Christmas night 1776, General George Washington led 2,500 Continental soldiers across the chilly river in boats launched from the Pennsylvania side. They landed at **Johnson's Ferry** (the site of today's park) around 4 AM, and began their march toward Trenton. Their successful surprise attack against British and Hessian troops would become a pivotal turning point in the Revolutionary War. Today, a network of trails for hiking and cross-country skiing includes a 3-mile paved roadway linking the park to the **Delaware and Raritan Canal trail.** Birders come to see a variety of migrating and wintering species, including hawks, owls, and bluebirds, and anglers fish the canal and river. Historic buildings throughout the park house an interpretive center, a visitors center and museum with hundreds of Revolutionary War–era artifacts, and the 18th-century **Johnson Ferry House** (restored as an 18th-century tavern). Playground and picnic area. Special events include **Christmas Day reenactments** of Washington's famous river crossing, a scene immortalized in artist Emanuel Leutze's 1851 painting *Washington Crossing the Delaware* (see *Special Events*).

✳ Green Space

PARKS Delaware and Raritan Canal State Park (732-873-3050; www.dandr canal.com), various access points along Rt. 29 from Frenchtown to Titusville. Open daily sunrise to sunset. Visitors bike, jog, hike, ride horses, and ski the 70-mile multi-use pathway running along the 19th-century shipping canal that connects the Delaware River to New Brunswick. The canal is also popular with paddlers and anglers. Not just a place for recreation, the canal provides New Jerseyans with 75 million gallons of water daily. A 22-mile feeder canal runs from Milford to Trenton, where it channels water to the main canal that continues east across New Jersey. A 92-acre tract outside Stockton, called **My Ben,** was added to the 4,470-acre state park in 2004; it is home to bog turtles, barred owls, and other threatened species. The park includes **Prallsville Mills,** a preserved 19th-century mill complex in Stockton (see *To See—Historic Sites*).

Bulls Island Recreation Area (609-397-2949), 2185 Daniel Bray Hwy. (Rt. 29), Stockton. An 80-acre state recreation area, especially popular with boaters, paddlers, and anglers, which includes a forested island surrounded by the Delaware River and the Delaware and Raritan Canal. A 24-acre natural area of floodplain forest protects several rare plant species. Camping (see *Lodging—Campgrounds*).

✳ Lodging

INNS

In Stockton 08559

❝❣❞ **The Stockton Inn** (609-397-1250; www.stocktoninn.com), One Main St. Rodgers and Hart's Broadway hit "There's a Small Hotel (with a wishing well)" was inspired by this elegant 18th-century inn near the Delaware River. The sheer number of weddings and equally special occasions set here is a nod to both the romantic atmosphere and the upscale American cuisine (see sidebar, page 237). Eleven guest rooms and suites in a series of historic buildings—the circa-1710 Main Inn, the elegant 19th-century Federal House, the 1832 stone Wagon House, and the charming Carriage House—are surrounded by lovely gardens and rambling stone walls. All rooms have private bath, phone, TV, and air-conditioning; some suites have fireplaces, canopy beds, and verandas. Continental breakfast. $95–195.

The Woolverton Inn (609-397-0802; 888-264-6648; www.woolvertoninn .com), Six Woolverton Rd. This elegant country estate high above the Delaware River is a lovely and romantic retreat on parklike grounds surrounded by 300 acres of picturesque farmland and forest. The 13 luxurious and stylish guest rooms and suites are spread among the magnificent 1792 stone manor house, the restored 1860s carriage house, and two converted barns at the edge of a sheep pasture, all uniquely equipped with luxe linens, featherbeds, fresh flowers, and plush robes; many have a fireplace, whirlpool tub, and private outdoor sitting area with rolling hills views. In the main house, Newell's Library boasts a stunning collection of antique mirrors and has 700 volumes to peruse. In the carriage house and barns, the Hunterdon Suite has a soaring windowed cupola,

fireplace, private screened-in porch, and split-level bathroom with whirlpool tub. The dramatic two-level Sojourn Suite has two fireplaces, a spacious spa bath with whirlpool tub, a king featherbed, and a hammock. A full gourmet breakfast that might include Grand Marnier French toast or apple-cranberry turkey sausage can be enjoyed by candlelight, in the gardens, or in your room. Rooms $145–315; suites $275–345; cottages $295–425.

In Lambertville 08530

❝❣❞ **The Lambertville House** (609-397-0200; 888-867-8859; www.lambert villehouse.com), 32 Bridge St. P.O. Box 349. A handsome 19th-century landmark downtown building built by Captain John Lambert in 1812 as an inn and stagecoach stop. The 26 guest rooms and suites are uniquely decorated with antiques and period reproductions. All have private baths, phones, TV, high-speed/wireless Internet access, and jetted tubs; some have fireplaces and private courtyard balconies. Two suites in the carriage house have fireplaces, refrigerators, and private entrances. **Left Bank Libations** is the hotel's convivial lounge with an elegant, clubby feel; relax with a specialty martini or a single-malt scotch in front of the fireplace or outside on the patio. $200–385.

Chimney Hill Farm Estate and the Ol' Barn Inn (609-397-1516; 800-211-4667; www.chimneyhillinn.com), 207 Goat Hill Rd. Terry Anne and Richard Anderson's elegant inn has graced the covers of *Colonial Homes* and *NJ Country Roads* magazines. Couples love this enchanting spot on a back road high in the wooded hills above Lambertville. The handsome 1820 fieldstone country house and barn are surrounded by fields and gardens, romantic and secluded yet less than a mile from town. There are eight guest rooms in the main house and four spacious luxury suites in the Ol' Barn Inn, all with private bath; many have fireplaces, Jacuzzi tubs, and canopied beds. The guest pantry is stocked with sweets and refreshments; a full gourmet country breakfast is served by candlelight in the Colonial dining room. $165–419.

"ᵀ" **The Inn at Lambertville Station** (609-397-4400; www.lambertville station.com), 11 Bridge St. A restored 19th-century train station is now a charming inn and restaurant. The grand stone building was the vision of architect Thomas Walter—who designed the U.S. Capitol dome in Washington—and was completed in 1865. An extensive restoration in the 1980s preserved many of this landmark structure's original details. Each of the 45 antiques-filled guest rooms looks onto the Delaware River, with unique décor inspired by the world's grand cities, and there's complimentary wireless Internet access throughout. Suites have fireplaces and sitting areas. The popular pub features live jazz and blues on weekends (see *Eating Out*). Continental breakfast. $125–305.

"ᵀ" **York Street House** (609-397-3007; 888-398-3199; www.yorkstreet house.com), 42 York St. Two years after George Massey built this grand brick manor house for his wife in 1909, it graced the cover of *House & Garden* magazine. Today, innkeepers Laurie and Mark Weinstein run the lovely Georgian Colonial Revival–style mansion as an in-town bed & breakfast. Original details—tile fireplaces and a stunning stained-glass window—and period décor, including a 1900 Waterford chandelier and local 19th- and 20th-century antiques, fill the common areas and seven guest rooms. Each room has a private bath, and some have canopied beds, a fireplace, a Jacuzzi tub, or a TV and complimentary Wi-Fi. Guests can stroll in the formal rose garden, relax by the fire in the cozy parlor or in a wicker rocker on the cool veranda, or cross the street to Sheridan Park to catch a free summertime concert. Lambertville's restaurants, galleries, and shops are a short walk from the house. Complimentary refreshments, and a full breakfast by candlelight featuring fresh local ingredients. $125–275.

CHESTNUT HILL ON THE DELAWARE

(908-995-9761; 888-333-2242; www.chestnuthillnj.com), 63 Church St., P.O. Box N, Milford 08848. A charming and old-fashioned Victorian-era mansion and cottage perched above the Delaware River. Linda and Rob Castagna's painstaking attention to detail is evident from the elegant common rooms to the tastefully decorated guest rooms and suites. Among the cozy guest rooms in the main house, the Summer Morning Room stands out—a light and airy retreat with fireplace, library, and Jacuzzi tub, and stained-glass windows in the bathroom, with a lovely river view. The spacious, private suites in the Country Cottage are sought after by couples, especially honeymooners. Guest like to congregate in the antiques-filled parlor, dining room, and drawing room, or claim one of the rocking chairs on the lovely wraparound veranda set above the river and gardens. At the river's edge is a long deck; tubes are available for those tempted to take a leisurely float on the river. Full breakfast. $115–275.

BED & BREAKFASTS

In Frenchtown 08825

🐾 ❝1❞ ✎ **Widow McCrea House** (908-996-4999; www.widowmccrea .com), Three Kingwood Ave. (Rt. 12). A beautifully restored 1878 Italianate Victorian built by Frances McCrea. Three guest rooms, two suites, and a private cottage boast period details, impeccable antiques furnishings, cozy featherbeds, and complimentary Wi-Fi. Some rooms have working fireplaces, marble Jacuzzi tubs, and private entrances. Innkeepers Lynn Marad and Burt Patalano will help plan activities or arrange dinner reservations. The inn is a short walk from Frenchtown's cafés, shops, galleries, and a bike path along the Delaware River. Continental breakfast is served during the week; full breakfast by candlelight on weekends. Complimentary evening cordials. $95–285.

In Lambertville 08530

❝1❞ **Bridgestreet House Bed and Breakfast** (609-397-2503; 800-897-2503; www.bridgestreethouse.com), 75 Bridge St. A tastefully decorated 19th-century Federal-style row house in Lambertville's historic downtown. Four guest rooms and one suite are furnished with Victorian-era antiques, all with private bath, air-conditioning, and TV; one has a claw-foot tub, another looks out on a private courtyard. Wi-Fi is available. Guests traveling on foot love the convenient location within walking distance of shops and restaurants and on the New York City bus line. Innkeeper Donna Herman offers complimentary wine and cheese, snacks, and refreshments. Continental breakfast is served in the parlor, outside in the courtyard, or in your room. $100–185.

❝1❞ **Martin Coryell House Bed & Breakfast** (609-397-8981; 866-397-8981; www.martincoryellhouse.com), 111 North Union St. An elegant and grand B&B in a brick, circa-1864 Federal-style house in downtown Lambertville. The interior is full of exquisite touches, like the hand-painted dining-room ceiling, silk drapery, and designer wall coverings. Two lovely guest rooms and three suites with private bath, Jacuzzi tub, antique claw-foot tub, fireplace, featherbeds, air-conditioning, TV, Wi-Fi, and phones. Innkeepers Rich and Mary Freedman serve a full breakfast on weekends, continental breakfast during the week. $155–279.

THE WIDOW MCCREA HOUSE, A CIRCA-1878 VICTORIAN BUILT BY FRANCES MCCREA, IS A QUAINT BED AND BREAKFAST, JUST OUTSIDE OF FRENCHTOWN'S CHARMING DOWNTOWN NEAR THE SCENIC DELAWARE RIVER.

Photo courtesy of Lynn Marad

In Sergeantsville 08557-0156

🐾 🌿 **Silver Maple Organic Farm and Bed & Breakfast** (908-237-2192; www.silvermaplebandb.com), 483 Sergeantsville Rd. (Rt. 523), P.O. Box 0156. A cozy and laid-back B&B in a 200-year-old stone farmhouse surrounded by 20 acres of woods, meadows, and organic gardens. Hosts Steve Noll and John Hendry offer three inviting guest rooms and two suites with country décor, air-conditioning, and down comforters. Guests are welcome to the in-ground pool, outdoor hot tub, sundeck, and tennis court. Indoors, guest can relax in the living room with stone fireplace and wide-plank floors, in the Colonial dining room, and in the rec room with TV, VCR, and stereo. The farm is home to ducks, chickens, goats, and pigs, and sells organic vegetables, berries, flowers, and herbs from spring until late fall. A full country breakfast features eggs fresh from the farm's chickens; complimentary refreshments available throughout the day. $99–175.

CAMPGROUNDS 🌿 **Bulls Island Recreation Area** (732-873-3050; www.dandrcanal.com), Rt. 29, Stockton. Open Apr.–Oct. A popular park along the Delaware River and the Delaware and Raritan Canal; 69 tent sites and trailer sites with picnic tables, fire rings, showers, and flush toilets. Sites $20.

🌿 **Washington Crossing State Park** (609-737-0623), 355 Washington Crossing–Pennington Rd. (Rt. 546), Titusville 08560. The campground is open Apr.–Oct. Four group sites with fire rings, picnic tables, and toilets. Sites $15–50.

✳ Where to Eat

DINING OUT

In Milford

Milford Oyster House (908-995-9411; www.milfordoysterhouse.com), 92 Water St. (Rt. 519). Open Wed.–Sun. for dinner; closed Mon. and Tues.; fish market open daily. A popular fish house that recently moved into a 19th-century stone mill near the banks of the Delaware River. The seasonal cuisine emphasizes creatively prepared seafood (oysters are on the menu from Sept.–Apr.), but meat and other dishes are also available. The daily specials reflect what's fresh in the in-house seafood market. Friday's special is crabcakes, which sell out early. The charming dining rooms are decorated with period antiques and artwork. $20–33.

In Frenchtown

The Frenchtown Inn (908-996-3300; www.frenchtowninn.com), Seven Bridge St. Open for lunch Tues.–Sat.; dinner Tues.–Sun.; Sun. brunch; closed Mon. This Bridge St. landmark was built in 1838 as a hotel. Today, lunch and dinner are served in a series of elegant dining rooms; the front porch allows alfresco dining in good weather. Saturday features a prix fixe menu with offerings like roast organic chicken breast over sautéed lobster and wild mushrooms. Business casual dress is required in the main dining room. The grill room offers casual dining and a lighter menu. $24–32.

Race Street Café (908-996-3179; www.racestcafe.com), Two Race St. Open for lunch and brunch Sat. and Sun.; dinner Thurs.–Sun.; closed Mon.–Wed. Reservations recommended. A charming little bistro in an enclave of historic downtown buildings where local artists' works adorn the walls and the Continental cuisine is upscale and creative. The menu changes weekly and features many vegetarian options; everything is homemade, including desserts. This small space gets rather crowded and noisy on weekends, but diners don't seem to mind. BYOB. $18–26.

In Lambertville

Andiamo Restaurant (609-397-6767; www.andiamonj.com), 13 Klines Ct. Lunch Fri.–Sun.; dinner Thurs.–Mon.; closed Tues. and Wed. Reservations are recommended. The menu is a mix of Italian, French, and American dishes served in an intimate ambience that's at once relaxing and elegant. Menu highlights include wild mushroom and goat cheese strudel or the caramelized-onion tart to begin, perhaps followed by grilled lamb chops rubbed with garlic, sage, and lemon. The house-made desserts change daily. Live classical guitar on Fri. night. BYOB. $18–25.

Anton's at the Swan (609-397-1960; www.antons-at-the-swan.com), 43 South Main St. Open for dinner Tues.–Sun.; closed Mon. Reservations suggested. Upscale New American cuisine in a chic, sophisticated setting at the stately Swan Hotel. Anton's candlelit antiques- and art-filled dining room is charming and romantic. The top-notch cuisine features fresh produce from local farms with offerings like baby pheasant with local chanterelles, or rack of lamb with curried chickpea *daal*. The wine list is extensive and well chosen. The **Swan Bar** (609-397-3552) is a historic pub known for its New York strip steak and seasonal outdoor dining; a light menu is available Tues.–Sun. $28–32.

Hamilton's Grill Room (609-397-4343; www.hamiltonsgrillroom.com), Eight Coryell St., in the Porkyard. Open daily for dinner. Reservations are strongly encouraged; call a month ahead for a table on Sat. night. A lovely country bistro on the historic Delaware and Raritan Canal that keeps pace with Lambertville's upscale dining scene.

The inventive Mediterranean menu has received glowing praise from the nation's top food critics. Fresh meats and seafood are expertly prepared on the open charcoal grill or in the wood-burning oven. In summer, you can dine outside around the fountain in the leafy courtyard, on the charming porch in the wine bar, or inside in view of the open kitchen. BYOB. $18–35.

Elsewhere

Sergeantsville Inn (609-397-3700; www.sergeantsvilleinn.com), 601 Rosemont–Ringoes Rd. (Rts. 523 and 604), Sergeantsville. Open for lunch Wed.–Sat., and dinner Tues.–Sun.; closed Mon. Reservations are recommended. A green-shuttered stone building from the early 1700s is a charming roadside country inn known for superior New American cuisine and romantic fireside dining. A top-notch menu of fresh seafood and exotic game, plus some vegetarian selections, is accompanied by an award-winning wine list and extensive selection of martinis and champagne. The rustic tavern is friendly and casual, with a lighter menu of appetizers, salads, pizzas, burgers, and ribs. $17–34.

The Café at Rosemont (609-397-4097; www.cafeatrosemont.com), Rts. 519 and 604, Rosemont. Open for lunch Tues.–Fri.; dinner Wed. and Fri.–Sun.; Sat. and Sun. brunch; closed Mon., Thurs. dinner. Reservations are suggested for dinner. An intimate café housed in a quaint 19th-century clapboard building—a former general store—in a cluster of historic homes on a quiet back road. The kitchen promises "fresh food at its simple best," and delivers with fish, chicken, and pasta, along with produce and cheeses from local farms. The American cuisine is sophisticated, earthy and wholesome. A must-do is the Wed.-night three-course prix fixe "global dinner," which spotlights the cuisine of a particular region (Indonesia, Scotland,

THE STOCKTON INN
(609-397-1250; www.stocktoninn.com), One Main St., Stockton. Open for lunch Tues.–Sat.; dinner daily; Sun. brunch. Reservations are recommended. Rodgers and Hart's "There's a Small Hotel (with a wishing well)" was inspired by this charming 18th-century 11-room inn at the center of this historic river town (see *Lodging—Inns*). There are charming dining rooms with fireplaces, and lovely murals depicting country life from centuries ago; a terraced slate patio surrounded by waterfalls, rocky outcroppings, and gardens; and an intimate, dimly lit bar. Many weddings and special occasions are set here, a nod to the romantic atmosphere. The seasonal menu features innovative takes on traditional and contemporary American dishes. Steamed littleneck clams and jumbo lump crabcakes with cilantro and mango butter highlight the starters. Many entrées feature roasted and grilled meats and fish, like salmon sautéed with sun-dried tomatoes, garlic, spinach and white wine, or full rack of lamb with pesto crumbs and red wine demi-glace. And, please, save room for dessert. $20–28.

West Africa, or New England, etc.). Desserts are made in-house. Rotating exhibits feature paintings, prints, and pottery by area artists. A local favorite. BYOB. $17–24.

It's Nutts (609-737-0505; www.itsnutts.com), 1381 River Rd., Titusville. Serving breakfast, lunch, and dinner daily. Reservations accepted for six or more. You'll easily mistake this place for a roadside burger joint, but—surprise—the menu reveals a fun combination of sophisticated fare and down-home comfort foods. Think pork roll, egg, and cheese sandwich for breakfast, and gourmet burgers, sandwiches, and salads for lunch. For dinner, there are remarkable tomato pies, homemade crabcakes, bacon-wrapped meatloaf, or pastas and seafood. Afterwards, the homemade ice cream from next door is a must. No credit cards. BYOB. $12–22.

EATING OUT

In Milford

The Ship Inn (908-995-0188; www.shipinn.com), 61 Bridge St. Open daily for lunch and dinner. A friendly neighborhood tavern with the convivial traditional English pub atmosphere. The stately circa-1860 Victorian building features the original pressed-tin ceiling, brickwork, and beams, and a long oak bar fashioned out of wood from a local bowling alley half a century ago. New Jersey's first brewpub has a colorful history: during Prohibition, it housed a speakeasy in the back of the building; later it was an ice-cream parlor and bakery. Today, authentic British and European specialties like fish-and-chips and steak and kidney pie are on the menu. More than 70 bottled and tap beers, including British ales and the pub's own brews. Ask about a tour of the brew house. Live entertainment on Sat. night. $13–22.

In Frenchtown

✐ **The Bridge Café** (908-996-6040; www.bridgecafe.net), Eight Bridge St. Open daily for lunch; breakfast Sat. and Sun.; dinner Fri. and Sat. A friendly and casual eatery on the banks of the Delaware River that has a full menu of fresh soups, salads, burgers, fried-seafood baskets with creative twists (such as Cajun seared shrimp and arugula salad with fresh mozzarella and smoked bacon) and homemade baked goods. $9–14.

Cocina del Sol (908-996-0900), 10 Bridge St. Open for lunch Fri.–Sun.; dinner Tues.–Sun.; closed Mon. Progressive Southern California–style Mexican cuisine in a laid-back, funky café in the center of town. The menu features burritos, enchiladas, and other mainstays of traditional Mexican restaurants, but here they're not slathered in sauce and cheese. Instead, they're prepared simply with the freshest seasonal ingredients. The guacamole and salsa are made in-house. Outdoor dining in-season. Children's menu available. BYOB. $13–18; credit cards not accepted.

Frenchtown Café (908-996-0663), 44 Bridge St. Open daily for breakfast and lunch. Maybe it's the motto that promises "Extraordinary food for ordinary people," or its convenient heart-of-town location. Whatever the reason, this friendly neighborhood eatery is an extremely popular breakfast and lunch place, a good stop before a bike ride along the canal trail or a break from browsing Frenchtown's shops and galleries. Creative and delicious daily specials and homemade desserts. $5–10.

In Stockton

Meil's (609-397-8033; www.meils restaurant.com), Rt. 29 and Bridge St. Open daily for breakfast, lunch, and dinner. This friendly family restaurant at the heart of town is a local favorite. They do a brisk take-out business with their homemade baked goods, but just as many customers dine in for the hearty and creative home cooking. Unique items include a chili and cheddar cheese omelet for breakfast; chicken potpie, for lunch; and crabmeat stuffed flounder for dinner. You can even get a Thanksgiving dinner with all

the trimmings, any time of the year. Breakfast $5–16; lunch $8–20; dinner $9.50–29. Credit cards not accepted.

In Lambertville

De Anna's (609-397-8957; www.de annasrestaurant.com), 54 N. Franklin St. Dinner Tues.–Sat.; closed Sun. and Mon. A casual and intimate eatery serving authentic regional Italian cuisine has been a local favorite for more than a decade. Many of De Anna's dishes are generations-old family recipes, including the delicious homemade pastas and sauces. In-season you can dine outdoors in the lovely garden. BYOB. $16–25.

Lambertville Station (609-397-4400; www.lambertvillestation.com), 11 Bridge St. Lunch Mon.–Sat.; dinner daily; Sun. brunch. A restored 19th-century train station is a casual and charming restaurant and inn on the Delaware River and the Delaware and Raritan Canal (see *Lodging—Inns*). Creative New American cuisine features fresh meats and seafood accompanied by the restaurant's signature homemade coconut bread. Downstairs, the spirited **Station Pub** features live jazz and blues on the weekends. $31–50.

Siam (609-397-8128), 61 North Main St. Open daily for lunch and dinner. Reservations recommended. Authentic Thai cuisine in a casual and unpretentious setting. Earthy spices and flavors enhance the noodle dishes, seafood, curries, and other familiar and exotic dishes. A small space that can get very crowded on weekends, but locals insist the food is well worth it. BYOB. $12–18; credit cards not accepted.

Tortuga's Cocina (609-397-7272; www.tortugascocina.com), 11-1/2 Church St. Open for lunch and dinner Sat.–Sun.; dinner Tues.–Fri. You need to hunt for this gem, half hidden on Church Street as it is, but the

Mexican/Tex-Mex cuisine is worth it. Appealing outdoor patio dining in season. $13–18.

Elsewhere

Café At Rosemont (609-397-4097; www.cafeatrosemont.com), County Rds. 519 and 604, Rosemont. Open for lunch Tues.–Fri. 11–3, brunch Sat.–Sun. 9–2, dinner Wed.–Sun. until 9; closed Mon. A small roadside spot serving an eclectic menu with daily specials. Thursday evening is tapas night, which shows a distinctive Asian flair. During income tax season, tax-free Wednesdays feature foods from countries with minimal or no income taxes. BYOB. $15–24.

SNACKS

In Milford

The Baker (908-995-4040; www.the-baker.com), 60 Bridge St. Open daily 6–5. Hearty old-fashioned whole-grain breads, rolls, and buns are hand-crafted using traditional baking methods and organic stone-ground wheat, raw honey, flax seeds, raisin juice concentrate, and other whole-some ingredients.

In Stockton

Errico's Market and Deli (609-397-0049), 12 Bridge St. Open daily 7 AM–8 PM. A bustling market occupying Stockton's red-clapboard former train station. Freshly made baked goods, soups, salads, and hot specials are made daily, along with gourmet sandwiches with ingredients like roasted red peppers and fresh mozzarella. A convenient rest stop for cyclists riding on the adjacent bike path. Drinks, snacks, and gourmet groceries. Sandwiches $5–8.

✍ **Cravings** (609-397-2911), 10 Risler St. Open daily in summer 7 AM–9 PM; shorter off-season hours. A popular locals' morning spot for coffee and breakfast-sandwiches during the week;

French toast, omelets, and pancakes are on the weekend menu. Eat at a patio umbrella table or inside the cheery eatery. From the grill, hot dogs, burgers, tuna melts, and cheesesteaks. Kids (and adults) love the ice cream, milk shakes, and banana splits. Sandwiches $5–8.

In Lambertville

✍ **Giuseppe's Ristorante and Pizza Bar** (609-397-1500; www.giuseppes ristorante.net), 40 Bridge St. Open Mon., Wed., Thurs., and Sun. 11–11; Fri. and Sat. 11–midnight; closed Tues. Eat-in or take-out gourmet pizza by the slice and traditional Italian cuisine, from chicken Parmesan and veal Marsala to calzones, pasta and authentic Italian desserts. $5–15.

Baker's Treat Café (609-397-2772; www.bakerstreat.com), 9B Church St. Open Thurs.–Sun. 9:30–5; closed Mon.–Wed. A small take-out bakery and café, a satellite of Nancy Baron's busy gourmet café in Flemington. Freshly made baked goods, sandwiches, salads, and soups, and a selection of prepared dinners to go. Proceeds benefit women in early recovery from substance abuse. $5–7.

✍ **Sneddon's Luncheonette** (609-397-3053), 45 Bridge St. Open for breakfast and lunch 6–2 daily. Good, simple food in a locals' atmosphere. Kids' menu. Cash only. $5–10.

In Sergeantsville

Sergeantsville General Store (609-397-3214), Rts. 523 and 604. Open daily. An old-fashioned general store with a twist—a full menu of home-made Chinese dishes. Try the hand-made dumplings stuffed with fresh vegetables, beef, and pork. There's also a regular deli menu, as well as drinks, snacks, and groceries. A general store has served this rural community at this busy intersection since the 19th century. $3–10.

COFFEE AND TEA *Buck's Ice Cream and Espresso Bar* (908-996-7258), 52 Bridge St., Frenchtown (also at 25 Bridge St. in Lambertville). Quick snacks like bagels, pastries, and ice cream, as well as biscotti for dunking in your espresso, cappuccino, or a variety of hot and cold coffee drinks.

Lambertville Trading Company (609-397-2232; www.lambertville trading.com), 43 Bridge St., Lambertville. Open daily. The region's first cappuccino bar serves hot and cold coffee drinks along with gourmet snacks and baked goods to a busy mix of locals and visitors. $3–7.

❋ Entertainment

ARTS CENTERS **Prallsville Mills** (609-397-3586), Rt. 29, Stockton. A beautifully preserved complex of historic mill buildings in Delaware and Raritan Canal State Park, with a full schedule of community events, concerts, art exhibits, and antiques shows. Just upstream from the center of Stockton. Call for event schedules and hours. (See *To See—Historic Sites.*)

Stockton Performing Arts Center (609-652-9000; www.stockton.edu/pac), Richard Stockton College, College Drive, Stockton. A variety of concerts and performances mounted year-round by local and touring artists and companies. Symphony, experimental theater, ballet, and opera are among the diverse offerings. Call or visit Web site for schedule.

MUSIC *Riverside Symphonia* (609-397-7300; 215-862-3300; www .riversidesymphonia.org), P.O. Box 650, Lambertville 08530. Professional orchestra and soloists in classical, pops, and chamber music performances at various locations in and around Lambertville. Holiday concerts, perform-ances especially for children, and world-renowned guest musicians and conductors are featured in a full year-round schedule of concerts.

THEATER **Washington Crossing Open Air Theatre** (609-737-1826), Washington Crossing State Park, 355 Washington Crossing–Pennington Rd. (Rt. 546), Titusville. A summer festival of musicals, dramas, comedies, and Shakespeare's plays performed in a 450-seat natural outdoor amphitheater in a historic state park (see sidebar, page 231).

River Union Stage (908-996-3685; www.riverunionstage.org), P.O. Box 333, Frenchtown 08825. A regional professional theater company launched in 2002. A variety of performances—from original plays to Shakespeare's works—staged at locations in and around Frenchtown.

❋ Selective Shopping

ANTIQUES

In Milford

Allen's Antiques (908-995-8868), 49 Bridge St. Open Wed.–Sun. 11–6; Tues. by appointment; closed Mon. Allen Hughes's cozy shop occupies a historic stone building in the center of town, distinguished by its front porch crammed with an eclectic jumble of antiques. The collection inside is equally diverse, from jewelry and furniture to art and decorative pieces. The relaxed and friendly atmosphere is inviting, and the prices are reasonable.

In Frenchtown

Stone and Company Antiques (908-996-4840), 12 Race St. A quaint shop in a row of historic downtown buildings sitting cheek by jowl along Race St. An absorbing variety of cottage-style antiques and home décor, from furniture to whimsical decorative pieces.

In Lambertville

Antique Center at the People's Store (609-397-9808; www.peoples store.net), 28 North Union St. Open daily 10–6. A 40-shop co-op offering a diverse selection of reasonably priced antiques, from vintage clothing and books to furniture, decorative pieces, and art. Lambertville's oldest and largest affordable antiques center.

Broadmoor Antiques (609-397-8802), Six North Union St. Open Wed.–Mon.; closed Tues. A riverside complex featuring 10 galleries selling decorative art, antiques, and fine art, from 19th- and 20th-century American paintings to Asian prints and bronze sculpture. One of the more notable antiques centers in the Delaware Valley region.

Jim's of Lambertville (609-397-7700), Six Bridge St. Open Wed.–Sun.; closed Mon. and Tues. A 7,000-square-foot showroom and separate gallery specializing in Pennsylvania impressionist and modernist paintings, primarily from the New Hope school of artists. In addition, a stunning collection of thousands of antiques, from American and European sculpture to vintage watches and art glass.

Mix Gallery (609-773-0777; www.mixgallery.com), 17 South Main St. Features an eclectic collection of 18th- and 19th-century antiques, vintage designer handbags from the 1940s to 1970s, and mid-20th-century modern lighting, furniture, and funky home décor.

ART GALLERIES

In Frenchtown

Gabriele's Art Gallery (908-996-6011), 57 Bridge St. A gallery specializing in aviation art, including original works and limited-edition prints depicting key scenes from World War I–, World War II–, and Vietnam War–era history; many pieces are signed by world-famous pilots. The gallery also carries original oils, photographs, and prints of sports, botanicals, and wildlife.

Mendham Gallery (908-996-2243), 33 Bridge St. An American crafts gallery representing more than 100 artists. A unique and diverse collection of fine crafts, including pottery, hand-blown glass, paintings, and jewelry.

In Stockton

Sunflower Glass Studio (609-397-1535; www.sunflowerglassstudio.com), 877 Sergeantsville Rd. A fascination with prisms and rainbows inspired Karen and Geoff Caldwell to open a stained-glass studio in 1978. Working from their historic 19th-century farmhouse, they collaborate on the design and crafting of everything from custom stained-glass windows for homes and churches to sculpture, bath accessories, and Christmas ornaments for the home. Their signature pieces are stunning hand-beveled glass and botanical renderings in bold hues and intricate designs.

DECOYS AND WILDLIFE GALLERY (908-996-6501; 888-996-6501; www.decoyswildlife.com), 55 Bridge St., Frenchtown. Open daily 10–6. A unique gallery featuring the area's largest selection of duck decoys and carvings made by artists from across the country. For centuries, hand-carved decoys have served a utilitarian purpose for hunters, fishermen, and trappers; today, many are works of fine art sought by collectors. The gallery also has wildlife art by nationally recognized artists, as well as bronzes and limited-edition prints.

In Lambertville

Artsbridge Gallery (609-773-0881; www.artsbridgeonline.com), 25 Bridge St. Open Thurs.–Sun.; closed Mon.–Wed. A nonprofit arts organization and gallery representing the work of hundreds of artists, performers, and writers in the river region of Lambertville and in New Hope, Pennsylvania. Call for a schedule of shows and exhibitions.

Coryell Gallery (609-397-0804), Eight Coryell St. Open Wed.–Sun. noon–5; closed Mon. and Tues. A fine-art gallery featuring the work of artists from the Delaware Valley region. Oils, watercolors, sculpture, printmaking, pottery, and other media. The gallery hosts an annual group show in summer.

Haas Gallery (609-397-7988; www.haasgallery.com), 71 Bridge St. Open Sat. and Sun. noon–5; Mon.–Fri. by chance or appointment. Gordon Haas's artist-owned gallery and working studio. Haas specializes in the area's rural landscape, from well-known historic sites, scenes along the Delaware River and the Delaware and Raritan Canal, and sculling. Original oils, drawings, and limited-edition prints.

Howard Mann Art Center (609-397-2300), 45 North Main St. Open Wed.–Sun. 12–5; closed Mon. and Tues. A fine-art gallery featuring the work of more than 100 internationally known artists, including some of the world's best. Works by Picasso, Miró, Dalí, Calder, and Remington on display.

BOOKSTORES Beasley's Bookbindery (908-996-9993; www.beasleys bookbindery.com), 106 Harrison St., Frenchtown. A small shop specializing in book restoration and conservation. An interesting selection of handmade books, fine personalized stationery, and book-related gifts.

Book Garden (908-996-2022; www.bookgarden.biz), 28 Bridge St., Frenchtown. Open Thurs.–Sun. 11–5; closed Mon.–Wed. Esther Tews's lovely shop occupies a charming 19th-century Victorian house. She sells a wide selection of bestsellers, art books, guides to local history, and books and games for children. The museum shop sells collections of fine-art cards, jewelry, and stationery, as well as handmade gifts from Russia, South Africa, Germany, and Egypt. A separate room features thousands of used paperbacks. Ask about book signings and other events.

Phoenix Books (609-397-4960), 49 North Union St., Lambertville. Open daily. An independent, full-service bookshop with a wide variety of titles. They also feature used, rare, first-edition, and out-of-print books, as well as classical and jazz records.

FLEA MARKET Golden Nugget Antique Market (609-397-0811; www.gnmarket.com), 1850 River Rd. (Rt. 29), Lambertville. Open Wed., Sat., and Sun. 6 AM–4 PM. One of the largest and best-known antiques markets in New Jersey, with more than 60 indoor shops and 250 vendors outside selling antiques, art, and collectibles.

SPECIAL SHOPS
In Milford

The Ginger Tree (908-995-0880), Two Bridge St. Open Wed.–Sat. 10–6; Sun. noon–5; closed Mon., Tues., and major holidays; closed Sun. in Jan. and Feb. Lucy Herman's whimsical shop occupies the former waiting rooms in the village's 1865 stone train station. In addition to her own original artwork, Herman sells lovely and unique gifts, fine stationery and note cards, and home décor.

In Frenchtown

Alchemy Artwear (908-996-9000), 17 Bridge St. Open daily 10–6. An original line of unique artist-made clothing, jewelry, hats, silk and velvet scarves, and accessories designed by artists. The dresses are popular among those seeking a creative alternative to traditional gowns for weddings, parties, and other events.

Treasures and Pleasures (908-996-0999), 111 Harrison St., Frenchtown. Open Tues.–Sun. 10–5; closed Mon. Carol Winnecki's enchanting shop in a charming old house is filled chockablock with a pleasing mix of items, from vintage lamps and linens to kitchen collectibles, unusual gifts, and decorative items for the home and garden.

In Lambertville

The Sojourner (609-397-8849; www .sojourner.biz), 26 Bridge St. Open daily 11–6; Wed. until 8. An interesting and unusual collection of exotic items from shopping excursions around the world. The shop features an ever-changing array of clothing, ethnic jewelry, artifacts, and textiles from China, Turkey, Bali, Japan, Guatemala, and other far-flung locales.

Chocolate Box (609-397-1920; www .chocolateboxusa.com), 39 North Union St. An elegant 19th-century shop featuring an enticing display of exquisite European and American chocolates, including organic and sugarless varieties. Buy them individually, by the box, or—for a lovely and unique gift—have them fill an antique container with the chocolates of your choice.

The Urban Archaeologist (609-397-9588), 63 Bridge St. and Seven Lambert Lane. Open Thurs.–Mon. 11–6; Tues. and Wed. by appointment. A unique shop in a historic downtown building, selling home and garden furnishings, handmade jewelry, and artifacts collected in Greece and Italy.

Hand-painted glass, Greek mahogany and Tuscan furniture, and reproductions of museum pieces are among the shop's more popular items.

FARMS AND GARDENS ✐ **Willow Creek Nursery** (908-237-2053), Rt. 579, Ringoes. Open Mon.–Sat. 9–6; Sun. 10–5. A full-service nursery and country store next to the Black River & Western Railroad. New Jersey–grown produce, freshly baked pies, local honey and apples, garden accessories, and seasonal gifts in the country store. All nursery products from hanging baskets to trees. Ask about autumn hayrides to the pumpkin patch and special holiday events for families.

Homestead Farm Market (609-397-8285; www.homesteadfarmmkt.com), 262 N. Main St. (Rt. 29), Lambertville. Open daily from Apr. 1 to Christmas. An extensive selection of New Jersey–grown produce fills this bustling farm market in a red barn just outside downtown. They also sell seasonal gift baskets, plants, honey, garden pottery, bedding plants, and organic meats and ice cream. The bake shop has freshly baked pastries, muffins, pies, and breads, and the **Take Away Café** features artisan cheeses and prepared gourmet dinners to go.

Fiddler's Creek Farm (609-737-0685), 188 Hunter Rd., Titusville. Open Mon.–Fri.; closed Sat. and Sun. A family farm in business for more than 60 years, it specializes in old-fashioned methods of curing and smoking fresh pork and poultry. All their products are made by hand without artificial ingredients or fillers; meats are cured with salt and brown sugar and smoked over hickory chips. Smoked turkey, chicken, bacon, and pork tenderloin.

✳ Special Events

January: ♪ **Lambertville–New Hope Winter Festival** (215-862-5067; 609-397-0055; www.winterfestival.net), in Lambertville and in New Hope, PA. A winter celebration hosted by two historic towns on opposite banks of the Delaware River. Ice-carving demonstrations, a parade, snow folk-art competition, wildlife seminars, concerts, and activities for families and children.

February: ♪ **George Washington Birthday Celebration** (609-737-0623), Washington Crossing State Park, Titusville. A popular event honoring George Washington at the site of his infamous crossing of the Delaware River during the Revolutionary War in 1776.

April: ♪ **Shad Festival** (609-397-0055; www.lambertville.org), Bridge, Union, and Lambertville Sts., Lambertville. For nearly a quarter century, Lambertville has celebrated spring and the return of spawning shad, a sea trout, up the Delaware River. Native American methods of shad preparation, riverside shad dinners, artisans, crafters, live music, and kids' entertainment. On nearby **Lewis Island,** the state's only commercial shad fishery demonstrates the old shad-hauling methods that Native Americans taught to the region's earliest European settlers.

June: **Hidden Gardens of Lambertville Tour** (609-397-2537), Lambertville. Self-guided tours of privately owned gardens tucked behind some of Lambertville's loveliest homes.

July: ♪ **Bastille Festival,** Frenchtown. An annual celebration honoring Frenchtown's founding father, Paul Henri Mallet-Prevost; food, crafters, entertainment, and art exhibits.

August: **Summer Antiques Show** (856-459-2229), Prallsville Mills, Rt. 29, Stockton. Some 40 exhibitors display their wares throughout this historic collection of restored mill buildings on the Delaware River.

September: ♪ **Celebration of Farming** (609-397-2752; www.holcombe -jimison.org), Holcombe-Jimison Farmstead Museum, Lambertville. A celebration of Hunterdon County's agricultural heritage. Demonstrations include wool spinning, beekeeping, blacksmithing, and sheep herding. Pony rides, wagon rides, and farm animals for children.

October: ♪ **Grand Harvest Wine Festival** (908-995-7800; www.alba vineyard.com), Alba Vineyard, Milford. New Jersey wineries feature several hundred wines for sale or to be sampled. Wine cellar tours, children's activities, live music, gourmet food, crafters, and antique cars. **Antiques Show** (609-397-3100), Lambertville. Dealers from around the country. **Autumn House Tour** (609-397-0770), Lambertville. Sponsored by the Lambertville Historical Society. Some of Lambertville's most magnificent Federal, Neo-Georgian, and Victorian private homes are open to the public. Visitors can also tour historic sites, including the Delaware and Raritan Canal.

November: **Thanksgiving in the Country** (908-996-4677; www.thanks givinginthecountry.com), Sergeantsville. A well-known guided historic house tour that benefits the Children's Hospital of Philadelphia.

December: ♪ **Washington's Crossing of the Delaware** (609-737-9303), Washington Crossing State Park, Titusville. Christmas Day reenactment of the famous 1776 crossing of General Washington and his Continental soldiers into New Jersey on their way to defeating Hessian troops in Trenton.

THE TRENTON AND
CAMDEN AREA

N ew Jersey's capital city—one of the oldest on the East Coast—sits on the
Delaware River midway between New York City and Philadelphia, about halfway
up the state's western border. The river was a vital travel and trade route for
Native Americans long before European settlers arrived in the early 1600s. The
Delaware is navigable by ship as far as Trenton, so it was inevitable that a trading
center bustled here with agricultural trade and, later, industrial trade before Trenton became the state capital at the end of the 18th century.

Downtown Trenton is a virtual living museum of Early American history. After
George Washington and his Continental troops crossed the Delaware River on
Christmas night 1776 they headed straight for the city, where they launched a surprise attack on Hessian soldiers occupying the Old Barracks that were built for
British troops during the French and Indian War. Trenton's landmark battle monument marks the spot where American artillery was placed before the pivotal battles
of Trenton, and commemorates Washington's first major victory against the British.
Trenton became the new nation's state capital in 1790; the 1792 statehouse is the
second-oldest in the nation in continuous use.

When the Industrial Revolution swept America after the Civil War, Trenton
became a major transportation hub and manufacturing center, especially in the
production of ceramics. In the late 1800s, potteries by the hundreds were in business in Trenton, which became known as the Staffordshire of America. The largest
operation, the Ceramic Art Company, was later succeeded by porcelain giant
Lenox. Relics from the city's famous industry are now on display in museums, galleries, and porcelain studios. Trenton's manufacturing heritage didn't end with
porcelain, however. Everything from steel and General Motors cars to American
Standard sinks and the Roebling wire rope used to make the George Washington
and Golden Gate bridges was produced here. The city's slogan, "Trenton Makes,
the World Takes," blazes in huge 1930s-era electric red letters on the bridge across
the Delaware River, a neon homage to the capital city's golden years as an industrial giant.

When industry waned in the 20th century, Trenton slipped into a decline and
much of the port city sadly fell into a state of neglect. In recent years, however,
revitalization efforts to shake its dreary urban image have been successful. Today
the city boasts top-notch museums, including the 1758 Old Barracks Museum, the

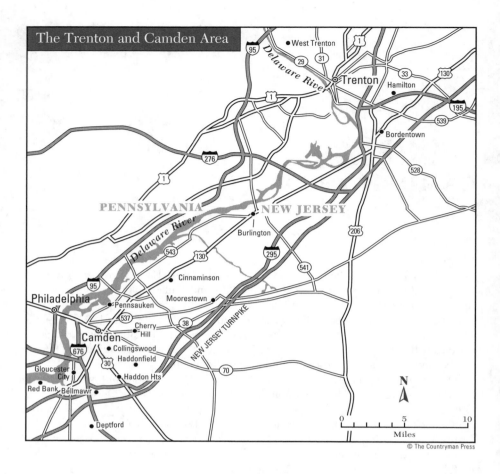

West Trenton

Trenton

Hamilton

Bordentown

PENNSYLVANIA   NEW JERSEY

Burlington

Cinnaminson

Moorestown

Philadelphia

Pennsauken

Cherry Hill

Camden

Collingswood

Haddonfield

Gloucester City

Red Bank Bellmawr

Haddon Hts

NEW JERSEY TURNPIKE

Deptford

N

0   5   10
Miles

© The Countryman Press

New Jersey State Museum, and the Trenton City Museum, a grand Italianate mansion in a park designed by the father of American landscape architecture, Frederick Law Olmsted. World-class musicians and performance artists play the Sovereign Bank Arena and the magnificent Patriots Theater at the historic Trenton War Memorial. Sports fans come to watch live minor-league baseball and hockey games in the city where the first professional basketball game in America was held in 1896.

Camden was settled in 1681, developed in large part because of its proximity to Philadelphia, just across the Delaware River. In the 18th century the Cooper family ran a ferry service between the two cities; a descendant, the great American novelist James Fenimore Cooper, was born in nearby Burlington. Another literary icon, the poet Walt Whitman, came to Camden in the 1800s to care for his ailing mother. The *Leaves of Grass* author grew to love the industrial riverfront city, and spent the remainder of his life in a modest home near the Delaware. Today, his house is open for tours, and an arts center and the suspension bridge over the Delaware River just south of Camden are named in his honor.

Like Trenton, Camden prospered at the turn of the 20th century, when it was a bustling transportation and industrial hub known as the Biggest Little City in the World. The Victor Talking Machine Company, later known as RCA Victor, as well as the Campbell Soup Company, were two giants based here. Unfortunately, the automobile eventually eclipsed trains and ferries as a major mode of transportation; the rail line to Philadelphia shut down in the 1950s; and the city started its 50-year steady slide, losing residents, jobs, and money. The city was hit hard, and the outlook was grim. For decades, Camden was plagued by urban problems, from scores of abandoned homes to blight, poverty, and crime. New Jersey's poorest city retained an image of a dangerous, drug-ridden place to avoid. In recent years, millions in state and county aid have been channeled to Camden to fund an economic recovery and ambitious redevelopment plans.

Today there's evidence of a budding renaissance, especially on the waterfront. With its major family-oriented attractions, the area has reemerged as a destination for families and visitors. The battleship *New Jersey,* the country's most decorated battleship, is a floating museum permanently berthed in the river. Nearby, the newly renovated Adventure Aquarium (formerly the New Jersey State Aquarium) is home to thousands of fish, two-dozen sharks, and rare South African penguins. The Susquehanna Center is the city's main venue for concerts, entertainment, and special events; the South Jersey Performing Arts Center offers regional and national theater and dance; and Rutgers University's Camden branch has an active arts center open to the public. The Riversharks play minor-league baseball at Campbell's Field, and musicians play under the stars at Wiggins Waterfront Park.

The baseball stadium is named for a longtime Camden industry whose products have found their way onto the shelves of most American kitchens for the past century. The Joseph A. Campbell Preserve Company began canning New Jersey–grown vegetables and condiments in 1869. In 1897, the Campbell Soup Company cooked its first batch of condensed soup; the ubiquitous red and white label was developed the following year. The original soup plant was demolished in the 1990s—the company's soups and other products are now manufactured in the Midwest—but the world headquarters still resides downtown, where a unique museum pays tribute to the iconic soup, of which millions of cans have been sold around the world.

You can explore the quieter historic towns of Haddonfield, Burlington, and Bordentown by visiting their historic districts, parks, small museums, and shops and restaurants. John Haddon was a wealthy Quaker businessman from London who bought a tract of wilderness in West Jersey (in the 17th century, New Jersey was divided into two colonies, "East" and "West") and sent his daughter, Elizabeth, to America to claim it. She named the settlement Haddonfield, a quiet Quaker community that became a significant crossroads during the American Revolution. British, Hessian, and American troops and generals—from Lafayette to Lord Cornwallis—marched through on The Kings Rd., the centuries-old route between Salem and Burlington laid out in the 1680s. Today Haddonfield's main street is called Kings Highway, and is lined with many well-preserved buildings and homes from the colonial era. In one of them, the Indian King Tavern, New Jersey was proclaimed a state and the state seal was formally adopted.

Today, Haddonfield is a lovely historic town with more than 200 antiques shops, cafés, boutiques, and galleries in a revitalized downtown of Federal and Victorian storefronts. The world's first nearly complete dinosaur skeleton was unearthed in a wooded ravine on a Haddonfield farm in 1858. The discovery of *Hadrosaurus foulkii* proved that massive reptile-like creatures—dramatically different from modern animals—roamed the planet long before the evolution of humans, a hotly debated topic in the 19th century. A tiny park at the end of a residential street marks the discovery site, now a national historic landmark. A sculpture of *Hadrosaurus foulkii* looking out onto Kings Highway is a beloved icon in Haddonfield's charming downtown shopping district.

Burlington was a colonial village in the 17th century; a young Benjamin Franklin worked as an apprentice in the printing trade here. Its charming historic district includes shops, restaurants, and several restored historic buildings. Two historical societies lead walking tours of Burlington's notable sites, including the home of Ulysses S. Grant and the birthplace of noted American novelist James Fenimore Cooper, whose frontiersman hero, Leatherstocking, is the stuff of literary legend. You can also catch a guided tour in Bordentown, which was settled as a river village in 1682 and was the first community in America to open a free public school.

Entries in this section are arranged in roughly geographic order.

AREA CODES 856, 609.

GUIDANCE The **Capital Region Convention and Visitors Bureau** (609-777-1770; www.trentonnj.com) is in the Old Masonic Lodge at Lafayette and Barracks Sts. Open Mon.–Fri. 9–4; Sat. and Sun. 10–4. They have an extensive selection of literature on lodging, dining, and cultural and sporting events.

Camden Waterfront Marketing Bureau (856-757-9400; www.camdenwaterfront.com) is at One Port Center, 2 Riverside Drive, Suite 102, Camden. The Web site offers an event calendar and map for waterfront attractions, plus links to dining, lodging, and other sites.

Haddonfield Information Center (856-216-7253; www.haddonfieldnj.org), 12 Kings Court, Haddonfield. Open daily noon to 4. A friendly and knowledgeable staff offers visitors guidance on area attractions, events, and activities, as well as public restrooms. Postcards and local books and gifts for sale.

In Burlington, the **Burlington City Historic District** (609-386-0200) and the **Burlington County Historical Society** (609-386-4773; www.burlingtoncounty historicalsociety.org), both at 451 High St., offer guided walking tours of the town's many historic homes, including the birthplace of novelist James Fenimore Cooper and the homes of Ulysses S. Grant and John Hoskins.

The Bordentown Historical Society (609-298-1740; www.bordentownhistory .org), 302 Farnsworth Ave., Bordentown, leads guided walking tours of the town's historic sites.

GETTING THERE *By air:* **Trenton–Mercer Airport** (800-644-3562), 5 minutes from downtown Trenton (off I-95), is currently open only to private aircraft and charter flights. **Newark Liberty International Airport** (973-961-6000; parking information: 888-397-4636; www.panynj.com) in Newark serves the entire state; it's about 45 minutes from the Trenton and Camden region. **Philadelphia International Airport** (215-937-6800; www.philadelphia-phl.com) in Pennsylvania is just across the Delaware River from Camden.

By rail: **New Jersey Transit's** Trenton to Camden River LINE light rail commuter service (973-275-5555; www.riverline.com) links 20 stations on a 34-mile route between Trenton and Camden, with connections to Amtrak, New Jersey Transit buses and commuter trains, and SEPTA rail service to Philadelphia. The line traces the historic route of New Jersey's first rail line, the Camden & Amboy Railroad, which was built in 1838 as part of a route for passengers traveling between Philadelphia and New York City.

Trenton Station, 72 South Clinton Ave. at Market St., is a regional rail hub served by Amtrak and New Jersey Transit. **Amtrak** (800-872-7245; www.amtrak .com) runs between Philadelphia and New York City. **New Jersey Transit** (973-275-5555; www.njtransit.com) connects Trenton with New York City. **SEPTA** (Southeastern Pennsylvania Transportation Authority) commuter trains (215-580-7800; www.septa.org) link Trenton to Philadelphia.

By bus: **Greyhound** (800-229-9424; www.greyhound.com) and **New Jersey Transit** (973-275-5555; www.njtransit.com) serve the Trenton and Camden region.

By car: The **New Jersey Turnpike** and **I-295** run just east of Trenton and Camden. Other major routes in the area are **I-195** from Trenton to the shoreline; **I-95** from Trenton to Philadelphia; and **Rt. 130** linking Trenton and Camden. Three toll bridges connect Camden to Philadelphia across the Delaware River; another links Trenton to Morrisville, Pennsylvania, on **US 1.**

GETTING AROUND *Taxis:* **King's Cab** (609-656-2400), **Yellow Cab** (609-396-8181), and **United Cab** (609-393-8778) serve the Trenton region. **Colonial Transport and Taxi Service** (856-854-5800) in Collingswood and **Best Taxi** (856-321-8294) in Cherry Hill serve the Camden area.

MEDICAL EMERGENCY
In Trenton
Capital Health Systems—Fuld Campus (609-394-6000; www.capitalhealth.org), 750 Brunswick Ave. The emergency number is 609-394-6063.

Capital Health Systems—Mercer Campus (609-394-4000; www.capitalhealth .org), 446 Bellevue Ave. The emergency number is 609-394-4022.

Saint Francis Medical Center (609-599-5000; www.stfrancismedical.com), 601 Hamilton Ave. The emergency number is 609-599-5210.

In the Camden area
Lourdes Medical Center of Burlington County (609-835-2900; www.lourdes net.org), 218A Sunset Rd., Willingboro. The emergency number is 609-835-3030.

Our Lady of Lourdes Medical Center (856-757-3500; www.lourdesnet.org), 1600 Haddon Ave., Camden. The emergency number is 856-757-3803.

Cooper University Hospital (856-342-2000; www.cooperhealth.org), Hadden Ave., Camden.

Kennedy Memorial Hospital (856-488-6500; www.kennedyhealth.org), Chapel Ave. and Cooper Landing Rd., Cherry Hill. The emergency number is 856-488-6816.

Underwood Memorial Hospital (856-845-0100; www.umhospital.org), 509 North Broad St., Woodbury. The emergency number is 856-853-2000.

THE DELAWARE RIVER VALLEY

✳ To See

AQUARIUM ✎ **Adventure Aquarium** (856-365-3300; 800-616-5297; www
.adventureaquarium.com), One Riverside Drive, Camden. Open daily 9:30–5.
Adults $18.95; children (ages 2–12) $14.95; children under 2, free. Adventure Pass
Combination (includes exhibits, live shows and one 4D Theater experience): adult
$23.95, children $19.95. The aquarium (formerly The New Jersey State Aquarium)
is a Camden landmark set on the Delaware River and home to more than 4,000
fish and other aquatic animals in 80 exhibits. Two-dozen sharks, as well as sea turtles, stingrays, and more than 1,500 fish reside in the huge 760,000-gallon Deep
Atlantic Open Ocean Tank. Other permanent exhibits include the Conservation
Outreach and Observation Lab, the Seal Shores exhibition, and the Inguza Island
exhibit of rare South African penguins. Daily seal and dive shows.

HISTORIC HOMES ✎ **William Trent House** (609-989-3027; www.william
trenthouse.org), 15 Market St., Trenton. Open daily 12:30–4 and by appointment for
group and individual tours; closed major holidays. The capital city's oldest dwelling is
a stately brick Georgian mansion—a national historic landmark—overlooking the
Delaware River. It was built around 1719 as a summer estate for prominent
Philadelphia merchant and justice William Trent, who laid out the original plans for
Trenton. During the battles of Trenton, the house was occupied first by Hessian soldiers, then later served as a supply depot for the Continental army. It was the official
governor's residence in the 19th century, and opened as a museum in 1939. Today
the house provides a glimpse at early-18th-century colonial life through period furnishings, exhibits, and hands-on activities for children (weekends only).

ADVENTURE AQUARIUM, FORMERLY THE N.J. STATE AQUARIUM, FEATURES A 40-FOOT
WALK-THROUGH SHARK TANK TUNNEL THAT TRAVERSES A SHARK TANK, AND A WEST
AFRICAN RIVER EXHIBIT WITH HIPPOS, EXOTIC BIRDS, AND CROCODILES.

Photo courtesy of Adventure Aquarium.

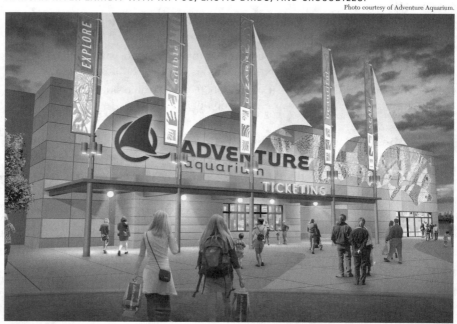

Kuser Farm Mansion (609-890-3630), 2090 Greenwood Ave., Hamilton. Open for tours Feb.–Apr., Sat. and Sun. 11–3; May–Nov., Thurs.–Sun. 11–3; closed Dec. and Jan. Grounds open daily. Free admission. This many-gabled Queen Anne–style mansion built in 1892 was the summer estate of the prominent Kuser family, an influential force in New Jersey politics and business. The first Kusers were Swiss immigrant farmers who came to New Jersey in the mid-1800s; their descendants founded such giants as the Prudential Life Insurance Company and Fox Films, which later merged with 20th Century Fox. Rooms contain original furnishings and memorabilia from the Kuser family, whose legacy includes the New Jersey Audubon Society and High Point State Park. Call for a schedule of exhibitions, demonstrations, and special events.

James and Ann Whitall House (856-853-5120), Red Bank Battlefield Park, 100 Hessian Ave., National Park. Open for tours Apr.–Sept., Wed.–Sun. 1–4; Oct.–Mar., Wed.–Fri. Sun. 9–noon and 1–4; closed weekends Nov.–Mar. Free admission. In the **Red Bank Battlefield Park,** site of the **1777 Battle of Red Bank** (see *Historic Sites*). The 1748 Georgian-style brick and stone house with distinctive red shutters is surrounded by a kitchen garden and orchard. The Whitall family lived here for 114 years, when it was the 300-acre Red Bank Plantation. During the Revolutionary War, American troops built **Fort Mercer** north of the house; and after the battle of Red Bank, the house was used as a field hospital, where Mrs. Whitall cared for wounded soldiers. After the war, the Whitalls ran a prosperous gristmill, an orchard, a shad fishery, and a ferry service across the Delaware River. The last Whitall descendant moved out in 1862. Call for a schedule of historical and cultural events.

HISTORIC SITES **Trenton Battle Monument** (609-737-0623), 348 S. Warren St., Trenton. Open Sat. 10–noon and 1–4; Sun. 1–4. The 150-foot-tall Beaux-Arts-style monument was built in 1893 to commemorate the 1776 battles of Trenton, George Washington's pivotal Revolutionary War victory. John H. Duncan, architect of Ulysses S. Grant's tomb, designed the granite Doric column topped with a viewing platform and a statue of the general standing with an outstretched arm. Washington's artillery was placed at this site during the surprise attack on three Hessian regiments, the day after the general and his Continental troops crossed the Delaware River on Christmas night and headed to the Hessian-occupied barracks in the city. A second battle was fought on January 2 before they moved on to the battle of Princeton. Visitors can climb to a balcony near the top for views of the city.

Trenton War Memorial (tours: 609-984-8484; box office: 609-984-8400; www.the warmemorial.com), Memorial Drive, in the state capitol complex, Trenton. Tours by appointment. This elaborate Italian Renaissance Revival and art deco–style city landmark was built in 1932 on the Delaware River to honor Trentonians who died in World War I. It's better known as the home to one of the region's top performing-arts venues—the **Patriots Theater**—and the place where New Jersey governors are inaugurated. A $35 million restoration in the 1990s transformed the historic theater into a stunning architectural gem, preserving the Memorial Court's blue terra-cotta ceiling and tile fountain, and the theater's ornate ceiling medallion. The acoustically superb theater hosts the **Greater Trenton Symphony Orchestra,** which has performed here since 1933 and has welcomed

WALT WHITMAN HOUSE

(856-964-5383), 328 Mickle Blvd., Camden. Open Wed.–Sun.; call for hours and admission prices. One of America's most distinguished writers, author of "Song of the Open Road" and "O Captain! My Captain!," didn't mean to spend his final years in Camden. "Camden was originally an accident," he once explained, "but I shall never be sorry I was left over in Camden. It has brought me blessed returns." He moved to the city in 1884 to care for his ailing mother, paid $1,750 for a modest Greek Revival–style house two blocks from the waterfront, and stayed for nearly 20 years. Whitman, then considered America's greatest poet, was fascinated by the bustling industrial city along the Delaware River, and was known to walk the streets and chat with people. During his years in Camden he befriended Philadelphia artist Thomas Eakins (who painted Whitman's portrait) and hosted literary gatherings at his house. Prominent literary figures, from Oscar Wilde to Charles Dickens, came from around the country and Europe to be in his company. While in Camden, Whitman revised his most notable work, *Leaves of Grass,* and completed his last volume of poetry. The six-room, wood-frame house—a national historic landmark—has been restored to its 1892 appearance, the way it was just before Whitman's death at age 72. Displays of personal belongings, original writings, and rare 19th-century photographs, as well as the death notice that hung on his door, share space with the bed Whitman died in. An excerpt from *Leaves of Grass,* which catapulted him to international fame, is etched in the stone tower of Camden's City Hall.

AMERICAN POET WALT WHITMAN LIVED THE LAST DAYS OF HIS LIFE ON MICKLE BOULEVARD NEAR THE CAMDEN WATERFRONT, WHERE HE HOSTED OSCAR WILDE, CHARLES DICKENS, AND OTHER 19TH-CENTURY LITERARY ICONS. TODAY THE MODEST CLAPBOARD HOUSE IS A NATIONAL HISTORIC LANDMARK.

Photo courtesy of the Camden Waterfront Marketing Bureau

world-class entertainers, from Bruce Springsteen and Frank Sinatra to Count Basie and Johnny Cash, to its stage (see *Entertainment—Arts Centers*).

Red Bank Battlefield (856-853-5120), 100 Hessian Ave., National Park (see *Green Space—Parks*). Open year-round, dawn to dusk. A historic park on the Delaware River at the site of the **1777 battle of Red Bank,** when the Continental army kept British supply ships from reaching Philadelphia. Near the park entrance is an exhibit containing remnants from the river defense system that protected the city from enemy attack during the American Revolution. A series of submerged obstructions, or *chevaux-de-frise,* were built of massive pine logs imbedded with iron spikes and hidden just below the surface in three locations on the river. The park also features Revolutionary War–era cannons, the remains of **Fort Mercer,** and the 1748 **Whitall House** (see *Historic Homes*), a Georgian-style home that served as a battlefield hospital. Monuments throughout the park denote historical events and key battle scenes.

Hadrosaurus Park (856-216-7253; www.hadrosaurus.com), Maple Ave., Haddonfield. The historic discovery site where the bones of *Hadrosaurus foulkii*—the world's first nearly complete dinosaur—were excavated in 1858 is a national historic landmark. Down a footpath into a ravine the actual excavation site sits in this suburban, wooded park. Here, local diggers led by scientist William Foulke uncovered the fossilized remains of a massive creature that resembled both a lizard and a bird. Since the 1700s, scientists had found random fossilized teeth and bones, but before the Haddonfield discovery, the idea that giant extinct creatures existed was hotly debated. With *Hadrosaurus foulkii,* paleontologists could study dinosaur anatomy and end the debate over whether the gargantuan reptile-like animals, or dinosaurs (from the Greek words meaning "terrible lizard"), were real. The bones are now in Philadelphia's Academy of Natural Sciences. A bronze *Hadrosaurus* sculpture stands in the center of Haddonfield.

RED BANK BATTLEFIELD PARK ON THE DELAWARE RIVER, IN NATIONAL PARK, CONTAINS THE 1748 JAMES AND ANN WHITALL HOUSE AND THE REMAINS OF FORT MERCER, TWO IMPORTANT SITES DURING THE REVOLUTIONARY WAR.

Photo courtesy of Gloucester County Parks and Recreation

MUSEUMS ✐ **New Jersey State Museum** (609-292-6464; www.nj.gov/state/museum), 205 West State St., Trenton. Open Tues.–Sat. 9–5; Sun. noon–5; closed Mon. and state holidays. Free admission; fee for planetarium and special events. This museum in the state capitol complex, established in 1895, is actually four individual museums. One features **Native American artifacts** from area Cherokee, Nanticoke, Powhatan-Renape, and Ramapough tribes. Another showcases **dinosaur relics,** including a cast of the locally excavated *Hadrosaurus foulkii,* the first nearly complete dinosaur skeleton found in America. **Artifacts from the Revolutionary War era** include a replica of Emanuel Leutze's famous painting of Washington and his troops crossing the Delaware on Christmas night 1776. Other galleries feature permanent and changing exhibits on archaeology, fine arts from the 19th and 20th centuries, natural science, and history. The **children's theater** hosts films, lectures, and special events; the 150-seat **Planetarium** features sky and laser shows on weekends.

✐ **Old Barracks Museum** (609-396-1776; 888-227-7225; www.barracks.org), Barrack St., in the state capitol complex, Trenton. Open daily 10–5; closed major holidays. Adults $8; seniors and students $6; children 5 and under, free. A museum (since 1902) that tells the story of colonial- and Revolutionary War–era New Jersey. The barracks, original buildings dating to the French and Indian War, are the only ones from that period still standing in the United States. The restored 1758 barracks and officers' house is near the site where George Washington won the battles

---

✐ **NEW JERSEY STATE POLICE MUSEUM AND LEARNING CENTER** (609-882-2000, ext. 6401; www.njspmuseum.org), State Police Headquarters, River Rd. (Rt. 175), West Trenton. Open Mon.–Fri. 10–4; Sat. group tours and **Lindbergh research library** by appointment. Free admission. The museum tells the story of the New Jersey State Police, formed in 1921 when 81 recruits completed training under **Colonel H. Norman Schwarzkopf** and became the first troopers to patrol on motorcycle and horseback. One collection centers on the kidnapping of aviator Charles Lindbergh's infant son. The **Crime of the Century** was the state police's biggest case; their apprehension of suspect Bruno Hauptmann made international headlines. A haunting exhibit features the wooden ladder used to snatch the baby, the ransom note, trial footage, the electric chair in which Hauptmann was executed, even hair and bone fragments recovered from the woods where the Lindbergh baby's body was found. Other exhibits feature videos on emergency response training and trooper training; interactive displays include a mock murder scene with clues and fingerprints that can be examined under a microscope. Law enforcement technology from radar guns to early models of the Breathalyzer, vintage police vehicles, and more than 100 confiscated rifles and handguns are also on display. An exhibit on the Crime Scene Investigation Unit shows how detectives handle a crime scene, with surveillance equipment, fingerprint-lifting devices, and forensic lab tools. A glass corridor is hung with portraits of New Jersey state troopers killed in the line of duty.

New Jersey State House (609-633-2709), 125 West State St., Trenton. Free tours every hour, Mon.–Fri. 10–3; Sat. noon–3; closed Sun. and state holidays. Advanced reservations required for groups of 10 or more. The **Welcome Center** is open Mon.–Sat. 9:30–4:30. Tours of the nation's second-oldest state capitol building in continuous use (Maryland's is first) trace the building's history and architecture, from the senate and assembly chamber galleries to the governor's reception room and the magnificent rotunda. The original capitol building—topped with a bell tower, not the massive gold dome seen today—was a simple stone structure built in 1792 for 250 English pounds— about $400. Various building projects in the 19th century expanded and renovated the capitol, which was nearly destroyed in a devastating 1885 fire. Today's building retains some of the original features—**the legislative chambers, the governor's office, and the circa-1792 Governor's Wing.** The most recent renovation was a $9 million dome face-lift in the 1990s. With help from funds raised by New Jersey schoolchildren, the 48,000 pieces of gold leaf that cover the massive cast-iron dome were replaced and polished to a high shine. It's no less impressive inside, with its lofty rotunda, portraits of New Jersey's early governors surrounded by stunning stained glass, polished marble and gleaming wood, and a landscaped plaza.

NEW JERSEY'S STATE HOUSE IN TRENTON, WHICH DATES TO 1792, IS AMERICA'S SECOND OLDEST STATEHOUSE STILL IN USE.
Photo courtesy of the New Jersey Commerce and Economic Growth Commission

Photo courtesy of the New Jersey Commerce and Economic Growth Commission

THE OLD BARRACKS MUSEUM IN TRENTON WAS BUILT IN 1758 TO HOUSE TROOPS DURING THE FRENCH AND INDIAN WAR. IT WAS LATER USED IN THE 1776 AND 1777 BATTLES OF TRENTON DURING THE AMERICAN REVOLUTION.

of Trenton. Visitors can see the cramped quarters where Hessian troops slept in bunk beds, and they can also watch daily living-history programs on military life that feature musicians, storytellers, and 18th- and 19th-century events. Changing exhibits display Revolutionary War–era clothing, furniture, and weapons. The battles of Trenton are reenacted annually, on the Saturday after Christmas.

✎ **Trenton City Museum at Ellarslie** (609-989-3632; www.ellarslie.org), Cadwalader Park, Stuyvesant and Parkside Aves., Trenton. Open Tues.–Sat. 11–3; Sun. 1–4; closed Mon. and major holidays. This elegant Italianate mansion, built as the summer home of a wealthy Philadelphian in 1848, has been a museum of Trenton memorabilia since 1889. Changing exhibits of fine contemporary art are in the first-floor galleries; special events include musical programs, art classes, and workshops for children in drawing, sculpture, and puppet making. Frederick Law Olmsted, the father of American landscape architecture, designed the parklike grounds to resemble a natural rolling landscape laced with trees and winding footpaths, much like his signature design project—Manhattan's Central Park.

✎ **The Battleship *New Jersey* Memorial and Museum** (866-877-6262 or 856-966-1652; www.battleshipnewjersey.org), 100 Clinton St. (on the Camden waterfront, next to the Susquehanna Center), Camden. Open Jan. and Feb., Fri.–Mon. 10–3; closed Tues.–Thurs.; Mar.–Apr., daily 9:30–3; May–Sept. 1, daily 9:30–5; Sept. 1–Dec., daily 9:30–3. Adults $17.40; seniors, veterans, and children 6–11, $13; children 5 and under, and active military, free. Guided tours extra. Self-guided and 2-hour guided tours aboard the USS *New Jersey,* the most highly decorated battleship in the U.S. Navy, which served in World War II, the Korean War, the Vietnam War, and in El Salvador and Beirut during the 1980s. Now it's permanently docked in Camden waterfront as a floating museum. The Iowa-class ship is one of the largest battleships ever built. Visitors can tour the battleship's upper and

lower sections, see military history displays and visit the museum shop.

Pomona Hall Park (856-964-3333; www.cchsnj.com), 1900 Park Boulevard, Camden. Library open Wed.–Sun. afternoons; house and museum tours Thurs. and Sun., noon until 3:30. The stately 1788 Georgian brick mansion on the outskirts of Camden was the home of prominent Quaker Joseph Cooper. Today it's the headquarters of the **Camden County Historical Society,** and offers a glimpse at the colonial-era life of one of Camden's most illustrious families. The adjacent museum has two floors of exhibits on local history and culture, from Lenape Indian artifacts and Civil War–era artifacts to relics of the city's industrial age. The research library contains three centuries' worth of books, genealogy materials, maps, and other historic memorabilia—some 20,000 items in all. Lectures and demonstrations on colonial life, living-history programs, traditional music, and other special programs; call for a schedule.

✔ **Garden State Discovery Museum** (856-424-1233; www.discoverymuseum .com), 2040 Springdale Rd., Cherry Hill. Open daily 9:30–5:30 year-round; open Sat. until 8:30 from Oct. to May; closed Thanksgiving and Christmas Day. Adults and children $9.95; seniors $8.95. *Child* magazine named this kid-friendly place one of the top 20 children's museums in America. Interactive and hands-on exhibits promote creative play for children aged 1 to 10, including a bubble play area, a make-believe diner, and a theater with costumes. Educational workshops and performances, from science experiments and multi-cultural arts and crafts to theater and crime scene investigation. The gift shop has a good selection of top-quality arts and crafts projects, books, and science experiments.

Indian King Tavern Museum (856-429-6792; www.levins.com/tavern), 233 Kings Hwy. East, Haddonfield. Open Wed.–Sat. 10–noon and 1–4; Sun. 1–4; closed Mon. and Tues. Tours of the refurbished first- and second-floor tavern rooms by appointment; it's recommended that visitors call 10 days in advance; for groups of seven or more, a reservation is required. Free admission. This Early American public house built in 1750 is New Jersey's first designated historic site. The state legislature reconvened at this colonial village tavern in 1777 during the American Revolution when clashes between British and American troops wreaked havoc on the capital city. In the Assembly Room, lawmakers adopted the state seal and passed legislation officially changing New Jersey's status from colony to independent state. Other rooms include a bar room, a keeping room, and a sleeping chamber with a bed slept in by Dolley Madison. Ask about the tavern's mysterious cellar (not open to visitors), the source of many myths and legends. Ongoing special programs include live traditional music and Christmas holiday concerts.

Greenfield Hall (856-429-7375; www.historicalsocietyofhaddonfield.org), 343 Kings Hwy. East, Haddonfield. Open Wed., Thurs., Fri. and first Sun. of the month 1–4; closed Aug. and major holidays. Admission $4. The headquarters of the **Historical Society of Haddonfield,** with collections of local pottery, glass, tools, and other artifacts that date to pre-colonial times. Rooms are furnished with 18th- and 19th-century pieces, as well as clothing and New Jersey glass from the early 1700s. Society members lead guided tours of Haddonfield's historic sites, from **Haunted Haddonfield,** held evenings in Oct., to tours of the village's Colonial and Victorian architecture. The adjacent **Samuel Mickle House,** an early-18th-century saddle shop, has an extensive library of historic and genealogical materials—maps, photos, books, postcards, and historic manuscripts—that is accessible to the public for research.

✳ To Do

AMUSEMENTS ✒ **Clementon Amusement Park and Splash World** (856-783-0263; www.clementonpark.com), 144 Berlin Rd., Clementon. Open late May–Sept. Admission $18–28; parking $8. A historic turn-of-the-20th-century family amusement park with more than 50 rides and attractions, from a classic Ferris wheel to extreme rides like the Inverter. The waterslides include a raft ride that goes through slides and splash pools, and a six-lane racing slide. The Tsunami roller coaster boasts the steepest vertical drop of any wooden roller coaster in North America—it plunges 105 feet over Clementon Lake. If you can pull the kids away from the rides, they'll love the live animal shows with tigers and lions.

BOATING (See also *Canoeing and Kayaking.*)

Boats can be launched at the following ramps on the Delaware River; most charge a fee: **Trenton Waterfront Park** (609-989-3169), 1595 Lamberton Rd. (off Rt. 29), Trenton; **Bordentown Beach** (609-298-0103, ext. 11), end of Park St., Bordentown; **Curtin Marina** (609-386-4657), 501 East Pearl St., Burlington, near the mouth of Assicunk Creek; **Hawk Island Marina** (856-461-5094), 130 Rancocas Ave., Delanco, near the mouth of Rancocas Creek; **Pennsauken Boat Ramp** (609-292-2965), Deronsse Ave., Delair; **Pyne Point Marina** (856-966-1352), North Seventh St., Camden; **West Deptford Municipal Boat Ramp** (856-845-4004), West Deptford.

GOLF Many 18-hole golf courses in the region are public or open to the public on a regular basis. Most have a pro shop, driving range, and clubhouse with a restaurant or snack bar. They include: **Mountain View Golf Course** (609-882-4093), Bear Tavern Rd., West Trenton; **Rancocas Golf Club** (609-877-5344), 12 Club Ridge Lane, Willingboro; **Willow Brook Country Club** (856-461-0131; www.willowbrookcountryclub.com), 4310 Bridgeboro Rd., Moorestown; **Pennsauken Country Club** (856-662-4961), 3800 Haddonfield Rd., Pennsauken; **Ramblewood Country Club** (856-235-2118; www.ramblewoodcc.com), 200 Country Club Parkway, Mount Laurel; **Indian Spring Country Club** (856-983-0222; www.indianspringgolf.com), 115 South Elmwood Rd., Marlton; **Westwood Golf Club** (856-845-2000; www.westwoodgolfclub.com), 850 Kings Hwy., Woodbury.

SPECTATOR SPORTS ✒ **Trenton Thunder** (609-394-3300; www.trentonthunder.com), Mercer County Waterfront Park, One Thunder Rd., Trenton. Games Apr.–Aug.; call or check the Web site for tickets and a schedule. This class AA minor-league affiliate of the New York Yankees plays at Trenton's old-fashioned 6,440-seat ballpark. It's the only minor-league stadium in New Jersey to use a hand-operated scoreboard. Kids love the silly contests staged between innings, and are particularly fond of Chase, the golden retriever that fetches bats and Frisbees.

✒ **Trenton Devils** (800-298-4200; www.trentondevils.com), Sovereign Bank Arena, 81 Hamilton Ave., Trenton. Call for a schedule and ticket prices. The Devils are an East Coast Hockey League AA affiliate of the New Jersey Devils. Home games are held in the city's 7,600-seat arena.

✒ **Camden Riversharks** (856-963-2600; 866-742-7579; www.riversharks.com), Campbell's Field, 401 North Delaware Ave., Camden. Games May–Sept.; call or see Web site for a schedule and ticket prices. The minor-league Riversharks baseball team plays at the 6,425-seat Campbell's Field on the Delaware River. Just beyond the outfield, the Benjamin Franklin Bridge rises dramatically, and downtown Philadelphia can be glimpsed from the right field grandstand. A game here is a fun family night out—entertainment like a Diaper Derby and an Elvis impersonator keep the fun going between innings. The park, with vintage-looking brick stadium and architecture, is named for the Camden-based soup giant, whose classic commercial jingle plays over the public address system whenever a Rivershark scores a homer.

✳ Green Space

GARDEN **Sayen Botanical Gardens** (609-890-3874; www.sayengardens.org), 155 Hughes Dr., Hamilton Square. Open daily dawn to dusk. Free admission. A 30-acre garden with more than 1,000 azaleas and 500 rhododendrons from around the world that explode in a profusion of springtime color. About 250,000 spring-flowering bulbs are also on display, as well as dogwoods, annuals, and perennials. Walking paths, fish ponds, and gazebos surround the historic Sayen House, the Arts and Crafts–style bungalow of avid gardener Frederick Sayen. Elaborate gardens feature the rare species Sayen collected in his excursions around the world, notably from England, China, and Japan. A popular **azalea festival** takes place here on Mother's Day (see *Special Events*).

NATURE CENTER ✍ **Paws Farm Nature Center** (856-778-8795; www.paws farm.com), 1105 Hainesport–Mt. Laurel Rd., Mount Laurel. Open Wed.–Sun. 10–4; closed Mon. and Tues. Adults $6, children $4. A nonprofit nature center whose goal is to interest young children in nature through fun hands-on activities. Visitors can explore the nature trails and butterfly garden, see domestic and wild animals in the barnyard, and view interactive exhibits in the restored 18th-century farmhouse, and natural-history exhibits in the dairy barn.

PARKS **South River Walk Park**, above the Rt. 29 tunnel, south of Waterfront Park, Trenton. This 6-acre park is a green space in the capital city, in a picturesque spot overlooking the Delaware River. Local river history is explained in a series of inscribed granite and bronze markers and plaques placed along a walkway that leads through a series of arches.

✍ **Dr. Ulysses S. Wiggins Waterfront Park** (856-795-7275), Mickle Boulevard at the Delaware River, Camden. Fireworks, evening concerts, and special events are held at this scenic 51-acre waterfront park. Stroll the promenade, take in a musical performance on the outdoor stage, or watch pleasure boats motor in and out of Wiggins Park Marina.

✍ **Camden Children's Garden** (856-365-8733; www.camdenchildrensgarden .org), Three Riverside Drive, on the waterfront, Camden. Adults $6; children ages 3–11, $5. A garden just for young green thumbs, next to Adventure Aquarium. Whimsical horticultural exhibits in the Storybook Garden include an Alice in Wonderland garden and a Giant's garden from the Jack and the Beanstalk story, as well as giant flowers, dinosaur eggs, and big pretend insects that encourage imaginative play. A 4-acre interactive garden includes a picnic garden, maze, butterfly garden, and dinosaur garden. Children can ride on the pint-sized train or the carousel.

✏ GROUNDS FOR SCULPTURE

(609-586-0616; www.groundsforsculpture.org), 18 Fairgrounds Rd., Hamilton (outside Trenton). Open Tues.–Sun.; closed Mon. Free weekday tours. A stunning 35-acre sculpture park at the former New Jersey fairgrounds is the vision of noted American sculptor **J. Seward Johnson Jr.**, a Johnson & Johnson heir who's known for his life-sized sculptures depicting famous 19th-century paintings and ordinary people in contemporary life. The **sculpture garden**—inspired by Claude Monet's 19th-century Giverny—features an eclectic collection of works by various artists in wood, bronze, stone, steel, and mixed media. Inside, a permanent collection and changing exhibits of sculpture, painting, and photography are on display in the **Toad Hall Shop and Gallery** (see *Selective Shopping—Art Galleries*). Poetry readings, musical events, lectures, gallery openings, exhibitions, special events for children, and workshops for adults are regularly scheduled. On the grounds is **Rat's,** a highly acclaimed gourmet restaurant (see *Dining Out*).

THE GROUNDS FOR SCULPTURE IS A UNIQUE, 35-ACRE, OUTDOOR SCULPTURE PARK AND MUSEUM JUST OUTSIDE OF TRENTON, FEATURING THE WORK OF AMERICAN AND INTERNATIONAL CONTEMPORARY ARTISTS.

⚓ Red Bank Battlefield (856-853-5120), 100 Hessian Ave., National Park. Open daily from dawn to dusk; pets are not allowed. This leafy 44-acre park on the Delaware River just south of Camden is a great place for history buffs (see *To See—Historic Sites*) and families looking for a place to spend the day. From the observation jetty or a park bench, you can enjoy the lovely view or watch the endless succession of planes flying to and from Philadelphia International Airport and the massive freighters pushing upstream toward the Philadelphia Shipyard. The picnic groves and pavilions are ideal for alfresco meals, riverfront pathways invite strolling, and the playground will delight the kids. Visitors can also see the remains of **Fort Mercer** and tour the 18th-century **Whitall House** (see *To See—Historic Homes*).

✳ Lodging

In addition to the listings below, there are numerous **chain hotels and motels** in this region. Many are clustered in **Mount Laurel,** close to the New Jersey Turnpike, I-295, and Rt. 73; in **Cherry Hill** on Rts. 70 and 38; and in **Bordentown,** near the New Jersey Turnpike.

HOTELS ⟁ **Lafayette Yard Marriott Conference Hotel** (609-421-4000; 888-796-4662; www.marriott .com), One West Lafayette St., Trenton 08608. The location can't be beat. The Trenton War Memorial and state capitol complex are steps away; restaurants and historic sites are also close by. With 193 guest rooms and four suites, this is Trenton's largest downtown hotel. A beautiful marble and glass lobby is full of local artwork and historic artifacts. **Archives Restaurant** features American cuisine at three meals, and the bar-lounge serves lunch and dinner. Fitness room. $119–209.

⟁ **Clarion Hotel and Conference Center** (856-428-2300; 800-424-6423; www.clarionofcherryhill.com), 1450 Rt. 70 East at I-295 Exit 34B, Cherry Hill 08034. A suburban hotel convenient to Camden and Trenton. The 204 guest rooms are clean and comfortable, with standard amenities from ironing boards to coffee makers; the two suites have refrigerators and microwave

ovens; there are eight themed "Utopia Exotic Suites." The **Elephant and Castle** is a friendly pub and restaurant serving British specialties and American fare. Fitness center and outdoor pool. $120–179.

BED & BREAKFASTS Fernbrook Bed & Breakfast (609-298-3868; www.fernbrookbb.com), 142 Georgetown Rd., P.O. Box 228, Bordentown 08505. You pass through brick columns and rows of ancient trees to reach this elegant circa-1750 Georgian mansion on 200 pastoral acres. The 7 rooms reflect 250 years of changing architectural tastes and styles. Guests can relax in the library, living room, and dining room—each with its own fireplace—or in the handsome billiard room with a 19th-century mahogany pool table. Stroll the flower and vegetable gardens, or roam the rolling fields. During the holiday season, guests can cut their own evergreen from the inn's private Christmas tree farm. The seven guest rooms boast private baths, luxe linens, and period antiques. $125–250.

The Victorian Lady (856-235-4988), 301 West Main St., Moorestown 08057. A clean and comfortable historic in-town Victorian. There are four guest rooms, each with a private bath. Three rooms have double beds; the other has a pair of twin beds. A full breakfast is served. $99-129.

✳ Where to Eat

DINING OUT

In West Trenton and Trenton

Erini (609-882-0303; www.erini restaurant.com), 1140 River Rd. (Rt. 29), Ewing. Open for lunch Mon.–Fri.; dinner Mon.–Sat.; closed Sun. Reservations are recommended. On the site of the former Diamond's Riverside, Erini serves diverse cuisine with Mediterranean influences—from Crabmeat Provençal to Greek Pasta—on the east bank of the Delaware River. Live music on Fri. and Sat. nights. $23–43; $19 three-course special daily until 6:15 and all night Mon.

&. **Lorenzo's Restaurant** (609-695-6868; www.petelorenzos.com), 66 South Clinton Ave., Trenton. Open for lunch Mon.–Fri.; dinner Mon.–Sat.; closed Sun. Late night menu served at the bar until 2 AM. Reservations are suggested. This capital city institution is known for its prime dry-aged steaks, hearty Italian-inspired seafood, and for the local movers and shakers who frequent it. Family-owned, it's been a downtown landmark since 1921. High-lights include the calamari appetizer, followed by porterhouse steak, or lobster stuffed with crabmeat. Its location—just steps away from the Trenton train station, and close to the state capitol, city hall, and Sovereign Bank Arena—makes for a diverse and colorful clientele. Lively bar and award-winning wine list. $11–39.

In Hamilton

&. **Rat's** (609-584-7800; www.rats restaurant.org), at the Grounds for Sculpture, 16 Fairgrounds Rd. Open for lunch and dinner Tues.–Sat.; Sun. brunch; closed Mon. Reservations are strongly suggested, and jackets are preferred at dinner. The French-inspired seasonal cuisine with international flavors gets high marks from critics and gourmands, and the 35-acre sculpture park (see sidebar, page 260) provides a beautiful backdrop. Dinner is pricey, so many dine here when the occasion is truly special. There's a variety of menus to choose from, with the option of à la carte or prix fixe; and there's lighter fare in **Kafe Kabul**. Seasonal dishes feature local organic produce. An entrée may include maple-smoked

---

🐾 ✐ &. HADDONFIELD INN

(856-428-2195; 800-269-0014; www.haddonfieldinn.com), 44 West End Ave., Haddonfield 08033. An elegant and intimate 19th-century home in a lovely residential neighborhood combines the charm and intimacy of a bed & breakfast with the amenities of a fine hotel. Innkeepers Fred and Nancy Chorpita offer concierge services, a guest elevator, spa treatments, even a gourmet candlelit dinner prepared by the inn's private chef. Nine guest rooms and suites are uniquely and tastefully decorated; all have private bath, fireplace, TV, and phone; and many have whirlpool tubs. Well-behaved children and pets can be accommodated in the suite. Guests like to congregate on the rambling wraparound porch, or by a fireplace in one of the antiques-filled common rooms. Complimentary snacks and refreshments are available all day, and the chef's gourmet breakfast might include belgian waffles, eggs florentine, or corn pancakes with chicken basil sausage. $219–369.

duck breast with parsnip puree, poached quince, braised red cabbage and port jus. Desserts are a must. The restaurant's unusual name derives from a main character in Kenneth Grahame's classic children's story *The Wind in the Willows*. $28–44.

In Collingswood
& **Sagami** (856-854-9773), 37 West Crescent Blvd. (Rt. 130). Open for lunch Tues.–Fri.; dinner Tues.–Sun.; closed Mon. Reservations are recommended. This extremely popular little spot in the suburbs has served authentic Japanese cuisine for more than 30 years. Even with reservations, be prepared to wait. On weekends, it can get rather noisy. The traditional flavors of Japan—at once delicate, smoky, and exotic—from ginger and cayenne to wasabi and sake, accent much of the cuisine. Standouts include the *edamame,* green seaweed salad, *osumashi* (clear broth soup), *unaju* (broiled eel), and an impressive roster of authentic sushi, sashimi, and tempura. Save room for the delicious green tea ice cream. BYOB. $16–22.

In Cherry Hill
& **La Campagne** (856-429-7647; www.lacampagne.com), 312 Kresson Rd. Open for lunch Tues.–Fri.; dinner Tues.–Sun.; Sun. brunch; closed Mon. and Sun. during July and Aug. Reservations are recommended. Elegant Provençal cuisine prepared with a global twist and served by a top-notch staff in a romantic and charming old country farmhouse. One of the four small dining rooms has a brick fireplace—try to reserve a table in front of it. Choose from the short but well-balanced menu or from one of the tasting menus. An appetizer like seared foie gras or duck confit can be a fine prelude to a dinner of meat or seafood, along with seasonal vegetables and exquisite sauces. Desserts that are well worth saving room for. BYOB. $26–39.

Caffe Aldo Lamberti (856-663-1747; www.lambertis.com), 2011 Rt. 70 West. Open daily for lunch and dinner. Reservations are recommended. The Lamberti family runs more than a dozen eateries in the Delaware Bay region; this is the flagship location. The elegant dining room is a pleasing, light-filled backdrop to excellent Italian-inspired seafood. Chef Bill Fischer was once a commercial fisherman, so naturally the fish and shellfish are as fresh as it gets. There's Australian rack of lamb, and the Italian fare includes homemade pastas paired with terrific sauces, and a changing daily selection of whole fresh fish. Excellent wine list. $16–33.

& **Melange Café** (856-663-7339; www.melangecafe.com), 1601 Chapel Ave. Open Tues.–Thurs. for lunch and dinner; Sat. and Sun. for dinner; closed Mon. Reservations suggested. A lively, upscale café serving an eclectic cuisine that mixes and matches authentic dishes from Italy with signature New Orleans cooking flavors. The results: starters like crawfish potato corn chowder and entrées like lobster gumbo, or Louisiana dirty rice and clams, concluded with a sweet Southern ending like bourbon bread pudding. A cookbook features one hundred of the café's most popular dishes, along with behind-the-scenes stories and anecdotes from the kitchen. BYOB. $18–29.

In Burlington
Café Gallery (609-386-6150; www.cafegalleryburlington.com), 219 High St. Open for lunch Mon.—Sat.; dinner daily; Sun. brunch. Reservations suggested. A charming eatery overlooking the Delaware River that has served contemporary French-Continental cuisine since 1979, such as escargot with garlic butter, sautéed rainbow trout en croûte with almond butter sauce; or braised pork loin in champagne with

baked apples and pineapple. You can eat indoors, where changing exhibits feature local artists' work; or outdoors, in view of the classical fountain on the lovely brick terrace. $17–25.

In Haddonfield

& **The Little Tuna** (856-795-0888; www.thelittletuna.com), 403 North Haddon Ave. Open for lunch Tues.–Fri.; dinner Tues.–Sun.; closed Mon. As this restaurant's name implies, the cuisine revolves around seafood—red snapper, shrimp, and salmon are among the expertly prepared fish and shellfish dishes (the menu also includes some meat and vegetarian choices). The tables in this charming and intimate space are placed close together, which means a bustling, convivial atmosphere, especially on busy weekends. BYOB. $21–30.

M Café (856-795-7232), 141 Kings Hwy. East. Open daily for lunch and dinner. Reservations suggested. An intimate café that's casual yet city-slick and sophisticated. The creative fusion menu combines contemporary American cuisine with global accents, particularly from Asian cooking. A lively and fun spot for dinner, when the dining room is filled with an interesting mix of locals and visitors. BYOB. $18–30.

EATING OUT

In Trenton

♂ & **John Henry's Seafood Restaurant** (609-396-3083; www.johnhenrys seafood.com), Two Mifflin St. Serving lunch Tues.–Fri.; dinner Tues.–Sun; closed Mon. John Henry's is a homey family restaurant in an Italian neighborhood, so naturally the menu is Italian influenced. Signature starters include clams casino and fried calamari; traditional dinners like veal parmesan and mussels *fra diavolo* are on the menu of seafood, chops, chicken, steaks, and pasta. $15–38.

Joe's Mill Hill Saloon (609-394-7222), 300 S. Broad. St. Open for lunch Mon.–Fri.; dinner Mon.–Sat.; closed Sun. A lively restaurant and brewery in a circa-1850 landmark building in the city's historic Mill Hill neighborhood. Chops, steaks, seafood, chicken, and daily blackboard specials, plus salads, burgers, and appetizers. The bar was saved from the razed Claridge's Hotel and Casino in Atlantic City. Downstairs, the **Brew Cellar** has a late-night menu with a good selection of ales, lagers, and local and regional microbrews. Live jazz. $12–25.

In Bordentown

♂ **Mastori's Diner** (609-298-4650; www.mastoris.com), Rts. 130 and 206. Serves breakfast, lunch, and dinner daily. In a state known as the unofficial Diner Capital of America, this spacious family-run establishment has been a South Jersey icon for decades. A long menu of dependable, classic diner fare, from steaks and chops to cheese blintzes, hearty sandwiches, and late-night snacks. Their New York–style cheesecake draws raves. $11–26.

♂ **Mario & Franks** (609-587-6958), 1580 Nottingham Way. Open Mon.–Sat., 11–10. This has been described as a "family-owned pizzeria with a sense of humor," where the Christmas décor remains year-round, and Italian soccer pennants and photos of Italian legends of all stripes (think Frank Sinatra and local politicians) cover the walls. Oh, and the food's a great value—hoagies and entrées like steak stromboli or eggplant parmesan. $7–15.

In Collingswood

♂ **Tortilla Press** (856-869-3345; www .thetortillapress.com), 703 Haddon Ave. Open daily for lunch and dinner; brunch Sat.–Sun. Creative and authentic gourmet Mexican cuisine in a chic and stylish storefront eatery. Artful dishes like barbecue salmon with chipotle mashed potatoes or broiled honey-lime scallops with poblano spinach rice are offered alongside traditional fare like enchiladas and fajitas. Children's menu. The fresh soups, sauces, and seasonings; the made-to-order guacamole bar; and the gourmet tacos and burritos make this café stand out among most Mexican restaurants. BYOB. $13–21.

✏ **Villa Barone** (856-858-2999; www.baronerestaurants.com), 753 Haddon Ave. Open daily for lunch and dinner. Authentic Italian-American cuisine features Barone family recipes from the old country. There's something on the menu to please everyone, with many dishes prepared to your liking. Try the broccoli rabe, roasted peppers, and sun-dried tomatoes—all served with your choice of grilled chicken or veal. The brick-oven pizzas or the hearty *panini* sandwiches make a light but satisfying meal. BYOB. $12–19.

✏ **The Pop Shop** (856-869-0111; www.thepopshopusa.com), 729 Haddon Ave. Open daily for breakfast, lunch, and dinner. With an imported old-time soda fountain as its centerpiece, this fifties-style soda fountain, decked out in bright turquoise, yellow, and pink with classic booths and chrome tables, serves breakfast all day, big burgers, PB&J, ten hot dog varieties, and 31 different grilled cheese sandwich variations, plus excellent milk shakes. It's noisy, and the service is sluggish, but the milk shakes are great; kids love it. $4–9.

In Haddonfield

🍸 ✏ **Villa Rosa** (856-428-9240), One E. Kings Hwy. Open daily for lunch and dinner. A traditional, reasonably priced Italian restaurant that's popular with families and those looking for a casual meal. A reliable menu of homey

Italian-American dishes, from pastas and pizzas to chicken and seafood. BYOB. $9–16.

&. **Melange at Haddonfield** (856-354-1333), 18 Tanner St. Open Mon. 7–5; Tues.–Sat. 7–9; Sun. 8–5. In a former diner, this locals' spot serves Greek-Mediterranean and American food for lunch and dinner, plus breakfast daily. Outdoor seating seasonally. The salads, *paninis,* and wraps are an especially good value. BYOB. $11–18.

Elsewhere

Cork Restaurant (856-833-9800; www.corknj.com), 90 Haddon Ave., Westmont 08108. Open Mon.–Fri. 11:30 AM–2 AM; Sat.–Sun. 4:30 PM–2 AM. A modern and hip place that features a huge drinks selection be it wine by the glass, beers or martinis. There's live jazz and an eclectic fusion fare that touches many bases. Small plates offer tapas-style dining; excellent solo pizzas allow the individualist various choices. Those seeking full dinners should order the large plates—pasta, seafood, or steak. There's a bar menu, too. $12–23.

✏ **Simply Radishing** (609-882-3760; www.simplyradishing.com), Lawrence Shopping Ctr., 2495 Brunswick Pike (Rt. 1), Lawrenceville 08648. Open Mon.–Sat. 11:30–9; closed Sun. A popular locals' spot on the highway serving a limited, traditional—but very good—Italian menu. Perfect for a quick lunch. Children's menu. BYOB. $7–15.

SNACKS Urban Word Café (609-989-7777), 449 S. Broad St., Trenton. A lively coffeehouse and bar in the Conduit Building, near Sovereign Bank Arena. The weekly poetry slams and open-mike nights are popular with the local arts community. The menu includes vegetarian dishes and light meals, and a good selection of microbrews on tap and in bottles. $5–10.

Café Ole (609-396-2233; www.cafe olecoffee.com), 126 S. Warren St., Trenton. Open Mon.–Fri. 7–4; Sat. 8–2; closed Sun. Across from the Lafayette Marriott Hotel (see *Lodging—Hotels*). A cheerful spot serving coffee, tea, and a light breakfast and lunch menu. $5–10.

Bayard's Chocolate House (856-663-2565; www.bayardschocolates.com) 2325 Rt. 70, Cherry Hill. Other locations in Cinnaminson (856-829-5195) and Pennsauken (856-663-2555). A confectioner famous for its chocolate-covered pretzels and assorted chocolates.

Diane's La Patisserie (856-767-8080; www.dianespatisserie.com), 405 Bloomfield Dr., Unit 1 West Berlin. A warm, friendly French and Italian bakery offering delectable pastries, homey breads, cookies, and scones, which can be enjoyed with a coffee or cappuccino. Diane Nussbaum is well known for her magnificent specialty and wedding cakes. The tiramisu and strawberry shortcake are works of art; the fresh fruit tarts and ricotta cheesecake are award winners.

✳ Entertainment

Trenton 2 Nite (609-393-8998; www .trenton2nite.com), S. Warren and Lafayette Sts., Trenton. Held on the second Fri. of every month from 5 to 9 PM. A monthly celebration featuring Trenton's restaurants and businesses, artists and crafters, live music, and food. Shops stay open late, and restaurants offer food and drink specials.

Sovereign Bank Arena (800-298-4200; www.sovereignbankarena.com), 81 Hamilton Ave., Trenton. The city's main venue for pop and rock concerts, sports contests (see *To Do—Spectator Sports*) and live entertainment, from the circus to World Wrestling Federation matches and professional hockey.

ARTS CENTERS

In Trenton
Patriots Theater (609-984-8400; www.state.nj.us/state/divisions/memorial), at the Trenton War Memorial, Memorial Dr. The city's major center for both local and touring performance artists and companies. The magnificent 1932 Italian Renaissance Revival theater in the auditorium of the War Memorial is a national historic landmark (see *To See—Historic Sites*). It reopened its doors in 1999 after a $35 million restoration. The venue hosts world-class artists and entertainers, including concert seasons by the **New Jersey Symphony Orchestra,** the **Greater Trenton Symphony Orchestra, Boheme Opera New Jersey,** the **Garden State Theatre Organ Society,** and the **American Repertory Ballet.**

Mill Hill Playhouse (609-989-3038), Montgomery and Front Sts. Performances Thurs.–Sat. at 8 PM, Sun. at 5 PM. Home of the **Passage Theatre Company** (609-392-0766)**,** the city's oldest professional theater company, performing in a historic and intimate 120-seat theater. A venue for concerts, dance performances, and world-premier contemporary plays by emerging and established playwrights.

In Camden
♪ **Susquehanna Bank Center and Walter Rand Theatre** (856-365-1300; www.tweetercenter/philadelphia), One Harbour Blvd. Formerly the Tweeter Center, Susquehanna Bank Center is the city's biggest venue, a 25,000-seat open-air amphitheater with a wide lawn hosting summertime concerts. In the fall and winter, the enclosed 1,600-seat Walter Rand Theatre is home to the **South Jersey Performing Arts Center** (856-342-6633; www.sjpac .com), with Broadway productions, dramas, family shows, and dance performances.

❧ Rutgers–Camden Center for the Arts (856-225-2700; www.rutgerscamdenarts.org), **Walter Gordon Theatre,** on the campus of Rutgers University—Camden, Third and Pearl Sts. Live dance, music, and drama; family shows; multicultural performances.

Walt Whitman Arts Center (856-964-8300; www.waltwhitmancenter.org), on the campus of Rutgers University—Camden, Second and Cooper Sts. What began in 1976 as the Walt Whitman International Poetry Center is now a literary performing-arts center in the neoclassical campus library, a national historic landmark. At the open-mike poetry nights on the second and fourth Tuesday of the month, poets gather to share their work. The center also presents art exhibits, author readings, live music, and plays.

In Moorestown

Perkins Center for the Arts (856-235-6488; 800-387-5226; www.perkinscenter.org), 395 Kings Hwy. An active community arts center and performance space in a 1910 Tudor-style mansion and 5-acre arboretum. Changing exhibitions showcase contemporary artists. Concert series include folk, jazz, bluegrass, musical storytellers, and blues in the **Moorestown DeCafe Coffeehouse**. Classical chamber music Family Concerts are presented periodically in the Perkins Center Memorial on Sunday afternoons. Classes and workshops in painting, sculpture, pottery, and drawing are taught by nationally recognized artists.

THE SUSQUEHANNA BANK CENTER IS A POPULAR SPOT FOR CONCERTS AND THEATER ON THE CAMDEN WATERFRONT, FEATURING AN OUTDOOR AMPHITHEATER DURING THE SUMMER AND AN ENCLOSED, INDOOR VENUE DURING THE REST OF THE YEAR.

Photo courtesy of the Camden Waterfront Marketing Bureau

MUSIC Greater Trenton Symphony Orchestra (609-396-5522; www.trentonsymphony.org), 28 W. State St., Ste. 202, Trenton. Performances Dec.–Apr. in various locations, including the acoustically superb Trenton War Memorial and Trenton's Trinity Cathedral. The symphony's Christmas Holiday Spectacular and New Year's Eve Concert, both held at the War Memorial's Patriots Theater, are major events.

✒ **Symphony in C** (856-963-6683; www.symphonyinc.org), One Market St., Ste. 1-C, Camden. Formerly the Haddonfield Symphony. Performances Oct.–Apr.; call for a schedule. One of three professional training orchestras in the U.S., the symphony performs a blend of widely known favorites and lesser-known works.

THEATER ✒ **Burlington County Footlighters** (856-829-7144; www.bcfootlighters.com), 808 Pomona Rd., Cinnaminson. Performances Sept.–May; call or see Web site for schedule. A nonprofit regional theater group founded in 1938 occupies a 19th-century brick schoolhouse, where they mount a popular series of comedies and dramas, from classics to little-known works. Acting workshops for children.

✒ **Haddonfield Plays and Players Performing Arts Center** (856-429-8139; www.haddonfieldplayers.com), 975 S. Atlantic Ave., Haddonfield. A nonprofit community theater founded in 1935. Professional-quality comedies, musicals, and mysteries are staged in their 150-seat theater (an intimate 50-seat space is used for new directors and experimental works). The center offers a variety of workshops—drama, dance, and music for kids; theater and film for adults.

✴ Selective Shopping

ANTIQUES Haddonfield is a renowned South Jersey antiques center. Many shops line Kings Hwy., the main thoroughfare, but others are tucked down quiet side streets. Among the notable are **Haddonfield Antique Center** (856-429-1929), Nine Kings Hwy. East; **The Owl's Tale** (856-795-8110), 140 Kings Hwy. East; and the **Haddonfield Gallery** (856-429-7722), Three Kings Ct.

ART GALLERIES

In Trenton
Artworks Gallery (609-394-9436; www.artworkstrenton.org), 19 Everett Alley. The gallery in this visual arts school run by the **Trenton Artists Workshop Association** has changing exhibits in contemporary painting, sculpture, and photography.

Boehm Porcelain Studio Gallery (609-392-2207; 800-257-9410; www.boehmporcelain.com), 25 Princess Diana Lane. Call for gallery hours and tours. A four-room gallery featuring Boehm's world-renowned fine porcelain collectibles, artwork, antiques, and limited-edition creations. Each piece is handcrafted at the Trenton studio.

Cybis Porcelain Gallery (609-392-6074), 65 Norman Ave. Call for tours. The country's oldest porcelain arts studio, founded by world-famous painter and porcelain artist Boleslaw Cybis in the 1940s. Fine handcrafted porcelain sculpture on display in the gallery and showroom. The motifs range from animals and children to weddings, holidays, sports, and music.

Gallery 125 (609-989-9119), 125 S. Warren St. Open Tues.–Fri. noon–6; Sat. 11–4; closed Sun. and Mon. A unique and progressive contemporary art gallery owned and operated by the **Trenton Downtown Association.** Changing juried exhibitions. Downtown's newest art gallery.

Elsewhere

Toad Hall Shop and Gallery (609-586-2366; www.groundsforsculpture .org), at the Grounds for Sculpture, adjacent to Rat's Restaurant, 18 Fairgrounds Rd., Hamilton. Open Tues.–Sun. 11:30–6; closed Mon. Changing gallery exhibits showcase the work of a variety of national and international contemporary designers and artists. The shop sells contemporary jewelry, unique glassware, leather accessories, and eclectic home décor.

Hopkins House Gallery (856-858-0040), 250 South Park Dr., Haddon Township. Changing exhibits feature the work of regional artists in a variety of media. The gallery is in a lovely 18th-century brick Georgian-style house, once the home of Ebenezer Hopkins, on the banks of the Cooper River. Run by the **Camden County Cultural and Heritage Commission.**

The College of New Jersey Art Gallery (609-771-2198), Holman Hall, at The College of New Jersey, 2000 Pennington Rd. (Rt. 31), Ewing. Tues.–Thurs. noon–7; Sun. 1–3. Biennial drawing and printmaking exhibits; student, faculty, and alumni shows; and an annual Mercer County juried photography exhibition.

SPECIAL SHOPS Rancocas Woods Village of Shops (856-235-1830; www .rancocaswoods.net), 114 Creek Rd., Mount Laurel. Open daily. A collection of quaint shops housed in old-fashioned buildings in a woodland setting. More than 25 shops sell gifts, collectibles, candy, furniture, toys, and crafts. Call or see Web site for a schedule of crafts fairs, antiques shows, and other special events, including the annual Christmas festival and candlelight tour.

Cherry Hill Mall (856-662-7440; www.cherryhillmall.com), 2000 Rt. 38, Cherry Hill. Open daily. This is where it all began: the East Coast's first enclosed shopping mall, with 165 moderate to upscale specialty shops anchored by three major department stores.

FARMER'S MARKETS Trenton has two active farmer's markets: **Trenton Farmers' Market** (609-695-2998; www.thetrentonfarmersmarket.com), 960 Spruce St., Lawrence Township. Open Thurs.–Sat. 9–6. A year-round market selling fresh produce, plants, flowers, artisan cheeses, cured meats, fresh ice cream, and other foods. **Capital City Farmer's Market** (609-393-8998), State & Broad Sts. Open Thurs. 11–2 from July to mid-Sept. Outdoor stands sell fresh produce from local farms; arts-and-crafts vendors and live music.

Collingswood Farmers' Market (856-858-2200; www.collingswood market.com), between Urban and Collings Aves., Collingswood. Open June–Oct., Sat. 8–noon. A downtown market under the PATHCO high-speed rail line. About a dozen farmers from South Jersey sell produce; other vendors offer herbal products, freshly baked goods, and homemade jams.

Columbus Farmers' Market (609-267-0400; www.columbusfarmers market.com), 2919 Rt. 206, Columbus. Indoor and outdoor markets open year-round. Indoor, Thurs. and Sat. 8 AM– 8 PM, Fri. 10 AM– 8 PM, Sun. 8 AM –5 PM; outdoor, Thurs. 7:30 AM –3 PM, Sat. 7:30 AM–2 PM, and Sun. 6:30 AM –3 PM. What began as a livestock and farm-equipment auction in the 1920s is a market selling vegetables, fruits, flowers, and much more. A sprawling complex with more than 70 indoor stores; outdoors, more than 1,200 vendors ply their wares.

✳ Special Events

March: ❧ **Saint Patrick's Day Parade** (609-777-1770), Trenton.
❧ **Shamrock Day Celebration** (856-216-7253), Haddonfield.

April: ❧ **Super Science Weekend** (609-292-6310), New Jersey State Museum, Trenton. The museum's annual celebration of science and technology. Science demonstrations, programs featuring the museum's own scientists, and special shows in the planetarium.

May: ❧ **Native American Festival** (609-261-4747; www.powhatan.org), Rankokus Indian Reservation, Rancocas. A celebration of New Jersey's American Indian heritage. Music and dance presentations on the 350-acre Rankokus Indian Reservation. **Haddon Fortnightly House and Garden Tour, Mayfest** (856-216-7253), Haddonfield. **Trenton Film Festival** (609-396-6966; www.trentonfilm festival.org), various locations, Trenton. Foreign, independent, documentary, animated, and experimental short- and feature-length films compete for prizes. **Sayen Gardens Azalea Festival** (609-890-3874; www.sayengardens .org), Sayen Botanical Gardens, Hamilton Square. An annual **Mother's Day celebration** at this 30-acre garden with more than 1,000 azaleas from around the world.

June: ❧ **Trenton Heritage Days Festival** (609-989-3628; www.trenton heritagedays.com), Trenton. New Jersey's largest cultural festival is a week-long celebration with arts and crafts, entertainment, ethnic foods, and children's activities.

July: **Haddonfield Crafts and Fine Art Festival** (856-216-7253; www .haddonfieldnj.org), Haddonfield. More than 200 professional artists and crafters from around the country in the historic downtown shopping district. **Camp Olden Civil War Reenactment** (609-585-8900; www.campolden .org), Veterans Park, Hamilton. Hundreds of reenactors camp in Veterans Park, 2 miles from the original Camp Olden, and reenact the **Battle of the Wilderness** between General Grant and General Lee. ❧ **Mercer County Fair** (609-989-6830), Mercer County Central Park, West Windsor. Animal exhibits, local crafters, flower and vegetable show, antique car show, hayrides, and live music.

October: ❧ **Native American Festival** (609-261-4747; www.powhatan.org), Rankokus Indian Reservation, Rancocas. ❧ **Fall Family Festival** (856-216-7253; www.haddonfieldnj.org), Tanner St., Haddonfield. Crafters, games, hayrides, scarecrow making, and trolley rides through town. **Haddon Fortnightly Antiques Show** (856-428- 9040), Grove St. and Kings Hwy., Haddonfield. A popular antiques show for more than 65 years.

November: ❧ **Thanksgiving Day Parade** (609-777-1770), Trenton.
❧ **Holiday Parade** (856-234-6265), Collingswood. The largest holiday parade in South Jersey.

December: **Reenactment of the Battles of Trenton** (609-777-1770), downtown Trenton. A soldiers' muster, battle reenactments, and a memorial service honor the two battles that took place in Trenton during the so-called Ten Crucial Days of the Revolution. **Holiday House Tours** in Burlington (609-386-4773) and Haddonfield (856-216-7253; www.firstnighthaddon field.org). ❧ **First Night Celebration** (856-429-4700, ext. 300; www.haddon fieldnj.org), Haddonfield. An alcohol-free celebration with family activities, live music, dance, theater, and fireworks on New Year's Eve.

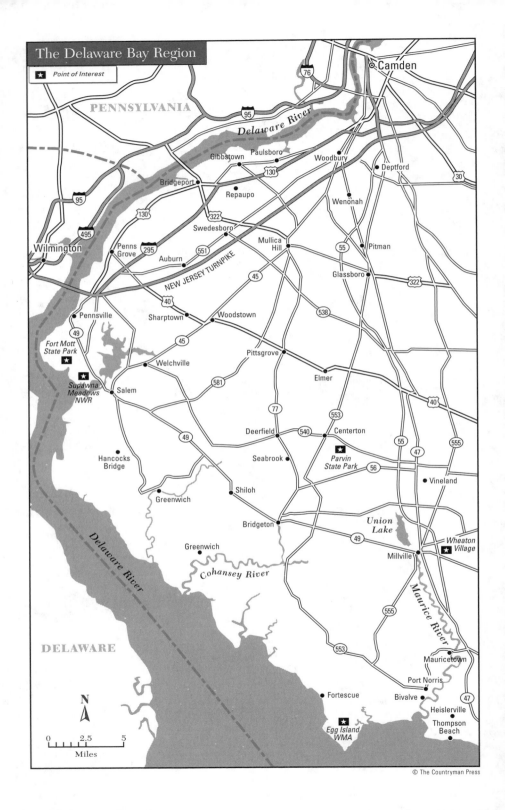

The Delaware Bay Region

★ Point of Interest

PENNSYLVANIA

Delaware River

Camden

Gibbstown
Paulsboro
Woodbury
Deptford

Bridgeport
Repaupo
Wenonah

Swedesboro
Mullica Hill
Pitman

Wilmington
Penns Grove
Auburn
NEW JERSEY TURNPIKE
Glassboro

Pennsville
Sharptown
Woodstown

Fort Mott State Park
Welchville
Pittsgrove
Elmer

Supawna Meadows NWR
Salem

Deerfield
Centerton

Hancocks Bridge
Seabrook
Parvin State Park
Vineland

Shiloh

Greenwich
Bridgeton
Union Lake

Greenwich
Wheaton Village

Delaware River
Cohansey River
Millville

Maurice River

DELAWARE

Mauricetown

Port Norris
Fortescue
Bivalve
Heislerville
Thompson Beach

N

Egg Island WMA

0   2.5   5
Miles

© The Countryman Press

THE DELAWARE BAY REGION

Cradled between the Delaware River and Delaware Bay, rural southern New Jersey—known as South Jersey—is noted for its vast stretches of farm fields and pristine tidal marshes, roadside produce markets and massive farming operations. The state's soil-rich southwestern bulge is considered some of the finest agricultural land on the East Coast. Unlike small-scale crop farms or dairies in northern parts of the state, here fields stretch to the horizon. Cumberland County is called New Jersey's Garden Spot, with 100,000 acres of farmland—orchards; wholesale nurseries; "truck farms" growing sod, corn, tomatoes, and eggplant— punctuated with silos, barns, and long straight ribbons of road that beckon to be explored.

South Jersey is also the least-visited and least-inhabited part of the state (not including, of course, the wildly popular southern shoreline, which merits its own chapter), a quiet, little-developed region of otherwise densely populated New Jersey. Salem County, on the Delaware River, is the state's least densely populated county, visited more by migrating birds than by tourists. Off-the-beaten-path travelers love the area because it affords a sense of discovery that's nearly impossible to find in places that cater to the masses. It may lack luxurious inns and fine restaurants, but it hangs on to an endearing old-fashioned charm that's lost in the polished, upscale suburbs.

The region is equally defined by the river and the bay. Cumberland County has more than 40 miles of intricate coastline cut with inlets and coves, and bordering vast expanses of grassy marshland and meandering tidal streams that stretch far inland. If the waterfront were a sandy beach, it would be crammed with motels, amusement parks, and resorts. Instead, people fish and hunt rather than parasail, living in villages born out of the maritime heritage of the oyster and shipbuilding industries. By the early 1900s, oystering, boat building, crabbing, and shad fishing were thriving in communities like Bivalve and Shellpile, until the rich oyster population was wiped out by a deadly parasite in the 1950s. Today in Bivalve, the Bayshore Discovery Project takes passengers sailing on the bay aboard New Jersey's official tall ship, the *A. J. Meerwald.* The nostalgic 1928 schooner is reminiscent of the days when a fleet of similar ships plied the bay in search of oysters. The water is still busy with commercial fishing boats and barges plying their way to and from Philadelphia, hauling freight through what is still a major shipping route.

Centuries-old towns scattered throughout the flat lowlands—Greenwich, Salem, Bridgeton, and Mauricetown among them—are rich in history, offering unique small museums and little-known yet significant historic sites. Students of American history often equate log cabins with the American frontier, but 17th-century Swedish settlers built the country's first log house in Gibbstown. Gloucester County, originally a Dutch settlement, is one of the oldest counties in America. During the Revolutionary War, as American and British warships skirmished for control of the Delaware River, local patriots took a small but defiant stand against growing British oppression in the colonies. Angered by a British tea tax—and perhaps inspired by news of a tea "party" in Boston—they gathered in Greenwich in Dec. 1774, dressed as Indians, and burned a cargo of Philadelphia-bound British tea that had recently arrived by ship. Greenwich—Cumberland County's oldest community—is one of only five tea-burning towns in America. A monument on "Ye Greate Street," the historic avenue laid out in 1684, commemorates their patriotic efforts.

After the Civil War, Fort Mott was built on the bay to protect Philadelphia and other river ports from enemy invasion. Remnants of the military base, today a state park, include officers' quarters and a massive concrete battery that hid guns positioned to fire upon enemy ships. A ferry shuttles history buffs to two other military forts—Fort Delaware and Fort DuPont—to see Civil War reenactments as well as the place where nearly 2,500 Confederate soldiers died while in captivity. They are laid to rest at Finns Point National Cemetery, the eerily peaceful burial ground at Fort Mott.

In the 17th century, Finnish settlers and Irish Quakers established plantations in Mullica Hill, named for the family who first settled here. In the next couple centuries a blacksmith shop, a pair of taverns, an iron foundry, and a woolen mill sprang up, along with dozens of homes, from Colonials to Queen Anne–style mansions. Today the entire village is on the National Register of Historic Places and is known for the plethora of antiques dealers occupying Main Street's well-preserved buildings.

Salem is the oldest English settlement in New Jersey, laid out in 1675 on the Salem River, a tributary of the Delaware. The brick downtown around Market Street and Broadway is a well-preserved national historic district, with small museums, historic churches, and an old county courthouse. The roads leading into town are lined with Colonial- and Victorian-era houses, some beautifully restored, others in various stages of repair. Visitors can tour the Hancock House, the site of a Revolutionary War–era massacre, and the Alexander Grant House, home to the Salem County Historical Society, an active organization since 1884.

The old glass-manufacturing town of Bridgeton boasts the state's largest historic district, with more than 2,200 registered Colonial-, Federal-, and Victorian-era historic landmarks. Its industrial heritage dates to 1686, when the first sawmill was built on the Cohansey River. By the 19th century, a fleet of schooners was based here, and the city boomed with glass factories, a woolen mill, a nail and iron industry, and half a dozen blacksmith shops. Those who profited from this success built elaborate mansions and grand commercial buildings. Despite this rich history, visitors shouldn't expect a polished, South Jersey version of colonial Williamsburg. Bridgeton is a workaday city, an architectural treasure trove with flaws typical of places that have seen better days. Declining industry in the 20th century, and the subsequent loss of jobs, led to poverty and decay, leaving neighborhoods that are weathered at best, in shambles at worst. Still, Bridgeton has a lot to offer visitors. The wooded 1,100-acre city park has a Native American village and museum, a restored 17th-century Swedish farmstead, and New Jersey's first public zoo. Summertime brings a farmer's market and a riverfront concert series.

Southern New Jersey has been a major glass-manufacturing center ever since German immigrant Caspar Wistar opened a factory in 1739. Wistarburgh Glass Works was colonial America's first successful glass factory, and not the last. A century later, Dr. Theodore Corson Wheaton built a facility in nearby Millville on the Maurice River. Today, Wheaton Village is a re-created 1888 glassmaking community about a mile from Wheaton's original factory. Visitors can watch sculptors and artisans in front of white-hot furnaces, shaping molten glass into works of art by using centuries-old glassmaking techniques. The Museum of American Glass, the largest collection of American glass in the country, draws collectors, artists, and dealers from around the world.

Millville's newest attraction is a small but thriving arts district, a creative effort to revitalize its deteriorating downtown by encouraging artists to relocate here and practice their craft. Today the Glasstown Arts District boasts more than two-dozen galleries and studios, and an arts education center with changing exhibits of work by regional artists. On the third Friday of the month the galleries, shops, and restaurants stay open late, and the town hosts live music and receptions for artists. Millville also offers a riverfront park along the Maurice River, an aviation museum at a World War II–era airfield, and fishing and swimming on New Jersey's largest artificial lake.

In the 19th century, sea captains navigated the Maurice (pronounced "Morris") River, docked their ships in Mauricetown, and built grand Victorian mansions, many of which still stand, their history noted on simple plaques. Among the historic buildings in this quiet town is the 1880 Mauricetown Methodist Church, whose soaring white steeple is reminiscent of a New England village. A handful of antiques shops and a peaceful riverfront park are worth a stop here, as are the festivals and historic-house tours hosted throughout the year.

South Jersey attracts birders, anglers, and other outdoors enthusiasts to the vast undisturbed natural surroundings that defy New Jersey's industrial image. Since 1955 the New Jersey chapter of The Nature Conservancy has preserved more than 13,000 acres in the Delaware Bay region. Cumberland County alone has some 50,000 acres of open space, from pine forest and marsh to mudflats, salt-hay meadows, and hardwood swamps protected in state wildlife management areas. The federally designated Wild and Scenic Maurice River and its tributaries wind through South Jersey on their way to the bay, the perfect place to meander in a kayak or a canoe. The Delaware Bay region is home to diverse songbirds, shorebirds, and waterfowl attracted to its tidal salt marshes, which are among the richest natural ecosystems in the world. In spring and fall, some 1.5 million migrating birds stop here to rest on their journey along the Atlantic Flyway. Birders know that the Maurice River is one of the East Coast's most important raptor wintering areas, where huge flocks of snow geese feed at the river's mouth. Gulls, egrets, herons, mute swans, and bald eagles wait out the cold months in ponds, tidal creeks, and marshes dotted with bayberry bushes and cedar trees. The annual migration of monarch butterflies happens in autumn, and hungry shorebirds pass through in May, when horseshoe crabs go ashore to lay thousands of eggs. When exploring in summer, it's wise to carry insect repellent to fend off the biting greenhead flies and deerflies that thrive in these wet, humid conditions.

Like all places worth exploring, South Jersey has its share of quirky surprises.

Fortescue bills itself as the Weakfish Capital of the World, with a marina full of charter boats that bring anglers onto the bay and the Atlantic Ocean. The remote fishing village hosts one of the East Coast's most popular fishing tournaments for its famous weakfish, a species of sea trout. Woodstown has been called the Cow Capital of the First Frontier, but to most folks it's simply home to the Cowtown Rodeo, where a Saturday-night rodeo has been held since 1929. Professional cowboys and cowgirls from around the country come here to rope steer, barrel race, and ride bulls at the longest-running weekly rodeo in America.

Entries in this section are arranged in roughly geographic order.

AREA CODES 856, 609.

GUIDANCE A New Jersey **state welcome center** in Deepwater (856-351-0194) is on I-295 northbound between Exits 2 and 4 at milepost 2.5, a mile from the Delaware Memorial Bridge.

An **information center** at Fort Mott State Park (856-935-3218), Fort Mott Rd. (Rt. 630), in Pennsville, is well stocked with regional tourism literature and has a helpful staff.

Cumberland County maintains a helpful Web site (**www.co.cumberland.nj.us**) for the entire region, with information on historic sites, recreation, shopping, lodging, and dining.

Mullica Hill (856-881-6800) has a top-notch Web site (**www.mullicahill.com**) for visitors and will send printed materials on request.

The **Bridgeton–Cumberland Tourist Information Center** (856-451-4802), at the junction of Rts. 77 and 49 (W. Broad St.), downtown Bridgeton, is a self-serve information center that's well stocked with tourism literature and maps.

GETTING THERE *By air:* **Newark Liberty International Airport** (973-961-6000; parking information: 888-397-4636; www.panynj.com) in Newark serves the entire state. **Philadelphia International Airport** (215-937-6800; www .philadelphia-phl.com) in Pennsylvania is close to the Delaware Bay area. **Atlantic City International Airport** (609-645-7895; 888-235-9229; www.acairport.com), Exit 9 on the Atlantic City Expressway, serves southern New Jersey through Spirit Airlines (800-772-7117).

By bus: **New Jersey Transit** (800-582-5946; www.njtransit.com) links Camden and Philadelphia to Millville, Gloucester, Swedesboro, Glassboro, Salem, Woodstown, and other communities in the Delaware Bay region. **Greyhound** (800-229-9424; www.greyhound.com) stops in Camden and Atlantic City.

By car: The **New Jersey Turnpike** is the only major highway through this rural area. In addition, **Rt. 55** runs along the northern edge of this region from Camden to Port Elizabeth; **Rt. 130** connects Camden to the New Jersey Turnpike just before the Delaware Memorial Bridge; **Rt. 40** travels from the New Jersey Turnpike east to the **Atlantic City Expressway;** and **Rt. 49** links the New Jersey Turnpike to Tuckahoe via Salem, Bridgeton, and Millville.

GETTING AROUND *Taxis:* **Yellow Cab** (856-825-2100) and **Landis Cab Co.** (856-293-9300) serve Millville and surrounding communities.

www.sjhealthcare.net), 333 Irving Ave., Bridgeton. Emergency and outpatient services.

SJH Regional Medical Center—Vineland (856-641-8000; www.sjhealthcare .net), 1505 West Sherman Ave., Vineland.

The Memorial Hospital of Salem County (856-935-1000; www.mhschealth .com), 310 Woodstown Rd., Salem. The emergency number is 856-339-6048.

SJH Elmer Hospital (856-363-1000; www.sjhealthcare.net), West Front St., Elmer.

✴ To See

CHURCHES **Old Swedes Trinity Episcopal Church** (856-467-1227; www .trinityswedesboro.org), 1129 Kings Hwy. at Church St., Swedesboro. The Swedish were some of New Jersey's first settlers, establishing agricultural and industrial communities as early as 1642 at the settlement of Raccoon, eventually re-named Swedesboro. To attend church, the Swedes had to cross the Delaware River to Philadelphia or Wilmington, a dangerous proposition in foul weather. At the turn of the 18th century they built a log cabin–style building to worship in, New Jersey's first Swedish church. Damaged during the Revolutionary War, the building was replaced with the current Georgian-style structure, completed in 1784. The church cemetery contains many Revolutionary War–era graves.

Old Broad Street Church (856-445-0809; www.fpcbridgeton.org), 119 W. Commerce St., Bridgeton. This stately brick 1792 meetinghouse is considered one of New Jersey's best-preserved 18th-century buildings. Bridgeton's first house of worship was patterned after the Georgian-style churches springing up in Philadelphia at the time. The church still boasts many original features, including the collection bags, brick flooring, pews, whale-oil lamps, and the Franklin stoves made at an iron furnace in the Pinelands. The dramatic Palladian window behind the pulpit is similar to one in George Washington's Virginia home, and in Philadelphia's Independence Hall. Revolutionary War veterans and slaves are buried in the church graveyard.

HISTORIC HOMES **C. A. Nothnagle Log House** (856-423-0916), 406 Swedesboro Rd., Gibbstown. Open by appointment only. Free admission. A circa-1638 log cabin built by Finnish-Swedish settlers shortly after they arrived from Europe has made the National Register of Historic Places for two reasons: it's the oldest such structure in America, and the oldest surviving log house in the Western Hemisphere. The original house would have had an earthen floor (pine floorboards weren't in use until the 18th century) and a chimney made of bricks imported from Sweden. Instead of nails, an ingenious system of pins and dovetails held the walls and roof rafters in place. Today the log house is attached to a private residence; the owners show visitors around.

Alexander Grant House (856-935-5004; www.salemcountyhistoricalsociety.com), 79–83 Market St., Salem. Call for hours; closed major holidays. A magnificent shuttered brick 1721 house at the heart of Salem's historic downtown is the headquarters of the **Salem County Historical Society.** The 20-room house, along with a rustic stone barn, contains the society's extensive collections of furniture, glass, textiles, china, and paintings from the colonial era to the mid-19th century. A research library contains genealogical and historic books, manuscripts, photographs, and other documents that visitors can view. From the library, there's a lovely view of the colonial garden behind the house.

Hancock House (856-935-4373), Three Front St., Hancocks Bridge. Wed.–Sat. 10–noon, 1–4; Sun. 1–4. Closed Mon.–Tues. Call ahead; sometimes meetings change the open hours. Free admission. The 1734 home of William Hancock, a Quaker judge, was the setting of perhaps the bloodiest chapter in Salem County's early history. Hancock built the brick mansion in a style popular in Essex, England, where the area's settlers came from. The exterior's unique herringbone pattern of red and blue bricks contains the initials of the judge, his wife, Sarah, and the construction year. During the Revolutionary War, Hancock allowed colonial militiamen to use the house as a barracks. In March 1778, some 300 British troops made up of Tories, Hessians, and Queen's Rangers staged a nighttime raid on Hancocks Bridge, killing everyone in the house, including Hancock. Today the well-preserved house, which has random-width floorboards, walls paneled in native pine, and a fireplace in every room, is a state historic site.

HISTORIC SITES Finns Point National Cemetery (609-877-5460; www .cem.va.gov), 454 Fort Mott Rd., at Fort Mott State Park, Pennsville. Open daily 8–sunset. Drive down a long, narrow lane past Fort Mott to reach the hushed burial ground of nearly 3,000 Civil War soldiers. Roughly 2,436 of the dead were Confederate prisoners held at Fort Delaware on Pea Patch Island; the rest were Union soldiers who served as prison camp guards. Many of the POWs were captured in 1863 during the battle of Gettysburg and brought to Fort Delaware, which had a dark reputation for dire conditions. Most of the prisoners died in 1863 and 1864 from disease, neglect, and malnutrition. Also in the cemetery is the **Confederate Monument,** a 50-foot granite obelisk etched with the names of the soldiers who

THE 1734 HANCOCK HOUSE IN HANCOCKS BRIDGE WAS THE SITE OF A BRUTAL MASSACRE OF LOCAL MILITIA MEMBERS BY BRITISH TROOPS IN A SURPRISE 1778 RAID, ONE OF THE MOST IMPORTANT EVENTS IN JERSEY'S REVOLUTIONARY WAR HISTORY.

Photo by Thomas E. Briglia / PhotoGraphics Photographpy

FORT MOTT STATE PARK

(856-935-3218), 454 Fort Mott Rd., Pennsville. Grounds are open daily 8 AM–dusk. Welcome center open daily 8–4, Mon.–Fri. in winter; call for interpretive programs schedule. Free admission. A sense of isolation pervades this former military post on the Delaware River, due perhaps to the miles of virtually unspoiled countryside you drive through to get here. It was built after the Civil War as part of a coastal defense system, along with Fort DuPont, and joining Fort Delaware, which had stood on Pea Patch Island since the 1820s. Along with fortifications on the riverbank at Finns Point, the trio of forts would protect the river from a future enemy attack, specifically, the threat of the Spanish-American War. A long concrete and earthen battery shielded the guns, and the fort itself, from the river. Fort Mott—named for decorated Mexican American and Civil War veteran General Gershom Mott—was an active military base until World War I; today, it's a serene state park (see *Green Space—State Parks*) where visitors can hike, picnic, stroll along the shoreline, take a self-guided tour of the batteries, or ride a ferry to the historic forts (see **Three Forts Ferry** under *To Do—Boat Excursion*). A staffed **welcome center,** part of the **New Jersey Coastal Heritage Trail,** is well stocked with tourism literature; check out the exhibits on South Jersey's maritime history and culture.

died in captivity. Union soldiers are memorialized at the domed **Union Monument.** Others interred here include German World War II POWs who died at Fort Dix, American soldiers who died while serving at Fort Mott, and others who served in World War I and the Spanish-American War.

Seabrook Educational and Cultural Center (856-451-8393; www.seabrook education.org), in the Upper Deerfield Township Municipal Building, 1325 State St. (Rt. 77), Seabrook. Open Mon.–Thurs. 9–2; closed Fri.–Sun. Free admission. In 1944, Charles Franklin Seabrook founded Seabrook Brothers & Sons, then the world's largest frozen-food factory. He needed a considerable workforce to can and freeze millions of pounds of vegetables. Simultaneously, more than 110,000 Japanese Americans were living around the country in World War II–era internment camps. Seabrook arranged for more than 2,000 to come to South Jersey, where they worked in food production and food processing or on the farms. When the camps were closed in 1945, Seabrook set up **Seabrook Village,** a multicultural community that thrived in the 1940s and 1950s with a mix of Japanese Americans and workers from around the world. The museum contains a large-scale model of the 1950s-era village and factory, exhibits on community life and farmwork, oral histories, photographs, cultural artifacts, and archives of published accounts.

Gibbon House Museum (856-455-4055; www.cchistsoc.org), 960 Ye Greate St., Greenwich. House open Apr.–Dec., Mon., Wed., and Sat. 12:30–4; closed Sun. Closed Jan.–Mar. Call for admission prices. A complex of historic buildings along Greenwich's oldest street is the headquarters of the **Cumberland County**

Historical Society. Nicholas Gibbon designed his circa-1730 home after an elegant London town house; the brick exterior has an intricate Flemish-style herringbone pattern typical of many 18th-century English homes. Today the formal dining room, paneled drawing room, and upstairs rooms are furnished in period antiques; the kitchen has a massive walk-in fireplace where demonstrations in colonial open-hearth cooking take place. The **Pirate House Library's** collection of old documents, deeds, and books is available to the public for research. The Red Barn is full of 19th-century farm implements, domestic artifacts, and tools for gardening, carpentry, and blacksmithing.

Potter's Tavern (856-451-4802), 49–51 W. Broad St., Bridgeton. Tours on summer weekends and by appointment. The restored 1776 building, now a national historic landmark and museum, was a popular gathering spot for local patriots. More notably, it was home to the *Plain Dealer,* believed to be New Jersey's first regularly published newspaper. It was certainly the first publication in the colony devoted exclusively to American liberty and independence; its articles urged Cumberland County residents to resist British domination. Publisher Ebenezer Elmer started out as a local tea burner and later distinguished himself as the last surviving officer from New Jersey in George Washington's Continental army. The original manuscript of the newspaper—printed in December 1775—is in the rare books collection at Rutgers University in New Brunswick.

LIGHTHOUSES **Tinicum Rear Range Lighthouse** (856-423-2545; www.tinicumrearrangelighthouse.org), Second and Mantua Sts., P.O. Box 176, Paulsboro. Open Apr.–Oct. on the third weekend of the month, Sat. 10–3, Sun. noon–4. Free admission. Since New Year's Eve 1880, this inland beacon has worked in sync with the Tinicum Front Range Light to guide ships up the Delaware River toward Philadelphia with a fixed red light that can be seen for 8.5 nautical miles. This historic lighthouse is in an unlikely place—surrounded by a sports complex, with no coastline in sight. It's equally unusual in appearance, an 85-foot tower of slate-gray steel, with 112 steps from the base to the lantern room. The lighthouse is still active, and maintained by the **Lighthouse Society of Paulsboro.**

Finns Point Rear Range Light (856-935-1487), 197 Lighthouse Rd. (Rt. 632), near Fort Mott State Park, Pennsville. Open Apr.–Oct. on the third Sun. of the month, noon–4. Free admission. The wrought-iron open frame is an unusual lighthouse design, built in Buffalo for $1,200 then shipped via train and mule wagon to New Jersey, where the lighthouse was first lit in 1877. Twice a day, the lighthouse keeper climbed 130 steps up a spiral staircase and wooden ladder to the lantern room to light and extinguish the flame. The lighthouse was decommissioned in 1950 when the Army Corps of Engineers dredged the channel. The **Finns Point Front Range Light,** a wooden tower that once stood on the riverbank, was moved in the 1930s.

East Point Lighthouse (856-327-3714), East Point Rd. (off Rt. 47), Heislerville. Open the third Sun. of the month, Apr.–Oct. and at special events; phone ahead. A beautiful red-roofed Cape Cod–style brick lighthouse built at the mouth of the Maurice River in 1849. Delaware Bay oyster schooners relied on the beacon to navigate their way to ports along the river, from Port Norris to Millville. It's one of the oldest lighthouses left standing in the state—its beacon is still an active navigational marker—and the last one remaining on the Jersey side of the bay. When the

WHEATON VILLAGE

(856-825-6800; 800-998-4552; www.wheatonvillage.org), 1501 Glasstown Rd. (off Rt. 552), Millville. Museum and glass factory: $10 adults; $9 seniors; $7 students; children 5 and under, free; admission is $1 less in winter. Admission to the village and shops is free. Hours vary by season. A reconstructed 19th-century glassmaking community in rural South Jersey—where America's glass industry began—is a mecca for glass artists and collectors. At the replica **T. C. Wheaton Glass Factory,** visitors can watch skilled glass sculptors use centuries-old tools and techniques in front of huge glass-melting and glass-reheating furnaces that burn at more than 2,000 degrees. Using a long, hollow steel tube, artisans blow and mold soft molten glass, which is later shaped with vintage grinding and polishing equipment into vases, bowls, and other works of art and function.

Other attractions here include the **Museum of American Glass** (see *Museums*), the largest museum in the country devoted to American glassmaking. A re-created village of elegant Victorian buildings includes shops, a general store, a one-room schoolhouse, and a restored train station. A research library contains 2,000 volumes on glassmaking history and technique. The **Down Jersey Folk Life Center** hosts programs on South Jersey's traditional arts and culture, including storytelling, music, and dance. Special events include workshops, lectures, and a major biennial international exhibition and symposium that attracts artists, collectors, and dealers from around the world.

ARTISANS DEMONSTRATE OLD-TIME GLASSMAKING METHODS IN THE GLASS STUDIO AT MILVILLE'S WHEATON VILLAGE, HOME TO THE MUSEUM OF AMERICAN GLASS AND THE DOWN JERSEY FOLK LIFE CENTER.

Photo courtesy of Wheaton Village, Millville NJ

Mauricetown Historical Society opens the lighthouse to visitors, you can climb to the lantern room for panoramas of the surrounding marshland.

MUSEUMS ✆ **Bridgeton Hall of Fame All Sports Museum** (856-451-7300), Bridgeton Recreation Center, Burt Ave. and Babe Ruth Rd., Bridgeton. Open Mon.–Sat. 10 AM –2 PM. Free admission. A unique collection of memorabilia that honors professional and amateur athletes from southern New Jersey. Permanent exhibits include a Cincinnati Reds bat collection, Hall of Famer Willie Mays's Golden Glove, and Philadelphia Phillies memorabilia from the 1980 World Championship. One large room is devoted solely to trophies, cups, and medals; another displays uniforms, equipment, and scrapbooks.

Nail House Museum (856-455-4100), Bridgeton City Park, One Mayor Aitken Dr., Bridgeton. Open Thurs.–Sun. 10–2. Free admission. Bridgeton was the hub of New Jersey's nail-manufacturing industry in the 19th century; today the office of the once-booming **Cumberland Nail and Iron Works** exhibits Industrial Revolution–era artifacts, including early iron tools, early Bridgeton glass, Nail Works artifacts, and the oldest public clock in South Jersey.

New Sweden Farmstead Museum (856-451-4802; 800-319-3379), Bridgeton City Park, Mayor Aitken Dr., Bridgeton. Currently closed except for pre-arranged tours by appointment. Most Swedish settlers came to America in the 19th century, except for a band of Swedes and Finns who arrived in South Jersey in 1638 and established the first permanent settlement in the Delaware Valley. Here, visitors see an exact replica of a 17th-century farmstead built by Scandinavian colonists. The authentic log buildings include a threshing barn, blacksmith shop, stable, sauna, smokehouse, and cabin. The complex was built in Bridgeton's 1,100-acre City Park to commemorate the 350th anniversary of the New Sweden Colony, the first Swedish settlement in America.

Woodruff Museum of Indian Artifacts (856-451-2620; 800-319-3379; www .bridgetonlibrary.org), Bridgeton Public Library, 150 E. Commerce St., Bridgeton. Open Mon.–Fri. 1–4, Sat. 11–2, or by appointment. Free admission. An excellent collection of artifacts from the Lenni-Lenape tribes that inhabited New Jersey's bay shore region for centuries. Tools, pottery, clay bowls, arrowheads, and other relics—in all, more than 30,000 objects—make this one of the largest collections of Native American artifacts in the state.

Museum of American Glass (609-825-6800, 800-998-4552; www.wheatonvillage .org), Wheaton Village, 1501 Glasstown Rd., off Rt. 552, Millville. Open Jan.–Mar., Fri.–Sun. 10–5; Apr.–Dec., Tues.–Sun. 10–5. Adults $10; seniors $9; students $7; children 5 and under, free. The nation's largest museum devoted to American glass is part of a South Jersey cultural center whose centerpiece is a replica of an 1888 glass factory (see sidebar, page 281). The museum chronicles the history of American glassmaking through more than 8,000 pieces dating from colonial times to the 20th century, with special focus on locally manufactured glass. Objects are positioned to take advantage of natural light, which highlights the fine details and brilliant color of each piece of glass.

Millville Army Airfield Museum (856-327-2347; www.p47millville.org), Millville Airport, One Leddon St., Millville. Open Tues.–Sun. 10–4. Guided tours by reservation only; please phone ahead. An excellent museum of World War II aviation history, focusing on Millville's role in the war and the history of the P-47

✎ COWTOWN RODEO

(856-769-3200; www.cowtownrodeo.com), 780 Rt. 40, Pilesgrove. Open Memorial Day–Labor Day. Call for admission prices. This popular Saturday-night professional rodeo is the longest-running weekly rodeo in the United States. The Harris family has operated this venerable South Jersey venue continuously since 1929, except for a hiatus during World War II. Hundreds of champion rodeo cowboys and cowgirls competing on the professional rodeo circuit come from around the country to perform in the 4,000-seat sta-dium, one of only two weekly rodeos in America sanctioned by the Profes-sional Rodeo Cowboys Association (the other is in Mesquite, Texas). Professional cowgirls, members of the Girls Rodeo Association, compete in barrel racing; a rodeo tradition since the 1960s. Other rodeo events are remi-niscent of the Old West, from bull riding, saddle bronc riding (most of the bucking broncs are raised here), and team roping to steer wrestling, bare-back riding, and calf roping. The **Cowtown Flea Market** on Tues. and Sat. is a well-known South Jersey tradition (see *Selective Shopping—Flea Market*).

THE COWTOWN RODEO IN PILESGROVE, A FAMILY-RUN RODEO IN SOUTH JERSEY SINCE 1929, IS THE LONGEST RUNNING SATURDAY NIGHT RODEO IN THE U.S

Photo by Joe Labolito

Thunderbolt fighter plane. The airfield was dedicated in 1941 as **America's First Defense Airport,** the first U.S. Army base built to defend our country. It served as a gunnery school for more than 1,500 fighter pilots, who received advanced training in P-40 Warhawks and P-47 Thunderbolt fighter planes. Some 10,000 men and women served at the base, whose headquarters now features exhibits of World War II–era aviation memorabilia and artifacts.

WINERY Heritage Vineyards of Richwood (856-589-4474; www.heritage stationwine.com), 480 Mullica Hill Rd. (Rt. 322), Richwood. Winery open daily 8:30–6 for tastings; wine and cheese tastings by reservation. Bill and Penni Heritage are fifth-generation farmers who started growing grapes on their 150-acre farm in 1998. Today they nurture six acres of vineyard grapes. Some of the farm's produce is used to make fresh fruit wines—sour cherry, blueberry, peach, apple—in addition to the Merlot, Chardonnay, Cabernet Sauvignon, and other traditional table wines. Their wines are sold at the farm's produce market (see *Selective Shopping—Farm Markets*).

ZOO 🐾 ✿ **Cohanzick Zoo** (856-453-1658), Bridgeton City Park, Bridgeton. Open daily 9–5; in winter, daily 8–4. Free admission. This is New Jersey's first public zoo—built in 1934—and one of the country's last remaining free zoos. The small facility in Bridgeton's wooded city park is home to more than 200 animals and birds, including white tigers, bears, monkeys, falcons, and leopards. Birds from around the world live in the walk-through aviary. The zoo's adopt-an-animal program helps to fund an animal's needs for a year; donors can choose the species they support. Gift shop and snack bar.

✳ To Do

BIRDING South Jersey is a birding hot spot, with thousands of acres of pristine marshland, meadows, and tidal wetlands that attract hundreds of species of native and migrating songbirds, waterfowl, and raptors. For more information, contact the **New Jersey Division of Fish and Wildlife** (609-292-3541; www.njfishand wildlife.com) or the **New Jersey Audubon Society** (908-204-8998; www.nj audubon.org).

Supawna Meadows National Wildlife Refuge (609-463-0994), 197 Lighthouse Rd., Pennsville, contains 2,800 acres of protected tidal marsh and grassland along the Delaware and the Salem rivers. It's considered a wetlands of international importance, where more than 250 species of local and migratory birds have been spotted. Large numbers of waterfowl feed and rest here during the spring and fall migrations. Sandpipers and other shorebirds frequent the area in summer. Bald eagles, ospreys, and others nest at the refuge, while hawks, kestrels, and owls hunt in the meadowland. Observation areas for wildlife viewing and photography.

Mannington Meadows Wildlife Refuge (609-292-2965), on Rt. 45 between Salem and Woodstown, is a rich habitat for local and migratory birds, including terns, swallows, ducks, and herons. In early spring, this is a good place to spot bald eagles.

In **Parvin State Park** (856-358-8616), on Rt. 540 in Pittsgrove, a boardwalk trail passes through a cedar swamp that's good for spotting owls, thrushes, and springtime migrating warblers.

Photo courtesy of the Supawna Meadows National Wildlife Refuge.

SUPAWNA MEADOWS NATIONAL WILDLIFE REFUGE IN PENNSVILLE, PRESERVES 2,800 ACRES OF TIDAL MARSHES ALONG THE DELAWARE RIVER ESTUARY, AN INTERNATIONALLY RECOGNIZED WETLANDS THAT IS A VITAL RESTING AND FEEDING STOP FOR THOUSANDS OF MIGRATING WATERFOWL AND SHOREBIRDS.

Harold N. Peek Preserve (856-825-9952), 2100 S. 2nd St., Rt. 47, Millville. Some 256 acres along the Maurice River, maintained by the **Natural Lands Trust,** include a variety of habitats, from scrubby pine forest to hardwood swamps and vast tracts of wild-rice marsh. The preserve is rich in wildlife, particularly ospreys, wild turkeys, bald eagles, great horned owls, and wintering waterfowl and raptors. A half-mile trail follows the river.

BOAT EXCURSION ✍ **Three Forts Ferry** (856-935-3218; 302-834-7941; www.threeforts.com), at Fort Mott State Park, 454 Fort Mott Rd., Pennsville. One-hour round-trip excursions; weekends and holidays, from late Apr. to late Sept.; Wed.–Fri., as well, mid-June–late Aug. Call or see Web site for a schedule. Adults $11; children $6. The *Delafort* takes history buffs on a tour of Delaware Bay's 19th-century three-fort coastal defense system. **Fort DuPont** in Delaware and **Fort Delaware** on Pea Patch Island, along with **Fort Mott** in New Jersey, were built to protect Delaware River ports after the Civil War. At the forts, visitors can watch authentic reenactments of Civil War scenes.

BOATING There are numerous public boat ramps in the Delaware Bay region, from the Delaware River and its tributaries to the many lakes and ponds that dot this vast rural area. Some charge a fee or require a New Jersey fishing license or boat ramp permit; it's best to phone ahead. They include **The Manumuskin River** in Port Elizabeth off Rt. 47; **Bridgeport Boat Yard** (856-467-0943), 118 Ferry Rd., Bridgeport, on Raccoon Creek; and **Pennsville Municipal Boat Ramp** (856-678-3089), Riviera Dr., Pennsville, on the Delaware River. **Penns**

Grove Wildlife Area (856-629-0090) in Oldmans Township has a 120-acre lake with five boat launches; **Fortescue State Marina** (856-447-5115) on Rt. 637 in Fortescue has a boat ramp on Delaware Bay.

Union Lake, off Rt. 49 in Millville, the state's largest artificial, and southern New Jersey's largest freshwater lake, is a popular destination for sailing and fishing, with two public boat launches.

FISHING Fortescue State Marina (856-447-5115; www.fortescue.com), on Rt. 637 in Fortescue, has a boat ramp on the bay. Most of the vessels docked here are charter boats or open (party) boats that take passengers fishing for blues, stripers, weakfish, and other species. Visit the Web site for comprehensive information on available boats, bait and tackle shops, marine services, fishing reports, launch ramps, and boat rentals.

Union Lake, off Rt. 49 in Millville. The **Union Lake Wildlife Management Area** surrounds this 898-acre lake, southern New Jersey's largest freshwater lake and the largest artificial lake in the state. Most anglers come here for the small-mouth and largemouth bass, as well as stripers and pickerel. Two public boat launches.

Menantico Sand Ponds Wildlife Management Area (609-292-2965), off Rt. 49 on the outskirts of Millville. Excellent fishing for largemouth bass and other species on a series of secluded small freshwater ponds and lakes at the head of the Menantico River. The state record for largemouth bass was recorded here 25 years ago. Public boat ramp.

Other prime fishing spots in South Jersey include **Fort Mott State Park** and **Supawna Meadows National Wildlife Refuge,** both in Pennsville; **Fortescue Wildlife Management Area** in Fortescue; **Mad Horse Creek,** a 5,826-acre tidal marsh on the Delaware River outside Hancocks Bridge; the **Cohansey River** in Bridgeton (there's a boat ramp on East Broad St.); and **Parvin Lake, Thundergust Lake, and Muddy Run,** all in Parvin State Park in Pittsgrove.

⚓ **BAYSHORE DISCOVERY PROJECT**

(856-785-2060; 800-485-3072; www.ajmeerwald.org), 2800 High St., Bivalve. Daytime and evening public sails: Adults $30; seniors $25; children 12 and under, $15; special sails: adults $25; seniors $20; children 12 and under, $15. The authentically restored 1928 oyster schooner *A. J. Meerwald,* New Jersey's official tall ship, is used by the Bayshore Discovery Project as a floating classroom to educate passengers on the maritime history and ecology of the Delaware Bay region. The majestic 115-foot ship harkens to the days when tall ships plied the waters of the bay in search of oysters. Day and evening sailing trips are staffed by a professional crew; passengers can help the crew set (raise) and furl (fold) the sails. Special programs include deck tours, lecture series, open-house events, birding sails, lighthouse cruises, and special cruises on Mother's Day and Father's Day.

GOLF Public 18-hole golf courses in South Jersey include **Cohanzik Country Club** (856-455-2122), 149 Fairton–Bridgeton Rd., Fairton; **Holly Hills Golf Club** (856-935-2412; www.hollyhillsgolf.com), 374 Friesberg Rd., Alloway; **Centerton Golf Club** (856-358-3325; www.centertoncc.com), 1016 Almond Rd., Pittsgrove; **Wild Oaks Golf Club** (856-935-0705; www.wildoaksgolfcourse.com), 75 Wild Oaks Dr., Salem; **Maple Ridge Golf Club** (856-468-3542), 1705 Glassboro Rd., Sewell; **Beckett Country Club** (856-467-4700; www.beckettgc.com), 2387 Old Kings Hwy., Woolwich Township.; **Town and Country Golf Links** (856-769-8333; www.tcgolflinks.com), 197 East Ave., Woodstown. All of these courses have a pro shop and a clubhouse with a restaurant or snack bar.

HIKING **Parvin State Park** (856-358-8616), 701 Almond Rd., Pittsgrove. Pick up a trail map at the park office before heading out on a hike (trails can be poorly marked), or ask about a schedule of guided hikes. More than 15 miles of trails wind through pine forest and swamp hardwood forest, including a 3.1-mile loop trail around **Parvin Lake,** short nature trails, and a mile-long trail circling **Thundergust Lake.** Other trails lace through a 465-acre natural area of cedar swamps, laurel thickets, and upland pine and oak forest, on the edge of the **Pine Barrens.**

SWIMMING ♂ **Greenwich Lake Park** (609-853-5120), Tomlin Station Rd., Gibbstown. A 20-acre lake with a swimming beach; lifeguards are on duty from mid-June–Labor Day.

♂ **Parvin State Park** (856-358-8616), 701 Almond Rd., Pittsgrove. On Parvin Lake—the only lake in the park that allows swimming—there's a beach at Parvin Grove that is staffed by lifeguards from Memorial Day to Labor Day. There's also a bathhouse, a first-aid station, and a concession stand that sells food and beach supplies. Picnic groves with tables and grills are near the beach.

✳ Green Space

WILDLIFE REFUGES One of the Delaware Bay region's most prominent characteristics is its seemingly endless expanse of pristine tidal marshland, thousands of acres protected as wildlife management areas or nature preserves. Most are ideal for bird-watching, canoeing, and fishing, and some have hiking trails and observation areas (see also *To Do—Birding*). Keep in mind that during the summer, these marshy areas can be swarming with biting greenhead flies and deerflies; carry insect repellent and wear protective clothing. Some of the more notable areas include the following:

Supawna Meadows National Wildlife Refuge (609-463-0994), 197 Lighthouse Rd. (Rt. 632), Pennsville. A vast expanse of tidal wetlands along the Delaware and the Salem rivers that's home to more than 250 species of birds, from waterfowl to migrating songbirds. Observation areas for photographers and birders; this area is also popular with hunters and anglers.

Egg Island Wildlife Management Area (856-629-0090), Maple St., Dividing Creek. Open daily dawn to dusk. A sizable expanse of windswept salt marsh laced with tidal creeks makes for excellent fishing, crabbing, and birding. Herons, marsh wrens, egrets, gulls, and wintering waterfowl love this wet habitat of tidal creeks and marsh surrounding a large pond. From the parking area, a footbridge leads to walking trails through the marsh.

Manumuskin River Preserve (609-861-0600), Schooner Landing Rd. (off Rt. 55), south of Millville. Open daily dawn to dusk. More than 3,500 acres of upland forest, tidal wetlands, mudflats, grassy meadows, and wild-rice stands, in the largest **Nature Conservancy** preserve in New Jersey. This pristine expanse is home to ospreys and bald eagles, and protects the largest concentration of rare joint vetch in the world, plus 30 other rare plant species. The remains of the 1790s settlement of **Fries Mill** are found in the preserve. Pick up the nature trail near the entrance at Schooner Landing Rd.

STATE PARKS Fort Mott State Park (856-935-3218), 454 Fort Mott Rd., Pennsville. Open daily 8 AM–dusk. A quiet 104-acre state park sits on the banks of the Delaware River where a post–Civil War military fort was built in anticipation of the Spanish-American War. Visitors can take a self-guided walking tour of the historic gun emplacements along the river, or ride the seasonal ferry to historic forts on the Delaware River (see **Three Forts Ferry** under *To Do—Boat Excursion*). The **Finns Point Interpretive Trail** is good for hiking, biking, and cross-country skiing; visitors head to the riverbank for fishing, crabbing, and picnicking. **Finns Point National Cemetery** (see *To See—Historic Sites*) contains the Civil War–era graves of 3,000 Confederate and Union soldiers (see page 278).

Parvin State Park (856-358-8616), 701 Almond Rd., Pittsgrove. A secluded state park on the edge of the Pine Barrens. Its 1,309 acres of pine forest surrounds picturesque Parvin Lake, with swimming, fishing, boating, and camping along the lakeshore (see *Lodging—Campgrounds*). The park was the site of several Native American encampments before Lemuel Parvin bought the land in 1796. He ran a sawmill on the banks of Parvin Lake, which he created by damming Muddy Run, the stream that flows through the park. During the Depression, the Civilian Conservation Corps built cabins and campsites; many of these original structures remain. Hikers love the trails in the 400 acres of hardwood swamp and oak and pine forest, and the groves of holly trees that reach upward of 40 feet in height. Close to 200 species of birds pass through during the fall and spring migrations.

PARKS ❀ ✿ **Riverview Beach Park** (856-678-6777), Rt. 49, Pennsville. Open daily. An expansive tree-lined town park on the river, in view of the Delaware Bridge. Plenty of tables for picnicking, pathways for strolling, and benches along the river for resting.

✿ **Bridgeton City Park** (856-455-3230), Mayor Aitken Dr., Bridgeton. A lovely 1,100 acre wooded city park, with canoeing, boating, and fishing on the Cohansey River. The Riverfront Promenade is lined with benches, lanterns, and brick walkways. Highlights include a museum of local industry, New Jersey's first public zoo, and an authentically re-created 17th-century Swedish village that honors the region's earliest settlers. A full schedule of free summertime concerts, theater, festivals, and family entertainment.

The Captain Buck Riverfront Park, Buck St., Millville. A pretty waterfront park named for Millville's 18th-century founder, Revolutionary War veteran and Cumberland County sheriff Joseph Buck. The park's 700-foot brick river walk invites strolling, the grounds are ideal for picnicking, and the downtown arts district is close by.

✷ Lodging

HOTEL ♿ ✐ ((T)) **Country Inn by Carlson** (856-825-3100; 888-201-1746), 1125 Village Dr., Millville 08332. A no-frills hotel with standard amenities adjacent to Wheaton Village and the Museum of American Glass, and a short drive from Millville's Glasstown Arts District. Guest rooms are clean and comfortable, with high-speed Internet access, TVs, and coffeemakers. A convenient place to stay when visiting Wheaton Village (see sidebar, page 281) or exploring the Delaware Bay region. The restaurant and lounge serve three meals. Continental breakfast. $75–100.

BED & BREAKFASTS Penny Royal Manor Bed and Breakfast (856-478-0236), 68 N. Main St., Mullica Hill 08062. A rose-colored Queen Anne–style Victorian at the heart of Mullica Hill's historic downtown. Comfortable and cozy, with five antiques-filled guest rooms, some with private bath. An ideal base for exploring the plethora of antiques shops tucked along Main St. Full breakfast. $75 shared bath; $90 with private bath.

Victorian Rose Farm Bed and Breakfast (856-769-4600; www.victorianrosefarm.com), 947 Rt. 40, Woodstown 08098. A beautifully restored 1887 Victorian farmhouse on a 6-acre horse farm. The three guest rooms are decorated with period antiques, fresh flowers, and other thoughtful touches; they also have private bath, air-conditioning, and TV. A quaint shop in the property's historic oak barn sells gifts and antiques. Full breakfast. $95–105.

CAMPGROUNDS 🐾 ✐ ♿ **Timberlane Campground** (856-423-6677; www.timberlanecampground.com), 117 Timberlane Rd., Clarksboro 08020. Open year-round. Nearly 100 open and wooded sites for tents and RVs on 20 acres. Kids love the playground, batting cage, and game room; there's also fishing, an outdoor pool, ball fields, and game courts. $34 and up.

✐ ♿ **Lake Kandle Campground** (856-589-2158; www.lakekandle.com), 250 Chapel Heights Rd., Sewell 08080. Open mid-Apr.–early Oct. A private family campground and swim club with 150 sites on 25 acres. A pleasant sandy beach on a 10-acre spring-fed lake, which offers swimming, boating, fishing, and a rope swing. Swimming pools, boat rentals, game room, and organized sports are among the many activities. Sites $45.

🐾 ✐ ♿ ((T)) **Old Cedar Campground** (856-358-4881; 800-582-3327; www.oldcedarcampground.com), 274 Richwood Rd., Monroeville 08343. Open mid-Mar.–Oct. A 180-acre working farm with domestic and wild animals. This is a family-friendly campground with lots of activities, from hayrides and tennis to horseshoes, swimming, and fishing. The 165 sites have full hookups. A camp store, laundry facilities, bathhouses, and other standard amenities. $25–55.

✐ ♿ ((T)) **Yogi Bear's Jellystone Park™ Camp-Resort at Tall Pines** (856-451-7479; 800-252-2890; www.jellystonenj.com), 49 Beal Rd., Elmer 08318. Open Apr.–Nov. A large family-friendly campground with 262 sites on 113 acres. A full range of options, from swimming and fishing to volleyball and other planned activities. The rental cabins, cottages, lodges, and chalets are ideal for families—amenities vary, and might include kitchens, TVs, screened-in porches, and wood-burning fireplaces. Sites $25–56; other lodging $75–159.

Parvin State Park (856-358-8616), 701 Almond Rd., Pittsgrove. Open year-round. Jaggers Point Campground has 56 tent and trailer sites on the south shore of Parvin Lake, with shower and laundry facilities and a boat launch for campers' use only. Four lakefront group tent sites, holding up to 25 campers each, are open Mar.–Nov. Cabins along the north shore of Thundergust Lake are available from Apr. to Oct., with a kitchen, a bathroom, a patio, and a living room with fireplace or wood-burning stove. Sites $20; cabins $45–65.

* Where to Eat

DINING OUT *blueplate* (856-478-2112; www.blueplatenj.com), 47 S. Main St., Mullica Hill. Open daily for breakfast, lunch, and dinner. A friendly eatery at the heart of Mullica Hill's antiques and shopping district, serving homey, satisfying American cuisine. It attracts locals, families with children, and out-of-town antiques hunters. Lunch is all about sandwiches. The dinner menu, which features offerings like mahimahi and handmade potato gnocchi, changes seasonally. Save room for the "chocolate sex on a plate" dessert specialty. $12–21.

& **Winfield's** (856-327-0909; www.winfieldsrestaurant.com), 106 N. High St., Millville. Open for dinner Tues.–Sun.; closed Mon. Reservations are recommended. In a region with few upscale dining options, this sophisticated eatery in Millville's arts district stands out. The atmosphere is relaxed and casual, and the tasteful contemporary décor in a century-old building lends an air of sophistication. Housed in a former Woolworth's store, the restaurant is named for founder Frank Winfield Woolworth, whose stores were synonymous with 20th-century small-town America. The American-Continental menu is well prepared with fresh seasonal ingredients. Featured are chicken, beef, seafood, and creative pasta dishes. $17–31.

Port of Call (856-327-5547), 3280 Rt. 47, Millville. Open for lunch Mon.–Fri.; dinner daily; Sat. breakfast; Sun. brunch. Reservations suggested. A casual family restaurant with simple, well-prepared dishes, including freshly made soups and desserts. The changing themed dinner menus make this eatery stand out. One night might spotlight oysters and barbecue; other nights feature clam pie, chicken potpie, or prime rib. BYOB. $11–20.

Franklinville Inn (856-694-1577; www.franklinvilleinn.com), 2526 Delsea Dr., Franklinville. Open for dinner Tues.–Thurs., 4–9; Fri.–Sat., 4-10. The building originated in the 1700s as a stage coach stop hotel for Philadelphia-to-Cape May travelers. Today it's a gem that's a locals' favorite for fine dining with a casual air of sophistication. The menu leans to steaks and seafood, but the quality is high and the service impeccable. $20–35.

EATING OUT

In Mullica Hill

⊗ * & **Harrison House Diner and Restaurant** (856-478-6077; www.harrisonhousediner.com), 98 N. Main Rd., at the corner of Rts. 45 and 322. Open daily for breakfast, lunch, and dinner. A bustling diner at an equally busy South Jersey crossroad is a local landmark. The original diner was traditional stainless steel; a brick façade was added to blend in with the nearby historic district. In true diner fashion, the extensive menu offers a little of everything: bacon, eggs, and hotcakes for breakfast; a Philly-style cheesesteak at lunch; for dinner, crabcakes or roast turkey with stuffing and cranberry sauce. Breakfast and lunch $4–10; dinner $8–20.

✍ **Naples Pizzeria** (856-478-6744), at The Old Mill Antique Mall, One S. Main St. Open daily for lunch and dinner. Nothing fancy, just well-prepared pizza-house fare: Sicilian- and Neapolitan-style pies, plus sandwiches, cheesesteaks, pasta dinners, calzones, and *stromboli*. A popular local spot that's ideal for grabbing a quick meal. $5–15.

In Millville
The Old Oarhouse Brewery (856-293-1200; www.oldoarhousebrewery .com), 123 N. High St. Open daily for lunch and dinner. A friendly, neighborhood Irish pub–style eatery in a circa-1883 building. The menu of traditional tavern fare is accompanied by an extensive selection of microbrews. The soups are homemade. Try the fish-and-chips or the crabcake sandwich. Generous and hearty portions. Very busy on weekends, with live entertainment on Thurs.–Sat. nights. $10–21.

The Looking Glass Coffeehouse and Café (856-327-1666), 16 N. High St. Open Mon.–Sat.; closed Sun. A friendly and funky coffeehouse a block from City Hall in Millville's arts district. Original artwork on the walls, live music, and cozy couches invite relaxation and lingering over the paper. A light menu of creative salads, sandwiches, burgers, and wraps at lunchtime. $5–10.

In Cumberland
✍ **Ike's Famous Crab Cakes** (856-825-2722; 888-302-2722), 5064 Rt. 49. Open daily for lunch and dinner. Reservations are recommended. This is the flagship restaurant and main pro-

duction facility for Ike's homemade crabcakes, lobster cakes, Cajun tuna bites, and garlic swordfish bites that are shipped around the country. This no-frills nautically themed seafood restaurant also offers steak, pasta, and chicken; a good place to bring the kids. Satellite locations along the Jersey shoreline. $12–20.

Elsewhere
Swede's Inn (856-467-2052; www .swedesinn.com),1301 Kings Hwy., Swedesboro. Open for dinner Mon.– Thurs., 4–midnight; Sat., 4 PM–2 AM; Sun., 3–10; lunch and dinner Fri., 11:30–2 AM. Built in 1771 as a tavern, you can still find evidence of this Colonial style building's original hand-pegged construction and historic features. The inn offers two dining options—a small, formal dining room and a café for casual, family dining with décor highlighted by large plate glass windows from a 1950's car showroom. Dining room offerings include steaks, scallops, and salmon. Café dining runs to appetizers, salads and quesadillas. A lively bar scene is augmented by live music on Thurs.–Sat. $20–35 dining room; $5–11 café.

S N A C K S **Mirenda's Bakery** (856-478-6800), 19B South Main St., Mullica Hill. Open Tues.–Fri. 8–5; Sat. 8–4; closed Sun. Homemade baked goods— from breads and rolls to cakes, pies, cookies, and brownies—in a charming barn-style building tucked off Church St.

Edible Art and Sweet Shoppe (856-825-2882), 226 North High St., Millville. Open Thurs.–Tues. 8–8; closed Wed. A little shop across from the historic Levoy Theater, with a tempting selection of pastries and other delicious treats.

✴ Entertainment

ARTS CENTER ♪ **Riverfront Renaissance Center for the Arts** (856-327-4500; www.riverfront center.org), 22 N. High St., Millville. The gallery is open Mon.–Thurs. 11–5; Fri. 11–8; Sat. 11–7; Sun. 11–5. This light and airy gallery is the centerpiece of the Glasstown Arts District. Solo and group shows feature emerging and established regional artists working in contemporary and traditional fine art and sculpture. Art classes for adults in many disciplines, and painting for kids. Every third Friday, the gallery stays open late, and visitors can meet the current exhibit's artist.

MUSIC AND THEATER Bay-Atlantic Symphony (856-451-1169; www.bayatlanticsymphony.org) is a Bridgeton-based regional professional orchestra that performs at several South Jersey venues, including **Stockton Performing Arts Center** (609-652-9000; www.intraweb.stockton .edu/pac) at Richard Stockton College of New Jersey in Pomona, and **Guaracini Performing Arts Center** (856-692-8499; www.cccnj.net/fpac) at Cumberland County College in Vineland.

Off Broad Street Players (856-451-5437; www.obsponline.org), P.O. Box 283, Bridgeton 08302. An amateur community theater group that performs a full schedule of Broadway shows, musicals, dramas, comedies, dinner-theater productions, and holiday performances.

✴ Selective Shopping

ANTIQUES

In Mullica Hill

Old Mill Antique Mall (856-478-9810), One S. Main St. (Rts. 45 and 322). Open daily 11–5. A 50-dealer co-op selling antiques and collectibles on three floors. A diverse selection of furniture, china, jewelry, vintage clothing, glass, toys, and textiles.

King's Row Antique Center (856-478-4361), 46 N. Main St. (Rt. 77). Open daily 11–5. Seven dealers selling furniture, china, glass, decorative items, and linens.

The Yellow Garage Antiquities Marketplace (856-478-0300; www .yellowgarageantiques.com), 66 S. Main St. Open Wed.–Sun. 11–5. Set in

---

♪ APPEL FARM ARTS AND MUSIC CENTER

(856-358-2472; 800-394-1211; www .appelfarm.org), 457 Shirley Rd., Elmer. In 1960, musicians Clare and Albert Appel converted their 176-acre farm into a summer arts camp for children. In nearly five decades, it has evolved into a multidisciplinary regional arts center, with year-round art classes and workshops. The grounds reflect the center's artistic spirit, with large-scale outdoor sculptures and whimsical murals covering the buildings. Saturday matinees for families; magic, comedy, and drama; and folk music, blues, and country music in the 250-seat **Clare Rostan Appel Theatre**. An **arts and music festival** is held every June (see *Special Events*).

a converted circa-1922 bus station, this is a collection of 35 dealers selling everything from Bakelite and toys to furniture and glass.

The Front Porch Antiques (856-478-6556; www.thefrontporchantiques .com), 21 S. Main St. Open Fri.–Sun. 11–5 or by appointment. Antique furniture and accessories on display in a 19th-century farmhouse.

In Repaupo and Mickleton
The antique center of Repaupo, a tiny community just east of the Delaware River, is a well-kept secret. Three auction companies here draw dealers and collectors from Canada to Florida to the huge Sun.–Tues. auctions held twice a month in sprawling warehouses. Thousands of antiques and collectibles trade hands during marathon all-day (and sometimes all-night) sessions. The auctions are haunted by dealers, but the public is welcome to participate in the frenetic business of peddling history. Many of the pieces found in antiques shops on the eastern seaboard passed through here. **S&S Auction** (856-467-3778; www.ssauction .com) and **South Jersey Auction** (856-467-4834; www.southjersey auction.com) are on Repaupo Station Rd. in Repaupo. **Dutch Auction Sales** (609-423-6800; www.dutch auctionsales.com) is at 356 Swedesboro Ave. in Mickleton.

In Millville
Treasures on High (856-825-3336), 204 N. High St. Open Wed.–Sat. Antiques, collectibles, and consignments.

ART GALLERIES Treen Studio Pottery Shoppe (856-223-2626; www.treenstudio.com), at The Mews, 43 S. Main St., Mullica Hill. Fine pottery, functional stoneware, and decorative glass. Open Wed.–Sun. 10–4.

Glasstown Arts District (856-0556; 800-887-4957; www.glasstownarts district.com), Millville. Millville's historic arts district near the riverfront is home to nearly 20 galleries, some with regular hours, others only open to the public during the regular third-Friday events or by appointment. **CCIA Gallery** (856-825-3700), at the corner of Main and High Sts., is open Mon.–Fri. 9–5; **Clay College** (856-765-0988), 108 N. High St., is a ceramics studio gallery open Mon.–Sat. **Fath Gallery** (856-825-0678), 120 N. High St., features the work of regional artists. Open Mon.–Fri. 9–4:30.

BOOKSTORES Murphy's Loft (856-478-4928), 53 N. Main St., Mullica Hill. Open Wed.–Sat. 11–5; Sun. 1–5. Used, out-of-print, and collectible books; magazines, maps, and prints.

Wind Chimes Book Exchange (856-327-3714), 210 N. High St., Millville. Open Mon.–Sat. 10–5; closed Sun. New and used books.

SPECIAL SHOPS

In Mullica Hill
Debra's Dolls (856-478-9778; www .debrasdolls.com), 20 N. Main St. Open Thurs.–Sat. noon–4; other times by appointment. A charming shop in Mullica Hill's oldest house, the circa-1704 **Mullica House,** featuring vintage, antique, and collectible dolls, plus several lines of new dolls and accessories.

In Bridgeton
Dutch Neck Village (856-451-2188; www.dutchneckvillage.com) 97 Trench Rd. Open Mon.–Sat. 10–5. Some shops open on Sunday; call for hours. A Colonial-style village of quaint shops and a café linked by brick walkways through landscaped grounds. Two small museums depict the area's rural early 20th-century farm life, with farming tools, World War II–era memorabilia, and

local Native American artifacts. The village hosts special events and festivals throughout the year.

By Our Hand (856-455-7693), 781 Shiloh Pike (Rt. 49). Open Tues.–Sat. 11–5; closed Sun. and Mon. A unique shop of handmade folk art, much of it created by owner-artist Alesia Farside.

In Millville

Rusty Heart (856-825-3002), 118 N. High St. Open Tues.–Sun. 10–6; closed Mon. Antiques, unique gifts, vintage jewelry, and dolls.

Secret Garden (856-825-3002), 116 N. High St. Open Tues.–Fri. 10–6; Sat. 10–5. Unique art and decorative accessories for the garden.

FARM MARKETS Cumberland County's Web site (www.co.cumberland.nj.us) includes a comprehensive list of the farms and produce markets that line roadsides all over South Jersey. They offer fresh Jersey produce in-season, which is May to Oct. in this region. Some have a unique specialty, such as fresh cider or eggs, local honey, organic produce, or pick-your-own strawberries—others seem to sell a little of everything.

In Richwood

✿ **Heritage Station** (856-589-4474; www.heritagestationwine.com), 480 Mullica Hill Rd. (Rt. 322). Open daily 8–6. A popular South Jersey farm market in an attractive barnlike building. Since 1850, five generations of the Heritage family have run Heritage Farm. Fresh produce includes peaches, pears, apples. A wide variety of home-baked goods, gourmet spreads, crafts, plants, and wines (see *To See—Winery*). Seasonal events like 5-acre corn maze, and pick-your-own.

In Bridgeton

Bridgeton Farmer's Market (856-455-3230), at the downtown Bridgeton waterfront, all summer on Fri. from 10 to 2. Local fruits and vegetables, honey, cut flowers, herbs, jams, and fresh crabs for sale.

Marlboro Farm Market and Garden Center (856-451-3138), 601 Rt. 49. Open daily year-round. In the market, fresh produce and flowers, jams, jellies, honey, and apple cider. In the nursery, bedding plants, shrubs, trees, and hanging baskets.

Adamucci Farms (856-451-4069), 152 Trench Rd. Self-service produce market open daily July–Nov. A fruit farm specializing in apples, peaches, and nectarines.

Elsewhere

Andy's Countryside Farm Market (856-447-5251), 939 Ramah Rd., Millville. Open May–Oct., daily 9–7. Sweet corn, tomatoes, cantaloupes, watermelon, and Jersey honey. Call ahead for a tour of the farm.

Fralinger's Cider Mill (856-455-0447), 24 Sheppards Mill Rd., Hopewell Township. Open Sept.–Dec., daily dawn to dusk. Freshly pressed apple cider made daily.

PICK-YOUR-OWN FARMS You can pick your own strawberries at the following farms in-season, usually mid-May through June: In Rosenhayn, at **Bisconte Farm** (856-455-3405) and **Sparacio's Strawberry Farm** (856-451-4142); in Newport, at **Woodbridge Farm** (856-447-4724), 100 Back Rd. You can pick blueberries at **Lebanon Creek Farm** (856-459-9428) in Rosenhayn in July and Aug. In the fall you can take a hayride and pick pumpkins at **Marlboro Farm Market** (856-451-3138) in Bridgeton. It's recommended that you phone ahead to check field conditions and availability.

FLEA MARKET Cowtown Flea Market (856-769-3200), 780 Rt. 40, Woodstown. Open Tues. and Sat. 8–4. "You name it, we sell it," goes the saying at this popular South Jersey flea market and **farmer's market,** with more than 550 vendors. Weekend regulars like to shop at the market during the day, then catch the Saturday-night rodeo, a tradition since 1929 (see *To See— Rodeo*).

✴ Special Events

February: **Cumberland County Winter Eagle Festival** (856-453-2177) Mauricetown Firehall, Noble St., Mauricetown.

April: **Farm Day** (856-455-4055; www.cchistsoc.org), Mauricetown Historical Society, Mauricetown.

May: **Antiques Street Fair** (856-881-6800), Mullica Hill.

June: 𝒮 **Appel Farm Arts and Music Festival** (800-394-1211; www.appel farm.org), Appel Farm Arts and Music Center, Elmer. A day-long outdoor concert on two stages, as well as a crafts fair and children's village. 𝒮 **Delaware Bay Day Festival** (856-785-2060), Port Norris, Bivalve, and Shellpile. A festival held in historic fishing villages along the Delaware Bay and the Maurice River. Highlights include a boat parade, an oyster-shucking contest, crab races, and family activities. **Strawberry Festival** (856-451-2188), Dutch Neck Village, Bridgeton. A celebration centering on strawberry-laden treats. **Cumberland County Weakfish Tournament** (856-447-5115), various locations. For nearly 20 years, thousands of anglers have participated in this popular competition. **Bridgeton Folk Festival** (856-451-9208; 800-319-3379), Sunset Lake, Bridgeton. Nationally known musicians, arts and crafts, and food.

July: 𝒮 **Cumberland County Fair** (856-825-3820; www.cumberlandcofair .com), Cumberland County Fairgrounds, Millville. Farm machinery, pony rides, tractor pull, petting zoo, 4-H exhibits, live music, and fireworks. 𝒮 **Gloucester County Fair** (856-478-2708), Rt. 77, Mullica Hill, with the **New Jersey Peach Festival,** 4-H exhibits, children's rides, crafts show, horse shows, and other animal shows.

August: **Midsummer Antiques and Collectibles Show** (856-825-6800), Wheaton Village, Millville. More than 80 dealers in glass, furniture, china, linens, and other collectibles. **Peaches N' Cream Festival** (856-451-2188), Dutch Neck Village, Bridgeton. A harvest celebration for more than 20 years. 𝒮 **Market Street Day** (856-935-7510; www.marketstreetday.com), Salem. Rides, children's entertainment, antique car show, live music, crafts, and food vendors. 𝒮 **Salem County Fair** (856-769-0414; www.salemcounty fair.com), Salem County Fairgrounds, Woodstown. Live music, pig races, and the popular ladies' skillet throw are among the activities at this traditional fair. **Downtown Car Show** (856-825-2600), Millville. Hundreds of antique and classic cars in the downtown arts district.

Labor Day Weekend: **Delaware Valley Bluegrass Festival** (302-475-3454; www.delawarevalleybluegrass .org), Salem County Fairgrounds, US 40, Woodstown. One of the top bluegrass festivals on the East Coast. Country, bluegrass, fiddling, and banjo playing.

September: **Cumberland County Sportsman's Jamboree** (856-692-3041), Union Rd. and Rt. 49, Maurice River Township. A 2-day festival with archery, skeet shooting, dog retrieving, turkey calling, activities for children, seminars on hunting, and an auction.

October: **Festival of Fine Craft** (856-825-6800), Wheaton Village, Millville. **Fall Festival** (856-451-2188), Dutch Neck Village, Bridgeton. ✐ **South Jersey Pumpkin Show** (856-765-0118; www.sjpumpkinshow.com), Cumberland County Fairgrounds, Millville. Contests for the largest pumpkin and best Halloween costumes, petting zoo, and pumpkin bake-off among the many fun events. **Fall Open House and Civil War Reenactment** (856-881-6800), Mullica Hill. Civil War–era military encampment, fashion show of historic clothing, family activities, tours, and a vintage-car show.

December: **Christmas Candlelight Tour** (856-785-0457), Mauricetown Historical Society, Mauricetown. **Christmas House Tour** (856-881-6800), Main St., Mullica Hill. A tour of historic homes decorated for the holidays. **Walk of Lights** (856-451-2188), Dutch Neck Village, Bridgeton. **Soul of the Season Celebration** (856-293-0556), Glasstown Arts District, Millville. Holiday music, Dickens actors, horse-and-carriage rides, entertainment, and fireworks.

Central New Jersey

THE PRINCETON REGION

THE PINELANDS REGION

THE PRINCETON REGION

I t's an amusing fact that of all the travelers who claim they've been to central New Jersey, few of them have actually exited the New Jersey Turnpike. Those who have know that this region is blessed with pleasant and unexpected surprises, from the rural landscape of horse farms, orchards, and sprawling state parks and forests to the small historic towns with downtown streets lined with antiques shops, inns, and cafés. Although acres of farmland are being carved into suburbs, the resulting patchwork of farm fields and subdivisions is still decidedly rural, dotted with as many barns and produce stands as shopping centers. The area is rich in Early American history, too, including two of the Revolution's most significant battles. For a time after the war, it was even the young nation's capital.

Central New Jersey is perhaps best known for the intellectually rich community of Princeton, home to one of the most prestigious Ivy League colleges in the country. Among its notable alumni are U.S. presidents James Madison and Woodrow Wilson, although Brooke Shields was probably more well known as a student here in the 1980s. Today, the university offers visitors world-class art, theater, and music. Student volunteers lead tours of the campus, which has a colorful history of its own. In 1776 New Jersey's first legislature met at Nassau Hall, where it adopted the state seal and inducted William Livingston as the colony's first governor. It served as a hospital and barracks during the American Revolution for both Continental and British troops; when Princeton was the temporary home of the Continental Congress, Nassau Hall was the capitol building. The façade still bears the scars of a cannonball fired by British troops during the Revolution.

Princeton's most famous 20th-century resident was arguably the iconic physicist and mathematician Albert Einstein, known as much for his shock of white hair as his revolutionary theory of relativity and his role in America's development of nuclear weapons. To the world he was a genius of mythical proportions, but to Princeton residents he was also a beloved local legend who could be seen sailing on Lake Carnegie and walking to his faculty post at the Institute for Advanced Study. He lived at 112 Mercer Street for two decades, until his death in 1955; his brain still resides at the University Medical Center at Princeton.

Princeton's downtown boasts all the expected accoutrements of a lively college town. Cafés, bars, shops, and coffeehouses line Nassau and Witherspoon streets, where eateries feature cuisine from around the globe. The historic neighborhoods of stately old homes around campus are ideal for strolling, notably along Library Place and Hodge Road. Woodrow Wilson resided at 82 Library Place, and Grover

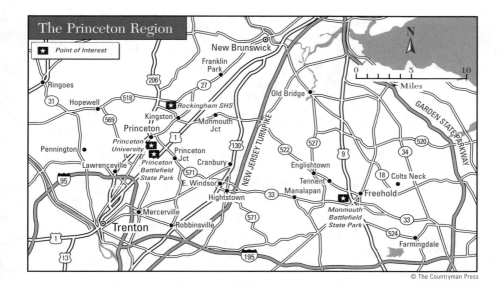

Cleveland lived in a stately yellow Georgian Revival house at 15 Hodge Road. Today both residences are private homes, but on Stockton Street visitors can tour Drumthwacket, the official governor's residence, and Morven, an 18th-century mansion built by a signer of the Declaration of Independence. The high-tech Princeton Public Library occupies the corner of Witherspoon and Wiggins streets, and stylish shops and bistros line Palmer Square, where the grand Nassau Inn has taken in lodgers since 1756.

Just outside downtown is Lake Carnegie, home to Princeton's crew team. In the 19th century, crews practiced on the Delaware and Raritan Canal, rowing alongside barges loaded with freight. The university ended this dangerous practice in 1886, and Princeton went without a crew program until wealthy industrialist Andrew Carnegie built the university its own private 3-mile-long lake in 1907. Today, visitors line the lakeshore to watch boats compete in springtime sprints and in longer races in the fall.

The lake is also popular with paddlers and anglers, as is the nearby Delaware and Raritan Canal. A towpath cutting between the canal and lake is a multi-use recreational trail for hikers, runners, and cross-country skiers. Farther afield, a restored 19th-century ironworks village is in Allaire State Park; still-rural historic towns like Hopewell and Ringoes have antiques shops, gourmet dining, and lovingly restored Colonials and Victorians. In the rolling hills beyond their quaint downtown streets are golf courses, wineries, orchards, and farms lining a network of scenic, lightly traveled back roads.

The longest battle—and largest land artillery battle—in the American Revolution took place in Manalapan. In 1778, the Continental army followed the British on their journey from Philadelphia to New York, and their violent meeting became the battle of Monmouth. On that scorching June day, by some accounts, General Washington and his Continental army defeated the British under General Sir Henry Clinton. Most historians agree, however, that the battle was a draw. Today the battleground is part of Monmouth Battlefield State Park, where visitors can see a landscape of forests and open fields as it was in the 18th century, as well as stirring reenactments of this major turning point in the Revolutionary War. Another battlefield preserves the site of the battle of Princeton, where a year earlier, American troops engaged the British and forced their retreat to New Brunswick, ending the military campaign known as the Ten Crucial Days that began with Washington's infamous Christmas-night crossing of the Delaware River.

Entries in this section are arranged in roughly geographic order.

AREA CODES 732, 609.

GUIDANCE The Molly Pitcher State Welcome Center (609-655-1610) is located in Cranbury at mile marker 71.9 on the New Jersey Turnpike southbound. It has public restrooms and is well stocked with tourism literature.

Monmouth County Department of Economic Development and Tourism (800-523-2587; www.visitmonmouth.com) publishes a visitor's guide and other information on travel in the region.

Western Monmouth Chamber of Commerce (732-462-3030; www.wmchamber .com) provides tourism information on Monmouth County.

Princeton Walking Tours (609-921-6748), 158 Nassau St., Princeton. Sun. at 2 PM; call ahead for group tours. Admission $7. The **Historical Society of Princeton** (www.princetonhistory.org) leads 2-mile guided walking tours of the Princeton University campus as well as two-dozen historical sites around town.

Princeton University Orange Key Campus Tours (609-258-3603; www .princeton.edu) leave daily (except during university holidays) from the welcome desk at the Frist Campus Center, Chancellor Green or from the Clio Center. Mon.–Sat. at 10, 11, 1:30, and 3:30; Sun. at 1:30 and 3:30. Arrive at least 5 minutes before the tour is scheduled to begin. Student volunteers lead informative 1-hour guided walking tours of the historic campus. Free.

GETTING THERE *By air:* **Newark Liberty International Airport** (973-961-6000; parking information: 888-397-4636; www.panynj.com) in Newark is New Jersey's largest airport, served by more than 40 major carriers.

By rail: **New Jersey Transit** (973-275-5555; www.njtransit.com) commuter trains on the Northeast Corridor Line between Trenton and New York City's Penn Station stop at Princeton and Princeton Junction. **Amtrak** (800-872-7245; www .amtrak.com) also stops at Princeton Junction, en route between New York and Philadelphia. A single-car train, known locally as the Dinky (www.gmtma.org), connects the Princeton Junction station to the southwestern corner of the Princeton University campus.

By bus: **New Jersey Transit** (973-275-5555; www.njtransit.com) links Trenton and Princeton, stopping at Princeton Forrestal Village; it also provides service from Port Authority Bus Terminal in New York City to Princeton Junction Railroad Station. Buses leave New York and Princeton every half hour during the day for the 2-hour trip. **Princeton Junction Shuttle** (609-443-4000, ext. 246) provides weekday local service between Princeton Junction and East Windsor and Hightstown. The Free-B, a free bus loops around Princeton Borough during commuter hours, making stops throughout the community and at the N.J. Transit Dinky train station.

By car: From the New York City metropolitan area, the **New Jersey Turnpike** cuts this region in half before drifting southwest toward Camden and Philadelphia on its way to Wilmington, Delaware. **I-195** connects the shoreline to Trenton. The **Garden State Parkway** traces this region's eastern border.

Many of Princeton's downtown streets have metered parking. A municipal parking garage can be accessed from Spring St. and at the Princeton Public Library at Witherspoon and Wiggins Sts. There's also an outdoor metered parking lot on Vandeventer Ave., behind Nassau St. Click on **www.princetonparking.org** for more information.

GETTING AROUND *Taxis:* **Princeton Taxi** (609-924-1400), **Nassau Taxi** (609-497-1800), and **Associated Taxi Stand** (609-924-1222) serve the Princeton area.

MEDICAL EMERGENCY University Medical Center at Princeton (609-497-4000; 888-742-7496; www.princetonhcs.org), 253 Witherspoon St., Princeton. The emergency number is 609-497-4431.

CentraState Medical Center (732-431-2000; www.centrastate.com), 901 W. Main St., Freehold.

✳ To See

UNIVERSITY Princeton University (609-258-1766; www.princeton.edu), Princeton. Pick up a map at the Frist Campus Center for a self-guided walking tour of the campus, or join one of the daily student-led tours (see *Guidance*). The College of New Jersey was chartered in 1746 in Newark, moved to Princeton in 1756, and became Princeton University in 1896. It's the fourth-oldest college in the United States (after Harvard, William and Mary, and Yale) and boasts a 500-acre campus with buildings rich in history and architectural diversity. Circa-1756 **Nassau Hall** is the oldest campus building. It was the onetime headquarters of the Continental Congress, when Princeton was the nation's capital after the American Revolution. During the war it was used as a hospital and barracks by British and American troops. The university's **art museum** is considered one of the best in the country, with an extensive collection of international works like Picasso's *Head of a Woman* (see *Museums*). The **university chapel** has wood paneling from England's Sherwood Forest and an 8,000-pipe Mander-Skinner organ; concerts are scheduled throughout the year. At the corner of Nassau St. and Washington Rd. is **Firestone Library,** Princeton's main research center, with two galleries and more than 4 million books.

CHURCH Old Tennent Presbyterian Church (732-446-6299; www.oldtennent church.org), 448 Tennent Rd., Manalapan. The original church—a tiny log building—was founded in 1692 by Scottish settlers. The current building—the **1751 New Scots Meeting House**—served as a field hospital after the battle of Monmouth in 1778. The church retains much of its original stark Georgian-style architecture, from the wavy glass panes and locally made iron fixtures to the wooden pews where wounded and dying soldiers were treated. Soldiers are buried in the churchyard.

HISTORIC HOMES Morven Museum and Garden (609-924-8144; www .historicmorven.org), 55 Stockton St., Princeton. Open for tours Wed.–Fri. 11–3;

Sat.–Sun. noon–4. The last tour begins 45 minutes before closing. Adults $5; seniors and students $4; group tours by reservation. A Princeton landmark built in the 18th century by Richard Stockton, founding father and signer of the Declaration of Independence. The stately mansion served as New Jersey's official governor's residence from 1953 to 1981. The mansion, gardens, and sweeping grounds reflect three periods of Morven's history. Inside are permanent and changing exhibits on New Jersey history. The old servants' quarters are now a visitors center with historic displays; a re-created historic garden is behind the house.

Bainbridge House (609-921-6748; www.princetonhistory.org), 158 Nassau St., Princeton. Open Tues.–Sun. noon–4; closed Mon. Free admission. This 1766 house was the birthplace of William Bainbridge, commander of the USS *Constitution* during the War of 1812. Today it's the headquarters of the **Historical Society of Princeton,** which mounts changing historical exhibits and leads guided walking tours of downtown Princeton on Sun. at 2 PM. Museum shop.

Covenhoven House (732-462-1466), 150 W. Main St., Freehold. Open May–Oct., Thurs.–Sat. 1–4. Free admission. Revolutionary War general Sir Henry Clinton used this Georgian house as British headquarters before the battle of Monmouth in 1778. The kitchen wing dates to circa 1710; the main section of the house was built decades later. Open-hearth cooking demonstrations and other programs illustrate what life was like for a prosperous local farmer in the 18th century.

HISTORIC SITES Princeton Battlefield State Park (609-921-0074), 500 Mercer Rd., Princeton. Open daily dawn to dusk. Free admission. An 85-acre state park and national historic landmark at the site of the January 1777 battle of Princeton, where George Washington's Continental soldiers defeated British troops in a surprise attack. Many historians consider this battle the fiercest fight of its size of the entire Revolutionary War. An Ionic Colonnade marks the common grave of 36 American and British soldiers killed in the battle. The **Thomas Clark House,** the

AMERICAN AND BRITISH TROOPS CLASHED HERE AT PRINCETON BATTLEFIELD STATE PARK ON JANUARY 3, 1777. THE BATTLE, CONSIDERED ONE OF THE FIERCEST OF THE AMERICAN REVOLUTION, WAS A VICTORY FOR GEORGE WASHINGTON'S CONTINENTAL ARMYS.

Photo courtesy of the New Jersey Department of Environmental Protection

DRUMTHWACKET

(609-683-0057; tour information: 609-683-0591; www.drumthwacket.org), 354 Stockton St. (Rt. 206), Princeton. Open to the public for tours on Wed. (except during Aug.); reservations are required and should be made at least a week in advance. Donations accepted. An elegant, pillared Greek Revival–style mansion is the official New Jersey governor's residence. Prominent businessman and politician Charles Smith Olden built Drumthwacket (the name is the Scottish term for "wooded hill") in 1835, and became the first governor to reside here. After nearly two centuries of private owners, state governors began living here in the 1980s. Docents lead 45-minute tours of six public rooms—including the music room, library, solarium, and governor's study—used for business meetings and receptions. Across the front lawn is the **Olden House,** a white 18th-century farmhouse that was the property's original residence. Gift shop and historic herb garden.

DRUMTHWACKET, SCOTTISH AND GAELIC FOR "WOODED HILL," IS AN ELEGANT 19TH-CENTURY GREEK REVIVAL–STYLE PRINCETON MANSION THAT SERVES AS THE OFFICIAL RESIDENCE OF THE GOVERNOR OF NEW JERSEY.

Photo courtesy of The Drumthwacket Foundation.

18th-century Georgian-style home of a Quaker farmer, was used as a field hospital; today it's a museum with period furnishings and colonial-era demonstrations. British troops used the **Stony Brook Friends Meeting House,** adjacent to the battlefield, as a barracks; it has displays featuring swords and Revolution-era firearms. (See *Green Space—State Parks.*)

Princeton Cemetery, (www.nassauchurch.org/cemetery) Wiggins and Witherspoon Sts., Princeton. Pick up a map at the cemetery office or print one from the Web site for a self-guided tour; call for a schedule of guided tours. An eclectic collection of colorful historical figures is laid to rest in what's known as the Westminster

MONMOUTH BATTLEFIELD STATE PARK

(732-462-9616), 347 Freehold–Englishtown Rd. (off Rt. 33), Manalapan. Grounds open daily 8–6; buildings open on a limited basis—call for hours. Free admission. The battle of Monmouth was a significant turning point in the American Revolution (see *Green Space—State Parks*). The June 1778 fight was the longest—and one of the bloodiest—in the 8-year war, and marked the last time Continental and British armies met on a battlefield. Revolutionary War buffs flock to the historic battlefield to see interpreters reenact camp life, military drills, and the scenes that took place here more than two centuries ago. Although the winner is still disputed, the Continental army forced the British to retreat to New York. George Washington's troops, using battle tactics gleaned during their long encampment at Valley Forge the previous winter, killed close to 300 enemy soldiers in heavy fighting. The battlefield is a national historic landmark that retains much of the original landscape and historic features, including the **Craig House**, the home of a local family, which served as a field hospital after the battle. The visitors center has exhibits and a gift shop; an annual reenactment commemorates the anniversary of the battle (see *Special Events*).

Abbey of America. They include George Gallup, creator of the ubiquitous public opinion poll; the fiery 18th-century preacher Jonathan Edwards, whose legendary sermon "Sinners in the Hands of an Angry God" fueled the Great Awakening; President Grover Cleveland and Vice President Aaron Burr Jr.; 19th-century businessman and Princeton native Paul Tulane; and novelist John O'Hara, along with an escaped slave, Civil War generals, and most of Princeton University's presidents.

Rockingham State Historic Site (609-683-7132; www.rockingham.net), 108 Rt. 518, Kingston. Open Wed.–Sat. 10–noon and 1–4; Sun. 1–4; closed Mon., Tues., and holidays. Free admission. Admission to the house is by guided tour only; call or see the Web site for a schedule. The circa-1702 house served as George Washington's final headquarters of the Revolutionary War. George and Martha Washington and some Continental soldiers lived here in the final days of the war, from August to November,1783. During that time Congress was set up in Princeton, the Treaty of Paris was signed in France, and the general wrote his famous "Farewell to Troops" orders. Rockingham is the second-oldest residence in the Millstone River valley, and was moved from its original hilltop location to the current site on the Delaware and Raritan Canal.

✍ **Allaire Village** (732-919-3500; www.allairevillage.com), Allaire State Park, 4265 Atlantic Ave. (Rt. 524), Farmingdale. Open Memorial Day–Labor Day, Wed.–Sun. 11–5; Labor Day–Nov. and in May, Sat.–Sun. 10–4; closed Dec.–Apr., except for special events. Free admission to the village; the park charges a parking fee during summer. A re-created 19th-century ironworking village is a living-history museum, complete with a general store, a carriage house, stables, trade shops, a chapel, and a bakery. Industrialist James Allaire bought the land in 1822 to supply the raw bog iron needed for his Howell Works Company. Demonstrations in 19th-century children's games, blacksmithing, leather making, carpentry, spinning, quilting, open-hearth cooking, and other skills by craftspeople in period dress. **Pine Creek Railroad,** the state's only live-steam narrow-gauge train, takes visitors through the 3,000-acre state park (see *To Do—Train Excursions*). Guided tours of the Allaire mansion, 19th-century militia reenactments, antique car shows, and Christmas lantern tours are among the special events in the village (see *Special Events*).

MUSEUMS 🦉 🚲 **Princeton University Art Museum** (609-258-3788; www .princetonartmuseum.org), McCormick Hall, Nassau St., Princeton. Open Tues.–Sat. 10–5; Sun. 1–5; closed Mon. and holidays. Free admission. The university's world-class art museum, founded in 1882, is considered one of America's leading art museums. More than 60,000 pieces ranging from French impressionist paintings and Greek antiquities to Roman mosaics from Antioch, medieval European stained glass, and contemporary art to ancient works from China, Europe, and Latin America. Of particular note is the collection of Chinese and classical art, as well as prints and drawings by the old masters. The museum offers a wide variety of special programs just for children, from docent-led talks during the school year to art-making workshops and family events. Museum shop.

🚲 **The Metz Bicycle Museum** (732-462-7363; www.metzbicyclemuseum.com), 54 W. Main St., Freehold. Open by appointment. Adults $5; seniors $4; students $3. The sign over the door says "Treasures of Years Gone By," and David Metz's extraordinary personal collections of antique bicycles dating from the 1850s to 1950s are just that. Children's riding toys, including a horse tricycle from the 1880s and a 1901 skateboard, 19th-century tandems, and unusual and one-of-a-kind bikes like circus-trick bikes, elegant high wheelers, and boneshakers. Among the more unusual pieces is an 8-foot-high "lamp lighter," ridden on New York City streets to light gas lamps, and a 19th-century "Zimmy" made at a Freehold bike factory in 1896. Displays of vintage bike equipment, from oil lanterns and seats to posters, tools, and other cycling accessories.

HISTORIC ROCKINGHAM, GEORGE WASHINGTON'S LAST WARTIME HEADQUARTERS DURING THE AMERICAN REVOLUTION, IS NOW A STATE HISTORIC SITE IN KINGSTON.

Photo courtesy of the New Jersey Department of Environmental Protection

Hopewell Museum (609-466-0103), 28 E. Broad St., Hopewell. Open Mon., Wed., and Sat. 2–5. Free admission. A small museum in an 1877 Victorian-era brownstone with period furnishings, toys, clothing, and antique weapons. Changing exhibits of crafts, farm tools, and other items illustrate the history and traditions of village life in America from colonial times to the present. One wing is devoted to Native American artifacts; a library is available for genealogy research.

WINERIES Silver Decoy Winery (609-371-6000; www.silverdecoywinery.com), 610 Windsor–Perrineville Rd., Robbinsville. Open Fri. 2–6, Sat.–Sun. 11–5; vineyard and production facilities tours by appointment. A 95-acre farm producing white and red table wine, as well as unique dessert wines from blueberries, raspberries, and other fruits.

Amwell Valley Vineyards (908-788-5852; www.amwellvalleyvineyard.com), 80 Old York Rd. (Rt. 514), Ringoes. Retail shop, tasting room, and tours Thurs.–Sun. noon–5 and by appointment. A winery known since 1978 for its handcrafted wines. Amwell uses traditional European methods, which means the grapes are grown here, picked by hand, and bottled on-site. Some 11 acres of grapes are made into 20 varieties of reds, whites, sparkling wines, and dessert wines. A picturesque site surrounded by the Sourland Mountain Range.

Unionville Vineyards (908-788-0400; www.unionvillevineyards.com), 9 Rocktown Rd., Ringoes. **Note:** at press time the winery was closed for renovations; call before visiting. A winery in a converted 19th-century dairy barn surrounded by 90 acres of vineyards planted in fields that were once part of the largest peach farm in the country. The wines have won more than 500 medals since Unionville opened in 1992. The winery adopted a fox-hunting theme that honors one of the oldest traditions in the Amwell Valley, a rural area of horse pastures and farm fields in the rolling hills of Hunterdon County. Call for a schedule of special events and festivals.

✶ To Do

BICYCLING The towpath along the historic 70-mile **Delaware and Raritan Canal** (732-873-3050; www.dandrcanal.com) is a beloved route among local cyclists. The flat, easy terrain is ideal for beginners, families with young children, and those who want to enjoy beautiful scenery with a minimum of effort. The state park is one of central New Jersey's most popular recreation corridors.

Bicycles can be rented from **Jay's Cycles** (609-924-7233; www.jayscycles.com), 249 Nassau St., Princeton.

BIRDING Assunpink Wildlife Management Area (609-259-2132), Robbinsville. Open daily dawn to dusk. Free admission. One of the top bird-watching areas in central New Jersey. More than 5,600 acres of woods, fields, and hedgerows surround three lakes where owls, hawks, sparrows, and other birds like to congregate in spring and summer. Ducks and Canada geese stop by on their annual fall migration.

Herrontown Woods (609-989-6530), Snowden Lane, Princeton. A popular local spot for birding. You can explore the woods on 3 miles of marked trails. Thrushes, warblers, and eastern screech owls and great horned owls live here year-round; many more species pass through during the spring and fall migrations.

CANOEING AND KAYAKING Popular areas for canoeing and kayaking in the Princeton region include Lake Carnegie, the Delaware and Raritan Canal, the Manasquan River in Allaire State Park, and the ponds and waterways in Upper Freehold's Assunpink Wildlife Management Area. The following outfitters rent boats and equipment:

⌇ **Griggstown Canoe and Kayak Rental** (908-359-5970), 1076 Canal Rd., Griggstown. Open daily Memorial Day–Labor Day; Apr.–Oct., open weekends and holidays only. Located next to Delaware and Raritan Canal State Park, about halfway along the 34-mile-long canal between Trenton and New Brunswick. Canoe and kayak rentals for the canal, where the gentle current is ideal for families and novice paddlers. Advanced paddlers should ask about trips on the Millstone River. Reservations are suggested for groups of five or more.

Princeton Canoe and Kayak Rental (609-452-2403), Turning Basin Park, 483 Alexander Rd., Princeton. Open mid-April–May, and Sept.–mid-Nov. on weekends and holidays; open daily June–Labor Day. A shop close to the train station that rents canoes and kayaks by the hour or by the day for excursions on Lake Carnegie and on the Delaware and Raritan Canal. Boaters first paddle to the canal then portage to the lake and Stony Brook.

GOLF Many 18-hole golf courses in central New Jersey are open to the public on a regular or limited basis (it's best to call ahead). Most offer a driving range, a clubhouse, a pro shop, and a restaurant or a snack bar, including: **Princeton Country Club** (609-452-9382), One Wheeler Way, **Cranbury Golf Club** (609-799-0341; www.cranburygolf.com), 49 Southfield Rd., and **Mercer Oaks Golf Course** (609-936-9603), 785 Village Rd.—all in West Windsor; **Pine Brook Golf Course** (732-536-7272), 1 Covered Bridge Blvd., Manalapan; **Colts Neck Golf Club** (732-303-9330; www.coltsneckgolfclub.com), 50 Flock Rd., **Hominy Hill Golf Course** (732-462-9222), 92 Mercer Rd. (considered one of the top public golf courses in New Jersey), and **Pebble Creek Golf Club** (732-303-9090; www.pebblecreek golfclub.com), 40 Rt. 537 East—all in Colts Neck; **Howell Park Golf Course** (732-938-4771), Preventorium Rd., Farmingdale; **Heron Glen Golf Course** (908-806-6804; www.heronglen.com), Rts. 202 and 31, Ringoes.

HIKING Many parks and natural areas in the Princeton region offer opportunities for short, easy hikes and longer excursions (see *Green Space*). Among the more notable: **Stony Brook–Millstone Watershed Nature Reserve** in Pennington has 8 miles of trails; **Charles H. Rogers Wildlife Refuge** in Princeton has trails in a 300-acre forest; **Princeton Battlefield State Park** and the adjacent 600-acre wildlife preserve have hiking paths; **Monmouth Battlefield State Park** in Manalapan has hiking throughout 2,000 acres.

SPECTATOR SPORTS **Freehold Raceway** (732-462-3800; www.freehold raceway.com), 130 Park Ave. (Rts. 9 and 33), Freehold. Live daytime harness racing for pacers and trotters from Jan.–May and Aug.–Dec.; closed after the first week in June and in July; post times, 12:30. Open daily year-round for simulcast harness racing and thoroughbred racing from racetracks around the country. The first track and grandstand were built here in 1853; today it's the oldest and fastest half-mile harness-racing track in America.

✔ **Old Bridge Township Raceway Park** (732-446-7800; www.racewaypark.com), 230 Pension Rd., Englishtown. Open Wed., and Fri.–Sun. A former 300-acre farm has hosted drag racing and motocross races, including national championships, since 1965. Practice courses for motorcycles and quads; one track is just for children.

SKY DIVING Skydive Jersey Shore (732-938-9002; 877-444-5867; www.sky divejerseyshore.com), Monmouth Executive Airport, Rt. 34, Farmingdale. Instruction and tandem jumps for beginner parachuters.

TRAIN EXCURSIONS ✔ **Pine Creek Railroad** (732-938-5524; www.njmt.org), Allaire State Park, Farmingdale. Open weekends mid-Apr.–June and mid-Sept.–Nov.; daily July–Aug. Tickets $4; call for special-event prices, which may be higher. A scenic 1.5-mile excursion through Allaire State Park on antique steam-powered trains. This is New Jersey's first operating steam-train exhibit, founded in 1952 and maintained by the **New Jersey Museum of Transportation.** It's also the oldest continuously operating steam preservation railroad in the world. The railroad's special trips are extremely popular, especially the Oct. fall foliage excursions, and the holiday rides at Halloween and Christmas (with Santa, of course). Visitors can tour the extensive collection of historic steam locomotives, boxcars, coaches, cabooses, and brake cars, and see some of the ongoing restoration projects. Model-train shows and other special events.

✔ **Black River & Western Railroad** (908-782-9600; www.brwrr.com), John Ringo Rd. (Rt. 579), Ringoes. Open May–Oct., Sat., Sun., and holidays; July–Aug., Thurs.–Sun. Adults $14; children 3–12, $7; children under 3, free. Nostalgic 1-hour trips (about 25 minutes one-way) on a restored steam train between historic rail stations in Ringoes and Flemington. The circa-1872 Ringoes Station has exhibits on historic railroad travel, a collection of old-time railroad cars, and a picnic area. Call or see Web site for a schedule of holiday and themed excursions.

✳ Green Space

STATE PARKS Princeton Battlefield State Park (609-921-0074), 500 Mercer Rd., Princeton. Open daily dawn to dusk. Free admission. An 85-acre national historic landmark preserving the meadows and woods that witnessed George Washington's first victory over British troops in the field (see *To See—Historic Sites*). The January 3, 1777, Revolutionary War battle is considered the fiercest of its size in the entire 8-year war. The surprise defeat came at the end of the pivotal "Ten Crucial Days" that began with the Continental army's infamous crossing of the Delaware River at Christmas. The battle stretched from here to the College of New Jersey (now Princeton University) a mile away. The park grounds are adjacent to **Institute Woods,** a 600-acre wildlife preserve of hardwood forest, fields, and wetlands. Together, they offer easy to moderate hiking trails, picnicking, and cross-country skiing.

Allaire State Park (732-938-2371), Rt. 524, Farmingdale. Open daily year-round; village buildings are open from spring to fall. $5 parking fee Memorial Day–Labor Day. Nature center open daily Memorial Day–Labor Day; Wed.–Sun., Sept.–May. A rural 3,000-acre park best known for **Allaire Village,** a restored early-19th-century ironworking village (see *To See—Historic Sites*). More than 23 miles of trails for hiking, mountain biking, and horseback riding.

Delaware and Raritan Canal Park (732-873-3050; www.dandrcanal.com), Trenton to New Brunswick. The historic 34-mile-long main canal opened in 1834 and bustled with barges shuttling freight between Pennsylvania and New York City. Today the old towpath is a 70-mile multi-use linear park popular with runners, strollers, and cyclists; fishing and canoeing in the canal. Along the way are historic wooden canal bridges, clapboard mills, and the houses where the lockkeepers and bridge tenders lived.

Monmouth Battlefield State Park (732-462-9616), 347 Freehold–Englishtown Rd. (off Rt. 33), Manalapan. The 1778 Battle of Monmouth was a turning point in the Revolutionary War. Molly Pitcher made a name for herself on the battlefield when she tended to soldiers and reportedly fired her husband's cannon after he was injured (see sidebar on this page). The battle is reenacted every June (see *Special Events*). Hiking trails, picnicking, and winter sports on more than 2,000 acres.

NATURAL AREAS Charles H. Rogers Wildlife Refuge, West Dr., Princeton. A rural 39-acre spread of hiking trails through a deciduous forest along Stony Brook. The sanctuary is a nesting ground for 90 species of birds attracted to the diverse habitat of marsh surrounded by woods and thickets.

MOLLY PITCHER

Molly Pitcher—real name, Mary Ludwig Hays—is New Jersey's famous Revolutionary War heroine who fought alongside her husband, William, in the Continental army during the battle of Monmouth on June 28, 1778. Traditionally, women on Revolutionary War–era battlefields served supportive roles—mainly nursing, cooking, and washing laundry. Hays was known to have cleaned uniforms and brought pitchers of water to General Washington's soldiers on the sweltering-hot battleground as they clashed with thousands of British troops during one of the war's bloodiest battles. Soldiers shouted "Molly, pitcher!" as she carried pitchers of water from a well onto the battleground. From there, the line between historic fact and legend becomes blurred. Stories credit her with all manner of battlefield heroics, from firing her husband's cannon after he collapsed either from heat exhaustion or injury, to likening her to an 18th-century Joan of Arc. Still others say the stories are just that, colorful bits of folklore woven over time. Regardless, Hays stayed with her husband until the war ended in 1782; 40 years later she became one of only three women in New Jersey awarded a military pension for her service during the American Revolution. Today she holds a dual honor in New Jersey: there's the **Molly Pitcher Inn,** a historic hotel overlooking the Navesink River in Red Bank (see *Lodging—Hotels* in "Sandy Hook to Belmar" in "The Central Seacoast"); and a rest stop on the New Jersey Turnpike that is named in her honor.

Mountain Lakes Nature Preserve (609-924-8720), 57 Mountain Ave., Princeton. A trail winds past the lakes that give this peaceful, 90-acre tract its name. This was a former farm that's being allowed to revert to a natural mix of open fields and woodlands. The lakes and surrounding wetlands attract a rich variety of birds, from herons and Canada geese to woodpeckers and warblers.

✧ **Stony Brook–Millstone Watershed Nature Reserve** (609-737-3735; www .thewatershed.org), 31 Titus Mill Rd., Pennington. Grounds open daily dawn to dusk. The **Buttinger Nature Center** is open Tues.–Sat. Call for a schedule of special events and programs. A 585-acre wildlife refuge with 8 miles of hiking trails, a wildflower area, a research pond, an arboretum, and an organic garden. The **Stony Brook Gallery** has changing exhibits in oil and acrylic painting, watercolors, woodwork, and photography, as well as live acoustic music and family matinees.

✳ Lodging

HOTELS

In Princeton 08549

&. **The Westin Princeton** (609-452-7900; www.starwoodhotels.com/westin), Princeton Forrestal Village, 201 Village Blvd. A handsome brick hotel set behind a classical fountain amid the shops and restaurants of Forrestal Village. The 294 guest rooms have all the usual amenities. Fee Wi-Fi available. Fitness room and indoor pool, another pool outdoors. Restaurant, sushi bar, and lounge. $150–320.

&. "🍴" **Princeton Marriott Hotel & Conference Center at Forrestal** (609-452-7800; 800-943-6709; www .doralforrestal.com), 100 College Rd. East. Newly renovated and now affiliated with Marriott, the lobby and 300 guest rooms and 11 suites with free Wi-Fi have the clean, elegant lines of Arts and Crafts design. The fitness center has a Jacuzzi, steam room, and sauna, and a full range of pampering spa services. The pool is enclosed in a glass atrium. Outside are four enclosed tennis courts, volleyball pits, and hiking trails through 25 acres of woodlands. Restaurant and pub. $139–329.

&. "🍴" **Hyatt Regency Princeton** (609-987-1234; www.hyatt.com), 102 Carnegie Center (off US 1). A soaring, skylit atrium lobby is nicely landscaped with a pond and dramatic plantings. The 347 Wi-Fi equipped guest rooms are clean and quiet, ranging from standard hotel rooms to others with lofty ceilings, spacious bathrooms, and balconies that overlook the atrium. The staff is friendly and helpful; the hotel runs a shuttle to the train station and downtown Princeton. Comedy club, bar, and restaurant. A solarium has an indoor pool and a whirlpool. $109–300.

In Freehold 07728

✧ &. "🍴" **Radisson Hotel Freehold Gardens Hotel and Conference Center** (732-780-3400; 888-201-1718; www.radisson.com), 50 Gibson Pl. and Rt. 537. Formerly the Freehold Gardens Hotel and Conference Center, the Radisson has undergone a major renovation, and now holds 121 luxury rooms and suites. Complimentary Wi-Fi is available throughout the hotel. Close to Six Flags Great Adventure and Freehold Raceway, and next to

♿ NASSAU INN

(609-921-7500; 800-862-7728; www.nassauinn.com), 10 Palmer Square, Princeton 08542. Since 1756, this elegant downtown landmark has been *the* place to stay for historical figures (Paul Revere), U.S. presidents (George Washington, John F. Kennedy), world leaders (Fidel Castro, Golda Meir), and various icons (Grace Kelly, Joe DiMaggio, Norman Rockwell, Bob Hope). Traditional and elegant Colonial décor with modern amenities like a fitness center and Internet access. The 203 guest rooms and five suites are popular with the university community and visiting luminaries. The rustic **Yankee Doodle Tap Room,** with rough-hewn beams, a stone hearth, and a Norman Rockwell mural above the bar, serves traditional American fare for three meals (look for the initials of Princeton University students carved into the oak tabletops). Close by are Palmer Square's upscale boutiques and gourmet restaurants. Rooms $199–229; suites $375–565; three-room suite $930.

THE HISTORIC NASSAU INN CAMPUS, DATES TO 1756, WHEN IT WAS A POPULAR PRE-REVOLUTIONARY WAR–ERA TAVERN ACROSS FROM THE PRINCETON UNIVERSITY CAMPUS. TODAY'S MODERN 200-PLUS ROOM COLONIAL-STYLE HOTEL PRESIDES OVER PALMER SQUARE IN DOWNTOWN PRINCETON.

Photo courtesy of Nassau Inn

Freehold Raceway Mall, the hotel has an outdoor pool, fitness center, restaurant, and offers a complimentary continental breakfast. $129–230.

BED & BREAKFASTS

Hepburn House (732-462-7696; www.hepburnhouse.com), 15 Monument St., Freehold 07728. A lovely circa-1885 Queen Anne Victorian, the inn is full of lovely period details like stained and leaded glass, a polygonal porch, and wood floors of inlaid parquet. The three cozy guest rooms have private bath, air-conditioning, TV, and phone. The two suites have private sitting areas; one has a private porch. Wireless Internet is available. The inn sits close to Monmouth Battlefield State Park (see *Green Space—State Parks*). Full breakfast. $115–175.

MOTEL 🐾 🖉 **Stage Depot—The Inn at Pennytown** (609-466-2000), 145 Rt. 31 N. Pennington 08534. Clean and simple motel-style lodging in a 23-acre complex of shops and restaurants. The 45 guest rooms are moderately priced, making this a favorite of families. One restaurant serves breakfast, another is open for lunch and dinner. Outdoor pool. $59–90.

CAMPGROUNDS 🐾 🖉 ᕕ **Turkey Swamp Park Campgrounds** (732-462-7286; www.monmouthcounty parks.com), 66 Nomoco Rd., Freehold 07728. Open Apr. 1–Nov. 15. Close to beaches and Six Flags amusement park. A 1,180-acre wooded campground with 64 sites—some with full hookups—for tents and tent trailers, and two cabins that sleep six. Canoeing, fishing, swimming, and hiking. Call for fees.

🐾 🖉 **Pine Cone Campground** (732-462-2230; www.pineconenj.com), 340 Georgia Rd., Freehold 07728. Open mid-April– mid-October. A quiet family campground on 34 acres with cabins, and 125 wooded and open sites with full services. Sports facilities; game room. Sites around $43; cabins $119–145.

Allaire State Park (732-938-2371), Farmingdale. Tent sites, yurts, and cabinlike shelters are available for year-round camping. $15–25.

✳ Where to Eat

DINING OUT

In Princeton (www.princetondining.com; www.princetonmenus.com)
Mediterra (609-252-9680), 29 Hulfish St. Open daily for lunch and dinner. Reservations suggested. A stylish and relaxed downtown eatery overlooking Palmer Sq., serving the cuisine of Spain, Greece, and the entire Mediterranean region. Look for seafood, chicken, and pasta among the entrées; a robust paella stands out, as does the award-winning wine list, house-made desserts, and artisanal breads from the nearby Witherspoon Bread Company (see *Eating Out—Snacks*). Outdoor dining in-season. $26–30.

ᕕ **The Ferry House** (609-924-2488; www.theferryhouse.com), 32 Witherspoon St. Open for lunch Mon.–Fri.; dinner daily. Reservations recommended. An elegant space in the heart of downtown, lauded by food critics for the creative French-American cuisine featuring locally grown produce, unique salads, and starters with a penchant for mushrooms. Rich desserts made in-house. BYOB. $25–29.

🖉 **Blue Point Grill** (609-921-1211; www.bluepointgrill.com), 258 Nassau St. Open daily for dinner. A casual and elegant seafood house with crisp, nautically themed décor, an open kitchen, and a popular raw bar. The American menu features a wide range of fish and shellfish, including a long list of daily specials that might include homemade bouillabaisse or whole crispy black sea bass. Children's menu available. BYOB. $16–30.

ᕕ **Lahiere's** (609-921-2798; www .lahieres.com), 5–11 Witherspoon St. Open for lunch and dinner Mon.–Sat.; closed Sun. Reservations recommended. Princeton's oldest restaurant has been a landmark for 90-plus years, and it's still considered one of the best for upscale fine dining. Contemporary American and European cuisine is matched with a stellar wine list. $17–39.

Main Street Bistro and Bar (609-921-2779; www.mainstreetprinceton .com), Princeton Shopping Ctr., 301 N. Harrison St. Open for lunch Mon.–Sat.; dinner daily. *Bon Appetit* magazine dubbed this European-style bistro one of America's Great Neighborhood Restaurants for its casual atmosphere, excellent service, and expertly prepared classic bistro fare. The seasonally changing menu features robust and hearty dishes in winter, fresh vegetables and herbs from local farms in summer. The stylish lounge and outdoor terrace are popular. A global wine list, a good selection of microbrews, and desserts from their own bakery round out the offerings. $16–22.

Witherspoon Grill (609-924-6011; www.jmgroupprinceton.com), 57 Witherspoon St., Princeton. Open daily for lunch and dinner. A classic American steakhouse that prides itself on serving all-natural Premium Gold Prime Angus beef raised by a co-op of small ranchers. Poultry and seafood dishes, as well. Children's menu. BYOB. $25–45.

In Ringoes

Harvest Moon Inn (908-806-6020; www.harvestmooninn.com), 1039 Old York Rd. (Rt. 179). Open for lunch Tues.–Fri.; dinner Tues.–Sun.; closed Mon. A three-course prix fixe dinner is available Tues.–Fri. Fine dining in a handsome 19th-century Federal-style stone farmhouse. The creative, seasonal New American menu includes exquisitely wrought dishes like sautéed sliced pekin duck breast. The rustic pub room offers a light-but-upscale menu of homemade pasta, pizza, and salads. Superb desserts. $20–35.

& **Main Street Bistro** (732-294-1112; www.bistro1.com), 30 E. Main St., Freehold. Open for lunch Mon.–Fri.; dinner daily. A trendy bistro complete with martini bar, sushi bar, and a menu

BROTHERS MOON

(609-333-1330; www.brothersmoon.com), Seven West Broad St., Hopewell. Lunch Tues.–Sat.; dinner Tues.–Sun.; Sun. brunch; closed Mon. Reservations are recommended. A legion of regulars frequent this village market-turned-chic French restaurant. The intimate 75-seat space is stylish and simple, the staff friendly and knowledgeable. The seasonal menu relies on local organic ingredients that accompany grilled and roasted meats and fish. Creative pasta dishes are among the vegetarian and vegan options. You might start with goat cheese and caramelized onion tart with arugula & aged balsamic vinaigrette. Dinner entrées might include Roasted masala spiced lamb rack, roasted vegetable bundle, couscous and honey mint sauce, or sautéed scallops with wild mushroom gnocchi and sweet peas in a white wine butter sauce. Save room for inventive desserts like vanilla cheesecake with pineapple chutney, or peanut butter mousse layered in chocolate cake. A tempting selection of salads, meats, bread, cheeses, and olives is available for a gourmet picnic or a special meal at home. BYOB. $17–31.

of classic American and Italian dishes accented with Asian influences. Dinner choices range from pork tenderloin to Szechuan ahi tuna. BYOB. $18–26.

&. **Basil's Legends Bar and Grille** (609-443-5565; www.basilslegends .com), at the Days Inn, 460 Rt. 33 E., E. Windsor. Open Tues.–Sun. for dinner; lunch Tues.–Fri.; closed Mon. Reservations recommended. This above-average chain hotel restaurant serves authentic Mediterranean dishes like roasted stuffed eggplant, or, Basil's Mixed Grill, a generous trio of petite filet mignon, bacon-wrapped shrimp, and lamb chops. *Tartufo,* baklava, and an assortment of gelati for dessert. $14–35.

EATING OUT

In Princeton (www.princeton dining.com; www.princeton menus.com)
Teresa's Café Italiano (609-921-1974), 23 Palmer Sq. E. Open daily for lunch and dinner. A casual, bustling trattoria-style café in Palmer Square, serving contemporary Italian cuisine like antipasti, gourmet brick-oven pizzas, and creative pasta dishes. Regional Italian wines dominate the list. Save room for the homemade desserts. $12–21.

&. **Triumph Brewing Co.** (609-924-7855; www.triumphbrewing.com), 138 Nassau St. Open daily for lunch and dinner. This lofty and modern brewery and restaurant, tucked down a long alleyway, is popular for its casual atmosphere, reasonable prices and house-brewed beer. The menu runs from a hearty pub fare of sandwiches, salads, and grilled pizzas, to creative dishes like coffee-crusted filet mignon. Specialty brews range from light and fruity to rich and stout. Late-night menu. $14–30.

Nassau Bagels and Sushi (609-497-3275), 179 Nassau St. Open daily for breakfast, lunch, and dinner. Bagels and sushi make for a unique combination, but it works in this small downtown shop. For breakfast, bagels are topped with traditional spreads or made into savory breakfast sandwiches; lunch is salads, wraps, and Asian boxed lunches. But, what shines here is the Korean and Japanese cuisine. Finish with red bean or green tea ice cream. Sushi $3–10; dinner entrées $10–17.

✎ ✐ **PJ's Pancake House** (609-924-1353; www.pancakes.com), 154 Nassau St. Open Sun.– Thurs. 7 AM–10 PM; Fri.–Sat. 7 AM–midnight. Their food promises to be "the way things used to taste." The setting is an old house as comforting as the homey food. It's always packed. Breakfast classics are served all day and night. For lunch and dinner, it's soups, buffalo wings, potato skins, shepherd's pie, and burgers and sandwiches. $6–10.

&. **Masala Grill** (609-921-0500), 19 Chambers St. Open daily for lunch and dinner. *Masala,* Hindi for "spice mixture," is an apt name for this restaurant where the air and the food are scented with the traditional flavors of Indian cuisine. The emphasis is on fresh and healthful ingredients, including vegetarian options, with food known to be prepared with less oil than most typical Indian dishes. Close to campus, popular with students. BYOB. $15–20.

The Original Soupman (609-497-0008; www.originalsoupman.com), 30 Palmer Square E., Princeton. Open daily 11–8. The soup shop made famous by *Seinfeld,* has expanded to many locations, including this small corner eatery. Soup menu changes daily. Sandwiches served, as well. $6–8.

Elsewhere
Blue Bottle Café (609-333-1710; www.thebluebottlecafe.com), 101 East Broad St., Hopewell. Open for lunch Wed.–Fri., 11:30–2; dinner

Tues.–Thurs. 5–9; Fri.–Sat. 5–10 and Sun. 4–8. Reservations recommended. A limited but sophisticated menu in a small house with minimalist décor and three small dining rooms. The food takes a Mediterranean slant, with the potato gnocchi entrée and the home-made desserts garnering rave reviews. The owners proudly support local farming, naturally raised meats and sustainable agriculture. BYOB. $18–34.

SNACKS Witherspoon Bread Company (609-688-0188), 74 Wither-spoon St., Princeton. Open daily from 6 AM. They take baking seriously here, from artisan breads like Italian *ciabat-ta*, tomato-basil focaccia, and crusty baguettes, to croissants, chocolate brioche, seasonal fruit tarts, and choco-late chip cookies. Hearty *panini* sand-wiches are made to order. Olive oil, gourmet coffees, and other specialty products for sale. Sandwiches $3–7.

❂ **Thomas Street Ice Cream and Chocolate** (609-683-8720; www .thomassweet.com), 179 Nassau St., Princeton (another take-out location at 33 Palmer Sq.). Open Sun.–Thurs. 11–11; Fri.–Sat. 11–midnight. Creative flavors like apple pie have made this little ice-cream shop a Princeton insti-tution for a quarter century. In warm weather, prepare to wait in a long line. The shop hosts live music and a popu-lar outdoor film festival in summer at the amphitheater in Petteronello Gar-dens.

Badger Bread Company (609-466-3666), 5 Railroad Pl., Hopewell. A bak-ery affiliated with Rat's restaurant in Hamilton (see *Dining Out* in "The Trenton and Camden Area" in "The Delaware River Valley"). Open Tues.–Sat. 7–4; Sun. 8–3; closed Mon. This stylish coffee shop and bakery with the look of an old-fashioned gen-eral store serves Old World–style breads, pastries, and decadent

desserts, along with a selection of cre-ative soups and sandwiches. A few café tables inside, and on the sidewalk when the weather allows. $4–10.

❂ **Old Monmouth Candies** (732-462-1311), 627 Park Ave. (Rt. 33 East), Freehold. Open daily. Home to what's billed as the "world's best peanut brit-tle," made of Virginia peanuts by the Old Monmouth Peanut Brittle Compa-ny since 1910. Cashew brittle is anoth-er customer favorite, along with thousands of chocolate bunnies sold at Easter.

Princeton Public Library (609-924-9529; www.princeton.lib.nj.us) 65 Witherspoon St., Princeton. The small snack bar in this most pleasant, mod-ern building serves sandwiches, pas-tries, and beverages in a congenial atmosphere. Or take your purchase outside to eat on the expansive public patio. Sandwiches $6–8.

COFFEE AND TEA Small World Coffee (609-924-4377; www.small worldcoffee.com), 14 Witherspoon St., Princeton. Open Mon.–Thurs. 6:30 AM–10 PM; Fri.–Sat. til 11; Sun. 7:30 AM–10 PM. Second location at 254 Nas-sau St. Go to one counter for fresh house-roasted coffee and espresso or an organic fruit smoothie, another for meals featuring local ingredients and organic produce, including hearty house-made muesli, an organic yogurt parfait, seasonal homemade soups, sal-ads and sandwiches. Changing exhibits of local artwork on display; live enter-tainment most Saturday nights. $4–9.

Chez Alice (609-921-6760; www .chezalice.com), 5 Palmer Sq., Prince-ton. Open Mon.–Thurs. 7–7; Fri.–Sat. 7–8:30; Sun. 8–6. A cozy bakery and coffee shop in the heart of things, offering delicious baked goods, good value sandwiches, coffees, teas, and juices. Sandwiches $6–9.

Kingston Bakery and Coffeehouse (609-921-2778), 56 Main St., Kingston. Open daily for breakfast, lunch, and early light dinner. A neighborhood spot for more than 20 years. Breakfast pastries and gourmet coffee in the morning, plus house-made breads, pies, cakes, and cookies. For lunch, soups, salads, and creative specialty sandwiches. Their frozen entrées—vegetable chili, chicken potpie, soups, and pasta sauces—are popular take-out items. $5–10.

✸ **Failte Coffeehouse** (609-466-6681), 9 E. Broad St., Hopewell. Open Mon.–Sat. 7–6; Sun. 9–5. *Failte* is Gaelic for "welcome," and a perfect name for this friendly and inviting community meeting place in an old white house in the center of town. The unhurried atmosphere and cozy furniture encourage lingering over the Sunday paper in the reading room, or enjoying a light meal or dessert. Changing exhibits of local artwork; also live entertainment, from traditional Irish music to acoustic rock. Especially popular are the special programs for children. Irish jewelry and apparel for sale. $4–9.

✷ Entertainment

MUSIC

In Princeton

✸ **Princeton Symphony Orchestra** (609-497-0020; www.princeton symphony.org), Richardson Auditorium, Alexander Hall, on the Princeton University campus. Princeton's award-winning professional orchestra presents classical and chamber series, world-renowned guest artists, holiday pops concerts, and performances for children. Free preconcert lectures.

Princeton University Concerts (609-258-9220), Richardson Auditorium, Princeton University. Chamber music and solo performances in a 900-seat concert hall.

Carillon Concert Series (609-258-3601), Cleveland Tower, on the historic Graduate College campus at Princeton University, Springfield Rd. Free Sunday-afternoon concerts in summer.

Westminster Choir College of Rider University (609-921-2663; www.rider.edu), 101 Walnut Lane. A year-round schedule of solo, choral, and ensemble concerts and recitals by students, faculty members, and guest artists. Westminster is the only music school in the world where all students perform with top conductors and orchestras, such as the New York Philharmonic.

THEATER Princeton Rep Company (609-921-3682), One Palmer Square, Princeton. Free admission. A professional theater company stages summertime performances of Shakespeare's plays at Pettoranello Gardens Amphitheatre in Community Park. Shows begin at 8 PM, rain or shine.

MCCARTER THEATRE CENTER FOR THE PERFORMING ARTS (609-258-2787; www.mccarter.org), 91 University Pl., Princeton. A Tony Award winner for outstanding regional theater with a full performance schedule of music, dance, and drama. For more than 75 years, Princeton's landmark theater has hosted world premieres, internationally acclaimed artists like Luciano Pavarotti and Mikhail Baryshnikov, and world-renowned dance companies.

✦ **Princeton Summer Theater** (609-258-7062; www.princetonsummer theater.org), Hamilton Murray Theater, on the Princeton University campus, Princeton. Performances mid-June–mid-Aug., Thurs., Fri., and Sat. at 8 PM; Sat. and Sun. at 2 PM. For more than 35 years, a summertime series of classic comedies, award-winning dramas, family entertainment, and Shakespeare's works. Drama workshops for children.

✦ **Kelsey Theatre** (609-570-3333; www.kelseyatmccc.org), Mercer County Community College, 1200 Old Trenton Rd., West Windsor. A full season of professional and semiprofessional productions for adults, children, and families in the college's 385-seat theater. Performing-arts workshops for students and children.

✳ Selective Shopping

ANTIQUES Tomato Factory Antique Center (609-466-9833; www .thetomatofactory.com), Two Somerset St., Hopewell. Open Mon.–Sat. 10–5; Sun. 11–5. More than 30 antiques dealers share space in a restored factory. Furniture, lighting, textiles, china, glass, dolls, and jewelry.

ART GALLERIES Gold Medal Impressions (609-606-9001; www .goldmedalimpressions.com), 43 Princeton–Hightstown Rd., Princeton Junction. Open daily 9–5. Sports photographer Dick Druckman's gallery contains hundreds of images he has taken of the Olympics, professional hockey, tennis, football, and basketball. Matted and framed photos for sale.

Gallery 14 (609-333-8511; www.photo gallery14.com), 14 Mercer St., Hopewell. Open Sat.–Sun. noon–5 or by appointment. A gallery devoted to fine-art photography.

FLEA MARKET Englishtown Auction (732-446-9644; www.english townauction.com), 90 Wilson Ave., Englishtown. Open weekends and some holidays 8–4. The family-owned auction originated in 1929 as a venue for farmers to buy, sell, and trade farm equipment and livestock. Today hundreds of vendors set up their wares outdoors or in five indoor buildings. Plants, toys, antiques, hardware, clothing, and other flea market finds.

SPECIAL SHOPS

In Princeton

Palmer Square (609-921-2333; www .palmersquare.com), downtown Princeton. Open daily. A charming tree-lined square, home to more than 40 upscale specialty shops, boutiques, and restaurants across from Princeton University and the Nassau Inn. Live music, theater, classic car shows, and other special events.

✦ **Labyrinth Books** (609-497-1600; www.labyrinthbooks.com), 122 Nassau St. Open Mon.–Fri. 9–8; Sat. 10–6; Sun. 11–6. Labyrinth replaces the longstanding Princeton institution Micawber Books, selling a full range of volumes from fiction to course textbooks to children's books.

Princeton Record Exchange (609-921-0881; www.prex.com), 20 S. Tulane St. Open daily. Tucked into a side street, here are thousands of new and used CDs, LPs and movies on tape and DVD.

✦ **Princeton Morning Glory** (609-252-9151, 20 Nassau St. Open daily. A cute little shop filled with toys, gifts, greeting cards, and novelty items.

MarketFair (609-452-7777; www .marketfairmall.com), US 1 at Meadow Rd. Open daily. More than 40 high-end shops like **Anthropologie, Smith & Hawken, Williams-Sonoma,** and

Restoration Hardware selling furniture, home accents, clothing, toys, and gardening supplies. Food court and movie theater.

Princeton Forrestal Village (609-799-7400; www.princetonforrestal village.com), College Rd. and US 1. Three-dozen factory-outlet shops and restaurants.

In Freehold

♪ **Freehold Raceway Mall** (732-577-1144; www.freeholdracewaymall.com), 3710 Rt. 9, Freehold. Open daily. More than 200 specialty shops and eateries, with high-end anchor stores like Macy's and Nordstrom. Kids love the indoor carousel.

FARMS AND GARDENS

♪ **Terhune Orchards** (609-924-2310; www.terhuneorchards.com), 330 Cold Soil Rd., Princeton. Store and farm open year-round, daily. Pam and Gary Mount's 200-acre farm grows 35 different fruits and vegetables, including 30 kinds of peaches and 35 apple varieties. Visitors can pick fruit and cut their own flowers. Kids love the horses, sheep, ducks, goats, and other farm animals they can feed and pet. A scenic 1-mile nature trail starts at the hay barn and leads through woods and open meadow, and past the pond and cherry orchard. The farm market is in a rustic century-old barn. Antique farm machinery on display. Special events.

♪ **Lee Turkey Farm** (609-448-0629; www.leeturkeyfarm.com), 201 Hickory Corner Rd., East Windsor. Open daily. A working farm in the Lee family since 1868. They raise 5,000 turkeys a year and sell them oven-ready, frozen year-round, fresh around the holidays. You can pick your own vegetables and fruits in the fields, or buy them in the produce market. Guided tours of the 54-acre farm include hayrides, pumpkin picking, and trips into the orchards.

♪ **Battleview Orchards** (732-462-0756; www.battlevieworchards.com), 91 Wemrock Rd., Freehold. The country store is open daily 9–6; call ahead for fruit-picking schedule. As in the name, Battleview is close to Monmouth Battlefield State Park. The country store sells fresh produce and homemade baked goods, including a popular summertime strawberry shortcake bar. Visitors pick their own strawberries, peaches, nectarines, and sour cherries in summer, apples and pumpkins in the fall. Call or see Web site to learn about farming demonstrations and special events.

♪ **Wemrock Orchards** (732-431-2668; www.wemrockorchard.com), 300 Rt. 33, Freehold. Open year-round. The country store sells more than a dozen homemade fruit pie varieties, freshly baked cider donuts, fruit preserves, New Jersey wines, and country crafts. Pick your own strawberries, pumpkins, and gourds in-season. Haunted hayrides and a corn maze in the fall.

♪ **Stults Farm** (609-799-2523; www.stultsfarm.com), 146 Cranbury Neck Rd. and 62 John White Rd., Cranbury. Open daily in-season. Pick your own fruits (strawberries, raspberries, blueberries, melons) and vegetables (tomatoes, lima beans, cukes, peppers, corn) in-season; call ahead or check Web site for picking schedules.

✳ Special Events

April: **Communiversity Day** (609-924-8777), Princeton. An annual festival of live entertainment, crafts, and art at locations around town; hosted by Princeton University and **the Arts Council of Princeton.**

May: **Manasquan River Canoe and Kayak Race** (732-842-4000), Howell Park Golf Course, Howell. For more than 35 years, advanced and intermediate paddlers have gathered here in the spring to race down an 8-mile stretch of the Manasquan River.

Summer: ♪ **Music-in-the-Park** (609-989-6899), Mercer County Park, West Windsor. Free outdoor Saturday-evening concerts; bring a picnic, lawn chair, or blanket. ♪ **Summer Concert Series** (732-946-2001), Main St., Freehold. Thurs.-evening free outdoor concerts.

June: **Carnegie Lake Regatta** (609-683-1618), Lake Carnegie, Princeton. High school crews and masters rowers in singles, doubles, fours, and eights compete in 1,000-meter sprints; sponsored by the Carnegie Lake Rowing Association. **Reenactment of the Battle of Monmouth** (732-462-9616), Monmouth Battlefield State Park, Manalapan. **Beacon Hill Horse Show** (609-332-0800), Beacon Hill Show Stables, Colts Neck. A Grand Prix competition for tens of thousands in prize money. **Princeton Festival** (609-537-0071), Princeton. Classical music, opera, jazz, and musical theater.

July: **Jersey Fresh Food and Wine Festival** (609-588-0085), East Windsor (sometimes produced in Aug.). ♪ **Independence Day Celebration** (732-793-3652), Freehold. ♪ **Monmouth County Fair** (732-842-4000), East Freehold Park Showgrounds, Freehold. Food, rides, amusements, a vintage car show, 4-H exhibits, a pie-eating contest, fireworks, horse shows, and a lumberjack show.

August: ♪ **Monmouth County Horse Show** (732-741-3847), East Freehold Park Showgrounds, Freehold. Riders come from around the country to compete in this prestigious event. ♪ **Hunterdon County Agricultural Fair** (908-782-6809), South County Park (off Rt. 179), Ringoes. A traditional country fair with agricultural exhibits, tractor pulls, a flower show, and bake-offs.

September: **Englishtown Swap Meet and Auto Show** (732-446-7800), Old Bridge Township Raceway Park, Englishtown. A 3-day swap meet featuring antique and classic cars, as well as trucks, hot rods, and custom cars. **Princeton JazzFest** (800-644-3489), Palmer Square, Princeton.

November: Collegiate rowers compete in two fall regattas on Lake Carnegie in Princeton. **The Belly of the Carnegie** is a 2-mile race for novice and freshmen crews; the following weekend, varsity rowers take part in the **Princeton 3-Mile Chase.**

December: **Christmas Lantern Tours** (732-919-3500), Allaire Village, Farmingdale. Guided tours along the lantern-lit streets of this historic village.

THE PINELANDS REGION

The Pinelands National Reserve is at once New Jersey's largest natural wonder and its best-kept secret, a 1.1 million acre semi-wilderness of oak and pitch pine forest and thick cedar swamps. Beneath its sandy ground is a massive underground aquifer holding 17 trillion gallons of pure water. It's a desolate landscape dotted with historic towns and villages, blueberry farms and cranberry bogs, and a vast network of lakes and streams. It's one of the largest tracts of open space east of the Mississippi River, and the first national reserve to be designated by Congress, which in 1978 recognized the importance of protecting its unique and natural balance.

Close-up, thick stands of mountain laurel, dogwood, and highbush blueberry provide refuge to hundreds of species of wildlife. In the swamps, rare bog plants like lady's slippers grow alongside others found no place else on earth. The Pine Plains is the largest pygmy forest in America, a 12,000-acre expanse of dwarf trees standing mostly at eye level.

Much of the Pinelands, or Pine Barrens, lies within rural Burlington, Gloucester, and Atlantic counties, where people work the cranberry bogs and harvest blueberries just as residents have done for centuries. New Jersey is second in the nation only to Michigan in blueberry growing. In 1840, South Jersey resident Peg Webb domesticated the cranberry, while another grower, Elizabeth Lee, is credited with making the first cranberry sauce, a venture that evolved into the Ocean Spray company. An annual festival in Chatsworth celebrates this famous Pinelands crop. The entire region is dotted with pick-your-own farms and produce stands. The mild climate and sandy soil are ideal for growing a variety of premium grapes, from Old World vines to hybrids, and support several vineyards and wineries that welcome visitors for tours, tastings, and festivals.

For centuries, South Jersey's pine forests have supported a variety of industry. In the 18th century, fishing, farming, and boatbuilding thrived as far inland as Mays Landing and Tuckahoe. Boats were built along the area's many tidal streams, then shipped to the coast. In the 19th century, the abundance of lumber supported many mills on lakes and rivers. In Wharton State Forest, Batsto Village is a re-created glass- and iron-manufacturing village that bustled in the northern Pinelands from 1766 to 1848. The village was a chief arsenal during the American Revolution, when Batsto Iron Works produced cannonballs for the patriots. Visitors can take guided tours of the blacksmith shop, general store, sawmill, wheelwright shop,

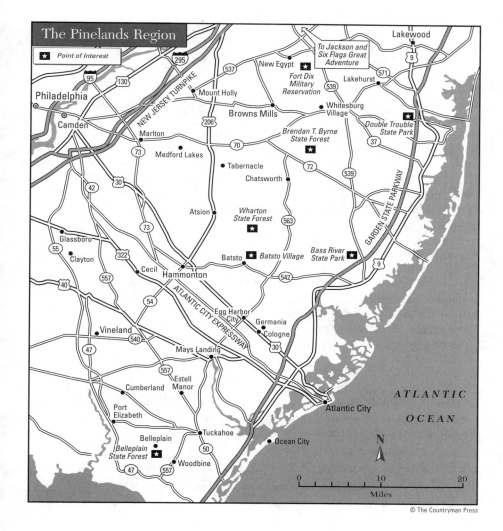

and the mansion where the ironmasters lived. Whitesbog Village is a restored agricultural village in Brendan T. Byrne State Forest where revolutionary methods of cultivating cranberries and blueberries were developed in the 1800s.

Outdoors enthusiasts and solitude seekers come to the Pinelands for the fishing, camping, hiking, and canoeing. Outfitters will rent you a canoe or kayak for the many waterways, from the Mullica and the Batsto rivers to Hammonton Lake and Lake Absegami—places that also attract anglers casting for pickerel, catfish, and largemouth bass. Wharton, Penn, Brendan Byrne, and other state forests provide ample opportunities for visitors to experience the isolated beauty of New Jersey's forestlands.

This desolation may have fueled the legends that have swirled about in the minds of Pinelands residents for generations. The fabled New Jersey Devil, a creature with a horse's face, a kangaroo's body, and a bat's wings, is believed to have lurked here since the 19th century. One popular explanation describes an exasperated mother of 12 children who, wishing to have a devil rather than another child, gave birth to a devilish creature that settled in the swamps. In South Jersey, he's as legendary as Bigfoot.

Small communities are scattered throughout the vast Pinelands region. Most visitors come to Jackson today for the rides and wild animals at Six Flags Great Adventure and Wild Safari, or to shop for bargains at the Jackson Outlet Village. In Lakehurst, the country's only inland naval base and the home of the U.S. Navy's Naval Air Engineering Center is the site of the famous 1937 *Hindenburg* air disaster, when the German dirigible crashed and burned, killing 36 people. Nearby, the sprawling Fort Dix Military Reservation was the first prisoner-of-war camp in New Jersey, holding World War II–era German prisoners, some of whom were soldiers in Rommel's Afrika Korps. A museum of military history at the base welcomes visitors.

In Lakewood, the BlueClaws minor-league baseball team plays at FirstEnergy Park, and the Garden State Philharmonic entertains in the restored 1922 Strand Theater. In 18th-century Mount Holly, specialty shops line Main Street, and its many historic sites include a prison museum, a historic Quaker meetinghouse that held Hessian soldiers during the Revolutionary War, and the oldest fire company in America. Well-preserved historic districts like those in Mount Holly, Mays Landing, and Allentown offer restaurants, art galleries, and antiques shops.

Entries in this section are arranged in roughly geographic order.

AREA CODES 732, 609, 856.

GUIDANCE **The Farley Plaza Rest Area** (609-965-6316) at mile marker 21 on the Atlantic City Expressway in Hammonton has a state-run welcome center stocked with travel literature.

Jackson Chamber of Commerce (732-833-0005; www.jacksonchamber.com) operates a visitor information center at the Jackson Outlet Village on Rt. 537.

The New Jersey Pinelands Commission (609-894-7300; www.state.nj.us/pinelands), P.O. Box 7, New Lisbon 08064, publishes a variety of information and literature on visiting the Pinelands National Reserve.

GETTING THERE *By air:* **Newark Liberty International Airport** (973-961-6000; parking information: 888-397-4636; www.panynj.com) in Newark serves the entire state. **Atlantic City International Airport** (609-645-7895; 1-888-235-9229; www.acairport.com), Exit 9 on the Atlantic City Expressway, serves southern New Jersey; carriers include Spirit Airlines (800-772-7117). **Philadelphia International Airport** (215-937-6800; www.philadelphia-phl.com) in Pennsylvania is convenient to central New Jersey.

By bus: **Greyhound** (800-229-9424; www.greyhound.com) stops in Mount Laurel at the bus station at 538 Fellowship Rd. (856-235-6030). **New Jersey Transit** (973-275-5555; www.njtransit.com) serves the Pinelands region between Newark and Philadelphia, with stops including Lakewood, Jackson, Fort Dix, Mount Holly, Marlton, Medford, and Vineland.

By car: The Pinelands region is accessed by several major highways. The **Atlantic City Expressway** and **I-195** cut across New Jersey from east to west.

The north–south **New Jersey Turnpike** runs along the western edge of the region, while the **Garden State Parkway** runs close to the shoreline.

GETTING AROUND *Taxi:* **Yellow Cab** (856-692-5555) in Vineland serves the southern Pinelands region.

MEDICAL EMERGENCY **Kimball Medical Center** (732-363-1900; www.sbhcs .com), 600 River Ave., Lakewood. The emergency number is 732-886-4525.

Virtua Memorial Hospital (609-267-0700; www.virtua.org), 175 Madison Ave., Mount Holly.

Virtua West Jersey Hospital (856-355-6000; www.virtua.org), Rt. 73 and Brick Rd., Marlton.

Kessler Memorial Hospital (609-561-6700; www.kesslerhospital.org), 600 S. White Horse Pike, Hammonton. The emergency number is 609-561-5200.

SJH Regional Medical Center (856-691-8000), 1505 W. Sherman, Vineland.

✳ To See

HISTORIC SITES **Prospertown Schoolhouse and Jackson Museum** (732-928-1200, ext. 200), 95 W. Veterans Hwy. (Rt. 528), Jackson. Open Mon.–Fri. by appointment. Free admission. A restored 1890 one-room schoolhouse with region-al memorabilia and artifacts from Jackson's gristmills and cranberry bogs. Changing art exhibits.

⌁ **Historic Batsto Village** (609-561-0024; www.batstovillage.org), Wharton State Forest, 31 Batsto Rd., Batsto. Visitor Center open daily 9–4; call or visit Web site for guided tour schedules and fees. Batsto is a restored historic Pine Barrens

BATSTO VILLAGE IN WHARTON STATE FOREST IS A PRESERVED 18TH- AND 19TH-CENTURY GLASSMAKING AND BOG IRON INDUSTRIAL CENTER IN THE PINELANDS.

Photo courtesy of the New Jersey Commerce and Economic Growth Commission

village that was a thriving industrial center producing iron, glass, and lumber as early as the 18th century. A general store, post office, sawmill, and the estate of the ironmaster, are among the restored village buildings. Interpreters in period dress lead tours and demonstrations.

MUSEUMS New Egypt Historical Society Museum (609-758-8111; www .newegypthistoricalsociety.com), 125 Evergreen Rd. (off Rt. 537), New Egypt. Open Wed. 11–1 and Sun. 1–4, except holidays. Admission by donation. An 1822 Federal-style farmhouse with local antiques and memorabilia on the region's cranberry production, farming, and equestrian sports, notably harness racing. The museum has an extensive collection of trophies, helmets, photos, and other racing memorabilia, mostly donated by local Hall of Fame harness racer Stanley Dancer.

Fort Dix Military Museum (609-562-2334), 6501 Pennsylvania Ave., Fort Dix. Open Mon.–Fri. 8–4. Free admission. An interesting collection of military memorabilia, including uniforms, military equipment, and firearms; archives of photos and lithographs. Museum shop.

Pemberton Station Museum (609-894-0546), 3 Fort Dix Rd., Pemberton. Open Wed., Fri.–Sun. 10–4; other times by appointment. Free admission. The 1892 North Pemberton Railroad Station was an active Pinelands station until rail service between here and Camden ended in 1969. Today the restored historic building is a regional-history museum with exhibits on railroad history, local industry, and the Pinelands. Among the permanent displays are fossils, Native American artifacts, and minerals found in southern New Jersey, as well as a pair of early-20th-century Pennsylvania Railroad cabooses.

Heritage Glass Museum (856-881-7468), 25 East High St., Glassboro. Open Sat. 11–2. Free admission. A small museum devoted to South Jersey's heritage as one of the nation's largest centers of glass manufacturing. Features 18th-century glassmaking memorabilia; historic glassware and glassblowing tools on display.

⚓ **Burlington County Prison Museum** (609-265-5476; www.prisonmuseum.net), 128 High St. (Rt. 541), Mt. Holly. Open Thurs.–Sat. 10–4; Sun. noon–4. Adults $4; students and seniors $2; under age 5, free. Built in 1811 as a state-of-the-art penal

---

⚓ **AIR VICTORY MUSEUM**

(609-267-4488; www.airvictorymuseum.org), South Jersey Regional Airport, 68 Stacy Haines Rd., Lumberton. Open Wed.–Sat. 10–4; Sun. 11–4; closed major holidays. Adults $4; seniors $3; children $2. An exciting history museum that strives to interest young people in aviation. A stunning collection of military aircraft, engines, uniforms, and artifacts. Most of the planes on display—including a Tomcat, Hawkeye, Corsair, Skyhawk, and Phantom—are on loan from the National Museum of Naval Aviation in Pensacola, Florida. The extensive collection of military uniforms includes all branches of the American military; uniforms from Russia, Great Britain, Thailand, and other foreign countries are represented as well. Kids love the hands-on exploration room, where they can learn about space exploration and airplane flight. Gift shop.

WHITESBOG VILLAGE

(609-893-4646; www.whites bog.org), Brendan T. Byrne State Forest, 120–130 Whites- bog Rd. (Rt. 530), Browns Mills. Open daily dawn to dusk. Free admission. A restored 19th- century agricultural village founded by farmer J. J. White, who developed revolutionary cranberry cultivation methods on his South Jersey farm. Following in his footsteps, his daughter Elizabeth produced the world's first domesticated blueberry here in 1916. Today, blueberries and cranberries are still grown and harvested in the fields and bogs. Fall visitors can watch the annual cranberry harvest. Special events include guided walks under the full moon, cranberry-industry tours, berry festivals, and tours to view wintering tundra swans.

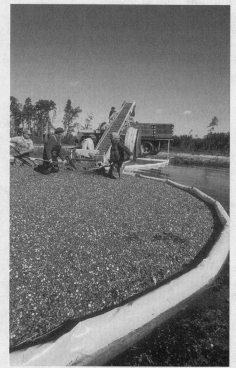

Photo courtesy of the Whitesbog Preservation Trust

HARVESTING CRANBERRIES AT WHITESBOG VILLAGE IN BROWNS MILLS IS A PINELANDS FARMING INDUSTRY THAT DATES TO THE 1800S.

institution, the formidable stone and brick building with the massive front door was in service until 1965. It provides a glimpse of imprisoned life, and of 19th-century progressive attitudes toward prisoners. Ghost tours, guided tours, and self-guided tours.

WINERIES **Cream Ridge Winery** (609-259-9797; www.creamridgewinery.com), 145 Rt. 539, Cream Ridge. Open daily for tastings; group tours by appointment. An award-winning, family- owned and -operated winery known for its unusual wines made from cherries, plums, apricots, cranberries, and other fruits. The wine shop sells gifts and gourmet food.

Valenzano Winery (609-268-6731; www.valenzanowine.com), 1320 Old Indian Mills Rd., Shamong. Tasting room open Thurs.–Fri. 11–6; Sat.–Sun. 11–4; other times by appointment. A winery on a 30-acre farm. Traditional wines as well as others made from locally grown fruits like strawberries and cranberries. The rustic and elegant tasting room has a fireplace, a mahogany bar, and a 1,000-bottle wine rack.

Tomasello Winery (800-666-9463), 225 White Horse Pike (Rt. 30), Hammonton. Open Mon.–Wed. 9–6; Thurs.–Sat. 9–8; Sun. 11–6; reduced winter hours. Three generations of winemakers have run New Jersey's highest-yield winery, and one of its oldest, since 1933. The shop and tasting room feature 40 wines—many of them medal winners—made from grapes as well as blackberries, cranberries, cherries, and raspberries. Special events like opera galas combine gourmet-wine dinners with live performances by internationally known opera singers.

Renault Winery (609-965-2111; www.renaultwinery.com), 72 N. Bremen Ave. (Rt. 674), Egg Harbor. Call or see Web site for a schedule of tours and tastings. Renault, founded in 1864, is one of the oldest continuously operating wineries in the country. Don't miss the extensive display of historic glassware, including wine glasses dating to medieval times. Gourmet restaurant (see *Lodging—Hotel*).

Sylvin Farms Winery (609-965-1548; www.sylvinfarmswinery.com), 24 N. Vienna Ave., Germania. Call or see Web site for tours and tastings. A noted vinifera winery owned by Sylvia and Franklin Salek for more than 30 years. Acres of vineyards grow around their farmhouse.

Balic Winery (609-625-2166; www.balicwinery.com), 6623 US 40, Mays Landing. Open daily for tastings in the Gallery Room; call ahead for tours. Savo Balic, a winemaker from Italy's Adriatic Sea region, crafts more than two-dozen varieties of wine using European wine-making techniques passed down from his family. Some of the 57-acre vineyard was planted by the descendants of Mays Landing's earliest settlers.

✷ To Do

AMUSEMENT PARKS ✍ **Clementon Amusement Park and Splash World Water Park** (856-783-0263; www.clementonpark.com), 144 Berlin Rd., Clementon. Open Memorial Day weekend–Oct. (daily in July only); call or see Web site for a complete schedule. Admission $25–35. A popular family amusement park for nearly 100 years. More than 50 rides and attractions, from the nostalgic antique carousel and 10-story Ferris wheel to the recently updated HellCat wooden roller coaster. Exciting thrill rides and one of the longest log flume rides in the country. Entertainment and wild-animal shows.

✍ **Storybook Land** (609-641-7847; www.storybookland.com), 6415 Black Horse Pike (Rts. 40 and 322), Cardiff. Open Apr.–Dec.; weekends spring and fall; daily in summer. Admission $21. A gingerbread house and a collection of storybook-themed buildings create the whimsical setting for a theme park just for children and their families. Rides and a petting zoo, picnic grounds and a snack bar.

BIRDING **Lester G. MacNamara Wildlife Management Area** (609-628-2103), 2201 Rt. 631, Tuckahoe. Open daily dawn to dusk. The 12,438-acre expanse of tidal creeks and salt marsh where the Tuckahoe River winds toward Great Egg Harbor Bay is home to a wide variety of birds. An 8-mile auto trail passes by a pine and oak forest on the edge of a salt marsh, a freshwater lake, and a hardwood swamp. The wetlands are a busy resting area and feeding ground; watch for peregrine falcons and bald eagles.

CANOEING AND KAYAKING Paddling is a popular activity in the Pinelands, with its myriad waterways winding through a swampy landscape of wild cranberry

✎ ♿ SIX FLAGS GREAT ADVENTURE AND WILD SAFARI

(732-928-1821; www.sixflags.com/greatadventure), Rt. 537, Jackson. Theme park and safari open Apr.–Oct.; daily mid-May–Aug.; Hurricane Harbor water park open Memorial Day weekend through Labor Day. Admission (including combination tickets to all three parks) $49–85; call or see Web site for exact schedule and pricing. New Jersey's Six Flags is the largest regional theme-park complex in the country, with more than 100 rides and a dozen roller coasters. Adrenaline junkies love extreme rides like the Superman-Ultimate Flight and the Medusa roller coasters; Bugs Bunny Land and the Looney Tunes Seaport offer tame thrills for young children and their families. Hurricane Harbor is the largest water park in the world, with nearly 20 waterslides, a family water playground, and the Blue Lagoon, a million-gallon wave pool.

Wild Safari is the largest drive-through safari outside Africa. A 4-mile paved auto road loops through the park, where 1,200 wild creatures live in a realistic setting that can't be found in a zoo. African elephants, kangaroos, bears, giraffes, white rhinos, baboons, and other exotic animals from around the world roam freely throughout a 350-acre natural landscape.

THE NITRO ROLLER COASTER AT SIX FLAGS GREAT ADVENTURE IN JACKSON WHISKS PASSENGERS ON A MILE-LONG TRACK WITH SEVEN DROPS AND SPEEDS UP TO 80 MILES PER HOUR.

Photo courtesy of Six Flags Great Adventure

bogs and pine forests, and riverbanks lined with cedars and thick with wild blue-berries. Some of the best places to canoe and kayak in the region are the Great Egg Harbor River (known locally as the Great Egg), the Batsto and the Mullica rivers, Rancocas Creek in Mount Holly, Cedar Creek in Double Trouble State Park, and the Oswego River in Penn State Forest.

The following outfitters are among the many who rent canoes and/or kayaks; some offer guide services. All can advise on planning a day trip or overnight trip.

Wading Pines Canoe Rentals (888-726-1313; www.wadingpines.com), 85 Godfrey Bridge Rd., and **Pine Barrens Canoe and Kayak Rental** (609-726-1515; 800-732-0793; www.pinebarrenscanoe.com), 3260 Rt. 563—both in Chatsworth. **Adams Canoe Rentals Inc.** (609-268-0189; www.adamscanoerental.com), 1005 Atison Rd., Shamong. Canoe and kayak rentals for the Batsto and the Mullica rivers. **Mick's Canoe Rental Inc.** (609-726-1380; 800-281-1380; www.micks canoerental.com), 3107 Rt. 563, Jenkins. **Bel Haven Canoe and Kayak** (609-965-2205; 800-445-0953; www.belhavenkayak.com), 1227 Rt. 542, Green Bank. Canoe and kayak rentals; guided trips on Pine Barrens rivers.

FISHING The many lakes, rivers, ponds, and streams in the Pinelands offer anglers virtually endless opportunities for fishing. *On lakes and ponds:* **Ocean County Park** in Lakewood; **Oswego Lake** in Penn State Forest; **Atison Lake** in Wharton State Forest; **Lake Lenape** in Mays Landing; and **Hammonton Lake** in Hammonton. *On rivers and streams:* the **Oswego River** in Penn State Forest; the **Mullica and the Batsto rivers** in Batsto State Forest; and the **Manamuskin River** in Cumberland.

GOLF Many 18-hole golf courses in the Pinelands are open to the public. Most have a clubhouse, driving range, pro shop, and restaurant or snack bar. They include **Harbor Pines Golf Club** (609-927-0006; www.harborpines.com), 500 St. Andrews Dr., and **McCullough's Emerald Golf Links** (609-926-3900; www .mcculloughsgolf.com), 3016 Ocean Heights Ave.—both in Egg Harbor; **Cream Ridge Golf Club** (609-259-2849), 181 Rt. 539, Cream Ridge; **Pine Barrens Golf Club** (877-746-3227; www.pinebarrensgolf.com), 540 S. Hope Chapel Rd., Jackson; **Eagle Ridge Golf Club** (732-901-4900; www.eagleridgegolf.com), 2 Augusta Blvd., Lakewood; **Golden Pheasant Golf Course** (609-267-4276; www.golden pheasantgc.com), 141 Country Club Rd., Lumberton; **Valleybrook Golf Course** (856-227-3171; www.valleybrookgolf.com), 200 Golf View Dr., Blackwood; **Blue Heron Pines Golf Club** (609-965-1800; www.blueheronpines.com), 550 West Country Club Drive, Egg Harbor; **Buena Vista Country Club** (856-697-3733; www.allforeclub.com/bvcc), Rt. 40, Buena; and **Mays Landing Golf Club** (609-641-4411; www.mayslandinggolf.com), 1855 Cates Rd., Mays Landing.

HIKING **Warren E. Fox Nature Center** (609-625-1897) in Mays Landing, and **Wells Mills County Park and Nature Center** (609-971-3085) in Waretown, each have more than 16 miles of hiking trails. At **Bass River State Forest** (609-296-1114) in New Gretna, hiking trails and gravel roads lead through a rare stunted forest. At **Double Trouble State Park** (732-341-6662) in Berkeley Township, you can hike past cranberry bogs.

THE BATONA TRAIL

(609-561-3262; 609-296-1114), from Brendan T. Byrne State Forest in Pemberton to Bass River State Forest in New Gretna. The 50-mile Batona Trail is the region's premier hiking trail, and the longest in New Jersey. It meanders through the Pinelands via three state forests, marked by telltale pink blazes starting near Ongs Hat in Brendan Byrne State Forest and ending near Lake Absegami in Bass River State Forest. The Batona Hiking Club—an active hiking organization since 1928—cut the trail in the 1960s and maintains it in cooperation with the Outdoor Club of South Jersey. The name is derived from the first two letters of the words *Back To Nature.* The route passes through a peaceful landscape of cranberry bogs, swamps, and forests thick with red maple and pitch pine. Part of the trail follows the Batsto River into the reconstructed 18th-century industrial village of the same name (see *To See—Historic Sites*) in Wharton State Forest. Trail maps are available at the Brendan Byrne and the Bass River forest offices, as well as at the Wharton State Forest visitors center.

SPECTATOR SPORTS ✍ **Lakewood BlueClaws** (732-901-7000; www.lakewoodblueclaws.com), FirstEnergy Park, Lakewood. Games played from Apr.–Aug. This minor-league baseball Class A affiliate of the Philadelphia Phillies plays in a 6,588-seat stadium that opened in 2001. Lots of fun entertainment for kids, and picnicking on the spacious outfield lawn. The gift shop sells BlueClaws souvenirs and memorabilia from most major- and minor-league teams in the country.

New Egypt Speedway (609-758-1900; www.newegyptspeedway.net), Rt. 539, New Egypt. A variety of races, from stock to sprint, on a half-mile clay track. Call or see Web site for a full schedule of special events.

✍ **Atco Raceway** (856-768-2167; www.atcorace.com), 1000 Jackson Rd., Atco. Jet dragsters, prostocks, funny cars, motocross, and thrill shows. One of three drag strips in the state.

SWIMMING In **Bass River State Forest** (609-296-1114), Stage Rd., New Gretna, there's swimming on Lake Absegami. **Ocean County Park** (732-506-9090), Ocean Avenue, Lakewood, has several lakes, one with a designated swimming area and beach.

THE LAKEWOOD BLUECLAWS, A MINOR LEAGUE AFFILIATE OF THE PHILADELPHIA PHILLIES, PLAY THEIR HOME GAMES AT FIRSTENERGY PARK IN LAKEWOOD.

Photo courtesy of Ocean Country Public Affairs

Photo courtesy of Atco Raceway/Kim Grant

DRAGSTERS, MOTORCYCLES, AND STREET
CARS RACE ON THE STRIP AT ATCO
RACEWAY IN ATCO.

✳ Green Space

GARDEN Lewis W. Barton Arboretum (609-654-3000), at the Medford Leas Retirement Community, Rt. 70, Medford. Open daily for self-guided tours (pick up a map at the Community Building); call ahead to arrange a guided group tour. Free admission. The garden-loving public is invited to this private retirement facility to enjoy its beautiful surroundings. The landscaped grounds feature a series of 36 unique courtyard gardens planted with trees, shrubs, annuals, and perennials, each one designed by landscape architects and horticulturalists from the University of Pennsylvania's Morris Arboretum. Guests can also stroll on nature trails through wildflower meadows and woodlands on the 160-acre property.

NATURAL AREAS The Pinelands (609-894-7300; www.state.nj.us/pinelands), New Jersey Pinelands Commission, P.O. Box 7, New Lisbon 08064. The Pinelands is a natural marvel: not only is it the largest tract of open space on the mid-Atlantic coast, it covers nearly 25 percent of the most densely populated state in America. Its vast underground aquifer pumps trillions of gallons of pure water into marshes and bays throughout South Jersey. More than 1.1 million acres of dense forests of pine, cedar, and oak are crisscrossed by the Toms, the Mullica, the Maurice, and the Great Egg Harbor rivers. Its many unique features include a 12,000-acre forest of pygmy pines, mature dwarf trees standing only a few feet tall.

Lester G. MacNamara Wildlife Management Area (609-628-3219), Rt. 631, Tuckahoe. Open daily dawn to dusk. More than 12,438 acres of tidal creeks, pine forest, and salt marsh around the Tuckahoe River's winding course toward Great Egg Harbor Bay. A freshwater lake and hardwood swamp is home to fish, beaver, and turtles.

Crossley Preserve (609-984-1339; 732-244-7400), Pinewald–Keswick Rd. (Rt. 530), Berkeley Township. A 1,200-acre preserve with pinelands, bogs, and white cedar swamps. Nature trails for hiking and biking.

NATURE CENTERS ⌀ Woodford Cedar Run Wildlife Refuge and Pine Barrens Education Center (856-983-3329; www.cedarrun.org), 4 Sawmill Rd., Medford. Open Mon.–Sat. 10–4; Sun. 1–4. Adults $5; children $3; children 2 and under, free. A 184-acre refuge surrounding Cedar Run Lake is the vision of James and Elizabeth Woodford, who founded the refuge in 1957 to rehabilitate native wildlife. Today the mission is threefold: preservation of the Pinelands habitat, environmental education, and wildlife rehabilitation. Visitors can hike the 1-mile nature trail around Cedar Run Lake to see the **Wildlife Compound,** where more than 3,000 injured animals are treated and rehabilitated every year. Kids love the education center, with its hands-on exhibits and small live animals to see and touch. Call about their yearlong schedule of special programs.

&. **Wells Mills County Park and Nature Center** (609-971-3085), 905 Wells Mills Rd. (Rt. 532), Waretown. Ocean County's largest park, with more than 16 miles of hiking trails through 910 acres of pine and oak forest in the Pinelands. Birding, trails for biking and hiking, and canoeing (you can rent a canoe here) and fishing on Wells Mills Lake. Nature center with exhibits, a library, and an observation deck. Full-moon hikes and other special events led by naturalists.

&. **Warren E. Fox Nature Center** (609-625-1897), Estell Manor County Park, 109 Blvd. (Rt. 50), Mays Landing. Open Mon.–Fri. 8–4:30; Sat.–Sun., 8–4. Tidal wetlands and upland forest in a 1,672-acre tract laced with 15 miles of hiking trails. Nature center; guided tours available. Activities include bird-watching, orienteering, guided nature walks, herb-garden talks, and a variety of classes and lectures.

Scotland Run Park (856-881-0845), 980 Academy St. (Rt. 610), Clayton. Grounds open daily, dawn to dusk. A 940-acre park of marshes, meadows, and an 80-acre lake for boating and fishing. The nature center has a year-round schedule of bird walks, nature hikes, and other environmental education programs for children and adults.

NJ Forest Resource Education Center at Jackson (732-928-2360), 370 E. Veterans Hwy., Jackson. A 660-acre facility with a 7.3-mile learning trail, outdoor learning stations with informational kiosks and "talking trees." Interpretive programs are offered free, and recreation includes hiking, hunting, fishing, horseback riding, and mountain biking. Open dawn to dusk.

STATE FORESTS Four major state forests in South Jersey protect hundreds of thousands of pristine acreage in the Pinelands. **Brendan T. Byrne State Forest** (609-726-1191), New Lisbon, has more than 100 miles of dirt roads and hiking trails through pine forests, cedar swamps, and cranberry bogs. **Wharton State Forest** (609-561-0024), Hammonton, has fishing and canoeing on Atison Lake. **Penn State Forest** (609-296-1114), Jenkin's Neck, has trails for mountain biking, hiking, and winter sports. **Bass River State Forest** (609-296-1114), New Gretna, has a rare stunted forest, and swimming and boating on Lake Absegami.

STATE PARK Double Trouble State Park (732-341-6662; www .state.nj.us/dep/parksandforests), Double Trouble Rd. (Rt. 530),

WHARTON STATE FOREST IN THE PINELANDS, NEW JERSEY'S LARGEST SINGLE TRACT OF STATE LAND, IS LACED WITH RIVERS AND STREAMS FOR CANOEING AND KAYAKING.

Photo by Thomas E. Briglia / PhotoGraphics Photography

Bayville. A variety of legends explain how this 8,000-acre tract of rural Pinelands habitat got its unusual name. It seems to have originated with the area's cranberry industry; an agricultural and industrial village has harvested timber and cranberries here since the 1700s. Today visitors can see cranberry bogs and historic buildings—including a schoolhouse and general store—dating to the 1800s. Fishing, canoeing, and kayaking on Cedar Creek—a bog-lined waterway that flows 9 miles from Bamber Lake to Barnegat Bay.

✳ Lodging

HOTEL ♿ Tuscany House Hotel

(609-965-2111; www.renaultwinery .com), 2111 N. Bremen Ave., Egg Harbor City 08215. An elegant Mediterranean-style villa is just beyond the vineyards of the renowned **Renault Winery** in the rural Pinelands (see *To See—Wineries*). Guests come to experience the sophisticated service and amenities of a European-style hotel. It's popular with golfers who come to play the area's championship courses, and with visitors to Atlantic City, just 20 minutes away. A fitness room, two outdoor pools, and an 18-hole golf course that opened in 2004. An elegant restaurant and bar serves Mediterranean cuisine. Rooms have Internet-ready computer ports. Breakfast. $189–399.

BED & BREAKFASTS ✒♿ Dancer Farm Bed & Breakfast Inn

(609-752-0303; 866-326-2376; www .dancerfarm.com), 19 Archertown Rd., New Egypt 08533. Fans of harness racing are familiar with the Dancer name; brothers Stanley and Vernon Dancer are both members of the Harness Racing Hall of Fame. The beautifully restored 19th-century Dancer-family homestead is a rustic and elegant inn on a 250-acre working farm. The spacious red-clapboard farmhouse with white columns and porches is surrounded by wildflower meadows, vineyards, and the paddocks and stables of the farm's standardbred racehorses. Innkeepers Jeri and Mike Robertson offer 10 tastefully decorated antiques-filled guest rooms and suites, each with a unique theme related to the farm. All

DANCER FARM BED & BREAKFAST INN OCCUPIES A 19TH-CENTURY FARMHOUSE ON A 250-ACRE WORKING FARM IN NEW EGYPT, SURROUNDED BY VINEYARDS, MEADOWS, ROLLING HILLS, AND RACEHORSE STABLES.

Photo by Mike Jones

& INN AT SUGAR HILL B&B

(609-625-2226; www.innatsugarhill.com), 5704 Mays Landing–Somers Point Road, Mays Landing 08330. An elegant Victorian B&B on the banks of the Great Egg Harbor River. The inn's name dates to the 18th century, when ships laden with rum, sugar, and other goods acquired in foreign lands were unloaded here to await shipment to Philadelphia and other cities. Entrepreneur and U.S. senator William Moore built the rambling, butter-yellow clapboard mansion in the 1840s. It has been a restaurant and bed & breakfast since 1987. Four antiques-filled guest rooms and one suite have air-conditioning and private bath, some also have fireplaces and lovely views of the river. A gift shop sells the work of local artisans. The restaurant serves innovative takes on classic fare (see *Dining Out*). Continental breakfast. $105–155; "Innkeeper's Rendezvous" includes a full course candlelight dinner for two on the night of arrival for an extra $65.

have private bath, phone, TV, Internet access, and air-conditioning; some boast private balconies, fireplaces, and sitting areas. Guests can relax on the front porch, in the cozy living room, or in the gazebo, or explore walking trails through the farm's gardens, meadows, and woods. Full breakfast. $155–310.

¹ʼ Iris Inn at Medford (609-654-7528; www.theirisinn.com), 45 S. Main St., Medford 08055. A lovely 1904 Victorian in the heart of a historic village. Edie Wagner has been the innkeeper since 2006 of this charming bed & breakfast, once the home of a local doctor. It retains many original features, from the rich chestnut woodwork to the elegant chandeliers. Nine antiques-filled guest rooms and one suite have private bath, TV, phone, Wi-Fi, and air-conditioning. Guests love the Butterfly Room, with its cozy sitting area and unique hand-painted walls done by a muralist from England. The inn is a short walk from Medford's shops and restaurants; you can also relax on a front-porch rocker or indoors by the fire. Full breakfast. $85–175.

CAMPGROUNDS

In Jackson 08527

✈ ʼ¹ʼ Butterfly Camping Resort (732-928-2107; www.butterflycamp.com), 360 Butterfly Rd. Open Apr.–Oct. A 125-acre campground with tent sites and cabin and deluxe cottage rentals. Clubhouse with video arcade; the camp store sells snacks and groceries. Playground and in-ground pool. Wi-Fi at every site. Sites $48–53; cabins $70–97; cottages $150.

✈ Indian Rock Resort (732-928-0034; www.indianrockresort.com), 920 W. Veterans Hwy. (Rt. 528). Open year-round with 200 sites plus trailer rentals and cabin rentals. A full-service campground close to Six Flags Great Adventure. A grocery store, laundry facilities, pool, and clubhouse. Sites $38–48; cabins $63.

🐾 ✈ Timberland Lake Campground (732-928-0500; www.timberlandlakecampground.com), 1335 Reed Rd., Cream Ridge; mailing: P.O. Box 48, Jackson. Open Mar.–Nov. 1. The campground has 200 sites on 54 acres. Fishing, swimming, and boating on a

5-acre lake. Many planned activities—
hourly during the summer—and special theme weekends. Playground,
pool, and mini golf. Sites $40.

🐾 ✎ "ⱦ" **Tip Tam Camping Resort**
(732-363-4036; 877-847-8261; www
.tiptam.com), 301 Brewers Bridge Rd.
Open mid-Apr.–Sept. Tent and trailer
sites with full hookups; rental cabins
and RVs. Amenities include two swimming pools, mini golf, volleyball, and
game courts. Limited Wi-Fi is available. Sites $44–50; cabins $70; RV
rentals $100.

In Mays Landing 08330
✎ ♿ **Yogi Bear's Jellystone Park**
(609-476-2811; 800-355-0264; www
.atlanticcityjellystone.com), 1079 12th
Ave. Open Apr.–Oct. Cabins and RV
trailers for rent, plus 150 tent and trailer sites, on 20 acres. Planned activities
and a playground for kids. Campsites
$37–55; cabins $100; RV trailers $200.

🐾 ✎ **River Beach Camp** (609-625-
8611; www.riverbeach.net), 4678
Somers Point Rd. Open May–Sept. A
20-acre campground with 135 sites on
the banks of the Great Egg Harbor
River. Boating, fishing, and swimming.
$30–40.

🐾 ✎ ♿ **Winding River Campground**
(609-625-3191; www.windingriver
camping.com), 6752 Weymouth Rd.
Open May–mid-Oct. A campground
on the Great Egg Harbor River with
132 camping sites and cabins for rent.
River activities include kayaking,
canoeing, and tubing. $37–42.

Elsewhere
🐾 ✎ "ⱦ" **Holly Acres RV Park** (609-
965-2287; 888-278-2267; www.holly
acresrvpark.com), 218 S. Frankfurt
Ave., Egg Harbor City 08215. Open
mid-Apr.–Nov. 1. A 60-acre campground on a private spring-fed freshwater pond for fishing and swimming,
with 235 full hookup sites and rental

cabins. Limited Wi-Fi access available.
Sites $39–41; cabins $70.

STATE FOREST CAMPGROUNDS
(www.state.nj.us/dep/parksandforests)
State forest campgrounds in the
Pinelands offer a variety of accommodations, from tent sites and cabins to
shelters, lean-tos, and group camping
areas, notably: **Bass River State Forest** (609-296-1114), New Gretna;
Wharton State Forest (609-561-
0024), Hammonton; and **Brendan T.
Byrne State Forest** (609-726-1191)
in New Lisbon.

✳ Where to Eat
DINING OUT

In Marlton
♿ **Food for Thought** (856-797-1126),
129 Rt. 73 S., Marlton Crossing Shopping Ctr. Lunch and dinner daily.
Reservations suggested. A charming
restaurant serving critically acclaimed
New American cuisine with an emphasis on fresh fish. Entrées range from
citrus-tarragon crusted tilapia to hand-
cut grilled filet mignon. BYOB.
$21–48.

In Medford
♿ **Braddock's Tavern** (609-654-1604;
www.braddocks.com), 39 S. Main St.
Open for lunch and dinner Tues.–Sun.;
closed Mon. Reservations suggested.
Traditional American cuisine served in
a charming colonial tavern. $15–30.

Ted's on Main (609-654-7011; www
.tedsonmain.net), 20 S. Main St. Open
Tues.–Sat. for dinner; closed Sun.–
Mon. Reservations recommended. A
small but graceful spot in the heart of
town with iron chandeliers highlighting
the décor and serving American cuisine
with strong New Orleans and Bahami-
an influences. Two such offerings are
tangerine-glazed salmon and jerk
grilled flat iron steak. BYOB. $22–30.

In Voorhees

Ritz Seafood (856-566-6650; www
.ritzseafood.com), 910 Rt. 561. Open
Tues.–Sat. for lunch; Tues.–Sun. for
dinner; closed Mon. An extensive
menu of creative Euro-Asian cuisine
with an emphasis on fresh fish and
shellfish. A signature appetizer is the
ahi tuna with a duo of caviars. Regulars
love the pizza with tuna, red onion,
tomato, and citrus vinaigrette on a
rice-cracker crust. A tasty Spanish
seafood paella and Thai-style jumbo
shrimp satay are among the stellar
entrées. BYOB. $17–35; daily four-
course special, $35.

& **Catelli Ristorante** (856-751-6069;
www.catellirestaurant.com), Plaza
1000, Main St. Open for lunch Mon.–
Fri.; dinner daily. Reservations recommended. Don't let the strip-mall
setting fool you; inside is upscale
northern Italian cuisine in a trio of
tasteful and elegant dining rooms. One
is formal and high-ceilinged, another is
a solarium full of lush greenery, the
third is a mellow wood-paneled room
with a clubby feel. Expert and attentive service by tuxedoed waiters adds
to the charm. A list of specials accompanies an extensive menu and well-
chosen wine list. Traditional
dessert-cart offerings include a decadent chocolate soufflé. Live music in
the bar. $14–32.

In Mays Landing

Inn at Sugar Hill (609-625-2226;
www.innatsugarhill.com), 5704 Mays
Landing–Somers Point Rd. Open
Wed.–Sun. for dinner; closed Mon.–
Tues. Reservations recommended.
Seafood and other American classics
with a creative twist, served in a waterfront Victorian B&B (see sidebar, page
333). The mansion's intimate dining
rooms have fireplaces, and the
enclosed verandas come with garden
and Great Egg Harbor River views.

Many of the exquisitely prepared dishes feature fish and shellfish, such as
emerald scallops and pepper seared
salmon. The meat and poultry dishes
are equally as delicious. The bistro
menu offers scallop risotto and other
lighter meals. The restored Victorian
bar was saved from a turn-of-the-20th-
century Philadelphia tavern. In summertime, the casual riverfront bar and
grill features live entertainment and
grilled seafood. $14.50–24.50.

EATING OUT

In Marlton

Marlton Tavern (856-985-2424; www
.marltontavernnj.com) 65 E. Main St.
Open daily for lunch and dinner. A
neighborhood tavern and restaurant
set in a historic house serving an eclectic menu ranging from standard appetizers like shrimp cocktail to elaborate
sandwiches and entrées of steak, chick-
en, and seafood. Extensive beer offerings and entertainment almost nightly.
$13–35.

In Medford

Izzie's Eatery (654-2121; www.izzies
eatery.net) 679 Stokes Rd. Open
Tues.– Thurs. 11–8, Fri.– Sat. 11–9,
Sun. 9–2; closed Mon. A locals'
favorite known for good food and service and a convivial atmosphere. Soups
are homemade and the crabcake plat-
ter is a best-seller. Sunday-only breakfast is highlighted by the belgian
waffles. $14–20.

Mulberry Tea House (609-714-
0640), 60 S. Main St. Open for lunch
and high tea Tues.–Sun. 10–3. A cozy
spot serving soups, salads, sandwiches,
and quiches, plus a wide variety of
teas. $12–15.

Zinc Café (609-953-9462), 679 Stokes
Rd. A popular spot with locals for
American fare. A 43-seat café with a
healthy orientation, offering natural
hormone-free chicken dishes, salads,

soups and even vegan choices. And, homemade desserts, too. $15–30.

In Jackson

Java Moon Café (732-928-3633; www.javamoon.com), 1022 Anderson Rd. and Rt. 537, next to Jackson Outlet Village. Three meals served daily. A good stop for lunch or coffee when you're shopping at the outlet stores. The take-out box lunches are popular among the many who want to spend their day shopping. A satisfying menu of salads, sandwiches, and healthy entrées. $6–15.

In Mount Holly

The Robin's Nest (609-261-6149; www.robinsnestmountholly.com), 2 Washington St. Open for lunch daily; dinner Tues.–Sat.; brunch Sun. A popular eatery in the historic Mount Holly shopping district with a charming old-fashioned bar and eclectic French-American cuisine, with seasonal offerings. Patio dining in warm weather. $18–29.

Island Taste (609-265-2233), 25 Madison Ave. Open for lunch and dinner Mon.–Sat.; closed Sun. A cute, informal place in the old Mt. Holly train station, decorated with art photographs and train artifacts, the menu includes genuine Jamaican fare like jerk chicken, curried goat, and daily specials like Jamaican stewed beef. BYOB. $9–14.

Bread From Heaven (609-261-4844; www.bfhsoul.net), 4 Mill St. Open Wed.–Sat. 9–8; Sun. -noon–6; closed Mon.–Tues. Real Southern and soul food from catfish three ways to oxtails and ribs in a casual, local eatery-style ambience. $10–15.

High Street Grill (609-265-9199; www.highstreetgrill.net) 64 High St. Open for lunch daily; dinner

Thurs.–Sun. A lively bar and grill with a mixed décor of modern and exposed brick, serving crafted beers and New American food. Entrées include Moroccan spiced duck and wild mushroom lasagna. Live jazz and folk music. $21–30.

Elsewhere

Huntzinger's American Food and Drink (609-625-4447), 6489 Harding Hwy. (Rt. 40), Mays Landing. Open daily for breakfast, lunch, and dinner. Sandwiches, salads, soups, and pasta dishes plus well-prepared American and European standards like herb-seared Atlantic salmon and steaks. The New England potpie is studded with lobster, scallops, shrimp, and salmon. Dinner specials most nights; Thursday's South Jersey clambake is a good opportunity to sample regional cuisine. Breads and desserts are baked in-house, and the bar features a large selection of American brews. $10–17.

SNACKS ✓ **Farley's Homemade Ice Cream** (732-370-4864), Bennetts Mills Plaza, 2275 W. County Line Rd., Jackson. Open daily in summer; shorter hours during the rest of the year. More than two-dozen flavors of homemade ice cream to choose from, on a cone or in a shake or sundae. They're known for their ice cream cakes, and there's always at least 100 of them in stock.

✓ **Yummy Tummy** (609-280-6681) 38 High St., Mt. Holly. Open daily. Ice cream, soups and sandwiches.

✓ **Swal Dairy** (609-259-8508), 33 S. Main St., Allentown. Open daily 11:30–9. Family- owned shop serving homemade ice cream made on premises. In winter, a menu of soups and chili, as well.

✳ Entertainment

ARTS CENTERS 𝒮 **Strand Theater**
(732-367-7789; www.strandlakewood
.com), 400 Clifton Ave., Lakewood.
This acoustically superb 1,000-seat theater opened in 1922 with silent films
and vaudeville acts. Lovingly restored
after years of neglect, the Strand
mounts a full schedule of Broadway-
quality plays and musicals, children's
shows, popular entertainers, and performances by the **Garden State Philharmonic.**

**Rowan University College of Fine
and Performing Arts** (856-256-4545;
www.rowan.edu/colleges/fpa), 201
Mullica Hill Rd., Glassboro. A wide
variety of visual and performing-arts
productions are open to the public,
including a concert series with student
and faculty ensembles, and student-
directed and -choreographed theatrical
and dance productions.

𝒮 **Mainstage Center for the Arts**
(856-227-3091; www.mainstage.org),
Dennis Flyer Theatre, Camden County College, College Dr. (off Rt. 168),
Blackwood. A popular South Jersey
arts center with a year-round schedule
of family entertainment and children's
shows, from magic and puppets to theater and performances by the **Garden
State Pops Youth Orchestra** and
other musical ensembles.

THEATER 𝒮 **Cumberland Players**
(856-692-5626; www.cumberland
players.com), 66 E. Sherman Ave. (Rt.
552), Vineland. Performances held
year-round. South Jersey's oldest community theater has been staging high-
quality amateur musicals, comedies,
and dramas since 1946. Plays and summer workshops for children.

LAKEWOOD'S ACOUSTICALLY SUPERB STRAND THEATER HAS BEEN ENTERTAINING
AUDIENCES WITH VAUDEVILLE SHOWS, LIVE COMEDY, CONCERTS, AND MUSICALS SINCE
1922.

Courtesy Strand Ventures Inc. Photo by Andrei Jackamets Photography

✳ Selective Shopping

ANTIQUES Red Barn Antiques
(609-758-9152; 800-400-8765; www
.redbarnnj.com), 56 Maple Ave., New
Egypt. One of the largest antiques
shops in New Jersey, with 18,000
square feet of dealer space. Furniture,
fine art, and collectibles.

Grist Mill Antiques Center (609-
726-1588; www.gristmillantiques.com),
127 Hanover St., Pemberton. Open
daily. A sprawling old mill on the banks
of Rancocas Creek. A huge selection of
antiques and collectibles, from fine art
and pottery to textiles, jewelry, china,
ceramics, and vintage dolls. Hosts an
annual flea market in the spring.

Gravelly Run Antiquarians (800-
451-3989; 609-476-4444; www.gravelly
run.com), 17 Estelle Ave., Dorothy.
Open by appointment only. A full-service used bookstore with more than
20,000 out-of-print, used, and rare
books in stock. Strong collections of
New Jersey, natural history, nautical,
and children's titles, as well as old photographs, prints, and maps.

ART AND CRAFTS GALLERIES
Millback Studio (609-208-0755), in
the Ol' Shoppes at Millback, 42 S.
Main St., Allentown. Oils, pastels, and
sculpture by area artists, as well as
interesting collectibles.

Off the Wall Craft Gallery (609-259-
0725), in the Ol' Shoppes at Millback
annex, 42 S. Main St., Allentown. An
eclectic crafts gallery attached to Allentown's 19th-century gristmill. The gallery
is known for its collection of finely crafted jewelry, and features the work of several hundred American studio artists.

Creative Genius (609-714-1131;
www.creativegeniusonline.com), 32-B
N. Main St., Medford. A wide-ranging,
high-quality collection of contemporary American fine arts, painting,
crafts, jewelry, and art photography.

**FACTORY OUTLETS Jackson Out-
let Village** (732-833-0503; www
.premiumoutlets.com), 537 Monmouth
Rd. (Rt. 537), Jackson. Open daily;
hours vary by season. Bargain hunters
flock here to shop more than 70 brand-
name outlet stores—including J.Crew,
Nine West, Tommy Hilfiger, Calvin
Klein, Banana Republic, and Brooks
Brothers—for high-end merchandise
at greatly discounted prices. **Java
Moon Café,** next to the village, is a
popular lunch stop with shoppers (see
Eating Out). Vintage-car cruise nights,
holiday sales, and other special events
are held throughout the year.

FLEA MARKETS AND AUCTIONS
Allen's Auction Barn (609-267-8382),
231 Landing St., Vincentown. Indoor
auctions on Wednesdays at 5 PM; pre-
view begins at noon.

Rova Farms (732-928-0928), 120
Cassville Rd. (Rt. 571), Jackson. An
outdoor flea market every Tuesday at
the ornate Russian Orthodox church
with its distinct gold onion dome. A
Russian community has been here
since the Russian Revolution, when
those loyal to the Czar fled Russia and
settled in Jackson.

**New Egypt Flea Market Village
and Auction** (609-758-2082), 933
Monmouth Rd. (Rt. 537), Cream
Ridge. Open year-round, Wednesday
and Sunday mornings.

FARMS AND GARDENS

In New Egypt
✐ **DeWolf's U-PICK Farms** (609-
758-2424), 10 W. Colliers Mills Rd.
(off Rt. 539). Call ahead for their picking schedule. Visitors can pick a wide
variety of fruits and vegetables—blackberries, strawberries, melons, pumpkins, raspberries—depending on the
season. The country store sells already-
picked produce.

*✔ **Emery's Blueberry Farms** (609-758-8514; www.emerysfarm.com), 346 Long Swamp Rd. Open daily 9–5; berry picking June–mid-August. A family-run farm growing certified organic blueberries, raspberries, and pumpkins. Take a weekend hayride to the pumpkin patch in the fall, or feed the farm animals. The farm store sells their famous homemade pies, jams, gift baskets, and just-picked produce.

Hallock's U-Pick Farm and Greenhouses (609-758-8847; www.hallocks upick.com), 38 Fischer Rd. (off Rt. 528). Open daily in season; phone or see Web site for picking schedule. Pick your own fruits and vegetables—strawberries and peas in the spring; eggplant, tomatoes, beets, and spinach in summer; pumpkins and sweet potatoes in the fall. Farm market.

In Jackson

Rare Find Nursery (732-833-0613; www.rarefindnursery.com), 957 Paterson Rd., Jackson. Open mid-Mar.–Nov., Wed.–Sat. 10–4; by appointment other days and during winter. A unique 11-acre nursery specializing in rare, exotic, and old-fashioned varieties. The spectacular 4-acre rhododendron display, with thousands of species and hybrids, is one of the largest on the East Coast. Try to visit in May and June, when the rhododendrons reach peak bloom.

✳ Special Events

January: **Fire and Ice Festival** (609-914-0811; www.fireandicefestival.com), Mount Holly. A winter festival with a chili cook-off (fire), and professional and amateur ice-carving contests (ice).

May: ✔ **American Indian Arts Festival** (609-261-4747; www.powhatan .org), Rankokus Indian Reservation, Mount Holly. A cultural celebration with more than 150 American Indian

artists and entertainers from around the country; held again in the fall.
Greek Festival (856-696-0917), Vineland. An annual Memorial Day weekend festival sponsored by St. Anthony's Greek Orthodox Church. Rides, traditional food, ethnic dancing.

June: ✔ **Whitesbog Blueberry Festival** (609-893-4646; www.whitesbog .org), Whitesbog Village, Rt. 530, Browns Mills. A celebration of the berry that was first cultivated in the Pinelands. Pick-your-own berries, Pineland folk music, children's activities and, of course, food: fresh berries, blueberry ice-cream sundaes, and berry-filled baked goods like traditional blueberry pie.

July: **South Jersey Canoe and Kayak Classic** (609-971-3085), Ocean County Park, Rt. 88, Lakewood. Canoe camping, kayak rolling, kayak fishing, ecotour paddling, basic canoeing and kayaking skills. ✔ **Burlington County Farm Fair** (609-267-2881; www .burlingtoncountyfarmfair.com), Lumberton Fairgrounds, Lumberton. Family fair featuring tractor pulls, horse shows, animal exhibits, pig and skunk races, and live country-and-western music. ✔ **Puerto Rican Festival** (856-696-1147), Landis Park, Vineland. The weeklong festival ends with a parade down Landis Avenue.

August: ✔ **Camden County Fair** (856-566-2900), 4-H Fairgrounds, Lakeland Rd., Blackwood. ✔ **Atlantic County 4-H Fair** (609-625-0056), Rt. 50, Egg Harbor City. Horse shows, rides, and agricultural exhibits at a traditional country fair.

September: **Renaissance Faire** (732-414-9639), Lakewood. Thousands come to this popular festival sponsored by the Lakewood Lions Club. Medieval dancers, full armor, fighting knights, jousting, period vendors, and a baronial parade.

October: **Cranberry Festival** (609-726-9237; www.cranfest.org), Chatsworth. **Medford Apple Festival** (609-654-2608), Medford. **Cranberry Industry Tours** (609-893-4646; www.whitesbog.org), Whitesbog Village, Rt. 530, Browns Mills. Tours of the cranberry harvest. **Witches Ball,** Mill Race Village, Mount Holly. A festival costume ball with ballroom dancing, costume contests, and scary stories. **Octoberfest** (609-965-2111), Egg Harbor City. ✧ **American Indian**

Arts Festival (609-261-4747; www.powhatan.org), Rankokus Indian Reservation, Mount Holly. A cultural celebration with more than 150 American Indian artists and entertainers from around the country; held again in the spring.

December: ✧ **First Night** (609-914-0811), Mount Holly. A traditional family-oriented New Year's Eve community celebration.

The Central Seacoast

SANDY HOOK TO BELMAR

SPRING LAKE TO BAY HEAD

BARNEGAT BAY

LONG BEACH ISLAND:
BARNEGAT LIGHT TO HOLGATE

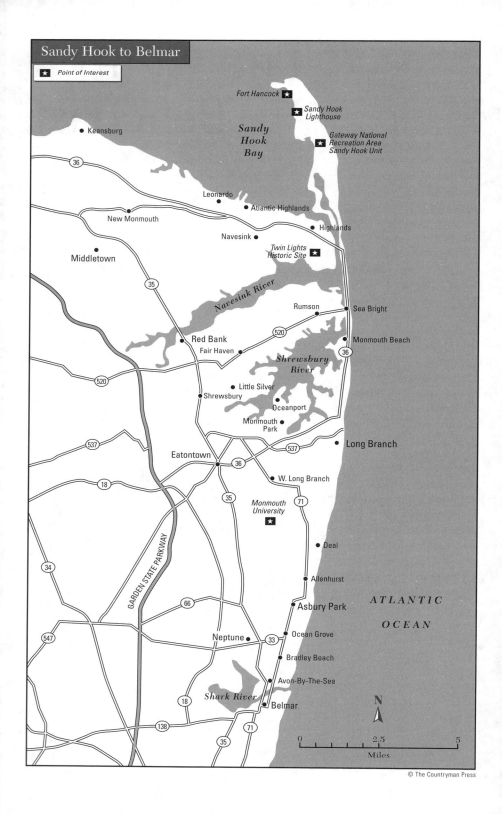

Sandy Hook to Belmar

★ Point of Interest

Fort Hancock ★
Sandy Hook Lighthouse ★
Gateway National Recreation Area Sandy Hook Unit ★

Sandy Hook Bay

Keansburg

36

Leonardo
Atlantic Highlands
New Monmouth
Navesink ●
Highlands

Middletown

35

Twin Lights Historic Site ★

Navesink River

Rumson
Sea Bright

520
Monmouth Beach

Red Bank
Fair Haven

36

Shrewsbury River

520

Little Silver
Shrewsbury
Oceanport

537

Monmouth Park

18

Eatontown
36

537
Long Branch

W. Long Branch

35
71

Monmouth University ★

34

Deal

Allenhurst

66

ATLANTIC

OCEAN

547

Asbury Park

Neptune ●
33
Ocean Grove

Bradley Beach

18

Avon-By-The-Sea

Shark River
Belmar

138
71
35

N

0   2.5   5
Miles

GARDEN STATE PARKWAY

© The Countryman Press

SANDY HOOK TO BELMAR

Perhaps more than any other state, New Jersey is defined by its shoreline. The Jersey Shore in this section is a coastal plain that stretches along the Atlantic Ocean from New York Bay to the southern tip of Long Beach Island. The entire 127-mile-long coastline, from Sandy Hook to Cape May, is a study in contrasts. Along the way is a string of beach towns that vary widely in style and flavor, each offering its own unique history and brand of Jersey Shore; and the eclectic variety holds something for every taste. It all depends on your idea of what a vacation at the beach should be. Is it an elegant Victorian inn with afternoon tea on a veranda full of white wicker rocking chairs? You will probably love Avon-By-The-Sea. A day spent along a lively boardwalk and a late night of loud music and nightclubbing? You'd be happier in Asbury Park. A walk through a natural landscape of dunes, pristine beaches, and a holly forest, with historic sites and wildlife along the way? Head to Sandy Hook, where thousands of birds wing through on their annual southern migration, and historic sites include America's oldest working lighthouse and a 19th-century military installation. Wholesome family fun and Victoriana reign in Ocean Grove, a Methodist seaside retreat that dates to the 1800s. Red Bank's oh-so-hip bistros and boutiques fill its historic downtown streets, while Belmar's marinas are full of charter boats and party boats waiting to show anglers where the trophy fish are. Beach cuisine runs the gamut from seafood shacks and boardwalk french fries to foie gras and black truffles. Visitors are presented with a similar variety when deciding where to spend the night. Choices range from grand historic mansions and no-frills motels to fanciful Victorian bed & breakfasts residing proudly behind white picket fences, neat as a pin.

Henry Hudson was the first to discover the beauty of New Jersey's long coast, when the famous navigator sailed his *Half Moon* into Sandy Hook Bay in 1609. Since then, many others have followed suit. First mariners and fishermen plied the waters; later, wealthy 19th-century vacationers hopped the trains from Philadelphia and New York City that whisked them off to Victorian seaside holidays in grand hotels. Today this portion of the shore from the Manasquan Inlet at Point Pleasant north to the Sandy Hook peninsula is sometimes called the North Shore. To the residents of New Jersey, New York, and Pennsylvania who visit here every summer, this is a place of surf, white-sand beaches, lively boardwalks, and just-off-the-boat seafood. It's also a place of traffic-clogged roads, blaring radios, and summertime crowds. Millions of people have figured out how wonderful the Jersey Shore is, and they all want a piece of it.

The shore officially begins in Sandy Hook, a spit of land reaching north into Raritan Bay and the Atlantic Ocean at the northernmost tip of the state's long coastline. It's part of the massive Gateway National Recreation Area, one of the country's first urban national parks and one of New Jersey's most natural and well-preserved areas of shoreline. The park receives about 2 million visitors a year who come to fish, hike, sunbathe, and beachcomb along 7 miles of ocean and bay beach; to check out the historic Fort Hancock military installation; and to tour the 1764 Sandy Hook Lighthouse, America's oldest working light station and the first to be powered by electricity.

First-time visitors to the peninsula are amazed and delighted to find this 1,600-acre expanse of maritime forests and salt marshes that has escaped the rabid development spreading along the rest of the shore. Despite heavy development and industry, the Sandy Hook and Raritan bays are vital rest stops for thousands of migrating birds. Sandy Hook is a prime bird-watching area; about 400 species of birds and butterflies have been identified, most passing through during the spring and fall migrations. The New Jersey Audubon Society runs the Sandy Hook Bird Observatory, where more than 300 species of nesting and migratory birds have been identified. The Manhattan skyline is visible on the clearest days, a reminder that you're not as far from civilization as you might feel here. Plans are under way to restore Fort Hancock's decaying buildings and to turn the historic complex into an active center for arts and culture, recreation, and education.

The shore towns closest to the park, Atlantic Highlands and Highlands, offer visitors the Twin Lights of Navesink, whose towers provide dramatic views of the New York City skyline and the Shrewsbury River. So does Mount Mitchell, which at less than 300 feet above sea level is the highest point on the Atlantic seaboard. The Highlands region is bordered by the Atlantic Ocean, Sandy Hook Bay, and the Navesink Hills. It's a community of marinas, beach cottages, and restaurants offering fine gourmet dining and all manner of seafood; many restaurants have boat slips for diners arriving by water. There's a high-speed ferry to New York City, and visitors will find plenty of places to spend the night.

Nestled away from the coast on the Navesink River is Red Bank, occupying a centuries-old site where the Navesink Indians, a tribe of New Jersey's Lenni-Lenape, once cultivated oysters on the riverbanks. The self-styled "hippest town in New Jersey" is sleek and trendy, with upscale boutiques and chic bistros in a Victorian-era downtown that is at once charming and progressive. An eclectic jumble of more than 300 shops and 60 restaurants fills a burgeoning arts and antiques district that also offers visitors two-dozen galleries and the Count Basie Theatre, a topflight performance venue and beloved town landmark.

From here, the Jersey Shore heads south, with resort towns, boardwalks, and beaches strung like jewels along the Atlantic. Sea Bright is one of Monmouth County's smallest communities, a narrow blink-and-you'll-miss-it kind of beach town, a mere slip of land just over half a square mile, tucked between the Atlantic Ocean and the Shrewsbury and Navesink rivers. Upscale restaurants, casual pubs, shops, a yoga studio, and a sleek SoHo-inspired club line Ocean Avenue, and homes here go for a cool million or two. It's a highbrow community in which local families keep several private beach clubs in business; but downtown has a nostalgic old-time feel, and beach bars, live music, tiki huts, and karaoke keep the oceanfront lively.

Monmouth Beach is a small and exclusive community that attracts the yachting set. In nearby Oceanport, the historic Monmouth Park Racetrack turned 140 years old in 2010. It offers live and simulcast thoroughbred racing and the Haskell Invitational, a famous summertime race (named for the first president of the Monmouth Park Jockey Club) whose $1.25 million purse makes it the richest invitational in North America.

Long Branch is an urban shore community with 5 miles of beaches, an oceanfront promenade, hotels and restaurants, and Monmouth University, whose Pollack Theater offers everything from dance performances to symphony orchestras. In the 19th century, wealthy business tycoons traveled here by stagecoach from New York City to frequent the gambling halls that bustled along the shore. It became known as the Summer Capital in 1869, when President Ulysses S. Grant set up a satellite White House here as a haven from Washington. It became a popular presidential retreat—seven U.S. presidents would vacation in Long Branch in the next 30 years, including William McKinley, Rutherford B. Hayes, and James Garfield, who was convalescing but ultimately died here in 1881 after having been shot during an assassination attempt in Washington. Today the city is undergoing a major revitalization, as old blighted buildings are being torn down to make room for new parks, businesses, homes, town houses, and condos.

Asbury Park has been part of America's collective consciousness ever since the album *Greetings from Asbury Park* launched Bruce Springsteen's career in 1973. The Boss got his musical start playing clubs on the shore, most notably the Stone Pony, Asbury Park's legendary rock club known for its rollicking bar bands. The public library boasts the world's largest collection of printed Springsteen material, from his first coming-of-age songs to his 21st-century releases, an impressive body of work. Asbury Park's history has been a roller-coaster ride, from early days full of promise, to hopes dashed by the mid-20th century (chronicled well in Springsteen's music), and now a sense of rebirth that is once again in the air.

Asbury Park was a premier seaside resort in the 19th century, founded in 1871 by New York City developer James Bradley, who wanted to create an exclusive retreat for the rich and famous of the day. By the turn of the 20th century, wealthy New Yorkers and Philadelphians were moving into Victorian mansions or staying in grand seaside hotels (more than 1,000 guesthouses were built for everyone else), strolling the mile-long boardwalk, and attending performances in a brand-new opera house. In the 1920s, the art deco–style Casino and Convention Hall were built along the waterfront. In its heyday after World War II, Asbury Park rivaled Atlantic City as a major resort destination. It was a getaway for hundreds of thousands of vacationers who crowded the boardwalk, the waterfront rides at Palace Amusements, and the majestic Paramount Theatre. By the 1960s and '70s, however, Asbury Park's run of good fortune was coming to an end. A devastating economic decline had taken hold, and suddenly the once-grand summer resort was a dingy and sadly beleaguered town, its buildings shuttered and deteriorating, the boardwalk deserted. Promises in the 1980s to resuscitate Asbury Park fell short, and the next glimmer of hope didn't come until quite recently.

Today the crumbling beachfront and downtown are enjoying an earnest resurgence—some refer to it as a renaissance—thanks to a $1.2-billion redevelopment plan that calls for a new entertainment complex, shops, parks, and housing, as well as the restoration of some of Asbury Park's historic landmarks. Shabby buildings have been razed, and freshly spiffed-up downtown storefronts are filling with galleries and bistros. The amusement rides are gone, but a newly restored boardwalk opened in 2004, and the iconic Paramount Theatre and Convention Hall arena have been brushed off and polished up, and once again they host top-name entertainers. Springsteen, a resident of nearby Rumson, is a prominent supporter of the city's revitalization; he and his E Street Band perform now and then to raise money for local organizations. The Palace—immortalized in "Tunnel of Love," "Born to Run," and other Springsteen tunes—has been demolished, but its painting of Tillie, Asbury Park's infamous grinning round-faced cartoon character, has been saved. There's good swimming, surfing, and fishing along its mile-long beach, and there's a lively after-dark scene of rock bands and dance clubs. Away from the historic boardwalk and ocean are the old working-class neighborhoods. The birthplace of Bud Abbott, of Abbott and Costello fame, is now a parking lot, but the Fourth Avenue boyhood home of 19th-century novelist Stephen Crane, of *Red Badge of Courage* fame, is a small museum and library that hosts literary programs and other events. The glory days may not be back in full force, but city leaders are hopeful and the future, for now, looks bright.

Just south of Asbury Park is Ocean Grove, a lovingly preserved Victorian town that began as a Methodist retreat in the 19th century. Passing through the gate of this picturesque little shore community is like stepping into a bygone era, and it's gaining a newfound popularity among families looking for a quaint and historic place to spend their summer vacations. Like the rest of the Jersey Shore, Ocean Grove comes alive during the summer, minus the glittery amusement rides and boisterous beach bars. The resort has a genteel air about it, compared to some of its bawdier neighbors up and down the shore. This is a dry town, a dictate that dates to its original 19th-century blue laws, which helps keep the atmosphere wholesome and family-friendly. The entire town is a national historic landmark. Its major attractions include the beach and old-time boardwalk, arts-and-crafts festivals, shops and upscale eateries along Victorian-style Main Avenue, and concerts in the Great Auditorium, the town's 1894 landmark assembly hall complete with dramatic bell tower and 9,000-pipe organ. It's still the community's social and religious hub; orchestras, folk concerts, choral performances, and worship services with the country's top preachers fill the 6,500-seat venue to capacity all year long. The annual Choir Festival draws upward of 1,500 choral singers from around the country to perform at the auditorium, an Ocean Grove tradition since the 1950s.

In 1869 the Reverend William Osborn and a dozen fellow ministers came to this pristine shoreline area, where they founded the Ocean Grove Camp Meeting Association, an offshoot of the Methodist Church. Followers hoped to attain a godly life on earth, or at least make the world a better place. It was an idyllic spiritual retreat where the faithful could spend the summer and renew themselves in beautiful natural surroundings of ocean views and rejuvenating salt air. They attended revival meetings in the Great Auditorium and stayed in the Camp Meeting Association's tents, a historic colony that still stands. They were progressive thinkers who believed in women's right to vote, rights for minorities, and other social causes—radical views in the late 19th century. In some ways, change has come slowly to Ocean Grove. Just a quarter century ago, vehicles were prohibited from the streets on Sunday, a rule enforced by blocking the entrances to town with chains. Lining the narrow leafy streets of this "Jewel of the Atlantic Coast" are hundreds of preserved houses from the late 1800s, an extraordinary collection of Victorian-era architecture, from modest white-clapboard bungalows to ornate gingerbread cottages. Many have been turned into charming bed & breakfasts, and the local historical society maintains a small museum and runs summertime house tours.

Farther down the shore, Bradley Beach is a small resort town that's popular with families, while Avon-By-The-Sea boasts clean white-sand beaches and an old-fashioned boardwalk that's perfect for strolling, complete with benches, Victorian-style lamps, and pavilions. Shops and restaurants line Main Street. Anglers who want to land a trophy fish, or at least something to grill for dinner, head to the marinas in Belmar, home to New Jersey's largest fleet of recreational fishing boats. Dozens of sportfishing boats go out every day on a quest for tuna, shark, bluefish, and other native species. This shore town is also popular with singles and young couples, who come for the dining, shopping, and lively after-dark nightlife. During the day they share space on the beach and boardwalk with hordes of families and retirees. Belmar's picturesque Silver Lake is home to a lovely park and the first flock of swans bred in America. Accommodations range from charming historic inns to reasonably priced family-friendly motels. A long calendar of special events includes the New Jersey Seafood Festival and Belmar's wildly popular sandcastle-building competition.

Entries in this section are arranged in roughly geographic order, from north to south.

AREA CODES 732, 609.

GUIDANCE Red Bank Visitors' Center (732-741-9211; www.visit.redbank .com) in the Red Bank Train Station, Monmouth St., Red Bank. Open Mon.–Fri., 9–5. This is a new visitors center, in the historic 1875 station built when the New York–Red Bank–Long Branch Line first opened; today it's one of the busiest rail stations on the North Jersey Coast Line that connects Manhattan to the Jersey

THE CULTURALLY RICH TOWN OF RED BANK ON THE NAVESINK RIVER BOASTS UPSCALE SHOPS, RESTAURANTS, ART GALLERIES, MUSIC FESTIVALS, AND A WORLD-CLASS THEATER.

Shore. The center is well stocked with travel literature (for Red Bank as well as Monmouth County), and run by a knowledgeable and friendly staff. They can provide bus, train, and ferry schedules, and information on Red Bank's many shops and galleries, special events, and performances. There's also an **Internet-connected information kiosk** in the train station for tourists and commuters to use. The center is run by a downtown business alliance, the **Red Bank RiverCenter** (732-842-4244; 888-447-8696; www.redbankrivercenter.org), 20 Broad St.

The town of **Belmar** (office: 732-681-2900; www.belmar.com) operates a **seasonal tourism booth** on the boardwalk at 10th Ave.; it's staffed 10–4 and it's stocked with literature on local attractions and events. Also, Belmar Tourism Commission (732-681-3700, press 9, press 214; www.visitbelmarnj.com).

The following chamber of commerce headquarters and local tourism offices can answer questions and supply brochures and other publications: **Belmar Chamber of Commerce** (732-681-2900; www.belmar.com); **Bradley Beach Tourism Commission** (732-869-1020; www.bradleybeachonline.com); **Ocean Grove Area Chamber of Commerce** (732-774-1391; 800-388-4768; www.oceangrovenj.com). Each maintains a Web site, listed here, with helpful information for visitors.

GETTING THERE *By air:* **Newark Liberty International Airport** (973-961-6000; parking information: 888-397-4636; www.panynj.com) in Newark serves the entire state. Those traveling to New Jersey also use **John F. Kennedy International Airport** (718-244-4168; www.kennedyairport.com) and **LaGuardia International Airport** (718-533-3850; www.laguardiaairport.com) in New York City. **Atlantic City International Airport** (609-645-7895; www.acairport.com), Exit 9 off the Atlantic City Expressway, Egg Harbor Township, is served by Spirit Airlines (800-772-7117; www.spiritair.com).

By rail: **New Jersey Transit's North Coast Line** (973-275-5555; www.njtransit.com) offers express commuter service connecting Penn Station in New York City (via Newark's Penn Station) to shore points in this region, including Red Bank, Little Silver, Monmouth Park, Long Branch, Elberon, Allenhurst, Asbury Park, Bradley Beach, and Belmar, continuing as far south as Bay Head. The stops are within walking distance of most beaches and attractions.

By bus: **New Jersey Transit** (973-275-5555; www.njtransit.com) and **Academy Bus Service** (800-442-7272; www.academybus.com) offer bus transportation throughout the region.

By ferry: **SeaStreak** (732-872-2628; 800-262-8753; www.seastreak.com) offers daily commuter ferry service via high-speed catamaran between New Jersey and Pier 11 (Wall St.) and East 35th St. in New York City. Ferries travel daily to and from Connor's Pier on Shore Dr. in Highlands, weekdays from Atlantic Highlands Municipal Harbor on Shore Dr. in Atlantic Highlands; during the summer, there is service to the beach at Sandy Hook.

By car: **The Garden State Parkway** connects the New York City and Washington, DC, regions to the Jersey Shore; from Philadelphia and Trenton, **I-195** East heads to the Belmar area. **Rt. 70** is a major secondary road that travels east across New Jersey from the Camden area, ending just west of Point Pleasant Beach. There are two major junctions along the way for shore destinations: **Rt. 37** heads to Seaside Heights, and **Rt. 72** goes directly to Long Beach Island.

GETTING AROUND *Taxis:* **Shore Transit** (732-222-6688), and **Paramount Cab Inc.** (732-222-5300) serve the Long Branch area. **Surf Taxi** (732-774-5500) and **Tops Taxi** (732-776-7711) operate out of Asbury Park. Red Bank cabs come from **Red Bank Yellow Car Company** (732-747-0747). **Belmar Car Service** (732-681-8294) serves the Belmar area.

MEDICAL EMERGENCY Riverview Medical Center (732-741-2700; www .riverviewmedicalcenter.com), One Riverview Plaza, Red Bank. The emergency number is 732-530-2204.

Monmouth Medical Center (732-222-5200; www.saintbarnabas.com), 300 Second Ave., Long Branch. The emergency number is 732-923-7300.

Jersey Shore University Medical Center (732-775-5500; www.jerseyshore medicalcenter.com), 1945 Rt. 33, Neptune. The emergency number is 732-776-4203.

✳ To See

HISTORIC HOMES AND SITES Allen House (732-747-6260; www.mon mouthhistory.org), Sycamore St. at Rt. 35, Shrewsbury. Open for guided tours May–Sept., Thurs.–Sat. 1–4. Free admission. This historic house at Shrewsbury's historic Four Corners is named for Dr. Edmund Allen, who ran a medical practice and pharmacy here from 1814 to 1867. The home's history dates well before him, however. The oldest section was built in 1740 by a wealthy Manhattan business-man; later it would serve a variety of roles, from dry-goods store, post office, and tearoom to hostelry, courthouse, and tavern. At the turn of the 20th century it was the prosperous Blue Ball Tavern, a community meeting place used by everyone, from the local Anglican Church to the Monmouth County circuit court. The historic taproom contains 19th-century barware, and the house features a pair of kitchen hearths—both with beehive ovens for baking cakes and breads—as well as period décor and household implements. Many of the artifacts on display were

---

FORT HANCOCK

(732-872-5970; www.nps.gov/gate), off Rt. 36 at the Sandy Hook Unit of Gateway National Recreation Area, Fort Hancock. Open daily year-round from dawn to dusk; park visitors center is open daily 10–5. Free admission. In the 19th century, the U.S. Army established this military fortification on the bay side of the Sandy Hook peninsula to defend New York Harbor and house the first artillery proving ground in the country. It was deactivated in 1974; since then, some buildings have been occupied, while many others remained vacant and sadly deteriorated over the years. Plans are under way to restore the historic complex to its former glory; part of it will be converted into a corporate retreat center, a marine research facility, an arts center, and a U.S. military museum. Visitors can explore the grounds, check out the 19th-century gun batteries and **Spermaceti Cove Lifesaving Station** (which contains the park's visitors center), and picnic in **Guardian Park.**

unearthed by the **Monmouth County Historical Association's Archaeology Camp,** which has found more than 25,000 objects at the site.

Monmouth University (732-571-3400; 800-543-9671; www.monmouth.edu), Cedar and Norwood Aves., West Long Branch. The university's 153-acre campus has two impressive historic buildings well worth seeing. There's the magnificent Beaux-Arts-style **Guggenheim Memorial Library,** the former summer residence of mining magnate and philanthropist Murry Guggenheim and his wife, Leonie. The white stucco mansion, which the Guggenheims called their "cottage," was built in 1903 and modeled after the Petit Trianon at Versailles; the architects, famed for their work on the New York Public Library, won awards for the design. The estate was donated to what was then Monmouth College in 1960. The library is open daily while the university is in session; pick up a visitor's permit from campus police headquarters or the greeter's booth off Cedar Avenue.

Woodrow Wilson Hall, on the Monmouth University campus, also has a unique history. The original estate, called Shadow Lawn, was destroyed by fire in 1927. That 52-room mansion served as President Woodrow Wilson's summer home—or summer White House, as it became known—while he campaigned in 1916. In 1929 the current 130-room mansion was built with limestone from the same Indiana quarry as the Empire State Building and filled with imported Italian marble and other opulent touches. The $10.5 million estate—a hefty sum in those days—was the private residence of Hubert Templeton Parson, president of F. W. Woolworth Co. Those who remember the 1980 motion picture *Annie* will recognize it as Daddy Warbucks' palatial digs; it's also a regular subject used in television and print advertising. Now home to the university's administrative offices and some classrooms, the building is listed on the National Register of Historic Places and as a National Historic Landmark.

Stephen Crane House Museum (732-775-5682; www.asburyradio.com/Crane house.htm), 508 Fourth Ave., Asbury Park. Open by appointment; call for a schedule of special programs. The 19th-century childhood home of one of America's premier novelists and author of *The Red Badge of Courage,* the magnum opus he published at the young age of 24. Crane was one of 14 children living in the house when he wrote his first short story there during his high school years. The 1878 house was narrowly saved from demolition and subsequently underwent extensive restoration to be converted into a "literary meeting place." Today it hosts a variety of literary events, including poetry readings, lectures, and discussions.

Great Auditorium (732-775-0035; 800-773-5689; www.ogcma.org), Pilgrim Pathway, Ocean Grove. Open to the public Mon.–Fri. from 1–2. The **Ocean Grove Camp Meeting Association** started with a few families that formed a seaside Methodist retreat here in 1869; the auditorium has been the center of life in Ocean Grove since the building went up in 1894. It's an impressive structure, about the size of a football field and accentuated with soaring steeples. The spectacular 9,000-pipe organ, installed in 1908, is the showpiece of the building; during the summer, free organ concerts are held on Wednesday evening and Saturday afternoon. Sunday worship services—open to visitors as well as church members—feature world-famous guest evangelists and preachers. A variety of music programs, including concerts, organ recitals, orchestras, and soloists is scheduled throughout the year (see *Entertainment—Music*).

Photo courtesy of the Ocean Grove Chamber of Commerce

THE GREAT AUDITORIUM, A 6,500-SEAT WOODEN HOUSE OF WORSHIP BUILT BY THE OCEAN GROVE CAMP MEETING ASSOCIATION IN 1894, IS STILL THE CENTER OF CULTURAL AND SPIRITUAL LIFE IN OCEAN GROVE.

Centennial Summer Cottage (732-774-1869), Central Ave. and McClintock St., Ocean Grove. Open July–Aug., Sat. 10:30–2:30. Adults $2; children 50 cents. This 1874 Victorian was built as a summer home and moved here from its original site in 1969. Today it's a museum devoted to the rich Victorian heritage of Ocean Grove, and preserves the turn-of-the-20th-century architectural style prevalent when the Ocean Grove Camp Meeting Association was organized (see previous listing). The rooms are filled with period furniture and artifacts; on the grounds is a late-19th-century flower and shrub garden and a religiously themed herb garden. The museum is maintained by the **Historical Society of Ocean Grove** and owned by the Ocean Grove Camp Meeting Association.

MUSEUM Army Communications and Electronics Museum (732-532-1682; www.monmouth.army.mil), Kaplan Hall, Fort Monmouth (off Rt. 35), Eatontown. Fort Monmouth is now a closed post with restricted access (since September 11, 2001); admission to the museum is by appointment only. Artifacts and photographs tell the story of the Fort Monmouth military post, especially its role as a research facility. New technology has been studied and developed here, including space communication, meteorological technology, and advanced radar equipment. Communications electronics dating to 1917 are on display; the Hall of Commanders is a tribute to each of the fort's leaders.

SCENIC OVERLOOK Mount Mitchell Scenic Overlook (732-842-4000; www .monmouthcountyparks.com), 460 Ocean Blvd., Atlantic Highlands. Open daily 8 AM–dusk. It may only be 266 feet above sea level, but it's the highest coastal peak on the Atlantic Seaboard (Maine's 1,532-foot-tall Cadillac Mountain in Acadia National Park is certainly taller, but it's on an island just off the coast). On a clear day you can see New York City; in the foreground are New York Harbor, the Atlantic Ocean, Fort Hancock, Sandy Hook Lighthouse, and the beaches of Sandy Hook. The Monmouth County parks system maintains the site, which also has a playground and picnic area.

✳ To Do

BICYCLING Gateway National Recreation Area—Sandy Hook Unit (732-872-5970; www.nps.gov/planyourvisit/sandy-hook), Fort Hancock. The park is open daily from dawn until dusk. The network of easy and scenic trails lacing through the 1,600-acre barrier island is open to cyclists—a mountain bike or hybrid is best. You'll be sharing the way with many hikers and birders, so use good trail etiquette when approaching and passing. A 5-mile paved multi-use path—popular with cyclists, walkers, and in-line skaters—connects the park entrance to the historic sites at Fort Hancock. Along the way you'll pass the Sandy Hook Visitors Center, housed in the former 19th-century Spermaceti Cove Lifesaving Station; the park's holly forest and southern beaches; and the old Nike missile radar site.

Hartshorne Woods Park (732-872-0336; www.monmouthcountyparks.com), Navesink Ave., Middletown. A lovely park near the Twin Lights of Navesink Lighthouse historic site (see sidebar on next page) occupies 736 acres of rolling woodland and open space. The 11-mile trail system is open to cyclists, as well as equestrians and hikers.

Most shore towns allow bicycling on their boardwalks in the early morning hours; you usually have to be off the boards by the time people are making their way to the beach.

BIRDING Sandy Hook Bird Observatory (732-872-2500; www.nj.audubon.org; rare bird alert: 732-872-2595), Gateway National Recreation Area, 20 Hartshorne Dr., Fort Hancock. Open Sept.–June, Tues.–Sat. 10–5; Sun. 10–3; closed Mon.; summer, Tues.–Fri. 10–5; closed Sat., Sun., Mon. One of New Jersey's newest birding centers, opened in 2001 and run by the **New Jersey Audubon Society.** Birds are active here year-round, but the best time to come is during the spring and fall migrations. Some 340 bird species and 50 types of butterflies—including many rare species—have been spotted here; there's even a hotline devoted to sightings of these seldom-seen birds. Springtime brings waterfowl, birds of prey, gulls, and songbirds. From August to October, shorebirds and songbirds wing through on their long migration south. In the winter months, expect to see gulls, ducks, loons, and other water birds. At the observatory, pick up a map of Sandy Hook birding spots, and check their updates on recent sightings. The nature store is well stocked with binoculars, nature and birding books, and bird-related gifts. There's a full schedule of special events and programs, from morning butterfly and bird walks and natural-history weekend events to birding workshops. The lush butterfly and hummingbird garden surrounding the observatory reaches peak bloom in midsummer and continues into fall. The annual **Sandy Hook Migration Watch** takes place at North Pond, near the northern tip of the peninsula. From the observation deck, an official bird counter monitors the activity of raptors—mainly kestrels, owls, and hawks—also egrets, loon, herons, and other species that appear in great numbers from mid-Mar.–mid-May.

THE SANDY HOOK AND TWIN LIGHTS OF NAVESINK LIGHTHOUSES

Sandy Hook Lighthouse (732-872-5970; www.nps.gov/gate), off Rt. 36 at the Sandy Hook Unit of Gateway National Recreation Area, Fort Hancock. Tours of the lighthouse are led by **New Jersey Lighthouse Society** volunteers from April–Nov., Sat.–Sun. from noon–4:30; grounds open daily sunrise to sunset. When the Sandy Hook Lighthouse was built in 1764 to guide mariners into New York Harbor, the tall white tower was perched 500 feet from the northern tip of the Sandy Hook peninsula. Thanks to three centuries of wave and water action, the historic light station now is more than a mile from the point. Today it's the oldest operational lighthouse in America and a national historic landmark. Visitors can climb to the top and enjoy the spectacular panorama of Sandy Hook, New York Harbor, the Atlantic Ocean, and the Manhattan skyline.

Twin Lights of Navesink Lighthouse (732-872-1886), Lighthouse Road (off Rt. 36), Highlands. Call for changes to hours due to state budget considerations. In the past, hours have been from Memorial Day–Labor Day, open daily 10–5; grounds open daily 9 AM–sunset; remainder of the year, lighthouse Wed.–Sun., 10–4:30; grounds daily 9 AM–sunset. Free admission. A lighthouse has guided ships into the lower bay of New York Harbor from the Navesink Highlands since 1828; this 256-foot double-beacon lighthouse was built of local brownstone in 1862 and sports a unique design. There are two light towers, as the name suggests, but they are not identical "twins." The north tower is octagonal and the south tower is square. The lights were extinguished in 1949, but a beacon still flashes from the north tower from sunset to sunrise. Today a small museum in the light station's generator building features maritime-history artifacts and the south tower's 9-foot-wide Fresnel lens. The view from the top of the north tower, at 246 feet above sea level, is well worth the 64-step climb.

THE SANDY HOOK LIGHTHOUSE, BUILT IN 1764, AT THE NORTHERN TIP OF THE SANDY HOOK PENINSULA, IS THE OLDEST OPERATIONAL LIGHTHOUSE IN AMERICA.

Photo courtesy of the New Jersey Lighthouse Society

BOAT EXCURSIONS (See also *Boating.*)

Let's Go Sailing (732-801-7472; www.charter-sails.com), Monmouth Cove Marina, Port Monmouth Rd., Port Monmouth. Daily sailing charters, half- or full-day. Excursions open to the public, Wed. 9 AM and 2 PM and Sun., 9 AM.

BOATING Marinas lining the shoreline offer slip rentals, boat ramps, bait and tackle, marine services, sometimes a restaurant. They include **Leonardo State Marina** (732-291-1333), 102 Concord Ave. (off Rt. 36), Leonardo; **Gateway Marina** (732-291-4400) 34 Bay Ave., Highlands; **Fair Haven Yacht Works** (732-747-3010), 75 DeNormandie Ave., Fair Haven; **Total Marine at Sea View** (732-775-7842), 120 Sea Spray Lane, Neptune; and **Main One Marina** (732-776-5992), One Main Street, Avon-By-The-Sea. (All these and more can be found at www.jerseymarinas.com; look for Monmouth County.)

FISHING The Jersey Shore is famous for its sportfishing opportunities; there are hundreds of party (or open) boats and charter boats based in marinas from Atlantic Highlands down to Belmar. In the spring, they head into the Atlantic for mackerel, cod, flounder, blackfish, sea bass, striped bass, and bluefish. Summer means fluke, bluefish, tuna, and shark, while day trips and night trips for tuna, striped bass, shark, bluefish, and porgy go out in fall and winter.

Belmar Municipal Marina (732-681-2266; www.belmar.com/marina), one of the biggest marinas in the region, is home base for the *Golden Eagle* (732-681-6144), a 100-foot party boat. *Ocean Explorer* (732-681-5005) and *Big Mohawk* (732-974-9606) are based at **Belmar Marine Basin** on Rt. 35 in Belmar; *Miss Belmar Princess* (732-681-6866) is docked on Rt. 35 in Belmar.

GOLF Old Orchard Country Club (732-542-9139), 54 Monmouth Rd., Eatontown. An 18-hole championship golf course established in 1929; facilities include a driving range, clubhouse, pro shop, snack bar, and restaurant.

Shark River Golf Course (732-922-4141; monmouthcountyparks.com for this and others), 320 Old Corlies Ave., Neptune. A historic 18-hole golf course—built after World War I by the city of Asbury Park—with a driving range and a clubhouse that has a restaurant, snack bar, and pro shop.

HIKING Gateway National Recreation Area—Sandy Hook Unit (732-872-5970; www.nps.gov/gate/planyourvisit/sandy-hook), Fort Hancock. If you're planning a summertime weekend hike, get here early. It's likely that the parking lot will fill up by 9 AM, especially if the forecast calls for a hot day. The nature trails range from easy to moderate in difficulty, and are a window to the peninsula's varied terrain, from holly forest and salt marsh to dunes and long stretches of beach. Sights along the way include the entrance to New York Harbor (and the Manhattan skyline beyond), the historic buildings of **Fort Hancock, Sandy Hook Lighthouse,** and 7 miles of protected ocean beaches, perfect for a posthike picnic or swim. Keep a close eye out for the many birds that call the barrier peninsula home.

HORSE RACING ✍ **Monmouth Park Racetrack** (732-222-5100; www.monmouthpark.com; Dawn Patrol tours: 732-571-5542), 175 Oceanport Ave., Oceanport. Open Apr.–Sept., Wed.–Sun.; simulcast thoroughbred and harness racing daily year-round. General admission $3; children 11 and under, free. Live thoroughbred racing by the top horses and jockeys in the country on a beautiful and historic mile-long oval. **Dawn Patrol tours** on Friday and Saturday mornings, late June–late Aug., are a must-do; there's no charge, but advance reservations are required. Get a rare glimpse at what goes on behind the scenes at one of America's top racetracks. This 2-hour tour goes through the stable, to the starting gate, and into the jockey room. If you miss the tour, then head to the **English Walking Ring** behind the clubhouse, where the public can watch as jockeys and trainers prepare for races, and the sleek horses are paraded around the ring. Every Sunday is **Family Fun Day,** with free activities for children, including music, clowns, pony rides, and face painting. In August, the million-dollar **Haskell Invitational**— the richest thoroughbred horse race in North America—draws more than 50,000 spectators who come to see the best horses and riders in the world (see *Special Events*). **New Jersey Transit** (973-275-5555; www.njtransit.com) operates a Pony Express train direct to the park on weekends and holidays.

ICE-SKATING ✧ **Red Bank Armory Ice Complex** (732-450-9001; www.red bankarmory.com), 76 Chestnut St., Red Bank. The public can skate at this figure skating and hockey center on Friday night and Saturday and Sunday afternoons; phone ahead for hours and admission prices. The pro shop sells hockey and skating equipment and can sharpen and repair skates.

SURFING In *Asbury Park*, the Seventh Ave. beach is a surfing-only beach, established by the city in 2003 after a 30-year ban on daytime surfing. Most communities allow surfing before and after regular beach hours, generally before 9 AM and after 5 PM, and on particular beaches. Local surf shops that sell surfboards, wetsuits, gear, and clothing include **Spellbinders Surf Shop** (732-870-2223; www .spellbindersurf.com), 200 Ocean Ave. N., Long Branch; and **Aloha Grove Surf Shop** (732-413-8575; www.alohagrove.com), 84 Ocean Ave., Pier Village, Long Branch.

✳ Green Space

BEACHES *Beaches are listed from north to south.* All require a beach badge, which can be purchased at various locations around town, including municipal halls or at designated spots at the beaches and along the boardwalks.

Sandy Hook (732-872-5970), off Rt. 36 at Gateway National Recreation Area, Highlands. Several ocean beach areas with restroom facilities. Surfing, scuba diving, windsurfing, and picnicking are allowed. Parking fee: day $10; season $50.

Sea Bright (732-842-0215; www.seabrightnj.org) has an oceanfront beach and boardwalk with fishing, rafting, surfing, and picnicking. Day $8; season $100.

Long Branch (732-571-6545; www.visitlongbranch.com) has an oceanfront beach and boardwalk with fishing, picnicking, scuba diving, and surfing. Day, adults (ages 18–61 years) $5; students (ages 13–17) $3; seniors and children 12 and under, free.

Seven Presidents Oceanfront Park (732-229-0924; www.monmouthcounty parks.com), on Ocean Ave. in Long Branch, has a mile-long oceanfront beach with picnicking, surfing, and fishing. Day $7, 12 and older; day parking $6.

Courtesy Ann. V. Loftus

LONG BRANCH WAS A POPULAR SUMMER RESORT AMONG WEALTHY NEW YORKERS AND SEVERAL U.S. PRESIDENTS IN THE 19TH CENTURY.

Deal Beach (732-531-1454; www.deal borough.com) at the foot of Phillips Ave. in Deal has picnicking, tennis, surfing, and after-hours fishing. Day $6; season $125.

Asbury Park (732-775-2100; www.city ofasburypark.com) is known for its historic boardwalk but also offers fishing and surfing. Day pass $5 for all. Season: adults, $60; seniors and teens $15.

Ocean Grove (732-988-5533; 732-775-0035; ww.oceangrove.org) has an oceanfront beach and charming boardwalk, as well as fishing, picnicking, rafting, tennis, and surfing. Day use costs $7 weekdays and $12 weekends; seven consecutive days, $35.

Bradley Beach (732-776-2999; www .bradleybeachonline.com) has an oceanfront beach with fishing, surfing, picnicking, and rafting; many beachgoers come back at night for the summertime concerts at the boardwalk band shell. Day $7; children under 14, free.

Avon-By-The-Sea (732-502-4510; www.avonbytheseanj.com) has a lovely old-time boardwalk along the beach. Day $8. The beach pavilion at Washington Ave. has an eclectic mix of shops and eateries.

Belmar (732-681-3700; www.visitbelmarnj.com) has a wide mile-long beach and boardwalk with fishing, picnicking, scuba diving, and after-hours surfing. Day $7; children 15 and younger, free.

GARDEN F. Bliss Price Arboretum and Wildlife Sanctuary (732-389-7621), Wycoff Rd., Eatontown. Open daily dawn to dusk. This wildlife sanctuary west of Long Branch is also known as the **Eatontown Arboretum.** Whatever you call it, the 55-acre wooded oasis is a peaceful spot that seems a world away from the nearby beaches and bustling boardwalks.

Walking paths pass through large white pines and a diverse variety of trees. Tanagers and owls are among the elusive species often spotted here in spring and fall, in addition to the more common woodpeckers and songbirds that call the arboretum home.

NATIONAL RECREATION AREA Gateway National Recreation Area— Sandy Hook Unit (732-782-5970; www.nps.gov/gate/planyourvisit/sandy-hook), Fort Hancock. The park is open daily year-round; the **Sandy Hook Visitor Center** is open daily 10–5. Admission to the park is free; beach parking fees are charged during the summer (see *Beaches*). One of America's first urban national parks is also one of the most pristine stretches along New Jersey's 127-mile-long coastline and one of its most popular shoreline destinations (see *Bicycling, Birding,* and *Hiking* under *To Do*). The park occupies a 1,600-acre peninsula that juts between the Atlantic Ocean and Raritan Bay, and offers sand dunes, salt marshes, long sweeping beaches, and a holly forest. Historic buildings include the **1764 Sandy Hook Lighthouse,** America's oldest continuously operating lighthouse, and **Fort Hancock,** a 19th-century military installation whose buildings are currently under restoration (see sidebar, page 349). Birders come for the spring and fall migration of thousands of shorebirds and songbirds; beachcombers and anglers (a fishing permit is required; contact the visitor center) come for the 7 miles of sand along the ocean and bay. Stop by the visitor center in the **1894 Spermaceti Cove Lifesaving Station** for a schedule of activities like guided nature walks, slide shows on local history, and birding programs, or to browse the bookstore and exhibits. Another bookstore and exhibit space at the **Fort Hancock Museum** and the historic guardhouse building are open Sat.–Sun. 1–5; daily 1–5 in July–Aug.

NATURE CENTER ✿ **Huber Woods Environmental Center** (732-872-2670; www.monmouthcountyparks.com), Huber Woods Park, 25 Brown's Dock Rd, in the Locust section of Middletown. A peaceful 258-acre park overlooking the Navesink River, the center has 7 miles of multi-use trails that pass through meadows, woodlands, and thick stands of mountain laurel that erupt into bloom in late spring. The trails—a mix of short and long loops—are open to hikers, cyclists, and equestrians. This was once a farm belonging to the locally prominent Huber family; their German-Swiss-style manor house is now an environmental center with hands-on displays of animals, plants, and the weather. There's also a weather station and a bird-viewing area, and a full schedule of classes and nature programs designed to increase the public's awareness of local environmental issues.

✳ Lodging

RESORT 🐾 ♿ "🍴" **Ocean Place Resort and Spa** (732-571-4000; reservations: 800-411-6493; www.ocean placeresort.com), One Ocean Blvd., Long Branch 07740. Open year-round. This is the only full-service resort between Manhattan and Atlantic City that has a private beach. The focus here is on rest and rejuvenation, accomplished through an extensive menu of luxurious European-style spa treatments and services. Guests head to one of the 15 treatment rooms for body wraps, massage therapies, mineral and seaweed baths, aromatherapy facials, self-tanning sessions, and facials designed especially for men. The menu of creative spa cuisine features lots of low-carb options and a variety of healthy drinks, from protein shakes and fruit smoothies to organic

juices. There's an oceanfront pool and a fitness center with an indoor pool, as well as Jacuzzi tubs, saunas, and steam rooms. Accommodations range from spacious oceanfront suites with parlors and private balconies to standard guest rooms, with a north-facing view toward Sandy Hook and the Manhattan skyline or a south-facing view toward Asbury Park, all with Wi-Fi. Rooms $189–339; inquire about suites and complete spa vacation packages and day-spa packages.

HOTELS ♿ "🍴" **The Oyster Point Hotel** (732-530-8200; out-of-state: 800-447-4136; www.mollypitcher -oysterpoint.com), 146 Bodman Pl., Red Bank 07701. Open all year. A full-service boutique-style hotel on the Navesink River with 54 guest rooms and four suites offering a variety of amenities. Double rooms have views of the river; king rooms are nice and spacious; and the suites have separate living areas and luxe bathrooms. . Downstairs, the handsome **Atrium Bar and Restaurant** serves American and Continental cuisine at breakfast, lunch, and dinner daily, as well as brunch on Sunday. Guests arriving by boat—whether to dine or to spend the night—can dock at the **Oyster Point Marina.** Fitness room; high-speed Internet access in all guest rooms. Standard rooms $129–229; suites up to $449.

& "ı" **Molly Pitcher Inn** (732-747-2500; out-of-state: 800-221-1372; www.mollypitcher-oysterpoint.com), 88 Riverside Ave., Red Bank 07701. Open year-round. Red Bank's landmark hotel was designed after Philadelphia's Independence Hall when it was built on the banks of the picturesque Navesink River in 1928. It's styled after an elegant 19th-century hotel and full of sophisticated Old World touches. The lobby makes a dramatic statement with fresh flowers and crystal chandeliers, and a roaring fireplace in the cool months. Rooms are nicely furnished and comfortable—some are on the small side; others are more spacious, with balconies overlooking the hotel's pool and marina. The suites are roomy and full of reproduction antiques. Wi-Fi available. Many locals come here for the dining room, which overlooks the river and serves top-rate American and Continental cuisine; Sunday brunch is especially popular (see *Dining Out*). The hotel is named for Revolutionary War heroine Molly Pitcher—real name Mary Hays—who fought beside her husband with the Continental army at the battle of Monmouth, which took place in nearby Freehold in June 1778. She earned her famous nickname for tirelessly supplying soldiers with pitch-

ers of water on the sweltering battlefield. The **Molly Pitcher Marina** has slips available for overnight guests arriving by boat. Standard rooms $129–229; suites up to $449.

& **The Berkeley Ocean Front Hotel and Conference Center** (732-776-6700; 888-776-6701; www.berkeley hotelnj.com), 1401 Ocean Ave., Asbury Park 07712. Open all year. A historic Jersey Shore landmark, across from the Asbury Park Convention Hall, that offers basic accommodations. Although it's nothing fancy, it is close to the shore. It opened as a hotel in the 1920s, housed the British navy during World War II, then served as a naval hospital before being fully restored to a hotel in the 1980s. There are 250 guest rooms and suites spread across eight floors. Standard rooms have no-frills traditional décor and basic amenities; other units boast upgrades like ocean views, king-sized beds, or extra-roomy bathrooms. The restaurant and bar serve American fare with an emphasis on seafood and steaks. $130 and up.

Shawmont Hotel (732-776-6985; www.shawmont.com), 17 Ocean Ave. (P.O. Box 27), Ocean Grove 07756. Open Memorial Day weekend through mid-Sept. A historic hotel with a casual, beachy feel, overlooking the Atlantic Ocean and Ocean Grove's charming boardwalk. The convenient location close to shops, restaurants, and the Great Auditorium is ideal for those who want to see everything Ocean Grove has to offer. Wide breezy verandas are furnished with rocking chairs and comfy chaise lounges for those who opt to just stay put. Guest rooms—ranging from half-bath singles to roomy efficiencies—are simply furnished, clean, and outfitted with TV and air-conditioning. Some have a private terrace. Starting at $65.

INNS & **"Ⅰ"** **Blue Bay Inn** (732-708-9600; www.bluebayinn.com), 51 First Ave., Atlantic Highlands 07716. Open all year. A sleek and stylish inn with 27 sophisticated rooms and suites, as well as furnished pieds-à-terre designed for extended stays. Its location within walking distance of the New York City ferry dock makes this an ideal choice for visitors coming from Manhattan without a car. The **Copper Canyon** is a popular upscale American restaurant and bar that moved into the hotel when it opened in the fall of 2004. Complimentary Wi-Fi. Continental breakfast. $159 and up.

✍ **Bradley Beach Inn** (732-774-0414; www.thebradleybeachinn.com), 900 Ocean Ave., Bradley Beach 07720. New Jersey Transit commuter trains stop at Bradley Beach Station, just a few blocks from the inn. Each of the eight uniquely decorated guest rooms comes with a view of the ocean, not to mention air-conditioning and a refrigerator. Some have a private bath with Jacuzzi tub, and others share bathrooms in the hallway. Complimentary

movies are shown every night in the inn's cinema room. Continental breakfast. $60–165.

BED & BREAKFASTS

In Highlands 07732

🐾 ✍ **SeaScape Manor** (732-291-8467; www.seascapemanorbb.com), Three Grand Tour. Open all year. A homey, family-friendly retreat overlooking the Atlantic Ocean. Four antiques-filled guest rooms, each with a private bath. Common areas include the cozy parlor with a fireplace that's appealing in the cooler months, and a large deck for reading, snoozing, and sunbathing. Full breakfast. $140–225.

✍ **Grand Lady by the Sea** (732-708-1900; 877-306-2161; www.grandlady bythesea.com), 254 Rt. 367. Open year-round. This 1910 brick home across from Sandy Hook has cozy guest rooms and beautiful views of the ocean. There are two nicely furnished rooms and one suite, each with private bath, TV, and mini-refrigerator. Guests are provided with complimentary beach passes and use of the inn's

OCEAN GROVE'S METICULOUSLY RESTORED VICTORIAN AND EARLY-20TH-CENTURY HOMES AND OTHER STRUCTURES THREADING THE LOVELY TREE-LINED STREETS IS THE LARGEST SUCH COLLECTION IN THE U.S.

Photo courtesy of the Ocean Grove Chamber of Commerce

bicycles. A full breakfast is served in the gazebo, when weather allows. $199–289.

In Long Branch 07740

✂ "ᵀ" **Cedars and Beeches Bed & Breakfast** (732-571-6777; reservations: 800-323-5655; www.cedarsand beeches.com), 247 Cedar Ave. Open all year. This historic Victorian mansion was the first of Long Branch's earliest homes to open its doors to travelers as a bed & breakfast. The grand three-and-a-half-story gem resides in the historic West End, a neighborhood of stately homes that were once the summer residences of U.S. presidents and tycoons. This one boasts Tiffany stained-glass windows, a dramatic staircase, and a beautiful wraparound veranda. Innkeeper Esther Cohen offers a dozen guest rooms (including one light and airy suite); all have private bath, TV, phone, air-conditioning, and hi-speed Internet access. Some have bay windows that overlook gardens; others occupy the inn's window-lined towers. Continental breakfast is available during the week, and a full breakfast is served on weekends. $100–400.

In Ocean Grove 07756

& ✂ "ᵀ" **Ocean Plaza** (732-774-6552; 888-891-9442; www.theinnsofocean grove.com), 22 Ocean Pathway. A family-friendly luxury Victorian-era bed & breakfast. Views of the Atlantic are especially dramatic from the top-floor guest rooms. The Ocean Grove Camp Meeting Association, one of the longest continually operating camp meetings in the country built a hotel on this site in 1870; today, the cheerful multicolored exterior and double wraparound porches make it hard to miss this landmark. Its 16 renovated guest rooms and two suites are bright and sunny, with private baths and Wi-Fi access. The beach is a block away. Continental breakfast. $100–425.

"ᵀ" **The Carriage House Bed & Breakfast** (732-988-3232; www .carriagehousenj.com), 18 Heck Ave. Open year-round. A typical, charming Ocean Grove Victorian with a wide porch and cheerful floral décor. Hosts Kathy and Phil Franco offer eight guest rooms and suites, all with private bath, phone, TV, free Wi-Fi, and air-conditioning. Some rooms come with nice extras, like a fireplace or a balcony with a view of the ocean, which is just a block away. In-season $125–180.

☀ ▼ **The Melrose** (732-774-5404; 800-378-9004; www.melroseog.com), 34 Seaview Ave. A cozy and comfortable, gay-friendly inn a block from the ocean. Eight guest rooms and two suites are spread across three floors, decorated with original art and equipped with private baths. Some rooms have a microwave and refrigerator, a fireplace, or a Jacuzzi tub. Guests like to congregate on the porches, in the garden, or in the TV room. Complimentary beach passes and towels are provided. Continental breakfast. $75–235.

In Avon-By-The-Sea 07717

"ᵀ" **Avon Manor Inn** (732-776-7770; www.avonmanor.com), 109 Sylvania Ave. Open all year. Innkeeper Greg Dietrich offers seven guest rooms and two suites, each tastefully and uniquely decorated. Some have a sleigh bed, a fireplace, or skylights; others are full of windows that let sunlight flood in. All have a private bath, TV, Wi-Fi, and air-conditioning. Guests are encouraged to make themselves at home. Outside there's a fireplace and barbecue grill, as well as a putting green. The rambling wraparound porch is shady, cool, and full of rocking chairs. Inside, the Victorian-style living room is lovely and relaxing. Bikes (including a tandem bicycle) are available for guests to use, as are complimentary badges, towels, and chairs to take to the beach. Complimentary tea and snacks are available most of the day, and a full breakfast is served in the morning. Ask about special packages for couples and golfers. $80–285.

🖋 **Cashelmara Inn** (732-776-8727; www.cashelmara.com; 800-821-2976), 22 Lakeside Ave. Open year-round. This former grand seaside private mansion–turned–charming inn boasts a unique amenity—**a private Victorian-era movie theater.** The 12 guest rooms and two suites all have a private bath as well as a mini-refrigerator and air-conditioning—some have a fireplace and a Jacuzzi tub. Nearly every room has a view of the Atlantic Ocean. Innkeeper Mary Wiernasz provides guests with badges, chairs, umbrellas, and towels for the beach. Full breakfast. $100–375.

Atlantic View Inn (732-774-8505; www.atlanticviewinn.com), 20 Woodland Ave. Open year-round. Innkeepers Chris and Debbie Solomita run a relaxed and comfortable inn in a restored early-20th-century summer home. Ten guest rooms and two suites are elegant and cozy, with featherbeds and carefully chosen antiques. Amenities include private baths, fireplaces, and TVs/VCRs. There are complimentary badges to take to the beach, which is just 200 feet from the inn. A full gourmet breakfast is served in view of the ocean, on the rambling wraparound porch in-season. $100–345.

In Belmar 07719

🖋 🌺 "I" **The Inn at the Shore** (732-681-3762; www.innattheshore.com), 301 Fourth Ave. Tom and Rosemary Volker's circa-1880 bed & breakfast near Silver Lake is pure Victoriana, from the period antiques and floral wallpaper to the white wicker and soaring tower. The interior is warm and cheery, with a library and a living room with a fieldstone fireplace and an entertainment center. Homey touches are everywhere, from the walls lined with family photos to the brick patio with barbecue grill and the veranda with antique gliders and rocking chairs. Ten guest rooms are quaint and cozy, and each has a phone, radio, air-conditioning, free Wi-Fi, and robes; some have a whirlpool tub and a fireplace. Four have a private bath; the rest share baths. The Volkers supply their guests with complimentary beach badges, chairs, towels, and bicycles. A full breakfast of home-baked goods, fresh fruit, and hot entrées might include Tom's homemade granola, crème brûlée French toast, or the inn's signature sunrise pancakes with vanilla-cream syrup. Ask about their romantic getaway and murder-mystery packages. $135–285.

Morning Dove Inn (732-556-0777; www.morningdoveinn.com), 204 Fifth Ave. Open all year. A late-19th-century home overlooking Silver Lake that's also close to the ocean. Each of the eight spacious rooms and suites has its own bath; some rooms have a clawfoot tub or a fireplace. Guests enjoy the open front porch in the summer, and the sunny solarium in the winter. There's a phone, refrigerator, and TV/VCR available for guests to use, as well as complimentary badges and chairs to take to the beach. Full breakfast. $125–290.

MOTEL 🐾 **Ocean Court Motel** (732-728-1505; www.oceancourtmotel.net), 170 Ocean Ave., Long Branch 07740. Open year-round. This is not a luxury property, and there are no special amenities or services, just 22 clean and comfortable units across the street from the ocean and boardwalk at bargain prices. It caters mainly to military personnel and businesspeople relocating to the area, but vacationers like the location and the value. Rooms come with a queen bed or a double bed, plus a futon or sofa bed, TVs and kitchenettes (with refrigerator, gas range, microwave, and coffeemaker). $95–125.

OTHER LODGING ♂ **Sandcastle Cottages** (732-681-0732; www.sand castlecottages.com), 211 Ninth Ave., Belmar 07719. Two adjoining housekeeping cottages offer simple, clean, and comfortable accommodations a block and a half from the beach. The fully furnished two-bedroom units are ideal for families or two couples vacationing together. The cottages come with barbecue grills and complimentary beach passes. $585–1,600 per week.

✳ Where to Eat
DINING OUT

In Highlands
♿ **Windansea** (732-872-2266; www .windanseanj.com), 56 Shrewsbury Ave. Open daily for lunch and dinner; Sunday brunch. Contemporary American cuisine at one of the northern shore's most highly acclaimed restaurants. Windansea is perched above the Atlantic on pilings; there's a dock for diners arriving by boat, and a porch that comes with sweeping ocean views. Wait for a table (no reservations) and watch the sunset from the lively outdoor tiki bar. The emphasis is on fresh fish and shellfish, be it grilled, broiled, seared, or fried, and shore standards are expertly done, with pastas, steaks, and chops keeping pace. Pub-style fare and homey house-made desserts, too. A hip crowd comes for the cocktails and late-night bands, and keeps the bar scene going. $14–22.

♂ **Bahrs** (732-872-1245; www.bahrs .com), Two Bay Ave. Open daily for lunch and dinner; outdoor dining from May–mid-Oct. A landmark seafood restaurant and marina, on the Shrewsbury River since 1917. It has all the hallmarks of a shore eatery—dockside dining, fresh seafood, nautical décor, and a family-friendly attitude. Bahrs doesn't take reservations, but they will put you on a waiting list if you call shortly before you arrive. If you're bringing kids, you might want to eat on **Moby's Deck,** a casual and seasonal outdoor dining area with a menu of seafood platters and sandwiches. $15–27.

In Red Bank
♿ **Nicholas** (732-345-9977; www .restaurantnicholas.com), 160 Rt. 35 South, Middletown (just outside Red Bank). Open for dinner Tues.–Sun.; closed Mon. Reservations are recommended. The superb service, romantic special-occasion atmosphere, and exquisitely rendered food keeps this stylish dining room at the top of critics' lists. The prix fixe menu changes seasonally, and is paired with a wine list offering hundreds of bottles. The sleek and polished setting is reminiscent of a contemporary Manhattan dining room, with prices to match. Chef-owner Nicholas Harary is renowned for his creative New American cuisine with French accents, exquisite sauces, and rich and vibrant flavors. The wonderful desserts require making a difficult choice. $38–75.

♿ **The Bistro at Red Bank** (732-530-5553; www.thebistroatredbank.com), 14 Broad St. Open for lunch and dinner daily. Reservations are required for groups of six or more. They call it world cuisine, an eclectic menu that ranges from sushi to brick-oven pizza. The crowd is hip and so is the exposed brick and other bistro-style décor. Many of the dishes are Asian-inspired, such as seafood in lobster broth over *udon* noodles. A good place for a far-better-than-average lunch. BYOB. $12–30.

DORIS & ED'S

(732-872-1565; www.dorisandeds.com), 348 Shore Dr., Highlands. Open daily for dinner July–Aug.; Sept.–June, open for dinner Wed.–Sun.; closed Mon.–Tues. Reservations are recommended. This traditional seafood house–turned–upscale eatery is widely considered the state's top seafood restaurant. It was the first restaurant in New Jersey to earn the prestigious **James Beard Foundation Award for Excellence** for its American regional cuisine. Executive Chef Russell Dare works magic in a quaint white house that fronts Sandy Hook Bay and the New York City skyline. He's been praised by *Gourmet, Bon Appétit,* and the *New York Times* for his eclectic mix of traditional shore fare and elegant innovations that make use of foie gras, truffles, and other highbrow ingredients. The classic menu starts with Manhattan clam chowder, steamers, and shrimp scampi and moves on to familiar dishes like stuffed flounder, filet mignon, and fried seafood platters. The eclectic portion of the menu has so many imaginative modern twists that it's hard to make a decision; each dish sounds more intriguing than the one before it. You might begin with baked oysters with spinach and foie gras, or rock shrimp risotto with chive oil, or duck confit and wild mushroom pizza before trying miso-glazed black sea bass, pine nut–crusted Atlantic halibut, grilled tuna on wasabi mayonnaise with ginger scallion sauce, or pan-seared Nantucket Bay scallops with creamy polenta and baby greens. Whatever you choose, the seafood will be fresh and prepared simply and perfectly. Award-winning wine list. $22–39.

Teak (732-747-5775; www.teak restaurant.com), 64 Monmouth St. Open daily for lunch and dinner. Reservations are suggested. This one is conveniently close to the **Count Basie Theatre** (see *Entertainment—Theater*), and is a popular stop before or after a performance. The atmosphere is high energy, and the eclectic pan-Asian cuisine is paired with a diverse wine list with many reasonably priced bottles. You can choose to dine among the main dining room, the sushi bar, the Caribbean-style porch, or the intimate and romantic lounge. $15–25.

& ⊙ **Molly Pitcher Inn** (732-747-2500; www.mollypitcher-oysterpoint .com; out of state: 800-221-1372), 88 Riverside Ave. Open for lunch Mon.–Sat.; breakfast and dinner daily; Sun. brunch. Reservations are recommended, and jackets are required at dinner. Creative twists on classic American and Continental dishes in Red Bank's historic waterfront hotel (see *Lodging—Hotels*). The elegant surroundings, replete with crystal chandeliers, white linen, and lovely views of the Navesink River, make this a popular setting for weddings and other special events. Weekends also draw in crowds for the lavish spread at the award-winning Sunday brunch. For a quiet meal, it's best to come during the week. The menu is built largely around fresh fish and shellfish, including lobster-studded chowder and excellent daily seafood specials. End with a decadent house-made dessert. Extensive wine list. $22–30.

Sogno Ristorante (732-747-6969; www.sognoredbank.com), 69 Broad St. Open daily for lunch and dinner. Reservations are recommended. A chic storefront eatery with lofty ceilings and a bustling bistrolike atmosphere sets the stage for innovative takes on upscale Italian cuisine. *Sogno* is Italian for "dream," and those who dine here often say it is a direct reference to the cuisine, such as classic osso buco, or sautéed red snapper in a green sauce with Manila clams. BYOB. $19–29.

In Rumson
David Burke Fromagerie (732-842-8088; www.fromagerie.com), 26 Ridge Rd. Open daily for dinner except Mon.; lunch available on Fri. Reservations are recommended. This charming and elegant eatery featuring contemporary French cuisine is a favorite for fine dining. There are extensive separate lists of hot and cold starters, and dinner features items like pan-seared venison, wild boar, and grilled yellowfin tuna. Stellar wine list. $24–39.

& **Salt Creek Grille** (732-933-9272; www.saltcreekgrille.com), Four Bingham Ave. Open daily for dinner; brunch on Sun. A pretty spot on the Navesink River is the setting for this chic and casual eatery serving innovative New American cuisine. Be prepared to wait for a table. Mission-style Arts and Crafts décor and the fire pit on the outdoor deck are inviting, as is the friendly bar and bustling open kitchen. The menu revolves around the mesquite grill, which turns out burgers, barbecued ribs, fresh seafood, chops, and hand-cut steaks. $15–27.

In Fair Haven
Raven and the Peach (732-747-4666; www.ravenandthepeach.net), 740 River Rd. Open for lunch Mon.–Sat.; dinner daily. Reservations are recommended.

A sophisticated and stylish dining room sets the stage for upscale Continental and American cuisine. Offerings like tempura fried shrimp with Asian vegetables and wasabi crème fraîche to start, followed by seared Angus steak with sake-marinated mushrooms, taro root puree, and sake demi-glace show a penchant for Asian flavors and techniques. Live piano on Fri. and Sat. nights. $26–34.

In Sea Bright
Anjelica's (732-842-2800; www .anjelicas.com), 1070 Ocean Ave. Open for dinner Tues.–Sun.; closed Mon. A popular eatery, the cuisine is classic Italian, from the house-made pasta to the grilled veal, chicken, and seafood. Windows adorned with cheerful flower boxes look out on the busy main thoroughfare through this little speck of a beach town. $15–30.

In Long Branch
Avenue Restaurant (732-759-2900; www.leclubavenue.com), 23 Ocean Ave., Open for lunch: Mon.–Fri., 11–3; dinner Sun.–Thurs., 5:30–11, Fri.–Sat. 5:30–midnight; brunch Sat.–Sun., 11–3:30. A chic and stylish locale serving French-American cuisine in the brasserie style. The emphasis is on seafood, but the menu includes boeuf Bourguignon or even a hamburger. Upstairs, you can dance the night away at Le Club $16–34.

In Asbury Park
& **Moonstruck** (732-988-0123; www .moonstruck.com), 517 Lake Ave. Open for dinner Wed.–Sun.; closed Mon.–Tues. A popular eatery that once resided in Ocean Grove has moved into a 19th-century Asbury Park Victorian with more dining space and a cocktail lounge. The wraparound porches (with tables for warm-weather dining) and bounty of windows boast views of Ocean Grove's Great Auditorium and trademark Victorian architec-

ture, just across Wesley Lake. The candlelit downstairs bar with gleaming mahogany (and signature martinis) has its own light menu; the upstairs dining room has a retro '50s feel, with white linen, potted palms, and soft lighting. American, Mediterranean, and Asian dishes come in well-prepared hearty portions. Live jazz on weekends. $14–28.

Bistro Ole (732-897-0048; www.bistro ole.com), 230 Main St. Open for dinner Tues.–Sun.; closed Mon. Spanish-Portuguese cuisine in a bright and sunny eatery that attracts an eclectic, lively crowd. The tapas menu is enticing. For dinner, paella comes studded either with fish and shellfish or a mix of seafood, chicken, and sausage. Sea bass topped with Spanish pesto sauce and bread crumbs with avocado salsa is a house signature dish. Ask about special events like cabaret night. Outdoor dining in-season. BYOB. $15–24.

In Ocean Grove

Bia (732-775-6100 www.majesticocean grove.com/bia), 19 Main Ave. Open daily for lunch 12–4, light fare 4–5 and dinner 5–10; Sun. brunch 11:30–4. A 60-seat European-style bistro with dining also available on a heated and enclosed side porch, the menu here changes seasonally with offerings like pan-seared Scottish salmon over potato gnocchi, appetizers such as duck crêpes. $18–30.

In Belmar

♿ **Matisse** (732-681-7680; www .matissecatering.com), 1301 Ocean Ave. Open Sept.–May, Wed.–Sat. for dinner and Sun. brunch; open nightly except Tues. in June; nightly July–Aug.; call to confirm hours. Reservations are recommended. Don't let the French name fool you—this stylish oceanfront eatery offers critically acclaimed innovative Continental cuisine. It also regularly racks up glowing

accolades from Zagat and food critics. Dining-room tables are set amid eclectic, neoclassical décor, and outdoor seating boasts ocean views. The creative fusion cuisine blends the exotic seasonings of South Africa and Asia, and changes with the seasons. Desserts change seasonally, as well. Live jazz on Wed. night. BYOB. $20–30.

♿ **Brandl** (732-280-7501; www.brandl restaurant.com), 703 Belmar Plaza, Ninth and Main Sts. Open daily for dinner except Mon. Reservations are recommended. Chef-owner Chris Brandl serves upscale New American cuisine with a flair for dramatic presentation. His stylish brick-storefront eatery is filled with original artwork and boldly hued sleek décor, and a charming courtyard patio complete with waterfall. The seasonal menu is an eclectic blend of seafood and meats flavored with exquisite sauces. Desserts are created by Brandl's on-site pastry chef. Live jazz on Friday night. $26–34.

Casa Solar (732-556-1144), 1104 Main St. Reservations strongly recommended. Open daily for lunch, 11:30–2:30; dinner from 5 PM. Superior Latin food with Asian-, French- and Spanish-inspired influences. An extensive tapas menu complements dishes such as sweet and spicy thai chicken and guava glazed ribs. Locals and regulars avidly recommend this change of pace from the ubiquitous shore seafood. BYOB. Dinner, $19–23; tapas, $9–15.

EATING OUT

In Highlands

🦞 ✑ **Inlet Café** (732-872-9764; www .inletcafe.com), Three Cornwall St. Open Wed.–Sun. in spring and fall; daily for lunch and dinner May–Sept.; call for exact hours. Reservations are suggested. A seafood eatery on the

Navesink River at the entrance to Sandy Hook Bay with reasonable prices and a casual atmosphere that attracts vacationing families. There's a raw bar, lobster specials, and a variety of low-carb entrées that revolve around seafood—fried, broiled, baked, stuffed, and grilled. But, the menu offers a light selection of creative salads and sandwiches. It gets very crowded during the summer. $12–25.

In Red Bank

& **Gaetano's** (732-741-1321; www .gaetanosredbank.com) 10 Wallace St. Open daily for lunch and dinner; Sun. dinner is served all day. A casual and busy eatery serving generous portions of rustic country-style Italian fare such as homemade lobster ravioli in a tomato-basil cream sauce, lamb osso buco, and gourmet pizzas from the brick oven. BYOB and New Jersey wines available. $17–24.

& **Basil T's Brew Pub & Italian Grill** (732-842-5990; www.basilt.com), 183 Riverside Ave. (Rt. 35). Open for lunch and dinner daily; late-night menu served until midnight. A friendly pub serving up authentic Italian cuisine based largely on family recipes, from hearty pastas to signature Neapolitan-style pizzas. Inventive dishes, such as oven-roasted organic chicken with lobster, mushrooms, and sweet potatoes, show the kitchen's creative side. A half-dozen beers are on tap fresh from their microbrewery. Live music on weekends. $30.

 No Joe's Café (732-530-4040; www.nojoescafe.com), 51 Broad St., Red Bank. Open Mon.–Wed. 6:30 AM–5 PM; Thurs.–Fri. 6:30 AM–9 PM; Sat. 7 AM–9 PM; Sun. 8–4, plus brunch. This friendly café is a good place to recharge during a busy day of shopping at Red Bank's stores and galleries. An extensive menu of gourmet coffee and hot and cold coffee drinks is accompa-

nied by freshly baked muffins, scones, and pastries for breakfast. Later on, creative soups, salads, pressed *panini* sandwiches, and wraps take over. A house specialty is chicken potpie soup, a hearty stew-like concoction. $4–11.

In Sea Bright

Ichabod's Bar & Grille (732-842-6154; www.ichabodsbarandgrille.com), One East Church St. Open daily for lunch and dinner. A lively pub with a friendly local crowd and better-than-average tavern fare. The menu runs the gamut from wings and other traditional appetizers to sandwiches, huge burgers, and grilled chicken and steak. Pies and other simple and satisfying desserts. $10–20.

In Long Branch

Charley's Ocean Grill (732-222-4499; www.charleysoceangrill.com), 29 Avenel Blvd. Open daily for lunch and dinner. This convivial spot just steps from the beach offers a cozy bar and an equally relaxed dining room. Most people come for the steaks, chicken, and pasta; but a light café menu features a daily homemade soup as well as burgers and sandwiches. $10–20.

 The WindMill (732-870-6098; www.windmillhotdogs.com), 200 and 586 Ocean Ave. Open daily for lunch and dinner. This chain is a Jersey Shore institution offering "gourmet fast food" at eight locations. If you've never heard someone wax nostalgic about a chili dog, then talk to a regular here. The grilled all-beef dogs are the stuff of legend, and come topped with sauerkraut, chopped onions, or slathered in chili or melted cheese. Other menu favorites are the burgers and cheesesteaks, accompanied by french fries or cheese fries. $4–8.

In Asbury Park

& **Carmines Asbury Park** (732-774-2222; www.carminesnj.com), 162 Main

St. Open for dinner Wed.–Sun. A lively bistro serving a classic Italian fare, it's one of Asbury Park's newer eateries. The brick oven turns out gourmet pizzas. Entrées range from veal *capricciosa* to grilled New York strip steak. $9–37.

In Ocean Grove

Raspberry Café (732-988-0071; www.theraspberrycafe.com), 60 Main Ave. Open for lunch Tues.–Sun.; dinner Fri.–Sat. This shuttered eatery is as quaint as its name suggests. Eclectic gourmet fare includes innovative takes on seafood (tilapia over couscous with coconut curry sauce) and scallops (pan seared over pineapple fried rice). BYOB. $19–24.

Seagrass (732-869-0770; www.seagrassnj.com), 68 Main Ave. Open seven days a week for lunch and dinner. Formerly Captain Jack's the new menu ranges from light salads and appetizers to fresh seafood, steaks, ravioli, and poultry. And, you can get a burger. $16–29.

In Neptune

&. ✑ **Pete & Elda's** (732-774-6010; www.peteneldas.com), 96 Woodland Ave. (Rt. 35). Open daily for lunch, dinner, and late-night meals. Pete & Elda's is famous on the Jersey Shore for their thin-crust pizza with traditional toppings, and for authentic Italian-American cuisine. They'll make you a thick-crust pie, if you wish, but the thin-crust one is what has made them a shoreline institution for nearly 50 years. Homemade Italian dinners make you feel like mom's in the kitchen. Casual and family-friendly. $8–13.

In Bradley Beach

&. ✑ **Vic's Bar and Restaurant** (732-774-8225; www.vicspizza.com), 60 Main St. Open Tues.–Sun. for lunch and dinner; closed Mon. Two words: tomato pies. They're what has made

this old-time Italian eatery a Jersey Shore institution for more than half a century. The winning combination here is a crisp crust topped with homemade tomato sauce. They offer, too, authentic Italian favorites, including eggplant parmigiana, stuffed manicotti, and such. $8–15.

In Avon-By-The-Sea

✿ **Schneider's Restaurant** (732-775-1265; www.schneidersrestaurant.info), 801 Main St. (Rt. 71). Open for lunch and dinner Tues.–Sat.; closed Sun.–Mon. Traditional German and Hungarian fare served in a no-frills casual setting. Hearty classics from the homeland include bratwurst, sauerbraten, wiener schnitzel, Hungarian beef goulash, potato pancakes, and huge sausage platters. Finish with apple and cherry strudel. BYOB. $11–20.

In Belmar

Kaya's Kitchen (732-280-1141; www.kayaskitchennj.com), 817 Belmar Plaza, Belmar. Open for lunch Tues.–Sat., 11:30–2:30; dinner 5–10; Sun. breakfast (Apr.–Oct.), 9–1, and all you can eat vegan buffet dinner 5–9. A small, casual, high-quality vegetarian establishment serving salads, soups, sandwiches, and main dishes with Asian, Indian, Caribbean, Mexican, and Mediterranean influences. $11–19.

&. ✑ **Klein's Fish Market & Waterside Café** (732-681-1177; www.kleinsfish.com), 708 River Rd. Open for lunch and dinner daily; Sun. brunch. Ollie Klein sold fresh seafood out of the back of his truck in Shore communities until 1927, when he opened a fish stand on the Shark River in Belmar. It evolved into today's multifaceted seashore landmark at the original location. Fresh fish is the mantra, whether it's in the casual alfresco dockside café, at the sushi bar, in the relaxed-yet-upscale Grill Room, or in the busy retail market. Boats unload their daily catch right at the dock. Most everything comes with coleslaw, veggies, and rice. A perfect place to end a day at the beach. $11–20.

Chef Ed's Seaside Grill (732-280-0444; www.shoreguide.info/chefeds), 400 Ocean Ave. Has traditionally been open Wed.–Mon. for breakfast, lunch, and dinner; closed Tues., but call to verify hours. A waterfront eatery specializing in vegetarian dishes and seafood with Latin American and Caribbean flair. Try the vegetable frittata for breakfast, grilled portobello sandwich with spinach and roasted-garlic mayo for lunch, or grilled chicken with mango sauce for dinner. The kitchen has a conscience—all vegetable scraps are composted and returned to the restaurant's own organic herb and vegetable garden. $13–22.

♪ **Connolly Station** (732-280-2266; www.connollystation.com) 711 Main St. Open daily 11 AM–2 AM. Named for a Dublin train station and its proximity to the Belmar Train Station, this Irish/railroad themed eatery offers a wide-ranging menu served in four dining areas. Selections run the gamut from steaks, seafood and wraps to corned beef, shepherd's pie and even an extensive sushi bar. Live entertainment. Children's menu. $11–25.

Elsewhere

♪ ᖴ **Mister C's Beach Bistro** (732-531-3665; www.jerseyshorerestaurant.com), Allen Ave. at Ocean Pl., Allenhurst. Open daily from 11:30. Mister C's serves contemporary Continental fare with an Italian emphasis. Dining is done in a tiered bar/lounge offering great beach views through panoramic windows, a warm and welcoming dining room with wood-lined walls, outdoors at the tiki bar, or a large separate bar set in the back. The menu ranges from pastas to filet mignon and

seafood. Children's menu available. $16–28.

SNACKS Old Monmouth Candies (732-462-1311; www.oldmonmouthcandies.com), 47 Broad St., Red Bank. This is a retail branch of the landmark Freehold candy factory that has been making old-fashioned confections since 1910. Their signature delicacy—sweet and crunchy peanut brittle—is still made with the original recipe that calls for fresh Virginia peanuts and other natural ingredients. Cashew brittle, crème-filled chocolates, nut bars, and other nostalgic treats.

♪ **Max's Famous Hot Dogs** (732-571-0248; www.maxshotdogs.com), Ocean Blvd. and Matilda Terrace, Long Branch. Open daily. The Jersey Shore is known for its hot dog institutions, and Max's grilled Schickhaus dogs are the best, according to their faithful regulars. This legendary eatery has enjoyed a run of success since 1928, and counts many a celebrity and politician among its fans (check out the framed and signed photos that line the walls). Grab a stool at the long counter. $4–9.

♪ **New Belmar Marina Coffee Shoppe** (732-681-3282), Belmar Marina, Rt. 35, Belmar. They open at 4 AM for the anglers and commercial fishermen heading in and out of this bustling marina. It's a good place for a hearty breakfast before a day at the beach or out on the water, or to pick up sandwiches and other picnic fixings. Your typical shoreline eatery—casual, reasonably priced, and family-friendly. $5–15.

✱ Entertainment

ARTS CENTERS Monmouth University Performing Arts Series (732-571-3483; www.monmouth.edu/arts), **Pollack Theater,** 400 Cedar

Ave., West Long Branch. Performances are scheduled during the academic year, from Sept. to May. Every year, the schedule runs the gamut from popular concerts and symphony orchestras to dance performances and theater.

✔ **Jersey Shore Arts Center** (732-502-0050; www.jerseyshoreartscenter .org), Main Ave. and Rt. 71, Ocean Grove. A year-round schedule of concerts, drama, and dance performances. Families love the children's performances, festivals, and holiday events.

MUSIC Paramount Theatre and Convention Hall (732-775-3533; www.asburyparkconventionhall.com), 1300 Ocean Ave., Asbury Park. Asbury Park's landmark art deco–style **Paramount Theatre** opened in 1930 with Ginger Rogers and the Marx Brothers on stage. Today the 1,600-seat acoustically superb performance space has

been saved from neglect, and once again resides proudly at the northern end of the boardwalk. It's the site of the annual **Garden State Film Festival** (see *Special Events*) and a full schedule of concerts and performances. It sits directly across the boards from the circa-1923 Convention Hall, designed by the architects whose work includes New York City's Grand Central Station.

Ocean Grove Great Auditorium (732-775-0035; 800-773-0097; www .oceangrove.org), 54 Pittman Ave., Ocean Grove. Open May–Sept. The grand auditorium and its 9,000-pipe Hope-Jones organ is the focal point of this historic resort town (see *To See— Historic Homes and Sites*). Summertime concerts ranging from symphony to doo-wop are held during the week and on Saturday night. Religious services are held on Sunday.

THE OCEAN GROVE CAMP MEETING ASSOCIATION ERECTED TENTS IN THE 1800S FOR FOLLOWERS TO SPEND THE SUMMER. TODAY THERE IS A SIX-YEAR WAITING LIST TO RENT THE HISTORIC STRUCTURES, 114 BEACH COTTAGE–STYLE CANVAS TENTS WITH MODERN AMENITIES CLUSTERED AROUND THE GREAT AUDITORIUM.

Photo courtesy of the Ocean Grove Chamber of Commerce

NIGHTLIFE Ashes Cigar Club (732-219-0710; www.ashescigarclub.com), 33 Broad St., Red Bank. Ashes calls itself a "cigar-lovers paradise," and the sleek walk-in humidor proves they indeed take their cigars seriously. But this hip spot on Red Bank's nighttime scene has something for everyone. Local blues and jazz bands play on Thurs.–Sat. nights; fresh seafood, prime steaks, and a raw bar are on the menu; and chic and sophisticated surroundings satisfy the see-and-be-seen crowd.

Elements (732-842-1100; www.elementslounge.com), 1072 Ocean Ave., Sea Bright. Open for dinner Tues.–Sun.; lounge Sat.–Sun. Much is made of feng shui in this steakhouse cum lounge's design, with each of the five elements—water, wood, fire, metal, and earth—represented in the décor, from the waterfalls and dramatic sculptures to the pervasive flickering candlelight. The young and beautiful have crowded this spot ever since partners Vincenzo Rizzo and Matthew Bongiovi (little brother to rocker Jon Bon Jovi) opened it in 2003. There are personal wine lockers for club members, VIP rooms, and DJ-spun '80s house music, rock, and hip-hop for all.

The Saint (732-775-9144), 601 Main St., Asbury Park. A mix of local acts and nationally known musicians, from Joey Ramone to Jewel, has taken the stage at this Asbury Park institution for more than a decade.

THEATER ♪ **First Avenue Playhouse** (732-291-7552; www.firstavenue playhouse.com), 123 First Ave., Atlantic Highlands. A unique dinner-and-dessert theater—dinner at a local restaurant, dessert at the playhouse—with a full schedule of comedies and dramas. The **Paper Moon Puppet Theatre** mounts shows for children using marionettes and other puppets to dramatize folktales, fables, and classic children's tales.

♪ **Count Basie Theatre** (732-842-9000; www.countbasietheatre.org), 99 Monmouth St., Red Bank. Open year-round. This landmark downtown theater opened in 1926 as the Carlton Theater, a film and vaudeville house. In 1984, the 1,500-seat performance space was restored and renamed in honor of jazz great, band leader, pianist, legendary composer, and Red Bank native (no, he's not from Kansas City) William "Count" Basie. Ballet, modern dance, and family productions as well as jazz, musicals, rock, and classical music performed by the New Jersey Symphony Orchestra.

New Jersey Repertory Company (732-229-3166; www.njrep.org), at the Lumia Theatre, 179 Broadway, Long Branch. The art deco–style **Lumia Theatre** is the setting for New Jersey premieres, classic plays, and world premieres of original works. Staged readings and short plays are presented in the intimate **Dwek Studio Theatre.**

✳ Selective Shopping
ANTIQUES AND ART

In Red Bank
The Antique Center of Red Bank (732-842-3393; www.redbankantiques .com), 195–226 West Front St. Open daily. This multi-dealer antiques showplace is a major focal point in Red Bank. More than 150 dealers occupy three well-preserved vintage factory buildings that produced parachutes during World War I.

Tower Hill Antiques (732-842-5551; www.towerhillantiques.com), 147 Broad St. Porcelain, lighting, furniture.

CEL-EBRATION! (732-842-8489; www.cel-ebration.com), 30 Monmouth St. Open Wed.–Sat., 11–5; closed

THE STONE PONY

(732-502-0600; www.stoneponyonline.com), 913 Ocean Ave., Asbury Park. Concertgoers must be 18 to enter, 21 to drink. Rock fans from around the world make the pilgrimage to this Asbury Park institution, the legendary rock club that was lyricized by Bruce Springsteen and subsequently became New Jersey's most famous rock 'n' roll club. It opened near the ocean on the corner of Second Street and Ocean Avenue in 1974, just when Springsteen was emerging onto the national scene and appearing here regularly with his E Street Band. The club shut its doors for most of the 1990s, then reopened in 2000 with a new state-of-the-art sound and lighting system, a permanent collection of Asbury Park and Stone Pony artifacts and memorabilia, and a full schedule of live music, from local musicians to national acts. Some nights feature live bands and solo artists; other times DJs spin hip-hop, house music, and reggae. In recent years the club has been involved in a variety of community causes, from art and music education in the Asbury Park public schools to throwing benefit concerts to support local charities and individuals in need. And, yes, Springsteen pops in and takes the stage time and again.

Sun.–Tues. Animation, cartoon, and rock- and pop-art gallery. Rare limited-edition prints and original works.

Art Alliance of Monmouth County's Studio Gallery (732-842-9403; www.artallianceofmonmouth.org), 33 Monmouth St. Open Tues.–Sat. noon–4; closed Sun.–Mon. Exhibits and receptions are open to the public.

In West Branch

Monmouth University (732-923-4786; www.monmouth.edu/arts), 400 Cedar Ave. Open Sept.–May. The **800 Gallery** and the **Rotary Ice House Gallery** mount changing exhibits of students', alumni's, and guest artists' work in ceramics, painting, printmaking, sculpture, photography, and other media.

In Belmar

Oceanside Gallery (732-280-2167; www.oceansidegallery.com), 1010 Main St., specializes in fine art by regional and national contemporary artists.

SPECIAL SHOPS

In Red Bank

The Galleria (732-530-7300; www.galleriaredbank.com), Two Bridge Ave. A former turn-of-the-20th-century uniform factory in Red Bank's arts and antiques district has been converted into shops, eateries, entertainment venues, and professional office space. One of the most significant historic landmarks in the downtown arts district.

CoCo Pari (732-212-8111; www.cocopari.com), 17 Broad St. A second location in Deal (732-517-1227), 270 Norwood Ave. (Rt. 71). Open daily. A chic women's boutique full of upscale beauty products, designer shoes, and clothing in an art deco–style town house. On par with the trendiest boutiques in SoHo.

Jay and Silent Bob's Secret Stash (732-758-0508; www.viewaskew.com), 35 Broad St. Open daily. A comic book outlet shop owned by independent film director and New Jersey native Kevin Smith, creator of such cult classics as *Chasing Amy, Clerks,* and *Dogma.* In addition to comics, there's an interesting selection of memorabilia and collectibles from his films.

In Shrewsbury

The Grove at Shrewsbury (732-530-1200; www.thegroveatshrewsbury .com), Rt. 35. Eclectic collection of clothing stores. Open daily. Billed as a "lifestyle center," The Grove combines residences and shopping. There are 34 shops ranging from regional to national retailers selling home furnishings, fashions, accessories, and jewelry.

✳ Special Events

March: **St. Patrick's Day Parade** (732-280-2648; www.belmarparade .com), Belmar. New Jersey's largest St. Paddy's parade, with floats, bagpipers and marching bands, and entertainers. **Garden State Film Festival** (877-908-7050), Paramount Theatre, Asbury Park. Premier of independent films, videos, and animated features from around the world. **Monmouth Festival of the Arts** (732-747-8278; www .monmouthfestivalofthearts.com), Tinton Falls. More than 250 artists and crafters on display.

May: **New Jersey Marathon Weekend at the Jersey Shore** (732-576-1771; www.njmarathon.org), Long Branch and Monmouth Beach.

Summer: **Sandy Hook Summer Beach Concerts** (732-291-7733; www.sandyhookfoundation.org), Sandy Hook Unit of Gateway National Recreation Area, Fort Hancock. Wednesday-evening free concerts on the beach.

June: **New Jersey Seafood Festival** (732-681-3700; 800-523-2587; www .belmar.com), at the oceanfront between Fifth and Sixth Aves., Belmar. Master chefs, artists, craftspeople,

New Jersey wineries, and live music draw close to 100,000 people. One of the top events in North America. ✐ **Red Bank Jazz and Blues Festival** (732-933-1984; www.redbank festival.com), Broad St. and Marine Park, Red Bank. An outdoor music festival with boat excursions on the Navesink River, food, crafts vendors, and children's activities. **Asbury Park Jazz Festival** (732-775-2100; www.city ofasburypark.com), Sunset Lake, Asbury Park. **Two Rivers Antiques Show and Garden Tour** (732-923-6886; www.tworivershow.org), in Rumson, Red Bank, and Fair Haven, benefits Monmouth Medical Center and offers a rare glimpse into some of the area's best private gardens and an antiques show with more than two-dozen dealers.

July: **Statue of Liberty Race** (www .fleet250.org), Atlantic Highlands. Sailors navigate high-tech racing catamarans on a 5-hour competition in New York Harbor and around the Statue of Liberty; sponsored by the Atlantic Highlands Hobie Cat club. ✐ **Oceanfest** (732-222-0400; www .longbranchchamber.org), on the Promenade, Long Branch. Fireworks, food, crafters, and sand-sculpting competitions; stilt walkers, clowns, live music, and other entertainment. ✐ **Independence Day Celebration in Red Bank** (732-530-2748; www .kaboomfireworks.org), with family activities and fireworks. ✐ **New Jersey Sandcastle Contest** (732-863-1900; www.njsandcastle.com), 18th Ave. at the beach, Belmar. For nearly 20 years, sand sculptors and sandcastle builders of all ages have filled Belmar's beaches with unique sand creations. **Summer House Tour** (732-774-1869; www.oceangrovehistory.org), Ocean Grove. The Ocean Grove Historical Society sponsors tours of some of the town's most historic homes.

August: **Haskell Invitational Handicap** (732-571-5548; www.monmouth park.com), Monmouth Park Racetrack, Oceanport. Thoroughbreds race for a million-dollar purse, the richest invitational in North America (see *To Do— Horse Racing*). ✪ **Clamfest** (732-291-4713; www.highlandsnj.com), Highlands. A week-long celebration with seafood, clam shucking, entertainment, rides, and a baby-costume contest. **Atlantic Highlands Historical Society's Arts and Crafts Fair** (732-291-1861; www.atlantichighlands history.org), Veterans' Park, Atlantic Highlands. A summertime fair for more than 30 years.

October: **Fort Hancock Day** (732-872-5970; www.nps.gov/gate), Fort Hancock, Gateway National Recreation Area—Sandy Hook Unit, Highlands. Military and living-history demonstrations at the 1895 fort built to protect and defend New York Harbor.

SPRING LAKE TO BAY HEAD

T he stretch of Jersey Shore between Spring Lake and Bay Head is an interesting mix of historic beach towns that offers everything from old-time gentility to noise and neon. By the late 1800s, fine summer hotels (this was the era before beach towns became year-round resorts), boardinghouses, and elegant Victorian mansions, or "cottages"—as wealthy vacationers preferred to call their lavish summer estates—were being built up and down the coast. Many of these historic buildings have been lovingly restored as charming inns and bed & breakfasts that welcome guests all year long. The late 1800s was also the era of the boardwalk, a destination for beachfront strolling that has transformed over time into today's rollicking amusement centers for which the Jersey Shore is famous.

Spring Lake is a Victorian seaside village with a quiet 2-mile-long boardwalk, stately 19th-century homes, and a charming Main Street lined with more than 60 specialty stores, upscale boutiques, and chic bistros. Resort towns on this part of the Jersey Shore get much of their clientele from Manhattan, and it shows in the level of sophistication and the caliber of restaurants, inns, and shops. *Travel + Leisure* magazine named Spring Lake one of the Top Ten Getaways in America. The town's namesake lake is just what you would expect it to be, a crystal-clean freshwater lake fed by numerous underground springs. The lakeshore is lined with weeping willows and laced with walking paths, making an evening stroll not just a popular pastime but a must for those who wish to savor the beauty and charm of this beach community.

In the early 1800s, the area was still an isolated farming and fishing outpost, home to a few rugged souls who welcomed a small number of summer visitors to an off-the-beaten-path destination. A new rail line that connected the region to the outside world in 1876 changed all that. Wealthy city folk began erecting vacation palaces, and as word spread of the area's beauty, the Spring Lake Beach Improvement Company took over a smattering of tiny settlements and incorporated them into the elegant resort town of Spring Lake. By 1903 there were grand hotels and opulent estates, and this once-undiscovered gem was a new stomping ground for the New York City and Philadelphia high-society scene.

Today's Spring Lake isn't relegated to the rich and famous, much to the delight of visitors who come to the shore with visions of lovely historic inns and gourmet fine dining rather than amusement piers, video arcades, and kitschy souvenir stands. There are fine family-oriented beaches, and the longest noncommercial

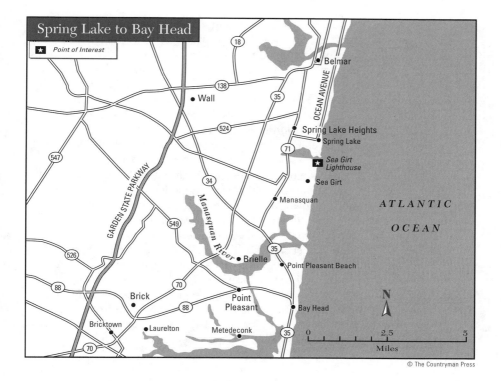

Spring Lake to Bay Head

Point of Interest

© The Countryman Press

boardwalk along the entire Jersey Shore. The Spring Lake Historical Society maintains a small local-history museum in the Victorian-era Borough Hall, and publishes walking-tour guides for the historic downtown and for Divine Park, which surrounds Spring Lake.

Brielle is a quiet residential community tucked away on the Manasquan River, just off the well-trodden tourist path. It stretches along 4 miles of riverfront but lacks an ocean beach, a fact that has staved off the summer crowds and traffic bottlenecks that plague nearby communities. In the 1700s, a small shipbuilding industry thrived along the riverbanks, and today Brielle offers boaters and anglers a few marinas with boat launch facilities and a decent number of party boats and charter fishing boats. The Brielle Yacht Club has a popular dockside seafood restaurant and bar, and the Mississippi-style *River Queen* takes passengers on scenic excursions along the river. In tiny Sea Girt, the slogan is "Where the Cedars Meet the Sea"; the 19th-century resort town boasts an old-time boardwalk, a mile-long beach, and America's oldest live-in lighthouse perched above Manasquan Inlet, the head of the infamous Intracoastal Waterway that continues inland all the way to Florida and Texas.

There was a settlement in Manasquan as early as the 1600s. The Unami Indians (a branch of New Jersey's Lenni-Lenape tribe) who fished and hunted along the Manasquan River and its tributaries for centuries gave it the name *Man-A-Squaw-Han,* meaning "stream of the island squaws." Today it's another of the state's lesser-known shore towns, with a young and lively summer scene, plenty of family activities, and clean, sandy beaches. The beachfront is packed with a string of summer houses, and it's one of the only communities along the shore that still allows group house rentals on a weekly, monthly, or seasonal basis. In surfing circles, Manasquan is known for its waves, and Inlet Beach offers some of the best surfing on the East Coast. Surfers come from around the country to ride the waves at the inlet jetty and compete in surfing competitions during Big Sea Day, the town's summertime festival that attracts hordes of tourists.

Families vacationing with children in tow head to kid-friendly Point Pleasant and Point Pleasant Beach. The latter boasts the area's liveliest boardwalk—especially on Friday and Saturday nights—packed with amusements, a fun house, midway-style games of chance, thrilling rides, live entertainment, food, souvenir shops, mini golf, beach bars, and an aquarium full of sharks, seals, penguins, and other creatures. Free entertainment, from classic-car cruises and fireworks to kiddie shows and concerts, keeps visitors busy all summer long.

Point Pleasant Beach first became a vacation destination in the 1870s, when local retired sea captain John Arnold built a road to the ocean (today's Arnold Avenue) and the first bridge over the Manasquan River to the coast, then lobbied successfully for passenger-train service from Philadelphia to Point Pleasant Beach. Since the first planks were laid in 1915, the boardwalk has evolved from a quaint beachfront walkway with a merry-go-round to a lively amusement park. In the 1920s, Orlo Jenkinson built his namesake pavilion, the precursor to today's amusement pier.

Point Pleasant Beach is the self-proclaimed state seafood capital, home to one of New Jersey's three commercial fishing fleets for generations. Many boats are owned by descendants of the region's earliest settlers, who fished these waters long before the first tourists arrived. They share space in Manasquan Inlet with a menagerie of sportfishing boats and recreational craft that ply in and out of the inlet on their way to the open waters of the Atlantic Ocean. Every September, the

SPRING LAKE'S STATELY VICTORIANS AND GRAND HOTELS ARE LASTING REMINDERS OF ITS 19TH-CENTURY AFFLUENCE. TODAY'S VISITORS COME FOR THE BOARDWALK, SAND DUNE BEACHES, AND CHARMING B&BS.

Festival of the Sea marks the end of the summer season in the Point Pleasant area.

The quaint and upscale 19th-century seashore village of Bay Head stands in stark contrast to the boisterous amusement scene in Point Pleasant Beach. The Bay Head Yacht Club, gourmet restaurants, art galleries, and elegant bed & breakfasts all lend a touch of polish to this classy-yet-casual beach town. Streets are lined with meticulously restored shingle-style Victorian houses, and regulations on development have kept the 2 miles of beachfront nicely preserved and relatively uncrowded, even in the height of summer. Bay Head is perched on a half-mile-wide spit of land that stretches between the Atlantic Ocean to the east and Barnegat Bay to the west. In the mid-1800s, this area was a patchwork of farmland, forest, and cranberry bogs. By the turn of the 20th century, a rail line from New York City was in place, and Bay Head blossomed into a tony summer resort favored by prosperous Manhattan industrialists and bankers. Today it's the last stop on New Jersey Transit's North Jersey Coast Line, and families, couples, and weekenders take full advantage of it.

Today that old air of exclusivity remains; Bay Head often draws comparisons to Martha's Vineyard, New England's famous enclave of the rich and famous. Its main draws are the ocean and the beach—there are no amusements, no boardwalk crowds, and no boisterous groups of people on the sand. Visitors looking for a party town are advised to go elsewhere. Along the ocean, East Avenue is popular with early-morning joggers, cyclists, and in-line skaters. Waterfront homes sit cheek by jowl, a mix of traditional cedar-shake beach cottages and newly built palatial multimillion-dollar homes squeezed into tiny beachfront lots. The year-round population of just over 1,000 swells to 20,000 during the summer, but much of Bay Head still closes down between October and May.

Entries in this section are arranged in roughly geographic order, from north to south.

AREA CODE 732.

GUIDANCE Greater Spring Lake Chamber of Commerce (732-449-0577; www.springlake.org), 1218 Third Ave., Spring Lake. The office is open in summer Mon.–Sun., 10–5 and stocked with general visitor information on Spring Lake; they also keep tabs on lodging availability in the town's bed & breakfasts. They will send a free map and vacation guide, on request. Their Web site contains lots of useful information on lodging, restaurants, shops, and activities.

Point Pleasant Beach Chamber of Commerce (732-899-2424; 888-772-3862; www.pointpleasantbeachnj.com), 517-A Arnold Ave., Point Pleasant Beach. The chamber's Web site is full of good information for visitors, including an events calendar and information on lodging, restaurants and bars, shopping, boating, and fishing.

Point Pleasant Chamber of Commerce (732-295-8850; www.pointpleasant online.com), 2808 Bridge Ave., Point Pleasant. They have brochures and information on local businesses and an online visitor's guide that covers Point Pleasant and the surrounding area.

The Bay Head Business Association (800-422-4323; www.bayhead.org), P.O. Box 135, Bay Head 08742. Write for information, or click on their Web site for tips on attractions, lodging, restaurants, and shopping.

THOUSANDS OF SPECTATORS FLOCK TO POINT PLEASANT BEACH EVERY SUMMER AS THE NEW JERSEY OFFSHORE POWERBOAT RACING ASSOCIATION HOSTS HIGH-SPEED BOAT RACES JUST OFF THE COAST.

GETTING THERE *By air:* Newark Liberty International Airport (973-961-6000; parking information: 888-397-4636; www.panynj.com) in Newark serves the entire state. Those traveling to New Jersey also use John F. Kennedy International Airport (718-244-4168; www.kennedyairport.com) and LaGuardia International Airport (718-533-3850; www.laguardiaairport.com) in New York City. Atlantic City International Airport (609-645-7895; www.acairport.com), Exit 9 off the Atlantic City Expressway, Egg Harbor Township, is served by Spirit Airlines (800-772-7117; www.spiritair.com).

By rail: New Jersey Transit's North Coast Line (973-275-5555; www.njtransit.com) offers express commuter service connecting Penn Station in New York City (via Newark's Penn Station) and shore points including Spring Lake, Manasquan, Point Pleasant, and the end of the line in Bay Head. The stops are within walking distance of most beaches.

By bus: **New Jersey Transit** (973-275-5555; www.njtransit.com) links the region to New York City, Atlantic City, and Philadelphia. **Academy Bus Service** (800-442-7272; www.academybus.com) busses connect the area to Port Authority terminal in New York City, with stops in Monmouth and Ocean counties, along Rt. 35 and Rt. 36, at the PNC Arts Center, from Toms River and Jackson Township and along the Garden State Parkway.

By car: The Garden State Parkway connects the New York and Washington, DC, regions to the Jersey Shore; from Philadelphia and Trenton, **I-195** east leads toward the coast, from which Rt. 138 continues directly to Belmar. Rt. 70 is a major secondary road that cuts east across New Jersey from the Camden area, ending just west of **Point Pleasant Beach.**

1414) and **Belmar Car Service** (732-449-2400) serve the region.

Water taxis: **Manasquan Water Taxi** (732-528-9248; www.manasquanwatertaxi
.com) is a boat taxi that provides transportation on the Manasquan River to various
restaurants, bars, and clubs in Point Pleasant, Point Pleasant Beach, and Brielle.
You can pick up the taxi at any of the waterfront establishments it serves (check
the Web site for a list). Special excursions include sightseeing cruises, fall hayrides,
and nature trips.

MEDICAL EMERGENCY **Ocean Medical Center** (732-840-2200; www.ocean
medicalcenter.com), 425 Jack Martin Blvd., Brick. The emergency number is 732-
840-3380.

✳ To See

AQUARIUM 𝄞 **Jenkinson's Aquarium** (732-899-1212; www.jenkinsons.com/
aquarium), 300 Ocean Ave., Point Pleasant Beach. Open year-round, Mon.–Fri.
9:30–5; Sat.–Sun. 10–5; closed major holidays. Adults, $10; seniors and children
3–12, $6; children 2 and under, free. An aquarium on the boardwalk with a bevy of
ocean creatures and thoughtful exhibits devoted to marine life and conservation.
The aquarium is open long after the amusements shut down for the season, making it a popular stop among parents traveling to the shore with children when summer is over. The touch tank is a pleaser with young visitors, who can feel all
manner of ocean critters, even a juvenile shark. For a real treat, stick around for
feeding time (ask about the schedule, which features specific times for each
species), when sharks, seals, alligators, and penguins get themselves into a frenzy.

HISTORIC HOUSE **Bailey-Reed
House** (732-223-6770), 105 South St.,
Manasquan. Open on the second Sunday of the month, 1–4, and by appointment. Admission by donation. The
Squan Village Historical Society
maintains this extensively restored
18th- and 19th-century home, one of
the oldest in southern Monmouth
County. Today it's an inviting small
museum and repository of local history. Rooms are furnished just as they
would have been in the mid- to late
1800s. The kitchen—the only original
remaining section of the house—
reflects domestic life in the 1700s.
Guided house tours and changing historical displays.

JENKINSON'S AQUARIUM ON THE
BOARDWALK IN POINT PLEASANT BEACH
IS A YEAR-ROUND ATTRACTION THAT'S
HOME TO SEALS, PENGUINS, SHARKS,
ALLIGATORS, REPTILES, AND OTHER
CREATURES.

Photo courtesy of Jenkinson's Aquarium

LIGHTHOUSE Sea Girt Lighthouse (732-974-0514; www.seagirtboro.com), Ocean Ave. and Beacon Blvd., Sea Girt. Guided tours Apr.–Nov., Sun. 2–4. At first glance, this handsome Victorian appears to be just that, another beautifully restored 19th-century house on the shore. A closer inspection reveals the two-story redbrick tower, the lantern and Fresnel lens, and the small sign welcoming you to the Sea Girt Lighthouse. This was America's last live-in lighthouse, a rarely seen departure from the traditional setup with a freestanding tower and separate keeper's house. The **Squan Inlet Light Station** was built in response to mariners' concerns over the 45-mile "blind spot" on the New Jersey coast between Barnegat Light to the south and the Twin Lights of Navesink to the north. Manasquan Inlet, known then as Squan Inlet, was a popular safe haven for boats traveling along New Jersey's long, unbroken shoreline, which made Sea Girt a perfect lighthouse location. With $20,000 in government funds, the land was purchased and the light station built. When its kerosene lamp was first lit on December 10, 1896, it could be seen from 16 miles out to sea. In 1921, the lighthouse was equipped with the first-ever radio fog beacon, at the time a revolutionary means of navigation. During World War II, the light was temporarily extinguished, and the building served as headquarters for the U.S. Coast Guard. It was active until 1955 and left empty until the **Sea Girt Lighthouse Citizens Committee** rallied together in 1981 to preserve it. The restored keeper's quarters are filled with period furnishings, artifacts, and vintage photographs.

MUSEUMS Historical Society Museum (732-449-0772; www.springlake.org), top floor of Borough Hall, Fifth and Warren Aves., Spring Lake. Open Sun. 1:30–3:30 and Thurs. 10–noon. Free admission. An elaborate former Masonic meeting room in Spring Lake's Victorian-era Borough Hall is home to a small local-history museum, run by the **Spring Lake Historical Society.** Collections include memorabilia, artifacts, and vintage photographs from Lenni-Lenape times to the present, all displayed in permanent and changing exhibits. The society publishes guides for two historic walking tours, one of downtown and another of Divine Park, which surrounds Spring Lake.

Militia Museum of New Jersey (732-974-5966; www.elktwp.org/military/museum), National Guard Training Center, Sea Girt Ave., Sea Girt. Summer season, open Mon.–Fri., 10–3 and the first and second weekends of the month, 10–3. Free admission. A small museum devoted to preserving New Jersey's military heritage through memorabilia and artifacts from the state's national guard units and militia units. Exhibits and displays have a special focus on the state's Naval Militia, Air National Guard, and Army National Guard.

Point Pleasant Historical Society Museum (732-892-3091), Point Pleasant Beach Borough Hall, 416 New Jersey Ave., Point Pleasant Beach. Open on the second Thurs. of the month 1–4, and by appointment. Free admission. A small but interesting collection of local artifacts and memorabilia mostly donated by area residents.

Bay Head Historical Society Museum (732-892-0223; www.bayhead.org/community), Bridge and Bay Aves., Bay Head. Open May–Oct., Sun., noon–2. The historic **Loveland House** doubles as the headquarters of the Bay Head Historical Society and a repository of local history. Memorabilia, photos, paintings, furniture, tools, and other artifacts collected from homes in Point Pleasant, Bay Head, and Mantoloking.

AMUSEMENT PARK 🖉 **Jenkinson's Pavilion and Amusement Park** (732-892-0600; www.jenkinsons.com), 300 Ocean Ave., Point Pleasant Beach. Open daily mid-June–Labor Day; weekends Easter–mid-June and Labor Day–Oct. An old-time family amusement park on the boardwalk—full of fun and thrills for all ages. There are 27 carnival rides and 13 kiddie rides, four video arcades, midway-style games of chance, bumper cars, mini golf, and beach volleyball. The aquarium is home to creatures from around the globe (see *To See—Aquarium*), and the food court offers everything from hot dogs and pizza to sushi. **Jenkinson's Sweet Shop** sells old-fashioned confections—candy apples, fudge, caramels, and such—in a quaint Victorian-style shop. Free weekly events in-season include live concerts and volleyball tournaments on the beach. **Jenk's Nightclub** is open until the wee hours.

BIRDING Manasquan Inlet (732-892-1118), at the north end of Ocean Ave., Point Pleasant Beach. The best times to visit this popular birding location are spring, fall, and winter, both for the prime bird activity and the absence of summer crowds. From the beach and the rock jetty at the southern tip of the inlet, you might spot rare species like snowy owls, harlequin ducks, loons, and Atlantic puffins, as well as a variety of gulls that like to congregate in the calm waters off the jetty.

BOAT EXCURSIONS (See also *Boating.*)

Manasquan Water Taxi (732-292-1159; www.manasquanwatertaxi.com), Brielle Yacht Club, Union Ln., Brielle. In addition to the popular water taxi service to local restaurants and bars (see *Getting Around*), they offer a variety of seasonal special excursions, such as afternoon lunch and sightseeing tours or ecology trips to **Treasure Island,** a pristine natural island in the Manasquan River that offers swimming, hiking, and fishing. **Fireworks cruises** depart on select summer evenings, and **Halloween "hayrides"** take place in Sept. and Oct.

> **THE *RIVER BELLE* AND THE *RIVER QUEEN***
> (732-528-6620; 732-892-3377; www.riverboattour.com), Broadway Basin, 47 Broadway, Point Pleasant Beach. Some weekends between Mother's Day and July. Daily sails July–Labor Day; reservations are recommended. Both boats are available for private charters mid-Apr.–Dec. For a memorable experience, hop on one of these replicas of authentic old-time Mississippi paddleboats as it drifts peacefully through the calm, quiet waters of Barnegat Bay, the Point Pleasant Canal, and the Manasquan and Metede-conk rivers. There's a variety of trips to choose from, including narrated sightseeing excursions; lunch, dinner, and dance cruises; murder-mystery trips; and seasonal trips on Mother's Day, Fourth of July (fireworks trips), and New Year's Eve. The *River Queen* sails out of Bogan's Basin, 800 Ashley Ave., in Brielle; the *River Belle* is based at Broadway Basin, 47 Broadway, Point Pleasant Beach.

Liberté **Cruise & Dine** (732-892-8894), Johnson Brothers Boat Works, 1800 Bay Ave., P.O. Box 117, Bay Head 08742. Reservations are required. Private cruises on Barnegat Bay aboard an elegantly restored 1957 56-foot wooden Chris-Craft. Parties of six can charter the boat for cocktail parties, overnight cruises to **Long Beach Island,** or private dinners featuring gourmet French and Continental cuisine. BYOB; inquire about rates.

BOATING (See also *Boat Excursions.*)

Dozens of full-service marinas occupy the shoreline between Spring Lake and Bay Head. They offer a range of marine services—repair, rentals, fuel, and boat slips— and many offer sportfishing and sightseeing excursions. Marinas in *Point Pleasant* include **Clark's Landing Marina** (732-899-5559; www.yachtworld.com/clarks landing), 847 Arnold Ave., and **Arnold's Yacht Basin** (732-892-3000; www.jersey marinas.com/clarkslanding), 1671 Beaver Dam Rd. *Point Pleasant Beach* marinas include **Southside Marina** (732-892-0388), 311 Channel Dr.; **Johnson Brothers Boat Works** (732-892-9000), 1800 Bay Ave.; and **Garden State Marina** (732-892-4222; www.yachtworld.com/gardenstateyachts), 101 Rt. 35. Others in the area include **Baywood Marina** (732-477-3322), 63 Pilot Dr., Brick; **Comstock Boat Works** (732-899-2500), 704 Princeton Ave., Brick; and **Strictly Marine** (732-223-4277), 381 Brielle Rd., Manasquan.

FISHING Charter boats and party (open) fishing boats run out of this region's marinas all year long. During the day, they go for flounder, porgies, sea bass, ling, and other species. Nighttime trips are a quest for tuna, bluefish, bonito, and albacore. *In Brielle,* sportfishing is available out of **Brielle Marine Basin** (732-528-6200), 608 Green Ave.; **Brielle Yacht Club Marina** (732-528-6250), 201 Union Ln.; **Hoffman's Marina** (732-528-6160), 602 Green Ave.; and **Bogan's Basin Deep Sea Fishing Marina** (732-528-5014), 800 Ashley Ave. *In Point Pleasant Beach,* **Broadway Basin** (732-892-4298), 47 Broadway, is home to numerous charter boats, as well as the *Dauntless,* an 85-foot party fishing boat. **Ken's Landing Marina** (732-892-9787; www.kenslanding.net), 35 Broadway, is home to the *Norma K III* (732-899-8868), *Norma K II,* and *Miss Point Pleasant,* party boats that go out year-round. The *Queen Mary* offers daily open trips from mid-April to Nov. from **Spikes Fishery** (732-899-3766), Broadway and Channel Dr.

GOLF ☙ **Ocean County Golf Course at Forge Pond** (732-920-8899; www .ocean.nj.us/parks/golf), 301 Chambers Bridge Rd., Brick. An 18-hole par-60 course in a scenic 300-acre conservation area, maintained by the Ocean County Parks and Recreation Department. It's an ideal course for beginners and experienced golfers, and rates are reasonable.

PARASAILING **Point Pleasant Parasail** (732-714-2359; www.pointpleasant parasail.org), Ken's Landing Marina, 35 Broadway, Point Pleasant Beach. Reservations are required. Single and tandem trips let passengers float 500 feet above the water. This company caters to all ages, including nervous first-timers and seasoned parasailers. The entire trip is about an hour, with everyone in the boat (usually six people) getting a turn in the air.

speedway.com), 1803 Rt. 34, Wall. Open Apr.–Nov. New Jersey's only remaining asphalt speedway hosts a NASCAR weekly racing series for stock cars, and smaller tracks for go-cart and small-car racing.

SURFING *In Spring Lake,* surfing in the summer months is generally confined to the Monmouth Ave. and Remsen Ave. beaches. *In Manasquan,* **Inlet Beach** (732-223-2514) is considered one of the best surfing beaches on the east coast. Surfers come from around the country to ride waves at the inlet and participate in the many surfing competitions that are held here, including the summertime surf contest in Manasquan's annual **Big Sea Day** (see *Special Events*). Surfers can go to Point Pleasant beaches in the off-hours, but most of them just head to Manasquan, where conditions are unmatched anywhere in the area.

Surf shops include **3rd Avenue Surf Shop** (732-223-7433; www.3rdavesurf.com), 1206 Third Ave., Spring Lake; **Inlet-Outlet Surf Shop** (732-223-5842), 146 Main St., Manasquan; and in Point Pleasant, **Baja East Surf Shop** (732-892-9400), 2600 Bridge Ave.; **Beach House Classic Board Shop** (732-714-8566), 517 Main Ave.; and **Brave New World Surf & Ski** (732-899-8220), 1208 Richmond Ave. South.

✳ Green Space

BEACHES

Beaches are listed from north to south.
Spring Lake (732-449-8005). Its innovative and environmentally friendly boardwalk—the Jersey Shore's longest noncommercial boardwalk—is made from recycled plastic. Spring Lake's 2 miles of family-oriented beaches are relatively quiet and peaceful during the week but fill up on weekends. Activities include rafting, fishing, scuba diving, and surfing. Day pass $7.

Sea Girt (732-449-9433). A mile-long stretch of white-sand beach is popular with anglers, surfers, and sunbathers. At one end of the boardwalk is the historic **Sea Girt Lighthouse** (see *To See—Lighthouse*); from there it follows the ocean to the south end of town. Picnicking, tennis, and other activities. Day $6.

&. **Manasquan** (732-223-1221). The beaches in Manasquan—from Sea Girt to the Manasquan Inlet—are named for the streets that you take to get to them. Manasquan's **Inlet Beach** has some of the best surfing waves on the east coast. There are designated areas for surfing as well as swimming, fishing, volleyball, and rafting. This is the only community on the Jersey Shore that has a beach dedicated to handicapped access, including parking, chairs, and an easily accessible beach platform. Day $6. Badges are sold at the beach office at Main St. Beach.

Point Pleasant (732-295-8850). Not to be confused with bustling and crowded Point Pleasant Beach on the ocean side. This one fronts the Manasquan River, and offers quiet, clean beaches and gentle water that is ideal for families with small children. There's a picnic area, playground, and fishing pier. Inquire about seasonal and daily badges; children are admitted free.

Point Pleasant Beach (732-899-2424). The beach is dominated by the famous boardwalk—lined chockablock with restaurants, shops, entertainment, and amuse-

THE WHITE SAND BEACH OFF OF JENKINSON'S BOARDWALK IN POINT PLEASANT BEACH IS ESPECIALLY POPULAR WITH FAMILIES.

ment rides—but there's also picnicking, surfing, scuba diving, and other pursuits off the boards. Point Pleasant Beach has a series of private beaches—including a popular one at **Jenkinson's Boardwalk**—that charge their own fees. Jenkinson's charge is $6.50 weekdays, $7.50 weekends.

Bay Head (732-892-0636; beach phone after May 15, 732-892-4179). There isn't much parking, so come early on summer weekends to avoid disappointment. There are no public restrooms or changing stations, so the beaches here are refreshingly clean and relatively quiet. Beach passes are sold by the Bay Head Improvement Association (Lake Ave. and Mount St.). Day $5.

NATURAL AREA Fisherman's Cove Conservation Area (732-922-3868), Third Ave., Manasquan. A 52-acre natural area consisting of beach, dunes, fields, woodland, and salt marsh along Manasquan Inlet. It's the last undeveloped tract of land along the inlet, and a haven for walkers and anglers as well as an active population of native and migratory gulls and waterfowl. An activity center offers a variety of nature programs.

✳ Lodging

RESORTS ⅃ "ṭ" ∞ **The Breakers on the Ocean** (732-449-7700; www.breakershotel.com), 1507 Ocean Ave., Spring Lake 07762. Open year-round. This is Spring Lake's only full-service oceanfront hotel, a hard-to-miss grand white building with a rambling wrap-around porch residing over the

Atlantic. The Breakers was built in 1905 and retains some of its charming Old World touches like cut-glass chandeliers and granite floors. It's a lovely spot across from the beach and boardwalk, and a popular venue for weddings (you'll likely see a wedding if you're here on a weekend). As in many historic seaside hotels, standard rooms here are on the small side. Opt for one of the suites if you need space; plus they come with a fireplace and a whirlpool bath. The 72 guest rooms and suites offer a variety of amenities that may include one or more of the following: king beds, fireplaces, whirlpool tubs, in-room ethernet-cabled Internet access (Wi-Fi in common areas), VCRs/DVDs, or ocean views. Guests congregate on the private beach, around the pool, and in the lounge. The elegant restaurant, with ocean views, serves exceptional Italian cuisine and fresh seafood (see *Dining Out*). $100–435.

🍴 ♿ ¶ **White Sands Oceanfront Resort and Spa** (732-899-3370; 888-558-8958; www.thewhitesands.com), 1205 Ocean Ave., Point Pleasant Beach 08742. Open all year. A beachfront resort with 130 guest rooms offering a range of standard and luxe amenities, including in-room ethernet-cabled Internet access (Wi-Fi in common areas), and a full-service spa and salon. The fitness center comes with a Jacuzzi tub, sauna, and steam room, and a variety of classes from aerobics and tai chi to yoga. Relax or do laps in one of the three indoor and outdoor pools. **Spano's Ristorante Italiano** serves steaks and Italian cuisine. There's live entertainment, planned summertime activities for children, and a private beach that's small but clean and uncrowded. $150–525.

HOTELS

In Spring Lake 07762
∞ **The Grand Victorian Hotel** (732-449-5327; www.grandvictorian springlake.com), 1505 Ocean Ave. Open all year. This is Spring Lake's only oceanfront Victorian hotel, making it a sought-after backdrop for weddings. It's on the beach and boardwalk, and a short walk to downtown shops.

There are 13 guest rooms, all with private bath, TV, and air-conditioning. Some can accommodate a family of four; others have an ocean view. Guests can relax on the wraparound porch. A restaurant serves breakfast, lunch, and dinner. Complimentary beach badges. $85–325.

¶ **Hewitt Wellington Hotel** (732-974-1212; www.thehewittwellington .com), 200 Monmouth Ave. Open year-round. Wealthy vacationers flocked to this grand Victorian-style inn at the turn of the 20th century for its lake-front location and views of the ocean. Recently closed for major renovations, it has been upgraded with modern amenities but has retained many of its original features and architectural details. Standard rooms and spacious suites have private baths, TVs/VCRs, mini-refrigerators, wireless Internet access, and phones with data ports. There's an outdoor pool, and complimentary badges to take to the beach. **Whispers** is the hotel's seasonal restaurant serving upscale contemporary American fare. $109–329.

In Bay Head 08742
♿ **Grenville Hotel** (732-892-3100; www.thegrenville.com), 345 Main Ave. Open all year. This elegant Queen Anne–style hotel overlooking the Atlantic Ocean—its fanciful pink and blue exterior is hard to miss—has been a shoreline landmark since 1890. The 29 guest rooms and suites were newly decorated in 2004 (coinciding with a change in hotel ownership) and are accessible by elevator. Guests can relax on the rambling wraparound porches or in the cozy common areas or head to the beach, which is an easy walk from the hotel. The award-winning on-site four-star restaurant tends to get higher marks than the rooms, and attracts many diners from outside the hotel. It's open daily in July and Aug. for lunch, dinner, and Sun. brunch. $109–299.

In Spring Lake 07762

&. *¶* **Chateau Inn and Suites** (732-974-2000; 877-974-5253; www.chateau inn.com), 500 Warren Ave. Open all year. This award-winning romantic inn is widely considered one of the best in the state. It has taken in travelers since 1888, and resides in a lovely nook tucked between two parks and overlooking the lake. The Smith family has run the historic inn for the past 50 years; today they offer 37 individually decorated guest rooms and one-bedroom suites, all recently redone and outfitted with marble bathrooms, two phones with voice mail, TVs/VCRs, Internet access, refrigerators, and airconditioning. Luxurious upgrades like soaking tubs for two, wood-burning fireplaces, and balconies are worth the extra splurge. Continental breakfast. $79–299.

✐ *¶* **Spring Lake Inn** (732-449-2010; www.springlakeinn.com), 104 Salem Ave. This year-round 19th-century Victorian inn a block from the beach was formerly the Spring Lake Hotel. The 16 spacious guest rooms and two suites all have private baths and air-conditioning, Wi-Fi, and might include a fireplace, sitting area, digital TV, or view of the ocean. The beach, boardwalk, and downtown shopping district are all close by, but the rambling rocker-filled porch—not to mention the relaxed and friendly atmosphere—keeps many guests from going anywhere. The inn welcomes children. A full breakfast is served in the elegant Victorian dining room. $99–499.

White Lilac Inn (732-449-0211; www.whitelilac.com), 414 Central Ave. Open year-round. A circa-1880 Victorian in a quiet Spring Lake neighborhood filled with historic homes. The triple-tiered porches give the inn an unusual and distinctive Southern flair, a dramatic statement in an area so defined by its classic Victorian architecture. The 10 uniquely themed guest rooms and suites all have private baths, TVs, air-conditioning, fireplaces, and Victorian country-style furnishings; some have whirlpool tubs, sitting rooms, and private porches or balconies. Complimentary bicycles and beach passes. Full breakfast is served in the garden room or on the enclosed porch. $179–359.

¶ **The Ocean House** (732-449-9090; www.theoceanhouse.net), 102 Sussex Ave. Open all year. This was one of the Jersey Shore's grandest resort hotels when it opened in 1878. There are 16 recently renovated guest rooms and four suites furnished in tasteful antiques and stylish fabrics, all with private bath, TV, Wi-Fi, and air-conditioning. Innkeepers Nancy and Dennis Kaloostian will provide you with the gear you'll need for a day at the beach (which is just across the street), including towels, umbrellas, and chairs. You can also take one of their bikes for a spin through town. Full breakfast. $100–375.

Elsewhere

Beacon House (732-449-5835; www.beaconhouseinn.com), 100 and 104 Beacon Blvd., Sea Girt 08750. Open year-round. An 1879 Victorian one block from the Atlantic Ocean. The inn is actually two adjacent guest houses, each with a rocker-filled wraparound porch. The 17 individually decorated guest rooms are bright, airy, and country-comfortable, furnished in white wicker and chintz, perhaps with a fireplace or a Jacuzzi tub—or both. Crystal chandeliers and other elegant touches lend an air of formality to the common areas, but they are still inviting places to unwind. A cottage and two studios offer more privacy and include a continental breakfast delivered to the doorstep every morning. Full breakfast is served in the dining room overlooking the pool and cabana. Complimentary beach passes. $165–385.

Inn on Main (732-528-0809; www .innonmainmanasquan.com), 152 Main St., Manasquan 08736. Open year-round. An upscale-yet-cozy country inn with the sleek style of a boutique hotel. Guest rooms are tastefully decorated in luxurious fabrics and furnishings; all have private baths and fireplaces, some have four-poster beds and balconies. The kitchen is open to guests around the clock for breakfast, afternoon tea, and late-night snacks. **Algernon's** is the inn's sophisticated dining room, which serves eclectic gourmet cuisine. $129–269.

BED & BREAKFASTS

In Spring Lake 07762

"♦" **Ashling Cottage** (732-449-3553; 888-274-5464; www.ashlingcottage .com), 106 Sussex Ave. Open Feb.– mid-Dec. Innkeepers Linda and Peter Foy welcome guests to their charming and elegant 1877 inn, a cozy and romantic retreat as well as an architectural gem. The inn has received kudos from *Travel + Leisure* magazine, which praised it for setting a standard in a town full of lovely places to spend the night. There are 11 guest rooms, all tastefully decorated in casual but elegant beach-inspired décor. Some rooms have a fireplace, and all but two have a private bath; all have Wi-Fi. If you like extra space, request one of the deluxe rooms, which are especially large, light, and airy. There are also two cottages with full kitchens; one sleeps three, the other four. Guests can take the inn's bikes for a spin, make use of the complimentary beach and

health club passes, or kick back on the white-wicker-filled porch. The Foys provide beverages and snacks, and a full breakfast served on the glass-enclosed porch. $105–285.

✔ **Normandy Inn** (732-449-7172; 800-449-1888; www.normandyinn .com), 21 Tuttle Ave. Open year-round. Mark and Christine Valari run this magnificently restored Italianate-style inn listed on the National Register of Historic Places. It was built for an illustrious Philadelphia family in 1888 as a summertime beach villa; today many of the original Queen Anne touches remain, yet the atmosphere is relaxed and casual. Guest rooms and common areas feature period antiques and reproduction Victorian-era wallpaper. There are 16 guest rooms and two suites, all with private bath, phone, and air-conditioning. A half block from the beach and close to the center of town. Full breakfast. $105–429.

"♦" **Victoria House Bed & Breakfast** (732-974-1882; 888-249-6252; www.victoriahouse.net), 214 Monmouth Ave. Open all year. Innkeepers Lynne and Alan Kaplan run this highly acclaimed B&B in a graceful 1882 Queen Anne–style waterside mansion. It's full of Old World charm, from the rambling porch out front to the antiques-filled rooms inside. The six guest rooms and two suites are nicely furnished with vintage pieces and country quilts. All have a private bath, Wi-Fi, TV/VCR, and air-conditioning; some have a fireplace, refrigerator, or Jacuzzi tub. Afternoon tea and refreshments and evening cordials are complimentary, as are bikes, health club passes, and beach badges, chairs, and towels. A full gourmet breakfast featuring home-baked goods and specialty dishes is served by candlelight. $199–399.

In Sea Girt 08750

Beacon House Inn (732-449-5835; www.beaconhouseinn.com), 100 and 104 Beacon Blvd. Open all year. A pair of carefully restored 19th-century Victorians near the ocean are reminiscent of the opulent Victorian age, from the antiques-filled formal parlors to the ornate crystal chandeliers and gleaming oak floors. Choose from a variety of accommodations to suit the space and privacy you require. The 17 guest rooms, suite, and three efficiencies all have air-conditioning, TV, and private bath; many have a fireplace. Guests are welcome to the in-ground pool and the lovely flower-filled verandas. Full breakfast. $100–325.

In Bay Head 08742

Bay Head Harbor Inn (732-899-0767; 800-899-7016; www.bayhead.biz/harborinn.htm), 676 Main Ave. Open May–Oct. An 1890s home a block from the beach has been a peaceful and relaxing retreat for the past 15 years. The décor is best described as country-casual, the kind of homey and pleasant place that makes you feel as if you're staying at a friend's beach house. Guest rooms and common areas are inviting and comfortable. Four guest rooms have porches; second-floor guest rooms have ceiling fans; and rooms on the third floor have air-conditioning. Bathrooms are shared, but most rooms have pedestal sinks. Full breakfast. $99–165.

Bay Head Sands (732-899-7016; www.bayheadsands.com), Two Twilight Rd. Open year-round. Hosts Mary and Ken Glass run a charming B&B in one of Bay Head's ubiquitous weathered shingle-style beach houses. This one was built in 1910 and boasts lovely stained-glass windows and other original features. Seven antiques-filled guest rooms have private baths and

views of either the ocean or Twilight Lake. Each is uniquely decorated with lots of bright pastels and floral prints; beds are topped with cozy quilts. A full breakfast is served by candlelight. $245.

The Bentley Inn (732-892-9589; 866-423-6853; www.bentleyinn.com), 694 Main Ave. (Rt. 35). Open all year. A 19th-century Queen Anne–style Victorian mansion with double porches near the beach and on Bay Head's main thoroughfare. Rooms are bright and cheerful, with walls painted in beachy pastels. Of the 20 guest rooms, some have a private bath; others share a bath or can be combined into a two-room suite. Some rooms have direct access to the porches. Common areas include the dining room, solarium, and living room, which is well-stocked with VCR and board games. Bikes, beach badges, towels, and chairs are complimentary—you can even take a metal detector to the water's edge to search for treasure. Wi-Fi available throughout the inn. Outdoor hot-water showers and dressing rooms are a welcome convenience after a long day at the beach. $125–289.

In Manasquan 08736

Nathaniel Morris Inn (732-223-7826; www.nathanielmorris.com), 117 Marcellus Ave. Open all year. Gail and Paul McFadden's lovely 1882 Victorian—built by one of Manasquan's founding fathers and surrounded by a white picket fence—is in the historic district. The perfectly restored interior is an homage to its turn-of-the-20th-century heritage. Victorian-era antiques and reproductions fill the parlor and the cozy living room, complete with a large-screen TV and an extensive library. There are four guest rooms and two suites, all bright and cheerful with private bath, TV, and air-conditioning. Second-floor rooms have access to a private balcony. Full breakfast. $155–275.

MOTELS

In Point Pleasant Beach 08742
"♦" **Surfside Motel** (732-899-1109; www.surfside-motel.com), 101 Broadway. Open all year. A clean and simply furnished motel three blocks from the beach and boardwalk. Accommodations range from standard rooms with one king bed to two-bedroom units and king rooms with nicely tiled baths. All come with TV, Wi-Fi, phone with voice mail, refrigerator, and air-conditioning. There's a heated outdoor pool, and beach badges are complimentary. Room rates vary by day of week and month of year.

♂ **Amethyst's Beach Motel** (732-899-3600), on Jenkinson's Beach, 202 Arnold Ave. A family-friendly motel near the boardwalk and amusement park. The pool and patio are newly renovated, and rooms and efficiencies are clean and comfortable. Suites and apartments rent by the week, month, or season. All rooms have a mini-refrigerator, and microwaves are available on request at no charge. Continental breakfast. $129–225.

In Sea Girt 08750
& **The Sea Girt Lodge** (732-974-2323; www.theseagirtlodge.com), 2168 Rt. 35 North. Open all year. A pleasant motel on Sea Girt's main drag with a heated pool and rooms with air-conditioning, TV, phone, and computer hookups. Common areas include a nicely furnished lobby (in the office building) with a TV and local daily newspapers. Every morning the guest breakfast nook is stocked with complimentary coffee, fresh fruit, and pastries. $100–159.

In Spring Lake
The Mill at Spring Lake Heights (732-449-1800; www.themillatslh.com), Old Mill Rd. (Spring Lake Heights). Open for dinner Wed.–Sun.; Sun. brunch. Reservations are accepted. An elegant Jersey Shore favorite since 1938, formerly the Old Mill Inn, occupies a renovated lovely lakeside setting. The menu emphasizes expertly prepared fresh seafood and aged steaks. Among the starters, lobster bisque is the house specialty. Entertainment Fri.–Sat.; ask about their big-band nights, wine dinners, and supper-club shows. $18–28.

The Island Palm Grill (732-449-1909; www.islandpalmgrill.com), 1321 Third Ave. Open Tues.–Sun. for lunch; Tues.–Sat. for dinner; closed Mon. Reservations for dinner are recommended. This cozy, family-run storefront eatery at the heart of Spring Lake's charming downtown is run by Larry and Deborah Cerrito. The ever-changing menu of creative New American cuisine—with a Latin flair—is brief, well balanced, and full of fresh seasonal ingredients. BYOB. $19–28.

& **The Breakers on the Ocean** (732-449-7700; www.breakershotel.com), 1507 Ocean Ave. Open daily for breakfast, lunch, and dinner. Reservations are suggested. This legendary century-old hotel on the Atlantic is one of the top places to dine and stay on the shore. In addition to classic northern Italian cuisine, the dinner menu offers fresh seafood specials, prime steaks and veal chops grilled to perfection. Cocktails, appetizers, and desserts are served in the piano lounge and, during warmer months, on the outdoor wrap-around porch overlooking the ocean. $12–38.

Whispers (732-974-9755; www
.whispersrestaurant.com), at the
Hewitt Wellington Hotel, 200 Monmouth Ave. Open daily for dinner.
Reservations are recommended. This
tiny gem (50 seats) is a haven for foodies, a romantic retreat for couples, and
a destination for chefs who have the
night off and know where to go for a
good meal. The menu is contemporary
American cuisine; the 19th-century
Victorian surroundings are elegant and
formal without being stuffy. Dinner is
an ever-changing selection from a few
appetizers; pan-seared ostrich filet is
one example. The short list of seafood
and grilled meats allows for serious
artistic attention from the chef. Try the
oven-roasted rack of lamb or the chef's
signature swordfish sautéed in a nori
crust, stuffed with jumbo lump crabmeat, and topped with shrimp and a
soy glaze. Service is gracious and attentive. BYOB. $26–36.

In Point Pleasant Beach
Europa South (732-295-1500; www
.europasouth.com), 521 Arnold Ave. (at
Rt. 35 South). Open for lunch Tues.–
Sat.; dinner Tues.–Sun.; closed Mon.
Reservations are suggested. Seafood is
the specialty at this bustling eatery
known for its authentic Spanish and
Portuguese cuisine. Starters include
garlic-marinated shrimp (the house
specialty) or grilled Spanish sausage.
For a traditional Basque region dish,
try the *mariscada,* a mélange of shellfish flambéed with Spanish brandy and
served with a green sauce. Or, try a
traditional Spanish paella. Live entertainment Fri.–Sat. might be acoustic
guitar, piano, DJ, or dancing. $17–28.

Spano's Ristorante Italiano (732-
701-1600), 719 Arnold Ave. Open daily
for dinner. Reservations are accepted.
Chef-owner Joseph Spano's elegant
Italian cuisine is one of the hallmarks
of the White Sands resort and spa.
Many dishes—like the homemade

meat and cheese ravioli topped with
marinara—are inspired by Spano's
southern Italian roots and family
recipes. The three-part menu is equally divided among pastas, meats, and
seafood. BYOB. $15–24.

In Manasquan
& **Mahogany Grille** (732-292-1300;
www.themahoganygrille.com), 142
Main St. Open daily for dinner. A very
popular restaurant serving innovative
global cuisine in plush, sophisticated
surroundings. Reservations accepted.
Enjoy the deliciously crusty artisan
bread while you peruse the menu that
revolves mostly around grilled fresh
seafood and meats. The large blue
point oysters and grilled Caesar Salad
make wonderful starters, and the
seafood specials are always a good
choice for dinner. Imaginative desserts
include a banana-chocolate spring roll
and a decadent chocolate soufflé cake.
Excellent wine list. $22–30.

In Brielle
✍ **Sand Bar Restaurant** (732-528-
7750; www.sandbarrestaurant.com),
201 Union Ln. Open year-round daily
for lunch and dinner. A popular dockside restaurant and bar at the **Brielle
Yacht Club** on the Manasquan River.
The extensive American menu of
steak, burgers, pasta, thin-crust pizza,
and seafood is paired with nightly dinner specials, such as surf and turf or
lobster dinners. Burgers and a huge
selection of pasta, seafood, chicken,
and steak. Live acoustic music
Fri.–Sat. nights. The convivial bar is
frequented by a colorful mix of locals,
boaters, and tourists. $12–20.

EATING OUT

In Spring Lake
✍ **Who's On Third** (732-449-4233),
1300 Third Ave. Open year-round daily
for breakfast and lunch; three meals
during the summer. A friendly family-

✒ ♿ THE GRENVILLE RESTAURANT

(732-892-3100; www.thegrenville.com), at the Grenville Hotel, 345 Main Ave. (Rt. 35), Bay Head. Lunch Mon.–Sat.; dinner Tues.–Sun. (daily July–Aug.); Sunday brunch. An elegant restaurant in a charming Queen Anne–style hotel known for its fine dining (see *Lodging—Hotels*). It's formal yet friendly, and the service is gracious and attentive. The American menu is a well-chosen mix of classics and innovative dishes that emphasize seafood. Crabcakes and seafood bisque are two popular starters that can be followed by fresh lobster, swordfish, or salmon, as well as beef, chicken, and other landlubber favorites. The Sunday brunch buffet of waffles, omelets, and other brunch standards is popular with families. New Jerseyans often put it at the top of statewide restaurant polls. $15–30.

owned eatery with a casual neighborly feel. Baseball is the theme here, from the décor to the menu; and just about everything is homemade, including the salads and soups—even the turkey used in the deli sandwiches is roasted in-house. You can get breakfast until 3 PM, burgers and sandwiches for lunch, and stuffed peppers, meatloaf, pot roast, or turkey with all the fixings for dinner. The take-out deli does a brisk business with made-to-order sandwiches and homemade salads. $8–14.

In Sea Girt

✒ **Rod's Olde Irish Tavern** (732-449-2020; www.rodstavern.com), 507 Washington Blvd. Open daily for lunch and dinner; brunch on Sun. A classic Irish pub in an old-time turn-of-the-20th-century saloon. The extensive menu of classic American tavern fare has something to please everyone, from pub-style appetizers and burgers and salads to fresh seafood, chicken, and hand-cut steaks. The bar is stocked with 10 televisions to satisfy all the sports fans. $12–22.

In Manasquan

🦞 ✒ Squan Tavern (732-223-3324; www.squantavern.com), 15 Broad St. Open for lunch Tues.–Sat.; dinner

Tues.–Sun.; closed Mon. A longtime family-run downtown eatery serving generous portions of southern Italian cuisine at very reasonable prices. The extensive menu of Italian standards includes pasta, steak, chicken, veal, and seafood. The potato gnocchi is homemade and served with marinara or cream sauce. There's also pizza and a kids' menu. $10–21.

In Point Pleasant Beach

Spike's Seafood (732-295-9400), 415 Broadway. A bustling waterfront seafood eatery with an adjoining fish market that stocks an impressive selection of just-caught fish and shellfish. Seafood is fresh and simply prepared, and the service is friendly; diners sit at plain wooden tables in a small room that seats just 50 patrons at a time. BYOB. $15–23.

Surf Taco (732-701-9000; www.surf taco.com), 1300 Richmond Ave. (Rt. 35 South). Plus seven other shore locations: Manasquan, Seaside Park, Belmar, Silverton, Jackson, Lacey, and Long Branch. Open daily for lunch and dinner. A casual spot that plays surfing movies and offers a fresh, California-style menu—enormous burritos stuffed with seafood, chicken, avocado, and other healthy ingredients. In addition to other Mexican fare, there's a decent selection of salads, wraps, and fruit smoothies. $3–10.

♪ **The Lobster Shanty** (732-899-6700; jackbakerslobstershanty.com), 81–83 Channel Dr. Open daily for dinner; closed Mon.–Tues. in winter. Reservations accepted for parties of eight or more. Fresh seafood has been the specialty at this popular seafood house for more than 40 years. This was the first location; today there are seven in New Jersey and Florida. Outdoor dining on the deck and patio, when the weather allows. $16–32.

Elsewhere

Red's Lobster Pot (732-295-6622; www.redslobsterpot.com) 57 Inlet Dr., Point Pleasant Beach. Open daily 12 noon–9 mid-May–mid-Sept.; closed Mon.–Tues. after Labor Day and in early spring; closed for season at the end of Sept. A very popular, tiny (12-table) dockside restaurant known for fresh lobster and seafood dishes, but they also do pasta and chicken. Parties of five maximum inside, but outdoor seating is available for lighter fare and appetizers from a separate menu. BYOB (beer and wine). $13–22; lobster at market prices.

SNACKS Tom Bailey's Market (732-282-0920; www.tombaileysmarket.com), 1323 Third Ave., Spring Lake. This upscale food market is a haven for cooks and gourmands. They stock high-end organic poultry and meats, fresh cheeses, top-notch aged steaks, truffles, pâté, and caviar, as well as delectable homemade muffins, pies, and cakes. Freshly prepared salads and other foods are ideal for taking home for dinner or to the beach for a picnic.

Bay Head Cheese Shop (732-892-7585; www.bayhead.org), 91 Bridge Ave., Bay Head. Open Mon.–Sat.

10–6; Sun. 10–4. Gourmet specialty foods, homemade hors d'oeuvres and desserts, and coffees and teas line shelves and display cases, but most customers come for the domestic and imported cheeses. They range from familiar Vermont cheddar, Italian provolone and mozzarella, and French Brie to more unusual varieties from Switzerland, Norway, and other noted cheese-making regions of Europe.

Susan Murphy's (732-449-1130; www.homemadeicecream.com), 601 Warren Ave., Spring Lake Heights. Open Apr. 1–Oct. 31. Hours vary by season. A quaint little white house is a mini ice-cream factory, where award-winning homemade ice cream and ice-cream cakes are made fresh daily. You can enjoy it on a cone or in a brownie sundae, in an apple crisp sundae, or in old-fashioned egg creams or banana splits. Sorbets, frozen yogurt, and fat-free and sugar-free varieties round out the tempting menu. Pints and quarts are available to take home.

The Beanery (732-295-9669; www.thebeanery.net), 516 Bay Ave., Point Pleasant Beach. Open Tues.–Thurs., 11–4; Fri., 11–5; Sat., 9–5; closed Sun.–Mon. A casual neighborhood spot with coffee and hot and cold coffee drinks, an espresso and tea bar, and a light menu of sandwiches, quiche, wraps, salads, and desserts. $5–10.

✳ Entertainment

THEATER ⅋ **Algonquin Arts Theatre** (732-528-9211; www.algonquinarts.org), 171 Main St., Manasquan. A 540-seat theater that stages live productions, films (from classic musicals to new releases by budding local filmmakers), dance, drama, concerts, musicals, storytelling, and an orchestra series. Professional touring companies like the Moscow Classical Ballet and the Chamber Music Society of Lincoln

Center make frequent appearances, and summertime features a popular outdoor film series.

Spring Lake Theatre Company (732-449-4530), Third and Madison Ave., Spring Lake. A popular local theater company that has presented high-quality classic musicals, musical revues, comedies, and dramas, even original works, to the community for the past 30 years. Performances are held in a 350-seat theater at the historic Tudor-style **Community House**. Six shows are put on each season—usually musicals. Each show's opening-night ticket sales—including the annual performance of the holiday classic *Scrooge*—are donated to local charities.

✳ Selective Shopping
ANTIQUES

In Point Pleasant Beach
Point Pleasant Antique Emporium (732-892-2222; 800-322-8002), Bay and Trenton Aves. More than 125 dealers spread across two floors in a historic landmark building. Antiques, collectibles, and memorabilia.

Point Pavilion Antique Center (732-899-6300), 608 Arnold Ave. A variety of dealers with a variety of specialties, in the old Woolworth building.

ART GALLERIES

In Spring Lake
Frederick Galleries (732-974-0376; www.frederickgalleries.com), 1405 Third Ave. Open daily except Wed. A gallery representing local and nationally known artists. They also sell framed art and do custom framing.

In Manasquan
Main Street Gallery (732-223-1268; www.mainstreetgallery.com), 131 Main St. A fine-art gallery, one of the largest on the Jersey Shore, specializing in

nautical scenes, beach images, and landscapes by local and regional artists.

In Bay Head
Anchor and Palette Art Gallery (732-892-7776; 866-813-7627; www.anchorandpalette.com), 45 Mount St. Shoreline landscapes and other images of the Jersey Shore by more than 20 local artists.

SPECIAL SHOPS

In Spring Lake
The Spot (732-974-0099), 1226 Third Ave. Open daily. Designer frocks from Nicole Miller, BCBG, and other upscale labels.

Whimsicality (732-449-9337), 1219 Third Ave. Chic home décor, bed and bath products, luxury linens, and unique garden décor.

Urban Details (732-282-0013; www.urban-details.com), 1111 Third Ave. Gifts, jewelry, glass, lighting, frames, and more.

In Point Pleasant Beach

Globetrotter (732-892-2001), 1809 Ocean Ave. (Rt. 35 South) and 300 Richmond Ave. (732-892-5554). Imported decorative pieces, antiques, and garden décor.

Coastal Creations (732-714-0606; www.coastalcreations.com), 405 Sea Ave. (Rt. 35). Coastal-themed home décor, from artwork and framed prints to rugs, lamps, mirrors, and other home accessories.

In Bay Head
Artisan's Galleria (732-892-7300), 41 Mount St. More than 50 area crafters.

✳ Special Events
Fireworks, classic-car cruises, and outdoor concerts are among the special events held regularly along the Jersey Shore all summer long. Contact the

local chambers of commerce (see *Guidance*) for a full events calendar.

January: **Wildlife Art and Decoy Show** (732-341-9622; www.ocymca .org), location within Ocean County changes each year. Seminars, competitions, and more than 100 exhibitors featuring decoys and wildlife carvings.

May: **Cherry Blossom Arts Weekend** (www.bayhead.biz/activities/ cherryblossoms), Bay Head. Exhibits of fine arts and crafts at galleries and shops, and an open-house tour of Bay Head's inns. **Authors and Inns Tour** (732-859-1465; www.historicinnsof springlake.com), Spring Lake.

June: **Art in the Park** (www.bayhead .biz/activities/artpark), Centennial Park, Bay Head. More than 40 professional artists sell their watercolors, oils, drawings, limited-edition prints, and other works.

Summer: ♪ **Summerfest** (www.brick townonline.com/Summerfest), Windward Beach, Brick. A popular summertime entertainment festival with music, fireworks, family activities, and food.

August: ♪ **Big Sea Day**, Manasquan. Held on the second Saturday, this is a beachy celebration featuring fishing, surfing, sandcastle building, and pie-eating contests, as well as children's activities and entertainment. **Art Show and Art Sale** (732-892-5926), Bay

Head at St. Paul's Methodist Church. Manasquan River Group of Artists and more. **Squan Tri-Sail Regatta** (732-899-0202; www.squantrisail.org), Manasquan. The state's biggest offshore sailing competition has been taking place off the coast here for more than a quarter century.

September: ♪ **Festival of the Sea** (732-899-2424; www.pointpleasant beachnj.org), Point Pleasant Beach. Food, live entertainment, arts and crafts, antiques, and children's activities. Point Pleasant Beach's premier annual event. **New Jersey Offshore Powerboat Race** (732-583-8501; www.njoffshore.org), Point Pleasant Beach. High-speed boats race from Manasquan Inlet to the ocean in front of Jenkinson's Pier; run by the New Jersey Offshore Powerboat Racing Association, the oldest such boat-racing club in the country. Spectators watch from Jenkinson's Pavilion or from their own boats. Part of a week-long festival.

December: **Christmas Inn Tours** (732-449-0577; www.historicinnsof springlake.com) Spring Lake. Candlelight tours of the town's inns and bed & breakfasts decorated for the holidays on two separate weekends—one features an afternoon tour and the other an evening candlelight tour.

BARNEGAT BAY

Thanks to a series of long, narrow oceanfront barrier beaches, Ocean County boasts a peaceful 40-mile-long bayside coastline, an intricate web of inlets, coves, and beaches protected from the wiles of the Atlantic. Barnegat Bay sits along the busy inland waterway that begins just to the north in Manasquan and provides boaters a safe passage on calm waters all the way to Texas. The bay region spreads out across a 450-square-mile oasis of islands, shallow tidal pools, pine and oak forests, vast stands of eelgrass, pungent mudflats, and gently lapping waves opposed to pounding surf. Acres of wild salt marsh are guaranteed to remain forever undeveloped. The bay is a haven for sailing, windsurfing, and parasailing, not to mention fishing—the combination of salt- and freshwater has created a rich ecosystem that is home to more than 100 plant and animal species. It's a world of kayaking, sailing, and crabbing off long docks for blue claws, unlike the other side of the barrier island, which draws personal watercraft and speedboats that thunder through the ocean waves. This laid-back summertime scene stands in stark contrast to the honky-tonk atmosphere on the oceanfront boardwalk in nearby Seaside Heights. The bay is considered the quiet shore, the less pricey alternative to the oceanfront resort towns. Together they are a prime vacation destination for thousands of New Jersey, New York, and Pennsylvania residents.

To the east, the lavish estates of Mantoloking—some of the most spectacular on the Jersey Shore—occupy just the thinnest strip of land along the ocean. Normandy Beach and Chadwick are quaint summertime communities of seaside bungalows crammed together along a network of narrow streets, many of them one-way lanes. Lavallette is named for navy Admiral Elie La Vallette, commander of the USS *Constitution*, or "Old Ironsides," the famous ship now berthed in Boston Harbor. Grand Central Avenue is lined with charming specialty shops, and free summertime concerts are held under the boardwalk's quaint gazebo.

Seaside Heights is popular with singles and families looking to live it up in a carefree town with a good beach and plenty to do. If you're planning an elegant, upscale shore vacation, stay away. But if clanging arcades, midway games, kid-packed entertainment centers, and nightclubs are your idea of fun, then this is the perfect place. The vintage Dentzel/Looff carousel at the boardwalk's Casino Pier is a gem. It's a living museum of sorts, a neoclassical-style relic of a bygone era whose elaborate hand-carved horses still carry delighted passengers, just as it has for nearly a century. The 60 or so gaily colored animals bob up and down in tune to New Jersey's only continuously operating Wurlitzer organ. There are plenty of

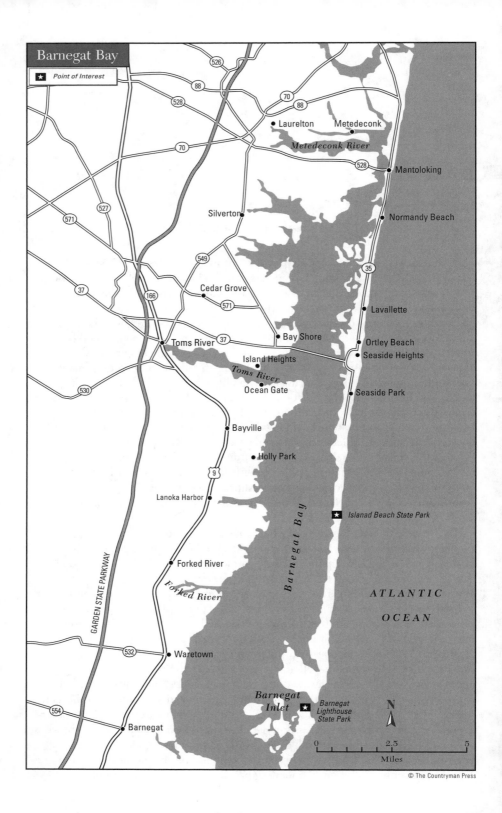

Barnegat Bay

★ Point of Interest

526

88

528

70

88

70

● Laurelton   ● Metedeconk

Metedeconk River

528   ● Mantoloking

527

571

● Silverton

● Normandy Beach

549

35

166

571   ● Cedar Grove

● Lavallette

37

● Bay Shore

37   Toms River ●

● Ortley Beach
● Seaside Heights

● Island Heights

Toms River

530

● Ocean Gate

● Seaside Park

● Bayville

● Holly Park

9

Lanoka Harbor ●

★ *Islanad Beach State Park*

B a r n e g a t   B a y

● Forked River

Forked River

A T L A N T I C

O C E A N

GARDEN STATE PARKWAY

532   ● Waretown

Barnegat Inlet

★ *Barnegat Lighthouse State Park*

N

554

● Barnegat

0   2.5   5
Miles

© The Countryman Press

motels that come in varying degrees of quality, some neat and clean, others a bit worn around the edges. When traveling here in May and June, be prepared to share space with hordes of teens that descend on the resort during prom season.

Neighboring Seaside Park was settled in 1874, and named for the oceanfront park that its founding fathers hoped to establish but never did. Instead, colossal Victorian hotels were built and filled every summer with vacationers coming to town on the Pennsylvania Railroad from New York City and Philadelphia. Today the grand buildings are long gone, replaced with reasonably priced motels and other family-friendly accommodations. Seaside Park's charming Borough Hall occupies the historic Coast Guard Life-Saving Service building, and the waters offshore are known for their exceptionally fine windsurfing conditions.

Nature lovers looking for sand dunes and a 10-mile-long stretch of pristine beaches that hasn't changed much in the past few centuries head to Island Beach State Park. The 3,000-acre undeveloped barrier beach is widely considered the crown jewel of the entire Jersey Shore. For visitors, it offers surf fishing, birding, and beaches for sunbathing, beachcombing, and swimming.

On the mainland, the bayside community of Toms River is the Ocean County seat; its columned 1850 Greek Revival–style courthouse still stands on Washington Street. Toms River was first settled in 1712, and thrived as a whaling, fishing, lumbering, and iron-making center for nearly a century. A brutal storm closed the inlet in the early 1800s, bringing the glory days of the bustling port to an abrupt end. The Ocean County Historical Society maintains a local-history museum with Native American artifacts, Victorian furnishings and clothing, and exhibits on the region's history as a major trading and industrial center. Also worth a visit is the Toms River Seaport Society Maritime Museum, with interesting exhibits and historic wooden boats under restoration. The 19th-century Toms River Yacht Club is one of the most active boating clubs in Barnegat Bay and holds regattas from

SAILBOAT REGATTAS ARE A COMMON SITE IN THE BARNEGAT BAY REGION FROM SPRING TO FALL, ESPECIALLY ON THE TOMS RIVER.

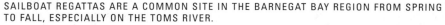

Photo courtesy of Ocean County Public Affairs

spring to fall. Ocean County's slogan, "Where the Sea Meets the Pines," is a nod to the presence of the vast Pinelands National Reserve, the million-plus-acre natural wonder that starts here and covers much of South Jersey in thick pine forest. By the end of the 19th century, throngs of vacationers were coming into the popular resort on trains from Philadelphia and New York City. It was a busy seasonal hot spot well into the 1920s. Today it's largely a residential community of commuters who jump on the conveniently close Garden State Parkway to points around New Jersey.

Island Heights is a charming historic town on the banks of the Toms River, another Ocean County hidden gem that delights first-time visitors who happen to stumble upon it. It's home to the active Ocean County Artists' Guild, the Island Heights Yacht Club, and a historic district of more than 375 restored Victorian homes and buildings. The town doesn't offer much for tourists, but it's a perfect destination for fishing, crabbing, or a leisurely stroll or bike ride around its quiet streets. From the town's picturesque waterfront, you might catch one of the many sailing regattas that take place on the river. Island Heights once hosted summer-time religious retreats; today the historic site is reminiscent of the famous camp meeting community in Oak Bluffs on Martha's Vineyard.

Entries in this section are arranged in roughly geographic order, from north to south.

AREA CODES 732, 609.

GUIDANCE Ocean County (732-929-2000; 800-365-6933; www.oceancounty tourism.com) maintains an online county directory that features a calendar of events, information on area attractions, lodging, and activities, and links to a variety of tourism Web sites. There is also a County Connections office at the Ocean County Mall (732-288-7777).

Seaside Heights Visitors Bureau (800-732-7467; www.seasideheightstourism .com), P.O. Box 43, Seaside Heights 08751. Seaside Heights's official tourism Web site has a host of information for visitors. They will send a free copy of their annual visitor's guide, on request.

Toms River–Ocean County Chamber of Commerce (732-349-0220; www .oc-chamber.com), 1200 Hooper Ave., Toms River. The chamber office is well stocked with tourism literature; their Web site has information on Toms River, Seaside Heights, and the rest of Ocean County.

GETTING THERE *By air:* **Newark Liberty International Airport** (973-961-6000; parking information: 888-397-4636; www.panynj.com) in Newark serves the entire state. Those traveling to New Jersey also use **John F. Kennedy International Airport** (718-244-4168; www.kennedyairport.com) and **LaGuardia International Airport** (718-533-3850; www.laguardiaairport.com) in New York City. **Atlantic City International Airport** (609-645-7895; www.acairport.com), Exit 9 off the Atlantic City Expressway, Egg Harbor Township, is served by Spirit Airlines (800-772-7117; www.spiritair.com).

By rail: **New Jersey Transit's North Coast Line** (973-275-5555; www.njtransit .com) offers express commuter service connecting Penn Station in New York City (via Newark's Penn Station) to shore points in this region, including Red Bank,

Little Silver, Monmouth Park, Long Branch, Elberon, Allenhurst, Asbury Park, Bradley Beach, and Belmar, continuing as far south as Bay Head. The stops are within walking distance of most beaches and attractions.

By bus: **New Jersey Transit** (973-275-5555; www.njtransit.com) and **Academy Bus Service** (800-442-7272; www.academybus.com) offer bus transportation throughout the region.

By car: The **Garden State Parkway** parallels the Jersey Shore from Cape May north to the Long Branch area; **I-195** connects Philadelphia and Trenton to the parkway just west of Belmar; **Rt. 9** branches off and heads directly to Toms River. **Rt. 70** is a major secondary road that starts in Camden and ends just west of Point Pleasant Beach. There are two major junctions along the way for shore destinations: **Rt. 37** passes through Toms River on its way to Seaside Heights, and **Rt. 72** goes directly to Long Beach Island.

Taxis: There is no taxi service in the area.

MEDICAL EMERGENCY Community Medical Center (732-349-8000; www.sbhcs.com), 99 Rt. 37 West, Toms River. The emergency number is 732-557-8080.

✳ To See

MUSEUMS Colonel Charles Waterhouse Historical Museum (732-818-9040; www.waterhousemuseum.com), 17 Washington St., Toms River. Call for hours. Colonel Charles Waterhouse—a veteran of the 5th Marine Division during World War II—is the U.S. Marine Corps' first and only artist in residence. His dramatic paintings, illustrations, and sculpture chronicle the history of the Marine Corps and the American military from the Revolutionary War period to the present. Colonel Waterhouse studied art and illustration after his World War II service, and since then has contributed thousands of military illustrations to books and magazines, in addition to his painting and sculpting. The museum's collection centers on close to 100 of Waterhouse's paintings and illustrations, including two bronze sculptures. The museum shop sells Marine Corps–related items, posters, limited-edition prints, and books.

The Ocean County Historical Museum and Research Center (732-341-1880; www.oceancountyhistory.org), 26 Hadley Ave., Toms River. Open Tues. and Thurs. 1–3; first Sat. of the month, 1–4. The 19th-century Victorian-style **Pierson-Sculthorp House** is headquarters of the Ocean County Historical Society and their collection of artifacts and memorabilia dedicated to Ocean County's rich maritime and cultural heritage, and the lives of Ocean County's earliest families. Permanent exhibits include period furnishings, artifacts of local industry, displays of hand-carved Barnegat Bay duck decoys, local Civil War– and Revolutionary War–era memorabilia, and relics of aviation history from the **Lakehurst Naval Air Station.** A library and research center is dedicated to Ocean County history.

Toms River Seaport Society Maritime Museum (732-349-9209; www.toms riverseaport.org), 78 East Water St., Toms River. Open Tues., Thurs., and Sat. 10–2. Admission is free. A boat-restoration museum devoted to the preservation of Barnegat Bay's rich maritime history. Displays of folk art, clothing, tools, maps, diaries, and photographs are reminiscent of the bygone era when schooners and fishing boats plied the protected waters of Barnegat Bay, and locally designed flat-bottomed skiffs trolled the shallow estuaries for bay scallops, clams, and blue crabs. Some of these boats are part of the museum's collections, either meticulously preserved or in the process of restoration. The museum hosts an annual **Wooden Boat Festival** in July (see *Special Events*) that is one of the largest such festivals on the East Coast.

PLANETARIUM ✿ **Robert J. Novins Planetarium** (732-255-0400, ext. 2111 for office; 732-255-0342 for recorded information; www.ocean.edu/campus/ planetarium), Ocean County College, Hooper Ave. North, Toms River. (**Note: The Planetarium** is closed for renovations until late 2009. There is some programming off-site. Call or check the Web site for exact re-opening dates.) Adults $6; seniors $5; children 12 and under, $4.50. Programs for children and adults. Ocean County College's planetarium is the only such astronomy facility in the area open to the public, and one of the most active in New Jersey. Shows in the 118-seat planetarium—covered by a 40-foot dome—re-create the night sky in presentations geared toward both adults and children. Friday-night planetarium shows are followed by outdoor sky–observing sessions, weather permitting, led by local amateur astronomers. The gift shop sells space- and astronomy-related souvenirs and other items. Call for a schedule of special stargazing events, like the **Summer Starwatch** and **Concerts Under the Stars.**

✳ To Do

AMUSEMENTS ✿ **Blackbeard's Cave** (732-286-4414; www.blackbeardscave .com), 136 Rt. 9, Bayville. Open daily 10 AM–midnight. An indoor-outdoor entertainment center that has just about anything a family could want. There's a 20-hole mini-golf course, a video arcade, a 40-tee driving range, batting cages, an archery range, pony rides, bumper boats, a paintball arena, and jousting. The Adventure Station has rides and games for little ones, including slides, face painting, a miniature train, a Ferris wheel, and a mini–roller coaster. Live bands and other special events.

THE WOODEN BOAT FESTIVAL IS AN ANNUAL SUMMERTIME EVENT ON THE TOMS RIVER AT HUDDY PARK IN DOWNTOWN TOMS RIVER.
Photo courtesy of Ocean County Public Affairs

BICYCLING Island Beach State Park (732-793-0506; www.island beachnj.org), Rt. 35, Seaside Park. There is a parking fee, but cyclists are admitted free. A popular cycling route through the undisturbed 3,000-acre park is the 16-mile out-and-back cruise on the park road that passes by a salt marsh, dunes, and freshwater bogs. If you ride in the spring or fall, you won't have to share the road with those heading to the beach.

BOAT EXCURSIONS *River Lady* **Cruise and Dinner Boat** (732-349-8664; www.riverlady.com), One Rob-

✎ POPCORN PARK ZOO

(609-693-1900; www.ahscares.org), Humane Way (at Lacey Rd.), Forked River. Open year-round daily 11–5; holidays 11–2. Adults $5; seniors and children $4. This 7-acre facility—the only one of its kind in the country—is more than just a home to 200 domestic, wild, and exotic animals and birds. It has been a refuge and last hope for abandoned, injured, abused, neglected, and unwanted creatures since 1977. The animals are rescued from a number of dire situations: some are circus animals abused by their trainers; others are taken from owners convicted on charges of animal cruelty; and more are found in the wild, too old (or young), sick, or injured to survive on their own. Of the zoo's injured and abandoned deer, many have been bottle-fed here since they were fawns. The wild menagerie includes American black bears, African lions, Bengal tigers, bobcats, cougars, monkeys, Australian wallabies, foxes, birds, and reptiles. There's a population of domestic animals, including goats, horses, sheep, and cows. The zoo runs spaying and neutering clinics, four animal-care centers, and a nationwide adoption program; they also investigate and prosecute animal-cruelty cases. And thanks to their concern and efforts, every police dog in New Jersey wears a bulletproof vest.

bins Parkway, Toms River. Public cruises May–Sept., Tues.–Thurs., and Sat.; private charters Apr.–Nov. Reservations are required. Narrated historical sightseeing tours and lunch-, dinner-, and dance cruises on the calm waters of the Toms River and Barnegat Bay aboard the *River Lady,* a Mississippi River–style 85-foot paddle wheeler. Traditional American cuisine is served in the Victorian dining room; there's also an open upper deck with lovely views of the bay's natural surroundings. This is the only boat operating on the river that's propelled by a paddle wheel. Call for pricing.

Barnegat Bay Sailing Charters (732-269-1351; www.sailingnj.com), Barnegat Bay Sailing School, 100 Harbor Inn Rd., Bayville. Chartered sunset cruises, half-day excursions, and personalized cruises in the bay aboard the *Margarita,* a 30-foot sailing sloop. Call for pricing.

Seaside Sailing (732-830-9285; www.seasidesailing.com), Pier One Marina, 3430 Adams Ave., Toms River. Daily summertime sailboat excursions aboard a 44-foot Hunter sailboat that carries up to six passengers on daytime, sunset, evening, and moonlight sails on the calm, protected waters of Barnegat Bay and the Toms River. Wednesday-night fireworks cruises leave from Seaside Heights. Snacks and soft drinks are provided. Call for pricing.

BOATING (See also *Boat Excursions.*)

Full-service marinas in the Barnegat Bay region include **Ocean Beach Marina** (732-793-7460; www.oceanbeachmarina.com), 3245 Rt. 35 South, Lavallette; **Lighthouse Point Marina and Yacht Club** (732-341-1105), Crabbe Rd., South

✍ SEASIDE HEIGHTS CASINO PIER

(732-793-6488; www.casinopiernj.com), 800 Ocean Terr., Seaside Heights. This rollicking amusement pier juts over the Atlantic Ocean on Seaside Heights's 1.5-mile boardwalk, one of the most-visited seaside promenades on the Jersey Shore. It's crammed with everything you would hope and expect to find—midway-style games of chance, clanging video arcades, thrill rides, a water park, mini golf, and a virtual smorgasbord of pizza, french fries, saltwater taffy, fudge, and all manner of boardwalk food.

For one of the most nostalgic rides on the Jersey Shore, head to the northern end of the boardwalk, where the historic **Dentzel/Looff Carousel** (732-793-6489; www.casinopiernj.com) is one of only two remaining vintage carousels in New Jersey. Dr. Floyd Moreland was instrumental in getting this rare American-made carousel not only restored but also up and running (daily in summer; weekends all year). Many of the ornate hand-carved animals date to the 19th century, and music is provided by the state's only continuously operating carousel organ, a 1923 Wurlitzer military-band organ. A gift shop sells music boxes and miniature carousels.

CASINO PIER ON THE SEASIDE HEIGHTS BOARDWALK OFFERS A DIZZYING ARRAY OF RIDES, GAMES, FOOD, A WATER PARK, AND OTHER AMUSEMENTS ALL SUMMER LONG.

Photo courtesy of Ocean County Public Affairs

Toms River; **Shorepoint Marina and Yacht Sales** (732-244-2106; www.shore pointyachts.com), One Corrigan Ave., Bayville; **Lanoka Harbor Marina** (609-693-2674;), Lanoka Harbor; **Forked River State Marina** (609-693-5045), 311 South Main St., Forked River; **Wilberts Marina** (609-693-2145; www.forked rivermarinas.com), 101 Bay Ave., Forked River; and **Cranbury Inlet Marina** (732-793-8554), Rt. 35 South, Seaside Heights.

FISHING **Casino Fishing Pier** (732-830-2252; www.casinofishingpiernj.com), Sherman Ave. and the Boardwalk, Seaside Heights. Seasonal fishing is allowed off the end of this ocean pier. Most anglers come here for the kingfish, fluke, striped bass, and bluefish. A fee is charged, and equipment rentals are available. Open 6 AM to midnight; lighted for night fishing.

Barnegat Bay is well known for its blue crabs, which are easily found up and down the bay shore. **Cranberry Inlet Marina** (732-793-4434), Rt. 35, Seaside Heights, offers crabbing and crabbing supplies, and rentals. Another option is **Dick's Landing** (732-269-0867), 1148 Island Dr. (off Rt. 9), Bayville, which offers crabbing and fishing as well as rowboat and motorboat rentals.

Island Beach State Park (732-793-0506; www.islandbeachnj.org) at the end of Rt. 35 in Seaside Park is a prime spot for surf fishing. Bluefish, weakfish, and striped bass are among the saltwater species often caught here. A permit is required to drive a vehicle on the fishing beaches; they can be purchased at the ranger station at the entrance to the park.

GOLF **Bey Lea Golf Course** (732-349-0566; 732-736-8889; www.usegolf.com), 1536 North Bay Ave., Toms River. An 18-hole course with a clubhouse, snack bar, pro shop, and restaurant.

Cedar Creek at Berkeley Municipal Golf Course (732-269-4460), Forest Hills Pky. and Tilton Blvd., Bayville. An 18-hole golf course with a practice driving range; the clubhouse has a pro shop and a snack bar.

HIKING **Island Beach State Park** (732-793-1698; www.islandbeachnj.org), Rt. 35, Seaside Park. An entrance fee is charged Memorial Day weekend–Labor Day; $6 weekdays, $10 weekends. The park's network of many self-guided **Discovery Trails** affords an up-close look at the diverse habitats, from sand dunes to marsh grass, in the 3,002-acre virtually undisturbed peninsula. Each trail is less than a mile long, and exhibit stations along the way explain various natural and environmental issues concerning the state park, which protects one of the only remaining undeveloped barrier beaches on the Atlantic Coast (see sidebar, page 404). Pick up a copy of the Discovery Trails map and brochure at the ranger station at the park entrance. Those guides and more material are also available at the park's nature center, where in the summer, there is usually someone who can answer questions, daily, 9 to 4.

WATER SPORTS Many outfitters along Rt. 35 in Seaside Heights rent Jet Skis, WaveRunners, paddleboats, kayaks, and just about any such boat imaginable. They include **Pedals and Paddles Rentals** (732-830-5757; www.pedalsandpaddles .com), Bayfront and Grand; and **Seaside Waverunners II** (732-830-4900; www .seasidewaverunners.com) on Rt. 35 South.

✳ Green Space

BEACHES **Normandy Beach** (732-341-1000). At low tide, the surf conditions are perfect here, thanks to the strategic positioning of an offshore sandbar. There is no boardwalk at this quiet beach; the closest one is a short drive south to Lavallette. Day pass $5.

Lavallette (732-793-7477; May–Sept. 732-793-2111; www.lavallette.org). Fishing, surfing, and tennis. Adults $5; children 11 and under, free.

Seaside Heights (732-793-9100). The mile-long boardwalk is considered one of New Jersey's best, with amusement rides, a water park, food, fishing, and nonstop

ISLAND BEACH STATE PARK

(732-793-0506; www.njparksandforests.com), Rt. 35, Seaside Park. Open daily dawn to dusk. There is a parking fee of $5 per vehicle in the off-season; $6 on weekdays and $10 on weekends and holidays between Memorial Day and Labor Day. This state park is considered one of the Jersey Shore's most prized attractions for good reason. It's one of the last remaining undisturbed barrier beach ecosystems in New Jersey, with more than 3,000 acres of salt marsh, dunes, and freshwater bogs, and 10 miles of pristine sand stretching between the Atlantic Ocean and Barnegat Bay. Millions of visitors flock here every year; if you plan to visit on a summer weekend, it's essential that you arrive early. Sunbathing and swimming reign in summer; in the off-season the quiet windswept beach is taken over by birders, beachcombers, and surf fishermen. Stop in at the visitors center.

ISLAND BEACH STATE PARK, JUST SOUTH OF SEASIDE PARK, IS CONSIDERED THE CROWN JEWEL OF THE JERSEY SHORE, NINE MILES OF NATURAL BARRIER ISLAND ALONG THE ATLANTIC OCEAN AND BARNEGAT INLET.

Photo courtesy of the New Jersey Department of Environmental Protection/Island Beach State Park

entertainment on the Casino Pier. In addition to swimming, beach activities include rafting, scuba diving, surfing, picnicking, and tennis. Bathhouses with showers and changing facilities are available. Day passes $5.

Seaside Park (732-793-0234; 732-830-2100; www.seasideparknj.org). The waters off Seaside Park's beaches are popular destinations for windsurfing and sailing. Beaches are wide, quiet, and beloved by families; the mile-long boardwalk offers beautiful views of the Atlantic Ocean. Day pass $7.

Island Beach State Park (732-793-0506; www.islandbeach.org). This is one of the few remaining undeveloped barrier island beaches on the North Atlantic coast. A pristine 10-mile swath of beaches and dunes contains guarded and unguarded beaches. Snorkeling and surf fishing are popular beach activities. The park closes once the parking spaces are filled, which happens early on summer weekends. Weekday parking $6; weekends $10; annual state park pass $50.

✴ Lodging

BED & BREAKFASTS ⁰**ĭ**⁰ **Victoria on Main** (732-818-7580; www .victoriaonmain.com), 600 Main St., Toms River 08753. A lovely bed & breakfast in Toms River's historic district occupies the historic **Mathis House,** a stately white 1897 Victorian mansion. This is the first bed & breakfast to open in town, and it offers six guest rooms nicely appointed with period furnishings. For instance, the Miss Megan Room has the home's original bathroom with claw-foot tub; the Lady Carolyn Room has a cozy sitting area and a king bed on a raised platform; and the Princess Erin Room has a four-poster bed and other elegant Queen Anne–style furnishings. Each room has a private bath, Wi-Fi, TV, and writing desk. The antiques-filled common areas include a living room, parlor, and wraparound porch. Summertime finds most guests on the garden patio. Full breakfast. $125–150.

Cottage on the River (732-270-8123; www.cottageontheriver.com), 10 Ocean Bend, P.O. Box 628, Island Heights 08732. Open year-round. A charming 1920s-era cottage on a bluff overlooking the Toms River is a stylish and tastefully furnished bed & breakfast in a quiet neighborhood that's just a short drive from ocean beaches, Island Beach State Park, Seaside Heights, and Point Pleasant. Philip and Sally Gauntt offer a quiet retreat in two bright and airy suites and two rooms. Each has a private bath, air-conditioning, and views of the marinas on the river. Common areas include a spacious outdoor deck, home-theater room, and screened porch. Guests are provided with complimentary badges for the bay beaches, as well as chairs, coolers, and towels. Bikes are available to take around town to see the river and Island Heights's lovely historic homes. Ask about using the local tennis courts. Full breakfast is served on the screened porch or outside on the deck. $95–270.

MOTELS

In Lavallette 08753
&. **Tradewinds Motor Lodge** (732-793-2100; www.tradewindsnj.com), 2000 Grand Central Ave. (Rt. 35 South). The 45 motel rooms are clean, decent-sized, and modern, with standard amenities that include TV, phone, and air-conditioning. The ocean is a short walk away, and guests can use their complimentary badges at Lavallette's beaches. For those who would rather stay behind, there's an in-ground heated pool and a sundeck with lounge chairs. $80–175.

In Seaside Heights 08751

🛏 ⁱⁱ **Cranbury Inn** (732-793-5117; 800-498-4233; www.cranburyinn.com), 201 Heiring Ave. Open mid-June–mid-Sept. A warm and friendly family-run motel in the quiet north end of town, two blocks from the beach and boardwalk. Rooms have standard amenities like TV, air-conditioning, and a mini-refrigerator, and basic, no-frills décor. For a little more room, ask for one of the deluxe units. These have small sitting areas, and some face the pool, where there's Internet access. The poolside **Cranbury Cove Restaurant** is open daily for breakfast. $100–180.

ⁱⁱ **Belmont Motel** (732-793-8519; www.seasideheightslodging.com), 120 Sheridan Ave. A family-owned and family-operated motel a block from the beach and boardwalk. There's a wide range of clean and roomy accommodations, including basic motel-style rooms, efficiency suites, and efficiency apartments with a full kitchen, bedroom, bathroom, and either a private porch or a balcony. Each comes with a recently remodeled ceramic tile floor and a new refrigerator as well as a TV, air-conditioning, microwave oven, and Internet access. The suites are the most up-to-date and pleasant accommodations; each has a living room, bedroom, and kitchenette. Outside there's a large in-ground pool surrounded by a sundeck with lounge chairs and a gas grill. Guests are provided with beach badges. In July and August continental breakfast is served by the pool. Ask about their golf specials and other packages. $109–229.

🛏 **Flamingo Motel** (732-793-0648; www.flamingomotel.com), 124 Kearney Ave. Open year-round. This no-frills family-friendly motel in the center of town was completely overhauled in 2004. Each of the standard rooms and efficiency units overlooks the in-ground pool. Shops, restaurants, and the boardwalk are less than two blocks away. Weekdays $70–120; weekends (2-night stay only) $250–300.

Village Inn (732-830-6777; www.villageinnnj.com), 314 Bay Blvd. Open all year. A short walk to the beach, boardwalk, and amusement rides on the pier. Basic motel-style rooms are clean and simply furnished. Outdoor pool. $50–200.

CAMPGROUND 🐾 🛏 **Cedar Creek Campground** (732-269-1413; www.cedarcreeknj.com), 1052 Rt. 9, Bayville 08721. Open year-round. A wooded family campground about 10 miles from Barnegat Bay and the Atlantic Ocean. There are 225 tent and RV sites, and fully equipped rental cabins that sleep up to 10 people. A full schedule of events is organized from spring to fall, from pancake breakfasts and arts and crafts to hayrides and a variety of lighthearted contests. You can rent a canoe or kayak here to take on Cedar Creek; better yet, hook up with one of their guided trips—from an hour to all day—that follows the creek through the Pinelands. A café serves casual breakfasts and lunches on weekends during the summer season. Sites $31–55; cabins $115–375.

✳ Where to Eat

DINING OUT This part of the Jersey Shore is known more for its casual family-friendly seafood houses rather than the upscale gourmet bistros found all over Cape May, Red Bank, Spring Lake, and other highbrow shore towns. While few restaurants in this region can claim to be truly gourmet, most serve decent meals at reasonable prices, taking full advantage of the abundance of fresh seafood. Most of the restaurants listed below are a perfect destination after a day on the beach when the kids are hungry and everyone's salty and all beached out. Most places are family-friendly, casual, and fun, but busy—especially the seaside ones. Be prepared to wait a while for a table if you come when everyone's getting off the beach.

In Normandy Beach

Labrador Lounge (732-830-5770; www.labradorlounge.com), 3581 Rt. 35 North. Open daily for lunch and dinner; phone ahead in the off-season. Reservations accepted. A casual, eclectic spot a block from the beach that's beloved by locals. The creative menu offers a world tour of exotic cuisines, from French and Asian to Mexican and Thai, plus some vegetarian dishes. Dinner features lots of fresh grilled fish, but if you hanker for meat, the baby back ribs are smoky, spicy, and flavorful. Kudos to the kitchen for innovative desserts. BYOB. $14–25.

In Lavallette

♪ **The Crab's Claw Inn** (732-793-4447), 601 Grand Central Ave. (Rt. 35 North). Open daily for lunch and dinner; brunch Sun. Reservations accepted. A local landmark and popular seafood house serving American cuisine with an emphasis on seafood, including crabs, or tuna, snapper, swordfish, or flounder broiled, blackened, or grilled with a variety of creative toppings, from garlic butter to salsa. There are steak and seafood combination platters, plus pasta, chops, steaks, and chicken dishes. The food is fresh and the price is right. The bar features 100 brands of beer and 100 different wines. Live entertainment nightly in-season. $12–25.

In Toms River

Hana (732-286-4465; www.hanasushi andsteak.com), 927 Rt. 166. Open daily for dinner. Reservations are accepted. A casual and relaxed place that's always crowded with fans of their fresh sushi. The menu also features a wide variety of teriyaki, tempura, and other well-prepared Japanese specialties. $12–23.

The Office Restaurant and Lounge (732-349-0800), 820 Main St. Open daily for lunch and dinner. Reservations are suggested. This downtown eatery is popular during the day with local businesspeople, at night with locals, and on weekends with visitors. The menu offers hearty seafood, steak, and pasta dishes, but you can opt for appetizers, sandwiches, or burgers if you're looking for something light. $10–20.

& **Basil T's Brew Pub & Italian Grill** (732-244-7566; www.basilts.com), 1171 Hooper Ave. Reservations are accepted. Open for lunch and dinner daily; brunch, Sun. Traditional Italian and Mediterranean cuisine in a casual yet inviting trattoria-style dining room. The thin-crust pizzas, wraps, and burgers are good choices, ditto for the appetizers like four-dip Mediterranean sampler—eggplant, roasted pepper and feta, cucumber-dill, and garlic— served with warm pita bread. Move on to grilled chicken in a warm herb vinaigrette, pan-seared pork tenderloin, or the vegetarian Greek sampler. $14–25.

EATING OUT

In Toms River

♪ **Linda's Pizza** (732-573-1906; www .trlindas.com), 932 Fisher Blvd. Open daily for lunch and dinner. This no-frills family eatery makes what many around here insist is some of South Jersey's best pizza. In addition to the popular pies, there's a full menu of subs, cheesesteaks, calzones, and Italian dinner specialties, from chicken parmigiana and veal scaloppine to baked ziti, plus a decent selection of Italian-style seafood dishes. $8–15.

🦞 **Apana II** (732-864-9100), Silverton Plaza, 1783 Hooper Ave. Open daily for lunch and dinner. Don't be fooled by the uninspiring strip-mall location. This authentic Indian restaurant is a local favorite. They offer a buffet at lunch (a real bargain) and dinner, as well as an à la carte menu. *Naan, poori,* and other traditional Indian breads are homemade. Try something from the clay tandoor oven, chicken or shrimp curry, or a seafood, lamb, or goat dish. Typical of Indian restaurants, there are many vegetarian choices. BYOB. $8–16.

In Forked River

🦞 **Forked River Diner** (609-693-2222), 317 Rt. 9. Open daily; 24 hours Fri.–Sat.; Sun.–Thurs. until 11 PM. A classic art deco–style diner and local landmark occupying one of New Jersey's quickly disappearing classic diner cars. This one was built in the 1960s by the Kullman Dining Car Company, a New Jersey–based firm established in 1927 that still makes ready-built diners like this one. The diner opens early for fishermen and stays open late for travelers and night owls. Low prices, hot coffee, generous portions of homestyle stick-to-your-ribs fare. $5–12.

SNACKS

In Toms River

🎭 **Mrs. Hanna Krause Candy** (732-270-9236; 888-657-2873; www.hanna krausecandy.com), 2220 Rt. 37. A family-owned business making old-fashioned confections by hand since 1929. Everything is made by hand, from the cordial cherries and nut bark, to the butter crunch and fudge. They cook all their own fillings—creams, marzipan, nougat, and jellies—then dip them individually in chocolate. The original store is still open in Paramus.

Natural Foods General Store and Vegetarian Café (732-240-9320), 675 Batchelor St. The general store is stocked with organic produce, wheat-free and low-carb products, and freshly baked goods. The café and deli area in back offers a healthy and tasty selection of daily lunch specials, vegetarian and vegan dishes, curries, tempeh, tofu, falafel, and refreshing fruit smoothies and fresh juices. A good place to pick up a boxed lunch to take to the beach.

In Lavallette

The Music Man (732-854-2779; www.njmusicman.com), 2305 Grand Central Ave. An ice cream shop with entertainment. The wait staff performs songs Vaudeville cabaret-style. Call or see Web site for the full performance schedule. Cash only.

✳ Entertainment

ARTS CENTERS 🎭 **Arts and Community Center at Ocean County College** (732-255-0500), College Dr. (off Hooper Ave.), Toms River. (**Note:** The center is undergoing renovation, and is scheduled to reopen in spring 2010.) A full schedule of children's programs, concerts, dance performances, and fresh takes on classic plays by the college's in-house theater company, the **Ocean County College Theatre Company,** as well as visiting repertory groups from around the country.

Ocean County Artists' Guild (732-270-3111; www.ocartistsguild.org), Ocean and Chestnut Aves., Island Heights. Exhibits, classes, and workshops for amateurs and professionals, as well as gallery shows featuring sculpture, paintings, and other works by local and regional artists and guild members. The **Gallery Gift Shop** has traditional and contemporary fine arts and crafts for sale. Ask about their schedule of cultural programs and demonstrations.

MUSIC Garden State Philharmon-

ic (732-451-0064; www.gardenstate philharmonic.org), Brick. Ocean County's professional symphony orchestra was created by local musicians in 1956, and features professional musicians as well as the youth orchestra and chorus. A subscription series of five concerts as well as other programs are held each performance season at a variety of venues throughout Ocean County, including Toms River High School and the Strand Theater.

✳ Selective Shopping
SPECIAL SHOPS

In Lavallette
Sama's Seashore Delights (732-793-5566; www.seashoredelights.com), 507 Grand Central Ave. (Rt. 35). Open Thurs. and Sun., noon–5; Fri.–Sat., noon–9. A quaint downtown candy shop a block from the beach. Confections come creatively wrapped in specialty gift baskets, or you can buy them individually. Fudge, chocolate-covered pretzels, nuts, and an ever-changing selection of seasonal treats. There's also Italian ice and homemade ice cream.

In Toms River
Ocean County Mall (732-244-8200; www.oceancountymall.com), 1201 Hooper Ave. at Bay Ave. (Rt. 37). Open daily. This is Ocean County's only enclosed regional shopping center. There are 115 specialty shops, restaurants, and a food court, anchored by a Macy's, JCPenney, and Sears. A good alternative to the beaches on a rainy day.

✳ Special Events
March: ⚓ **Ocean County St. Patrick's Day Parade** (732-830-1847), Seaside Heights. A parade of floats, marching units, and bands that draws more than 50,000 spectators.

May: ⚓ **New Jersey State Chili and Salsa Championship** (732-341-8738; www.downtowntomsriver.com), Toms River. An International Chili Society–sanctioned chili competition with live music, food, crafts vendors, children's entertainment, and more than 50 cooks. **Toms River Canoe and Kayak Race** (609-971-3085; oceancountyparks.org), Toms River. Races on the Toms River in solo and tandem boats.

July: ⚓ **Independence Day Celebrations** in Lavallette (732-793-3652; www.lavallette.com) and Seaside Heights (732-854-8000; 800-732-7467; www.seasideheightstourism.com), with fireworks and family activities. ⚓ **New Jersey State Ice Cream Festival** (732-341-8738; www.downtowntoms river.com), Washington St., Toms River. Ice cream—both homemade and gourmet name brands—plus music, crafters, food vendors, and children's entertainment. **Ocean County Fair** (732-914-9466; www.ocean countyfair.com), Robert Miller Air Park, Berkeley Township. **Wooden Boat Festival** (732-349-9209; www.tomsriverseaport.org), Toms River Seaport Society Maritime Museum, Toms River. This 25-year-old festival is one of the largest events of its type on the East Coast and draws thousands of visitors to see restored vintage wooden boats.

August: **Barnegat Lighthouse Fine Art Sale** (609-361-6186), Barnegat Lighthouse State Park, Barnegat Light.

September: ⚓ **Seafood Festival** (732-854-8000; 800-732-7467; www.seaside heightstourism.com), Seaside Heights. ⚓ **ClownFest** (732-854-8000; 800-732-7467; www.seasideheightstourism.com), Seaside Heights.

October: ⚓ **Halloween Parade** (732-929-2138; www.oceancountytourism.com), Toms River. **Italian Street**

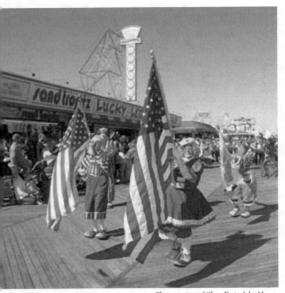

Photo courtesy of ClownFest—John Maurer

Festival (732-854-8000; 800-732-7467; seasideheightstourism.com), Seaside Heights. Italian food, exhibits, and entertainment.

December: ♪ **First Night Celebration** in Seaside Heights (732-854-8000; 800-732-7467; www.seaside heightstourism.com) features family entertainment and activities on New Year's Eve.

CLOWNFEST IS A POPULAR SEPTEMBER EVENT IN SEASIDE HEIGHTS. IT'S A NATIONALLY KNOWN CLOWN CELEBRATION WITH PUBLIC PERFORMANCES, BALLOON AND MAKEUP COMPETITIONS, AND A CLOWN PARADE.

LONG BEACH ISLAND:
BARNEGAT LIGHT TO HOLGATE

L ong Beach Island is the aptly named fingerlike barrier island about midway along the Jersey Shore that protects Barnegat Bay and Little Egg Harbor from
the vagaries of the Atlantic Ocean. The Lenni-Lenape were the island's first summer visitors, making annual pilgrimages from the mainland for the rich fishing and
clamming grounds. Rooming houses and rambling hotels sprang up on the 18-
mile-long island in the early 19th century as vacationers came in droves by stagecoach and train to the ferries waiting to shuttle them across the bay. Today, beach
towns that are quiet in the off-season swell with summer tourists who come for the
silver-sand beaches, amusements, water sports, and marinas.

The 19th-century lighthouse standing sentry at the northern tip of Long Beach
Island—known affectionately by islanders and visitors as Old Barney—marks the
entrance to one of the most dangerous inlets on the east coast of the United
States. Before it was first lit in 1858, more than 200 sailing ships ran aground while
trying to navigate the shifting Barnegat Shoals. Today it's the showpiece of
Barnegat Light State Park—New Jersey's smallest state park—and one of the Jersey Shore's most famous landmarks. Pictures of this much photographed and painted lighthouse, one of the best known in America, appear on postcards, in
calendars, and in the vacation scrapbooks of thousands of tourists. Visitors can
climb the 217 steps to the top, where they are rewarded with a magnificent
panorama of the Atlantic Ocean, Long Beach Island, and much of the Jersey
Shore. The beacon that once guided countless mariners to safety is now extinguished, and the multifaceted glass lens is on display at the Barnegat Light Historical Museum, just south of the park in the town of Barnegat Light.

Barnegat Light is a quaint beach town whose population of less than a thousand
permanent residents swells to several thousand during the summer. Its specialty
shops and seafood restaurants are good places to visit after exploring Old Barney.
The community is also known for its commercial fishing fleet based out of the
Viking Village dock complex on the bayside. Barnegat Light is considered the tilefish capital of the world as well as a major East Coast center for scallops. Thanks to
the rich offshore fishing grounds, Viking Village is the island's largest employer.
Boats catering to sightseers and fishermen also leave from here; there are shops,
boutiques, and dock tours for those who opt to stay ashore.

Loveladies and Harvey Cedars are side-by-side pricey enclaves, the latter

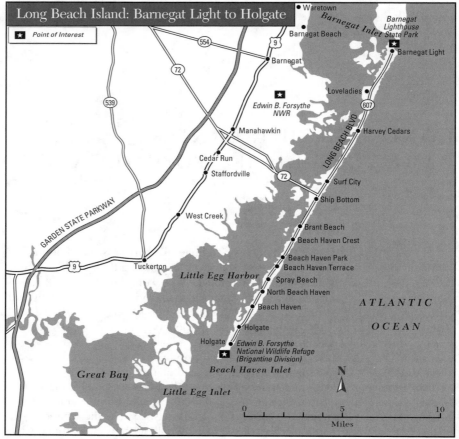

© The Countryman Press

named for the tall red cedars that once covered this part of the island. Whaling was big business here in the 1600s; New England fishermen were enticed south by tales of riches and an abundance of whales that they depleted in short order. Both are quiet communities that offer visitors lovely beaches, fishing, family-friendly seafood eateries, and outdoor concerts and other events during the summer. The annual Blue Claw Festival in Harvey Cedars features crab races, activities for children, and lots of fresh seafood. In Loveladies, the Long Beach Island Foundation of the Arts and Sciences is an active arts center and gallery open to the public for lectures, concerts, art exhibits, and even guided nature walks.

Surf City is a family-oriented resort town that boasts some of the best surf on the shoreline, as the name implies. At the busy junction where Route 72 connects the mainland to Long Beach Island is Ship Bottom, the crowded and heavily trafficked beach town named after a 19th-century shipwreck just offshore. (According to local legend, the upside-down vessel washed ashore after being pummeled by the dangerous Barnegat Shoals during a dense fog. When townspeople approached the wreckage, they found a young woman on board, the ship's lone survivor.) This clogged commercial sprawl of stores and gas stations is ideal for stocking up on vacation supplies or souvenirs, but the towns north and south of it are far more desirable.

Beach Haven was founded in 1874 as one of two planned resort communities on the island. Today, it is the island's busiest and most popular vacation destination, full of restaurants, shops, nightlife, and a variety of accommodations. Its beaches are lovely, and its historic district of meticulously restored Victorian homes is perfect for strolling—several of these structures have been turned into charming antiques-filled bed & breakfasts that pamper overnight guests. Fantasy Island Amusement Park, the island's only amusement center, has thrill rides, midway games, live entertainment, a video arcade, and a vintage carousel in an old-time Victorian-style village setting, not to mention a water park next door.

Concerts, crafts shows, and flea markets are held in Bicentennial Park all summer long. Surflight Theatre has been a legendary Long Beach Island venue since it opened as a summer stock theater in 1950 and began presenting high-quality renditions of classic musicals. Bay Village in Beach Haven is a unique complex of shops and attractions designed to resemble a historic fishing village. The Long Beach Island Historical Society runs an excellent local-history museum, whose informative exhibits cover the island's early whaling days, destructive coastal storms, and the region's evolution into one of New Jersey's top seaside resorts. From here, pick up a self-guided walking map of Beach Haven's Victorian homes and explore the historic district just outside the door.

Bayside communities on the mainland include Barnegat and Barnegat Bay—not to be confused with Barnegat Light, 5 miles across the water on Long Beach Island. Antiques hunters cruise through Barnegat along Route 9, a main thoroughfare dotted with shops selling an eclectic jumble of antiques and collectibles. In Waretown, the legendary Albert Music Hall has been the scene of lively Saturday-night folk and bluegrass concerts for more than three decades. Its roots lie in the Pinelands hunting cabin of brothers George and Joe Albert, who hosted informal weekend gatherings of local fiddlers and other musicians. Word of the rousing jam sessions spread, and the crowds quickly outgrew the cabin, known affectionately as the Home Place. The backwater vibe may fool you into thinking you're the first to discover this place, but it has been a mainstay for more than three decades; features in *National Geographic,* the *New York Times,* and other equally top-notch and widely read publications have put the hall on the international map. Today a variety of live bands plays short sets every Saturday night.

Settlements were established on Barnegat Bay as early as 1699, and a century later Tuckerton was named for Revolutionary War veteran Ebenezer Tucker and soon became one of the country's first official colonial-era ports of entry. Tuckerton was a significant hub for shipbuilding, lumbering, iron making, and salt manufacturing. Today, it's best known as home to the Tuckerton Seaport and Museum, a 40-acre re-created village on the banks of Tuckerton Creek. Thoughtful exhibits and displays are devoted to the area's unique history and maritime heritage. There's a collection of restored historic houses to explore, and a full schedule of presentations on oystering, boatbuilding, decoy carving, and many other skills that figure prominently in the region's culture.

A spectacular natural landscape of tidal marshes, creeks, and inlets teeming with shorebirds and waterfowl is protected under the auspices of several vast sanctuaries. The 40,000-acre Edwin B. Forsythe National Wildlife Refuge maintains a wildlife observation area in Barnegat, and protects the entire southern tip of Long

Beach Island in Holgate. The dunes and beaches are off-limits during the summer to shelter the refuge's population of endangered piping plovers while they are busy nesting. From fall to spring, however, the beachfront is open to anglers, birders, and beachcombers. Great Bay Boulevard Wildlife Management Area, Manahawkin Wildlife Management Area, and the Jacques Cousteau National Estuarine Research Reserve protect thousands of acres along the mainland, as well as the tiny islands dotting Little Egg Harbor.

Entries in this section are arranged in roughly geographic order, from north to south.

AREA CODE 609.

GUIDANCE Southern Ocean County Chamber of Commerce (609-494-7211; 800-292-6372; www.discoversouthernocean.com), 265 West Ninth St., Ship Bottom 08008. The chamber maintains an informative Web site and publishes a variety of travel publications on attractions, restaurants, activities, and lodging in the Long Beach Island area, from the communities on the island to those across Little Egg Harbor on the mainland. They'll send a copy of their free annual vacation planner, on request.

GETTING THERE *By air:* **Newark Liberty International Airport** (973-961-6000; parking information: 888-397-4636; www.panynj.com) in Newark serves the entire state. Those traveling to New Jersey also use **John F. Kennedy International Airport** (718-244-4168; www.kennedyairport.com) and **LaGuardia International Airport** (718-533-3850; www.laguardiaairport.com) in New York City. **Atlantic City International Airport** (609-645-7895; www.acairport.com), Exit 9 off the Atlantic City Expressway, Egg Harbor Township, is served by Spirit Airlines (800-772-7117; www.spiritair.com).

By rail: **New Jersey Transit's North Coast Line** (973-275-5555; www.njtransit.com) offers express commuter service connecting Penn Station in New York City (via Newark's Penn Station) to shore points in this region, including Red Bank, Little Silver, Monmouth Park, Long Branch, Elberon, Allenhurst, Asbury Park, Bradley Beach, and Belmar, continuing as far south as Bay Head. The stops are within walking distance of most beaches and attractions.

By bus: **New Jersey Transit** (973-275-5555; www.njtransit.com) and **Academy Bus Service** (800-442-7272; www.academybus.com) offer bus transportation throughout the region.

By car: The **Garden State Parkway** connects the New York and Washington, DC, regions to the Jersey Shore; from Philadelphia and Trenton, **I-195** east leads toward the coast, where **Route 138** continues to Belmar. **Route 70** is a major secondary road that heads east across New Jersey from the Camden area, ending just west of Point Pleasant Beach. **Route 72** goes directly to Long Beach Island; it's the only route onto the island. **Long Beach Boulevard (Route 607)** runs the length of Long Beach Island from Barnegat Light to Holgate.

GETTING AROUND *Taxis:* **Express Taxi** (609-597-5106), Manahawkin, serves Long Beach Island.

MEDICAL EMERGENCY Southern Ocean County Hospital (609-978-8900; www.soch.com), 1140 Rt. 72 West, Manahawkin. The emergency number is 609-978-2205.

✳ To See

HISTORIC SITE Heritage Village and Museum (609-698-5284; www.barne gathistoricalsociety.com), 575 East Bay Ave., Barnegat. Open Memorial Day–Labor Day, Sat. 1–4. Free admission. A collection of 18th-century buildings and shops dedicated to preserving the maritime heritage of Barnegat, a quiet bayside town that was once a world-famous seafaring port. The **Edwards House** and **Lippincott-Falkenburgh House** are the two main buildings; there's also a barbershop, corncrib, and butcher shop. On display are vintage maps, authentic captains' logs, and other artifacts that tell the story of the sea captains and baymen who made a living off the bay and the waters far beyond New Jersey. Docents from the **Barnegat Historical Society** are available to answer questions. Ask about a schedule of special events and programs that are held at the village throughout the year.

MUSEUMS Long Beach Island Historical Museum (609-492-0700; www .lbimuseum.org), Engleside and Beach Aves., Beach Haven. Summers, daily 10 AM–4 PM, plus Wed. 7 PM–9 PM. Exhibits and displays of island artifacts, photographs, and memorabilia, maintained by the **Long Beach Island Historical Association.** The museum is housed in a former 1882 Episcopal church. A full schedule of guest speakers and special programs includes guided walking tours of Beach Haven's Victorian architecture (see *To Do—Sightseeing Tours*). $3.

✳ To Do

AMUSEMENTS ✧ Fantasy Island Amusement Park (609-492-4000; www .fantasyislandpark.com), 320 W. Seventh St., Beach Haven. Open weekends May–June, daily mid-June–Labor Day, and weekends through mid-Sept. Open 5 PM–midnight weekdays; 2 PM–midnight weekends. The arcade is open weekends and holidays through the winter. Long Beach Island's only amusement park is modeled after an old-fashioned Victorian-style village, complete with ornate lampposts, oak benches, brick walkways, Tiffany glass, and a classic turn-of-the-20th-century carousel. There are rides for all ages, traditional midway games, a video arcade, live entertainment, and food. The park works hard to project a wholesome family-friendly environment, which is made evident by the lineup of special programs, from illusionists and DJs to live reptile shows.

✧ Thundering Surf Water Park (609-492-0869; www.thunderingsurfwaterpark .com), Taylor and Bay avenues, Beach Haven. Open late-May–early Sept., daily 9–7:30. A variety of low- and high-thrill water rides and slides, Cowabunga Beach interactive water games, and the Crazy Lazy River water ride. The park has snack bars, an old-fashioned ice cream parlor, and two 18-hole mini-golf courses.

BICYCLING Wells Mills County Park and Nature Center (609-971-3085; 877-627-2757; www.oceancountyparks.org), 905 Wells Mills Rd. (Rt. 532), Waretown. Open daily 10–4. More than 16 miles of easy-to-moderate off-road trails open to cyclists.

Surf Buggy Center of LBI (609-361-3611), 1414 Long Beach Blvd., Surf City. They carry just about every kind of rental bike imaginable, from tandems and hybrids to comfortable cruisers, high-end road bikes, and mountain bikes.

BIRDING Barnegat Light State Park (609-494-2016; www.njparksandforests .com), Broadway and the Bay, Barnegat Light. Open year-round. Free admission. The park is ideal for observing the many species of waterfowl that stop here to rest

---

BARNEGAT LIGHTHOUSE

(609-494-2016), Barnegat Light State Park, Barnegat Light. Open daily Memorial Day–Labor Day 9–4:30; daily 9–3:30 during the rest of the year. Free admission. You'd be hard-pressed to find a Jersey Shore vacation album without a photograph of "Old Barney," the venerable light tower presiding over Barnegat Inlet at the northern tip of Long Beach Island. It was under construction from 1856 to 1858 and was built by George Meade, who also designed Atlantic City's Absecon Lighthouse and later became a major general in the Union army. For nearly a century it guided mariners through the notoriously dangerous inlet, whose shifting sandbars, strong currents, and hard-to-navigate offshore shoals were the demise of many ships and fishing boats. Its distinct and handsome red-and-white light tower soaring 165 feet above the sea makes it the second-tallest lighthouse in the country, and a beloved landmark for both locals and tourists. In the summer, for a small fee, you can enter the tower and climb the 217 steps to the top, where the views of the Atlantic Ocean, Barnegat Bay, and Long Beach Island are spectacular. Old Barney makes regular appearances on calendars, postcards, T-shirts, and those glossy, beautifully photographed coffee-table books that feature American lighthouses. The beacon was extinguished when the light station was decommissioned in 1944, but the tower is dramatically floodlit at night.

Just south of the lighthouse is the **Barnegat Light Historical Museum** (609-494-8578; www.bl-hs.org), Fifth Street and Central Avenue, Barnegat Light. The museum is open during June and Sept., Sat.–Sun., 2–4; July–Aug., daily 2–4; grounds are open daily from dawn to dusk. Artifacts from shipwrecks, fishing and nautical memorabilia, and vintage photographs of Barnegat City (the former name of Barnegat Light) are housed in the 1903 one-room **Barnegat Light Elementary School.** After the school closed in the 1950s it became a museum and has since been filled with mostly donated items, from a Revolutionary War–era iron pot used to extract salt from ocean water, to shark teeth and a whale's skull. Many visitors come to see Old Barney's 5-ton lighthouse lens made of over 1,000 pieces of glass. The museum is surrounded by the lush and lovely **Edith Duff Gwinn Gardens,** maintained by the Long Beach Island Garden Club.

and feed during the spring and fall migrations. Egrets, herons, pelicans, and other wading birds are often seen, as are a great number of shorebirds.

Edwin B. Forsythe National Wildlife Refuge (609-652-1665; www.fws.gov/ northeast/forsythe), Bay Shore Dr., Barnegat. This 300-acre freshwater marshland with an observation platform is a perfect spot for birding. This is just a small pocket of the entire refuge, a vast 40,000-acre undisturbed tract of salt marsh that extends south to Atlantic City, covering islands, coves, and inlets, as well as the mainland. The refuge's **Holgate Unit** (609-698-1387) covers the entire southern tip of Long Beach Island and, because it's such an important wildlife habitat and an extremely fragile environment, visitor access is strictly limited. Beach nesting birds, especially the endangered piping plovers and black skimmers, are active generally from April to August. The refuge is open to visitors only from Sept.– Mar., when pedestrians and four-wheel-drive vehicles (a permit is required to drive on the sand) are allowed on the beachfront for birding and wildlife observation. It's a rewarding place for birding: the beach area is full of waterfowl and shorebirds, including terns, gulls, sandpipers, plovers, herons, egrets, marsh hawks, and many other species.

BOAT EXCURSIONS **Black Whale Cruises** (609-492-0333; www.blackwhale cruises.com), Centre St. and the Bay, Beach Haven. Open May–Oct. The *Crystal Queen* is a double-decker paddle wheeler offering 1-hour sightseeing cruises on the bay. They also operate a water shuttle to Atlantic City's Trump Marina.

BOATING (See also *Boat Excursions.*)

Full-service marinas in the area include **Bob's Bay Marina** (609-698-7264), 459 East Bay Ave., Barnegat; **The Marina at Barnegat Light** (609-494-6611; www .fishgear.net), 1501 Bayview Ave., Barnegat Light; **Ship Bottom Marine Center** (609-494-8100), 2601 Central Ave., Ship Bottom; **Beach Haven Yacht Club Marina** (609-492-9101), 20 West Ave., Beach Haven; **Morrison's Beach Haven Marina** (609-492-2150; www.morrisonslbi.com), 525 Second St., on the Bay, Beach Haven; **Sportsman's Marina** (609-492-7931; www.sportsmansmarina.com), 20th St. and the Bay, Beach Haven; and **Cedar Cove Marina** (609-296-2066), 458 South Green St., Tuckerton.

CYCLISTS AT THE BEACH IN HOLGATE, A QUIET RESIDENTIAL COMMUNITY THAT SHARES THE SOUTHERNMOST TIP OF LONG BEACH ISLAND WITH PART OF THE MASSIVE EDWIN B. FORSYTHE NATIONAL WILDLIFE REFUGE.

Photo courtesy of Ocean County Public Affairs

HE CENTRAL SEACOAST

Photo courtesy of the Tuckerton Seaport Collection

TUCKERTON SEAPORT IS A RE-CREATED WORKING SEAPORT AND MARITIME
MUSEUM ALONG TUCKERTON CREEK IN TUCKERTON, DEDICATED TO PRESERVING
THE MARITIME HERITAGES, ENVIRONMENT, AND FOLKLORE OF BARNEGAT BAY.

✍ TUCKERTON SEAPORT

(609-296-8868; www.tuckertonseaport.org), 120 West Main St. (Rt. 9), Tuckerton. Open Apr.–Oct., daily, 10–5; Nov.–Dec., weekends, 11–4; Jan.–Mar.,
weekends, 10–5. Adults $8; seniors $6; children 6–12, $3; children 5 and
under, free. A re-created working maritime village on 40 acres along Tuckerton Creek, dedicated to the rich history and maritime heritage of Barnegat
Bay and the baymen who worked its quiet waters for centuries. The seaport
complex features 16 replicated sheds, shacks, clam and oyster houses,
decoy-carving shops, a lighthouse, and a boatworks. Permanent and changing exhibits feature items from the seaport's collection of memorabilia,

The following **municipal boat ramps** are open to the public; for hours and fees
see: www.longbeachisland.com. *In Barnegat Light* on 10th St. *In Harvey Cedars*
(609-494-2843) on Bay Terrace. *In Surf City* (609-494-3064) on Division St. *In
Ship Bottom*, 10th St. *In Beach Haven* on Taylor Ave.

FISHING Barnegat Light is a major sportfishing hub on Long Beach Island.
Charter boats and party boats operate out of many marinas, including **Viking Vil-
lage** (609-494-0113; www.vikingvillage.net), 19th St. and the Bay; **Lighthouse
Marina** (609-494-2305), Sixth St. and Barnegat Bay.

Big party boats (100 to 130 passengers) operating out of Barnegat Light include
Miss LBI (609-361-2250), 14th St.; *Doris Mae IV* (609-494-1692), 18th St.; *Carolyn Ann III* (609-693-4281), 18th St.; and *Miss Barnegat Light* (609-494-2094),
18th St. and Bayview Ave.

GOLF Ocean Acres Country Club (609-597-9393; www.allforeclub.com), 925
Buccaneer Ln., Manahawkin; **Ocean County Golf Course at Atlantis** (609-296-

regional crafts, vintage tools, and restored boats. There are more than 5,000 maps, documents, and photographs; oyster rakes, shrimp nets, hay forks, crab traps, and other tools that baymen worked with; more than 45 restored boats, from duck-hunting boats and recreational sailing vessels to skiffs, charter-fishing boats, and a dugout canoe; and some 300 hand-carved decoys and shore-birds from various regions along the eastern seaboard. For many, a highlight of their visit here is the variety of live programs on historic maritime trades. Watch as baymen demonstrate old-time methods of clamming, and local artisans take part in boatbuilding and decoy carving (see **Baymen's Seafood and Music Festival** under *Special Events*).

The visitors center is home to the **Jacques Cousteau Coastal Education Center** (609-812-0649; www.marine.rutgers.edu), a series of interactive exhibits that serves as a virtual tour of the nearby 110,000-acre **Jacques Cousteau National Estuarine Research Reserve,** one of 26 such reserves around the country that protect coastal estuaries. An estuary is the point at which a river flows into the sea; the combination of fresh water and salt water creates a rich ecosystem for a wide variety of plants and wildlife. The refuge—managed by the Department of Marine and Coastal Sciences at Rutgers University—encompasses habitats ranging from pinelands and open ocean to coastal plain, forest, bay, and barrier island. Only about 1 percent of the tract is developed, making it one of the least-disturbed estuaries in the Northeast.

Among the historic buildings is the circa 1699 **Andrews-Bartlett Homestead,** the oldest home in Ocean County. There's a restaurant, a gift shop, and docks available for visitors arriving by boat. Docent-guided boat trips during the summer along Tuckerton Creek and Little Egg Harbor Bay.

2444; www.oceancountyparks.org), 261 Country Club Blvd., Little Egg Harbor; and **Sea Oaks Golf Club** (609-296-2656; www.seaoakscc.com), 99 Golf View Dr., Little Egg Harbor—all offer public 18-hole courses, each with a driving range and a clubhouse with a restaurant, snack bar, and pro shop.

KAYAKING New Jersey Kayak (609-698-4440; www.njkayak.com), 409 East Bay Ave., Barnegat. A full-service kayak shop with kayak rentals, instruction, and guided and self-guided ecotours for novices and experienced paddlers. Their slogan is "Adventure in your own backyard"; here that means the open waters of Barnegat Bay or the shallow coves, tidal pools, salt marshes, and meandering creeks of the **Edwin B. Forsythe National Wildlife Refuge.**

First Bridge Marina and Kayaks (609-296-1888; www.fbkayak.com), 500 Great Bay Blvd., Tuckerton. Reservations are required for tours. A full-service kayak shop with sales and rentals (single and tandem kayaks), plus a variety of guided kayak nature tours, from educational nature tours to overnight and sunset excursions through the vast **Great Bay Boulevard Wildlife Management Area.**

They take beginners and seasoned paddlers, and you can go out for a couple hours or a couple days. Their most popular guided tour, for individuals or groups, is the 2-hour excursion through the salt marshes. Birders love this trip for the rich variety of wildlife along the way, including nesting ospreys. Other customized guided tours include kayak fishing tours, and sunset, moonlight, and camping tours.

PARASAILING Beach Haven Parasailing (609-492-0375; www.bhparasailing .com), Bay Haven Marina, 2702 Long Beach Blvd., Beach Haven. Reservations are required. From 500 feet above the bay, the views of Long Beach Island, Beach Haven, and Little Egg Inlet are spectacular. All ages are welcome, and no experience is necessary. You can take off and land on the boat platform, or they will dip you in the water during your ride, on request.

SIGHTSEEING TOURS Dock Tours at Viking Village (609-494-7211; www .vikingvillageshows.com/historic_viking), 19th St. and Bayview Ave., Barnegat Light. Reservations are required; call for a schedule. Guided tours of Barnegat Light's commercial fishing docks are enlightening to those who have never realized that New Jersey has a commercial fishing fleet. Much of the fresh seafood on the menu of seafood restaurants up and down Long Beach Island—and the Jersey Shore, for that matter—comes off boats that dock here.

✐ **Alliance for a Living Ocean** (609-492-0222), 2007 Long Beach Blvd., North Beach Haven. Call for a schedule. A popular series of summertime environmental programs includes **Inherit the Earth tours** to local natural points of interest, children's stories and crafts programs, beach cleanups, ecocruises on Long Beach Island via trolley, and beach walks at Barnegat Light State Park.

Beach Haven Guided Walking Tours (609-492-0700), Beach and Engleside Aves., Beach Haven. Tours Tues. and Fri. morning, late-June–Labor Day weekend; call for hours. Groups meet on the front porch of the Long Beach Island Museum, where volunteers with the **Long Beach Island Historical Association** lead visitors on an informative tour of more than 30 historic buildings in Beach Haven's Victorian downtown.

The Belmar Environmental Commission (732-681-3700, press 9, press 214) offers a popular series of free nature walks/talks at Silver Lake, Shell Beach, and Shark River. The town's Treasure Trail highlights noteworthy local environmental and historical aspects like the Mast of the Malta, the remains of an 1865 shipwreck. There's also a self-guided 11-mile walk-bike-drive around Shark River that passes the first lunar radio signal, unique architecture and ecological highlights.

SURFING *In Surf City* (609-494-3064) there's a designated surfing area on the beach between First and Third Sts. The waves are at their best in the morning and late afternoon. **Ron Jon's Surf Shop** (609-494-8844), Ninth St. and Central Ave., Ship Bottom, has gear, clothing, and advice.

WATER SPORTS Outfitters all over Long Beach Island rent a variety of water toys, from Jet Skis and WaveRunners to windsurfing boards and ski boats. They include **Island Surf and Sail** (609-494-5553; www.islandsurf-sail.com), 3304 Long Beach Blvd., Brant Beach; **George's Boat Rentals** (609-492-7931, www.sports

mansmarina.com), 20th St. and the Bay, North Beach Haven; and **Beach Haven Parasailing** (609-492-3518), 2702 Long Beach Blvd., Beach Haven.

✳ Green Space

BEACHES Barnegat Light (609-494-9196; www.barnlight.com). Wheelchair access to the beach is available at 9th and 29th Sts. Day $5. Beach badges can be purchased any day from the beach badge booth at West 11th St. or from badge checkers at the beaches.

Harvey Cedars (609-494-2843; www.harveycedars.org). Harvey Cedars beaches are on the ocean side, except for the bayside beach at 75th St. Day $6.

Surf City (609-494-3064). There is a designated surfing area between First and Third Sts. Fishing is allowed from North 23rd to North 25th Sts. There is a bayside beach near 15th St. and Barnegat Ave. Day $8; seniors, and children 11 and under, free.

Ship Bottom (609-494-1614; www.shipbottom.org). Day $7; children 12 and under, free; senior 65 and older, $3 lifetime; disabled, free.

Brant Beach (609-361-1000). Day $6; children 11 and under, free. If you're looking for a wide beach and smooth sand, head to the beaches at the southern end of town; the northern beaches are much narrower. There's a bayside beach at **BayView Park** on 68th St.

Beach Haven (609-492-0111; www.beachhaven-nj.gov). There's a wheelchair ramp at the Centre St. beach. On the bayside, there's a small kiddie beach with a play area and basketball court at Taylor Ave. Day $5; seniors, and children 11 and under, free.

PARKS ♿ Barnegat Lighthouse State Park (609-494-2016), Broadway, off Long Beach Blvd., Barnegat Light. Open year-round. Free admission. Most people come here to see 165-foot-tall Old Barney (see sidebar, page 416), but this small and picturesque 32-acre park offers picnicking along the Barnegat Inlet, jetty fishing, and a short self-guided nature trail through one of Long Beach Island's last remaining tracts of maritime forest. It's typical of the kind of woodland that blanketed the island centuries ago, a mix of holly, red cedar, sassafras, and black cherry. Anglers at the park's south jetty—which is handicapped accessible—fish for flounder, bluefish, and striped bass.

Wells Mills County Park and Nature Center (609-971-3085; www.ocean.nj .us/parks/wellsmills), 905 Wells Mills Rd. (Rt. 532), Waretown. Open daily 10–4. Free admission. This 910-acre park—the largest in Ocean County's park system—protects a trail-laced oak and pine forest surrounding Wells Mills Lake, a picturesque freshwater lake where you can launch a canoe or go fishing. The observation deck atop the nature center affords views into the vast Pinelands National Reserve that blankets much of South Jersey in a million-plus-acre sandy pine forest. Inside the center, check out the nature displays and ask about their schedule of nature programs offered throughout the year, including the very popular full-moon hikes. The park hosts the annual **Pine Barrens Jamboree** (see *Special Events*).

✳ Lodging

Long Beach Island and the mainland across the bay offer a bounty of vacation rentals, from houses and cottages to apartments and luxury condominiums. Contact the **Southern Ocean County Chamber of Commerce** (609-494-7211; 800-292-6372; www.discover southernocean.com), 265 West Ninth St., Ship Bottom 08008, for a list of real estate agents in the area that specialize in vacation rentals.

HOTELS ♂ ♿ **Surf City Hotel** (609-494-7281; www.surfcityhotel.com), Eighth St. and Long Beach Blvd., P.O. Box 250, Surf City 08008. A renovated beachfront hotel with no-frills but clean motel-style rooms outfitted with standard amenities. There are newer rooms and a brand new apartment-style unit. Roomier suites are in the cottage, including one that is wheelchair accessible. The hotel restaurant is casual and beachy, serving American cuisine like seafood, prime rib, and award-winning clam chowder. The **Beach Club** lounge has live music, reggae, and karaoke. Light meals are served in the pub (see *Dining Out*). $105–375.

♿ ¹⁰ **daddy O** (609-494-7051; www.daddyohotel.com), 4401 Long Beach Blvd., Brant Beach 08008. Open year round. A Long Beach Island landmark, now a modern, full-featured, boutique hotel within walking distance to beaches on the Atlantic Ocean and Barnegat Bay. The place was shut down for a time during World War II when the U.S. Army used the building as a barracks; other than that, it has been home to generations of vacationers year after year. The on-site seafood restaurant is popular for lunch and dinner. During the season there's live entertainment Fri. and Sat. in the bar. Wi-Fi throughout. $250–450.

♂ ¹⁰ **St. Rita Hotel** (609-492-9192; www.stritahotel.com), 127 Engleside Ave., Beach Haven 08008. Open late-May–Sept. Long Beach Island's oldest operating hotel is also one of the few remaining grand hotels—ones that are more than a century old—left standing along the Jersey Shore. Guests first started staying in the circa-1840 home in the 1870s, when the local couple residing there added a few rooms to make a little extra cash. At first the rooms were rented out only to clergy members; later the invitation was extended to families and tourists. Vintage photographs in the lounge tell the hotel's long and colorful story, from the fierce coastal storms it weathered to its stint as Beach Haven's turn-of-the-20th-century post office. Today it's on the National Register of Historic Places and in the hands of the Coates family, who have been at the helm for more than 50 years, offering one- and two-room air-conditioned hotel accommodations; some rooms have a private bath, whereas others have a sink in the room but share a bath in the hall. All have basic amenities, Wi-Fi, and are clean and simply furnished. There are also two apartments (for families only) that sleep four to six people and are rented by the week. The front porch is cozy and inviting, full of wicker furniture; the lounge has antiques, old photographs, and memorabilia. Bicentennial Park is across the street, and beaches, shops, and restaurants are within walking distance. Children 12 and older welcome. Rooms, $75–300, per night; two apartments rented weekly, $1,060–1,310.

INNS

In Beach Haven 08008

♿ ¹⁰ **Julia's of Savannah** (609-492-5004; www.juliasoflbi.com), 209 Centre St. Open Feb.–Dec.; closed Jan. A meticulously restored elegant Victorian inn, a romantic retreat at the heart of Beach Haven. Common areas, including a cozy sitting room and a breezy wraparound porch, have authentic period details. Six charming guest rooms and three luxurious suites offer unique features, and most have a fireplace, canopy bed, or private veranda. All have carefully chosen period antiques. Two of the suites have a Jacuzzi tub; the other has a charming claw-foot bathtub. Complimentary Wi-Fi, bicycles, as well as towels, chairs, and badges for the beach. Afternoon tea and full breakfast. $275–350.

"ᵀ" Green Gables Inn and Restaurant (609-492-3553; www.gableslbi .com), 212 Centre St. Closed Jan.– mid-Feb., open daily May–Oct.; Fri.– Sun. during the off-season. A romantic 1880 Victorian with five cozy guest-rooms, two with private bath, all with air-conditioning, Wi-Fi, and charming décor. Tucked into their tiny inn is one of Long Beach Island's most highly acclaimed gourmet restaurants (see *Dining Out*), whose five-course dinners are enjoyed outdoors or in the tearoom. Beach badges are complimentary, as is continental breakfast in-season. $100–180.

✦ "ᵀ" Windward Manor Inn (609-492-4468; www.windwardmanorinn .com), Atlantic Ave. and Amber St. Open Memorial Day weekend–mid-Oct. A historic seaside inn with a variety of accommodations, from studios with kitchenettes to one- and two-bedroom efficiencies with full kitchens and dining areas. All rooms have TV, Wi-Fi, phone, private bath, and air-conditioning. Guests have use of the library, the Garden Lounge, and outdoor barbecue grills. Complimentary badges for the beach, which is just 200 feet from the inn. Continental breakfast. $130–339.

"ᵀ" J. D. Thompson Inn (609-294-1331; www.jdthompsoninn.com), 149 East Main St. (Rt. 9). Open year-round. An 1823 Gothic Revival–style inn at the heart of Tuckerton, within walking distance (two blocks) of the Tuckerton Seaport (see sidebar, page 418). Lorenzo and Catherine Lauro have filled their charming inn with authentic Victorian décor. The six uniquely decorated guest rooms and one suite are fitted out with handsome period antiques. Each has private bath, TV, Wi-Fi, phone, and air-conditioning; some have a fireplace. There's an outdoor spa, open in-season. Guests can make use of the complimentary beach badges and the inn's bicycles (early spring through late fall). Continental breakfast is available during winter season; a full breakfast is served spring through fall and on weekends. $130–210.

BED & BREAKFASTS

In Beach Haven 08008
✦ "ᵀ" The Victoria Guest House Bed and Breakfast (609-492-4154; www.lbivictoria.com), 126 Amber St. Open May–Oct. Side-by-side restored late-19th-century homes offer warm and homey accommodations a half block from the ocean. **Victoria** is the main house, where breakfast is served and wicker furniture fills rambling wraparound porches. There are 8 guest rooms here—some small, others spacious—that might feature an antique armoire or Victorian claw-foot tub; some overlook the garden, all have Wi-Fi access. The adjacent house, **Victoria Too,** has 6 guest rooms, including an extra-spacious room with a private porch overlooking the pool. Of the 14 guest rooms, all have a private bath, two outside the room. Two shaded wicker-filled porches invite relaxation,

as does the parlor and the backyard in-ground heated pool. There is a cottage with two rooms, each with its own entrance. Explore the island on one of the inn's bicycles, or take the complimentary badges and chairs, towels, bags and bottled water to the beach. Afternoon tea and continental breakfast. $165–300.

Elsewhere

♿ ⁙ **The Sand Castle Bed & Breakfast** (609-494-6555; 800-253-0353; www.sandcastlelbi.com), 710 Bayview Ave., Barnegat Light 08006. Open Feb.–mid-Dec. Romantic and private accommodations ideal for couples in a luxury bed & breakfast on the bay. It's part B&B, part mini-resort. The five guest rooms and two suites come with a private bath, fireplace, TV, Wi-Fi, phone, and private entrance—some have a whirlpool tub. Common areas include an enclosed sunporch and a parlor that doubles as a music room. Outside is an inviting in-ground heated pool and whirlpool spa as well as a cabana and patio with lounge chairs, umbrella tables, and a barbecue grill. The rooftop deck offers magnificent sunsets. Beachgoers will appreciate the complimentary badges, chairs, and towels. Full breakfast. $295–450.

MOTELS

In Beach Haven 08008

♿ ✎ **Coral Seas Oceanfront Motel** (609-492-1141; www.coralseasmotel.com), 21 Coral St., P.O. Box 1175. Open May–Oct. There are 50 guest rooms and suites, all clean and cozy with standard amenities. Standard units have a refrigerator, coffeemaker, and TV. Oceanfront rooms have private balconies. The third-floor suites have a bedroom, a living room with pullout sofa, and a private balcony overlooking the ocean. The heated outdoor pool is surrounded by plenty of lounge chairs. $175–260.

🐾 ✎ ♿ ⁙ **The Engleside Inn** (609-492-1251; reservations: 800-762-2214; www.engleside.com), 30 Engleside Ave. Open year-round. This is the oldest family-run motel on Long Beach Island. Accommodations range widely in amenities and price, from basic motel-style rooms and efficiencies with kitchenettes to oceanfront suites with private balconies. Hi-speed Internet connection is available. The **Leeward Room** restaurant offers steak and seafood in pleasant surroundings, and there's a casual beach bar by the heated outdoor pool. Pets are allowed in the off-season. $250–453.

🐾 ✎ **The Sea Shell** (609-492-4611; www.seashellclub.com), 10 South Atlantic Ave. A motel right on the beach that offers 55 units, including standard motel rooms, deluxe oceanfront rooms with private balconies, and spacious two-room suites, all with air-conditioning, TVs, phones, and refrigerators. There's an outdoor tiki bar, a restaurant serving Caribbean-style cuisine, and a nightclub with live entertainment. Bands and DJs draw big crowds to the nightclub, from the early poolside happy hour to the wee hours. Pets permitted in the off-season. $65–335.

Elsewhere

✎ ⁙ **North Shore Inn** (609-494-5001; www.northshoreinn.com), 806 Central Ave., Barnegat Light 08006. Open mid-Apr.–Dec. 1. Accommodations range from motel-style rooms to efficiency units with kitchenettes and dining areas. Extensively remodeled in 1998, all rooms have TV, Wi-Fi, phones with voice mail, and private bath. Complimentary badges for the beaches that are a block away—a quick walk or hop on the beach tram that stops here. Barnegat Light State Park and Old Barney are conveniently close (see sidebar, page 416). $135–165.

Buccaneer Motel (609-492-4582; www.buccaneermotel.com), 2600 North Bay Ave., Spray Beach 08008. Open Feb.–Oct. A no-frills motel with a great bayside location. Guest rooms have a refrigerator and TV; the two-room waterfront suites have whirlpool tubs, refrigerators, microwave ovens, TV/VCRs, and a view of the bay from a private balcony. An indoor pool and whirlpool tub are open in the off-season; in-season, opt for the waterfront outdoor pool (both pools are heated), and the rooftop sundecks with spectacular views of the bay and ocean, especially at sunset. The motel has a private dock available for guests who arrive by boat, and a waterfront picnic area complete with gas grills. Summer rates for two adults and two children under 12, $160–285.

CAMPGROUNDS *Long Beach RV Resort* (609-698-5684; www.care freervresorts.com), 30 Rt. 72, Barnegat 08005. Open Apr.–Oct. There are 165 seasonal RV sites, 20 transient sites, seven one- and two-bedroom rustic cabins and 30 tent sites. Long Beach Island is a 10-minute drive away, but there's plenty to do here, from mini golf and hiking to daily activities and bikes for rent. Call for rates.

Sea Pirate Campground (609-296-7400; reservations: 800-822-2267; www.sea-pirate.com), 154 Rt. 9, P.O. Box 271, West Creek 08092. Open May–Oct. A 300-acre campground located just across Little Egg Harbor from Long Beach Island. There's a swimming pool, a video arcade, ball fields, a stocked pond for fishing, and many other amenities. Indoor accommodations include rustic cottages that are handicapped accessible. They rent motorized boats that will take you into the creeks and salt marshes surrounding the campground, part of the vast **Edwin B. Forsythe**

National Wildlife Refuge. Sites $37–55; cabins and cottages $64–159.

Baker's Acres Campground (609-296-2664; 800-648-2227; www .bakersacres.com), 230 Willets Ave., Parkertown 08087. Open May–Oct. A 240-site full-service family campground on 60 wooded and pleasantly landscaped acres just north of Tuckerton on the edge of the vast **Pinelands National Reserve.** There's a busy schedule of planned activities in addition to boating, fishing, hayrides, and swimming. The Victorian-style camping cabins are a unique alternative to pitching a tent. Sites $34–44; cabins and cottages $85–115.

"T" Atlantic City North Family Campground (609-296-9163; 888-229-9776; www.campacn.com), Stage Rd., Tuckerton 08087. Open Apr. 1–Nov. 1. The campground offers 191 sites, boating, fishing, swimming, cabin rentals, and full services. In-season there's a full-time recreation director who plans daily activities; they offer complimentary beach passes for those venturing to Long Beach Island. Mini golf, outdoor pool, beach volleyball, game courts. Wi-Fi access. Sites $45–57; cabins $89–109.

✳ Where to Eat
DINING OUT

In Manahawkin
Mud City Crab House (609-978-3660; www.mudcitycrabhouse .com), 1185 East Bay Ave. (off Rt. 72). Open daily for lunch and dinner in summer; weekends in spring and fall. Arrive early at this seafood grill and fish market, or be prepared to wait. The house specialty is crabs, as one might guess, and they're done in a variety of ways. The mussels steamed in white wine and garlic butter, as a starter, comes with bread for sopping

up the savory juice. Seafood bisque is generously studded with scallops, shrimp, and crab. Fresh fish of the day is prepared grilled, blackened, broiled, however you like. Save room for their signature homemade key lime pie. BYOB. $12–25.

In Harvey Cedars
Plantation Restaurant and Bar (609-494-8191; www.plantation restaurant.com), 7908 Long Beach Blvd. Open year-round for lunch and dinner. Reservations are recommended. This lovely gourmet fine-dining spot prepares innovative contemporary American cuisine with Southern and Caribbean accents served in a sleek dining room and casual bar. Starters include West Indies–style ceviche with conch, shrimp, sea bass, and scallops in a cilantro-lime marinade. Entrées— like coriander-and-chili-glazed pork chop with hearts of palm and molasses- whipped yams; or jerk-grilled mahimahi with soft fried plantains— really show the kitchen's creativity. There's also a light menu of sandwich- es, burgers, and pasta dishes. $15–35.

In Surf City
& **Blue** (609-494-7556), 1016 Long Beach Blvd. Open daily in summer only for dinner. Reservations strongly recommended. Contemporary Ameri- can and global cuisine with interna- tional accents in stylish yet relaxed surroundings. The kitchen's emphasis is on fresh seafood, grilled meats, and fruits and vegetables from local mar- kets and the restaurant's own garden. Desserts are downright elegant. BYOB. $20–35.

Surf City Hotel (609-494-7281; 800- 353-3342; www.surfcityhotel.com), Eighth St. and Long Beach Blvd. Open daily for lunch and dinner, Memorial Day–Labor Day; weekends, May–June, Sept.–mid-Oct. Contempo- rary American cuisine, from prime rib

and steak to fresh seafood. Don't miss their award-winning clam chowder. Summertime means live entertainment in the action-packed lounge, light fare and late-night snacks in the pub, and fresh shellfish in **Shucks clam bar.** (See also *Lodging—Hotels.*)

In Beach Haven
& **Green Gables Inn and Restau- rant** (609-492-3553; www.gableslbi .com), at the Green Gables Inn, 212 Centre St. Open daily for lunch, after- noon tea, and dinner in summer. Open Fri.–Sun. in the off-season. Reserva- tions are required for dinner. A hidden gem serving acclaimed gourmet Amer- ican, Continental, and Mediterranean cuisine in a charming and romantic Victorian inn (see *Lodging—Inns*). Dinners are memorable, albeit pricey. This is a restaurant without a menu, so meals are always a surprise, and change daily. Dinner might begin with lobster soup, then a salad of baby greens, or fresh fruit and herbs. It could follow with butternut squash gnocchi, then fresh seafood or grilled duck, and might end with sorbet or fresh fruit with crème anglaise. Dine alfresco, in the quaint tearoom, or in the antiques-filled formal dining rooms. BYOB. Prix fixe (for two) $150.

Sweet Vidalia (609-207-1200), 122 North Bay Ave. Open daily for dinner in summer; in the off-season, Thurs.–Sun.; closed Mon.–Wed. Reservations are recommended. You might think that the menu revolves around onions, and thankfully it does- n't. The famously sweet and earthy Vidalias do appear in a couple dishes (like the sweet Vidalia onion soup, or roasted Vidalia onion stuffed with French lentils), but the remaining menu is creative and well-prepared New American cuisine. Save room for Valrhona chocolate mousse cake with vanilla crème anglaise. BYOB. $16–29.

In Barnegat Light

Kubel's Bar (609-494-8592), Seventh St. and Bayview Ave. Open daily year-round for lunch and dinner. This bayside seafood house has sat at the quiet northern tip of Long Beach Island for 80-plus years. During the Jazz Age it was a speakeasy and guesthouse; today, its fresh local seafood is popular with families, who crowd in here after a day at the beach. Contemporary dishes like blackened yellowfin tuna and baby back ribs with Asian barbecue sauce are featured alongside crab pie and fish cakes based on an old family recipe. $15–25.

In Surf City

Panzone's Pizza (609-494-1114), Long Beach Blvd. at 22nd St. Offers pizza and sandwiches year-round. A second location at 11th St. and Bay Ave. (609-492-5103) in Beach Haven. Open seasonally for lunch and dinner. Most people come for the award-winning pizza, but there's a full menu of subs, chicken steaks, steak sandwiches, and enormous hoagies. A good place to grab a quick bite. $5–15.

In Beach Haven Terrace

Terrace Tavern (609-492-9751), 13201 Long Beach Blvd. Open daily for lunch and dinner; phone ahead in the off-season. $10–22. A lively bar that's popular with the surfing set, and a fun place to hang out after a day at the beach or on the water. The menu features lots of local seafood, including oysters and clams from Great Bay and Barnegat Bay.

In Beach Haven

The Chicken or the Egg (609-492-3695; www.492fowl.com), 207 North Bay Ave. Open late Apr.–Oct. daily for breakfast, lunch, and dinner; open around the clock Memorial Day–Labor Day. This is some of the best breakfast food on the island, and you can get it anytime. Standards like omelets, pancakes, and French toast accompany specialties like country-fried steak and eggs, sausage gravy and buttermilk biscuits, breakfast burritos and quesadillas, and creamed chipped beef on toast. For lunch and dinner, chicken wings come with your choice of 14 sauces; signature dishes include chicken potpie and old-fashioned meatloaf with mushroom gravy. Kids love the menu just for them. Those in the know gladly wait in line. $4–14.

In Ship Bottom

Ship Bottom Shellfish (609-494-0088), 1721 Long Beach Blvd. Open for lunch and dinner daily mid-Apr.–Oct. A popular mom-and-pop seafood shop where the fish is fresh and the cole slaw homemade daily. BYOB. $10–20.

SNACKS

In Barnegat Light

Off the Hook (609-361-8900; www.vikingoffthehook.com), 20th St. and Bayview Ave. Loyal patrons line up at the door of this old-fashioned seafood shack for fish fresh off the boats at Viking Village, the nearby commercial fishing pier. They offer a delicious to-go menu of New England–style and red Manhattan–style clam chowder; cucumber, potato, and artichoke salads; fried clam strips, clams casino, and crabcakes. $7–20.

In Surf City

Surf Side Coffee (609-494-3345; www.surfsidecoffeehouse.com), 1901 Long Beach Blvd. Open year-round daily: winters, 6:30 AM–2 PM; summers, 6:30 AM–10 PM. A busy coffee shop with a full menu of coffees and coffee drinks, and espresso. Baked goods are made fresh every morning, and might include cheesecake, tarts, scones, and freshly baked pastries and muffins.

Coffee beans come from a New Jersey roaster. The perfect end to a hot day at the beach is a fruit smoothie or yoguccino, a fat-free yogurt drink with a double shot of espresso. $1–8.

Country Kettle Fudge (609-494-2822; www.countrykettlefudge.com), 20th St. and the Boulevard. Other locations in Beach Haven and Ship Bottom. Open mid-May–Oct.; weekends mid-Feb.–mid-May, and Oct.–Dec. Old-fashioned hand-whipped fudge comes in more than two-dozen flavors. Customers can watch as it's made the old-fashioned way in big copper kettles.

In Ship Bottom

❝❢❞ **How You Brewin?** (609-494-2003; www.howyoubrewin.com), 2020 Long Beach Blvd. Open year-round except Jan.–Feb., daily from 7 AM. A coffeehouse and Internet café serving gourmet coffees, tea, espresso drinks, fruit smoothies, Italian sodas, and egg creams. Pastries are popular at breakfast, and the decadent desserts make this a good after-dinner dessert stop. Use one of their computers to surf the Net, or bring your own laptop.

In Beach Haven

✐ **Show Place Ice Cream Parlour** (609-492-0018; www.surflight.org), 204 Centre St., next to **Surflight Theatre** (see *Entertainment—Theater*). Open Memorial Day–Labor Day. This old-time ice cream parlor is known around the country, not so much for the ice cream (which is excellent) but for the singing waiters and waitresses. They're all professional performers from the Surflight Theatre, and they serenade you while they serve cones, banana splits, even colossal sundaes that feed 10 people. Customers are often asked to perform (sing, dance, etc.) for their dessert.

✳ Entertainment

ARTS CENTER ✐ **Long Beach Island Foundation of the Arts and Sciences** (609-494-1241; www.lbi foundation.org), 120 Long Beach Blvd., Loveladies. Open year-round. A very active arts center and gallery mounting art exhibitions and crafts shows, and hosting lectures, film and book discussions, concerts, other entertainment, and art classes for adults and children. Call about a schedule of nature walks.

THEATER ✐ **Surflight Theatre** (609-492-9477; www.surflight.org), Beach and Engleside Aves., Beach Haven. Open May–Dec.; call or see Web site for a schedule of evening and matinee performances. A professional musical

SURFLIGHT THEATRE IN BEACH HAVEN, FOUNDED IN 1950, IS OCEAN COUNTY'S ONLY PROFESSIONAL THEATER, PRESENTING CONCERTS, CLASSIC MUSICALS, AND NEW WORKS FOR ADULTS AND CHILDREN.

Photo courtesy of Ocean County Public Affairs

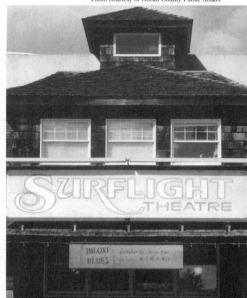

theater with a New York cast performing classic musicals. The Surflight has been a Long Beach Island institution since it opened as a summer stock theater in 1950. **Surflight Children's Theatre** mounts a series of classic works from mid-June–mid-Sept.

Joe Pop's Shore Bar and Restaurant (609-494-0558; www .joepops.com), 2002 Long Beach Blvd., Ship Bottom. A hip, happening nightclub open seasonally with live bands and DJs six days per week. Restaurant serves pub fare, steaks and seafood, and a limited late-night menu nightly until 1 AM.

🎵 ALBERT MUSIC HALL

(609-971-1593), 131 Wells Mills Rd. (Rt. 532, www.alberthall.org), Waretown. Concerts are held year-round on Saturday night from 7:30 to 11:30. Adults $5; children 11 and under, $1. More than three decades ago, a small group of local musicians and friends would gather at Joe and George Albert's remote hunting cabin in the woods outside town to play and listen to traditional Pinelands music. When word spread and the crowds at the "Home Place" got too big, the concerts were staged in town at an auction hall. Today a 350-seat auditorium is the setting for popular Saturday-night live concerts featuring the old-time sounds of bluegrass, country, and folk. Musicians playing banjo, fiddle, mandolin—even spoons and washtubs—take the stage for 20-minute sets. You can also watch as musicians participate in free jam sessions in the adjoining **Pickin' Shed.** The music hall hosts the annual **Ocean County Bluegrass Festival** (see *Special Events*).

SATURDAY NIGHT CONCERTS FEATURING BLUEGRASS, ACOUSTIC, COUNTRY, FOLK, AND TRADITIONAL PINELANDS MUSIC HAVE BEEN A SATURDAY NIGHT EVENT IN WARETOWN FOR MORE THAN 30 YEARS.

Photo courtesy of the Pinelands Cultural and Historical Preservation Society

✳ Selective Shopping
ANTIQUES AND ART

In Barnegat
Barnegat Antique Country (609-698-8967), 684 East Bay Ave. Open Wed.–Mon., 10:30–5; closed Tues. Three floors full of antiques and collectibles.

Bay Avenue Antiques (609-698-3020), 349 South Main St. (Rt. 9). Open daily 10–5. Fri.–Sat. until 9. Multi-dealer shop.

Recycling the Past (609-660-9790; www.recyclingthepast.com), 381 North Main St. Open daily except Mon., 10–5. Unique home and garden finds at this shop that sells the rare, the unique, and the unusual. They specialize in architectural salvage, collecting the remains from dismantled estates, farms, and public buildings and bringing them here. One-of-a-kind finds, from fountains and statuary to stained glass, fireplace mantels, and ornate wrought-iron gates.

Unshredded Nostalgia (609-660-2626; 800-872-9990; www.unshredded nostalgia.com), 323 South Main St. (Rt. 9). Open daily 10–5. A fine collection of rare film posters, casino chips, and memorabilia, as well as autographed celebrity photos, antiques, and animation cels from Disney, Hanna-Barbera, and Warner Bros.

In Barnegat Light
Americana by the Seashore (609-494-0656; www.americanaseashore.com), 604 Broadway, Barnegat Light. Open seasonally. An antiques shop specializing in decoys and wildlife carvings as well as 19th-century oyster plates.

In Surf City
Long Beach Island Art Studios and Gallery (609-494-4232), 2001 Long Beach Blvd. Open year-round; call for hours. Wildlife carvings, original paintings, art supplies and art classes.

FLEA MARKET Manahawkin Mart (609-597-1017), 657 East Bay Ave., Manahawkin. Open Fri.–Sun., 8–5. A popular indoor and outdoor flea market.

SPECIAL SHOPS

In Tuckerton
Tuckerton Emporium (609-296-2424; www.tuckerton.com), Two East Main St. (Rt. 9). Open daily, 10–5. You can make a day out of exploring this collection of 10 unique specialty shops. They include a historical-paintings gallery, a contemporary gifts store, Coastal Fireplace Showroom, an antiques shop, a women's clothing store, a shop selling Victorian and country gifts, and a country-furniture and home-décor store. The charming **Debra's Daydream Café** serves lunches.

In Beach Haven
Bay Village and Schooner's Wharf (609-492-2800; www.bayvillagelbi.com), Ninth St. and Bay Ave. Open daily. A quaint collection of gift stores and specialty shops styled after an old-fashioned fishing village. Shops selling everything from candy to jewelry are linked by brick paths and boardwalks. The *Tivoli* is a replica of a 19th-century schooner that houses a gift shop.

Foster's Farm Market (609-492-1360), 400 North Bay Ave. Open July–Sept, 8–7. An old-fashioned local farm market with produce, nursery plants, and a full-service deli with made-to-order sandwiches, fresh salads, butcher meats, desserts, and ice cream. Most of the fruits and vegetables come from New Jersey farms, including tomatoes, corn, eggplant, blueberries, and zucchini.

✳ Special Events

February: **Ocean County Bluegrass Festival** (609-971-1593; www.albert hall.org), Albert Music Hall, Waretown. Bluegrass bands from all over have been playing at this wintertime music festival for more than 20 years.

April: **Spring Art Show and Sale** (609-494-8861; www.stfranciscenter .org), St. Francis Center, Brant Beach.

June: ♪ **Baymen's Seafood and Music Festival** (609-296-8868; www .tuckertonseaport.org), Tuckerton Seaport, Tuckerton (see sidebar, page 418). Jersey Fresh shrimp, clams, and crabs, plus live entertainment, children's activities, and crafters.

July: **Red Wine and Blues Festival** (609-296-8868; www.tuckertonseaport .org), Tuckerton Seaport, Tuckerton. Annual festival. Food, New Jersey wines, and live blues.

Independence Day fireworks (800-292-6372; www.discoversouthern ocean.com), Schooner's Wharf and Bay Village, Beach Haven. **Arts and Crafts Festival** (609-494-1241; www .lbifoundation.org), sponsored by the Long Beach Island Foundation of the Arts and Sciences, Loveladies. An annual juried show and sale featuring the work of nationally recognized artists and craftspeople. **Festival of the Sea** (609-494-8861; www.stfrancis center.org), Brant Beach.

August: **Seashore Open House Tour** (609-494-1241; www.lbifoundation .org), Long Beach Island. Always held the first Wednesday of August. A tour of the island's most magnificent waterfront homes; sponsored by the Long Beach Island Foundation of the Arts and Sciences in Loveladies. ♪ **Blue Claw Festival** (800-292-6372; www .discoversouthernocean.com), Harvey Cedars. Crab races, food, entertainment, crafts show.

September: **Ocean County Decoy and Gunning Show** (609-296-5606), Tip Seaman Park, Tuckerton. A festival celebrating the heritage of the bay, with hundreds of exhibitors and vendors selling wildlife art, decoys, and maritime crafts on the banks of Lake Pohatcong. Food, live music, and contests in carving, retrieving, and skeet shooting. ♪ **Ocean County Bluegrass Festival** (609-971-1593; www .alberthall.org), Albert Music Hall, Waretown (see sidebar, page 429). Live bluegrass music. Held twice a year, Feb. and Sept. **18-Mile Run** (609-494-8861; www.stfranciscenter.org), Long Beach Island. A point-to-point minimarathon along the entire length of Long Beach Island, from Holgate to Barnegat Light.

October: ♪ **Chowderfest Weekend** (609-494-7211; www.discoversouthern ocean.com), Beach Haven. An end-of-the-season celebration with entertainment, activities, food, and music. On Sunday, local restaurants vie for the title King of Clams in the Chowder Cook-off Classic. ♪ **Pine Barrens Jamboree** (609-971-3085; www .oceancountyparks.org), Wells Mills County Park, Waretown. A celebration of the Pinelands, with live music, entertainment, children's activities, food, historical displays, and canoe trips. **LBI Surf Fishing Tournament** (609-494-7211), Long Beach Island. A month-long competition for striped bass and bluefish has been a tradition for half a century. Anglers compete for thousands of dollars in prizes on beaches up and down the island.

December: ♪ **Ship Bottom Island Christmas Parade** (609-494-1614), Long Beach Blvd., Ship Bottom. **Christmas House Tour** (609-494-3752), various Long Beach Island locations. Festively decorated homes open their doors to visitors; sponsored by the Long Beach Island Garden Club.

The Southern Shore:
Atlantic City to
Cape May

THE ATLANTIC CITY REGION

OCEAN CITY TO WILDWOOD

THE CAPE MAY PENINSULA

THE ATLANTIC CITY REGION

No other place on the Jersey Shore—in the entire state, for that matter—has the instant name recognition of Atlantic City. From the early days as a turn-of-the-20th-century seaside vacationland to its current role as an East Coast gambling hot spot, it has enjoyed a worldwide reputation as a one-of-a-kind place. Over the years, "A.C." has continually reinvented itself, from glamorous resort town to faded has-been to the largest casino city outside Nevada. It's known as the Queen of Resorts, the World's Playground, the Gem of the Jersey Shore, and America's Favorite Playground. Whatever you call it, it's still one of the biggest tourist destinations in America, much like it was in the 1800s. In a sense, one could argue, the more Atlantic City changes, the more it stays the same.

Atlantic City sits on Absecon Island, a 25-mile-long sandy barrier island about two-thirds of the way down New Jersey's 127-mile shoreline that also includes the quieter "down beach" communities of Ventnor City, Margate City, and Longport. Atlantic County's largest city occupies a spit of sand that's a mere 10 blocks wide and 48 blocks long. Its casinos and hotels punctuate the sky, and together they twinkle at night along the dark Atlantic Ocean like a miniature big-city skyline.

For all its changes, nothing altered the face of Atlantic City quite like the legalization of gambling in 1976. Today nearly a dozen casino resorts stay open around the clock, and this town of 40,000 residents receives more than 32 million visitors every year, mostly day-trippers who rumble into town on one of those ubiquitous casino tour buses that everyone (or at least their Aunt Sally) has been on. The casinos are less than a day's drive from a third of the nation's population, a few short hours from New York City, Philadelphia, and Washington, DC—not to mention millions of New Jerseyans.

Atlantic City turned 150 years old in 2004. Of all New Jersey's resort towns strung along the Atlantic Ocean from Sandy Hook to Cape May, this is where it all began. The Lenni-Lenape made a living on the island centuries ago by making wampum out of the abundance of clam shells. The first European settlement came in 1793, but Absecon Island remained a rural backwater until the steam-powered Camden and Atlantic City Railroad line was completed in 1854, to whisk tourists in from Philadelphia. It flourished as a rail-terminal resort, rooming houses quickly sprang up, and crowds started coming. Some were looking for fun, and others hoped that the ocean and tangy salt air would relieve a host of ailments, from pneumonia to consumption, as resort developers claimed. A mile-long boardwalk, designed to keep sand out of both tourists' shoes and hotel lobbies, was completed

The Atlantic City Region

★ Point of Interest

ALT 561

Smithville
Leeds Point

9

Oceanville

Edwin Forsythe NWR ★

ATLANTIC CITY EXPRESSWAY

563

561

Little Bay

Absecon Highlands
Conovertown

Reeds Bay

Absecon

Absecon Bay

Pleasantville

30

87

ALT 559

GARDEN STATE PARKWAY

585

9

Lakes Bay

Northfield

40

322

563

Sculls Bay

Atlantic City

Ventnor City

ATLANTIC

OCEAN

Margate City

559

Somers Point

152

Longport
Ocean City–Longport Bridge (toll)

52

N

Ocean City

0   2.5   5
Miles

in 1870 (it was replaced in 1896 with the 4-mile-long and 40-foot-wide promenade that stands today). Men pushed tourists up and down the boardwalk in wicker rolling chairs, a nostalgic pastime that has been recently brushed off and revived. Atlantic City's boardwalk was the country's original above-ground wooden walkway, and in 1882 the first of several amusement piers was built and packed with midway games, rides, vaudeville shows, novelty acts, and food, including a sweet confection with a colorful history. David Bradley opened Atlantic City's first candy stand on the beach in 1880. Soon after, a storm-driven high tide soaked his merchandise and inspired the original saltwater taffy, or so the story goes. At its height of popularity in the 1920s, the chewy pastel candies were as synonymous with Atlantic City as the gambling halls are today, and they are still sold up and down the boardwalk.

Atlantic City's popularity peaked in the early 1900s. For Americans not familiar with leisure travel, it had a larger-than-life mystique; it was a fascinating place like no other they had ever seen. By the 1920s it glittered enough to attract the rich and famous to its grand hotels. Plays and musicals debuted to audiences here

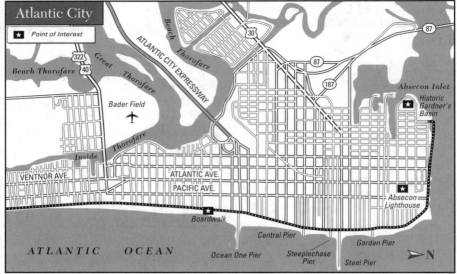

before heading to Broadway. In 1921, a "mermaid contest" or "bather's revue" was held on the boardwalk, a competition that evolved into the Miss America Pageant. Atlantic City's most famous event was held every September at the city's historic Boardwalk Hall. In January 2006 the pageant moved to Las Vegas, Nevada.

In the days before television and radio advertising, major companies like Heinz and Goodyear came to Atlantic City, where marketing campaigns could reach larger crowds than elsewhere in America. Nationally known products were traditionally launched on Central Pier. Shrewd businessmen knew that the public was drawn to the new and the bizarre, so the phenomenon of "World's Largest (fill in the blank)" was a popular boardwalk gimmick. The Underwood Company built the World's Largest Typewriter, a colossal two-story replica of their famous office product, on Garden Pier. The world's largest electric sign—some 27,000 bulbs strong—advertised Chesterfield Cigarettes on Steeplechase Pier. Henry J. Heinz (think ketchup) recognized this potential and opened Heinz Pier in 1898, where the public could visit a museum filled with his personal art collection, ogle the latest household appliances in a top-of-the-line demonstration kitchen, snack on free Heinz products, and go home with a complimentary Heinz pickle pin. His pier was known as the Crystal Palace by the Sea before it was demolished by a 1944 hurricane.

In the 1930s the greats of the day performed at the old Steel Pier, built in 1898 at the boardwalk and Virginia Avenue. Tourists flocked to the 2,000-foot-long pier, billed as the Showplace of the Nation to watch circus acts, concerts, and especially the famous diving horses that would plunge—with girls astride—from a high platform into a pool of water. The old Steeplechase Pier was known as the Funny Place—patrons reached its amusements through the giant gaping mouth of a clown. World-famous illusionist Harry Houdini performed on Million Dollar Pier, which also hosted the Miss America Pageant for a time, and boasted a mansion with lush gardens and a conservatory. The Garden Pier was an entertainment center, with live music and boxing matches. Today, it is home to the Atlantic City Historical Museum and the Atlantic City Art Center.

Another boardwalk landmark was Club Harlem, where legendary black entertainers like Ray Charles, Sarah Vaughan, Sammy Davis Jr., and Pearl Bailey played until the wee hours. The iconic 500 Club hosted world-famous comics and crooners, from Frank Sinatra and Dean Martin to Jerry Lewis. Atlantic City still draws world-class entertainers to its casinos and performance halls, a colorful mix of old legends and the hottest new stars that cater to the wide range of generations that come here. Tom Jones, Dolly Parton, Tony Orlando, and Wayne Newton still take the stage, as does REM, Bon Jovi, Sting, Elton John, and Cher.

Another famous landmark, recognizable even by those who've never been here, is its grid of city streets. Generations of board-game fans across the country remember the names: Park Place, Marvin Gardens, and Atlantic, Pacific, and Baltic avenues, as well as Pennsylvania, New York, Virginia, and the rest of the streets assigned state names. They're all part of Monopoly, the real estate game that's so deep in the American consciousness that most people can still recall whether their favorite game piece was the car, the top hat, or the worn-out shoe. Remember the elation of plunking down a couple hotels on Pacific Avenue (and taking that crisp play money from your opponents), or the dread of going directly to jail without passing Go or collecting $200? Charles Darrow was one of many Philadelphians who vacationed in Atlantic City, and during the financially strapped Depression-era 1930s (while, like many Americans, he was out of work) he dreamed up a board game based on Atlantic City real estate. He sold Monopoly to Parker Brothers and made a fortune, and his brainchild is still one of the most popular board games in the world.

The crippling effects of the Depression and World War II would eventually leave their collective mark on the crown jewel of the Jersey Shore, as they did on vacation spots around the country. In the 1940s, 20th Century Fox released *Three Little Girls in Blue,* a musical film set in the turn-of-the-20th-century that introduced the popular tune "On the Boardwalk in Atlantic City," a nostalgic homage to the carefree summer days when the boards flourished with lights, noise, people, and music. It was a lively destination that appealed to the working class, a burgeoning group that was America's first generation to have leisure time and money to perpetuate it. But as air travel became affordable and tourists jetted off to more exotic locales, it was the beginning of a long, sad slump that continued into the 1970s; and the city didn't bounce back. Atlantic City needed something new.

The idea of casinos was bandied about in the 1960s, but the promise of a revival didn't come until 1976, when New Jersey passed the Casino Control Act, which legalized casino gambling and allowed state-authorized casinos to open in what had become a faded and foundering seaside resort. Atlantic City became the first place in the nation outside Nevada to legalize gambling. Steve Lawrence, half of the world-famous Steve and Eydie singing duo, was the first to roll the dice (and lose $10 at craps) when Resorts International—the city's first casino—opened its doors on Memorial Day weekend in 1978. Ecstatic gamblers lined up on the boardwalk to get in—for the first time ever, they didn't have to jet west to Las Vegas to pursue their hobby. The following decades marked a whirlwind period of tearing down the old to pave way for yet another new Atlantic City. The extravagant 900-room Traymore Hotel was an Egyptian-themed art deco–style hotel on the boardwalk, one of many grand hotels and vintage Beaux-Arts buildings demolished to make way for a new casino city of soaring glass and modern hotel towers. Some casinos like Resorts and Bally's have incorporated old landmarks into the design of their casinos.

Today, the East Coast's biggest gaming resort feeds a $4-billion-a-year industry, luring high rollers and fledgling gamblers with dreams of quick returns. A dozen casinos offer round-the-clock access to acres of slot machines and table games, from blackjack to poker, roulette to baccarat. Casinos here are required by law to have hotels, and Donald Trump owns three of them: Trump Marina (the former Trump Castle), Trump Taj Mahal, and Trump Plaza. There's also Bally's, the Atlantic City Hilton Casino, Harrah's, Caesars, the Tropicana, Showboat, and Resorts. The newest jewel in Atlantic City's crown is the upscale Borgata Hotel Casino and Spa, which attracts the kind of young, hip crowd that Atlantic City has always been after. Like all the casinos, the Borgata offers nightclubs, big-name entertainment, boutique shopping, and a variety of restaurants under its roof.

Whether Atlantic City's over-the-top and fast-paced world of high-stakes gaming is glamorous or gaudy is a matter of personal taste. While some places pump millions into creating enclaves of upscale luxury, others maintain a tawdry atmosphere that can be described at best as faux glamour. The mix of schlock and splash is anything but dull, even if you don't gamble. The frenetic world of greed, chance, and luck, of money changing hands at a dizzying pace, and the sense that fortune can be had or lost with the next poker chip, card, roll of the dice, or spin of the wheel certainly makes for good drama.

The city's transformation from old-time seaside resort to Vegas-style casino strip is portrayed in Louis Malle's 1981 film *Atlantic City,* starring Burt Lancaster and (New Jersey native) Susan Sarandon, about a seedy, fading resort town that has seen better times. Bruce Springsteen's song of the same name is a haunting look at the sad, losing side of gambling. In the 1990s, Atlantic City's grandeur had faded, and the resort was in danger of foundering in a big way. Atlantic Avenue, one of the city's main thoroughfares, was dotted with vacant lots and abandoned buildings, and attractions along the famous boardwalk were closing. Not far from the glamorous casino world, residents were living in abject poverty.

The Casino Reinvestment Development Authority channels tens of millions annually into Atlantic City to polish up, revamp, and expand, and the past couple years have seen a lot of it. When the $1.1-billion Borgata opened in the summer of 2003, it was the first new casino-hotel to open in Atlantic City in 13 years. Its luxury spa, haute cuisine, big-name entertainment, more than 2,000 boutique-style guest rooms, and 3-acre casino floor not only gave Atlantic City a much needed shot of coolness, it has had a ripple effect on those who want to keep pace. Older casino hotels are sprucing themselves up with sushi bars, martini lounges, and trendy nightclubs. In late 2004, the Tropicana unveiled The Quarter, an upscale retail, dining, and entertainment complex with a sleek classic Havana theme and Atlantic City's first IMAX theater. Resorts Atlantic City completed a $125 million expansion in 2004 that includes more gaming space, a new 27-story tower with luxury guest rooms and suites, and a spiffed-up art deco–style façade. The Pier at Caesars replaced the aging Ocean One shopping mall on the historic Million Dollar Pier with luxury boutiques (Armani, Louis Vuitton, Gucci, and HUGO BOSS, among them) and highbrow restaurants. And on the casino floors, the mantra is change—newer shops, hotter nightclubs, more slot machines—whatever it takes to keep people coming back.

For many years, Las Vegas and Atlantic City were America's two gambling destinations. Now that casinos are springing up all over the country, from Native American reservations to riverboats, Atlantic City is cleaning up and luring the visitors it once isolated—families and nongamblers. Family-style attractions like the Ripley's Believe It or Not Museum on the boardwalk, amusements on the revitalized Steel Pier, dolphin-watching excursions, and minor-league baseball at Sandcastle Stadium are turning Atlantic City into a kid-friendly vacation spot. Historic Gardner's Basin offers a waterfront park, restaurants, shops, party boat fishing, boat excursions, and a marine museum and aquarium. The spirit of old-fashioned fun lives on along the historic boardwalk. T-shirt shops, souvenir stands (Atlantic City introduced the world to the kitschy trinket and the tradition of sending postcards to the folks back home), games of chance, fortune-tellers, arcades, restaurants, and amusements stretch along the shore for 4 miles. Some of the original 2,500 rickshaw-like rolling wicker chairs have been refurbished and are once again whisking tourists up and down the boards. Of course, there's the beach. It's one of only two (Wildwood is the other one) along the entire Jersey Shore that is free, and the only one where you can swim and sunbathe with a casino skyline as a surreal backdrop.

The communities in the shadow of Atlantic City offer their own attractions worth exploring. Brigantine is a residential shoreline town, with beaches, restaurants, and motels, just north of Atlantic City. From here the bustling casino city is a silent miniskyscape that glints in the sun by day and glitters with neon and twinkling lights at night. Smithville was settled as a stagecoach stop in 1787 but fell off the map when it was bypassed by the railroad in the mid-1800s. Today, the Historic Towne of Smithville is a quaint shopping village of some 60 restored Colonial buildings lining cobblestone pathways. There's a Colonial-style bed & breakfast, paddleboating on an artificial lake, and a historic inn serving traditional American fare. The Noyes Museum of Art in Oceanville is the largest fine-arts museum on the Jersey Shore, known for its extensive permanent collection of hand-carved shorebird decoys. The town sits on the edge of a natural attraction that couldn't contrast more with Atlantic City—the vast 43,000-acre swath of tidal marshes, saltwater meadows, and barrier beach in the Edwin B. Forsythe National Wildlife Refuge. More than 200 species of birds use the refuge as a stopover during the busy spring and fall migrations along the Atlantic Flyway. It's also home to bald eagles, peregrine falcons, owls, and water birds, and the breeding ground for the rare piping plover and other endangered bird species. Visitors can explore the refuge via an 8-mile auto loop or a pair of nature trails; together they offer a unique look at New Jersey's pristine bird-filled coastal wetlands, a little-known side of the Jersey Shore.

Ocean Drive is a magnificent scenic route that begins at Atlantic City's Absecon Lighthouse and heads south through the residential towns of Ventnor City, Margate City, and Longport, the last stop on Absecon Island before the toll bridge over the Great Egg Harbor Inlet leads to Ocean City and south to the "end" of the Jersey shore at Cape May Point. These towns offer an interesting mix of shops, restaurants, and beaches, but nothing quite so wonderfully weird as Lucy the Elephant, a six-story, 90-ton pachyderm-shaped building that's a beloved local treasure as well as a national historic landmark. To local residents it's much more than a throwback to America's era of goofy roadside oddities. In her heyday, Lucy was an internationally known tourist attraction that hosted the likes of Henry Ford and Woodrow Wilson.

Visitors can enter a door in her back leg and climb to her back for spectacular panoramas that include the Atlantic Ocean and the Atlantic City skyline.

Entries in this section are arranged in roughly geographic order, from north to south.

AREA CODE 609.

GUIDANCE The Boardwalk Information Center (609-348-7100; 888-228-4748; www.atlanticcitynj.com), Boardwalk Hall at Kennedy Plaza, between Mississippi and Georgia Aves. Open 9:30–5:30; extended hours Thurs.–Sun. from Memorial Day to Labor Day. The **Atlantic City Convention and Visitor's Authority** staffs this information center that offers room reservations and ticket sales, local maps, and general tourist information on events, attractions, restaurants, and casinos. They also sell a full line of Atlantic City souvenirs.

The Atlantic City Expressway Visitor Welcome Center (609-383-2727; 888-228-4748; www.atlanticcitynj.com) is a state-run facility on the Atlantic City Expressway at mile marker 3.5 (accessible from both directions), 2 miles outside Atlantic City. Open 9–5; extended hours Thurs.–Sun. from Memorial Day to Labor Day. The staff is extremely knowledgeable and helpful; they can provide tourism literature, directions, and information on attractions, and they can make same-day lodging reservations.

GETTING THERE *By air:* **Atlantic City International Airport** (609-645-7895; www.acairport.com), Exit 9 off the Atlantic City Expressway, Egg Harbor Township. Spirit Airlines (800-772-7117; www.spiritair.com) has direct and connecting service from points around the country. **Philadelphia International Airport** (215-937-6800; www.philadelphia-phl.com), about 60 miles west on the Atlantic City Expressway, is served by most major carriers.

By rail: The **Atlantic City Rail Terminal** (800-228-7246) is located within the Atlantic City Convention Center, One Miss America Way, Atlantic City. Free shuttles connect the train station with all the casinos. The **New Jersey Transit** (973-275-5555; www.njtransit.com) Philadelphia–Atlantic City Rail Line offers daily commuter service between Atlantic City and Philadelphia's 30th Street Station, where there are connections to **Amtrak's** Northeast Corridor lines (800-872-7245; www.amtrak.com).

By bus: While most visitors reach Las Vegas by air, they travel by car or by bus to reach Atlantic City, which is about 100 miles from New York City and 60 miles from Philadelphia.

Greyhound (800-231-2222; www.greyhound.com) and **Academy** (201-420-7000; 800-442-7272; www.academybus.com) operate buses from Port Authority bus terminal in New York City to the casinos; Greyhound also offers round-trip service from Philadelphia, Baltimore, and Washington, DC. **New Jersey Transit** (973-275-5555; www.njtransit.com) connects Atlantic City with points all over the state, as well as New York City and Philadelphia. The Atlantic City Municipal Terminal on Atlantic and Michigan avenues is close to the hotels and casinos.

By car: The major route into Atlantic City from the west is the **Atlantic City Expressway;** the Garden State Parkway runs north and south and connects to the expressway just west of Atlantic City. When driving to Atlantic City, keep in mind a truism about roads leading to the Jersey Shore—traffic is the unfortunate by-product of the region's popularity. Traffic tie-ups on the southbound Garden State Parkway on summer weekends are inevitable. Try to avoid heading to Atlantic City by car late on a Friday afternoon, or leaving late on a Sunday afternoon.

If you're not in a big hurry, or if the expressways are clogged, there are also a few secondary roads—old highways that are scenic and relaxing—that pass leisurely through small towns in the Delaware Bay and Pinelands regions. **Rt. 40** leads directly from the Delaware Memorial Bridge to Pacific Avenue in Atlantic City; on the way it joins **Black Horse Pike,** or **Rt. 322,** which is a busy but viable alternative to the Atlantic City Expressway. **Rt. 49** isn't so direct, but you can pick it up east of the Delaware Memorial Bridge and follow it through historic towns like Salem, Bridgeton, and Millville before it ends south of Atlantic City; you can finish the journey on the parkway and expressway. **Rt. 30** starts in the Camden area and roughly parallels the Atlantic City Expressway before ending on Virginia Avenue in Atlantic City. You may have to endure the traffic lights, but in many situations this route can be a quicker, saner option.

Once you arrive in Atlantic City, keep in mind that public parking is at a premium. The casinos have their own parking garages, but you must either stay at the hotel or at least patronize the casino to park in them. You can find some metered parking spots and outdoor parking lots; prices vary widely.

By ferry: **The Cape May–Lewes Ferry** (800-643-3779; www.capemaylewes ferry.com) connects Lewes, Delaware, to North Cape May, New Jersey—close to the Garden State Parkway. The ferry accepts both car and foot passengers; the one-way trip takes about 70 minutes. Reservations are recommended when traveling during peak summertime periods, especially Friday afternoon and evening, Saturday morning, and Sunday afternoon and evening.

GETTING AROUND 🐚 **Atlantic City Jitney Association** (609-344-8642; 877-928-7246; www.jitneys.net), 201 Pacific Ave., Atlantic City. Office open Mon.–Fri. 9–5; closed Saturday and Sunday. Tickets $2; book of 10 tickets, $17.50. Nearly 200 independently owned and operated blue minibuses circumnavigate Absecon Island year-round, 24 hours a day. The 13-passenger buses stop at every block on Pacific Avenue, which runs parallel to the boardwalk. Look for the color-coded and numbered signs on every corner near the casinos—they outline the four bus routes (pink, blue, orange, and green) the jitneys follow. They stop at most major attractions, the casinos in particular. The buses are safe, reliable, and affordable, and are used by locals as well as millions of visitors.

Atlantic City Trolley Tours (609-884-7392; 866-872-6737; www.gatrolley.com). Adults $17–25; children 5–10, $15–20; rates vary depending on the tour; call for a schedule. Tours leave from the **Boardwalk Visitors Center** and the Holiday Inn on the boardwalk. The **Great American Trolley Company** leads tours of Atlantic City landmarks on old-fashioned trackless trolleys. The Splash of Atlantic City tour goes to Absecon Lighthouse, to the Ocean Life Center at Historic Gardner's Basin, and to Lucy the Elephant. The Grape Vines and Vintage Shopping tour takes passengers to Renault Winery, to the Noyes Museum of Art, and to the Historic Towne of Smithville. Custom tours for groups can be arranged.

Taxis: **Yellow Van** (800-224-9945) services Atlantic City and the entire South Jersey region; **Atlantic City Airport Taxi** (609-383-1457; 877-568-8294; www.actaxi.com)

ATLANTIC CITY ROLLING CHAIRS

(609-347-7500), on the boardwalk, Atlantic City. Six-block tours, $5; up to 13 blocks, $10; 10 blocks, $20 round-trip; a half-hour tour is $30; an hour costs $40. Rolling chairs have been a boardwalk tradition since the 19th century, when the wheeled chairs that were originally used to transport handicapped visitors quickly caught the attention of tourists who wanted a leisurely tour of the boards. At their peak in the 1920s, there were some 2,500 rolling chairs, charging 75 cents for an hour-long tour. Today men (sometimes women), many of them college students, push one or two passengers in the ubiquitous wicker chairs up and down the boardwalk. You can pick one up anywhere on the boardwalk. **Royal Rolling Chairs** (609-347-7500), 114 S. New York Ave., Atlantic City, opened in 2002; their chairs comfortably hold up to three adults on tours of the boardwalk. Call for rates.

and **Royal Airport Shuttle/Galloway Limousine** (609-748-9777; 888-824-7767; www.royalairportshuttle.com) serve airports in Atlantic City, Newark, New York City, and Philadelphia; **AA Action Car Service and Limousine** (609-839-9797) in Atlantic City offers local and airport service in vans, limos, and sedans; **Ace Luxury Car Service** (609-646-4796; 800-660-9766) provides service to airports and the Atlantic City area.

MEDICAL EMERGENCY Atlantic City Medical Center (609-345-4000; www.atlanticare.org), 1925 Pacific Ave., Atlantic City. The emergency number is 609-441-8050.

Health Med (609-345-6000; www.healthmedassociates.com), 24 South Carolina Ave., Atlantic City. An urgent-care facility and family medical center.

Shore Memorial Hospital (609-653-3500; www.shorememorial.org), 1 E. New York Ave., Somers Point. The emergency number is 609-653-3515.

Burdette Tomlin Memorial Hospital (609-463-2000; www.caperegional.com), Stone Harbor Blvd., Cape May Court House. The emergency number is 609-463-2138.

✳ To See

& **THE BOARDWALK** The first boardwalk in the world opened in Atlantic City on June 26, 1870, to serve a dual purpose. The 10-foot-wide wooden planks set a foot or so above the sand allowed tourists to stroll leisurely along the ocean without trudging through soft beach sand. Likewise, the sand remained on the beach and out of elegant hotel lobbies and the railcars shuttling people home from their vacations. Today it's over 4 miles long and 60 feet wide, and has four massive steel and concrete piers that jut out over the Atlantic Ocean. It's lined with arcades, shops, restaurants, and hotels, and stretches from the Atlantic City Inlet south to Ventnor City. Along the way it passes most of the casino resorts and historic **Boardwalk Hall,** the city's 1929 convention hall where the Beatles once played and Miss America was crowned every September. Today there's a new convention center at the entrance to the Atlantic City Expressway, but Boardwalk Hall was spiffed up to the tune of $90 million and hosts championship boxing, professional wrestling and ice-skating, world-class entertainers, and other sports events.

Cyclists are allowed on the boardwalk early in the morning, and several shops rent all manner of bikes. For a more leisurely tour, hire one of the restored old-fashioned wicker rolling chairs to whisk you along the boards (see *Getting Around*), a nostalgic experience as synonymous with Atlantic City as the boardwalk itself. Many prefer to just sit on an oceanfront bench with some saltwater taffy and watch the parade of tourists and joggers, families and gamblers. The boardwalk is handicapped accessible via ramps at the end of each street; pets are not permitted on the boardwalk at any time.

At the pre-casino turn of the 20th century, the boardwalk was Atlantic City's centerpiece, the link between the grand hotels and the bustling amusement piers. It was lined with stands selling saltwater taffy and just about every imaginable trinket emblazoned with "Atlantic City," and photographers jockeying to take portraits of tourists. The first amusement pier was built off the boardwalk in 1882, but it was Captain John Young's impressive **Ocean Pier,** built a decade later, that set the standard for the rest to follow. It jutted 2,000 feet over the ocean and featured midway games, thrilling rides, vaudeville shows, and a trolley that shuttled visitors to the end, where they could hop on a pleasure boat or cast a fishing line into the Atlantic. Hoping to bank on his success, Young built the **Million Dollar Pier** in 1906, with an opulent Italianate villa (he dubbed it Number One Atlantic Ocean) surrounded by lavish gardens for himself, and a variety of entertainment—amateur variety shows, dramatic high-diving acts, Harry Houdini stunts, and early Miss America pageants—for the masses. When the **Garden Pier** was built in 1913, it attracted an upscale crowd to its lavish flower gardens and elegant Spanish Renaissance–style buildings. It was a definite notch of class above the middlebrow

THE ATLANTIC CITY BOARDWALK WAS THE WORLD'S FIRST. IT WAS BUILT IN 1870 TO KEEP VACATIONERS FROM TRACKING SAND INTO HOTEL LOBBIES AND PASSENGER TRAINS. TODAY, MANY OF ATLANTIC CITY'S 30 MILLION ANNUAL VISITORS STROLL THE HISTORIC 4-MILE STRETCH OF BOARDS ABOVE THE SAND.

Photo courtesy of the Atlantic City Convention and Visitors Bureau

atmosphere of the other amusement piers. The **BF Keith's Theatre** mounted Broadway-caliber shows, and a young Rudolph Valentino taught tango lessons at the pier's ballroom before he became a silent-film star. At Missouri Avenue, there's a street sign marking "500 Club Lane," a nod to Paul D'Amato's iconic **500 Club,** also known as the Five, where showbiz legends like Frank Sinatra crooned, and Jerry Lewis and Dean Martin first took the stage together.

Crowds went to **Heinz Pier,** where the national condiment manufacturer promoted his 57 products, ran a cooking school, and gave away free food samples and pickle pins. George C. Tilyou's **Steeplechase Pier** debuted in 1908, designed after his world-famous amusement park at New York's Coney Island. In the 1920s and '30s, the world's largest billboard advertised Chesterfield Cigarettes; below it were Tilyou's thrilling rides, including flying chairs that sent riders soaring out over the ocean. In the mid-20th century, the **Steel Pier** was built atop massive pillars, and featured films, vaudeville shows, circus acts, ballroom dancing, famous singers of the day, and the famed High-Diving Horse, who, along with a bareback rider, would take the dramatic and crowd-pleasing 40-foot plunge off a platform on the pier into an above-ground pool.

Unfortunately, the golden era of Atlantic City's amusement piers came to an eventual end. Some were destroyed by fire and storms; others were sadly reduced to hulking eyesores. Today work is under way to restore them to their original grandeur. The Garden Pier is home to the **Atlantic City Art Center,** with changing displays of regional and national artists, and the Atlantic City Historical Museum and Cultural Center, with fascinating exhibits on the Queen of Resorts' colorful history, including an extensive collection of old-time photographs. As a sentimental nod to condiment king Henry Heinz and his long-gone pier, museum visitors receive a free pickle pin. Today's Steel Pier, across from the Taj Mahal at Virginia Avenue, lacks the formality of its early days, but families with kids love the carnival-like mix of games, rides, activities, and free concerts. In 2005 the colossal Ocean One Shopping Mall on the old Million Dollar Pier became The Pier at Caesars, an upscale mix of glitzy boutiques, trendy restaurants, and entertainment.

HISTORIC HOMES AND SITES **Somers Mansion** (609-927-2212), 1000 Shore Rd., Somers Point. Open Fri.–Sat., 10–noon and 1–4; Sun., 1–4. Free admission. This three-story brick gambrel-roofed mansion is the oldest intact house in Atlantic County, as well as one of the oldest in all of New Jersey. It was built by harbormaster Richard Somers between 1720 and 1726 on Somers Plantation, his prominent family's 3,000-acre spread. The Somers family was among the region's earliest European settlers, and descendants occupied the home on Great Egg Harbor for 200 years, until it was turned over to the **Atlantic County Historical Society** and extensively renovated in the 1940s. The house has been restored in keeping with its 18th-century appearance. Ten rooms added on during the Victorian era were eliminated; the remaining were furnished with 18th- and 19th-century artifacts, original furnishings, and 18th-century antiques—china, paintings, handmade quilts—from various Atlantic County homes.

✧ **Historic Gardner's Basin** (609-348-2880; www.gardnersbasin.com; www.acaquarium.com), 800 N. New Hampshire Ave., Atlantic City. In the 1700s, pirates and rumrunners were said to have hidden out in this cove off Absecon Inlet. In the next century, fishing docks bustled with whaling boats coming and

✐ LUCY THE ELEPHANT

(609-823-6473; www.lucytheelephant.org), 9200 Atlantic Ave., Margate City. Open daily mid-June–Labor Day; hours vary during Apr.–May and Sept.; closed Nov.–Mar.; call or visit Web site for exact hours. Guided tours every 30 minutes. Adults $6; children 11 and under, $3. Lucy isn't a real elephant. She's an architectural oddity and beloved gem, a 65-foot-high elephant-shaped building just south of Atlantic City off Margate Beach. In 1881 real estate developer James V. Lafferty needed a promotional strategy (i.e., a gimmick) to interest potential buyers in some scrubby Atlantic City beachfront home lots. Eschewing traditional advertising methods, Lafferty wanted to build something that would pique people's curiosity and lure them to his remote real estate. So he built a giant walk-in pachyderm. He hired a Philadelphia architect and acquired a patent for the design, which was based on a photo of one of P. T. Barnum's elephants that he saw in a magazine. Not only did people come to see the six-story, 90-ton marvel (the world's largest elephant) standing at the edge of the Atlantic Ocean, she became an international phenomenon. It took several tons of bolts and nails to hold her together, and more than a million pieces of wood and sheet metal and nearly $40,000 (a sizable sum in the late 19th century) to complete the structure. Her proportions are impressive: legs 20 feet tall and 10 feet in diameter, a 36-foot-long trunk, a 26-foot-long tail, and 22-foot-long tusks. Lafferty tried to bank on his success by building the Light of Asia in Cape May and The Elephantine Colossus in Coney Island. By 1900 they had both burned down, and Lafferty was broke. He sold the Atlantic City building to John Gertzen, whose wife, Sophie, reportedly named her Lucy. She has been a tourist attraction, tavern, private residence, and campground centerpiece. In the 1960s she was vacant and got pretty shabby, until a Save Lucy Committee moved her in the 1970s to her current home at the intersection of Atlantic and Decatur avenues and pumped thousands into polishing her up. You can enter a stairway in her hind legs and climb six stories to her howdah, learn about Lucy's history, and marvel at the panorama and the fact that you're standing atop the only elephant of this size in the world—and the only surviving relic of zoomorphic architecture in America. The gift shop sells Lucy stuffed animals, T-shirts, and the like.

going from the Atlantic's deep fishing grounds into Absecon Island's calm-water back bays. Today, it's a waterfront fishing, boating, shopping, and dining complex at the confluence of Clam Creek and Absecon Inlet, across from the Coast Guard Station and Farley State Marina. It's a hub for all manner of boat excursions, from sightseeing and fishing cruises to dolphin- and whale-watches. Restaurants and bars serve up fresh-off-the-boat seafood and offer outdoor dining and live music in-season; a Crafter's Village holds more than a half dozen shops selling art, jewelry and crafts; and the **Atlantic City Aquarium** is a first-rate marine-life education facility (see *Museums*). From the waterfront park you can watch an endless parade of boats, including ultra-luxe yachts and New Jersey's largest fleet of commercial fishing vessels. Special events and festivals throughout the year.

LIGHTHOUSES Absecon Lighthouse (609-449-1360; www.abseconlighthouse .org), 31 South Rhode Island Ave., Atlantic City. Open July–Aug., daily 10–5; Sept.–June, Thurs.–Mon. 11–4, closed Tues., Wed., and major holidays. Adults $7; seniors $5; children 4–12, $4; children 3 and under, free. Visitors can climb 228 steps up an iron spiral staircase to the top of New Jersey's tallest lighthouse (the Twin Lights of Navesink in Highlands is shorter but sits higher above sea level) for panoramic views of the Atlantic Ocean and the Atlantic City skyline. The majestic 171-foot-high lighthouse was built in 1856 at the northern end of Atlantic City to warn ships of the dangerous shoals in the inlet between Absecon Island and Brigantine, nicknamed Graveyard Inlet for the high incidence of shipwrecks. Like Long Beach Island's Barnegat Light, or "Old Barney," this one was designed and built by Lieutenant George Gordon Meade—who would later go on to command the Union army at Gettysburg. This is the only lighthouse in New Jersey to retain its original first-order Fresnel lens, a massive lens of 36 plates that was custom made in Paris. The kerosene flame cast a beam that could be seen for nearly 20 nautical miles. The lighthouse was converted to operate with electricity in 1925, then decommissioned and extinguished in 1933. It's just a few short blocks from the boardwalk; look for the yellow tower with a thick black band. While the lighthouse was undergoing extensive renovations in 1998, the original keeper's house was destroyed in a fire. The reconstructed red-roofed keeper's house is gleaming white and neat as a pin, and open to visitors as a museum and gift shop.

Atlantic City Laser Lighthouse (www.iloveac.com/laser-light) Grand Blvd., between Arkansas and Missouri Aves. Free shows nightly. No, this isn't a real lighthouse, but a free laser show that takes place every night on Grand Boulevard that can be seen from all over the city. During the day it's an unusual-looking white structure that is visible to motorists approaching on the Atlantic City Expressway; but at dusk, it puts on a spectacular multi-hued performance, as lights are projected both on and from the lighthouse. It was built to commemorate Atlantic City's latest revitalization efforts.

MUSEUMS Atlantic City Historical Museum and Cultural Center (609-347-5839; www.acmuseum.org), Garden Pier, the Boardwalk at New Jersey Ave., Atlantic City. Open daily 10–4; phone ahead on major holidays. Free admission. The story of Atlantic City as it used to be, told in a permanent exhibition of historic kitsch—souvenirs, seashells, costumes, Kewpie dolls, vintage postcards, playbills, posters, and other artifacts—dating to the 1800s. Changing exhibits chronicle big entertainers who visited Atlantic City over the decades, the history of gambling, and lots of Miss America memorabilia, such as snow globes with tiny beauty queens inside. One of the museum's founders is Vicki Gold Levi, and the museum's treasure trove of memorabilia and artifacts is based on her personal collection that spans decades. Her father, Al Gold, was Atlantic City's first chief official photographer from 1939 until his death in 1964. Like many Philadelphians, Gold came to the shore for health reasons, and photographed the first Miss America pageant in 1921. Goldie, as he was known, was one of the biggest news photographers on the East Coast. Hundreds of his photographs are featured in rotating displays in the museum's **Al Gold Photography Gallery.** Don't miss the historical video *Boardwalk Ballyhoo: The Magic of Atlantic City,* a documentary that traces the resort's colorful history through old footage of the high-diving horses, Miss America pageants, and throngs of tourists roaring down the boardwalk. The permanent exhibition **Atlantic City: Playground of the Nation** includes costumes, postcards, song sheets, souvenirs, a collection of original sand art, and a miniature boardwalk and beach. The museum hands out complimentary Heinz pickle pins, a nod to Atlantic City's turn-of-the-20th-century heyday.

✿ **Ripley's Believe It or Not! Museum** (609-347-2001; www.ripleys.com), New York Ave. and the Boardwalk, Atlantic City. Open daily; call for hours. Adults $14.99; seniors $11.99; children 5–12, $9.99; students, AAA members, and military $12.99. As befitting a museum that's devoted to all things bizarre, Ripley's collection is housed in a building whose façade appears to be collapsing into the street, the victim of a globe-shaped wrecking ball. Robert Ripley traveled the globe and amassed a collection of oddball items that define strange and unusual; they are on display here and in his other similar museums around the world. Over 400 exhibits in 13 themed galleries feature the imaginable and unimaginable, from a shrunken head to a lock of George Washington's hair to a life-sized wax replica of Robert Wadlow, who at an inch shy of 9 feet tall not only towered over others, but was the tallest person in the recorded history of the world. The museum shows films throughout the day, and has an interactive fun house. The latest addition? A gumball Obama.

✿ **Atlantic City Aquarium** (609-348-2880; www.acaquarium.com), Gardner's Basin, 800 N. New Hampshire Ave., Atlantic City. Open daily 10–5; closed Thanksgiving, Christmas Day, and New Year's Day. Adults $7; seniors $5; students and children, $4; children 3 and under, free. A marine museum and educational science center with more than 100 varieties of fish and marine animals, including Groman, a 100-pound loggerhead turtle, and Octavia the octopus. Nearly 50,000 gallons of live exhibits in 17 aquariums. One aquarium is devoted to nurse sharks, weakfish, northern stingrays, and other fish that live off the New Jersey coast; others contain jellyfish, sea horses, giant moray eels, and tropical fish. There's one tank with a coral reef exhibit, another on the local freshwater tributaries of the Pinelands. A 250-gallon touch tank contains shrimp, mussels, knobbed whelks, sea urchins, hermit crabs, and horseshoe crabs. A 16-station computer learning center and other interactive exhibits encourage thoughtful exploration. The third-floor observation deck is a prime spot for watching commercial fishing boats, luxury yachts, and sightseeing boats ply back and forth between the Atlantic Ocean and the marinas.

Noyes Museum of Art (609-652-8848; www.noyesmuseum.org), Lily Lake Rd. (off Rt. 9), Oceanville. Open Thurs.–Sat. 10–4:30; Sun. noon–5; closed Mon., Christmas Day, and New Year's Day. Adults $3; seniors and students $2; children 11 and under, free; admission by donation on Friday. South Jersey's largest art museum is just a few miles north of Atlantic City, next to the **Edwin B. Forsythe National Wildlife Refuge** (see sidebar, page 457). It showcases a permanent collection of fine art, contemporary arts and crafts, and 19th- and 20th-century American folk art, with an emphasis on artists from the mid-Atlantic region and an extensive collection of some 200 vintage North American shorebird decoys. The galleries mount a dozen or so changing exhibits on photography, painting, graphic design, and mixed media by regional and national artists. The museum was founded by Fred and Ethel Noyes, the husband-and-wife entrepreneurial team who also developed the Historic Towne of Smithville (see *Selective Shopping—Special Shops*); they sold the shopping village to fund a museum of American arts and crafts. Mrs. Noyes died in 1979, just a few years before the museum was complete. The collections are displayed in an inviting airy space with lovely views of the surrounding coastal wetlands area.

✍ **Sea Life Museum and Marine Mammal Stranding Center** (609-266-0538; www.mmsc.org), 3625 Brigantine Blvd., Brigantine. Open daily Memorial Day–Labor Day, 10–4; open Sat. only 10–2, Sept.–May; call before you visit, as hours can change due to the center's daily operations. Admission by donation. The Sea Life Museum occupies a 1930s-era Coast Guard boathouse and includes life-sized replicas of marine mammals, sea turtles, and game fish that are found in New Jersey. A hands-on exhibit features the bones of whales and other marine mammals. Displays educate visitors on the dangers faced by these creatures when they come in contact with—or ingest—debris from the ocean. The Marine Stranding Center, founded in 1978, is a private nonprofit center that rescues and rehabilitates stranded sea turtles, whales, dolphins, seals, and other marine creatures before returning them to the wild. The center responds to thousands of calls for mammals stranded on New Jersey beaches—mostly dolphins and seals, but they've also rescued a 25-ton whale. This is the only authorized facility in New Jersey that can rescue stranded sea turtles and marine mammals. Visitors can watch from the observation area as the animals are resting and being treated. From May to September, a 1,000-gallon outdoor observation pool is stocked with local fish, which are released in the fall to area waters. This small facility relies on donations and membership fees for support; it can take several months—and thousands of dollars—to rehabilitate one animal. The gift shop sells stuffed animals, T-shirts, trinkets, and quality books and games for children.

Atlantic Heritage Center (609-927-5218; www.atlanticheritagecenter.org), 907 Shore Rd., Somers Point. Open Wed.–Sat. 10–3:30. Free admission. The historical-society headquarters preserves the history and culture of Atlantic County and southern New Jersey with maritime artifacts, Victorian clothing, photographs, weapons, and memorabilia. The museum's entire collection contains more than 20,000 objects dating from 1770 to 1980. The main collections feature household, decorative, and utilitarian objects—particularly from the Victorian era—with smaller collections of historic weaponry, fine art, and relics from Atlantic County's heritage as a 19th-century shipbuilding center. The research library contains thousands of old manuscripts, books, deeds, and documents as well as vintage photographs, tintypes, and daguerreotypes.

✷ To Do

AMUSEMENTS ✍ **Steel Pier** (609-345-4893; www.steelpier.com), across from the Trump Taj Mahal Casino and Resort, on the Boardwalk at Virginia Ave., Atlantic City. Open Mon.–Fri. 3 PM–midnight; Sat.–Sun., noon–1 AM; hours subject to change due to weather and season. Free admission. Atlantic City's historic boardwalk pier—first built in 1898—was a world-renowned entertainment mecca from the 1920s to the 1950s. Thousands of visitors came every day to see the famous high-diving horses, circus performers, and other novelty acts, as well as the Miss America Pageant and the world's top entertainers—Mae West, Bob Hope, Frank Sinatra, Charlie Chaplin—play the Steel Pier. After years of neglect—ending with a devastating fire in 1982—it was restored in 1993 into a family entertainment center. Today there are two-dozen amusement rides, games, prize wheels, a food court, and an old-fashioned double-decker carousel. Circus-style "thrill shows" are performed regularly, and future plans call for a water park and bigger, faster, extreme rides.

✔ **Atlantic City Boardwalk Arcade** (609-345-3710), 1315 Boardwalk and Ocean Ave., Atlantic City. Atlantic City's largest arcade is a block down the boardwalk from Resorts Casino Hotel.

✔ **Central Pier Arcade and Speedway** (609-345-5219), 1400 Boardwalk at Tennessee Ave., Atlantic City. Paintball, laser tag, race-car speedway, along with more traditional carnival rides, booths, and arcade games on a 19th-century boardwalk pier.

✔ **Playcade Amusements** (609-345-8260; www.playcade.com), 2629 Boardwalk, between the Convention Hall and the Tropicana. Open daily from 10 AM. Billed as Atlantic City's "longest established arcade," it features video games, slots, and the usual arcade pastimes.

✔ **Storybook Land**, (609-646-0103; www.storybookland.com), 6415 Black Horse Pike, Egg Harbor Township. Open Apr.–Dec.; call or see Web site for exact hours. An amusement park for little ones that uses classic stories and nursery rhymes as its theme, and tosses in exciting family rides. $20.95, plus tax for each child or adult includes all attractions and unlimited rides; children under 1 year, free.

BICYCLING In Atlantic City, bicycles are allowed on the boardwalk daily from 6–noon. On Ventnor City's 1.7-mile boardwalk, you can ride daylight hours all year round. Bikes can be rented from **AAAA Bike Shop** (609-487-2453; www.aaaabike shop.com), 5300 Ventnor Ave., Ventnor City, and from **B&K Bike Rental** (609-344-8008), 1743 Boardwalk, Atlantic City.

Edwin B. Forsythe National Wildlife Refuge (609-652-1665; www.fws.gov/ northeast/forsythe), Great Creek Rd. (off Rt. 9), Oceanville. You can ride along **Wildlife Drive,** the scenic 8-mile auto road that loops through the refuge. Bikes are not permitted on the nature trails. (See also sidebar, page 457.)

BIRDING **Edwin B. Forsythe National Wildlife Refuge** (609-652-1665; www.fws.gov/northeast/forsythe), Great Creek Rd. (off Rt. 9), Oceanville. The refuge is open daily sunrise to sunset; the headquarters is open Mon.–Fri. 10–3. This pristine 43,000-acre swath of grassy tidal marshes and coastal woodlands and waterways (see sidebar, page 457) sits along the Atlantic Flyway, the busy flight path of tens of thousands of birds traveling north and south during the spring and fall migrations. The mix of islands, bays, and inlets just north of Atlantic City forms a natural buffer between the barrier islands along the Atlantic Ocean and the mainland. Egrets, sandpipers, terns, ducks, geese, shorebirds, wading birds, and bluebirds inhabit the wooded and marshy areas. Bald eagles, peregrine falcons, owls, water birds, and endangered piping plovers are among the species that are also often seen here. Birders can explore on two interpretive trails, or bike or drive along **Wildlife Drive,** an 8-mile auto road through the refuge; pick up a brochure at the refuge headquarters. An **observation tower** is outfitted with a high-powered telescope, which enables visitors to focus not only on the abundant wildlife but also the glimmering towers of the nearby Atlantic City casinos. Call about a schedule of special events related to bird migration. Be sure to use insect repellent while visiting in summer, when swarms of biting greenhead flies are abundant.

BOAT EXCURSIONS Atlantic City Cruises (609-347-7600; www.atlantic citycruises.com), Gardner's Basin, 800 N. New Hampshire Ave., Atlantic City. Open late-May–Sept. A wide variety of bay and ocean excursions aboard *Cruisin 1* leave daily from spring through fall. Dolphin and marine-mammal sightseeing excursions are led by an onboard marine naturalist. Call for a schedule of morning skyline tours, late-afternoon harbor tours, sunset cocktail cruises through the back bays, and moonlight dance-party trips.

Atlantus Charters (609-408-3564; www.atlantuscharters.com), Gardner's Basin, 800 N. New Hampshire Ave., Atlantic City. Full- and half-day charter fishing trips, scuba-diving excursions, and special events.

The *Atlantic Star* (609-348-8418; 800-353-8418; www.atlanticstarcharters.com), Kammerman's Atlantic City Marina, 447 Carson Ave., Atlantic City. A variety of charter trips, from sportfishing to dinner cruises and sightseeing excursions aboard a 46-foot luxury yacht.

BOATING (See also *Boat Excursions.*)

Kammerman's Atlantic City Marina (609-348-8418; www.atlanticstarcharters .com), 447 Carson Ave., Atlantic City. Open year-round. This marina has a ship's store and Atlantic City's largest fuel dock.

Senator Frank S. Farley State Marina (609-441-8482; 800-876-4386; www .trumpmarina.com), Huron Ave., next to the Coast Guard Station, Atlantic City. The 640 slips can accommodate yachts up to 300 feet in length. Bathrooms, private showers, and laundry facilities as well as fuel, repair, and other marine services. Next door, Trump Marina Casino Resort has restaurants and a ship's store. The marina has an interesting interpretive exhibit on the region's maritime history.

DOLPHIN-WATCHING ♪ **Atlantic City Cruises** (609-347-7600; www .atlanticcitycruises.com), Gardner's Basin, 800 N. New Hampshire Ave., Atlantic City. Trips run on Wed., Sat., and Sun. in May, and from mid-Sept.– mid-Oct. They run daily, Memorial Day weekend to mid-Sept. Adults $34; seniors 60 and up, $29; children 5–15, $18. Daily dolphin and marine-mammal observation excursions aboard *Cruisin 1.* The 2-hour open-ocean trips are accompanied by a marine naturalist.

FISHING The ocean waters off Absecon Island are known for their flounder, tuna, swordfish, and striped bass, as well as crabs and clams in the bays. A variety of charter boats and party boats (below are just a few) dock at marinas in the Atlantic City region. Charter boats are small, usually carrying private groups of a few people; party boats carry large numbers of passengers on a first-come, first-served basis. Pontoon boats take guests on fishing trips in the calm-water bays that separate the barrier island from the mainland.

Many sportfishing boats are based at **Gardner's Basin** (800 N. New Hampshire Ave., Atlantic City), at the confluence of Absecon Inlet and Clam Creek. **Stray Cat Sportfish** (609-391-9630; www.captmikesstraycat.com) offers back-bay fishing excursions and ecotours aboard *Highroller*, a 50-foot pontoon boat. **Shore Bet Fishing** (609-345-4077) takes passengers deep-sea fishing on daily half-day trips, Memorial Day–Sept.; 6-hour trips run April–Memorial Day, and Oct.–mid-Dec., Fri.–Sun.; and night fishing runs, from Memorial Day–Sept.

The *Atlantic Star* (609-348-8418; 800-353-8418; www.atlanticstarcharters.com), Atlantic City Marina, 447 Carson Ave., Atlantic City. A variety of charter trips, from sportfishing to corporate fishing tournaments.

Keeper Back Bay Fishing (609-823-6428; www.keeperfishing.com), 9605 Amherst Ave., Margate City. Four-hour, morning and afternoon back-bay fishing excursions aboard a 50-foot pontoon boat. They also offer evening charters and party cruises.

Duke O'Fluke (609-926-2280; www.dukeoffluke.com), Higbee Ave., at the Bay, Somers Point. Open May–Nov. Daily 4-hour party boat excursions in the back-bay area for fluke, weakfish, snapper, bluefish, flounder, and sea bass.

Anglers can also cast a line off fishing piers in the Atlantic City region. In Ventnor City, the **Ventnor City Fishing Pier** (609-823-7944) is on the boardwalk at Cambridge Ave. In Brigantine, **Old Brigantine Bridge** is at Absecon Inlet. The **Edward Klingener Fishing Pier** is off Rt. 152 between Somers Point and Longport. **Margate Fish Pier** is at the Angler's Club in Margate City.

Edwin B. Forsythe National Wildlife Refuge (609-652-1665; www.fws.gov/northeast/forsythe), Moss Mill Rd., Oceanville. There is a public boat ramp at Scott's Landing. Anglers can launch boats at the Scott's Landing ramp to fish the refuge's shallow coves and bays.

Birch Grove Park (609-641-3778; 800-354-6201), Burton Ave. and Mill Rd., Northfield. A municipal park with 21 interconnected finger lakes that offer a variety of fishing experiences. The front lakes are easily accessible by the park's network of boardwalks. You must hike through heavily wooded trails to reach the back lakes. Largemouth bass, trout, pike, and catfish are among the resident species; the state stocks the lakes with trout in winter and spring, and it's stocked during the year for a variety of fishing tournaments. The park has a family campground (see *Lodging—Campgrounds*). Fishing supplies and live bait are sold in the park, and a New Jersey fishing license is required (you must obtain an additional stamp for trout fishing).

GAMING There are eleven casino resorts in Atlantic City, open 24 hours a day, every day of the year (see *Lodging—Casino Resorts*). Most are clustered along the boardwalk, with the exception of Trump Marina, The Borgata, and Harrah's, which are in the Marina District at the northern end of the city. All offer a wide variety of table games and slot machines that cater to both high rollers and new gamblers. The slots are decidedly user-friendly—all you need to know is where to insert your money and which button to push. Old-school gamblers, however, can still crank the handle of the "one-armed bandits," as in the early days. Serious players crowd the green-felted roulette, blackjack, craps, poker, and baccarat tables. Older folks like to play keno and wager on simulcast races.

You don't have to stay off the gaming floor if you're not a gambler. It's always interesting to just sit back and observe the rich pageantry of people from around the world and all walks of life who are lured to the betting action by the promise of instant fortune. "Bet with your head, not over it," is always a good rule to follow, and the casinos all urge guests to gamble sensibly and within their means. Keep in mind that New Jersey state law requires gamblers to be at least 21 years old; no one under 21 is permitted on the casino floor. When luck or money is running low, there's always something else to do without leaving the casino.

Atlantic City Hilton Casino and Resort (609-347-7111; 888-224-4586; www .hiltonac.com), Boston Ave. and the Boardwalk, is the farthest south along the boardwalk, and has a decidedly intimate and elegant feel. At 66,000 square feet, its casino floor is smaller than many of the others in town, and the chandeliers and Italian marble lend an air of sophistication. There are 2,260 slot machines, and 13 varieties of table games including Big Six, roulette, and blackjack.

Bally's Atlantic City (609-340-2000; 800-772-7777; www.ballysac.com), 1900 Park Pl. and the Boardwalk. Four casinos with a combined 220,000 square feet of gaming space are devoted to slot machines, poker, simulcast wagering, and more than a dozen kinds of table games. The California gold rush–themed Wild Wild West Casino has a 19th-century frontier façade and a western motif inside, where a youngish crowd flocks to Billy's Poker Parlor and Coyote Kate's Slot Parlor.

Borgata Hotel Casino and Spa (609-317-1000; 866-692-6742; www.theborgata .com), One Borgata Way. Atlantic City's newest casino is off the boardwalk at Renaissance Point in the Marina District. The gaming floor boasts 200 tables and 4,100 coinless slot machines. The Borgata gets the usual high rollers but also attracts a clientele that is younger than the gamblers who traditionally frequent the casinos. (See also sidebar, next page.)

Caesars Atlantic City Hotel Casino (609-348-4411; 800-443-0104; www.caesars ac.com), 2100 Pacific Ave. Caesars sports a bold ancient-Rome motif, from the classical artwork and statues to the massive replicas of Caesar Augustus and Michelangelo's *David*. Six gaming areas with more than 3,400 slot machines and 20 varieties of table games are spread across two floors, including Palace East, an Asian gaming area featuring more than 25 table games. The Palace Court slot parlor is designed after the Roman Pantheon.

Harrah's Atlantic City Casino Hotel (609-441-5000; 800-242-7724; www .harrahsresort.com), 777 Harrah's Blvd. This was the first of three casinos to opt for a quieter bayfront location away from the venerable boardwalk. The 112,000-square-foot casino floor has 3,712 video-poker and slot machines, including the high-limit Diamond Cove slot area; blackjack, roulette, craps, and mini-baccarat at 65 tables; the poker room has Texas Hold'em, 7 Card Stud, and other variations on the game.

Resorts Atlantic City (609-344-6000; 800-336-6378; www.resortsac.com), 1133 Boardwalk at North Carolina Ave. This is where it all began. Atlantic City's first casino opened on Memorial Day weekend in 1978; Steve Lawrence rolled the dice and lost $10 at craps. Its 100,000-square-foot casino features the usual gaming tables, an art deco–style baccarat room, and slot machines at which you can bet $100 or a penny a pop.

"ℹ" ♿ BORGATA HOTEL CASINO AND SPA
(609-317-1000; 866-692-6742; www.theborgata.com), One Borgata Way, Atlantic
City. Atlantic City's newest hotel, casino, and spa is the first to come on the
scene in more than 10 years. Everything about it is impressive, including the
$1.1-billion price tag. This sleek gold glass tower soars 43 stories above the
bay, where it keeps company with
Harrah's and Trump Marina away from
the boardwalk. The ultrachic lobby
has bold sculpture and reproductions
of works by Matisse and Klimt, and
the 2,002 tastefully decorated guest
rooms and suites boast floor-to-ceiling
windows and contemporary European-style décor. The classic rooms
have marble baths with showers for
two and high-speed Internet access;
the suites have upscale amenities
such as deep soaking tubs, wet bars,
plasma TVs, multimedia entertainment
centers, and powder rooms. Eleven
restaurants offer trendy haute cuisine,
homey diner fare, sushi, and dim sum.
There are a dozen upscale shops and
boutiques, and a hip collection of bars
and clubs. The 1,000-seat **Music Box
Theater** and larger **Event Center** have
a full schedule of top-flight entertainment (see *Dining Out* and *Eating Out,*
and *Entertainment*). The **Pump Room**
is a state-of-the-art fitness center
with high-tech cardio stations, and
Spa Toccare offers massage, facials,
and body and bath treatments. Rooms
$129–650; suites $209 and up.

THE BILLION-DOLLAR BORGATA HOTEL,
CASINO, AND SPA BECAME THE
LARGEST HOTEL IN NEW JERSEY
HISTORY WHEN IT OPENED IN 2003.

Photo by Scott Francis Photography

Showboat—The Mardi Gras Casino (609-343-4000; 800-621-0200; www
.showboatac.com), 801 Boardwalk at Delaware Ave. A turn-of-the-20th-century
New Orleans–themed casino with live Dixieland jazz, authentic Southern cuisine, a
festive Bourbon Street atmosphere, and a House of Blues on-site. The gaming
floor features simulcast horse racing, 80-plus table games, 3,500 slot machines, and
everything else from video poker to Caribbean stud poker. The luxe high-roller
lounge is a recent $5.3 million addition.

Tropicana Casino and Resort (609-340-4000; 800-843-8767; www.tropicana .net), Brighton Ave. and the Boardwalk. Watch simulcast thoroughbred and standardbred racing on more than 100 monitors, or play in one of Atlantic City's largest poker rooms, or at one of more than 4,400 slot machines. The Crystal Room is a luxurious space devoted exclusively to slots, and Jade Palace has authentic Asian table games, from Sic Bo and mini-baccarat to Pai Gow Tiles.

Trump Marina Casino Resort (609-441-2000; 800-777-1177; www.trumpmarina .com), Huron Ave. and Brigantine Blvd. More than 2,100 slot machines and 90 gaming tables on a 80,000-square-foot casino floor. This casino tends to attract a young and energetic crowd that also comes here for the lively nightclubs on Absecon Inlet.

Trump Plaza Hotel and Casino (609-441-6000; 800-677-7378; www.trump plaza.com), Mississippi Ave. and the Boardwalk. Traditional table games from craps and blackjack to baccarat and roulette. The casino is tucked onto the boardwalk next to historic Boardwalk Hall, and gets high marks for the impeccable service and classiness that's several notches above the norm.

TRUMP MARINA HOTEL AND CASINO, FORMERLY KNOWN AS TRUMP CASTLE, ADJACENT TO THE SENATOR FRANK S. FARLEY STATE MARINA, IS ONE OF REAL ESTATE MOGUL DONALD TRUMP'S THREE ATLANTIC CITY CASINOS.

Photo courtesy of the Atlantic City Convention and Visitors Bureau

Trump Taj Mahal Casino Resort (609-449-1000; www.trumptaj.com), 1000
Boardwalk at Virginia Ave. More than 4,000 slot machines, 210 table games, a baccarat pit, and simulcast racing. The smoke-free poker room, the largest smoke-free poker room on the East Coast, is home to the United States Poker Championship. The Taj is either a temple of opulence or gaudiness, depending on whom you ask. Either way, it's impressive—not only for the $14 million in crystal chandeliers, but also for having the largest casino floor in Atlantic City.

GOLF There are more than 20 golf courses in the greater Atlantic City region. While some, as in Brigantine, are very close, most are a short distance inland. Look in "The Pinelands Region" in "Central New Jersey" to find more courses that are convenient to Atlantic City. The **Greater Atlantic City Golf Association** (800-465-3222; www.acgolfvacations.com), 1742 Mays Landing–Somers Point Rd., Egg Harbor Township, has information on courses in the area and can arrange golf vacation packages with area hotels or book tee times.

Seaview Marriott Resort and Spa (609-748-7680; 800-205-6518; www.sea viewgolf.com), 401 S. New York Rd., Galloway. A historic golf resort dating to 1914 (see *Lodging—Resort*), with two 18-hole championship-caliber courses spread across the resort's 670 wooded acres. The PGA Championship was held here in 1942, and the resort hosted the prestigious Shoprite LPGA Classic for years.

Brigantine Golf Links (609-266-1388; www.brigantinegolf.com), 1075 North Shore Dr., Brigantine. A Scottish links–style golf course built in 1927 with views of the ocean and 18 holes spread across flat, open terrain 4 miles north of Atlantic City. The clubhouse has a restaurant, snack bar, and pro shop.

SCENIC DRIVE **Ocean Drive** This scenic road passing through a string of barrier islands is a famous seashore route from Atlantic City to Victorian Cape May. A chain of six bridges links 14 seaside communities along 40 miles of southern New Jersey shoreline, with spectacular ocean views along the way.

SPECTATOR SPORTS ⚓ **Atlantic City Surf** (609-344-8873; www.acsurf.com), Bernie Robbins Stadium at Bader Field, Black Horse Pike (Rt. 322), Atlantic City. Games May–Sept. Atlantic City's Atlantic League professional minor-league baseball team plays its home games—about 70 a season—at the 5,900-seat **Sandcastle Stadium,** located about a half mile from the casinos. From the stands, spectators enjoy a spectacular view of the beachfront skyline. Weekly fireworks shows take place when the team is in town. A picnic area is available to ticket holders.

WATER SPORTS In Brigantine, **Bayside Marina** (609-264-0900), 4401 Atlantic–Brigantine Blvd., and **Jolly Roger Marina** (609-266-3131), 3101 Bayshore Ave., rent Jet Skis and Sea-Doos. **Brigantine Island Water Sports** (609-266-9330), North Point Marina, 1225 East Shore Dr., rents powerboats for fishing, cruising, tubing, and waterskiing.

✳ Green Space

BEACHES ♿ **Oceanfront beaches** in Absecon Island's shore communities are open to the public. With the exception of Atlantic City, whose 4-mile beach is free, visitors are required to purchase a beach badge, or tag, as some towns call them.

Prices are generally reasonable, ranging from around $5 for a day badge, $10–15 for a weekly pass, and between $10 and $25 for the entire season. All beaches offer swimming, and most allow rafting, fishing, and surfing; some have tennis courts and playgrounds. In **Atlantic City** (609-449-7166) the boardwalk and its amusements are a welcome diversion when the kids get too much sun or the sky clouds over. From Memorial Day to Labor Day—all summer long—there are beach bars, volleyball courts, and live beach concerts. About a dozen handicapped-access ramps lead from the boardwalk to the beach. There are no public bathhouses, but outdoor showers at South Carolina Ave., Virginia Ave., and Albany Ave. are available for rinsing off sand.

Other public oceanfront beaches are in **Brigantine** (609-266-1122; www .brigantinebeachnj.com), **Ventnor City** (609-823-7900; www.ventnorcity.org), **Margate City** (609-822-2605; www.margate-nj.com), and **Longport** (609-823-2731; www.longport-nj.us/). In **Somers Point** (609-927-9088), there's a municipal beach on Bay Ave. facing Great Egg Harbor Bay.

PUBLIC GARDEN Civil Rights Garden (609-347-0500), next to the Carnegie Library, Pacific Ave. and Dr. Martin Luther King Blvd., Atlantic City. A public sculpture garden honoring the 20th-century civil rights movement is a tranquil retreat from the boardwalk and casino crowds. A series of 11 columns made of black African granite are inscribed with tributes to the key historical figures and milestone events that helped black Americans achieve equal rights. Walking paths lace through a manicured landscape of flowers, plants, and ginkgo trees that surrounds a reflecting pool topped with a bronze bell, encircled by excerpts from Dr. Martin Luther King Jr.'s famous "I have a dream" speech.

ATLANTIC CITY'S WIDE EXPANSE OF SAND ALONG THE ATLANTIC OCEAN BOASTS SOME OF THE ONLY BEACHES ON THE ENTIRE JERSEY SHORE THAT ARE FREE.

Photo courtesy of the Atlantic City Convention and Visitors Bureau

EDWIN B. FORSYTHE NATIONAL WILDLIFE REFUGE

(609-652-1665; www.fws.gov/northeast/forsythe), Brigantine Division head-quarters, Great Creek Rd. (off Rt. 9), Oceanville. The Wildlife Drive auto road and nature trails are open daily from sunrise to sunset; the headquarters is open Mon.–Fri. 10–3. Admission $4 for cars; $2 for cyclists and pedestrians. Pets are allowed but must remain on a short leash; bikes are permitted on Wildlife Drive only. This 43,000-acre refuge is named for New Jersey congressman and conservationist Edwin Forsythe, and it receives more than 200,000 visitors a year. Nearly all of it is tidal marsh and salt meadow dotted with shallow bays, tidal wetlands, and coves. A pristine 6,000-acre barrier beach and undeveloped woodlands make for rich coastal habitats and a vital resting place for tens of thousands of migratory birds. The refuge stretches some 70 miles, from Atlantic City to the Bay Head area; islands and fingers of land jut into numerous shallow coves and ponds, as well as into Absecon Bay at the southern tip of the refuge and Barnegat Bay to the north. The quiet waters are feeding grounds for fish, shellfish, and birds and a popular destination for birders and photographers (see *To Do—Birding*) who know that dawn and dusk are the best times to spot wildlife. Visitors can see the refuge's marshes and woodlands from the 8-mile **Wildlife Drive** auto road; pick up a map and a bird checklist at the self-service information area, where reports of recent wildlife sightings and other news are posted. Descriptions in the brochure correspond with signposts along the road; visitors in spring and fall often see large groups of migratory birds along the way. **Leeds Eco-Trail** is a half-mile loop through the woods and over a boardwalk in the salt marsh. **Akers Woodland Trail** is a quarter-mile easy footpath through woodlands, a good place to spot migratory warblers. Biting insects thrive here from mid-May to mid-October; bring insect repellent and wear protective clothing.

✳ Lodging

When trying to find a place to spend the night in Atlantic City, the question isn't so much "if" as "where." There are 14,000 hotel rooms in the casinos alone, and the city streets as well as the outskirts are filled chockablock with reasonably priced chain hotels and motels of varying degrees of age, quality, and cleanliness. As a rule, the Atlantic City region isn't synonymous with quaint bed & breakfasts, but there are a few sprinkled around Absecon Island. The **Atlantic City Convention and Visitor's Authority** (888-228-4748; www.atlanticcitynj .com) offers online booking of casino hotels, resorts, and bed & breakfasts; **A.C. Central Reservations** (888-227-6667; www.acrooms.com) is a reservation service for casino hotels and resorts in Atlantic City and surrounding communities; **Acenet Hotel Reservations** (800-511-5741;

www.acenethotels.com) can arrange discount lodging in Atlantic City.

RESORT ✆ ♿ "ṭ" **Seaview Marriott Resort and Spa** (609-652-1800; 800-205-6518; www.seaviewmarriott.com), 401 S. New York Rd., Galloway 08205. An elegant resort-style hotel close to Atlantic City and famous for its championship golf facilities opened in 1914 as the exclusive Seaview Country Club. Today it's a member of the **National Trust Historic Hotels of America,** and the only full-service resort and spa in southern New Jersey. There are 297 well-appointed, newly renovated guest rooms and one- and two-bedroom suites that are tastefully decorated and come with standard amenities such as voice mail, in-room coffee and movies, and a minibar. In-room wired Internet and public areas' Wi-Fi available. The **Elizabeth Arden Red Door Spa** is a luxurious full-service spa for men and women, complete with an indoor lap pool, heated outdoor Jacuzzi tubs, therapeutic steam rooms, saunas, and nearly 20 rooms for facials, massage, body treatments, and other pampering services. Two 18-hole championship golf courses—and six all-weather tennis courts—are spread across 670 wooded acres. Other amenities include indoor and outdoor pools, a health club, a gift shop and newsstand, and a fully equipped business center. Child care, dry cleaning, and secretarial service can be arranged. Rooms $89–369; suites $179 and up.

CASINO RESORTS Nothing embodies Atlantic City's never-ending transformation quite like its casino resorts. Within their glittering confines, multimillion-dollar face-lifts are de rigueur—shops and restaurants come and go at a dizzying rate; guest rooms and lobbies are revamped and redesigned; and gaming halls are constantly adding better slots, bigger poker rooms, new baccarat pits, and hotter nightclubs. As the casinos reinvent themselves, they like to change—or at least tweak—their names. Since Resorts International opened in 1978 it has been known as Merv Griffin's Resorts, Resorts, and now Resorts Atlantic City. Atlantic City Hilton used to be the Golden Nugget, Bally's Grand, and The Grand-A Bally's Casino Resort. The Tropicana Casino and Resort opened as the Tropicana Hotel and Casino and was also known as Trop World. And so on. Most casinos are referred to in tourism literature with a maddening array of name variations.

All listings are in Atlantic City 08401.

♿ "ṭ" **Atlantic City Hilton Casino Resort** (609-347-7111; 888-224-4586; www.hiltonac.com), Boston Ave. and the Boardwalk. This southernmost boardwalk casino resort is known for its elegant décor and professional and attentive staff. It's a little smaller than most of the hotels, so there's an intimate atmosphere that many visitors find appealing. Most of the 604 guest rooms—and all the 200 suites—have a view of the Atlantic and fee-based Internet access. World-class entertainers play the 1,200-seat **Grand Theater** (where Frank Sinatra used to perform) and the **Dizzy Dolphin**'s nautically themed beach lounge features a bar made from an actual schooner. Amenities include an exercise room, a health spa, and an indoor pool in a lush garden setting. Seven restaurants and eateries include an Asian noodle bar, a coffeehouse, a 24-hour diner, an all-you-can-eat buffet, an upscale steakhouse, and the elegant and sophisticated **Peregrine's** (see *Dining Out*). Rooms $65–375; suites $265 and up.

& **Bally's Atlantic City** (609-340-2000; 800-772-7777; www.ballysac.com), Park Pl. and the Boardwalk. This is Atlantic City's biggest casino resort, and one of the first to open along the boardwalk. When the resort' was built, it was designed to incorporate one of Atlantic City's architectural relics at a time when most old buildings were demolished to make way for the new. The Dennis Hotel, a mansard-roofed Beaux-Arts building that dates to 1860, has been completely restored, and the stately **Dennis Lounge** harkens to the Old World charm of Atlantic City's grand hotels. There are more than 2,000 guest rooms and suites, 14 restaurants, four lounges, two pools, more than a dozen specialty shops, four casinos, and a fitness center with indoor pool and spa. Guest rooms are spread across four distinct areas: the historic **Dennis Hotel,** the **North Tower Casino,** the **Garden Rooms,** and the **Claridge Tower.** Décor ranges from traditional to modern, room size from standard to spacious. An enclosed walkway connects all sections of this mammoth resort. Rooms $69–455; suites $279 and up.

& **'¶' Caesars Atlantic City Hotel Casino** (609-348-4411; 800-443-0104; www.caesarsac.com), 2100 Pacific Ave. and the Boardwalk. The glory of the Roman Empire is the theme of Atlantic City's second casino hotel to rise from the boardwalk strip. The décor of ancient Rome includes an 18-foot-tall, 9-ton marble replica of Michelangelo's *David,* and a towering statue of Caesar Augustus at the corner of Arkansas Ave. and the boardwalk. Bubbling fountains and imported marble fill the dramatic four-story atrium in the **Temple Lobby,** and 1,144 guest rooms are spread throughout four towers. Rooms in the **Temple Tower** are closest to the hotel and

casino, and the Ocean Tower has spacious suites. All have fee-based Wi-Fi. **The Piers** has 100 Retail Shops, plus dining. The **Qua Baths and Spa** has 14 treatment rooms, and there's a seasonal outdoor pool and a fitness center. A bevy of restaurants (no, they're not all Italian), five bars and lounges, and top acts at the **Circus Maximus Theater.** Rooms $75–375; suites $400 and up.

& **'¶' Harrah's Atlantic City Casino Hotel** (609-441-5000; 800-242-7724; www.harrahsresort.com), 777 Harrah's Blvd. Harrah's was the first casino to open on the "quiet" side of Absecon Island, away from the venerable boardwalk. Gamblers and overnight guests can arrive by boat at the hotel's own full-service marina by the Brigantine Bridge. Five shimmering towers overlooking the bay have 2,588 guest rooms ranging from comfortable and standard to elegant and richly furnished. All have fee-based Wi-Fi. Families traveling with older children appreciate the supervised teen center with video games and activities. Amenities include a spa, an indoor pool, a sauna, and an interesting mix of boutiques, restaurants, and bars. The **Fantasea Reef Buffet** is piled high with all manner of fresh seafood, surrounded by tropical fish in thousands of gallons of aquariums. $72–400.

& **Resorts Atlantic City** (609-344-6000; 800-336-6378; www.resortsac.com), 1133 Boardwalk at North Carolina Ave. In 1978 Resorts International was the first casino in Atlantic City to open under New Jersey's Casino Control Act, which legalized gambling. It was built at the site of an Atlantic City landmark, the grand Chalfonte-Haddon Hall Hotel, and a subsequent $50 million renovation spiffed up the façade and casino, securing Resorts' place as a leading contender along the boardwalk. The 942 guest rooms and suites (suites are for guest upgrades only) in the Ocean and new Rendezvous towers, range from standard accommodations to luxe digs, many with art deco–style décor. Championship boxing matches and top-flight entertainment take place in the 1,700-seat state-of-the-art **Superstar Theatre.** The resort has its own beach on the ocean, as well as an indoor and outdoor pool, a health club, and a spa. **Asian Spice** is a far eastern noodle bar, and **Capriccio** (see *Dining Out*) offers upscale and authentic Italian cuisine; there's also a **Gallagher's Burger Bar**, a medieval-style banquet hall, and a **Starbucks**. Rooms $75–350.

& **Showboat—The Mardi Gras Casino** (609-343-4000; 800-621-0200; www.showboatac.com), 801 Boardwalk. This New Orleans–themed casino resort's signature Bourbon Street and Mississippi riverboat style, along with its Southern hospitality, are complemented now by the **House of Blues** tower, which holds a House of Blues Restaurant, Spirit Bar and concert venue, plus its own poker room. Live Dixieland jazz is still here, and authentic Southern cuisine is served at the **French Quarter** buffet, while the upscale **Rib & Chophouse** serves steaks, seafood, and more. The 1,309 guest rooms have the usual hotel amenities, and most come with a view of the ocean. $56–400.

♂ & "1" **Tropicana Casino and Resort** (609-340-4000; 800-843-8767; www.tropicana.net), Brighton Ave. and the Boardwalk. Of all the resorts in Atlantic City, this one is known for being especially family-friendly. Tropicana's bold multi-leveled geometric design includes 17-story towers (with 2,124 rooms and suites) and a glass-

enclosed elevator that goes to the **Top of the Trop,** a lounge and observation area with live entertainment and a spectacular panorama of the city. The 2,000-seat **Tropicana Showroom** is the only Broadway-style theater in an Atlantic City casino. **The Quarter**— the resort's lineup of shops, restaurants, and nightclubs—bustles day and night with live jazz, reggae, traditional Irish music, stand-up comedy, and Atlantic City's first IMAX theater. The upscale complex is reminiscent of the sultry and exotic style of old Havana, where the original Tropicana Casino and Resort stood. The outdoor pool has a prime view of the beach and boardwalk; inside is a health club with an indoor pool, a Jacuzzi, and a sauna. Most of the rooms have standard amenities with views of the ocean or boardwalk; suites have upgrades like king beds, mini-refrigerators, and Jacuzzi tubs. All have fee-based Wi-Fi. The two-level townhouse-style suites have a spiral staircase, living and dining areas, and two bathrooms. Rooms $29–400; suites $129 and up.

& **Trump Marina Casino Resort** (609-441-2000; 800-777-1177; www .trumpmarina.com), Huron Ave. and Brigantine Blvd. When Trump Castle first opened here, The Donald parked his yacht outside to entertain the highest high rollers. Today Trump Marina is popular with yachters and boaters, as well as a hip young crowd that packs its restaurants and bars. The **Harbor View** serves fresh seafood and Italian cuisine, and when the weather allows, you can party at **The Deck,** an outdoor bar overlooking the bay and the sprawling Farley State Marina. The **Bay Tower** offers clean and comfortable standard rooms with the usual amenities; its 57 suites have lovely views, a parlor area, and two bathrooms. The **Crystal Tower** suites are ultra-luxe, with elegant décor, crystal chandeliers, Italian marble, and Jacuzzi tubs. The resort's **Crimzen Health Spa** is top-flight, and there's an outdoor pool, a running track, and tennis courts. Rooms $49–429; suites $149 and up.

🔥 "🍽" **Trump Plaza Hotel and Casino** (609-441-6000; 800-677-7378; www.trumpplaza.com), Mississippi Ave. and the Boardwalk. Trump Plaza is widely considered one of the most elegant and luxurious of Atlantic City's casino resorts. It's connected to the historic **Boardwalk Hall.** Some of the 904 guest rooms and suites are airy and bright; others are done in rich bold hues. All have fee-based Wi-Fi. An Olympic-sized pool occupies the seventh floor; the spa has steam rooms, saunas, Jacuzzis, and a fitness center. **Max's Steak House** has an old-time clubby feel; and **China Café** serves Asian fusion fare. Rooms $59–350; suites $350 and up.

🔥 "🍽" **Trump Taj Mahal Casino Resort** (609-449-1000; www.trump taj.com), Virginia Ave. and the Boardwalk. The Taj, as it is affectionately known here, was the world's largest casino until the MGM Grand opened in Las Vegas. Nevertheless, it's duly impressive, from the massive elephant statues guarding the front door to the collection of rare art and sculpture and the $14 million worth of crystal chandeliers adorning the ceilings. Its 147,000-square-foot gaming floor is the largest in Atlantic City. **Il Mulino New York** reflects a traditional, white-table-cloth, old New York Italian style, with tuxedo clad waiters. **Dynasty** has a sushi bar and authentic Asian cuisine. The 2,050 guest rooms and luxury suites, including 800 rooms in the new Chairman Tower, are spacious and well appointed. All have fee-based Wi-Fi. Rooms $69–400; suites $250 and up.

HOTELS 🐾 🦆 ♿ "🍽" **Sheraton Convention Center Hotel** (609-344-3535; 800-325-3535; www.starwood hotels.com), Two Convention Blvd., Atlantic City 08401. An elegant 502-room hotel with the world's largest collection of Miss America Pageant memorabilia. It's connected to the Atlantic City Convention Center and the commuter-rail station via an enclosed skywalk, which makes it convenient to convention goers, and just a few blocks from the casinos and the boardwalk. The stylish art deco–inspired lobby is done in sumptuous tones and centers on a grand staircase. The guest rooms and suites are clean and comfortable, and offer contemporary décor in pleasing neutral colors with gold, burgundy, and plum accents. Voice mail and in-room movies are among the usual amenities; upgrades like ergonomic desk chairs and oversized work desks, robes, and fee-based high-speed Internet access are available. The indoor pool is surrounded by potted palms, comfy chairs, and umbrella tables; there's also a fitness center and a seasonal outdoor whirlpool and a sundeck. **Boulevard Café** serves three meals and has a spectacular ocean view; the sleek **Shoe Bar** lounge offers a light menu, and the **Tun Tavern Brewery & Restaurant** next door is a replica of a 17th-century Philadelphia brewhouse (see *Eating Out*). Rooms $79–299; suites $200 and up.

♿ "🍽" **The Water Club at the Borgata** (800-800-8817; www.thewater clubhotel.com), One Borgata Way. Among AC's newest upscale properties, The Water Club promotes itself as the town's "first cosmopolitan lifestyle hotel." Its 43 stories hold 800 rooms and suites, most with water and city skyline views. Wi-Fi available throughout. There are five swimming pools;

the Immersion Spa on the 32nd floor and the fitness center on the 33rd floor present 360-degree panoramic views through floor-to-ceiling windows. Bobby Flay and Wolfgang Puck both have signature restaurants here. $129–559.

Pier 4 Hotel on the Bay (609-927-9141; 888-927-9141; www .pier4hotel.com), Six Broadway Ave. and the bay, Somers Point 08244. A family-run hotel located just off the traffic circle in Somers Point, on the bay and close to Atlantic City. The 70 rooms with contemporary décor are spread across four floors. The standard units are equipped with a microwave, mini-refrigerator, and coffeemaker; the suites also have in-room movies, Wi-Fi, king beds, and comfortable living areas. Each room has its own balcony, some with a nice view of the Great Egg Harbor Bay and the skyline of Ocean City. A seasonal pool and sundeck are outside on the landscaped grounds. The **Crab Trap** restaurant is a traditional shore seafood house open daily for lunch and dinner; there's live entertainment and a raw bar on the outdoor deck during the summer. Continental breakfast. $69–289.

The Chelsea (800-548-3030; www.thechelsea-ac.com) 111 S. Chelsea Ave. Converting a Holiday Inn and an adjacent Howard Johnson's, The Chelsea is an upscale, non-gaming boutique hotel that makes attempts to return to the city's more storied past. Its 208 luxury rooms and 12 suites display sweeping ocean and bay views, all with the expected amenities and complimentary Wi-Fi. There's a 15,000 square-foot rooftop pool with private cabanas, a spa, and a fifth-floor "social area" replete with a lounge, bar, game room, and living room. Dining includes Chelsea Prime (see *Dining Out*), an upscale steakhouse. $95–275 off-peak; $225–450 peak.

BED & BREAKFASTS **The Colonial Inn at Historic Smithville** (609-748-8999; www.colonialinnsmithville .com), 615 E. Moss Mill Rd., Smithville 08205. A newer B&B with the feel of a centuries-old country inn is tucked amid the quaint shops on the village green in the Historic Towne of Smithville shopping village. The eight cozy guest rooms are furnished with Early American period reproductions; all have private bath, television with DVD, phone, and turndown service. Five of the rooms have a lovely view of Lake Meone. Continental breakfast and afternoon refreshments. $99–199.

Dr. Jonathan Pitney House B&B (609-569-1799; 888-774-8639; www.pitneyhouse.com), 57 Shore Rd., Absecon 08201. The former home of Dr. Jonathan Pitney, "the Father of Atlantic City," is a charming bed & breakfast just a few miles from the city he worked tirelessly to build. Jonathan Pitney came to this once-remote area as a young country doctor, but he would be immortalized for his key role in developing Atlantic City as a seaside resort. Notably, he got a rail line built across New Jersey from Philadelphia to Absecon Island in the 19th century. He also lobbied the federal government to fund the construction of Absecon Lighthouse at the northern tip of the island, an area of dangerous shoals and so many shipwrecks that mariners dubbed it Graveyard Inlet. The doctor bought this 18th-century Colonial-style mansion in 1833, and built an Italianate-style addition in 1848. Six antiques-filled guest rooms in the manor house all have private bath, most with early-1900s claw-foot soaking tubs with showers, and some have a working fireplace. The **Doctor's Quarters** is a separate building boasting four elegant and uniquely themed suites with whirlpool tub, fireplace, TV/VCR, Wi-Fi, and either a private veranda or a cozy sitting area. The common rooms include a country kitchen with hearth, a Victorian parlor, and a Colonial dining room. Complimentary tea and refreshments are served in the afternoon. Full buffet breakfast. $69–225.

🍴 **Carisbrooke Inn B&B** (609-822-6392; www.carisbrookeinn.com), 105 S. Little Rock Ave., Ventnor City 08406. The best of both worlds: quiet surroundings close to the beach and a short mile away from the casinos. The B&B is named after a 19th-century grand hotel in the resort town of Ventnor on England's Isle of Wight. Seven uniquely appointed guest rooms and one suite are cozy and comfortable, with floral wallpaper and other decidedly English-style accents. All have private bath, cable TV, Wi-Fi, ceiling fans, air-conditioning (June through Labor Day), and either a king or a queen bed, or two full beds. The parlor suite has its own entrance and a private deck overlooking the lovely back patio. Guests can relax on the quiet landscaped patio or on the second-floor deck overlooking the ocean. The complimentary beach towels and badges are a nice touch. Afternoon tea in the formal main parlor is served in front of a fire during the winter. Full breakfast might include banana-nut French toast or multigrain pancakes. $95–230.

CAMPGROUNDS For a complete listing of the 20 or so campgrounds in the Atlantic City region, contact the **New Jersey Campground Owners Association** (609-465-8444; 800-222-6765; www.newjerseycampgrounds .com), 29 Cook's Beach Rd., Cape May Court House 08210. They have an online directory and will send you a free color guide, on request. In addition to the campgrounds featured

below, see "The Pinelands Region" in "Central New Jersey," and "Ocean City to Wildwood" in this region, for others that are close to Atlantic City.

🐾 🦴 🍴 **Blueberry Hill Campground** (609-652-1644; reservations: 800-732-2036; www.morganrvresorts .com), 283 Clarks Landing Rd. (Rt. 624), Port Republic 08241. Open Apr.–mid-Dec. A 30-acre family campground with 178 sites for tents and RVs, plus some vacation cottages and rental RVs. Amenities include a coffee shop and an ice cream shop, an Olympic-sized pool with a diving board, whirlpool spa, playground and limited Wi-Fi access. The campground runs shuttles to the casinos, for a fee. A full schedule of activities such as antique car shows, hay rides, and progressive dinners. $30–107.

🐾 🦴 ♿ **Birch Grove Park and Family Campground** (609-641-3778; 800-354-6201; www.cityofnorthfield.org), Burton Ave. and Mill Rd., Northfield 08225. Open Apr.–mid-Oct. Birch Grove offers 51 wooded tent sites and sites with full hookups on 271 acres. Full services. A lovely park centered on 21 interconnected finger lakes (see To Do—Fishing), it started as a 19th-century brickyard and became a municipal park in the 1950s. Egrets, herons, and ospreys are often spotted around the lakes. Walking trails through the park are linked by wooden footbridges. Pick up a trail map at the **Children's Nature Center,** which is stocked with activity sheets for kids; kids love the mural inside, painted by local fourth-graders. Ball field, picnic area, and boccie courts. An **outdoor concert series** is held in the park's bandstand in July and August. $18–24.

✷ Where to Eat

There is no shortage of places to eat in Atlantic City. Dining establishments, cuisines, and price ranges run the gamut, from expensive haute cuisine to local sub shops and authentic ethnic eateries. You can dine at an old-time supper club, lounge in a martini bar, or listen to a crooning balladeer while munching on fish-and-chips in an Irish pub. Fresh-off-the-boat seafood is everywhere, of course, at upscale waterfront dining rooms to a 19th-century seafood house. You can wander the boardwalk and graze on saltwater taffy, french fries, pizza, fudge, frozen custard, and pretzels, or pay far too much for a trendy meal at an overpriced tourist trap. There's **Planet Hollywood, Hard Rock Café, Hooters, Rainforest Café,** and the other themed chains. The **casinos** offer everything from middlebrow all-you-can-eat buffets and gourmet bistros to sushi bars and New York–style delicatessens. Casinos boast their share of big-name eateries, but fine dining isn't relegated to the gaming halls. The idea that the best dining is in the casinos is a myth. Many of Atlantic City's independent restaurants are still in business after more than a century and offer a refreshing dose of local color, not to mention an excellent meal.

DINING OUT
In Atlantic City

Café 2825 (609-344-6913; www.cafe 2825.com), 2825 Atlantic Ave., a block from Tropicana Casino and Resort. Open Tues.–Sat. for dinner; closed Sun.–Mon. Reservations are recommended. A family-run storefront café with elegant northern Italian cuisine. The 48-seat corner space is cozy and intimate. Regulars rave about the attentive service and excellent food. Signature dishes include osso buco (when available), whole fish, and calamari stuffed with crabmeat, Italian herbs, and bread crumbs. The fried calamari and *pasta fagioli* are excellent starters. Classic Italian side dishes like artichoke hearts and broccoli rabe are ordered separately. $17–32.

Knife and Fork Inn (609-344-1133; www.knifeandforkinn.com), 29 S. Atlantic Ave. Open for dinner daily; lunch Fri. Reservations are suggested. An Atlantic City landmark, serving traditional shore cuisine in surroundings that feel like a private European club. The building's gleaming-white Flemish-style façade, with golden weathervane and leaded windows, is an icon in Atlantic City's former Chelsea District. It opened in 1912 as a private gentlemen's club, and continued as a Prohibition-era speakeasy. Its present incarnation is a seafood restaurant, in the same family since 1947. Generations of family photos lining the walls add an air of warmth and nostalgia to the Tudor-style décor. Service is attentive and professional, and the menu is full of comfort food and simply prepared classics, such as oysters Rockefeller, clams casino, or clam chowder. The seafood bouillabaisse is a family recipe. Lobster is served several ways. Extensive wine list. $25–52.

Chef Vola's (609-345-2022), 111 S. Albion Pl. at Pacific Ave. Open for dinner Tues.–Sun.; closed Mon. Reservations are required and should be made well in advance. This tiny restaurant is one of Atlantic City's best-kept secrets, a beloved local treasure that's easy to miss but well worth finding. Getting a table can be a challenge—a testament to just how outstanding this family-run restaurant is—and if you're not a regular customer, you might not get in on a Friday or Saturday night. The dining room consists of a dozen or so tables tucked away in a basement beneath a little white house—a former boardinghouse—on a residential street in the heart of the city. A restaurant has occupied the space since 1921, and in keeping with an old tradition, Michael and Louise Esposito don't advertise—the phone number isn't listed, and there's no sign out front (look for the statue of the Virgin Mary marking the entrance)—but it's obvious from the perpetually packed tables that word of mouth is working just fine. Celebrities know about this place, too, and sightings aren't unusual. Tables are packed into a small space, but regulars say the superb Italian cuisine and intimate ambience is well worth it. The Espositos serve generous portions of Sicilian and Neapolitan dishes that are based on old family recipes. Just about everything is exceptional; but the signature dish is the veal sausage broiled with mushrooms, peppers, and onions. The check is delivered to your table in a music box; credit cards are not accepted. BYOB. $20–30.

Jonathan's on West End (609-441-1800), 672 N. Trenton Ave. at West End Ave., across from the Sandcastle Stadium. Open daily for dinner. Reservations are recommended on weekends. An intimate eatery with a friendly and relaxed atmosphere and eclectic contemporary American dishes. The inviting dining room offers a lovely Absecon Bay view from most tables. Chef-owner Jonathan Karp serves creatively prepared and presented gourmet cuisine in an extensive menu of steak, pork, chicken, seafood, and pasta dishes. Service is friendly and top-notch, and prices are reasonable. Convivial bar. $16–30.

Peregrine's (609-236-7870; 888-224-4586; www.hiltonac.com), at the Atlantic City Hilton Casino Resort, Boston and Pacific Aves. Open for dinner; hours vary by season; call or check the Web site. Reservations are recommended and jackets are required. An elegant five-star dining room named

for the peregrine falcons that spend the summer on the ledge of the Hilton's penthouse suites. It's one of the priciest and most sophisticated dining rooms in Atlantic City. Peregrine's features exquisitely prepared and presented regional and international contemporary cuisine with an emphasis on gourmet seafood, an extensive selection of wines, and impeccable service. Desserts are equally exceptional; the kitchen is known for its delicate vanilla and chocolate soufflés. $40–75.

Cuba Libre Restaurant & Rum Bar (609-348-6700; www.cubalibrerestaurant.com), in the Quarter, Tropicana Casino and Resort, Brighton Pl. and the Boardwalk. Open daily for dinner; late-night menu until 1 AM, Fri.–Sat.; brunch Sat.–Sun. The second location for one of Philadelphia's best-known Cuban restaurants, serving contemporary Cuban dishes with the bold colors and flavors typical of Latin cuisine. The restaurant, like the Philadelphia original, celebrates Cuban culture, from the artwork on the walls to the music and, of course, the food. Together they re-create the exotic and urbane feel of 1940s-era Havana. The menu of seafood, beef, chicken, and pork is accentuated with exotic fruits, vegetables, and spices. The appetizer sampler platters offer a good introduction to the diverse flavors of Cuban cooking. The late-night menu offers light meals, Cuban coffees, exotic after-dinner drinks, and an extensive variety of rum. $15–28.

Ombra (609-317-1000; 866-692-6742), at the Borgata Hotel Casino and Spa, One Borgata Way. Open for dinner Wed.–Sun.; closed Mon.–Tues.; the bar is open until 1 AM, Fri.–Sat. A Venetian-style trattoria and wine bar in an intimate, subterranean space with a 14,000-bottle brick wine cellar, reminiscent of an Old World wine-making estate. There are 50 varieties of artisanal cheeses and excellent antipasti to begin with before delving into the rustic Italian country menu. Among the signature creations is beef short rib ragu. Other good choices are whole roasted fish and the rustic pasta dishes. $20–44.

&. **Capriccio** (800-932-0734), at Resorts Atlantic City, 1133 Boardwalk at N. Carolina Ave. Open for dinner Wed.–Sun; brunch Sun; closed Mon.–Tues. Reservations are highly recommended. An elegant fine-dining restaurant that has earned the coveted Zagat award for excellence yet manages to make guests feel relaxed. Magnificent views of the Atlantic Ocean are accompanied by top-notch northern and southern Italian cuisine—even tableside singing! Desserts are made in-house. $18–48.

Chelsea Prime (609-428-4545; www.thechelsea-ac.com) 111 S. Chelsea Ave. Fifth Fl., in the Chelsea Hotel. An upscale steakhouse that evokes a 1940s supper club, replete with white piano and black-and-white photos of the city in the '40s. This restaurant is among Atlantic City's newest entries into sophisticated fine dining, and it's not cheap. But, the food and service are fine, and the setting offers a break from the big casinos. $29–45; side dishes extra.

In Galloway

Ram's Head Inn (609-652-1700; www.ramsheadinn.com), 9 W. White Horse Pike. Lunch Tues.–Fri.; dinner Tues.–Sun.; closed Mon. Reservations are recommended. Lunch is casual, but jackets are required at dinner. A charming white-clapboard inn whose exceptional American cuisine and spectacular country setting earn it a consistent spot at the top of statewide dining polls. Each candlelit dining room is unique in atmosphere and décor, and each has a fireplace. The grand ballroom is an opulent, celebra-

tory kind of place, while the cozy veranda is perfect for a quiet, romantic dinner. The pretty brick courtyard with bubbling fountain surrounded by manicured gardens makes for a lovely alfresco lunch. An airy gallery doubles as a piano lounge and displays the work of local artists. The menu includes traditional fare like creamy chicken pot pie with dumplings, plus offerings such as beef Wellington. Chateâubriand for two is carved tableside, a nod to the long-ago era when restaurants were formal and refined. $24–39.

In Smithville

Historic Smithville Inn (609-652-7777; www.smithvilleinn.com), 1 N. New York Rd. Open daily for lunch and dinner; Sunday brunch. Reservations are accepted. A restored 1787 inn at the Historic Towne of Smithville colonial shopping village (see *Selective Shopping—Special Shops*) is a romantic and elegant restaurant serving classic American and Continental cuisine. The historic building and lavish landscaped grounds are a popular setting for weddings and other special events. The menu ranges from roasted chicken and various pastas to pan-seared grouper and filet mignon. The inn's signature appetizer is crabcakes with rémoulade sauce. Save room for the excellent desserts. Friday-night diners select from a prix fixe multi-course seafood menu. $17–42; prix fixe $28.

In Margate City

Melissa's Bistro (609-823-1414), 9307 Ventnor Ave. Open daily for dinner in summer; call for winter hours. Reservations accepted. A relaxed family-run 40-seat neighborhood bistro on Margate City's main drag that is a locals' favorite, especially during low-season. The creative American cuisine is considered gourmet comfort food, with entrées like pecan-crusted Idaho rainbow trout, and Mediterranean-style chicken. The décor is quaint country, with dried flower arrangements, lacy curtains, and meals served on mismatched china, among other charming touches. Desserts are house-made and shouldn't be missed. BYOB. $20–30.

Mojo (609-487-0300), 223 N. Washington Ave. Open daily for dinner. Reservations are suggested. Sleek and chic with a sophisticated SoHo vibe, and a gourmet seasonal menu to match. Seafood is what many people come here for—potato-crusted Atlantic salmon in a ginger-soy reduction, or soft shell crabs. For a lighter meal, try one of the inventive pasta dishes. Definitely save room for dessert. Live jazz, a young crowd, and an extensive martini menu make for a lively bar scene. $18–35.

♭ **Tomatoes** (609-822-7535; www .tomatoesmargate.com), 9300 Amherst Ave. Open daily for dinner. Reservations are recommended. A stylish corner eatery overlooking the bay that has blossomed into a chic and casual multilevel restaurant with hip, modern décor—a star in Margate City's increasingly upscale collection of gourmet restaurants. Tomatoes attracts a sophisticated year-round clientele. The California-style menu of Mediterranean, Latin, and Pacific Rim dishes is known for its fresh sushi and seafood, and quality vegetarian options. A good selection of wines and martinis, and a lively scene at the bar. $18–31.

Manna (609-822-7722; www.manna ventnor.com), 8409 Ventnor Ave. Open for dinner Tues.–Sat., 5–9. Reservations recommended. They call this New American cuisine, but with offerings like organic Lancaster County chicken, paella, and blood-orange sorbet it's something more. This food is lovingly made, to the point of hand-

rubbing the smoked baby back ribs. Desserts get the same loving touch. BYOB. $12–33.

In Brigantine

♭ **Steak 38** (609-266-4400; 866-782-2538), 3700 Atlantic–Brigantine Blvd. Open daily for dinner; lunch daily in the raw bar. Reservations are recommended. An old-school steakhouse on Brigantine's main drag, a satellite of the popular Cherry Hill steakhouse. Huge slabs of aged beef, fresh seafood, and live lobster fill the menu. DiAmore favors the dying tradition of tableside service, so that's where Caesar salad is tossed, meats are carved, and the bananas Foster for two is dramatically flambéed. The daily seafood specials are an excellent bet, but the regular menu has some fine dishes, too. The clam bake is a full pound of steamed shellfish—lobster, clams, mussels, shrimp, and fish—served in its own pot. The island-themed **Mickey's Raw Bar,** centered on an unusual wooden schooner bar, offers casual lunch and dinner fare. Live music and dancing every night. $15–39.

EATING OUT

In Atlantic City

The Metropolitan (609-317-1000; 866-692-6742; www.theborgata.com), at the Borgata Hotel Casino and Spa, One Borgata Way. Open 24 hours for breakfast, lunch, and dinner; closed Wed. 11:30 PM–Thurs. 7 AM. A round-the-clock café that offers something for everyone, be it breakfast, oysters from the raw bar, or a freshly made triple-decker sandwich. The décor is reminiscent of an old-school European bistro. Traditional and contemporary renditions of bistro classics include meatloaf and steak *frites*. The gelato bar is a good option for dessert. $8–30.

Pickles Deli (609-340-2320; 800-772-7777; www.ballysac.com), Bally's

Atlantic City, Park Pl. and the Board-walk. Open daily from late morning to late evening. A classic New York–style deli known for its hearty stacked sand-wiches and moderate prices. The kitchen churns out sandwiches piled high with savory pastrami or corned beef, hot Reubens, and steaming bowls of matzo ball soup at a Manhattan-style pace. Tempting desserts include their famous strawberry tall cake. Be prepared for a line at mealtimes, but it moves fast. $5–12.

& **Girasole** (609-345-5554; www .girasoleac.com), 3108 Pacific Ave. Open for lunch Mon.–Fri.; dinner nightly. Reservations are recommend-ed. A stylish eatery serving homemade pasta, fresh seafood, and other casual Italian fare. Especially popular are the individual brick-oven pizzas that come with a wide variety of gourmet top-pings. You can start with a light salad; a dish of shrimp, clams, squid, and octo-pus with roasted vegetables; or the homemade soup of the day. Entrées include veal Milanese, salmon with pesto, or homemade pastas made fresh daily. $14–29.

Atlantic City Bar and Grill (609-348-8080; www.acbarandgrill.com), 1217 Pacific Ave. Open daily for lunch and dinner. What began as a little pizzeria more than a quarter century ago is now a family-owned Atlantic City institution that's perpetually packed. The crowd is lively and fun, the service is friendly, and the menu is moderately priced. Some people come here for a quick bite en-route to some-place else; many spend the entire evening. Appetizers include pub-fare standards like chicken wings, stuffed mushrooms, and fried calamari. Move on to the extensive menu of ribs, pizza, homemade pasta, sandwiches, or seafood. $10–46.

Dock's Oyster House (609-345-0092; www.docksoysterhouse.com), 2405 Atlantic Ave. Open daily for lunch and dinner. A family-owned seafood restau-rant and shore institution since 1897. Four generations of the Dougherty family have run the place for an astounding 108 years. The venerable menu—once a temple of fried seafood—today features a mix of clas-sics like oysters Rockefeller and clams casino alongside Maine clam chowder and lime-cured shrimp ceviche. Exten-sive wine list. $20–63.

& **Tun Tavern Brewery & Restaurant** (609-347-7800; www.tuntavern.com), Two Miss America Way, next to the Sheraton and across from the Atlantic City Convention Center. Open daily for lunch and dinner; reservations are rec-ommended. Atlantic City's first and only brewery-restaurant is a casual pub with roots dating to the American Rev-olution. The original Tun Tavern opened in 1685 on the Philadelphia waterfront, where it stood for more than a century. It was one of America's first breweries and the birthplace of the U.S. Marine Corps in 1775. Like the original, this shoreline replica (*tun* is an Old English term for a barrel or keg of beer) serves handcrafted brews and American pub fare, but with a gourmet twist, including starters like Maryland crab soup, or littleneck clams steamed in white wine, garlic, and butter. Signa-ture dishes are chicken and shrimp marsala and filet mignon. Or, go easy with a burger or crabcakes. Desserts are delicious. The bar has live enter-tainment, and the outdoor deck boasts casino skyline views. Ask about brewery tours. $17–32.

& **Tony's Baltimore Grill** (609-345-5766; 609-345-9461; www.balti moregrill.com), 2800 Atlantic Ave. The kitchen is open daily 11 AM–3 AM; the bar stays open 24 hours. An Atlantic

City old-time institution, this is a casual, convivial spot with a legion of regulars, serving reasonably priced, old-school Italian fare and thin-crust pizza regarded as Atlantic City's best. Diners can watch as cooks toss pizza dough in the open kitchen. The menu of standards includes fried crabcakes, spaghetti and meatballs, sandwiches, Italian-style seafood dishes, antipasti, and pizzas with traditional toppings—no gourmet concoctions here. Service is friendly; a good place to bring the kids. Credit cards are not accepted. $7–13.

The Irish Pub (609-344-9063; www.theirishpub.com), 164 Saint James Pl. at the Boardwalk. Open 24 hours. This isn't Absecon Island's first tavern—that one opened in 1839—but this pub's history dates to 1900. It's a friendly and casual spot just off the boardwalk, and among Atlantic City's top bars. Though bustling and noisy, the polished dark paneling makes the place warm and inviting. The food is hearty and satisfying—fish-and-chips, homemade chili, crabcakes, burgers—and the prices are ridiculously low. Live Irish music and a good selection of brews on tap. A good place to mingle with the locals. $4–7.

Back Bay Ale House (609-449-0006; www.backbayalehouse.com), 800 N. New Hampshire Ave. Open daily for lunch and dinner. Eat and drink on the upstairs enclosed waterfront deck. Pub appetizers like cheese fries, grilled Polish kielbasa, and jerk chicken wings. Sandwiches are hearty, including the New Orleans–style crabcake po'boy. From the grill, hand-cut steaks, chicken, burgers, and seafood. Live Irish ballads sung by a local balladeer. Sandwiches $8–9; entrées $11–18.

Ducktown Tavern (609-449-1212; www.ducktowntavernac.com), 2400 Atlantic Ave. Open daily, 24 hours.

WHITE HOUSE SUB SHOP

(609-345-1564), 2301 Arctic Ave., Atlantic City. Open Mon.–Thurs. 10 AM–11 PM; Fri.–Sat. 10–midnight; Sun. 11–10. Three blocks from the boardwalk and close to the Atlantic City bus station; there's free parking across the street for customers. The self-styled "Home of Submarines" is an old-time Atlantic City culinary landmark. They claim not only to have invented the submarine sandwich but also to have sold more than 15 million subs. The White House was featured in the remake of *Ocean's Eleven* and has served luminaries, including former president Clinton and Frank Sinatra, for more than 50 years. The walls boast a mishmash of photos of celebrity patrons, from Joe DiMaggio to the Beatles, Liberace, Ol' Blue Eyes, and countless other celebrities. It's perpetually packed with regular patrons and tourists; there are a few booths for eating in, but most just take a ticket and wait (you can phone in your order). As when it opened in the 1940s, the shop bakes its own bread, and their house-made relish is an original recipe. Hundreds of colossal sausage sandwiches, Philly-style cheesesteak subs, and hot and cold subs (or hoagies, or grinders—depending on where you're from) piled high with salami, bologna, roast beef, and other meats are made fresh every day. Half subs (they're huge) around $7.

A locals' hangout that never closes. Dinner options include Steak and Cake—a steak "cooked to temp with a broiled or fried crab cake"; or, a bowl of linguine. $9–21.

In Margate City

Steve and Cookie's By the Bay (609-823-1163; www.steveandcookies .com), 9700 Amherst Ave. Open Thurs.–Sun. for dinner. In the 1930s this was Strotbecks, a venerable private supper club similar to many that dotted the shore in Atlantic City's heyday. The rambling white-clapboard building has been restored, and today it's known for its relaxed and casual atmosphere and signature seafood, steaks, and dressed-up comfort food. Lobster-studded macaroni and cheese, rack of lamb, and Maine lobster are among the house favorites. Nightly live jazz, two working fireplaces, a friendly bar, and a view of the bay all make this a local haunt. $17–40.

In Ventnor City

& **Sage** (609-823-2110), 5206 Atlantic Ave. Open for lunch and dinner Tues.–Sun.; closed Mon. Reservations accepted. A tasty treat with an Italian bent, the offerings here include appetizers like eggplant gallo and entrées in a wide selection of seafood and pastas. Good desserts, too. BYOB. Cash only. $18–30.

In Pleasantville

Gary's Restaurant (609-383-9980; www.go2garys.com), 831 New Rd. Open daily 7–3. A real locals' spot not far from the airport, serving breakfast and lunch—hot and cold sandwiches, salads, soups. Kids menu. Breakfast, $4–8; lunch, $5–8.

BOARDWALK FOOD Steel's Fudge (609-345-4051; 888-783-3571; www .steelsfudge.com), 2719 Boardwalk. A southern shore icon, both here and in Ocean City. Elizabeth Steel opened a

fudge shop on the Atlantic City boardwalk in 1919. She later added saltwater taffy to the menu, and her family continues the tradition of selling huge quantities of both. Steel's is the oldest continuously operating family-owned fudge company anywhere.

Boardwalk Peanut Shoppe (609-272-1511; www.boardwalkpeanuts .com), four boardwalk locations. A sweet shop selling roasted peanuts, chocolate-covered pretzels, caramel corn, saltwater taffy, and chocolates on the boardwalk since 1972. You can buy treats by the piece, or stuffed into a miniature lifeboat or beach pail.

Boardwalk Bistro (609-347-7194), 1523 Boardwalk. Open daily for lunch and dinner. A pizzeria where you can pick up a couple slices to take on a stroll of the boards. You can also eat in or phone for delivery.

✳ Entertainment

All listings are in Atlantic City. For a complete listing of entertainment in Atlantic City—including the casinos—see the **Atlantic City Convention and Visitor's Authority** Web site (www.atlanticcitynj.com), or visit their information center at **Boardwalk Hall** (see *Guidance*). Most of the casino resorts have their own theaters offering a full schedule of world-class entertainment, including music, comedy, and sporting events. They include **Circus Maximus Theater** (800-677-7469; www.caesarsac.com; tickets: 888-241-8545) at Caesars Atlantic City Hotel Casino; **Superstar Theatre** (800-336-6378; www.resortsac.com; tickets 800-736-1420) at Resorts Atlantic City; **Tropicana Showroom** (800-345-8767; www.tropicana.net; tickets 800-745-3000), a 2,000-seat Broadway-style theater at Tropicana Casino and Resort; **Grand Cayman Ballroom and Shell Showroom**

JAMES' CANDY COMPANY & FRALINGER'S ORIGINAL SALT WATER TAFFY

(609-344-1519; www.jamescandy.com), James' and Fralinger's, now combined, offers four boardwalk locations. Enoch James was a well-known shoreline confectioner at the turn of the 20th century. In 1905 he began to sell "Salt Water Taffy by James," a recipe based on the original taffy from the 1880s. Supposedly, James added vegetable oil to cut down on the stickiness and fashioned the candy into smaller pieces to make chewing more enjoyable. In the early days, a nickel would buy a half-dozen pieces of taffy. Today there are 17 flavors of the sweet, chewy confections: some dipped in chocolate, others filled with marzipan, nuts, or fudge—even sugar-free flavors. Other nostalgic treats include coconut and almond macaroons, creamy fudge, mint sticks, butter toffee, peanut butter chews, and molasses pops dipped in dark chocolate.

Joseph Fralinger sold his first batch of chewy taffy in 1885. Their chocolate molasses lollipops have been made since the late 19th century. Taffy is made with lots of sugar, but no salt water, and comes in a pastel palette of blues, yellows, and pinks—16 different flavors in all. Boxes of individually wrapped taffies are packaged just as they were sold in the 1890s. Taffy also comes in nostalgic tins that are reproductions of the original containers from the 1930s. Old-fashioned fudge, almond macaroons, and peanut butter chews round out the menu. James' and Fralinger's taffy is still manufactured in Atlantic City and sold in shops along the southern shore, including Cape May, Stone Harbor, and Wildwood.

(609-449-6595; 888-310-6782; www.trumpmarina.com) at Trump Marina Hotel and Casino; the 5,000-seat **Mark G. Etess Arena** (609-449-5150) and 1,400-seat **Xanadu Showroom** (609-449-1000; 800-825-8888; www.trumptaj.com) at Trump Taj Mahal Casino Resort; **Grand Theater** (888-224-4586; www.hiltonac.com; tickets 609-340-7200) at Atlantic City Hilton; **Main Ballroom** (609-340-2000; 800-772-7777; www.ballysac.com) and the intimate 550-seat **Palace Theater** at Claridge Tower at Bally's Atlantic City; **Music Box** (609-317-1000; 866-692-6742; www.theborgata.com) at Borgata Hotel Casino and Spa; and **Plaza Showroom** (609-441-6000; 800-677-

7378; www.trumpplaza.com) at Trump Plaza Hotel and Casino.

Atlantic City Convention Center (609-449-2000; www.accenter.com), One Miss America Way. The $268 million state-of-the-art convention space was built in 1997 at the site of the city's old rail terminal. At 500,000 square feet, it's the largest convention center in the mid-Atlantic region, and hosts a nonstop schedule of sporting events; political and corporate conventions; home-, boat-, and car shows; and a variety of expos. A **New Jersey Transit** rail station (973-275-5555; www.njtransit.com) is located within the convention center and offers commuter service to Philadelphia's 30th

Street Station, with connections to **Amtrak's** Northeast Corridor lines.

Boardwalk Hall (609-348-7000; www.boardwalkhall.com; tickets: 800-736-1420), 2301 Boardwalk. This *was* the brand-new Atlantic City Convention Hall, built during the year of the stock market crash on Wall Street in 1929. Today it's a national historic landmark called Boardwalk Hall, a 13,800-seat arena that hosts big-name concerts and events throughout the year. Its $90 million face-lift completed in 2001 was grand enough to grab the attention of New Jerseyan Bruce Springsteen, whose Boardwalk Hall concert was his first-ever Atlantic City appearance. It boasts the largest pipe organ (with nearly 33,000 pipes) in the world.

ARTS CENTERS

In Atlantic City

Atlantic City Art Center (609-347-5837; www.acartcenter.org), Garden Pier, the Boardwalk at New Jersey Ave. Open Tues.–Sun. 10–4; closed Mon.

Free admission. Changing exhibits in three galleries by regional and national artists in media ranging from painting and sculpture to graphic art and photography. The art center has been on the pier since 1953.

Dante Hall Theatre of the Arts (609-344-8877; www.dantehall.org), 14 North Mississippi Ave. Call or see Web site for a schedule of performances. A 1926 Italian-style building that was once an active local community center has been renovated and is now a 250-seat state-of-the-art performing arts facility.

NIGHTLIFE

All listings are in Atlantic City. **Mixx** (609-317-1000; 866-692-6742; www.theborgata.com), Borgata Hotel Casino and Spa, One Borgata Way. Night club Fri.–Sat.10 PM until whenever. A hot South Beach–style dance spot playing high-energy music all night. Upstairs a lounge with plush furnishings has a posh, clubby ambience.

CHICKEN BONE BEACH JAZZ SERIES

(609-441-9064; www.chickenbonebeach.org), Kennedy Plaza, on the boardwalk between Mississippi and Georgia avenues, Atlantic City. Thursday-night jazz concerts in July and Aug. are sponsored by the Chicken Bone Beach Historical Foundation, an organization dedicated to preserving local African American history and culture. The thousands of African American tourists who came to Atlantic City's beaches in the first half of the 20th century were segregated to the waterfront around Missouri Avenue, which became affectionately known as Chicken Bone Beach for the chicken dinners beachgoers toted in their picnic baskets. Music was an integral part of the Chicken Bone Beach community. Sammy Davis Jr., the Club Harlem Showgirls, "Moms" Mabley, and other top African American entertainers of the day performed at the beach. Today's concerts draw hundreds to the boardwalk to hear vocalists, pianists, and ensembles perform classic jazz standards, eclectic blends of jazz and Latin and Cuban sounds, contemporary jazz, Afro-Caribbean jazz, or tributes to Duke Ellington, Count Basie, and other legendary jazz greats.

It also overlooks the dance floor, an ideal vantage point for people-watching.

Gypsy Bar (609-317-1000; 866-692-6742; www.theborgata.com), at the Borgata Hotel Casino and Spa, One Borgata Way. Dinner daily; bar open Sun.–Wed. until 1 AM; Thurs. 2 AM; Fri.–Sat. 3 AM. The bar is fun and lively while the dance floor pulsates with energetic Latin music. Extensive drink menus feature gourmet tequilas, exotic beers, and eclectic martinis.

Casbah (609-449-1000; 800-234-5678; www.trumptaj.com; www.casbahclub .com), Trump Taj Mahal Casino Resort, 1000 Boardwalk at Virginia Ave. Open Fri. 10:30 PM–5 AM; Sat. 10:30 PM–6 AM; closed Sun.–Thurs. Avid club goers gladly wait in line for over an hour to get into this cavernous nightclub, with catwalks above the dance floor, an exclusive VIP area, and special themed events like Latin Night and Battle of the DJs. The **Star Bar** on an outdoor deck provides a respite from the action on the dance floor.

The Wave (800-777-1177; www.trump marina.com), Trump Marina Hotel and Casino, Huron Ave. and Brigantine Blvd. Open Fri.–Sat. from 9 PM. The dance floor is always packed, as are the tables and comfy chairs that surround it. DJs spin house music when live bands aren't on stage. It's a smaller club and known to get notoriously overpacked.

Blue Martini Lounge (609-340-2000; 800-772-7777; www.ballysac.com), Bally's Atlantic City, Park Pl. and the Boardwalk. An upscale lounge adjacent to Bally's main casino floor, with a menu of more than 100 martinis and a chic and trendy crowd. Big-screen TVs and live jazz and other entertainment on Friday and Saturday nights. The bar has a unique built-in frosted ice railing.

Déjà Vu Nightclub (609-348-4313), 245 S. New York Ave. Open daily 1

PM–8 AM. A multi-level dance club just off the boardwalk that's packed just about every night. Latin, hip-hop, house music, reggae, and disco classics are spun by as many as five DJs a night. Six bars; the kitchen serves a light menu until late.

The Quarter at Tropicana Casino and Resort (800-345-8767; www .tropicana.net) hosts a variety of venues. **Cuba Libre Restaurant & Rum Bar** has DJs playing salsa and other Latin music on weekends (see *Dining Out*); **Ri Ra** is an authentic Irish pub with traditional Irish dancing, clogging, and music; **32° Luxe Lounge** is sleek and hip, with a private VIP section; **Tango's** has live salsa, jazz, and reggae bands. There's also a karaoke bar and comedy club.

THEATER South Jersey Regional Theatre (609-653-0553), Gateway Playhouse, Bay Ave., Somers Point. Professional theater, also known as **Broadway by the Bay,** offering a year-round schedule of live plays and Broadway musicals.

✳ Selective Shopping

ANTIQUES Elliot's (609-348-9526), 1329 Boardwalk, Atlantic City. A family-owned and family-operated antiques shop on the boardwalk for 85 years. The impressive variety of unique antiques and kitschy collectibles, and the warm and friendly staff, invite long-term browsing. The ever-changing inventory might include antique statuary, Oriental rugs, imported European furniture, figurines, clocks, and an exceptionally large collection of handkerchiefs and tablecloths.

The Black Horse Pike (Rt. 322), from Atlantic City south to Cape May, is a renowned antiques alley featuring everything from small shops to sprawling multi-dealer complexes.

ART GALLERIES Belrose Galleries (609-345-2279), 1505 Boardwalk, Atlantic City. Open daily 10–5. Original fine art, estate and contemporary jewelry, bronze sculpture, and hand-crafted furniture.

Great Bay Gallery (609-653-4991), 829 Bay Avenue, Somers Point. Call for times.

Roslyn Sailor Fine Arts (609-847-2401), 8401 Ventnor Avenue, Margate City. Open daily in summer; reduced off-season hours. One of the world's largest private art galleries.

SPECIAL SHOPS

In Atlantic City

Atlantic City Outlets–The Walk (609-872-7002; www.acoutlets.com), Michigan and Arctic Aves. A $76 million upscale retail outlet center, the massive 320,000-square-foot shopping district—which stretches along Michigan Ave. between the Boardwalk and the convention center—features brand-name outlets like Tommy Hilfiger, Guess, Coach, and Liz Claiborne, as well as restaurants and entertainment.

The Quarter at Tropicana (800-345-8767; www.tropicana.net), Tropicana Casino and Resort, Brighton Ave. and the Boardwalk. A three-story Havana-themed shopping, entertainment, and dining complex with specialty shops, restaurants, a spa, and Atlantic City's first IMAX theater. The original Tropicana Casino and Resort was a Havana hot spot in the 1940s.

The Pier at Caesars (609-345-3100; www.thepiershopsatcaesars.com), across from Caesars Atlantic City, on the boardwalk. Another Atlantic City landmark on the historic boardwalk has undergone a dramatic multimillion-dollar transformation. This time it's the historic Million Dollar Pier, home for years to the aging Ocean One shopping mall. Re-opened, now it's The Pier at Caesars, a three-level enclave of world-class boutiques, restaurants, and entertainment. Louis Vuitton, Armani, Gucci, hugo boss, and other upscale boutiques, with trendy gourmet eateries and a unique multimedia presentation of light, water, fire, and sound.

In Smithville

✄ **Historic Towne of Smithville** (609-652-7777; www.smithvillenj.com), 1 N. New York Rd. Open daily year-round. A quaint colonial-style shopping village with more than 60 restored historic buildings surrounding a village green lined with brick and cobblestone paths, selling crafts, candles, kitchen gadgets, gifts, wines from Tomasello Winery, collectibles, and memorabilia. A handful of eateries serve light meals and treats, while the **Historic Smithville Inn** (see *Dining Out*) offers gourmet dining. Kids love the paddleboats and ducks on Lake Meone, along with the miniature-train ride and puppet theater. Stay overnight at the **Colonial Inn** (see *Lodging—Bed & Breakfasts*). Special events include Civil War encampments, antiques shows, summer concerts, Native American festivals, and cruise nights.

✳ Special Events

February: **Atlantic City Classic Car Show** (856-573-6969; 800-227-3868; www.acclassiccars.com), Atlantic City Convention Center, One Miss America Way, Atlantic City. America's largest indoor classic-car show, with more than 1,000 antique-, custom-, and collectible cars; a live car auction; and a swap meet. A flea market and antiques show attract hundreds of vendors.

Atlantic City International Powerboat Show (609-449-2000; www.ac boatshow.com), Atlantic City Convention Center. A wintertime boat show has taken place here for more than a quarter century. Some 700 powerboats, including the latest yachts, cruisers, and fishing boats.

March: **Atlantique City Spring Antiques and Collectibles Show** (800-526-2724; www.atlantiquecity .com), Atlantic City Convention Center, Atlantic City. The world's largest indoor antiques, art, and collectibles show is spread over more than 10 acres of exhibit space. Dealers come from around the country, Canada, Europe, and Asia with their wares. **St. Patrick's Day Parade** (609-290-7723), on the boardwalk, Atlantic City.

June: **Virginia Civil War Re-encampment** (609-652-7777; www.smithvillenj.com), Historic Towne of Smithville, Smithville. Marching drills, military and civilian camp, and musket-firing demonstrations as Company K invades Smithville. **Brigantine Spring FestivalCraft Show** (856-297-0639; www.brigantine.atlnet.org), Brigantine. ✿ **Jersey Genesis Triathlon and Bambino Biathlon For Kids 5–12** (609-652-6154; www.jerseygenesistriathlon.com), Port Republic.

July: **Chicken Bone Beach Jazz Series** (609-441-9064; www.chicken bonebeach.org), Kennedy Plaza, Atlantic City. Free Thursday-night concerts on the boardwalk (see sidebar, page 472). **Offshore Powerboat Racing** (732-

583-8501), Atlantic City. High-powered speedboats race up and down the coast; sponsored by the New Jersey Offshore Powerboat Racing Association.

August: **Thunder Over the Boardwalk** (609-317-1000), the Atlantic City Airshow brings aerobatics to the beach; **Atlantic City Around-the-Island Marathon Swim** (609-653-7033; 888-228-4748), Historic Gardner's Basin, Atlantic City. A 22.5-mile open-water ocean marathon around Absecon Island draws top competitors from around the world. A **Living History Encampment** (609-652-7777; www .smithvillenj.com) is staged at the Historic Towne of Smithville, Smithville.

September: **Atlantic City In-Water Powerboat Show** (215-732-8001; www.acinwaterboatshow.com), Farley State Marina, Atlantic City. More than 800 boats and 200 vendors. **Atlantic City Festival Latino Americano** (609-412-7421; www.haac.org), Atlantic City.

October: **Atlantique City Fall Antiques and Collectibles Show** (800-526-2724; www.atlantiquecit y.com), Atlantic City Convention Center, Atlantic City. The largest indoor art, antiques, and collectibles show in the world. **Atlantic City Marathon** (609-822-6911; www.atlanticcity marathon.org), on the boardwalk, Atlantic City.

OCEAN CITY TO WILDWOOD

The narrow barrier islands stretching along New Jersey's southern shore between the famous resorts of Atlantic City to the north and Cape May to the south are dotted with a handful of seaside towns, each with a unique history and flavor. The old-fashioned charm of family-friendly Ocean City and Sea Isle City, the upscale beach towns of Avalon and Stone Harbor, and the carnival-like atmosphere on the Wildwood boardwalk—each appeals to a particular type of visitor and offers a one-of-a-kind Jersey Shore experience.

Ocean City is a quaint boardwalk resort just 20 minutes south of the glitz and glitter of Atlantic City, on a 7-mile-long barrier island that protects the islets and bays of Great Egg Harbor from the Atlantic Ocean. It bills itself as America's Greatest Family Resort, a slogan that seems to be everywhere in town, proudly splashed across banners, posters, and tourism brochures. It's one of the few remaining dry towns in New Jersey—dating to one of the blue laws created by its Methodist founding fathers—which means no alcohol is sold or consumed anywhere, not even a glass of wine at dinner. Instead, there's lots of wholesome, clean fun, which seems to suit those who visit and live here just fine.

Ocean City sponsors hundreds of special events that keep the hordes of vacationing families with young children in tow busy all summer long. In June, lovelies from around the Garden State compete here in the Miss New Jersey Pageant. In July, Night in Venice is a boat festival on the back bays that just about every resident and visitor attends. Some 100,000 lavishly decorated pleasure boats parade past the shoreline, where spectators watch from bleachers or one of the many waterfront homes that throw festive celebrations. Baby parades are a popular tradition on boardwalks up and down the shore, and Ocean City's version is New Jersey's first—and one of the oldest in the world—dating back more than a century. A crowd of thousands watches as floats and bands accompany kids on bikes and toddlers in wagons, strollers, and carriages, all decorated to the nines. Other events include a parade of floppy basset hounds, a hermit crab beauty pageant, and Weird Week, which can feature just about anything.

Ocean City is an old-time boardwalk town, where the amusements lining the boards are tame rather than tawdry. The Gillian family owns and operates Ocean City's three amusement piers, whose rides and games are geared mostly toward youngsters and preteens. Those expecting an adrenaline rush whenever they step onto a carnival ride should most definitely head south to Wildwood. The Ocean City Pops orchestra plays summertime concerts at the historic Music Pier, and 8

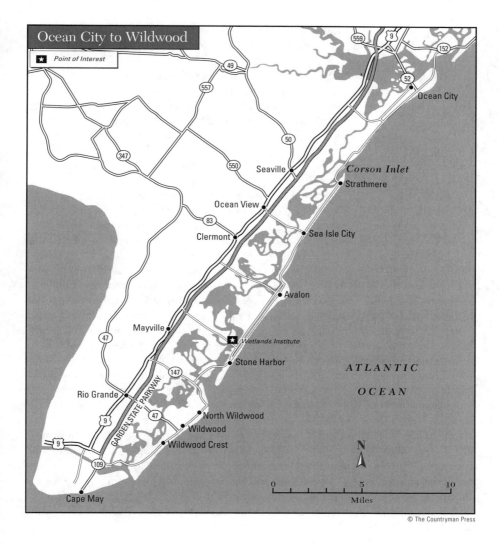

559
9
152
49
557
52
Ocean City
50
550
Seaville
Corson Inlet
Strathmere
Ocean View
83
Clermont
Sea Isle City
Avalon
Mayville
47
★ *Wetlands Institute*
Stone Harbor
147
Rio Grande
ATLANTIC
OCEAN
9
47
North Wildwood
9
Wildwood
Wildwood Crest
N
109
Cape May

0   5   10
Miles

miles of sandy beaches are wide and clean—even the waves here are gentle, thanks to the offshore sandbars that temper the mighty force of the Atlantic Ocean. There are a few beachfront mansions, but Ocean City is decidedly understated, unpretentious, and middle class.

Brothers and Methodist ministers James, Ezra, and Samuel Lake were seeking a location to start a bucolic seaside resort and summertime religious retreat when they settled Ocean City in 1879. Later on, grand hotels and Victorian mansions were built for wealthy Philadelphians who summered on the Jersey Shore. Among them was Grace Kelly, who vacationed here with her family. Most of the historic homes have been replaced by tightly packed two-family vacation duplexes, but many modern houses are being built in the Victorian style as a nod to the town's heritage. Many vintage buildings are preserved in the historic district, which can be seen in guided walking tours sponsored by the Ocean City Historical Museum or by hopping on one of the many trolleys that pass through town. Downtown offers an interesting mix of specialty shops and eateries, mostly on Asbury Avenue between 6th and 14th streets.

Sea Isle City used to be a favorite haunt among retirees; today there's still an older crowd, but it's also become a popular family resort. In many ways it's a scaled-down version of Ocean City, with white-sand beaches frequented by young families and children during the day. After dark is a different matter—the resort isn't a dry town, so it morphs into a party town at night, with bars and nightclubs hopping until the wee hours. There are few motels and hotels in town, so most visitors rent a cottage for a week or longer. Lots of activities keep vacationers busy, from surf contests and crafts shows to concerts and dance parties.

Sea Isle City's 5-mile stretch of beach is lovely and clean, and a 1.5-mile paved promenade is the town's version of a boardwalk. It may lack the charm of traditional weathered boards, but cyclists, joggers, and in-line skaters appreciate the smooth surface. Party boats and charter fishing boats, as well as commercial fishing and lobstering vessels, are lined cheek by jowl in the bayside marinas. Fun City's amusement rides may not be quite spine-tingling, but they're ideal for young thrill seekers. Sara the Turtle is Sea Isle City's beloved mascot, created to raise public awareness about the local population of diamondback terrapins, the only species of turtle to inhabit the coastal salt marshes. In June and July, female terrapins travel from the quiet bayside marshland to lay their eggs in the sand along the coast, navigating their way across a busy street to reach their nesting grounds. One of the resort's most popular summertime activities is the series of "beachcombing" environmental programs in which young and old explore the shoreline with a naturalist and learn about the fragile coastal environment.

Avalon and Stone Harbor are Sea Isle City's upscale neighbors on Seven Mile Beach Island, a three- to four-block-wide barrier island about 40 miles south of Atlantic City. These are the priciest towns on the southern shore, with upper-middle-class families living in grand million-dollar-plus homes dotting the beaches and back bays. The two communities have remained deliberately low-key by gladly forgoing the amusements of Ocean City and Wildwood—and are definitely not for shore visitors seeking bright lights and around-the-clock excitement. There is no boardwalk in Stone Harbor, and Avalon's is a modest half-mile plankway along the sand—no thrill rides and arcades here. But the beaches are clean and relatively uncrowded, the surfing is decent, and there are plenty of places for better-than-average eating and shopping. Tourists who come here looking for a quiet, family atmosphere and beautiful surroundings return for their summer vacations year after year.

Avalon's slogan "Cooler by a Mile" is a reference to geography rather than attitude—the northern tip of the barrier island juts a mile farther out to sea than the southern end. In the 18th century, it was a pristine 2,725-acre swath of untouched woodlands and dunes known as Leaming's Island. Charles Bond bought it all for 70 pounds, 10 shillings—about $380—in 1722. Avalon—named for King Arthur's fabled island paradise—and Stone Harbor were both incorporated around the turn of the 20th century. They're often thought of as a single community, since they blend into each other with no obvious boundary and share a main drag. Avalon stretches from Townsend's Inlet to 80th Street; from there, Stone Harbor continues to the island's southern tip at Hereford Inlet. Avalon has more restaurants and bars, while Stone Harbor has better shopping, with more than 100 specialty shops and eateries in the heart of town. Women's clothing boutiques, jewelry stores, cafés, and the requisite shops selling T-shirts, souvenirs, and beach towels stretch along busy 96th Street.

Naturally, people come here for the beaches, and the fees in Avalon and Stone Harbor are reasonable, given the upscale surroundings. The island is deeply committed to protecting its natural beauty. The World Wildlife Fund owns and preserves more than 1,000 acres of marshland and wetlands in Avalon, which is also famous for its pristine sand dunes. From 49th to 72nd streets a dramatic series of dunes is covered in bayberry bushes, dune grass, and cedar trees. Stone Harbor has a national reputation as a leading birding center. Sandwiched between the barrier island and the mainland, the Wetlands Institute encompasses 6,000 acres of islands, tidal marshes, lagoons, and bays—a rich habitat for thousands of butterflies, migrating and nesting birds, and other wildlife. The Stone Harbor Bird Sanctuary is America's only municipal heronry, one of only two such facilities in the world (the other one is in Japan).

Across Hereford Inlet is Five Mile Beach Island, a barrier island that's better known as the Wildwoods—Wildwood and its sister communities of North Wildwood and Wildwood Crest. In the 1963 pop smash "Wildwood Days"—Bobby Rydell's ode to the Jersey Shore—he proclaims "every day's a holiday and every night is a Saturday night." The mishmash of arcades, thrill rides, souvenir shops, and food stands that inspired Rydell still line Wildwood's famous 2-mile boardwalk, one of the oldest and most popular boardwalks in the country.

Before the era of high-tech theme parks and mega-mall food courts, there were amusement-packed boardwalks lined with boardwalk food—a sweet, salty, spicy, hot, and frosty smorgasbord of delights that people steadfastly avoid, except while vacationing on the shore. And though they have adapted to the changing times, boardwalks remain decidedly low-tech and maintain an allure that's steeped in nostalgia for a bygone era of innocence. People-watching is an American pastime unto itself, and there's perhaps no better place to observe the spectacle than at Wildwood, whose retro, sentimental charm appeals to older generations as well as children. Summertime in Wildwood—like Ocean City—is boardwalk season, but on a bigger, louder, more garish scale. The 38-block boardwalk buzzes with energy all day and well into the night, when the amusement piers thump with music and blaze in electric neon. It's lined with a funky jumble of old-fashioned pastimes—carnival rides, games of chance, tacky souvenir shops, humming arcades, and old-time treats—funnel cakes, cotton candy, saltwater taffy, fudge, crisp curly fries, and frozen custard, to name just a few. It also boasts one-of-a-kind attractions, like the only boardwalk chapel in America and what has been called the tallest Ferris wheel in the Northeast. The Morey family runs Wildwood's three action-packed amusement areas, which attract millions of visitors every summer to 150 rides—no other boardwalk in the country has as many. The oceanfront piers are crammed with midway-style games, kiddie rides, looping roller coasters, familiar Tilt-A-Whirls, the newest thrill rides, and a pair of water parks. The boardwalk has many different things to offer many different people—perhaps the only thing it lacks is peace and quiet. Unless, of course, you wake up while the rest of the island is sleeping off the good times of the day before. In the early hours you can pedal a bike along the boards or wander the tranquil coastline, and enjoy the peaceful side of Wildwood that few visitors experience.

Long before the amusement piers were built, New Jersey's southern coastline was a desolate outpost. Lenni-Lenape tribes lived and fished on the barrier islands, establishing a network of trails that would later be used by offshore livestock farmers and, eventually, European settlers. The explorer Robert Juet, who sailed with English navigator Henry Hudson on a 17th-century expedition for the Dutch East India Company, described the barrier island in his journal as "a very good land to fall in with, and a pleasant land to see" when he first spotted it in 1609. He wasn't supposed to see it, originally: Hudson's *Half Moon* sailed up the Atlantic Coast from Cape May only after aborting a plan to explore the Delaware River's potential as a passage to China. Juet's observations of the white-sand beach and dense pine forest are the first known recorded references to the barrier island. In the 1870s fishermen began settling at the northern tip of the island; the small community of shacks called itself Angle-sea and was a major East Coast fishing center in the 19th century. In 1874 a lighthouse was built to warn local mariners of the treacherous shifting shoals in Hereford Inlet. A rail line connected the island to Cape May Court House, and by the late 1800s, word was spreading about its lovely beaches and refreshing salt air. Soon after, the first bridges were built, including one to carry automobiles. Wildwood was incorporated in 1895, and the original boardwalk was built on the sand (by carpenters earning 25 cents an hour) for the tidy sum of $2,400.

Tourists came along with the railroad, but it wasn't until the 1950s that Wildwood experienced its heyday as a seaside resort. It was the era of the American Dream, when for many the ritual of driving to the beach for summer vacation began. Wildwood's 200-plus motels symbolize America's postwar automobile culture, when a growing middle class was enjoying a new phenomenon—leisure time and money to spend on it. Some are nautically themed (the Buccaneer, the Quarter Deck, the Mariner), while others (Acropolis, Bird of Paradise, Isle of Capri, Montego Bay, Aztec, Riviera) celebrate far-flung locales with décor to match. Kitschy though it may seem, they appealed to vacationers who wanted an ersatz version of an exotic vacation, one that they could drive to and park in front of.

The biggest change in Wildwood in recent years is a stylized new look that's actually a nostalgic step back to that mid-20th-century era. It's called a doo-wop revival, an effort to preserve the bold, outlandish architecture and pastel-and-neon flamboyance that defined Wildwood in the 1950s and '60s. The island was filled with sleek and showy motels inspired by the space age and exotic travels, painted in gaudy teals and pinks, and decorated with wildly colored neon signs, plastic palm trees, shag carpets, and other campy touches. The past decade has seen a tireless movement to restore and preserve these relics, many of which were tired and faded by the late 20th century. Wildwood's collection of "doo-wop architecture"—named for the popular a cappella group singing style of the '50s—is the largest in the country. The revival has caught on all over town, giving the streets and boardwalk a stylishly retro appeal.

Between Wildwood and its sister cities of Wildwood Crest and North Wildwood, there are close to two hundred 1950s-era motels still in business. Along with guesthouses, inns, and resorts—even some bed & breakfasts—the island has about 14,000 rooms that offer a variety of price ranges and degrees of quality. Finding a place to stay is usually easy; nevertheless, it's a good idea to book a room ahead during the summer. Most visitors come to Wildwood for a week or two, whereas in beach towns like Avalon and Stone Harbor, it's not unusual for vacationers to spend the entire summer.

Wildwood isn't all about thrill rides. The island offers local-history museums and a 19th-century lighthouse, sportfishing, surfing, parasailing, and, of course, the beach. Its 5-mile stretch of sugar-fine sand is clean, wide, and best of all, free. Wildwood and Atlantic City are the only towns on the Jersey Shore than don't require beach badges. Off the boardwalk there's a variety of eateries, from martini bars and weathered seafood houses to gourmet cuisine and all-you-can-eat family-style joints. Like the motels, they're all locally owned, and many have been in the same family for generations.

While families love the beach, young partiers love Wildwood's nightclubs and bars that bustle till 3 AM. This is where everyone heads for nightlife, especially if they don't want to venture north to Atlantic City. The music ranges from live Jimmy Buffett–esque acoustic beach bands to DJs spinning house music. Nightclubs run the gamut from trendy to tacky.

For all that Wildwood has to offer, there are some things that simply don't exist here. You won't find the amenities of a luxury inn, or a centuries-old bed & breakfast on the national register. But motel rooms are generally clean and moderately priced, and families adore Wildwood because the kids won't get bored. In fact, between the rides, the beach, and the boardwalk, it couldn't get easier to keep children entertained. During the summer, Thursday in Wildwood brings Family Fun Night, with parades, music, and clowns; fireworks light up the sky above the beach every Friday night.

At the southern end of Five Mile Beach, Wildwood Crest is the quieter, family-oriented part of the Wildwoods. It's a community with a laid-back beach-town feel, and more seasonal cottage renters than visitors spending a week in a motel. You can catch beautiful sunsets from the bayside in Wildwood Crest, especially from aptly named Sunset Lake and its lovely park.

Entries in this section are arranged in roughly geographic order, from north to south.

AREA CODE 609.

GUIDANCE **The Ocean View Travel Plaza** (609-624-0918) is a **state welcome center** located between Exits 17 and 20 on the Garden State Parkway in Ocean View, west of Sea Isle City. Open daily year-round, 9–5.

The Ocean City Regional Chamber of Commerce (609-399-1412; 800-232-2465; www.oceancityvacation.com) staffs an information center on the Ninth St. causeway just before you enter town. It is well stocked with tourism literature, and the knowledgeable and courteous staff will offer advice on Ocean City's attractions, events, restaurants, and activities. The center also has a computerized system providing information on lodging vacancies. Other information centers are located on the boardwalk at the Music Pier (summer only) and at the old municipal building at West Ave. and 46th St. The chamber will send tourism literature on request, including their annual vacation guide.

Sea Isle City Tourism Development Commission (609-263-8687; www.seaislecity.org), P.O. Box 622, Sea Isle City 08243, publishes an annual visitor's guide and events schedule, and will send them on request. A **tourist information center** (609-263-8900), on the promenade at 40th St., is open May–Sept. from 10–6.

The **chambers of commerce** *in Avalon* (609-967-3936; www.avalonbeach.com), 30th St. and Ocean Dr. and *Stone Harbor* (609-368-6101; www.stoneharborbeach .com), 212 96th St., maintain online community directories with information for visitors. The Stone Harbor chamber publishes a free vacation guide that they will send on request.

North Wildwood has several seasonal information centers: a **Boardwalk Information Center** (609-729-8686) at 22nd Ave. and Boardwalk; a **Tourism Information Center** at Fourth and New Jersey Aves.; and the **Hereford Inlet Lighthouse** (609-522-4520) on First and Central Aves. is stocked with tourism brochures.

In Wildwood, the **Greater Wildwood Chamber of Commerce** operates two visitor information centers. The **Downtown Visitor Information Center** (609-729-4000; 888-729-0033; www.gwcoc.com), 3306 Pacific Ave., Wildwood (mailing address: P.O. Box 823, Wildwood 08260), is open year-round Mon.–Fri. 9–4:30; and a seasonal **Boardwalk Information Center** (609-522-1507), 3601 Boardwalk at Schellenger Ave., from May–Sept., open weekends in spring and Sept., and daily in summer, 10–4. The friendly staff provides information and tourism literature on dining, lodging, activities, attractions, and events.

The Greater Wildwood Hotel and Motel Association (609-522-4546; 800-786-4546; www.wildwoods.org), 1 S. State Hwy. 47, Wildwood 08260 staffs an information center on Rt. 47, just before the bridge to the Wildwoods. Ask them to send you a copy of their visitor's guide, which includes information on Wildwood's huge array of accommodations.

The Wildwood Crest Information Center (609-522-0221) is on Rambler Rd. at the beach in Wildwood Crest. Open seasonally.

GETTING THERE *By air:* **Atlantic City International Airport** (609-645-7895; www.acairport.com), Exit 9 off the Atlantic City Expressway, Egg Harbor Township. Spirit Airlines (800-772-7117; www.spiritair.com) has direct and connecting service from points around the country.

By bus: **New Jersey Transit** (973-275-5555; www.njtransit.com) buses connect the region to bus terminals in Philadelphia and New York City, and provide local service between Cape May and Atlantic City, with stops in Sea Isle City, Avalon, Stone Harbor, North Wildwood, and Wildwood.

By car: The **Garden State Parkway** runs north to south along the southern shoreline; the **Atlantic City Expressway** links Philadelphia to the Atlantic City region; from the Delaware Memorial Bridge, **Rts. 40 and 49** head toward the shore. The four barrier islands from Ocean City to the Wildwoods are connected by a series of toll bridges.

By ferry: **Cape May–Lewes Ferry** (800-643-3779; www.capemaylewesferry.com) connects Lewes, Delaware, to North Cape May, New Jersey—close to the Garden State Parkway. The ferry accepts both car and foot passengers; the one-way trip takes about 70 minutes. Reservations are recommended when traveling during peak summertime periods, especially Friday afternoon and evening, Saturday morning, and Sunday afternoon and evening.

GETTING AROUND *Taxis: In Wildwood,* **Yellow Cab** (609-522-0555), **Coastal Cab Company** (609-523-8300), **Wildwood Cab** (609-729-1911), and **Checker**

Cab Company (609-522-1431) serve the Wildwoods. **Atlantic City Airport Taxi** (609-383-1457) operates between the airport and the southern shore. **Aart's Cape May Taxi** (609-898-7433) serves Cape May County.

The Great American Trolley Company (609-884-5230; 800-487-6559; www .gatrolley.com) operates a summertime trolley in Ocean City daily from mid-June to Labor Day. The driver will stop on any corner along the route, which runs along the beach from 59th St. to Battersea Rd. Year-round trolleys run on several routes linking North Wildwood, Wildwood, and Wildwood Crest.

Sightseer Boardwalk Tram (609-523-8726), on the boardwalk, Wildwood. A seasonal battery-operated tram shuttles visitors from one end of the 2.5-mile-long boardwalk to the other. You can get on and off anywhere along the boards. In Wildwood, the tram runs from 9 AM–1 AM, and in North Wildwood from 10 AM–5 PM.

Doo Wop '50s Trolley Tours (609-884-5404; 800-275-4278), Wildwood. Tours leave from the Greater Wildwood Chamber of Commerce; call for a schedule and prices. A 45-minute narrated tour of more than 60 buildings sporting Wildwood's famously flamboyant 1950s doo-wop architecture, from bold boomerang rooflines and Jetson fins to plastic palm trees and thatched roofs. The **Mid-Atlantic Center for the Arts** (609-884-5404; 800-275-4278; www.capemaymac.org) and the **Doo Wop Preservation League** (609-729-4000; www.doowopusa.org) run the tours, which are accompanied by 1950s- and '60s-era music. A **Doo Wop Museum,** long in planning, opened in 2008.

MEDICAL EMERGENCY Atlantic City Medical Center (609-345-4000; www.atlanticare.org), 1925 Pacific Ave., Atlantic City. The emergency number is 609-441-8050.

Health Med (609-345-6000; www.healthmedassociates.com), 24 South Carolina Ave., Atlantic City. An urgent-care facility and family medical center.

Shore Memorial Hospital (609-653-3500; www.shorememorial.org), 1 E. New York Ave., Somers Point. The emergency number is 609-653-3515.

Cape Regional Medical Center (609-463-2000; www.caperegional.com), 2 Stone Harbor Blvd., Cape May Court House. The emergency number is 609-463-2130.

Convenient Medical Care of Ocean City (609-525-0008), on the 900 block of Haven Ave., Ocean City. A walk-in medical clinic open daily 8–8.

For marine emergencies, contact the **U.S. Coast Guard—Cape May** at 609-884-3491.

✳ To See

HISTORIC HOMES AND SITES Ocean City Tabernacle (609-399-1915; www.octabernacle.org), 500 Wesley Ave., Ocean City. Aside from the beach and boardwalk, the Ocean City Tabernacle is among the top tourist attractions. It replaced the original 1881 church built by the Methodist clergymen who founded Ocean City as a seaside religious retreat. Today it's a nondenominational summer-community church (vacationers are welcome) with world-renowned preachers and a full schedule of concerts and lectures, all open to the public. Guest musicians, community choirs, classical soloists, and others perform in the tabernacle's 1,000-

seat state-of-the-art auditorium. Visitors are also welcome to walk the lovely grounds, which feature a fountain and historic bell tower, whose set of 13 bells was created in 1893 to symbolize America's 13 original colonies. Some programs offer admission by donation; others require tickets. Call or see Web site for a schedule.

J. Thompson Baker House (609-522-8914), 3008 Atlantic Ave., Wildwood. Guided tours June–Aug.; group tours May–Dec. by appointment. The only house in the Wildwoods on the National Register of Historic Places has been home to the Wildwood Civic Club since 1936. The grand 1904 Classical Revival–style home, with elegant white columns, was built by J. Thompson Baker, one of the organizers of the Wildwood Beach Improvement Company that developed Five Mile Beach Island into a seaside resort. Baker served as Wildwood's first mayor in 1911 and 1912 before serving a term in Congress. Visitors can see two refurbished bedrooms decorated with period antiques and furnishings, as well as original details like the foyer's stained-glass windows and oak staircase.

Sunset Lake and Turtle Gut Park and Memorial (609-522-0221), New Jersey and Miami Aves., Wildwood Crest. Wildwood Crest is the only town in Cape May

---

✐ THE WILDWOOD BOARDWALK

Wildwood's boardwalk is a virtual feast for the senses, an oceanfront amusement park with more rides than Disneyland, as well as T-shirt shops, souvenir stands, video arcades, and just about anything you could possibly want to eat. It begins in North Wildwood at 16th Ave. and heads south along the shore through Wildwood before ending at Cresse Ave. in Wildwood Crest, nearly 3 miles and 36 blocks later.

The Great White ranks among the fastest and tallest wooden roller coasters on the East Coast, and the 140-foot-high Ferris wheel is among the tallest on the East Coast. The Nor'Easter and the Sea Serpent are as spine-tingling as they sound. Battery-powered tram cars shuttle visitors up and down the boardwalk from early in the morning until late at night. The amusement rides are generally open on weekends from Easter to Memorial Day, daily Memorial Day through Labor Day, then weekends until Columbus Day. Wildwood's specialty is family entertainment, and the boardwalk's calendar of special events keeps visitors busy all summer long. Every Monday is **Doo Wop '50s Night,** with vintage cars, parades, and 1950s-era live music. **Family Fun Night** happens every Thursday, with clowns, and more live music and parades. Friday night means movies on the beach at 9 PM and at midnight, with a break in between for fireworks at 11 PM.

Wildwood is a different world in the morning, before the amusements and food stands open. If you didn't stay up too late the night before, get up early and go for a bike ride on the boards. Cycling is allowed until 10:30 AM on weekends and until 11 AM on weekdays, and affords a rare glimpse at the quiet and peaceful side of Wildwood that few visitors ever see.

County to have seen action in the American Revolution. On June 29, 1776, the **battle of Turtle Gut Inlet,** a little-known naval encounter, was fought between British warships and the brigantine *Nancy.* As British ships pursued and attacked the American boat—loaded with a Philadelphia-bound cargo of gunpowder for the Continental army—Captain John Barry of the frigate *Lexington* stepped in to assist the *Nancy,* which had run aground in the inlet and was under heavy enemy fire. Barry and his men boarded the *Nancy,* manned its guns to fend off the warships, and unloaded the cargo. They left some gunpowder behind, which was ignited as British troops boarded the ship. The massive blast, according to documented accounts, was "heard 40 miles above Philadelphia." The cargo was shuttled safely up the Delaware River by the frigate *Wasp,* and Barry would later be known as Commander Barry, "the Father of the American Navy." The inlet has since been filled in, but a marker across from the park at New Jersey and Miami avenues commemorates the battle site.

MUSEUMS ✍ **Discovery Sea Shell Museum and Shell Yard** (609-398-2316), 2721 Asbury Ave., Ocean City. Open Apr.–Nov. Free admission. Shell collectors and beachcombers love this unique family-run seashore museum, which features more than 10,000 varieties of seashells from oceans around the world. Among the exotic varieties on exhibit are rare golden cowries and a record-sized Siamese helmet shell. Other displays feature coral, shark teeth and shark jaws, and an extensive variety of specimen shells. An interesting selection of shells and nautical gifts for sale, from puzzles and books to fossils, hermit crabs, shell lamps, and jewelry.

Ocean City Historical Museum (609-399-1801; www.ocnjmuseum.org), in the Ocean City Cultural Arts Center, 1735 Simpson Ave., Ocean City. Summer hours: Mon.–Fri. 10–4; Sat. 2–4; closed Sun. Winter hours: Tues.–Fri. 10–4; Sat. 11–2; closed Sun.–Mon. Admission is pay what you will. The story of Ocean City is told through an extensive collection of artifacts and treasures in this well-stocked local-history museum. The *Sindia* Room contains cargo, photos, and artifacts salvaged from the famous **shipwreck of the *Sindia,*** a 392-foot four-masted ship that sank off the coast of Ocean City during a fierce storm in 1901. Visitors can see a scale model of the ship and a dramatic stained-glass window depicting the *Sindia* as she looked under sail. Period rooms display Victorian furniture and clothing, a collection of exquisite vintage dolls, memorabilia from the families of Ocean City's founding fathers, and a collection of vintage photos and postcards. Gift shop.

✍ **The Bayside Center** (609-525-9244), 520 Bay Ave., Ocean City. Open daily in summer. A vintage 1910 home is an environmental education and historical center with a popular series of nature programs throughout the summer. Among the displays are museum-quality classic model ships, hand-carved decoys, and photographs and memorabilia that chronicle the 100-year-old history of Ocean City's beach patrol. Many visitors come here simply to picnic on the grounds and see the butterfly garden and lovely views of Great Egg Harbor Bay from the third-floor observation area. This is one of the best places in town from which to view the annual **Night in Venice** summertime boat parade (see *Special Events*).

Sea Isle City Historical Museum (609-263-1772; www.seaislecityhistorical society.org), 4208 Landis Ave., Sea Isle City. Open July–Aug., Mon.–Sat. 10–1; closed Sun.; open Sat. 10–1 in spring and fall; other times by appointment. Admission by donation. A small museum featuring memorabilia, artifacts, furniture,

HEREFORD INLET LIGHTHOUSE

(609-522-4520; www.herefordlighthouse.org), 111 North Central Ave. (at First Ave.), North Wildwood. Open mid-May–mid-Oct., daily 9–5; open mid-Oct.–mid-May, Wed.–Sun. 10–4. Adults $4; children 11 and under, $1. This Victorian-style lighthouse was built at the northern tip of Five Mile Beach in 1874 to safely guide local fishermen and mariners through the inlet's dangerous shoals and strong currents on their trips from the back bays to the fishing grounds in the Atlantic Ocean. The lighthouse's **ornate turret and Swiss Gothic–style architecture**—the only lighthouse design of its kind on the East Coast—was the vision of architect Paul Pelz, who also designed the Library of Congress in Washington, DC. The lighthouse was decommissioned in 1964, when an iron light tower with a modernized automated beacon was built on the property. The keeper's house and tower deteriorated for two decades before restoration efforts began in 1983. The modern beacon was returned to the historic tower, where it once again guides boats through the inlet. Today the stately lighthouse is surrounded by old-fashioned **English-style cottage gardens** with more than 170 varieties of perennials and herbs that bloom from spring to late fall. The antiques-filled keeper's quarters contains a small **nautical museum and gift shop.** A full schedule of crafts shows and other special events are held on the grounds every summer. The lighthouse interior is undergoing restoration, and plans are under way to turn the historic Coast Guard station next to the lighthouse into a living-history museum.

clothing, and photographs that chronicle Sea Isle City's history as a seaside resort. The Military Room has a collection of artifacts from both world wars, and the gift shop sells prints, photographs, souvenirs, and books. Call about **guided walking tours** of Sea Isle City's historic downtown area, Townsend Inlet, and the old boardwalk.

 Wetlands Institute and Museum (609-368-1211; www.wetlandsinstitute.org), 1075 Stone Harbor Blvd., Stone Harbor. Open mid-May–mid-Oct., Mon.–Sat. 9:30–4:30, Tues.–Thurs. until 8; mid-June–Labor Day, also Sun. 10–4. From mid-Oct.–mid-May, open Tues.–Sat. 9:30–4:30; closed Sun.–Mon. Adults $7; children 2–11, $5; children under 2, free. This nationally known nonprofit research center is an environmental classroom devoted to raising public concern and knowledge about the region's fragile ecosystem. A boardwalk trail and 40-foot observation tower provide close-ups and panoramas of the 6,000-acre salt marsh. Inside are interactive touch tanks, a saltwater aquarium filled with marine animals, and exhibits on native diamondback terrapins, bird life, and the institute's natural surroundings. A lecture series is held in the auditorium, and research is conducted in the institute's laboratories. The **Tidepool Museum Shop** has quality nature books and unique gifts, clothing, and prints. Special events for children and families include guided bird walks, kayaking trips, back-bay boat tours, and the annual

Wings 'n Water Festival (see sidebar, page 490; also *To Do—Canoeing and Kayaking* and *Special Events*).

The Boyer Museum (609-523-0277; www.the-wildwoods.com), 3907 Pacific Ave., at the Holly Beach Station Mall, Wildwood. Open May–Sept., Mon.–Fri. 9:30–2:30 (until 8:30 on Fri.), Sat.–Sun. 10:30–2:30; Oct.–Apr., daily 10:30–2:30. Admission by donation. The **Wildwood Historical Society** runs this museum, which tells the story of Wildwood through an eclectic collection of artifacts, memorabilia, and vintage photographs and films. Here you can learn about Wildwood's evolution as a seaside resort town, from the early days of the boardwalk and beach patrol to the famous entertainers who performed in Wildwood's clubs. It has had a colorful history, as when **Tuffy the Lion** escaped from his cage and wreaked havoc upon the boardwalk in 1938, killing a bystander; and when local leaders destroyed Wildwood's original promenade in a midnight raid so a new boardwalk would be built closer to the water. The **National Marbles Hall of Fame** is devoted to the historic sport of shooting marbles, and contains trophies, photos, memorabilia, and exhibits on the game's top players, and, of course, an interesting variety of marbles. Wildwood has hosted the **National Marbles Tournament** every summer since 1922 (see *Special Events*).

Photo courtesy of the Wetlands Institute

THE WETLANDS INSTITUTE IN STONE HARBOR IS A MUSEUM AND EDUCATIONAL AND RESEARCH FACILITY SURROUNDED BY 6,000 ACRES OF COASTAL WETLANDS TEEMING WITH BIRDS AND OTHER WILDLIFE.

Wildwood Crest Historical Society and Museum (609-729-4515; www.cresthistory.org), in the Crest Pier Building, 5800 Ocean Ave., Wildwood Crest. Admission by donation; phone ahead for hours. A unique collection of historic artifacts, photographs, memorabilia, and antiques tells the history of Wildwood Crest. The museum was founded when the historical society acquired historic documents belonging to Philip Baker, one of the 19th-century founders of the Wildwoods. The collection has grown over the years through donations of artifacts and special objects from local families.

✳ To Do

AMUSEMENTS 🎨 **Gillian's Wonderland Pier** (609-399-7082; www.gillians .com), Sixth St. and the Boardwalk, Ocean City. Open daily, mid-June through summer; phone ahead or see Web site for spring and fall hours. The Gillian family has been offering family-style amusements in Ocean City for more than 70 years. Wonderland Pier is the boardwalk's landmark amusement complex, with close to 40 classic rides that cater to families with young children. It's a pay-as-you-go park—rides are $1–3 a pop—with everything from a Tilt-A-Whirl and a Ferris wheel to bumper cars. Some of the rides are historic—the ornately carved carousel was built in 1926, the train ride dates to the 1940s, and the monorail has circled the park since 1965.

✿ **Gillian's Island Water Theme Park** (609-399-0483; www.gillians.com), Plymouth Pl. and the Boardwalk. Open daily mid-June–Labor Day 9:30–6; admission $16 and up. A family water park with 35 rides, slides, and activities, including an 18,800-square-foot water playground. Older kids will love the 6-foot drop on the Shotgun Falls slide; younger ones enjoy the tame Gangslide that they can ride with their parents. The jungle-themed mini-golf course features a unique landscape of rock ledges and waterfalls with challenging holes.

✿ **Playland's Castaway Cove** (609-399-4751; www.boardwalkfun.com), 1020 Boardwalk (at 10th St.), Ocean City. In May, open Fri. evenings and weekends from 1 PM; in June, Mon.–Fri. from 6 PM, Sat.–Sun. from 1 PM; late June–Labor Day, open daily at 1 PM. A pirate-themed amusement park that has catered to families since 1959. More than 30 rides range from mellow to bone-tingling, including an old-time train, bumper cars, a log flume, a Tilt-A-Whirl, and the adrenaline-charged Double Shot. There are go-carts, mini golf, and four roller coasters, including the Python, Ocean City's only looping coaster.

✿ **Morey's Amusement Piers and Raging Waters** (609-522-3900; www.moreys piers.com), on the boardwalk at 25th Ave., Schellenger Ave., and Spencer Ave., Wildwood. Open from Memorial Day–Labor Day, daily noon–midnight; call or see Web site about reduced hours in spring and fall. Morey's offers a variety of admission options, including day passes and season passes, amusement pier–water park combination pricing, family packages, and tickets for individual rides. This family-owned amusement and water park complex has been a Wildwood institution for more than 35 years. It's also considered one of the best amusement parks on the Jersey Shore. It boasts three ride-packed piers and two beachfront water parks with kiddie rides, waterslides, win-a-prize midway-style games, go-carts, boardwalk food, a colossal Ferris wheel, and seven roller coasters, including the Great White—one of the largest wooden coasters on the East Coast. All told, there are 150 rides, described as "Mild Thrill" (the familiar carousel), "Moderate Thrill" (the classic Tilt-A-Whirl), and "High Thrill" (the Sea Serpent's 12-story free fall). Generally speaking, Mariner's Landing Pier is the most family-friendly; Adventure Pier is for thrill seekers; and Surfside Pier has a nostalgic '50s theme, including a doo-wop-style roller coaster.

✿ **Splash Zone Water Park** (609-729-5600; www.splashzonewaterpark.com), 3500 Boardwalk at Schellenger Ave., Wildwood. Open daily, Memorial Day–Labor Day, with limited hours in late spring and early fall. Call or see Web site for ticket prices. With 16 water rides and attractions, you can laze slowly down Adventure River or stand under the Giant Bucket as it lets loose 1,000 gallons of water. The Beast of the East features family-sized whitewater rafts, and the Speed Dominator is as fast as it sounds.

BICYCLING Ocean Drive (Rt. 619), is a 40-mile-long scenic route between Cape May and Atlantic City that makes for a spectacular and challenging bike tour. It passes over a string of barrier islands connected by a series of toll bridges (no charge for cyclists) and through a natural landscape of ocean, back bays, marshland, and seaside resort towns. This route is heavily trafficked in summer, and is recommended for experienced cyclists only.

You can ride a bike on the *Ocean City boardwalk* every day from 6 AM–noon. *In Sea Isle City,* bicycling is allowed on the promenade Mon.–Fri. from 5 AM–3 PM, and Sat.–Sun., 5 AM–noon. *In Avalon,* bikes are permitted on the boardwalk from 5–10 AM. *In Wildwood,* you can pedal the boards Mon.–Fri. from 5–11 AM, and weekends and holidays from 5–10:30 AM. In *North Wildwood,* a bike path follows Surf Ave., and a second path follows the beach from Fifth Ave. to the boardwalk at 16th Ave. In *Wildwood Crest,* a bike path starts at the boardwalk at Cresse Ave. and goes south to Rambler Rd. Another bike path *in North Wildwood* follows Surf Ave.

Numerous shops rent a variety of bikes, from tandems to surreys, including: **Annarelli's Bicycles** (609-399-2238), 1014 Asbury Ave., Ocean City; **12th Street Bike Rentals** (609-399-2814), 12th St. and the Boardwalk, Ocean City; **Surf Buggy Center** (800-976-5679), JFK and Pleasure Blvds., Sea Isle City; **Hollywood Bicycle Center** (609-967-5846; www.hollywoodbikeshop.com), 2544 Dune Dr., Avalon; **Harbor Bike and Beach Shop** (609-368-3691; www.harborbike.com), 9828 Third Ave., Stone Harbor; **Casino Pier Bike Rentals** (609-522-0070), 340 East Oak Ave., Wildwood; **Crest Bike Rental** (609-522-5763), 500 E. Heather Rd., Wildwood Crest.

BIRDING In Ocean City, **Cowpens Island Bird Sanctuary** is on Rt. 52, near the information center. Birds flock to this string of tiny marsh-covered islands, especially at dawn and dusk. Herons, ibis, and egrets are among the commonly spotted species.

Corson's Inlet State Park (609-861-2404), Rt. 619 (Ocean Dr.), Ocean City. This small 341-acre state park (see *Green Space—State Park*) is a pristine swath of marshland on Corson's Inlet that protects one of the few remaining undeveloped tracts of land along New Jersey's shoreline. Least terns, black skimmers, and endangered piping plovers nest on the beach and undisturbed sand dunes in the **Strathmere Natural Area.** The estuaries and uplands are prime nesting and feeding grounds for sandpipers, gulls, ducks, and herons. This is a good spot to observe the annual migration of monarch butterflies, shorebirds, and waterfowl.

Stone Harbor Bird Sanctuary (609-368-5102), 114th St. and Third Ave., Stone Harbor. Open year-round. This spectacular 21-acre sanctuary, founded in 1947, is the only municipally funded heronry in America and a federally designated national landmark (see *Green Space—Natural Areas*). During the nesting season, birders gather at dawn to watch for stick-legged wading birds like ibis, herons, egrets, and other avian species. You can rent binoculars and find information on the birds at the observation area adjacent to the parking lot. July and August are the peak viewing times, when some 10,000 birds are busy nesting in the sanctuary and traveling (often in large groups) to the marshes to feed.

BOAT EXCURSIONS *Silver Bullet* **Speedboat and Dolphin Watch** (609-522-6060; www.silverbullettours.com), Wildwood Marina, Rio Grande Ave. and the bay, Wildwood. Trips daily, May–Oct. Reservations are recommended. Dolphin- and whale-watch excursions aboard a superfast 70-foot speedboat. Adults $28; children $15.

✐ WETLANDS INSTITUTE

(609-368-1211; www.wetlandsinstitute.org), 1075 Stone Harbor Blvd., Stone Harbor. Open mid-May–mid-Oct., Mon.–Sat. 9:30–4:30; Tues.–Thurs. until 8, mid-June–Labor Day; Sun. 10–4. From mid-Oct.–mid-May, open Tues.–Sat. 9:30–4:30; closed Sun.–Mon. Adults $7; children 2–11, $5. Some 6,000 acres of coastal wetlands and upland marsh form a natural barrier between the mainland and the narrow barrier islands along the Atlantic Ocean (see *To See—Museums*). Pick up a map at the front desk and set out on the self-guided nature trail through the salt marsh, where you'll see a variety of birds flitting about. At the trail's end, a 125-foot pier juts out over the tidal creek, which is home to one of the world's largest colonies of **laughing gulls.** Don't leave without climbing the spiral staircase to the observation tower for an expansive panorama. The **bird and butterfly gardens** are other good spots for bird-watching. During the summer, **guided walks** begin at 10 AM, noon, and 2 PM, Mon.–Sat., and at 11 AM and 1 PM on Sun. Ask about a schedule of bird-watching events, including the popular **Wings 'n Water Festival** every September, which features exhibits of wildlife paintings and bird-carving demonstrations.

✐ **Captain Sinn's Sightseeing Center** (609-522-3934), 6006 Park Blvd., Wildwood Crest. Dinner and sightseeing cruises, and whale- and dolphin-watching excursions, aboard the *Dixie Queen*.

✐ **Starlight Fleet** (609-729-3400; www.jjcboats.com), 6200 Park Blvd., Wildwood Crest. Several trips daily, May–Oct. Dolphin- and whale-watching excursions aboard the *Atlantic Star*, a 100-foot whale-watcher. Several trips a day leave during the summer: dolphin cruises in the morning, which include continental breakfast; afternoon whale- and dolphin-watch trips; dolphin-watch trips at sunset with a dinner buffet.

BOATING (See also *Boat Excursions.*)

In Ocean City, a **public boat ramp** on Tennessee Ave. provides access to Great Egg Harbor Bay; **Corson's Inlet State Park** (609-861-2404), Rt. 619 (Ocean Dr.), has a public boat launch that provides access to Corson's Inlet. The ramp is open daily year-round, and a launch fee is charged from Memorial Day weekend to Labor Day.

In Sea Isle City, you'll find the following: **Sea Isle Municipal Ramp** (609-263-0009), 42nd St. and the bay; **Larsen's Marina** (609-263-1554), Old Sea Isle Blvd.; **Pier 88 Marina** (609-263-5260), 88th St. and the bay; and **Sunset Pier** (609-263-8174), 86th St. and the bay.

In Avalon, you can launch a boat at **Avalon Anchorage Marina** (609-967-3592; www.avalonanchorage.com), 885 21st St. and the bay, and at **Avalon Bay Park** (609-967-8200), Ocean Dr. and 54th St.

In Stone Harbor, the **Stone Harbor Municipal Marina** (609-368-5102) on 81st St. has a boat ramp.

In *the Wildwoods,* there are public boat ramps at Leaming Ave. and the Boardwalk in *North Wildwood;* on Fifth St. in *Wildwood;* and in *Wildwood Crest* at Park Blvd. and Sweet Briar Rd., and at New Jersey Ave. and Orchid Rd. Visitors can launch boats from most marinas.

CANOEING AND KAYAKING **Bay Cats** (609-391-7960; www.baycats.com), 316 Bay Ave., Ocean City. Two-hour, morning, guided tours by kayak of Ocean City's tranquil back-bay channels and pristine Cowpen and Bird islands—the busy feeding and nesting grounds of egrets, ibis, and herons. Bay Cats also rents single-, double-, and three-person kayaks that you can launch on the bay or take to the ocean. Rentals include life jacket and paddle.

Harbor Outfitters (www.harboroutfitters.com) rents single and double kayaks and leads guided tours from two locations. *In Sea Isle City* (609-263-0805) from Pier 88, 88th Street and the bay; *in Stone Harbor* (609-368-5501) from 354 96th St.; and in *North Wildwood* at 501 Ocean Dr. (609-522-6568).

T I Kayaks (609-391-8700; www.tikayaks.com), 190 34th St., Ocean City rents kayaks by the hour, day, or week; they can be used either in the bay or in the waves.

FISHING There is no shortage of opportunities to fish along New Jersey's southern shore. Many shops rent equipment and sell bait and tackle, and a number of fishing tournaments are held up and down the coast from spring to fall. And best of all, no fishing license is required. You can rent a skiff and fish the back bays on the inland side of the barrier islands. These quiet waters are home to striped bass, flounder, bluefish, and weakfish, not to mention local blue claw crabs. For shore fishermen, a large number of piers, marinas, jetties, bridges, and beaches are open to anglers. The ocean holds sea bass and bluefish inshore, marlin, mahimahi, bluefish, tuna, shark, and a variety of other big species offshore. Charter boats and party boats can take you to them.

In Ocean City, fishing is permitted at Longport Beach, at the northern tip of the island and on the fishing jetty at Fifth St. and the Boardwalk. *In Sea Isle City,* there's a fishing pier on the bay at 59th St. and Sounds Ave. Corson Inlet State Park (609-861-2404) on Rt. 619 *in Strathmere* is known for its striped bass, weakfish, kingfish, and bluefish. A public fishing pier *in North Wildwood* is at the municipal parking lot at Inlet and Spruce Aves. There is excellent surf fishing *in Wildwood* from several town jetties.

From Ocean City to Wildwood Crest, numerous charter boats (smaller boats that take individual groups on private fishing trips) and party boats (larger vessels that take passengers on regularly scheduled offshore trips) are available on a first-come, first-served basis.

In Ocean City, **Rainbow III** (609-391-6446; www.rainbowdeepseafishing.com), 228 Bay Ave., offers both party and charter half-day fishing trips. The **Laura Marie III** (609-653-9164), Second St. and Bay Ave., offers half- and full-day charter trips.

In Sea Isle City, party boats include **Captain Robbins** (609-263-2020; www
.captainrobbins.com), Old Sea Isle Blvd.; **Starfish** (609-263-3800; www.starfish
boats.com), 42nd Pl. and the bay; and **Ursula** (609-263-9326), 42nd Pl. and the
bay. *In Avalon,* **Miss Avalon II** (609-967-7455; www.missavalon.com) is a 60-foot
party boat offering half-day fishing trips out of the Avalon Sport Fishing Center at
14th St. and Ocean Dr. from Apr.–Dec. *In Wildwood,* **Adventurer II** (609-729-
7777) leaves from Wildwood Marina Fishing Center on daytime and evening cruises for bluefish. The **Capt. Carlson** (609-522-0177; www.captcarlson.com), Rio
Grande Ave., offers charter trips from June–Sept. *In Wildwood Crest,* party fishing
boats include **Royal Flush Sport Fishing** (609-522-1395), 6100 Park Blvd., which
leads three trips daily; and the **Starlight Fleet** (609-729-7776 www.jjcboats.com),
6200 Park Blvd., which offers half- and full-day fishing, depending on the season.

GOLF If you're planning to take a golf vacation along the southern shore, the
Greater Atlantic City Golf Association (800-465-3222; www.acgolfvacations
.com) can help arrange hotel and golf packages, and can book tee times. For other
golf courses in the region, see "The Atlantic City Region" and "The Cape May
Peninsula" in this region, and "The Pinelands Region" in "Central New Jersey."

Ocean City Golf Course (609-399-1315), 2600 Bay Ave. at 26th St., Ocean City.
This bayside 12-hole course may not challenge the pros, but it's ideal for novice
and intermediate players. A series of golf tournaments is held here during the
summer.

Shore Gate Golf Course (609-624-8337; www.shoregategolfclub.com), 35
Schoolhouse Lane, Ocean View. *Golf Magazine* rated Shore Gate one of the top 10
new daily-fee golf courses in the country.

NATURE WALKS Corson's Inlet State Park (609-861-2404), Ocean Dr. (Rt. 619), Ocean City. Guided nature walks July–Aug. Call for schedule. Adults $1; children 50 cents. Volunteers with the park's Beachwalk program lead fact-filled hour-long tours along the paths that cut through the dunes to the beach. Guides specialize in various areas, from marine life to beach ecology.

PARASAILING Atlantic Parasail (609-522-1869; www.atlanticparasail.com), 1025 Ocean Dr., Wildwood Crest. Reservations are required. No experience is needed to soar 500 feet above the ocean, just a healthy dose of courage. They also operate trips in Sea Isle City at **Sea Isle Parasail** (609-263-5555; www.seaisleparasail.com) at Sunset Pier on 86th St. and the bay.

⚓ BEACHCOMBER WALKS (609-263-9643), on the 29th St. and 94th St. beaches in Sea Isle City. Guided walks are held from mid-June–Aug., Tues. and Thurs. at 10 AM. The hour-long Treasure Hunt walks, sponsored by the Sea Isle City Environmental Commission, cover a variety of marine environmental issues, including the plight of local endangered diamondback terrapins. As you look for beach treasure, learn interesting facts about seashells, dunes, plants, birds, and the ocean. A fun and educational family activity.

SCENIC DRIVE **Ocean Drive** This famous 40-mile-long scenic seashore route, which follows Rt. 619 and stretches from Atlantic City at the northern tip of Absecon Island all the way to Cape May Point, is the Jersey Shore at its finest. Along the way you'll cross six toll bridges, maintained by the Cape May Bridge Commission, that link a string of barrier islands and more than a dozen seaside communities. This is a pristine region of marshy lowland, back bays, and tidal inlets—and seaside amusement resorts—with the Atlantic Ocean providing a spectacular backdrop. The route, marked with Follow the Gull signs, enters this region from Absecon Island on the Ocean City–Longport Bridge that crosses Great Egg Harbor Inlet, passes through Ocean City and Corson's Inlet State Park, crosses another bridge over Corson's Inlet and passes through Strathmere and Sea Isle City before taking the Townsend's Inlet Bridge to pass through Avalon and Stone Harbor on Seven Mile Beach. From there you'll cross Hereford Inlet on the Grassy Sound Bridge to Five Mile Beach, where the Wildwoods are located. South of Wildwood Crest, the Middle Thorofare Bridge crosses Cape May Inlet into the Victorian seaside resort at the tip of the Cape May peninsula.

SURFING *In Ocean City,* surfing is permitted at Seventh St. and the boardwalk. Surfing beaches *in Sea Isle City* are at 33rd, 42nd, 48th, 52nd, 63rd, and 74th Sts. *In Avalon,* surfing is allowed on 30th St. between 10th and 11th Sts. Nun's Beach at 114th St. *in Stone Harbor* is a popular spot that offers some of the best surfing conditions on the southern shore. Surfing is allowed *in North Wildwood* between 8th and 10th Aves.; *in Wildwood* on Diamond Beach; and in *Wildwood Crest* at Rambler Rd.

It's always a good idea to call a local surf shop for a wave report before you head to the water. Shops along the southern shore include **7th Street Surf Shop** at 654 Boardwalk (609-391-1700; www.7thstreetsurfshop.com) and at 654 Asbury Ave. (609-398-7070), Ocean City; **Surfers Supplies** (609-399-8399; www.surfers supplies.com), 3101 Asbury Ave., Ocean City; **Heritage Surf and Sport** (609-263-3033; www.heritagesurf.com), 3700 Landis Ave., Sea Isle City or 744 West Ave., Ocean City (609-398-6390; **Wetsuit World** (609-368-1500; www.wetsuitworld .com), 9716 Third Ave., Stone Harbor; **Suncatcher** (609-368-3488; www.suncatcher surf.com), 9425 Second Ave., Stone Harbor; **Sand Jamm Beach and Surf Company** (609-522-4650; www.sandjamm.com), 2701 Boardwalk, Wildwood; **Wild Ocean Surf Shop** (609-729-0004), 5011 Ocean Ave., Wildwood; and **Ocean Outfitters** (609-729-7400; www.newjerseysurfcamps.com), 6101 New Jersey Ave., Wildwood Crest.

SWIMMING (See *Green Space—Beaches* for a list of public beaches along the Atlantic Ocean that allow swimming.)

✳ Green Space

BEACHES With the exception of the Wildwoods—where beaches are free—a beach badge, or tag, is required. Prices vary from town to town, but in *Ocean City* (609-399-1412; 800-232-2465; www.oceancityvacation.com), *Strathmere* (609-263-1151), *Sea Isle City* (609-263-1771; 1-866-546-4466), *Avalon* (609-967-3936), and *Stone Harbor* (609-368-5102), expect to pay around $5 for a day badge, $8–10 for a weekly pass, and between $15 and $20 for a season badge. In Sea Isle City, beach tags are not required on Wednesday. The tags can be purchased at various locations around town, including information centers, municipal halls, and locations right on the beach (and many lodging establishments offer complimentary beach tags to their guests). Most of the beaches allow fishing, rafting, and surfing; some have tennis courts, beach volleyball, and picnic areas, and allow beach buggies on the sand, with a permit.

In *North Wildwood* (609-729-8686), *Wildwood* (609-729-4000; 888-729-0033; www.gwcoc.com), and *Wildwood Crest* (609-522-0221) lifeguards are on duty from Memorial Day to Labor Day from 10–5. At the beach's widest point, it's a half-mile trek from the boardwalk to the water. It's wise to bring sandals—the sand can get sizzling-hot. Alcohol, glass containers, and barbecues are not permitted; leashed pets are allowed on Wildwood's beaches from October to May.

In Ocean City and Sea Isle City, the beach gets packed, especially on summer weekends and holidays. Families with young children appreciate the gentle waves and gradual slope into the water. Ocean City's best family beach is at 34th St. The least-crowded beaches are in Avalon and Stone Harbor. Wildwood's beaches are the widest, with unbelievably fine soft white sand. North Wildwood's beaches are especially family-friendly—all of them have playgrounds. Beachcombers know that Wildwood Crest's southernmost beach is a great spot to find shells.

NATURAL AREAS **The Wetlands Institute and Museum** (609-368-1211; www.wetlandsinstitute.org), 1075 Stone Harbor Blvd., Stone Harbor. Open mid-May–mid-Oct., Mon.–Sat. 9:30–4:30; Tues.–Thurs. until 8, mid-June–Labor Day; Sun. 10–4. From mid-Oct.–mid-May, open Tues.–Sat. 9:30–4:30; closed Sun.–Mon. Adults $7; children 2–11, $5; children under 2, free. An education and research center surrounded by a spectacular living laboratory—a pristine 6,000-acre tract of coastal marshland that forms a natural buffer between the mainland and the narrow barrier islands along the Atlantic Ocean. The salt marshes and tidal creeks that spread out beneath the causeway coming into Stone Harbor are prime spots for birding—there's a boardwalk trail and an observation pier in the salt marsh—and the nonprofit facility has educational exhibits and special programs (see sidebar, page 490; also *To See—Museums*).

Stone Harbor Bird Sanctuary (609-368-5102; www.stone-harbor.nj.us), 114th St. and Third Ave., Stone Harbor. Ornithologists and animal lovers flock to this scenic 21-acre wildlife refuge at the southern end of town that is home to hundreds of species of shorebirds (see *To Do—Birding*). It's the only municipal heronry in the country, one of only two such facilities in the world (the other is in a small Japanese town on the outskirts of Tokyo), and a federally designated national landmark. Thousands of nesting herons have been recorded here since the sanctuary was established in 1947. From the observatory at 114th St. and Third Ave., you're likely to catch a glimpse of glossy ibis, green herons, Louisiana herons, cattle egrets, snowy egrets, and many other species.

STATE PARK **Corson's Inlet State Park** (609-861-2404), Rt. 619 (Ocean Dr.), Ocean City. Open daily, dawn to dusk. This virtually undeveloped 341-acre state park has no visitors center or campground, just spectacular coastal wetlands and a pristine stretch of beach and sand dunes, one of the few such landscapes remaining along the coast between Atlantic City and Cape May. The **Strathmere Natural Area** occupies a thin strip of barrier island and protects close to 100 acres of beach and sand dunes, an important nesting site for endangered piping plovers (see *To Do—Birding*). The park is home to hundreds of wildlife species, and a haven for resident and migrating birds. The public boat launch is used by paddlers, anglers, crabbers, and boaters on Jet Skis, sailboards, and motorboats. Scenic nature trails lead through the sand dunes to the beach, and a popular series of beach walks takes place during the summer (see *To Do—Nature Walks*).

✳ Lodging

It's strongly advised to have lodging reservations before visiting this area, especially in the summer. But if you happen to be in Ocean City without a place to stay, stop at the information center on the Ninth Street causeway just before entering town. It's staffed by the **Ocean City Regional Chamber of Commerce** (609-399-1412; 800-232-2465; www.oceancityvacation .com) and has an automated phone line that enables you to check for last-minute availability in hotels, motels, apartments, guesthouses, and bed & breakfasts. **The Greater Wildwood Hotel and Motel Association** (609-522-4546; 800-786-4546; www.wild woods.org), 1 S. State Hwy. 47, Wildwood 08260, will send, on request, a copy of its visitor's guide, which includes a listing of accommodations. The **Greater Wildwood Chamber of Commerce** (609-729-4000; 888-729-0033; www.gwcoc.com), 3306 Pacific Ave., Wildwood (mailing address: P.O. Box 823, Wildwood 08260), publishes an accommodations directory. The options below are only some of the multitude of places to stay, especially in Ocean City and the Wildwoods. **Wildwood Reservations** (800-729-7778; www.stayinwildwood.com) is a free reservation service for hotels, motels, bed & breakfasts, and guesthouses in the Wildwoods. In Wildwood, Ocean and Atlantic Aves are packed with motels.

Contact local chambers of commerce for information on renting a house, cottage, or condo. Internet sites have information on long-term lodging options, with links to local chambers of commerce and rental agencies. Make your plans as early as possible; the best places get booked quickly. Sometimes discounts are offered on properties if a particular week remains vacant.

RESORTS

In Avalon 08202

✐ ᵴ "ᵀ" **Golden Inn Hotel and Resort** (609-368-5155; www.golden inn.com), oceanfront at 78th St. Open year-round. An elegant oceanfront resort with 154 tastefully decorated guest rooms, efficiencies, studios, and one-bedroom suites. Wi-Fi available in the conference center. Guests can relax by the beautifully landscaped outdoor pool or on the beach (beach tags are complimentary). Daily planned activities, airport transportation, and babysitting and laundry services are available. The Dining Room features an upscale seasonally changing menu of seafood and American cuisine; Luigi's Pasta and Vino serves Italian regional specialties in a casual setting overlooking Avalon's spectacular sand dunes, and light meals and cocktails are served poolside in-season. A variety of live entertainment is scheduled from spring to fall. Rooms and efficiencies $99–395; studios and suites $325–495.

In Wildwood 08260

✐ ᵴ **Bolero Resort and Conference Center** (609-522-6929; www.bolero resort.com), 3320 Atlantic Ave., Wildwood 08260. Open year-round.

A resort with motel-style rooms and spacious suites and efficiencies, and a state-of-the-art fitness center in an airy atrium with a pool, whirlpool tubs, and a panoramic view of the ocean. An attractive restaurant serves three meals, while the martini lounge has live music on Fri. and Sat. nights and a light menu served until midnight. Rooms and suites are clean, comfortable, and equipped with standard amenities; luxury suites are upgraded with a Jacuzzi and steam bath. Rooms $77–175; suites $98–188.

In Wildwood Crest 08260

❧ Aqua Beach Resort and Beachcrest Condominiums (609-522-6507; 800-247-4776; www.aqua beach.com), 5501 Ocean Ave. Open April–mid-Oct. An oceanfront resort with 132 guest rooms and suites spread across two buildings, on the beach and a block from the boardwalk. Aqua Beach Resort's rooms are simple and comfortably furnished. The Beachcrest Condominiums feature bright, spacious, fully equipped condos and suites with attractive furnishings, and up to four bedrooms. Largo Suites are new for 2009 and done in a Caribbean theme. The sixth-floor penthouse suites boast upscale décor, four bedrooms and bathrooms, lofty 9-foot ceilings, a spa tub, a large-screen TV, and a fully equipped and stocked kitchen. All guests have access to two outdoor heated pools, a poolside Jacuzzi, gas grills, and a rooftop sundeck. For kids, there's a game room, planned summertime activities, and a heated baby pool. The beachfront café serves breakfast and lunch. Rooms $48–252; suites $146–770; inquire about rates for the penthouse suites.

❧ ᵭ ❦ El Coronado (609-729-1000; 800-227-5302; www.elcoronado.com), 8501 Atlantic Ave. (at E. Preston Ave.). Open May–mid-Oct. A beachfront resort with large, nicely furnished rooms, a friendly staff, and spectacular views of the Atlantic Ocean. Rooms and efficiencies were all updated in 2008, and have refrigerators, microwaves, TVs, and ocean views from the private balconies; two- and three-bedroom suites also have a full kitchen. Wi-Fi access in the lobby. The brick sundeck has heated pools and a poolside Jacuzzi tub. Other amenities include a gift shop, a beach volleyball area, barbecue grills, free in-room movies, and a casual café with an outdoor patio. During the summer, there is plenty for kids to do, from daily planned activities to a kiddie pool and game room. Rooms $58–225; efficiencies $88–220; suites $98–450.

HOTELS

In Ocean City 08226

❧ ᵭ ❦ Flanders Hotel (609-399-1000; 800-866-624-6835; www.the flandershotel.com), 719 E. 11th St. This Spanish mission–style hotel was one of the top luxury spots on the southern shore when it opened in 1923, hosting the likes of Grace Kelly, Jimmy Stewart, and other luminaries. Today the hotel, with its distinctive red-tile roof, is a beloved Ocean City gem on the boardwalk. The lovely antiques-filled lobby is reminiscent of 1930s and '40s Jersey shore grand hotels. Renovations transformed the rooms into spacious two- to five-room suites with kitchens, dining areas, Wi-Fi, and elegant décor; some have views of the bay or the ocean. There's an outdoor heated pool and sundeck, and complimentary beach tags. The hotel is named for Belgium's Flanders Field, where American soldiers were buried in World War I. Ask about Emily, "the Lady in White"—a ghost who is rumored to wander the halls. An image of Emily in a portrait on the second floor is based on descriptions by hotel workers and guests. $149–960.

✐ ⁗⁗ **Beach Club Hotel** (609-399-8555; www.ocbeachclub.com), 1280 Boardwalk, P.O. Box 929. Open May–mid-Oct. An oceanfront hotel on the boardwalk, ideal for families and anyone looking for a convenient location. The heated oceanfront pool is surrounded by a sundeck filled with lounge chairs. Rooms are clean and nicely decorated, with amenities like refrigerators, Wi-Fi, cable TV, and private balconies. The **Café Beach Club** serves breakfast, lunch, and dinner in an oceanfront dining room and outside on the patio. Complimentary morning coffee. $91–346.

✤ ⁗⁗ **Watson's Regency Suites** (609-398-4300; 888-397-4673; www.watsonsregency.com), 901 Ocean Ave. Open year-round. The 79 spacious and tastefully decorated one-bedroom suites have full kitchens, living and dining areas, Wi-Fi, cable TV with VCR, wireless Internet access, and private balconies. An indoor pool and hot tub reside in a bright and airy glass-enclosed atrium. The beach is close by, and beach tags are complimentary. $109–309.

In Avalon 08202

✐ ✤ **Windrift Hotel** (609-368-5175; 800-453-7438; www.windrifthotel.com), 80th St. and the beach. Open mid-March–Nov. A variety of accommodations, from motel-style rooms and efficiencies with kitchenettes to condominiums with kitchens, dining areas, and up to four bedrooms. Outside, there's a heated pool, a kiddie pool, and a sundeck overlooking the ocean. A casual restaurant serves three meals daily, brunch on Sun., and has a raw bar. There's nightly live music and DJs all summer, as well as a piano bar and a lounge. Rooms and efficiencies from $94; condominiums from $245; some accommodations available only weekly during high season.

✤ ⁗⁗ **Desert Sand Resort** (609-368-5133; reservations: 800-458-6008; www.desertsand.com), 7888 Dune Dr. A 91-room hotel a block from the beach. Accommodations are clean and comfortably furnished, ranging from small motel-style rooms with one bed to spacious three-bedroom suites with fully equipped kitchens, all with Internet access. The **Mirage** restaurant serves contemporary cuisine at breakfast and dinner. The health club has sun beds and an indoor pool; outside there's a heated pool, kiddie pool, patio, and sundeck. Bike rentals and complimentary beach tags. Rooms $77–234; efficiencies and suites $118–429.

✐ ✤ ⁗⁗ **Concord Suites** (609-368-7800; reservations: 800-443-8202; www.concordsuites.com), 7800 Dune Dr. Open May–mid-Oct. The Concord is Avalon's only all-suite hotel; each unit has a bedroom, living room, kitchenette, and free wireless Internet. Outside, sundecks surround two pools. The hotel's casual and friendly restaurant serves pizza and pub fare. The beach is one block away; guests receive complimentary beach tags. $89–216.

In the Wildwood Crest 08260

✐ ✤ **Pan American Hotel** (609-522-6936; www.panamericanhotel.com), 5901 Ocean Ave. Open May–mid-Oct. A family-friendly hotel on the beach offering rooms and one-bedroom efficiencies with private balconies, air-conditioning, and TV. A uniquely designed circular pool and adjacent kiddie pool, and an elevated sundeck overlook the ocean. There's a full schedule of supervised children's activities during the summer. Alosi's Bistro is a casual BYOB eatery that serves three meals daily. Rooms $93–247; efficiencies $124–319.

✐ ✤ **Bal Harbour Hotel** (609-522-3343; www.balharbourhotels.com), 508 E. Stanton Rd. Open Apr.–Oct.

&. THE STARLUX

(609-522-7412; www.thestarlux.com), 305 East Rio Grande Ave., Wildwood 08260. Open year-round. This stylish boutique hotel is a neon-and-glass homage to Wildwood's glory days of doo-wop, complete with plastic palm trees, 1950s décor, and a kidney-shaped pool. The 20 guest rooms, 16 suites, and cottage—some with kitchenettes and private balconies—are individually furnished in bold geometric prints, pastels, and other retro touches. For the ultimate '50s flashback, stay in one of the **authentic silver Airstream trailers,** each fully restored with a living area, wet bar, double bed, and sofa bed. The all-glass and convex-shaped lobby and **Astro Lounge** feature a coffee bar, games, and a fireplace. Exercise room, guest laundry facilities, heated outdoor pool, and whirlpool tub. A block from the beach and boardwalk. $69–325.

WILDWOOD'S STARLUX BOUTIQUE HOTEL IS PART OF THE REVIVAL OF THE RESORT'S RETRO DOO-WOP ARCHITECTURE, COMPLETE WITH COLORFUL NEON, ALL-GLASS LOUNGE, AND PLASTIC PALM TREES.

Photo courtesy of the Mid-Atlantic Center for the Arts

A sprawling family resort that occupies a full block along the beach. A wide range of rooms, suites, and efficiencies—accommodating up to six people—spread across six floors; some with kitchenettes, private balconies, and lovely views of the pool or the ocean. Guests have use of four pools and an expansive sundeck. Restaurant, gift shop, and video arcade. $86–398.

♂ &. **Port Royal Hotel** (609-729-2000; www.portroyalhotel.com), 6801 Ocean Ave. Open May–mid-Oct. A beachfront hotel on a beautiful stretch of sand in Wildwood Crest that gets many repeat customers, especially families. Rooms are simple and clean, and have ocean views, refrigerators, air-conditioning, and TV with VCR. Efficiencies and suites are spacious, face the ocean, and boast upgraded amenities like kitchenettes and private balconies. The heated hourglass-shaped pool and snack bar are surrounded by a sundeck with enough lounge chairs to handle a crowd. There is a pool, a game room, and supervised planned activities just for the kids. The **Royal Grille Café** (609-729-2211) has a 1950s doo-wop theme and serves breakfast, lunch, and dinner. Rooms $102–247; efficiencies and suites $142–325.

Elsewhere

⁰T⁰ **Colonnade Inn** (609-263-8868; www.thecolonnadeinn.com), 4600 Landis Ave., Sea Isle City 08243. Open year-round. This 19th-century seaside property, formerly a B&B, is now a full-amenity modern hotel with one- to three-bedroom units and efficiencies. The suites boast fireplaces, kitchens, cable TV, Wi-Fi, and Jacuzzi tubs. Guests like to congregate on the wraparound porch, in the garden, and in the Victorian parlor. Continental breakfast. $109–290.

BED & BREAKFASTS

In Ocean City 08226

Atlantis Inn Seaside Bed & Breakfast (609-399-9871; www.atlantis inn.com), 601 Atlantic Ave. Open year-round. A luxurious B&B in the former Croft Hall Hotel, a grand Victorian built in 1905 by the Reverend James Lake, one of Ocean City's founding fathers. Today, under innkeepers Bob and Kristina Doliszny, it's a high-style B&B a block from the beach and boardwalk. The common areas are bright and elegant; guests can relax in front of the fireplace in the cozy sitting room, in a wicker rocking chair on the veranda, or on the magnificent mahogany roof deck with lovely views of the ocean. Ten guest suites and two villa-style apartments are tastefully

decorated with ornately carved 18th- and 19th-century reproduction furnishings and rich imported fabrics. All have a private bath and amenities that might include a working fireplace, whirlpool tub, spa shower, sitting room, or private entrance to the roof deck. The Bordeaux Suite has a whirlpool tub, spa shower, and a king sleigh bed; the Fiorenza Suite has a lovely marble working fireplace; the Biarritz Suite occupies one of the bay-facing tower turrets; and the Barcelona is the only two-room suite. Two beautifully furnished apartments have full kitchens, sitting areas, screened-in porches, and private entrances. They're available by the week during the summer and on a daily basis in the off-season. A full gourmet breakfast and afternoon tea are served in the dining room or on the veranda. Suites $175–475; apartments $265–575.

⁰T⁰ **Ocean City Mansion Bed & Breakfast** (609-399-8383; www.oc mansion.com), 416 Central Ave. Open year-round. Innkeeper Nancy Aiken's extensively renovated 1896 mansion combines elegant historic touches with modern comforts. The seven guest suites, two apartments, and a three-bedroom condo are individually decorated with lavish touches, which might mean a crystal chandelier in one room, a canopy bed in another. All suites have TVs, Wi-Fi, private baths, Internet access, and air-conditioning; some have upgraded amenities like towel warmers, fireplaces, Jacuzzi tubs, balconies, and private entrances. Two rooms and the apartments are dog-friendly. Complimentary beach tags. Full gourmet breakfast. $251–521.

✐ ⁰T⁰ **Plymouth Inn** (609-398-8615; www.plymouthinn.com), 710 Atlantic Ave. An authentically restored 1898 Victorian, a block from the boardwalk and beach. Common areas and guest rooms present gracious details, from hand-carved fireplaces to vintage furnishings. Guest rooms and family suites have private bath, air-conditioning, wireless Internet and cable TV, and include complimentary beach tags. A continental breakfast of freshly baked muffins, cobbler, and fruit might also feature belgian waffles, French toast, or blueberry pancakes. $119–159.

✿ **Scarborough Inn** (609-399-1558; 800-258-1558; www.scarboroughinn .com), 720 Ocean Ave. Open May–Oct. A 19th-century European-style inn tucked behind a charming white picket fence and flower garden. It's in the center of town and just a short walk from the beach and boardwalk. Innkeepers Gus and Carol Bruno offer 24 guest rooms and suites, all with private bath, air-conditioning, TV, and other amenities. The standard suites have DVD/VCR players; the king suites have plush robes. Some of the rooms can be connected, an arrangement that suits families and couples traveling together. There's also a one-bedroom apartment that rents by the week. Guests can relax on the wraparound porch, or inside in the living room, the library, or the card room, made cozy with family photos, mementos, and homey furnishings. Complimentary extras include beach tags, afternoon refreshments, and a full gourmet breakfast. $110–255.

Brown's Nostalgia (609-398-6364; 866-223-0400; www.brownsnostalgia .com), 1001 Wesley Ave. The charming 1900 B&B sits in the center of town, close to the boardwalk and beach, where you can use your complimentary beach tag and bikes. The eight guest rooms and one apartment are quaint and cozy; all have a private bath and air-conditioning; some have a private deck, fireplace, or Jacuzzi tub. The two-bedroom apartment sleeps six and is available by the week. Guests are welcome to the roomy hot tub, table games, and exercise equipment in the game room, and the rockers on the wraparound porch. Full breakfast. Rooms $117–185; apartment $900–1,400 weekly.

ⓘ **Northwood Inn Bed & Breakfast** (609-399-6071; www.northwood inn.com), 401 Wesley Ave. Open year-round. A lovely many-gabled Victorian that has won numerous awards for historic preservation and community beautification. The 1894 Queen Anne–style mansion resides in Ocean City's historic district, and was one of the first homes to be built in this 19th-century resort town. Innkeepers Marj and John Loeper completed a total restoration in 1990. Their painstaking efforts are evident in the well-preserved details throughout their elegant inn, from the gleaming hardwood floors to the grand sweeping staircase. The five rooms have air-conditioning and TVs with VCRs and wireless Internet access; in addition, the two suites are outfitted with Jacuzzis. Rockers line the circular wraparound porch, and the rooftop whirlpool spa is a lovely spot at sunset and later on under the stars. Inside, guests have full use of the library, video collection, and pool table. The boardwalk and beach are within walking distance (three blocks), but you can also borrow a bike to get there faster. The Loepers provide their guests with beach tags, and will make dinner reservations if you need them. Continental breakfast is served during the week; on weekends, a full breakfast. $130–305.

In North Wildwood 08260
ⓘ **Candlelight Inn** (609-522-6200; 800-992-2632; www.candlelight-inn .com), 2310 Central Ave. Open year-round. Innkeepers Bill and Nancy Moncrief's beautifully restored red-roofed 1905 Queen Anne Victorian

offers seven lovely guest rooms and three suites (two suites are in an adjacent carriage house) filled with period antiques and unique décor. All have private bath, TV, Wi-Fi, and air-conditioning; some suites boast fireplaces and whirlpool tubs for two. The fresh flowers, chocolates, and sherry in each room are nice touches. Guests can laze in a hammock or claim a rocker or swing on the wraparound front porch, or relax in the antiques-filled parlor; the hot tub on the backyard sundeck is another option. Close to beaches, shops, and restaurants. Afternoon refreshments and a full breakfast are included. Rooms $115–185; suites $115–265.

&. "I" **Summer Nites** (609-846-1955; 866-762-1950; www.summernites .com), 2110 Atlantic Ave. Open year-round. Rick and Sheila Brown's cheerful B&B—a few blocks from the beach and boardwalk—sports a nostalgic and fun 1950s atmosphere. Each of the five guest rooms and two suites is decorated with a unique theme—Elvis, Marilyn Monroe, the beach, and movies, television, and music from the early rock 'n' roll era—and vintage furnishings. All rooms have newly tiled private baths, TV with DVD/VCR, Wi-Fi, and air-conditioning; some also have a Jacuzzi tub. There's wireless Internet access, a hot tub, a billiards room, and bikes for guests to use. A full breakfast is served in a '50s diner, complete with vintage jukebox and vinyl booths. $105–275.

In Wildwood 08260

The Sea Gypsy Bed & Breakfast (609-522-0690; www.theseagypsy.com), 209 E. Magnolia Ave. Open year-round. A handsomely restored 1900 Queen Anne Victorian, complete with gables, fanciful architecture, and wraparound porch a few blocks from beach and boardwalk. The four individually decorated guest rooms, one suite, and

a cottage have private baths and well-chosen antiques; some have original artwork and handmade quilts. The charming two-bedroom cottage is ideal for families and others wishing for privacy. Guests can help themselves to the candy, cookies, popcorn, and other treats in the old-fashioned candy cupboard. A full breakfast with homemade baked goods is served in the dining room or on the veranda. $100–185; cottage $1,000 weekly.

Elsewhere

Sea Lark Bed & Breakfast (609-967-5647; www.sealark.com), 3018 First Ave., Avalon 08202. Open year-round. Innkeepers Patricia Ellis and John Oldham run this B&B. A block from the beach and boardwalk, it feels like a family beach house. The lovely Victorian was built in 1891 and was a guesthouse in the 1940s. Light and airy rooms are furnished with antiques and family heirlooms; hardwood floors are covered in Oriental rugs. Guests have full use of the living room with TV and video library, and the screened-in wraparound veranda. Six guest rooms—four with private bath—and two lofts are cozy and simply furnished. Some of the guest rooms have separate sitting areas and ocean views. The two lofts have kitchenettes and share a private deck; the third-floor Artist's Loft is decorated with the work of local artists; and the Lighthouse Loft faces the ocean and has a separate bedroom. A full breakfast buffet with homemade hot entrées is served on the veranda in summer, and by the parlor fireplace in cooler weather. $50–260.

✎ **Risley House Bed & Breakfast** (609-368-1133; www.risleyhouse.net), 8421 First Ave., Stone Harbor 08247. Open mid-May–late Sept. Reese Risley, who founded Stone Harbor along with his two brothers, built this historic Victorian in the early 1900s. Today it's

a cozy bed & breakfast offering 11 guest rooms. Afternoon refreshments and continental breakfast featuring home-baked goods are included. $85–245.

MOTELS

In Stone Harbor 08247-0306

⚓ "1" **The Lark Motel** (609-368-2500; www.larkmotel.com), 9800 Second Ave. Open Apr.–Oct. A family-owned and family-operated motel close to beaches and Stone Harbor's shop-filled downtown. Two-room units and efficiencies have private bath, air-conditioning, cable TV, Internet access, microwaves, and refrigerators. The heated pool is surrounded by a sun-deck with a gas grill. Complimentary beach tags. $45–170.

In Wildwood 08260

⚓ **Eden Roc Motel** (609-770-1484; 888-373-1930; www.edenrocmotel .com), 5201 Atlantic Ave. Open Apr.–Sept. This renovated vintage motel built in 1958 is a family-friendly establishment across from the board-walk, amusement piers, and water parks. Standard rooms and efficiency units are clean and simply furnished; all have air-conditioning, cable TV, refrigerators, and microwaves. There's a heated pool, a gas grill, and shuffle-board. $65–114.

In Wildwood Crest 08260

⚓ ♿ **Coliseum Ocean Resort Motel** (609-729-4444; 866-752-3224; www .coliseumoceanresort.com), 416 East Miami Ave. Open May–Sept. A new beachfront family resort with cozy and nicely furnished efficiency rooms and suites. Amenities include an ocean-front pool and sundeck, a patio with barbecue grills, and outdoor showers and changing rooms. $59–179; three-night minimum stays on holidays.

⚓ ♿ "1" **Lotus Inn** (609-522-6300; reservations: 800-822-6306; www .lotusinn.com), 6900 Ocean Ave. Open May–mid-Oct. A family-style motel next to the beach, boardwalk, and bike path. Accommodations range from simple motel-style rooms to two-level town houses with three bedrooms and private oceanfront balconies; all have a refrigerator, microwave, free in-room movies, and a complimentary daily newspaper. Outside there's a heated pool, kiddie pool, oceanfront sun-deck, and patio, where there are complimentary hot dog barbecue parties during the summer. Free Wi-Fi in the activities room and pool area. Discounted passes to Wildwood's amusement piers and water parks are available. Rates include continental breakfast. Rooms $59–175; efficiencies $64–232; town houses $110–455.

⚓ **Bel-Air Motel** (609-522-4235; reservations: 800-528-7991; www .belairmotel.net), 5510 Ocean Ave. Open May–mid-Oct. A family-owned and family-operated motel whose thatched-roofed gazebos, palm trees, and wooden shutters give the surroundings a tropical feel. Outside is a heated pool with poolside picnic tables and grills. All first-floor rooms are poolside, and each second-floor room has a view of the pool from above. Rooms, suites, and efficiencies all have a refrigerator, cable TV, air-conditioning, and a microwave; some rooms boast a view of the ocean. Within walking distance to amusement piers, restaurants, and shops—the boardwalk and beach are a short block away. $59–190.

CAMPGROUNDS The campgrounds closest to the shoreline resort towns are a few miles inland; many are along Rt. 9. All the facilities listed below provide sewer, water, and electric hookups as well as the usual campground amenities. Look under *Lodging—Campgrounds* in "The Cape May Peninsula" in this region, and in "The Pinelands Region" in "Central New Jersey," for other nearby camping options.

In Marmora 08223

🐾 ⚲ "📍" **Whippoorwill Campground** (609-390-3458; 800-424-8275; www.campwhippoorwill.com), 810 S. Shore Rd. (Rt. 9). Open Apr.–Oct. Whippoorwill offers 288 wooded sites for tents and RVs on 28 acres, three miles from the Ocean City beaches. Rental cabins with screened porches, TV, microwave, refrigerator are available, limited Wi-Fi access, plus fully equipped trailers. An Olympic-sized pool, a kiddie pool, a playground and volleyball and tennis courts. Activities and games for kids, tennis tournaments, bingo, festivals, and other activities. Sites $52; cabins $92; trailers $145.

In Clermont 08210

🐾 ⚲ "📍" **Avalon Campground** (609-624-0075; reservations 800-814-2267; www.avaloncampground.com), 1917 Rt. 9 N. Open mid-Apr.–Sept. Avalon has 360 sites on 85 wooded acres. One- and two-bedroom log cabin and three-bedroom trailer rentals; planned activities as well as special weekend events. Two outdoor pools, mini golf, a playground, volleyball, game courts, Wi-Fi access, and a game room. Sites $36–54; cabins $55–90; trailers $1,025 weekly.

🐾 ⚲ **Hidden Acres Campground** (609-624-9015; 800-874-7576), 1142 Rt. 83. Open mid-Apr.–mid-Oct. A family campground with 200 sites on 50 acres. The spring-fed freshwater swimming lake has a pleasant sandy beach. Mini golf, playgrounds, shuffleboards, and a game room. Sites $31–35; cabins $50–65.

⚲ **Frontier Campground** (609-390-3649; reservations: 800-277-4109; www.frontiercampground.com), 84 Tyler Rd. (Rt. 50). Open mid-Apr.–early Oct. Tent and RV sites in a quiet, wooded setting about 10 minutes from the Ocean City and Sea Isle City beaches. For a unique experience, stay in one of their secluded tree houses. Game room, camp store, playground, fishing and crabbing. Pets not permitted. Sites $35–45; tree houses $100.

🐾 ⚲ "📍" **Ocean View Resort Campground** (609-624-1675; www.ovresort.com), 2555 Rt. 9. (mailing address: P.O. Box 607). Open mid-Apr.–late Sept. This is billed as the state's largest campground, and with 1,173 sites on more than 180 wooded acres, it's so big that it features a tram car to shuttle people around. A freshwater spring-fed lake boasts a white-sand beach and paddleboats for rent; another pond is stocked for fishing. There's an Olympic-sized pool, a kiddie pool, game courts, mini golf, two arcades, and four playgrounds. Limited Wi-Fi access. A full schedule of family activities includes crafts shows, teen dances, and games for kids. Five minutes from the beach in Sea Isle City. An 18-hole golf course is next door (see *To Do—Golf*). Sites $39–77; cabins $69–125.

✳ Where to Eat

DINING OUT As a rule, the dining scene along this part of the southern shore isn't fancy. This is the land of the seafood house, the beach bar, and casual family-friendly joints whose patrons are looking for a no-frills satisfying meal after a day at the beach. Remember that Ocean City is a dry town, which means not only do restaurants not serve alcohol, but they also don't allow you to bring your own.

In Ocean City

The Culinary Garden (609-399-3713), 841 Central Ave. Open daily for breakfast, lunch, and dinner. The exterior of this eatery, painted a bold purple and blue, is a hint at the creative goings-on in the kitchen. It may be a little pricier than the usual Ocean City eatery, but it's among the few places in town to offer the kind of fine dining you usually have to go to Cape May for. It's a perennial favorite with friendly service and an inviting atmosphere; some regulars are known to eat here several times a week. People flock here in the morning for the gourmet breakfasts and the inventive seafood, chicken, and pasta dishes later on. $14–26.

In Marmora

⌁ ♿ **Tuckahoe Inn** (609-390-3322; www.tuckahoeinn.com), One Harbor Rd. (Rt. 9). Open daily for lunch and dinner in summer; Wed.–Sun., Jan.–Mar. This bayside tavern on Beesley's Point is a casual family-friendly eatery offering lovely views of the bay, a convivial bar, and well-prepared American standards with an emphasis on seafood (crabcakes are the house specialty). Diners love the outside tables for light meals and live music, in-season. $19–27.

In Strathmere

⌁ **Deauville Inn** (609-263-2080; www.deauvilleinn.com), 201 Willard Rd. Open daily May–Sept. for lunch, dinner, and late-night snacks. Closed Tues.–Wed., Oct.–Apr. Reservations are recommended. This restored shoreline inn is a local landmark at the foot of the Corson's Inlet Bridge, between Ocean City and Sea Isle City. The building's colorful history includes stints as a Prohibition-era speakeasy, a gambling casino, and a rum-running station; it even hosted former president Teddy Roosevelt when it was a hotel. Today locals and tourists come for the fresh seafood and lovely views of the back bays and Corson's Inlet, especially at sunset. Slips are available for diners who arrive by boat. An extensive menu of shore seafood standards is served in a casual and friendly setting, but there's also a list of pastas, steaks, and poultry. You can eat in the dining room, in the casual sports bar, or on the long outdoor deck. Live entertainment in the evening. $11–40.

In Sea Isle City

⌁ ♿ **Busch's Sea Food** (609-263-8626; www.buschsseafood.com), 8700 Anna Phillips Lane. Open May–Oct.; dinner Tues.–Sun.; closed Mon. A classic shore seafood restaurant that has resided at the southern tip of Sea Isle City since 1882, serving generous portions of classic down-home shore fare with an emphasis on local seafood. Five generations have run the kitchen. Just about everything is homemade, from the salad dressing to the soup. Don't miss their signature homemade onion rings, deviled crabs, crabcakes, and she-crab soup, of which more than 40 gallons a day are sold on Tuesday and Sunday only. The list of entrées is long and consists primarily of fish and shellfish. The sprawling restaurant seats more than 400 in a series of dining rooms; order takeout or come early for a quieter and quicker meal. $20–40.

Braca Café (609-263-4271; www.bracacafe.com), 18 41st St. (at Kennedy Blvd.). Open daily for lunch and dinner. The Braca family has been a prominent fixture in town since Lou and Madelena Braca opened a barbershop here in 1901. Since then, the family has run a café, a grocery store, and many other pursuits. Their friendly café is a beloved local landmark known for its generous portions of authentic Italian cuisine. The long list of pastas is complemented by dishes like veal parmigiana and broiled flounder. $17–30.

🍴 ♿ **Basilico's Ristorante** (609-263-1010), 27 43rd St. Open daily for lunch Mon.–Thurs.; lunch and dinner Fri.–Sun. A charming and casual Italian eatery that is very popular with vacationing families, who come for the delicious pizza and authentic Italian dishes after a day at the beach. Pasta, seafood, chicken, and steak dishes are well prepared and nicely presented. $16–25.

In Avalon
The Sea Grill (609-967-5511; www.seagrillrestaurant.com), 225 21st St. Open daily year-round for lunch and dinner. One of Avalon's top restaurants in a turn-of-the-20th-century building (formerly a garage) that has been beautifully converted into an open-air dining room. From a window at the kitchen, customers order their meals directly from the chef. A loyal following of regulars come for the friendly atmosphere and extensive menu of seafood, steaks (ordered by the ounce), grilled meats, and chops, not to mention the tempting list of homemade cakes and pies for dessert. Award-winning wine list. $19–50.

In Stone Harbor
Kuishimbo (609-967-7007), 330 96th St. In summer, open for dinner Wed.–Mon.; closed Tues. In spring and fall, open for dinner Sat.–Sun. Reservations are recommended. Traditional Japanese cuisine served in a peaceful, relaxed setting that's frequented by couples, families, and tourists. The sushi and sashimi are fresh and expertly prepared, but most patrons come for authentic Japanese dishes like tempura, grilled fish, and shellfish. Credit cards are not accepted. $14–30.

In North Wildwood
Claude's Restaurant (609-522-0400; www.claudesrestaurant.com), in Anglesea Village, 100 Olde New Jersey Ave. Open daily for dinner in summer; closed Tues.–Wed. in the off-season. Reservations are recommended. Classic French restaurants are a dime a dozen in northern New Jersey—not so on the southern shore. Claude's is an intimate bistro in a quaint yellow-clapboard building, where you can dine on bouillabaisse, coq au vin, and other French specialties. You'll forget you're in the Wildwoods. $23–35.

In Wildwood
♿ **Beach Creek Oyster Bar and Grille** (609-522-1062; www.beachcreek.net), 500 West Hand Ave. Open daily for dinner. Fine dining in lovely surroundings of stained-glass windows and gleaming hardwood floors. The menu changes regularly, but often includes signature dishes like strawberry barbecue salmon and grilled trout. Oysters make frequent appearances throughout the menu and at the raw bar, especially in appetizers like the classic oysters Rockefeller, or baked with andouille sausage and Brie. There's also a martini bar with an extensive wine list and live jazz on Fridays. $19–40.

🍴 **Café jonpaul** (609-729-4600; www.cafejonpaul.com), 2501 New Jersey Ave. Open daily in spring through early autumn for lunch and dinner. A 43-seat café where the emphasis is on healthy, meal-sized salads, soups, *paninis*, wraps and sandwiches, as well as sushi. Or, if you like, a PB&J from the kids' menu. $6–12.

In Wildwood Crest
Two Mile Landing (609-522-1341; www.twomilelanding.com), Ocean Dr., at the Cape May drawbridge. Open daily for lunch and dinner. Classic shore dishes served in a lovely water-

front setting next to Two Mile Marina. Starters are a traditional lineup of clams casino, steamed mussels, oysters Rockefeller, and fried calamari. Entrées include regional specialties, for example, a variety of seafood combinations and the Seafood Feast, a huge bouillabaisse. There's a short menu of steaks, chicken, and veal for landlubbers. The **Tiki Bar** offers a raw bar menu; the upstairs lounge is an ideal spot for watching sunsets over the back bays. $17–24.

Marie Nicole's (609-522-5425), 9510 Pacific Ave. Open daily in summer for lunch and dinner. In the off-season, dinner is served Wed.–Sun. Reservations are recommended. This intimate and romantic spot offers the caliber of elegant gourmet dining for which patrons usually must travel to Cape May. The inventive menu of fresh seafood and top-notch meats with Asian and Caribbean influences is enthusiastically hailed by restaurant critics and gourmands, including starters like duck spring rolls with Asian plum dipping sauce and organic greens, or quesadilla with freshly roasted lobster, spinach, caramelized onions, and mango guacamole. Move on to the lemongrass encrusted Ahi tuna or Chilean sea bass. Desserts are well worth saving room for. A menu of light meals, desserts, and coffee is available until midnight. Outdoor patio dining in-season. Extensive wine list. $21–35.

EATING OUT

In Ocean City

✐ **Brown's** (609-391-0677), St. Charles Pl. and the Boardwalk. Open daily in-season for breakfast and lunch. Everyone comes to Brown's for the homemade donuts, which are rated by locals and various New Jersey readers' polls among the best on the shore.

Watch as donuts roll hot off the press, then try to resist ordering a dozen. Harmon and Marjorie Brown also run a charming bed & breakfast in the center of town (see *Lodging—Bed & Breakfasts*).

🍴 ✐ **The Chatterbox** (609-399-0113), 500 Ninth St. (at Central Ave.). Open daily year-round for breakfast, lunch, and dinner. A local gathering spot since 1937 that vacationers love, too, especially if they have children in tow. The atmosphere is family-style and casual; the extensive menu of steaks, seafood, pasta, soups, sandwiches, and burgers has something to please everyone; and the prices will please those who are feeding a brood. During the summer, The Chatterbox stays open 'round the clock and offers a late-night menu of light meals. Some people come just for the old-fashioned ice cream sundaes and thick, frosty milkshakes. Portions are large and reasonably priced. $5–15.

In Sea Isle City

🚺 ✐ **Dock Mike's Pancake House** (609-263-3625; www.dockmikes.com), 4615 Landis Ave. Also in Cape May at 1231 Rt. 109. Open daily for breakfast and lunch. Mike's menu says "We have over 30 years experience in making pancakes and still love it!" It's a locals' favorite and great for kids. Pancakes, of course, and most other breakfast favorites, and burgers, etc., for lunch. $5–10. Cash Only.

Mike's Seafood Restaurant and Takeout (609-263-3458), 43rd St. and Park Rd. Open May–Oct., daily 10–10. Mike Monichetti's friendly and casual spot on the docks is very popular with locals. Pick from the delicious and fresh seafood on the menu or the blackboards (if it's not on the menu, just ask—they might be able to make it), order it yourself right from the kitchen, then bring it outside to a picnic table on the deck and watch the sunset over the bay. The raw bar has won local dining awards. BYOB. $9–25.

Vince's Restaurant (609-263-4567; www.vincesrestaurant.net), 25 JFK Blvd. Open daily for breakfast, lunch, and dinner. Dependable breakfast fare in the morning, with a few nice surprises thrown in—like an excellent omelet stuffed with asparagus and crabmeat—pasta, steak, and seafood later on. $19–41.

In North Wildwood

❡ **Cool Scoops Ice Cream Parlor** (609-729-2665; www.coolscoops.com), 1111 New Jersey Ave. Open mid-June–Labor Day, daily 2 PM–midnight; Sept.–mid-June, Fri.–Sun. 7–10 PM. A fun-filled chrome-and-neon 1950s-style diner serving up nostalgia along with old-fashioned sundaes, creamy malts, and soft-serve and hand-dipped cones. Grab a '57 Ford Fairlane or '59 Caddy car booth, watch oldies on the vintage television, put a quarter in the jukebox, and play a game of pinball. There's also a light café menu of curly fries, pizza, hot dogs, burgers, and appetizers. $5–10.

In Wildwood

Key West Café (609-522-3433), 4701 Pacific Ave. Open daily for lunch and dinner. A casual and friendly café serving tropical specialties with an emphasis on fresh seafood. Among the standouts: homemade crawfish bisque, conch fritters and entrées like Greek-style shrimp scampi with feta cheese and kalamata olives, and a hearty fisherman's stew. House-made island desserts prepared daily. BYOB. $11–16.

❡ **Tucker's Pub** (609-846-1110; www.tuckers-pub.com), 3301 Atlantic Ave. Serving lunch, dinner, and a late-night menu year-round. A lively Irish pub

housed in a restored 1913 bank building. Homemade specialties include fish-and-chips, crabcakes with roasted red pepper cream, and hearty sandwiches. There's a raw bar during the summer, and dining on the enclosed outdoor deck year-round. The bar features a dozen beers on tap and big-screen TVs for watching the game. $7–15.

❡ **Urie's Waterfront Restaurant** (609-522-4189), 588 West Rio Grande Ave., at the foot of the Rio Grande Bridge. Open daily for lunch and dinner. This bustling seafood house has been serving steamed mussels, broiled crabcakes, fried scallops, and other seafood for more than 50 years. Other entrées include chicken, steak, and veal. The waterfront deck is a convivial spot for dinner or drinks. Kids love the video arcade and Treasure Cove gift shop, which sells an interesting selection of knickknacks, clothing, and nautically themed crafts. $13–30.

❡ **Groff's Restaurant** (609-522-5474; www.groffsrestaurant.com), Magnolia Ave. and the Boardwalk. Open daily for dinner June–late Sept. Groff's is a Wildwood landmark, serving reasonably priced homey comfort food to vacationing families since 1925. They don't accept reservations, so be prepared to wait in line along with many others. Pies—including coconut cream, lemon meringue, and blueberry—are among the signature homemade desserts. BYOB. $14–32.

In Avalon

❡ **Sylvester's Fish Market and Restaurant** (609-967-7553; www.sylvesters-avalon.com), 21st St. and Fifth Ave. Open May–Oct.; lunch Fri.–Sun. until July 1, daily after that; and dinner daily. Sylvester's has been a local institution for more than 30 years, the kind of laid-back place people stumble upon while on vacation and

end up eating at every night. Regulars rave about the crabcakes, she-crab soup, clams, and the extensive selection of well-prepared seafood dinners. You can eat inside or on the covered patio, or take some fresh or prepared seafood home. BYOB. $11–27.

In Stone Harbor

Green Cuisine (609-368-1616), 302 96th St. Open May–Sept., daily for breakfast, lunch, and dinner. A vegetarian eatery with an emphasis on fresh, natural ingredients. A healthy menu of gourmet sandwiches and creative soups and salads. $6–13.

✔ **Uncle Bill's Pancake House** (609-368-8129), 304 96th St. Open daily for breakfast and lunch spring–late Nov. An institution along the southern shore—there's an Uncle Bill's in just about every town from Ocean City to Cape May. Although they serve a decent lunch, each is known for its belgian waffles, French toast, bacon and eggs, and, of course, light and fluffy pancakes in every variation imaginable. $5–10.

BOARDWALK FOOD *✔* **Mack and Manco Pizza** (609-399-2548; www.mackandmancos.com), three locations along the Ocean City boardwalk: 758 Boardwalk (seasonal), 920 Boardwalk (year-round), and Boardwalk at 12th St. (seasonal). A boardwalk institution since 1956. The Ocean City locations—as well as others in Wildwood and Atlantic City—are all run by family members. Their trademark thin and crispy crust comes with sauce and mozzarella, or a variety of other toppings, from traditional pepperoni and mushrooms to fresh Jersey tomatoes. Legions of loyal fans come to watch pizza makers stretch dough the old-fashioned way—twirling and spinning it in the air until it's impossibly uniform and thin.

TLC's Polish Water Ice (609-399-2662), 1068 Boardwalk and three other Boardwalk locations, Ocean City. Tourists line up on the boardwalk for this tasty treat, a creamy version of traditional Italian ice that comes in a rainbow of flavors, from mango and lemon to cherry and watermelon. Try some of their specialties, like the Polish Ice Cap (mixed with soda) or the Polish Freeze (mixed with soft-serve ice cream).

Shriver's (609-399-0100; 877-668-2339; www.shrivers.com), Ninth St. and Boardwalk, Ocean City. This candy store is the oldest continuously operating business on the Ocean City boardwalk, and a crowd favorite since 1898. They sell old-fashioned confections like fudge, saltwater taffy, and mint rolls, all made fresh on the premises every day.

Johnson's Popcorn (609-398-5404; 800-842-2676; www.johnsonspopcorn.com), three locations along the boardwalk, Ocean City. Johnson's has been selling "world-famous" caramel corn since 1940. It's still made the old-fashioned way—hot kernels of corn are tossed with sweet melted caramel in a huge copper kettle. Buy it by the cup, bag, or in one of their trademark plastic tubs or collector's tins.

James' Candy Company (609-368-0505; www.jamescandy.com), 255 96th St., Stone Harbor and on the Wildwood boardwalk at Oak Ave. This is where it all began: Enoch James, the famous 19th-century Atlantic City confectioner, developed a recipe for saltwater taffy, and a boardwalk phenomenon was born. In addition to the signature taffy, crowd favorites include macaroons, chocolate-covered taffy pops, butter toffee, creamy fudge, and cream mints. Boardwalk strollers can still be seen munching on James' chewy taffy, just as they did in the

1880s. Today taffy comes in more than a dozen flavors—some are sugar-free, others have marzipan, fudge, or nut centers.

Curley's Fries (609-729-3131), Morey's Piers, boardwalk at 25th St., North Wildwood. Open daily in-season. A fixture on Morey's Piers since 1978. Curley's sells all the boardwalk standards, but a bucket of crispy fresh-cut fries and a fresh-squeezed lemonade top them all.

Maui's Dog House (609-846-0444; www.mauisdoghouse.com), 2116–2118 Boardwalk, North Wildwood. Open daily from 11 AM. An old-fashioned mustard-colored hot dog joint known for its 25 varieties of creative toppings, many of which are not for the faint of heart. Finish off one or two with fresh-cut cheese fries and an old-fashioned vanilla crème. $4–9.

Douglass Fudge (609-522-3875; www.douglasscandies.com), 3300 Boardwalk at Wildwood Ave., Wildwood. Open mid-May–mid-Oct. Of course you can get all varieties of creamy homemade fudge, but don't overlook the chocolate-covered saltwater taffy, cream mint sticks, butter toffee, chocolate-covered strawberries, and molasses paddles. In business on the boardwalk for more than 85 years.

The Original Fudge Kitchen (609-522-4396; 800-233-8343), Boardwalk at Roberts Ave., Wildwood, and also in Ocean City, Stone Harbor, and Cape May. Watch as fudge, saltwater taffy, chocolates, and other confections are made before your eyes. There are 18 flavors of hand-whipped fudge, and old-time candy like marzipan and molasses paddles.

Kohr Brothers Frozen Custard (609-522-1029; www.kohrbros.com), 2518 Boardwalk in North Wildwood, 3500 Boardwalk in Wildwood, and on the boardwalk in Ocean City and in Cape May. Their frozen custard is a light and silky concoction of cream, eggs, milk, and sugar that's based on the recipe Archie Kohr developed in 1919. Kohr started delivering his homemade ice cream to his milk customers via horse-drawn wagon. Its rousing success inspired the Kohr brothers to open an ice cream shop on the Coney Island boardwalk. Today more than a dozen shops throughout New Jersey sell Archie's custard, along with smoothies, malts, shakes, and sundaes.

✳ Entertainment

ARTS CENTER Ocean City Arts Center (609-399-7628; www.ocean cityartscenter.org), in the Ocean City Cultural Arts Center, 1735 Simpson Ave. (between 17th and 18th Sts.), Ocean City. Free admission. A non-profit arts organization hosts a busy year-round schedule of concerts, art exhibits, lectures, workshops, and fine-arts classes, including pottery, sculpture, dance, and music. The work of local and regional artists is exhibited monthly (see *Selective Shopping—Art Galleries*). The arts center mounts juried art and photography shows, and an annual art show on the boardwalk.

CONVENTION CENTER Wildwoods Convention Center (609-729-9000; www.wildwoodsnj.com/cc), 4500 Boardwalk, Wildwood. Wildwood's convention center hosts a year-round schedule of concerts, crafts shows, sports competitions, and other special events in a 7,000-seat arena.

MUSIC In July and August, summertime concert series—most of them outdoors and free—are as much a shore tradition in New Jersey as boardwalks and amusement rides.

The **Ocean City Pops Orchestra** (609-398-9585; www.oceancitypops .org) presents a diverse music series at Ocean City's historic boardwalk Music Pier (609-525-9291). *In Sea Isle City,* **Concerts Under the Stars** (609-263-8687) are held on Mon. and Wed. nights on the promenade, beginning at 7:30. *In Avalon* (609-967-3936), noon-time concerts take place on the 30th St. beach. At the **Lou Boothe Amphitheater** (800-882-7787) *in North Wildwood,* live concerts and musical revues—from doo-wop and swing to big band and vaudeville—are held on Thurs. and Sat. at 8 PM. Summertime means music and dancing on the **Wildwood Crest Pier** (609-522-5176), 5800 Ocean Ave., on Mon. at 7:30 PM; on Wed., *Wildwood Crest's* gazebo at Miami Ave. and Sunset Lake features jazz, reggae, country-and-western, and other music starting at 7 PM.

✳ Selective Shopping

ART GALLERIES The **Gallery at the Ocean City Arts Center** (609-399-7628; www.oceancityartscenter .org), 1735 Simpson Ave. (between 17th and 18th Sts.), Ocean City. A variety of individual and group exhibitions showcase the work of local and regional artists. The **Boardwalk Art Show** and **Fine Craft Show** (both in August), a juried art show in the fall, and a springtime juried photography show are among the gallery's many annual events. Lectures and "meet the artist" receptions are open to the public (see *Entertainment—Arts Center*).

Ocean Galleries (609-368-7777; www.oceangalleries.com), 9618 Third Ave., Stone Harbor; another location in Avalon (609-967-4462), 297 22nd St. Changing exhibits of works by local and national contemporary artists, including fine-art paintings, prints, nautically themed crafts, and furniture.

OCEAN CITY'S HISTORIC MUSIC PIER, A LANDMARK VENUE ON THE BOARDWALK THAT REACHES OUT OVER THE ATLANTIC OCEAN, FEATURES PERFORMANCES BY THE OCEAN CITY POPS ORCHESTRA AND A VARIETY OF SPECIAL EVENTS THROUGHOUT THE YEAR.

Photo by Donald B. Kravitzs/DBKphoto

DOO-WOP

Like many communities along the Jersey Shore, Wildwood slid into a decline during the 1970s and '80s, when tourists vacationed elsewhere, and storefronts and motels were vacant and dilapidated. The once-vibrant boardwalk resort had become faded and seedy, and needed to reinvent itself. By the mid-1990s a local preservation league adopted the term doo-wop, a nod to the popular 1950s-era a cappella music, to describe Wildwood's flamboyant pastel-and-neon architecture, similar to that in Southern California, where it's called populux, or coffee-shop modern; and in Miami, where it's termed MiMo. Redevelopment efforts were under way to preserve the vintage architecture popular here during the resort's giddy heyday as a seaside hot spot—the post–World War II 1950s and '60s—when it boomed with upward of 200 motels. Wildwood boasts the largest collection of exuberantly kitschy doo-wop architecture (also known as midcentury architecture) in the country. It's an architectural treasure trove of boomerang rooflines, sleek chrome and glass, kidney-shaped swimming pools, plastic palm trees, and other campy touches. These mementos of a bygone era line both sides of Ocean Avenue for a dozen or so blocks, taking visitors back in time to America's golden era, when middle-class families had money to burn on the pursuit of leisure and took their automobiles on vacation. Bill Haley and his band the Comets performed their hit "Rock Around the Clock" for the first time live in Wildwood. Liberace and Sam Cooke were among the stars that played Little Las Vegas, as Wildwood was known. Narrated trolley tours feature Wildwood's doo-wop motels and buildings (see *Guidance*), and a museum has opened that's dedicated to the resort's pop-culture history of the '50s, from its signature architecture and retro heritage to its rock 'n' roll legacy. The **Doo Wop Preservation League** (609-729-9000; www.doowopusa.org) publishes a self-guided walking-tour map; it's best to take the tour at night, when the neon is dramatically aglow.

SPECIAL SHOPS *In Ocean City,* the **Shops at Asbury Avenue** (609-398-4662) is an interesting collection of 100 shops, restaurants, and galleries that stretches along Asbury Ave. between Sixth and 11th Sts. *On the boardwalk* at 11th St. is **The Flanders**, a retail area with specialty shops. *In downtown Stone Harbor,* there are more than 100 specialty shops—from women's clothing boutiques to surf shops—mostly on Third Ave. and 96th and Feeder Sts.

FARMER'S MARKET OCEAN **City Farmer's and Crafters Market** (609-399-1412) on the grounds of the Ocean City Tabernacle, Sixth St. and Asbury Ave., Ocean City. A seasonal outdoor market is held in July and Aug. every Wed. from 8 AM–1 PM. Locals and tourists come for the fresh fruits, vegetables, and herbs, fresh-cut flowers, and handmade crafts.

❋ Special Events

The resort towns along the southern shore—particularly Ocean City, Sea Isle City, and Wildwood—make sure that visitors and vacationers have plenty to do all summer long. In addition to the events listed below, there is a full schedule of family-friendly activities and events that take place along the boardwalks, from classic-car shows and fishing tournaments to professional wrestling, talent shows, family-fun nights, and free music concerts (see *Entertainment—Music*). In Wildwood, crafts shows are held on the boardwalk and at Hereford Inlet Lighthouse in July and August. Friday-night fireworks on the beach light up the sky in Wildwood all summer. Contact local tourism bureaus for their complete events listings.

New Year's Day: **First Day at the Beach** (609-525-9300), Ocean City. Ocean City kicks off the new year with an icy plunge into the ocean at the Music Pier.

THE ANNUAL INTERNATIONAL KITE FESTIVAL ON THE WILDWOOD BEACH IN MAY IS AMERICA'S LARGEST KITE FESTIVAL, WITH WORLD RENOWNED KITE BUILDERS AND COMPETITORS, AND THE EAST COAST STUNT KITE CHAMPIONSHIPS.

Photo courtesy of Greater Wildwood Tourism

February: **Polar Bear Plunge** (609-263-8687), at the 41st St. beach, Sea Isle City.

March: **Ocean Drive Marathon** (609-523-0880; www.odmarathon.org), Sea Isle Promenade, Sea Isle City. The 26-mile race follows the scenic Ocean Dr. coastal route between Cape May and Sea Isle City and includes the entire Wildwoods boardwalk. ❧ **St. Patrick's Day Celebration and Parade** (609-729-4000), North Wildwood. The parade route follows Atlantic Ave., from Ninth to Second Aves.

April: ❧ **Doo Dah Parade** (609-525-9300), Ocean City. When basset hounds get together for a parade, it's called a waddle, and this procession features hundreds of the comically droopy hounds.

May: **Boardwalk Spring Family Fun Fest** (609-525-9300), Ocean City. Features 350 crafters, food vendors, and entertainers. ❧ **Wildwoods International Kite Festival** (609-729-4000), on the beach, Wildwood. The Memorial Day weekend festival includes the **East Coast Stunt Kite Championships** (the world's largest sport-kite competition and America's largest kite festival), the **World Indoor Kite Competition** at the Wildwoods Convention Center, and an **illuminated nighttime kite fly.** Kite makers and flyers come from around the world for the weekend. **Spring Thunder in the Sand Motocross Race** (609-523-8051), on the beach, Wildwood.

June: **Miss New Jersey Pageant** (609-525-9294), on the boardwalk at Music Pier, Ocean City. Beauties compete for scholarships and the Miss New Jersey crown. Festivities include a boardwalk parade of pageant contestants, high school bands, dancers, and local youth groups. **Ocean City Flower Show** (609-525-9300), Ocean

City. **Skimmer Festival Weekend** (609-263-8687), on the Promenade, Sea Isle City. Food court, live entertainment, dance contest, antique-auto show, and free trolley tours. **Mummer's Brigade Weekend** (609-729-4000), North Wildwood. ✍ **National Marbles Tournament** (301-724-1297; 609-729-4000), Ringer Stadium, Wildwood. The official national marbles competition for children ages 8–14; a Wildwood tradition for more than 80 years.

July: **New Jersey Shuffleboard Championships** (609-525-9300); different disciplines staged on various dates through the summer in Ocean City. **Freckle Contest** (609-525-9300), on the boardwalk, Ocean City. **Night in Venice** (609-525-9300), Ocean City. The city's annual boat parade—one of the largest in the world—attracts 100,000 spectators to Great Egg Harbor Bay. ✍ **Sand Sculpting Contest** (609-525-9300), Sixth St. beach, Ocean City. ✍ **Sara the Turtle Festival** (609-263-8687), on the Promenade at JFK Blvd., Sea Isle City. ✍ **Independence Day Fire-**

works and Parade (609-522-2955), parade along Surf Ave. in North Wildwood, fireworks display on the boardwalk in Wildwood. **Anglesea Blues Festival** (609-523-6565), Old New Jersey Ave., North Wildwood. Blues fans come to hear live music and eat authentic barbecue. **Christmas in July Boat Parade** (609-729-5501), Wildwood.

August: ✍ **Baby parades** *in Ocean City* (609-525-9300), *Avalon* (609-463-6415), *Wildwood* (609-729-4000) and *Sea Isle City* (609-263-8687). The Ocean City parade—nearly a century old—is one of the first in the world. ✍ **Miss Crustacean Hermit Crab Beauty Pageant** (609-525-9300), Sixth St. beach, Ocean City. A beauty contest for crustaceans. ✍ **Weird Week** (609-525-9300), Ocean City. A variety of wacky family events. **Greater Wildwood Yacht Club Regatta** (609-522-0969), Sunset Lake, Wildwood Crest. A boat race more than 70 years old. **Stone Harbor Arts and Crafts Show** (609-368-4112), 80th St. and First Ave., Stone Harbor. A popular show with more than 350

FIREWORKS ABOVE THE ATLANTIC OCEAN ARE PART OF WILDWOOD'S ANNUAL WEEK-LONG 4TH OF JULY CELEBRATION.

Photo courtesy of Greater Wildwood Tourism

artists, craftspeople, and vendors. **Wildwoods Classic Cup** (609-729-4000), Wildwood. Ocean sailing competition. **Greater Wildwood Yacht Club Regatta** (609-729-4000), Wildwood. **Boardwalk Craft Show** (609-729-4000), on the boardwalk, Wildwood.

September: **Wings 'n Water Festival** (609-368-1211; www.wetlandsinstitute.org), Wetlands Institute, Stone Harbor. **Ocean City Airport Festival & Boardwalk Aerobatic Airshow** (609-525-9300) at the Municipal Airport and over the boardwalk, Ocean City. **Street Rod Weekend** (609-525-9300), Sports and Civic Center, Sixth St., Ocean City. ♪ **Fall Family Festival Weekend** (609-263-8687), on the promenade, Sea Isle City. Live entertainment, fireworks, a sand-sculpting contest, trolley tours, and an antique-car show. **Irish Fall Festival** (609-729-0075), North Wildwood. A piper competition and traditional Irish food, music, and dancing. **Boardwalk Classic Car Show** (609-523-8051), on the boardwalk and at the Wildwoods Convention Center, Wildwood.

October: ♪ **Surf Fishing Tournament** (609-522-2955), North Wildwood. Divisions for kids and adults. **Thunder on the Beach Truck Com-** **petition** (609-523-8051), Wildwood. **Indian Summer Weekend** (609-525-9300), Ocean City. A seafood festival on the boardwalk with hundreds of vendors and events. **Sunset Lake Hydrofest Powerboat Races** (609-886-8156), Sunset Lake, Wildwood Crest. A powerboat racing series that features hydroplanes and flat-bottomed boats skimming the surface at speeds of up to 140 miles an hour. ♪ **Halloween Parade and Fun Fair** (609-729-1934), Wildwood. The parade goes along Atlantic Ave.; the fair is at the Wildwood Convention Center. **Great Fall Classic Surf Fishing Tournament** (609-729-4000), Wildwood.

November: **Boardwalk Kennel Club Dog Show** (609-729-4000), Wildwoods Convention Center, Wildwood.

December: **Carol Fest** (609-525-9300), at the Music Pier, Ocean City. ♪ **First Night Celebration** (609-525-9300), Ocean City. Family-oriented activities to celebrate New Year's Eve, wrapping up with fireworks at midnight. **Hereford Inlet Lighthouse Christmas Tree Lighting Ceremony** (609-522-4520), North Wildwood. ♪ **Christmas parades** in Ocean City (609-525-9300) and Wildwood (609-729-4000).

THE CAPE MAY PENINSULA

The Victorian era has been charmingly reborn in Cape May, which bills itself as the oldest seaside resort town in America. It's certainly one of the country's best-known Victorian towns, and one of only four restored Victorian seaports, along with Mendocino, California, Port Townsend, Washington, and Galveston, Texas. Cape May sits at New Jersey's southernmost tip, on a peninsula nestled between the Atlantic Ocean and Delaware Bay. The region is known as the Jersey Cape and is part of Cape May County, which stretches north to Ocean City, just below Absecon Island and Atlantic City. The historic district actually sits on a little island cut off from the rest of the peninsula by the Cape May Canal.

The entire town is a national historic landmark; with more than 600 authentically restored homes and buildings—most built between 1850 and 1910—it has one of the most extensive collections of late-19th-century structures in the United States. People come from around the world to see this virtual treasure trove of Victorian architectural richness, wander the lovely gas-lit historic streets, eat at some of the top gourmet restaurants on the East Coast, and spend the night in one of the many old mansions converted into quaint bed & breakfasts, luxurious inns, and grand hotels. A visit to Cape May is a trip to a long-gone era of elegance, charm, and romance, which is perhaps why visitors find it so appealing and return year after year.

Cape May earned the prestigious "One of America's Prettiest Places" designation twice in recent years—the only place in the country to do so. Once the town received national landmark status in the 1980s, restoration efforts reached a feverish pitch. Victorians all over town underwent painstakingly meticulous restorations, and many of the newly polished gems became inns, guesthouses, and B&Bs. Not surprisingly, Cape May is one of the most popular locations for destination weddings in the country. These historic lodgings mix old-time elegance and charm with modern amenities like air-conditioning and private baths. You can book a luxury suite at a grand 19th-century hotel, sip afternoon tea on the wraparound veranda of a stately inn, or lounge in one of Cape May's ubiquitous wicker rocking chairs on the front porch of a gingerbread house sporting a bold multihued color scheme.

Cape May is the epicenter of gourmet fine dining for New Jersey's entire southern shore. And since Cape May Harbor is one of the largest commercial fishing ports on the East Coast, naturally there's lots of fresh seafood, from traditional lobster dinners to blue claw crabs, and just about every restaurant has its own special recipe for crabcakes. Even though Cape May is considered the Restaurant Capital

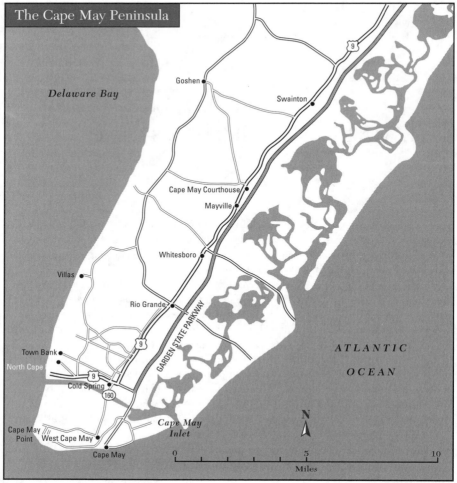

The Cape May Peninsula

Delaware Bay

Goshen

Swainton

Cape May Courthouse

Mayville

Whitesboro

Villas

Rio Grande

GARDEN STATE PARKWAY

Town Bank

North Cape

Cold Spring

ATLANTIC

OCEAN

Cape May Point

West Cape May

Cape May Inlet

Cape May

N

0   5   10

Miles

of New Jersey, some of the best restaurants are open only on weekends during the off-season, while others close altogether from Thanksgiving to spring. If you visit Cape May in the quiet season with a particular restaurant in mind, it's wise to phone ahead to avoid disappointment.

In the 1600s the only ones summering here were the Lenni-Lenape, the local Algonquin Indians who set up seasonal camps and hunted and fished along the shore; the Lenape's Kechemeche tribe inhabited the peninsula until the mid-18th century. Henry Hudson anchored his *Half Moon* off Cape May Point in 1609, but the famous English navigator continued his journey up the Delaware River without starting a settlement at Cape May. Dutch sea captain Cornelius Jacobsen Mey sailed along the coast in 1621 while exploring the region for the Dutch East India Company. He named the desolate land of sand dunes and thickly wooded rolling hills Cape Mey; the spelling would change as English settlers arrived later to be close to the region's busy whaling routes. Many who came for a piece of the profitable whale oil trade were *Mayflower* descendants from New England. They created the first whaling settlement on the cape around 1685 on the banks of the Delaware River, which is now the Townbank area of North Cape May. Many of the residents were laid to rest in the cemetery at "Old Brick," the historic Cold Spring Presbyterian Church; excepting Massachusetts, more *Mayflower* descendants are buried in Old Brick than elsewhere in the country.

Cape May was known as America's First Seashore Resort when it was discovered by wealthy Philadelphians who summered here as early as the 1700s, persuaded by their physicians that the salt air and pleasant weather would cure a variety of ailments. The first waves of vacationers came to Cape May, then known as Cape Island, by steamship, stagecoach, and private schooner in the 1800s. The Pennsylvania Railroad and the Reading Line began shuttling passengers here in 1879. Several U.S. presidents who vacationed in Cape May used Congress Hall as a summer White House, while dozens of hotels and inns catered to illustrious guests like Henry Ford, Louisa May Alcott, John Philip Sousa, and circus impresario P. T. Barnum. A devastating fire in 1878 destroyed most of the seaside resort, and the homes that rose from the ashes were bedecked in gingerbread trim, ornate latticework, and daring color schemes. The Victorian era had arrived, and it gave Cape May an identity that would define it for more than a century to come.

Today the entire resort is a nod to the era when Queen Victoria reigned and homes were adorned with magnificent wraparound verandas, stained-glass windows, turrets, gables, and all manner of fanciful fretwork and curlicue trim and painted in a showy palette of cheerful colors. Cape May's famous "Painted Ladies" line main thoroughfares like Jackson Street and Beach Drive, but it's even more rewarding to stroll the picturesque neighborhoods, like Hughes and Gurney streets, where the fairy-tale-like Victorian homes reside in quiet splendor as they have for more than a century.

The Emlen Physick Estate, an authentically restored 18-room Victorian mansion built in the 1880s, is Cape May's only Victorian house museum, a fact that surprises many first-time visitors, who expect to find such places on every corner. It's a fine museum with period furnishings and lots of seasonal events; it's also home to the Mid-Atlantic Center for the Arts, or MAC, an active local arts organization that runs everything from the Cape May Lighthouse and the annual music festivals to the old-fashioned trolley tours that run through town.

Travel writers and vacationers have been raving about Cape May for decades, and perhaps that's why it has become a year-round resort. This small town of 4,200 residents hosts half a million or so visitors every year, mostly between June and August, when families arrive for summer vacation. Summertime sunset parades are held at the Coast Guard Training Center, a training facility and active search-and-rescue center in Cape May Harbor. The former World War II–era naval base is the only Coast Guard training center in the country. Cape May Stage performs dramas, comedies, and holiday productions, and the East Lynne Theater Company stages revivals of classic American plays and literary works. Autumn's glorious Indian summers lure beachgoers well past Labor Day, when couples take romantic weekend escapes and music lovers come to hear world-class entertainers headline the Cape May Jazz Festival. Victoriana reaches its zenith every October during Victorian Week, with house tours, dancing, mystery dinners, lectures, and other activities celebrating Cape May's famous heritage. The Christmas season bustles with tours of gaily decorated inns and homes, horse-drawn carriages sporting jingle bells, a hugely popular Christmas parade, and merry wassail parties. Springtime brings the Cape May Music Festival, 6 weeks of music performances—jazz, folk, chamber music, pop music, and other styles—in venues around town. No matter what season it is, you'll need at least a full day or two to explore the town and experience a worthwhile share of all Cape May has to offer.

Cape May has 2 miles of public beaches and a boardwalk lined with arcades, stores, eateries, and souvenir shops. Here it's called the Promenade, not world-famous like those in Atlantic City and Wildwood, but a pleasant place to stroll along the ocean or ride a bike in the early-morning hours. At the southern tip is a lovely gazebo; from there, postcard views include St. Mary's by the Sea, the Cape May Lighthouse, and a beach where you can watch the sunrise at dawn and return at the end of the day to witness an equally spectacular sunset. Cape May's beaches are small—erosion is unfortunately diminishing them even further—but popular with sunbathers, surfers, and families. Offshore, you can take an excursion by boat to spot schools of bottlenose dolphins as well as whales, harbor seals, and other marine animals.

Many visitors never leave Cape May's historic district, but those who do are justly rewarded with quiet bayside beaches, lovely parks and gardens, wineries, historic sites, and a diverse collection of unspoiled natural areas well worth finding. Active visitors take advantage of the first-rate golf, fishing, and kayaking. Historic Cold Spring Village is a re-created 19th-century South Jersey farming community with seasonal festivals, military encampments, concerts, and other special events. Leaming's Run Botanical Gardens is one of the best-known public gardens in the East, and its 25 uniquely themed gardens boast the largest display of annuals in the country. The Cape May County Park and Zoo—open daily and free of charge—is home to more than 400 exotic animals, from monkeys to camels, and even zebras and lions roaming a natural setting that simulates the savanna of eastern Africa. Cape May Court House, as its name suggests, is the county seat; and its historic courthouse and centuries-old homes and churches are national historic landmarks. The 18th-century John Holmes House contains the Cape May County Historical Museum, with relics and artifacts spanning centuries of local history.

Cape May Point is a tiny community of less than 300 year-round residents that was founded in 1875 as a religious retreat. There are no places to eat or stay, but visitors come to see its tiny 19th-century gingerbread church, the 1859 Cape May Lighthouse, and some of the finest sunsets in New Jersey. The bayside beaches face west, and Sunset Beach naturally draws crowds that gather along the water to watch the day's-end spectacle. During the summer, a flag-lowering ceremony is held here at sunset to honor the wreckage of the SS *Atlantus*, a World War I–era concrete ship that broke loose from its moorings and ran aground off the beach in 1926. Its decaying hull still protrudes from the surface, a permanent reminder of the U.S. government's experimental "Concrete Fleet," an unsuccessful and rather odd solution to the country's wartime steel shortage. Children comb Sunset Beach for "Cape May diamonds," tiny gemlike nuggets of quartz that sparkle in the sand. West Cape May has earned the distinction of Lima Bean Capital of the World, and hosts a lighthearted autumn festival devoted to the broad, flat legume, which features food, contests, songs, and the crowning of the Lima Bean Queen.

The Cape May peninsula is known as the Birding Migration Capital of North America, and birding enthusiasts from around the world come to watch as hundreds of thousands of raptors, shorebirds, and songbirds pass through Cape May during spring and fall migrations. The peninsula is home to the country's second-highest concentration of shorebirds and is an important stopover for the migratory species—some 400 of them—that rest and feed here before winging their way across the 13-mile expanse of Delaware Bay and beyond to their wintering grounds.

Famous birding locations like the Cape May Migratory Bird Refuge, Cape May Point State Park, and the Higbee Beach Wildlife Management Area protect thousands of acres of pristine salt marsh, tidal creeks, and coastal forest that attract waves of songbirds and shorebirds in the spring, and waterfowl, seabirds, and raptors in the fall. Dragonflies, bats, and monarch butterflies also pass through. Reeds Beach and Kimbles Beach are well worth a stop in late May and early June, when female horseshoe crabs come ashore to lay up to 80,000 eggs in shallow pits in the sand. The enormous flocks of seabirds that descend on the beach to feast on the protein-rich eggs are indeed a sight to behold.

Entries in this section are arranged in roughly geographic order.

AREA CODE 609.

GUIDANCE Cape May Region Welcome Center (609-624-0918), at the Ocean View Service Plaza at mile marker 18 on the Garden State Parkway. Open year-round, daily 9–5. A full-service visitors center staffed by the Cape May County Chamber of Commerce is stocked with brochures, menus, maps, and information on lodgings, restaurants, attractions, and events.

Cape May County Chamber of Commerce (609-465-7181; www.capemaycounty chamber.com), 13 Crest Haven Rd. (Garden State Parkway Exit 11), Cape May Court House. The information center is open mid-Apr.–mid-Oct., daily 9–5; and mid-Oct.–mid-Apr., Mon.–Fri. 9–5.

Cape May County Department of Tourism (609-463-6415; 800-227-2297; www.thejerseycape.net) can provide information on the Cape May region and will send a vacation planning package, on request.

GETTING THERE *By air:* **Atlantic City International Airport** (609-645-7895; www.acairport.com), Exit 9 off the Atlantic City Expressway, Egg Harbor Township. Spirit Airlines (800-772-7117; www.spiritair.com) has direct and connecting service from points around the country.

By bus: **New Jersey Transit** (973-275-5555; www.njtransit.com) buses connect the region to bus terminals in Philadelphia and New York City, and provide regularly scheduled bus service from Philadelphia and Atlantic City with stops in Cape May, North Cape May, Villas, and Rio Grande.

By car: Cape May is at the southern end of the **Garden State Parkway,** 3 hours south of New York City and about an hour east of Philadelphia. A more scenic alternative is Cape May County's **Ocean Drive,** which follows the Atlantic Ocean along a series of barrier islands linked by five toll bridges. The 40-mile route is marked with Flight of the Gull signposts from Atlantic City to Cape May.

By ferry: **Cape May–Lewes Ferry** (800-643-3779; www.capemaylewesferry.com) connects Lewes, Delaware, to North Cape May, New Jersey—close to the Garden

TROLLEY TOURS OF CAPE MAY'S HISTORIC DISTRICT, U.S. COAST GUARD BASE, AND THE BEACHFRONT ARE OFFERED YEAR-ROUND BY THE MID-ATLANTIC CENTER FOR THE ARTS.

State Parkway. The ferry accepts both car and foot passengers; the one-way trip takes about 70 minutes. Reservations are recommended when traveling during peak summertime periods, especially Friday afternoon and evening, Saturday morning, and Sunday afternoon and evening.

GETTING AROUND The best way to explore Cape May is on foot or by bicycle. There is a metered municipal parking lot on Jackson and Perry streets, and metered parking around town. There are many ways to explore the historic district, from trolley tours and horse-drawn carriages to self-guided walking tours; stop in at one of the information centers for guidance.

Five Mile Beach Electric Railway Company (609-884-5230; 800-422-8366; www.gatrolley.com) shuttles visitors around Cape May and Rio Grande via an old-fashioned open-air trolley. Call or see Web site for a schedule.

Taxis: **Aart's Cape May Taxi** (609-898-7433); **AA Plus Cab** (609-889-9595); and **Villas Taxi** (609-889-8799) all serve the Cape May region.

MEDICAL EMERGENCY Cape Regional Medical Center (609-463-2000; www.caperegional.com), 2 Stone Harbor Blvd. (at Rt. 9), Cape May Court House. The emergency number is 609-463-2138.

For marine emergencies, contact the **U.S. Coast Guard—Cape May** at 609-884-3491.

✳ To See

HISTORIC HOMES AND SITES Emlen Physick Estate (609-884-5404; 800-275-4278; www.capemaymac.org), 1048 Washington St., Cape May. Open year-round, daily 10–5. Adults $10; children $5. Cape May's only Victorian house museum is the headquarters of the **Mid-Atlantic Center for the Arts,** an extremely active local arts organization that organizes everything from Victorian heritage celebrations to seasonal festivals and sightseeing tours. Renowned architect Frank Furness designed this elegant Stick-style 18-room mansion in 1879 for Philadelphia doctor Emlen Physick. Today it's authentically restored and open for guided tours. You might see Dr. Physick's Model T Ford parked on the front lawn. The **Carriage House Gallery** mounts changing exhibits on Victorian history and culture; it's also home to the **Carriage House Tearoom & Café,** where you can have a spot of tea in high Victorian style (see *Where to Eat—Coffee and Tea*), then browse the gift shop for tea and specialty tea items.

The Colonial House (609-884-9100; www.capemayhistory.org), 653 Washington St., Cape May. Open mid-June–mid-Sept., Mon.–Sat. 10–2; closed Sun. Admission by donation. This preserved circa-1775 house behind City Hall is the oldest structure in Cape May and the only colonial-era house in Cape May open to the public for tours. Memucan Hughes built this austere clapboard house in the days before the American Revolution, on what was then known as Cape Island. Today it's the headquarters of the **Greater Cape May Historical Society,** which mounts changing exhibits.

Cold Spring Presbyterian Church (609-884-4065; www.oldbrickpresbyterian .com), 780 Seashore Rd. (across from Historic Cold Spring Village), Cape May. Tours are led of both the church and the historic cemetery during the summer. A stately 1823 church, affectionately nicknamed Old Brick for its crimson brick exterior, is one of the oldest churches in America and on the National Register of Historic Places. The site dates to 1718, when a log structure served as the first church before it was replaced by a frame meetinghouse in 1762. The headstones in a centuries-old cemetery by the church tell the story of Cape May's early history. The oldest grave dates to 1742, and many of the dead are descendants of the Pilgrims who arrived in New England on the *Mayflower*. They were lured here in the 1600s by tales of whaling riches; in fact, more *Mayflower* descendants are buried in the Cape May region than anyplace else outside Massachusetts. A marker in the cemetery is a haunting memorial to the local residents who died during the global cholera epidemic in 1832 and were buried at night in unmarked graves.

THE EMLEN PHYSICK ESTATE IS CAPE MAY'S ONLY VICTORIAN HOUSE MUSEUM, AND HOME TO THE MID-ATLANTIC CENTER FOR THE ARTS.

Photo courtesy of the Mid-Atlantic Center for the Arts

⌗ HISTORIC COLD SPRING VILLAGE

(609-898-2300; www.hcsv.org), 720 Seashore Rd. (Rt. 9), Cape May. Open Memorial Day–mid-June, Sat.–Sun. 10–4:30; mid-June–Labor Day, Tues.–Sun. 10–4:30; Labor Day–mid-Sept., Sat.–Sun. 10–4:30; closed mid-Sept.–Memorial Day. Adults $8; seniors $7; children 3–12, $6; children 2 and under, free. A unique open-air living-history museum that depicts life in an 1850s South Jersey farming community. Stop first at the welcome center, where there's an exhibit on Cape May County history and a short orientation video about the village. The 25 restored antique buildings were moved to this 22-acre wooded site from places all over Cape May County. There's a country store with a bakery and restaurant, a county jail, barns, a pottery store, train stations, shops, and historic homes. You can talk with historical interpreters dressed in period garb, from innkeepers and blacksmiths to farmers and schoolmasters. Watch crafts- and tradespeople demonstrate their skills—basketry, decoy carving, spinning, open-hearth cooking, and many other arts—using traditional tools and methods from the era when everything was made by hand. Every weekend brings Revolutionary War encampments, festivals, holiday candlelight walks, concerts, and other events (see *Entertainment—Music and Special Events*).

Battery 223 and Fire Control Tower No. 23 (609-884-5404; 800-275-4278; www.capemaymac.org), Sunset Blvd., Cape May. There were eleven concrete fire control towers on the Delaware side of the bay and four in New Jersey, constructed for World War II homeland defense. Fire Control Tower No. 23 is the only surviving New Jersey tower. Now fully restored, visitors can ascend to the 6th floor spotting gallery to relive the era. The ground floor of the tower is fully accessible. Hours vary. Adults, $6; children (ages 3–12), $2.50.

LIGHTHOUSE Cape May Lighthouse (609-884-5404; 800-275-4278), Cape May Point State Park, Lighthouse Ave., Cape May Point. The tower is open from Apr.–Nov. for self-guided tours, daily 9 AM–8 PM; weekends only during the rest of the year. Phone ahead when visiting during the off-season. Free admission. The Cape May Lighthouse was built at the southernmost tip of New Jersey in 1859 and restored late in the 20th century, when the 157-foot structure was repainted in its original color scheme—a crimson lantern room atop a beige tower. This is where the Atlantic Ocean meets Delaware Bay, and the automated beacon reaches 24 miles out to sea to guide ships that rely on the light, as mariners have done for close to 150 years. Climb the 199 steps up a cast-iron spiral staircase to the **Watch Room Gallery** for a panoramic view of the ocean and the bay. From the top you can see the decaying remains of the SS *Atlantus*, a concrete ship that sunk offshore in 1926, and the gun emplacements that were part of New Jersey's World War II–era coastal defense system. The restored **Oil House** has a visitors orientation center and a museum shop with nautical gifts and memorabilia. The lighthouse is maintained by the **Mid-Atlantic Center for the Arts,** which offers guided beach walks, educational programs, and special tours like **Stairway to the Stars,** which includes a narrated trolley ride from Cape May and a nighttime climb to the lantern room for a panoramic view of the night sky. This is one of Cape May's most historic landmarks; more than 100,000 visitors a year climb up for the view.

MUSEUMS Cape May County Historical Museum (609-465-3535; www .cmcmuseum.org), in the John Holmes House, 504 Rt. 9, Cape May Court House. Open June–Sept., Tues.–Sat. 10–3; Oct.–May, Fri., 10–2, Sat. 10–3. Free admission. A fine museum run by the **Cape May County Historical and Genealogical Society** in a historic house that was built before the Revolutionary War. The grand white-clapboard house looks like it was plucked out of New England; it's one of the oldest buildings in Cape May County. The collection of artifacts and documents tells the story of three centuries of Cape May County history, from the early Lenni-Lenape to the

THE 1859 CAPE MAY LIGHTHOUSE AT CAPE MAY POINT STATE PARK TOWERS 157 FEET ABOVE THE SOUTHERNMOST TIP OF THE CAPE MAY PENINSULA. VISITORS CAN CLIMB THE 199 STEPS FOR A PANORAMIC VIEW THAT INCLUDES THE ATLANTIC OCEAN AND DELAWARE BAY.

European settlers who lived in fishing communities along the Delaware Bay and later filled Cape May with Victorian mansions. The extensive collection includes costumes, furnishings, decorative and utilitarian objects from the 17th to the 20th centuries, and special marine, toy, and medical exhibits. Authentic period rooms include a Victorian sitting room and an 18th-century kitchen and bedroom. Guns, uniforms, and swords fill the Military Room; vintage carriages, including a peddler's wagon and a stagecoach, are on display in a 19th-century barn. Museum gift shop.

Carriage House Gallery (609-884-5404), Mid-Atlantic Center for the Arts, Emlen Physick Estate, 1048 Washington St. Gallery hours vary; phone ahead. A restored 1876 carriage house is a lovely setting for a full schedule of changing exhibits at Cape May's only Victorian house museum (see **Emlen Physick Estate** under *To See—Historic Homes and Sites*). Past exhibits have featured Victorian costumes and household objects, Cape May history, art, and local historic figures, including Dr. Physick himself.

Naval Air Station Wildwood Aviation Museum (609-886-8787; usnasw.org), Cape May County Airport, 500 Forrestal Rd., Rio Grande. Open daily Apr.–Sept. 9–5; Oct.–Nov. 9–4; Dec.–Mar. 9–4, Mon.–Fri. Adults $6; children 3–12, $4; children 2 and under, free. A nostalgic collection of vintage aircraft and military memorabilia dedicated to the 38 airmen who lost their lives while training at the air station during World War II, when it was used to train dive-bomber squadrons. At its peak in 1944, there were more than 200 planes stationed here, and nearly 17,000 training flights a month. Special year-round events include dances, veterans' ceremonies, historical lectures, and fly-ins. Vintage aircraft are on display in a historic hangar, including Vietnam War–era helicopters, jet trainers, a navy Skyhawk jet, a Coast Guard helicopter, a World War II–era biplane, a World War II–era fighter-bomber, and a Korean War–era Russian fighter plane. The historic all-wooden hangar, on the National Register of Historic Places, contains military memorabilia, jet engines and helicopter engines, and aviation artifacts. The county airport is still active, but open only to private planes.

WINERIES Cape May Winery and Vineyard (609-884-1169; www.capemay winery.com), 709 Townbank Rd., Cape May. The tasting room is open daily year-round June–Sept. noon–6; Oct.–May noon–5. Established in 1995, this is New Jersey's southernmost winery, whose sandy soil and location between the Atlantic Ocean and Delaware Bay provide ideal conditions for growing pinot grigio, chardonnay, cabernet sauvignon, and other vinifera grapes.

Turdo Vineyards and Winery (609-884-5591; www.turdovineyards.com), 3911 Bayshore Rd., North Cape May. Open year-round. Tastings Jan.–Mar., Fri.–Sun. 12–4; mid-Apr.–Dec., Fri.–Sun. 1–5. Owner and winemaker Sal Turdo started making wine in Italy many years ago and was crafting wine at home for decades before he planted more than 5,000 acres of vineyards in North Cape May. The vinifera grapes benefit from the perfect combination of sandy soil, breezes off Delaware Bay and the Atlantic Ocean, and the peninsula's long growing season. The winery produces a dozen varieties—pinot grigio, sauvignon blanc, and merlot are among the Turdo wines that have won awards.

✿ ❦ CAPE MAY COUNTY PARK AND ZOO
(609-465-5271; www.capemayzoo.org), Rt. 9 and Crest Haven Rd., Cape May Court House. Open summer, Thurs.–Tues. 10–4:45; Wed. 10–6:45; winter, daily 10–3:30. Free admission. Nearly 400 mammals, birds, and reptiles—some 180 species—live in this 85-acre county zoo surrounded by a 128-acre woodland park. Between the park and the zoo, a family can easily spend an afternoon here. Take the boardwalk through the forest to see the vast 57-acre African savanna, where zebras, ostriches, and a giraffe roam in a natural setting. The Reptile House has Asian turtles, anacondas, pythons, and other reptiles and amphibians from around the globe. Snowy owls, flamingos, and 75 other species of exotic and native birds reside in the aviary. It's an interesting place to be during feeding time, and the antics of the monkeys are always amusing. The barnyard is home to ducks, pigs, goats, and other domesticated animals that can be fed. The park is laced with tree-lined paths that lead to picnic pavilions and barbecue grills as well as ball fields, a playground, and a freshwater fishing pond.

BICYCLING Cape May offers some of the flattest terrain in New Jersey, ideal for those who want to leisurely glide along the Atlantic or pedal down tree-lined side streets to check out Victorian mansions. The historic district's easy-to-navigate streets make for a good outing, but if you really want to explore, get on **Sunset Blvd.** The straight-as-an-arrow street—also called Rt. 606—links Cape May to Cape May Point. Other options include the bike path following **Seashore Rd. (Rt. 626)** from West Cape May to the Cape May Canal, and a **paved bike lane** that stretches from Rio Grande to Historic Cold Spring Village. Of course, there's Cape May's 2-mile-long **Promenade,** which is open to cyclists May–Oct. every morning until 10 AM.

A host of shops rents cruising bicycles, children's bikes, tandems, even surreys for the whole family. They include Village Bicycle Shop (609-884-8500), 605 Lafayette St., Cape May; Shields Bike Rentals (609-884-2453; 609-898-1818), 11 Gurney St., Cape May; and Cape Island Bicycle Center (609-884-8011; reservations: 609-898-7368), at Howard St. at Beach Ave. and 135 Sunset Blvd. in West Cape May.

BIRDING The Cape May peninsula is one of the top 10 birding hot spots in North America. Vast undisturbed tracts of saltwater wetlands, coastal woods, marshes, and upland meadows are an important stopover for more than 400 species of migrating shorebirds, raptors, waterfowl, and songbirds. The best viewing times are spring and fall, when waves of birds—sometimes numbering in the hundreds of thousands—pass through on their way to and from their wintering grounds far to the south. Thousands of novice birders and experienced spotters from around the country come to Cape May in May and September for the **World Series of Birding,** a 24-hour birding contest sponsored by the **New Jersey Audubon Society** (see *Special Events*). There are numerous prime bird-watching sites around the cape, including the ones listed below. Most of these facilities offer guided bird walks, workshops, tours, and bird-watching programs. To accommodate all the birders who descend on Cape May during the annual migrations, the Audubon Society runs the **Cape May Birding Hotline** (609-884-2736), a 24-hour information line with up-to-the-minute news on avian activity in the region.

✿ **Cape May Bird Observatory: Northwood Center** (609-884-2736; www
.birdcapemay.org), 701 E. Lake Dr. (off Sunset Blvd.), Cape May Point. Open daily Apr.–May and Sept.–Nov. 9:30–4:30; June–Aug. and Dec.–Mar., Wed.–Mon. 9:30–4:30, closed Tues. This chapter of the **New Jersey Audubon Society** at the northern end of Lily Lake offers a popular series of birding and nature workshops and programs for adults and families. There are guided walks along beaches, and through coastal woods and wetlands, that focus on wildflowers, butterflies, and birding. They also host the **World Series of Birding,** a 24-hour birding contest in May and September. The raised viewing platforms perched above swamps are ideal for spotting the hundreds of species that nest here during the summer. The nature shop has gifts, books, and birding equipment; the research center has information on birding, nature, and travel.

Higbee Beach Wildlife Management Area (609-628-2103), north of Sunset Beach off Bayshore Rd. (Rt. 607), Cape May. Open daily, dawn to dusk. A half-mile stretch of undisturbed beach on Delaware Bay hosts a springtime natural spectacle of dramatic proportions. In late May, horseshoe crabs come in on the high tide and lay their eggs on the beach. When the tide goes out and the eggs are exposed, shorebirds descend and the feast begins; birders come from around the country to witness the event. Spring is also a good time to spot ruby-throated hummingbirds, cardinals, warblers, and indigo buntings. A marked dune trail with observation platforms winds through the dunes, bayberry thickets, brushy fields, and a rare coastal dune forest of cedar, holly, and beach plum. The freshwater marsh and ponds, dense forest, and hardwood swamp form a rich habitat for many species of migrating birds and butterflies.

Cape May Migratory Bird Refuge (609-861-0600), at Cape May Point State Park, Cape May Point. Open daily from dawn to dusk. A 180-acre nature wildlife refuge on the Atlantic Ocean with a nature museum, trails, and birding programs. Many species live at the refuge, and many others rest and feed here during their annual journey south. Some of the oft-spotted species include shorebirds, songbirds, and waterfowl (spring and fall) and ducks, loons, songbirds, and hawks (fall and winter). Tens of thousands of raptors and more than a million seabirds fly over the refuge.

Cape May National Wildlife Refuge (609-463-0994), headquarters: 24 Kimbles Beach Rd., Cape May Court House. This undeveloped refuge is open year-round, daily from dawn until dusk; the headquarters is open Mon.–Fri. 8–4:30. This is one of the newest refuges—established in 1989—in the national wildlife refuge system. The **Delaware Bay Division** is an undisturbed tract of coastal forest, dunes, salt meadows, tidal marsh, and beach that supports more than 300 native and migratory bird species. Viewing areas at **Kimbles Beach** and **Reeds Beach** are good vantage points for spotting huge concentrations of shorebirds and gulls. The best time to visit is mid-May, when horseshoe crabs come ashore to lay their eggs, attracting thousands of migrating shorebirds as well as laughing gulls, red knots, and ruddy turnstones that feast on the protein-rich eggs.

BOAT EXCURSIONS **Cape May–Lewes Ferry** (800-643-3779; www.capemay lewesferry.com). *Cape May terminal:* Sandman Blvd. and Lincoln Dr., North Cape May. Call or see Web site for prices. The ferry operates daily, year-round; shuttles

THE CAPE MAY HAWK-WATCH
(609-884-2159), Cape May Point State Park, Lighthouse Avenue, Cape May Point. The hawk-watch platform is open year-round daily from dawn to dusk, but most people come in the fall, when some 16 raptor species—including peregrine falcons, bald eagles, red-tailed hawks, ospreys, vultures, and American kestrels—migrate through Cape May. Thousands of hawks ride the prevailing westerly winds toward the East Coast and down the length of the peninsula. They rest here before making the long crossing over Delaware Bay on their annual winter journey south. From September through November the viewing platform is staffed everyday from 9 to 5, and receives more than 100,000 visitors. Spotters maintain a daily raptor tally and help novice birders with their spotting skills.

✒ CAPE MAY WHALE WATCHER

(609-884-5404; 800-786-5445; www.capemaywhalewatcher.com), Miss Chris Marina, Second Ave. and Wilson Dr., Cape May. Trips run mid-May–mid-Oct. Reservations are recommended; call for a schedule and pricing. The popular **Lighthouse Adventure cruise** heads up the Delaware Bay to see half a dozen historic lighthouses built between the late 19th and early 20th centuries. Most are built on offshore pedestals and are visible only from the water. They are still active aids-to-navigation for boaters making their way through the bay's treacherous channel. A narrated tour includes interesting facts about the history and lore of the bay.

run daily from mid-June to September, and weekends from May to mid-June and in October. Sure, it's a practical means of transportation between Lewes, Delaware, and Cape May, New Jersey, but the 3-hour round-trip across the mouth of Delaware Bay is also a fun excursion. Along the way you can relax in an indoor salon, or find a spot on the open deck and watch for dolphins. Some people bring their bikes to the opposite shore, while others take the seasonal shuttles that run to stores, restaurants, and attractions in the historic seaside resorts.

✒ **Harbor Safari** (609-884-3100; www.skimmer.com) Dolphin Cove Marina, Ocean Dr., Cape May. Two trips daily from spring to fall; three in summer. Reservations are recommended. Salt marsh safaris aboard *The Skimmer,* a stable 40-foot catamaran that carries 41 passengers. Explore the vast back bays and coastal salt marshes surrounding Cape May for an up-close look at resident wildlife, from ospreys, peregrine falcons, and horseshoe crabs to terns, egrets, and herons. The springtime bald eagle cruises are also a good opportunity to spot loons as they prepare to migrate north after spending the winter in the marshes. The trips are popular with birders, nature enthusiasts, and families.

DOLPHIN- AND WHALE-WATCHING ✒ **The Cape May Whale Watch and Research Center** (609-898-0055; www.capemaywhalewatch.com), 1286 Wilson Dr., Cape May. Trips daily, mid-Apr.–mid-Nov. Reservations are accepted; call or see Web site for prices. This is the only research facility in the state that takes the public to sea on its vessels. An onboard naturalist answers questions and helps with spotting techniques as cruises head into the Atlantic to look for frolicking dolphins, breaching whales, and other marine life. You'll watch for humpback whales, and Nubby, Tippy, and other bottlenose dolphins. There's a variety of trips lasting 2 to 3 hours, from breakfast and dolphin excursions at sunset to offshore whale trips and a unique trip that looks for birds, dolphins, and whales.

✒ *Cape May Whale Watcher* (609-884-5445; 800-786-5445; www.capemay whalewatcher.com), Miss Chris Marina, Second Ave. and Wilson Dr., Cape May. Two trips a day, weekend late-Mar.–mid-Apr., daily from mid-Apr.–Oct., weekends Nov.–Dec. Call or see Web site for prices. Two- and 3-hour excursions for bottlenose dolphins and the finback and humpback whales that are common in the Cape May region. Finbacks—baleen whales once hunted for the oil in their thick blubber—are known as the Greyhounds of the Sea for their cruising speed, which can reach 30 miles an hour. The distinctive red 290-passenger boat is the largest and fastest whale-watcher in southern New Jersey. There's seating outside on the upper deck and inside in the main salon, where there's a snack bar.

FISHING Many charter boats and party boats depart from Cape May's docks and marinas. Anglers head offshore for trophy fish like shark, marlin, and tuna; they fish closer to shore for mackerel, weakfish, bluefish, flounder, and other species. The **Cape May Rips** at the southernmost tip of the peninsula is a world-renowned fishing spot. It's the land's end where the Atlantic Ocean meets Delaware Bay, and winds and tides clash where the powerful, deep tidal waters hit the calm shallows of the bay. The strong currents deposit an ever-changing series of sandbars during the twice-daily tides. The area is especially known for its striped bass, bluefish, and weakfish. The powerful currents and irregular sea bottom make for treacherous conditions, so it's best to fish here with an experienced guide.

South Jersey Sport Fishing Marina (609-884-3800; www.southjerseymarina .com), 1231 US 109, Cape May. This marina offers a wide variety of half- and full-day and nighttime inshore and offshore deep-sea fishing trips.

Other marinas in Cape May with party boats and charter boats include **Miss Chris Marina** (609-884-3351), Third Ave. and Wilson Dr.; **Utsch's Marina** (609-884-2051; www.capemayharbor.com), 1121 Rt. 109 ; and **Bree Zee Lee Marina** (609-884-4849) on Ocean Dr.

For surf fishing, anglers head to **Cape May Point State Park** (609-884-2159) in Cape May Point for striped bass, flounder, bluefish, and weakfish. The park is open year-round, daily from dawn until dusk. Surf fishing is also permitted from October through March at the Two Mile Beach Unit of the **Cape May Wetlands Wildlife Management Area.**

GOLF Southern New Jersey is world-renowned for its golf courses, which are considered among the best on the East Coast. *Golf Magazine* designated Cape May and Atlantic counties as one of the country's best golf destinations, and many of the courses here are open to the public. See "The Pinelands Region" in "Central New Jersey," and the rest of "The Southern Shore," for other golf courses in this region. The **Greater Atlantic City Golf Association** (800-465-3222; www.acgolf vacations.com) will help arrange golf-hotel packages and can book tee times.

The Pines at Clermont (609-624-0100; www.pinesatclermont.com), 358 Kings Hwy., Clermont. A nine-hole course in northern Cape May County featuring sand traps, pleasantly rolling greens, bunkers, and water areas. This is an ideal course for novices or those looking for a short practice session.

Sand Barrens Golf Club (609-465-3555; www.sandbarrensgolf.com), 1765 Rt. 9 North, Swainton. Ranked by *Golf Digest* as one of the top courses in New Jersey. There are three sets of nine 36-par holes on tree-lined fairways and greens with challenging scrub bunkers.

Avalon Golf Club (609-465-4653; www.avalongolfclub.net), 1510 Rt. 9, Swainton. The 18-hole course—one of the most popular in the region—is in a lovely setting dotted with several lakes and ponds. Amenities include a driving range, a putting green, and a clubhouse with pro shop, snack bar, and restaurant.

Cape May National Golf Club (609-884-1563; www.cmngc.com), Rt. 9 and Florence Ave., Cold Spring. Close to the Cape May–Lewes Ferry, 2 miles outside Cape May. This award-winning golf course is called The Natural for its pristine landscape of ponds, woodlands, natural grasses, and expansive wetlands, designed around a private 50-acre bird sanctuary. *Golf Digest* has called it one of the "top 50 places to play in America."

Cape May Par 3 Golf Course and Driving Range (609-889-2600; www.cape maypar3.com), Fulling Mill Rd., Rio Grande. Open daily, year-round. A family-friendly 18-hole links-style course that's ideal for expert and novice players, a good place to learn the subtleties of the game.

HIKING ✔ **Cape May Point State Park** (609-884-2159), Lighthouse Rd. (off Rt. 606), Cape May Point. Open year-round, daily from dawn to dusk. A small and scenic state park at the tip of the Cape May peninsula that offers marked hiking trails through a variety of habitats, from salt marsh and coastal dunes to forest, beach, and ponds. Several observation areas and wildlife blinds are found along the way for viewing ducks, swans, and wading birds in the ponds, and shorebirds along the beach and dunes. The peninsula is a significant migratory route for birds and monarch butterflies, and one of the top birding destinations in North America. Shorebirds and songbirds fly through in spring; monarch butterflies rest here in late summer before journeying across Delaware Bay; and raptors pass through in the fall. Many other species nest and feed here throughout the year. Ask about a schedule of guided nature walks.

KAYAKING Aqua Trails Kayak Nature Tours (609-884-5600; www.aquatrails .com), 1600 Delaware Ave., Cape May. Reservations are suggested. Guided tours leave twice daily, May–Sept. Guided kayaking tours explore the inland salt marshes around Cape May. A 1.5-hour paddle cuts through the salt marshes and narrow waterways surrounding Cape May, a natural sanctuary for hundreds of wildlife species, including egrets, gulls, turtles, and ospreys. Special excursions, such as sunset tours and full-moon trips. They also rent single-, double-, and surf kayaks.

PARASAILING East Coast Parasail (609-884-8359; www.eastcoastparasail .com), South Jersey Marina, 1121 Rt. 109, Cape May. Reservations are required. Trips leave every 90 minutes, in-season, starting at 8 AM. The entire boat trip is about an hour and a half; passengers parasail for about 10 minutes, when they're treated to a bird's-eye panorama of Cape May and the Atlantic Ocean.

SIGHTSEEING EXCURSIONS The Mid-Atlantic Center for the Arts (MAC) (609-884-5404; 800-275-4278; www.capemaymac.org), offers a variety of year-round narrated tours by trolley and boat on Cape May's Victorian history, architecture, and heritage. MAC's newest tour, the World War II Trolley Tour, explores the war's impact on the Cape area, visiting coastal fortifications at Battery 223 and Fire Control Tower No. 23, the Cape May Canal, and the Naval Air Station Wildwood Aviation Museum, Hangar #1. Other tours include a Cape May Family Treasure Hunt, the Cape May by Moonlight, and the Artists and Studios Tour.

Great American Trolley Company (609-884-5230; 800-487-6559; www.gatrolley .com). **Victorian Gingerbread of Cape May tours** leave from various hotels and locations in Atlantic City. Learn about the history and grandeur of Cape May and its vibrant turn-of-the-20th-century architecture. Award-winning narrated sightseeing trolley rides connect Atlantic City to Cape May, where passengers can stroll through the historic streets and shop at the outdoor **Washington Street Mall.**

Cape May Carriage Company (609-884-4466; www.capemaycarriage.com). The carriage stop is at the Washington Street Mall on Ocean St., Cape May. Open daily, June–Sept.; open Apr.–May, Oct.–Nov., Fri.–Sun. Tickets can be purchased at the carriage stop; phone reservations are not accepted for tours; call or see Web site for rates. Nostalgic horse-drawn carriage tours through Cape May's charming historic streets, day or night.

Haunted Cape May Tours (609-463-8984; www.hauntednewjersey.com), Cape May. Tours meet on the Promenade across from the Hotel Macomber, 727 Beach Dr., at 7 and 9 PM (in Nov. at 7 PM only). Tours are offered May–Nov.; nightly in summer; reduced schedule in the off-season. A ghost walking-tour featuring extensively researched true tales of paranormal phenomena in Cape May's past.

Fisherman's Wharf (609-884-5404; 800-275-4278; www.capemaymac.org), Schellenger's Rd., Cape May. Call or see Web site for schedule. Tickets are sold 15 minutes before the start of the tour. Adults $10, children 3–12, $7. The **Mid-Atlantic Center for the Arts** offers 45-minute guided tours of Cape May's famous **Lobster House Restaurant** dock and fish-packing plant. Cape May is one of the busiest fishing ports on the East Coast, and Fisherman's Wharf is home to Cape May's commercial fishing fleet.

SWIMMING (See *Green Space—Beaches*.)

TENNIS **The Cape May Tennis Center** (609-884-8986; www.capemaytennis club.com), 1020 Washington St., Cape May. There are 14 hard-turf and 2 all-weather courts that are open to the public (for a fee) daily 8 AM–dusk.

✳ Green Space

BEACHES There are 2 miles of public beaches in Cape May on the Atlantic Ocean and Delaware Bay. Beach tags (609-884-9525) are required for adults and children ages 12 and older from Memorial Day weekend to mid-Sept. every day from 10–5. Daily, weekly, and seasonal tags are sold at various locations around town, including the city hall information desk at 643 Washington St., the information center at the Washington Street Mall on Ocean St., the Cape May Convention Hall on Beach Dr., and at all beach entrances. Ask about beach wheelchairs, which are available at no charge.

In Cape May (609-884-9520), lifeguards are on duty daily in-season from 10–5:30. Day pass $4; weekly tag $11; seasonal beach tag $17. **The Promenade** is a 2-mile-long beachfront walkway lined with shops, arcades, and eateries. Surfing is allowed at **Colonial Beach and Jefferson Beach. Cove Beach** is known for its view of the Cape May Lighthouse.

Cape May Point Beach (609-884-8468) is at the southernmost tip of the Cape May peninsula, where the Atlantic Ocean meets Delaware Bay in Cape May Point. Day pass $5; weekly tag $10; seasonal tag $17. Lifeguards are on duty in-season

On Delaware Bay, **Sunset Beach** is a pretty little stretch of sand, the southern-most of Cape May's bayside beaches. Swimming is not permitted; instead, people come here to watch the sun dip below the horizon at sunset and to search the sand for **Cape May "diamonds."** The cloudy nuggets of quartz resemble milky stones, and when they're polished up they glitter like diamonds, and are often made into rings and pendants. Just a few yards offshore are the hulking remains of the **SS *Atlantus,*** a World War I–era concrete ship that broke loose from its moorings during a storm and ran aground in 1926. The 250-foot freighter was one of 12 experimental concrete ships made by the federal government—their solution to a wartime shortage of steel. During the summer, a patriotic flag-lowering ceremony takes place on the beach every evening at sunset, and includes the playing of taps and other patriotic American music. The flag ceremony is more than 40 years old and held daily, May through September.

GARDENS Leaming's Run Botanical Gardens (609-465-5871; www.leamings rungardens.com), 1845 Rt. 9, Swainton. Open mid-May–mid-Oct., daily 9:30–5. Adults $8, children 7–14, $4; children 6 and under, free. This is the largest annuals garden in America and one of the top public gardens in the East, planted on property once owned by Christopher Leaming, one of Cape May County's founding fathers. From late spring to fall, 30 acres of magnificent gardens attract nature lovers, world-renowned horticulturalists, and fledgling gardeners who come for inspiration or quiet reflection. A walking path across lawns, over bridges, and around ponds connects 25 individually designed lush gardens. Birds and butterflies are often seen hovering around the drifts of bright color; in August, ruby-throated hummingbirds come to the gardens to feed in preparation for their annual migration south. You'll regret not bringing a camera here. In addition to the showy annuals, there's a small re-created farm site planted with crops like cotton and tobacco that grew here in the 18th century. A re-created one-room log cabin is typical of the ones 17th-century whalers lived in alongshore; next to it is a historic herb and vegetable garden. The property also boasts the last remaining uncut forest in Cape May County, a holly forest, and an extensive collection of cinnamon ferns.

NATURAL AREAS Cape May National Wildlife Refuge (609-463-0994), headquarters: 24 Kimbles Beach Rd., Cape May Court House. This undeveloped refuge is open year-round, daily from dawn until dusk; the headquarters is open Mon.–Fri. 8–4:30. This wild and beautiful tract of salt marsh, maritime forest, grassland, forested wetland, and other unique habitats, is one of the newest refuges in the national wildlife refuge system. Since it was established in 1989, the refuge (which comprises many tracts of land around the Cape May peninsula, each with a unique habitat) has protected thousands of acres, and is still growing. The **Delaware Bay Division** protects a string of Delaware Bay beaches, where shorebirds feast on horseshoe crab eggs every spring. Rare stands of Atlantic white cedar fill the 5,000-acre **Great Cedar Swamp Division.** The foot trails are good spots for observing birds and other wildlife, especially in spring and fall.

Dennis Creek Wildlife Management Area (856-629-0090), Jake's Landing Rd. (off Rt. 47), North Dennis. Open year-round, daily from dawn to dusk. A vast expanse of undisturbed marsh grasses, reeds, and tidal creeks that's home to herons, egrets, and wintering hawks, eagles, and other raptors. Anglers go to the freshwater lake to fish for sunfish and perch (a New Jersey fishing license is required). There's a parking area and boat ramp on Dennis Creek.

NATURE CENTERS ✿ **Nature Center of Cape May** (609-898-8848), 1600 Delaware Ave., Cape May. Open Mar.–May, Tues.–Sat. 10–3; June–Aug., daily 9–4; Sept.–Nov., Tues.–Sat. 10–3; Dec.–Feb., Tues.–Sat. 10–1. This center run by the **New Jersey Audubon Society** in Cape May Harbor comprises 18 acres of meadow, marshland, and beach. The focus is on environmental education, with exhibits on Cape May ecology and lots of programs for children, adults, and families, from beachcombing at low tide, winter duck-watches along the harbor to nature crafts and drawing workshops. Classrooms, themed display gardens, and a nature store with nature books, T-shirts, and children's items.

Cape May Bird Observatory: Center for Research and Education (609-861-0700), 600 Rt. 47, Goshen. Open year-round, daily 9–4:30. A **New Jersey Audubon Society** center whose focus is on backyard bird-watching and natural landscaping. There's a full schedule of nature programs, tours, bird-watching programs, workshops, and lectures. The center has an observation deck and demonstration models of backyard habitats (a good place to spot birds and butterflies) surrounded by 26 acres of salt marsh and upland. Inside there's a wildlife art gallery and a nature shop stocked with bird feeders and supplies, nature books, and binoculars and other optics.

PARK ✿ **Cape May Point State Park** (609-884-2159), Lighthouse Ave. (off Rt. 606), Cape May Point. Open year-round, daily from dawn to dusk. Free admission. Most visitors come to this small state park to see the **Cape May Lighthouse** (see *To See—Lighthouse*), but it's worth spending time exploring the pristine natural surroundings. Freshwater coastal marsh, dunes, ponds, shoreline, and wooded uplands are a haven to resident wildlife and thousands of migratory birds, butterflies, and raptors in spring and fall. There's a hawk-viewing platform, 3 miles of hiking trails, guided nature walks, and aquatic wildlife shows and talks for children. The beach is a good place for surf fishing, but swimming is not allowed.

The park's stone tower was once part of the Harbor Defense Project of 1942, a World War II–era coastal defense system that included 15 such towers along the southern New Jersey coast, built to protect Delaware Bay from enemy attack. It's on the National Register of Historic Places and has recently been opened to the public. The submerged concrete bunker was once 900 feet inland, surrounded by earth and covered by sod; from the sea or air it once looked as if it were a hill. Today it's in the water—thanks to erosion—but at low tide you can still see the gun turrets at the front of the bunker.

✳ Lodging

Cape May has more than 80 bed & breakfasts, not to mention a host of motels, hotels, inns, and guesthouses. Finding a place to fit your needs and budget shouldn't be a problem, but arrangements should be made well in advance, especially in summer, on spring and fall weekends, or during major events like the Cape May Music Festival, the World Series of Birding, or Victorian Week. If you arrive in town without a reservation, or want to plan a spur-of-the-moment visit, there are a few lodging services you can turn to. **Historic Accommodations of Cape May** (hotline: 609-884-0080; www.capemaylodging.com), P.O. Box 83, Cape May 08204, is an association of more than 70 guest apartments, guesthouses, and bed & breakfast inns that can help with last-minute reservations. The hotline is available daily, 11 AM–7 PM. The **Greater Cape May Chamber of Commerce** (609-884-5508; www.capemaychamber.com) maintains an up-to-date online listing of lodging vacancies. **Cape May Reservation Service** (800-729-7778), 1382 Lafayette St., Cape May 08204, has a helpful staff that will provide information and guidance. Most lodgings are smoke-free—especially inns and B&Bs—but many allow guests to smoke outside on their porches. Keep in mind that while some B&Bs allow young children, many do not. Innkeepers are virtual treasure troves of information for planning activities, and many will gladly arrange dinner reservations, on request. Many lodgings offer special packages that might include gourmet dinners, spa treatments, or sightseeing tours.

HOTELS

All listings are in Cape May 08204.

꒰ᵀ꒱ **Hotel Alcott** (609-884-5868; 800-272-3004; www.hotelalcott.com), 107–113 Grant St. Open year-round. Cape May's second-oldest operating hotel has been welcoming guests since 1878, when it was known as the Arlington House. It was eventually renamed in honor of frequent visitor and icon of American literature Louisa May Alcott. At the turn of the 20th century, this grand Italianate villa-style hotel bus-

tled with vacationers arriving by train—as most did then—from the rail station that once stood across the street. An extensive restoration has preserved many of the hotel's original historic features, from the dramatic hanging staircase to the chestnut-paneled lobby and elegant dining room. Today it offers the amenities found in a full-service hotel combined with the charm of a historic inn. There are 31 custom-decorated guest rooms and suites. Standard rooms are small but nicely furnished; suites are more spacious. All have TV, Wi-Fi, phone, individual climate control, wireless Internet, and private baths done in granite and tile. A complimentary continental breakfast and afternoon refreshments are included. Guest like to savor the views from the breezy second-floor veranda, relax in the lush fountain courtyard, or claim a rocking chair on the handsome rambling porch. **La Verandah** restaurant offers fine dining outdoors and in an elegant high-ceilinged 19th-century dining room. Complimentary afternoon refreshments and continental breakfast. $100–340.

꒰ᵀ꒱ ꧁ **Carroll Villa B&B Hotel** (609-884-9619; 877-275-8452; www.carroll villa.com), 19 Jackson St. Open year-round. A warm and friendly family-owned and family-operated B&B hotel offering reasonably priced accommodations at the heart of the historic district. The circa-1882 national historic landmark structure was built as a seaside villa for vacationing families. Today it is one of only a small handful of Victorian hotels remaining in Cape May. The 22 guest rooms are comfortable and nicely decorated with floral wallpaper and Victorian antiques. The rooms are on the small side—many have just one double bed—but they retain a homey rather than a cramped feel. All have private bath (some are in the hallway), air-conditioning, free Internet access, TV/VCR, phones, and ceiling fans. Guests have use of the warm and cozy Victorian parlor. The **Mad Batter** restaurant serves innovative gourmet cuisine at three meals, but the breakfasts are legendary (see *Dining Out*). The beach, ocean, and promenade are a convenient half block away. $75–215.

❝1❞ The Virginia Hotel (609-884-5700; 800-732-4236; www.virginia hotel.com), 25 Jackson St. Open year-round. An elegant Victorian-era mansion transformed into a stylish boutique hotel with the amenities and attentive service of a full-service luxury facility and the personal touches found in an intimate B&B. The 24 custom-furnished guest rooms are tastefully appointed, and all have private baths, air-conditioning, phones, TVs/VCRs, CD players, complimentary wireless hi-speed Internet, plush robes, and down comforters. Some have private balconies overlooking historic Jackson Street. Guests can relax in the bar, in the intimate library lounge complete with fireplace and baby grand piano, or on the cozy front porch. The highly acclaimed **Ebbitt Room** (see *Dining Out*) is one of the hottest dining spots in town. Continental breakfast is served on the front veranda or delivered to your room; complimentary beach chairs and umbrellas, and the daily *New York Times*, are among the thoughtful extras. $89–455.

The Queen's Hotel (609-884-1613), 601 Columbia Ave. Open year-round.

❝1❞ CONGRESS HALL

(609-884-8421; 888-944-1816; www.congresshall.com), 251 Beach Ave. at Perry St., Cape May 08204. Open year-round. This 19th-century white-pillared Cape May landmark underwent an impressive $25 million overhaul that returned the stately beachfront hotel to its original grandeur. Today, the hotel's common areas and 109 guest rooms and suites boast custom furnishings, luxurious amenities, and modern upgrades combined with the old-fashioned ambiance and hospitality it was known for when it premiered in 1816. U.S. president Benjamin Harrison used Congress Hall as his summer White House in the 1890s; he was one of four presidents to vacation here while they ran the country. Composer John Philip Sousa stayed here, too. The lobby is classic and elegant, with dark wicker furniture, white columns, buttery yellow walls, a grand staircase, and the original black-and-white tile floor. The guest rooms are bright and airy, spruced up with simple-yet-stylish furnishings and updated bathrooms, and filled with an eclectic blend of antiques and family heirlooms. The five suites have private sitting areas and offer lovely ocean views; all rooms have a private bath, a flat-screen TV, hi-speed wireless Internet access, two phones, a daily newspaper, and twice-daily housekeeping service. Some accommodations have upgraded luxuries like soaking tubs and private balconies. Amenities include a spa, an outdoor pool, a fitness room, a lounge, a nightclub, and shops. The **Blue Pig Tavern** serves breakfast, lunch, and dinner (see *Dining Out*). $115–395.

This charming hotel occupies two meticulously restored Victorian buildings. The 1876 hotel used to house a gambling casino; today it has guest rooms with Victorian décor and modern amenities. The Queen's Cottage is a fanciful multi-hued gingerbread Victorian with two romantic and private guest rooms overlooking a lovely perennial garden. The nine guest rooms and three suites come with private baths and amenities like TV, telephone, and a mini-refrigerator and coffeemaker, plus luxurious touches like duvets, custom window treatments, whirlpool tubs for two, and private balconies that overlook the ocean or Cape May's historic streets. Guests often congregate on the porches and balconies, which are filled with rockers and boast views of the ocean. Bikes are available for guests to pedal around town. Complimentary refreshments and continental breakfast. $75–270.

✔ **The Chalfonte Hotel** (609-884-8409; 888-411-1998; www.chalfonte.com), 301 Howard St. Open Memorial Day–Columbus Day. The Chalfonte has been taking in guests since 1876, making it the oldest continually operating hotel in Cape May. It's certainly a hard-to-miss landmark—the rambling white building is dressed in ornate gingerbread trim, an Italianate cupola, and close to 200 shutters. Comfortable rocking chairs line a long front porch shaded by a snazzy green-and-white-striped awning. The old-fashioned lobby is furnished with antiques, as are many of the guest rooms, which occupy the main building and three cottages. Guest rooms are simply furnished and do without modern amenities like TV, phone, and air-conditioning. Many have shared baths, which are either adjacent to the room or down the hall. The setup gets mixed reviews—where some guests see old-fashioned charm, others see outdated

sparseness. The **Magnolia Room** serves authentic Southern-style cuisine (see *Dining Out*), and the **King Edward Bar** has a warm, pubby feel. Kids can eat breakfast and dinner in the supervised **Children's Activity Room.** The hotel's popular summertime cultural series features art exhibits, cabaret, and the **Concerts by Candlelight** classical concert series, all open to the public. $130–499.

🌸 ✔ **Hotel Macomber** (609-884-3020; www.hotelmacomber.com), 727 Beach Ave. Open Apr.–Dec.; closed Jan.–Mar. A landmark shingle-style hotel on the Atlantic Ocean offering clean and comfortable accommodations at bargain prices. Longtime patrons come back for the old-fashioned charm and the friendly and helpful staff. Families especially like the laid-back homey feel. The charming wraparound front porch is a favorite with guests, who flock to the rockers to watch the sunrise and the superb ocean view. Of the 36 guest rooms, the oceanfront units are the largest, and many have balconies. Other rooms are smaller but cozy and bright, with white wicker furnishings and standard amenities. There is no air-conditioning, and some rooms have shared baths. The **Union Park Dining Room** offers gourmet dining (see *Dining Out*). $65–275.

INNS

All listings are in Cape May 08204.

Inn at 22 Jackson (609-884-2226; 800-452-8177; www.innat22jackson.com), 22 Jackson St. Open year-round. This 1899 Queen Anne–style Victorian is a charming and romantic inn on the most historic street in town. The four tastefully decorated suites boast a variety of amenities that might include a claw-foot tub, fireplace, or private porch. Each suite has a private bath, a TV, a wet bar, air-conditioning, and a ceiling fan. There's also a cottage that's ideal for families with children. At night the inn's twinkling lights put on a festive display. Guests can use the complimentary bikes and beach chairs, or relax on one of the three verandas that overlook Jackson Street. Refreshments and home-baked snacks in the afternoon, and a full buffet breakfast in the morning. Suites $175–400; inquire about cottage rates.

Peter Shields Inn (609-884-9090; www.petershieldsinn.com), 1301 Beach Dr. Open year-round. This elegant Georgian Revival–style mansion with soaring white columns and rambling screened porch is a real gem of an inn, tucked into a quiet neighborhood a block from the ocean. Each of the nine guest rooms is furnished in tastefully chosen period antiques and comes with private bath, TV, Wi-Fi, and air-conditioning; some have working fireplaces. The Restaurant serves top-notch gourmet American cuisine in five oceanfront dining rooms. Guests can take the inn's bikes around town, or take their beach chairs, umbrellas, and towels to the sand. Complimentary tea and snacks are offered in the afternoon, wine and cheese in the evening, and a full breakfast. $99–395.

Inn of Cape May (609-884-5555; reservations: 800-583-5933; www.innofcapemay.com), 7 Ocean St. Open daily Apr.–mid-Oct; weekends, mid-Oct–mid-Dec.; closed mid-Dec.–Mar. Built in 1894, this family-run grand white landmark hotel sits across the street from the Atlantic Ocean. Guest accommodations come in a variety of sizes, from small rooms with one double bed to suites with bedrooms and sitting rooms; many face the ocean. All are individually furnished with antiques or wicker décor; all have private bath, Wi-Fi, air-conditioning, and TV; VCR/DVD players are available for guests to use. Rooms do not have phones. The original elevator is still in use and staffed around the clock. **Aleathea's Restaurant** serves traditional American cuisine in a charming Victorian parlor and on the inn's front porch. Outdoor pool, antiques shop, and live piano music nightly during the summer. Full breakfast. $115–380.

Leith Hall Historic Seashore Inn (609-884-1934; 877-884-1400; www.leithhall.com), 22 Ocean St. Open year-round. A nicely restored 1884 Victorian a half block from the beach, the guest rooms and common areas boast elegant Victorian touches, from carefully chosen antiques to Oriental rugs and lace curtains. There are eight stylishly furnished and uniquely themed guest rooms and generously sized suites, all with private baths and air-conditioning, some with refrigerators, whirlpool tubs, fireplaces, and lovely ocean views. Common areas include the wraparound porch and beautifully restored parlor and library. Afternoon English tea and a full breakfast are served on antique china and silver. $165–275.

Queen Victoria (609-884-8702; www.queenvictoria.com), 102 Ocean St. Open year-round. This lovely inn occupies two restored 1880s Victorian homes surrounded by a fanciful wrought-iron fence and lovely perennial borders. The 32 well-appointed rooms and six suites are furnished with period antiques and handmade quilts. All have air-conditioning, TVs, mini-refrigerators, and private baths; some have a gas fireplace, a whirlpool tub, or both. There is a staggering collection of some 50 rocking chairs on the porches and in the gardens. Guest can use the inn's bicycles and beach chairs. Afternoon tea and refreshments, and a full buffet breakfast. $115–460.

All listings are in Cape May 08204.

♪ **Poor Richard's Inn** (609-884-3536; www.poorrichardsinn.com), 17 Jackson St. Open all year. Innkeeper Harriett Sosson's 1882 colorful Second Empire–style gingerbread house is a charming and inviting retreat located a mere quarter of a block from the beach. Guest rooms and common areas are filled with a nice mix of homey furnishings and fine antiques. Each of the eight guest rooms has air-conditioning; most have a private bath. Some rooms are decorated in a casual, country Victorian-style with painted furniture and patchwork quilts, less austere and formal than the traditional period décor that fills other rooms. Rocking on the porch is a popular pastime here, as is relaxing in the courtyard garden or inside in the cozy sitting rooms. A garden apartment is available by the week; phone for rates. Continental breakfast. $110–180.

⁰↑⁰ **The Fairthorne Bed & Breakfast and Cottage** (609-884-8791; 800-438-8742; www.fairthorne.com), 111–115 Ocean St. (mailing address: P.O. Box 2381). Open year-round. Innkeepers Ed and Diane Hutchinson's 1892 Colonial Revival–style inn was once the home of a whaling captain. Today it's a charming and romantic B&B in the heart of the historic district and close to restaurants, shops, and the beach. There are nine antiques-filled guest rooms—six in the main house and three in the cottage—all with TV, Wi-Fi, mini-refrigerator, air-conditioning, and private bath; some have updated amenities such as a whirlpool tub, fireplace, or VCR. Afternoon refreshments might be lemonade or tea and coffee with snacks and fresh-baked cookies. Guests have full use of the inn's bicycles and beach chairs. Full breakfast. $265–280.

♿ **Wilbraham Mansion Bed & Breakfast Inn** (609-884-2046; www .wilbrahammansion.com), 133 Myrtle Ave. Open year round. This 1840 mansion on Wilbraham Park, built for a prominent Philadelphia industrialist, is the only bed & breakfast in Cape May that boasts an indoor heated pool. It also offers 9 lovely guest rooms and 13 suites, an elegant and relaxed atmosphere, and lots of splendid Victorian flourishes, from authentic period-style wallpaper to some of the home's original furnishings. Some rooms have antique armoires, Victorian slipper chairs, dry sinks, and claw-foot tubs. All have private bath and air-conditioning; some have ceiling fans. Common space includes two dining rooms, a pair of Victorian parlors, a TV room, and the mansion's open porches. Guests can help themselves to the inn's bikes. Afternoon tea and full breakfast. The Wilbraham Mansion Suites fill a new building complementing the design and décor of the mansion. Each suite features an LCD-TV, DVD player, Satellite TV service, gas fireplace, two-person Jacuzzi, whirlpool bath, Salon Spa, two-person shower, mini refrigerator, ceiling fan, and individual temperature control. The suite building is fully handicapped accessible. $110–270.

The Humphrey Hughes House (609-884-4428; 1-800-582-3634; www .humphreyhugheshouse.com), 29 Ocean St. Open year-round. Humphrey Hughes, a sea captain, was one of the first to settle in 17th-century Cape May. A Hughes descendant built this elegant turn-of-the-20th-century summerhouse, and it stayed in the family until 1980. Today it's Terry and Lorraine Schmidt's charming B&B with seven individually decorated guest rooms and three suites, all with private baths, air-conditioning, and TV. Guests have use of the antiques-filled common rooms, the glass-enclosed sunporch, and the spacious rocker-lined wraparound veranda. Afternoon tea and full breakfast. $145–350.

& **The Mainstay Inn** (609-884-8690; www.mainstayinn.com), 635 Columbia Ave. Open year-round. This elegant Victorian inn started out in 1872 as a private men's gambling club. It later became Cape May's first bed & breakfast. Today it's a museum-like Cape May treasure, painstakingly restored and full of original period details and luxurious furnishings. It offers nine guest rooms, three suites, and four luxury fireplace suites spread across three buildings—the original inn, a refurbished cottage, and the Officer's Quarters, a World War I–era building once used as housing for naval officers. All rooms have private baths; some suites have whirlpool tubs, fireplaces, and private verandas with rockers. One of the suites is handicapped accessible. Afternoon tea and snacks and a hearty breakfast (buffet in summer, served family-style in winter) are included. Rooms $175–360; suites $195–360.

The Southern Mansion (609-884-7171; 800-381-3888; www.southern mansion.com), 720 Washington St. Open year-round. In 1863, this elegant summer mansion was built for a wealthy Philadelphia family. The house remained in the Allen family for a century before it was sold, used as a boardinghouse, and sadly neglected. Since then, an impressive top-to-bottom restoration has transformed the dilapidated building into an architectural showcase with boutique hotel style and Old World antebellum charm. Today the lovingly restored mansion with fanciful green-and-red trim has graced many a magazine cover, and is one of Cape May's most popular bed & breakfasts. It's surrounded by 2 acres of Italian gardens;

rocking chairs line the rambling gleaming-wood porch, and museum-quality antiques and ornate furnishings fill the genteel common areas. The guest rooms and suites are nothing short of opulent—spacious accommodations full of fine antiques and dressed in bold colors and rich fabrics. Each has private bath, TV, and phones with computer ports; most have king beds. Afternoon refreshments are served in the ballroom, and a full breakfast is served each morning in the plant-filled solariums. $130–415.

The Mason Cottage (609-884-3358; www.themasoncottage.com), 625 Columbia Ave. Open year-round. This spectacular mansion was built in 1871 as the summer "cottage" of a wealthy Philadelphia entrepreneur. The Mason family started welcoming guests in the 1940s when they opened the house as an inn, and today's innkeepers are only the third owners of this historic property. Many impressive Victorian features are found throughout the house, from the elegant floor-to-ceiling windows to the wide veranda and many of the original furnishings. The five guest rooms and four suites are cozy and charming. All have private bath, air-conditioning, and TV; some have whirlpool tubs, fireplaces, and other upgraded amenities. Each afternoon, guests are treated to tea, seasonal drinks, and homemade sweets, and a full breakfast is served in the morning. A gourmet coffee bar with more than 15 kinds of coffee and coffee drinks is available around the clock. $115–269.

❝❞ **Angel of the Sea** (609-884-3369; 800-848-3369; www.angelofthesea .com), 5 Trenton Ave. This lovely property holds 27 guest rooms, each uniquely furnished in Victorian style and with private bath. About a quarter of the rooms have ocean views, and every room has cable TV and wireless

Internet access. A full breakfast, an afternoon tea, and evening wine and cheese are served. $95–315.

MOTELS

In Cape May 08204

✂ ⅚ "I" Avondale By The Sea (609-884-2332; 800-676-7030; www.avondalebythesea.com), Beach Dr. and Gurney St., P.O. Box 2382. Open Apr.–mid-Nov. A modern oceanfront inn that has clean and comfortable rooms and a warm and friendly staff. Innkeepers Sheila and Herb Weiner offer standard motel-style guest rooms and spacious suites with separate sitting areas and sofa beds. All rooms have private baths, TV, Wi-Fi, air-conditioning, phones, and refrigerators; some have private balconies. Outdoor pool and separate kiddie pool. Continental breakfast. $80–245.

✂ ⅚ "I" **Atlas Inn** (609-884-7000; 888-285-2746; www.atlasinn.com), 1035 Beach Ave. Open Apr.–early Nov. Beach Avenue runs between the inn and the beach, but the views are pleasant and the rooms are clean and comfortable. Modern rooms and efficiency suites have standard amenities including TV, telephone, wireless Internet, refrigerator, and an oceanfront deck or balcony. There's an outdoor pool, barbecue grills, fitness room, and laundry facilities. **Bloody Mary's Bar & Grill** serves casual fare. Continental breakfast. $83–208.

Victorian Motel (609-884-7044; www.victorianmotelnj.com), 223 Congress Pl. Open year-round. The location is as good as it gets—close to Cape May's beaches, shops, and restaurants—and the price is reasonable, even in the high season. Standard rooms and one- and two-room efficiencies are no-frills but are comfortable and simply furnished. In-ground pool. $50–210.

"I" **La Mer Beachfront Motor Inn** (609-884-9000; 800-644-5004; www.capemaylamer.com), 1317 Beach Ave. Open mid-Apr.–Sept. An oceanfront motor inn with 93 recently redecorated rooms and efficiencies; all have private baths, TV, phones, and Internet access. The large heated outdoor pool is surrounded with plenty of lounge chairs, and an outdoor terrace is lined with umbrella tables. Restaurant and lounge. $62–339.

In West Cape May 08204

✂ **West Cape Motel** (609-884-4280; www.westcapemotel.com), 307 Sunset Blvd., West Cape May 08204. Open May–Oct. Nothing fancy, just clean and comfortable accommodations that are reasonably priced, and popular with the many birders who come for the nearby refuges and sanctuaries. Rooms, efficiencies, and two-room suites have TVs, phones, air-conditioning, and refrigerators. Outdoor pool. $60–185.

CAMPGROUNDS

In Cape May 08204

🐾 ✂ ⅚ **Cape Island Resort** (609-884-5777; www.capeisland.com), 709 Rt. 9. Open May–Oct. This is the closest full-service campground to Cape May's historic district, beaches, and the Cape May–Lewes Ferry. There are 75 sites spread across 175 acres of meadows and forest. Two full-sized pools plus one just for kids, mini golf, volleyball and tennis courts, and playgrounds. During the summer there's a full schedule of activities, from hay rides and movies to bingo and organized casino trips. $26–46.

🐾 ✂ "I" **Beachcomber Camping Resort** (609-886-6035; reservations: 800-233-0150; www.beachcombercamp.com), 462 Seashore Rd. Open mid-Apr.–Nov. 1. A 100-acre family campground that's convenient to the Cape May and Wildwood beaches and offers plenty of its own attractions. Stay at one of the 750 tent and RV sites, or rent a rustic cabin on a wooded or lakefront site. There are two spring-fed lakes, six swimming pools, and daily planned activities during the summer. Golf carts, paddleboats, and kayaks for rent. Limited, fee-based Wi-Fi. Sites $28–66; cabins $60–186.

In Cape May Court House 08210
♪ "I" **Big Timber Lake Camping Resort** (609-465-4456; reservations: 1-800-542-2267; www.bigtimberlake.com), 116 Swainton–Goshen Rd. (Rt. 646). Open mid-Apr.–mid-Oct. A full-service campground with 515 sites on 90 wooded acres. Daily summertime activities include crafts, holiday celebrations, water carnivals, live music, and a variety of contests—even a beauty pageant. There's a heated pool; freshwater lakes for fishing, canoeing, and swimming; hiking; game courts; and two playgrounds. Rustic one- and two-room cabins with double beds and bunk beds for rent. Complimentary morning coffee. Wi-Fi. Sites $44–65; cabins $73–120.

✴ Where to Eat
DINING OUT

All listings are in Cape May, unless otherwise indicated.
Union Park Dining Room (609-884-8811; www.unionparkdiningroom.com), Hotel Macomber, 727 Beach Ave. Open daily for dinner during the summer; reduced off-season hours. Reservations are recommended. Acclaimed Cape May restaurateur J. Christopher Hubert's fine-dining venue in the historic Hotel Macomber (see *Lodging—Hotels*), offers expertly prepared American cuisine served in charming antiques-filled and candlelit

dining rooms by an attentive and courteous staff. The seared salmon with dill yogurt vinaigrette is a standout. BYOB. $18–45.

♪ **The Magnolia Room** (609-884-8409; www.chalfonte.com), at the Chalfonte Hotel, 301 Howard St. Open daily, Memorial Day–Columbus Day, for breakfast and dinner. Sisters and cooks Lucille Thompson and Dot Burton have worked at Cape May's oldest continually operating hotel (see *Lodging—Hotels*) since the 1940s, when their mother, Helen, was the kitchen's longtime cook. The Virginia natives brought their homey Southern-style cooking to Cape May; today's menu still features Southern classics like fried chicken, spoon bread, corn pudding, and lemon meringue pie. Families with young children are encouraged to dine before 7; there's also a supervised **Children's Activity Room,** where young dinner guests can eat and play with their peers while Mom and Dad enjoy a quiet meal alone. $18–30.

The Ebbitt Room (609-884-5700; 800-732-4236; www.virginiahotel.com), at the Virginia Hotel, 25 Jackson St. Open year-round for dinner. Reservations are recommended. This is fine hotel dining at its best (see *Lodging—Hotels*), one of only four establishments in Cape May to earn the prestigious Five-Star Diamond designation. The atmosphere and décor is elegant and sophisticated, from the white linen and candlelight to the impeccable service. The flawless New American cuisine has delightful Southern touches, and the menu changes often. Live piano in the lounge. $24–35.

♿ **Tisha's Fine Dining** (609-884-9119; www.tishasfinedining.com), 714 Beach Dr. Open Apr.–Oct. for dinner. Reservations are recommended.

A lovely and intimate dining room on the beach and boardwalk with an ever-changing menu of inventive New American cuisine. The emphasis is on fresh local seafood and steaks, and the many dishes are prepared with an Italian flair. Starters might include fried calamari with roasted peppers and capers and a garlic cream sauce, instead of the standard marinara. Move on to Tuscan grilled chicken and shrimp or veal au poivre. BYOB. $19–31.

Frescos Ristorante (609-884-0366), 412 Bank St. Open Apr.–Oct. for dinner. Reservations are recommended. A fine-dining restaurant serving authentic and well-prepared Northern and regional Italian standards, from seafood and veal to pasta. This quaint clapboard house tucked behind a picket fence is a bring-your-own-bottle local favorite and a magnet for accolades and critical acclaim. Try to get one of the coveted tables on the porch. BYOB. $15–30.

410 Bank Street (609-884-2127), 410 Bank St. Serving dinner daily May–Oct. Reservations are recommended. Gourmet American cuisine with the exotic flavors of New Orleans, French, and Caribbean cooking. The restaurant is especially known for its slow-smoked meats and mesquite-grilled seafood, paired with creative sauces and local fresh ingredients. The 18th-century wisteria-covered cottage provides an elegant backdrop for the kitchen's creative flair and the dining room's impeccable service. BYOB. $23–33.

The Mad Batter (609-884-5970; www.madbatter.com), at the Carroll Villa Hotel, 19 Jackson St. Open for breakfast, lunch, brunch, and dinner—daily in summer, reduced hours (long weekends) in winter. Reservations are suggested. A local favorite in the his-

toric Carroll Villa B&B Hotel (see *Lodging—Hotels*) for more than 30 years. Breakfast is their trademark, from the thick slices of orange-almond French toast to their signature omelet stuffed with jumbo lump crab, sun-dried tomatoes, fresh herbs, and Gruyère cheese. Dinner is equally good, offering contemporary American and regional cuisine. Their "championship" Maryland crabcakes come with a tasty sweet potato hash, and ordering their unique rendition of clam chowder is a must. You can dine on the intimate garden terrace, on the European-style porch overlooking the sidewalk, or in the bright and airy dining room. The bar has a nice selection of wines and interesting microbrews, and there's always something special going on, such as live music or their popular trivia night. Breakfast $7–10; dinner $19–27.

The Blue Pig Tavern (609-884-8422; www.congresshall.com), at the Congress Hall Hotel, 251 Beach Ave. Open daily for breakfast, lunch, and dinner. Reservations are accepted. An American tavern tucked away in one of Cape May's most spectacular 19th-century hotels (see *Lodging—Hotels*). The Blue Pig has a colorful history of its own. It occupies the site of Cape May's first tavern—frequented by whalers in the 1700s—and takes its name from a gambling parlor that opened after the hotel was built in 1816. Today it serves well-prepared classic cuisine in the light and airy garden room or in the cozy tavern. Dinner could begin with clam chowder with smoked bacon and thyme, or calamari with wasabi aioli and beet oil. The daily blue plate entrée special, with soup or salad, is a bargain. The **Boiler Room** has a late-night menu. Full bar. Dinner $11–28.

Freda's Café (609-884-7887; www .fredasgourmet.8m.com), 210 Ocean

St. Open Thurs.–Mon. for lunch and dinner. Reservations are accepted for dinner. This intimate and charming gem is a local favorite, housed in Cape May's historic former post office building. The menu of international dishes is mixed with an ever-changing list of seasonal specials. Appetizers sometimes include baked Brie in puff pastry, followed by entrées like grilled chicken with artichoke hearts and tarragon, barbecue spareribs, or the fresh fish of the day. Service is friendly and efficient, and the deli behind the restaurant offers excellent sandwiches and salads to go. BYOB. $15–30.

EATING OUT

In Cape May

✿ �& **Lobster House** (609-884-8296; www.thelobsterhouse.com), on Fisherman's Wharf, 906 Schellenger's Landing Rd. Open year-round for breakfast, lunch, and dinner; hours vary with the seasons; phone ahead once summer is over. This famous local landmark on Cape May Harbor attracts huge crowds and doesn't take reservations, so lines get long, especially on summer weekends when the wait can stretch beyond an hour. Inside is a casual seafood house with traditional nautical décor and a menu of shore seafood standbys, much of which arrives by boat at Fisherman's Wharf. When it's super-crowded, some like to order takeout from the raw bar and eat outside on the wharf, or bring home some of the market's fresh seafood and prepared dinners. There's a raw bar, a coffee shop, a gift shop, a fish market, and cocktails aboard the **schooner *America*.** $19–48.

✿ **Cape Orient** (609-898-0088; www.capeorient.com), in the Washington Commons Mall, 315 Ocean St. Open year-round, daily for lunch and dinner. Asian cuisine is hard to come by in Cape May, surprising for a town that's packed with restaurants. This friendly and casual eatery serves authentic and reasonably priced Chinese, Thai, and Japanese specialties, and it's the only place on the entire Cape May peninsula where you can get sushi. There's a

---

WASHINGTON INN

(609-884-5697; www.washingtoninn.com), 801 Washington St., Cape May. Open daily for dinner. Reservations are recommended. The gourmet American cuisine, romantic and elegant surroundings (a 19th-century plantation house), and numerous "best of" accolades and awards make dinner here an experience not to be missed. This was one of Cape May's first fine-dining establishments, and continues to raise the bar for the many that have followed its lead. Chef Mimi Wood's menu changes seasonally to take full advantage of the freshest ingredients. Starters could include bruschetta with roasted apples, chestnuts, and herbed mascarpone cheese, or a Tuscan salad of roasted peppers, olives, capers, and sourdough croutons in a tomato-basil vinaigrette. Move on to fig-and-hazelnut-crusted rack of lamb, herb-roasted organic chicken in a pesto-parmesan broth, or butter-poached lobster tail with a blood orange vinaigrette. End with vanilla bean crème brûlée or one of the house-made ice creams or sorbets. There's a full bar and an impressive 500-bottle wine cellar. $20–40.

large selection of sushi, sashimi, and hand rolls, and a whole section of the menu is devoted to tempura and teriyaki dishes. $10–20.

Louisa's Café (609-884-5882), 104 Jackson St. Reservations are essential. Open daily from early spring to late fall for dinner. A charming European-style eatery on Cape May's oldest street. Eclectic cuisine and reasonable prices make this intimate café a local favorite. It's a tiny word-of-mouth kind of place with a menu that changes according to what's fresh and available, which might be locally caught weakfish or shad, or a salad of vine-ripe Jersey tomatoes. Start with the signature crab soup, and end with a satisfying wedge of homemade pie. BYOB. $15–25.

McGlade's (609-884-2614), 722 Beach Ave. Open daily for breakfast, lunch, and dinner. Reservations are accepted. The location can't be beat—a screened-in deck on a beachfront pier overlooking the ocean—and the food is just as pleasing. For more than a quarter century, this has been a popular spot for breakfast, with a long list of omelets with creative fillings (think crabmeat, asparagus, cream cheese, sprouts), plus French toast, waffles, and other breakfast classics. Later on, regulars come here for the fresh and well-prepared seafood, the fried lobster tail in particular. BYOB. Breakfast and lunch $5–12; dinner $17–22.

&. **Jackson Mountain Café** (609-884-5648), 400 Washington St. Open daily for lunch and dinner. The menu of standard tavern fare is decent—burgers, sandwiches, salads, and Mexican dishes—and the bar is casual and friendly. The big draw at this lively eatery, however, is the collection of outdoor tables, which offers a perfect vantage point for people-watching on the Washington Street Mall. $9–15.

&. **Cucina Rosa** (609-898-9800), 301 Washington Street Mall. Open for dinner mid-Feb.–Dec., Thurs.–Tues.; closed Wed. Reservations are suggested. Traditional Italian cuisine—most everything homemade—served in a casual storefront eatery that's beloved by locals and a lucky find for visitors. You can eat outside on the patio or in one of the charming dining rooms. Expertly prepared and nicely presented signature dishes like seafood *fra diavolo,* chicken Florentine, and veal scaloppine are complemented by seasonal specialties like locally caught fish. Cannoli and espresso pair up for the perfect sweet ending. Pick up a bottle of Cucina Rosa marinade, specialty sauce, or spice mix and try to replicate their culinary brilliance at home. BYOB. $14–26.

&. **Carney's** (609-884-4424), Beach Dr. and Jackson St. Open daily for lunch, dinner, and light late-night meals. A laid-back beachfront pub that is a favorite haunt of both locals and visitors. The extensive menu is a something-for-everyone mix of pub fare—pizza, quesadillas, wings, and such—as well as their signature crabcakes and New England clam chowder, seafood, steaks, and homemade desserts. Nothing fancy, but fun and friendly. Carney's caters to a busy crowd that comes for the live music, lively bar, and dancing. If you're looking for a mellow evening, you can listen to jazz musicians perform in **The Other Room.** $14–22.

&. ✿ **Lucky Bones Backwater Grille** (609-884-8646; www.luckybonesgrille.com), 1200 Rt. 109. Open daily for lunch, dinner, and late night snacks. A good spot for brick-oven pizza, seafood, and steaks. The name comes from the Cape's whaling village days when superstitious sailors would carry a lucky bone (an odd hook-like claw found only on male horseshoe crabs) to stay safe at sea. Children's menu. $8.50–25.

Zoe's Beachfront Eatery (609-884-1233; www.zoescapemay.com), 715 Beach Dr. Open daily in summer 7 AM–10:30 PM; call for nonpeak season hours. This may be one of Cape May's best bargains. Set across from the Convention Hall, Zoe's serves full breakfasts, burgers, sandwiches, salads, and seafood baskets. It's very kid-friendly, and even welcomes dogs on the patio. Breakfast $5–8; lunch (dinner), $5–10.

In West Cape May

Vanthia's (609-884-4020; www.vanthias.com), 106 Sunset Blvd. Open for breakfast, 8–noon; lunch, noon–3; dinner, 3–until late. An upscale but family-friendly and reasonably priced bistro where the food reflects Greek, Italian, and Mediterranean influences. Breakfast, $3.75–9.50; lunch, $6–12; dinner, $14–25.

SNACKS AND SWEETS The Lemon Tree (609-884-2704), 101 Liberty Way, on the Washington Street Mall. A friendly deli serving up authentic Philadelphia-style cheesesteaks, Italian ice, and homemade lemonade that has been locally famous for nearly three decades. $5–8.

Fralinger's Original Salt Water Taffy (609-884-5695; www.jamescandy.com), 326 Washington St., Cape May. Open year-round. Fralinger's has been a beloved Jersey Shore institution since Joseph Fralinger began making saltwater taffy on the Atlantic City boardwalk in 1885. They adapt with the changing times—mango, mocha latte, and cookie dough are some of the newer flavors—but still cater to nostalgia seekers with sweet-filled replica 1915 gift tins.

The Fudge Kitchen (609-884-4287; 800-233-8343; www.fudgekitchens.com), on the Promenade at 728 Beach Dr., and 513 Washington Street Mall (609-884-2834), Cape May. The classic summer vacation indulgence of creamy fudge is made fresh every day, whipped by hand in old-time copper kettles. Traditional recipes like penuche, chocolate, and maple walnut along with new-fangled flavors like cookies-and-cream and mint chocolate chip for a total of 18 yummy varieties. These family-run shops—with additional locations in Stone Harbor, Ocean City, and Wildwood—also make saltwater taffy, truffles, almond bark, and other old-fashioned confections.

Nothing says summer at the beach quite like **ice cream,** and parlors abound in Cape May, where they dish out waffle cones, thick milkshakes, and colossal sundaes to a hungry vacation crowd. They include **Dry Dock Ice Cream Bar and Grill** (609-884-3434; www.capemaydrydock.com), 1440 Texas Ave.; **Cold Spring Village Ice Cream Parlor** (609-884-0392), Cold Spring; **Uncle Charley's Ice Cream** (609-884-2197), 310 Washington St.; and **Jennie's Ice Cream Parlor** (609-884-1953), 313 Beach Dr.

COFFEE AND TEA Rick's Coffee Café (609-898-9776; 888-884-3181; www.rickscoffeecafe.com) 414 Washington Street Mall and 315 Beach Drive (609-884-3181). A pair of locally run coffeehouses with the kind of relaxed and friendly atmosphere coffeehouses should have and often don't. A menu of coffee, tea, hot and cold drinks, and espresso accompanies house-made pastries, cakes, pies, and made-to-order sandwiches. $5–7.

⟁ CARRIAGE HOUSE TEAROOM & CAFÉ

(609-884-5111; 609-884-5404; www.capemaymac.org), at the Emlen Physick Estate, 1048 Washington St., Cape May. Open daily in-season; phone ahead in the off-season; luncheon is served from 11:30, afternoon tea begins at 2 PM. Reservations are recommended. Afternoon tea and tea luncheons are served in the beautifully restored 1876 Carriage House or under the tent in the Garden Patio on the grounds of Cape May's only Victorian house museum. Tea is served with the elegant formality typical of the Victorian age. Luncheon includes delicate tea sandwiches—cucumber, smoked salmon, and the like—along with an assortment of salads, tea breads, scones with clotted cream, and dessert. Afternoon tea features finger sandwiches, pastries, and scones. Both the luncheon and the afternoon tea are accompanied by a selection of hot and cold teas. Be sure to leave time to browse in the Gallery Shop, where there is a fine selection of tea, china, and tea-related gifts. Luncheon $18.50; afternoon tea $15.50.

✳ Entertainment

ARTS CENTERS ♂ Mid-Atlantic Center for the Arts (MAC) (609-884-5404; 800-275-4278; www.cape maymac.org), at the Emlen Physick Estate, 1048 Washington St., Cape May. This extremely active nonprofit local arts organization was founded in 1970 to restore the historic Physick Estate, Cape May's only Victorian house museum. Since then it has grown to 3,000 members and promotes Cape May's Victorian heritage through an impressive year-round schedule of festivals, workshops, family activities, events, and tours. They maintain and operate the Cape May Lighthouse, run the 19th-century Physick Estate (along with its Carriage House Gallery and Tearoom), offer year-round walking, boat, and trolley tours, and organize Victorian Week, the Cape May Music Festival, and a host of other major events.

Middle Township Performing Arts Center (609-463-1924; www.middle pac.com), 1 Penkethman Way, Cape May Court House. Cape May County's only performing-arts center, located in Middle Township High School, offers a year-round schedule of world-class performances, from dance, plays, and musicals to well-known orchestras and musical groups, like the Metropolitan Opera Guild and the New Jersey Pops.

MUSIC

In Cape May
The Cape May Music Festival and **Cape May Jazz Festival** (609-884-5404; 800-275-4278; www.capemay mac.org) are two world-class music festivals that draw huge crowds of music fans to Cape May (see *Special Events*). The 6-week music festival features classical, pop, jazz, folk, and chamber music in May and June. The jazz festival brings well-known names in the music world to town in April and November, with blues, reggae, jazz, and gospel.

The Chalfonte Hotel (609-884-8409; 888-411-1998; www.chalfonte.com), 301 Howard St., hosts a popular annual cultural-events series that runs May–Sept. Cabaret, opera, fine-art exhibits, and classical concerts in one of Cape May's most historic hotels are open to the public. Call for a schedule.

Historic Cold Spring Village (609-898-2300; www.hcsv.org), 720 Rt. 9. Free Saturday-evening concerts in July–Aug. at the museum village's outdoor gazebo. Performances begin at 6:30 PM, light rain or shine.

THEATER

In Cape May

⚓ **Cape May Stage** (609-884-1341; www.capemaystage.com), Lafayette and Bank Sts. Performances from May–Dec.; curtain rises at 8 PM. Reservations are strongly recommended. A professional equity theater presenting fine renditions of classics and original works. Performances are held in an intimate 75-seat theater housed in Cape May's former welcome center. Call for the season's lineup of dramas, comedies, family programs, and holiday shows.

East Lynne Theater Company (609-884-5898; www.eastlynnetheater.org), First Presbyterian Church, 500 Hughes St. Performances June–Oct. Professional actors stage high-quality renditions of American stage classics and adaptations of works by Mark Twain, Stephen Crane, Louisa May Alcott, and other famous American literary figures. The company takes its name from a popular 19th-century American play, and is the only professional nonprofit theater devoted to preserving the country's theatrical and literary history. Ask about dinner-theater packages.

✳ Selective Shopping

ART AND ANTIQUES

In Cape May Court House

Anthony Hillman Antique and Fine Wood Carvings (609- 536-2738; www.hillmanart.com), 980 West Hand Ave. Open by appointment. Anthony Hillman has been making hand-carved traditional bird decoys and waterfowl miniatures for more than 30 years. He also buys and sells antique decoys, and has written more than two-dozen how-to guides for artists and carvers. His shop, **The Decoy,** is open to the public by appointment.

In Cape May

Victorious Antiques (609-898-1775; www.victoriousantiques.com), Congress Hall Hotel, 301 Howard St. Antiques, gifts, and estate jewelry.

Cape May County Art League (609-884-8628; www.capemaycountyart league.com), P.O. Box 2195, Cape May. This has been an active county art league since 1929, which makes it the oldest such organization in America. They have a full schedule of programs that are open to the public, from poetry nights and art appreciation events to guest lectures and art classes. Major annual events include a spring-time members' exhibition, a children's summer art camp, and a juried fine-arts show at the Washington Street Mall every September.

MALL Washington Street Mall (609-884-0555; www.washington streetmall.com), 429 Washington St., Cape May. Open daily year-round. This Victorian-style open-air pedestrian mall at the heart of the historic district is Cape May's main shopping center. The car- and bicycle-free stretch of independently owned and family owned specialty boutiques,

candy stores, souvenir shops, and sidewalk cafés is just a block from the ocean. It's especially charming at Christmastime, when candles, wreaths, and garland transform the mall into a festive holiday scene reminiscent of the Victorian era.**SPECIAL SHOPS**
Mother Grimm's Bears (609-886-1200; www.mother grimmsbears.com), in the Hotel Macomber, 727 Beach Dr., Cape May. Ellen and Jennifer Grimm's delightful shop is a small-scale teddy bear factory. You give them a garment with sentimental value, such as a wedding gown, and they will create a unique custom-designed "memory bear" out of it. The mother-daughter team has made hundreds of bears out of fur coats, baby blankets, military uniforms, bridesmaid dresses, even flannel shirts and blue jeans. A unique way to preserve special memories.

Sunset Beach Gift Shops (800-757-6468; www.sunsetbeachnj.com), 502 Sunset Blvd., Cape May Point. A family-owned group of gift shops that's best known for its collection of Cape May diamonds and other unique stones. The infamous "diamonds"—gemlike pieces of quartz scattered all over nearby Sunset Beach—are sold in their natural state or polished and fashioned into rings, pendants, and other jewelry. The shops also sell the usual selection of vacation souvenirs, from lighthouses and clocks to coffee mugs, books, candles, and Cape May T-shirts.

The Cape May Cottage (609-463-1685), 1339 Rt. 9, Swainton. Call for hours. An inviting shop with an interesting collection of antique furniture, vintage linens, and unique home décor, as well as candles, lotions, bath soaps, and other gifts.

✳ Special Events

February: **Crafts and Antiques in Winter** (609-884-5404; 800-275-4278), Cape May Convention Hall, Cape May. Antiques and collectibles dealers and craftspeople from the Mid-Atlantic region. One day of folk-art, jewelry, Victorian pieces, and other crafts; another featuring silver, glass, porcelain, and other antiques and collectibles.

March: Sherlock Holmes Weekend (609-884-5404; 800-275-4278).

April: **Cape May Jazz Festival** (information: 609-884-7277; tickets: 800-595-4849), Cape May. A weekend-long festival of jazz, blues, gospel, and reggae at venues around Cape May. Some 30 events feature well-known jazz musicians and singers performing in afternoon jam sessions and evening concerts. **Cape May Spring Festival** (609-884-5404; 800-275-4278), Cape May. Two weeks worth of special events throughout town, from self-guided tours of Victorian homes and gardens to concerts, glassblowing demonstrations, a garden and crafts show, and murder-mystery dinners. **Tulip and Garden Festival** (609-884-5404; 800-275-4278), Cape May.

May: **Crafts and Antiques at Memorial Day** (609-884-5404), Cape May Convention Hall, Cape May. More than 50 craftspeople, artisans, and dealers. **World Series of Birding** (609-884-2736), Cape May. A bird-tallying contest sponsored by the New Jersey Audubon Society; proceeds benefit various conservation groups. **Great Cape May Foot Race** (609-884-5508), Cape May. A 5K and 10K race through Cape May's historic streets.

May into June: **Cape May Music Festival** (609-884-5404; 800-275-4278), Cape May. A 6-week-long music festival—one of Cape May's premier events—featuring concerts at a variety of venues. Jazz bands, a chamber music series, and an orchestra series, as well as doo-wop, Celtic, Dixie, Flamenco, opera, and more.

Summertime: **Sunset Parades** (609-898-6969), Coast Guard Training Center parade grounds, Cape May. A series of free military parades scheduled May–Sept. are open to the public on a first-come, first-served basis. The parades begin around 8 PM and feature the Coast Guard drill team and recruit band, cannon fire, marching troops, and a low-level flyover by a Coast Guard helicopter.

June: **Victorian Fair** (609-884-5404), Emlen Physick Estate, Cape May. Traditional Victorian-era crafts, activities, and food. **Strawberry Festival** (609-884-8382), Wilbraham Park, West Cape May. **Boardwalk Craft Show** (609-884-9565), on the Promenade, Cape May. **Military Timeline Weekend** (609-898-2300), Historic Cold Spring Village, Cold Spring. Military encampments and demonstrations re-creating soldier life from Viking warriors to the American Revolution to the Korean War.

July: ♪ **4-H Fair** (609-465-5115), Cape May County Fairgrounds, Middle Township. An old-time country fair with agricultural exhibits and a chicken barbecue. **Promenade Art Show** (609-884-9565), Cape May. **Independence Day Parade** (609-884-9565), Cape May. **Antique Auto Show** (609-884-5508), Washington Street Mall, Cape May.

August: ♪ **Railroad Days** (609-898-2300), Historic Cold Spring Village, Cold Spring. ♪ **Sand Sculpture Contest** (609-884-9565), Cape May boardwalk. **Hummingbird Extravaganza** (609-465-5871), Leaming's Run Botanical Gardens, Swainton. **Promenade Craft Show** (609-884-9565), Cape

May. ♪ **Baby Parade** (609-884-9565), on the Promenade, Cape May. A tradition on the Promenade for more than 70 years.

September: **Air Fest** (609-886-8787), Naval Air Station Wildwood Aviation Museum, Rio Grande. **World Series of Birding** (609-884-2736), locations throughout Cape May. Teams of bird-watchers look for more than 700 bird species in a 24-hour competition. **Wine and Food Festival** (609-884-5404; 800-275-4278), Cape May. A culinary celebration featuring restaurant tours, cooking seminars, wine tastings, and multicourse gourmet meals. **Washington Street Mall Art Show** (609-884-8628), Washington Street, Cape May. **Civil War and Revolutionary War weekends** (609-898-2300), Historic Cold Spring Village, Cape May. **Tomato Festival** (609-884-8382), West Cape May. **Arts and Crafts Show Weekend** (609-898-2300), Historic Cold Spring Village, Cape May.

October: **Victorian Week** (609-884-5404), Cape May. Historic-house tours, old-time dancing, mystery dinners, lectures, and other activities celebrating Cape May's Victorian heritage. **Coast Day New Jersey** (732-872-1300), Cape May. A celebration of the state's marine and coastal heritage with ship tours, live music, ecotours, and family activities. ♪ **Pumpkin Festival** (609-898-2300), Historic Cold Spring Village, Cape May. **Antique Auto Show** (609-884-2133), Washington Street Mall, Cape May. ♪ **Lima Bean Festival** (609-884-8382), Wilbraham Park, West Cape May. Lima bean dishes, lima bean tossing contests, and the crowning of a Lima Bean Queen are among the activities at this lighthearted festival celebrating the town's agricultural past. **New Jersey Audubon Autumn Weekend and Bird Show**

(609-884-2736), Cape May Bird Observatory, Cape May Point. Boat trips and field trips to observe the fall bird migration; artists, crafters, workshops, live birds, and more.

November: **Cape May Jazz Festival** (609-884-7277), Cape May. World-class jazz, gospel, reggae, and blues all weekend; afternoon jam sessions and evening concerts. **Cape May New Jersey Film Festival** (609-884-6700), Cape May. A celebration of New Jersey films and filmmakers.

December: **Christmas Candlelight House Tours** (609-884-5404), Cape May. A Victorian Christmas celebration with more than 20 Victorian churches, inns, and bed & breakfasts decorated for the holidays and open to the public. **Dickens's Christmas Extravaganza** (609-884-5404), Cape May. A holiday celebration featuring traditional 19th-century festivities. **Community Wassail Party** (609-884-5404), Cape May. ✪ **West Cape May Christmas Parade** (609-884-1005), West Cape May.

INDEX

A

AA Plus Cab, 520
AAAA Bike Shop, 449
Aart's Cape May Taxi, 483, 520
Abbott, Bud, 69, 346
ABC Taxi (New Brunswick), 124
ABC Taxi Limo (Newark), 72
Abram S. Hewitt State Forest, 156
Absecon Island, 434–74; beaches, 455–56; map, 435. See also Atlantic City
Absecon Lighthouse, 31, 446
Absegami, Lake, 329, 331
A.C. Central Reservations, 457
Academy Bus Service, 348, 378, 399, 414
Ace Luxury Car Service, 442
Acenet Hotel Reservations, 457–58
Acorn Hall, 189
Action Car Service and Limousine, 442
Adams Canoe Rentals Inc., 328
Adamucci Farms, 294
Adega Grill, 81–82
Adventure Aquarium, 19–20, 24, 250
Adventure Sports, 174
Adventurer II, 492
Aeroflex, Lake, 152, 157
African American Arts and Heritage Festival, 142
African Art Museum of the Society of African Missions, 20, 44
Afro-American Historical Society Museum, 73
Ag-Field Day, 141
Agricultural Fair Association

of New Jersey, 18
agricultural fairs: overview, 18. *See also specific fairs*
Agriculture, New Jersey Museum of, 128–29
air (aviation) museums, 46, 282, 284, 324, 523–24
air shows, 475, 514, 548
Air Victory Museum, 324
airports (airlines), 18–19. *See also specific airports*
AirTrain Newark, 18, 43, 70, 92–93
A.J. Meerwald, 23, 286
Akers Woodland Trail, 457
Alba Vineyard and Winery, 34, 228, 244
Albert Music Hall, 429
Alchemy Artwear, 243
Aldrin, Buzz, 46, 69
Aleathea's Restaurant, 536
Alexander Adams Homestead, 178–79
Alexander Grant House, 277–78
Alexandria Balloon Flights, 195–96
Algonquin Arts Theatre, 392–93
Alice Ransom Dreyfuss Memorial Garden, 74, 76
Aljira, A Center for Contemporary Art, 88
Allaire State Park, 308, 312
Allaire Village, 29, 304–5, 308
Allamuchy Mountain State Park, 148, 157; biking, 154; cross-country skiing, 156; fishing, 152, 197; horseback riding, 175
Allamuchy Pond, 152, 197
Allen House, 349–50
Allenhurst: eating, 368

Allen's Antiques, 240
Allen's Auction Barn, 338
Allentown: eating, 336, 338; shopping, 338
Alliance for a Living Ocean, 420
Alloway: golf, 287
Aloha Grove Surf Shop, 355
Alpine: sights/activities, 45, 48, 49, 51
Alpine Boat Basin, 49
Alpine Haus Bed & Breakfast, 159–60
Alpine Picnic Area, 45, 48
Alstede Farms, 217
Amanda's, 55
Amateur Astronomer, Inc., 102
American Family Immigration History Center, 77
American Hungarian Foundation Museum, 128
American Immigrant Wall of Honor, 77
American Indian Arts Festival (Mount Holly), 270, 339, 340
American Indians. *See* Lenni-Lenape Indians; Powhatan Indians
American Labor Museum, 97
American Repertory Ballet Company, 140, 266
American Revolution: overview, 13; reenactments, 244, 270, 319, 548. *See also specific figures and sights*
American Taxi, 124
Americana by the Seashore, 430
Americana Festival of Sails, 142
Amethyst's Beach Motel, 389
Amici's Restaurant, 84

Amtrak, 34. *See also specific destinations*

amusement parks (amusements): overview, 19, 24. *See also specific amusement parks*

Amwell Valley Vineyards, 306

Anchor and Palette Art Gallery, 393

Anderson House Seafood Festival, 219

Andiamo Restaurant, 236

Andover: lodging, 160–61; shopping, 163, 164; sights/ activities, 151, 152, 154, 157

Andre's Restaurant & Wine Boutique, 161

Andrews-Bartlett Homestead, 419

Andy's Countryside Farm Market, 294

Angel of the Sea, 538–39

Anglesea Blues Festival, 513

Anjelica's, 364

Annandale: golf, 197

Annarelli's Bicycles, 489

Anthony David's Gourmet Market, 64

Anthony Hillman Antique and Fine Wood Carvings, 546

Antique Bakery (Hoboken), 60

Antique Center at the People's Store, 241

Antique Center of Red Bank, 370

Antique Fire Apparatus Muster and Flea Market, 165

Antique Station (Keyport), 141

antiques (antiquing), 19; Andover, 163; Atlantic City, 473, 475; Barnegat, 430; Cape May, 546, 547; Chester, 215; Dorothy, 338; Frenchtown, 240; Haddonfield, 268, 270; Hope, 181, 183; Keyport, 141; Lafayette, 163; Lambertville, 241, 244; Long Valley, 215; Mickleton, 293; Milford, 240; Millville, 293; Montclair, 120, 121; Morristown, 218; Mullica Hill, 292–93, 295; New Egypt, 338; Pemberton, 338; Point Pleasant Beach, 393; Princeton, 317; Red Bank, 370–71; Repaupo, 293; Stockton, 244; Washington, 214–15

Anton's at the Swan, 236

Apana II, 408

Appalachian Trail, 19, 29, 144, 159, 164; Hewitt State Forest, 156; Upper Delaware River, 174–75, 177, 179; Wawayanda State Park, 153

Appalachian Trail Conservancy, 19

Appel Farm Arts and Music Festival, 31, 292, 295

Apple Festival (Medford), 340

Apple Harvest Festival (Chester), 219

Apple Mountain Golf and Country Club, 152, 174

Apple Valley Inn Bed & Breakfast, 159

Aqua Beach Resort, 496

Aqua Trails Kayak Nature Tours, 529

aquariums, 19–20, 24, 250, 379, 447, 459, 486

Architects Golf Club, 174

Archives Restaurant, 261

area codes, 18. *See also specific destinations*

Arielle's Gallery, 63

Army Communications and Electronics Museum, 351

Arnold's Yacht Basin, 382

Art Across the River (Delaware River), 184

Art Alliance of Monmouth County's Studio Gallery, 371

Art Center on First (Jersey City), 88

Art in the Park (Bay Head), 394

Art in the Park (Upper Montclair), 121

art museums: overview, 20. *See also specific art museums*

art/craft galleries, 25; Allentown, 338; Atlantic City, 474; Bay Head, 393; Bedminster, 215; Belmar, 371; Blairstown, 183; Branchville, 183; Cape May, 546; Clinton, 215; Demarest, 63; Englewood, 63; Ewing, 269; Frenchtown, 241; Haddon Township, 269; Hamilton, 269; Hoboken, 63; Jersey City, 88, 89; Lambertville, 242; Lyndhurst, 63; Madison, 119–20; Mahwah, 119; Manasquan, 393; Medford, 338; Millville, 293; Montague, 183; Montclair, 119; Morristown, 215; Mullica

Hill, 293; Newark, 88; Ocean City, 510; Princeton, 317; Rahway, 88; Red Bank, 371; Ringwood, 164; Sparta, 164; Spring Lake, 393; Stockton, 241; Stone Harbor, 510; Summit, 119; Surf City, 430; Sussex, 164; Trenton, 268; Wayne, 119; West Branch, 371

art/craft shows and festivals, 89, 121, 141, 142, 184, 218, 219, 270, 296, 339, 373, 394, 431, 475, 513–14

Arthur's Landing, 57

Artisan's Galleria (Bay Head), 393

arts councils, 20. *See also specific arts councils*

Arts Guild of Rahway, 88

Artsbridge Gallery, 242

Artworks Gallery (Trenton), 268

Asbury Park, 345–46; beaches, 356; eating, 364–65, 366–67; entertainment, 369, 370, 371; events, 372; lodging, 358; nightlife, 370; sights/activities, 350, 354, 355; transportation, 349

Asbury Park Jazz Festival, 372

Ash Brook Golf Course, 101

Ashes Cigar Club, 370

Ashling Cottage, 387

Associated Taxi Stand, 301

Assunpink Wildlife Management Area, 21, 306

Atco Raceway, 329

Atelier Gallery, 119–20

Atison Lake, 328, 331

Atlantic City, 434–75; beaches, 455–56; casinos, 23, 437–39, 451–55, 458–61; eating, 463–66, 467–70; emergencies, 442; entertainment, 470–73; events, 474–75; history of, 434–40; information, 440; lodging, 457–62; map, 436; nightlife, 472–73; shopping, 473–74; sights/ activities, 442–57; transportation, 440–42

Atlantic City (movie), 438

Atlantic City Airport Taxi, 441–42, 483

Atlantic City Airshow, 475

Atlantic City Aquarium (Ocean Life Center), 20, 24, 447

Atlantic City Around-the-Island Marathon Swim, 475

Atlantic City Art Center, 444, 472

Atlantic City Bar and Grill, 468

Atlantic City Boardwalk, 22, 434–35, 440, 442–44; eating, 470, 471; Information Center, 440, 441; shopping, 473–74

Atlantic City Boardwalk Arcade, 449

Atlantic City Classic Car Show, 474

Atlantic City Convention and Visitor's Authority, 440, 457, 470

Atlantic City Convention Center, 471–72

Atlantic City Cruises, 450

Atlantic City Expressway, 29, 322, 440–41, 482; Visitor Welcome Center, 440

Atlantic City Festival Latino Americano, 475

Atlantic City Golf Association, 455, 492, 528

Atlantic City Health Med, 442, 483

Atlantic City Hilton Casino and Resort, 23, 452, 458, 465

Atlantic City Historical Museum and Cultural Center, 446–47

Atlantic City International Airport, 18, 276, 322, 348, 378, 398, 414, 440, 482, 519

Atlantic City International Powerboat Show, 474–75

Atlantic City In-Water Powerboat Show, 475

Atlantic City Jitney Association, 441

Atlantic City Laser Lighthouse, 446

Atlantic City Marathon, 475

Atlantic City Medical Center, 442, 483

Atlantic City North Family Campground, 425

Atlantic City Outlets-The Walk, 474

Atlantic City Rail Terminal, 440

Atlantic City region, 434–75; campgrounds, 463; map, 435

Atlantic City Rolling Chairs, 442

Atlantic City Steel Pier, 24, 444, 448–49

Atlantic City Surf, 455

Atlantic City Trolley Tours, 441

Atlantic County 4-H Fair, 339

Atlantic County Historical Society, 444

Atlantic Flyway, 21, 42, 48, 275, 439, 449

Atlantic Heritage Center (Somers Point), 448

Atlantic Highlands, 344, 351–52; entertainment, 370; events, 372–73; lodging, 359–60

Atlantic Highlands Historical Society's Arts and Crafts Fair, 373

Atlantic Parasail, 492

Atlantic Star, 450, 451

Atlantic View Inn, 361

Atlantique City Fall Antiques and Collectibles Show, 475

Atlantique City Spring Antiques and Collectibles Show, 475

Atlantis Inn Seaside Bed & Breakfast, 499

Atlantus Charters, 450

Atlantus, SS, 518, 522, 531

Atlas Inn, 539

Atrium Bar and Restaurant, 358

Audubon Society. See New Jersey Audubon Society

Augusta: events, 145, 165

Augustino's, 54

Authors and Inns Tour, 394

auto racing, 132, 308, 319, 329, 383

auto (car) shows, 295, 319, 474, 514, 548

Avalon, 478–79; activities, 489, 490, 492, 493; beach, 493; eating, 505, 507–8; entertainment, 510; events, 513; information, 482; lodging, 495, 497, 501; shopping, 510

Avalon Anchorage Marina, 490

Avalon Bay Park, 490

Avalon Campground, 503

Avalon Golf Club, 528

Avenue Restaurant, 364

Aviation Hall of Fame and Museum of New Jersey, 46

Avis Campbell Gardens, 102

Avon Manor Inn, 360–61

Avon-By-The-Sea, 347, 354; beaches, 356; eating, 367; lodging, 360–61

Avondale By The Sea, 539

B

Baby parades, 476, 513, 548

Back Bay Ale House, 469

Badger Bread Company, 315

Bahrs, 362

Bailey-Reed House, 379

Bainbridge House, 302

Baja (Hoboken), 59; (Jersey City), 85

Baja East Surf Shop (Spring Lake), 383

Baker, The (Milford), 239

Baker's Acres Campground, 425

Baker's Treat Café, 239

Bal Harbour Hotel, 497–98

Balic Winery, 326

Ballantine House, 74

ballet, 140, 266

Balloonatics and Aeronuts, 172

ballooning, 20, 172, 195–96, 218–19

Balloons Aloft (Pittstown), 196

Bally's Atlantic City, 23, 452, 459; eating, 467–68; entertainment, 471, 473

Balthazar Bakery, 61

B.A.M.A. Galleries, 63

Bamboo Brook Outdoor Education Center, 199, 202

B&B Innkeepers Association of New Jersey, 21

B&K Bike Rental, 449

Bangkok City, 58–59

Barn Gallery, 164

Barnegat, 413; campground, 425; shopping, 430; sights/activities, 415, 417, 419

Barnegat Antique Country, 430

Barnegat Bay, 395–410; beaches, 404–5; campground, 406; eating, 406–8; emergencies, 399; entertainment, 408–9; events, 409–10; information, 398; lodging, 405–6; map, 396; shopping, 409; sights/activities, 399–405; transportation, 398–99

Barnegat Bay Sailing Charters, 401

Barnegat Historical Society, 415

Barnegat Light, 411; activities, 416–18; beaches, 421; eating, 427; lodging, 424; map, 412; shopping, 430; tours, 420

Barnegat Light Elementary School, 416

Barnegat Light Historical Museum, 416

Barnegat Light Marina, 417

Barnegat Lighthouse, 30, 416, 421; Fine Art Sale, 409

Barnegat Lighthouse State Park, 416–17, 420, 421

Barnert Hospital, 93

Barron Arts Center, 87
Barton Arboretum, 330
baseball, 23; Atlantic City,
455; Bridgewater, 102;
Camden, 258–59; East
Rutherford, 49; Lakewood,
329; Little Falls, 102;
Newark, 75; Trenton, 258
Basil Bandwagon, 212
Basil T's Brew Pub & Italian
Grill, 366, 407
Basilico (Millburn), 111–12
Basilico's Ristorante (Sea Isle
City), 505
Basil's Legends Bar and
Grille, 314
Basking Ridge: lodging, 108;
sights/activities, 101–2, 104,
105
Bass River State Forest, 331;
campground, 334; hiking,
328, 329; swimming, 329
Bastille Festival, 244
Batona Hiking Club, 329
Batona Trail, 29, 329
Batsto River, 328, 329
Batsto Village, 29, 320–21,
323–24
Battery 223 (Cape May), 522
Battleship *New Jersey* Memo-
rial and Museum, 31,
256–57
Battleview Orchards, 318
Bay Avenue Antiques
(Barnegat), 430
Bay Cats, 491
Bay Head, 377; beaches, 384;
eating, 391, 392; events,
394; information, 377;
lodging, 385, 388; map,
375; shopping, 393; sights/
activities, 380, 382
Bay Head Business Associa-
tion, 377
Bay Head Cheese Shop, 392
Bay Head Harbor Inn, 388
Bay Head Historical Society
Museum, 380
Bay Head Sands, 388
Bay Village and Schooner's
Wharf, 430
Bayard's Chocolate House,
266
Bay-Atlantic Symphony, 292
Baymen's Seafood and Music
Festival, 431
Bayonne, 70; eating, 84, 85;
emergencies, 72
Bayonne Hospital, 72
Bayshore Community Hospi-
tal, 124
Bayshore Discovery Project,
286
Bayside Center (Ocean City),
485

Bayside Marina (Brigantine),
455
BayView Park, 421
Bayville: campground, 406;
sights/activities, 400–401,
403
Baywood Marina, 382
Beach Club Hotel (Ocean
City), 497
Beach Creek Oyster Bar and
Grille, 505
Beach Haven, 413; beaches,
421; eating, 426, 427, 428;
entertainment, 428–29;
events, 431; lodging,
422–24; shopping, 430;
sights/activities, 415–21
Beach Haven Guided Walk-
ing Tours, 420
Beach Haven Parasailing,
420, 421
Beach Haven Terrace: eat-
ing, 427
Beach Haven Yacht Club
Marina, 417
Beach House Classic Board
Shop, 383
Beachcomber Camping
Resort (Cape May), 539–40
Beachcomber Walks (Sea
Isle City), 492
Beachcrest Condominiums,
496
beaches, 20–21; tides, 34;
Asbury Park, 356; Atlantic
City, 455–56; Avalon, 493;
Avon-By-The-Sea, 356;
Barnegat Light, 421; Bay
Head, 384; Beach Haven,
421; Belmar, 356; Bradley
Beach, 356; Brant Beach,
421; Brigantine, 456; Cape
May Peninsula, 530–31;
Deal Beach, 356; Gateway
National Recreation Area,
355; Harvey Cedars, 421;
Lavallette, 404; Long
Beach Island, 421; Long
Branch, 355; Longport,
456; Manasquan, 383; Mar-
gate City, 456; Normandy
Beach, 404; Ocean City,
493–94; Ocean Grove, 356;
Point Pleasant, 383; Point
Pleasant Beach, 383–84;
Sea Bright, 355; Sea Girt,
383; Sea Isle City, 493–94;
Seaside Heights, 404–5;
Seaside Park, 405; Ship
Bottom, 421; Somers Point,
456; Spring Lake, 383;
Stone Harbor, 493–94;
Strathmere, 493; Surf City,
421; Ventnor City, 456
Beacon Hill Horse Show, 319

Beacon House Inn, 386–87,
388
Beanery, The, 392
Bear Creek Berry Patch, 165
Bear Rock, 158
Bear Swamp Lake, 101
Beasley's Bookbindery, 242
Beaver Brook Country Club,
197
Beckett Country Club, 287
bed & breakfasts (B&Bs):
overview, 21. *See also specif-
ic B&Bs*
Bedminster, 187, 201; eating,
210; shopping, 215
Bee's Knees, 163
Bel Haven Canoe and Kayak,
328
Bel-Air Motel, 502
Belgiovine's Italian Deli-
catessen, 116
Bella Montagna, 162
Belleville: eating, 85
Belly of the Carnegie, 319
Belmar, 347; beaches, 356;
eating, 365, 367–68; events,
372; fishing, 354; informa-
tion, 348; lodging, 361–62;
map, 342; shopping, 371;
transportation, 348–49
Belmar Car Service, 349, 379
Belmar Chamber of Com-
merce, 348
Belmar Environmental Com-
mission, 420
Belmar Marine Basin, 354
Belmar Municipal Marina,
354
Belmont Motel, 406
Belmont Tavern, 85
Belrose Galleries, 474
Belvidere, 169; eating, 181;
entertainment, 181; events,
184; farms, 183; informa-
tion, 146; sights/
activities, 152, 171–74
Belvidere & Delaware River
Railroad, 176, 225
Ben Shahn Galleries, 119
Bentley Inn, 388
Bergen County Historical
Society, 45–46
Bergen County Zoological
Park, 24, 47
Bergen Performing Arts
Center, 62
Bergen Regional Medical
Center, 44
Berkeley Heights: eating,
114, 116
Berkeley Municipal Golf
Course, 403
Berkeley Ocean Front Hotel
and Conference Center,
358

Berkeley Township: events, 409; sights/activities, 328, 330
Bernards Inn, 205, 209
Bernardsville, 187; eating, 208–9; lodging, 205; shopping, 215; sights/activities, 196, 200, 201
Berra, Yogi, 69, 75, 90; Museum and Learning Center, 98, 102
Berrie Center Art Galleries, 119
Berta's Chateau, 161
Best Taxi, 249
Best Western Morristown Inn, 204–5
Best Western Westfield, 108–9, 110
Beth Israel Memorial Park, 77
Bey Lea Golf Course, 403
Beyti Kebab, 59–60
BF Keith's Theatre, 444
Bia Ocean Grove, 365
Bible Gardens of Israel, 77
Bickford Theatre, 194, 214
Big Flat Brook, 174, 177
Big Mohawk, 354
Big Sea Day, 376, 383, 394
Big Timber Lake Camping Resort, 540
biking, 21; Central New Jersey, 306; Central Seacoast, 352, 357, 400, 415–16; Delaware River Valley, 229; Northeastern Gateway, 47–48, 73–74, 131; Northern New Jersey, 154, 196; Southern Shore, 449, 488–89, 525
Birch Grove Park and Family Campground, 451, 463
birding, 21–22; Central New Jersey, 306, 309–10, 326, 331; Central Seacoast, 352–53, 381, 384, 416–17; Delaware River Valley, 231, 275, 284–85; Northeastern Gateway, 47, 58, 74–75, 101–2; Northern New Jersey, 151, 152, 173, 201; Southern Shore, 449–50, 457, 489, 490, 494, 518–19, 525–26, 529–32; World Series of Birding, 22, 525, 547, 548
Bischoff's Ice Cream, 62
Bisconte Farm, 294
Bistro at Red Bank, 362
Bistro Ole, 365
Bivalve, 273, 286
Black Creek Sanctuary, 155, 158
Black Forest Inn, 163

Black Horse Pike, 473
Black Horse Tavern, 211–12
Black Maria, 27, 41, 130
Black River, 197
Black River & Western Railroad, 23, 199, 308
Black River Candy Shoppe, 216
Black River Gorge, 198, 203
Black Whale Cruises, 417
Blackbeard's Cave, 400
Blackwells Mills, 127
Blairstown: activities, 175; lodging, 178; shopping, 183
Blauvelt Art Museum, 20, 44–45
Bloody Mary's Bar & Grill, 539
Bloomfield: eating, 117
Blue (Surf City), 426
Blue Bay Inn, 359
Blue Bottle Café, 314–15
Blue Claw Festival, 431
Blue Fish Grill, 210
Blue Heron Pines Golf Club, 328
Blue Martini Lounge, 473
Blue Pig Tavern, 541
Blue Point Grill, 312
Blueberry Hill Campground, 463
blueplate, 290
blues festivals, 89, 372, 431, 513
boardwalks: overview, 22. *See also specific boardwalks*
Boardwalk Bistro (Atlantic City), 470
Boardwalk Classic Car Show (Wildwood), 514
Boardwalk Hall (Atlantic City), 472
Boardwalk Peanut Shoppe (Atlantic City), 470
boat excursions: Atlantic City, 450; Bay Head, 382; Beach Haven, 417; Brielle, 381–82; Cape May, 526–27; Jersey City, 75; Long Beach Island, 382; Pennsville, 285; Perth Amboy, 131; Point Pleasant Beach, 381; Port Monmouth, 354; Toms River, 400–401; Weehawken, 48; Wildwood, 489–90. *See also* ferries
boat shows, 89, 141, 165, 474–75
boating, 22; Central Seacoast, 354, 382, 401, 403, 417–18; Delaware River Valley, 229, 258, 285–86; Northeastern Gateway, 75; Northern New Jersey, 151, 173, 196–97; Southern

Shore, 450, 490–91. *See also* canoeing/kayaking; sailing
Bobolink Dairy and Bakeyard, 165
Bob's Bay Marina, 417
Boehm Porcelain Studio Gallery, 268
Bogan's Basin Deep Sea Fishing Marina, 382
Boheme Opera New Jersey, 266
Bolero Resort and Conference Center, 495–96
Bonnie Brae Polo Classic, 218
Book Garden (Frenchtown), 242
Book Worm, The, 215
Bookends Bookstore, 120
Boonton, 144, 145; emergencies, 147; entertainment, 163; events, 165; museum, 149
Boonton Historical Society and Museum, 149
Bordentown, 247–48; eating, 264; lodging, 261
Bordentown Beach, 258
Bordentown Historical Society, 248
Borgata Hotel Casino and Spa, 23, 452, 453; eating, 465–66, 467; entertainment, 471, 472–73
Botto House National Landmark, 97
Boulder Gorge Trail, 198
Bovella's Pastry Shoppe, 117
Bowcraft Playland, 100
Bowling Green Golf Club, 152
Boxwood Hall State Historic Site, 72
Boyer Museum, 487
Braca Café, 504–5
Braddock's Tavern, 334
Bradley Beach, 347; beach, 356; eating, 367; information, 348; lodging, 359
Bradley Beach Inn, 359
Bradley Beach Tourism Commission, 348
Braff, Zach, 27, 69
Branch Brook Cherry Blossom Festival, 89
Branch Brook Park, 78, 89
Branchburg: entertainment, 213
Branchville: campground, 179; shopping, 183; sights/activities, 174–77
Brandl Restaurant, 365
Brant Beach, 421; events, 431; lodging, 422; water

sports, 420
Brasilia Grill, 82
Brave New World Surf &
    Ski, 383
Bread Company (Montclair),
    116
Bread From Heaven, 336
Breakers on the Ocean,
    384–85, 389
Bree Zee Lee Marina, 528
Brendan T. Byrne State For-
    est, 325, 329, 331, 334
breweries, 114, 149–50, 228,
    314, 468
Brick: activities, 382; emer-
    gencies, 379; events, 394
Bridge Café, 237–38
Bridgeport Boat Yard, 285
Bridgestreet House Bed and
    Breakfast, 234
Bridgeton, 274–75; emergen-
    cies, 277; entertainment,
    292; events, 295–96; shop-
    ping, 293–94; sights/
    activities, 277, 280, 282,
    284, 286, 288
Bridgeton City Park, 282,
    284, 288
Bridgeton Farmer's Market,
    294
Bridgeton Folk Festival, 31,
    295
Bridgeton Hall of Fame All
    Sports Museum, 282
Bridgeton Public Library,
    282
Bridgeton-Cumberland
    Tourist Information Center,
    276
Bridgewater: information,
    92; sights/activities, 101,
    102
Brielle, 375; eating, 390;
    sights/activities, 381, 382
Brielle Marine Basin, 382
Brielle Yacht Club, 375, 381,
    382, 390
Brigantine, 439; beach, 456;
    eating, 467; events, 475;
    sights/activities, 448, 455
Brigantine Golf Links, 455
Brigantine Island Water
    Sports, 455
Brigantine Spring Festival-
    Craft Show, 475
Briggs Transportation, 379
Broadmoor Antiques, 241
Broadway Basin, 381, 382
Brookdale Park Rose Gar-
    den, 103, 121
Brothers Moon, 313
Brown's, 506
Brown's Nostalgia, 500
Brownstone Diner & Pan-
    cake Factory, 85

Buccaneer Motel, 425
Buccleuch Mansion Muse-
    um, 125–26
Buck Garden, 200
Bucks County Carriages, 230
Bucks County River Country,
    230
Buck's Ice Cream and
    Espresso Bar, 240
Budd Lake: eating, 211;
    entertainment, 214; events,
    219
Budget Limo & Taxi, 72
Buena Vista Country Club,
    328
Bugs Bunny Land, 24, 327
Bula World Cuisine, 161
Bulls Island Recreation Area,
    230, 231; boating, 229;
    campground, 235
Bumblebee Taxi, 189
Burdette Tomlin Memorial
    Hospital, 442
Burlington, 247–48; eating,
    263–64; events, 270; infor-
    mation, 248; marina, 258
Burlington County Farm
    Fair, 339
Burlington County Foot-
    lighters, 268
Burlington County Historical
    Society, 248
Burlington County Prison
    Museum, 324–25
Burr, Aaron, 43, 97
bus services, 22. *See also spe-
    cific destinations*
Busch's Sea Food, 504
Butler: brewery, 149–50
Butler's Pantry Trackside,
    212
Butterfly Camping Resort,
    333
Buttinger Nature Center,
    310
By Our Hand, 294
Byram, 229
Byrne State Forest, 325, 329,
    331, 334

C

C. A. Nothnagle Log House,
    277
Cadwalader Park, 256
Caesars Atlantic City Hotel
    Casino, 23, 452, 459, 474
Café 2825, 464
Café Angelique, 60
Café at Rosemont, 236–37,
    239
Café Beach Club (Ocean
    City), 497
Café Beethoven, 117
Café Eclectic, 116–17

Café Gallery (Burlington),
    263–64
Café Matisse, 56
Café Ole, 266
Café Panache, 113–14
Café Verde, 181
Caffe Aldo Lamberti, 263
Califon: lodging, 207; shop-
    ping, 217–18
Camden, 246–47; emergen-
    cies, 249; entertainment,
    266–68; information, 248;
    lodging, 261; map, 246;
    sights/activities, 250, 252,
    256–59; transportation,
    248–49
Camden Children's Garden,
    259
Camden County Cultural
    and Heritage Commission,
    269
Camden County Fair, 339
Camden County Historical
    Society, 257
Camden Riversharks, 23,
    258–59
Camden Waterfront Market-
    ing Bureau, 248
Camp Olden Civil War
    Reenactment, 270
Camp Taylor Campground,
    180
Campbell Gardens, 102
Campbell Soup Company,
    247
Campbell-Christie House,
    45–46
Campbell's Field, 258–59
Campgaw Mountain Ski
    Center, 33, 155
camping (campgrounds), 22;
    Andover, 161; Atlantic City
    region, 463; Bayville, 406;
    Branchville, 179; Cape
    May, 539–40; Clarksboro,
    289; Clermont, 503; Clin-
    ton, 207–8; Delaware
    Water Gap, 179–80; Egg
    Harbor, 334; Elmer,
    289–90; Farmingdale, 312;
    Freehold, 312; Glen Gard-
    ner, 208; Hackettstown,
    161, 208; Hope, 179–80;
    Jackson, 333–34; Jersey
    City, 80; Lebanon, 207;
    Long Beach Island, 425;
    Marmora, 503; Matawan,
    135; Mays Landing, 334;
    Monroeville, 289; Newton,
    160; Ocean View, 503;
    Pinelands Region, 333–34;
    Pittsgrove, 290; Sewell,
    289; Stockton, 235; Sussex,
    160, 179; Swartswood, 161;
    Titusville, 235; Upper

Delaware River, 179–80
C&C Collectibles and Antiques, 183
Candlelight Inn, 500–501
Candlewood Suites-Exchange Place, 80
canoeing/kayaking, 22–23; Central New Jersey, 307, 326, 328, 339; Central Seacoast, 403, 419–20, 421; Delaware River Valley, 229–30; Northeastern Gateway, 49, 131; Northern New Jersey, 151–52, 173–74; Southern Shore, 491, 529
Cape Island Bicycle Center, 525
Cape Island Resort, 539
Cape May, 515–49; beaches, 530–31; campgrounds, 539–40; eating, 540–45; emergencies, 520; entertainment, 545–46; events, 547–49; history of, 516–18; information, 519; lodging, 532–39; map, 516; shopping, 546–47; sights/activities, 520–32; tours, 529–30; transportation, 519–20
Cape May 4-H Fair, 548
Cape May Antique Auto Show, 548
Cape May Bird Observatory, 22, 525, 532; Weekend and Bird Show, 548–49
Cape May Birding Hotline, 525
Cape May Carriage Company, 530
Cape May Cottage, 547
Cape May County Airport, 523–24
Cape May County Art League, 546
Cape May County Chamber of Commerce, 519
Cape May County Department of Tourism, 519
Cape May County Historical and Genealogical Society, 523
Cape May County Historical Museum, 523
Cape May County Park and Zoo, 24, 524
Cape May Court House, 480; campground, 540; entertainment, 545; shopping, 546; sights/activities, 523–24, 526, 531
Cape May "diamonds," 531
Cape May Hawk-Watch, 526
Cape May Jazz Festival, 545, 547, 549
Cape May Lighthouse, 31, 522–23, 532
Cape May Migratory Bird Refuge, 22, 526
Cape May Music Festival, 31, 545, 547–48
Cape May National Golf Club, 529
Cape May National Wildlife Refuge, 526, 531
Cape May New Jersey Film Festival, 546
Cape May Par 3 Golf Course and Driving Range, 529
Cape May Peninsula, 515–49; beaches, 530–31; map, 516
Cape May Point, 518; beaches, 530–31; sights/activities, 522–32
Cape May Point State Park, 532; birding, 526; fishing, 528; hiking, 529; lighthouse, 522–23
Cape May Promenade, 518, 525, 530; events, 548
Cape May Region Welcome Center, 519
Cape May Reservation Service, 533
Cape May Rips, 528
Cape May Spring Festival, 547
Cape May Stage, 546
Cape May Tennis Center, 530
Cape May Whale Watch and Research Center, 35, 527
Cape May Whale Watcher, 35, 527–28
Cape May Wine and Food Festival, 548
Cape May Winery and Vineyard, 524
Cape May-Lewes Ferry, 27, 441, 482, 519–20, 526–27
Cape Orient, 542–43
Cape Regional Medical Center, 483, 520
Capital City Farmer's Market, 269
Capital Health Systems-Fuld Campus, 226, 249
Capital Health Systems-Mercer Campus, 226, 249
Capital Region Convention and Visitors Bureau, 248
Capriccio (Atlantic City), 466
Capt. Carlson, 492
Captain Buck Riverfront Park, 288
Captain Robbins, 492
Captain Sinn's Marine Center, 35, 490
car racing. *See* auto racing
car shows. *See* auto shows
car travel: highways, 29. *See also specific destinations*
Caravan Traders, 216
Cardiff: amusement park, 19, 24, 326
Carillon Concert Series, 316
Carisbrooke Inn B&B, 463
Carlo's Bake Shop, 60–61
Carmines Asbury Park, 366–67
Carnegie Lake, 299, 307; Regatta, 319
Carney's, 543
Carol Fest, 514
Carolyn Ann III, 418
Carriage House Bed & Breakfast (Ocean Grove), 360
Carriage House Gallery (Cape May), 523
Carriage House Tearoom & Café (Cape May), 545
Carroll Villa B&B Hotel, 533–34, 541
Casa Dante Restaurant, 82
Casa Giuseppe, 84
Casa Solar, 365
Casbah Club, 473
Cashelmara Inn, 361
Casino Fishing Pier, 403
Casino Pier Bike Rentals, 489
casinos, in Atlantic City, 23, 437–39, 451–55, 458–61. *See also specific casinos*
Catelli Ristorante, 335
Cathedral Basilica of the Sacred Heart, 72
Catherine Lombardi, 136
CCIA Gallery, 293
Cedar Cove Marina, 417
Cedar Creek Campground, 406
Cedar Run Lake, 330
Cedars and Beeches Bed & Breakfast, 360
Cedars Restaurant, 138
CEL-EBRATION! Gallery, 370–71
Celebration of Farming, 244
Centenary Stage Company, 214
Centennial Summer Cottage, 351
Center Gallery, 63
Centerton Golf Club, 287
Central New Jersey, 298–340. *See also specific destinations*
Central Pier Arcade and Speedway, 449
Central Railroad of New Jersey Terminal, 77, 78–79

Central Seacoast, 343–431. *See also specific destinations*
CentraState Medical Center, 301
Chairman's Grill and Bar (East Rutherford), 53; (Edison), 134
Chakra Restaurant, 58
Chalfonte Hotel, 535, 540, 546
Chamberlain Canoes, 174
Chamot Gallery, 88
Charles H. Rogers Wildlife Refuge, 307, 309
Charleston Springs Golf Course, 131
Charley's Ocean Grill, 366
charters. *See* fishing
Chateau Inn and Suites, 386
Chateau of Spain, 82
Chatham: eating, 112, 113, 117; entertainment, 119; events, 121
Chatham Bookseller, 120
Chatham Community Players, 119
Chatterbox, The, 506
Checker Cab Company, 482–83
Cheesequake State Park, 135; biking, 129, 131; campground, 135; canoeing/kayaking, 131; fishing, 131; hiking, 132; swimming, 132
Chef Ed's Seaside Grill, 368
Chef Vola's, 464–65
Chef's Table, The, 110
Chelsea Hotel, 462, 466
Chelsea Prime, 466
Chengdu 46, 58
Cherry Blossom Arts Weekend (Bay Head), 394
Cherry Blossom Festival (Newark), 89
Cherry Hill: eating, 263, 266; emergencies, 249; lodging, 261; museum, 257; shopping, 269; transportation, 249
Cherry Hill Mall, 269
Chester, 187–88; eating, 211, 213; events, 218–319; shopping, 215–17; sights/activities, 190, 197, 199–200, 202
Chester Antique Center, 215
Chester Antique Mall, 215
Chester Craft Show, 219
Chester Crafts and Collectibles, 216
Chestnut Hill on the Delaware, 233
Chez Alice, 315

Chez Catherine, 110
Chicken Bone Beach Jazz Series, 472, 475
Chicken or the Egg, 427
children, especially for, 23–24; child-friendly symbol, 6. *See also specific sights and activities*
children's museums, 23–24, 46, 73, 257
Chilton Memorial Hospital, 93
Chimney Hill Farm Estate, 232–33
China Café, 461
Chocolate Box (Lambertville), 243
Chowderfest Weekend, 431
Christie's Steakhouse, 134
Christmas Candlelight House Tours (Cape May), 549
Christmas Craft Market (Hope), 184
Christmas House Tours, 296, 431
Christmas in July Boat Parade (Wildwood), 513
Christmas Inn Tours (Spring Lake), 394
Christmas Lantern Tours (Farmingdale), 319
Christmas parades, 270, 431, 514, 549
Christopher's Restaurant & Bar, 134
Cinnaminson: eating, 266; entertainment, 268
Circle Line Statue of Liberty Ferry, 23, 27, 75, 76
Circus Maximus Theater, 459, 470
Citispot Coffee and Tea House, 213
City Bistro (Hoboken), 54–55
Civil Rights Garden, 456
Civil War: reenactments, 218, 270, 285, 296, 319, 475, 548. *See also specific sights*
CK's Steakhouse, 53
Clamfest, 373
clamming, 28, 419
Clara Maass Medical Center, 44
Clarion Hotel and Conference Center, 261
Clark's Landing Marina, 382
Clarksboro: campground, 289
Classic Sail, 48
Classic Taxi, 146
Claude's Restaurant, 505
Clay College, 293

Clementon Amusement Park, 19, 24, 258, 326
Clerks (movie), 27, 69, 371–72
Clermont: campground, 503; golf, 528
Cleveland, Grover, 224, 298–99; House, 95
Clifton, 41; eating, 58, 60, 61; sights/activities, 46, 50
Clifton Municipal Sculpture Park, 50
climate, 24–25
Clinton, 187; campground, 207–8; eating, 210–13; events, 218; lodging, 205, 206; shopping, 215; sights/activities, 191, 192, 195–97, 199, 202
Clinton Book Shop, 215
Clinton Falls Frame and Art, 215
Clinton Inn Hotel, 52–53
Closter: eating, 57–58
Clothes Call, 216
Cloves, 211
ClownFest, 409
Club Harlem, 437, 472
Clydz, 136
Coast City Cab, 379
Coast Day New Jersey, 548
Coast Guard Training Center, 548
Coast Guard-Cape May, 483, 520
Coastal Cab Company, 482
Coastal Creations, 393
Cocina del Sol, 238
Coco Luxe, 212–13
CoCo Pari, 371
Cohansey River, 286, 288
Cohanzick Zoo, 24, 284
Cohanzik Country Club, 287
Cold Spring Presbyterian Church, 521
Cold Spring Railroad Days, 548
Cold Spring Village, 518, 522, 546, 548
Cold Spring Village Ice Cream Parlor, 544
Colgate Clock, 68
Coliseum Ocean Resort Motel, 502
College of New Jersey Art Gallery, 269
colleges: overview, 25. *See also specific colleges*
Collingswood: eating, 263, 264–65; events, 270; shopping, 269
Collingswood Farmers' Market, 269
Collingswood Holiday Parade, 270

Colonel Charles Waterhouse Historical Museum, 399
Colonial Beach, 530
Colonial House (Cape May), 520–21
Colonial Inn at Historic Smithville, 462
Colonial Park Arboretum, 132
Colonial Transport and Taxi Service, 249
Colonnade Inn, 499
Colts Neck: events, 319; golf, 307
Colts Neck Golf Club, 307
Columbia: campground, 180; sights/activities, 171–72, 174, 175, 177, 179
Columbus Farmers' Market, 269
Comfort Cab, 189
Commerce Bank Ballpark, 102
Common Greens Farmer's Market, 88
Community Medical Center (Toms River), 399
Community Wassail Party (Cape May), 549
Communiversity Day, 318
Comstock Boat Works, 382
Concord Suites, 497
Confederate Monument, 278–79
Confucius Asian Bistro, 82
Congress Hall, 534, 541, 546
Connolly Station, 368
Convenient Medical Care of Ocean City, 483
Cook College, 128–29, 133, 141
Cool Scoops Ice Cream Parlor, 507
Cooper Gristmill, 190
Cooper, James Fenimore, 246, 248
Cooper University Hospital, 249
Copeland Restaurant, 204
Copper Canyon Restaurant, 359
Cora Hartshorn Arboretum and Bird Sanctuary, 105
Coral Seas Oceanfront Motel, 424
Cork Restaurant, 265
Cornelius Low House, 125
Cornucopia Cruise Line, 131
Cornwallis, Charles, 45, 46, 50, 51
Corrado's Family Affair, 64
Corson's Inlet State Park, 494–95; birding, 489; boating, 490; nature walks, 492
Coryell Gallery, 242

Cottage on the River (Island Heights), 405
cottage rentals: overview, 25. *See also specific destinations*
Count Basie Theatre, 370
Country Gate Players, 181
Country Griddle (Flemington), 212
Country Inn By Carlson, 289
Country Kettle Fudge, 428
Country Pancake House (Ridgewood), 116
Cousteau National Estuarine Research Reserve, 419
Cove Beach, 530
Covenhoven House, 302
covered bridge, Green Sergeants, 227, 230
Cowpens Island Bird Sanctuary, 489
Cowtown Flea Market, 283, 295
Cowtown Rodeo, 23, 283
Crab Trap Restaurant, 462
Crab's Claw Inn, 407
Craft Education Center, Peters Valley, 25, 182, 184
crafts. *See* art/craft galleries
Crafts, Museum of Early Trades and, 25, 99
Craftsman Farms, 195
Craig House, 304
cranberries (cranberry bogs), 320, 324, 325, 340
Cranberry Festival (Chatsworth), 340
Cranberry Industry Tours (Whitesbog), 340
Cranberry Inlet Marina, 403
Cranberry Lake, 152
Cranbury: farm, 318
Cranbury Cove Restaurant, 406
Cranbury Golf Club, 307
Cranbury Inlet Marina, 403
Cranbury Inn, 406
Crane (Israel) House Museum, 98
Crane, Stephen, 69, 346; House Museum, 350
Cranford: eating, 117
Cravings, 239
Crawfish Fest, 165
Cream Ridge: campground, 333–34; shopping, 338; sights/activities, 325, 328
Cream Ridge Golf Club, 328
Cream Ridge Winery, 34, 325
Creative Genius, 338
Crescent Theater, 163
Crest Bike Rental, 489
Crimzen Health Spa, 461
Cross Estate Gardens, 200
cross-country skiing, 33, 155–

56, 176, 199, 202, 231
Crossed Keys Inn, 160
Crossley Preserve, 330
Crossroads Theatre, 141
Crowne Plaza Edison, 134
cruises. *See* boat excursions
Cruisn 1, 35, 450
Crystal Queen, 417
Crystal Springs Golf and Spa Resort, 152, 158, 162
Cuba Libre Restaurant & Rum Bar, 465, 473
Cucharamama, 56
Cucina Rosa, 543
CulinAriane, 110–11
Culinary Garden, 504
Cumberland: eating, 291
Cumberland County Fair, 295
Cumberland County Historical Society, 279–80
Cumberland County Sportsman's Jamboree, 295
Cumberland County Weakfish Tournament, 295
Cumberland County Winter Eagle Festival, 295
Cumberland Nail and Iron Works, 282
Cumberland Players, 337
Curley's Fries, 509
Curtin Marina, 258
Cushetunk Trail, 198
Cybis Porcelain Gallery, 268
Cycle Corner of Frenchtown, 229
cycling. *See* biking

D

daddy O, 422
Dancer Farm Bed & Breakfast Inn, 332–33
Dancer, Stanley, 324, 332
Dani & Jonny's Cappuccino, 213
Dante Hall Theatre of the Arts, 472
Darlington Golf Course, 100
Darress Theatre, 163
Daughters of the American Revolution, 125–26, 189
Dauntless, 382
David Burke Fromagerie, 364
De Anna's, 238
Deal Beach, 356
Deauville Inn, 504
DeBaun Auditorium, 62
Debra's Dolls, 293
Decoys and Wildlife Gallery, 241
Déjà Vu Nightclub, 473
DeKorte Park, 50–51; art gallery, 63; birding, 48; hiking, 49

Delafort, 285

Delaware and Raritan Canal State Park, 123–24, 133–34, 231, 309; arts center, 240; biking, 129, 229, 306; boating, 131, 229–30, 307; fall foliage, 26; fishing, 131, 230; hiking, 132, 230, 231

Delaware Bay Day Festival, 295

Delaware Bay Region, 273–96; eating, 290–91; emergencies, 277; entertainment, 292; events, 295–96; information, 276; lodging, 289–90; map, 272; shopping, 292–95; sights/activities, 277–88; transportation, 276

Delaware River, 167, 223–24, 259, 273, 288; boating, 173–74, 229, 258, 285–86; campgrounds, 235; canoeing/kayaking, 229–30; fishing, 174, 230; tubing/rafting, 173–74, 230. *See also* Upper Delaware River

Delaware River Family Campground, 180

Delaware River Tubing, 230

Delaware River Valley, 223–96. *See also specific destinations*

Delaware Valley Bluegrass Festival, 295

Delaware Water Gap National Recreation Area, 32, 167, 176–77; boating, 173; campgrounds, 179–80; hiking, 19, 174–75

Demarest: shopping, 63

Demarest Farm, 64

Demarest House, 45–46

Dennis Creek Wildlife Management Area, 531–32

Dentzel/Looff Carousel, 402

Denville: activities, 156; emergencies, 147

Desert Sand Resort, 497

Destiny, 131

DeWolf's U-PICK Farms, 338

Dey Mansion, 94

Diablo Freeride Park, 154

Diane's La Patisserie, 266

Dickens's Christmas Extravaganza, 549

Dickie-Dee Pizza, 84

Dick's Landing, 403

Dimaio's Cucina, 116

diners: overview, 25. *See also specific diners and destinations*

Dingmans Campground, 179

Dining Room at Anthony David's, 55

dinosaurs, 128, 247–48, 253, 254, 259

Discovery Sea Shell Museum and Shell Yard, 485

Dizzy Dolphin's, 458

Dock Mike's Pancake House, 506

Dock's Oyster House, 468

Dr. Jonathan Pitney House B&B, 462–63

Dr. Ulysses S. Wiggins Waterfront Park, 259

dolphin-watching, 35, 450, 490, 527–28

Dom's Bakery Grand, 60

Donaldson Farms, 218

Donna Toscana, 117

Doo Dah Parade, 512

doo wop: about, 511

Doo Wop '50s Night, 484

Doo Wop '50s Trolley Tours, 483

Doo Wop Museum, 483

Doo Wop Preservation League, 483, 511

Dora Restaurant, 210

Doris & Ed's, 363

Doris Mae IV, 418

Double D Guest Ranch, 175

Double Trouble State Park, 328, 331

Doubletree Club Hotel, 79–80

Douglass Fudge, 509

Dover: entertainment, 214

Dover Flea Market, 216

Dover Little Theatre, 214

Down Jersey Folk Life Center, 281

downhill skiing. *See* skiing

Downtown Car Show (Millville), 295

Drew University, 93, 103, 120, 121

Drew's Bayshore Bistro, 138

Dreyfuss Planetarium, 74

driving: highways, 29. *See also specific destinations*

Drumthwacket, 303

Dry Dock Ice Cream Bar and Grill, 544

Dryden Kuser Natural Area, 177

Ducktown Tavern, 469–70

Due Terre, 208

Duke, Doris, 188, 203

Duke Farms, 196, 203

Duke O'Fluke, 451

Dunnfield Creek Natural Area, 174, 175

Durand-Hedden House and Garden, 95–96

Dutch Auction Sales, 293

Dutch Neck Village, 293–94

E

Eagle Ridge Golf Club, 328

Eagle Rock Reservation, 101, 106, 111

Eagles Taxi Service, 93

E&V Ristorante, 114

East Brunswick: entertainment, 140; events, 142; golf, 131; information, 124; lodging, 134–35

East Brunswick Chamber of Commerce, 124

East Brunswick Municipal Complex, 140

East Coast Car Company, 44

East Coast Parasail, 529

East Coast Stunt Kite Championships, 512

East Japanese Restaurant, 60

East Jersey Olde Towne Village, 126–27

East Lynne Theater Company, 546

East Millstone: events, 142; sights/activities, 132, 133

East Orange Golf Club, 101

East Point Lighthouse, 31, 280, 282

East Rutherford: eating, 56–57; events, 64, 65; lodging, 53; shopping, 64; sights/activities, 49–50

East Windsor: events, 319; farm, 318

Eatontown: sights/activities, 351, 354, 356

Eatontown Arboretum, 356

Ebbitt Room, 540

Echo Lake Stables, 154

Eclectic Grill, 204

eco-friendly symbol, 7

Eden Roc Motel, 502

Edgewater: biking, 47–48; shopping, 64

Edible Art and Sweet Shoppe, 291

Edison: eating, 138; entertainment, 139, 140; events, 141–42; lodging, 134; sights/activities, 96, 130

Edison, Thomas, 27, 41; Memorial Tower, 130; National Historic Site, 90, 130

Edith Duff Gwinn Gardens, 416

Edward Klingener Fishing Pier, 451

Edwards House (Barnegat), 415

Edward's Steak House (Jersey City), 83

Edwin B. Forsythe National Wildlife Refuge, 439, 457; biking, 449; birding, 21, 417, 449–50; campground, 425; fishing, 451; kayaking, 419; map, 412

Egg Harbor: campground, 334; events, 339, 340; lodging, 332; sights/activities, 326, 328

Egg Island Wildlife Management Area, 287

18-Mile Run (Long Beach Island), 431

18th Century Living History Weekend (West Milford), 165

Einstein, Albert, 298

El Artesano Restaurant, 59

El Coronado, 496

Electric Brook, 198

Elements Lounge (Sea Bright), 370

Elements Spa (Vernon), 158

Elephant and Castle, 261

Elizabeth, 68, 70, 72; eating, 87; emergencies, 72; shopping, 88

Elizabeth Arden Red Door Spa, 458

Elliot's Antiques, 473

Ellis Island Immigration Museum, 76–77

Elmer: campground, 289–90; emergencies, 277; events, 295; shopping, 292

Elysian Fields, 40, 52, 53

Elysian Park, 52

emergencies, 25. See also specific destinations

Emery's Blueberry Farms, 339

Emlen Physick Estate, 517, 520, 545, 548

Engleside Inn, 424

Englewood: eating, 61; emergencies, 44; entertainment, 62; shopping, 63; sights/activities, 49, 50

Englewood Boat Basin, 49

Englewood Cliffs, 49

Englewood Hospital and Medical Center, 44

Englishtown: events, 319; raceway, 308; shopping, 317

Englishtown Auction, 317

Englishtown Swap Meet and Auto Show, 319

Enjou Chocolat, 216–17

entertainment. See specific destinations

Epernay, 111

equestrian sports: overview, 26. See also horse racing

Equestrian Team, U.S., 26, 198

Erini Restaurant, 262

Errico's Market and Deli, 239

Estell Manor County Park, 331

Europa South, 390

events, 26. See also specific events and destinations

Ewing: eating, 262; shopping, 269

Express Taxi, 124, 414

F

F. Bliss Price Arboretum and Wildlife Sanctuary, 356

factory outlets: Elizabeth, 88; Flemington, 215–16; Jackson, 338; Secaucus, 63–64

Failte Coffeehouse, 316

Fair Acres Farms, 164

Fair Haven: eating, 364

Fair Haven Yacht Works, 354

Fair Lawn, 90; eating, 117; historic site, 96–97

Fairleigh Dickinson University, 94, 118

fairs: overview, 18. See also specific fairs

Fairthorne Bed & Breakfast and Cottage, 537

Fairton: golf, 287

Fairview Farm Wildlife Preserve, 201

Fairview Lake Ski Touring Center, 33, 156

Fall Family Festival Weekend (Sea Isle City), 514

fall foliage, 26, 308

Fall Sugarloaf Crafts Festival, 142

Family Farm (Lafayette), 164

Family Film and Fun Festival (Flemington), 219

Family Scoops, 62

Famous Trials Theater, 213–14

Fantasea Reef Buffet, 459

Fantasy Island Amusement Park, 19, 415

Fantasy Theater, 119

Far Hills, 187; eating, 212; sights/activities, 194, 200

Farley Plaza Rest Area, 322

Farley's Homemade Ice Cream, 336

Farm Day, 295

farmer's markets, 26; Bridgeton, 294; Collingswood, 269; Columbus, 269; Jersey City, 88–89; Newark, 88; Ocean

City, 511; Trenton, 269

Farmer's Wife, The, 164

Farming Celebration, 244

Farmingdale: campground, 312; events, 319; sights/activities, 304–5, 307, 308

farms (farm markets; pick-your-own farms), 32; Andover, 164; Belvidere, 183; Bridgeton, 294; Califon, 217–18; Chester, 217; Cranbury, 318; Cumberland County, 294; Delaware, 183; East Windsor, 318; Freehold, 318; Glenwood, 164–65; Hackettstown, 218; Hillsdale, 64; Lafayette, 165; Lambertville, 243; Long Valley, 217; Millville, 294; Montague, 183; Morristown, 218; New Egypt, 338–39; Newton, 165; Pittstown, 218; Princeton, 318; Richwood, 294; Rosenhayn, 294; Titusville, 243; Upper Delaware River, 183–84; Wantage, 164

Fascino, 110

Fath Gallery, 293

Feltville, 101, 106

Fernbrook Bed & Breakfast, 261

ferries, 27; Cape May-Lewes, 441, 482, 519–20, 526–27; Highlands, 348; Hoboken, 44; Jersey City, 70–71; New York City, 44, 70–71; Statue of Liberty, 75, 76

Ferry House (Princeton), 312

Festival of the Sea (Brant Beach), 431; (Point Pleasant Beach), 394

festivals, 26. See also specific festivals and destinations

Fiddler's Creek Farm, 243

55 Main (Flemington), 208

film festivals, 27. See also specific film festivals

Finns Point Interpretive Trail, 288

Finns Point National Cemetery, 278–79, 288

Finns Point Rear Range Light, 31, 280

Fiore House of Quality, 61

Fire & Oak, 80

Fire and Ice Festival, 339

Fire Control Tower No. 23, 522

Firestone Library, 301

First Avenue Playhouse, 370

First Bridge Marina and Kayaks, 419

First Day at the Beach (Ocean City), 512
First Night: Haddonfield, 270; Montclair, 121; Morristown, 219; Mount Holly, 340; Ocean City, 514; Seaside Heights, 410; South Orange, 121; Summit, 121
FirstEnergy Park, 329
fish hatchery, 27, 195
Fisherman's Cove Conservation Area, 384
Fisherman's Wharf (Cape May), 530
fishing, 27–28; Central New Jersey, 328; Central Seacoast, 354, 382, 403, 418; Delaware River Valley, 230, 286; Northeastern Gateway, 75, 131; Northern New Jersey, 152, 174, 197; Southern Shore, 450–51, 491–92, 528; tournaments, 295, 431, 514
Five Mile Beach Electric Railway Company, 520
Five Mile Beach Island, 479–81; map, 477. See also Wildwood
500 Club, 437, 444
Flamingo Motel, 406
Flanders Hotel, 496
Flanders Valley Golf Course, 197
Flat Rock Brook Nature Center, 49, 50
Flatbrook Farm, 183
flea markets: Boonton, 165; Cream Ridge, 338; Dover, 216; East Rutherford, 64; Englishtown, 317; Jackson, 338; Lambertville, 242; Manahawkin, 430; Vincentown, 338; Woodstown, 295
Flemington, 187; eating, 208, 210, 212; emergencies, 189; entertainment, 213–14; information, 188; lodging, 205–306; map, 186; shopping, 215–16, 219; sights/activities, 191, 196, 197, 199
Florence and Robert Zuck Arboretum, 103
Florham Opera, 118
Florham Park: lodging, 107
flower shows, 141, 512–13
Flying Pig Gallery, 164
Flyway Gallery, 63
Food for Thought, 334
football, 49
Ford Mansion, 192–93
Forked River: eating, 408; sights/activities, 401, 403

Forked River Diner, 408
Forked River State Marina, 403
Forno's of Spain, 81
Forsythe National Wildlife Refuge. See Edwin B. Forsythe National Wildlife Refuge
Fort Delaware, 274, 278, 279, 285
Fort Dix Military Museum, 324
Fort Dix Military Reservation, 322, 324
Fort DuPont, 274, 279, 285
Fort Hancock, 32, 344, 349, 354, 357; Day, 373
Fort Lee, 41, 49, 50; entertainment, 63
Fort Lee Historic Park, 50
Fort Lee-Rockefeller Lookout, 51
Fort Mercer, 251, 253, 261
Fort Monmouth, 351
Fort Mott State Park, 274, 279, 288; boat excursions, 285; fishing, 286; information center, 276
Fortescue, 276, 286
Fortescue State Marina, 286
Forum Theatre Company, 119
Foster-Armstrong House, 170
Fosterfields Living Historical Farm, 29, 191
Foster's Farm Market, 430
Four Sisters Winery, 34, 172, 183
410 Bank Street, 541
Fourth of July celebrations. See Independence Day celebrations
Fox Nature Center, 328, 331
Fralinger's Cider Mill (Hopewell), 294
Fralinger's Original Salt Water Taffy (Atlantic City), 471; (Cape May), 544
Francis Byrne Golf Course, 101
Frank and Sheri's, 212
Frank Sinatra Park, 62, 65
Frankie & Johnnie's, 56
Franklin Inn, 127
Franklin Lakes: eating, 110; sights/activities, 100, 105
Franklin Mineral Museum, 24, 149
Franklinville Inn, 290
Freckle Contest, 513
Freda's Café, 541–42
Frederick Galleries, 393
Freehold: campgrounds, 312; eating, 313–14, 315; emergencies, 301; events, 319;

lodging, 310–12; shopping, 318; sights/activities, 302, 305, 307
Freehold Raceway, 26, 307
Freehold Raceway Mall, 318
Frelinghuysen Arboretum, 199, 201, 218
French Quarter Buffet, 460
Frenchtown, 224; eating, 235–38, 240; entertainment, 240; events, 244; information, 226; lodging, 234; shopping, 240–43; sights/activities, 229–31
Frenchtown Café, 238
Frenchtown Inn, 235
Frenchtown Visitors Bureau, 226
Frescos Ristorante, 541
Fries Mill, 288
Frog and the Peach, The, 135–36
Frogmore Country Store, 164
Frontier Campground, 503
Fudge Kitchen (Cape May), 544
Fusion, 208

G

Gabriele's Art Gallery, 241
Gaetano's, 366
Gallagher's Burger Bar, 460
Galleria, The (Red Bank), 371
galleries. See art/craft galleries
Gallery 14, 317
Gallery 125, 268
Gallery at the Ocean City Arts Center, 510
Galloway: eating, 466
Galloway Limousine, 442
gaming, in Atlantic City, 23, 437–39, 451–55, 458–61. See also specific casinos
Garden Club of Montclair, 102
Garden Conservancy's Open Days Program, 28
Garden Pier, 437, 443–44, 472
Garden State (movie), 27, 69
Garden State Discovery Museum, 23, 257
Garden State Exhibit Center, 139
Garden State Film Festival, 369, 372
Garden State Home Show, 141
Garden State Horse Show, 165

Garden State Marina, 382
Garden State Parkway, 29, 44, 70, 90, 93, 124, 301, 323, 348, 378, 399, 414, 482, 519; information centers, 30, 43, 92, 481, 519; west of, 90–121
Garden State Philharmonic, 31, 337, 409
Garden State Pops Youth Orchestra, 337
Garden State Wine Growers Association, 34
gardens: overview, 28. *See also specific gardens*
Gardner's Basin, 439, 444–46, 450–51
Gardner's Pond, 152, 157
Garretson Farm County Historic Site, 96–97
Gary's Restaurant, 470
Gateway Marina, 354
Gateway National Recreation Area-Sandy Hook Unit, 32, 344, 356–57; beaches, 21, 355; biking, 352; birding, 352; events, 372, 373; Fort Hancock, 344, 349; hiking, 354; lighthouses, 353
George, Lake, 197, 198
George Street Playhouse, 140–41
George Washington Birthday Celebration, 244
George Washington Bridge, 44
George's Boat Rentals, 420–21
Geraldine Dodge Poetry Festival, 165
German Festival, 142
Germania: winery, 326
Ghost Lake, 174, 178
ghost tours, 257, 325, 530
Giant Stairs, 51
Giants Stadium, 49
Gibbon House Museum, 279–80
Gibbstown: sights/activities, 277, 287
Gillian's Island Water Theme Park, 488
Gillian's Wonderland Pier, 24, 487–88
Ginger Tree, The, 242
Ginsberg, Allen, 69, 92
Girasole, 468
Giuseppe's Ristorante and Pizza Bar, 239
Gladstone, 198
Glass Woods Tavern, 134
Glassboro: entertainment, 337; museum, 324
Glasstown Arts District, 293, 296

Glen Gardner: campground, 208; sights/activities, 199, 202
Glenmont, 130
Glenwood: farm, 164–65; lodging, 159
Glenwood Mill Bed & Breakfast, 159
Globetrotter, 393
Gloucester County Fair, 295
Gold Medal Impressions, 317
Golden Bean, 108
Golden Eagle, 354
Golden Inn Hotel and Resort, 495
Golden Nugget Antique Market, 242
Golden Pheasant Golf Course, 328
golf, 28; Central New Jersey, 307, 328; Central Seacoast, 354, 382, 403, 418–19; Delaware River Valley, 258, 287; Northeastern Gateway, 48, 100–101, 131; Northern New Jersey, 152, 174, 197; Southern Shore, 455, 492, 528–29
Golf Association Museum and Archives, U.S., 28, 194
Gourmet Pantry (Hackensack), 61
Grace Fine Art Gallery, 215
Grain House Restaurant, 108
Grand Banks Restaurant, 83
Grand Café (Morristown), 209
Grand Cascades Lodge, 158
Grand Cayman Ballroom and Shell Showroom, 470
Grand Harvest Wine Festival, 228, 244
Grand Lady by the Sea, 359–60
Grand Summit Hotel, 107–8
Grand Theater (Atlantic City), 471
Grand Victorian Hotel (Spring Lake), 385
Grandma's Olde and New Shoppe, 141
Grant (Alexander) House, 277–78
Gravelly Run Antiquarians, 338
Great American Railway, 191
Great American Trolley Company, 441, 483, 529–30
Great Andover Antique Company, 163
Great Auditorium, 346, 350, 369
Great Bay Boulevard Wildlife Management Area,

414, 419–20
Great Bay Gallery, 474
Great Cape May Foot Race, 547
Great Egg Harbor River, 328
Great Fall Classic Surf Fishing Tournament, 514
Great Falls Festival, 121
Great Falls National Historic Landmark District, 96–97
Great Gorge Country Club, 152
Great Swamp National Wildlife Refuge, 101–2, 104, 105
Greater Atlantic City Golf Association, 455, 492, 528
Greater Cape May Chamber of Commerce, 533
Greater Cape May Historical Society, 521
Greater Spring Lake Chamber of Commerce, 377
Greater Trenton Symphony Orchestra, 251, 253, 266, 268
Greater Wildwood Chamber of Commerce, 482, 483, 495
Greater Wildwood Hotel and Motel Association, 482, 495
Greater Wildwood Yacht Club Regattas, 513, 514
Greek Festival, 339
Green Cuisine, 508
Green Gables Inn and Restaurant, 423, 426
Green Knoll Golf Course, 101
Green Park, 74
Green Sergeants Covered Bridge, 227, 230
Green Valley Beach Campground, 160
Greenfield Hall, 257
Greenville Public Library, 73
Greenwich, 274, 279–80
Greenwich Lake Park, 287
Greenwood Gardens, 103–4
Greenwood Lake, 151, 154
Greenwood Observatory, 176
Grenville Hotel, 385, 391
Grenville Restaurant, 391
Griggstown Canoe and Kayak Rental, 131, 307
Grist Mill Antiques Center, 338
Groff's Restaurant, 507
Grounds for Sculpture, 260
Grove at Shrewsbury, 372
Grove Taxi, 72
Grover Cleveland House, 95
Growing Stage, The, 214
Guaracini Performing Arts Center, 292
Guardian Park, 349

Guggenheim Memorial Library, 350
Gypsy Bar, 473

H

Haas Gallery, 242
Hackensack, 41–42, 47; eating, 57, 58, 60, 61; emergencies, 44
Hackensack University Medical Center, 44
Hackettstown: campground, 161, 208; emergencies, 189; entertainment, 214; farm, 218; lodging, 158; sights/activities, 197, 203
Hackettstown Community Hospital, 189
Hacklebarney State Park, 197, 198, 202–3
Haddon Fortnightly Antiques Show, 270
Haddon Fortnightly House and Garden Tour, 270
Haddonfield, 247–48; eating, 264, 265; entertainment, 268; events, 270; information, 248; lodging, 262; shopping, 268; sights/activities, 253, 257
Haddonfield Antique Center, 268
Haddonfield Crafts and Fine Art Festival, 270
Haddonfield Gallery, 268
Haddonfield Historical Society, 257
Haddonfield Information Center, 248
Haddonfield Inn, 262
Haddonfield Plays and Players Performing Arts Center, 268
Hadrosaurus foulkii, 247–48, 253, 254
Hadrosaurus Park, 253
Hageman Farm, 127
Haledon: museum, 97
Half Moon Lounge, 80
Half Pint Harbor, 24, 150
Hall of Fame All Sports Museum, Bridgeton, 282
Hallock's U-Pick Farm and Greenhouses, 339
Halloween Parades, 409, 514
Hambletonian Festival of Racing, 26, 50, 65
Hamburg: eating, 162; golf, 152
Hamilton: eating, 262–63; events, 270; shopping, 269; sights/activities, 251, 260
Hamilton, Alexander, 43, 72, 96–97; Schuyler-Hamilton

House, 189
Hamilton Farm (Gladstone), 198
Hamilton House Museum (Clifton), 46
Hamilton Park Hotel & Conference Center, 107
Hamilton's Grill Room, 236
Hammonton: emergencies, 323; information, 322; sights/activities, 326, 328, 331
Hammonton Lake, 328
Hampton Inn, 205
Hana Sushi and Steak, 407
Hancock House, 278
handicapped access, 6, 29
Harbor Bar and Brasserie (Weehawken), 54
Harbor Bike and Beach Shop (Stone Harbor), 489
Harbor Pines Golf Club, 328
Harbor Safari (Cape May), 527
Hard Rock Café, 464
Harding Historical Society, 99
Harmony: fair, 168, 184
harness racing. *See* horse racing
Harold N. Peek Preserve, 285
Harrah's Atlantic City Casino Hotel, 23, 452, 459
Harrison: eating, 83–84, 85
Harrison House Diner and Restaurant, 290–91
Harsimus Cove Bar and Grill, 80
Hartshorne Woods Park, 352
Harvest Bistro, 57–58
Harvest Festival (Chester), 219; (Hoboken), 65; (Mountainside), 121
Harvest Moon Brewery and Café, 139
Harvest Moon Inn, 313
Harvest Square Farmer's Market, 89
Harvey Cedars, 411–12; activities, 418; beaches, 421; eating, 426; events, 431
Hasenclever Iron Trail, 148
Haskell Invitational Thoroughbred Race, 26, 355, 373
Haunted Cape May Tours, 530
Haunted Haddonfield, 257
Hauptmann, Bruno, 187, 213, 254
Have Balloon Will Travel, 172
Hawk Island Marina, 258

Hawk Migration Association of North America (HMANA), 48, 173
Hazzard's Launching Ramp, 49
Headley Overlook, 154
Hedden County Park, 199, 200
Heinz Pier, 436, 444
Heislerville: lighthouse, 280, 282
Heldrich Hotel & Spa, 134
Hemlock Falls, 101
Hendricks Field Golf Course, 49
Henry Hudson Drive, 47–48
Hepburn House, 311–12
Hereford Inlet Lighthouse, 31, 482, 486; Christmas Tree Lighting Ceremony, 514
Heritage Glass Museum (Glassboro), 324
Heritage Station, 294
Heritage Surf and Sport, 493
Heritage Village and Museum (Barnegat), 415
Heritage Vineyards of Richwood, 284
Hermitage, The, 95
Heron Glen Golf Course, 307
Herrontown Woods, 306
Hewitt: campground, 161; sights/activities, 151, 152, 154, 156
Hewitt State Forest, 156
Hewitt Wellington Hotel, 385, 390
Hidden Acres Campground, 503
Hidden Gardens of Lambertville Tour, 244
Hidden Valley, 33, 155
Higbee Beach Wildlife Management Area, 21, 525–26
High Bridge Hills Golf Club, 197
High Mountain Golf Club, 100
High Point Cross Country Ski Center, 33, 155–56
High Point Monument, 175
High Point State Park, 26, 174–75, 177, 179
High Point Wheat Beer Company, 149–50
High Street Grill, 336
Highland Park: eating, 137–38
Highlands, 344; beaches, 355; eating, 362, 363, 365–66; events, 373; ferries, 27, 348; lodging, 359; sights/activities, 353, 354

Highlands Conservation Act, 146
Highlands Trail, 29, 153, 154
Highlawn Pavilion, 106, 111
hiking (walking trails), 29; Central New Jersey, 307, 308, 328–32; Central Seacoast, 354, 357, 384, 403, 421; Delaware River Valley, 230, 259, 287–88; Northeastern Gateway, 49, 50–52, 101–2, 132; Northern New Jersey, 152–54, 174–75, 198; Southern Shore, 492, 529. *See also* Appalachian Trail; Batona Trail; Highlands Trail
Hills of Istanbul, 137–38
Hills, the, 185–219; campgrounds, 207–8; eating, 208–13; emergencies, 189; entertainment, 213–14; events, 218–19; information, 188; lodging, 204–7; map, 186; shopping, 214–18; sights/activities, 189–203; transportation, 188–89
Hillsborough: sights/activities, 196, 197, 203
Hillsborough Country Club, 197
Hillsdale: shopping, 64
Hilton at Short Hills, 107
Hilton East Brunswick, 134–35
Hilton Newark Penn Station, 79
Hilton Woodcliff Lake, 52
Hiram Blauvelt Art Museum, 20, 44–45
Hispanic State Parade of New Jersey, 65
Historic Cold Spring Village, 518, 522, 546, 548
Historic Gardner's Basin, 439, 444–46, 450–51
Historic New Bridge Landing Park, 41, 45–46
historic sites: overview, 29. *See also specific historic sites*
Historic Smithville Inn, 466, 474
Historic Speedwell, 190
Historic Towne of Smithville. *See* Smithville
Historical Society of Princeton, 300, 302
Hobby's Delicatessen and Restaurant, 84
HoBiken, 48
Hoboken, 39–65; eating, 54–56, 58–62; emergencies, 44; entertainment, 62–63; events, 64–65; information,

43; lodging, 54; map, 38; shopping, 63–64; sights/activities, 44–52; transportation, 43–44
Hoboken Arts Music Festival, 64
Hoboken Chamber of Commerce, 43
Hoboken Gourmet Company, 61
Hoboken Historical Museum and Cultural Center, 47
Hoboken House Tour, 65
Hoboken Italian Festival, 65
Hoboken Taxi, 44
Hoboken Yellow Taxi, 44
hockey, 75, 200, 258
Hoffman's Marina, 382
Ho-Ho-Kus, 90, 95
Holcombe-Jimison Farmstead Museum, 227, 244
Holgate, 417; map, 412. *See also* Edwin B. Forsythe National Wildlife Refuge
Holiday Inn Select (Clinton), 205
Holiday Light Spectacular (Holmdel), 142
Holland American Bakery, 163
Holland Tunnel, 44, 70
Holly Acres RV Park, 334
Holly Hills Golf Club, 287
Holly Thorn House Bed and Breakfast, 206
Holly Walk, 219
Hollydell Ice Arena, 200
Hollywood Bicycle Center, 489
Holmdel, 122; emergencies, 124; entertainment, 140; events, 142; sights/activities, 126, 127, 129, 132
Holmdel Arboretum, 132
Holmes (Sherlock) Weekend, 547
Holmes-Hendrickson House, 126
Holsten's Brookdale Confectionery, 117
Homestead Farm Market (Lambertville), 243
Homestead Restaurant (Sparta), 162
Hominy Hill Golf Course, 307
Hooked on the Hudson, 64
Hooks Creek Lake, 131, 132, 135
Hooters, 464
Hopatcong Boathouse, 151
Hopatcong Lake, 157; boat show, 165; boating, 151; fishing, 152; swimming, 155

Hopatcong State Park, 149, 155, 157
Hope, 168–69; campground, 179–80; eating, 181; events, 184; lodging, 178; shopping, 181, 183; sights/activities, 172, 174–78
Hope and Dreams Film Festival, 184
Hopewell, 299; eating, 313–16; shopping, 317
Hopewell Museum, 306
Hopewell Valley Vineyard, 228
Hopkins House Gallery, 269
Horizon Cruises, 48
Horse Park of New Jersey, 26
horse (harness) racing, 26; East Rutherford, 49–50, 65; Freehold, 307; Oceanport, 354–55, 373
horse shows, 165, 319
horseback riding, 132, 154, 175
hospitals, 25. *See also specific hospitals and destinations*
hot-air ballooning, 20, 172, 195–96, 218–19
Hotel Alcott, 533
Hotel Indigo Basking Ridge, 108
Hotel Macomber, 535, 540
Hotel Westminster, 106–7
Hotoke Restaurant, 136
Houdini, Harry, 436, 443
House of Blues, 460
How You Brewin?, 428
Howard Mann Art Center, 242
Howell Living History Farm, 23, 228
Howell Park Golf Course, 307
Huber Woods Environmental Center, 357
Hudson County Chamber of Commerce, 70
Hudson, Henry, 343, 480, 516–17
Hudson River: boat excursions, 48; ferries, 44, 70–71
Hudson River Performing Arts Center, 62
Hummingbird Extravaganza, 548
Humphrey Hughes House, 537–38
Hunt Club, 108
Hunterdon Ballooning Inc., 196
Hunterdon County Agricultural Fair, 319
Hunterdon County Arboretum, 199

Hunterdon County Chamber of Commerce, 226
Hunterdon Hills Playhouse, 214
Hunterdon Historical Museum, 191
Hunterdon Medical Center, 189
Hunterdon Museum of Art, 20, 192
hunting, 30, 295
Huntley Taverne, 115
Huntzinger's American Food and Drink, 336
Hutcheson Memorial Forest, 133
Hyatt Morristown at Headquarters Plaza, 204
Hyatt Regency Jersey City, 79
Hyatt Regency New Brunswick, 134
Hyatt Regency Princeton, 310

I

Iberia Peninsula, 82
ice fishing, 152
ice hockey, 75, 200, 258
ice-skating, 200, 355
Ike's Famous Crab Cakes, 291
Il Capriccio (Whippany), 110
Il Mondo Vecchio, 113
Il Mulino New York, 461
Import and Low Rider Summer Slam, 132
In Flight Balloon Adventures, 195
Independence Day celebrations: Beach Haven, 431; Cape May, 548; East Brunswick, 142; Freehold, 319; Lavallette, 409; Long Branch, 372; Maplewood, 121; Morristown, 219; North Plainfield, 121; Piscataway, 142; Red Bank, 372; Seaside Heights, 409; Wildwood, 513
Indian Head Canoes, 174
Indian King Tavern Museum, 257
Indian Rock Resort, 333
Indian Spring Country Club, 258
Indian Summer Weekend, 514
Indians. See Lenni-Lenape Indians; Powhatan Indians
Indigo Smoke, 115
information sources, 30. See also specific destinations
Inlet Beach, 376, 383

Inlet Café (Highlands), 365–66
Inlet-Outlet Surf Shop, 383
Inn at 22 Jackson, 535–36
Inn at Lambertville Station, 233, 238
Inn at Millrace Pond, 178, 181
Inn at Panther Valley, 158
Inn at Sugar Hill, 333, 335
Inn at the Shore (Belmar), 361
Inn of Cape May, 536
Inn on Main (Manasquan), 387
Institute Woods, 308
Iris Inn at Medford, 333
Irish Fall Festival, 514
Irish Pub (Atlantic City), 469
Ironbound District, 66, 81–82
Iselin: eating, 84, 85
Island Beach State Park, 21, 397, 404, 405; biking, 400; fishing, 403; hiking, 403
Island Dragway, 198
Island Heights, 398; lodging, 405
Island Palm Grill (Spring Lake), 389
Island Surf and Sail (Brant Beach), 420
Island Taste (Mount Holly), 336
Israel Crane House Museum, 98
Italian Street Festivals, 65, 89, 409–10
It's Nutts, 237
IZOD Center, 50
Izzie's Eatery, 335

J

J. D. Thompson Inn, 423
J. Thompson Baker House, 484
Jack Cooper's Celebrity Deli, 138
Jackson, 322; campgrounds, 333–34; eating, 336; information, 322; shopping, 338–39; sights/activities, 323, 327, 328, 331
Jackson Chamber of Commerce, 322
Jackson Mountain Café, 543
Jackson Museum, 323
Jackson Outlet Village, 338
Jacques Cousteau National Estuarine Research Reserve, 419
James A. McFaul Environmental Center, 104
James and Ann Whitall

House, 251
James' Candy Company, 471, 508–9
James Rose Center, 102
Jane Voorhees Zimmerli Art Museum, 20, 128
Java Moon Café, 336, 338
Jay and Silent Bob's Secret Stash, 371–72
Jay's Cycles, 306
jazz festivals, 87, 89, 121, 319, 372, 472, 475, 545, 547, 549
Jefferson Beach, 530
Jenkinson's Aquarium, 20, 24, 379
Jenkinson's Boardwalk, 384
Jenkinson's Pavilion and Amusement Park, 24, 381
Jenk's Nightclub, 381
Jennie's Ice Cream Parlor, 544
Jenny Jump Mountain, 177–78
Jenny Jump State Forest, 177–78; campground, 179; cross-country skiing, 176; fishing, 174; stargazing, 176
Jerry's Hot Dogs, 87
Jersey Arts, 20
Jersey City, 66–89; campground, 80; eating, 82–83, 85–87; emergencies, 72; entertainment, 87; events, 89; information, 70; lodging, 79–80; map, 67; shopping, 88–89; sights/activities, 72–79; transportation, 70–72
Jersey City Artists Studio Tour, 88, 89
Jersey City Jazz for Lunch, 87
Jersey City Medical Center, 72
Jersey City Museum, 73
Jersey Fresh Food and Wine Festival, 319
Jersey Gardens, 88
Jersey Genesis Triathlon and Bambino Biathlon For Kids 5-12, 475
Jersey Shore: Central Seacoast, 343–431; Southern Shore, 434–549. See also specific destinations
Jersey Shore Arts Center, 369
Jersey Shore University Medical Center, 349
Jersey Voices, 119
Jimmy Buff's, 117
Jim's of Lambertville, 241
Jitterbugs Nightclub, 205
Jockey Hollow, 193, 198

Joe Pop's Shore Bar and Restaurant, 429
Joe's Mill Hill Saloon, 264
John F. Kennedy International Airport. *See* Kennedy International Airport
John Henry's Seafood Restaurant, 264
Johnny & Hanges, 117
Johnson Brothers Boat Works, 382
Johnson Ferry House, 231
Johnson Gallery, 215
Johnson's Ferry, 231
Johnson's Popcorn, 508
Jolly Roger Marina, 455
Jonathan's on West End, 465
Jose Tejas Restaurant, 85
Journal Square Farmer's Market, 88
Julia's of Savannah, 422–23

K

Kafe Kabul, 262–63
Kammerman's Atlantic City Marina, 450
kayaking. *See* canoeing/ kayaking
Kaya's Kitchen, 367
K.C.'s Coffee Place, 213
Kearney House (Alpine), 45, 51
Kearny Cottage (Perth Amboy), 125
Keeper Back Bay Fishing, 451
Kelsey Theatre, 317
Kenilworth Inn, 108
Kennedy International Airport, 18, 43, 93, 124, 146, 170, 188, 348, 378, 398, 414
Kennedy Memorial Hospital, 249
Ken's Landing Marina, 382
Kerouac, Jack, 92
Kessler Memorial Hospital, 323
Key West Café, 507
Keyport, 123; eating, 138; events, 142; shopping, 141
Keyport Antique Emporium, 141
Keyport Antique Market, 141
Keyport Fall Festival, 142
Keyport Harbor, 123, 142
Kilmer, Joyce, 126
Kimball Medical Center, 323
Kimbles Beach, 519, 526
King Edward Bar, 535
King, Martin Luther, Jr., 456
King's Cab, 249
King's Row Antique Center, 292

Kingsland Overlook Trail, 49
Kingston: eating, 316; sights/ activities, 304
Kingston Bakery and Coffeehouse, 316
Kinnelon: activities, 156, 196
Kirby Shakespeare Theatre, 120
kites (kiting), 512
Kittatinny Beach, 173
Kittatinny Canoes and Rafts, 174
Kittatinny Point Visitor Center, 176
Kittatinny Valley State Park, 157; biking, 154; birding, 151; canoeing/kayaking, 152; fishing, 152; hiking, 153–54
Klein's Fish Market & Waterside Café, 367–68
Knife and Fork Inn, 464
Knowlton Riverfest, 31, 184
Knowlton Welcome Center, 30, 170
Kohr Brothers Frozen Custard, 509
Krogh's Restaurant and Brew Pub, 162
Krueger Collection of Agricultural, Household, and Scientific Artifacts, 129
Kubel's Bar, 427
Kuishimbo, 505
Kuser Farm Mansion, 251
Kymer's Camping Resort, 179

L

La Campagne, 263
La Casa Bianca, 210
La Festa Italiana, 89
La Mer Beachfront Motor Inn, 539
La Riviera Trattoria, 60
La Sierra Coffee Roasters, 213
La Verandah Restaurant, 533
Labrador Lounge, 407
Labyrinth Books, 317
Lackland Performing Arts Center, 214
Lafayette: birding, 151; eating, 163; farms, 164; shopping, 163–65
Lafayette Clayworks, 183
Lafayette Mill Antiques Center, 163
Lafayette Yard Marriott Conference Hotel, 261
LaGuardia International Airport, 18, 43, 93, 124, 146, 170, 188, 348, 378, 398, 414

Lahiere's, 312–13
Lake Hopatcong Historical Museum, 149
Lake Hopatcong Yacht Club Antique and Classic Boat Show, 165
Lake Kandle Campground, 289
Lake Mohawk Gallery, 164
Lakehurst Naval Air Station, 322, 399
Lake's End Marina, 151
Lakewood, 322; emergencies, 323; entertainment, 337; events, 339; sights/ activities, 328, 329
Lakewood BlueClaws, 23, 329
Lakota Wolf Preserve, 171–72
Lambert Castle Museum, 98
Lambertville, 224–25; eating, 236, 238–40; entertainment, 240; events, 244; information, 226; lodging, 232–34; shopping, 241, 242, 243; sights/activities, 227–30; transportation, 226
Lambertville Area Chamber of Commerce, 226
Lambertville Historical Society, 226, 228, 244
Lambertville House, 232
Lambertville Trading Company, 240
Lambertville-New Hope Winter Festival, 244
Land of Make Believe, 19, 24, 172
Landis Cab Co., 276
Lanoka Harbor Marina, 403
L'Appetito, 213
Lark Motel, 502
Larsen's Marina, 490
Laura Marie III, 491
Lavallette, 395; beach, 404; eating, 407, 408; events, 409; lodging, 405; shopping, 409; sights/activities, 401, 404
Lawrenceville: eating, 265
Layton: crafts, 25, 182, 184
Lazy River Outpost, 173
LBI Surf Fishing Tournament, 431
Le Petit Château, 208–9
Leaming's Run Botanical Gardens, 28, 531, 548
Lebanon: campground, 207; sights/activities, 196–99, 202
Lebanon Creek Farm, 294
Lee Turkey Farm, 318
Leeds Eco-Trail, 457
Lee's County Park Marina, 151

Left Bank Libations, 232
Leith Hall Historic Seashore Inn, 536
Lemon Tree, 544
Lenape Lake, 328
Lenni-Lenape Indians, 13, 66, 90, 129, 144–45, 148, 167–68, 225, 257, 282, 344, 375, 411, 434, 480, 516
Leonard J. Buck Garden, 200
Leonardo State Marina, 354
Leo's Grandevous Restaurant, 58
Les Saisons, 109
Lester G. MacNamara Wildlife Management Area, 21, 326, 330
Let's Go Sailing, 354
Lewes-Cape Ferry, 27, 441, 482, 519–20, 526–27
Lewis Island, 244
Lewis Morris County Park, 202; biking, 196; cross-country skiing, 199; ice-skating, 200
Lewis W. Barton Arboretum, 330
L'Hommedieu House, 190
Libby's Lunch, 116
Liberté Cruise & Dine, 382
Liberty Boat Show, 89
Liberty Hall Museum, 99
Liberty Harbor Marina & RV Park, 80
Liberty House Restaurant, 83
Liberty Landing Marina, 75, 89
Liberty Park Water Taxi, 27, 70–71
Liberty Rhythm & Blues and Jazz Festival, 89
Liberty Science Center, 23–24, 31, 73
Liberty State Park, 68, 73, 78–79; biking, 73; birding, 74–75; boat excursion, 75, 76; boating, 75; events, 89; fishing, 75; welcome center, 30, 70
Liberty Village Premium Outlets, 30, 215–16
Liberty Walk, 74, 75, 78
Lighthouse Point Marina and Yacht Club, 401, 403
lighthouses: overview, 30–31. See also specific lighthouses
Lima Bean Festival, 548
Lincoln Park Music Festival, 89
Lincoln Tunnel, 44
Linda's Pizza, 407
Lindbergh, Charles, 69, 187, 213, 254

Ling, USS, 42, 47
Lippincott-Falkenburgh House, 415
Lisa's Deli & Restaurant, 212
Little Egg Harbor, 411; golf, 418–19
Little Falls: sights/activities, 98, 102
Little Food Café, 85
Little Tuna, The, 264
Livingston: eating, 114–15; lodging, 106–7
Lloyd's, 141
Lloyd's French Shop, 141
Loantaka Brook Reservation, 106
Lobster House (Cape May), 542
Lobster Shanty (Point Pleasant Beach), 392
Lodi: eating, 61–62
Loew's Jersey Theatre, 87
Long Beach Island, 411–31; beach, 421; campgrounds, 425; eating, 425–28; emergencies, 415; entertainment, 428–29; events, 430–31; information, 414; lodging, 422–25; map, 412; shopping, 430; sights/activities, 382, 415–21; transportation, 414
Long Beach Island Art Studios and Gallery, 430
Long Beach Island Foundation of the Arts and Sciences, 428
Long Beach Island Historical Museum, 415
Long Beach RV Resort, 425
Long Branch, 345; beaches, 355; eating, 364, 366, 368; emergencies, 349; entertainment, 368–69, 370; events, 372; lodging, 357, 360–62; sights/activities, 350, 355, 356; transportation, 349
Long Path, 51
Long Pond Ironworks Historic District, 148
Long Pond Ironworks State Park, 148, 151, 152
Long Valley, 188; eating, 211; entertainment, 213; lodging, 206–7; shopping, 215–17; sights/activities, 197, 198
Long Valley Antiques, 215
Long Valley Pub and Brewery, 211
Longport, 439; beach, 456; fishing, 451
Longstreet Farm, 127
Looking Glass Coffeehouse

and Café, 291
Lookout Point, 101
Looney Tunes Seaport, 24, 327
Lopatcong: golf, 174
Lorena's Restaurant, 113
Lorenzo's Restaurant, 262
Lorrimer Sanctuary, 105
Lost Brook Preserve, 50
Lotus Inn, 502
Lou Boothe Amphitheater, 510
Louisa's Café, 543
Lourdes Medical Center of Burlington County, 249
Loveladies, 411–12; entertainment, 428; events, 431
Loveland House, 380
Low (Cornelius) House, 125
Lua Restaurant, 56
Lucey's Berry Farm, 165
Lucky Bones Backwater Grille, 543–44
Lucy the Elephant, 24, 439, 445
Lumberton: sights/activities, 324, 328
Luna Stage Company, 117–18
Lyndhurst: events, 63, 89; sights/activities, 48–51

M

M Café, 264
McAfee: golf, 152
McCarter Theatre Center for the Performing Arts, 316
Macculloch, George P., 186, 194
Macculloch Hall Historical Museum, 194–95
McCullough's Emerald Golf Links, 328
McFaul Environmental Center, 104
McGlade's Restaurant, 543
Mack and Manco Pizza, 508
Mackey's Orchard, 183–84
MacNamara Wildlife Management Area, 21, 326, 330
Mad Batter Restaurant, 541
Mad Horse Creek, 286
Madeleine's Petite Paris, 57
Madison: eating, 113; entertainment, 118–20; events, 121; shopping, 119–20, 120; sights/activities, 99, 103
Madison Hotel, 204
Madison Jazzfest, 121
Madison Livery, 93
Magnolia Room, 540
Mahlon Dickerson Reserva-

tion, 154, 156, 161
Mahogany Grille, 390
Mahwah: shopping, 119; sights/activities, 94, 100, 101, 155
Main Ballroom (Atlantic City), 471
Main One Marina (Avon-By-The-Sea), 354
Main Street Bistro (Freehold), 313–14
Main Street Bistro and Bar (Princeton), 313
Main Street Gallery (Manasquan), 393
Main Street Manor Bed & Breakfast (Flemington), 205–6
Mainstage Center for the Arts, 337
Mainstay Inn, 538
Maize Restaurant, 81
Mall at Short Hills, 120
malls: Atlantic City, 474; Cape May, 546–47; Cherry Hill, 269; Jersey City, 88; Princeton, 317–18; Short Hills, 120; Toms River, 409
Manahawkin: eating, 425–26; emergencies, 415; golf, 418; shopping, 430
Manahawkin Mart, 430
Manalapan, 301–2, 307; events, 319; sights/activities, 301, 304, 307, 309
Manamuskin River, 328
Manasquan, 375–76; beaches, 383; eating, 390, 391; entertainment, 392; events, 394; lodging, 387–89; shopping, 393; sights/activities, 379, 382–84
Manasquan Inlet, 381, 384
Manasquan Inlet Beach, 376, 383
Manasquan Lake, 378
Manasquan River, 375, 383; canoeing/kayaking, 307, 318–19; water taxi, 379, 381
Manasquan River Canoe and Kayak Race, 318–19
Manasquan Water Taxi, 379, 381
Mangel's Homemade Chocolates, 216
Manna, 467
Mannington Meadows Wildlife Refuge, 284
Manor Restaurant, 112
Manumuskin River, 285
Manumuskin River Preserve, 288
Manville: events, 141

Maple Falls Cascade, 101
Maple Ridge Golf Club, 287
Maple Sugaring Festival, 121
Maplewood: eating, 113; events, 121; lodging, 109; sights/activities, 95–96, 106
Maplewood Garden Club, 96
marathons, 372, 431, 475, 512
Marbles Hall of Fame, 487
Marcia, Lake, 176, 177
Marco & Pepe, 82
Margate City, 439; beach, 456; eating, 466–67, 470; shopping, 474; sights/activities, 445, 451
Margate Fish Pier, 451
Marie Nicole's, 506
marinas. See specific marinas
Marine Mammal Stranding Center, 448, 451
Mario & Franks, 264
Mark G. Etess Arena, 471
Market Street Bar and Grill, 79
Market Street Day, 295
MarketFair, 317–18
markets. See farmer's markets; flea markets
Marlboro Farm Market and Garden Center, 294
Marlton: eating, 334, 335; emergencies, 323; golf, 258
Marlton Tavern, 335
Marmora: campground, 503; lodging, 504
Marshall House Museum, 227–28
Marshall's Farm Market, 183
Martin Coryell House Bed & Breakfast, 234
Masala Grill, 314
Mason Cottage, 538
Mason Gross Performing Arts Center, 139–40
Mastori's Diner, 264
Matarazzo Farms, 172, 183
Matawan: campground, 135; sights/activities, 129, 131–32
Mathis House, 405
Matisse, 365
Matt's Red Rooster Grill, 208
Maui's Dog House, 509
Mauricetown, 275; events, 295–96
Mauricetown Historical Society, 280, 282, 295, 296
Max's Bistro, 210
Max's Famous Hot Dogs, 368
Max's Steak House, 461
Maxwell's, 59
Mayflower, 517, 521
Mayo Center for the Per-

forming Arts, 214
Mays Landing: campgrounds, 334; eating, 335, 336; lodging, 333; sights/activities, 326, 328, 331
Mays Landing Golf Club, 328
Meadowlands Environment Center, 48, 49, 50–51
Meadowlands Exposition Center, 62
Meadowlands Flea Market, 64
Meadowlands Hospital Medical Center, 44
Meadowlands Liberty Convention and Visitors Bureau, 43
Meadowlands Museum, 46–47
Meadowlands Plaza Hotel, 53–54
Meadowlands Racetrack, 26, 49–50
Meadowlands Sports Complex, 42, 49–50
Meadowlands State Fair, 18, 64
Meadows Foundation, 127
Meadows Golf Club, 101
Mead-Van Duyne House, 94
Medford: eating, 334, 335–36; lodging, 333
Medford Apple Festival, 340
medical emergencies, 25. See also specific hospitals and destinations
Mediterra, 312
Mehndi, 209
Meil's Restaurant, 238
Melange at Haddonfield, 265
Melange Café (Cherry Hill), 263
Melick's Town Farm, 217–18
Melissa's Bistro, 466–67
Melrose, The, 360
Memorial Hospital of Salem County, 277
Menantico Sand Ponds Wildlife Management Area, 286
Mendham: eating, 211–12
Mendham Gallery, 241
Menlo Park Museum, 130
Mercer County Community College, 317
Mercer County Fair, 270
Mercer Oaks Golf Course, 307
Mesob Restaurant, 111
Metropolitan, The, 467
Mettler's Woods, 133
Metuchen: entertainment, 119
Metz Bicycle Museum, 305

Mickleton: antiques, 293
Mick's Canoe Rental Inc., 328
Mid-Atlantic Center for the Arts (MAC), 520, 529, 545
Middle Township Performing Arts Center, 545
Middlesex County Cultural and Heritage Commission, 124
Middlesex County Museum, 125
Middletown, 352, 357; eating, 362
Midsummer Antiques and Collectibles Show, 295
Mie Thai, 85–86
Mignon Steak House, 57
Mike's Seafood Restaurant and Takeout, 506–7
Milford, 223–24; eating, 235, 237, 239; events, 244; lodging, 233; map, 222; shopping, 240, 242; sights/activities, 228, 231
Milford Oyster House, 235
Military Timeline Weekend, 548
Militia Museum of New Jersey, 380
Mill at Spring Lake Heights, 389
Mill Hill Playhouse, 266
Millback Studio, 338
Millburn, 92; activities, 101, 106; eating, 111–12, 114, 116; entertainment, 119
Millburn Deli, 116
Million Dollar Pier, 436–37, 443, 474
Millside Café, 163
Millstone, 128, 131
Millstone River, 307
Millville, 275; eating, 290, 291; entertainment, 292; events, 295–96; lodging, 289; shopping, 293–94; sights/activities, 281, 282, 285–88; transportation, 276
Millville Airport, 282, 284
Millville Army Airfield Museum, 282, 284
Milton: golf, 152
Mine Brook Golf Club, 197
Minerals Resort & Spa, 158
Minerals Sports Club, 158
Mining Museum, Sterling Hill, 24, 150
minor-league baseball. See baseball
Mirenda's Bakery, 291
Miss Avalon II, 492
Miss Barnegat Light, 418
Miss Belmar Princess, 354
Miss Chris Marina, 527–28

Miss Crustacean Hermit Crab Beauty Pageant, 513
Miss LBI, 418
Miss New Jersey Pageant, 512
Mister C's Beach Bistro, 368
Mitsuwa Marketplace, 64
Mix Gallery (Lambertville), 241
Mixx (Atlantic City), 472–73
Moby's Deck, 362
Mohawk House Restaurant, 162
Mojo, 467
Molly Pitcher Inn, 309, 358, 363–64
Molly Pitcher Marina, 358
Molly Pitcher State Welcome Center, 30, 300
Monksville Reservoir, 151, 152
Monmouth Battlefield State Park, 299–300, 304, 309, 319
Monmouth Beach, 345
Monmouth County Department of Economic Development and Tourism, 300
Monmouth County Fair, 319
Monmouth County Horse Show, 319
Monmouth Cove Marina, 354
Monmouth Executive Airport, 308
Monmouth Festival of the Arts, 372
Monmouth Medical Center, 349
Monmouth Park Racetrack, 26, 354–55
Monmouth University, 350, 371
Monmouth University Performing Arts Series, 368–69
Monroe Center for the Arts, 62
Monroeville: campground, 289
Montague: farms, 183; sights/activities, 170–71, 183
Montague Historical Society, 170–71
Montclair, 92; eating, 110–11, 114–17; emergencies, 93; entertainment, 117–18; events, 121; shopping, 119–20; sights/activities, 94, 98, 102–3; transportation, 92–93
Montclair Antique Center, 120
Montclair Art Museum, 20, 94
Montclair Book Center, 120

Montclair State University, 94, 98, 102, 119
Montrose in May, 121
Montville, 158; eating, 161
Montville Inn, 161
Moonlight Lounge, 139
Moonstone Mystery Bookstore, 215
Moonstruck, 364–65
Moorestown: entertainment, 267; golf, 258; lodging, 261
Moorestown DeCafe Coffeehouse, 267
Morey's Amusement Piers and Raging Waters, 24, 488
Morning Dove Inn, 361
Morris Canal, 145, 186–87, 203
Morris County Fair, 219
Morris County Historical Society, 189
Morris County Parks Commission, 196
Morris County Visitors Center, 188
Morris Museum, 31, 194
Morrison's Beach Haven Marina, 417
Morristown, 185, 187; eating, 209, 212, 213; emergencies, 189; entertainment, 214; events, 218–19; information, 188; lodging, 204–5; map, 186; shopping, 215–18; sights/activities, 189–203; transportation, 188–89
Morristown Antiques Show, 218
Morristown Community Theatre, 214
Morristown Fine Arts and Crafts Festival, 218
Morristown Holiday Crafts, 219
Morristown Memorial Hospital, 189
Morristown National Historical Park, 32, 185–86, 192–93; biking, 196; events, 219
Morse, Samuel F. B., 190
Morven Museum and Garden, 301–2
Mother Grimm's Bears, 547
Mother's Day Celebration, 270
Mount Holly, 322; eating, 336; emergencies, 323; events, 339–40; museum, 324–25
Mount Kemble, 193, 198
Mount Laurel: activities, 258, 259; lodging, 261; shopping, 269

Mount Mitchell Scenic Overlook, 351–52
Mount Tammany, 175
mountain biking. *See* biking
Mountain Creek Ski Resort, 33, 155, 158
Mountain Creek Waterpark, 19, 24, 150
Mountain Lake, 174
Mountain Lakes: eating, 161–62
Mountain Lakes Nature Preserve, 310
Mountain View Golf Course, 258
Mountainside: eating, 115; events, 121; sights/activities, 101, 104–5, 121
Movies and Music Under the Stars (Fort Lee), 63
movies, set in New Jersey, 27. *See also specific movies*
Movies Under the Stars (Hoboken), 63
Mrs. Hanna Krause Candy, 64, 408
Mud City Crab House, 425–26
Muddy Run, 286
Mulberry Tea House, 335
Mulhockaway Creek, 197
Mullica Hill, 274; eating, 290–91; events, 295–96; information, 276; lodging, 289, 291; shopping, 292–93
Mullica River, 328
Mummer's Brigade Weekend, 513
Murphy's Loft, 293
Musconectcong River, 148, 157, 197, 203
museums: overview, 31. *See also specific museums*
Museum of American Glass, 281, 282
Museum of Early Trades and Crafts, 25, 99
Museum of the American Hungarian Foundation, 128
music: overview, 31–32. *See also specific destinations*
music festivals: overview, 31–32. *See also specific festivals*
Music Man, The, 408
Music-in-the-Park (West Windsor), 319
My Ben, 231
Myhelan Cultural Arts Center, 213

N

Nail House Museum, 282

Nancy, 485
Naples Pizzeria, 291
Nassau Bagels and Sushi, 314
Nassau Hall, 301
Nassau Inn, 311
Nassau Taxi, 301
Nast, Thomas, 186, 194–95
Nathaniel Morris Inn, 388–89
National Marbles Hall of Fame, 487
National Marbles Tournament, 487, 513
national park areas: overview, 32. *See also specific national park areas*
Native American Festival (Mount Holly), 270, 339, 340
Native Americans. *See* Lenni-Lenape Indians; Powhatan Indians
Natural Foods General Store and Vegetarian Café (Toms River), 408
Nature Center of Cape May, 532
Nature Conservancy, 32, 275
nature preserves: overview, 32. *See also specific nature preserves*
nature trails. *See* hiking
Naval Air Station Wildwood Aviation Museum, 523–24, 548
Naval Museum, 47
Navesink Lighthouse, 30, 353
Needmore Farm, 164
Neighbour House Bed & Breakfast, 206–7
Neldon-Roberts Stonehouse, 171, 183
Neptune: activities, 354; eating, 367; emergencies, 349
Nest, The (Hope), 183
Netcong: entertainment, 214; theme park, 151
New Belmar Marina Coffee Shoppe, 368
New Bridge Landing Park, 41, 45–46
New Brunswick, 122; eating, 135–37, 139; emergencies, 125; entertainment, 139–41; events, 141, 142; information, 124; lodging, 134–35; sights/activities, 125–34; transportation, 124
New Brunswick Cultural Center, 140
New Egypt: lodging, 332; shopping, 338–39; sights/activities, 324, 329
New Egypt Flea Market Vil-

lage and Auction, 338
New Egypt Historical Society Museum, 324
New Egypt Speedway, 329
New Gretna: campground, 334; sights/activities, 328, 329, 331
New Jersey Astronomical Association, 199
New Jersey Audubon Autumn Weekend and Bird Show, 548–49
New Jersey Audubon Society, 22, 105, 156, 173, 201, 284, 352, 525, 532, 547
New Jersey Boat Show, 141
New Jersey Campground Owners Association, 22
New Jersey Children's Museum, 23, 46
New Jersey Coastal Heritage Trail, 279
New Jersey Colonials, 200
New Jersey Commission on Higher Education, 25
New Jersey Convention and Exposition Center, 139
New Jersey Daffodil Show, 201, 218
New Jersey Department of Transportation, 21
New Jersey Devil (creature), 321–22
New Jersey Devils (hockey), 75, 258
New Jersey Division of Fish and Wildlife, 27
New Jersey Division of Parks and Forestry, 23, 33
New Jersey Division of Travel and Tourism, 29
New Jersey Festival of Ballooning, 20, 218–19
New Jersey Film Festival, 125, 141, 142
New Jersey Flower & Garden Show, 141
New Jersey Folk Festival, 141
New Jersey Historical Society, 29
New Jersey Historical Society Museum, 72–73
New Jersey International Film Festival, 27
New Jersey Jackals, 23, 102
New Jersey Kayak, 419
New Jersey Lighthouse Society, 30, 353
New Jersey Marathon Weekend at the Jersey Shore, 372
New Jersey Meadowlands Commission, 42, 51
New Jersey Memorial and

Museum, 31, 256–57
New Jersey Museum of Agriculture, 128–29
New Jersey National Golf Club, 101
New Jersey Naval Museum, 47
New Jersey Nets, 50
New Jersey Office of Travel and Tourism, 26
New Jersey Offshore Powerboat Race, 394
New Jersey Peach Festival, 295
New Jersey Performing Arts Center, 86, 87
New Jersey Pinelands Commission, 322
New Jersey Quilt Convention, 141
New Jersey Renaissance Festival and Kingdom, 121
New Jersey Repertory Company, 370
New Jersey Sandcastle Contest, 372
New Jersey School of Dramatic Arts, 118–19
New Jersey Seafood Festival, 372
New Jersey Shuffleboard Championships, 513
New Jersey Spring Home Show, 64
New Jersey State Botanical Garden, 28, 156, 157
New Jersey State Chili and Salsa Championship, 409
New Jersey State Fair, 18, 165
New Jersey State Golf Association, 28
New Jersey State House, 255
New Jersey State Ice Cream Festival, 409
New Jersey State Museum, 31, 254, 270
New Jersey State Police Museum and Learning Center, 254
New Jersey state symbols, 170
New Jersey Symphony Orchestra, 31, 86, 87, 266
New Jersey Theatre Alliance, 33
New Jersey Trailer and Camping Show, 141
New Jersey Transit, 22, 34. See also specific destinations
New Jersey Transportation Heritage Center, 171
New Jersey Turnpike, 29, 44, 70, 71, 93, 124, 249, 276, 301, 323
New Jersey Vietnam Veter-

ans' Memorial, 129
New Lisbon, 330, 331
New Sweden Farmstead Museum, 282
New York City, 39, 66; ferries, 44, 70–71
New York Giants, 49
New York Jets, 49
New York Water Taxi, 27, 70–71
New York Waterway, 27, 44, 71
New York-New Jersey Trail Conference (NYNJTC), 29, 153
Newark, 66–89; eating, 81–82, 84, 86; emergencies, 72; entertainment, 86, 87; events, 89; information, 70; lodging, 79; map, 67; shopping, 88; sights/activities, 72–79; transportation, 70–72
Newark Bears, 75
Newark Black Film Festival, 89
Newark Fire Museum, 76
Newark Food and Brew Festival, 89
Newark Jazz in the Garden Summer Concert Series, 87
Newark Liberty International Airport, 18, 43, 70, 72, 92–93, 124, 146, 170, 188, 248, 276, 322, 348, 378, 414
Newark Liberty Marriott, 79
Newark Museum, 20, 74
Newark Open Doors, 89
Newark Symphony Hall, 87
Newport Centre Mall, 88
Newport Pavonia Farmer's Market, 89
Newton, 145; activities, 152, 154, 156; campground, 160; eating, 161–63; emergencies, 147, 170; farms, 165; lodging, 160
Newton Memorial Hospital, 147, 170
Nicholas Restaurant, 362
Night in Venice, 476, 513
9/11 Monument, 68
NJ Forest Resource Education Center at Jackson, 331
No Joe's Café, 366
Norma K, 382
Normandy Beach, 395, 404; eating, 407
Normandy Inn, 387
North American Wetlands Aviary, 47
North Brunswick: eating, 139
North Jersey Rose Society, 103

North Plainfield: events, 121
North River Antiques, 141
North Shore Inn, 424
North Wildwood, 480–81; beaches, 494; eating, 505, 507, 509; entertainment, 510; events, 512–13, 514; information, 482; lodging, 500–501; sights/activities, 484, 486, 489, 491, 493, 509
Northeastern Gateway, 39–142. See also specific destinations
Northern Highlands, 144–65; campgrounds, 160–61; eating, 161–63; entertainment, 163; events, 165; information, 146; lodging, 158–60; map, 145; shopping, 163–65; sights/activities, 147–58; transportation, 146–47
Northern New Jersey, 144–219. See also specific destinations
Northfield: campground, 463; park, 451
Northlandz, 23, 191
Northvale: eating, 57
Northwood Center, 525
Northwood Inn Bed & Breakfast, 500
Norvin Green State Forest, 156
Nothnagle Log House, 277
Novins Planetarium, 400
Noyes Museum of Art, 20, 447–48

O
Oak Ridge Golf Course, 101
Oakland: sights/activities, 151, 152, 153, 157
Ocean Acres Country Club, 418
Ocean Beach Marina, 401
Ocean City, 476–78; beaches, 493–94; eating, 504, 506, 508–9; emergencies, 483; entertainment, 509–10; events, 512–14; information, 481; lodging, 496–97, 499–500; map, 477; shopping, 510–11; sights/activities, 483–95; transportation, 482–83
Ocean City Airport Festival & Boardwalk Aerobatic Airshow, 514
Ocean City Arts Center, 509
Ocean City Boardwalk, 22, 476, 489, 512; eating, 508–9

Ocean City Farmer's and Crafters Market, 511
Ocean City Flower Show, 512–13
Ocean City Golf Course, 492
Ocean City Historical Museum, 485
Ocean City Mansion Bed & Breakfast, 499
Ocean City Pops Orchestra, 510
Ocean City Regional Chamber of Commerce, 481, 495
Ocean City Tabernacle, 483–84
Ocean County Artists' Guild, 408
Ocean County Bluegrass Festival, 431
Ocean County College, 408
Ocean County Decoy and Gunning Show, 431
Ocean County Fair, 409
Ocean County Golf Course at Atlantis, 418–19
Ocean County Golf Course at Forge Pond, 382
Ocean County Historical Museum and Research Center, 399
Ocean County Mall, 398, 409
Ocean County Park, 328, 329
Ocean County St. Patrick's Day Parade, 409
Ocean Court Motel (Long Branch), 361–62
Ocean Drive, 439, 455, 493, 519; biking, 488–89
Ocean Drive Marathon, 512
Ocean Explorer, 354
Ocean Galleries (Stone Harbor), 510
Ocean Grove, 346–47; beaches, 356; eating, 365, 367; entertainment, 369; events, 372; information, 348; lodging, 358, 360; sights/activities, 350–51
Ocean Grove Area Chamber of Commerce, 348
Ocean Grove Boardwalk, 22, 352, 356
Ocean Grove Camp Meeting Association, 346, 350, 351
Ocean Grove Great Auditorium, 346, 350, 369
Ocean House (Spring Lake), 386
Ocean Life Center (Atlantic City Aquarium), 20, 24, 447
Ocean Medical Center (Brick), 379
Ocean Outfitters (Wildwood Crest), 493

Ocean Pier (Atlantic City), 443
Ocean Place Resort and Spa, 357
Ocean Plaza (Ocean Grove), 360
Ocean View Resort Campground, 503
Oceanfest (Long Branch), 372
Oceanport, 345; horse racing, 354–55, 373
Oceanside Gallery (Belmar), 371
Oceanville: sights/activities, 447–49, 451
Ocquittunk, Lake, 173, 174, 177
Octoberfest, 340
Off Broad Street Players, 292
Off the Hook, 427
Off the Wall Craft Gallery, 338
Office Restaurant and Lounge, 407
Offshore Powerboat Racing, 475
Ogdensburg: museum, 150
Ol' Barn Inn (Lambertville), 232–33
Old Alpine Trail, 51
Old Barney. See Barnegat Lighthouse
Old Barracks Museum (Trenton), 31, 254, 256
Old Bay Restaurant (New Brunswick), 136
Old Book Shop (Morristown), 215
Old Bridge Township Raceway Park, 132, 308, 319
Old Brigantine Bridge, 451
Old Broad Street Church (Bridgeton), 277
Old Cedar Campground, 289
Old Dutch Parsonage (Somerville), 128
Old Man Rafferty's, 139
Old Mill Antique Mall (Mullica Hill), 292
Old Millstone Forge Museum, 128
Old Mine Road, 169
Old Monmouth Candies, 315, 368
Old Oarhouse Brewery (Millville), 291
Old Orchard Country Club, 354
Old Riverhouse (Clinton), 211
Old Swedes Trinity Episcopal Church (Swedesboro), 277
Old Tennent Presbyterian

Church, 301
Olde Lafayette Village, 164
Olde Mill Inn (Basking Ridge), 108
Olden House (Drumthwacket), 303
Oldwick: shopping, 217
Oldwick General Store, 217
Olmsted family, 78, 92, 177, 256
Ombra, 465–66
Omni Theater, 73, 79
On Location Tours, 40
On the Waterfront (movie), 27, 40, 52, 56
opera, 118, 266
Oradell: museum, 44–45
Orange: eating, 115. See also South Orange; West Orange
orchards. See farms
Origin Thai, 137
Original Fudge Kitchen, 509
Original Soupman, The, 314
Ort Farms, 217
Oskar Schindler Performing Arts Center, 118
Osteria Giotto, 111
Oswego Lake, 328
Oswego River, 328
Our Lady of Lourdes Medical Center, 249
Outdoor Store (Montclair), 120
outlet malls. See factory outlets
Overpeck Golf Course, 49
Owl's Tale, The, 268
Ox Restaurant, 83
Oxford: events, 218; sights/activities, 193, 195
Oxford Furnace, 193
Oyster Point Hotel, 357–58
Oyster Point Marina, 358

P

Paine, Thomas, 41, 46
Palace Theater, 471
Palisades, 39–65; map, 38
Palisades Interstate Park, 42–43, 51; biking, 47–48; birding, 48; canoeing/kayaking, 49; Hooked on the Hudson, 64; Kearney House, 45, 51
Palisades Interstate Parkway, 44
Palmer Square, 317
Palmer's Crossing, 53
Pals Cabin, 115
Pan American Hotel, 497
P&P Taxi, 189
Panico's, 136
Panther Lake Camping Resort, 161

Panzone's Pizza, 427
Paper Mill Playhouse, 92, 119
Paper Moon Puppet Theatre, 370
Paramount Cab, 349
Paramount Theatre, 369
Paramus: eating, 58; emergencies, 44; shopping, 64; sights/activities, 46, 47
parasailing, 382, 420–21, 492, 529
Park & Orchard Restaurant, 56–57
Park Performing Arts Center, 63, 64
Park Ridge, 41, 45
Parsippany: museum, 195
Parvin Lake, 286, 287, 288
Parvin State Park, 288; birding, 284; campground, 290; fishing, 286; hiking, 287; swimming, 287
Pascack Valley Hospital, 44
Passage Theatre Company, 266
Passaic County 4-H Fair, 121
Passaic County Golf Course, 101
Passaic County Historical Society, 98
Passion Play, 63, 64
Paterson, 90–92; eating, 114, 116; emergencies, 93; information, 92; map, 91; sights/activities, 93–106; transportation, 92–93
Paterson Area Taxi, 93
Paterson Museum, 96
PATH (Port Authority Trans Hudson), 34, 44, 70, 93
Patriot's Path Recreation Trail, 196, 199, 201
Patriots Theater, 266
Paul Robeson Gallery, 88
Paul Robinson Observatory, 199
Paula at Rigoletto, 57
Paulinskill Valley Trail, 151, 153–54, 157, 175
Paulsboro, 27, 280
Paws Farm Nature Center, 259
Pax Amicus Castle Theatre, 214
Pazzo Pazzo, 209
Pea Patch Island, 278, 279, 285
Peaceful Valley Orchards, 218
Peaches N' Cream Festival, 295
Peapack: eating, 212–13
Pebble Creek Golf Club, 307
Pecoraro Bakery, 86–87

Pedals and Paddles Rentals, 403
Peek Preserve, 285
Pegasus Antiques, 215
Pemberton Station Museum, 324
Penn State Forest, 328, 331
Pennington: lodging, 312; sights/activities, 230, 307, 310
Penns Grove Wildlife Area, 285–86
Pennsauken: activities, 258; eating, 266
Pennsauken Boat Ramp, 258
Pennsauken Country Club, 258
Pennsville: information, 276; sights/activities, 278–80, 284–88
Pennsville Municipal Boat Ramp, 285
Penny Royal Manor Bed and Breakfast, 289
Pequest Trout Hatchery and Natural Resources Education Center, 27, 195
Peregrine's, 465
Perkins Center for the Arts, 267
Perryville: eating, 209–10; entertainment, 214
Perryville Inn, 209–10
Perth Amboy, 123; events, 142; sights/activities, 125, 131
Perth Amboy Waterfront Festival, 142
Pete & Elda's, 367
Peter Pan, 22
Peter Shields Inn, 536
Peters Valley Craft Education Center, 25, 182, 184
pets, traveling with, 7, 32
Phi Restaurant, 108
Philadelphia International Airport, 18–19, 226, 248, 276, 322, 440
Philadelphia Phillies, 282, 329
Phillipsburg, 169; eating, 180, 181; emergencies, 170; sights/activities, 171–74, 176
Phillipsburg Boat Ramp, 173
Phoenix Books, 242
Pickles Deli, 467–68
pick-your-own farms. See farms
Pier 4 Hotel on the Bay, 462
Pier 88 Marina, 490
Pier A Park, 51, 63
Pier at Caesars, 474
Pierson-Sculthorp House, 399

Pilesgrove: rodeo, 283
Pillars of Plainfield, 109
Pinch Brook Golf Course, 101
Pine Barrens Canoe and Kayak Rental, 328
Pine Barrens Education Center, 330–31
Pine Barrens Golf Club, 328
Pine Barrens Jamboree, 431
Pine Brook Golf Course, 307
Pine Cone Campground, 312
Pine Creek Railroad, 23, 305, 308
Pinelands National Reserve, 26, 32, 320, 330; campgrounds, 425
Pinelands Region, 320–40; campgrounds, 333–34; eating, 334–36; emergencies, 323; entertainment, 337; events, 339–40; information, 322; lodging, 332–33; map, 321; shopping, 338–39; sights/activities, 323–32; transportation, 322–23
Pines at Clermont, 528
Piscataway: events, 142; sights/activities, 125–27, 131
Pitcher, Molly, 309, 358
Pittsgrove: campground, 290; sights/activities, 284, 286–88
Pittstown: ballooning, 195–96; events, 218; shopping, 218
PJ's Pancake House, 314
Plain Dealer, 280
Plainfield, 92; entertainment, 118; lodging, 109
Plainfield Garden Club, 104
Plainfield Shakespeare Garden, 104
Plainfield Symphony, 118
Planet Hollywood, 464
planetariums, 74, 105, 254, 400
Plantation Restaurant and Bar, 426
Playcade Amusements, 449
Playland's Castaway Cove, 488
Plays in the Park (Edison), 140
Pleasant Acres Farm Campground, 160
Pleasantville: eating, 470
Pluckemin Inn, 210
Plymouth Inn, 499–500
PNC Bank Arts Center, 140, 142
Pochuck Valley Farm, 164–65

Point Pavilion Antique Center, 393
Point Pleasant, 376; beaches, 383; information, 377; sights/activities, 382–83
Point Pleasant Antique Emporium, 393
Point Pleasant Beach, 376–77; beaches, 383–84; eating, 390, 391–92; events, 394; information, 377; lodging, 385, 389; shopping, 393; sights/ activities, 379–84; transportation, 378
Point Pleasant Beach Boardwalk, 383–84
Point Pleasant Beach Chamber of Commerce, 377
Point Pleasant Chamber of Commerce, 377
Point Pleasant Historical Society Museum, 380
Point Pleasant, PA: activities, 230
Point Pleasant Parasail, 382
Polar Bear Plunge, 512
Police Museum and Learning Center, New Jersey State, 254
Pollack Theater, 368–69
Pomona Hall Park, 257
Pompton Plains: emergencies, 93; golf, 101
Poor Richard's Inn, 537
Pop Shop, The, 265
Popcorn Park Zoo, 24, 401
population, 33
Port Authority Trans Hudson (PATH), 34, 44, 70, 93
Port Authority Transit Corporation (PATCO), 34
Port Murray: shopping, 218
Port of Call (Millville), 290
Port Republic: campground, 463; event, 475
Port Royal Hotel, 498–99
Porto Leggero, 83
Potter Library Galleries, 119
Potter's Tavern, 280
Powhatan Indians, 254; festival, 270, 339, 340
Prallsville Mills, 227, 240, 244
Presby Memorial Iris Gardens, 28, 103
Princess, 131
Princeton, 298–319; eating, 312–15; emergencies, 301; entertainment, 316–17; events, 318–19; information, 300; lodging, 310; map, 299; shopping, 317–18; sights/activities, 301–10; transportation, 300–301

Princeton 3-Mile Chase, 319
Princeton Battlefield State Park, 300, 302–3, 308
Princeton Canoe and Kayak Rental, 307
Princeton Cemetery, 303–4
Princeton Country Club, 307
Princeton Festival, 319
Princeton Forrestal Village, 318
Princeton JazzFest, 319
Princeton Junction Shuttle, 300
Princeton Marriott Hotel & Conference Center at Forrestal, 310
Princeton Morning Glory, 317
Princeton Public Library, 315
Princeton Record Exchange, 317
Princeton Rep Company, 316
Princeton Summer Theater, 317
Princeton Symphony Orchestra, 316
Princeton Taxi, 301
Princeton University, 298, 301; Art Museum, 20, 305; concerts, 316; events, 318–19; Orange Key Campus Tours, 300; theater, 317
Princeton Walking Tours, 300
Printmaking Council of New Jersey, 213
Proprietary House, 123, 125
Prospertown Schoolhouse, 323
Prudential Center, 75, 87
Prudential Hall, 86
Puccini's Restaurant, 82–83
Puerto Rican Festival, 339
Pumpkin Festival (Cape May), 548
Pumpkin Show (Millville), 296
Pumpkins and Petunias, 120–21
Pyne Point Marina, 258
Pyramid Mountain Natural Historic Area, 158

Q

Qua Baths and Spa, 459
Quail Brook Golf Course, 131
Quarter at Tropicana, 465, 473, 474
Qube Lounge, 204
Queen Victoria, 536
Queen's Hotel, 534–35
Quick Chek New Jersey Festival of Ballooning, 20, 218–19

R

Raagini, 115
Raccoon Ridge, 173
Race Street Café, 235–36
Radisson Hotel Freehold Gardens Hotel and Conference Center, 310–11
rafting, 173–74, 230
Rahway: eating, 84; emergencies, 72; shopping, 88
Rainbow III, 491
Rainforest Café, 464
Ramapo College, 94; Art Galleries, 119
Ramapo Lake, 152
Ramapo Lake Natural Area, 157
Ramapo Lake Trail, 153
Ramapo Mountain State Forest, 157; biking, 154; boating, 151; cross-country skiing, 156; fishing, 152; hiking, 153
Ramapo Valley County Reservation, 101
Ramblewood Country Club, 258
Ram's Head Inn, 466
Ramsey: eating, 113–14
Rancocas: events, 270
Rancocas Golf Club, 258
Rancocas Woods Village of Shops, 269
Rankokus Indian Reservation, festival, 270, 339, 340
Rare Find Nursery, 339
Raritan Inn at Middle Valley, 207
Raritan River: fishing, 197
Raritan River Music Festival, 218
Raritan River Railway, 191
Raspberry Café, 367
Rat's Restaurant, 262–63
Raven and the Peach, 364
Raymond's, 116
RCA Victor, 130
Readington: ballooning, 20, 187, 218–19
Recycling the Past, 430
Red Bank, 344; eating, 362–64, 366, 368; emergencies, 349; entertainment, 370; events, 372; ice-skating, 355; information, 347–48; lodging, 357–58; nightlife, 370; shopping, 370–72; transportation, 348–49
Red Bank Armory Ice Complex, 355
Red Bank Battlefield Park, 251, 253, 261
Red Bank Jazz and Blues Festival, 372

Red Bank Visitors' Center, 347–48
Red Bank Yellow Car Company, 349
Red Barn Antiques, 338
Red Mill Museum Village, 191, 218
Red Wine and Blues Festival, 431
Red's Lobster Pot, 392
Redwoods Grill & Bar, 211
Reeds Beach, 519, 526
Reeves-Reed Arboretum, 28, 103
regattas, 319, 394, 513, 514
Renaissance Faire (Lakewood), 339
Renaissance Festival and Kingdom (South Orange), 121
Renaissance Meadowlands Hotel, 53
Renault Winery, 34, 326, 332
Repaupo: antiques, 293
Resorts Atlantic City, 23, 452, 459–60; eating, 466; entertainment, 470
restaurants: overview, 33. *See also specific restaurants and destinations*
Restaurant David Drake, 84
Restaurant Latour, 162
Restaurant MC, 114
Restaurant Serenade, 112
Restaurant, The (Hackensack), 58
Revolutionary War: overview, 13; reenactments, 244, 270, 319, 548. *See also specific figures and sights*
Riamede Farm, 217
Rib & Chophouse, 460
Richard Robbins, 48
Richard W. DeKorte Park, 50–51; art gallery, 63; birding, 48; hiking, 49
Richwood, 284, 294
Rick's Coffee Café, 544
Rider University, 316
Ridgewood: eating, 116; emergencies, 93; garden, 102; shopping, 120
Rinehart Brook, 197
Ringoes, 299; eating, 313; events, 319; sights/ activities, 199, 243, 306, 308
Ringwood, 144; eating, 162; shopping, 164; sights/ activities, 147–48, 152–57
Ringwood Manor, 147–48
Ringwood State Park, 144, 157; attractions, 147–48; biking, 154; canoeing/kayaking, 151; cross-

country skiing, 156; fishing, 152; hiking, 153; swimming, 155
Rio Grande Air Fest, 548
Ripley's Believe It or Not! Museum, 24, 447
Risley House Bed & Breakfast, 501
Ritz Diner (Livingston), 114–15
Ritz Seafood (Voorhees), 335
River Beach Camp (Mays Landing), 334
River Belle, 381
River Edge, 45–46
River Horse Brewery, 228
River Lady Cruise and Dinner Boat, 400–401
River Queen, 375, 381
River Union Stage, 240
River Vale Country Club, 49
Riverfront Renaissance Center for the Arts, 292
Riverfront Stadium, 75
Riverside Symphonia (Lambertville), 240
Riverside Victorian (Clinton), 206
Riverview Beach Park (Pennsville), 288
Riverview Medical Center, 349
Riviera Bakery, 86
Rivoli Theater, 62
Robbinsville, 306
Robert J. Novins Planetarium, 400
Robert Treat Hotel, 80, 81
Robert Wood Johnson University Hospital, 72, 125
Robeson, Paul, 69, 122
Robin's Nest, 336
Robongi, 55
Rockingham State Historic Site, 304
Rod's Olde Irish Tavern, 391
Rogers Wildlife Refuge, 307, 309
Rolling Greens Golf Club, 152
Ron Jon's Surf Shop, 420
Roosevelt Park Amphitheater, 140
Roots Steakhouse, 113
Rose Day, 142
Rosemont: eating, 236–37, 239
Rosenhayn: farms, 294
Roslyn Sailor Fine Arts, 474
Rotary Ice House Gallery, 371
Round Valley Recreation Area, 202; biking, 196; boating, 196; campground, 207; cross-country skiing, 199; fishing, 197; hiking, 198;

swimming, 199
Round Valley Reservoir, 196, 197, 199, 202, 207
Rova Farms, 338
Row Your Boat Rentals, 152
Rowan University College of Fine and Performing Arts, 337
Royal Airport Shuttle, 442
Royal Flush Sport Fishing, 492
Royal Rolling Chairs, 442
Royce Brook Golf Club, 197
Rudolf W. van der Goot Rose Garden, 132, 142
Rumson, 346; eating, 364
Rusty Heart, 294
Rutan Farm, 148
Rutgers Gardens, 133
Rutgers University, 122, 125; arts center, 139–40; events, 141–42; gardens, 133; golf course, 131; museums, 128–29
Rutgers University Geology Museum, 128
Rutgers University-Camden, 267
Rutgers-Camden Center for the Arts, 267
Rutherford: eating, 56–57, 60; entertainment, 62; lodging, 53; sights/ activities, 46–47
Rutt's Hut, 61
Ryan's Parkside, 181

S
Saddle River: eating, 109–10; shopping, 121
Saddle River Inn, 109–10
Sagami, 263
Sage, 470
sailing, 75, 154, 286, 354, 401; regattas, 319, 394, 513, 514
St. Ann's Italian Street Festival, 65
St. Clair, Arthur, 186, 193
Saint Clare's Hospital, 147, 170, 189
Saint Francis Medical Center, 226, 249
St. Joseph's Regional Medical Center, 93
St. Mary Hospital, 44
Saint Michael's Medical Center, 72
St. Patrick's Day Parades: Atlantic City, 475; Belmar, 372; Hoboken, 64; Newark, 89; North Wildwood, 512; Seaside Heights, 409; Trenton, 270

St. Rita Hotel, 422
Saint, The (Asbury Park), 370
Salem, 274; emergencies, 277; events, 295; sights/activities, 277–78, 287
Salem County Fair, 295
Salem County Historical Society, 277–78
Sally Lunn's, 211
Salt Creek Grille, 364
saltwater fishing. See fishing
Sama's Seashore Delights, 409
Samuel Mickle House, 257
Sand Bar Restaurant, 390
Sand Barrens Golf Club, 528
Sand Castle Bed & Breakfast (Barnegat Light), 424
Sand Jamm Beach and Surf Company, 493
Sand Sculpting Contest (Ocean City), 513
Sand Sculpture Contest (Cape May), 548
Sandcastle Contest (Belmar), 372
Sandcastle Cottages (Belmar), 362
Sandcastle Stadium, 455
S&S Auction, 293
Sandy Hook, 343–44; beaches, 355; map, 342; sights/activities, 349, 352–57; transportation, 348
Sandy Hook Bird Observatory, 344, 352
Sandy Hook Lighthouse, 30, 32, 344, 353
Sandy Hook Migration Watch, 352
Sandy Hook Summer Beach Concerts, 372
Sandy Hook Unit. See Gateway National Recreation Area-Sandy Hook Unit
Sandy Hook Visitor Center, 356
Sara the Turtle, 478; Festival, 513
Sarah Vaughan Concert Hall, 87
Sarandon, Susan, 27, 69, 438
Saw Mill Creek Wildlife Management Area, 49
Sawmill Lake, 179
Sayen Botanical Gardens, 259, 270; Azalea Festival, 259, 270
Sayreville: horseback riding, 132
Scalini Fedeli, 113
Scandinavian Fest, 219
Scarborough Inn, 500
Scarlet Oak Pond, 101

Scherman-Hoffman Sanctuary, 201
Schnackenberg's Luncheonette, 59
Schneider's Restaurant, 367
Schooley's Mountain County Park, 197, 198, 202
Schooley's Mountain General Store, 216
Schuyler-Hamilton House, 189
Scotch Plains: activities, 100, 101; eating, 113
Scotland Run Park, 331
Scott's Mountain Hawk Watch, 173
scuba diving, 202, 355–56, 383–84, 450
Sea Bright, 344; beaches, 355; eating, 364, 366; nightlife, 370
Sea Girt, 375; beaches, 383; eating, 391; lodging, 386–89; sights/activities, 379–80
Sea Girt Lighthouse, 30, 380, 383
Sea Girt Lodge, 389
Sea Grill (Avalon), 505
Sea Gypsy Bed & Breakfast, 501
Sea Isle City, 478; beach, 493–94; eating, 504–7; entertainment, 510; events, 512–14; information, 481; lodging, 501–2; sights/activities, 485–86, 489–93
Sea Isle City Historical Museum, 485–86
Sea Isle City Tourism Development Commission, 481
Sea Isle Municipal Ramp, 490
Sea Isle Parasail, 492
Sea Lark Bed & Breakfast, 501
Sea Life Museum (Brigantine), 448
Sea Oaks Golf Club, 419
Sea Pirate Campground, 425
Sea Shell Club, 424
Sea Shell Museum, 485
Seabrook Educational and Cultural Center, 279
Seafood Empire (North Brunswick), 139
seafood festivals, 219, 372, 373, 409, 431
Seagrass, 367
SeaScape Manor, 359
Seashore Open House Tour, 431
Seaside Heights, 395, 397; beaches, 404–5; events,

409–10; information, 398; lodging, 406; sights/activities, 401–3
Seaside Heights Boardwalk, 22, 24, 402, 404–5
Seaside Heights Casino Pier, 402
Seaside Heights Seafood Festival, 409
Seaside Heights Visitors Bureau, 398
Seaside Park, 397, 405
Seaside Sailing, 401
Seaside Waverunners II, 403
SeaStreak, 27, 348
Seaview Marriott Resort and Spa, 455, 458
Secaucus: emergencies, 44; entertainment, 62; events, 64; lodging, 53–54; shopping, 63–64
Secaucus Outlets, 63–64
Secret Garden, 294
Selden Rodman Gallery of Popular Arts, 119
Senator Frank S. Farley State Marina, 450
SEPTA (Southeastern Pennsylvania Transportation Authority), 34, 249
September 11th Monument, 68
Sergeantsville, 225, 227; eating, 236, 239; events, 244; lodging, 235
Sergeantsville General Store, 239
Sergeantsville Inn, 236
Seton Hall Pirates, 75
Seton Hall University, 94
Seven Mile Beach Island, 478–79; map, 477. See also Avalon; Sea Isle City; Stone Harbor
Seven Presidents Oceanfront Park, 355
7th Street Surf Shop (Ocean City), 493
Sewell: campground, 289; golf, 287
Shad Festival, 244
Shaker Café, 210
Shakespeare Theatre of New Jersey, 120
Shamong: sights/activities, 325, 328
Shamrock Day Celebration, 270
Shanghai Jazz, 118
Shark River Golf Course, 354
Shawmont Hotel, 358–59
Shea Center for the Performing Arts, 118
Shepherd Lake Recreation

Area, 157; boating, 151; fishing, 152; hiking, 153; swimming, 155
Sheraton Convention Center Hotel, 461
Sheraton Edison Hotel-Raritan Center, 134
Sheraton Meadowlands Hotel and Conference Center, 53
Sheraton Suites on the Hudson, 54
Sherlock Holmes Weekend, 547
Shields Bike Rentals, 525
Ship Bottom, 412; activities, 417, 418, 420; beaches, 421; eating, 427, 428; events, 431; information, 414; lodging, 422; nightlife, 429
Ship Bottom Island Christmas Parade, 431
Ship Bottom Marine Center, 417
Ship Bottom Shellfish, 427
Ship Inn, 237
Shippen Manor Museum, 193
Shoe Bar, 461
shopping. *See specific shops and destinations*
Shops at Asbury Avenue, 511
Shore Bet Fishing, 451
Shore Gate Golf Course, 492
Shore Memorial Hospital (Somers Point), 442, 483
Shore Transit, 349
Shorepoint Marina and Yacht Sales, 403
Short Hills: lodging, 107; shopping, 120; sights/ activities, 101, 103–5
Show Place Ice Cream Parlour, 428
Showboat-The Mardi Gras Casino, 23, 453, 460
Shrewsbury: historic site, 349–50; shopping, 372
Shriver's, 508
Shumi, 138
Siam, 238
Silas Condict County Park, 156, 196
Silver Bullet Speedboat and Dolphin Watch, 35, 489
Silver Decoy Winery, 306
Silver Lake, 347, 420
Silver Maple Organic Farm Bed & Breakfast, 206, 235
Simplicity Café, 181
Simply Radishing, 265
Sinatra, Frank, 40, 58, 69, 444, 458
Sindia, 485

Six Flags Great Adventure, 19, 24, 327
SJH Elmer Hospital, 277
SJH Health Center-Bridgeton, 277
SJH Regional Medical Center-Vineland, 277, 323
skiing, 33, 155. *See also* cross-country skiing
Skimmer Festival Weekend, 513
Skimmer, The, 527
sky diving, 308
Sky Manor Airport, 195–96
Sky Sweeper Balloon Adventures, 195
Sky View Golf Club, 152
Skydive Jersey Shore, 308
Skylands. *See* Northern Highlands
Skylands Manor, 147
Skylands of New Jersey Tourism Council, 146, 170, 188
Sky-View Taxi, 124
Small World Coffee, 315
Smith, Kevin, 27, 69, 371–72
Smithville, 439; eating, 466; events, 475; lodging, 462; shopping, 474
Sneddon's Luncheonette, 239
Sogno Ristorante, 364
SoHo on George, 136–37
Sojourner, The, 243
Solstice Stones, 158
Somers Mansion, 444
Somers Point: beach, 456; emergencies, 442, 483; lodging, 462; shopping, 474; sights/activities, 444, 448, 451; theater, 473
Somerset: eating, 138; entertainment, 139, 141; events, 141, 142; sights/ activities, 127, 128, 131
Somerset Art Association, 215
Somerset County Chamber of Commerce, 92
Somerset County Environmental Education Center, 104
Somerset Hills Hotel, 108
Somerset Medical Center, 124
Somerset Patriots, 23, 102
Somerville, 122; eating, 137, 138; emergencies, 124; events, 141; historic site, 128; shopping, 141
Sophie's Bistro, 138
Sopranos, The (TV show), 39, 40, 69
Soul of the Season Celebra-

tion, 296
South City Grill (Mountain Lakes), 161–62
South Jersey Auction, 293
South Jersey Canoe and Kayak Classic, 339
South Jersey Cultural Alliance, 20
South Jersey Performing Arts Center, 266
South Jersey Pumpkin Show, 296
South Jersey Regional Theatre, 473
South Jersey Sport Fishing Marina, 528
South Mountain Reservation, 100, 101, 106, 121
South Orange, 94; entertainment, 118; events, 121
South Orange Performing Arts Center, 118
South River Walk Park, 259
South Shore Marina (Hewitt), 151, 154
Southeastern Pennsylvania Transportation Authority (SEPTA), 34, 249
Southern Gateway, 122–42; eating, 135–39; emergencies, 124–25; entertainment, 139–41; events, 141; information, 124; lodging, 134–35; map, 123; shopping, 141; sights/ activities, 125–34; transportation, 124
Southern Mansion, 538
Southern Ocean County Chamber of Commerce, 414
Southern Ocean County Hospital, 415
Southern Shore, 434–549; maps, 435, 477, 516. *See also specific destinations*
Southside Marina, 382
Sovereign Bank Arena, 266
Space Farms Zoo and Museum, 24, 150
Spanish Pavillion, 83–84
Spano's Ristorante Italiano, 385, 390
Sparacio's Strawberry Farm, 294
Sparta: eating, 162; shopping, 164; sights/activities, 151, 152
special events, 26. *See also specific events and destinations*
Speedwell Iron Works, 190
Spellbinders Surf Shop, 355
Spermaceti Cove Lifesaving Station, 349, 357

Sperry Observatory, 102
Spikes Fishery, 382
Spike's Seafood, 391
Spirit Cruises, 48
Spirit of New Jersey, 48
Splash World Water Park
  (Clementon), 19, 258, 326
Splash Zone Water Park
  (Wildwood), 488
Spooky Brook Golf Course,
  131
Sportsman's Marina, 417
Spot, The (Spring Lake), 393
Spray Beach: lodging, 425
Spring Art Show and Sale
  (Brant Beach), 431
Spring Chester Craft Show,
  218
Spring Lake, 374–75; beach-
  es, 383; eating, 389–92;
  entertainment, 393; events,
  394; information, 377;
  lodging, 384–87; map, 375;
  shopping, 393;
  sights/activities, 380,
  382–83; transportation,
  378–79
Spring Lake Historical Socie-
  ty Museum, 380
Spring Lake Inn, 386
Spring Lake Theatre Compa-
  ny, 393
Spring Thunder in the Sand
  Motocross Race, 512
Spring Valley Equestrian
  Center, 154
Springsteen, Bruce, 69, 345,
  346, 371, 438
Spruce Run Creek, 197
Spruce Run Reservoir, 197
Spruce Run State Recreation
  Area, 202; biking, 196;
  boating, 197; campground,
  207–8; cross-country skiing,
  199; fishing, 197; swim-
  ming, 199
Squan Inlet Light Station,
  380
Squan Tri-Sail Regatta, 394
Squan Village Historical
  Society, 379
Stage Depot-The Inn at Pen-
  nytown, 312
Stage House Restaurant and
  Wine Bar, 113
Stage Left, 137
Stanhope, 144; eating, 163;
  events, 165; historic site,
  148; lodging, 160
Stanhope Area Taxi Service,
  146
Stanhope Spring Festival,
  165
Star Tavern & Pizzeria, 115
Starfish, 492

stargazing, 102, 176, 199
Starlight Fleet, 490, 492
Starlux, The, 498
State Fair Meadowlands, 18,
  64
State House, 255
State Line Hawk Watch, 48
state parks and forests:
  overview, 33. *See also specif-
  ic state parks and forests*
state symbols, 170
State Theatre (New
  Brunswick), 139
Staten Island Expressway, 70
Statue of Liberty Ferry, 23,
  27, 75, 76
Statue of Liberty National
  Monument, 76–77, 78
Statue of Liberty Race, 372
Steak 38, 467
Steel Pier, 24, 444, 448–49
Steel's Fudge, 470
Steenykill Lake, 179
Steeplechase Pier, 436, 444
Stephen Crane House Muse-
  um, 350
Stephens Farm, 164
Stephens State Park, 157,
  203; biking, 154; camp-
  ground, 161, 208; cross-
  country skiing, 156; fishing,
  197
Sterling Hill Mining Muse-
  um, 24, 150
Steuben House, 41, 45–46
Steve and Cookie's By the
  Bay, 470
Stevens Institute of Technol-
  ogy, 40, 62
Stickley Museum at Crafts-
  man Farms, 195
STIR Bar, 107
Stockton, 224; campground,
  235; eating, 237–39; entertainment, 240; events, 244;
  lodging, 232; shopping,
  241; sights/
  activities, 227, 229–31
Stockton Carriage Tours, 230
Stockton Inn, 232, 237
Stockton Performing Arts
  Center, 240, 292
Stokes State Forest, 177;
  birding, 173; boating, 173;
  campground, 179; cross-
  country skiing, 176; fishing,
  174; hiking, 174–75; swimming, 176
Stone and Company
  Antiques, 240
Stone Harbor, 478–79;
  beach, 493–94; eating, 505,
  508, 509; events, 513–14;
  information, 482; lodging,
  501, 502; shopping,

  510–11; sights/
  activities, 486–87, 489–91,
  493–94; transportation,
  482–83
Stone Harbor Arts and
  Crafts Show, 513–14
Stone Harbor Bird Sanctu-
  ary, 21, 489, 494
Stone Harbor Municipal
  Marina, 491
Stone House at Stirling
  Ridge, 114
Stone Pony, 345, 371
Stoneyfield Orchards, 184
Stony Brook, 177, 309
Stony Brook Friends Meet-
  ing House, 303
Stony Brook-Millstone
  Watershed Nature Reserve,
  307, 310
Stony Hill Farm Market and
  Gardens, 217
Stony Hill Inn, 57
Stony Lake, 174, 176, 177
Storybook Land (Cardiff),
  19, 24, 326; (Egg Harbor),
  449
Strand Theater, 337
Strathmere: beach, 493; eat-
  ing, 504
Strathmere Natural Area,
  489, 494–95
Strawberry Festival
  (Bridgeton), 295; (Lynd-
  hurst), 89; (West Cape
  May), 548
Strawberry Hill Farm, 184
Stray Cat Sportfish, 451
Street Rod Weekend, 514
Strictly Marine, 382
Strip House, 107
Stuff Yer Face, 139
Stults Farm, 318
Summer Enchanted Evening
  Concert Series (Hoboken),
  62
Summer Nites (North Wild-
  wood), 501
Summerfest (Brick), 394;
  (Jersey City), 87
Summit: eating, 113, 115,
  117; events, 121; garden,
  103; lodging, 107–8; shop-
  ping, 119
Summit Cheese Shop, 117
Sunfish Pond Natural Area,
  174, 175, 177
Sunflower Glass Studio, 241
Sunrise Lake, 200
Sunrise Mountain, 173, 175
Sunset Beach, 531
Sunset Beach Gift Shops,
  547
Sunset Lake, 484–85
Sunset Lake Hydrofest

Powerboat Races, 514
Sunset Parades, 548
Sunset Pier, 490
Sunset Valley Golf Course, 101
Supawna Meadows National Wildlife Refuge, 284, 286, 287
Super Nationals, 132
Super Science Weekend (Trenton), 270
Superstar Theatre, 460, 470
Surf Buggy Center, 489
Surf Buggy Center of LBI, 416
Surf City, 412–13; beaches, 421; eating, 426–28; lodging, 422; shopping, 430; sights/activities, 416, 418, 420
Surf City Hotel, 422, 426
Surf Fishing Tournament (Wildwood), 514
Surf Side Coffee, 427–28
Surf Taco, 391–92
Surf Taxi, 349
Surfers Supplies, 493
surfing, 355, 383, 420, 493
Surflight Theatre, 428–29
Surfside Motel (Point Pleasant Beach), 389
Surprise Lake, 101
Susan Murphy, 392
Susquehanna Bank Center, 266
Sussex, 145; campgrounds, 160, 179; eating, 162–63; emergencies, 147, 170; entertainment, 163; shopping, 164; sights/activities, 148–50, 155, 175–77
Sussex Branch Trail, 153–54
Sussex County Fairgrounds, 165
Sussex County Farm and Horse Show, 165
Sussex County Strawberry Farm, 164
Swainton: events, 548; lodging, 547; sights/activities, 528, 531
Swal Dairy, 336
Swartswood Lake, 152, 157
Swartswood State Park, 152, 157, 161
Swede's Inn, 291
Swedesboro: church, 277; eating, 291
Sweet Basil's Café, 115
Sweet Vidalia, 426
swimming: Central New Jersey, 329; Delaware River Valley, 287; Northeastern Gateway, 132, 135; Northern New Jersey, 154–55,

176, 199. *See also* beaches
Sylvester's Fish Market and Restaurant, 507–8
Sylvin Farms Winery, 326
symbols key, 6–7
Symphony in C, 268
Symposia Bookstore, 63

T

T I Kayaks, 491
Taco of the Town, 162
Take Away Café, 243
Tamarack Golf Course, 131
Tap Room (Basking Ridge), 108
Tea Hive, The, 162–63
Teacup, the, 175
Teak Restaurant, 363
Teaneck: eating, 60, 62; sights/activities, 49, 94
Ted's on Main, 334
Tenafly: eating, 60; lodging, 52–53; sights/activities, 44, 50
Teresa's Café Italiano, 314
Terhune Orchards, 318
Terrace Tavern (Beach Haven Terrace), 427
Teterboro Airport, 46
Tewksbury Balloon Adventures, 196
Thai Chef (Montclair), 114; (Somerville), 138
Thanksgiving Day Parade (Trenton), 270
Thanksgiving in the Country (Sergeantsville), 244
theater: overview, 33. *See also specific theaters and destinations*
Theater Square Grill, 81, 86
3rd Avenue Surf Shop (Spring Lake), 383
Thisilldous Eatery, 181
Thomas Clark House, 302–3
Thomas Street Ice Cream and Chocolate, 315
Three Forts Ferry, 27, 285
Three Pillar Rock, 158
Thunder on the Beach Truck Competition, 514
Thunder Over the Boardwalk, 475
Thundergust Lake, 286, 287, 290
Thundering Surf Water Park, 415
Tick-Tock Diner, 61
Tidepool Museum Shop, 486–87
tides, 34
Tillman Ravine, 175
Timberland Lake Campground, 333–34

Timberlane Campground, 289
Tinicum Rear Range Lighthouse, 31, 280
Tip Tam Camping Resort, 334
Tisha's Fine Dining, 540–41
Titusville, 223; campground, 235; eating, 237; events, 244; map, 222; shopping, 243; sights/activities, 228–31; theater, 240
TLC's Polish Water Ice, 508
Toad Hall Shop and Gallery, 260, 269
Tom Bailey's Market, 392
Tomahawk Lake, 19, 151
Tomasello Winery, 34, 326
Tomato Factory Antique Center, 317
Tomato Festival, 548
Tomatoes Margate, 467
Tommy's Hot Dogs, 87
Toms River, 397–98; eating, 407–8; emergencies, 399; entertainment, 408; events, 409; information, 398; lodging, 405; shopping, 409; sights/activities, 399–403; transportation, 398–99
Toms River Canoe and Kayak Race, 409
Toms River Seaport Society Maritime Museum, 399–400, 409
Toms River-Ocean County Chamber of Commerce, 398
Tony's Baltimore Grill, 468–69
Tops Diner, 85
Tops Taxi, 349
Tortilla Press, 264–65
Tortuga's Cocina, 238–39
Total Marine at Sea View, 354
Tour of Hoboken's Secret Gardens, 65
Tour of Somerville Cycling Series, 141
tourist information, 30. *See also specific destinations*
Tourne Park, 156
Tower Hill Antiques, 370
Town and Country Golf Links, 287
Towne Deli (Summit), 117
Traction Line Recreation Trail, 196, 199
Tradewinds Motor Lodge, 405
Trailside Nature and Science Center, 101, 104–5, 121
train services, 34. *See also*

Trans-Bridge Lines, 226
Transportation Heritage Center, 171
Trap Rock Restaurant and Brewery, 114
Treasure Island, 381
Treasures and Pleasures, 243
Treasures on High, 293
Treen Studio Pottery Shoppe, 293
Trent (William) House, 250
Trenton, 245–70; eating, 262, 264, 265–66; emergencies, 226, 249; entertainment, 266, 268; events, 270; information, 248; lodging, 261; map, 246; shopping, 268–69; sights/activities, 250–61; transportation, 248–49
Trenton 2 Nite, 266
Trenton Artists Workshop Association, 268
Trenton Battle Monument, 251
Trenton City Museum at Ellarslie, 256
Trenton Devils, 258
Trenton Farmers' Market, 269
Trenton Film Festival, 270
Trenton Heritage Days Festival, 270
Trenton Station, 249
Trenton Thunder, 23, 258
Trenton War Memorial, 251, 253
Trenton Waterfront Park, 258
Trenton-Mercer Airport, 248
Trinitas Hospital, 72
Triple Brook Family Camping Resort, 179–80
Tripod Rock, 158
Tri-State Actors Theater, 163
Triumph Brewing Co., 314
Tropicana Casino and Resort, 23, 454, 460; eating, 465; entertainment, 460, 470, 473; shopping, 474
Tropicana Showroom, 460, 470
Trout Brook, 197
trout hatchery, 27, 195
Trump Marina Casino Resort, 23, 454, 460–61; nightlife, 473
Trump Plaza Hotel and Casino, 23, 454, 461; entertainment, 471
Trump Taj Mahal Casino Resort, 23, 455, 461; entertainment, 471, 473
Trumpets Jazz Club, 118

tubing, 173–74, 230
Tuckahoe Inn, 504
Tucker's Island Light, 30–31
Tucker's Pub, 507
Tuckerton, 413; campground, 425; events, 431; lodging, 423; shopping, 430; sights/activities, 417–19
Tuckerton Emporium, 430
Tuckerton Seaport, 418–19, 431
Tulip and Garden Festival, 547
Tun Tavern Brewery & Restaurant, 468
Tunis-Ellicks Historic House and Museum, 99
Turdo Vineyards and Winery, 524
Turkey Swamp Park Campgrounds, 312
Turkey Trot and Cross Country Race, 142
Turntable Junction, 216
Turtle Back Zoo, 24, 100, 106
Turtle Gut Park and Memorial, 484–85
Tuscany House Hotel, 332
TV shows, set in New Jersey, 27. *See also specific TV shows*
12th Street Bike Rentals (Ocean City), 489
12 Miles West Theatre Company, 118–19
27 Mix, 81
Twice Told Tales, 215
Twin Lights of Navesink Lighthouse, 30, 353
Two Mile Landing, 505–6
Two Rivers Antiques Show and Garden Tour, 372

U

Uncle Bill's Pancake House, 508
Uncle Charley's Ice Cream, 544
Underwood Memorial Hospital, 249
Union: eating, 115; emergencies, 93; events, 121; museum, 99
Union City: eating, 59–60; entertainment, 63
Union County Art Show, 88
Union Hospital, 93
Union Lake, 286
Union Lake Wildlife Management Area, 286
Union Monument, 279
Union Park Dining Room, 540

Union Station Grill (Phillipsburg), 180
Unionville Vineyards, 34, 306
United Cab (Trenton), 249
United States Equestrian Team, 26, 198
United States Golf Association Museum and Archives, 28, 194
United Taxi (Hoboken), 44
universities: overview, 25. *See also specific universities*
University Art Galleries (Montclair), 119
University Medical Center at Princeton, 301
Unshredded Nostalgia, 430
Upper Delaware River, 167–94; campgrounds, 179–80; eating, 180–81; emergencies, 170; entertainment, 181; events, 184; information, 170; lodging, 178–79; map, 166; shopping, 181–84; sights/activities, 170–78; transportation, 170
Upper Montclair, 92, 103; events, 121
Urban Archaeologist, 243
Urban Details, 393
Urban Word Café, 265
Urie's Waterfront Restaurant, 507
Ursula, 492
Utsch's Marina, 528

V

Vail House, 190
Valenzano Winery, 325
Valley Brook Golf Club, 49
Valley Hospital (Ridgewood), 93
Valley Shepherd Creamery, 217
Valleybrook Golf Course, 328
Van Bunschooten House and Museum, 148–49
Van Gogh's Ear Café, 115
Van Liew-Suydam House, 127
Van Riper-Hopper House, 94
Van Slyke Castle, 153
Van Vleck House and Gardens, 102
Van Vorst Farmer's Market, 88–89
Van Wickle House, 127
Vanthia's, 544
Ventnor City, 439; activities, 449, 451; beach, 456; eating, 470; lodging, 463
Ventnor City Fishing Pier, 451

Verjus Restaurant, 113
Vernon, 146; farm, 165; lodging, 158–60; sights/ activities, 150, 154, 155
Verona Park Fine Art and Crafts, 121
Vic's Bar and Restaurant, 367
Victoria Guest House Bed and Breakfast (Beach Haven), 423–24
Victoria Hall of Science (Newark), 74
Victoria House Bed & Breakfast (Spring Lake), 387
Victoria on Main (Toms River), 405
Victoria Theater (Newark), 86
Victorian Days (Belvidere), 184
Victorian Fair (Cape May), 548
Victorian Gingerbread Of Cape May Tours, 529–30
Victorian Lady (Moorestown), 261
Victorian Motel (Cape May), 539
Victorian Rose Farm Bed and Breakfast (Woodstown), 289
Victorian Week (Cape May), 548
Victorious Antiques, 546
Victory Taxi Association, 124
Vienna Bake Shop, 212
Vietnam Era Educational Center, 129
Viking Village, 411, 418, 420
Vila Nova do Sol Mar, 82
Villa Barone, 265
Villa Rosa, 265
Village Bicycle Shop (Cape May), 525
Village Gourmet (Rutherford), 60
Village Inn (Seaside Heights), 406
Villagers Theatre (Somerset), 141
Villas Taxis, 520
Vince Lombardi Travel Plaza, 43
Vincentown: shopping, 338
Vince's Restaurant, 507
Vineland, 34; emergencies, 277, 323; entertainment, 337; events, 339
vineyards. See wineries
Virginia Hotel, 534, 540
Virtua Memorial Hospital, 323
Virtua West Jersey Hospital, 323
visitor information, 30. See

also specific destinations
Visual Arts Center of New Jersey, 119
Vitamia & Sons, 61–62
Voorhees: eating, 335
Voorhees State Park, 202; biking, 196; campground, 208; stargazing, 199

W
W Hotel, 54
Wabun C. Krueger Collection of Agricultural, Household, and Scientific Artifacts, 128
Wading Pines Canoe Rentals, 328
Walk of Lights, 296
walking trails. See hiking
Wall Township Speedway, 383
Wallace House State Historic Site, 128
Walpack Inn, 180
Walt Whitman Arts Center, 267
Walt Whitman House, 252
Walter Gordon Theatre, 267
Walter Rand Theatre, 266
Wanaque: eating, 161
Wantage: farms, 164
Waretown, 413; entertainment, 429; events, 430–31; sights/activities, 328, 331, 415, 421
Warren: eating, 114; lodging, 108
Warren County Antiques Fair & Festival, 184
Warren County Convention & Visitors Bureau, 146
Warren County Farmers' Fair, 18, 184
Warren County Heritage Festival, 218
Warren County Historical Society Museum, 171
Warren E. Fox Nature Center, 328, 331
Warren Hospital, 170
Wasabi (Clinton), 212
Wasabi Asian Plates & Sushi Bar (Somerville), 137
Washington Antique Center, 214–15
Washington Crossing Open Air Theatre, 240
Washington Crossing State Park, 224–25, 231; campground, 235; events, 244; fishing, 230; hiking, 230
Washington, George, 41, 46, 50, 94, 95, 106, 122, 128, 185–86, 198, 227, 245, 251,

254, 256, 299–300, 302, 304, 308; Birthday Celebration, 244; Crossing State Park, 224–25, 231, 244; Morristown National Historical Park, 32, 192–93
Washington Inn, 542
Washington Riding Stables, 132
Washington Street Mall, 530, 546–47; Art Show, 548; eating, 543, 544
Washington Township: sights/activities, 197, 200, 202
Washington's Crossing of the Delaware, 244
Watchung Arts Center, 118
Watchung Booksellers, 120
Watchung Reservation, 101, 104–5, 106
Water Club at the Borgata, 461–62
water parks, 19, 24, 150, 258, 326, 415, 488
Waterford Gardens, 121
Waterhouse Historical Museum, 399
Waterloo Village, 148, 157, 165
Watson's Regency Suites, 497
Wave, The (Atlantic City), 473
Wawayanda Lake, 151, 152, 154–55, 157
Wawayanda Mountain, 152–53
Wawayanda State Park, 157; boating, 151, 152; campground, 161; cross-country skiing, 156; fishing, 152; hiking, 152–53; swimming, 154–55
Wayne: emergencies, 93; entertainment, 118; events, 121; shopping, 119; sights/activities, 93–94, 101
Wayne General Hospital, 93
Wayne Historical Commission, 94
Wayne Taxi & Limo, 93
weather, 24–25
Weehawken, 43; boat excursions, 48; eating, 57; entertainment, 62; lodging, 54
Weird Week, 513
Weis Ecology Center, 156
Wellmont Theatre, 118
Wells Mills County Park and Nature Center, 328, 331, 415, 421
Well-Sweep Herb Farm, 218
Wemrock Orchards, 318
West Berlin: eating, 266
West Branch: shopping, 371

West Cape Motel, 539
West Deptford Municipal Boat Ramp, 258
West Milford: events, 165; sights/activities, 148, 151, 152
West Orange, 90; eating, 111, 112, 115, 117; entertainment, 118; sights/activities, 100, 101, 106, 130
West Orange & Orange Taxi, 93
West Trenton: eating, 262; sights/activities, 254, 258
West Windsor: entertainment, 317; events, 270, 319; golf, 307
Western Monmouth Chamber of Commerce, 300
Westfall Winery, 171
Westfield: eating, 110, 117; entertainment, 118; lodging, 108–9; shopping, 120–21
Westfield Symphony Orchestra, 118
Westin Governor Morris, 204
Westin Jersey City Newport, 80
Westin Princeton, 310
Westminster Choir College of Rider University, 316
Westmont: eating, 265
Westwood Golf Club, 258
Wetlands Institute and Museum, 21–22, 486–87, 490, 494; Wings 'n Water Festival, 487, 490, 514
Wetsuit World, 493
whale-watching, 35, 489–90, 527–28
Wharton State Forest, 331; Batsto Village, 29, 320–21, 323–24; campground, 334; fishing, 328; hiking, 329
Wheaton Village, 281, 282; events, 295, 296
Whimsicality, 393
Whippanong Valley Railroad, 99
Whippany: eating, 110; sights/activities, 99, 201
Whippany Railway Museum, 99
Whippoorwill Campground, 503
Whispers (Spring Lake), 390
Whispers Lounge (Edison), 134
Whistling Elk, 216
Whistling Swan Inn, 160
Whitall House, 251
White House Sub Shop, 469
White Lilac Inn, 386

White Manna Hamburgers, 60
White Sands Oceanfront Resort and Spa, 385
Whitehouse Station: ballooning, 196; eating, 210; lodging, 206
Whitesbog Blueberry Festival, 339
Whitesbog Village, 29, 325; events, 339, 340
Whitman, Walt, 246; House, 252
Who's On Third, 390–91
Wick Farm, 193
Widow McCrea House, 234
Wiggins Waterfront Park, 259
Wightman's Farms, 218
Wilberts Marina, 403
Wilbraham Mansion Bed & Breakfast Inn, 537
Wild Oaks Golf Club, 287
Wild Ocean Surf Shop, 493
Wild Safari, 327
Wild West City, 19, 23, 151
Wildlife Art and Decoy Show, 394
Wildlife Drive, 449, 450, 457
Wildwood, 479–81; beaches, 494; eating, 505, 507; entertainment, 509–10; events, 512–14; information, 482; lodging, 495–96, 501, 502; map, 477; sights/activities, 484–95; transportation, 482–83
Wildwood Boardwalk, 22, 479–80, 484; eating, 508–9; events, 512–14; Information Center, 482; tram, 483
Wildwood Cab, 482
Wildwood Crest, 480–81; beaches, 494; eating, 505–6; entertainment, 510; events, 513, 514; information, 482; lodging, 496–99, 502; sights/activities, 484–85, 487, 489–94
Wildwood Crest Historical Society and Museum, 487
Wildwood Crest Pier, 510
Wildwood Historical Society, 487
Wildwoods Classic Cup, 514
Wildwoods Convention Center, 509
Wildwoods International Kite Festival, 512
Will, August, 73
William G. Mennen Sports Arena, 200
William L. Hutcheson Memorial Forest, 133

William Paterson University, 93–94, 118, 119
William Trent House, 250
Williams Center for the Arts, 62
Williams, William Carlos, 62, 69, 91–92
Willingboro: golf, 258
Willow Brook Country Club, 258
Willow Creek Nursery, 243
Willowwood Arboretum, 199, 200
Wilson, Woodrow, 80, 298; Hall, 350
Wind Chimes Book Exchange, 293
Windansea, 362
Winding River Campground, 334
WindMill Hot Dogs, 366
Windrift Hotel, 497
Windsor: eating, 314; shopping, 318. See also West Windsor
Windward Manor Inn, 423
Windy Brow Farms, 165
wine festivals, 228, 244, 319, 431, 548
wineries, 34; Belvidere, 172; Cape May, 524; Cream Ridge, 325; Egg Harbor, 326; Germania, 326; Hammonton, 326; Lambertville, 228; Mays Landing, 326; Milford, 228; Montague, 171; Pennington, 228; Pinelands Region, 325–26; Richwood, 284; Ringoes, 306; Robbinsville, 306; Shamong, 325
Winfield's, 290
Wings 'n Water Festival, 487, 490, 514
Winter Sugarloaf Crafts Festival, 141
Witches Ball, 340
Witherspoon Bread Company, 315
Witherspoon Grill, 313
Wolf Preserve, Lakota, 171–72
Woodbridge, 77; eating, 85–86; entertainment, 87
Woodbridge Farm, 294
Woodbury: golf, 258
Woodcliff Lake: lodging, 52
Wooden Boat Festival, 400, 409
Wooden Duck Bed & Breakfast, 160
Woodford Cedar Run Wildlife Refuge, 330–31
Woodrow Wilson Hall, 350
Woodruff Museum of Indian

Artifacts, 282
Woodstown: events, 295; golf, 287; lodging, 289; shopping, 295
Woolverton Inn, 232
World Indoor Kite Competition, 512
World Series of Birding, 22, 525, 547, 548
Wortendyke Barn, 45
Worthington State Forest, 168, 177; boating, 173; campground, 179; cross-country skiing, 176; fishing, 174; hiking, 174–75
Wyanokie High Point, 153
Wyanokie Wilderness Area, 156
Wyckoff: nature center, 104
Wyckoff-Garretson House, 127

X

Xanadu Showroom, 471

Y

Yankee Doodle Tap Room, 311
Yellow Cab (Millville), 276; (Pinelands), 323; (Trenton), 249; (Wildwood), 482
Yellow Garage Antiquities Marketplace, 292–93
Yellow Van (Atlantic City), 441
Yogi Bear's Jellystone Park (Mays Landing), 334
Yogi Bear's Jellystone Park Camp-Resort at Tall Pines, 289–90
Yogi Berra Museum and Learning Center, 98, 102
Yogi Berra Stadium, 23, 102

York Street House, 233
Yummy Tummy, 336

Z

Zimmerli Art Museum, 20, 128
Zinc Café, 335–36
Zoe's Beachfront Eatery, 544
zoos: overview, 24. *See also specific zoos*
Zuck Arboretum, 103

New Jersey